"A stunning achievement."

—Meryle Secrest

"An epic Hollywood narrative about the craft, politics, and business of the industry, with Stanwyck at its center. A compelling, if complicated, read . . . worth the journey."

—Bill Desowitz, *USA Today*

"One hopes that the wait for Ms. Wilson's second volume won't be as long as World War II, since *Steel-True* is so readable, and as direct as its subject. I couldn't put it down."

—Cathy Horyn, *The New York Times*

"I am loving your Barbara Stanwyck—you bring that whole period of time so brilliantly to life. I am already in love with her and so so angry at Frank Fay! Thank you for this wonderful, delicious book!"

—Susan Cheever

"In *A Life of Barbara Stanwyck* the accretion of detail, told simply and unemotionally, builds a living thing. *Steel-True, 1907–1940,* does detail her life. . . . But the book is also a life of Hollywood during the 1930s and America during the Depression and the way the dream factory and reality interact."

—Aljean Harmetz, *Indiewire*

"Monumental in every sense . . . sweeping and authoritative . . . written with verve and with great empathy and relish for her subject. The author is shrewd about the actress's complexity and human limitations . . . she is smart about the films and about the history and business of Hollywood in the Golden Age. Not the least of her achievement is leaving the reader eager to read volume two."

—Foster Hirsch, author of *The Dark Side of the Screen* and
A Method to Their Madness

"A fabulous and expansive examination of the life of an iconic American actress."

—*Booklist* (starred review)

"I had a great time reading about Miss Stanwyck . . . what a fabulous endeavor. I marveled at the work involved. You gave me a terrific read, and I thank you sincerely."

—Art Garfunkel

"*Steel-True* courts the definitive. . . . The voice is passive, reportorial, almost choral. Applied to Wilson's landmark recovery and synthesis of 1920s and '30s Broadway and Hollywood history, it works beautifully. . . . Wilson is a bold and determined architect, and ultimately succeeds in tracing, via some of Hollywood's most brilliant minds and celebrated careers, the evolution of both an industry and an art form during one of its most hallowed and productive periods."

—Michelle Orange, *Slate* magazine

"Wilson's book is indeed a monument of research. . . . *A Life of Barbara Stanwyck* will unquestionably remain the biography of record; beyond Wilson's excavation of so much that would otherwise have been lost, her book has a deep sensitivity to the seriousness and subtlety of Stanwyck's craft. This is the biography not of a Hollywood phenomenon but of a serious artist."

—Geoffrey O'Brien, *Bookforum*

"What you have done is extraordinary. It is an amazing book, brilliantly written, enhancing the whole life, Barbara's life, happenings around her—people of the industry, people in the theater and in politics. The way you have shown her life to include other situations, all that you interject . . . it makes her life, to me, more historically important. . . . You have brought her wonderful career magnificently to life, and as her friend, I thank you."

—Nancy Sinatra, Sr., Barbara Stanwyck's closest friend

A fulsome embrace of Victoria Wilson's
A Life of Barbara Stanwyck: Steel-True, 1907–1940

"You'll love this book. The story is full of flavor with details that create a kind of chiaroscuro, painted deftly with a soft brush, of our life at that time . . . Wilson's scholarliness on the subject of the life of a movie actress, a movie star whose career ran (she worked) for six decades, is awesome. . . . If you are a movie fan, a filmmaking fan, a fan of Hollywood history, or a filmmaker, or would be, should be, could be one, or even just a person who is completely a *TCM* addict, this book you should be reading. . . . I finished reading, much to my disappointment (wanting more), after 860 pages."

—David Columbia, *New York Social Diary*

"A large, thrilling, and sensitive biography. . . . Wilson brilliantly sets the movies Stanwyck made against a whole period of American history, from the Roaring Twenties to the fast-changing coming-of-age motion picture industry at the dawn of World War II. . . . What Wilson discovered—and shares in this book—is an artist's extraordinary transformation from homeless child to one of the most magnetic stars in the history of Hollywood."

—Michael Lindsay-Hogg, *Town & Country*

"Eight hundred sixty glittering pages. . . . It ends with a cliffhanger, creating eager anticipation for Ms. Wilson's concluding volume. . . . *A Life of Barbara Stanwyck: Steel-True, 1907–1940* is not about the actress alone. It's bigger and splashier. Stanwyck knew the most notable directors, writers, actors, studio chiefs and Broadway impresarios of her day, and Ms. Wilson is interested in all of them. . . . Regarding Ms. Wilson's follow-up, no studio's publicity department could offer a better set of coming attractions."

—Janet Maslin, *The New York Times*

"Barbara Stanwyck was one of the very great loves of my life, and Victoria Wilson's book told me so much more than Barbara herself could tell anybody. Wilson has captured her loyalty; her professionalism; her anger and her undeniable will to stay in the game of life; and, perhaps most importantly, her loneliness. Victoria has been 'steel-true' to her."

Robert Wagner

"If ever there was an actress who was ready for prime time, it is Stanwyck, and this enormously informative tribute—juicy, yet dignified, admiring yet detached—is the book to bring her to center stage."

—Molly Haskell, *New York Times Book Review*

"Your book is wonderful! The no-nonsense, hardworking woman that was Missy is so well described. The Hollywood history and the stories behind her individual movies were so interesting and illuminating. I can't wait to start watching the movies again and will do so with your book on my lap. From cover to cover, it was entertaining, informative, and just good reading. . . . This will be a treasure for our family and for many generations to come."

—Christine Presley, Barbara Stanwyck's great-niece

"I was blown away, absorbed, riveted. What great smooth style, what brilliance, what depth. This is huge and wonderful and rich. What an achievement!"

—Anne Rice

"I finished your book last night with a SIGH. I wanted volume two immediately. What a wonderful book. I didn't really know much about Barbara Stanwyck, and now I can't wait to see all her movies, having seen only a very few. Many congratulations on writing such a good, good book."

—André Bishop, Artistic Director of Lincoln Center Theater

"This biography, when completed, will be the last word on Stanwyck."

—Leonard Maltin, *Indiewire*

"Altogether magnificent and, one might argue, different in kind from everything available about others in her sisterhood. And that's true even though it stops in 1940, before so many of Stanwyck's greatest achievements in *The Lady Eve, Meet John Doe,* and *Double Indemnity.*"

—Jeff Simon, *The Buffalo News*

"Wilson's take on Stanwyck's life and era is so commanding and delightful, I would happily read as many pages again and more. A riveting history of vaudeville and early cinema, and refreshingly inclusive of women—not only the actresses, but the writers, directors, studio executives, and designers who were integral to both industries. . . . Victoria Wilson's *Steel-True* allows our imaginations to flourish."

—Jenny McPhee, *Bookslut*

A LIFE OF

BARBARA STANWYCK

STEEL-TRUE

1907–1940

VICTORIA WILSON

Simon & Schuster Paperbacks
New York   London   Toronto   Sydney   New Delhi

For Helen Wilson, Nina Bourne, and Bob Gottlieb

Simon & Schuster Paperbacks
An Imprint of Simon & Schuster, Inc.
1230 Avenue of the Americas
New York, NY 10020

First Simon & Schuster trade paperback edition November 2015

SIMON & SCHUSTER PAPERBACKS and colophon are registered
trademarks of Simon & Schuster, Inc.

For information about special discounts for bulk purchases,
please contact Simon & Schuster Special Sales at
1-866-506-1949 or business@simonandschuster.com.

The Simon & Schuster Speakers Bureau can bring authors
to your live event. For more information or to book an event,
contact the Simon & Schuster Speakers Bureau at
1-866-248-3049 or visit our website at www.simonspeakers.com.

Designed by Joy O'Meara

Manufactured in the United States of America

10 9 8 7 6 5 4 3 2 1

The Library of Congress has cataloged the hardcover edition as follows:

Wilson, Victoria, date.
    A life of Barbara Stanwyck. Volume 1: Steel-true, 1907–1940. / Victoria Wilson.—First
Simon & Schuster hardcover edition.
        pages   cm
    1. Stanwyck, Barbara, 1907–1940. 2. Motion picture actors and actresses—United States—
Biography. 3. Entertainment & Performing Arts. 4. Biography and autobiography / Women.
I. Title.
    Includes illustrations, bibliographical references, and index.
    PN2287.S67 W55 2013
    791.43'028092

ISBN 978-0-684-83168-8
ISBN 978-1-4391-9406-5 (pbk)
ISBN 978-1-4391-9998-5 (ebook)

Trusty, dusky, vivid, true,
With eyes of gold and bramble-dew,
Steel-true and blade-straight,
The great artificer
Made my mate.
—Robert Taylor on Barbara Stanwyck, quoting Robert Louis Stevenson

She was the greatest emotional actress the screen has yet known.
—Frank Capra

I only met her once. She was introduced to me by, of all people,
Gertrude Lawrence . . . Stanwyck was gracious and laconic; very
tiny; very chic; very controlled. But I met her! I saw the eyes, the lips.
Contact was made.
—Tennessee Williams

When John Ashbery was asked where he turned for consolation, he
replied, "Probably to a movie, something with Barbara Stanwyck."
—Deborah Solomon, *The New York Times Magazine,* January 14, 2007

CONTENTS

.

PART FOUR | A Larger Reach

PART ONE

Up from Under

Life beats down and crushes the soul, and art reminds you that you have one.

—Stella Adler

Ruby Stevens, 1923, age sixteen. Note the spelling of her name: "Rubye."

ONE

Family History

My grandparents on both sides were probably horse-thieves. No one ever told us anything about them. Therefore I suspect the worst. I imagine they were born and raised in Ireland. But wherever the family tree is planted, whether its branches are rotten or sound, I'll never know.

—Barbara Stanwyck, 1937

It has been written about Barbara Stanwyck, born Ruby Stevens, that she was an orphan. Her mother, Catherine Ann McPhee Stevens, Kitty, died in 1911, when Ruby was four years old. Following Kitty's death, Ruby's father, Byron E. Stevens, a mason, left his five children and set sail for the Panama Canal, determined to get away and hoping to find work at higher wages than at home.

The story goes that Ruby and her older brother, Malcolm Byron, then six years of age, were passed from Brooklyn home to home, from tenement to tenement, to whatever family would take them in for the few dollars the family would be paid for their care. Ruby would earn her keep scrubbing toilets, doing whatever she could to stay alive. Her three sisters, who were much older, two of whom were married, were busy with their own lives. One sister was in show business, a dancer who frequently traveled and was barely able to care for herself, but who looked out for Ruby and Byron and earned enough money to keep both children off the street.

In and around that story is the notion that Ruby Stevens came from nowhere, that she was a tough Brooklyn girl, educated on the streets, who never finished high school, who became a showgirl as a young teenager, hoofing her way from one club to another, from one musical revue to another, until she landed a job in a play, got her big break, and was a sensation on Broadway.

And some of this story is true.

Ruby Stevens from the streets of Brooklyn, who danced in cabarets and clubs, a Broadway star at twenty, was a daughter of the American Revolution.

The Stevens family can be traced in America as far back as 1740. Ruby's great-great-grandfather Thomas Stephens Sr. was from New England—Georgetown, Maine. Her great-great-grandmother Mary Oliver was from Marblehead, Massachusetts, and married Thomas Stephens when he was nineteen and she sixteen.

Stephens established a business in maritime shipping. During the Revolutionary War, his ships were used against the Crown in a massive seaborne insurgency that helped to win the War of Independence.

Thomas junior, Ruby Stevens's great-grandfather, one of five Stephens children, was born in Georgetown, Maine, nine years before America won its war of independence. Her grandfather Joseph, one of ten children, was born on July 4, 1809, and married three times—first to Isabelle Morgan, who died soon after; then to her sister, Arzelia Morgan, two years later (together they had four sons); and then to a young woman from Derby, Vermont, living in Lowell, Massachusetts. Joseph Stephens, at almost six feet tall, dark with dark hair and blue eyes, was fifty years old; Abby Spencer, twenty-seven. The Stephens family bought farmland on the main road of Lanesville, Massachusetts, near Gloucester, which, with a voting population of 350, was the largest town in Massachusetts. The Stephens house at 16 Langsford Street between Lanes and Folly Coves was built with the compactness of a ship's interior. Behind it was a carriage barn with an old cherry tree that dominated the Stephenses' front lawn. Off to the parlor side the branches of a mulberry tree spread out over the wooden fence that surrounded the property.

Cod and mackerel fishermen used Lanes Cove, taking their pinkies and schooners out before dawn and returning by three to unload their catches. They kept their nets and tackle and pots in wooden sheds that faced the water along the curve of the beach.

In 1862, almost a year after the shelling of Fort Sumter in Charleston Harbor, and at the age of fifty-three, Joseph Stevens (spelling now changed) traveled to Boston and enlisted in the U.S. Army, a private in Company L of the First Massachusetts Heavy Artillery Volunteers. Months later, Stevens, as a sergeant, was engaged in the Second Battle of Bull Run and was discharged in mid-October 1863, days before two of his sons, Melville and Sylvanus, enlisted.

Stevens returned to Lanesville and found work as a ship's navigator and caulker, putting jute rope between the joints of the ship's boards and sealing the joints with tar. His wife, Abby, gave birth on July 16, 1864, to their only child, Byron, Ruby Stevens's father.

On April 9, 1865, General Robert E. Lee surrendered the Confederate Army of Northern Virginia to Lieutenant General Ulysses S. Grant. The people of Lanes Cove celebrated by blowing fish horns and decorating their ships. Six days later, a horse and rider galloped into the village with the shocking news of President Lincoln's assassination. Churches were draped in mourning cloth. Mourning flags flew with black-and-white stripes and white stars on a black background. Women sewed black-and-white ribbon rosettes and wore them on the left shoulder as mourning badges.

Byron Stevens grew up in the small fishing village of Lanesville and came to love the sea. His mother was a favorite of the fishermen who passed her house on their way home from Lanes Cove and offered Abby lobsters from their daily catches. The Stevens family wasn't rich, but by 1870 Joseph Stevens had amassed a great deal of land, and they were comfortable.

The Stevenses were careful in their rearing of Byron. Joseph and Abby

Loading Stone, Lane's Cove, Lanesville, Mass.

The Stevenses lived in Lanesville. Their house on Langsford Street was a short distance from the main harbor of Lanes Cove, pictured above.

were formal people, strict Methodists. Each Sunday they traveled the mile by horse and carriage to the neighboring town of Bay View to attend the Bay View Church and often invited the minister to dinner.

By 1881, Byron had started college with the hopes of studying law. When his father died of consumption, Byron was forced to quit school and found employment a block away from his house, learning a trade in one of the great granite quarries as a mason and a stone setter. The towns of Bay View and Lanesville had grown up around the quarries.

During the winter months, the local fishermen worked at the Eames and Stimson (later Lanesville) Granite Company cutting paving blocks. Iron-rimmed wagons carried the blocks through the fields, up Langsford Street to Lanes Cove, where granite schooners and stone sloops were docked. Paving stones, as many as forty thousand, were loaded onto ships and delivered to New York, Boston, Philadelphia, and other cities being built up along the seaboard.

On a trip to Boston, Byron met a young girl from Canada who had come to visit her aunt Mary and cousin Mary Gallis.

Catherine Ann McPhee, from Sydney, Nova Scotia, was of Scotch-Irish descent. Her forebears had left Scotland in the seventeenth century like thousands of other Scottish Lowlanders who migrated to Ulster for a grant of land and a long lease. They were Presbyterian in faith and stayed in Northern Ireland until the mid-eighteenth century, when, with thousands of others who left in waves during the famine of 1740–1741, they came to the United States and Canada.

Kitty McPhee grew up in a large family that included a twin brother, Malcolm, who died when he was a boy. Their father, George, died when both children were young, and their mother, Elizabeth, remarried and had another family.

Byron Stevens and Kitty McPhee married in 1886 and stayed in Lanesville, boarding at 876 Washington Street, half a mile down the road from Byron's boyhood home. Byron was twenty-one years old; Kitty was fifteen and carrying their child. On April 23, six weeks after their marriage, Kitty gave birth to a girl, Laura Mildred. After Mildred was born, Abby Stevens frequently visited Byron and her daughter-in-law to make sure things were done properly.

During the next four years, Byron and Kitty had two more daughters: Viola Maud in 1888 and Mabel Christine in 1890.

Byron found temporary work as a mason in New York City, but once the work was completed, the family returned to Massachusetts and decided to leave Lanesville to follow his older half brothers who had moved to the town of Lynn, on Massachusetts Bay.

Chelsea, Massachusetts, eight miles south of Lynn, had originally been part of Boston until it became a separate township made up of Chelsea, Revere, and Winthrop. The city of roughly thirty thousand people boasted of being fifteen minutes by iron steamboat from Boston as well as a twenty-minute ride from the sea along Revere Beach Reservation.

Lumber warehouses, rubber works, and bone-black factories lined the industrial heart and main street of the city, Marginal Street, which ran along the Charles River. Shipyards still produced schooners there as well as pilot boats and steamboats. The Stevenses lived in the rear of 106 Essex Street, a brick two-family building, like many of the houses of the city, a few blocks north of Marginal Street.

Each summer the family traveled the thirty-five miles to Lanesville to spend a portion of July or August with Byron's mother, who stayed in the house on Langsford Street after Joseph's death. The sun and sea air of Lanesville felt different, and the three young Stevens girls were happy to be in the village where they had grown up and in their grandmother's house with its daunting parlor of horsehair-and-mahogany-backed chairs used only for special occasions and its marble-top tables displaying family albums. In the winter the parlor was heated by a small round stove at the room's center.

Byron Stevens was a strict father with a fierce temper and frequently lashed out at his daughters. The girls would have preferred he beat them than punish them with such harsh scolding. Abby expected her daughter-in-law to be equally strict with the girls. Kitty tried to follow Abby's dictum when her mother-in-law was around, but on her own, when Byron left for work and his mother wasn't in the house, Kitty, who had talent and dreams of being on the stage, would sing and put on playlets with her girls. She longed to be a dancer.

Byron and Kitty were soon able to afford a house on Spruce Street, a step up, a modest two-family structure away from the water, closer to the center of town.

Byron found work in New Hampshire, and the Stevens family closed up their house and took the Boston-and-Maine train to Dover, a small but once busy port with ships from all over the world traveling the ten miles up the narrow Cochecho River to tie up at Dover Landing. Brick schooners carried cargo from the twenty-three Dover brickyards that stood along the clay

The Stevens family, Chelsea, Massachusetts, circa 1901. Left to right: Mabel Christine, age ten; Catherine Anne ("Kitty") MacFee Stevens, thirty-three; Viola Maud, twelve; Byron, thirty-eight; Laura Mildred, fourteen. (COURTESY GENE VASLETT)

banks of the Cochecho and Bellamy Rivers to eastern cities like Philadelphia and Boston. Dover brick was being used to build row houses along Copley Square. Dover was also a mill town, supplying cotton for soldiers' uniforms and blankets during the war. Now, thirty years later, the town's mills produced dress cloth—organzas, sateens, ruffles, and calicoes. The largest of the mills, the Cochecho Plant Works, employed more than a thousand people and produced eighty million yards of cotton a year.

A year before the Stevenses' move to Dover, the town was devastated by the worst disaster in its history. In March 1896, a late winter storm came in, bringing rain so driving that the Cochecho River rose more than six feet, causing huge ice floes to break loose and destroying the town's five bridges as well as its central avenue and a row of stores. Carloads of lumber were swept off the wharves at Dover Landing; more than a thousand barrels of lime ignited a fire that raged through the buildings.

Dover as a port was devastated. The silt that had taken fifty years to be dredged out of its harbor was swept back in by the furious waters in thirty-six hours. The harbor's 140-foot schooners were destroyed.

Byron had been hired to help rebuild the town, and the Stevenses lived

Maud Stevens, age ten, circa 1898.
(COURTESY JUNE D. MERKENT)

on a street of white clapboard houses that ended a block from the Cochecho River. During the days, Millie, Maud, and Mabel, eleven, nine, and seven, played hide-and-seek in the storage trunks of a factory that was close to the house.

Soon the family returned to Chelsea, and Abby Stevens, sick with heart disease, died on February 14, 1898. She was sixty-six years old.

Kitty and Byron and the three girls traveled back to Lanesville for the funeral but were barely able to make it through the February southwester that had started the night before. Snow squalls were raging through the town; the main street was strewn with live wires and downed telephone poles. Coasters, sloops, and fishing vessels still in the water made a tangled chain.

Abby's funeral was held later that day at 16 Langsford Street with the service led by the Stevenses' pastor, the Reverend Nicklin of the Bay View Church. The snow was so deep it was impossible for a horse pulling a carriage with a casket to make its way to the Lanesville Cemetery; the burial was postponed a day. Abby was buried in pastureland that had once belonged to the Stevens family.

Kitty Stevens was free. With the death of Byron's mother, she no longer had to withstand her mother-in-law's instructions on the correct way to raise children, keep her house, comport herself and her family. Kitty had lived through twelve years of Abby's iron rule, and she could now give her daughters the things she wanted for them.

Dancing classes topped the list. She worried that Byron would disapprove, knowing that his mother would have been aghast at the idea that her granddaughters were learning to dance. But her resilience and spirit were hard to resist, as was her determination. Finally, she had her way; Byron agreed to let the girls attend dancing classes, and Kitty, an expert seamstress, sewed dresses for them of organdy, challis, and Lansdowne silks in case they should be asked to attend any balls.

The Stevens girls gathered in their kitchen to rehearse their dance lessons as Kitty whistled the songs and Byron accompanied them on the violin. Millie danced the "French dance"; Maud, the "Highland Fling"; and Mabel, "the Sailor's Hornpipe."

The Stevenses were a proud family. Byron was a man whose bearing bespoke austerity, strength, and formality, but things weren't right in the house. Byron's drinking was unsettling, and one day he left and didn't return. Kitty had three daughters to care for and no money. Her eighteen-year marriage was all she had known.

Kitty soon learned that Byron was living in Brooklyn and sent sixteen-year-old Maud, the second of the three daughters, whose authority and fierceness made her seem as if she were the oldest, to bring him back. Maud made her way to Brooklyn, found Byron living in a boardinghouse, and persuaded him to return with her to Chelsea.

Shortly after, Kitty gave birth to a son, Malcolm Byron, on February 26, 1905, the name Malcolm from Kitty's twin brother who had died as a boy in Nova Scotia. Millie, Maud, and Mabel were eighteen, sixteen, and fifteen.

The Stevens girls had grown into proper young women, each as accomplished a seamstress as her mother. Millie, the oldest, had a tender fey quality, a softness that surrounded the even features of her face. Her blue eyes were large and sharply defined. Millie was a dreamer like Kitty and, with her mother's prompting, intended to be an actress and a dancer.

Maud was practical and grounded, proud and haughty. She made sure things got done in a way that Millie never quite could. Maud was proud of her family heritage, of her handsome papa and stalwart mother, and proud as well of her own position as a clerk in a dress shop. Maud cared about the way she looked and loved to wear the finest dresses and suits with fur stoles, fur muffs, and grand hats that were adorned with veils, feathers, and flowers.

Mabel, the quietest of the three, was soft-spoken and shy but a hard worker. The family was back together, but work was hard to find in Chelsea.

Flatbush, circa 1900.

Byron realized that employment was available in Brooklyn, New York, where buildings were being constructed in brick. Within the year he and Kitty left Chelsea with Millie and her husband, Maud, Mabel, and Malcolm to make a new life across the river from Manhattan.

Flatbush in 1906 was a small town, similar to Lanesville and Chelsea, with row and clapboard houses and narrow tree-lined streets. Thirty years before, large farms ran along the avenues to Coney Island.

With the opening of the Brooklyn, Flatbush, and Coney Island Railroad in 1878, the area began to be developed. Sixty-five acres of land that had been a potato farm of the Vanderveers was transformed into a grid of streets. By 1906, when the Stevenses moved to Brooklyn, Flatbush was becoming a fashionable section that included Vanderveer Park, Ditmas Park, Fiske Terrace, Manhattan Terrace, and Slocum Park. Landowners had resisted dividing their fields into city lots, and the lush green lanes and country roads of Flatbush turned into wide avenues and boulevards, but once it became part of the City of Brooklyn, new tax rates made it impossible for farmers to hold on to the land.

Within thirty years Flatbush was transformed from a small village into a busy, thriving town.

The Stevenses moved to 312 Classon Avenue between DeKalb and Lafayette Avenues. Millie, Maud, and Mabel, twenty, eighteen, and sixteen,

The Stevens girls, now young women, Brooklyn, New York, 1907. Millie Stevens, age twenty-one (top left), Maud Stevens Merkent, age nineteen (top right), Mabel Stevens, age seventeen (left). (ALL COURTESY GENE VASLETT)

and Millie's husband were living with their mother and father and year-old brother. Classon Avenue was a narrow, quiet, dark cobblestoned street of three-story brownstones two blocks south of Myrtle, with its grocery shops and vegetable stores crowded together.

Malcolm was two years old when Byron and Kitty had another child—a girl, who was born on July 16, 1907, the same birth date as her father, who had been born in 1864.

Maud and Mabel were employed as sales clerks at the Abraham & Straus dry goods store on Fulton, Hoyt, and Livingston Streets. Maud had be-friended one of the other clerks there, a woman her age called Ruby Merkent Joppeck, and Maud wanted her mother to name the baby girl after her friend Ruby. Kitty and Byron liked the name and called their fifth child Ruby Catherine Stevens.

Millie, Maud, and Mabel, now young women, were embarking on their own lives.

In December 1907, Maud Stevens and Albert Merkent were married and moved to a house at 1330 Rogers Avenue. The Merkent family owned a well-established butcher shop, Merkent's Meat Market, but Albert took a job as a chauffeur and was considered an excellent driver.

Millie had been married for three years and was struggling as an actress. She had always been thought of as the beauty of the family, with a softness and light that drew people to her. Her mouth was full, and the set of it with its slight smile was both an invitation and a warning of a determined spirit. The fullness of her face and violet eyes were similar to those of her mother, her proud stance that of her father.

In October 1907, Millie found work in a show and was on the road in the Midwest, appearing in a political comedy called *A Contented Woman* by the successful Broadway playwright Charles Hoyt. Millie Stevens was being singled out in reviews and was soon on tour in a production of *The Road to Sympathy* and traveling with the show as far as Columbus, Ohio.

In April 1910, Maud, age twenty-two, gave birth to a boy, Albert Mortimer Merkent. While Maud was being a new mother, Kitty, forty-one, and Byron, forty-six, were rearing two young children. Malcolm Byron was five years old and had just started kindergarten at P.S. 45; Ruby was three. Work was steady, but times were not easy: Byron drank, and money was scarce. And in 1911, Kitty became pregnant with her sixth child.

Toward the end of July, the intense summer heat had settled in the city. Kitty was late into her pregnancy. She and Ruby and Byron were on a trolley when a drunk fell and kicked Kitty in the stomach. She lost her footing and was thrown from the car. Byron and Ruby watched as their mother fell to the street and people rushed to her side. A mounted policeman moved through the crowd and helped Kitty to her feet, and she and the children were brought home.

Kitty had started to hemorrhage. Five-year-old Malcolm saw blood everywhere as he waited for what seemed a long time before Mabel came to help. The doctor was called. Kitty had gone into labor. During the day and

Ruby Stevens, age four, with her brother, Malcolm
Byron, age five or six, circa 1911.
(MARC WANAMAKER/BISON ARCHIVES)

throughout the night she continued to lose blood and was overtaken by fever
and chills. Byron, Millie, Maud, and Mabel were with her. Blood poisoning
set in from an incomplete miscarriage. She fought to stay alive, but by the
following evening septicemia had overtaken her body. Kitty was dead at age
forty and was buried two days later in Green-Wood Cemetery.

Byron and Kitty had been married for twenty-five years, had raised a family together first in the village of his childhood and then made a new life in a
small city. They had raised three girls and made a fresh start in a strange new
place with a new family. Without his wife, Byron was lost, undone.

He couldn't take care of his young son or daughter. Six-year-old Malcolm
didn't return to school in September. Byron Stevens moved out of the apartment. What happened next to Byron, Malcolm, and Ruby is unclear; there
are variations to the story.

In one version, Malcolm, then six, and Ruby, four, were placed in orphanages and were moved to a series of institutions. In another, Millie took Ruby,
tightly holding her hand and carrying a box that contained what bare essen-
tials Ruby owned, to a tenement flat and, unable to care for her sister, left her

with a family. Malcolm and Ruby were taken in by friends of the Stevenses. In another version, the children were taken in by a series of strangers, families who were paid to care for the children as they were moved from house to house. And in yet another version, Malcolm went to live with one sister, Mabel, and her husband of two years, Giles Vaslett, an accountant from Pawtucket, Rhode Island, and Ruby went to live with Maud and her husband, Bert Merkent, and their year-old son, Al.

Byron Stevens took a room in a run-down hotel, similar to the one he was living in when he had left Kitty years before. He continued to work through the early fall and into the winter until he was laid off. He wept for the loss of his wife, continued to drink, and found himself in one brawl after another.

During Christmas 1911, six-year-old Malcolm Stevens was brought to his father's room. The boy sat on the edge of the steel bed, with father and son having little to say to each other. Malcolm was frightened and became even more so when his father left the room to go down the hall. The room was dark. One corner housed a pole for clothes with nothing on it but a few hangers. A chest of drawers had cigarette burns on it.

The boy sensed his father was going to go away, but he didn't know what to do or say to stop him.

Byron Stevens left Brooklyn after the New Year. There were extra dollars to be made on a massive U.S. government project south of Costa Rica with food, living expenses, and medical services being paid for and written off to national defense. U.S. military engineers had taken over from the French government the massive construction of a waterway that was to be a new route joining the Atlantic and Pacific Oceans by way of the Isthmus of Panama.

Stevens found work on a freighter going south. He was headed for Panama, a long way from Lanesville, Massachusetts, and a longer way from the wife who had died and the children he was leaving behind.

TWO

The Perils

1911–1915

My father loved my mother madly and when she died, he went gypsy. I was raised by strangers, farmed out. There were no rules or regulations. Whoever would take me for five dollars a week, that's where I was. So I really didn't have any family.

—Ruby Stevens

Ruby, at four years old, and her brother, Malcolm Byron, were on their own. They had a family of grown-up sisters who loved them but couldn't care for them, who lived in houses that were warm with their own families. For Ruby and Byron it was a world of loneliness. They were placed with different families. Ruby often slept at the houses of friends of Maud's and Millie's and would be given a cot in the dining room or parlor. During the day, she ate meals with her sister Maud and Bert Merkent. Millie paid to keep Ruby with families in the neighborhood, thinking it would be good for her.

Ten or twelve families took Malcolm and Ruby in, perhaps more. "There was never a family that had room for the two of us, Byron and me," said Ruby. "That was the tragedy of it." The names of the families became a blur, but the feelings remained sharp and clear: Ruby didn't belong to anyone.

She came first only to Byron. There was no mother or father to love or comfort her; no one bothered about her clothes. Byron was everything to Ruby, and she, everything to him. He was a little boy, but to Ruby, Byron was a "little man" and she idolized him.

Ruby (top row, second from left) and Malcolm Byron Stevens (middle row, far left), Brooklyn, New York, circa 1912. (COURTESY NANCY BERNARD)

• • •

Ruby learned to live on the streets and to make the best of it. "We never played games," she said. "I never cared for games anyway. The only game I can remember playing," she said, "is the game of fighting." She learned at a young age that her survival was based "on self-preservation . . . When you live like that you always take care of yourself first, because there's no one else to do it."

Malcolm Byron was a quiet boy, never loud or outspoken in the way Ruby was. "He was always a loner," she said. Malcolm never teased his little sister and was protective of her.

Ruby was the "leader of any gang" she and Malcolm played with. "Despite her quietness," said Malcolm, "the other children would turn to Ruby when they were hurt, or bullied. She never failed them."

The Dutch Reformed Church was a short walk from Rogers Avenue. Ruby found a world at the church deep within herself, "a world of . . . beauty and music and laughter and dancing," without scorn or mistrust.

Ruby thought the church was beautiful and on Sundays went there by herself. Its clock and steeple stood over the old maple and oak trees on the avenue. On either side of the church along Flatbush Avenue were large white gabled houses that had been built during the previous century.

Ruby was enrolled in P.S. 152 and "hated school, hated arithmetic." The teachers called her a "dunce" and wondered what was wrong with her. Literature was the first thing she could do well and the only thing she paid attention to. One teacher was gentle and understanding and warned her student who "hated so many things so earnestly" and lived in a fantasy world, "Life will deal you an awful blow, Ruby, unless you come out of the clouds." Ruby acted as if she weren't listening, but she heard her teacher's words.

Ruby watched boys playing catch on the street. They tolerated her and allowed her to play football with them. Their games seemed more exciting than the girls'. It was the girls who resented Ruby's easy companionship with the boys. A ring of girls one day closed in around her. "She's an orphan," one girl said, making it sound as if it were the worst thing anyone could be. "They were branding me an outcast," said Ruby. She kept her eyes level with theirs and stared them down. With the exception of the football team, Ruby "hated everything about school. I hated the teachers, the other kids and the enforced obedience." She signed her own report cards and envied the other children who had parents to sign theirs.

Ruby's three sisters did the best they could to care for her, but they could never be mother or father to her or Malcolm. Millie, Maud, and Mabel had known an upbringing that was formal, where tradition and propriety were important. The girls had known the love, protection, and care of a mother whose magnetic, determined spirit and raucous laugh were their sources of hope and strength; they had grown up with a sometimes remote father who would drink and get angry but whose sense of fun and love saw them through their years together. Though they struggled, the Stevenses had had each other. Millie, Maud, and Mabel carried that inside them, and they tried the best they could to pass that on to Ruby and Malcolm.

He did his best to look out for Ruby, to take care of her and make sure she was safe. When Malcolm was to be moved to another family, Ruby tried to lock him up so they couldn't take him away. She screamed and cried and promised she would be easy to look after if they would only take her too. "I promised everything," she said, "if they would only keep us together. I couldn't believe they were taking him, and I was being left behind. Afterwards all sorrow died away." Ruby felt only "a terrible fighting anger." If she needed to get in touch with her brother during the times they lived apart, a boy their age would act as the go-between and somehow get a message to Malcolm.

Ruby associated the women around her, she later said, with working at washtubs, at kitchen sinks, hanging clothes outside streaked, dirt-covered tenement windows. She remembered women whose backs were bent from exhaustion, whose stomachs were swollen from giving birth too many times, who were in an endless battle against poverty.

"I used to dream," said Ruby, "that somebody got me all mixed up, that I belonged to nobility. That my parents had been rich, and one day they would come and take me out of all this muck and mire."

It hurt Maud when, years later, Ruby described herself as a child who was "shifted from pillar to post." Maud and Ruby, separated in age by nineteen years and worlds of experience, argued about what those early years had been like for Ruby. Maud described how she had raised her baby sister; Ruby understood that Maud didn't want to hear the truth.

Millie didn't have a home, much less a place where Ruby could live with her, but she took her to work with her as much as possible when Millie wasn't on the road and had work as a showgirl.

Millie was the most beautiful woman Ruby had ever seen, with all the talent and emotion an actress should have. She was finding work in shows that played in New York and traveled the northeastern and midwestern circuits, opening for a few days in one city and moving on to the next, from Syracuse and Columbus to Toledo and Pittsburgh and back again. Her work continued to be noticed and get strong mention in local reviews in town after town.

When Millie spoke to Ruby of their mother, her "eyes were soft and dreamy." She described Kitty as "beautiful, with long, raven-black hair and violet eyes," and a voice Shakespeare would have called "soft, gentle and low." And, said Millie, "she had a wonderful lilting laugh." She could still hear her mother's laugh.

In 1913, when Ruby was six years old, the movie serial was sweeping the country. It started as a circulation battle among newspapers—the *Chicago Tribune* and six other Chicago papers—originally a promotional gimmick thought up by *McClure's Magazine* to coincide with its publication in *The Ladies World* of a group of stories called What Happened to Mary. The idea was to publish a story and release a screen version of it as a two-reeler for the nickelodeons. Each story was self-contained but was connected by the same set of characters.

These serials were so successful that in 1914 Pathé Frères made a serial of

Pearl White, star of Pathé's serial, *The Perils of Pauline,* renowned for her hair-raising adventures and for doing her daring stunts herself. (PHOTO-FEST)

its own—*The Perils of Pauline*—at Pathé's newly built studios in Jersey City at One Congress Street. The story was printed simultaneously in the Hearst papers.

The Perils of Pauline featured a young actress called Pearl White, a Missouri farm girl—part Italian (her father), part Irish (her mother)—who had joined the circus, tumbling and riding bareback, getting her nerve and her training. Pearl joined a touring stock company at five years old, appearing as Little Eva in *Uncle Tom's Cabin.* Three years later she was in New York acting with the Powers Film Company. By 1914 she had starred in more than 120 one-reelers.

Occasionally, Millie Stevens would take Ruby to see Pearl White "in her perils." "There wasn't much money for anything," Ruby recalled. There were times when, in order to get a hot meal, Ruby would go into a diner, order hot water, and add ketchup to it. Ruby "tended children, washed dishes, ran errands," she said, anything to earn enough money to go to the serials.

The heroine of the *Perils* was a young modern woman of 1914. Pauline's parents, like Ruby's, were dead. Pauline is alone in the world and lives in a grand mansion with servants who attend to her needs and drive her about in her town cars and roadsters. Pauline is not stuffy, nor does she put on airs. She is simple, trusting, free-spirited, bursting with the possibilities of life, and hell-bent on experiencing its adventures. A devoted suitor asks for her hand in marriage, but Pauline laughs off the proposal. Marriage and its obligations are of no interest to her. Pauline intends to "realize life's greatest thrills" and then describe them in a book that she will write herself, a romance of adventures.

Pauline's new trustee is determined to get her money and plots to lure her to certain death, from which she manages to free herself. She is drawn into outrageous exploits, blissfully, innocently. In each episode, a surefire inescapable trap is set for her. And while Pauline's reliable fiancé seems to be her rescuer, it is Pauline who withstands all forms of torture, somehow figuring out an escape from the most treacherous circumstances, defying the odds like an agile escape artist, avoiding death from gunshot, drowning, or falling from great heights. Whether she is kidnapped on horseback, pursued by Indians, tossed down the side of a mountain, ducking boulders, or bound and gagged and left in a cave, Pauline—quick, undaunted—always prevails. Or does she?

Tune in to the next episode . . .

The Perils of Pauline became a huge sensation. Even Madame Sarah Bernhardt requested an audience with the young Pearl White, telling her how she had longed to meet her, how the screen adventuress was worshipped by the soldiers back in France fighting in the war against Germany.

Pearl White supported women's suffrage. By 1916 eleven states, mostly in the West, had ratified the right of women to vote. A referendum for suffrage had been defeated in New York, Pennsylvania, Massachusetts, and New Jersey. White was performing a publicity stunt to show how "fearless, peerless" she really was. The eighteen-year-old "lady daredevil of the fillums" stood on a scaffolding twenty-two stories in the air, painting her initials in four-foot letters on the brick wall of the Gregory Building on Seventh Avenue. Her manager was sure she would fall and be killed. But Pearl painted on. Draped over her shoulders was a scarf that said in large red letters, "VOTES FOR WOMEN."

It was often mentioned in newspaper accounts that Pearl White, along with Paul Panzer (Pauline's nefarious guardian), refused the help of a double to perform the hair-raising escapes that mesmerized audiences: jumping off cliffs, bridges, railroad trains, yachts; being chased by wild animals; being bound and gagged and left in dangerous positions; going over embankments locked in a car. Pearl had a fondness for reckless living; the more danger involved, the more pleasure it gave her.

She was called a modern Joan of Arc, the empress of the Pathé serials, an actress without temperament who believed that "working ten hours a day took the edge off of artistic emotion." The press described her as being "frank" and "having common sense to an unusual degree," someone who "disliked flattery" and thought of her acting "more as work than as art." She understood that "pantomime alone" was the way to the camera and the audience, that even if you had an effective voice, you couldn't use it, and that in front of the camera the emotion was located in the play of the eyes, especially in close-ups.

Pearl White was a girl from the West who loved to do wild, daring things. She was a goddess whose sense of freedom appealed to Ruby Stevens. After watching Pearl in one picture be thrown down a deep well with a cobra lying at the bottom, Ruby walked through Prospect Park hoping to find a similar well with a cobra coiled at the bottom lying in wait.

During the summer of 1915, when Ruby was eight years old, Millie left to go on the road with a vaudeville show described as "high class vaudeville at low prices" and took her youngest sister with her. They traveled by train and lived in dressing rooms and railroad hotels in town after town, the show continuing in the fall and winter months in cities like Buffalo, Rochester, Pittsburgh, Indianapolis, and beyond.

Ruby stood in the wings watching each performance. She had a place to be, and people let her be there. She "loved the music and the lights. Everyone looked so happy out there dancing and singing for the audience," she said. She became the heroine of her own plays.

When the show played the Lyric Theatre, *The Indianapolis News* called Millie Stevens "the hit of the bill." The *Pittsburgh Leader* described her as "an expressive comedienne" whose portrayal was "so vital in spirit that her characterization compels admiration by the very human qualities through which she clothes it . . . the equal of Miss Stevens has not appeared in popular priced vaudeville in a great while."

Ruby watched as the performers came offstage, removed their spangles and makeup, and turned into young women who worked hard and had problems and concerns like anybody else.

"I couldn't have cared less about the birds and the bees in the park," she said. "All I wanted to do was watch the actors and talk to the stagehands."

The applause thrilled her. Ruby experienced an ecstasy just being in the theaters and made up her mind that she was going to be "a great dancer."

THREE

Starting Life Anew

1916–1923

The Reverend William Chamberlain "was the only person outside of my family whom I loved," said Ruby, who had fallen under the spell of the pastor at the Protestant Dutch Reformed Church.

The following year, the Reverend J. Frederic Berg became the pastor and spoke to the congregation about public spirit and ways to cultivate it. Ruby came to admire Reverend Berg as much as she had Reverend Chamberlain. "During one Sunday sermon, Reverend Berg asked us if we knew what love was," said Ruby. "I thought he was going to expose my feelings for him to everyone." The pastor talked about different kinds of love, about forgiveness, about the power of love and how it could save you and make you strong. "The hate was drained out of me," said Ruby. "It was vague and strange but something happened in my heart."

Ruby was inspired by the work of the church and wanted to become a missionary, to walk the world finding lost souls and save them from their unhappiness. On a spring day early in June 1916, Ruby was baptized in the sanctuary of the Protestant Dutch Reformed Church. Without any family members present, Ruby and Reverend Berg stood below the pulpit with the baptismal font between them. Ruby promised to be brought up a Christian, to avail herself of the church, and to renounce evil. Afterward, he gave her the testament, in which he had written on the flyleaf, "In all thy ways acknowledge him." Many years later, Ruby still had the little testament.

Mabel and Harold Cohen, good friends of the Merkents' who lived two blocks north of their home at 2586 Bedford and agreed to let Ruby live with them. The Cohens were poor, but their house was clean, and they knew how to prettify poverty.

They had meals together as a family, eating food that was plain but good. Mrs. Cohen thought children should have something hot in their stomachs before school and served oatmeal for breakfast. For dinner, she stewed chicken with cooked carrots and gave them soft little balls that tasted like dumplings. Ruby noticed that Mr. Cohen kissed his four children and wife when he came home each night.

He taught Ruby how to use a knife and fork. At first she was ashamed, but no one laughed, and Mr. Cohen, whose voice was soft and melodious, was patient with her. "They tried to teach me manners. They tried to stop me from swearing."

The Cohens were the first people ever to brush Ruby's hair or care how she looked. She learned to play jacks and marbles and to jump rope. "They were the first to give me affection," she said later.

Ruby marked off the days of the calendar until Millie came to see her.

Whatever unhappiness Ruby may have suffered, it was compensated for when Millie and her fiancé, Gene Salzer, called for her and took her to the city for weekends.

Gene Salzer conducted the orchestra in the theater in which Millie was acting, and Millie and Gene looked forward to being married and making a home that would include Ruby. After performance Gene took Ruby to get something to eat; "if they didn't have cream puffs," said Ruby, "we would get up and walk out." Millie would take Ruby to a vaudeville show, and Ruby would return to the Cohens and act out what she'd seen on the stage, dancing and singing and imitating the comics.

There was talk of war. The Germans had sunk three American ships, resulting in the death of fifteen men.

President Wilson pronounced, "The world must be made safe for democracy," and demanded a declaration of war with Germany. A draft was created, the largest since the Civil War, that called for ten million unmarried men between the ages of twenty-one and thirty-one to sign up.

Ray Merkent, Bert's brother and the youngest of the six Merkents, volunteered for service, enlisting in the navy with its fleet of modern battleships second in the world only to England. War bond rallies were organized. Factories were on call twenty-four hours a day to produce artillery, tanks, and ammunition. The Brooklyn Navy Yard, the largest government shipbuilder in the country, had two years before produced the battleships *Arizona* and *New Mexico* and was now building the battleship *Tennessee*.

The country was calling on its citizens to go a day without wheat, meat, fat, and sugar and to use Sundays as a day to ration gas. Even the president went to church on Sunday in a horse-drawn carriage rather than in a car. Broadway theaters were closed in an effort to save coal. In Malcolm's and Ruby's schools—in all public schools—teachers had to take an oath of allegiance, solemnly swearing to support the Constitution of the United States of America and the Constitution of the State of New York, an oath that had to be certified by the schools' principals.

By November 1918, General Pershing's troops had triumphed in France; Germany and Austria-Hungary surrendered. More than a hundred thousand American men lost their lives, as had ten million European soldiers. The armistice was signed; the war was over. Celebrations were organized for returning war heroes, among them a parade down Fifth Avenue for General John Joseph Pershing and his army.

Mrs. Cohen was going to have a baby, and Ruby knew there would no longer be room in the house for her. She understood that these were her circumstances, and she was determined to change them rather than be their victim.

She went to live with Maud and Bert and their son, Al. Malcolm was living with Mabel, her husband, Giles Vaslett, an accountant, and their new baby, Eugene, on Eastern Parkway with Giles's parents, Esther and Fayette Vaslett. Giles Vaslett was a difficult man and a heavy drinker, and Malcolm spent hours walking the Brooklyn docks, watching the tramp steamers and cargo ships from Latin America and elsewhere enter the harbor and leave, heading for the upper New York Bay and out to sea. He dreamed of the day when he himself would set out to sea, heading south. He would somehow work his way to Panama, where he would find his father and bring him back to Brooklyn, and he and Ruby would be together again as a family. At fourteen, Malcolm, big and blond and resembling his father, looked more like a man than a boy.

Millie Stevens found work in the chorus of a John Cort production called *Glorianna* and in October 1918 opened at the Liberty Theatre on Forty-Second Street, west of Broadway.

At thirty-two years old she was one of eighteen dancers of "Dolores' Dancing Class of Debutantes and Maids," a chorus described in the opening paragraphs of the *New York Times* review as "well accounted for" and "indispensable to the proceedings." She was living at the Palace Hotel, and Ruby occasionally stayed there with her and accompanied her big sister to "haunt the wings" of the Liberty Theatre.

Also in *Glorianna* was Buck Mack, part of the dance team Miller and

Mack. Mack was newly returned from the war and was living at the Princeton Hotel, five doors down the street from the Palace. On his days off, he would "mosey up" to see Millie and Ruby.

"Millie was a swell girl," said Mack. "A pretty blonde doll herself and crazy about her kid sister." Mack encouraged Ruby to dance and often took her out to a delicatessen on Broadway. Ruby began to call him Uncle Buck. "We had a regular routine," she said. "Uncle Buck would ask me what I wanted and I'd always answer, 'A turkey leg.' 'Turkey leg, huh?' as if it were a surprise. Then, he'd say, 'Well, Joe, give the little lady the finest you got.' "

In 1919, Malcolm and Ruby were living with Maud, Bert, and Al on Bedford Avenue. Malcolm at fourteen graduated from eighth grade at P.S. 152 and began working at Merkent's Meat Market delivering meat, still haunting the docks and dreaming of hiring out on a boat. In his nine years of education, he had attended nine different schools and lived in fourteen different homes, some belonging to family members, others to strangers.

Ruby was twelve and in the sixth grade. She lived near the old Vitagraph studios and often went there to wait for her favorite movie idols to emerge. One day she saw two beautiful little blond girls at the entrance of the studio, looking like angels, each wearing a coat and hat made of white rabbit fur. They were Dolores and Helene Costello waiting for their father, Maurice. Ruby would have given anything for the girls' clothes.

Soon after Malcolm's graduation, he told Ruby he was leaving Brooklyn on a ship going to South America. Ruby had always counted on her brother being there for her. They had talked many times about running away together, and this was their chance. When Malcolm told her that everything would be all right, she believed him. She pleaded with Malcolm to take her with him; they could take care of each other. Malcolm knew it wouldn't work and said no. Ruby didn't belong to anyone except Malcolm. As a little girl, she felt safe with her brother and wanted to hide behind him. Ruby believed that had she been a boy, he would have taken her with him. She acted as if nothing could hurt her but cried long after he left.

Malcolm told his older sister nothing of his plan. One day, Maud expected her brother home early for dinner and didn't see him for the next year and a half.

The Merkents soon moved again to a quiet pristine street away from the noise and crowds of Flatbush and Bedford Avenues. Vanderveer Place was a street of well-tended two-story brick row houses. Mabel, Giles, and their three-year-old son, Gene, moved in with the Merkents.

Ruby slept in Al's bedroom; her cousin slept on the couch in the living room. Behind the Merkents' house was a large tomato farm where Gene and Al would go to play baseball, steal tomatoes, and try to outsmart the farmer, who shot poachers with a pepper gun.

Ruby entertained her nephew Gene with her favorite record, "The Japanese Sandman" ("Here's a Japanese sandman/Sneakin' on with the dew/Just an old secondhand man/He'll buy your old day from you"), playing the song over and over on the phonograph while Gene built model planes of the Great War. Ruby was packing her trunks to join Millie in Chicago for the summer. The song of the sandman reassured her ("He will take every sorrow of the day that is through/And he'll give you tomorrow just to start a life anew").

Ray Merkent, the Merkent with the most spirit and ambition, was back from the war and was an active member of the Masonic Temple as well as most of the clubs in Brooklyn. Ray, who spent a good deal of time at his brother Bert's house, was seven years older than Ruby and liked her, maybe too much. Through his intervention, Ruby was given a part in a dance recital to be held at the Masonic Temple in Brooklyn.

The night of the performance—the first time Ruby danced in public—her gold-tasseled short skirt could have been ruined by heavy rains had she not been carried to the car. Her debut was a big occasion, and the whole family was there to see it: Mabel and her son, Gene, Maud, Bert, and Albert.

Ruby began appearing in pageants and amateur theatricals that were put on in neighborhood movie houses. She became part of an amateur dramatic group that rehearsed in Maud's living room and was drawn to one young man, Frank Chauffeur, who lived in Flatbush, was Ruby's age, and was equally taken with her.

In one of the productions at the Rialto Theatre on Flatbush Avenue, Ruby was given a line to speak: "Be careful with that knife."

The Merkents bought a larger house at Avenue L and Thirty-Sixth Street, a couple miles from Vanderveer Place. The house was newly built and more spacious than anything the Merkents had lived in before, with a porch, living room, dining room, kitchen, and three bedrooms upstairs. The house had a finished basement with a bathroom and was heated by a coal furnace, which Bert Merkent stoked each night.

Ruby's school, P.S. 152, was six blocks from the Merkents' house. From her classroom she could see the tops of the trees of Prospect Ridge and beyond it a small patch of ocean. She could see the spire of the Dutch Reformed Church. At school Ruby suffered through a hundred or so crushes, though the boys never paid any attention to her. She had crooked teeth and straight hair. "And," she said, "not one of the hundred knew I was around."

Ruby was able to get a job at the five-and-dime working in the novelty department. When the counter got busy with customers and the pressure was on, she had trouble making change. The other girls working alongside her would vanish, and Ruby became even more flustered as customers called to her to take their money.

Gene Vaslett loved his aunt Ruby and thought her special. To him, Ruby at the age of thirteen was a woman of the world. Gene would look over his aunt's shoulder as she wrote and try to identify the letters and words he saw on the page, with Ruby correcting him when he got them wrong. On Sunday mornings Gene and Ruby sat on the floor and read the comics together, Ruby showing her nephew the letters of the alphabet.

Malcolm sent Ruby postcards of places he had visited and dreamed about, which she carried in her schoolbooks to show her classmates until she put them away in a box, looking at the photographs of faraway places only at night.

When Ruby graduated, her class at P.S. 152 put on a pageant to celebrate its commencement, with Ruby as the month of September.

She had decided that she was not going to go to Erasmus Hall High School. She was going to get a full-time job.

FOUR

Heart and Nerve and Sinew

1921–1926

In 1921, Ruby Stevens was fourteen but looked older, with a deep voice that sounded from childhood as if she had perpetual laryngitis.

Now that she'd finished school, she answered a telephone company ad—telling the interviewer she was sixteen—and was hired as a switchboard operator at 15 Dey Street. She made it clear to the other operators that she was working there temporarily; she was going to be a dancer.

Ruby "talked back to a caller" and "got their wires so jammed up," she said that she was transferred to the billing department as a clerk, packing cards and getting paid $13 a week, a lot of money to her. After the switchboard job Ruby hated hearing a telephone and would answer it within the first or second ring. When she learned that secretaries in the telephone company earned $25 a week, Ruby enrolled in a night school to study shorthand and typing.

As a file clerk she sat all day long, "fiddling with little pieces of paper, and folding envelopes," matching subscribers' numbers with the calls made—"a job that could be done by an idiot," she said. "I couldn't stand the idea of sitting so long." After many months "of this [nothingness]," she took "the pieces of paper and all the blasted envelopes and threw them into the air, which made a great paper shower." The superintendent came rushing over and told Ruby to "sort them into order." Ruby would have none of it and walked out of the telephone company. "It got me nowhere, that loss of temper," she said.

Frankie Chauffeur would come to Maud and Bert Merkent's house to take Ruby to dances at Erasmus Hall High School or to parties in the two-family houses around Flatbush. Sometimes they would go to the pictures and hold hands as they watched Rudolph Valentino or Ramon Novarro or

Wallace Reid and Gloria Swanson. When Frank mentioned marriage, Ruby backed away from the idea of it. She didn't see herself as a wife or mother. She was intent on being a dancer or an acrobat.

Bert Merkent and his brother Ray went to baseball games together at Ebbets Field, and some of the Brooklyn Robins often stopped by the house. Everyone seemed to like Ray, the youngest of the six Merkents, except Ruby. Ray was a man of nineteen; Ruby a girl of fourteen. She was uncomfortable around him and made sure not to be at the house when he was there. One day Ray showed up when Ruby was home alone and began to force himself on her and wouldn't stop. Ruby was horrified and shaken and told Maud what had happened. "Oh, well, dear," said Maud, "I think you're making too much of it . . . You imagined a lot of it."

"I hate him," said Ruby, furious that Maud didn't believe her story. "You know that son of a bitch raped me. You know he did." She became all the more wary and determined to get out and live on her own.

Ruby wasn't any beauty. She "didn't have a great figure," she said, but she was intent on finding a place for herself as a dancer in the theater.

Isadora Duncan, the interpretive dancer, was performing at the Century Opera House, Carnegie Hall, and the Brooklyn Academy of Music. Ruby was fascinated by her free dancing. Isadora danced with her pupils without corsets or high-heeled shoes, barefoot and bare legged. Duncan's free dancing was revolutionary, inspirational; "a return to simplicity, beauty and truth." Ruby was equally enchanted by the great ballerina Anna Pavlova but knew she would never have enough money for ballet training. She needed a job to pay for her food and board at Maud's and got a job as a package wrapper at Abraham & Straus, where Mabel and Maud had worked a decade before. Next she worked at the Vogue Pattern Company on Fifth Avenue in New York City. She needed a job so badly that she lied and told the interviewer that she knew how to sew and cut patterns. She was hired at $18 a week.

Each morning Ruby left Maud and Bert's house on Avenue L, boarded a trolley car to Flatbush Avenue, and took the subway into Manhattan.

At her job with Vogue patterns, Ruby discovered reading. She read "nothing good," but she read "books on all subjects," she said, "lurid stuff about ladies who smelled sweet and looked like flowers and were betrayed, about gardens and ballrooms and moonlight trysts and murders." She began to be aware of herself in a new way, how she looked, the clothes she wore. "I bought awful things at first, pink shirtwaists, artificial flowers, tripe."

Soon she was reading Conrad, Hardy, Hugh Walpole, Edith Wharton,

John Galsworthy, and Kipling, including *Rewards and Fairies,* in which Ruby came across what became one of her favorite poems. "If," published in 1910, was a guidepost for her. To "hold on when there is nothing in you/Except the Will which says to them: 'Hold on.' "

It was a way of being that Ruby understood, that seemed true for her. Kipling's poem offered a standard of courage, balance, and strength that she embraced. She had lived with that kind of determination, with the desire to fight wholeheartedly. Kipling's words "Meet with Triumph and Disaster/And treat those two impostors just the same" summed up for her the belief that nothing was permanent, that nothing could be taken for granted.

Reading Hugh Walpole's novel *Fortitude,* published in the United States in 1913, Ruby recognized the truth of the book's opening lines: " 'Tisn't life that matters! 'Tis the courage you bring to it." Walpole's words inspired and comforted her and gave her strength.

She read Sarah Bernhardt's *Memories of My Life,* in which the actress described "the debut of [her] artistic life," when she attended the theater and watched as the curtain went up and the stage was revealed, "as though the curtain of [Bernhardt's] future life were being raised." Ruby read of the moment when Bernhardt at age fifteen, in order to be admitted to the conservatoire, recites the unlikely choice of the La Fontaine fable "Les deux pigeons."

She read of the change that began to take place in the young French actress, whose "soul remained childlike" but whose "mind discerned life more distinctly." And about how, years later, the Divine Sarah, with a hostile French and English press relentlessly at her, was consoled by a friend who said to her, "You are original without trying to be so . . . [Y]ou have a natural harp in your throat . . . [Y]ou never accept any compromise, you will not lend yourself to any hypocrisy, and all that is a crime of high treason against society."

Ruby was reading a book a day and "felt a sense of doors opening."

She was made a hostess at the Vogue Pattern Center, a showplace for *Vogue* magazine, owned by Mr. Condé Nast, and met a young salesman in the advertising department.

Edwin Kennedy was in his early twenties and was working his way up through the company. He thought Ruby was "a knockout, sultry but wary." He knew that Ruby was a girl who didn't have love affairs, and he said "it was quite a feather in my cap" when she agreed to go out with him.

Their first date was at the Biltmore hotel, where, because of Prohibition, "tea dances" were held from five in the afternoon to seven in the evening with actual tea as refreshments. Ruby loved to dance, and she'd never been to the Biltmore, with its Palm Court, Italian garden, ice-skating rink, and sliding roof where diners could eat under the stars.

Ruby and Ed began to see each other often. After their evenings together, he accompanied her back to Avenue L. Sometimes there were extravagant evenings that ended with his bringing Ruby back to Flatbush by taxi.

Ed was falling in love with Ruby. She was fond of him and felt comfortable enough to confide her plans of becoming a dancer. He told her about how he was going to be a magazine publisher like Mr. Nast.

Women went to the Vogue center to buy patterns and to learn how to put them together. Ruby one day gave a woman incorrect instructions. The customer returned and complained to the manager, who asked Ruby how to put the pattern together. "Of course I was stumped," she said. "And then there were too many complaints from people who put paper patterns on cloth and expected a sleeve and got a belt."

Ruby was fired and began to study acrobatics with a young man who was willing to instruct her for $2 a week.

One night Ed took Ruby to a large party. "I loved to show her off," he said. "She was so beautiful." At the party was an executive of a music publishing company. At the end of the evening Ed brought Ruby back to Flatbush, but he kept thinking about the party and how the music executive might know someone who would be able to help her. "Ruby had a driving ambition," said Kennedy. "And I was so in love that above all things I wanted to help her." It was after one in the morning when Ed returned to New York and went back to the party. The music executive promised to help Ruby get a job.

The Jerome Remick music publishing company was located at 219 West Forty-Sixth Street, in the heart of Tin Pan Alley. Inside its offices, the sound of pianos being played and "all the hub-bub and noise" scared Ruby. "Girls and fellows singing and dancing in every direction." But Ruby felt at home after all the years with Millie: being around chorus girls who joked and kidded; watching dance routines; good-natured stagehands; lights and costumes.

It occurred to Ruby that these singers and dancers were trying out for an opportunity on the stage. "In a fraction of a second," she said, "I forgot what I had really come for."

A man from the Remick music company asked her what she wanted. "I made no mention of the job, but instead I told him that I could sing and dance and wanted to have a tryout."

Ruby was brought into a crowded office. Against the background music of pianos coming from other cubicles, she showed Jerry Cripp how she could dance and sing. She didn't know any routines, but after studying acrobatics she made it up as she went, high kicking and cartwheeling.

The audition was over before she knew it. "If I had gone [to the Remick music company] with a try out in mind I would have been too self-conscious. But I had so little time to think about the change in my plans." Cripp thought Ruby's dancing was "okay." He was not impressed with her singing. "In fact," she said, "he made some mention of it being terrible." He could see that she wasn't an inspired dancer but she had something; she was young and she had an appeal, and he thought he could get her a job "with a friend of his who was looking for some girls for his club." Cripp sent Ruby over to the Strand Roof, a supper and after-theater club on top of the Strand Theatre on Broadway between Forty-Seventh and Forty-Eighth Streets, and told her to speak to Earl Lindsay, the dance director there. Ruby told Lindsay that she'd been on the stage, that she'd danced at the Marigold Café in Chicago, a club where Millie had danced, and that she sang as well. She was hired.

She was now in the chorus of Earl Lindsay's Revue.

The Strand Roof was a large dance hall with a balcony around its upper reaches. It had opened during the public craze for dancing in 1913 and was the creation of Mrs. William K. Vanderbilt and other society women who conceived of it as an alternative to the usual form of charity work and saw its cafeteria-lunch-dansant as a place where the working girl could go during lunch hour. No liquor was served; admission was fifty cents plus twenty cents for lunch.

The Strand Roof was popular; stenographers went there to dance the hoochie coochie, eat lunch, and be served by Mrs. Vanderbilt and her friends, who, for a brief stint, were the Strand's waitresses.

Over time the Strand was used in other ways. The New York Drummers held a competition there with Jerome Kern as one of the judges. Two years later the Strand was raided in a vice cleanup that swept across major cities. It was charged with solicitation taking place under its auspices: women were soliciting men via the waiters, and the supper club temporarily lost its dance license.

In 1921, the Strand Roof offered a dinner deluxe for $2 with a revue "twice nightly" at 7:15 and at 11:30 following the theater. Diners could dance "on the city's largest, perfect floor" with forty massive floor-to-ceiling windows that opened out on New York's Great White Way.

There were eight cast members in the Strand revue, including a comedian, a male singer, and a young woman equal to the singer who would appear in love scenes and be a foil for the comedian. Ruby was put in the back row of the chorus and figured she could get by "with giving something less than my best." Lindsay caught her at it and "gave her hell."

With her salary at the Strand Roof, Ruby could afford to move out of Maud and Bert's house on Avenue L in Flatbush and move in with the family of one of the other Strand chorus girls, Claire Taishoff, who lived in Manhattan on 135th Street and Riverside Drive.

Florenz Ziegfeld was opening a new *Follies* and was looking for dancers. The Ziegfeld girls were from all over the country: waitresses, runaway debutantes, escapees from convent schools, file clerks, and beauty contest winners from county fairs and beaches.

At the Ziegfeld audition, the women in the front were told to come forward in an orderly line and walk toward the footlights. Mr. Ziegfeld sat in the first row and looked at the women before him, discussing their qualities with his stage manager and secretary, who sat behind him. Ziegfeld pointed from right to left those women he wanted. The stage manager called out their numbers, and those chosen walked down a small flight of stairs into the theater and were told when to report for rehearsals. Out of five hundred or so women trying to find parts in a Ziegfeld show, fifty would be chosen.

Earl Lindsay helped Ruby get a job in Ziegfeld's 1922 *Follies*. She was fifteen years old, just under age, and was hired, using the name Dolly Evans, for the sixteenth production of the *Follies*.

Skits and songs in the show were written by Gene Buck, Ziegfeld's right-hand man. Buck hired many of the performers who became synonymous with the *Follies:* Will Rogers, Lillian Lorraine, Ed Wynn, W. C. Fields. Ziegfeld's set designer, Joseph Urban, who was trained as an artist and an architect—he had designed a new Viennese town hall as well as a bridge in St. Petersburg for the czar—had worked with Ziegfeld since 1915.

It was assumed that Florenz Ziegfeld found the dancers who made his shows so famous, but it was his dance director, Ned Wayburn, and ballet dancer/choreographer, Pearl Eaton, who hired the *Follies'* dancers. Wayburn had produced revues, musical comedies, and vaudeville acts and had taught Ann Pennington, Marilyn Miller, Fanny Brice, and Fred and Adele Astaire at his studios on West Forty-Fifth Street between Broadway and Eighth Avenue.

The girls of the *Follies* made up an enormous ensemble, a hundred dancers with a class system all their own. There were twenty-five showgirls, many of whom were six feet or taller, who performed the famous Ziegfeld walk

Florenz Ziegfeld, Follies and musical comedy producer, known as the "glorifier of the American girl," with his wife, Billie Burke, New York, circa 1910.

first introduced by Ned Wayburn in the *Midnight Frolics* at the roof of the New Amsterdam Theatre: it was straight backed, shoulders squared, chest out; a step with a slide, arms outstretched, bodies draped in magnificent costumes, balancing elaborate large hats. The showgirls who were courted offstage were disdainful of the other dancers.

The chorus dancers, approximately twenty-five of them and five feet three, performed in the production numbers; sixteen ballet dancers, five feet tall, performed the works of Ned Wayburn and Michel Fokine (the dancers thought Fokine flighty and wanted to quickly learn his choreography so "they could get rid of him"). Sixteen ponies, five feet to five five, tap-danced; ten girls were in musical numbers or comedy numbers with a specialty act, singing or dancing, and eight girls were understudies. Ruby was one of the ponies.

The 1922 production of the *Follies* opened on June 5. Ruby danced in a number, "Bring on the Girls," that appeared late in the first act, following "Frolicking Gods," a ballet composed and produced by Fokine in which a young man and woman in the mid-nineteenth century are mistakenly locked overnight in a Paris museum and watch spellbound as the marble statues of Greek gods on display come to life and dance. Will Rogers was on next and talked to the audience about his "Yankee philosophy." Ruby's number, "Bring on the Girls," followed. Then "Sure-Fire Dancers of Today" built up to "The English Pony Ballet" with Ruby again dancing in the number that brought down the curtain on act 1.

Ruby stayed with the *Follies* through July, was out of the show in August and back in September, through Christmas and New Year's of 1923 as it traveled to Boston, Washington, Cleveland, Chicago, and Detroit.

The sixteenth edition of the *Follies* cost Ziegfeld $265,000 to produce; Ziegfeld cut the cost of the top ticket from $5 to $4.

When the tour was over, Ruby returned to New York and to the Strand Roof.

Malcolm had worked his way to Panama and asked everyone he met if they knew his father. Frequently the answer would be yes; Byron Stevens, or Big Mike, as he was called, had worked on the canal, and when it opened in 1914, he'd stayed on. Most said they didn't know where he was until Malcolm met two men who told him that Byron was dead, that they themselves had buried him.

Malcolm was two years older than Ruby, but he worried about her as if she were his child. He returned from Panama and made his way to the East Coast and to Brooklyn to tell Ruby about their father and went to see her at the Strand. He was in New York for a short time; he had signed up with the merchant marine and was going back out to sea as soon as he could. He told Ruby only that their father was dead, deciding it would be better for her not to know the rest, which he told his older sisters; that there had been an epidemic in Panama; that Byron had fallen ill from it; that Big Mike had been buried in the "dirt without a casket." Malcolm's dream of the Stevenses being together again as a family was over.

Ruby worked hard at the Strand Roof. "I learned how to dance . . . and hoofed my feet off" performing an acrobatic dance, and she was soon promoted to the front line. "I tried to outdo myself by kicking higher than any of the other girls." Lindsay once again pulled Ruby out of the line. "Who do you think you are to be constantly out of step?" he asked her. "You've got to learn right now that your job on the stage consists of teamwork. If you want to last, remember that."

Ruby's costumes were ill fitting, either too big or too small, and she was frequently concerned that her underpants would fall down around her ankles while she was onstage. The dancers changed in the bathroom, sweating, struggling to use the one small mirror on the wall. Ruby thought it was a wonder the dancers got onstage at all and didn't look worse than they did.

The eighteenth edition of the *Follies* starred Fanny Brice, Bert and Betty Wheeler, the husband-and-wife comedy team who sang and danced, Ann

Pennington, Eddie Cantor, the dancer Lina Basquette, and Paul Whiteman and His Orchestra. Al Jolson used to stand in the wings so he could be close to the pretty girls.

One of Ruby's dance partners, Dorothy Van Alst, was a featured specialty dancer with the 1923 edition of the *Follies* and before that a dancer in Ned Wayburn's *Demi-Tasse Revue* at the Hotel Shelburne in Brighton Beach. Dorothy, nineteen and three years older than Ruby, came from Brooklyn (her father was a vice president of a fleet of tugboats with the Gowanus Towing Company) and was at work on a ukulele act in the hopes of auditioning for a spot in Earl Lindsay's Revue. By December 1923, Dorothy was dancing at the Strand Roof with Ruby and another dancer who was engaged to Jack Dempsey.

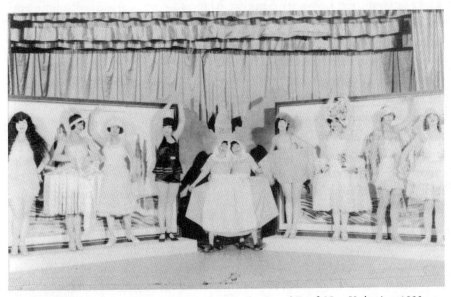

Ruby Stevens (second from right) in a revue at the Strand Roof, New York, circa 1923.
(COURTESY DOROTHY VAN ALST COLLECTION)

FIVE

Keeping Kool

Nils Granlund began working for Marcus Loew as an advance man and publicist several years after Loew had given up manufacturing furs for the acquisition of second-string movie houses and down-and-out vaudeville theaters. Granlund started to broadcast over the new medium of radio and was stunned when listeners thirty miles away in New Jersey heard him speak through it. In 1922, Loew bought the radio gadget that became WHN, which broadcast from a one-room studio in the new Loew State Building on Times Square. The room was large enough to accommodate a small orchestra and an announcer. During the broadcasts, the door to the room and all of the windows except for one were sealed; after a short time the walls felt as if they were closing in from lack of air, so programs were kept to fifteen-minute intervals.

Harry Richman was playing piano for Mae West at the RKO-Colonial and went to the station to sing and play the piano on the air, as did Al Jolson and Eddie Cantor. Helen Morgan was earning $60 a week performing at Billy Rose's Backstage Club but went to the station to sing on the show. Ethel Merman was working as a stenographer for the adventurer, aviator, car and boat racer Caleb Bragg, getting $35 a week, and would sing on the air on Tuesdays and Thursdays.

Ruby was interested in radio and thought it would give her some experience in dramatic speaking. She stopped by the station several times a week to see Granlund, who liked her and felt she had a dignity and honesty he found unusual. Sometimes he took her to a restaurant downstairs called Yohalem's.

During the intervals of Granlund's regular programming or when performers would fail to show up, he would read poetry over the air—Kipling or Poe—and occasionally he would let Ruby read in his place.

It was the work of the English-born poet Robert W. Service that interested her. Granlund let her read one of his poems several times on the radio. It was Service's long poem "Cocotte," about the effects of the war, that Ruby read most frequently:

When a girl's sixteen, and as poor as she's pretty,
And she hasn't a friend and she hasn't a home,
Heigh-ho! She's as safe in Paris city . . .

The eight-stanza poem would have been a challenge for Ruby to read and catch its drama and richness; its sense of danger and joy with life's opening up; its fullness of heart at finding "a lover who loved me only"; an abandon from the happiness of being together and bereavement, from the young man's leaving to fight and from his death, "sword in hand on the field of glory." The poem captures a defiance, an anger, a refusal to bend to convention as "women fix me with eyes of scorning/Call me 'cocotte,' but I do not care"; a return to a solitary self as "men look at me with eyes that borrow/The brightness of love" that moves to a feeling of regeneration: "There is wonderful work to be done."

Ruby had no training as an actress, but she was a reader and knew how to use the words. Her inflections, spirit, and deep familiarity with sorrow allowed her to give the poem a power that carried over the airwaves. Granlund

Nils Thor ("Granny") Granlund, also known as N.T.G., circa 1920.

was impressed and saw in her an intensity that he didn't see in most show-girls. He thought her deep voice had dramatic promise.

Granlund put together a vaudeville show in Brooklyn for Loew's Metro-politan Theatre and put Ruby in it, watching her work. He thought she was beautiful but couldn't understand why she was wasting herself on an acro-batic dance for which she did splits and rolled around on the floor. Despite that, when he put together shows for nightclubs, cabarets, and benefits, he made sure to hire Ruby, who would perform her specialty number, her acro-batic dance.

The moral outrage against alcohol, jazz, sex, and women who smoked ciga-rettes was at its height. Nightlife was forced underground—and thrived. New speakeasies opened daily in New York. Along Fifty-Second Street, owners of brownstones put signs in front of their houses that warned, "This Is Not a Speakeasy."

There were five thousand speakeasies in New York, a thousand of them along Broadway running north from Fortieth to Fiftieth Streets between Sixth and Eighth Avenues. There was the Club Lido, the Café de Paris, the Mirador, the Club Richman, Club Anatol, Ciro's. There were cabarets and theaters and dance clubs, as well as the *Ziegfeld Follies, Earl Carroll's Vanities, George White's Scandals,* Minsky's Burlesque, and the vaudeville circuit with the Palace Theatre on Broadway and Forty-Seventh Street as the pinnacle of vaudeville success.

Texas Guinan was the hostess at the El Fay Club, owned by a notorious bootlegger, Larry Fay, who started out as a taxi driver and amassed a fleet of taxis distinguished by their extra nickel trim, tuneful horns, and black swas-tikas (for good luck) painted on the sides of the cab doors.

Once Prohibition was passed, Larry Fay used his cars to run liquor from Montreal to New York City until his fleet of taxis gave way to a fleet of trucks and then a fleet of boats. Soon he was bringing vast quantities of liquor into the country. Fay opened a nightclub and joined the other bootleggers who owned clubs, like Owney Madden, who had the Cotton Club in Harlem and the Silver Slipper on Broadway, and Legs Diamond, who owned the Hotsy Totsy Club. Granlund finally figured out that the curious but regular requests made by Fay's men for poems by Kipling, Poe, Service, and others to be read over the WHN airwaves were coded messages intended to help Fay's bootleg-ging boats elude the coast guard and make it—stash intact—to Fay's ware-house in Hoboken. The authorities soon caught on to the ruse, and Fay was listed as New York's public enemy No. 3.

Mary Louise Cecilia ("Texas") Guinan (center; in britches) from Waco, Texas. She played a gunslinger and rode bareback in pictures and claimed (inventively) that she'd ridden broncos, herded cattle, and was the product of a Virginia finishing school.

· · ·

The El Fay Club was on Forty-Sixth Street, east of Broadway, above a restaurant on the ground floor. It was at the top of a narrow staircase that led to a door with a peephole that opened up to a small room that could hold eighty patrons. The silks on the walls and a tentlike draping over the dance floor gave the room an even more intimate feeling.

Texas Guinan was forty years old and back from Hollywood with more than thirty five-reelers to her name, first from Triangle Studios and Frohman Amusement Corporation and then from her own Texas Guinan Productions and Victor Kremer Features. Texas—she was born in Waco—had created a Western heroine on the screen in shorts like *Two-Gun Girl* and *The Lady of the Law;* she could ride and shoot like a man but was all woman and became famous as the female version of the cowboy star William S. Hart.

There were dancers and entertainers at the El Fay Club, but it was Texas Guinan as mistress of ceremonies whom patrons came to see. She was loud, flamboyantly dressed, full of Irish wit—the all-around life of the party. There was only room enough on the small stage for a chorus of six women; most were from Ziegfeld's *Follies*.

The Ziegfeld girls arrived at the El Fay Club in time for the midnight show after the curtain went down at the New Amsterdam Theatre; performances at the club followed every couple of hours until 5:00 a.m.

The El Fay's watered-down liquor, which cost $10.00 a case, was sold for $1.25 a drink (Fay got a hundred drinks per quart); the champagne cider, spiked with alcohol, was $35.00 a bottle.

While the doctored liquor made the club profitable, it was the irresistible energy of Texas Guinan that made the club a success. ("Give the little girl a big hand," she would say to the packed audience about her entertainers.) She promised her guests "a fight a night or your money back." She played to the men in the audience who spent large sums of money at the club. "Hello, sucker," she would call out to them. As the evening wore on, Texas would invite those audience members who had just arrived and who she knew would be lavish spenders to come sit down by the stage to be near her. Chairs were brought forward and placed on the edge of the dance floor. By the second show there was hardly any dance floor.

Ruby Keeler at fourteen was one of the six who danced in the chorus at the El Fay; George Raft tap-danced on the small stage for $75 a week. Ruby Stevens was hired by Granlund to perform her acrobatic dance.

On the first night of her dance, Texas had invited a number of men to sit down in front with her. The remaining stage space was small. Ruby began her acrobatic routine. Her splits and rolls carried her beyond the small stage, out from the spotlight, and she landed under the table, between the legs of the chairs. After that, for her own protection, Ruby did a constrained tap dance.

Often the two Rubys—Keeler and Stevens—went out on dates together, Ruby Keeler introducing Ruby Stevens to the many gangsters she knew.

At the Strand Roof, Earl Lindsay often asked Ruby to watch out for newcomers to the show. One was Mae Klotz. Lindsay said to Ruby, "Look, I've got a little kid coming in, but she's a cute dancer, and I think she's got potential. I want you to watch over her and teach her the ropes."

Mae Klotz was fourteen; Ruby, seventeen.

Like Ruby, Violet Mary "Mae" Klotz had graduated from the eighth grade and didn't go on to high school. Mae studied dance, first toe, then interpretive dance. Soon she was one of Dawson's Dancing Dolls. It was when Mae Klotz was onstage in a disastrous solo that Earl Lindsay saw her during his annual summer holiday with his wife and his mother and asked Mae to come to New York to be a showgirl.

Ruby said to Mae when they were introduced, "First of all, kid, those curls gotta go." Mae said later, "[Ruby] talked real low and real tough. I think she put it on to make me feel that she was my superior." But Mae was thrilled to be around one of the girls who had so much experience; she was even more thrilled to be dancing in New York and be paid for it.

Mae came from Atlantic City, though she was born in Philadelphia. ("Our name was a very honored name. We had Klotzes in Philadelphia who were millionaires.") Mae was a family girl, close to her parents, and she hated to leave them in Atlantic City. Her father was "Atlantic City's Premier Organist," the accompanist for two-reelers and then for ten-reel photoplays ("He managed to perform in every theater in Atlantic City"). Father and daughter went to work together: he to play the organ; she to watch the pictures his music punctuated. Mae's family needed extra money, and she had a dream of New York, "where all the theaters were one after another . . . one great stream of white."

Mae and Ruby became close friends and soon went everywhere together. Ruby taught Mae about sex and sophistication.

"This is going to make you look older than what you are," Ruby said as she taught Mae to smoke. "And make you appear sexier."

"I'm not sure how to do it," Mae said.

"Don't be silly. You put it in your mouth. You light it up and the rest just comes natural."

Ruby told Mae about men.

"There's a big difference between boyfriends and lovers," said Ruby. "You've had little boyfriends, but that's all over now."

Ruby taught Mae how to charm men, how to woo them, how to get what she wanted from them. "If 'once over lightly' is what it took to do the job, we'll do the job. No emotions attached."

Mae needed a new coat and saw the one she wanted. Ruby told her how to get it.

"You say to your date, 'Oh, I really love that coat, but I can't afford it now. But it would mean so much to me.' Unless he's stupid, he's going to say, 'Oh, let me get it for you.' And then you're going to play it like this: 'No, no, I don't want to be indebted to you.' Look forlorn. Put it in the face. Use the voice a little bit, tremble the voice about how you certainly need it but there's no way you can afford it, but wouldn't it be wonderful. He's going to say, 'Come on, let me do it as a favor to you.' Play it that way and you'll get the coat. Don't come on too strong. He can't know what you're doing."

Mae tried it out. She and her date went into the store. Mae did as Ruby told her and wore the coat back to her room. Once in the door her date said, "And now . . ."

Mae said, "Oh no, I can't do that." The coat was yanked from Mae's body, and her date walked out.

"Listen, stupid," Ruby said. "Part of the deal is if you want something, you've got to give out."

Ruby brought Mae home to Maud and Bert's for Sunday suppers; at other times Mae brought Ruby home to Atlantic City and her family. When Ruby's friend Claire Taishoff announced that she was getting married to a violinist from the New York Philharmonic Society, Mae and Ruby decided to move in together and found a small apartment, above a Chinese laundry on Forty-Sixth Street between Fifth and Sixth Avenues. Ruby described it as "a cute place. The first real home I ever had. We never admitted that we lived there, though."

When they went out on dates, they were dropped at the Knickerbocker or Astor hotel and would "run like the dickens to get home," Ruby said.

They were earning $35 each per week and "put every cent on our backs. We did our own washing, ironing, dry-cleaning," said Ruby. "Each night we washed our stockings and lingerie. I never had more than one of anything. We shampooed and manicured each other. We did our own cooking, many times, over the old reliable gas-jet."

In the winter the windowsills were used as iceboxes. In the summer the bathtub was filled with water for fruit.

Ruby and Mae went to Gray's Drugstore to buy makeup and get "cut" tickets on a professional discount for the theater. They went to see musical comedies on Wednesdays and Saturdays and dramas—"legit"—on Tuesdays and Thursdays.

"We couldn't wait to get together and say, 'Hey, what'd you see last night?' 'Well, I went over to the so-and-so, and I saw such and such. Gee, there's a scene in there, let me tell you about it.' And that's how we learned, by telling each other stories of what we saw."

Most chorus girls learned from watching one another—mannerisms, how to dress, put on makeup, manage men. Lucille LeSueur from San Antonio, Texas, with wide blue eyes, generous mouth, clean freckled face, and frizzy auburn hair, who danced in the chorus at Detroit's Oriole Terrace for eight weeks and made "end girl," was new in town, dancing at the Winter Garden in the Shubert musical *Innocent Eyes,* which starred Mistinguett, the unrivaled star of the French musical, who was making her debut in America at age forty-nine. Lucille got help with her costumes from the other girls who lent her their clothes, lipstick, and powder. Lucille—some called her Freckles, others, Billie—was confident at nineteen, plump, garish, shy, with a restless seeking energy; her frenzied dancing was spontaneous; what she didn't know, she made up. Lucille lived in a tiny brownstone on Fiftieth Street, just off Seventh. She was consumed with becoming a stage star, a musical-comedy favorite. There wasn't anything she wouldn't do if it helped make her a success and carry her away from the shame and drudgery of her ugly childhood past in Lawton, Oklahoma, and Kansas City.

It had been said of LeSueur that when waitressing in Detroit, between shows at the Oriole Terrace, the town's biggest nightclub, she had spilled a glass of water onto Jake Shubert's lap as he was dining with his star Mistinguett. LeSueur soaked up the water with a napkin, promising Shubert that she gave "good head" and was as well a "capable dancer." Shubert had smiled and given her his card. Afterward, Mistinguett whispered in the ear of the youngest Shubert, "She'll go a long way in life, but she'll eat you whole, cock first, and spit out the pips!"

On days when the stars performed benefits for each other, Ruby and Mae and the others went to the Winter Garden. Their one main benefit was for the Actors Fund. "At intermission," Mae said, "lights came up and all the actors in plays would pass the hat . . . and those hats would come back full. Most of the audience were actors."

The dinner show at the Strand Roof began at eight. The girls checked in at seven. The dressing rooms were large and took up the whole space on top of the theater. Ruby and Mae would dress for the show before they left the apartment, go to dinner, and then leave for the theater in time. At the theater someone would check to see if they had arrived. "If you weren't there, look out," Mae said. "But the final was 'half-hour, half-hour.' And you'd have to answer back so he knew you were there."

After the last show, Earl Lindsay wanted the dancers "in bed immediately following a little something to eat," said Mae. "He wanted us healthy. And not only that, but in each of his productions he had at least three who were under age. And they had to be protected."

When the run ended at the Strand, Mae and Ruby were out of work and didn't think another job would be coming their way. Finally, because of Lindsay's connections as a producer and choreographer, Mae got a part in a show called *Sitting Pretty*, a musical comedy by Guy Bolton and P. G. Wodehouse with music by Jerome Kern.

For the new part Mae had a new name: Mae Clarke. "I only changed it because they laughed at Klotz. They laughed publicly, in a nightclub called the Silver Slipper across the street from the Everglades Cafe. Nils T. Granlund . . . worked as a dirty comic [there] under the name 'N.T.G.' "

Granlund invited girls from a show to his nightclub for free. He got up on the stage as the master of ceremonies. A spotlight was directed to the girls sitting at the table while Granlund commented on how beautiful they were and mentioned the show they were appearing in. Mae was there one night with some of the girls from the show when NTG put the spotlight on her and walked over to her table. "I was thrilled to death," she said. When Granlund asked her name, she answered, "Mae Klotz." "Here she is! Folks, I've found her. We've been looking everywhere for you." Mae thought she had been discovered. Granlund said, "Here she is, Minnie Klutz!" The audience roared. Mae didn't know what to do, where to look. "I didn't have a comeback," she said. "I couldn't get up and leave . . . [W]e went through the rest of the evening and went back to do our own show."

Afterward, Mae said to her friends who were trying to console her, "That's my father's name and I love it. I love him. And I don't like people laughing at him. Or me." One friend suggested she change her name to Mae Hughes; another to Mae Gray. "It's too—it's like a burlesque queen," Mae said. She wanted it to be as close to her father's name as possible. She thought of Klotz and then Clarke. "And right there, I saw the 'e' . . . [W]hen I don't get the 'e,' I take it as a personal insult."

Sitting Pretty opened at the Fulton Theatre on Forty-Sixth Street, west of Broadway, and then moved to the Imperial Theatre.

In the program notes Mae Klotz was listed as May Clark; no *e* was at the end of either name.

Earl Lindsay was staging a new show and gave Ruby a part in it, as he did Dorothy Van Alst. It was a musical revue in two acts called *Keep Kool;* the title was inspired by the presidential campaign slogan making its way across the country, "Keep Cool with Coolidge." ("The business of America is business," Coolidge said.) The show was scheduled to run during the summer months, traveling around the Northeast in early May, coming to the Montauk Theatre in Brooklyn before it opened in New York at the Morosco Theatre on May 22, 1924.

Ruby appeared in two numbers and was one of sixteen in the chorus. The curtain went up on the Keep Kool Cuties in the opening number called "The Broadway Battle Cry." One critic described the dancers as "the hoofiest chorus seen in ages," the audience applauding them throughout. Hazel

Dawn's first number was a monologue parody of "Gunga Din"; Bill Frawley, of vaudeville's Frawley and Louise, sang a duet with Jessie Maker. Frawley did a fast-talking back-and-forth comedy routine with Hazel Dawn in a prop taxi.

Ruby's number, "With Apologies To," was a sketch satirizing the work of George M. Cohan; the new heroic playwright of realism, Eugene O'Neill; William Squibes and Avery Hopwood, or, as Alexander Woollcott described him, the "inexhaustible Avery." Hopwood said he "wrote for Broadway to please Broadway," and he did. Hopwood ("the Playboy Playwright") wrote a new hit play on Broadway every year and had for the past ten years, including 1920 when five of his plays were running on Broadway simultaneously, among them *The Bat*. His plays such as *Fair and Warmer* and *Nobody's Widow* Americanized French farce. It was Hopwood's play *The Gold Diggers* that made the term part of the American language.

Reviewers singled out Ruby's sketch and described it as the centerpiece of the show. *Variety* said it was the "high spot" of the evening.

Ruby appeared onstage when the curtain went up on act 2, with the Keep Kool Cuties accompanying Hazel Dawn and Charles King in a number called "Gypsy Ann," and was back again in a song called "Beautiful but Dumb" as a mannequin wearing an evening gown who comes to life modeling in a window.

Keep Kool was more than three hours long. The final curtain came down at 11:25.

The New York Times called the show "excellent"; Alexander Woollcott said in the *Sun* that it was "gay and good looking and reasonably bright"; Arthur Hornblow in his column "Mr. Hornblow goes to the play" declared it "too good to be missed."

A block south of the Morosco Theatre at the Broadhurst was *Beggar on Horseback* with Roland Young; the Marx Brothers were at the Casino Theatre on Thirty-Ninth Street in a musical called *I'll Say She Is;* Mary Boland was in a farce called *Meet the Wife;* John Barrymore's picture *Beau Brummel* was running at the Strand Theatre on Broadway, and three blocks away was D. W. Griffith's *America*.

Once *Keep Kool* opened, Ruby arranged for Maud and Mabel and Gene to see a matinee. It was Gene's first musical and the first time Maud and Mabel had seen Ruby perform on a Broadway stage. In one number Gene proudly spotted his aunt Ruby dancing at the far right of the chorus line. After the show Ruby's sisters and nephew went backstage to her dressing room upstairs.

During the summer *Keep Kool* moved to the Globe Theatre; by the fall it had moved again to the Earl Carroll Theatre on Seventh Avenue and Fiftieth Street.

Ruby and Ed Kennedy were still seeing each other; they would argue and make up and argue again.

When the show moved to the Earl Carroll Theatre, some of the Keep Kool Cuties left and five new dancers were brought in to replace them. Among them was Dorothy Sheppard, who in high school had modeled hats and shoes ("I didn't take it seriously") and was now a dancer in the chorus line ("I didn't go to dancing school. I never learned to dance. I just followed whatever they did"). After finishing high school, she was hired for a show called *Battling Buttler* and at seventeen went into *Keep Kool.*

Dorothy—her stage name was Dotty—liked Ruby immediately; they were both from Flatbush. Ruby had confidence, "a lot more than I had," said Dorothy.

During the summer, through Granlund's intervention, Ruby appeared on the cover of *The National Police Gazette* as "one of the famous kuties in 'Keep Kool.' "

He also helped Lucille LeSueur (known in Kansas City, Missouri, as Billie Cassin) get a job earning extra money at Harry Richman's club in between her appearing in the chorus at the Winter Garden in the Shuberts' new musical revival, *The Passing Show of 1924.* For all of LeSueur's shyness and lack of confidence, she was winning dance contests up in Harlem clubs, cutting loose with wild abandon, stomping her way through the Charleston, spanking herself through the black bottom. LeSueur was becoming synonymous with "man killer" and was walked in on by a Ziegfeld dancer late one night in the bedroom at a party making love to a well-known actress. Nothing surprised people about Billie.

Florenz Ziegfeld agreed with the assessment of *The Billboard*'s critic Gordon Whyte, who, when *Keep Kool* opened, called it "smart and dashing and thoroughly entertaining . . . the only revue I remember which has the 'Follies manner' . . . it has the color and the speed and what the Follies generally lacks, a number of humorous scenes. In fact, its comedy . . . is incomparably higher than that."

In October 1924, Ziegfeld incorporated *Keep Kool* into the eighteenth edition of the 1923 *Follies,* the same edition Ruby had appeared in two years before. It had been such a success it was still on the road.

See Review of Renault-Madden Bout on Page 10

INTERNATIONAL EDITION

The NATIONAL

POLICE GAZETTE.

THE LEADING ILLUSTRATED SPORTING JOURNAL IN THE WORLD.

NEW YORK: SATURDAY, AUGUST 30, 1924.

BEAUTY IN A PENSIVE MOOD IS BEAUTY MOST ADORABLE.

Ruby Stevens (cover), *The National Police Gazette,*
August 30, 1924. The caption reads: "Judging by her
gravely meditative expression, Miss Ruby Stevens, one
of the famous kuties in 'Keep Kool,' current revue at
the Globe Theater, possesses fine qualities of mind in
addition to her exceptional physical loveliness."

Ruby was a principal in the show, earning a salary of $100 a week; the
girls in the chorus were receiving a weekly salary of $50. Hazel Dawn was
paid $1,000 per week; the Mosconi family, $1,250.

The *Follies* road show with *Keep Kool* in it opened in Chicago at the Illinois Theatre and in the Motor City at the New Detroit on October 13, 1924.
Dorothy Sheppard didn't want to leave New York and decided not to travel
with the show; Dorothy Van Alst did.

One of Van Alst's big numbers, "The Shadowgraph," followed Ruby's

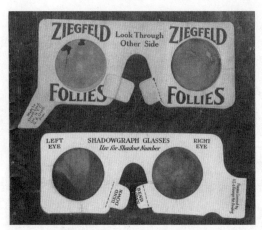

Three-D audience glasses for the Shadowgraph Number from *Keep Kool*.

sketch "With Apologies To." For "The Shadowgraph" each member of the
audience was given a pair of Follies-Scope cardboard glasses to wear. The
right lens was a red filter; the left, blue.

The number opened with the silhouette of two women onstage (Dorothy Van Alst and Hilda Ferguson) behind a thick screen. When looked at
through the Follies-Scope glasses, the women onstage seemed to be throwing
snowballs directly out at the audience and then gathering them up from the
tops of the heads of people in their seats. The number builds to Van Alst (still
behind a screen, on a ladder) undressing (she is wearing a bathing suit), toss-
ing out each garment, it seems, into the face of the theatergoers.

The number was a sensation. Audiences loved the effect of the three-
dimensional optical illusion.

After opening in Detroit, the show toured for eight months to Cleveland,
Buffalo, Boston, and Newark, traveling from city to city by train with the
Ziegfeld office reserving three Pullman cars for the company.

Nancy Bernard, one of the dancers in the chorus, became good friends
with Ruby, and they shared a room. Ruby called her Billy for no reason other
than she had liked the name. While on the road, the two were having a few
drinks one night when Ruby confided that she had been raised in a convent.
She also told "Billy" that her mother was Jewish and her father gentile. "But
I'm a Christian," said Ruby. "I believe in Christianity." Nancy was Jewish,
as was Maud's friend Mabel Cohen, with whom Ruby had lived. For a short
time Ruby had been placed in a Catholic home. Nancy didn't question what
Ruby was telling her; she was a great girl, and whatever her religion or back-

ground may have been, it was fine with Nancy, though she kept Ruby's confidence a secret.

After months of working together and long hours on the train and in between shows, Ruby told Nancy that she couldn't have children. A couple of years before, Ruby said, she was seeing the son of a man who owned a chain of famous restaurants. Ruby had a "problem" and had it "fixed." It was a bad abortion with complications, and she would never be able to get pregnant again.

Ruby returned to New York and was sharing a hotel suite with Mae Clarke. Earl Lindsay was working on another show, this time with J. J. Shubert as director and producer.

Gay Paree opened in Atlantic City early in August at Nixon's Apollo Theatre. It starred Billy B. Van, Chic Sale, George LeMaire, Jack Haley, and the singer comedian Winnie Lightner, who had just finished a six-month run in the 1924 edition of *George White's Scandals*. Earl Lindsay hired Ruby and Mae, as he usually did, after the show opened so they could avoid the dead time of rehearsals. Ruby, Mae, and Dorothy Sheppard of the *Keep Kool* chorus became part of the "Ladies of the Ensemble."

SIX

The Prevailing Sizzle

*G*ay *Paree* was conceived in the style of *George White's Scandals,* with the dancers wearing fewer clothes. It was billed as a "continental revue filled with Greenwich Village's most dazzling models, snappy music and sparkling wit and the spirit of Paris," with music by Alfred Goodman, Maurie Rubens, and J. Fred Coots and lyrics by Clifford Grey.

Winnie Lightner sang; Chic Sale told jokes, performed monologues, and told stories from an imaginary place called Hicksville. There were spectacular numbers such as "A Vision of Hassan" and "Baby's Baby Grand" with Jack Haley and Alice Boulden. The show was fast paced with minute-long scenes and thirty-two quick blackouts.

The women of the *Gay Paree* chorus wore beaded or spangled bras and pants. Many were bare breasted. The Paris of *Gay Paree* was nowhere evident in the show, but Venice, Florida, Times Square, and Sheba were. Burns Mantle of the *Daily News* called *Gay Paree* "a naked show" and compared it to *Artists and Models,* then the most successful show along with the *Follies,* the *Vanities,* and the *Scandals.* The chorus of *Gay Paree* danced the American crawl and the South Seas wiggle. "There are girls and girls and still more girls, duly assembled in graduated sizes," said Gilbert Gabriel of the New York *Sun,* "drilled to the last damp vestment, all of them cheerfully, many of them handsomely energized against the prevailing sizzle . . . There are seven times seven variations on the theme of the seventh commandment."

Artists and Models had caused a sensation when it opened on Broadway in the late summer of 1923. It was the first time in the history of the American revue that a chorus of twenty models paraded from the back wings to center stage nude from the waist up. The audience was stunned but was soon swept up by the cleverness of the show's writing and performances. There were burlesque satires by James Montgomery Flagg on the mindlessness of the Critic; skits by Winsor McCay and Rube Goldberg; a raucous satire about

From the J. J. Shubert revue *Gay Paree,* a giant fan hung with curling feathers and "beautiful maidens," circa 1925.

Henry Ford and his presidential cabinet; and a savage takeoff of *Rain.* Marie Dressler appeared as Queen Tut-ti and danced across the stage from one tomb to the next.

The master of ceremonies of the evening was the actor turned singer and dancer Frank Fay, considered for years a Broadway institution. Fay was a former headliner on the Keith and Orpheum Circuits who was discovered there by Elisabeth Marbury, the grande dame of producers, and J. J. Shubert. Fay's rare timing, control, and amiability made him a whirlwind of laughter without him ever telling a joke.

Artists and Models was instantly sold out with lines half a block long extending past the Hotel Astor. The Shuberts opened four additional box offices to cope with the demand for tickets. George Jean Nathan in *Judge* described the revue as "the most original; the brightest show of its kind," containing "more fresh humor, sound burlesque and genuine observant comedy than any other music show in town at the moment."

Despite the efforts of the churches and the Society for the Suppression of Vice and Crime to shut down *Artists and Models,* the production was a great success, and many other revues and shows followed its style and content.

Gay Paree opened at the Shubert Theatre on August 18, 1925.

Michael Arlen's play *The Green Hat,* starring Katharine Cornell, Leslie Howard, and Margalo Gillmore, was next door at the Broadhurst; Al Jolson

Ruby Stevens (third from left) in a scene from the
Gay Paree revue.

was east of Broadway, performing in *Big Boy,* another Shubert show; Laurette
Taylor, who the season before had starred in a pantomime called *Pierrot the
Prodigal,* was now starring—and speaking—in Philip Barry's *In a Garden*
with Frank Conroy and Louis Calhern; Ann Harding was in *Stolen Fruit;*
down a few blocks at the Maxine Elliott Theatre was Noël Coward's play *Hay
Fever* with Laura Hope Crews. In mid-September Coward's play *The Vortex,*
starring the playwright, opened at Henry Miller's Theatre. Its caricature of
well-mannered, light-headed moderns, "flowers of evil" nourished on a civilization that made rottenness so easy, amused audiences until the third act,
when playgoers were stunned by mother and son—Lilian Braithwaite and
Coward—and revelations of sexual excess and drug addiction.

Gay Paree ran for 181 performances to much fanfare and publicity. Nils
Granlund put together the "First Annual Outing of the Ziegfeld Chorus
Girls" at the Schencks' Palisades Amusement Park and a month later organized an event publicizing *Gay Paree.* Sixty girls from the show, wearing bathing suits, sat in open limousines and traveled up Broadway like a caravan

with a circus calliope leading the parade. As they crossed Times Square, the lead car broke down; the procession came to a halt. Noontime traffic from both directions stopped. Cars honked, and drivers shouted; photographers captured the bedlam, and Granlund made sure they photographed Ruby and Mae, whom he'd placed on the front fenders of the first car.

During the run of *Gay Paree,* Dorothy Sheppard was living in Astoria with the family of Ruby's friend Claire Taishoff.

After the show late one night Dorothy took the train back to Astoria. The streets were still. Dorothy became aware that someone was walking behind her. She quickened her pace and began to run. The footsteps behind her quickened. Dorothy made it to the house. She was safe but frightened. The next day she told Ruby and Mae what had happened, and they suggested that she come and live with them. They were near the Shubert Theatre at the Knickerbocker Hotel and had a two-bedroom suite. Dorothy, whose mother was living in Florida, was happy to make the move.

The suite at the Knickerbocker had an extra room across the hall, a maid's room. The three drew lots to see who would get the small room. It was Mae, and she was just as happy about it. She liked the idea of having her own room.

Ruby, Mae, and Dorothy were together most of the time. They looked after one another. When the girls thought one of the three was being hoity-toity, the other two would look at each other and say, "Oh, dear, pardon my forty-button-glove."

Mae was a blonde, Dorothy a redhead. "They were both beautiful girls," said Ruby, who felt she "wasn't any beauty. In fact, all I was was a fairly good chorus girl." But she loved the work. "I thought I was the star—the other 15 girls didn't matter."

Ruby, Mae, and Dorothy scoured the town for jobs. "We worked nights, but we saw a lot of movies in the daytime," said Ruby, pictures such as *We Moderns, The Big Parade, The Merry Widow,* and *Sally, Irene, and Mary* with Constance Bennett, Sally O'Neil, and Joan Crawford. Sally O'Neil called Billie "Freckles," though Joan had long wanted to be called "Butch."

They shopped for clothes; went to the theater together to see Helen Hayes in *Dancing Mothers,* Katharine Cornell in *The Green Hat,* or Ina Claire in *The Last of Mrs. Cheyney;* and rarely went to parties.

On Sundays, Ruby, Mae, and Dorothy slept, washed, and ironed. Ruby and Mae would often accompany Dorothy to church, usually to St. Patrick's Cathedral. During the service that called on parishioners to rise and sit, Ruby

The triumvirate left to right: Mae Clarke, Dorothy Shepherd, and Ruby Stevens, circa 1925.

and Mae would both lean in to Dorothy and whisper, "I wish you'd make up your mind about when you're going to sit. Stand; sit; what are you going to do? Whatever you're gonna do, let us know. We'll catch up to you."

On Sundays they rode horses in Central Park. Ruby was the most natural rider of the three; she and Mae wore proper riding habits: jodhpurs, boots, and a hacking jacket. Dorothy was content to wear a pair of old pants and a sweater.

Ruby was seen about town with three or four girls from the Strand Roof.

Ruby with Dorothy Shepherd, New York, circa 1923. (COURTESY LARRY KLENO)

Dana O'Connell, a young dancer of nineteen in the *Midnight Frolics,* Ziegfeld's supper club entertainment on the roof of the New Amsterdam Theatre, regularly went to Schrafft's in the afternoons and saw Ruby sitting at a table, dressed in her riding habit. "Ruby was always with girls," said Dana. "I never saw her out with men. I never saw her out with anyone except those afternoons when I would be going into Schrafft's. It was just a casual Hello, how have you been? 'Fine.' One of those things. She always wore her riding suit. Someone asked her why. And she said, 'I feel more comfortable in pants.' " In 1923 chorus girls and dancers wore dresses and stockings and gloves when not on the stage or going to and from the theater. "It was a smart-looking suit," said Dana, "with a little jacket and the boots and the little hat. It was quite saucy."

Ruby and Mae pooled their money to buy Dorothy a formal riding habit for her birthday. Dorothy was overwhelmed by the pair of black broadcloth jodhpur pants, broadcloth jacket, and jodhpur boots. "Oh, but these are so expensive," she said, embarrassed by the extravagance of the gift. Her concern about the gift's expense hurt Ruby's feelings; Dorothy knew Ruby's feelings were easily ruffled.

The triumvirate went out together to Reuben's after the show for coffee and a sandwich; they hoped desperately to be taken out to dinner, and if they weren't, they knew they could get a meal for thirty-five cents ("We ate a lot of ham and eggs"). When they had enough money, they ate at La-Hiff's chophouse, on West Forty-Eighth Street down the block from their hotel.

LaHiff's, or the Tavern, as it was known, was one of the best restaurants around Broadway, named after its owner, Billy LaHiff, a well-known Broadway figure. LaHiff's Tavern was the kind of restaurant where, said Mae, "the latest boxing champion, or the contenders, on the night of the fight or right after it" would eat. "It was *the* gathering place and we thought of it as our place as well."

Everyone went to LaHiff's: Broadway performers, chorus girls, politicians, studio executives like Gradwell Sears, sports figures, Broadway reporters such as Damon Runyon, Mark Hellinger, and Walter Winchell. Hellinger was thought to be the first of the Broadway reporters; his Broadway column appeared each week in the New York *Daily News;* Winchell was called the first of the Broadway columnists. Winchell's column, Your Broadway and Mine, was running in Bernarr Macfadden's *New York Evening Graphic,* a newspaper for the "masses not the classes," written in first-person rather than hard-news stories to "dramatize and sensationalize the news." Winchell and Hellinger were so linked that the saying was: "If Hellinger comes, can Winchell be far behind?" Winchell said, "The gintellectuals named us the Damon and Pythias of Broadway."

Ruby, Mae, and Dorothy knew they could go to the Tavern, "stony, and be sure of a welcome," Ruby said. "We could eat anything we wanted, any time we wanted, on the cuff. That broad white cuff of Billy La Hiff's. It knew more kindly erasures than any endowed Charity will ever know."

LaHiff's night manager was the former nightclub bouncer Toots Shor, a huge hunk of meat and potatoes of a man, called by Hellinger "the classiest bum in town."

"La Hiff and his waiter Jack Spooner were great friends to all kinds of people," said Ruby. "Down and out fighters, chorus girls on their uppers, the broken and the bent of Broadway. LaHiff'd feed us and slip us a ten or a fifteen besides, just to be sure we'd be okay. He had his and was grateful for it. So grateful, that he had his heart and his hand and his pocketbook open for those who hadn't got theirs yet or who had had it and lost it."

The three girls were on "the lookout" for their next opportunity, "our chance to step up to a dramatic part," said Mae.

Ruby was ambitious and determined to do things. Dorothy saw Ruby as strong, attractive, "full of life." To Mae, Ruby was the most disciplined and ambitious girl she'd ever met. Ruby was an "entity" who went after what she wanted. Mae was serious about dancing; Dorothy wanted to make money, but show business wasn't everything to her. She was interested in getting married and having a family.

Ruby told Dorothy about the death of her mother when Ruby was four and about her father's leaving to go to Panama. "Ruby acted like an orphan," said Dorothy. "And talked about it a lot. She liked feeling sorry for herself."

"You seem as if you are proud of it," Dorothy said to Ruby. "You almost brag about it."

"Well, I am," said Ruby. "So I might as well make the best of it."

"You think about it too much," Dorothy said. "Get on with life, you can do something about it." Ruby replied, "Maybe some people can do that, but it's difficult for me."

Dorothy believed that life for Ruby was "an enemy, not a friend."

Mae missed her mother's cooking and her father's love. Ruby didn't want to hear about it and told Mae to stop going on about them. Dorothy was an occasional reader, but Ruby read constantly: the just-published *Manhattan Transfer, An American Tragedy, The Great Gatsby.* "Ruby would finish books really fast," Dorothy said.

Ruby didn't speak much about her sisters Maud and Mabel, but she talked lovingly to Dorothy and Mae about her oldest sister, Millie. It was clear that Ruby thought she was wonderful.

Millie was married again and living in New York's Tudor City. Her husband, Arthur Smith, was a copywriter for Benton & Bowles. Ruby was fond of Maud's husband, Bert Merkent, who she felt was down to earth, a quiet man who got along with everybody. While Maud always put on airs, Bert was content to be in the background. Ruby admired that in Bert, but she didn't like Millie's husband and made it known.

One Christmas the whole family was gathered at the Merkents' house in Flatbush to exchange gifts and have dinner: Maud and Bert and their son, Al; Mabel and her son, Gene; Millie, Art, and Ruby. At the end of the evening, Ruby said her good-byes and left to go back to Manhattan. Millie's husband opened the door after her and threw the present Ruby had given him onto the street at her.

Earl Lindsay's new revue was at the Everglades Café. *Gay Paree* was two months into its run when Lindsay hired Ruby, Mae, and Dorothy to be in the floor show of the Everglades' *Ship Ahoy.* The Everglades Café was transformed into a nautical setting, from the menus and furniture to the sailor suit costumes.

The Everglades Café was a gangsters' haunt. "Bootlegging, speakeasies, murder, dope," said Mae Clarke. "No gangster hurt anybody except another gangster . . . There were no accidental killings. They were good shots. They kept to their own reasons and their own people."

The dancers' dressing rooms were underneath the stairs, separated from the rest of the club by a huge door made of concrete and iron. Gus the bodyguard was stationed there to protect the performers. "He loved every one of us," said Mae. "He used to write poems and put them in pretty frames and present one to each little girl."

Ruby and Mae and the others were in the dressing room getting ready for the next number when one night they heard the sound of the concrete stage door being rolled shut. They knew Gus was locking them in. "Something was happening on the outside . . . [A] murder. Or a raid," said Mae. It happened so frequently that Ruby and the other dancers thought nothing of it and continued with their conversation. After it was over, Gus refused to tell them what had happened.

Mae noticed a man sitting at a corner table each night and found out he was the head of the New York narcotics squad assigned to the Everglades Café to monitor who entered and left and what went on in between. He and Mae became friends. He knew she was fifteen and that each weekend her mother took the train to New York to see if her daughter was all right and if Mae was still smoking cigarettes.

The second show ended each evening at eleven. Often, Mae, Ruby, and Dorothy would go out after the show, "hopping from one [supper club] to another," said Mae, "like the Silver Slipper, where Texas Guinan was," or the Yacht Club. Mae's escort became the head of the narcotics squad, who promised Mae's mother that he would watch out for her daughter.

Mae and Ruby were frequently guests of Billy Rose, with the head of the narcotics squad along as well.

At other times Ruby and Mae went out with gangsters for a steak dinner and an occasional gift of a bracelet or necklace, which they quickly sold for extra money. To Mae the gangsters were nice men who happened to be in an illegal business. For the most part they behaved like gentlemen and treated Ruby and Mae to dinners. "Where else were we going to get steak dinners?" Mae said.

Being in two shows a night seemed manageable to Ruby and Mae. The

Everglades Café was a block away from the Shubert on Forty-Fourth Street. After a few evenings of doing both shows Ruby and Mae had the run figured out: they finished their numbers at the Shubert Theatre, got out of their costumes, threw on their coats (Ruby had bought hers on the installment plan and prayed the two jobs would hold out until the coat was paid for), ran out into the cold winter nights and down Forty-Fourth Street wearing nothing but a coat and a pair of shoes, "stark naked in freezing weather, and the coats were not so hot either. Papier-mâché." They got to the Everglades Café in time for their *Ship Ahoy* numbers, performed their routines, stripped off their sailor suit costumes, put on their coats, rushed back to the Shubert, and were there in time for their next number in *Gay Paree*. Working in two shows, they averaged as many as thirty-eight dance routines a night.

"We worked like dogs and were as strong as horses," said Ruby, who danced even when she had pleurisy. "You can't take a deep breath with pleurisy," said Ruby, "so you take a short breath. And you go on, until you run out of breath. I danced with blisters on my heels because I didn't want an understudy to take my place."

Ruby learned discipline to avoid being fired.

"I couldn't sing worth a darn," she said. "It didn't matter as long as [I] could belt it out so they could hear [me] in the back row." Although Ruby "was far from [being] a singer," she had a sultry look, a defiant gaze combined with an unadorned quality that was unusual for a showgirl.

Al Jolson stood in the wings during the ensemble numbers, smoking a cigar. As Ruby came off the stage, she slid by him on her way to the dressing room and tried to ignore his sexual remarks.

After one performance Ruby attempted to slide by him as usual. Jolson blocked her way and cornered her against a wall. Ruby was worried about the costume. It didn't fit that well and was pinned to stay on. She tried to laugh off Jolson's comments and hurry by, for fear of losing her job. Jolson told her he was going to take her home that night. Ruby forgot to make a joke of it. She became furious and struck him. He pushed her against the wall and ripped open her costume. She couldn't scream out; there was a show going on. He took his lit cigar and held it up to her skin with its red-hot tip burning into her breast and held it there until she blacked out.

"Ruby was tough," Mae said. "She was cool, very, very cool. She played men like she would any scene. She had a gentle side that she used to play up to men, but it could also be genuine." Ruby could be cruel to Mae, but at other times she could be protective of her, almost motherly. She was becoming more of a mother to Mae than Mrs. Klotz, and Mae's mother resented it. Ruby had a strength and toughness that Mae and Dorothy counted on. She advised them about what to wear and would lend them her clothes, even her shoes.

If they were entertaining, Ruby could be curt with guests. If she wanted to go to bed, she would say, "This is it. Get the hell out." She had a child-like gentleness that surprised her friends. "It was a sweet side that few people saw. If I was sick or tired, a warm, almost mothering side of Ruby came out," said Mae. "It wasn't what Ruby showed most people. She didn't like standing naked before people."

Ruby told Dorothy and Mae that for their next shot, their next oppor-tunity, they had to "wangle it, but do it legitimately, and always maintain [their] independence."

"I wouldn't have known that," said Mae, "but [Ruby] did. [Dorothy] and I listened to her. [She] was smart. We were harum-scarum kids, mad-caps who did crazy things but I never knew Ruby to do an unrefined thing."

"She was the Duchess," Mae said. "Always."

SEVEN

On Being Actresses, Not Asstresses

1926–1927

Pleasure was the color of the time.
—Harold Clurman

Ruby remained with *Gay Paree* until the end of the year, when the Shuberts put on a new edition of the show. During its run, Anatol Friedland, songwriter, composer, and producer of revues, went to see the show and noticed her. Friedland had earlier collaborated with Lee Shubert on the music for a show at the Winter Garden and thought the Misses Stevens, Clarke, and Sheppard talented and hired them for the Club Anatol on West Fifty-Fourth Street between Sixth and Seventh Avenues, next to Texas Guinan's. Throughout the next few months, Ruby, Mae, and Dorothy performed their specialty dances: Ruby, the Charleston; Mae, a buck dance; and Dorothy, something Hawaiian.

Friedland, who knew his way around Broadway and Tin Pan Alley, became protective of the trio and advised each about what she should do and whom she should see. Although he'd planned to become an architect after graduating from Columbia University, Friedland had drifted into vaudeville and appeared as the lead in musical productions, performing at the piano singing his own songs, and during the next two decades performed in or produced lavish revues. A year before he opened the Club Anatol, he was headlined on the Keith Circuit in *Anatol's Affairs of 1924.*

Dorothy Sheppard said of him: "Whatever he did was all right. He was like a father to us."

• • •

Barbara's brother, Malcolm, was back from the sea and was living with Maud and Bert on Avenue L, working at Merkent's Meat Market.

Malcolm at twenty-one was in love with Elizabeth Zilker, the daughter of the Ecuadoran consul, and was about to be married. His sister Mabel was about to be divorced. She had had it with her second husband coming home at the end of each day from his job at Condé Nast to their apartment on Church Avenue, taking out his handkerchief, and running it along the molding to see how meticulously his wife had dusted.

To get out of the house and out of the heat (moving picture theaters and the big vaudeville houses were installing refrigeration at a cost of $100,000 per theater), Mabel took Gene to the pictures as often as she could. After nine months of trying to get away from her second husband, Mabel had had enough of Darse Griffiths; she and Gene were going back to Avenue L to be with Maud and Bert and Al, she was returning to her job at Best & Co.

Ruby visited her sisters and brother in Brooklyn and asked Dorothy or Mae to come along. They took the subway to the end of the line at Nostrand Avenue and the trolley to Avenue L, walking the three blocks to Thirty-Sixth Street. Gene would watch for his aunt Ruby, and when he saw her a couple of blocks away walking toward his street, he would run out of the house and down the block and throw himself in her arms.

Each time Ruby came to visit, she carried with her a pile of ten or twelve books tied together to give to Gene, among them a series of stories about the Great War called Boy Allies with the Army—*The Boy Allies at Liege; or, Through Lines of Steel* and *The Boy Allies on the Firing Line*—and another series called The Motion Picture Boys as well as Robert Louis Stevenson's *Kidnapped* and *Treasure Island*. Gene was thrilled to have them.

In late April, Malcolm was married to Elizabeth at the Kings Highway Methodist Episcopal Church in a ceremony officiated by Norman Vincent Peale. A few friends were there, as were Elizabeth's brother, Frank, and Malcolm's family. Ruby's arrival with Mae and Dorothy caused a stir. On a whim the three had decided to dye their hair, and Ruby's hair, naturally a reddish auburn, as was Dorothy's—Mae's was brown—was now in a flame of spectacular red. Maud was not pleased at the color nor the disruption of decorum.

Bert and Mabel teased Maud about her grandness; she expected only the best, and it was often beyond her means. Maud wanted things to look right, to be just so, and it annoyed Ruby, who hated any pretense.

"My sister thinks she's high society," Ruby said of Maud. "And I always say to her, 'Look at me, am I high society? And I come from the same loins you do.' "

Elizabeth Zilker and Malcolm Byron Stevens, Brooklyn, New York, circa 1926. (COURTESY GENE VASLETT)

Maud's son, Albert, would raise his eyes and gesture in his mother's direction and say, "Oh . . . Queen Marie," referring to the queen of Romania, who had arrived in New York on the *Leviathan* and was being written about daily in the newspapers.

Ruby was delighted that her sister Mabel was now seeing a wonderful man: Roland Munier, a traveling salesman for Masury Paints whose sales territory was the northern part of New Jersey and who lived in a small apartment in Flatbush with his mother. He was welcomed into the Merkent family; Gene called him Uncle Rol. Each Saturday night, the Merkents, Mabel, and Roland played cards at Avenue L.

As spring turned into summer, Anatol Friedland let go of most of the dancers in the revue but invited a few—among them Ruby, Mae, and Dorothy—to the Ritz-Carlton Grille in Atlantic City, where Mae's family lived. The three stayed with the Klotzes.

While working for Anatol, the three girls met Carter De Haven, who had been around Broadway for a long time, first as a successful child actor, then as a headliner in vaudeville on the Orpheum Circuit as a singer and dancer. He had the reputation of being the most correctly dressed man on the American stage. De Haven had built a theater on Hollywood Boulevard between Vine Street and El Centro, Carter De Haven's Music Box, and wanted Ruby, Mae, and Dorothy to join him in a show he was putting together there.

He tried to sell Ruby on California, talking to her about its beauty and about how the girls should see it firsthand. Dorothy was tempted; Los Ange-

Ruby (left) with Jerry Dryden and Dorothy Shepherd (right), Atlantic City, 1926.

les sounded interesting; in fact she was sold on the idea. But Dorothy was too fond of Anatol to leave.

During the summer months, Ruby, Mae, and Dorothy modeled for various magazines—even modeling swimsuits on the beach—and swam in the ocean as often as they could. Ruby and Dorothy were swimming along the shore one day and didn't realize that they were being pulled out to sea until they noticed how small the boardwalk looked. Ruby, the better swimmer, began to make her way back to the beach. Dorothy swam along but struggled against the tide, tired quickly, and began to call for help. Anatol heard the calls from the boardwalk, made his way out to the swimmer, and was surprised to find he was rescuing Dorothy. Ruby made it back to shore on her own.

At the end of the 1926 summer season, the triumvirate returned to the Club Anatol in New York City.

James J. Walker was in his first eight months as the mayor of New York. Nightclubs and cabarets were more popular than ever; vaudeville's draw was beginning to fade. Between the Keith-Albee and the Orpheum Circuits, there were fewer than fifteen two-a-day vaudeville houses in New York. Most theaters that carried vaudeville with continuous shows throughout the country featured them with a moving picture like the sensational *Torrent,* which presented Greta Garbo in her first American picture; *Ben-Hur* with Francis X. Bushman; *Dancing Mothers* with Clara Bow; Lillian Gish as Hester Prynne in *The Scarlet Letter;* Garbo and John Gilbert in *Flesh and the Devil;* or *The Sea Beast* with John Barrymore and Dolores Costello. By late summer, theaters were giving moving pictures top billing over their stage shows.

In the first week of August at the Warner Theatre, on Broadway and Fifty-Second Street, Warner Bros. released its most expensively made picture ever, *Don Juan,* with John Barrymore, offering the greatest sensation of the decade since radio: sound that was recorded and synchronized to moving pictures. If movies were taking business away from vaudeville, radio was taking audiences away from movie theaters.

Ruby, Dorothy, and Mae were dancing onstage at Anatol's one night when Mrs. Henry B. Harris, wife of the late producer, came to see the revue. With her was the much-admired and successful actor, writer, director, and producer Willard Mack.

Mrs. Harris and Mack were casting a contemporary play that she and Martin Sampter were producing and that Bill Mack had co-written and was to direct. Mrs. Harris and Mack were looking for girls to fill the parts of cabaret singers in the play's second act. She liked the way Ruby, Dorothy, and Mae looked and arranged for them to come to her office at the Hudson Theatre on West Forty-Fourth Street.

When they arrived, three other young women were there as well. Mrs. Harris talked about the play and described the roles. The play was called *The Noose,* a contemporary drama about bootlegging and gangsters, the recklessness and violence of Prohibition, and capital punishment. The roles were cabaret girls with lines for them to speak. "This made all the difference," Ruby said. "This was big time stuff."

Without Mack's knowledge, Mrs. Harris had them read a few lines and hired them.

The Noose was based on a story by H. H. Van Loan, who began as a newspaperman and short story writer and who went on to become a screenwriter, selling his scripts to Maurice Tourneur, Norma Talmadge, William Desmond, and others. By 1920, Van Loan was the director of publicity for the Universal Film Company.

Bill Mack, successful Broadway playwright, was interested in capturing life as it was reported on the front pages of the newspapers, "with human frailties and hopes at the play's center." The realism of his characters and consistency of setting and action were central to his notion of the successful contemporary play.

By the time *The Noose* was to go into production, Bill Mack, then forty-eight, had written more than forty Broadway plays. Mack was rugged, romantic, swashbuckling, a heavy drinker, an outlaw of sorts, and a scorner of conventions. He wrote plays visualizing people as they were, "their ways of living, their home, their associates, conversations and ambitions."

At the center of *The Noose* is a young man who has murdered a notorious bootlegger and nightclub owner and is hours away from execution by hanging. The setting is a back room in a nightclub. Cabaret girls and bootleggers are in a swirl of hot jazz. In the third act, the governor's daughter, in love with the boy, goes before the governor to plead for the body of the young man following his execution.

Rex Cherryman played the part of the young man. He was a "handsome, wonderful actor," said Mae Clarke. Cherryman, then twenty-nine had already had a career in the theater, though he began as a bank clerk in his hometown of Grand Rapids, Michigan.

Lester Lonergan played the governor; Ann Shoemaker, the governor's wife; George Nash, the gangster club owner. "George Nash was the villain," said Mae. "And there was no worse one, but he was a great guy and a wonderful actor. We used to ask him, 'How do you act?' He would say, 'Now you girls, I'm not going to talk to you unless you get one thing straight with me. Are you serious about this business? Because I want you to be "actresses," not "asstresses." ' "

Ruby played a cabaret girl called Dot. Dorothy Sheppard was Frances, and Mae Clarke, Georgie. When the script was handed out, each had the same-size role.

Mrs. Harris was amazed at the way Ruby read and asked Mack to enlarge her part in act 2.

Bill Mack wanted to rehearse with Ruby in private, as he had Marjorie Rambeau before she became the second Mrs. Willard Mack; as he had with the great film star Pauline Frederick before she became the third Mrs. Mack.

Miss Rambeau had forcefully urged Mack to rehearse with her alone; Miss Frederick, stately and magnificent, had simply expected it. Ruby Stevens wanted the work but had no such expectations and was grateful to have the director's help whenever he could spare the time.

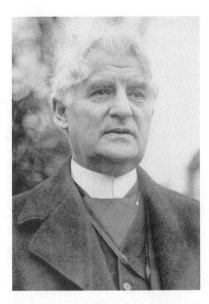

David Belasco, playwright, producer, director, stage genius, the "Wizard of the American Theater."

Mack one day took Ruby to see his longtime associate David Belasco, the maestro, the old master whose name was synonymous with the theater. By 1926, Belasco at seventy-three was considered eternal, a god.

He had produced hundreds of plays and helped to establish even more careers, from Mrs. Leslie Carter and Ina Claire to Maude Adams.

Belasco was seen as a force; he'd led the theater from the nineteenth century into the modern world, from the old Madison Square Theatre on Twenty-Fourth Street to the theater that carried his name on Forty-Fourth Street.

Belasco had started in the theater of gaslight flares forty years before and worked in a time when footlights were the dominant source of illumination on the stage, casting false shadows without control. Belasco had a notion about lighting and saw it as a way to dramatize the mood of a play. His experiments resulted in diffused light. He took a mica slide frosted with emery and oil, placed it on a series of coins, over a beam of light, and, by using silver reflectors, was able to control the spread of a beam of light. The harshness and unreality of footlights were banished from the Belasco stages.

By 1915, Belasco was able to re-create the different lights of a day, from a morning sunrise to the light of dusk, from the threatening light of a storm to the light of the moon. By using manually operated spotlights, sometimes with up to twenty electricians working at the same time, and nonreflecting spotlights, Belasco found a way to project differently colored lights that didn't clash on any number of people standing side by side on the stage.

Belasco and Willard Mack had just finished work on a play about a Yiddish vamp that starred Fanny Brice in her first drama. The play, produced as well by Belasco at the Lyceum, had opened in September and closed soon thereafter.

Belasco's office on West Forty-Fourth Street was above the theater. Ruby and Mack climbed a set of winding golden oak stairs that led to the cranium of the theater. Mack opened a small door with the name Belasco on it. He wanted the great director to hear Ruby read from her expanded part.

Belasco was then a silver presence with a white mane and piercing eyes staring out from under shaggy brows. Though he was born a Jew (the name was Velasco, his father had been a Harlequin in the London theaters), he wore the clothes of a cleric, and his manner was that of a mystic.

Belasco's private office was at the end of a series of rooms, fourteen in all. One held his many collections—of rosaries, rare and ancient glassware, vases, silver, urns, precious stones, armor standing against the walls, jester's sticks made of ivory and encrusted with jewels. Another housed the book-lined walls of his library, with a grand fireplace and a mantelpiece that had belonged to Stanford White. A Japanese room had bamboo walls; an Italian room, old velvet and an indoor garden with a fountain. Another room had only a crucifix. And then, finally, Belasco's office itself, with a simple desk given to him thirty-two years before by his mother and now held together with string.

Ruby was "scared pink," she said. "Scared of the office that looked like a cathedral, scared of the priest's collar, the white hair, the terrific power and prestige of the great impresario of the theater." Mack had Ruby read through her expanded scene from *The Noose.* "I kept wondering what the hell I was doing here," she said. "Me, Ruby Stevens."

Belasco told Ruby that she didn't know how to walk, that most women didn't know how to walk. "Go to the zoo!" he said. "Watch the animals!"

After Ruby's audition with Belasco, she sat in the visitors' room, waiting. She heard Mr. Belasco and Bill Mack talking. Belasco spoke slowly. He was telling Mack that she would have to change her name, that "Ruby Stevens" was too much like that of a burlesque queen.

"He sounded as though he was spitting my name right out on the floor," she said.

As Ruby tells the story, Belasco was looking through old theater programs, one from a quarter of a century before of a Clyde Fitch play of the Civil War, *Barbara Frietchie,* starring a Jane Stanwyck, about a Southern woman in love with a Union soldier, loosely based on the life of a real Barbara Frietchie of Maryland, "bravest of all in Frederick town," wrote John Greenleaf Whittier in his poem about her. Frietchie had been a fierce supporter of the Union, and as legend tells it, at ninety-five years of age, with rebel soldiers approaching her house, "took up the flag the men hauled down." ". . . To show that one heart was loyal," Frietchie waved the Stars and Stripes from her attic window as Brigadier General Jesse Reno and his troops passed by on the road to Washington County and the Battle at Antietem.

Fitch's play was fresh in the public's mind since Thomas Ince had made it into a two-hour movie—one of the big hits of 1924—that starred Florence Vidor and Edmund Lowe.

Julia Marlow had created "The Frederick Girl" in the original production that opened in Philadelphia on October 10, 1899, at the Broad Theatre and two weeks later in New York at the Criterion.

When the play returned to Broadway the following year, Effie Ellsler, "the uncommonly efficient and sympathetic actress," was the "ravishing young creature" of Frederick town.

Jane Stanwyck may have appeared in a touring production of the Fitch play, but there doesn't seem to be a record of it—or of her.

It might have been another theater program that caught Belasco's eye, one of Victor Herbert's comedy opera, *Dream City,* which opened in New York in 1906 for a three-month run. Among those listed in the ensemble: Addison Stanton and Dorothy Southwick. America's great theatrical wizard might simply have conflated the last two names, the Stan from Stanton; the Wick from Southwick, thrown in a 'y' to make it appear more regal and come forth with Jane Stanwyck as a new name for Ruby Stevens.

Mack said, "Jane Stanwyck won't do because of Jane Cowl," one of the great ladies of the theater, revered with the same passion as Laurette Taylor and Eleonora Duse. A few years earlier, Cowl had astounded audiences in her twenty-week run of *Romeo and Juliet* and triumphed over Ethel Barrymore's Juliet. On the last day of Cowl's run, three thousand people had stood outside Henry Miller's Theatre in the hope of catching a glimpse of the great actress; a thousand people who hoped to see her in her final performance as Juliet were turned away from the theater. Cowl was due to come to New York at the beginning of the New Year—1927—with Philip Merivale in a debut play by Robert E. Sherwood called *The Road to Rome.*

Mack and Belasco looked at the *Frietchie* program again. "As one man, they said, 'Barbara Stanwyck,' " said Ruby. "I was rechristened with Mr. Belasco and Mr. Mack as my second sponsors in baptism."

Later, when Ruby signed her contract, she wrote "Barbara" but had to be reminded of how to spell her new last name.

At Mrs. Harris's suggestion, it was to be Ruby's character, Dot, in *The Noose*, who was in unrequited love with the young man rather than the governor's daughter. Mrs. Harris cast and staged her plays and had been producing this way a decade before *The Noose*. She'd learned from her brother, Edgar Wallach, and her husband, Henry B. Harris, both successful showmen and theatrical producers.

Henry Harris was from a theatrical family: his father, William Harris Sr., began as a blackface comedian and became a famous minstrel man and was one of the founders of the Theatrical Syndicate. The younger Harris had learned the business from his father and set out on his own to produce shows and manage theaters, among them the Hudson Theatre. In 1911, Harris, with Jesse Lasky, built the Folies Bergère dinner theater. Shortly before Harris and his wife left on a tour of the Continent, the dinner theater was converted into the Fulton Theatre.

The Harrises' journey abroad ended with a tour of North Africa. Mrs. Harris broke an arm, and both Harrises were happy to be returning to America on the White Star liner *Titanic,* bound for New York from Southampton. On the fourth day out to sea, four hundred miles south of Newfoundland, the Harrises were in their cabin playing a game of double Canfield when Mrs. Harris felt the ship's engines stop.

The *Titanic*'s captain, Edward J. Smith, realized the ship had struck an iceberg and was taking in water. The crew sent up distress rockets to radio CQD signals, to which the Cunard liner *Carpathia* signaled back; it was making its way northward toward the *Titanic*. The *Carpathia* was fifty-eight miles away when it radioed back and would take four hours to reach the *Titanic*. The more than twenty-two hundred passengers of the *Titanic* were not going to be rescued in time. Women and children were loaded into the twenty lifeboats for eleven hundred passengers.

Henry Harris, then forty-five years old, escorted his wife of fourteen years to the crew that had formed a ring around one of the lifeboats. The boat sat forty-seven; there were sixteen hundred people left on board. Renée (listed on the ship's manifest as Irene) Harris was helped onto lifeboat collapsible D, the last boat to be lowered from the *Titanic*.

Following a long period of mourning, Mrs. Henry B. Harris, as she was thereafter referred, took over the estate of Henry B. Harris, brought suit against the White Star Line for $1 million for the loss of her husband, and,

Willard Mack, who before becoming a playwright
and director was a stock actor touring America's
West. (*NEW YORK TRIBUNE*)

rather than "living the life of an idle rich woman," began to produce plays
herself. One of the first to be presented was a play called *Damaged Goods* with
Richard Bennett, about the taboo subject of syphilis, that became one of the
most controversial plays of the 1913 season.

Renée Harris became a theatrical manager, designer, and technical director; she understood that producing and directing were not as romantic as appearing on the stage, but at the age of thirty-seven she felt strongly that hers
was a profession to which women ought to belong and one that in the long
run would prove more profitable than acting.

Willard Mack assembled *The Noose*'s cast for rehearsals. Instead of the actors reading their parts aloud, Mack read to them as he wanted each part to
be played, using the power of his voice to virtually hypnotize his company.
Mack was tough and demanding and wanted perfection, and for him that
meant a naturalism, a realism.

His desire as a playwright to capture realism came from his decades-long
association with Belasco, who had acted in more than 130 plays before starting to write and direct. Belasco was a stickler about realism, not just with the
lighting and the look of the play, but with the actors.

Mack's notion of realism came as well from his work as a reporter in Chicago and from the many lives he'd lived before he became a full-time playwright: sailing to the South Seas with Jack London; prospecting for gold in
Alaska; being an officer in the Northwest Mounted Police. He'd worked in

The cabaret girls of *The Noose*. Left to right, top row: Mae Clarke, Dorothy Shepherd. Left to right, bottom row: Erenay Weaver, Ruby, Maryland Jarbeau. (PHOTOFEST)

vaudeville, become a stock actor in his own play, *In Wyoming*, and toured with it out west for more than two years on the John Cort "tank town" circuit.

Mack believed that his new play, *The Noose*, defied all conventionality in construction, speech, and action. He wanted the nightclub owner to sound like a gambler and bootlegger and the governor to sound the opposite. To Mack the world war had changed everything. Established standards had been thrown out: delicacy of speech had been prostituted by modern convention; the belief in chastity, the reverence for parental guidance, and the intimacies of domesticity were being talked about in ways that would have been considered an affront prior to the war. Mack wanted Dot to act and sound like thousands of other cabaret dancers, and he worked with Ruby during rehearsals to get that sense of truth in the part.

"He threw the gestures out of all of us," Ruby said. "Mack would say if we can't come on stage without screwing up our faces or waving our hands . . . we'd just better make the next exit permanent."

Following Mr. Belasco's command that Ruby learn how to walk, she traveled to the Bronx Zoo, where she watched the animals in their cages pacing back and forth. It was the panther's stride with its purpose and beauty that captured her eye, and Ruby copied it until it became somewhat natural for her. "It is a way of walking that holds off fatigue," she said.

The Noose went on the road for three weeks, opening first in Buffalo at the Shubert-Teck Theatre. The *Buffalo Courier* called the play "superb" and went on to say of the cast that it was as "fine and polished as we've seen in the theater in many a moon." Cherryman's performance was described as "remarkable . . . never once does he overplay the part."

Despite the positive reviews, there was a problem with the last scene of the third act. The society girl's plea to the governor for the young man's body was supposed to build to a pitch, but it had no emotional payoff. "It was a big nothing," said Mae Clarke. The governor "granted it and the curtain came down."

Mrs. Harris called a meeting with Mack to try to solve the problem. She realized that the wrong woman was pleading for the boy's body and told Mack to use "the girl who has the unrequited love that he doesn't know about," Mae said, describing Mrs. Harris's vision. "They're just friends as far as he's concerned, but she's nuts about him. Let her be the one to ask for the body."

Mrs. Harris told Mack to rewrite the part and give the scene to the cabaret girl. Mack finished the new dialogue and gave Ruby the additional pages. He told her in front of the cast to go home and learn the lines. "You've got a great voice," he said. "If you can do the part, take it, you've got it for out-of-town until we can find an actress to play it."

Bill Mack left for New York that night to try to find a major actress for the role.

Renée Harris worked with Ruby and Rex Cherryman on Mack's new pages.

"I was no actress," said Ruby. "I was a dancer, not a great one but I knew left from right."

The next morning, Ruby rehearsed with the entire company, and Mrs. Harris thought her work was "dynamic." Mack called several times from New York to suggest various names of actresses he thought would be right for the part, among them the Broadway star Francine Larrimore, niece of Jacob Adler, founder of the Yiddish Theater. Larrimore was traveling to Buffalo to meet up with the show.

Mack returned from New York to Mrs. Harris's excitement about Ruby's work in the new role. That afternoon he watched Ruby in rehearsal and told Mrs. Harris that her work with the cabaret girl was an inspiration. Mack "proceeded to go on a drinking binge from sheer joy."

During the remainder of the week's run in Buffalo, the director worked with Ruby, training her "hours upon hours upon hours," said Ruby. "It was a living hell." Except for catnaps backstage, Ruby didn't sleep at all. Toward the end, she broke down and stormed and yelled that she couldn't act—

couldn't and, what's more, wouldn't—and, weeping, said, "It's no use. I can't act. I don't know how."

Up to this point, Mack had flattered and encouraged Ruby. Now he yelled back at her in front of the entire company that she was "dead right." She was a chorus girl, "would always be a chorus girl, would live and die a chorus girl and be damned."

"Mack completely disarranged my mental make-up," said Ruby. "The bejesus was scared out of me."

She fought back, said she could act, would act. "I told him I was Bernhardt, Fiske, all the Booths and Barrymores rolled into one."

Mack had seen temperament around the theater and fire, but he had never seen a performance to equal Ruby's that afternoon. Then he hammered "every line, every inflection, every gesture of the part into my memory," teaching Ruby how to read, how to walk, what tricks to use and not to use, and how to sell herself by entrances and exits.

"Mostly he taught me to think," said Ruby. "Acting is thinking."

Mae and Dorothy worked as Ruby's coaches, sitting with the script and helping her run her lines. "We kept telling her," Mae said, "you're going to do it! You're going to do it! Come on!"

After rehearsals, Ruby and Rex Cherryman would go out for a sandwich and coffee.

"Everything about him was so vivid," said Ruby. "Or perhaps it was because he was an actor and knew how to project."

Rex was handsome and young. He had great talent and good humor. Ruby adored him, but Rex was married and had a small boy.

Cherryman had recently appeared on Broadway in a play called *Down Stream*. He was from the Midwest, which he left to become an actor. He'd traveled to Los Angeles, where he found work in various stock companies traveling from Pasadena to San Diego to Denver, and then appearing in Alla Nazimova's early 1920s pictures *Madame Peacock* and *Camille*.

The Noose left Buffalo for Pittsburgh, where it was to open at the Pitt Theatre on October 11. This was to be Ruby's first performance in front of an audience with the new third act.

The cast rehearsed that day down the block from the Pitt Theatre at the William Penn Hotel.

The evening of the performance the curtain went up on acts 1 and 2 as the company had rehearsed and played them before. Ruby, Dorothy, and Mae went on in the second act as they had in Buffalo. "We were little chorus girls," said Mae. Ruby had a few more lines than the others "but not by much."

Then Ruby went into the third act.

"When I came out on the stage," she said, "I was all alone. The farther I walked from the wings, the more frightened I became; each step I took toward the governor's desk out there in the center of the stage the weaker I grew."

The governor's secretary met Ruby halfway and escorted her to him.

"The governor looked up at me," said Ruby. "I was supposed to be frightened, hopeless, desperate. My hands were clammy. I had that awful feeling that the muscles in my throat were paralyzed, and that when it came time for me to speak, I wouldn't be able to utter a sound."

The governor spoke his line: "Are you the young lady that wanted to see me?"

Ruby said her lines in response and "didn't recognize her own voice."

"I've come to ask you," she said as Dot, "if we could have his body because we'd like to give it a real funeral . . . You see he ain't got no relatives, ain't even got a father and mother, he told me—so nobody wants it but us . . . That's what I came for, ain't no reason why I can't have it—is there—if nobody wants it."

Then Dot sinks her head on the desk and begins to sob softly. The governor tells her there is no reason why she shouldn't claim the boy except that he is not dead, he was not executed. Dot asks, "He ain't dead?" and then asks the governor not to tell the boy she was here.

The governor pauses. "You love him don't you?"

Dot confesses she was "always crazy about him—even if he never gave me a tumble. But—there's a girl—somewhere—'cause Nickie told me he wanted to have a wife. And if he lives, I'll find out who she is—and fix it up between them . . . You see, caring about him—that was the reason I came. He never gave me a break while he was out and around so I thought that when he was dead I could take the body away somewhere to a little cemetery I know and then I could go there once in a while and tell him the things I couldn't say when he was alive—see?"

The governor asks her if she wants to see the young man, and she is taken offstage by his secretary.

Mae and Dorothy grabbed hold of Ruby in the wings; they "didn't say a word because nothing was happening," said Mae. "Usually they give a little polite applause when an actor leaves the stage. Nothing. And there was nothing else to be said . . .

"Then, the heavens broke loose," said Mae. "The people screamed. They stomped their feet. They stood up. She was so terrific!"

The Pittsburgh Post called the play "a simple melodrama dressed up in modern accoutrements . . . there were times," said the *Post* critic, "when the sound of a pin hitting the carpet would have resembled the advent of a small boy's new Fourth of July," and reported that "the house lights put an end to the curtain calls."

Mack had assured Ruby during the endless hours of rehearsals that she would be able to "do it when the time comes."

Ruby said later, "I did it. Somehow I did it."

The Noose went to New York and opened at Mrs. Harris's Hudson Theatre on October 20, 1926. Ruby was nineteen years old and had worked on and around Broadway, just barely getting by, for five years. Now she was earning $100 a week.

She wasn't sure how she felt about being a dramatic actress. "It's noisy back stage in a musical or a night club," she said. "But in a dramatic show you don't even whisper for fear the people out front will hear you. Where before there'd been kidding and laughs, the silence made me nervous."

The Noose was being compared to another play that had opened five weeks before at the Broadhurst Theatre, Jed Harris's hit production, *Broadway,* by Philip Dunning and George Abbott.

Sam N. Behrman, a young press agent for the production, described *Broadway* as being as "realistic as a metronome without a grain of sentimentality," a "gutter play about the lowest forms of human life, set in a degraded cabaret frequented by rival bootlegger gangs with guns at the ready." The play received strong notices and was a big hit, bringing in as much as $31,000 a week, making its writers and producers rich. It was also making a name for its star, Lee Tracy.

Broadway was considered gritty and real, and *The Noose* "melodrama of a slightly old model," though tough and thrilling. The word was out that the second act of *The Noose* was almost identical to *Broadway,* with only minor differences.

On opening night of *The Noose,* following the second act, Bill Mack went in front of the curtain to make a statement to his audience. He assured them that *The Noose* had been written a year before *Broadway* opened and that his play had remained largely unchanged from the initial draft.

The reviews for *The Noose* ran the following day. The New York *Sun,* in a review by Stephen Rathbun, warned that the play would "grip you if you don't watch out!" The reviewer mentioned "a moving scene in the last act" by "Miss Barbara Stanwyck," who "played it well enough to make first nighters wipe tears from their eyes." The New York *Telegraph* called *The Noose* "sentimental" but described Cherryman's performance as "splendid" and, in the final line of the review, said that "Barbara Stanwyck brings the handkerchiefs forth with expediency." The *Telegram* said it was "the most authentically teary play of the season" and that "there is an uncommonly fine performance by Barbara Stanwyck who not only does the Charleston steps of a dance hall girl gracefully, but knows how to act . . . After [she] breaks down and sobs out her unrequited love for the young bootlegger in that genuinely moving scene . . . there was nothing for the Governor to do but reprieve the boy. If he hadn't, the weeping audience would probably have yelled at him until he did." *The New York Times* described the play as "good entertainment when it gets going" with "several good performances." After singling out the work of its star and praising George Nash's "characteristic performance," the *Times* mentioned the "further good work of Dorothy Stanwyck."

There were moments when even Ruby had to ask "Clarke (Mae) what my name was." Another time Ruby heard someone calling "Miss Stanwyck, Miss Stanwyck" around the Hudson Theatre and said, "Where is that dame? Why doesn't she answer?"

Ruby sent wires to her family in Flatbush inviting them to come to the show. On the day of the performance, when Ruby went onstage in the second act, she looked out at the front row expecting to see her sisters and nephew, but instead the seats she had paid for were empty. She felt "utterly forlorn and friendless," she said.

After the performance Ruby found out that her family had come to the theater, claimed their tickets, taken their seats, and, full of pride, looked through the program in search of Ruby's name. When they didn't find "Ruby Stevens" listed, they assumed they were in the wrong theater and had been given tickets that were meant for others. They were sure the management would ask them to leave and were so uncomfortable they left before they could be ejected.

Ed Kennedy frequently went to see Ruby in the show. It was during the run of *The Noose* that their romance began to fall apart. Their working hours were diametrically opposed. Ed finished his work at the office as Ruby was getting ready to go to the theater.

"We both had these terrible driving ambitions, which conflicted," Ed said. Ruby was serious about her work, and Ed about his. "And we'd get impatient with each other." The relationship cooled for a while, but Ed had

Ruby with Rex Cherryman, February 1927, Mineola,
New York.

not yet given up. He was jealous of Bill Mack, but "he was wrong there," said
Ruby. "He should have focused on Rex [Cherryman]. I adored him." She
and Rex began to spend more time together, and she brought him home to
Avenue L for everyone to meet.

"I think she was in love with him in her way," said Dorothy.

Despite *The Noose*'s mixed reviews, the play ran through the winter months,
into 1927 and through part of the spring. Its competition during the 1926–
1927 season included Anita Loos's adaptation of her best-selling comic novel
Gentlemen Prefer Blondes, with June Walker as Lorelei Lee and Frank Morgan
as Henry Spoffard, the famous Philadelphia Presbyterian (and moralist) who
preferred "a witless blonde." In November, Gertrude Lawrence opened in
George Gershwin's *Oh, Kay!* by P. G. Wodehouse and Guy Bolton; Ethel
Barrymore was playing in *The Constant Wife,* Somerset Maugham's comedy
about infidelity; and Eva Le Gallienne as director, actress, and founder of the
Civic Repertory Theatre in its revival of *The Three Sisters.*

A number of plays that opened that year were considered sexually outrageous, decadent, not fit for the stage.

When *The Captive* opened early in the season, many theatergoers were prepared to be shocked. Édouard Bourdet's play *La prisonnière* had first appeared in Paris, and word of its audacious theme had reached New York. The play was about a woman struggling against her passion for another woman who marries in a desperate attempt to save herself and escape her terrifying feelings. Ultimately, she abandons her marriage in pursuit of the woman whose love for her has held her captive. It opened at the Empire Theatre and starred Helen Menken (who had just married another Broadway actor, Humphrey Bogart) and Basil Rathbone.

Many critics who expected the worst were surprised by the deftness of Arthur Hornblow's translation and adaptation of the play, produced and directed by Gilbert Miller. Brooks Atkinson thought its treatment of "the theme and the austere quality of the performance cleared the humid air like a northwestern breeze." Alexander Woollcott in the New York *World* saw the play as "unprecedented . . . a study of an abnormal erotic passion, made with infinite tact and reticence." George Jean Nathan called *The Captive* "profoundly wrought." Other critics, many under the auspices of William Randolph Hearst, were outraged by the subject and the play.

Hearst had a personal bias against *The Captive*. His mistress's niece Pepi Lederer was an avowed lesbian. Marion Davies was unfazed by her niece's sexual preferences, but Hearst was made furious by Pepi's refusal to adhere to what he believed was moral and decent; Hearst was made even more enraged by Pepi's public display of her liaisons.

Articles condemning *The Captive* appeared in the Hearst morning and afternoon New York newspapers, the *Journal,* the *American,* and the *Daily Mirror.* Despite the bad press, the play was having a successful run. But Hearst's campaign began to take hold. Public outcries of obscenity and calls for censorship reached a pitch, and the Citizens' Play Jury, formed several years before, made up of theater managers, playwrights, actors, and civic associations, was pressured into putting the play on trial for indecency. *The Captive* was tried and cleared of its charges. It continued with the run, as did the campaign against it.

The Society for the Suppression of Vice, under the leadership of John Sumner, who saw Broadway as a "sewer," was determined to rid the theater of the indecency and filth that had overtaken the New York stage. Sumner was joined in his relentless campaign by the Catholic Church and other religious organizations. The result was the newly passed Padlock Bill that allowed the police to raid any "obscene, indecent, immoral or impure drama." Theater owners, directors, agents, and actors were all to be held accountable for any indecent productions in which they were a part. They could be arrested, tried, and imprisoned. In response to the hysteria, Texas Guinan began to wear a necklace of miniature gold padlocks.

At the heart of the furor was a play written by and starring Mae West that had opened the previous April. *Sex* had been written under the name Jane Mast. When it opened at John Cort's Daly's Theatre, it was a sensation. Tickets sold for the extraordinary price of $10.00 a seat when the top-priced ticket in the 1926–1927 season was $2.80. The play was making $10,000 a week. No newspaper, including *The New York Times,* would carry an ad for it; the word "sex" was taboo unless it was used to refer to "the opposite sex" or "the fair sex." Out of desperation to get the word around, ads were placed on top of taxicabs that read: "HEATED—Mae West in SEX—Daly's 63rd Street Theatre."

Sex was about a prostitute who allows a young society boy, unaware of her past, to fall in love with her and is brought home to meet his family. The boy's mother is shocked when she finds out the truth about her son's intended, and a battle of wits ensues between the mother and the prostitute/fiancé.

Audiences found shocking the open declaration of a woman as a sexual being. The play dared to challenge the accepted standards of marriage, respectability, and convention. (Mae West to the boy's mother: "I'm going to dig under the veneer of your supposed respectability and show you what you are . . . the only difference between us is that you could afford to give it away.") At the play's end the Mae West character is neither transformed, punished, nor spiritually redeemed.

Forty-four weeks into the run of *Sex,* in February 1927, under the jurisdiction of the Padlock Law, the police raided the theaters in which *Sex, The Captive,* and a play called *The Virgin Man* were running. The charge: obscenity.

The cast of *Sex* was placed under arrest. Mae West was held overnight at the Jefferson Market Women's Prison on Sixth Avenue and Ninth Street ("It was no rose," she said of it, "the very young and perhaps foolish, but certainly some innocent were mixed with foul and decaying old biddies who knew every vice and had invented a few of their own").

The twelve actors from *The Captive,* as well as the writer, Arthur Hornblow, and the producer, Gilbert Miller, were taken from the Empire Theatre to the nearest police station, where they were fingerprinted but not booked.

Another play, *The Shanghai Gesture,* was given two weeks to revise its script. The play was written by John Colton, co-author of *Rain,* was directed by Guthrie McClintic, and starred Florence Reed. *The Shanghai Gesture* was about an Oriental madam of a Shanghai whorehouse seeking revenge through her drug-addicted son on the Englishman who had promised to marry her.

The raids were reported on the front page of *The New York Times;* the headline in the *New York Herald Tribune* read: "Three Shows Halted, Actors Arrested in Clean-Up of Stage." Mae West chose to stand trial rather than close down the play. A month later a grand jury indicted her, the cast of *Sex,* and the theater's owner, John Cort, on grounds that they had produced "an obscene, indecent, immoral and impure drama." The jury handed down a verdict of guilty. The judge applauded the decision, saying, "Obscenity and immorality pervaded this show from beginning to end," and told West that she had gone "to extremes to make the play as obscene and immoral as possible." She was sentenced to ten days in prison at the Welfare Island Women's Workhouse and had to pay a fine of $500.

The Captive reopened and closed soon after the raid; it was shut down by Adolph Zukor, whose Famous Players owned Charles Frohman Inc., which had brought *The Captive* to Broadway. *The Captive*'s translator and adapter, Arthur Hornblow, was fed up with civic-minded groups censoring the theater and left New York altogether to work in Hollywood as a writer for Samuel Goldwyn.

The Noose ran for 197 performances through the first week of April. Each night onstage Ruby broke down and pleaded for the young man she loved and held audiences in thrall. Mae and Dorothy teased Ruby about her emotional performance. "She cried and she screamed," said Dorothy, "and we got to kidding her about it. But Ruby said, 'Well, it's getting me someplace,' and we couldn't argue with that."

During the run of the play Bill Mack gave Barbara some advice. "He didn't exactly tell me—he dinned it into me. He said, 'It's wonderful to be good on the stage and to be aware of your talent and not be shy about it. If someone gives you a compliment about your work, learn to accept it graciously. But—always remain aware that you are expendable, that nobody is so great they can't be replaced.' "

Each time Ruby went onstage, she had to "start from scratch," to prove herself again. There was nothing about her work she could take for granted; if she faltered, she knew she could be fired.

EIGHT

Formerly Ruby Stevens of the Cabarets

1927–1929

During the run of *The Noose* a new picture called *Broadway Nights* was being cast at Cosmopolitan Studios on 125th Street. The picture follows the rise of a jazz-singing chorus girl from vaudeville to nightclubs to Broadway musical star, a story set against Manhattan's nightlife (it promised to present to audiences "the heart of the great White Way—the bright lights and broken hearts. Night clubs! Cabarets! Speak-easies!").

The producer of *Broadway Nights,* Robert Kane, and his production manager, Leland Hayward, who was casting the picture, were still looking for a leading lady days before they were to begin to shoot. Ruby tested for the part along with a hundred other actresses from Broadway and the screen.

Ruby's test didn't go well. The cameraman, Ernest Haller, turned against her after she rebuffed his flirtation. One of the producer's press agents who watched the test said Ruby "wasn't in the market for cameramen, producers or press agents."

"She was handicapped further," he said, "because the scene called for her to cry. The director had the old stand-by method of starting the tears [by using] an onion, a rasping violin and a cracked piano."

While Ruby was trying to cry, Ruth Chatterton, also testing for the part, came on the set accompanied by her maid. As they watched the director's efforts with the onion and the music, Chatterton, the great stage star, began to laugh at the notion of any serious stage actress needing to resort to such methods.

Ruby "hissed between sobs" for silence. Robert Kane's press agent walked over to Miss Chatterton and informed her that the girl before the camera was Barbara Stanwyck, whose big scene in *The Noose* was "bringing the critics back night after night just to have a good cry."

From *Broadway Nights,* 1927. Left to right, center: Sam Hardy, Lois Wilson, unidentified, Ruby in large hat, ruffled dress, and dark bob.

Miss Chatterton was quiet after that until it was time for her test.

Ruby didn't get the part; nor did Ruth Chatterton. Lois Wilson starred in the picture.

Ruby as "Barbara Stanwyck" appeared in the film in a small part as a nightclub dancer and friend of the Lois Wilson character. Kane was so impressed with the way Ruby came across on the screen that he announced to the press he had put Barbara Stanwyck under contract as a "new find." The picture introduced other new faces of Broadway, among them Sylvia Sidney, who was starring in A. H. Woods's play, *Crime.*

The Noose closed in New York the first week in April and opened in Chicago ten days later, for a ten-week run at the Selwyn Theatre. Business was slow, and the decision was made to close the play a month early; by June 4, *The Noose* was shut down.

Ruby, Dorothy Sheppard, and Mae Clarke went back to New York, out of work, and daily made the rounds of all the agencies, going in and out of agents' offices on Forty-Second Street "as regularly as I breathed and ate my meals," said Ruby. "I don't know which there were more of, parts I hoped for that didn't happen, or parts that happened in shows that closed." Ruby tried to dress well, to be seen about, to "keep my chin up," she said.

After *The Noose* closed, Bill Mack told Dorothy Sheppard she needed a different name and came up with "Walda" and suggested "Mansfield" to go with it. Dorothy thought the two sounded "so pretty together." Dorothy Sheppard was now "Walda Mansfield."

Mae's moods took hold and tended to last for weeks at a time. During these "spells" she thought too much about herself and "lost all sense of proportion and values."

Once her mood abated, Mae enlisted the help of an agent to get her work. Louis Shurr was a top agent in New York who worked with Sophie Tucker and Fanny Brice, among others. Shurr was a short, funny-looking man who went out with beautiful women, giving his escort an ermine coat to wear at the start of the evening and expecting it to be returned at its end.

Shurr suggested that Mae put together an act and said he would see what he could do with it. Mae went to Tin Pan Alley, to Irving Berlin's building, with its row of songwriters and song pluggers, to pick out a song as the basis of the number. She was put in a little cubbyhole with a piano player who sat at "a little straight piano [on] a little seat."

Walter Donaldson was a self-taught pianist turned songwriter whose hit songs of the decade included "How Ya Gonna Keep 'Em Down on the Farm," "Carolina in the Morning," and "My Blue Heaven." Donaldson played song after song for Mae until she picked one she liked, which he then taught her.

Ruby helped Mae "put a few steps together" and choreographed her dance: "a cartwheel, a click of the heels together on the top, a ring of the bell, ring, a bum-buh. A little step to get you around the floor. Then pull yourself back."

Next Mae called her friend Claire Taishoff Muller, now married with a daughter and living on Long Island, and asked to borrow a dress ("Yellow's good," Claire said) with little diamonds all over it.

Shurr arranged for Mae to perform the number one time only at the Club Madrid and brought George White to watch. George White "*owned* New York," said Mae. "Besides, he was cute—very cute." White liked what he saw and hired Mae for his new show, *Manhattan Mary*, which was to star Elizabeth Hines and Ed Wynn. Mae was given two dance numbers with Harland Dixon, considered, said Mae, "one of the ten best tap dancers of the world."

After *The Noose* closed, Rex Cherryman and Ruby saw less of each other. Ruby was looking for work and was seeing Ed Kennedy again.

Ed was no longer working for Condé Nast; he had a bigger job at a relatively new magazine, a weekly, called *Liberty,* similar in size and content to *The Saturday Evening Post* and *Collier's. Liberty* paid higher fees for stories and for art and was attracting the best writers and illustrators—Scott Fitzgerald, Ben Hecht, Peter Arno, and Ralph Barton. The magazine's circulation was growing, and Ed Kennedy's job was growing with it.

Ruby and Ed talked about getting married, but they couldn't come to an understanding about how their lives would work together. Ed could easily have supported Ruby, but he would never suggest to her that she give up her work. Her ambitions of being an actress were as big as his of becoming a magazine publisher.

Ruby rarely let it show when she was depressed. "The surface was beautiful," said Ed Kennedy, "but there was depth to this girl." During difficult times Ruby showed her strength and will to survive, but weeks had passed without her finding work, and Ed saw how upset she was. It was at lunch one day at the Piccadilly restaurant that Ed finally asked Ruby why she wanted "to go through all this[.] Come on," he said, "let's go down to City Hall and get married." They left the restaurant mid-lunch, hailed a cab, and were on their way.

"This is crazy," said Ruby, with the cab stopped at a red light. "Our marriage wouldn't last a week. You have to make your success and I have to make mine."

During the spring of 1927, George Manker Watters went to see a performance of *The Noose.* Watters had been a manager of stock companies and was now managing the Astor movie theater. He'd written a play, *Burlesque*—his first—that, like so many other plays of the time, was about backstage life, about the world Watters knew so well, the world of vaudevillians, hoofers, and down-and-out comics.

Burlesque had been sent around to producers for several years until Lawrence Weber read the script and, despite its problems, agreed to put it on. The play was given a tryout but was shelved for a few months until August.

The producer sent the script to Arthur Hopkins, one of the most distinguished and daring directors and theatrical producers of his time. Hopkins thought the play was a muddle but was taken with the two central characters, a burlesque comedian and his soubrette wife, and agreed to work with Watters to fix the script. Hopkins's experience as a young playwright and staff reporter for a small-town newspaper had taught him how to construct a story.

Hopkins saw that for most playwrights realism was flat, mediocre. Writing and acting, to Hopkins, were explorations of the unknown self. He yearned for a return to the unconscious, to a poetic dream state, and helped to accomplish this through his long association with the great stage designer Robert Edmond Jones. Jones moved away from photographic and realistic stage designs toward a visual interpretation of mood and meaning using line, color, and light in his stage backgrounds. If theater was going to deal with everyday life, Hopkins wanted it to bring "some new illumination, some new understanding."

Hopkins saw the legitimate theater as being in transition and was the first to open a nickelodeon in a rented storeroom on the corner of Eighth Avenue and Thirty-Second Street in New York. To Hopkins, the theater was no longer the "palace of dreams, of unreality, that lifted people far out of themselves . . . with the actors as liberators, guides to exalted places," as it had been for more than a century. It was Ibsen who'd changed the rules by giving birth to the intellectual drama and elevating the theater "from the unconscious to the conscious mind." Ibsen was a poet, and to Hopkins, unlike most playwrights following in his path, the realism Ibsen portrayed was imbued with a symbolism that could touch the unconscious.

Together Hopkins and Watters worked out a different second act for *Burlesque*. When Watters came back with something other than what was discussed, Hopkins wasn't satisfied, and together they outlined another second act. Watters returned with something that Hopkins thought still wasn't right. After Watters's sixth rewrite, Hopkins was ready to abandon the play. His notion of the second act was so clear that he finally wrote it himself and, to free up Watters's response to the material, told him that he had hired a collaborator. Watters was delighted with the new second act, and he and Hopkins entered into an agreement, with the director ultimately rewriting the first and third acts as well.

Both men went in search of the principals, Skid Johnson and Bonny Kane, each role requiring actors who could play comedy as well as drama and who could sing and dance.

Skid Johnson is a heavy-drinking comic in a down-and-out song-and-dance group whose talents are being eaten away by too much liquor and too little ambition. Skid is a tall, rawboned, hard-dancing, singing clown in checked baggy trousers, bulbous red-putty nose, trick collar and tie who's seen it all in musical-comedy road shows. As the play opens, he's traveling in the sticks in a burlesque show, getting by—barely—with any job that comes his way.

His wife, Bonny, is hot-tempered. She is young and pretty with golden-red hair, born on the road to an entertainer mother and sent off to her aunt's to get away from the world of dingy hotels and cold railroad stations only to run away, at sixteen, to join a third-rate musical show. Bonny's talent and freshness as a singer and dancer propel her out of the chorus into Skid's troupe as the leading lady, into Skid's arms, and into marriage. Her sole ambition: to get for Skid the break and recognition he deserves in a Broadway show. Bonny pushes Skid in his work, ignoring his infidelity with a showgirl in the company. When the long-sought offer comes from Charles Dillingham, Skid leaves for New York, leaving Bonny behind, who watches as her husband's fame, and New York speakeasies, almost destroy him, body and soul.

Bonny sets her divorce in motion and begins a new life with a devoted, loving cattleman until she is drawn back to New York and to Skid when she is asked to help sober him up for an important opening. Skid finds redemption in his need for his wife and her willingness "to stick" with him.

On opening night he goes onstage with Bonny watching in the wings, calling to him between numbers, "Atta boy, Skid. Keep it up, Skid. You're knockin' 'em cold." And then she is with him on the stage, dancing with him in the spotlight before a full house, doing a soft shoe together, side by side, hearing Skid's labored breath, seeing his straining eyes, and, as they dance, asking him if he can make it.

"I can; if you stick."

Bonny to Skid: "I'll stick."

"For good?" he asks.

Her yes almost stops him, and then they are in the wings after an encore. Bonny says, "I guess it's like the guy that spliced us said, 'For better or for worse.'"

"Yeah," Skid says. "Better for me and worse for you."

For the role of Skid, Hopkins hired Hal Skelly, a musical comedian with little experience in serious drama. Hopkins saw in him an "engaging, lovable quality which was essential to the part."

Skelly's life resembled Skid's. He had toured the circuits beginning at age fourteen; he was studying to be a priest at St. Bess College near Davenport, Iowa, when he'd run away with a troupe of actors. Skelly performed in comic operetta and became a leading comedian, getting to know life on the circuit touring in Honolulu, Shanghai, Tokyo, and the Philippines with Raymond Teale's musical comedy company. He'd worked as a barker and traveled from Iowa to Oregon with Dr. Rucker's All-Star Comedians medicine show, selling an elixir for a dollar a bottle that he concocted from port wine, Rochelle salts, and water, while the company performed *Hamlet* and *The Banker's Daughter.*

• • •

George Watters had seen Barbara Stanwyck's performance in *The Noose* and told Hopkins about her. She had the "sort of rough poignancy" Hopkins wanted for Bonny.

The director called Barbara and asked her to come to his office on the mezzanine of the Plymouth at 236 West Forty-Fifth Street, a theater the Shuberts had built ten years before in collaboration with Hopkins, who wanted to use it to showcase his more serious productions. Hopkins had since leased the theater from the Shuberts.

Ruby had been warned that Hopkins was a man of few words. She entered his austere cubicle, sat down, and waited. Hopkins was sitting behind a rolltop desk. He leaned back in his swivel chair and told Ruby the name of the play and gave her a copy of the script, but didn't offer her the part.

"He looked me over and asked me what my salary was," she said. Ruby had not made more than $100 a week but summoned the courage to reply, "Three hundred dollars." She waited for Hopkins's outraged response. Instead, he agreed to pay the, to her, enormous amount of money.

"Hopkins told me his terms and his production schedule. It was up to me to find out when the rehearsals started and to show up on the first day."

Hopkins thought Hal Skelly and Barbara Stanwyck were "the perfect team" for his new show.

Mae, Walda, and Ruby moved to the Empire Hotel on West Sixty-Third Street between Broadway and Columbus Avenues.

Mae Clarke was in rehearsals during the long summer months for *Manhattan Mary*. "It was hot and heavy and sweaty," she said.

Burlesque went into rehearsals in the dead of summer in July 1927.

Ruby had lunch regularly with Nancy "Billy" Bernard, her friend from *Keep Kool* days. Nancy had married a traveling salesman and moved to Long Island. When she came into New York, it was to see Ruby and to stay with her at the Empire. "It was no Waldorf Astoria or anything like that."

Nancy and Ruby ate lunch at the Broadway Schrafft's near the hotel and spent afternoons shopping. "We would spend the evenings together and laugh," said Nancy.

Ruby needed clothes, and Billy took her to a shop on Broadway called Merl's, owned by a designer for whom Billy occasionally modeled. "It was like Cartier's, very expensive," said Nancy. "Ruby saw a dress with a jacket that she wanted. She asked me if I would get it for her and said she would pay me back. I had Merl wrap it up for her."

Soon after, Ruby telephoned Billy on Long Island to tell her that she had arranged for her friend to have "a spot" in *Burlesque*. Nancy's husband didn't want his wife working in the theater. He was often away for two or three months at a time selling men's clothes, and Nancy was trying to wean herself away from the stage, but she wanted the part in *Burlesque*. She reasoned that if she went into the show when her husband was away, he would be "all right with my working in it when he returned," and she accepted the part. Four days into rehearsals with the cast, Nancy's husband unexpectedly returned and insisted that she drop out of *Burlesque*.

"Ruby never paid for the suit," said Nancy. "I asked her, and she said she would, but she never did. I had to pay for it myself from modeling, $5 a week."

Hopkins's rehearsals were known for their intense quiet and calm, the mood almost monastic. The cast sat in a semicircle reading their lines as if they were chanting a prayer. A portable stage light was center stage. Next to it at a table sat Hopkins's general stage manager, Paul Porter, with the book of the play for line cues.

Hopkins stayed in the shadows at the upper stage and paced back and forth, never interrupting a scene to give instructions or suggestions, nor speaking to the actors before or after, his silences communicating the force of his ideas. Hopkins believed in letting it just happen, in letting the actor come to his or her own interpretation, even the beginning actor, not yet cluttered with old clichés, who Hopkins felt could work well this way. Hopkins sought naturalness onstage, no unnecessary movement and simplicity, and the following morning would whisper the most minimal comments.

Oddly, it was during Hopkins's days working as a press agent for Keith's Columbus Vaudeville Theatre in Cleveland, watching vaudeville actors establish their characters immediately, that he came to understand what would be most useful for the actor on the legitimate stage.

He saw vaudeville as a severe test; vaudeville audiences could quickly become restless; any letdown—the curse of the legitimate theater—was not possible. Hopkins saw that even if an act had been played for years, the vaudevillian could not afford to be bored; the act had to remain fresh to him. The vaudeville actor could get the effect of being new not by trying but by being. His only safety was in submerging himself completely in the character.

Hopkins watched Ruby work and began to have great plans for her. She "displayed more sensitive, easily expressed emotion" than he had encountered since Pauline Lord.

Hopkins's distinguished productions and his knowing direction had helped to bring the careers of many to the fore. He'd first seen Pauline Lord in a small part in *The Talker;* Katharine Cornell, as a young girl in *A Bill of Divorcement;* Ruth Chatterton in *The Rainbow;* Lynn Fontanne in a small role in a play with Laurette Taylor. Through their work with him, they became the most admired and celebrated actresses of their time. Hopkins worked as well with actors whose legend preceded them by many decades—Mrs. Fiske and John Drew among them—and still other actors who were at the peak of their careers: he cast John Barrymore in Tolstoy's *Living Corpse* and directed him again in *Richard III* and *Hamlet;* he cast Alla Nazimova, acclaimed as the first "modern" actress in the American theater, at the age of thirty-nine, in the part of the fourteen-year-old girl in the first English-speaking production of Ibsen's *Wild Duck.* Nazimova, long a theatrical star in her native Russia as well as in Europe and New York, was then under contract to Metro, having made two pictures at its New York studio at Sixty-First Street near Broadway: *Revelation* and *Toys of Fate.*

During the summer months, rehearsals for *Burlesque* began at ten in the morning and went until ten at night, heat or no heat.

Barbara and Skelly began to sense that the ties between Bonny and Skid would evoke strong sympathy with the audience.

Skelly saw Skid Johnson as "a big drunken lout with good intentions, blundering into misfortune, raising hell, but no Romeo, just faithful to one love." Like Skid, Skelly was a blunderer and a hell-raiser: he'd spent a week in jail; he'd been a prizefighter and manager and first baseman for the Boston Braves. Skelly knew life in burlesque and understood what it was to be a comedian/clown; he'd played one for two years. Like Skid, Skelly got his first break from the theater owner John Cort and began his career on the New York stage in a series of musical comedies.

Barbara described Bonny as the one "elected for the job of loving this poor clown. They say pity is akin to love and I suppose that has a great deal to do with Bonny's feeling for her husband . . . How can you explain love anyway? You can't . . . You know it exists but seek the reason, and you are up a tree."

Hopkins's rewrite of *Burlesque* included the character of a songwriter. During the second act, Skid's songwriter and piano player, Jerry Evans, plays a piano onstage, punctuating the scene. Hopkins wanted a musician who, like Skelly and Stanwyck, could be himself and hired the young pianist and composer Oscar Levant, whose song "Keep Sweeping the Cobwebs off the Moon" was having success in New York.

Levant had just returned from England, where he was the piano accompaniment for Rudy Wiedoeft, the classical saxophonist, and Frank Fay, who was then appearing at the Palladium.

Levant was a classically trained pianist who'd come to New York from Pittsburgh at fifteen to study music with the dream of becoming a concert pianist. In between, to earn a living, he'd found work as a flash pianist, "full of technical ornamentation, appoggiatura and cascading frills," as he described it, "but in the jazz lexicon signifying absolutely nothing."

Levant was a talker who was funny, and Barbara loved to laugh. Levant could go on a talking jag and not know what he was saying; he was unpredictable and easily unhinged.

His life was split between the discipline of musical study and the excess of boozy parties and dangerous nights; he attended the concerts of pianists appearing in New York and went to hear symphony orchestras. He studied the work of New York's permanent and guest conductors Arturo Toscanini, Siegfried Wagner, Maurice Ravel, Walter Damrosch, and Leopold Stokowski; he spent time with songwriters and jazz musicians. By night Levant fell into the company of bookies and showgirls, prizefighters and gangsters. When he played the piano, his music was tough, animated, honest.

During rehearsals for *Burlesque* he and Ruby became good friends.

Hopkins worked with Levant to score the music for the second act to create a party atmosphere. Levant was to set the mood throughout the scene: at first, it was to be jazzy and playful, soft and sentimental. He was to play popular songs like "Ain't She Sweet," "Here in My Arms," and "In the Gloaming," which Bonny sings for her Wyoming cattleman but directs to Skid ("Best to leave you—best for you, and best for me"). Levant was to follow with Gershwin's "Someone to Watch over Me" and then a few bars from *Rhapsody in Blue.*

As the scene moves toward its final desperate moments, and Skid realizes that Bonny is through with him forever, that she is about to marry her Wyoming cattle rancher, he calls for Jerry/Levant to play the wedding march with "pep and ginger." "Come on, Jerry, play it fast. It's a dancin' weddin'. Here comes the Minister, here comes the bride." Skid is laughing, drunk. He offers to give the bride away. He begins to dance, all arms and legs like a puppet being pulled by a madman to the rhythm of Levant's frenzied playing. Skid dances faster and faster. "Here comes the bride. Here comes the groom. Do you take this gal? Do you take this gal? Do you take this man? Do you take this man? Till death do you part. Till death do you part . . . Man and wife— Man and wife. Come on, sing, everybody. Here comes the bride."

Bonny can't take any more and pounds on the piano top, screaming,

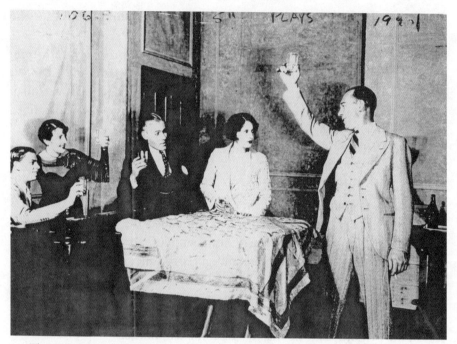

The second act curtain scene from *Burlesque*. Left to right: Oscar Levant, Eileen Wilson, Charles D. Brown, Ruby (now Barbara Stanwyck), and Hal Skelly, New York, 1927. (CULVER PICTURES)

"Stop him! Stop him! Stop, all of you!" Skid dances out of the room. "I'm goin'," he yells as he leaves. The curtain comes down as the door slams shut and the music stops with a crash.

Mae Clarke was out front in the audience almost every night watching Ruby and never "got through marveling at her performance." During the scene where they "jazzed up" the wedding march, Mae said of Ruby's cry that she'd "never heard one person get as many vibrations into her voice as Barbara got into hers. As she beat her hands on the piano, screaming, 'Stop it! Stop it' . . . it was like [listening to] a symphony chorus . . . instead of just one person speaking."

Burlesque went into the Plymouth in August. It was the first production with music ever to play the theater.

President Coolidge announced in Rapid City, South Dakota, that he would "not choose to run for President in 1928." Herbert Hoover, secretary of commerce (and "Under-Secretary of Everything Else"), accepted the nomination for president at the Republican convention in Kansas City, Missouri.

In his acceptance speech, Hoover, called "the Wonder Boy" by Coolidge, reassured the delegates on the convention floor, "We have not yet reached the goal, but given a chance to go forward with the policies of the last eight years, and we shall soon, with the help of God, be within sight of the day when poverty will be banished from the nation."

Burlesque opened on September 1, 1927. The opening night audience was enraptured by it. Brooks Atkinson in *The New York Times* compared the play unfavorably to *Broadway,* the hit of the previous year, saying that *Broadway* did "the trick first and with infinitely more skill in both drama and producing." Atkinson went on to say that Skelly "gives a glowing performance of fleeting character portrayal amid a whirl of eccentric make-ups and bits of hoofing and clowning." And "Miss Stanwyck plays with genuine emotion."

Walter Winchell compared *Burlesque* favorably to *Broadway,* saying *Burlesque* was the "more touching piece . . . even if it isn't as thrilling. [It] is a finer dramatic effort and a lovelier story . . . a simple love tale but so moving, effective and so tenderly told that even the men's kerchiefs were conspicuously employed at the Plymouth where it promises to remain for ever so long a spell.

"Hal Skelly, a veteran of tent shows, small and big time vaudeville and comical attractions crashed the star division . . . Miss Stanwyck's performance . . . is adroit and sympathetic; she toys with your heartstrings . . . [and] made you fear that you were effeminate . . . [S]ome of us wept . . . There is no competition in town right now and even when there is, *Burlesque* will survive it all, for it is poignant stuff, rich in plot and life."

Alexander Woollcott called it a "no account and palpably synthetic play in which the skill and unfailing taste of our foremost producer had been lavished." But Woollcott praised the two central roles as "beautifully played," describing "Miss Stanwyck" as "touching and true" who "brought much to those little aching silences in a performance of which Mr. Hopkins knows so well the secret and sorcery."

A critic from *Variety* said, "Young Barbara Stanwyck, who used to be Ruby Stevens of the cabarets . . . is a fine ingénue and in her dramatic moments, gleams. Her chief virtue is poise, and her salvation is restraint. That girl has a big future."

After the play's opening, Bill Mack presented Barbara with a diamond bracelet. She thought he'd waited to see if she was "any good" before giving it to her. The diamonds were small, but Barbara thought they were "the

Barbara as Bonnie with Hal Skelly as Skid, in *Burlesque*, New York, 1927. She is twenty years old.
(© CONDÉ-NAST ARCHIVE/CORBIS)

greatest." Every time she moved her hand she thought she was "blinding the public."

Burlesque was a success. It was the first production at the Plymouth to charge the top weekday ticket price of $4.40—$5.50 on Saturdays—the highest ticket price for a Broadway nonmusical.

The play opened on Thursday. The following day, ticket sales broke all house records, netting more than $3,000. Saturday's matinee took in more than $2,000 after expenses. The first four performances brought in $12,000 in gross receipts. The 650-seat theater had an eight-week advance sale of 570 orchestra seats. The show was grossing $29,000 per week.

Audiences considered *Burlesque* racy. In one scene Ruby appeared in a teddy that covered her from neck to thigh. "Chorus girls stripped," said she, but never stars, and "the audience gasped."

Ruby's nephew Gene was taken to see the show for his eleventh birthday. Barbara sang a song to him, the hit song of the show, in his first-row center seat. "She just looked at me," he said. "I'll never forget it."

Barbara Stanwyck was being talked about and photographed. She posed for a sitting with Hal Skelly for *Vanity Fair*'s photographer Edward Steichen. She was being asked to parties, but she rarely accepted. When she did attend, Walda Mansfield said, "she sat there and wasn't terribly friendly with anybody." When she entered a room, Barbara found where she was to sit and sat there. Her head was up, her shoulders squared. She looked neither to the

right nor to the left, but even so, in a crowded room, Barbara was the first woman to be noticed.

After each evening's performance Oscar Levant made the rounds of night-clubs, parties, and all-night delicatessens. Ruby was invited along, but she "couldn't abide going," said Levant. "She was the rage of Broadway but Barbara was wary of sophisticates and phonies."

Among the invitations was a request for her to attend a big party given by Mr. Condé Nast, owner of *Vogue, Vanity Fair, The American Golfer,* and his pattern publishing.

Walda said, "Oh, that'll be fun. What are you wearing?"

Ruby said, "I'm not going."

The party was at Mr. Nast's thirty-room apartment at 1040 Park Avenue.

"You're not going? That'll be good for you to go to a party and meet all these people."

"I'm not going. I'm not ready for it." Ruby didn't attend. "I didn't know what the hell to say to them—they all talked verry, verry English. Can you imagine me . . . acting up the part of a lady with those dames? I knew it was going to be one of those ritzy affairs. I wanted to go, but, honestly I was scared stiff. I just couldn't get up my nerve."

Ruby sent a note to Mr. Nast declining and told him in so many words that she "couldn't make the grade."

With the success of *Burlesque,* Ruby was able to buy a mink coat on credit.

"It was beautiful. Dark mink." She felt as if she were "the only girl who'd ever had a mink coat and wore it all the time. It was a uniform."

Ed Kennedy went to see Ruby in her new play. He thought she was heartbreaking in the role of Bonny. Ed and Ruby hadn't seen much of each other, but he was proud of her success and went backstage to congratulate her and say hello. Ruby was thrilled to see him, and they made a date for dinner. Ed picked up Ruby at the Empire Hotel in his new Hupmobile touring car to drive out to the country for a Sunday evening. Ruby rushed through the hotel lobby as several young men whistled at her. The catcalls so agitated Ed that when he opened the car door for her, he pulled the door off its hinges. They went to a garage, had the door fixed, and then drove off to have dinner in the country. Their romance did not start up again.

Mae was touring with *Manhattan Mary*. The play wasn't doing well in Pittsburgh; the heat and the popularity of moving pictures were eroding theatrical profits.

Manhattan Mary was about to come into New York as George White was still changing the cast. Ona Munson was brought in to replace Elizabeth Hines. The cast was rehearsing until two and three in the morning and then proceeding to the author's hotel room to learn the new songs that had just been written.

Rex Cherryman was starring with Ann Harding in Bayard Veiller's new play, *The Trial of Mary Dugan*, which opened on September 19, 1927, at the National Theatre on West Forty-First Street.

The play was based on the sensationalized Long Island trial of Ruth Snyder, who murdered her husband. Stories of the Snyder trial filled the newspapers; spectators who didn't reserve seats paid $100 to sit in the courtroom and watch the trial unfold. Veiller had written two successful plays, *Within the Law* and *The Thirteenth Chair*, and the screenplay of *Unseeing Eyes*. He had written screenplays for Metro and Hearst's Cosmopolitan Pictures, and watching the spectacle of the Snyder trial, Veiller decided to give the public what it wanted, a courtroom drama with every scene taking place in the courtroom.

Alexander Woollcott described the opening night audience as "enthralled" by Veiller's play, a play that no one liked before it was produced, including Veiller's agent, who refused to read it. Rex Cherryman, Woollcott said, "held the play taut by his own skill and intensity"; Ann Harding, who also hated Veiller's play from the beginning, was, Woollcott said, "true and sensitive" in the starring role.

The Trial of Mary Dugan was the hit of the fall 1927 season, bringing in a weekly gross of $25,000 in ticket sales. *Burlesque* was right behind it as the season's runner-up hit.

Two weeks after *Burlesque* opened, the name Barbara Stanwyck in electric lights went up on the marquee of the Plymouth Theatre, next to Hal Skelly's.

Manhattan Mary opened at the Apollo on West Forty-Second Street one week after *Mary Dugan.* The book, lyrics, and music were by B. G. DeSylva, Lew Brown, Ray Henderson, William K. Wells, and George White. *The New York Times* called *Manhattan Mary* "a gorgeous presentation of everything a musical comedy should have. Great dancing, fine singing . . . catchy tunes and a great glitter and wealth of costumes, sets and backdrops that dazzle, and Ed Wynn."

Mae Clarke in her red silk Annette Kellerman bathing suit danced her "five-step," as she described it. "There-it-is, one, two, there-it-is, one-two-three. Can't you see we're the merriest? One, two, three, four—one, two, three, four—five-step!"

A couple of weeks later, on October 6, a new picture starring Al Jolson opened at the Warner Theatre on Broadway, a little more than a year after the first Vitaphone picture was shown there. The Warner Bros. talking picture was considered a triumph. In New York, audiences began to stand on line at six in the morning to see and hear the picture. The lines went around the block.

The Broadway play of *The Jazz Singer* starring George Jessel was a great hit. Sam Warner saw it and optioned it for Warner Bros.

Darryl Zanuck, the general manager of production for the studio, thought the play was "a real piece of schmaltz . . . pure corn. What makes it go is the music, and the songs." It was Zanuck's wife, Virginia, who thought of using the new system being tested by Warner Bros. to put the songs on the soundtrack so "that when the guy opens his mouth to sing, you actually let him sing—and the movie audience hears him."

Zanuck agreed. "If we can get him to sing on the sound track we'll have [the audience] bawling in the aisles."

Warner Bros. approached Jessel for the part, but he asked for too much money. Jack Warner then went to Al Jolson, who'd been touring in *Big Boy.* Jolson agreed to make the movie, which also starred Warner Oland and May McAvoy.

In the picture, directed by Alan Crosland, who also directed Warners' earlier picture with sound, *Don Juan,* Jolson's voice was heard on the sound track as he sang "Dirty Hands, Dirty Face," "Toot, Toot, Tootsie," "Blue Skies,"

"Mother of Mine (I Still Have You)," "Kol Nidre," and "Mammy." During a rehearsal of the scene when Jolson sings to his mother, the actors and crew were standing around, as was Zanuck, waiting for the music to be played. The microphones were still on. Zanuck came up with an idea: why not have Jolson talk to his mother? Jolson was to turn to her and say, "Mamma, I wanna sing a song for you." When the engineers played it back, the sound was clear; Jolson's words were recorded exactly as he'd said them. Talking scenes—four in all—were written into the script and added to the picture.

Ethel Barrymore's response to talking pictures: "The public won't put up with them. People don't want their ears hurt or their intelligence insulted."

NINE

Broadway's Favorite Son

Several months after *Burlesque* opened, Oscar Levant told Ruby he knew a "fellow" he thought she should meet. "You'll get a lot of laughs out of him."

"Frank Fay's a great guy," said Levant, though he thought Fay suffered from "a total self-enthrallment." Fay was brilliant, spontaneous, smart; what he was doing onstage no one had done before.

Of course Ruby had heard of Frank Fay; he was legendary, a Broadway institution and had been for more than a decade. He was called "the Great Fay," "the King," "Broadway's Favorite Son," "America's Greatest Master of Ceremonies," and "the Great Faysie"—names Fay mostly gave himself.

He had headlined at the Palace Theatre, had been held over for weeks at a time, earning the record-breaking salary of $5,000 a week.

The Keith-Albee Palace in New York was considered "the big time," "the house that housed two a day": a matinee and an evening performance. It was a big theater that seated just under eighteen hundred people. Fay had the star position in the lineup; he was "next to shut." He came onstage in the second half of the show, before the last act.

Fay was so successful at the Palace and was held over for so many consecutive weeks that he became known as "Albee's Irish Rose." He also came to be called "the Chairman." After a run of eight weeks, Fay celebrated his hundredth consecutive performance on the Palace stage and set a new record. He was credited by many with the theater's great success.

Fay had a rich baritone voice and in the beginning saw himself as a ballad singer and teamed up with another singer called Gerald Griffin. It was impossible for them to find bookings, and Griffin & Fay broke up.

Fay joined up with an older vaudeville comedian, Johnny Dyer. Dyer was the straight man, while Fay, dressed in baggy pants and false nose, skated back

Frank ("Faysie") Fay, circa 1920, monologist, actor, writer, singer, supreme comedian, who came from a family of stock company troupers and first appeared on the stage at four years old in a production of *Quo Vadis*. By the time he was fifteen, he boasted that he'd played in every Shakespeare drama except *Titus Andronicus*.

and forth onstage, making wisecracks. Slapstick was not the comedy for Fay. He wanted to perform onstage the kind of smart comedy that Wilson Mizner personified at the Lambs Club. For Fay, the true wits were Mizner, George Nash, and Eddie Foy. He was in awe of their skill and spontaneity and learned from them. "They never went after anyone," Fay said. "But if you got in their way or tried to outsmart them, the Lord help you—you were dead."

Fay had wanted to work in an elegantly tailored double-breasted suit and began to work alone as Frank Fay, Nut Monologuist. At first he told a long story about saving a piece of string. Soon he performed "Darktown Strutters' Ball" as an opera singer.

The importance of any act was measured by the amount of time a performer was given onstage. The young comedian George Burns said, "You'd meet a vaudevillian on the street and ask him how he was doing, and he'd answer 'seventeen minutes' if he were a top act." Fay was onstage for more than twenty.

Prohibition was in effect when Fay first played the Palace; he was onstage alone for twenty-two minutes telling satiric stories, such as the one about a drunk regaling a group of people at a soda fountain about how he became a grapejuice fiend. The number was called "The Face on the Drug Store Floor" and became the talk of Broadway.

Fay's notion of being the "Chairman" and introducing and remarking on each act before it appeared was not exactly new. In England almost a century earlier, a "chairman" presided at every music hall and announced the acts in a similar manner.

By the late 1920s, Fay felt that laughs were "not what they used to be when people were not so wise to everything. They do not roar anymore," he said, "or even scream; they just laugh like human beings who never go insane." "The public will not stand for overacting any more. The comedian who used to get his laughs by exaggerating everything has died, right on the stage, quite often."

Fay thought the stage had once been "all camouflage." But by the end of the 1920s it was "wide open with no secrets."

When Fay was performing in more than two shows a day, he would walk out onstage for the morning show with a toaster under his arm and plug it into the footlights. Then, as he was doing his act, he would sit down at a table and have a cup of coffee and a piece of toast.

He was thought of as a wise guy who brilliantly improvised his lines through each performance, never saying the same line twice. When he came onstage, Fay had only a "faint idea" of what he was going to do or say, but he trusted "inspiration" and "always finished up with the cue." He didn't tell jokes, use props, or resort to comic makeup. He had "an aversion to clowning." His comedy worked because he was what he called "natural; a human character, true to life."

George Burns once saw Fay do an impression of John Barrymore dancing the Charleston and another of his doing Caruso singing "Stutterin' Bill." Burns also saw Fay use the first stooge act ever. In it Fay told the audience that he'd learned some card tricks on a train ride and wanted to demonstrate them, asking for some volunteers from the audience. Three woebegone people came up on the stage to assist him, George Haggerty, Lew Mann, and little Patsy Kelly.

Fay presented Mann with a deck of cards and asked him to pick one and then replace it. Fay shuffled the deck and picked what was supposed to be Mann's card. It was an altogether different card. Fay then took a bow. When Haggerty objected that it was the wrong card, Fay dismissed him and went on with the next trick. In another bit, Patsy Kelly would walk out on the stage, disheveled, and stand there looking a mess and slightly lost. Fay would say, "Good heavens, where've you been?"

"The beauty parlor."

"I see," Fay would answer, "and they didn't wait on you."

Fay called Haggerty, Mann, and Kelly his "stock company."

Patsy Kelly said that Fay's "tutelage was the most valuable in the world for an amateur" but that Fay "could be cruel." He didn't want her to wear makeup, would yell at her onstage, and fired her weekly. "Fay never had a script and would just spring lines on [me]," she said. "He might start talking about anything from pears to presidents. It always seemed to me that I was standing on the stage with my hand out waiting for my cue to drop. I led with my chin because my knees were helpless."

After *Burlesque* opened on Broadway, Fay wanted to meet Barbara and told Levant to bring her to the show and he would leave tickets for them at the box office, one of the few times Fay was willing to pay for tickets for anyone to see his show. Fay was "penurious," said Levant. He "crossed himself whenever he spent money."

Walda went with Barbara and Oscar to see Fay's performance. "We got hysterical at everything he did," Walda said. "The way he talked, and his hands were beautiful." Fay conducted the audience with his hands as if he were conducting a symphony orchestra. He felt he had an advantage over other comedians because of his eyes and his hands. Others watching Fay said, "He could give you an inferiority complex just watching him light his cigarette."

Fay underplayed his lines. He spoke slowly, pausing, lifting his eyebrows, with a slight touch of irony around his mouth and a slightly feminine stance. He had a way of making his eyes sparkle.

Fay's work was new with its own style.

His walk onstage was distinctive. It was a conceited swagger, an effeminate saunter that made a strong impression on young comedians watching him work. Bob Hope and Jack Benny adopted Fay's walk and used it as part of their onstage personae.

J. J. Shubert and Elisabeth Marbury had taken Fay from the vaudeville stage and put him in his first legitimate role in a show called *Oh, Mama*. Fay described Shubert's direction of comedy as "unerring," saying that Shubert could "put his finger on the sore spot every time and show us how to get the punch into our work." Fay called Miss Marbury "one of nature's noblewomen." In *Oh, Mama*, Fay had the part of an ex-bartender prizefighter who marries the divorced wife of a New York millionaire. He was a hit on opening night and became featured in the show. In it Fay introduced what became known as the "wristwatch" comedian who appeared to be effeminate in his walk, his stance, and his deadpan stare at the audience.

"He always worked a little effeminate," said Milton Berle. "He had a hauteur about him, but he talked to his audience in a way that made them feel that what he was talking about could happen to them. He never did jokes in which he was the butt."

The London critics called him "the wistful comedian."

If Fay wanted, he could verbally destroy any performer or act; he would simply introduce the act by saying with a slight smile, in his soft voice, "The next gentleman is very, very popular. They *say*—that he is very funny." Then he would raise an eyebrow; the act didn't have a chance with the audience.

Fay didn't use one-liners. He talked conversationally, unemotionally. He might take a song and say to the audience, "The music to most songs is generally good, but the lyrics are awful. I can prove it to you. Now here's a song. Vincent Youmans's. He was one of the best." Fay would sing a few lines of a song and deliberately interrupt himself to comment on the lyrics.

" 'Just picture me upon your knee, just tea for two and two for tea.' " He would stop, and pause. He might scratch the back of his neck, then his head. Then say to the audience, " 'Ain't that rich? Now, here's a guy, he's probably got enough tea for two so he's going to have two for tea. If the third person walks in, they stab him.' "

Then he would continue. He called it "breaking up" songs. "Just me for you and you for me alone." Fay might stop there; play with his chin or suddenly point to someone and say, "Alone. I remember that old one about 'C'mon up to the room, I want to show you my etchings.' " Then continue singing, "But nobody near us, to see us or hear us." Fay would say, "Who wants to listen to two people drinking tea?" The music would start up again and Fay would continue. "No friends or relations on weekend vacations. If I have—well, a vacation without a relation. We won't have it known dear that we own a telephone here."

Fay would be slow and charming. Then he might comment, "Makes a big thing out of it. Now all this guy has is a broken down cup of tea and a telephone he won't let you use." The music starts up; Fay would sing, "Day will break and you'll awake and start to bake a sugar cake." "The poor woman. What a future," Fay would comment. "She hops out of bed, washes her teeth and bang, right to the oven. Nobody up but her, feeling around in the dark for flour."

Audiences loved these pieces, and Fay became identified with them.

"We just fell in love with him," said Walda. "He had to have the whole floor. He was every inch a star. Barbara thought he was wonderful."

Performers—comics, actors, singers—saw Fay as the greatest master of ceremonies in vaudeville. Young comedians like George Burns thought Fay was "something to see." Milton Berle thought he was "incomparable. There was no one like him." Eddie Cantor said Fay had a knack of making love to his audience and making them like him at the same time that he identified with them. Other comedians, like the young Jack Benny, watched Fay and modified his act. Benny stopped telling jokes; he dropped the use of a prop, a violin, onstage; he built his humor around everyday occurrences to make it seem more immediate, less rehearsed, and, like Fay, Benny slowed up his delivery.

Following Fay's years at the Palace, the master of ceremonies became common in vaudeville.

While Ed Wynn and Raymond Hitchcock acted as masters of ceremonies in musical shows, no one had Fay's finesse or brilliant comedic patter.

He often shepherded more than seventy stars who appeared on the bill with him. "Fay would comment on the acts that preceded him," said Milton Berle. "He'd say, 'I just want to say, you remember, the acrobat, the lady acrobat in the first act? In the first half that came on? Nobody knows this, only *I* do—' Fay would look off to the wings as if it was a secret, and nobody knew what he was about to reveal. Then he would say, 'She goes with the fellow in the third act. I don't know if they fool around or not.'

"Fay was on his feet by himself, talking, unprepared," Berle said. "He would come on, in the early years, he would be seventh on the show—there were eight acts between an intermission. And Fay looked at the orchestra leader, and said, 'How has the show been up to now?' The leader, in the pit, would say, 'Wonderful.' Then Fay would take a couple of beats, and say, 'Really? Well I'll change that.' Like a throwaway. And the audience would laugh, because of his style. He had a point of view when he was talking. He worked with an honest method. He talked to an audience like it was private, between himself and the audience."

Women saw Fay as a young Greek god. He was five feet ten, 150 pounds, with florid skin and blue Irish eyes. For a while he was known as the "blonde young comic"; soon after he became the "auburn haired" comic and kept his shock of rusty hair. He had been a boxer years before and carried two pairs of gloves with him. He said of himself, "I was a pugilist at one time. And what a ham. I was so poor that I myself realized that I was no good. And when a boxer knows he is no good, he is terrible."

Fay could ad-lib in any dialect, sing, dance with an unrestrained abandon, and direct dog tricks. "A master of ceremonies must be willing to undertake anything," he said.

• • •

Oscar Levant said that Fay "had an aura of shabby worldliness. He was extremely xenophobic and disliked Jewish comedians especially."

Fay was one day headlining the bill at B. F. Keith's Bushwick Theatre in Brooklyn. Milton Berle was "doing twelve minutes of something, including my Eddie Cantor." After Berle finished his act, he would stand in the wings to watch Fay work, breaking his rule that no one was to watch him from the wings. Performers were forbidden to watch the other acts from the audience in order to protect their material.

Fay came off the stage of the Bushwick from his first bow, to much applause. Berle thought he heard Fay say to the stage manager, "Get that little Jew bastard out of the wings. I don't want him standing there." A few days later, Berle was back in the wings watching Fay. When Fay came offstage, Berle heard him say something about "that little kike" that made Berle so angry he took a stage brace made of wood and metal used to hold scenery together and hit Fay across the face with it, causing "the Great Faysie" to be taken to Brooklyn Hospital.

After Fay's show at the Palladium, Levant brought Barbara and Walda backstage. They entered Fay's dressing room as he was removing his makeup. He was charming and beguiling. He announced he was hungry and said that as soon as he finished taking off his makeup, he was going to a restaurant where, he said, they served the best food in town.

"They really know how to serve food in this place," Fay went on. "A little table in a quiet corner, soft music . . ."

Barbara was ready to accept the invitation when the dressing room door opened and in walked a beautiful woman who said, "Are you ready for dinner, Frank?"

"Be with you right away," Fay said as he put on his coat. He turned to his guests and said, "You must try this place, the food is really delicious." Fay put on his hat, reached for the door, and, as he walked out of the dressing room, said to Barbara and the others, "Drop around again sometime," and closed the door behind him.

Barbara was stunned. She assumed that she, Walda, and Oscar would be invited to join him for dinner. Barbara turned to Walda and Levant and said, "Let's get out of here. But for heaven's sake let's not go where there is good food. The very idea of it chokes me."

Barbara was angry. She thought Fay might call the next day, but he didn't, nor the next. The idea that Fay had hurt her made her all the angrier.

Three days later Fay phoned and asked her to dine with him at Longchamps that Sunday evening. In her most polite voice, Barbara said she would be delighted and thanked him for his call. At seven that evening Barbara was home, not at Longchamps, pleased at the thought that Fay was waiting for her at the restaurant.

She expected to hear from him the following morning. Days went by without a word from him. After two weeks of silence, Barbara asked Levant to invite Fay to a dinner that was being given at the Flippens Club in honor of the cast of *Burlesque*. Fay said he would attend and asked who would be there.

"Barbara and the others," Levant said.

"Oh. I'm playing cards at the club until late tonight, but I'll try to make it if I can. If I can't make the dinner, I'll meet you at Reuben's afterward."

Barbara and Levant waited for Fay at the Flippens Club and then at Reuben's until dawn. He didn't show up.

During the next two weeks, Barbara saw Fay around town, each time with a different woman. Fay seemed enthralled with each of his dinner partners and bowed politely when he saw Barbara. Levant was Barbara's sole escort as she tried to keep track of Fay's whereabouts. Barbara and Levant were seen together so frequently it was believed that they were a couple.

One night they had just been seated at the Silver Slipper. Fay appeared at the table with Harry Delmar, the producer of *Harry Delmar's Revels,* in which Fay was starring, and sat down at Barbara and Oscar's table.

"Let me congratulate you both on your engagement," he said.

"You know everything, don't you?" Barbara said. They began to argue.

Levant suggested they stop fighting with each other. "You know you like one another. Try and be nice—you know you'll get around to it sooner or later. You might as well start now."

Barbara and Fay danced. Back at the table, they sat close together and talked. Fay revealed that the many occasions of their spotting each other at restaurants had not been coincidence: each time Fay had found out Barbara's evening plans and quickly arranged for someone to accompany him to the restaurant or club where he knew she would be. He revealed as well that the first time Barbara met him in his dressing room, Fay's excessive charm, the talk of a restaurant, the beautiful woman coming in at the last moment to take him to dinner had been a setup; Fay had planned it all.

Barbara and Walda began to meet Fay at Reuben's each night after the show. Fay loved to tell stories. "And we loved to listen to them," said Walda. Barbara hung on Fay's every word, as they all did. "He was so funny and amusing," said Walda. "We thought he was grand; he was so graceful with his hands, those beautiful gestures that only actors can use and get away with.

Sometimes Harry Delmar would join us, but mostly it was the three of us. Barbara was mad about him," Walda said. "Frank was crazy about her but he didn't show it as much as she did. He wasn't demonstrative."

She would do anything to please Fay. Walda recalled, "Barbara had a beautiful crepe green afternoon dress made with a green velvet collar that she loved and one day put on to go downstairs to meet Frank. A few minutes later, she came back up and said, 'Frank can't stand this dress. He hates me in green.' When Frank didn't like something, that was it; it was out."

Frank disliked Barbara in green, though it was the preferred color for his own suits.

Barbara gave Walda the dress and said, "Do whatever you want with it." "I took it," said Walda, "and I liked the dress twice as much when it was mine."

Barbara decided to give a dinner party for Frank. She had neither silverware nor table linens and asked her former roommate and beloved friend, Claire Taishoff Muller, if she might borrow them for the evening. Claire was only too happy to lend them to Barbara and said, "Leave it all to me. I will arrange everything." Claire brought the silver and glassware to Barbara's.

A few days after the dinner party, Barbara returned the silver and linens to Claire and thanked her. Claire phoned soon after, and Barbara refused to talk with her. Claire phoned again, and again Barbara refused to talk. Claire was baffled. She couldn't understand what she had done to hurt or offend Barbara. They had been friends for years; Barbara had lived with Claire's family when the two young women had started out together as dancers. She, Walda, and Mae had spent years together. Claire adored Barbara and didn't know what happened.

Barbara's good friend from Ziegfeld days Nancy Bernard met Fay with Barbara and didn't particularly like him. Fay "thought he was the one and only person in the world," said Nancy.

Fay traveled with an entourage. He had his own tailor, his private barber, manicurist, secretary, typist, songwriter, composer, piano player, set of chauffeurs, handymen, messenger boys, and literary advisers.

When Barbara and Walda met Frank at Reuben's each night after their shows, "nobody drank because Frank was on the wagon," said Walda.

Fay's drinking was legendary. When he was drunk, it was known that he would wend his way to St. Patrick's for confession, though he claimed he went to Mass every day. He was known to tip his hat each time he passed a church. Fay kept a poem pasted in the inside cover of one of his scrapbooks that read as follows:

The wonderful love of a beautiful maid,
And the staunch true love of a man.
The love of a baby unafraid
Which hath existed since life began.
But the greatest love, the love of love
Transcending e'en that of a mother,
Is the tender, the passionate, the infinite love
Of one drunken bum for another.

Damon Runyon said that the word for Fay was "puckish," that Fay "had always been an addict and a master of whimsy on the stage and off," that he lived "in a world of fantasy pretty much his own, starry-eyed and never worrying a great deal." "Faysy boy," as Runyon said Fay generally referred to himself, "had a streak of good old Smithfield ham in him a mile wide. He was always an individualist who was happier putting on his own little vaudeville shows Sunday nights and wandering up and down the aisles chatting with the customers than when he was knocking them dead at the Palace." "Fay was extremely well groomed and suave," Runyon said, "and one of the greatest squires of dames that ever hit Broadway. He had a pair of marvelous hands and some astonishingly expressive eyebrows and it was always a good show to watch Frank pitch to the gals, using both with great skill."

Fay was Barbara's senior by sixteen years. He was thirty-seven; she, twenty-one. Barbara was aware of the stories about Frank's drinking and recklessness, of his smashing up cars and being charged with driving under the influence of alcohol, of his missing any number of performances and his declarations of bankruptcy. She had heard of his barroom brawls and dice games, of the many claims brought by actors against Fay for nonpayment when his productions were abandoned for lack of funds. She was aware of his three previous marriages. The first was to Lee Buchanan, an actress, who worked with him in vaudeville. The second, two years later, was to Frances White, a comedienne and dancer who, because of her five-foot two-inch height, became known as "the Diminutive Star of Broadway" and was a sensation on the stage of the Keith Palace. Frances White appeared in Ziegfeld's *Midnight Frolics* and was a star at London's Palace Theatre, earning the vast sum in 1921 of $3,500 a week. After only two months of being Mrs. Frank Fay, Frances White had had enough of Fay's flirtations with other women and of supporting his extravagances and, two months later, was granted a divorce. Three months after that, Fay was in the Ludlow Street Jail for nonpayment of alimony.

Frances (Caples) White, the second Mrs. Frank Fay, musical comedy star, one of Ziegfeld's big draws in his *Follies* of 1916 and his *Midnight Frolics,* circa 1916. (MUSEUM OF THE CITY OF NEW YORK)

Barbara had heard about Fay's return to his first wife and their remarriage, that on becoming Mrs. Frank Fay for the second time, Lee Buchanan at Frank's urging announced her retirement from show business.

Fay's arrogance, sardonic humor, and meanness were as much a part of his legend as were his Irish humor and his ability to make an audience wild with laughter. It was said of Fay that he loved to make people suffer, that while he was stabbing someone onstage, he would have a smile on his face, enjoying it so much. Because of his cruelty he was feared.

The vaudevillian Bert Wheeler, who appeared at the Palace on the same bill with Fay, was a sketch comedian and a big star. He knew he was no match for Fay onstage. Wheeler said of Fay that he had "the fastest mind in the business" and could "chase any comic bar none."

During one of Wheeler and Fay's appearances together, Wheeler asked Fay not to bring him back out after his act. Fay honored Wheeler's plea until one important performance—a matinee—when the talent bookers were in the audience with stopwatches in hand to time the laughs.

Wheeler finished his act to great applause and left the stage. Fay came on as he had throughout the show and called Wheeler back onstage. For whatever reason, Fay began to talk to the audience at Wheeler's expense. Fay was calm, controlled; he spoke in his soft, easy, slow delivery with his deadpan stare. Wheeler stood on the stage, unable to think of anything to say that could equal or stop Fay's sarcasm. Finally, Wheeler said, "Frank, you're a very funny man, but I predict that I am going to get the biggest laugh ever heard at The Palace." Fay said, "Oh, really, Bert? How are you going to do that?"

Wheeler pulled back and hit Fay in the face. The audience laughed, thinking this was part of the act.

Years before, when Fay was appearing at the Orpheum in Brooklyn, four minutes into his scheduled performance he was still in his dressing room fixing his tie. When the stage manager went to Fay's dressing room to find out what was going on and to say the audience was becoming impatient, Fay's response was "Let them wait." As a result of Fay's attitude, the United Booking Office canceled the rest of his engagements and fined him $100.

Fay was known to look in the mirror and say, "Who do I love? Me."

Fay smoked constantly and carried a gold cigarette case with him onstage. A sign backstage said, "No Smoking in the Theater." Also backstage was a big Irish fireman. Fay went onstage and would immediately light the cigarette. When he came offstage the fireman called him "a fag." Fay punched him.

Barbara didn't care about any of Fay's past.

"He was a joy in our lives," said Walda. "We thought he was the funniest man we ever saw. But Frank became possessive. He wanted Barbara all to himself. I thought it was awful that she put up with it, but she didn't mind."

What appeared to be possessiveness to others was love to Barbara, mother love, father love, romantic love. As long as "she and Fay were together," she said, "everything would be alright."

Barbara was willing to convert from Protestantism to Catholicism because it meant so much to Fay. She began to wear a large silver cross around her neck. Fay's concern for every aspect of her being was like experiencing love almost for the first time. If Fay uttered a wish, Barbara obeyed.

Barbara wasn't comfortable wearing makeup, and Fay preferred her without it. She wore only lipstick. He suggested she not wear nail polish; she removed it. Fay didn't like it when she smoked; she quit, except to light his cigarettes and to take a couple puffs before passing the cigarette over to him. He preferred her in clothes that were black and white; her clothes were white with an accent of black.

In certain respects, Frank's background was similar to Barbara's. His formal education ended in the fifth grade; like Barbara, he'd taught himself to act, write, and sing. Fay, though, composed songs and wrote his own lyrics. Unlike Barbara, he came from the West; he was born in San Francisco in 1891 and grew up in a family of sorts. His parents were vaudevillians, and the Fay family traveled together from city to city. Fay's mother, Marie, had

had a brief career on the stage. His father was a lyric poet who had worked as a conductor on the Southern Pacific Railroad, fought Indians, and prospected in a mine. But it was as a comedian and actor that he was known as "Chicago" Billie Fay.

Frank Fay made his debut on the stage at the age of four, appearing as a potato bug in Victor Herbert's *Babes in Toyland*, and was carried onstage by his father in *Quo Vadis*.

Long before Fay was a vaudevillian, he was part of Henry Irving's farewell American tour, traveling with the company for two years, playing with Irving in *The Merchant of Venice, Richelieu, Louis XI*. "All my early training," Fay said, "was in the classic drama." He appeared in every Shakespearean play except *Titus Andronicus* and had a part in Ibsen's *Enemy of the People*.

Fay "looked forward to playing the big classical roles some day, but times changed," and he went into vaudeville to earn a living. He still wanted to play Shakespeare and Ibsen and try his hand at the plays of Oscar Wilde. He had appeared at the old Daly's Theatre in *The Catch of the Season* with Edna May and played the Savoy, the Garrick, and the Hackett Theatres. Fay understood acting, timing, simplicity. He felt he had been branded "a comedian" because of his red hair. "For that reason," he said, "neither the public nor the managers take me seriously when I claim I would be a great dramatic actor."

Fay took Barbara seriously. He knew she was a great dramatic actress.

TEN

Having a Hunch

First National Pictures released *The Noose* at the end of January 1928. The picture starred Richard Barthelmess as the young man condemned to die. Barbara had been asked to play Dot in the picture, but it was early in the run of *Burlesque*. She was in the midst of a great success and had no interest in traveling to Hollywood to appear in the movie. Lina Basquette, the Ziegfeld dancer and actress, got the role of the young dancer secretly in love with the doomed man. Some thought Lina and Barbara resembled each other.

They'd appeared in the same edition of the *Ziegfeld Follies;* Lina, a featured dancer by the time she danced for Ziegfeld, had already been under contract to Carl Laemmle and starred in sixteen Lina Basquette Featurettes for Universal. A few years later, when dancing with the *Follies,* Lina was spotted by Pavlova and was urged to break her contract with Ziegfeld and accompany the great dancer, then in her forties, on a tour and become her possible successor. Lina resisted the invitation to leave Ziegfeld, but when the youngest of the four Warner brothers saw her on the stage, fell in love with her, and proposed, Lina accepted. She was eighteen years old; Sam Warner was twice her age. Ziegfeld was furious that Lina had wed "a third-rate picture man." By the time Lina got the part of Dot in *The Noose,* she had a reputation and a name all her own, but now she was also Mrs. Sam Warner.

The Noose, just released, was breaking attendance records around the country and bringing in tens of thousands of dollars each week in admissions. Paramount Famous Lasky had just bought the screen rights to *Burlesque* from Arthur Hopkins for $75,000.

Louis B. Mayer, the general manager of the newly merged Metro-Goldwyn-Mayer, was married to the daughter of an Orthodox butcher and cantor. Margaret Shenberg Mayer was also related to Oscar Levant's mother. When

Louis B. came to New York, he stayed with Levant's aunt and uncle. Mayer had heard about Barbara and was interested in meeting her. Oscar introduced them. "Fay was irate" that Oscar intruded on his "domain and exclusivity of property" and told Levant he was going to "punch [him] in the nose for bringing Mayer . . . here." Fay's concern was baseless. Barbara wasn't interested in Mayer's offer to go into moving pictures.

Mae was having a successful run in *Manhattan Mary* and one evening was introduced at a cocktail party to Lew Brice, brother of Fanny.

"It was instantaneous," said Mae. "He was so funny and so cute . . . He was tall and slender, agile, a wonderful dancer . . . He carried himself like royalty, without being snobbish."

Lew Brice was considered one of the ten best tap and ballroom dancers in the world but had no interest in show business. He was "a handsome dresser," Mae said. "He was a club man. He was a gambler, and he played cards all night long."

Brice left for Chicago and called Mae in New York. "It's snowing here," he said. "And I'm cold. And I want you."

Mae said, "Under what terms?"

"Mrs. Brice."

"I'll be right there."

Mae was seventeen. She wrote a note to her mother saying, "I'm in love. I'm going to marry him no matter what you do, or say . . . I will scrub floors . . . go through fire . . . I have got to be with him."

She wrote to the show's producer, George White, saying, "I'm in love . . . I can't think. I can't do anything without him. He's waiting for me in Chicago. And yet, if I give you my two-weeks I'll miss the whole thing. I'll be unhappy the rest of my life. What'll I do?"

White answered her on the play's program. "Get on that train," he wrote. "You are dismissed. God bless you. G.W."

Mae said good-bye to Barbara, to Walda, to White's *Manhattan Mary*, and left for Chicago. When she got to the hotel, the front desk had no word of her arrival. A bellboy opened the door to let Mae into Lew Brice's room. He was asleep on the bed. "You could see he had been drinking. Old, half-filled glasses, cigarette butts." Mae's impulse was to turn around and go back to New York, "but I couldn't face George White then. And my mother . . . I was disgusted . . . I thought . . . 'I've got to marry this fool and get tired of him and get divorced from him in order to get rid of him.' "

Mae and Lew were married in Chicago that day, February 6, 1928, "even with his hangover and the snow and the wind." For a wedding present, Fanny

Lew Brice (1938), brother of Fanny, with whom he appeared at the Palace. He knocked around as tap dancer and singer and beginning in 1909 as part of various vaudeville acts, appearing at the Winter Garden in *The Passing Show* (1915) and the Shuberts' *Maid In America*. He didn't have his sister's talent or focus and was undone by gambling.

Brice had Billy Rose write a vaudeville act for her brother and new sister-in-law. The act was a musical comedy with "songs, dances and dialogue" and a cyclorama, "hung just so," and a horse race was projected onto the screen. The Brice and Clarke act was about bookmakers and long shots with singing and dancing and gags, though "not too gaggy," *Variety* said, and went on to call the whole playlet "first-rate class Vaudeville." "Our whole act was our own personalities and how funny and cute we were," said Mae. "And how beautifully we danced together."

Barbara signed a contract with the J. Walter Thompson Company in conjunction with Lever Brothers for the use of her name and photograph in advertisements for Lux Toilet Soap. In exchange for the publicity, the ad would show a photograph of Barbara Stanwyck, co-starring in *Burlesque;* accompanying her picture was a block of type that read: "People are especially critical of your appearance if you are on the stage, which makes a smooth, youthful skin doubly important. I care for mine faithfully with Lux Toilet Soap—it keeps my skin so beautifully smooth."

Barbara was now an endorsement.

• • •

Walda had made up her mind; she was leaving for California. She had been thinking about it for three years, and now she was going west. She didn't know what she would do there, but she was ready to take the chance.

Fay had recently been signed by the Skouras Brothers to a twenty-week run at the Missouri Theatre in St. Louis. He asked Barbara to marry him and gave her a ring made from his Master of Arts pin.

One night they began to argue about nothing. In the midst of the argument Frank said, "If that's the way you feel, perhaps it is just as well that I'm leaving town next week." Fay was set to begin his tour.

"In view of that," Barbara said, "it would be silly for us to keep up any pretense of an engagement. You go around with other women—I'll go with other men."

"You mean it's all over with us?" said Frank.

"Why not?"

"We aren't going to write—or telephone each other—or anything?"

"It would be silly under the circumstances," Barbara said.

Frank took the train to St. Louis.

Barbara stopped going out with friends. Those who had seen her with Frank telephoned her repeatedly, but she didn't answer and declined all invitations.

The curtain for *Burlesque* went up each evening at 8:30. Each night Barbara, as Bonny, said, "It's got to be that way with me. For I've only loved one man and I've got a hunch that I won't ever love anyone else." After the performance Barbara walked home, made some coffee, and read for an hour or two. What she said as Bonny was true for Barbara. Her friends told her to go out and meet other men.

"Not for me," she said.

In mid-July, Hopkins closed *Burlesque* because of record heat. The show was set to go on tour in late August. *The Trial of Mary Dugan* also shut its doors in New York to begin its national tour. Rex Cherryman had been with the show for more than ten months and was exhausted; he had recently divorced his wife and needed to take a few weeks' leave to travel abroad.

Cherryman boarded a steamer to Le Havre on August 1 to tour the Continent with plans to return to the show in September, when it was to begin its run in Chicago. During the crossing he became ill; he had missed the last performance of *Mary Dugan* due to a mild flu the night before he left New

York, but it was a small wound that was the cause of his illness, a wound that could easily have been operated on and cleared up. When the boat docked in Le Havre, Cherryman was taken to a hospital and died there of septic poisoning at the age of thirty-one.

"Barbara's relationship with Rex had ended, but she was shocked when she learned of his death," said Walda. "We never thought of him dying. He was so young, so alive."

The 1928 presidential race was in full force. After the overwhelming vote at the Republican convention in Kansas City, Missouri, Herbert Hoover, the Republican candidate, was running against Governor Al Smith. Smith was the first presidential candidate of the Catholic faith; Hoover, the first Quaker. Their platforms were distinct: Hoover had been secretary of commerce for seven years under President Harding and, after Harding's death, under President Coolidge. Coolidge was a conservative as well as a religious fundamentalist whose puritan New England upbringing informed the way he governed. His sense of thrift was embodied in his tight hold on government expenditure and in his unwillingness to take action to ward off trouble. Coolidge believed that "if you see ten troubles coming down the road, you can be sure that nine will run into the ditch before they reach you and you have to battle with only one."

Hoover, as secretary of commerce, had warned Coolidge about the easy money policies that encouraged stock speculation; the president dismissed Hoover's concerns and said the administration should not interfere with the stock market.

Some worried that if Al Smith was elected along with a Democratic Congress, there would be a depression the following year. Others felt there was no cause for worry; the "Coolidge prosperity" would continue.

Hoover was concerned about a depression as well; he'd been born a year after a great depression and began his career in the midst of another. As secretary of commerce, he'd warned the Federal Reserve Board that it was a mistake to allow speculators to buy stocks on mostly margin—ten cents down for a dollar's worth of stock. He'd written to the Senate Banking and Currency Committee in 1925 that the continued wild stock speculation "would bring inevitable collapse which will bring greatest calamities upon our farmers, our workers, our legitimate business." The secretary of the Treasury, Andrew Mellon, pronounced Hoover "alarmist," his comments "unwarranted."

"Leave it alone," Mellon told Coolidge. Mellon's simple formula: "Liquidate labor, liquidate stocks, liquidate the farmers, liquidate real estate."

• • •

It was two o'clock in the morning when Barbara's phone rang. It was a long-distance call from Ace Beery, a theater manager and friend of Fay's. Beery was calling to say that Frank was drinking himself to death.

"Let him drink as much as he likes," Barbara said, though she was worried about him. Ace called the following morning to tell Barbara that Frank was in terrible shape. "He can't work or sleep."

"If he's near the phone, I want to talk to him."

Frank sounded drunk.

Barbara pleaded with him to stop drinking.

Fay, in a drunken voice, said, "Can't shhtop drinking. Can't shtop. My heart is broken."

"So is mine," said Barbara. "Please stop drinking, and everything will be all right. We'll be engaged again."

"You mean we'll start all over again? Mean you'll marry me?"

"Sure."

"Then listen, you can catch a train out of New York at nine tomorrow morning. You'll be in St. Louis by one. We'll be married. You can leave here at four and be in Newark at eight for the evening show." Fay's words weren't slurred. He sounded cold sober.

Barbara boarded the train for St. Louis on a hot August Sunday morning and arrived at Union Station by 1:00 p.m. Fay was there to meet the train. Instead of looking wasted and alcoholic, as Barbara feared, Fay looked fit and trim. Despite his drunken calls at two o'clock in the morning and the concern for his well-being, Fay "hadn't had a drink in four months."

Barbara and Frank rushed off to Magnolia Avenue in south St. Louis, to the home of William Tamme, the recorder of deeds, and were issued a license. Harry Pfeifer, the justice of the peace, performed the ceremony. With them was Spyros Skouras, one of the producers of Fay's show. Margaret and Harry Niemeyer of the *St. Louis Post-Dispatch* were witnesses. Margaret Niemeyer was Barbara's matron of honor. Spyros Skouras stood up for Fay.

Ruby Stevens was now Mrs. Frank Fay. Before leaving St. Louis, Barbara announced to reporters that she would retire from the stage as soon as *Burlesque* had finished its winter run in Chicago, as had the first Mrs. Fay when she became the third Mrs. Fay. By 5:00 p.m., Barbara was on the train back to New York and to *Burlesque,* which was to begin its road tour the following night.

Barbara couldn't have cared less that Arthur Hopkins said his star's wedding to Fay was "a bad marriage." She believed she was "nothing" until Fay had come into her life. Everything she knew "of etiquette and the niceties of life, the correct way to talk and walk and meet people and entertain: everything [she knew] of books and art and people and the world around [her]" she learned from Fay.

The tour was due to begin in Newark. Hal Skelly had stayed with the show, as did Levant, but many in the company were new, including Barbara Robins, who played the "other" girl, and Marjorie Main, who played Gussie, "a Beef Trust girl."

Barbara and Fay had their honeymoon via airmail, telegraph, and telephone, and, she said, "it was no way to conduct a honeymoon."

Burlesque played in cities across the country from New Jersey to Pittsburgh and St. Louis, never playing longer than two or three weeks in each city. The physical demands of the show and the tour began to affect Barbara's health.

The troupe was traveling by train from Kansas City on its way to its run in Detroit, where *Burlesque* was set to open at the Shubert Theatre. The train was derailed, and Barbara was thrown from her berth. Her head grazed the side of the metal compartment, but she was only slightly scratched. It was an icy-cold night; men were in their nightclothes, and women with curling papers frantically ran through the vestibule of the car shouting about how they were going to sue the train company. Barbara was in a nightgown and thin robe and stood in the corridor of the partially destroyed car attending to her understudy, who had had the flu when they set out from Kansas City and was hurt in the wreck.

The train got under way again. Barbara took care of the young actress and ignored the symptoms of her own oncoming illness. By the time the train reached Detroit, Barbara had influenza and a high fever and was so ill she was taken off the train and driven to the Book-Cadillac Hotel in downtown Detroit. The doctor advised her to skip the evening performance, but she was determined to get to the theater. When it was time to leave, Barbara descended the grand staircase leading to the hotel's lobby and began to feel light-headed from the fever. When she came to, she had fallen to the bottom of the stairs. "It was very dramatic," said Barbara. "Unfortunately, I didn't get up in time to hear the applause."

Barbara had weighed 118 pounds at the start of the *Burlesque* tour; now, in the Detroit hospital, she weighed 98 pounds. It was clear she wasn't strong enough to return to *Burlesque*. After staying in the hospital for five days, she, along with her German maid, took the train back to New York and to Fay, who met her at the station and was "wild" with worry about how his wife might look. Barbara said that when she got off the train, Fay thought she "looked more like a corpse than a bride" and took her back to his hotel on Fifty-Seventh Street. A doctor and a nurse were in attendance for the next few weeks as Barbara regained her strength and the weight she had lost. *Burlesque* was due to close, and Barbara's understudy finished the run of the play.

During the next three months as Barbara recuperated, she felt strong enough to accompany Fay on his tour of the Keith Circuit. He was about to play in Chicago for three weeks, and Barbara prevailed upon him to let them appear together in his act. It was agreed that Fay would bring Barbara on-stage late in the show, and with a piano accompanist Mr. and Mrs. Frank Fay would perform the final number. Word of the success of their act got back to the New York Keith office, and they were hired to perform at the New York Keith-Albee Palace Theatre.

Walda had found work in the movies, as a featured player at Metro-Goldwyn-Mayer Studios. Eddie Mannix, one of the executives at Metro, and his wife welcomed Walda into their family and invited her to live in their guesthouse.

Mae Clarke and her husband, Lew Brice, had finished playing the Fox Theatre in Philadelphia and were set to come into New York with the now successful act that Mae's sister-in-law, Fanny, had built for her brother and his bride.

Back in New York, Mae received a telegram from a Hollywood agent telling her to "report to the studio on Long Island and make a test . . . there's something cooking there." It was a picture called *Big Time*, a backstage story that needed "a girl who could sing and dance but who'd never done one of these films before because they were all too much alike."

Lew realized "it was the beginning of the end for Jewish comedians," though he thought he might be able to get work if he went to Hollywood with Mae. Mae was adamant; she was not going to go to Hollywood for a picture if it meant breaking up the act. Lew called his sister Fanny and asked her to intervene.

"Are you out of your mind?" Fanny said to Mae. "You have to do it, my dear. There isn't any question about it. You're big time now. And I'm coming with you!"

At Fanny Brice's suggestion, for the screen test Mae sang a torch song, "My Man," with Fanny telling Mae how to sing it. Fanny said, "I lean against the post, but my eyes aren't seeing. They don't go directly to the middle of the audience or to any one person, but they pick a spot and never leave it.

Fanny Brice with Julius W. "Nicky" Arnstein, mostly cropped from the photograph, circa 1918.

That's who I'm talking to . . . Then you have your audience concentrating. When is she going to look away? The only way you get their involvement is through the eyes. Think it first and don't blurt the words out just because they are there."

For the test, Fanny lent Mae one of her long dresses and pinned it to fit Mae's body. Fanny suggested that Mae dance in short velvet pants and perform a dramatic skit. Mae couldn't think of anything and used Barbara's big scene from *The Noose*.

The test was put on the train west. It took four days to get to Los Angeles. The word came back that Mae was to report to Fox Studios on Western Avenue to sign a contract.

Mae and Lew and their wirehaired terrier, Max, traveled cross-country on the Chief for three days before they reached California. Mae was frightened of what she was leaving behind and of what she was going toward, but Lew assured her that if she failed in pictures, he would bring her back to New York.

Fanny had traveled west ahead of them. She was living in a suite at the Roosevelt Hotel and had another suite reserved for her brother and his wife. When the Chief pulled in to the Pasadena station, Fanny was there to greet her family. Mae ate her first dinner in Los Angeles at the Blossom Room of the Roosevelt Hotel.

Barbara was concerned for her brother, now called by his middle name, Byron, when she learned that his wife, Elizabeth, had contracted "the great white plague," tuberculosis, and was being treated in a sanitarium in the Bronx. Byron was devoted to Elizabeth and spent every hour he could with her. Gene, Mabel, and Maud traveled there to visit Elizabeth, who looked wasted. They left the sanitarium thinking it would be the last time they would see her.

Barbara had brought Frank Fay to Avenue L to meet her family. It was a big event for the Merkents and for Mabel. Gene, who was eleven, had never heard of Frank Fay, but he was excited about his aunt Ruby's marriage.

Both families were charmed by Fay's storytelling. Fay called Ruby "Barbara," and Maud, Mabel, and Bert tried hard to remember to address Ruby by her new name.

The moment Gene saw his aunt, he couldn't stop noticing the large pendant she was wearing. At the end of the evening, after Barbara and Fay went back to Manhattan, Gene asked his mother and Maud why his aunt was wearing a large silver cross on her neck. Gene attended Kings Highway Methodist Episcopal Sunday school each week; neither the Vasletts nor the Merkents were Roman Catholic, and he was upset by the religious object and by the size of it. Maud and Mabel didn't want to make too much of it and tried to assuage Gene's concerns by telling him that their mother had worn a cross around her neck, and that was the end of it.

Fay was so devout in his own ways he was known as a professional Catholic, and Barbara had tried to please him by wearing the cross to show her conversion to Catholicism.

Barbara found out that her brother had contracted tuberculosis from proximity to his wife and wanted to do what she could, but Byron refused to take money from his sister. The sanitarium in the Bronx was large and impersonal. By and Elizabeth traveled cross-country to a sanitarium in a small town in northwestern Arizona in the Hualapai valley, between the Cerbat and the Hualapai mountain ranges near Kingman. The small city of Kingman, Arizona, had been put on the map the year before when Charles Lindbergh and Amelia Earhart stopped over on the first forty-eight-hour airmail service run between New York and Los Angeles and dedicated Port Kingman airport.

The dry air and altitude of Kingman, at more than three thousand feet, were conducive to a full recovery from tuberculosis. The small town, west of Flagstaff, south of Las Vegas, Nevada, reinforced the isolation of those suffering from tuberculosis. After a stay there, Byron was almost recovered, and he was sure Elizabeth was getting better. Once she was strong enough to travel, By planned to take her to the Grand Canyon, something she'd always wanted to see. But Elizabeth's doctor told him that she was not going to get well; she was dying.

Just after Christmas, Barbara was approached by a Mr. Ginsberg, who wanted to know if she had a recent film test he might see and if she would be available for motion picture work in Hollywood. Mr. Ginsberg was making the inquiry on behalf of Al Lichtman, a vice president in New York of United Artists. Lichtman was following the directive of Samuel Goldwyn, whose pictures were distributed by United Artists and who had become interested in Barbara after hearing about her from Johnny Considine, a young producer at Metro who'd worked with Valentino on two pictures. Goldwyn had sent a wire to Lichtman giving him instructions about getting the test and finding out about Barbara's availability.

Barbara responded to Goldwyn's interest by letting it be known that she would not work without her husband.

Despite Barbara's feelings about working in Hollywood, word was around that she was to be in a picture for Fox Studios called *Mr. Broadway*, opposite the writer and performer Joe Frisco of Ziegfeld's *Follies* and currently *Earl Carroll's Vanities*. Barbara's name was mentioned in the same column with those of William Powell, "of the movies," who was in New York for two weeks, and Robert Benchley, Donald Ogden Stewart, and Jock Whitney, who were in New York "taking in the fast places for laughs."

Elizabeth Stevens died of consumption. Byron was heartbroken and arranged to have his wife brought back from Arizona to Brooklyn to be buried in Brooklyn's Green-Wood Cemetery, next to his mother, Catherine Stevens.

Barbara wanted Byron back in her world. She felt that he had married up. He had traveled in a world in which she didn't feel comfortable, and now that there was no one to stand between them, she wanted her brother to be with her. By loved his sister and was protective of her, but he wanted a life separate from hers.

Barbara and By looked alike; their features were so similar that they were often called "the twins." Unlike Barbara, By was at ease with himself and fit in many worlds. Barbara longed to be as free as he with people. Byron Stevens was seen as a gentleman who spoke impeccably, whose charming manner was rarely marred by anger, and whose sincerity was reflected in the direct gaze of his blue eyes. Barbara admired those qualities in her brother, almost envied him. She was wiry and shy and tense and only too aware of how quick to anger she could be.

ELEVEN

Invitation West

Fay opened at Keith's Palace in the beginning of February 1929. He came on with two male pianists and "broke up" his songs. "Let's build a stairway to the stars," Fay sang. The music stopped while he spoke to the audience: "Let's build a stairway to the stars. This is of course the craziest, and the guy that's singing it is the worst. Oh, when you stop to think, well, he has a girl no doubt. And probably the poor thing has a brand-new dress on, and she figures that later on maybe he'll take her out to eat, drink, and be merry. But he says: 'No, my dear. Let's climb this stairway to the stars.' Naturally, she gets, well, tired pretty quick and you know building and climbing. But he says, 'Keep going, honey. Keep going, baby, we got to get to those stars.' So the poor kid changes her gown for pants and he throws her a shovel and she throws him a kiss and bang they're in business."

Fay's speaking voice onstage was low and smooth and easy; its richness combined with a fullness and clarity that registered somewhere deep within his audiences. Fay's voice was capable of the most subtle variations and control. He used its softness to caress and seduce, a warmth overtaking his listeners. He used its harshness and street gruffness to punctuate his stories and to catch his listeners up short.

The first week that Frank and Barbara were at the Palace, Fay came on late in the mostly all-male bill and was onstage for thirty minutes or so ("and could have made it a weekend," said *Variety*) before introducing his wife.

Barbara had a choice, she said, "of merely walking to the footlights and uttering a silly, meaningless speech or of cooperating with my husband in an act that offered real entertainment."

She and Fay bantered back and forth with Fay getting most of the laughs. Barbara said, "[Fay] is essentially a comedian. I am not. Therefore, to provide entertainment, I played 'straight man' and he supplied the laughs. Audiences appeared to enjoy the act."

During their second week at the Palace, as part of Frank's act, he and Barbara appeared on the bill in Vincent Lawrence's short play, *The Conflict,* in which Ruth Chatterton had regularly starred in variety shows. Barbara's clothes reflected the colors Fay preferred for her: early in the show, she wore a pair of black-and-white satin and velvet pajamas and then, as Fay's "straight man," a white crepe dress with pleated trimming and gold buttons.

The New York Times called the "playlet" "of chief interest" on the bill and referred to Barbara as "the beauteous Miss Stanwyck." The reviewer described Fay's "easy style of performing" and commented that it "carried him over one or two rough places," and went on to single out the "quality of tenderness, of femininity," that Barbara's acting "so definitely transmits."

Burlesque was about to be made into a movie. Paramount Famous Lasky offered the role of Skid Johnson to Hal Skelly and the role of Bonny Lee to Barbara. She refused to leave Fay behind in New York.

"Frank comes first with me and always will," she said. Nancy Carroll, the niece of Barbara's champion Billy LaHiff, was hired for the role of Bonny Lee.

Barbara was in her dressing room one night when one of the actors who worked with her in a skit knocked on the door and introduced her to an old friend of his.

Barbara looked at the friend and said, "You don't remember me." The gentleman couldn't say that he did. She twisted one side of her hair into a pigtail.

"Remember Millie Stevens?"

"Sure I do."

"Well, Uncle Buck, I'm Millie's kid sister, Ruby."

Barbara hadn't seen Buck Mack since the days when Millie was in *Glorianna* and Ruby was eleven. Buck had drifted away and become part of a dance team with Skins Miller. He'd lost track of Millie Stevens and Ruby as Miller and Mack "rattled all over the country" performing in vaudeville shows and then performed in Europe.

The day after Buck saw Barbara in her dressing room, she invited him and Skins Miller to join up with them. "Things look good for your routine—how about it?" she said over the phone. Buck had always been kind to Barbara.

Mack was thrilled at the chance to work at the Palace and with Millie Stevens's little sister, who was now "a smart looking, young lady with plenty of style."

Barbara and Frank's run at the Palace was followed by a new floor show at the Club Richman featuring the Fays. The Richman was one of the most exclusive—and expensive—clubs in the country. Harry Richman, the nightclub king, had the room designed to look like a patio with fake windows that opened out onto painted scenery. The club's ceiling was painted to give the impression of a sky with stars that lit up when the sun—a spotlight—was on the performers.

Oilmen and Texas cattlemen showed up at the Club Richman, as did Vanderbilts, Whitneys, and Morgans. Performers like Eddie Cantor and Al Jolson went as well. As did gangsters, Al Capone among them, and financiers, "Sailing" Baruch, and great ladies of the American stage like Ethel Barrymore. Damon Runyon met his future wife there; Willie K. Vanderbilt, one of the Warburton girls. And Marion Davies made drinks for "the Chief" (William Randolph Hearst) from every variety of liquor that she had Richman stash for her in the ladies' room.

The Fays' show opened February 20 to large audiences. The Club Richman, when packed, seated 240, and it was packed every night with people wanting to see Frank Fay and his wife.

Fay's humor was broad, original, funny. Bob Hope thought Fay was "the most economical comedian" he had ever seen. "Fay could get more out of an attitude than anybody." Hope marveled at his "complete audience control."

Hope saw Fay one time alone on a "darkened stage with the spotlight on him. For the longest time Fay just stood there. He said absolutely nothing, and he did absolutely nothing. Then he said, 'I think I'll go play the piano.' He walked slowly across the stage to the other side. As he got there, the spot, which had followed him, showed a piano with a stool and a fellow sitting on it. Frank just looked at it and then, just as slowly, walked back to exactly where he had been standing. 'There's somebody there.' That was the whole thing," said Hope, "but it was one of the funniest acts I ever saw."

Fay thought it was unnecessary to struggle to be funny. "All anyone has to do is stand in the subway station and watch people." Onstage, Fay talked about things people did that were recognizable. He would talk about his uncle, the string saver who was working his way up to rope, or his aunt Agatha, a paper bag putter-awayer.

"Everyone knows string savers, and paper bag puttersaway," Fay would remark. "That's why those people are funny to the rest of us. Talk about those people and everyone laughs. Take the mustache fixer. You have seen him twist his mustache for half an hour or so and at the end of that time, it looks worse than ever. But because you have seen mustache fixers, you laugh when I talk about it. That's all there is to being funny."

People noticed that Fay was different onstage now, and much of the change was attributed to his marriage to Barbara. One critic noted that he had "changed muchly from the old days; for the betterment of his impression. And the draw of the Fay-Stanwyck combination cannot be gainsaid." Fay did a dramatic skit in the act with Barbara, who also sang and danced.

Variety's critic called Barbara's "dramatic moment with her husband, superb," and said, "Miss Stanwyck so splendidly faded it in and out that the merit of the bit could not be overlooked." Barbara was described by the critic as "very nifty, in looks, figure, dress and work." It was noted how much the audience liked her, and the critic advised Fay to "divide the entire routine with his wife on the floor."

Barbara and Fay were held over an additional three weeks at the Club Richman. Fay was billed as the International Laugh Provoker; in addition to Barbara, the show featured Joey Ray and Adia Kuznetzoff.

The Fays' run followed that of Libby Holman and Irene Bordoni. Ruth Etting was to appear at the club following the Fays at a salary of $1,000 a week. Barbara and Frank's new manager, Lou Irwin, arranged for them to receive a weekly minimum of three and a half times Etting's salary; in order for the club to break even, it had to bring in $9,000 worth of business each week. The Richman was paying Fay $3,500 a week; Barbara, $2,500. Frank was also appearing at the Fox Academy and Audubon being paid $2,500 per week. His radio commercials for *The Palmolive Hour* paid $1,000 a commercial. Fay and Barbara were earning $9,500 a week.

Fay had written a new act with Nick Copeland and Buck Mack and was trying it out in a theater in New Jersey. The plan was to spend a month perfecting it and then bring it into New York in mid-April.

In March, Joseph Schenck, the head of United Artists, went to see Barbara and Fay at the Club Richman. After the show, he went back to talk with the Fays to suggest they consider going to the West Coast to work in talking pictures as Schenck had twelve years before, when he left New York to produce pictures in Hollywood. The new technology was coming into its own, even though, of the twenty thousand movie theaters in the United States, only slightly more than six thousand were equipped to show pictures with sound.

Schenck, before becoming president of United Artists, had been a successful independent producer in New York, making pictures for his wife, Norma Talmadge, and her sister Constance in an old warehouse on East Forty-Eighth Street. Schenck, Russian-born, had grown up in a New York ghetto in the 1890s. He'd earned his first dimes with his good friend Irving Berlin as an unsuspecting delivery boy for a shady neighborhood drugstore, dropping off packages containing dope and rising to become a messenger for the underworld. He and his younger brother, Nicholas, built up a small chain of New York drugstores and then developed an amusement park across the river from New York City in New Jersey. Within a few years Palisades Amusement Park had made both men rich.

The Schenck brothers became partners with Marcus Loew in Consolidated Enterprises, whose movie house and theater chain had been built from nickelodeons. Joe Schenck booked Loew's films, met the three Talmadge sisters, decided to leave the Loew company to promote Norma's career, married his star, and went to work making pictures. In 1917, Schenck left for California with his wife; his sister-in-law; his screenwriter, Anita Loos; and his director, Loos's husband, John Emerson. Schenck's pictures that starred his wife were released through First National Exhibitors Circuit. He produced pictures as well for D. W. Griffith, Fatty Arbuckle, and his brother-in-law Buster Keaton, husband of Natalie, the third Talmadge sister.

Schenck had seen Barbara in *The Noose* and *Burlesque* and was interested in offering her a contract to star in a remake of a picture he'd originally produced in 1921 for Norma. A few years later in 1924, Schenck became a partner with Douglas Fairbanks, Mary Pickford, Charlie Chaplin, and D. W. Griffith in the cooperative company United Artists. As chairman of the board, Schenck set about reorganizing it, creating a finance company, and creating Feature Productions Inc., whose films were to be released through United Artists.

Schenck understood from Samuel Goldwyn, whose films United Artists distributed, that Barbara would not go to Hollywood without Fay.

(The other Schenck brother, Nicholas, stayed with Loew, who was still buying up theaters. Soon Loew's profits were large enough to enable him to buy an independent producing and distributing company called Metro; his intent: to make the pictures himself that were exhibited at his theaters and improve their quality. Loew then bought Goldwyn Pictures Corporation and soon after an independent producing unit run by Louis B. Mayer. In 1924 the companies were merged; Metro-Goldwyn-Mayer Studios became a subsidiary of Loew's Inc.

When Marcus Loew died in the summer of 1927, leaving an estate of $10 million, Nicholas Schenck became the president of Loew's Inc.

Barbara wasn't interested in going to Hollywood to make pictures with or without Fay; it all seemed crazy to her. She knew the stage and New York, and she was up for the lead in a play inspired by the life of the convicted murderer Ruth Snyder, called *Machinal*, that Arthur Hopkins was producing and directing.

But Fay was intrigued by Hollywood. Talking pictures interested him; he wanted to try them out, and was eager for Barbara to go to Hollywood with him. Even though she didn't want to leave New York, Fay had consented to go west, and she was going with him. Barbara agreed to make one picture for Schenck, a remake of his film based on Channing Pollock's successful play, *The Sign on the Door,* which had been produced on Broadway nine years earlier.

During the Fays' extended run at the Club Richman, Barbara was asked to approach the table of one of the guests.

"My name is Irving Thalberg," a young man said. "I am from Hollywood. Your work interests me and I wonder if you have ever thought of doing something in pictures."

Barbara cut him short. "Thank you, Mr. Walberg. My husband, Frank Fay, and I have just signed contracts to make pictures for Joseph Schenck and Warner Bros."

"Ah, when you come to Hollywood, drop in to see me."

Barbara nodded and walked away.

The Fays packed their trunks and boarded the 20th Century for an overnight journey that took them from Grand Central Station to Dearborn Station, Chicago. There the Chief left for Los Angeles in the twilight of the afternoon.

On the train, Barbara recognized the man from the Club Richman who had called her over to his table and asked her if she had any interest in going to Hollywood.

For the next two days and three nights, the Chief ("Extra Fast—Extra Fine—Extra Fare") crossed the prairies, the Rocky Mountains, and the Mojave Desert, making its way through the mountain ranges of San Gabriel and San Bernardino, passing groves of oranges, and finally steaming into Pasadena. Amid the luxury of the transcontinental train, Fay and Barbara were surrounded by polished mahogany, mirrors, brass, and crystal. The Chief was carrying them from the East, away from the solid, familial life Barbara had worked so hard to make on the stage, to a place she didn't know and didn't care to be, farther west than she'd ever traveled before.

Walda Mansfield read an announcement in the paper that Barbara and Fay were coming to Los Angeles and were to arrive in Pasadena. She had been living in Los Angeles for more than a year and working steadily in small parts for Metro-Goldwyn-Mayer. She found out when the train was due in and drove to the station to welcome her friends and take them to their hotel.

Barbara and Walda hadn't seen each other in more than a year. Walda saw

Barbara on the platform. Frank was busy with the porters gathering together their luggage and said a quick "Hello, Wally," and went on attending to the trunks. Walda was all set to throw her arms around her friend. Instead of the warm welcome she expected, Barbara's hello was oddly cool. Barbara was usually so warm; Walda was surprised, but decided that Barbara was just distracted by the excitement of her arrival and the bustle of passengers getting off the train.

Among those disembarking was the small young man from the Club Richman. It became clear to Barbara that while "in New York, he might have been another night-club guest," he must have been "something pretty celestial out here. Two-thirds of Hollywood was there to meet him."

Walda told Barbara that she had come to pick them up and give them a ride to wherever they were staying. Barbara replied that they were staying at the Roosevelt Hotel and already had a ride.

"I'll call you there in a few days," said Walda.

"Do that," said Barbara.

Left to right: Mr. and Mrs. Frank Fay, Joe
Schenck, and Irving Berlin, circa 1929.

TWELVE

Panic of Self-Doubt

1929–1931

Pictures have only scratched Barbara's surface. If she ever lets go and gives herself to pictures as I know her, she'll be the biggest star on the screen. Her personality is as dominant, as vital, as Mae West's or Garbo's. Oh, go and laugh but you don't know her.

—Mae Clarke

T he first day Barbara saw Los Angeles she hated it.

She wanted to turn right around and take a train back to New York. Instead, she sent a Western Union to Maud, Bert, Mabel, and Gene telling them that she and Fay had arrived safely.

She had no desire to be in Los Angeles. She was willing to stay for the duration of *The Locked Door,* but after that she planned to return to New York. Pictures were insane, she thought, and everyone connected to them "tetched."

Barbara had asked Fay to sign a contract for only one picture, and to oblige his wife, he signed a letter of agreement with Warner Bros. for *So Long Letty.*

Fay was expected to report to work on May 5 to star with Charlotte Greenwood and was being paid $27,500 for seven weeks of work—what he was making in New York.

A few days after Fay signed the agreement for *So Long Letty,* Warner Bros. decided they wanted him instead to appear in *Under a Texas Moon,* the studio's first all-talking, singing picture, to be filmed outdoors on the Warner Bros. Ranch in the all-natural two-color process called Technicolor. It was one of forty all-color pictures for which the studio had contracted with the newly operating Hollywood plant of the Boston-based Technicolor Motion Picture Corporation. Warner Bros. was hoping this new enhanced effect would lure audiences away from radio.

Walda telephoned Barbara at the hotel. "She was very cool," said Walda of Barbara's response to hearing her friend's voice on the phone. Walda didn't know what to make of it, "whether Fay was there, or she didn't want to see me. I didn't think of her changing that much. But I certainly got the message that that's the way it was going to be."

Walda didn't phone Barbara again.

Barbara and Fay continued their stay at the Roosevelt Hotel. It "looked the nearest thing to Broadway," Barbara said.

Fay was waiting to begin work for Warner Bros. and was happy to appear around town as the master of ceremonies at different hotels, including the Monday night celebrations of their hotel, and Sid Grauman's midnight show. He performed next to closing for an actors' club at the Warner Bros. Theatre in Los Angeles. The show started at midnight and let out at 3:45 in the morning. Barbara put on a gown, wore no makeup, and sat at a corner table while Fay performed onstage.

Fay came home one day and said that he'd seen "the most attractive house" and had "leased it for a year." Barbara was horrified. The idea of living in one place for a year, and in a house, was almost unimaginable.

From the time Barbara and Frank were first married, neither had "wanted a home. Being installed in a house, weighed down by possessing household goods and a feeling of permanence was revolting to both of us," Barbara said. "We wouldn't consider even an apartment. We lived in hotel suites and lived in our trunks." The attitude about going to Hollywood was "don't buy anything you can't put on the Chief"; everything was rented.

The large, comfortable house Fay rented on Holly Mont Drive belonged to Harry Langdon, the comedian who, in less than a year, had become as famous and beloved as Chaplin and almost as rich. The Langdon character that won America's heart was the baby-faced, moon-cheeked little man whose goodness triumphed over adversity. It had been created by Frank Capra, then a Mack Sennett gag writer, who figured out how to make use of Langdon's winsome childlike personality. After Langdon made it big in a series of Sennett's pictures, he left Sennett and signed a million-dollar contract with First

National for three features, with an option for a fourth. Three of the four pictures were directed by Capra. Within two years Langdon became one of the most famous comedians in pictures. As soon as he insisted on directing his own movies, the critics dismissed them, audiences didn't like them, and Warner Bros. let him go. The once famous comedian who'd been on top of the world was now broke and scrambling for work and was relieved to lease his house to Frank Fay and his wife.

Barbara was to share equal billing for *The Locked Door* with Rod La Rocque. La Rocque and his wife, Vilma Banky, one of the great stars of silent pictures, cut quite a figure as the Hollywood couple. La Rocque had come from the stage and, like Barbara, had worked as a child with Willard Mack. He had grown rich playing the romantic hero in more than fifty pictures and had starred as well in Cecil B. DeMille's *Ten Commandments.*

La Rocque was an award-winning photographer and an inventor and was awaiting a patent from the U.S. Patent Office for one of his creations that he planned to manufacture: a self-answering telephone that automatically answered a call after a certain period of time. *The Locked Door* was the first picture in which La Rocque, as the seducer, was the heavy.

Barbara was to be paid $1,500 a week, a good deal less than what she'd been making in New York.

The director of *The Locked Door* was George Fitzmaurice, one of the three highest-paid directors in Hollywood.

Many of the studios had spent the previous two years converting their equipment to speaking likenesses, each studio setting up different recording equipment. Technical problems hampered the making of pictures. What had taken almost three decades of silent movie making to develop—the freedom of the camera, the richness of the lighting, and the unhampered ability of the director and actor to tell a story in delicate, moving nuance—was undone by the technical advancement of putting words to storytelling. George Fitzmaurice, and other directors, had had great freedom with silent pictures; they could just roll camera and didn't have to worry about the dialogue fitting in to the scene, or the picture.

Movies could now talk; silent pictures were dying out quickly, but it was the actors and directors who had to pay the price of the new technology.

The camera now had to be fixed in place, its lens fitted through the booth's glass panel, which flattened the image, despite the quality of the lens being used. It was locked in a soundproof, airless booth to avoid the microphone's recording of the noise as it turned, with the cameraman wearing long black robes to prevent reflection from the inside glass of the booth. The camera crews came out of the booths in between takes, gasping for air.

Lighting on the set was affected as well. What was good for one camera angle didn't necessarily work for another. The front lights of the sets were competing for space with the bulkiness of the camera booth. The microphones were unwieldy and difficult to move from actor to actor; they were heavy and clumsy and encased in bronze. Scenes were ruined when different camera setups didn't correspond to the microphone's proximity to the actor or when the microphone picked up the sound made by the klieg lights, which were soon replaced by silent incandescent lights. The problem with incandescent lights was the amount of heat they gave off. One technician said the lights were so hot "you could light a cigar a hundred yards away."

During the shooting of one scene in *The Locked Door,* the temperature on the soundstage reached 118 degrees. There was a heat spell in Los Angeles, and two hundred extras on a close set crowded together didn't help. The thirty-four incandescent lamps beating down on Barbara and La Rocque and the others made the temperature unbearable.

The Locked Door was a remake of Joe Schenck's 1921 picture that had starred his wife, Norma Talmadge. The story involved blackmail, a shooting that isn't accidental, and the virtue of a stepdaughter who becomes unknowingly involved with the blackmailer.

Barbara "staggered through" the filming of the picture. Fitzmaurice had been making pictures since 1914, and had directed the biggest stars of silent

Circa 1929.

George Fitzmaurice rehearsing with Vilma Banky for *The Night of Love,* 1927. (PHOTOFEST)

pictures, Pola Negri, Betty Compson, Anna Q. Nilsson, Marie Prevost, and Colleen Moore among them. He'd directed Valentino's final movie, *The Son of the Sheik,* and actors who were starting out, among them Gary Cooper and Ronald Colman.

Several of Fitzmaurice's pictures had been accompanied by synchronized sound, but *The Locked Door* was his first talking picture. Fitzmaurice understood what was required of silent pictures, and though he said publicly that with the talkies "pictures had entered the second great stage of their development, socialization," he, along with many others, was struggling to find a way to work with actors in this new realm and to tell a story as effectively and as simply as before.

Fitzmaurice's heavy French accent—he was born and raised in fin de siècle Paris—made it difficult to understand what he was saying. It was "all one big mystery," said Barbara.

Fitzmaurice was portly with a face so red that one of the technicians on the picture called it "a magnificent example of a bourbon blush."

"He was used to working with the beauties of the silents," Barbara said. "Norma Talmadge, Vilma Banky, Billie Dove. He kept arranging all kinds of drapery and tapestries behind." He had trained in Paris as a painter, and he was known as a director whose strong visual style and elaborate sets were his own production designs. For one set in *The Locked Door* he reproduced every detail of his Beverly Hills living room, from the oak paneling on the walls to the rugs on the floors, the furniture in the room, and the lamps on the tables. Finally, Fitzmaurice shook his head in despair about Barbara and screamed, "Dammit, I have tried everything! Look at the way you look! I can't make you beautiful no matter what I do."

Barbara didn't think of herself as a beauty. She saw herself "as an average-looking person." Two of her teeth were crooked, and she wanted them left that way, despite the United Artists executives who insisted she straighten them.

"Look," Barbara said to Fitzmaurice, "they sent for me, I didn't ask to come to Hollywood."

It wasn't beauty that interested Barbara. She'd learned from working with Willard Mack and Arthur Hopkins, and from watching Fay onstage and off, that what mattered was being natural. What interested Barbara as an actress was being believable.

Fitzmaurice was trying to get at the same freedom of movement and naturalness of the silent screen. It was United Artists' new equipment that allowed the cast to be scattered over a wide area ten or fifteen feet apart and still shoot a scene. Its achievement was a selling point for the movie.

Edward Bernds was one of the few men who understood the new equipment that made sound work, and he spent ten days working on the last third of *The Locked Door* as the head of the sound crew. Bernds saw Barbara as an unusual beauty, and he watched as Fitzmaurice became frustrated by the constraints of the new technology. "Fitzmaurice seemed at quite a loss with sound," said Bernds. "He fussed and complained about the camera, about the fact that it was in the camera booth, and that the cameraman couldn't give him what he wanted. Well, he had to cope with that, that's what sound did."

Barbara in *The Locked Door* was the young wife of a rich society man; the couple is on the verge of celebrating their first anniversary when her past invades and threatens to undo their marriage. Husband and wife are unwittingly drawn into a web of deception and betrayal, seemingly to protect his adored younger sister but in fact for self-sacrificing reasons to protect each other.

Barbara was able to find the innocence of the character and play her with a simplicity and softness.

"Fitzmaurice didn't direct the way a director should," said Bernds. "He didn't let the actors do what seemed right to them."

Barbara's frustration that Fitzmaurice was not helping was obvious; in addition, it was difficult for her to get used to acting out of sequence.

La Rocque's lumbering acting and slow singsongy way of speaking were offset by his commanding physicality. He was more than six feet tall and solidly built. Barbara's husband in the picture, William Boyd, was known in Hollywood as William "Stage" Boyd, to distinguish him from William Boyd, the Pathé star and leading man of Cecil B. DeMille's *Volga Boatman.*

La Rocque and Boyd were both much larger and taller than Barbara, who was five feet three inches. On film her stature and presence equaled theirs.

Betty Bronson, Boyd's younger sister in the picture, was five feet tall and lithe. Bronson's movements and facial expressions in *The Locked Door* didn't need dialogue to carry her scenes. It was acting that suited the silent camera. Bronson, who was twenty-two, had been an extra in pictures until Herbert Brenon chose her to star at eighteen as Peter Pan. The following year, she appeared in the 1925 production of *Ben-Hur* and went on to act in more than twenty silent pictures.

Barbara was comfortable relying on dialogue to carry the narrative; the naturalness of her body movements would have been lost in silent pictures. She was used to the constraints of the stage; the camera's lack of mobility didn't affect her. The simplicity of her acting worked well in sound pictures. Her deep and resonant voice recorded well.

Barbara completed work on *The Locked Door* as Fay began the first week of shooting *Under a Texas Moon.* The picture was set in the 1830s. Fay was playing the part of a whimsical, fast-riding Don Juan, a two-gun seducer who, with his guitar-strumming companions, travels the old Southwest promising devotion to every woman he meets, fighting hard, and capturing cattle rustlers.

The picture's director, Michael Curtiz, ordered Fay's red hair dyed black. Curtiz was an experienced, urbane man who had directed pictures for almost two decades. As Mihály Kertész, he had made more than forty pictures in his native Budapest. Curtiz had worked in Berlin, Rome, Paris, and Copenhagen before coming to America to direct Dolores Costello in Warner Bros.' *The Third Degree.* He'd been with the studio for three years and during that time had directed thirteen pictures. *Under a Texas Moon* was his seventy-fifth picture. He was jovial, friendly, but with a will of iron. Curtiz was a martinet on the set; Fay took an instant dislike to him.

Fay's leading woman was the Mexican actress Raquel Torres, just starring in Metro-Goldwyn-Mayer's newly released part-talking picture, *The Bridge of San Luis Rey.* Torres, who was educated in a convent, made her debut as the lead in *White Shadows in the South Seas.* One of the other women seduced by

Myrna Loy as Lolita Romero with Frank Fay as
Don Carlos, *Under a Texas Moon,* 1930.

Fay's character was played by Myrna Loy, who was becoming an intermediary
on the set between Fay and Curtiz and would intervene when Curtiz got angry
and stormed around the set shouting in Hungarian. Curtiz hated actors. Each
day when they broke for lunch, he never ate; it cost him an hour's shooting.

Under a Texas Moon was being shot in the Mojave Desert in Technicolor;
the picture should have been designed from the beginning with color in
mind. The color lights had to be changed for Technicolor. The regular heavy
makeup used for black-and-white film should have been replaced with less
artificial-looking makeup. The company suffered from temperatures that were
frequently above 120 degrees. Fay began to lose weight. There were wind-
storms; the whistling of the wind was picked up by the microphones, and
scenes had to be reshot. The company was forced to work at odd hours due
to the constant stream of airplanes, though aeronautics was a new industry.

Pictures that had been made in the previous twenty-five years were being
re-released with sound, among them D. W. Griffith's *Birth of a Nation,* even
Edwin S. Porter's *Great Train Robbery.* While Warner Bros. was making color
pictures with sound, other movie studios, like Paramount, were still releasing
large numbers of silent pictures.

Stage actors were being wooed to Hollywood for the quality of their
voices. Colleen Moore saw it as "the gold rush of '49 all over again, only this
time the gold lay in the mouths of silent movie actors who were looked down
upon as a disgrace to the acting profession."

Actors who had been looked at by casting bureaus for their physical appearance and the color of their hair and eyes were now being considered in terms of their vocal abilities as well as vocal peculiarities. A man with a stutter could be lifted out of the ranks of extras to become a "character voice" and receive a raise in salary.

Stage directors were reconsidering working in moving pictures in the belief that the technical advancement of sound would result in a new school of writers and artists.

Willard Mack was in Los Angeles to make a Metro-Goldwyn-Mayer picture of Bayard Veiller's play *The Trial of Mary Dugan.* The new world of sound to Mack had "no precedents, no rules laid down, no experts to bow to." He believed that talking film produced "a greater range of expression than had been previously possible."

Mae Clarke was at Fox Studios making her first picture, *Big Time,* with Lee Tracy, directed by Kenneth Hawks. For the few musical numbers in the film, she was being coached by Sidney Lanfield, the film's dialogue director. While Mae was at the studio working, her husband, who'd made several two-reel comedies in Hollywood before he and Mae were married, was trying to find work. In between, Brice spent his days gambling and drinking. "It killed the time," said Mae, "but it also killed his heart." Lew (who was twice Mae's age) said to her, "I guess you're going to find somebody new soon." She couldn't convince him that their age difference didn't matter.

During the making of *Big Time,* the studio promised Mae that great things were going to happen to her.

Mae and Barbara met for lunch. Mae talked about *Big Time.* John Ford was in it as himself, a Hollywood director.

During the lunch, Mae felt an inexplicable tension from Barbara, that she couldn't reach her. Mae sat there "with the dearest friend I've ever had," she said. "There was a constraint between us as though we were strangers." In New York, Mae and Barbara had been inseparable; they'd shared the same bed, eaten together, worked together. Mae couldn't understand what was wrong. She felt that if she could "just bridge those silences everything would be all right." There was nothing else to talk about, so Mae talked about the plans the studio had for her. "The picture didn't mean half as much to me as getting close to Barbara again. But she didn't understand.

"Barbara thought I was getting 'high-hat.' And all I could think of was that now that Frank Fay was going to be a big success out here, Barbara didn't want to have anything to do with me. I'm a link that binds her to

With Mae Clarke, New York, circa 1927.

the past. In New York we were harum scarum kids, madcaps, who did crazy things."

Mae was upset by the lunch. She experienced emotions in extremes. She was either high with happiness or "floundering in the depths." She called them "spells," and they usually lasted a couple of weeks. "I'm just not good for anything when I'm in the throes of one," she said. "My mother has them. So does my father. I worry over every word I utter for fear of not expressing myself clearly. I think I must educate myself. I start reading a history. There are allusions to something that preceded the era I'm studying. I get another history to look up those references and find that alludes to something else. And before I know it, I'm in a hopeless muddle. So I throw down the books and wonder what in the world I can ever make of myself."

Mae made another lunch date with Barbara, and they spoke occasionally on the phone. After that, Barbara told Mae she was busy, that life had taken them in different directions. "This is my direction and that is yours," Barbara said.

Mae talked to Walda about what had happened with Barbara and went over and over it in her mind in an effort to try to make some sense of it.

"Forget it," said Walda. "If that's the way Barbara feels, maybe her husband has gone to her head."

Mae felt that it "was an entire new game for Barbara, a game she took very seriously. Barbara Stanwyck Fay didn't want any part of the old Ruby Stevens."

In August the movie of the Arthur Hopkins play *Burlesque* opened under the title *The Dance of Life*. The original title had been changed to avoid confusing the moviegoer who might think he or she was going to see a burlesque show. *The Dance of Life* was a title taken from the Havelock Ellis book, published six years before, and was also owned by Paramount Pictures.

The Dance of Life was a talking picture with Technicolor sequences, directed by the theater director John Cromwell and the movie director Eddie Sutherland, both of whom appeared in small parts. Cromwell called the concerns about sound that "old devil dialogue."

The picture was to have been shot on Paramount's brand-new stage. The night before shooting was to begin, the interior of the newly built stage went up in flames. Cromwell had to shoot the picture at night with the dance numbers choreographed by Barbara's former producer Earl Lindsay.

Hal Skelly repeated his role from the stage version. Nancy Carroll was Bonny. The young actress was being groomed by Paramount to be a star. The studio wanted vehicles for her that were "on the emotional side with a little comedy of the precious type." David O. Selznick, acting as assistant producer to Hunt Stromberg, thought that the actress was best in "dramatic and wistful moments" and had assigned her leading roles in *Manhattan Cocktail*, with Richard Arlen, directed by Dorothy Arzner; *The Shopworn Angel*, with Gary Cooper; the studio's first all-talking picture, *Close Harmony*, with Buddy Rogers; and *The Wolf of Wall Street*.

. . .

Barbara was having a hard time living in Los Angeles; she was scared. No studio was interested in her. And Frank didn't want her to work, just as he had his two previous wives, each of whom retired from the stage after becoming Mrs. Frank Fay. Frank wanted Barbara to stay at home; he would support her. Barbara was in love, and Fay's thinking sounded reasonable.

Harry Cohn of Columbia Pictures saw Barbara dancing at a Celebrity Night at the Hollywood Roosevelt Hotel and offered her a part in a movie. Frank told Barbara not to take it; she turned down the role.

She tried to pretend that she was happy being idle and was gallant about it; being idle was not her natural state, and she felt trapped. Work was essential to her. She'd worked since she was thirteen: dancing on the stage for seven years from the time she was fifteen; starring on Broadway when she was twenty; and playing the Palace Theatre in New York City with the biggest draw in vaudeville, her husband. And now here she was clear across the country, in a place she didn't want to be, married to a man she loved and who loved her but who wanted her to give up what she needed most, work.

Fay continued to appear around Los Angeles at various theaters as master of ceremonies. Barbara sat "in a corner attracting no more attention than the furniture," she said, "listening to all the bright and easy sophisticated conversation, while Frank sprinkled his magic over everything; watching other women glow under the spell of his charm."

She felt the way she had all those years ago when she was in Brooklyn watching the neighborhood kids playing games and not letting her be a part of it. "I was still the child who cringed when not being accepted," still "in a panic of self-doubt."

After the completion of *Under a Texas Moon,* which cost $486,000 to make, Frank was offered an exclusive contract by Jack Warner, vice president of Warner Bros., for three Vitaphone talking and singing pictures. Each was to be made within a year, beginning in March 1930; each was to take no more than eight weeks to make, with the studio having the option to make a fourth or fifth picture within the same year. Fay was to receive $35,000 a picture and first billing.

Eventually Frank realized his arrangement with Barbara wasn't going to work. She tried to pretend she was content to be at home and to "feel cherished and sheltered and protected," but "it was too late"; the life of the homemaker was not for her.

Fay went to see Harry Cohn at Columbia Pictures and told him that if he offered Barbara a part in a picture, "with some opportunity in it," Fay would pay half of the picture's production costs and all of Barbara's salary plus the cost of her costumes.

Columbia Pictures Corporation was a minor studio with run-down facilities that produced eighteen pictures a year to Fox's or Universal's annual release of fifty films or more.

"Barbara is unhappy," Fay told Cohn. "And it is worth that much money to cheer her up a little."

Harry Cohn didn't take Fay up on his offer, but early in October Cohn called Barbara on his own to offer her a part, this time the lead role in a picture called *The Gamblers*. Margaret Livingston, originally signed to the picture, had become ill. Livingston was a beauty who became popular as a vamp in silent pictures, reaching her apotheosis as the siren in F. W. Murnau's *Sunrise*, and had won a whole new audience in talking pictures.

In the previous two years she'd starred in more than twenty pictures. That spring she'd been the voice double for Louise Brooks in Paramount's picture of the S. S. Van Dine novel *The Canary Murder Case*.

Cohn couldn't hold up production for Livingston. Did Barbara want the part? Production was to start the next day.

Barbara's agent, Arthur Lyons, thought she should take it; he insisted that any footage was good for a new actress. Barbara wasn't as sure. She wanted to work, but she thought the script was terrible, and she wouldn't accept the part without Frank's consent. Fay wanted Barbara to be happy, and he knew she would be happiest doing something. He agreed that she should take the role.

Cohn gave Barbara a contract for *The Gamblers* with an option for Columbia Pictures to use her again.

Columbia Pictures, at North Gower Street and Sunset Boulevard, was a studio that had started up only five years before, in 1924, located on land that a decade earlier had been lined with corrals for the horses used in western pictures. In the intervening years the strip became known as Gower Gulch, the gathering place for cowboys looking for work as extras. The studio had emerged from a production company called CBC, headed by Jack Cohn, his brother Harry, and Joe Brandt.

Harry Cohn still operated the way he had when he first went from two-reelers to producing features. As a fly-by-nighter, the producer often acted as writer, creating a story around whatever sets had just been used by the larger studios that could be borrowed. The pictures were shot in short takes using discarded unexposed negative strips from the ends of film reels thrown away by the bigger studios. Cameras and equipment were rented; the cameraman

set up his own lights; one assistant loaded the film and took the still photographs. There were no wardrobe men or women; the leading actors came
with their own makeup. While the large studios were investing millions in
sound equipment, Cohn continued to rent sound cameras and the facilities
to process the new technology.

Harry Cohn was crude and rough, argumentative, brassy. He could be a
gambler who played long shots. Sam Bischoff, who lost his studio to Cohn,
called him "the wandering Jew without a soul." The agent Louis Shurr described Cohn as "a great friend and a great enemy."

Cohn's credo for Columbia was "Just plain common sense, determination
and concentration." Cohn learned that the big circuit bookers looked at a
reel or two of a picture, and if they weren't won over by the early footage, they
wouldn't finish watching the picture. As a result, Cohn put a punch in the
first reel of each picture in order to win immediate attention. "Our scenarios
run about two hundred and seventy five scenes," he said. "The big studios use
five hundred scenes in their scripts. We never waste time and money filming
scenes we don't really need."

Cohn could be tyrannical and petulant, but he had taste, and he bet on
people. He said of the actors he employed, "We get 'em on the way up and the
way down." Columbia's big stars were men and women whose careers were on
the wane, actors and actresses who'd been released from their contracts by the
big studios and who could be had for not much money. Many of the studio's
supporting actors were borrowed from the same large studios, actors whose
careers were not yet established and could be had for even less money.

Barbara began filming *The Gamblers,* now called *Mexicali Rose,* at the end
of the first week of October.

"It was Margaret Livingston's picture," Barbara said, "but I inherited the
red, red 'Rose.' " She described the character Rose as a woman who "poisons
everyone in sight and those I don't poison, I knife."

Sam Hardy, a former stage actor and twice Barbara's age, was the lead in
the picture. Hardy was a graduate of Yale, a Belasco discovery, and the peren-
nial heavy in Columbia's pictures.

Erle Kenton, another former actor, was directing the picture. Kenton had
directed for Mack Sennett and, like George Fitzmaurice, had worked in silent
film and wasn't interested in dialogue or how it was spoken. To Kenton, the
spoken word merely replaced the title cards used in silent pictures.

Ed Bernds, sound technician on Barbara's first picture, had left United
Artists for Columbia and had just finished *Song of Love,* also directed by
Kenton, starring Belle Baker.

Bernds thought Kenton was patronizing and pompous. During the filming of *Song of Love*, "he seemed overbearing and arrogant and seemed to talk down to everybody." In addition to George Fitzmaurice, Bernds had worked with directors such as Herbert Brenon and D. W. Griffith; "the manner—of all of them—was far less pompous than Kenton's." Kenton addressed Bernds during *Song of Love* like a "landowner talking to a peon."

Bernds reminded Barbara that they had worked together on *The Locked Door* at United Artists. She made a face at the thought of how awful the picture was and said she had "added little or nothing to it."

Here she was, in another bad picture, with an even weaker script. Barbara had learned about constructing a character on the stage, but in *Mexicali Rose* there wasn't much to be done with Rose. Barbara said that as an actress she "didn't even know how to make an entrance and exit," let alone work from within to find a way to make Rose real. Barbara sauntered about, hands on the back of her hips, dressed in light chiffon, seducing any man who would have her, and then being kicked about.

The script in its own way was daring. Rose, a seductive, sexual, faithless woman, marries and is soon found out to be cheating on her husband, who throws her out. She seeks her revenge by marrying his young ward. The young man is unaware of his new wife's conjugal relation to his guardian, the man he worships. Since the men are not biologically related, the element of father and son sleeping with the same woman is skirted, though the young man falls in love with Rose because she reminds him of his guardian.

Kenton's seeming condescension toward Barbara made working on the picture even more difficult for her. Bernds said, "She knew she was a good actress, she tried to do her best with poor material, but to have Kenton talk down to her hurt her and made it a painful ordeal."

Barbara struggled to make something out of nothing. One moment stands out in the film and shows her, in an instant, as an actress. Rose, now married to the young man, has been found back at the casino/bar in a tryst with another man and has been called up to the room she once lived in with her first husband, owner of the casino. He tells her that he is sending her home, that she is going to live a decent life with his ward. Hardy's swaggering voice drones on, as does Barbara's, as she says to him, "Who do you think you are, to tell me what to do? I'm going to do exactly what I want." She brings a beat of humanity to a clichéd portrait of the Evil Woman, in a world of men who care only about themselves, just as she does, and who don't take kindly to being two-timed by their women.

Barbara's hard, grinding voice turns soft; her body is quiet. Rose is not redeemed, but the moment shows that the young actress has something that can touch an audience.

Bernds had trouble with Sam Hardy's voice. "But Stanwyck's voice was good, as always. It always recorded well."

On Monday of the final week of shooting on *Mexicali Rose,* the papers were full of the news that the stock market had fallen sharply as the result of a massive $5 billion sell-off; one stock declined ninety-six points. People were nervous, but the market rallied by the end of the day, and the economy was pronounced by experts "fundamentally sound." By midweek, stocks were still falling; Tel and Tel lost fifteen points; General Electric, twenty. More than two million shares changed hands. Reports came back that speculators were told to post more collateral; thousands of margin calls were sent out.

During the final day of shooting on *Mexicali Rose,* October 24, the floor of the New York Stock Exchange was in chaos; more than twelve million stock shares changed hands. The word was out that eleven speculators had committed suicide. Stock exchanges were closing in Chicago and Buffalo.

On Sunday, thousands of Wall Street bankers and brokers went to work to try to cope with what had happened the previous week. The following day, the stock market did not recover. Losses in quote values exceeded $10 billion. On Tuesday, October 29, the drop in prices was almost as great as on Monday. At the end of the day sixteen million sales had been recorded on the exchange, more than three times the number of a strong day. Stock prices virtually collapsed, swept downward with gigantic losses in the most disastrous trading day in the stock market's history.

Fourteen billion dollars was lost on all of the exchanges; the New York Stock Exchange declined $10 billion.

So many stocks were traded during the week that New York State stood to gain more than $1 million in stock transfer tax, with two cents per $100 of par value.

At first, the major motion picture studios seemed untouched by the market collapse. Paramount Pictures was particularly strong, with no outstanding loans against the studio; it was set to post a profit in the last quarter of the year. Fox's stock was equally strong, with the company making a profit of $4 million for the year. During the market collapse the Loew directors had raised their dividend from $2 to $3 and threw in an additional seventy-five cents. As a result, Fox, which owned more than 700,000 shares of Loew stock, was to receive $1 million during the final quarter of the year. In addition, Warner Bros. had just paid Fox $10 million for the sale of its minority interest in First National Pictures. A merger that was to take place between Warner Bros. and Paramount was postponed indefinitely.

THIRTEEN

A Test in Technicolor

Barbara was certain that she and Hollywood "had nothing in common." She was playing with the notion of returning to New York and the stage. Fay spoke to Jack Warner about her. Out of deference to him, Warner arranged for Fay's wife to make a test. And as a gesture to her husband, Barbara agreed to make it.

Barbara was to arrive at Warner Bros. in the evening. The test was for *Song of the Flame*. Warner was considering Barbara for the part of a dancer. She was told it was ever so much more important than the prima donna. "They didn't fool me with that one," said Barbara. "I have been on Broadway a few years. No dancer is better than any prima donna."

The test, Barbara said, "was stuck off on some stuffy little sound stage down the alley."

When she arrived, there was no director, no makeup man.

Finally, a man came in and introduced himself to her as Alexander Korda and told Barbara he had "been asked to do a test" and could she "suggest something"?

Barbara was furious. There was no script to read. But she didn't want to get angry with him; he was clearly in a spot as well.

"I can do a scene from *The Noose* without a script," she said.

Barbara thought the test was going to be wasted motion but said, "What the hell," and decided to give it her best.

The Warner front office called the set of *King of Jazz* and told the production manager that they needed a cameraman to shoot a test for a foreign director and a young girl from New York. The test was to be in all-natural Technicolor to see if there was any motion picture potential.

Ray Rennahan, the cameraman on *King of Jazz* had worked with the Technicolor lab for eight years, shooting the first Technicolor sequences in

1923 for Cecil B. DeMille's *Ten Commandments* and five years later for *Love at First Flight* and *The Swim Princess*. Rennahan went over to the stage to shoot the test.

Korda had just finished directing Myrna Loy in a silent, also for First National, called *The Squall*.

He set the lights and gave Barbara a few suggestions. She performed the scene from *The Noose*. When she finished, Korda seemed to be searching for words. At last, he spoke. "I want to apologize for the way this studio has treated you tonight. It doesn't mean anything coming from me. I'm leaving Hollywood."

Korda was a Hungarian who'd directed pictures in his country for more than a decade and who had been in Hollywood for two years with a contract at First National Pictures. In Hollywood, Korda had directed his wife, the European stage actress and film star María Corda, in two pictures and Billie Dove in three silent pictures.

"I want you to know," said Korda, "that it's been a privilege to make this test with a real actress—a privilege I won't forget."

He kissed Barbara's hand as if she were "Sarah Bernhardt," she said. Barbara and Korda talked about the "injustice of it all," about how someday "Hollywood would come to terms with [them] on its palmy, balmy knees."

A few days later, Ray Rennahan asked the production manager how the test had come out. "The front office group ran the test," the production manager said. "Neither the director nor the girl had anything to offer for motion pictures."

The stock market crash was all anyone was talking about. Investors who, two weeks before, had bought blocks of stock of Radio-Keith-Orpheum in five-thousand-share lots and paid $34–$36 a share, with the expectation that the stock would reach $50, were looking at a stock that was now worth $20.

Some of the country's leading industrial and political leaders who'd been out of the market for months began buying railroad and industrial stocks in huge quantities at bargain prices. People were reassured that the effects of the collapse would last only two or three months.

A week or so after the completion of *Mexicali Rose*, Barbara got a call from Columbia Pictures. A young director wanted her to come into the studio to talk about a part in a picture called *Ladies of the Evening*, based on a 1924 play by Milton Herbert Gropper. Harry Cohn wanted Frank Capra to interview Barbara about the leading part; the rest of the cast was already set. Capra had another actress in mind, but Cohn had yet to sign her for the role.

Barbara went over to Columbia Studios angry that she was there.

Frank Capra's office was on the ground floor and looked out on a waterless fountain filled with cigarette butts.

Barbara didn't want to meet with the director. She was fed up with interviews and tests, with Hollywood in general. She'd already been tested eleven times. She didn't like the people she'd met since she and Fay had arrived in Hollywood. And she sensed that they didn't like people from the East.

She went to the meeting looking as plain as she could and wore no makeup. She sat on the edge of her chair and looked sullen. The director thought this chorus girl was not the actress he wanted. To the usual questions he asked, "What plays have you been in?" "What movies have you made?" Barbara's answers were curt.

The director was annoyed that he was interviewing her at all and thought Barbara was a "drip." Finally, he told her what he thought of the two pictures she had made and of her performances in them. Barbara listened and took the criticism "without a flicker." He was impressed when she "frankly admitted her failure, offered no alibis or excuses."

The director said he would need to make a test with her. It was as if he had "waved a red flag before a sore bull."

"Either I'm qualified to play the role or I'm not," she said. "I'd like to play it, but I won't make a test if I never do another picture. I've already made tests, and, with one exception, they were a complete waste of everybody's time, including mine."

Capra said, "No test . . . no picture."

Screw it, she thought, she wasn't going to make it in pictures; she was going back to New York, back to where she had made it.

Barbara got up and said, "Oh, hell, you don't want any part of me," and left Capra's office.

The director called Cohn. "Forget it, Harry," said Capra. "She's not an actress, she's a porcupine."

When Barbara got home, she told Fay what had happened. She was going back to Broadway or go home and just sit.

Fay telephoned Capra to find out what had gone so wrong that his wife had come home upset and in tears. "Nobody can do that to my wife," Fay said.

"Listen, funny man," said Capra, "I don't want any part of your wife, or of you. She came in here with a chip on her shoulder, and went out with an ax on it."

Fay explained that Barbara was "young and shy" and that she'd "been kicked around out here." He told Capra about the three-minute test Barbara had made for Warner Bros. Capra was surprised to hear of it. "You gotta see it before you turn her down," Fay said. "I'm coming right down with it."

The test that Korda directed was the scene from *The Noose* in which Barbara, as the nightclub dancer, pleads with the governor for the body of the man she secretly loves and believes to have been executed. Capra watched Barbara on the screen.

Playing this each night at the Hudson Theatre, for 197 performances, Barbara had brought audiences to a pitch of emotion as the frightened, hopeless young woman learns from the governor that the man she thought was dead is still alive. Out of relief she breaks down and weeps, confessing her love for the condemned man, who is unaware of her feelings.

As Capra watched Barbara on the screen, he was stunned by the raw power of her emotion and by the burst of feeling stirring in him. Capra saw that "underneath her sullen shyness smoldered the emotional fires of a young Duse or a Bernhardt."

He sent for Barbara a few days later and offered her the part of Kay Arnold. Capra described Barbara's reaction as "the most surprised girl" he'd ever seen. "If I'm against a girl and she can still reach me," Capra said, "she's got the power I want."

Fay's intervention worked. Barbara wouldn't be leaving for New York, at least for a while. She was being paid $2,000 a week as the lead in *Ladies of the Evening.*

Fay took the train to New York for the premiere of Warner Bros.' *Show of Shows,* opening at the Winter Garden with Fay as master of ceremonies, as he was in the film.

Barbara's first picture, *The Locked Door,* was released in mid-November, heralded by United Artists as "all-talking."

"A better bilge you never saw," is how Barbara described it.

Reviewers called the picture "tense and dramatic"; the *Detroit Daily* called it "thrilling"; *Variety* praised the picture's "fine taste and elegance in handling and settings" but saw the film as "a straight transcription from stage to screen of a formal play" with "no great story distinction." Chief among the film's assets, *Variety* said, was "Barbara Stanwyck, an actress of much character" who "saved the picture from dullness."

Barbara's sisters and nephew went to see *The Locked Door* in Times Square at the Rialto. The theater was crowded. The lights dimmed. The credits rolled by. She appeared on the screen. Gene, then twelve, said, "Oh, boy, there's Aunt Barbara." Mabel at thirty-nine was watching her baby sister, now twenty-two, starring in a moving picture. At the end of the film, Mabel was teary-eyed and left the theater saying, "That was just wonderful."

FOURTEEN

Trying to Make a Living

1930

Frank Fay's first picture premiered days later and was set to open across the country in December. *The Show of Shows* was a musical revue with hundreds of dancers and elaborate costumes and sets. Warner Bros. was re-creating for moviegoers an extravagant Broadway musical revue, with segments filmed in Technicolor.

The picture was framed by a grand stage with curtains. It featured Warner Bros.' stars and starlets under contract—among them Dolores Costello, Sally Blane, Loretta Young, Rin Tin Tin, Chester Morris, Myrna Loy, Richard Barthelmess, Patsy Ruth Miller, Viola Dana, Noah Beery, Louise Fazenda—appearing in a series of lavishly produced musical numbers.

Fay as master of ceremonies is the one constant in the picture.

He first sidles around the proscenium dressed in a WWI doughboy's uniform, with crushed cap slightly lopsided, holding a gun that seems too large for him to handle. He is unsure, unassuming (Fay to audience in a halting delivery with bent wrists and hands punctuating the air: "I was supposed to appear as a sad soldier, but after the Warners heard me, they said, 'He's about as sad as you can get.' I could probably sing a sad song for you now, but I've forgotten the lyrics").

After one number, Fay comes back out from the curtain, now dressed in white tie and tails. He loves "old-fashioned songs. In fact," he says, "I tried to prevail upon the Warners to let me sing an old-fashioned melody. I don't suppose they'd object to my pushing in a little ol' number now." He pauses and looks down at the orchestra pit, then back at the camera. "They have all left."

His gestures are hardly noticeable, his voice is low, resonant, and smooth.

"Still that won't stop Fay," he says softly. He pronounces his words slowly. He turns to the curtain to find the right key and turns back, ready.

Fay begins to sing, without an accompaniment. In an exaggerated, loud voice, he sings: "She was only a bird in a gilded cage, but she loved a man."

His delivery is a combination of female intonation and controlled masculine anger. His body is perfectly still; the movement and fluidity are in his voice.

In between routines the running gag throughout the picture is Fay's attempt to perform between acts and his being thwarted every time.

One of the musical routines features eight pairs of sister acts (among them the Costello sisters, Dolores and Helene; Sally Blane and Loretta Young; Peanuts Torres and sister Renee), each dressed in the clothes of a different nationality. They come onstage singing a verse ("Here's me, Raquel Torres, and Sister from Spain/We're proud of our old Spanish name/Remember it's *Torres*, not *Toro*—that's *bull*!/To think it was that would be a shame"). Myrna Loy follows, in full Technicolor, with flaming red hair and green eyes, in a Chinese fantasy, dressed in Oriental garb singing "Li-Po-Li." John Barrymore as the Duke of Gloucester is in a scene from Shakespeare's *Henry VI*. ("And yet I know not how to get the crown,/For many lives stand between me and home: And I,—like one lost in a thorny wood,/That rends the thorns and is rent with thorns, Seeking a way and straying from the way,/Not knowing how to find the open air . . .).

Fay on-screen isn't simply a comedian, or matinee idol, or singer. The controlled, pent-up feelings, the soft, beautiful, commanding voice, the hint of feminine gesture and underlying male assurance, create a presence that is slightly odd, though winning, charming, unsettling. In the end, his hold over the stage and his uncanny timing are irresistible, and the edgy reaction to his work gives way: he seduces his audience. Onstage, the immediacy of watching him and the power of his presence could obscure much of the oddness about him; on-screen, the camera hints at his low-lying anger and reveals a murky sexuality.

At the premiere, Fay introduced many from the film, including Rin Tin Tin and Ted Lewis.

Jim Cagney, a much-admired young actor and song-and-dance man in New York, often saw Fay at the Palace and thought he was an "utter revelation." Cagney had had a small part in the run of *Broadway*. He had choreographed the large numbers of the Neighborhood Playhouse's annual satiric revue *The Grand Street Follies* and was teaching acting and dance with his wife in New Jersey.

Cagney had seen monologuists before—Julius Tannen, Walter C. Kelly, James J. Morton—"and they were great." To Cagney, "monologuists were the bravest vaudevillians . . . they went out there all alone—no gimmicks, no costume, no funny makeup—and they didn't sing, dance, or do cartwheels. They just *talked* . . . in such a whimsical way they made you roar . . . But they couldn't touch Frank."

Of all the great vaudevillians, Cagney admired Fay the most. Fay "was the funniest, and . . . he had the most control." Through watching vaudevillians, Cagney came to understand their true command over the audience. Fay "never made an unnecessary move or facial grimace. He didn't need to wave a cigar around as a prop . . . [He] let us see only *himself* . . . I tried to keep in mind that constant composure he maintained. A dynamic composure, if that's not a contradiction in terms. That was his secret. I tried to learn that."

Fay returned to Los Angeles by train with his parents, who were planning to spend the winter with their son and daughter-in-law.

After renting a house for a year, Barbara was still surprised that she could live in any one place for that long and that she wasn't living out of hotel rooms. She and Fay began to talk about owning their own house and soon bought one outside Los Angeles on the beach at Malibu Lake. She sent a photograph of it back east to show her family, Millie and Art, the Merkents, Mabel and Gene.

Barbara found her lack of home feeling curious since she thought frequently about having a baby. Her thoughts about having a child were always present; in fact, she described their constancy as "a complex, a phobia."

And while she told reporters that there was "no medical reason why Frank and I can't have a child," Barbara had been left sterile by the brutal abortion she'd had at fifteen.

"When I dream," she said, "I dream that I have a baby in my arms—I can see its little face and *feel* it."

In the first week of December, President Hoover gave his annual message to Congress. He was convinced confidence had been reestablished and declared business sound. He promised an overall $160 million cut in income taxes but believed "wages should remain stable." He told Congress, "A very large degree of industrial unemployment and suffering has been prevented."

Christmastime in Los Angeles was strange. It was hot, but on Hollywood Boulevard people were lined up on the sidewalks watching a parade led by four stuffed reindeer on floats, followed by another float with Santa Claus, followed by another float with a wind machine and a man throwing confetti into it.

The Locked Door was being shown at theaters around the country but was not doing well. In Boston's State Theatre, the picture brought in $15,700 during the week of Thanksgiving, compared with $24,000 in earned receipts from MGM's *The Kiss,* which had opened the same day in November. It was difficult to top the lure of Greta Garbo.

Fay was on to his next picture for First National, *Bright Lights,* about a hula dancer from the African Kohinoor who performs in a waterfront café in the Congo and rises to become a hula queen on Broadway. The story involved murder, the underworld, the law, and the press. Fay played the protector and secret lover to Dorothy Mackaill's hula star. Once again Fay was given the role of master of ceremonies but wasn't being cast as the Latin lover.

For the third time, Fay's director was Michael Curtiz.

Warner was selling *Bright Lights* as "500 horsepower entertainment . . . the strangest and most entertaining picture the talking screen has brought." The picture was again made in all Technicolor (the studio even painting the feathers of the tropical birds—parrots, peacocks, and canaries—to heighten the intensity of their color on film).

Mexicali Rose premiered the day after Christmas. The picture was to be officially released at the end of January 1930. Columbia sold the picture as "A drama that will stir your soul . . . Life and love on the Mexican border portrayed with artistry by a cast of capable favorites."

"The main flaw in the picture, among others," said Barbara, "was that somebody didn't knife me before I began."

The Locked Door was "a terrible flop," said Barbara. After the premiere of *Mexicali Rose,* she felt "the true pulse of Hollywood."

She was honest about her feelings for the town. She hated it. She hated the pretense of the people; they were "so starry" and "so self important." She and Fay avoided Hollywood socializing as much as possible.

"When you're a failure," said Barbara, "you're just so much scum."

"In the eyes of the Hollywood crowd, I was nothing," said Barbara. "They couldn't see me for dust."

FIFTEEN

A Primitive Emotional

Columbia Pictures' newly released *Flight* was its most ambitious film yet, an adventure story about Marine Corps fliers sent to Central America to destroy Nicaraguan guerrilla rebels. The picture, using U.S. government fighter bombers and top marine fliers, showed spectacular flying sequences.

It opened in New York in September 1929, six months before *Ladies of the Evening* was set to be filmed.

Flight was a major success for the struggling studio, as well as for the picture's young director, Frank Capra. It was Capra's second big success for the studio in ten months, the follow-up to *Submarine,* his, and Columbia's, first big success and the studio's most expensive picture to date, filmed with a budget of $150,000, five times the cost of most Columbia pictures.

Capra was thirty-one years old. He'd worked for Jack Cohn at CBC Film Sales Company on Screen Snapshots when the company was jokingly known as "Corned Beef and Cabbage." Before that, he had drifted for a couple of years, knocking on doors as a salesman when he needed money, selling books, appearing as a "naive, . . . shy, scared little guy," then selling phony mining stocks to unsuspecting farmers and their wives. He'd traveled across the country and "got a real sense of small towns . . . of America."

He taught ballistics mathematics as an army instructor during the Great War, and worked in a film lab for a year and a half, developing, printing, drying, and splicing as he "ate, slept, and dreamed celluloid."

Capra had worked as a gag writer and comedy director. He'd worked for a few weeks as a writer for the Hal Roach Studios inventing plots for the Our Gang series, using his own background from the Los Angeles streets, and watching other directors like Leo McCarey work.

Fired by Roach, Capra went to Mack Sennett studios. Sennett was a disciple of D. W. Griffith's.

Frank Capra, circa 1930. (PHOTOFEST)

During the year and a half that Capra stayed with Sennett, he wrote twenty-five pictures and learned everything he could about comedy: "timing, construction, the building of a gag, the surprise heaping of 'business on business' until you top it all off with the big one—the 'topper.' " He wrote gags for every type of Sennett picture: the chase, the romantic melodrama, the mock adventure story, the romantic comedy.

Harry Cohn had heard about Capra from the former Sennett leading man Ralph Graves, then directing pictures at Columbia. Graves had starred in five adventure comedies written or co-written by Capra and thought him "a delightful guy" and "a wonderful director" and let Cohn know. But Capra was told that Cohn found him on a list of unemployed directors when he came upon Capra's name, beginning with *C,* near the top.

Capra saw from the outset that Columbia was "not a place for the weak or the meek." It was a place that "measured you not by what you could do," Capra said, "but by how you did it under Cohn's bullying."

Cohn was a new type of moviemaker Capra hadn't met before: "tough, brassy, [an] untutored buccaneer." Cohn may have been a boor whose "faults were legion," Capra said, but "he was not stupid."

During the two years Capra and Cohn worked together, they were constantly at odds with each other. Capra never let Cohn win "one single argument," knowing that if Cohn got the better of a person, "[Cohn] would throw you out . . . It was a crude way to run a studio but it got results . . .

on the simple theory that an artist with courage and guts should know more about what he's doing than the sensitive ones who are unsure. Cohn didn't want any unsure people around him."

In the months that Capra was at Columbia before *Submarine,* he'd directed six inexpensive quickies, as well as a picture starring Ben Lyon for First National, *For the Love of Mike,* that lost most of the money invested in it, and two successful Harry Langdon pictures, *The Strong Man* and *Long Pants.* In the quickies for Columbia, Capra pulled away from comedy and "experimented with heavy drama" in an effort to learn how to convey on film "the delicate nuances [and] moods of dramatic conflict."

Cohn's crudeness and gambler's instincts and Capra's cockiness, storytelling know-how, understanding of people, and determination to "master the new, universal language of film" combined to turn around the fortunes of Columbia Pictures.

When Capra took over the shooting of *Submarine,* he hadn't had much experience directing feature-length dramas or adventures. He'd put together short films for amateurs—cutting film, teaching himself how to tell a story. He'd worked as a propman, a "magician who grabs things out of the air . . . producing the impossible *now.*" He trusted that D. W. Griffith's advice to Erich von Stroheim—"Take the job but don't do it the way they tell you. Do what you want"—was the way for him to go.

On his first day as director of *Submarine,* Capra insisted on a realism actors were hardly used to. The studio's pasty makeup was removed from the actors' faces. Jack Holt's hairpiece was taken off; the pristine uniforms of "musical comedy actors" were replaced with what looked like the real thing. Right away Capra brought a natural look to the picture that the camera intensified.

Ladies of the Evening was Capra's eleventh picture for the studio within two years.

Harry Cohn was worried about how Barbara would photograph. He thought she wasn't pretty enough, and certainly not at all glamorous. Cohn had Joseph Walker, Columbia's head cameraman and the cameraman on *Ladies of the Evening,* make an "all-out" test of Barbara and do everything he could to glamorize her. "*Glamour* was a key word with [Cohn]," Walker said. "And little wonder. He found it paid off handsomely at the box office."

Walker had been with Columbia for two years, since 1927. He expected the worst from Cohn. When he was first brought to the studio by the director George Seitz to replace Columbia's cameraman, J. O. Taylor, on *The Warn-*

ing, Walker was told by Taylor in Harry Cohn's office, "Regardless of how fast you work, this guy [Cohn] wants you to work faster. He sees the rushes, takes every scene to pieces, an' gives you hell. Believe me, when I finish this picture I'll never set foot in this studio again. If you can work for this son-of-a-bitch, more power to you."

Walker was impressed with Cohn and agreed to take the job. Six pictures later he told Capra what Cohn had in mind with Barbara's test. Capra asked Walker to make the test using a sequence from *Ladies of the Evening.*

Barbara "had everything in her favor," said Walker. "High cheek bones, a face that responded to light, and she was young." Walker made the test, "shooting several tight close-ups, and made her look beautiful." He thought Barbara looked "gorgeous" and ran the test for Capra.

The director was silent.

"I thought she looked great," Walker said. "What's wrong?"

"Joe, she looks marvelous. But I've an idea we're losing something." Capra went on. "With the right handling, she could come forth with a lot of fire and talent. I'm afraid we're hiding it under all that beauty. Let's throw out the test and make another—one without the glamour; show her as she really is and I think she will be great."

Walker was concerned that when Cohn saw the test of a simple, unadorned Barbara Stanwyck, he would be "right out on Gower Street looking for a job."

"If that happens," Capra assured him, "I'll be right out there with you."

Walker went ahead and made the test. In it Barbara looked natural *and* beautiful and much more dramatic than she did with all of the makeup.

Capra had written the script for *Flight* and adapted Gropper's *Ladies of the Evening.* He sent out copies to the studio's staff writers hoping that the responses to the script would offer "little 'hints' . . . offhand first impressions" about consistency and character that would be more useful to him "than ten-page critiques."

A meeting was called in Cohn's office.

Harry Cohn resembled Mussolini. In fact, he was an admirer of the Fascist leader and modeled his large office after the dictator's. On one side of Cohn's desk was a screen that led to a door of a steam room. On the other side was a screen that went to various dressing rooms where Cohn could visit with his stars.

During the meeting in Cohn's office, someone started to read aloud Capra's script in a singsong voice; no one appeared to be listening. Cohn was telephoning, looking out the window, writing on a pad. At the end of the

Jo Swerling, 1939. Columbia brought him to Hollywood with three other writers, Paul Harvey Cox; Elmer Harris; and Herbert Ashton, Jr., none of whom knew what they "were in for. The money looked good and [they] figured it was a reasonably promising gamble." (PHOTOFEST)

reading, Cohn asked for reactions. Everyone thought the script was great. Capra was sitting next to Cohn and was clearly pleased. One of the newly hired writers, a newspaperman and playwright from New York who hadn't yet been introduced to Capra, said he thought the script was "terrible; [that] it was the worst piece of drivel he had ever heard in his life."

"The piece stunk when Belasco produced it as [a play]," the writer said. "And it will stink [as a movie]. The script is inane, vacuous, pompous, unreal, unbelievable—and dull."

Capra looked at the writer and saw "a squat, heavy-set, seething young man, furiously chain-smoking strong White Owl cigars . . . His thick glasses so enlarged his watery blue eyes he looked like a mad white owl himself." Jo Swerling had been brought out from New York by Columbia Pictures under a six-week contract and had been at the studio for only a couple of weeks. Swerling read aloud from the fifty notes he'd made about Capra's script. Silence followed. After the meeting, Cohn called out Swerling's name; he was sure he would be fired.

Swerling looked at the man who had been sitting next to Cohn. "Meet Mr. Capra," Cohn said. "It was his script you were criticizing."

Cohn asked Swerling if he thought he could improve Capra's script.

Swerling, a playwright, said he could. He'd been a reporter, editorial writer, columnist, and critic working for Hearst newspapers for twelve years. He started at the *Chicago Herald and Examiner,* sitting at a desk which adjoined that of Charles MacArthur, both on rewrite battery. At the *Herald and Examiner,* Swerling wrote a popular comic strip, *Gallagher and Shean,* based on the famous vaudeville stars.

Once Swerling was in Hollywood and got to the studio, he was "ignored as completely as the forgotten man."

Swerling took Capra's script and went to his hotel, locked himself in his room, and "pounded out a rewrite story of the plot he heard" as he would "a newspaper yarn with a longer deadline than usual." He interrupted his writing "long enough for [only] black coffee, sandwiches and brief snatches of sleep." Five days later Swerling brought his revised pages to the studio. Capra thought they were "magnificent—human, witty, poignant."

Swerling knew how to take a story and tell it.

The premise of Milton Herbert Gropper's 1924 play takes its cue from *Pygmalion*: a rich sculptor and idealist makes a bet with his fellow club members that he can transform the ways of a prostitute through kindness. The artist believes that a prostitute is only a victim of circumstances and environment and can be saved if treated with love and care; his colleagues scoff at the idea. To win the bet, he hires a streetwalker as a model, brings her to his studio, and sets out to prove his theory by ignoring her as a sexual being. The artist's best friend, with the artist's consent and with no break in their friendship, tries to lure the model back into her old life. The model instead falls in love with the sculptor and becomes spiritually uplifted; eventually, her love is returned. She finds out she is the subject of a wager and goes back to prostitution, until the fourth act, when the two lovers are reunited.

The play, staged and produced by David Belasco, was regarded as a "curry of sensationalism" but one that gave audiences what they wanted. It followed the trend that began two years before with *Rain,* which starred Jeanne Eagels, and continued with Robert Edmond Jones's production of *Desire Under the Elms,* starring Walter Huston and Mary Morris.

Ladies of the Evening "went the limit as far as vocabulary, characterizations and story are concerned." Some thought the play was a "violation of the canon of propriety," written in "the language of the gutter; tawdry, cheap, sensational." One critic wrote, "Things were said and done in *Ladies of the Evening* that should not be said and done in private, much less in public"; another called it a "shrewd frame-up calculated to hook the sex-tourist."

The play was about sex and redemption. Capra was drawn to its idea of hope and change.

Swerling kept the basic idea of the rich artist as idealist, got rid of the girl as prostitute, and made her a "party girl" ("Brother, that's my racket. I'm the one you call if you need a filler-in. That's how I make my living"). He took out the notion of the wager and framed the script in more straightforward human terms.

The two main characters in the script are transformed by each other: she wishing she "could be born all over again so I could wait for you to come along"; he finding the inspiration in her to break out of his rigid society with its ideas and expectations of right and wrong and follow his heart and dreams.

Swerling knew how to write dialogue and make it human and poetic and, at the same time, sound real.

He saw the *Ladies of the Evening* script as "the old Camille story [that needed] a new twist." He has the railroad magnate father demand of his son that he give up the girl ("I've gone to the trouble of looking you up," the father says to her. "You're not a model at all") and has the young man's mother go, unbeknownst to her son, to the girl's apartment ("I must fight for him. That's what mothers are for") and implore the girl to consider what will happen once people know the truth about her past ("I'm not here to judge you . . . I understand that you love him . . . but people won't. His friends will all slip away. He won't blame you but you'll think it's your fault").

Swerling, like Capra, used class and hypocrisy to show what they could do to people. Capra had grown up in a Sicilian ghetto in Los Angeles and hawked newspapers as a boy; he'd come to this country with his parents by boat when he was six. He saw his way out of the ghetto through education: he finished grammar school, earned his way through Manual Arts High School in Los Angeles by playing the banjo, and studied chemical engineering at Throop College of Technology, which "changed his whole viewpoint on life, from [that] of an alley rat . . . to that of a cultured person."

Jo Swerling was an immigrant like Capra who came to America when he was four years old. Swerling's Russian-born family had barely escaped a religious massacre and had been forced to flee their village of Berdichev. Like Capra's, his family in America was poor. Swerling also sold newspapers as a boy: New York's dailies in the old Tenderloin district, on Broadway and Forty-Sixth Street.

Capra thought himself "a rebel against conformity" who saw "the individual as the hope of the world"; his "goal as a youth was to leap across the tracks—to rise above the muck and meanness of peasant poverty" and to achieve "freedom from established caste systems."

Swerling saw hope and goodness in the individual and despised what the rich did to their own and to others. He saw them as a closed society that imprisoned and stultified those in it, that allowed little chance for the individual to get at what was honest and real and good in himself and others.

In the script for *Ladies of the Evening,* Swerling played up the element of the rich and powerful who allow their boundaries to be threatened for only so long and then, in the name of love, swoop down to crush those individuals, even their own, who dare to upset the rules.

The young model, after telling the artist's mother that her son is the only man she has ever loved and being told in response that her love for him will ruin him, agrees to give him up. "You win," the girl tells his mother. "You always win. You won a long time before I met Jerry. Long before any of us were born, you won."

Kay Arnold is the party girl, the lady of the evening, a tart. To Jerry Strong's idealism and dreaminess, Kay Arnold's view of the world is grounded, hard, literal.

The painter is drawn to the openness he sees on her face as she sleeps against his shoulder early one morning driving back from Long Island and is inspired to "see if he can put it on canvas." ("She was a strange sort of girl," he tells his mother. "She had a mask on like everybody else but underneath she had hope.")

When Kay is posing, Jerry asks her to "look up, higher and higher, [to] imagine the stars" in order to capture the look he saw on her face the night she slept against his shoulder. Kay can't imagine the stars; she only sees the ceiling.

"Look through the ceiling," he tells her. "And visualize the sky, the universe, stardust."

Kay can't afford to imagine. She has to make money to eat and have a roof over her head.

Jerry Strong is an idealist who follows his own instincts, isn't at all taken with the goings-on of his set, but understands it, has grown up with it, and plans to marry inside it. His apartment is a perfect blend of both worlds: a modest painter's space and a Fifth Avenue penthouse with an expansive terrace garden and a full wall of skylight windows for the best northern light.

Capra was drawn to the individuality of the young man, his impulse to dream, his romanticism, his refusal to embrace the pragmatic route, business, power, and influence, for what appears to be the half-baked notion of earning a living as an artist.

He was drawn to the toughness of the girl, her spirit, her streetwise grit that allows her to see right through the high-hat ways of Jerry Strong's world, her tenderness and purity of feeling that come through full throttle once allowed to be seen. Capra saw Barbara in Kay Arnold. He saw her as "a natural actress" and "a primitive emotional" and "let her play herself, no one else."

Barbara's initial prickly interview with Capra, and her powerful emotional screen test, showed the director how much of the Kay Arnold character was in the young actress.

Capra had what he thought was a fine cast for his picture. Ralph Graves, Capra's romantic six-foot-tall leading man from *Submarine* and *Flight,* was to play the young artist. Graves was the strong, silent, sensitive hero. "A renegade who got on a freight train from New York and high-tailed it to Chicago," is how he described himself. There he met Louella Parsons, a Chicago newspaperwoman who helped Graves get a contract with the Essanay Film Manufacturing Company. Graves, like Capra, trained as an engineer, turned actor, director, and writer. He'd become famous as an actor when he appeared in D. W. Griffith's *Dream Street* and starred in Capra's first picture for Columbia, *That Certain Thing.* It was Graves's story about Marine Corps fliers that was used as the basis for *Flight.*

Also in the cast of *Ladies of the Evening* from Capra's Sennett days was the comedienne Marie Prevost as Kay Arnold's roommate and party pal, just one piker after another ("In our flat, we ain't got much of a library: the phone book and Bradstreet"). Prevost was a former *Follies* girl who went from the New York theater to Mack Sennett two-reelers as a Sennett bathing beauty along with Gloria Swanson and Bebe Daniels. Marie Prevost made her mark a year later in 1924 in dramatic features such as *Daughters of Pleasure, Cornered,* and George Fitzmaurice's *Tarnish.* She was first noticed as a comedienne when Ernst Lubitsch directed her in a feature-length sophisticated comedy, the first of its kind ever filmed, called *The Marriage Circle,* and then in *Kiss Me Again.* Marie Prevost had appeared in more than seventy pictures before *Ladies of the Evening.*

The urbane, polished Lowell Sherman had a leading role in *Ladies of the Evening:* the hero's best friend, ever inebriated and out for a high time, usually still in white tie and tails at nine in the morning from the night before.

From *Ladies of Leisure*, 1930. Left to right: Ralph Graves, Barbara, Lowell Sherman. The handwriting on the photograph is Barbara's. (AMERICAN HERITAGE CENTER, UNIVERSITY OF WYOMING)

Lowell's character was to lure Kay Arnold back to her party girl days and then maybe on a sojourn to Havana.

Sherman was one of the most sought-after feature actors around and as a result was one of the highest paid. He came from generations of theater people, his father having arranged stage effects for David Belasco. Sherman had been on the stage from the time he was a child and made his debut in pictures in 1914 in James Kirkwood's *Behind the Scenes,* which starred Mary Pickford.

Joe Walker used diffusion and tricks of lighting. Most of the stars who went to Columbia were "asked to play roles much younger than their own age," Walker said, and "soft lighting and a light diffusion [could] work wonders."

Capra and Walker had made three silent and two talking pictures together before *Ladies of the Evening.* On their first picture, a comedy called *That Certain Thing,* Capra wanted "clear, sharp lighting, clear all the way to the corners," but once Walker explained his reasons for the "arty effects," Capra came to trust the cameraman. "It was the first time I met a cameraman who understood his camera," Capra said. "He understood how it worked and he understood *why* it worked . . . I'd say a couple of words and he knew what the hell I wanted. He knew what I was thinking."

Walker was much more free to move his camera about and had been since

Flight. Cameras were out of their booths, housed in padded "blimps," and were set on wooden frames and rollers, although film was still shot through glass plates. The cameras themselves had been quieted, and for exterior shots only padded camera covers were used to reduce noise.

For his work at Columbia, Walker had had to be inventive; the diffusion and tricks of lighting he used may have looked affected, but his reasons for using them were practical: the studio's sets were "cheap and phony [and] photography had to make them look like something."

The difference for Capra between making silent and sound pictures was enormous, and not just because of the use of dialogue.

"Suddenly [with talking pictures] we had to work in the silence of a tomb," said Capra. "No one, while a silent picture was being shot, was quiet. Shooting of silent scenes had gone on with hammering and sawing on an adjacent set, the director yelling at actors through a megaphone, cameramen shouting, while everybody howled if the scene was funny.

"With sound, when the red light went on, everyone froze in his position—a cough or a belch would wreck the scene. To the nervous snit of the non-stage silent actors—over having to memorize lines for the first time—the funereal hush added the willies. They shook with stage fright."

One silent-picture star said, "The silence from the studio was unbearable. There wasn't that help from the director saying, 'You're doing fine, now a little faster.' Nothing."

Shooting on *Ladies of the Evening* began in mid-January 1930.

Barbara loved the role of Kay Arnold "from the start. It was so human and real," she said.

The first time she heard her own voice on the screen she said, "My God! Who is that?"

Barbara had a great range of loudness and softness in her voice, which was a challenge to the soundman. Ed Bernds, the sound mixer on *The Locked Door* and *Mexicali Rose,* took over for Harry Blanchard as Capra's sound mixer on *Ladies of the Evening.*

Barbara "was perfectly accustomed to sound, and used it," said Bernds. "When she had a very loud scene, she would distance herself from the mike a little bit. Of course my mike man had instructions to pull the mike away from *her.*"

On the second day of shooting, someone asked Barbara if she was going to the rushes. She didn't know what "rushes" meant.

"Well, you see yesterday's work."

Barbara thought that sounded wonderful and went off to see them. Once she saw what had been shot the day before, she looked at herself on the screen and "didn't see anybody else, I just looked at me. I don't know what the hell the other actors were doing, but I was fascinated with me. It was a dramatic scene." But the cords in her neck were standing out; her hands looked odd. She thought, "*Jesus,* that's an ugly thing.

"I was sick. My gestures seemed abrupt. My hands looked awkward. And I pulled my mouth to one side when I talked fast.

"The next day I waved my hands around in elaborate gestures and delivered my lines carefully."

She was "absolutely gorgeous. There were no veins standing up, my hands were lovely and my mouth was just so."

Capra was quiet. He didn't make any comment. Finally, he asked Barbara if she'd been to see the rushes.

"Oh, yes. And I've corrected all those faults—"

"Don't you ever dare look at yourself again. I forbid you right now to go in to see yourself. Only go later, when the thing is done. We're going to do this morning's work all over again."

Capra was confident on the set. He acted as if "it was fun to make motion pictures," Joe Walker said. "His attitude was contagious"; "in his lighthearted 'lets-get-with-it' manner, he knew what he wanted . . . Capra kept us hustling; he remained alert and fired with energy." Walker was impressed with "Frank's enthusiasm . . . his confidence in himself, the ease with which he was able to tell people what he wanted."

When Walker and Capra began working together on their first picture, two years before *Ladies of the Evening,* Capra had made three feature-length pictures to Walker's thirty-six. Capra was "different from any other director" Walker had worked with. He didn't tell Walker what to do. But "he understood what the lens would do and what the angle was." Capra wouldn't tell Walker what lens to use; "he'd just say, 'I want a couple of big heads,' and he knew what it would look like . . . Capra wanted [the camera] to keep close on people . . . He left it to me."

Capra was different from the two directors with whom Barbara had worked. Where George Fitzmaurice and Erle Kenton were interested in making their actresses beautiful rather than what they did in front of the camera, Capra wanted his actors and actresses to be real, "to let a person play himself or herself," he said. Capra talked to them about the scene and let them do what felt natural. For Barbara it was like working again with Willard Mack and Arthur Hopkins.

Where Fitzmaurice and Kenton used the camera as a recorder of a set piece, Capra saw the camera as a "ubiquitous phantom eavesdropper" on what was to seem as real as the real world. Capra used the camera to help tell his story and to punctuate it with heightened moments, just as he used sound as a critical part of the narrative.

Barbara "left her best scene the first time she did it, even in rehearsal." What she did "was just wonderful," Capra said. "But then she could never reproduce that scene again." The more times Capra shot the scene, the further away Barbara got from it. "She just left it," he said. "She was just drained. She gave it all in that one scene."

Capra sensed that "Barbara was rehearsing mentally [and] she threw it all out at once . . . Most people get better in rehearsal," Capra said. "She got worse." He was amazed by this; he'd never seen it before. "Fires were bursting out of her, but they burned too fast."

For Barbara, it was the result of hundreds of performances given before a theater audience.

"The curtain [goes] up at 8:30 and you better be good," she said. "You don't get a retake. You shoot for the first time. If you have an emotional scene you only have so much water in you to come out!" About the third or fourth take she was "drying up," not because she wanted to; "it's a physical thing that happens."

Capra liked to rehearse his cast and crew. But to help Barbara give her best performance, he went about shooting the picture differently. Instead of a full rehearsal with cast, cameras, and sound moves worked out, the scenes with Barbara were to be rehearsed at a low level of intensity. Capra had her go through the motions with the other actors so the camera could follow their moves, but she was not "to utter one word of the scene until the cameras were rolling."

This presented a problem for the soundmen, who didn't get a chance to rehearse the scene for sound; somehow they managed.

Capra had Barbara's hairdresser, Helen, give her the cues from the other actors. He went to Barbara's dressing room before each scene to talk with her about its meaning, "the points of emphasis, the pauses."

He talked to her about the character. " 'You would speak out?' 'No, I don't think she would.' 'Well, why don't you?' "

If he agreed with Barbara, he said, " 'Yes, that's good, that's the way we'll do it.' It was always 'We.' It was never 'I, I, I,' " Barbara said. "It was never 'I don't want you to do this.' "

"Barbara was silent, somber," said Capra. "She act[ed] like she [wasn't] listening, but she hear[d] every word."

Capra talked softly in order not to "fan the smoldering fires that lurked beneath that somber silence." He stressed honesty; he didn't want any emotional tricks.

Barbara felt how much Capra liked actors. She'd worked with two directors who didn't. "You can almost smell it," she said. She sensed that Capra liked women as well, "not in a lecherous way . . . and he didn't demean them. If you were a hooker [in the picture], you were a hooker, but you better be a good one. That's how you made your living."

Barbara appreciated that when Capra came to discuss the scene, he didn't say, "Psychologically, do you think she would—?" That was much too analytical for Barbara. "It has to be from the gut. His role was not to probe people but to watch them."

From the quiet rehearsal sessions between Capra and Barbara, Bernds "could see a performance coming to life. A lot of times Capra didn't even include Ralph Graves. He didn't slight Graves, but he really worked with [Barbara]."

Capra saw in Barbara's original test from *The Noose* an honesty, a power, a force, that had reached down inside and deeply stirred him. He wanted to do whatever he could to help her get to that again, and he wanted his cameras to capture it on film, to use the camera to feel the glow of her emotion as if from the inside.

Capra "attempted only one thing," said Barbara. "To preserve the intense honesty" he saw in her test.

Ed Bernds said that Capra could make a scene better than it was written. He encouraged Barbara "to show how really deeply she felt things" and to "develop a dramatic personality which, if it hadn't been real, might have been melodramatic. But it was real."

As they shot, Bernds saw that "something was happening. The scenes as they were played really came to life."

Barbara was "so happy" in her work that she "began to be reconciled to Hollywood" and to the reviews she was receiving for *The Locked Door* and *Mexicali Rose*.

As Capra went along, he shot a silent version of the picture with slight variations of a number of scenes.

Two weeks into the shooting of *Ladies of the Evening,* they were to film the opening scene, where Jerry Strong stops along a Long Island shore road because of a flat tire and meets Kay Arnold after she has fled a shipboard party. The shooting was to take place at night.

It was a long drive to Malibu Lake near Barbara and Fay's where the scene was to be shot.

Capra didn't say much to Barbara that night, but he communicated what he wanted. "Somehow," said Ed Bernds, "he was really giving her her character."

It was a cold February night. The scene called for a long shot of Barbara rowing ashore.

Barbara was to call out to Ralph Graves onshore. She was wearing only an evening gown. ("I blew that cattle boat in such a hurry," says Kay Arnold, "I left my wrap.")

The crew was bundled up. The wardrobe lady covered Barbara's shoulders with blankets.

When Barbara was needed, "she exposed her arms and shoulders and never complained," said Ed Bernds. "When it was over, the wardrobe lady was ready with blankets that had been warmed by the spotlights to put over Barbara."

They shot throughout the long night until four in the morning.

Instead of telling Barbara what to feel in a scene, Capra taught her that "if you can *think* it," she said, "you can make the audience know it. You can make them know what you are going to do."

The centerpiece of *Ladies of the Evening* follows a scene in which Kay has posed for Jerry until the early hours of the morning. After days of his not seeing her as a woman, in fact "looking right through her" as if she were just part "of his routine like his paints and brushes," she gets angry and says to him, "Miss Arnold, Miss Arnold, can't you call me Kay? What am I, a statue, or a hunk of furniture? I'm a human being," and he lovingly wipes away her tears of frustration. Once she feels his attention, her face is infused with happiness, and he sees the look he's been longing to capture since the night they met. The first day at his studio, he tells Kay, "I can't paint you unless I can see you. And I can't see you with all this camouflage."

As he takes off her makeup and peels off her eyelashes, she asks, "You want me to be homely?"

"I want you to be yourself."

Jerry has been painting her for hours. The sound of the rain on the roof and the fire in the fireplace make the room seem warmer, safe.

It is early in the morning. Jerry suggests to Kay that she spend the night in his studio rather than go out at this late hour. Barbara is standing in front of the fire, the silhouette of her small lithe body against the light of the flames. "Oh no, I don't want to put you out." Her face is still, serious. Without her

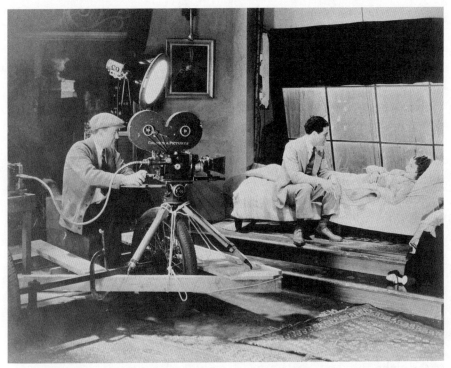

With Frank Capra on chaise longue; Joseph Walker on camera, during production, *Ladies of Leisure,* 1930. (PHOTOFEST)

moving, a shadow crosses her face. She is on guard, about to bolt, but perfectly still. Jerry is carrying the sheets to make up the couch. The only sound is that of the rain. It washes down the full wall of glass of the studio.

Jerry makes up the bed.

"We can get to work first thing in the morning," he says. "But I'm glad we got started."

Kay, in her tough way, "Yeah, we got started."

He ignores the comment. "You're the first young lady to spend the night in this studio."

Kay says, "Yeah, now tell me the one about the traveling salesman; that sure would get a laugh out of me."

The camera sees Jerry and Kay from the outside of the studio, two silhouettes seen through the rain. Then from the inside. Jerry goes to his bedroom and comes back with a pair of pajamas for her. He puts another log on the fire as he leaves and says good night. The camera is on the bedroom door as it closes.

Kay is seen against the white moonlight and the rain-washed window.

Barbara betrays nothing on her face. It is still, but her manner has changed. For Kay, it's business. She slowly walks to the light and turns it off and begins to undress against the window. She removes her skirt.

On the other side of the living room wall, Jerry has taken off first his shirt, then his pants.

Kay is seen almost in darkness in profile against the light from the window. Viewed from the outside of the studio, her figure is blurred by the rain against the windows. She removes her sweater and is in her slip.

Jerry is in his room, pacing. He walks to the door, gets a book from the shelf, and turns off the overhead light.

Kay is putting on the pajama top Jerry has given her and is getting in between the white sheets on the couch. The white light from the window bathes her, and her childlike body is made even smaller by the size of his pajama top.

Jerry is in bed and tosses aside the book; the only sound that of the wood burning in the fireplace.

Kay stares ahead, waiting, still.

The scene fades. It opens up again on Kay, awake in the dark.

The sound of the clock chiming is heard three times against the stillness of the night.

Kay hears a sound. She turns her eyes toward the bedroom door; the heat behind her eyes is palpable. The doorknob to Jerry's bedroom is turning. She is lying still, as if her stillness will ward off his making a move toward her. The camera follows Kay's vantage point from the couch. Jerry in slippers, robe, and pajamas walks toward her.

The camera is on Kay's face. She closes her eyes, pretending to be asleep, almost holding her breath. Jerry walks over to the couch lit against the window. He takes a satin throw and places it over her and gently touches her.

He walks back to his room. Barbara's face fills the screen. Her eyes are shimmering. Jerry closes the door behind him. She turns her head slightly toward the window, burying the edge of the throw against her mouth. Jerry is on his bed, leaning against the wooden carved headboard. Barbara's face barely moves, but her eyes are full of happiness and wonder—and hope.

The scene is five minutes long and silent except for the sounds of the rain and the fire and the chime of a clock, each of which Capra used for mood.

Capra used rain in a love scene as "an exciting stimulant, an aphrodisiac." The rain enfolds Kay Arnold and Jerry Strong and washes away the sins of her past.

Capra had his leading characters reveal their fears, their longings, and the discovery of their love for each other without a word of dialogue. Barbara conveyed it all with hardly a trace of movement. This is the beginning of the love scene, a turning point that is completed two fraught scenes later when Jerry takes her in his arms.

Shooting was completed on February 15, 1933. The picture was renamed *Ladies of Leisure*.

SIXTEEN

Life, Liberty, and the Pursuit of Love

Fay and Michael Curtiz had stopped speaking during the production of *Under a Texas Moon*.

Curtiz was smart and fast and known for his wicked tongue. Jack Warner said of him, "Curtiz is a director, not a man; when he goes out the [studio] gate, he's nothing." But on a picture Curtiz had a sense of rhythm and pace and knew how to get things done. He had an enormous flair for cinematic values, and Fay agreed to be directed by him again. He was getting ready to make *Broadway Playboy*.

He was under contract as well to produce six song and monologue recordings a year for Brunswick Records, a Warner subsidiary.

Fay was busy at the studio but was not among those like Al Jolson, Rin Tin Tin, George Arliss, and John Barrymore who ranked as Warner stars. His name was last in a listing of Warner featured players that began with Conrad Nagel and included H. B. Warner, Noah Beery, and Chester Morris.

Barbara's work in *Ladies of Leisure* was so strong that Capra was sure she would receive an Award of Merit from the Academy of Motion Picture Arts and Sciences. The academy was three years old, the notion of Louis B. Mayer, production head of Metro-Goldwyn-Mayer; Conrad Nagel, the actor; Fred Niblo, the director; and Fred Beetson, the producer, who, while dining at Mayer's Santa Monica beach house one Sunday night, began to talk about forming a group that could represent the motion picture industry. The idea was to create an organization that would help solve problems affecting the entire industry: technological problems, labor disputes, and the coming of censorship from outside forces. A week later, at a dinner at the Ambassador Hotel in Los Angeles, thirty-six leaders of the film industry listened as the plan was put forward for a new organization to represent all branches of the industry. The idea was wholeheartedly embraced. The guests included Richard Barthelmess, George Cohan, Cecil B. DeMille, Douglas Fairbanks, Harold Lloyd, Mary Pickford, Joseph Schenck, Irving Thalberg, Raoul Walsh, and Jack Warner.

The organization was incorporated two months later. By May the State of California granted the group its nonprofit charter. To celebrate, a banquet was held at the Biltmore Hotel in Los Angeles that three hundred guests attended. Two hundred and thirty of them joined the academy, each writing out a check for $100. The following year, 1928, the academy asked Cedric Gibbons, art director at Metro-Goldwyn-Mayer, to design an award that would be given annually by the academy to each of the main branches of the industry in recognition of outstanding work in a motion picture. Gibbons designed an art deco statuette of a sleek, perfectly proportioned figure, thirteen and a half inches tall, weighing eight and a half pounds.

In 1929 the academy presented an evening of awards at a dinner held at the Roosevelt Hotel. The nominees and the winners were voted on by a handful of judges; the recipients had been told three months before who would be receiving the statuettes.

For the 1930 awards ceremony, Capra was sure *Ladies of Leisure* would receive an award for Best Picture and that he would be the recipient of an Award of Merit for Best Director.

At the beginning of April, Harry Cohn offered Barbara a three-year contract at Columbia with a starting salary of $2,000 a week that would increase to $4,000 a week by the third year.

Despite the collapse of the stock market in November, people across the country were paying to go to the movies, in New York, Chicago, Baltimore, Kansas City, Los Angeles, Seattle, to see box-office successes like *Romance of the Rio Grande, Untamed, So This Is College, Applause, Gold Diggers of Broadway, The Taming of the Shrew, The Virginian, Sunnyside Up,* and *Rio Rita.* The weekly box-office receipts for most theaters were down from their high, but business was steady.

As a result of the crash, several million jobs had been lost. From the spring of 1929 to December, the Ford Motor Company reduced the size of its staff by twenty-eight thousand. By March 1930, businesses had folded, construction had stopped, and banks had tightened up on credit.

"I Don't Want Your Millions, Mister" was a song heard around the country:

I don't want your Rolls-Royce, mister
I don't want your pleasure yacht.

All I want is food for my babies;
Give to me my old job back.

In the spring of 1930, Columbia was proceeding with its next roster of pictures. Harry Cohn and the board had agreed on a $10 million budget for its next twenty features and shorts that included the cartoon series Disney's *Silly Symphonies* and *Mickey Mouse,* as well as *Krazy Kat.*

Among the feature pictures to go into production was *Rain or Shine,* a Broadway musical-comedy hit that Capra wanted Cohn to buy for him. Cohn had balked at the cost of the "blowsy acrobatic musical comedy," as Charles Brackett described it in his review in *The New Yorker,* but Capra wanted to work with the play's star, Joe Cook. Cook had been described by Brooks Atkinson as "one of the great comic spirits . . . practiced and letter perfect"; Capra thought Cook was "mad, unique."

Capra's plan was to drop the show's musical numbers, have Jo Swerling write the script with Dorothy Howell, and make the picture for "peanuts" using "only one set, a small two-ring circus tent." Cohn relented and purchased the film rights to the play.

The studio had also bought the rights to a play called *Bless You, Sister* by the playwright John Meehan and the theater producer Robert Riskin, as well as an original story by Lynn Root called "Lover, Come Back to Me," whose title was taken from a hit song from the Sigmund Romberg and Oscar Hammerstein II 1928 musical hit, *The New Moon.*

With the signing of Barbara's new contract, she advanced from Columbia "featured player" to "star."

Columbia's roster of stars and players, in addition to Jack Holt and Ralph Graves, included Evelyn Brent, Margaret Livingston, Sally O'Neil, Molly O'Day, Sam Hardy, Aileen Pringle, George Sidney, and Marie Prevost.

Fay's second picture, *Under a Texas Moon,* opened to the public in Los Angeles on April 1 at the Warner Bros. Downtown Theater. Louella Parsons called the picture "a delicious bit of satire" and wrote, "In all the years the prolific and debonair Fay has been acting, including those 10 consecutive Sunday night concerts which Fay presented alone at the Cort theatre in New York, I doubt whether Broadway's playboy ever thought of playing a Mexican! Not only does Fay play an adventurous Mexicano in appearance, but with an accent—and what's more, he does it well. The subtle Fay plays his character with his tongue in his cheek and does so cleverly."

Fay traveled to Texas to open the picture with Myrna Loy and Raquel Torres.

His next picture for Warner was to have been *Captain Applejack;* instead, the studio hired John Halliday as its star. Warner was considering having Fay star in *The Gay Caballero,* a sequel to *Under a Texas Moon,* but decided against it.

Fay, in preparation for whatever picture the studio decided would be next, had his teeth recapped.

Ladies of Leisure opened in Los Angeles on April 2, 1930, at the Orpheum Theatre and in New York on April 23 at the Capitol Theatre on Broadway. *Variety* saw the picture as "great box office." The headline of the review in the *New York American* read: "Stanwyck Scores in Movie of *Ladies of Leisure*"; in the *New York Times* review, "Miss Stanwyck Triumphs."

The censors gave the picture a pink slip ("adults only"). *The New Yorker* described it as having been made "with a good deal of taste . . . excellent . . . funny, touching, always alive." The *New York Evening Journal* thought the censors so toned down the picture from the play "that the screen version [could] best be described as a . . . conventional modern-clothes 'Camille' with a happy ending." But Louella Parsons, in the *Los Angeles Examiner,* thought the "talkie version of David Belasco's flaming play very much better than the original stage version . . . with enough punch to make it exceptionally good entertainment." And she said that Barbara's performance was "remarkable . . . and you understand that underneath all that hardened exterior there is a real soul. Miss Stanwyck, I prophesy, will be one of the most sought after actresses on the screen after producers see her performance."

The *New York Herald Tribune* ran an article about the Fays with a headline that read: "Barbara Stanwyck's Career Matches That of Husband; Indeed Friends Believe She Will Surpass Frank Fay."

Barbara was devoted to Fay. "Frank is a big actor with a following and I'm just nobody. He deserves top billing."

In Los Angeles, the Fays were about town, attending parties and dining at the Mayfair, as were the most fashionable couples in Hollywood: Norma Shearer and her husband, Irving Thalberg; the Hunt Strombergs; Mr. and Mrs. Jack Warner; the Harry Cohns; the Darryl Zanucks; Lady Peel, Corinne Griffith, Constance Bennett, and Harry Rapf. Barbara and Frank attended a party given by Howard Hughes for two hundred people, following the premiere of his picture *Hell's Angels* and the debut of Jean Harlow.

Barbara was spending her days in Malibu, furnishing their cottage and spending long afternoons swimming in the ocean and walking on the beach. She had gained weight and had a glow of health from being in the sun. Those who knew her from New York said she never looked better.

Barbara read two books that she wanted to make into movies: Theodore Dreiser's *Gallery of Women,* published the year before by Horace Liveright; and Helen Grace Carlisle's new novel just out by Harper & Brothers.

Dreiser's two-volume book was a series of portraits—or studies, as Dreiser called them—of modern women in and around his life caught in the grip of painful love affairs.

Carlisle's *Mothers Cry* was written in a colloquial, stream-of-consciousness first-person narrative. It portrayed the life of a simple, good, uneducated woman, from girlhood at the time of the Spanish-American War; her court-ship with the man who works at the counter next to hers at a department store; their happy marriage; the births of their two boys and two girls; her years as devoted wife, mother, and widow after her husband dies in a trolley accident (like Barbara's own mother), when the woman is left with four children to raise (as was Barbara's father) and no means of earning a living. The novel opens out as she struggles, against all odds, to prevail on behalf of her children.

One son grows up to be an acclaimed architect; one daughter, like her mother, marries and settles down; the other, a modern woman with mod-ern ideas about sex and marriage, becomes a Bolshevik, determined to be a writer, who has an affair with a married man, travels alone to Europe, and returns to America to write the great American novel. The older son, always in trouble with the law, becomes involved with gangsters, shoots his sister in a quarrel, and is put to death in the electric chair.

"Full to the brim with life," said *The New York Times.* "[It] leaves an un-broken spell out of which the reader comes away feeling that he has pen-etrated beneath the surface of something rich and beautiful."

Barbara loved the book and its vitality and thought it would make a strong picture. First National bought it for $15,000. Lenore Jackson Coffee, who'd written almost forty pictures beginning in 1919, when she was twenty-three and sold her first story to the movies, adapted Helen Carlisle's novel.

Barbara didn't get to play the devoted, hardworking mother. The part went to a thirty-three-year-old stage actress, Dorothy Peterson, making her debut in pictures. David Manners was the sensitive, talented architect son; Edward Woods, the troubled boy who becomes a killer.

During the spring of 1930, Barbara mostly enjoyed being apart from Holly-wood's social life and refused most invitations to go into town. She saw herself as not fitting in with Hollywood, a place she called "the papier-mâché town." She was "used to having a good time" alone with Fay "or with a few close friends and, after encountering Hollywood society, preferred it that way."

She and Fay spent time on the beach and would wander over to Budd Schulberg's tennis court and watch him play and make jokes. They attended a party because they were told "it was good business policy to be seen out socially." It was given at the home of "a big executive," said Barbara. "The cream of Hollywood society was there.

"Almost immediately after our arrival, the men went into the card room." Barbara was left with a group of executives' wives and some famous stars who went into a gossip huddle and "left me sitting by myself."

Barbara sat there "thinking the evening would never end" and that she'd "never been treated so rudely." The following week, she and Fay were invited back. This time Barbara brought a book.

"I never demanded anything from anyone," she said. But "I do expect courtesy and honesty. Every day was a struggle, but when people entered our home, they were our guests. We had little to offer but we made them welcome. Our people were terribly poor, but they had better manners than those in Hollywood. I've never seen people so artificial and insincere."

Barbara's work was being hailed in the press as superb, miraculous. She was being mentioned in glowing terms in the same newspapers and magazines that had previously ignored her. One magazine described her performance in *Ladies of Leisure* as "astonishing . . . she has the spirit of a great artist."

She was described in *Photoplay* as "a new sensation in the world of pictures . . . A star's been born . . . a real, beautiful, thrilling wonder. Only a few years ago, Barbara Stanwyck was just one of Texas Guinan's pretty children. Into her lap tumbled the leading role in *Burlesque* and she caught New York's heart and fancy . . . So good luck Barbara. You're in a fair way to be one of the truly greats. Keep your head!"

During Barbara and Fay's first months in Hollywood, "we felt our unimportance and were pretty much out of it. Every place we would turn there would be stars, Rolls Royces and all that goes with it. Frank and I [have] never found all this necessary for our happiness."

With Barbara's success in *Ladies of Leisure*, the J. Walter Thompson Company renewed her contract for Lux soap through December 31, 1932.

The advertisement's tagline read: "A stage star's charm depends so much on the beauty of her skin. She never lets anything interfere with regular care of it. Lux Toilet Soap is certainly wonderful for keeping the skin smooth. And when you do a 'talkie,' the glaring lights of the close-up would show up even the tiniest flaw."

In the early spring of 1930, in cities across America, the unemployed held demonstrations. Daily breadlines in New York's Bowery were made up of two thousand people.

On the outskirts of Detroit, three thousand unemployed workers set out for the Ford River Rouge plant in Dearborn and were met at the city limits by the Dearborn police, who ordered the crowd to turn back. The marchers continued to move forward up the road toward the Ford employment office building. Shots were fired into the crowd from behind a gate and from a submachine gun on an overpass. Four marchers were killed, and more than fifty were injured. Hundreds of "radicals, communists and suspected communists" were rounded up. To honor the men who'd been shot to death during the riot, six thousand people marched through the streets of Detroit in a funeral procession.

Fay's studio, Warner Bros., wanted Barbara for a picture from a recently written, as yet unproduced play by Edith Fitzgerald and her companion, Robert Riskin; the studio had not yet purchased the script. The plan was to produce it as a play in New York after the film was released in key cities.

Barbara was under contract to Columbia for three pictures. During the contract negotiations, she had made it clear to Columbia that she didn't want to make more than three pictures a year.

Fox Film Corporation approached Barbara to make a picture. Columbia's Sam Briskin, assistant general manager, reminded Barbara that she was under contract to the studio and legally had no right to be in negotiation with another company. As long as production plans didn't interfere with Columbia's plans, Barbara thought it would be financially beneficial for her to work for another studio. Briskin discussed it with Cohn, and the studio agreed to let her make a picture with Fox.

Warner Bros.–First National called Columbia to ask if Barbara could appear in one of its pictures. Darryl Zanuck of Warner Bros. wanted Barbara for the role of Anne Vincent in *Illicit*. Zanuck at twenty-eight was fierce and wily, with an unbeatable eye for a good story that could get to an audience and make them react. Barbara had read the script months before she was offered the movie and knew it was a "natural."

She told Briskin to tell Warner Bros. she would do the picture for $50,000, $30,000 more than she was getting from Columbia. Briskin negotiated, and

Zanuck agreed to pay Columbia $35,000 for Barbara's services in the picture, $7,000 a week from mid-July through mid-August; Columbia agreed to pass on the $35,000 in its entirety to Barbara.

Zanuck, in addition to writing scripts, supervised many of the early Warner pictures and acted as a talent scout, bringing actors and directors to the studio—among them Michael Curtiz and Ernst Lubitsch along with Lubitsch's assistant, Henry Blanke.

Illicit was a twist on boy meets girl, boy loses girl, boy gets girl.

The movie begins with the young romantic lead imploring his girl to marry him; she loves him, but she refuses his offer; she isn't the marrying kind ("I know we're very much in love," she tells him. "It's marriage I want to be sure of").

She's a Park Avenue society girl, an unconventional, free-spirited modern young woman, the daughter of divorced parents, with her own theories about love and the institution of marriage. ("It's disastrous to love," she pronounces. "There's too much about it that's all wrong. The awful possessions people exert over each other—the intimacy—duties. Love can't stand the strain.") "Illicit" means illegal and unlicensed. But to Anne Vincent, it is "merely being modern."

Barbara saw Anne Vincent as someone who "believes in the new declaration of women's sex independence—Life, Liberty and the Pursuit of Love." She wants freedom and love but not a husband. She wants to be a playmate of love, not a prisoner of marriage. "Anne Vincent is a girl deeply in love. She is the girl who thinks the wedding ring will kill love."

"Her drama," said Barbara, "is that of the 'advanced or new woman' who has made her position in society more secure through the freedom women had abrogated to themselves during the war."

Anne Vincent's beau, Dick, is as in love with her as she is with him. He, though, is ruled by convention and wants desperately to get married. Dick's father begs Anne to do as society demands. "You can't lick the marriage institution," he says to her. "You've been within the gates [of the good opinion of society], so you don't know what it is to be on the outside. The moment you desecrate those sacred marriage laws, you'll find out. They'll pounce, Anne. They've already pounced."

Anne reluctantly agrees to marry Dick after being blissfully with him in sin and freedom for six months. She sends away her former suitor; Dick reassures his former girlfriend that she will find "someone to love—much more than you did me"; and Anne and Dick's wedding is the "social event of the season."

The picture begins with the couple living happily ever after. They winter in New York in their East Sixties town house and summer at the family estate in Glen Cove, Long Island. They no longer spend their evenings alone; instead, they give formal dinners in their perfectly appointed dining room or attend the theater with friends.

After two years, everything Anne feared has come to pass: she is bored; Dick has wearied of marital ties. She chafes under his simultaneous husbandly devotion and neglect; he begins to have an affair. She feigns indifference to his constant late-night, early-morning "business dinners," his lies about his dinner companions, until she catches him in a lie and hates herself more that she has deliberately caught him. ("It's all come true, Dick, just as I said it would. It's living together in the same house, going to the same places, doing the same things, the intimacy that makes you helpless and dependent on one another.")

Rather than live in a burned-out marriage, Anne decides to take back her maiden name, move out, reopen her apartment, become an individual again, and win back her husband as her lover.

Columbia's agreement with Warner Bros. stipulated that Barbara's name was to be two-thirds the size of the film's title; no name was to precede hers in the billing or be larger than hers.

Illicit was to be directed by the talented Archie Mayo, who had overseen musicals, dramas, and comedies and who'd been at Warner Bros. for three years. Mayo before that had worked as a gagman and an extra in films and as a director of shorts.

Barbara was to start work on *Illicit* a week after the agreement between Columbia and Warner was signed. A telegram came from her sister Maud telling her that their sister Mabel had been taken to Hackensack hospital due to an intestinal blockage.

Barbara followed Mabel's progress. The surgery was a success, but an infection developed. Gene stayed close to his mother's bed. Mabel hoped to be going home soon, but the infection lingered. Peritonitis set in.

Barbara came home from her first day of shooting to a telegram from Maud saying that Mabel had died earlier in the day.

Fay wired back to Gene and Mabel's husband, "Barbara's heart is broken."

Because she had just started shooting *Illicit* she wouldn't be able to go to the funeral service.

Barbara's grief over the loss of her sister went deep. Mabel was gentle and the quietest of the Stevens family. Barbara was convinced that her sister had been "butchered in [the] operation," that the doctors had perforated her gastrointestinal tract. "[Mabel] was young. She had so much to live for," Barbara said.

Mabel had died at forty. Their mother, Catherine Stevens, had died at the age of forty-one, when Mabel was twenty-one years old and Barbara was four. Their father had left home when Barbara was five. Barbara was now twenty-three. Her parents were dead, and the youngest of her three older sisters was gone.

Barbara somehow got around her deep feelings of grief and showed a new ease and confidence in her work in *Illicit*.

She arrived at the studio each morning at seven o'clock to go through her lines with a script girl. Whenever Barbara thought the dialogue was slow and in need of a "good place for a wise-crack," she added one. Mayo didn't object, and much of Barbara's witty dialogue in the picture was written in those early morning sessions.

To help the actors record their voices, Mayo used a pitch pipe during the shooting to test the note at which the words recorded at their best. He had shot sixteen pictures for the studio (many of them silents; Zanuck thought Mayo was one of the best titlers in the business) and directed such actresses as Belle Bennett, Pauline Frederick, Betty Bronson, Dolores Costello, Irene Rich, and Myrna Loy.

Before shooting a scene, Mayo blew the correct pitch for each actor, who used the note as the starting-off place to begin to speak.

The stage actor James Rennie, then married to Dorothy Gish, played Barbara's husband, Dick Ives.

Adding a comedic element to *Illicit* was Joan Blondell as Anne's rough-neck playgirl pal, Dukie. ("[Joan's] career was pre-determined," said Barbara. "She was born to the stage; her father was Eddie Blondell, the Katzenjammer Kid. Her mother, brother and sister helped her father in what constituted the family act and as soon as Joan was able to toddle, she too was initiated.")

Joan was blond and blue-eyed with a big smile and played a blowsy, knowing, good-hearted party girl who's seen it all.

Like Barbara, Joan, at seventeen, had made her debut in New York in the *Ziegfeld Follies*. Joan had seen Barbara in *Burlesque*. "I was never so overcome in my life," she said of Barbara and Hal Skelly. "Never again have I experienced anything like it. [She] made me cry, laugh, want to hug her."

During the shooting of *Illicit*, Joan and Barbara became friends.

When Jack Warner first began to consult with Zanuck about the kinds of movies the studio should make and who should star in them, Raymond

Virginia and Darryl Zanuck, 1925. He left his hometown of
Omaha, Nebraska, a discharged soldier of sixteen who'd survived
the Great War with dreams of being a writer. By the age of twenty-
five, he was made head of production of the four-year-old Warner
Bros. (PHOTOFEST)

Schrock, then Warner's head of production, told the Warners that they
needed to choose between himself and Zanuck. They chose Zanuck, offering him in 1925 the position of supervisor of pictures and meeting his demand for a salary of $260,000 a year. In addition, Zanuck wanted to be
given screen credit on all Warner Bros. productions. The credit was to read:
"Warner Bros. Presents A Darryl F. Zanuck Production." Warner agreed and,
given the new title, advised the twenty-three-year-old Zanuck: "Even if you
don't need glasses, get some window panes and grow a mustache. It'll give
you a little age."

Mayo kept his crew amused on *Illicit* and was able to get a lighthearted
quality in the work. He was appealing, clever at gags, with a light touch, and
loved to make people laugh. He was round with thick glasses, a graduate
of Columbia University, who'd worked on the stage, trying his hand at jazz
songs and melodies and writing the book and lyrics for a Broadway musical
revue, *Hello, Paris*.

He relied on the actor to know his or her job, just as he relied on the cameramen and the engineers to know theirs.

Barbara had little direction, but Mayo knew how to time a line and a
scene, and Barbara responded well. His sense of light sophisticated comedy

came through in her work and in the picture, and Barbara puts across a playfulness in the simplest manner. Joan Blondell said of Barbara's work, "What she did, she did on her own." She takes her time, and a strength from deep down comes through. The self-assurance of the character is clear, as is her wit and belief in her own ideas.

Barbara was able to draw upon herself and what she'd learned from Bill Mack, Arthur Hopkins, Fay, and Capra to achieve simplicity on the screen. In its own quiet way, *Illicit* was a defining picture of Barbara's style. The work was stripped down, but it had feeling, humor, and depth.

Several weeks into production, Warner purchased the rights to Fitzgerald and Riskin's play, *Illicit,* for $30,000. The picture cost the studio $249,000 to make.

During the weeks that Barbara shot *Illicit* at Warner Bros., the studio embarked on a massive $4 million renovation. The Warner plant on Sunset Boulevard was being consolidated with its new acquisition from Fox West Coast Theatres, First National, whose stars included Colleen Moore, Richard Barthelmess, Loretta Young (first discovered by Colleen Moore), Billie Dove, Kay Francis, and Conrad Nagel.

The Warner studio was not being dismantled, but $400,000 of its electrical equipment was being moved to Burbank. In the future, Warner's original stages were to be used for filming shorts, recording on Warner's Brunswick label, and rehearsing ensembles.

Eleven new stages were being built at First National Studios in Burbank in addition to the studio's ten, Warner's five, and Vitagraph's six (two of them outdoors). Warner was building what would be the biggest electrical plant in the industry. It was putting up a building for additional dressing rooms, as well as buildings for pre-duping, a two-story scene dock, a staff shop, a foundry, and a paint shop. A new restaurant was being built on the First National lot to accommodate more than eleven hundred people and would be catered by Herb Sanborn, owner of the Brown Derby.

A bridge was designed to connect the First National lot of 85 acres to the Warner Bros. Ranch (formerly, the Lasky Ranch) of 116 acres, along with the Warner studio, which sat on 12 acres of land.

The new Warner Bros.–First National Studio would be made up of more than 130 buildings—with thirty-two soundstages—on 231 acres of land. Warner Bros. in 1932, formally incorporated seven years earlier, would be the biggest of all the studios in stage space and acreage, with a value of $30 million.

SEVENTEEN

On Her Own

During the early weeks of shooting *Illicit,* Warner released Frank Fay's third picture, *The Matrimonial Bed.* Michael Curtiz directed Seymour Hicks's screen adaptation of Yves Mirande and André Mouëzy-Éon's French farce. In it were also Lilyan Tashman, Florence Eldridge, and James Gleason.

Fay played a French gentleman about town who five years before was believed to have died in a train wreck and now, as a hairdresser, is the double of a Parisian widow's former husband. At a dinner party at her house, one of the guests, a doctor, hypnotizes the hairdresser, who, when he is brought out of his trance, it is revealed, is indeed the first husband. He recognizes his wife, is unaware of his present life as a hairdresser, and is equally unaware that he is the lover of both servant girls in his first wife's house.

A series of whirlwind triangles unfold as the picture races to its "uproarious, rollicking" conclusion. Warner Bros. tried to sell *The Matrimonial Bed* as a bedroom romp for adult and sophisticated moviegoers: a gay French farce set in Paris, "the city of beautiful nonsense, where only the river is Seine."

For the most part, the critics thought the picture "missed fire." *The New Yorker* described *The Matrimonial Bed* as "preposterous and grotesque and disappointing."

Barbara was worried about her nephew now that Mabel was gone. Gene was motherless. Barbara knew what it felt like to be motherless, and she kept up with Gene's comings and goings. He was staying with his stepfather in an apartment in Flatbush, and enrolled in Erasmus Hall High School.

Barbara was living life in Hollywood her own way, trying to block out as much of it as she could, and Hollywood didn't know what to make of her. She was being talked about as "the coming big star, another Norma Talmadge," with her work being embraced by the town. In her own way, she made it clear she didn't want to belong; she'd never felt she belonged anywhere and was uncomfortable around most people except when she was working.

She quietly tried to evade most of the town's customs. She wasn't interested in a large social life and stayed away from parties, where she felt for the most part like a "frozen rabbit." Whatever trappings of Hollywood life she was expected to take on she tried to minimize. She didn't glamorize herself and wasn't interested in getting into evening gowns. She wore no makeup, only lipstick. The flaunting of money and the Hollywood custom of excluding people of a seemingly lesser class—those who worked on her pictures as assistants and hairstylists and technicians—frustrated her. The expectation that she would adhere to this caste system made her all the more defiant. In truth, Barbara saw herself as part of the working class, who were more often than not, to her, free from pretension and social affect.

"The two best friends I have in this town are a young married couple who haven't a dime," she said. "They probably never will have. Their names will never twinkle in electric lights. But they're real. I'd rather spend an evening with them than go to the best Mayfair party ever given."

Barbara had no illusions about the art of moving pictures; to her it was "a racket," and she had every intention of getting to the top of it. And she wanted Fay to be part of it with her.

She and Fay were well matched. They kept to themselves and were even more tightly bound to each other by what they saw as Hollywood's "exclusive" ways.

Frank was an erratic but heavy drinker. And Barbara's flashes of temper and moodiness could be just as erratic as his drinking.

Barbara felt a deep gratitude for Fay's love and guidance and for the way in which she believed he'd educated her. "Everything I know of etiquette, of books and art and people and the world around me," she said. "I was nothing until Fay came along and I would have been nothing a great deal longer if he had never come along."

Fay had appeared on the same vaudeville bill with Fred and Adele Astaire, Judith Anderson, Ethel Barrymore, Lahr and Mercedes, Señor Angel Cansino performing with Helen Dobbin and Rita Mayon, as well as Johnny Dooley, Bobby Dale, and Barbara's champion Buck Mack from her days traveling with her sister Millie. Hal Skelly had appeared on the same bill with Fay at the Palace in 1926, the year before he began to work with Barbara in *Burlesque.* Fay had appeared on the stages of most New York theaters—the Winter Garden, the Shubert, the Alvin, the Cort—and in theatrical productions from *The Passing Show of 1918* and *Oh, What a Girl!* to *Jim Jam Jems* and *The Smart Alec.*

Barbara loved to read. It had always been both a great escape for her and the way to educate herself. She read a book a day, and now that they had the money, she and Frank began to collect first editions.

Fay agreed at the last minute to return to New York to appear at the Palace Theatre for two weeks. Included in the RKO contract was an agreement to appear free of charge on its Friday night NBC radio broadcast. Fay failed to show up for rehearsal at 10:30 a.m. RKO threatened to cancel his contract, but Frank was able to talk the studio out of it, claiming laryngitis.

Fay's last movie, *The Matrimonial Bed,* had not been a success. The picture cost $208,000 to make and grossed just more than $241,000 in box-office sales.

Fay phoned Barbara from New York each night. He could afford the large telephone bill; he was being paid $4,000 a week for the two-week booking, but the effects of the stock market crash were beginning to be seen around New York.

Playhouses along Forty-Second Street had been forced to convert to movie theaters. The legitimate theaters were empty. Five thousand Broadway theater actors were out of work. The Shubert brothers, seemingly untouched by the fall of the stock market, were coming to the rescue of producers such as Al Woods, Charles Dillingham, and the Selwyns, each of whom was losing vast amounts of money.

The Shubert brothers were putting on more than twenty new productions for the season, but the number of unemployed was growing.

To help those out of work, the International Apple Shippers Association came up with the idea of selling apples on credit for $1.75 a crate. The apples were to be sold individually on the street at a nickel apiece; if all of the apples in a crate were sold, the hawker could make $1.85. Soon six thousand people were on New York's streets selling apples.

The first of Barbara's three pictures for Columbia, *Roseland,* was to be directed by Lionel Barrymore. Barrymore's work in silent pictures had been waning, but talking pictures helped to resurrect his career. Of his early work in Hollywood, Barrymore said, "In the years between 1912 and 1917 I made an enormous number of motion pictures. I am, it suddenly occurs to me, a pioneer and possibly a kind of landmark in the industry. I was in Hollywood before a number of people, including Douglas Fairbanks, came and had their careers and finished, and I'm still here."

Barrymore's voice was rich, theater trained. He had no fear of the microphone, nor of talking pictures. His first talking picture, *The Lion and the Mouse,* was made on loan to Warner Bros. and was a big hit. Barrymore's studio, Metro, was one of the last to incorporate sound.

Louis B. Mayer saw how confident Barrymore was about his voice and the new technology and asked him to direct a picture rather than act in it. Barrymore said that Mayer and Thalberg probably reasoned, "Well, this fellow ran with that theatrical crowd in New York. Maybe he knows a thing or two. We will make him a director."

The first picture Barrymore directed was a remake of the French melodrama *Madame X.* The picture was a success. Barrymore was nominated for the academy's Award of Merit for his direction, and Ruth Chatterton was nominated for her performance as Jacqueline Floriot.

Next, Mayer assigned Barrymore to direct the great matinee idol John Gilbert in his second talking picture, *His Glorious Night.* Gilbert was one of the biggest stars on the Metro lot. But Mayer and Gilbert had had a terrible row on Gilbert's wedding day when his bride-to-be, Greta Garbo, stood him up.

Gilbert and Garbo were to have been married in a double wedding at the Beverly Hills home of Marion Davies. The director King Vidor and Eleanor Boardman were neighbors of Gilbert's and had long planned to be married. Two weeks before the wedding, both couples were having dinner together. Gilbert, who frequently proposed to Garbo in public, did so again. This time Garbo had said yes. She'd said yes once before but had got as far as the steps of city hall before she'd changed her mind. This time she'd consented in front of witnesses and suggested that the double wedding be kept a secret from the press.

On the morning of the wedding, Gilbert saw Garbo pulling out of the driveway. Later in the day, when it was time to leave for Marion Davies's, Garbo had not yet returned from her morning outing. Gilbert drove to Davies's Spanish hacienda hoping Garbo would have driven directly there. Garbo had not yet arrived.

While the wedding guests stood around talking, waiting for Garbo, Vidor stalled and made phone calls for as long as he could. Eleanor Boardman asked the photographer to take pictures, but finally she quietly told Gilbert they would have to go ahead with the ceremony. Gilbert was beside himself. Mayer, who'd been in the guest bathroom, came out and walked over to Gilbert, slapped him on the back, and said, "What's the matter with you, Gilbert? What do you have to marry her for? Why don't you just fuck her and forget about it."

Mayer's remark gave Gilbert the perfect outlet for his fury. Gilbert went for Mayer, who fell backward through the door of the bathroom, knocking his head on the wall and losing his glasses. Gilbert was hitting Mayer's head against the tile wall as Eddie Mannix, a New Jersey Irish tough and former bouncer and Mayer's general manager, second in command, and keeper of the peace at Metro, quickly pushed his way into the room and separated the men. Mannix, who had the seemingly jovial manners of a police chief but could just as easily put a bullet in one, picked up Mayer's glasses and wiped his face with a towel.

"You're finished, Gilbert," Mayer shouted. "I'll destroy you if it costs me a million dollars."

Mayer was a great hater, and the full force of his hatred would now be focused on John Gilbert and destroying the studio's romantic idol.

Mayer wanted Barrymore to direct Gilbert's first full-length talking picture, *Redemption*. Barrymore was in constant debt to Mayer. He frequently borrowed money against his salary and relied on Mayer to bail him out of tight financial circumstances. Midway through the filming of *Redemption*, Barrymore was replaced by Fred Niblo. When Gilbert saw the finished product, he tried to buy the prints and negatives with the intention of destroying them in the waters off Catalina Island. The studio refused to scrap the picture but agreed to postpone its release.

Mayer asked Barrymore to direct Gilbert in the movie that the studio now planned to be Gilbert's first talking picture.

His Glorious Night was based on *Olympia*, a light comedy by Ferenc Molnár, about Viennese society, in which Gilbert was to play an elegant, romantic cavalry officer, a dashing figure equally adept with women and horses. The screenplay, which was largely Molnár's script, was written by Willard Mack.

His Glorious Night received positive reviews from the critics, who said Gilbert "was to be congratulated on the manner in which he handles his speaking voice"; that Gilbert "could not have found a more entertaining vehicle for his talking debut than this delightful comedy"; and that "Mr. Gilbert . . . can speak the English language and speak it beautifully."

But women in moving picture audiences weren't as accepting of Gilbert's performance. Instead of inspiring women to fantasize as they watched Gilbert on-screen, "the love scenes are so intense," one critic wrote, that "they make the women let out nervous giggles."

Gilbert was being laughed at by female audiences across the country. In silent pictures he had been looked upon as the essence of male virility. Now, in his first sound picture, he was provoking laughter and discomfort. In addition, some thought his voice didn't sound masculine; this was ruining his image as the world's greatest lover.

Those who worked with Gilbert knew his demise began with the aborted Vidor-Gilbert double wedding and continued with Louis B. Mayer's choice of Lionel Barrymore as the director of Gilbert's first two talking pictures.

Hedda Hopper, an actress in *His Glorious Night,* said, "I watched John Gilbert being destroyed on the sound stage by one man, Lionel Barrymore. Barrymore had plenty of experience on the stage; Gilbert had none.

"During the picture, Lionel was in physical misery. He had a bad hip and took drugs to ease the pain. Around four p.m. when he'd inch himself out of his chair, it took a good minute before he could start the locomotion of his legs."

Gilbert's opening speech in the second reel began with "Oh, beauteous maiden, my arms are waiting to enfold you. I love you. I love you. I love you."

By then in pictures, said Hopper, "love was a comedy word. Use it too freely," Hopper said, "and you get a belly laugh. Whether by diabolical intent or accident, Jack's speech was 'I love you, I love you, I love you.' Jack was young and virile. He was handsome but his face didn't fit those words. When sound came on the screen from his lips, a strange meeting took place between his nose and mouth and made him look more like a parrot than a lover. In silent pictures you never noticed."

Of his supposedly high voice, Colleen Moore, a good friend of Gilbert's, said, "Jack's voice was not a deep one, but neither was it a high pitched one. His voice was in the middle register—the same register as that of Douglas Fairbanks and many other male stars. What ruined Jack Gilbert were three little words."

To Colleen Moore, it was the discomfort of the women in the audience actually hearing John Gilbert say, " 'I love you, I love you, I love you,' right out loud for all the world to hear, [that] disconcerted and embarrassed [them]; those most ordinary but still most profound words that can be spoken between a man and a woman. In their embarrassment they giggled."

Louise Brooks said of Lionel Barrymore, he "was taking heavy doses of morphine . . . and was hardly responsible for what went on. Anyone could have manipulated [Barrymore] and someone did. It was common talk at the studio before the picture came out. Everyone knew it but Jack." In the picture Gilbert's speech was stiff; the pronunciation of his words, exaggerated.

Leatrice Joy, Gilbert's former wife, saw *His Glorious Night* and said, "I don't know whether Barrymore deliberately did Jack in, but he couldn't have done much worse if he tried. Jack's scenes with Catherine Dale Owen were dreadful. All that kissing and saying 'I love you' looked all the more ridiculous with her because she was such a cold fish . . . She made Jack look ridiculous and Barrymore allowed it."

Douglas Shearer, the sound engineer for *His Glorious Night,* told the director Clarence Brown that the engineers "never turned up the bass when Gilbert spoke; all you heard was treble. Of course it was a mistake." A mistake ordered by Mayer?

After the Gilbert picture, there were to be no more love scenes in Metro's pictures; movies had to show a man or a woman in love without saying "I love you."

Barrymore directed two pictures in 1929: *Confession* and *The Rogue Song,* a musical made in color with a script by Frances Marion and John Colton from a Franz Lehár, A. M. Willner, and Robert Bodansky 1911 play called *Gypsy Love.*

The Rogue Song was released in May 1930, and Harry Cohn thought Lionel Barrymore would be just the right person to direct *Ten Cents a Dance,* originally called *Roseland.*

Metro temporarily released Barrymore from his contract.

Ten Cents a Dance began shooting in mid-September 1930. The picture's title was taken from a song from the musical comedy *Simple Simon,* written by Ed Wynn and Guy Bolton. Lorenz Hart had written the lyrics for the show; Richard Rodgers, the music.

The song "Ten Cents a Dance" had been created for a number designed by Ed Wynn and was first performed when *Simple Simon* was still in tryouts in Boston.

For the number in the play, Ed Wynn mounted a piano on wheels to be ridden like a bicycle. The idea was for him to ride the bicycle-piano while a singer sat atop it and sang. A new song was needed for the number, and Rodgers and Hart quickly wrote one about a beleaguered dance-hall hostess.

> *Ten cents a dance, that's what they pay me*
> *Gosh, how they weigh me down*

Lee Morse, a featured singer in the show, was to introduce the song on the final night of the Boston tryout. Morse went onstage sitting on top of Ed Wynn's bicycle-piano but was so drunk she couldn't remember the song's words or music and was fired that night. The show went on to New York,

As Barbara O'Neill at the Palais de Dance ("I'm here because my brains are in my feet") with Victor Potel and James Ford (far right). From *Ten Cents a Dance,* shot in September and early October of 1930. (PHOTOFEST)

and Morse was replaced by a thin blond singer called Ruth Etting. Etting sang "Ten Cents a Dance" for the first time when the show opened in New York.

Harry Cohn had Jo Swerling write the picture's story and dialogue. Swerling used the idea of the song's dance-hall hostess and created the character of a smart, tough girl, Barbara O'Neill, who, like Kay Arnold in *Ladies of Leisure,* has seen nothing of the world but who's seen it all. She's the most popular dancer at the Palais de Dance. "When you dance with them as long as I have, they all sort of blend into one," says Barbara O'Neill.

Swerling wrote a Jazz Age fairy tale. He took the idea of the fine innocent young woman living in a lonely metropolis who is forced by circumstances into a tough, white-knuckle world where wisecracking and street smarts are the only way to get by and is taught a lesson in love.

("What's a guy gotta do to dance with you gals?" asks a loutish sailor through a wad of chewing tobacco tucked up into his cheek. "All you need is a ticket and some courage," Barbara O'Neill tosses off as they move to the dance floor.)

She quietly dreams of a sweet marriage but nightly earns a living by dancing with any man who "mauls you around and steps on your toes and tears your dresses and breathes into your face. He's got a pocketful of dimes and only one idea in his head."

The matron of the Palais de Dance "keeps the place hot enough to avoid bankruptcy and cold enough to avoid raids." Barbara O'Neill is the most frequently picked dancer in the place ("If I get any more rhythm, I'll dislocate a hip," she says to the dance-hall matron, who complains about her recent lackluster work).

Barbara O'Neill knows how to keep her dancing partners at a distance and knows how to take care of herself. Her dream of romantic love prompts her to embrace the man who has no money or job but who appears to love her without conditions and to turn away from the man with money who is more than willing to openly buy her love.

Jo Swerling's ideas about money came to the fore: that the rich were of weak character and deserved everything bad that befell them. Swerling differentiated between those who were old moneyed and those whose money was new and had been made fast and furious.

Class was once again at the heart of Swerling's story. Barbara leaves her job and takes up her life as a loving, steadfast housewife who doesn't want or need more than a few dollars to make their patched-together household feel like a palace, at least to her.

One evening, her husband is on his way home from the office. He runs into an old college chum and his sister, who are about to get into their limousine to go off for a night of high-stakes bridge. Eddie flirts with his friend's sister, whom he's always liked. When invited to come along for the evening, he admits neither that he can't afford to gamble nor that he is married and is on his way home to the dinner his wife has prepared for him. Instead, he appears to be carefree, a man on his way up, and agrees to join his friends for the evening.

It is the first of many such evenings for Eddie. As he is seduced into the world of his rich friends, he is drawn deeper and deeper into debt, first from bridge and then from playing the market on margin. When he finally admits to Barbara that he has taken $5,000 from the office owned by the other man who loves her and that the books are to be examined within the next two days, she has no choice but to go to the man from whom she has asked nothing for herself to ask for the money for her husband.

At first he praises Barbara because she never asks for anything of him ("You're the only woman I know who doesn't want something"), but when he finds out what she needs and why (she offers to pay him back every penny; "Ten cents a dance," he says to her. "That's fifty thousand dances"), he gives her the money and realizes how unselfish her love is for her husband.

Eddie takes the money without a thank-you, returns it to the office, doesn't go to jail, and then accuses his wife of being unfaithful.

Finally she realizes who and what Eddie is.

"I've listened to you and now you're going to listen to me," the Stanwyck character says in the explosive moment in the picture where she shows she's no patsy and where Stanwyck shows she can electrify an audience. "You're a coward, Eddie. You were running away from something the first time I met you, and you're a thief. You stole money from your employer. You're a liar . . .

"You're not a man. You're not even a good sample."

She leaves Eddie and goes back to the Palais de Dance where she meets the newly married man again and realizes that he loves her and she loves him. He asks her to go with him to Paris, where she can get divorced and be free to begin a whole new life together.

Monroe Owsley was the mousy, nondescript Eddie Miller. Owsley, who'd graduated from Yale and worked on a newspaper until he left it for the stage, had appeared in productions that called for a young man of his breeding. He'd appeared in *The Great Gatsby* and in Philip Barry's 1928 stage production of *Holiday*, in which he played the alcoholic Seton brother, Ned, the same sort of weak character he was playing in *Ten Cents a Dance*. Owsley had just finished re-creating the role of Seton in the film version of *Holiday* that starred Ann Harding, Mary Astor, Edward Everett Horton, and Hedda Hopper.

Ricardo Cortez was Bradley Carlton in *Ten Cents a Dance*. Cortez had worked with Barbara in *Illicit* as her former admirer and beau. Cortez, whose real name was Jacob Krantz, had been spotted by Adolph Zukor seven years before, dancing with a society girl in a hotel ballroom. Zukor was so impressed by Krantz's looks and demeanor that he gave him a five-year contract. The young actor went from being Jacob Kranze, Viennese émigré and New Yorker, to Jacob Krantz to Ricardo Cortez, Latin lover, supposed successor to Rudolph Valentino. Cortez, who was to make love to Barbara in the picture—his thirty-ninth—had appeared opposite Garbo in her first American film, *Torrent*, with Cortez's name above Garbo's.

Two weeks into the filming of *Ten Cents a Dance*, Barbara slipped from a parallel and fell ten feet. She was backing away from Monroe Owsley. "In my desire to be vehement," she said, "overacting, I think people would call it," she fell down the stairs and fainted. One of the men working on the production picked her up and was carrying her when he tripped and fell. Barbara landed on her head and was taken to the hospital.

The newspapers reported the incident but were told there was no serious injury from the fall. But the base of Barbara's spine had been dislocated, and

John, Ethel, and Lionel Barrymore, circa 1932.

as a result her right leg was three inches shorter than her left. It was agony for her to walk, to stand, to sit. The doctor prescribed rest for the next few weeks; work was out of the question.

The company faced a big loss without her, and she was determined not to hold up production.

Barbara defined her days by work, study, and long hours with Fay. She didn't drink, rarely smoked or attended parties, and so despite doctor's orders of rest to heal from the fall, she went back to work.

She kept quiet about the injury and went to the set each day, whether she was working or not, with her spine strapped and braced. Specially designed shoes were made by the studio to compensate for the three-inch difference in her legs. The hours between scenes were punctuated by intense pain, but when Barrymore said, "Okay, we'll shoot the scene," Barbara came alive.

With the help of physicians and studio technicians and mostly Barbara's will, the effects of the injury were hidden on-screen. As they shot the picture, Barbara unobtrusively leaned on furniture, sat whenever she could, and wasn't seen walking for long stretches in front of the camera.

In addition to working with severe pain from her spine, Barbara, along with the rest of the company, had to cope with a director too ill to direct.

Barrymore was fifty-two. As an actor, he was inspired. He could turn himself into any character he played. John Barrymore once said of his older brother, whose artistry he so admired, "[Lionel] seems to check his personality like an overcoat whenever he goes into a part." Ethel Barrymore said that of the three Barrymores, "Lionel was the real one. He has none of those tricks of the theatre. His acting comes out of his head. If he had to be a *dwarf,* he would make you think he was one."

At heart, Barrymore had never wanted to act. "The theatre was not in my blood," he said. "I was related to [it] by marriage only; it was merely a kind of in-law of mine which I had to live with."

As a director of more than ten pictures, Barrymore was only workman-like. He would "labor for months ahead of his picture, casting, approving costumes, approving scenery, and conferring with the producer." He worked "early in the morning, before anybody else start[ed], getting scenes ready for the day's shooting, and stayed late at night examining his rushes, deciding which scenes he [would] have to retake." But Barrymore, from boyhood, had wanted only to paint and draw and ended up in the theater and in motion pictures simply because, as he said, he "had nothing else to do." He knew that directing pictures "was totally unsuited to a man like me, whose admiration for mañana is only exceeded by his yearning for more mañana." The morphine Barrymore was taking to offset the debilitating pain from arthritis made him even more interested in mañana and less capable of focusing on the work at hand—overseeing the actors and having a feel for the tempo of the scenes being shot and the overall shape of the picture.

"The poor man was in so much pain," said Barbara. "I couldn't warm up to him. It was a very impersonal relationship. I don't think he ever objected to anything I did. He tried his best. As a performer, you just had to try harder."

Cortez said that Barrymore was charming, but making *Ten Cents a Dance* was "very trying. You'd start a scene and look around and find [Barrymore] asleep."

Barbara's frustration with Barrymore's lack of direction only intensified as she worked with Cortez.

Cortez admired Barbara "for her dignity. She was a perfect lady at all times. Perfect."

Barbara was not as admiring of her co-star, whom she privately referred to as "old fish eyes."

"He gave me nothing to work with," she said of Cortez. "I was on my own in every scene." And without a director to help her out, playing against nothing was even more frustrating.

Once again, Barbara found her way. Despite the flatness of the picture, in part due to Barrymore's lack of control over the scenes, Barbara has a radiance about her and a strength that comes through between both of the weak, unseeing men her character chooses to love. She found a rhythm to Barbara

O'Neill and is by turns prickly and soft, hopeful and pure, funny and wise. And once again, she conveys emotion, large and small, and creates a dimensional woman trying to make her way in a tough world.

In the midst of shooting *Ten Cents a Dance* for Columbia Pictures, Barbara signed a letter of agreement with Warner Bros. detailing the terms of her new contract.

The contract was for $100,000 for three pictures, at a time when more than one thousand banks had failed and almost $900 million had been lost in deposits.

Barbara's name was now to appear above the title of any Warner picture she made. The script, story, or play the studio proposed for each picture was to be mutually agreed on within a thirty-day period. If Barbara refused a script or idea, the studio could then submit two additional ideas or stories. If all three were rejected, the studio had the right to submit three additional ideas or stories. If all six were rejected, the studio would pick one of the six ideas already submitted, and Barbara would appear as the star.

The contract went on to state: "It is further agreed that any delay or additional time consumed, caused by your failure to approve of one of the subjects, plays or stories submitted to you in excess of sixty day period herein fore mentioned, shall be added to the yearly period of employment hereunder which may be then in force, and such period shall be deemed extended to such extent."

The contract was to go into effect on August 1, 1931, when Barbara's contract with Columbia was to run out, or begin earlier, if her contract with Columbia expired before and she was available to work.

Under the terms of the Warner agreement, Barbara was to be paid $33,333.33 per picture, payment to be made in seven weekly installments of $4,761.90 for each picture.

The studio had the option to renew the contract for four successive years. If the studio picked up the option, Barbara was to be paid $150,000 for the first year; $175,000 for the second; $225,000 for the third; and $275,000 for the fourth.

Fay's three-picture contract with Warner Bros. was due to expire, with one picture still to be made. After the reception of his latest picture, *The Matrimonial Bed,* the studio had decided not to renew his contract and to hold off making his last picture until the following spring. If Fay needed money, the studio would give him an advance against his salary.

Zanuck insisted, however, that Fay be given a new three-picture contract, each to be made within a year with an option for another year for three additional pictures. Fay was to be paid $35,000 per picture, with first billing. No name in the cast was to be as large as Fay's. The contract specified that first billing was not star billing. Unlike Barbara's arrangement with the studio, there was no mention of Fay's name appearing before the title of the picture.

In an interoffice memo, Zanuck wrote that Fay's new contract was to start "on exactly the same date as the Barbara Stanwyck (Mrs. Fay) contract." The contract department was told not to make the connection in drawing up the contract but to merely refer to the date.

Ten Cents a Dance was completed late in October 1930. It took another six weeks for Barbara's spine to heal. The straps were removed, and she was finally able to walk without limping.

"I couldn't believe that this injury would be permanent," she said. "Whether it was or not, I would have gone on anyway. There are other things in my life that bring me happiness. I'm not afraid. I am not afraid of anything that life can do to me."

Mr. and Mrs. Frank Fay, September 1932. (CULVER PICTURES)

PART TWO

Undertow

I hate whiners. You have to fight life and make it work for you.

—Barbara Stanwyck

ONE

"Hot Speel in the Blood"

When she wasn't in front of the camera, she was almost mousy . . . But when the camera rolled, she turned into a huge person.

—Frank Capra

In 1930, the Academy of Motion Picture Arts and Sciences had four hundred members. The academy's nominations and Awards of Merit were no longer voted on by a small panel of judges; each branch of the academy (producers, actors, writers, directors, technicians) selected five nominees for an award, and members of the academy voted on each of the categories. The academy kept secret the selection of the five members from each of its branches until its awards dinner.

The awards for the year ending July 31, 1930, were announced at the academy's meeting at the Ambassador Hotel on November 7. For the first time the academy combined its awards dinner with its annual business meeting to elect officers for the coming year.

Despite Capra's prediction, Barbara's name for *Ladies of Leisure* was not among those actresses singled out for their work for 1930. Nominated were Nancy Carroll (*The Devil's Holiday*), Ruth Chatterton (*Sarah and Son*), Greta Garbo (*Anna Christie*), Norma Shearer (*The Divorcee*), and Gloria Swanson (*The Trespasser*). Shearer received the award for Best Actress. It was rumored that Metro had asked its employees in a memo to vote for Norma Shearer, Mrs. Irving Thalberg since 1927. Joan Crawford, Mrs. Douglas Fairbanks Jr., was quoted as saying, "What chance have I got? She sleeps with the boss."

Capra's name was also not among those nominated for Direction, nor

Irving Thalberg with his wife, Norma Shearer, on Nick Schenck's yacht off Catalina Island, July 1936.

was Jo Swerling's for Writing. Capra was "galled. The major studios had the votes," he said. "I had my freedom" in working at Columbia Pictures, "but the 'honors' went to those who worked for the Establishment," not those who worked on Poverty Row.

Columbia didn't have a large roster of popular stars, but the success of *Ladies of Leisure,* despite its not being singled out by the academy, put Barbara at the top of the list of Columbia's big female leads, followed by Dorothy Revier, femme fatale veteran of some sixty silent and talking pictures, and the sultry, beautiful Evelyn Brent, former WAMPAS Baby Star of 1923, von Sternberg's original exotic smoldering-eyed, feather-drenched Queen of the Underworld.

Barbara's fourth picture, *Illicit,* was about to be released; for the first time, her name was to appear over the title.

When Barbara and Fay weren't working, they spent time together at home, with their Irish terrier, Shanty, and their Boston terrier, Punky. Barbara turned over her money to Frank as it came in, and together they'd bought four cars—two Fords, one open and one closed, a Lincoln, and a Cadillac.

Fay's new picture, *The Devil Was Sick,* was intended to help make him into a kind of tongue-in-cheek romantic lead and to put across his onstage presence: his personality, mannerisms, expressions, and seductive humor. The picture was based on Jane Hinton's unproduced play of the same name. The script was another whirlwind Continental farce that centers on a notorious rich young man-about-Paris in love with every woman he meets, and with several in particular, who squabble and misbehave as they try to win his affections. The women in the cast who see him as God's gift to women included Laura La Plante, Joan Blondell, Louise Brooks, and Margaret Livingston.

Fay began filming in the first week of January 1931. Once again Michael Curtiz directed, terrorizing the cast and demanding endless retakes for tempo, tempo, tempo. In one scene in which Fay follows a woman from room to room on his knees, Curtiz asked for so many retakes that Fay's patellas were damaged and a doctor was called in to attend to him.

Louise Brooks was amused by Curtiz's Hungarian accent. He addressed one of the actors in the company, the jovial stage actor and comedian Charles Winninger, as "Mr. Vinegar. Mr. Vinegar, get outdt where ve can see you und vatch the cue! Go aheadt, Frank."

Before *Illicit* could be released, censors around the country wanted all references to premarital sex taken out and any mention of an adulterous marriage. Censorship statutes existed in many states, including Ohio, Pennsylvania, Maryland, Virginia, Kansas, and Florida. Zanuck refused to make the changes or to alter the picture's title.

The Motion Picture Producers and Distributors of America, beginning eight years earlier, in 1922, had managed to keep control of the content of motion pictures in the hands of the Hollywood studios rather than in the hands of censor-minded religious groups, local politicians, and civic organizations. Five years later, the Association and its president, Will Hays, who sold the studio heads on "self-control and self-censorship" as something "manly and democratic," had devised a set of guidelines, a list of "Don'ts and Be Carefuls," that were optional but were to be used in the writing of scripts, all in an effort to avoid a storm of censorship from the public. Hays's "Don'ts and Be Carefuls" opposed the use of profanity "either by title or by lip," including the use of words such as "God," "Lord," "Jesus," "Christ," "hell," and "damn." It opposed any licentious or suggestive nudity; any inference of sexual perversion; white slavery; miscegenation; sex hygiene and venereal diseases; children's sex organs; and ridiculing the clergy.

To the studio heads, desperate to thwart all outside efforts of censorship, Will Hays was the perfect choice to head the self-regulating MPPDA. Hays had served as postmaster general under President Harding and headed the National Republican Committee for three years. Hays was a Hoosier, an Indiana lawyer, a member of the Masonic Order, as well as the Shriners and the Elks. His "Don'ts and Be Carefuls" came from his own Christian upbringing. He was taught by his father "to drink no kind of intoxicating liquors, and

William Harrison Hays, called by *Variety* the "Czar of all the Rushes," circa 1926. (PHOTO-FEST)

never speak evil of anyone." Hays was a man who had "faith in God, in folks, in the nation and in the Republican party," in that order.

The studio heads reasoned that Hays would know how to enlist the confidence of the public and help the industry to work with women's clubs and churches and civic organizations instead of battling them. His national political experience would give him the authority to galvanize producers, actors, directors, and technicians in an effort to improve motion pictures and ward off legal censorship. Soon Hays, through the MPPDA, put together a force of 600,000 volunteers who were engaged in an organized campaign to help improve motion pictures that in Hays's eyes had to be held to a stricter standard of taste, morality, and merit than other forms of entertainment. Eighty million people went to the movies; to Hays, motion pictures represented the American way of life. He saw moving pictures as a force for good, but to Hays, pictures could "easily become a corrupting influence on future generations." The "licentious mood of books and stage plays was bound to work its way into movie scripts." The MPPDA's fight was not simply to make the industry self-governing and help distributors "overcome fraud and loss"; its fight had to be "against filth" and to improve the quality of pictures, and quickly.

To create "accepted standards of morality and good taste," Hays put his system of "Don'ts and Be Carefuls" to work in 1927. But Hays had something else in mind, a production ethic "capable of uniform interpretation, based not on arbitrary 'do's' and 'donts' but on principles," something he called "a corpus of philosophy" of right and wrong.

Hays wanted a code to "govern the making of talking, synchronized and silent motion pictures," and he knew he would need the right time to put it forward; preaching "morality" in the panic of 1929 was like a voice "crying in the wilderness." In early January 1930, Hays felt the moment had come. Talking pictures had made the industry "as cosmopolitan as international diplomacy." Hays thought the industry was ready to accept "a philosophy as opposed to more prudent rules." He came up with a nineteen-page booklet written by his friend the magazine publisher Martin Quigley and the Reverend Daniel A. Lord, a Jesuit priest of Saint Louis University. Quigley and Lord's document was based on, as Quigley said, "the rules on which all moral laws are based: the Ten Commandments, and the Natural Law written into the heart of every human being of sound reason and morals."

Hays met with a committee of the MPPDA to review the contents of a draft of the code. The committee was made up of the heads of studios, including Irving Thalberg, Carl Laemmle Jr., B. P. Schulberg, J. L. Warner, and Joseph M. Schenck. They argued about the definition of words such as "vulgarity" (they defined it as the "treatment of low, disgusting, unpleasant though not necessarily evil, subjects"); they differentiated "vulgarity" from "obscenity" and forbade both in motion pictures, along with scenes of carnal passion, immodest costumes, and improper dances. The code was presented to the West Coast branch of the MPPDA; it was applauded and quickly adopted. Even Pope Pius in Rome heard about the code and exhorted its observance.

Despite the one-year existence of the code, the censors in New York state had problems with *Illicit* and made cuts throughout.

The picture's world premiere was in San Francisco at the Embassy, a new Warner theater. Barbara traveled north with Jack Warner and Mervyn LeRoy, the thirty-year-old triumphant director of the moment whose latest picture, *Little Caesar,* had opened in New York weeks before and whose first weekend grosses broke the all-time record for Warner Bros.' Strand Theatre, bringing in $50,000 in only eleven performances. The picture was being hailed as a new kind of movie and LeRoy as a "masterly" director. *Little Caesar* was based on a novel by W. R. Burnett and dared to portray the relentless brutality of a Chicago gangster crime lord, Caesar Enrico "Rico" Bandello, "a little punk trying to be big," a self-exile, a man without family, romantic attachment, and church, who kills without remorse and dies unrepentant.

Will Hays's newly approved MPPDA code prohibited the use of the word "God" in pictures. As a result, the last moment of *Little Caesar* had to be changed. Caesar's final words in the picture, "Mother of God, is this the end of Rico?" had to be changed to "Mother of Mercy, is this the end of Rico?"

Illicit was criticized by reviewers who called attention to the "bad cuts" made by the censors in New York, who "deleted many subtle touches which would have done much to give the film a sophisticated flair," particularly "the deadly first reel." They commented on Barbara's clothes as well. Cecelia Ager wrote in *Variety* that Barbara Stanwyck "belongs in subdued, conventional clothes but weathers as furiously striking a series of costumes as pictures can produce [including] a black velvet suit with cocoa ermine flared sleeves and collar tied with an ermine bow . . . Miss Stanwyck would never wear one long black glove and one long white one, just because her dress is black and white printed chiffon. That's going a bit too far, even for picture representation of a 'society woman.' "

Illicit opened in Los Angeles at both the Warner Bros. Downtown Theatre and Warner's Hollywood, where Frank Fay acted as the evening's master of ceremonies and introduced the picture's supporting cast as well as his wife; it was Barbara's first local stage appearance.

Louella Parsons in the *Los Angeles Examiner* called *Illicit* "as smart as next year's frock, as modern as television and as sophisticated as a Parisian hotel clerk." She said that Barbara "proves herself every inch a star in her portrayal of the modern 'Anne Vincent.' [She is] delightful in her gay moments and very telling, indeed, in her emotional ones." And she went on to praise Barbara's "naturalness . . . beauty, and poignant sincerity."

Illicit was opening around the country, as was Fay's *Bright Lights.* Although many of the reviews commented on the tired genre of Technicolor backstage pictures, *Bright Lights,* which cost Warner Bros. $385,000 to make, was doing well at the box office.

Ten Cents a Dance, Barbara's fifth picture, was set to open with almost a year to go on her Columbia contract. She was to star in *Lover, Come Back to Me,* the second film of her three-picture contract with the studio. At the last minute, instead of making *Lover, Come Back to Me,* Barbara was to work with Frank Capra in his next picture, *The Miracle Woman.* Her salary: $16,000.

Following *The Miracle Woman,* Barbara was to be lent to Warner Bros. for a picture called *Night Nurse.* Warner had considered using Constance Bennett but hired Barbara instead. *Night Nurse* was to be directed by William Wellman, the thirty-five-year-old who made the daring spectacle *Wings,* the first major picture to show the epic role of the airplane in the Great War, and

"What is the real truth about this modern genera-tion's attitude toward the once sacred convention of marriage?"

also *Beggars of Life.* Wellman had just finished shooting *The Public Enemy* weeks before.

The supporting cast of *Night Nurse* was to include Ben Lyon, Joan Blondell, with whom Barbara had worked in *Illicit,* Charles "Vinegar" Win-ninger, James Cagney, and Mildred Harris, the former child bride of Charlie Chaplin. Cagney was to play the small part of an intern, but after *The Public Enemy* he was replaced by Allan Lane. The former Mrs. Chaplin, Mildred Harris, was out of the picture as the society mother, and Charlotte Merriam was in, although Warner had considered Louise Brooks, Evelyn Brent, and Virginia Valli for the part.

Once *Night Nurse* was completed, Barbara's contract at Columbia would be fulfilled, and she could begin her five-year contract with Warner. Harry Cohn let Barbara make *Night Nurse* only if she agreed to make one extra picture for Columbia, in addition to the optional picture the studio already had. Jack Warner drew up a letter freeing Barbara to make the additional picture for Columbia without being in violation of her new Warner contract. Despite all this, Columbia still had the option of recalling Barbara to make two pictures during the first year of her Warner contract.

Before Barbara was to start work on *The Miracle Woman,* she and Fay, along with others, were asked to appear in a two-reel comedy to help the National Variety Artists in their fund-raising drive for their tuberculosis sanitarium in Saranac Lake, New York. The picture was being produced by the Hollywood

Masquers Club, a charitable organization for which actors and actresses volunteered their services.

The film's premise: Norma Shearer's pearls are stolen (hence the title, *The Stolen Jools*, or *The Slippery Pearls*) at a picture ball. The detective Eddie Kane is sent by the station sergeant (Wallace Beery) to unravel the mystery of the missing pearls; to do so, Kane interrogates the guests who attended the ball.

More than forty actors agreed to be in the fund-raiser. Each scene was shot with different actors on a different studio lot and directed by a different director. All services were donated, from those of the actors and directors and the various studios involved, to the theaters projecting the picture, even the film company supplying the celluloid—Eastman.

Detective Kane begins his search for the "stolen jools" with Norma Shearer herself, who tells the story of what happened to her ("Well, let me see, I was with Billy Haines, Jack Gilbert, Joan Crawford . . .") as she is consoled by fellow actress Hedda Hopper.

Detective Kane goes off to question those who were at the fete: Joan Crawford (Kane overhears her describing something she's taken, something she wanted, something she couldn't resist: a Pekingese puppy), Douglas Fairbanks Jr., Loretta Young, and Maurice "Chandelier," who, when told about the mystery of the missing jewels and asked what he thinks, sings, "It's a great life if you don't weaken." Irene Dunne is stopped by Kane about the "stolen jools."

She asks him, "Were they wrapped in a purple box?"

"Yes," says Kane.

"With a silver padlock?"

"Yes."

"And a gold ribbon wrapped around them?"

"Yes, yes."

"Well, I never saw them," says Miss Dunne.

Kane is next seen in a living room where Frank Fay is seated, leisurely reading a newspaper. Barbara appears, in dark suit, white open-necked silk blouse, and white cloche. She stands between Fay and Detective Kane. Kane introduces her to Fay, who assures Kane that they know each other; they are married.

Kane is about to interrogate them when Barbara looks lovingly into Fay's eyes and announces she's just written "the most beautiful piece of poetry." With the promise of a poem about to be read, Kane announces he must be going. "Really, just a second," says Fay. "Let's hear it."

Barbara reads the first stanza, then announces, "There's more." She reads on:

In a year or so the girl returned
And mighty proud was she
She told how she'd done her duty
In the great war o'er the sea
She told how she'd picked up the wounded
And held each one to her breast
So the woodworkers got together
And made her a cedar chest.

Fay shakes Barbara's hand and says, "I'll see you around sometime, I guess."

Detective Kane to Barbara, "Kindly come in the garden please," and escorts her out.

Fay tucks his newspaper under his arm as he puts his fingers to his ears. The sound of a gunshot is heard off camera. Fay winces.

It was the only peculiar segment in the picture.

Liggett & Myers's Chesterfield cigarettes absorbed $200,000 of the picture's cost in exchange for being mentioned three times and twice having a pack of Chesterfields shown on the screen during the twenty-two-minute film to raise money for a tuberculosis sanitarium.

Ten Cents a Dance opened in New York at Warner Bros.' Strand days before Barbara was to begin filming *The Miracle Woman*. The reviews were mostly tepid. *The New York Times* described Barbara as "out of place in the Palais de Dance" and criticized the film for its "too leisurely" pace. *Variety* said that "Columbia should be grateful to Barbara Stanwyck for breathing life" in the picture; that she "strikes to the heart of a simple story . . . her acting is compellingly simple and direct." But the reviewer went on to say, "Her figure should receive more careful consideration than it appears to be getting from camera and costume departments. Avoidance of long camera shots in profile would soften defects." No doubt referring to her long waist and low flat rear that widened and jutted out.

The Miracle Woman was based on a 1927 farce by John Meehan and Robert Riskin called *Bless You, Sister,* inspired by Sinclair Lewis's satire *Elmer Gantry* about the church and sectarian religion and a Baptist-Methodist preacher. Lewis's novel was published to much fanfare in March 1927. *Gantry* had followed Lewis's *Babbitt* and *Arrowsmith,* novels that portrayed America's vulgarity and grotesqueness. *Gantry* was described by one critic as "a sort of cathedral in which every stone is a gargoyle"; other reviewers were less taken with Lewis's vision of America's organized religion and commercial preachers.

Meehan and Riskin's play was influenced as well by the popular evangelist preacher Aimee Semple McPherson, who was denounced as a "twentieth-century Jezebel," and hailed as a "miracle woman" faith healer who brought the message to millions and whose Church of the Foursquare Gospel in Los Angeles had been saving sinners who had experienced the electric shock of her power for more than a decade. McPherson, a farmer's daughter, served God by becoming "a winner of souls" and nightly spread the Gospel of Christ ("Jesus Christ is the same yesterday, today, and forever"), praying for forgiveness, speaking in tongues, first building up a ministry in a "canvas cathedral," crisscrossing the United States and Canada, and then establishing the Church of the Foursquare Gospel, Angelus Temple—a five-thousand-seat facility—in Los Angeles, next to Echo Park.

"We all know what hell is," preached McPherson. "We've heard about it all our lives . . . the less we hear about hell the better . . . Let's forget about hell. Lift up your hearts. What *we* are interested in, yes, Lord, is *heaven,* and how to get *there!*"

Capra considered Meehan and Riskin's play about the big business of religion and fakery "the most controversial idea" he could think of, a movie that could win him an Oscar. Cohn thought Capra was "nuts." "You can't kid religion," Cohn said to Capra. "The Christers'll murder you."

Robert Riskin loved the theater and as a boy, one of five children of Russian immigrants, used to sneak into shows in Brooklyn and try unsuccessfully to memorize the jokes he heard onstage. Once he'd saved enough money to buy Isaac Pitman's shorthand book, he learned the system of dots and hooks and was able to copy down every joke he heard.

Riskin, like Barbara, went to school up to the age of thirteen. At fifteen, he bought a typewriter, taught himself to type, and went to work as an office boy in a textile mill. The mill owner had invested money in a few short comedies to be released by Famous Players–Lasky and asked Riskin, always a joke teller, to look at the two-reelers before he showed them to Famous Players. Riskin told his boss that "a moron could write better, a blind man could direct better," and that even he, Riskin, a non-actor, "could be funnier." Famous Players–Lasky shared Riskin's opinion and declined to distribute the pictures.

Riskin's boss was determined to make short comedies one way or another and formed a new company to do so. At seventeen, Riskin became executive producer of a company in Jacksonville, Florida, making two-reel comedies without the use of scripts, "off the cuff, progressing as circumstances and light allowed." Riskin did "everything, not only producing the picture, but taking care of business details and worrying how the darned thing would do in Waukegan." In two years, he wrote and produced more than a hundred Klever Komedies.

After a stint in the navy in the Great War, Riskin made a series of shorts about muscle building, called Facts and Follies, in which "the guy with the biggest muscles got the girl." A year into it Riskin realized his films were getting him nowhere, and he went to work in a series of jobs, first in the linoleum business, then in the spark plug business, and then the teething ring industry. Finally, he decided to work for himself and, with his brother Everett, opened an office at 220 West Forty-Second Street, and together they became moderately accomplished theatrical producers.

Frank Capra's recent successes allowed him to prevail with *Bless You, Sister;* Harry Cohn bought the rights to Meehan and Riskin's play, which had opened in New York four years earlier, in December 1927.

The Broadway production of *Bless You, Sister* was directed by Riskin's co-writer, John Meehan, as well as George Abbott. Alice Brady was the loving daughter of a small-town minister who turns Gospel merchandiser after her father is kicked out of his pulpit by vestrymen who see his religious fervor as dull and "out of step." Charles Bickford was the tough salesman who enlists the young woman into the fold of the Bible business, telling her that "if she can sell the Book as well as she can roast it," they'll "clean up a cool million." Together they go on the road, playing religion across the board; he as the organization's racketeer business manager overseeing the tents and props and hiring the false cripples who, town after town, are converted and saved; she becoming a national figure as an evangelist healer, performing miracle after miracle, saving souls by the score in the name of the Lord, knowing she is a fake, a swindler of souls, and that her miracles are nothing more than a moneymaking dodge.

With Columbia Pictures owning the rights to *Bless You, Sister,* Riskin was asked to come to the studio for a story conference. He entered Harry Cohn's office with a meeting already in progress; the room was filled with writers and executives. Capra was telling a story. Riskin thought Capra looked like "a mug" and that he was telling the story "badly." Riskin soon "recognized" the story Capra was telling as Riskin and Meehan's own *Bless You, Sister.* "The recognition was painful," Riskin said.

Harry Cohn said, "Since this was Riskin's play, we'll call on him first for suggestions. Mr. Riskin." Riskin stood and said, "I wrote that play. My brother and I were stupid enough to produce it on Broadway. It cost us almost every cent we had. If you intend to make a picture of it, it proves only one thing: You're even more stupid than we were." The room was silent.

Left to right: Harry Cohn, Grace Moore, and Robert Riskin, 1936.
(PHOTOFEST)

Capra said he thought the picture's subject matter was "dynamite," that it had worked like gangbusters with a play on a similar subject (religion and fakery) by George M. Cohan called *The Miracle Man,* produced on the stage in 1914 and then made into a successful picture five years later with Lon Chaney and Betty Compson.

The Miracle Man involved a gang of crooks on the run from the law who hide out in a small town, encounter a faith healer, and use him to con his parishioners, until they witness a real healing and find their own souls transformed. Capra was so inspired by the success of *The Miracle Man* that he changed the title of *Bless You, Sister* to *The Miracle Woman.*

Riskin argued that *Bless You, Sister* had failed on the New York stage because sophisticated Broadway audiences were offended by the subject matter of religion and that surely less knowing moviegoers would be more offended by it. He was adamant about not writing the script; he knew in advance the picture would be a failure at the box office. Capra was impressed by Riskin's honesty and integrity, but if Riskin wouldn't write the script, Capra would hire Jo Swerling to write it.

The play *Bless You, Sister* flopped, as Riskin described it, because its subject matter was offensive to theatergoers. But it may have been the writers' own discomfort with the subject that lay at the heart of the play's failure. Some opening night critics had described the play's two central characters as turning soft, saying that the playwrights had been unwilling to go the distance with them. The critics were frustrated by the waning element of satire, which, they said, was replaced by melodrama.

Jo Swerling took up Riskin's concern with middle-class hypocrisy, God, faith, innocence, about what's real and what's fake, what's pious and what's not. In the script Swerling was tough on merchandising and the shills and come-ons, and rather than put down those who believe in the exploiters and swindlers, he and Capra showed a respect for ordinary people.

Swerling changed the young evangelist's name from Mary MacDonald to Florence Fallon, a name seemingly inspired by another preacher, Sharon Falconer, Sinclair Lewis's preacher in *Elmer Gantry*. In adapting the Riskin-Meehan script, Swerling kept Riskin's natural ways of speech, but Riskin's toughness is muted by the poetic incantation of Swerling's dialogue. In Swerling's script for Capra, the large turns of the play are born of sentiment instead of cynicism. Capra believed audiences liked sentiment ("always have, always will," he said).

In the play, the young man who is the romantic interest comes from Sister's hometown. In Swerling's script, the young man is a struggling composer down on his luck, an aviator blinded in the war who is now alone in the world. John Carson is well-heeled, Harvard educated, and at the end of his dreams. Much like Sister Fallon before she joins up with the swindler, he is a lost soul who has run out of hope and belief in himself.

John Carson is contemplating jumping to his death (he's written a suicide note to his elderly landlady, who watches out for him), when he hears the strident voice of a woman on the radio talking to anyone within hearing distance: "I bring you the promise and pledge that God is in heaven and all's well with the world. Oh, my dear ones, I can't see you, but I can feel you all around me." Carson shuts the window to keep out the insistent noise coming from across the air shaft, where a mother is seen rocking her baby and listening in on station "G-O-D, GOD."

Carson opens the window again to look down at the courtyard, in preparation for the jump that will end his life. The woman on the radio is still talking. "The trouble with most people," she is saying, "is that they're quitters. They're yellow. The moment they go through any sort of test, they cave in. The difference between a man and a jellyfish is the fact that a man has backbone. What did God give him a backbone for? To stand up on his feet. That's what real men do." Carson is caught off guard by the power of the words, by the beauty and strength of their sounds. "Beethoven wrote his greatest symphony when he was deaf; Oscar Wilde wrote his greatest poem in jail; and

Milton, a blind man, gave us *Paradise Lost*. It's easy to forgive sinners, but it's hard to forgive quitters."

When Carson turns to his landlady to ask the name of that "coon shouter that broadcasts over the radio every day," he learns she is Sister Florence Fallon of the Temple of Happiness Tabernacle.

Carson's love for Sister Fallon—a love and faith as blind as his eyes—and his self-sacrifice for that love bring Sister Fallon back to herself and cause her rebirth. And for each soul, lost but now found, once blind but now able to see, the message is that love will lead us home.

To avoid the fate of the Riskin-Meehan play, Capra wanted to make clear that *The Miracle Woman* was in no way poking fun at religion. The credits were followed by a quotation that read: "Beware of false prophets, which come to you in sheep's clothing." Another title read, " 'The Miracle Woman' is offered as a rebuke to anyone who, under the cloak of Religion, seeks to sell for gold, God's choicest gift to Humanity—faith."

Capra worked closely with Swerling on the script. "I have to absorb [the script]," the director said, "and like it in order to interpret it on the screen. Even though somebody else wrote it, it becomes yours before you're through with it."

To be at the studio each morning at 7:00, Barbara left her house in Malibu at 5:00 a.m. to drive the forty miles to Gower Street. It took a full hour to put on makeup and another hour for hair; by 9:00 a.m., the company was ready to start shooting.

For the picture's opening scene, Florence Fallon comes before the parishioners to give her father's farewell sermon. Barbara walks quietly, hesitating a beat before those in the pews. She is wearing a black dress with wide white cuffs and collar. The church her father preached in is a simple white-clapboard building, and Florence has the stark look of a Puritan, perhaps a Hester Prynne.

Barbara looks out at the men and a few women, simple folks, sitting and waiting to hear what she has to say. Her face has a set expression. She begins to read from the notes before her on the pulpit.

Her voice is quiet: "This morning my father was to deliver his farewell sermon to you. But he has been ill as you all know. And today he cannot be with you." Barbara's voice is soft; she is holding herself together; not looking directly at the churchgoers.

"I have it here and I am going to read it to you."

She speaks as the dutiful daughter whose voice is young, reading the sermon her father had dictated to her, as he had for so many years. The camera pulls back to the rear of the church and shows Sister Fallon in front of the room, still, alone, sorrowful, but proud.

"I have baptized many of you in the Lord's grace." She continues to read, her voice a monotone, making it clear she is reading by rote; the words are of little value to her.

She raises her eyes now to look out at those around her. "And though I leave you, I do not leave the Lord." The camera looks up at her as one of those listening to her father's words. "Surely goodness and mercy will follow me all the days of my life, and I will dwell in the house of the Lord forever. When the heart is thirsty, there is drink." Her voice softens; there is love in her words, the love she feels for her father and for the familiar words that will comfort her and carry her through this difficult time. "The Lord is my shepherd I shall not want. He maketh me to lie down in green pastures. He leadeth me beside the still waters. He restoreth—" She lifts her eyes, and stops speaking, and looks out at the parishioners, wary.

"That's as far as he got. This is his farewell message to you." She stiffens. "You see that he stopped in the middle of a sentence.

"My father is dead." Whatever restraint she was able to find gives way to a quiet power. "He died in my arms five minutes ago before he could finish his message to you. But I am going to finish it for him." Her words are an indictment.

She comes out from behind the lectern. The flatness of her words is gone as her voice rises up against the parishioners. "My father preached to empty hearts. I don't mind talking to empty pews." She is crying, her words piercing the sanctity of the room. "My father is dead and you killed him. You crucified him just as surely as He was crucified." The camera is behind her as we see her fragile girl's arm pointing to a stained-glass window that shows Christ on the cross.

Her words reverberate throughout the room as members of the congregation stand up to get away from her berating and the truth. Her tirade is shocking, hard to listen to. Her eyes are ablaze. "This isn't a house of God. This is a meeting place for hypocrites. Go on, get out." She is fighting with everything she's got, screaming at the church deacon, "You've been running this church, but I'm going to run it for the next hour. I'm going to preach the sermon my father should have preached. The Bible says the laborer is worthy of his hire." She is following the parishioners in the aisle, walking after them, her words like fire as they try to get away from her. "But you wouldn't pay your pastor what you pay your children . . . I was brought up

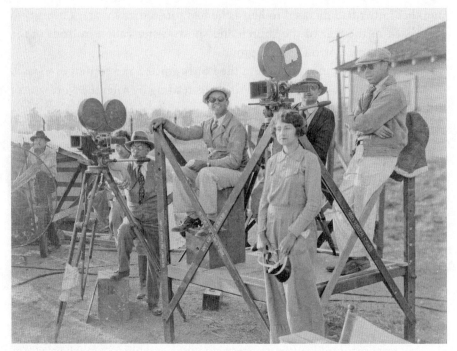

Frank Capra (center, in light suit) filming *Broadway Bill,* 1934. (PHOTOFEST)

on the Bible and I know it by heart. I'm going to take my text this morning from chapter 23 of the Gospel of Matthew." She is beating them down with the force of her words: "And I say unto you, as Christ said to the scribes and the Pharisees, 'Woe unto you hypocrites for you devour widows' houses and as a pretense you . . . make long prayers.' "

Those who are trying to get out of the church look back and call out that she is crazy. She *is* crazy; she has become crazy before the parishioners, but she won't stop talking as she advances toward them. "Go on, get out, all of you. Get out so I can open these windows and let some fresh air into this church."

The parishioners have fled her rage. She shuts the church doors, sobbing, exhausted, alone in the house of the Lord. A man (Sam Hardy) applauds her performance. She looks up at him. He tries to sell her a line of how magnificent she was. She is all business; the softness is gone. She tells him she isn't interested in what he has to offer.

Capra decided to get to the heart of the scene, the vital close-ups of Barbara, first. Multiple cameras were set up on her. If different shots, different setups were used, he'd "never get the same scene again," and with multiple cameras Barbara only had to do the scene once.

COLUMBIA PICTURES
presents
BARBARA
STANWYCK
in
"THE MIRACLE WOMAN"
A
FRANK CAPRA
Production

David Manners as John Carson, the lonely, blind songwriter who's given up on life and is reawakened by Sister Fallon, charming her with "Sambo, the Hoofer," a dancing whirligig, as Pagliacci the clown (not shown) plays a mechanical xylophone and pounds out "Farmer in the Dell."

Because of the two or three cameras, Capra shot a close-up of Barbara in profile. When he wanted to have her full face, to see both eyes and have a stronger impact of her performance with the close over-the-shoulder two-shot, the camera was moved deep into the set, and Barbara did the scene again, performing it with the same emotional power that she had before. Using two or three cameras made it more difficult for the crew. "Multiple cameras aggravate the difficulties of lighting and recording," Capra said. "Four times as complex with two cameras, eight times with three cameras." But Capra made it clear to the crew that "they were working for the actors. They're not working for you."

Capra blocked out the scene with the actors and crew and shot Barbara's close-ups first instead of the establishing shot. "It's all right if you have one or two people," said Barbara. "But if you have four or five people in a scene, working backwards is very difficult for a director, because he's got to remember all the places. But Mr. Capra made it easy for me."

In the next shot Barbara is with her deceased father, sitting on the floor at his feet as he, undisturbed, sits in a wingback chair with its back turned toward the camera. Her body is caressing the sleeve of his jacket, her body almost like a pietà. The swindler has come to the door to search her out. As she rises, startled, and asks, "Who's there?" the softness in her face disappears. She is guarded and shuts the door to the sacred room of love.

From scene to scene Capra alternately showed Barbara's steeliness, her playfulness and softness, her tenderness and openness, her sense of what is love and what isn't.

David Manners, a twenty-nine-year-old contract player, was lent from Warner–First National to Columbia for the part of John Carson, the young blind songwriter. Manners had appeared in *Mothers Cry* and in the just-released *Dracula* as John Harker. As John Carson of *The Miracle Woman,* Manners, a romantic who'd dreamed of becoming a sea captain from his boyhood in Nova Scotia, came through as a man of deep feeling, of artistic temperament and sensitivity. Even his real name conjured up wilder shores: Rauff de Ryther Duan Acklom. While Manners had longed to be an actor, he'd graduated from the University of Toronto with a degree in forestry and somehow made it to New York, found work in the Theatre Guild, and went out to Hollywood.

Capra used Barbara's scenes with John Carson at his apartment to reveal the unfettered Florence Fallon: childlike, loving, touched by the innocence of Carson's soul, and transformed by his kindness into the real miracle woman, able to bring happiness and love to a man who has given up on life. It is in his apartment that John Carson's sincerity and maladroitness open her up and show her to be soft and true.

As she preaches to her thousands of followers in the lions' cage at the Temple of Happiness with her arms open and outstretched, looking diaphanous in the stream of her white chiffon robes that seem like the wings of an angel, Sister Fallon is seemingly lit from within. She stands with the lions pacing behind her in "a cage of fear, [with] bars of doubt . . . among beasts that tear and destroy," and assures her flock that "behold they cannot hurt me . . . if you come into this cage with love and understanding in your heart" because finally "there is no fear in God's kingdom." Florence knows it is a fake but draws her boundaries ("When I'm out there talking to those people, I've got to make it seem real, or I can't put it over").

It isn't until she leaves the tabernacle one night on her way to a party— a week after John Carson has gone to see Sister Fallon for himself and has come forward from the bleachers to enter the lions' den with her, sincere, willing, giving—"Blessed are the blind who cannot see fear," Sister Florence

Sister Fallon with Carson at her Temple of Happiness, preaching to
her followers that she and her fellow believer, "among the beasts that
tear and destroy," are unharmed, from *The Miracle Woman*, 1931.
(PHOTOFEST)

intones to him as he stands with her in the cage with lions behind them
both . . . "Faith, you have shown it brother, by coming up here with me tonight, and I solemnly promise when the day will come and your faith will
be rewarded"—that Florence is shown the way out from her deceit and from
being truly tainted.

It is raining heavily late at night. John Carson is standing at the stage door
waiting for a chance to talk with Sister. She leaves the building, dressed to go
out for the evening, sees that it's raining, and asks a man standing near her to
run to tell her chauffeur to escort her with an umbrella. She doesn't recognize
the man who a week before had come forward out of the audience to stand
with her in the lions' den. She realizes that he is blind and, embarrassed, asks
if she can give him a lift in her car. She bundles him under her umbrella and
takes him in out of the rain.

When they arrive at his apartment and step out of her limousine, she is
wearing his fedora and overcoat to protect herself from getting wet; he stands
shyly at the door of his building. She insists on going up to his apartment,
and when they reach the top floor, she asks if she may take off his hat and
stay awhile. Shyly, he begins to entertain her with his two "friends," which
he takes out of a cedar chest: "Pagliacci the clown" that plays a mechanical
xylophone, and "Sambo the hoofer," a dancing whirligig.

"What would you like to hear?" John asks Florence. "Ballads, songs, symphonies?" When she responds, "A bit of opera," the little clown begins to pound out "Farmer in the Dell"; Sambo dances along in accompaniment to the music of the xylophone. With the second chorus, Florence joins in and sings along. The camera is close in on her. Her eyes are full of the pleasure of the moment, and Barbara looks radiant.

Florence and John banter back and forth interrupted only by his landlady, Mrs. Higgins (played by Beryl Mercer, an actress born to British parents in Spain, a leading lady of Sir Herbert Tree's, and a celebrated actress of the London stage before she was twenty). Mrs. Higgins, plump, birdlike, dowdy, kindly, has brought John a large box. She is surprised to see he has a guest and even more surprised when she is introduced to Sister Fallon. "Oh, sure," Mrs. Higgins says, "and I'm Martha Washington . . . But I know Sister's voice as well as her face, so speak up and I'll tell you if you're Sister or not." Sister is dressed in an evening gown, in fur trim. She looks glamorous, worldly, and in response to Mrs. Higgins's dare that Sister "say a few words," Florence says, looking like a great sophisticate and almost in a monotone: "Eeny, meeny, miny, moe." It's what people say when they speak to hear back their voices and say the minimal amount, but instead of it sounding silly or thin, or like a throwaway, the richness and dimensionality of Barbara's voice make it sound like a benediction, a piece of wisdom spoken from the worldly elegant lady.

Mrs. Higgins opens the box she's brought John, and inside is a life-size plaster bust of Sister Fallon. John is embarrassed and admits to Sister, "I wanted to know what you looked like."

John begins to work dummy, Al, who speaks the words to Florence John doesn't have the nerve to say to her directly. ("I'll say I'm getting personal," John says through Al. "It's about time somebody was getting personal around here.") The magic of the evening is enfolded by the steady sound of the rain (the same sound Capra used for the love scenes of *Ladies of Leisure* and for effect in his silent pictures, including *The Matinee Idol*). The clock's cuckoo bird calling the hour is all that is heard above Florence and John's talk.

It is the end of the evening, and Florence has said her good night. She is about to go back to the real world. John is standing there, part of the enchanted but circumscribed room. He looks sweet, yearning, almost unable to move from the sadness of her leaving. She walks over to him, stands on her toes, and kisses his lips. She who has lost touch with her heart begins to feel it again.

With Florence Fallon and John Carson, Capra reversed convention. She is the one who knows the ways of a man's world with its deceits and dirty deal-

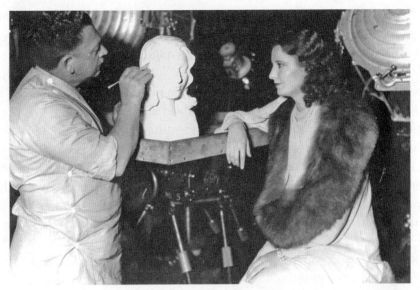

Richard Cromwell, former actor who starred in Columbia's 1930 *Tol'able David* and became an artist, making a bust of Barbara as Sister Fallon for the blind John Carson to feel what she looks like.

ings, who's fast-talking and has the trappings of success and luxury and the pretense of power that supposedly heals the sick and the deformed and can change lives. He is the innocent spirit, brought in from the rain, who allows Sister to enter his simple world, where things are domestic and orderly and safe, whimsical and childlike and shielded from the ugliness beyond its walls. When Capra has Barbara kiss the David Manners character, she is the more worldly of the two, the one who knows the truth of life. In the safety and innocence of Carson's room both spirits are reborn.

Florence returns to the gritty truth of her life at the party of freaks where she was originally headed. Circus performers and contortionists drinking and mostly drunk are singing around a piano; a crazed hilarity rings throughout. Florence is clearly disgusted with the ugliness that surrounds her. Barbara's bearing as she strides across the room ("Where did you collect all this garbage?" she asks) is angry and hard and shut off, the opposite of the openness and innocence she shows when she is with Carson.

"She could suffer from her toughness," Capra said. "And really suffer from the penance she would have to pay."

Capra was so deft with Barbara there were times she felt she wasn't being directed. "But of course you were," she said.

As Capra left her dressing room, he would say, "Remember, Barbara. No matter what the other actors do, whether they stop or blow their lines—you continue your scene right to the end. Understand?"

Capra wanted to make it easy for Barbara. What Willard Mack did for her on the stage, Frank Capra was doing for her in pictures. "He wanted me to be great and made me know it." She felt "babied and pampered" by him. And in his understanding of her, she knew, "he wanted me to be free," and made it possible for her to reach deep into herself.

The notion of innocence in a far from innocent universe intrigued Capra, as did the process of redemption. He'd used the idea of the innocent afoot in a careless, indifferent world early in his pictures: as the basis of the Harry Langdon character and again at the heart of *Ladies of Leisure*. Capra saw in Barbara a childlike innocence that he could help her to find. He felt the depth of the pain still inside her and gave her room for her to reach it. Hers was a passion and purity of feeling that deepened his own heart.

"He sensed things that you were trying to keep hidden," Barbara said. "He'd been kicked around [and] he understood it. And without probing and asking a lot of intimate questions, he knew. He just knew."

To Capra, Barbara was "naïve" and "unsophisticated." She lacked pretension, vanity. She wasn't interested in the things that most actors and actresses were: "makeup, clothes, or hairdos." When she went to work, "this chorus girl," he said, "could grab your heart and tear it to pieces."

In one emotionally pitched scene, David Manners was supposed to remain calm while Barbara became upset. During the shooting of the scene, Barbara's work so carried Manners away he had to turn his back to the camera so his tears wouldn't spoil the take.

As the days passed, Capra saw that Barbara "knew nothing about camera tricks: how to 'cheat' her looks so her face could be seen, how to restrict her body movements in close shots. She just turned it on and everything else on the stage stopped."

Capra was falling in love with her.

When production started on *The Miracle Woman*, stories began to appear in the newspapers that Barbara and Fay's marriage was over. Both denied the rumors. Fay told the *Los Angeles Examiner*, "You'd better speak to my wife about it; she's in the kitchen." Barbara said to the reporter, "I'm making a pot of tea and a bit of shortcake for him this moment. Does that sound like we're separated? Would any wife do that much for a husband she was mad at?"

It was Fay who was upset and drinking heavily. Barbara felt a profound

With Frank at home in the Malibu Colony, June 1932.

loyalty to him. They were in this together, and she was determined to tough out whatever problems they were having.

During the shooting of *The Miracle Woman,* Barbara and Frank had attended the opening of Capra's new action-adventure picture, *Dirigible,* starring Jack Holt and Ralph Graves. It was Columbia's most expensive picture, costing

Circa 1931. (CULVER PICTURES)

$650,000, and the studio's first picture to have its world premiere at Grauman's Chinese Theater on Hollywood Boulevard, the fulfillment of a seven-year dream for Harry Cohn. Capra called an opening at Grauman's "the zenith of recognition in Filmland. The searchlights lit up Hollywood's sky," he said.

Barbara and Frank had come home late from the studio and were so tired they decided not to put on evening clothes for the premiere. They arrived at the theater in street clothes to the disapproval of the other guests in full dress, who were put off by the impropriety of the Fays' casual attire and assumed they were drunk, partially from the stories around town about Frank's drinking binges.

Barbara was furious. The pomp and pretense of the evening only intensified her dislike of Hollywood. "I saw many there in evening clothes who really were drunk," Barbara said. The evening "soured [them both] on Hollywood night-life" and made Barbara all the more bound to Fay in her determination that husband and wife would stand together—authentic and true—against Hollywood and its hypocritical standards and righteous gossipmongers.

Production ended on *The Miracle Woman* in early April. For the final explosive scene in the movie, the tabernacle goes up in flames as in *Elmer Gantry,* whose scathing portrait of the Bible Belt ministry had sold more than half a million copies in its first few months. The book was banned in Boston as "obscene and indecent literature," as had been *An American Tragedy* and, four decades before that, *Leaves of Grass.*

The day after completing *The Miracle Woman,* Barbara began work at Warner Bros. on a picture called *Night Nurse,* to be directed by the thirty-five-year-old flinty William A. Wellman, who, two months before, had finished making *The Public Enemy* for Warner.

TWO

Idealism and Fight

William Wellman admitted he was "a son of a bitch" and could be hard on actors. "I like to keep them guessing. Never tell them anything," he said. He was known for being tough. "Wild Bill," he was called.

Wellman was under a two-year contract with Warner Bros.–First National—a contract he'd signed in 1930—getting paid $2,500 a week and, for directing *The Public Enemy*, $2,750.

Wellman was boyish, lean, wiry, quick-tempered. He was rugged, hard drinking, often in fights. At twenty-one, he'd run off to France to join the Norton-Harjes Ambulance Corps, then the French Foreign Legion and the Lafayette Flying Corps formed by William Vanderbilt, an offshoot of the Lafayette Escadrille.

Wellman was a fighter pilot in the Black Cat Squadron, crashing five of his own planes (the Nieuports he flew were equipped with only four instruments, "none of which worked, and no parachutes," said Wellman. "It was wonderful"). He christened each of the five planes Celia, after his mother. During General Pershing's historic first over-the-top attack on the "Huns," Wellman was the only American serving in the air guard while the famous Rainbow Division of Yankee troops received its baptism by fire on the ground.

During Wellman's months fighting, he shot down seven German planes in air battles over enemy lines before he himself was shot down over the forest of Parroy by anti-aircraft guns (Wellman called them "the most useless [guns] in the entire war"). When Wellman left the Flying Corps a year later, he was awarded a Croix de Guerre with two palms by the French army.

"Wild Bill" Wellman and Warner's Darryl Zanuck were kindred spirits. Zanuck admired Wellman's recklessness and daring. The young director was equally admiring of Zanuck and his way "of grabbing a headline and generat-

William Wellman, circa 1932. He couldn't stand being an actor and became a director instead. As a boy— "a crazy bastard"—he was kicked out of high school for throwing "a stink bomb on the principal's bald head. A direct hit," he said, and had to report to the Newton, Massachusetts, probation officer—his mother—for six months.

ing the speed and enthusiasm . . . to make a good picture quickly." Wellman said, "Whatever you say about Zanuck, he would back you up. He'd give you your head. If he decided you could do something, he'd be right behind you." Wellman thought Zanuck was "the hardest-working little guy . . . When you wanted an answer, you got it right then and there; if [Zanuck] shook hands on a deal, it was a deal, period."

Zanuck's early years in Los Angeles, to which he came from the sand hills of Wahoo, Nebraska, began with a series of jobs, first as a rivet catcher in a shipyard earning seventy-five cents an hour. "Miss one of those rivets," Zanuck said, "and it could burn a hole right through you. Even when I bought the heavy reinforced apron and gauntlets, I was in a constant muck sweat thinking I was going to fumble a red-hot rivet and get my balls burned off." Zanuck worked as a dishwasher, car polisher, and barbershop sweeper. He became a publicity man for a laundry and a press agent for Yuccatone Hair Restorer (Zanuck's tagline for the yucca-based, alcohol-enhanced tonic— "You've never seen a bald-headed Indian"—worked; the tonic sold).

Wellman and Zanuck drank together. They loved each other one day and the next were fighting and knocking each other down.

Wellman had promised Zanuck, who had been hesitant to make *The Public Enemy*, believing that gangster pictures had had their run, that if he were given the chance to direct *Beer and Blood*, he would make it "the toughest goddamn [gangster picture] of them all."

The Public Enemy was taken from an unpublished novel called *Beer and Blood* by Kubec Glasmon and John Bright: one a Chicago druggist and boot-legger whose drugstore was a hangout for gangsters; the other, his nineteen-year-old protégé, who delivered the store's diluted prescription whiskey.

Beer and Blood was a portrait of the Chicago underworld—"Italians, Irish, Jewish, Polish," said John Bright, "with each group's particular methods and interests specified." Zanuck bought the book and had the story streamlined. The script was about two young boys, street pals, who grow up to be thugs controlling the beer racket for the Chicago speakeasies. The picture came in the wake of the violence from Prohibition and the bootleg wars that were in the headlines every day and followed two other Warner Bros. gangster pictures, *The Doorway to Hell* and *Little Caesar*.

The country was still shaken from Al Capone's attempted murder of the mobster and beer baron Bugs Moran in Chicago on Valentine's Day while Moran's men were in a warehouse about to drive two empty trucks to Detroit to pick up Canadian whiskey smuggled into the country. Moran's men were lined up against the rear wall of a garage and sprayed with machine gun bullets.

Moviegoing audiences flocked to see gangster pictures. Bertolt Brecht was fascinated by them, seeing in them the mechanism of capitalist enterprise. Zanuck had first assigned *The Public Enemy* to Archie Mayo, who directed *The Doorway to Hell,* but Mayo wanted to get away from gangster pictures. He wanted to make a woman's picture, to which Zanuck said, "You do what you're told, you toad."

Zanuck was drawn to Wellman's toughness and ultimately agreed to re-assign the picture to him.

James Cagney was under contract to Warner Bros. for $400 a week. In *The Public Enemy,* Edward Woods was originally cast in the leading role of Tom Powers, and Cagney was to be his quiet boyhood pal. Woods was engaged to Louella Parsons's twenty-five-year-old daughter, Harriet, and Zanuck liked the proximity to Hearst. But as the picture's childhood scenes were shot, the script's writers, Glasmon and Bright, realized that the roles had been given to the wrong actors, and both writers pushed Wellman to give Cagney the lead.

Cagney was a street-smart, raw spirit and could easily project what he himself described as a "gutter quality" more powerfully than Woods. He had the spitfire energy and strut that were right for the vicious underworld gangster. After three days of shooting, Wellman went to Zanuck and told him, "We got the wrong man playing the wrong part. This Cagney is the guy."

Zanuck sent out an executive summons saying he'd had a great idea and was changing the casting; the role of Tom Powers would be played by Jimmy Cagney. Wellman had already shot the picture's childhood sequences of Matt Doyle and Tom Powers as young street kids drinking beer and stealing. The Powers character was Woods as a boy—tall and gangly with dark hair. His quiet pal, Matt Doyle, was a young Cagney—light-haired, short, and stocky. Wellman kept the footage as it was, despite the switch in actors and the stark differences in appearance.

The part of Powers's girlfriend, Gwen Allen, was first offered to Louise Brooks (Wellman had directed her three years before in *Beggars of Life*), who turned it down to go to New York. Wellman then offered the part to Jean Harlow, who accepted it.

In the cast as well was Mae Clarke. Mae had just finished appearing as Molly Malloy in Lewis Milestone's *Front Page,* a picture produced by Howard Hughes. When Mae's agent called to say he had another Molly Malloy for her, "that's all [she] had to hear." She and Joan Blondell were to play a "couple of whores . . . on the town."

Blondell had just finished working with Cagney in a picture called *Other Men's Women,* also directed by Wellman. In it, Blondell, a former Miss Dallas, played a smart-talking waitress who, when a customer says to her, "Gimme a slice of you on toast and some french-fried potatoes on the side," replies, "Listen, baby, I'm APO. Ain't puttin' out."

Mae was concerned about playing a "night-on-the-town whore [who] enjoys it." She wanted to play a woman who "fell into it, couldn't help it, couldn't get out and hated it." She thought the role of Tom Powers's girl in *The Public Enemy* "didn't sound right." She wanted to "advance in her career and play ladies—nice people, exciting people. Versatility was my goal." But if she had to "sacrifice a little bit in motive," she could still try to "get something in there," and so she accepted the offer to play Kitty. It was her first picture for Warner Bros., and it was a way to get work in other Warner pictures.

Mae's was a small part, just the scene with Tom Powers in a nightclub, first with Blondell sitting at a table with their two gentlemen escorts, both of whom are passed out, and then a breakfast scene the morning after with Cagney's Tom Powers character.

Mae had a sense that the director "might be difficult. Wellman didn't seem very sympathetic or kind," Mae said. "He'd have a joke at anybody's expense, which was funny and amused most people," but Mae "didn't want to be on the receiving end of Wellman's wit." Wellman thought this was the way to keep his crew lively. "Anyone working in one of my pictures knows what they're going to get before they even start!"

Wellman was making *The Public Enemy* with the same "quiet sadism" in front of the camera that Louise Brooks described him practicing "behind the camera" when he directed her in *Beggars of Life*. He had been fired from Paramount for goosing a female extra and ruining a camera.

Zanuck told Wellman that the characters in the picture had to be "tough, tough, tough. People are going to say the characters are immoral, but they're not . . . they don't have any morals. They steal, they kill, they lie, they hump each other because that's the way they're made and if you allow a decent human feeling or a pang of conscience to come into their makeup, you've lost 'em and changed the kind of movie we're making."

With Cagney's jangled taut energy and the feel about him of violence about to explode, Wellman was aiming for an assault on the nerves, a gritty realistic portrait of a vicious, sadistic man. Wellman thought Cagney "as tough as they come, but he knew ballet and all the rest of it. He was a wonderful dancer." Wellman used that quality of Cagney's in the picture. He allowed the actor to bring a dimensionality to Powers without using sentimentality.

Robert Sherwood wrote about Cagney's portrait of Powers, "I doubt there is an actor extant who could have done what James Cagney does . . . He does not hesitate to represent Tom Powers as a complete rat—with a rat's sense of honor, a rat's capacity for human love, and when cornered, a rat's fighting courage . . . Although his role is consistently unsympathetic, Mr. Cagney manages to earn for Tom Powers the audience's affection and esteem."

Wellman shot Mae's breakfast scene at the end of the day.

She'd had little to do with Cagney during their two scenes together. She could "hear him [and] smell him—he was a man who knew his business and his business [didn't] stop within himself. He was interested in the whole picture," Mae said. He gave time in rehearsal and took Mae aside "when the director didn't do it."

Mae "felt an empathy with Jimmy" that she didn't feel with Wellman. "It didn't matter that I wasn't getting anything from the director. I didn't need anything from him. I had it within myself" and, with Cagney's help, was all right.

The scene with Tom Powers and Kitty was to take place in the bedroom. Powers was to say to her, "Shut your mouth and open your legs, for God's sake." Zanuck and Wellman knew the line couldn't be used and instead set the scene the next morning at a breakfast table.

In the rewritten scene, Powers sits down and asks for a drink. Kitty was to say, "Not before breakfast, Tom." His response: "I didn't ask for any lip,

I asked for a drink." Kitty says, out of a longing for a gentler response, "I wish . . ." Powers cuts her off by saying, "You're always wishin'. You got the gimmes for fair! I'm going to get you a bag of peanuts."

Cagney changed the line and said instead, "I wish you was a wishing well so I could tie a bucket to you and sink you."

"That was enough," Mae said. "It showed [Powers's] hatred of me" and his violence.

In the Glasmon and Bright novel, the scene ends with Mae Clarke's character throwing a glass of water at Tom Powers.

After they finished shooting the scene, Mae went back to her dressing room to change into her street clothes. Cagney appeared in the doorway and asked if he could come in. "Bill [Wellman] and I have been talking," Cagney said. "We thought of a heck of an idea. We'd like to do [the scene] again to give the guys a kick. This is really something you won't forget."

Cagney told Mae that he'd heard of a gangster in Chicago, Hymie Weiss, who, listening to his girlfriend "endlessly yakking away at breakfast one morning," took an omelet she had just prepared and shoved it in her face. Cagney said the omelet would be too messy, so they were thinking of using a grapefruit.

"Wouldn't it be fun?" Cagney asked. "Would you mind if we tried it?"

Mae "couldn't believe [her] ears." She asked Cagney if he was kidding.

"No, come on back," he said. "We'll do the scene again, just like we forgot something and we want to improve it. They haven't broken the set yet. The lights are still there. And then I'll pick up this grapefruit and push it in your face and the guys will go crazy."

Mae had struggled to get this far as an actress—working at Warner and with Wellman. If she refused Cagney, she feared all her work would "be out the window." She thought of calling her agent, but she couldn't get to a phone. "Jimmy was sitting right there and being persuasive."

"I'll do it. Once," she said. "I'll trust you not to hurt me and that's all. Just for the guys. Okay."

Wellman was ready to reshoot the scene. Mae and Jimmy sat down at the breakfast table again, she in a negligee, he in striped pajamas. Cagney asks her for a drink. Once again Kitty says, "I wish . . ." and is cut off by Powers: "I wish you was a wishing well so I could tie a bucket to you and sink you."

Cagney picked up the half grapefruit on Mae's plate and pushed it into the side of her face. Mae knew what was coming, but she was still shocked by it. The men yelled at Cagney. "They thought he had lost his mind," said Mae.

Cagney kept his promise and didn't hurt Mae, but she instantly regretted

Mae Clarke and James Cagney pose for a still photograph from Wellman's *Public Enemy*, 1931. "I was a good sport," said Mae about shooting the scene. "I could have sued [the studio] and won."

doing the retake. She assumed "that was the end of it" until she was told the scene was going to be shown in the projection room the following day.

Mae drove home that evening. She got to her house and felt she "was no longer Mae, the actress." Her mother opened the door and told Mae what they were having for dinner. "I put my head on her shoulder and broke down crying. 'Mother, something happened today that I will never, ever, get over.' I told her I felt so used, I wished to God I'd never done it, and she sat me down to a good meal and got me to stop crying. My father . . . went quietly to the piano and consoled me by playing. That was the way he talked to me. [The studio] had no right to put that in the picture without my permission. I gave no permission. I signed no release."

"We needed something big right there in the picture," Wellman said. "Well, that grapefruit on the table looked inviting—and I didn't like the dame much anyhow. So I told Jimmy to try socking her with it—but hard. He did."

Wellman went to work directing *Night Nurse*, which was planned as a big picture for Warner Bros., based on the novel by Dora Macy and purchased by the studio the year before for $4,000. Dora Macy (Grace Perkins Oursler) was the author as well of *Ex-mistress*.

Bill Wellman had worked his way up from being a messenger at the Goldwyn studios, watching contract directors like Maurice Tourneur and Frank Lloyd (he "stole scripts, new ones, old ones and pored over them, always from a director's point-of view"), to a position of assistant propman, then assistant director, working first for Goldwyn's Alfred Green and others. He then moved on to Fox, where he worked for directors like Bernard J. Durning, who taught Wellman "more than anybody in the business—action, pacing, stunts." When Durning got drunk during *The Eleventh Hour,* Wellman took over and was made a full director. He made a series of low-budget Buck Jones melodramas and at Metro was given a slapstick comedy with Joan Crawford, *I'll Tell the World,* which was released as *The Boob.*

Wellman had tried acting; he was in *The Knickerbocker Buckaroo,* a part given to him through Douglas Fairbanks Sr., and he'd appeared in Raoul Walsh's *Evangeline.* Acting for Wellman was not a self-respecting job, and he didn't like the way he looked in front of a camera. At the premiere of *The Knickerbocker Buckaroo,* Wellman "stayed for half the picture and went out and vomited for no reason at all."

Wellman told Fairbanks, "I don't mean any disrespect, but I'm no actor." Fairbanks asked him what he wanted to be. Wellman pointed to a director and asked how much he made. Fairbanks told him, and Wellman said, "That's what I want to be."

Wellman was becoming known as a fast, efficient director; he'd shot *When Husbands Flirt* from a Dorothy Arzner script in four days and was capable of bringing in a picture days in advance of its schedule—and under budget. *The Public Enemy* was shot in twenty-six days at a cost of $151,000.

In *Night Nurse,* Barbara was an idealistic young woman, Lora Hart, who makes her way to a big city hospital, is trained as a nurse, and in the process learns about life, death, and the workings of love and power.

She is hired by a society doctor of impeccable reputation to be the private-duty night nurse for two rich children suffering from malnutrition and anemia. She soon realizes that the children are being starved to death by their boozed-up mother and her chauffeur, who keeps his employer plied with bootlegged liquor. The sadistic chauffeur also oversees the children's "care."

The night nurse pieces together that the doctor is in league with mother and chauffeur. At stake are the children's lives; for mother, chauffeur, and doctor, what matters is the children's trust fund left them by their father. In proving malpractice, Lora Hart comes up against the medical establishment and the power of the rich and helps to shatter the facade of the seemingly perfect American family.

Wellman had twenty-four days to shoot the picture. Barbara was on loan from Columbia, or, as Sam Briskin wrote in an agreement letter to Warner Bros., "we are renting her to you" for three and a half weeks, for which the studio was being paid $35,000. Columbia threw in an additional half week's time. Jim Cagney was to play the young intern at the hospital who flirts with Lora Hart. A month later Cagney was replaced by Eddy Nugent. Wellman began shooting on April 4, 1931.

Most of the scenes were shot fast. Wellman knew exactly what he wanted. "I had a script and I worked like hell at home. I never slept—four hours of sleep was a big night—so I did a lot of the work then."

In *Night Nurse*, Wellman continued the pace and toughness of *The Public Enemy*. It was almost the Tom Powers story, showed from the flip side of his world: those who buy Powers's "dirty liquor" and the havoc it can wreak in their lives. *Night Nurse* has the same menacing threat of violence as *The Public Enemy*. Lora Hart's idealism and fight have the same tough raw spirit as Cagney's character in *The Public Enemy*.

The Public Enemy was Wellman's portrait of American madness, of a society out of control through greed, power, and booze. *Night Nurse's* party scenes with the children's mother are a grim portrait of Prohibition and the manic fever it spread. The mother, in a low-cut white evening dress, is seen passed out on a bear rug, her slippers dangling upside down on the chandelier; across the hall in her penthouse duplex her two daughters are dying from lack of food. The scene is as shocking as the one in *The Public Enemy* when Cagney is shot and falls facedown into the rain-soaked street, his blood spilling out onto the wet gutter as he mumbles to himself, "I ain't so tough."

In *The Public Enemy*, the shooting of Nails Nathan's prize horse (off camera) at the bucolic equestrian stables is comparable in shock value in *Night Nurse* to the society doctor's refusal to call the police or change the children's feeding orders when he's told by Lora Hart that his young patients are being starved and won't last another month.

Wellman's portrait of a medical profession bound by stringent rules and etiquette, even at the cost of a patient's life, is summed up when Lora Hart says, "Ethics, ethics, ethics. That's all I've heard since I got into this business. Isn't there any humanity?"

The part of Nick, the chauffeur, was played by Clark Gable, a young freelance actor, who was paid $750 a week for the part. Mervyn LeRoy had pursued the actor for the part of the racketeer in *Little Caesar*, but Jack Warner wanted Douglas Fairbanks Jr. LeRoy had seen Gable onstage in a production of *The Last Mile* put on by a touring company at the old Majestic Theatre in

With Clark Gable, *Night Nurse,* 1931. He was from Cadiz, Ohio, born
in 1901, the son of an oil-field contractor from Pennsylvania Dutch
stock who worked on the Oklahoma derricks until he rode blind baggage west in a freight car. It was Pauline Frederick's personal dentist—
Gable played a small part in one of her companies—who fixed his
teeth. His ears stuck out even more until he had them pulled back.

Los Angeles. LeRoy wanted "a real tough guy, not somebody who looked as
though he'd just stepped out of some elegant drawing room," as Fairbanks did.

When Clark Gable came onstage in *The Last Mile,* as a convict, stripped
to the waist, LeRoy saw the tough guy he was looking for. "He was powerful,
brutal, animal-like," said LeRoy, who arranged to test the actor at Warner.
Gable did scenes from *The Last Mile* and read some lines from *Little Caesar.*
LeRoy thought the actor had "the same quality on screen that he had on
stage, only magnified." Zanuck didn't see Gable's power. "Do you know what
you've done," Zanuck told LeRoy. "You've just thrown away five hundred
bucks on a test. Didn't you see the size of that guy's ears?"

Wellman said, "They [the powers that be at Warner Bros.] forgot to look
at [Gable's] dimples and listen to his voice and see his smile."

Bill Wellman saw the power in Gable's presence and wanted him for the
part of "Nick, the black-clothed chauffeur." Gable, listed as "Gables" in the
production reports, was "one of the most despicable heavies imaginable," said
Wellman. "The instant Clark walked onto that set," Barbara said, "I knew,
we all knew, that here was a striking personality. He commanded attention."

Marjorie Crawford, Wellman's fourth wife and a member of the Ninety-Nines whose first president was Amelia Earhart, circa 1930.

In one scene Wellman has Gable (Nick) slug Barbara (Lora Hart) in the chin and in another push her so hard she is slammed against a door and falls to the floor. The scene was originally written for the chauffeur to push the doctor (Charles Winninger) into the door as he is about to perform a transfusion to save the children. Wellman shot the scene with Nick first punching the doctor almost into the camera and then throwing Lora Hart across the room.

Gable pushed Barbara with such force that she went through the door. "That was okay," said Barbara. "That was how great Clark was."

Despite the violence aimed at women in *The Public Enemy,* Wellman saw women as capable of the same kind of two-fistedness, fearlessness, and passionate idealism as men—able to hold their own—and showed that in Barbara's character in *Night Nurse.*

Louise Brooks said that Bill Wellman was "shy in conversation" with women; he "resembled an actor [with women] . . . uncertain of his part, more than he did a director."

Wellman was married to a "beautiful polo-playing aviatrix," a kind of Tommy Hitchcock, Wellman's good pal, with whom he had flown in the Lafayette Flying Corps. "Tommy Hitchcock was the roughest, toughest, most fearless and best [polo player] in the world," said Wellman. "A 10-goal player—that's as high as you can get. Marjorie Crawford [Wellman's wife] wasn't in Tom's class but [she] was awfully good for a woman. As graceful on horseback as [she was] in the air," said Wellman. She was "rough and tough. With the face of an angel, a beautiful blonde angel. And a figure, amen."

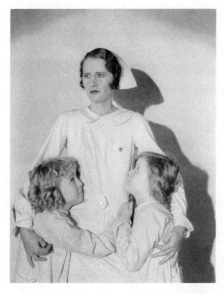

With Betty Jane Graham as Desney Ritchey and Marcia Mae Jones as Nanny. *Night Nurse,* 1931. (PHOTOFEST)

Wellman married Marjorie Crawford twice, the first time when he was not yet legally divorced from his third wife, Margery Chapin. The silent-film star Helene Chadwick, Wellman's second wife, great-granddaughter of Lord Chadwick, was described in the 1920s as "intelligent; womanly, and, at the same time, a good comrade; the best-fellow-in-the-world."

In one of Wellman's silent pictures, *Beggars of Life,* he shows a young girl (Louise Brooks) on the run from the law (she kills her father when he tries to rape her) who joins up with a young tramp. Together they ride the rails and sleep in haystacks, she disguised as a boy, wearing shirt, jacket, pants, boots, and cap to hide her girlish bob.

In *Night Nurse,* Wellman makes Barbara the kind of woman he delights in. She is almost as "rough and tough" as Nick, the chauffeur, and, like Wellman's own wife, had "the face of an angel," with passion and idealism as well.

The psychic assault of *Night Nurse* continues when Barbara's character slams the mother's leering, hopped-up boyfriend in the neck with the full force of her arm. He falls over backward and crawls away. When he peers out at Barbara from behind the bar, she throws an ice bucket at him from across the room, just missing his head but shattering bottles of champagne. The children for whom the night nurse is caring are near death, and she finds their mother, Mrs. Ritchey, draped over the bar, dead drunk, almost passed out.

Barbara yells at Mrs. Ritchey, "You're a cruel, inhuman mother. You're a rotten parasite. Don't blame it on the booze. It's you. You're going up to that nursery with me if I have to drag you by the hair of your head." Mrs. Ritchey drops off the bar stool. Barbara drags her by the neck until Mrs. Ritchey falls at Barbara's feet. Lora Hart stands there, hands on her hips, looking down at Mrs. Ritchey passed out on the floor. With all of the steeliness and street grit of *The Public Enemy*'s Tom Powers, Barbara speaks the ultimate indictment, "You mother," steps over Mrs. Ritchey, grabs a champagne bucket full of ice water, and dumps it on her face.

Barbara next squares off against Nick. "You think just because you can strong-arm a couple of women," she says, "you have the brains to put over a racket like this. I had you numbered the minute I stepped into this house. They use the electric chair for the kinds of things you're responsible for."

At the end of each day's shooting, Barbara asked the assistant director how many pages had been shot. "I was happy when we had covered more than scheduled and unhappy if we fell short," she said. The crew kidded her, asking if she had money in the production.

Wellman finished *Night Nurse* on May 6, two days earlier than scheduled. The picture was budgeted at just over $260,000. Wellman brought it in at just over $139,000 and was paid $27,000 to do the job.

Fay's picture *God's Gift to Women* opened in Los Angeles at the Warner Bros. Hollywood Theatre and in New York at the Strand on Broadway. Warner was heralding Fay as the "It Man"; "the 1931 Model Lover—built for Speed, Style, Endurance." He went east for the opening and stayed for the picture's first week, appearing at the Strand doing four shows a day, performing twenty minutes of gags, songs, and imitations (among them his uncanny imitation of John Barrymore), and chatting onstage about Hollywood and his wife.

The reviews for *God's Gift to Women* were poor. *Variety* said, simply, "It's no gift to audiences," but the reviewers commented on how Fay's presence carried the picture. *The New York Times* called Fay "the whole show. He softens the banality of dialogue that would be better left unspoken and . . . tricks his audiences into believing that the stock farce situations are both amusing and fresh, which they are not."

The lure of "the Great Fay," "Broadway's Favorite Son," and the studio's promise of beautiful women, sexual sophistication, hilarity, and high jinks failed to be enough of a draw for an audience struggling to keep the Depression at bay. More than two million men crisscrossed the countryside in search of jobs that weren't to be found. In New York City families were being supported by tens of millions of government relief dollars. Despite that, 60 percent of Americans still faithfully paid the few cents it cost to escape their troubles and go to the movies.

After a six-day run, *God's Gift to Women,* which cost $220,000 to make, had brought in $12,000. The following week, *The Public Enemy* grossed $60,000 without the appearances of its cast members or Cagney, its new star.

Fay was obligated to make one more picture for the studio. In early June, Warner Bros. decided to buy out the last remaining months of his contract for $27,500 and let it be known in the press. The Broadway sensation seemed unaffected by the studio's decision and bought a new car and hired a driver. Fay wasn't the only actor dropped by the studio: within a two-week period Warner had let go more than forty actors, writers, and directors. Barbara was reshooting the end of *The Miracle Woman.* She was not happy about the way Warner had treated Fay and was just as publicly letting it be known how much she disliked Hollywood and "the Hollywood attitude."

She was keenly aware of how in Hollywood "you were loved for success and success alone." When the Fays first came to Hollywood two years earlier, Barbara was known as "the girl Frank Fay married" and was barely tolerated by the Hollywood royals, even though she'd experienced the thrill of her name in electric lights on Broadway. After the critical and financial failure of *God's Gift to Women,* the town began to refer to Frank as "Barbara Stanwyck's husband."

Barbara put no faith in fame. "When you are up in Hollywood, you are accepted; when you are down, it is as though you do not exist."

She told the press she was in it for the money, even though of course she was happy when she made a good picture. And, unlike most of the other "poor women in the octopus-like grip of the studios," Barbara had made sure that she was free from studio control.

She wanted to remain outside studio life and Hollywood society. Fame and work were not her gods, she said. What Barbara had was Frank Fay. And when they'd made enough money, they planned, she said, to live in Europe as they pleased, have a couple of children, and possibly do a play in London and bring it into New York. Life would be rich and full for them, and, she told the press, if she never saw Hollywood again, that would be fine with her.

THREE

On Being "Barbaric"

Barbara was obligated to make one more picture—her third—for Columbia and agreed to star in *Forbidden* with Frank Capra directing. She also approved a story by Houston Branch to be the basis of her first picture under her new Warner contract. *Safe in Hell* was a dark, twisted story about a New Orleans prostitute who believes she's killed a former trick, her first, in a fire she accidentally starts. She flees the city and is stowed away by her seaman fiancé (Donald Cook), who loves her no matter whom she's been with or what she's done. The ship is bound for Tortuga in the Caribbean, the only island in the world without an extradition law. The plan is to lie low until the hunt for her quiets down and the law gives up its search.

Tortuga—hot, close, infested with insects and disease, separated by weeks of travel from the nearest body of land—is full of desperate, violent characters who long ago sought refuge there. The newly arrived Gilda Karlson, now Erickson, is the only "white woman" to be found on the island.

Gilda can hardly believe her sailor fiancé has married her. When he goes off on months-long voyages, Gilda keeps her promise to him and rebuffs each crazed man who behaves like a starved dog trying to devour her. The desperate men of Tortuga come to respect Gilda and leave her alone, except for the island's jailer-executioner, who wants her and will do anything to get her, including stealing the adoring letters her husband writes to her from every port and setting her up to kill the man she thought she'd already murdered. On Tortuga the laws are strict. The executioner tells Gilda, "As long as you behave yourself here, you are safe from jail and gallows." And adds under his breath, "Safe in hell."

The Houston Branch story was as daring as the law allowed. The story combined elements of Bill Wellman's *Beggars of Life:* a girl on the run from the law who escapes its wrath only to find her way into a parallel society, a

Barbara's sister, Laura Mildred Stevens Smith. She was buried in Brooklyn in Green-Wood Cemetery near her mother, Catherine; her younger sister, Mabel; and Byron Stevens's wife, Elizabeth. (COURTESY JUNE D. MERKENT)

dark underworld, governed by the dispossessed, beggars and thieves whose own twisted laws and conventions, and desire for her, eventually seal her fate.

Gilda keeps her vow to be faithful to her husband to the end and chooses hanging by the executioner rather than be at his mercy for the six months she is to serve in his prison camp.

In the picture were elements of Maugham's *Sadie Thompson,* in its sexual combustion and repression and in its story of redemption and purity. In the script were Darryl Zanuck's hard-edged notions about story, drama, and character—the requisite fall from grace and the spiritual rebirth—fed by Zanuck's boyhood love of dime novels and tabloid journalism. *Safe in Hell* for Warner was to go into production in mid-September after the completion of Barbara's next picture for Columbia.

Barbara's sister Millie died suddenly of a heart attack at the age of forty-five. Millie was Barbara's "tall, beautiful" sister who had taken care of her, brought her to New York City, given her the world of theaters and performers, and been the closest thing to a mother to her. "She was gorgeous," said Barbara.

The funeral was in Flatbush at Moadinger's, where Mabel's funeral had been held almost a year earlier. Laura Mildred Stevens Smith was buried in Brooklyn in Green-Wood Cemetery near her mother, Catherine, her younger sister Mabel Stevens Vaslett Munier, and By's wife, Elizabeth Stevens. Barbara and Fay were unable to go east for the service.

Barbara "nearly went crazy" over the sorrow from Millie's death. "Where the hell am I going to go from here?" she said.

It was just the three Stevenses now: Maud, at forty-three years old, in Flatbush; Byron, twenty-six, recuperating from tuberculosis in Arizona; and Ruby, at twenty-three, making pictures in Hollywood.

Barbara and Fay rarely entertained and refused most invitations. Fay often became annoyed with Barbara's friends and didn't want her to go out. The Fays were thought of as reclusive, and people resented their standoffishness.

Barbara's deep feelings of loss for Millie, as with the death of Mabel the year before and those of her mother and father so long ago, coupled with Hollywood's fickleness that made her so angry, fueled her desire to carve her way against all circumstances. "The trouble is I so love a good fight," she said. "I just can't help it."

Barbara "got to thinking one day," soon after Millie's death, "about how much money Constance Bennett was making and Ann Harding and people like that," she said. Constance Bennett had signed with Warner for a large sum of money, as had Ruth Chatterton; Ann Harding had just renewed her contract at Pathé for an equally large salary. "Good for Ann," said Barbara. "She's a wonderful person and a grand actress." Barbara concluded that the reason she wasn't making that kind of money was because she hadn't asked for it.

Columbia Pictures was to pay Barbara $20,000 for her next film, *Forbidden.* This at a time when more than thirteen million Americans had lost their jobs.

Frank Capra had discussed with Barbara in detail the story of *Forbidden.* She was delighted with it and with the opportunity to have such an unusually fine part. Now that Barbara's pictures with Columbia were successful, and the studio had exercised all of its options without increasing her salary, she decided to call Harry Cohn and remind him of their agreement.

Barbara had come to Hollywood with a written contract and a verbal understanding. "I [was to] be paid more money if I proved popular with movie fans," she said. "I had had such verbal agreements with New York stage producers, and I never experienced difficulty."

Before the conversation with Cohn went far, Barbara got angry.

"Fifty thousand dollars a picture," Barbara said to Cohn, "or I won't work."

"You have a contract," Cohn told her, and she had to live up to it.

"Listen, I don't have to do anything," Barbara said to Cohn. "And nobody can tell me I do."

Fay told Barbara that she "couldn't go around tearing up contracts," that the studio would sue her. "You'll have to stick to it," said Fay. "And fight the suit. You can't win, you know. You shouldn't win. But you'll have to fight. When will you learn not to do things like that?"

Consequences didn't stand in Barbara's way.

Like Sister Fallon in *The Miracle Woman,* Barbara was a young woman living surrounded by con artists. "In the theatre we had our sharpees," said Jim Cagney. "But when you got to Hollywood you knew you had arrived in the big league for con men and frauds."

There was a fragility in Barbara as well as an unworldliness. Her attitude toward Harry Cohn and most of Hollywood was Sister Fallon's: "I'm going to get up there and read you my father's last sermon and then I'm going to tell you sons of bitches what I think of you. And if you walk out of the church, so what? I don't care. Damn the consequences."

Barbara said nothing more to Cohn about the salary increase.

Each day she went to Columbia and worked with Capra on costumes, wigs, and makeup for *Forbidden:* her character was to age from a twenty-five-year-old to a sixty-year-old. Columbia had hired a special makeup artist—Monte Westmore—to design the look of the aging process.

Sam Briskin, Columbia's assistant general manager, told Barbara that shooting would start within the week. She was ready to report on whatever date he gave her. Three days later, Barbara called Briskin's office. Briskin called her back an hour later. Barbara got on the phone and said, without any small talk, "I'm not doing the picture." Briskin was surprised. After a moment, he asked, "What in the world are you talking about?"

"I mean exactly what I say. I will not do the picture unless you pay me $50,000. It is nothing against Columbia," said Barbara. "I have simply decided that no matter who the producer is, I will not appear in a picture for anybody unless I get $50,000 for my services. You can talk it over with Mr. Cohn and let me know."

Briskin said there was nothing to talk over. Barbara was under contract to Columbia, and, he said, "we expect you to live up to the contract and perform your services for us. I think it extremely unfair," he went on, "for you to take such an attitude only a couple of days before we are to start production on a picture when there's been such extensive preparation and so much money has been spent."

Columbia so far had spent $50,000 getting ready to start production.

"Well, think it over and you can let me know later," said Barbara.

Briskin told Capra that Barbara was refusing to do the picture. Capra was stunned. Having made extensive plans and devoted his best energies in preparation for the picture, he was "greatly disappointed. Barbara is the only actress," he said, "who could perform this part to my satisfaction."

Later that day, Columbia drew up a letter that said the studio expected Barbara to report on July 20 for the start of *Forbidden;* it "expected her to perform her services according to her contract."

Briskin called Barbara two days later to ask if she'd decided to come to work and do the picture. "My mind is made up," she said. "Unless I get $50,000 for the picture, I won't appear in it and that's all there is to it."

Night Nurse premiered in New York City at the Strand on Barbara's twenty-fourth birthday, July 16, 1931. Of the movie *The New York Times* wrote, "Barbara Stanwyck's quiet charm and rare trouping evidence themselves from time to time. Like *The Public Enemy,* [*Night Nurse*] has an air of repellent fascination . . . [W]hile condemning Wellman for what he chooses to palm off as entertainment, it would be unfair not to recognize his uncanny ability for creating realistic drama out of environment. Even a slugger may be an artist with a blackjack." The review singled out Clark Gable's "brutally sinister" portrayal of the "chauffeur-baron."

Moviegoers wanting to see *Night Nurse* at the Strand formed lines around the block.

The critic for the *Los Angeles Evening Herald* described Barbara as "one of the most natural actresses [on] the screen" and said that she "delivers another of her superb performances." Clark Gable was described as "one of the screen's biggest moment[s] at the present time, [with] a small but vital part."

Barbara watched Gable emerge from *Night Nurse* as a star from his small role as Nick, the chauffeur. On the picture's first day in New York at the Strand, the theater marquee read: "NIGHT NURSE STARRING BARBARA STANWYCK." "The second day," said Barbara, "the marquee read, 'NIGHT NURSE Barbara Stanwyck Co-starring Clark Gable.' The third night," she said, "it read 'NIGHT NURSE Barbara Stanwyck Clark Gable.' "

Fay and Barbara ran into Capra at the Brown Derby Café in Hollywood, and Capra told Barbara he was personally hurt that she'd refused to do the picture. "I consider it a reflection of my own ability as a director," he told her.

"There's nothing personal about it," said Barbara. "I have great respect for you as a director, but I've made up my mind that unless I'm paid $50,000 I won't appear in any more motion pictures."

"You can tell Cohn and Briskin," Fay said to Capra, "that if Columbia cancels its option for the other pictures, Barbara will do this picture for nothing."

"Absolutely," Barbara said, "and I will even work until six o'clock every day."

Capra reported the conversation to Cohn and heard nothing else from Barbara, who was scheduled to report to the studio on July 20. Barbara stood firm and didn't show up.

A few days after the premiere of *Night Nurse,* Frank Fay emceed the opening of *The Miracle Woman* at the Orpheum in Los Angeles, telling the audience that vaudeville was making a big comeback and that he, Fay, was there not because of Columbia but because of his regard for RKO, owner of the Orpheum chain of theaters.

The critics called *The Miracle Woman* "Miss Stanwyck's most effective role"; "Capra can do more with Miss Stanwyck than any other director she has worked with . . . her performance is splendid in unfolding plenty of fire, balanced by undertones of instinctive character softness and mood."

Cohn was furious about his star's demands and announced to the press that Barbara Stanwyck was in breach of contract and that she couldn't work for Warner Bros. until she finished her picture for Columbia. Her contract with Columbia was due to expire in a month, on August 14, and, contract or no contract, Cohn said, Barbara was not legally allowed to work for Warner until she completed her picture for his studio.

Night Nurse and *The Miracle Woman* were both doing well at the box office. Each was mentioned in *Photoplay*'s Best Pictures of the Month along with DeMille's *Squaw Man* and von Sternberg's *An American Tragedy. Photoplay* singled out Barbara for both pictures in its Best Performance of the Month.

Stories in the press announced that Barbara was returning to New York, that she was leaving pictures forever now that Frank Fay's contract was not being renewed, and that she would go wherever Fay went. Barbara was quoted as saying that she was "overworked, turning out picture after picture on the double contract," and that her doctor told her she could not last another year without a complete collapse if she kept it up. Barbara's lawyer, Charles Cradick, denied the stories. Barbara made it clear that neither she nor Fay was through in pictures.

The press wrote about her as "barbaric," as defined by the dictionary: "rudely splendid, striking, picturesque," and called her "splendidly rude."

Harry Cohn offered Barbara's part in *Forbidden* to Helen Hayes, who refused it. He then decided to abandon *Forbidden*. Frank Capra went to work instead on *Gallagher,* a newspaper picture originally to be directed by the actor and writer Eddie Buzzell.

The press continued to cover the Frank Fays and their troubles: Fay was accused in print of being the force behind Barbara's unreasonable demands with Columbia and of being jealous of his wife's success, of trying to persuade her to leave Hollywood with him and go back to vaudeville. Barbara's response: if she were ever forced to choose one or the other—her career or her marriage—she would "turn to her husband without a moment's hesitation."

Barbara received a letter from the publisher of a trade paper for motion picture exhibitors called *Harrison's Reports* telling her that "many of the exhibitors have bought the Columbia program with the understanding that they were going to get two pictures with you as the star . . . [The exhibitors] will not get what they bargained for. And they have no redress . . . I don't know what your troubles with the Columbia production executives are. But I don't believe they are such as can not be adjusted so that innocent persons may not suffer."

Barbara responded in a telegram:

I ASKED FOR FIFTY THOUSAND A PICTURE FOR MY THREE REMAINING PICTURES . . . STOP . . . [COLUMBIA] REFUSED . . . STOP . . . I THEN OFFERED TO MAKE THE FIRST PICTURE FOR THIRTY FIVE THOUSAND AND SECOND FOR FIFTY AND THE THIRD FOR FIFTY FIVE AND I WOULD MAKE ONE PICTURE FOR TWENTY THOUSAND IF COLUMBIA WOULD RELEASE ME FROM MAKING THE LAST TWO PICTURES STOP I BELIEVE THIS IN VIEW OF ALL CONDITIONS TO BE FAIR TO ALL PARTIES AND UNLESS COLUMBIA COMPLIES WITH MY REQUEST I WILL NEVER APPEAR IN A COLUMBIA PICTURE AGAIN STOP KINDEST.

During one of Barbara's heated arguments with Cohn, he let it be known that without Fay's belief in her and his persistence she wouldn't even be on the screen.

"What do you mean?" Barbara asked.

Cohn told her what Fay had kept from her for years, that after *Mexicali Rose,* Fay had offered to pay Barbara's salary if Cohn would give her another chance. Cohn had told Fay that she'd spoil any picture she was in.

"I tell you she's a great emotional actress," Fay had said to Cohn. "You take up the option and I'll not only pay her salary, I'll pay half the production cost."

"That won't make the picture any better," Cohn had said. "I don't want her for nothing. She's rotten."

"That's a damned lie," Barbara said to Cohn when she heard the story. Cohn shrugged. "Ask him."

Fay admitted the truth of the story. "I knew you had great stuff. I was afraid if Columbia fired you, you might never let go in front of a camera again."

Night Nurse was a standout at the box office along with *Dirigible, The Smiling Lieutenant,* and *A Free Soul. The Miracle Woman* wasn't faring as well, along with *An American Tragedy, Daddy Long Legs,* and *Pardon Us,* Laurel and Hardy's first full-length picture.

Louella Parsons wrote in the *Los Angeles Examiner:*

> This town of supreme sophistication and hardboiled philosophy has been busy analyzing the Barbara Stanwyck case. A scattered few think it just sweet that Barbara is willing to give up a flourishing career for her husband. The more thoughtful, practical souls are frankly worried over the future of the little red-haired girl who is so content to bask in the shadow of Frank Fay's fame . . .
>
> Frank was the fairhaired lad of Warners. He took his wife's devotion as a matter of fact, as his due. Then . . . Frank was through and Barbara was sitting on top of the world, in demand by two studios and working picture after picture. If Frank Fay is as devoted to Barbara as she is to him, he will urge her to fulfill her contracts. I do not mean to imply that Frank Fay is selfish and self-centered. But from all I gather it is Barbara who is making all the sacrifices.

"If you only knew what [Fay] has gone through," said Barbara in response, "helping me to finish what I started by myself—and then taking the blame for most of it." Some of Barbara's friends "cut me cold," she said, "as if afraid to contaminate themselves by speaking to me."

Fay's picture *Bright Lights* was released and barely broke even. Despite that and Barbara's own troubles, and Fay's dislike of Hollywood, they were around town, even playing in the Los Angeles Tennis Club Pacific Southwest Tournament with the Clive Brookses, Bill Wellman and Marjorie Crawford, Richard Dix, Phillips Holmes, and William Powell.

Fay's drinking was getting him into trouble with the law. While driving, he hit a man and his wife when his car drove across the white line, and he was later arrested on suspicion of driving while intoxicated.

With Frank Fay, arrested at home and booked at Central Police Station on charges of suspicion of drunk driving and a hit-and-run—driving on the wrong side of the road on Beverly Boulevard and crashing his car into another in midafternoon. He was released on $1,500 bail. August 1932.

He got into a fight with Eddie Mannix at the Brown Derby. Both men were separated by the state boxing commissioner, who happened to be dining with Fay. Fay's anger and vindictiveness were well-known from his days in New York. When he had appeared in *Harry Delmar's Revels* and the show ran into financial trouble, he decided to get rid of the producers and take it over himself. Billy Rose had yet to be paid any royalties and complained to the Dramatists Guild; the guild threatened to close the show if Fay didn't pay Rose the $1,100 owed him. Fay went to the bank, got a sack filled with 110,000 pennies, brought it to Rose's apartment, and emptied its contents on the floor of his living room.

Fay's drinking was making him more violent. During one of his spells, Barbara called his doctor to ask him to come to the house to help her. When Dr. Willis arrived, Fay flew into an angry rage, got a large knife, and threatened to kill the doctor. He was so violent and unruly that Willis had him committed to the Osteopathic Hospital in Los Angeles. As soon as he was released, he began to drink again.

• • •

Warner Bros. was drawn into the fray between Barbara and Columbia Pictures. Warner's official position was that Barbara would have to resolve her differences with Columbia before she could begin her new Warner contract. The studio issued a statement saying that it did not want to be in the same bind that Columbia was now in with actors breaking their contracts and demanding salary increases. Barbara's refusal to work cost Columbia money in lost bookings and in preparations of other stories.

Capra lost four weeks before starting to direct *Gallagher*. Cohn was adamant about Barbara's salary: the actress was under contract to make *Forbidden* for $20,000, and Cohn wasn't going to let her arbitrarily demand and receive additional money, and certainly not an additional $30,000.

Despite Warner's public stance with regard to her new contract, Barbara went into rehearsals for *Safe in Hell*. Columbia filed an application for an injunction saying that Barbara had jumped her contract to work for Warner Bros. and asked the court for a temporary restraining order preventing her from working for any company other than Columbia.

As part of the injunction, Columbia gathered the forces of many of the other studio heads, getting sworn affidavits from each, including Irving Thalberg, in charge of production at Metro-Goldwyn-Mayer; Louis B. Mayer, chief executive of Metro-Goldwyn-Mayer; Joseph Schenck, managing head of United Artists Corporation; Winfield Sheehan, chief executive in charge of production at Fox Film Corporation; and Jesse Lasky, chief executive of Paramount Publix Corporation. Each affidavit, attached to the complaint for an injunction, stated that the deposed executive knew the work of Barbara Stanwyck and was familiar with her ability and how "it would be difficult, if not impossible, to successfully replace her."

Barbara was twenty-four years old. Powerful men—the Hollywood establishment, except for Warner Bros.—were allied against her. Right or wrong, Barbara stood her ground and refused to concede.

An emissary from Columbia Pictures was sent to Malibu to reason with her. Barbara made it clear that if she didn't get her price, she was quite contented to sit on the sands in front of her house with her two terriers. "What are you going to do, Miss Stanwyck, if the studios blacklist you for breaking your contract?" asked the studio representative. "You can't go back to the theater because Wall Street is behind both stage and screen and you can't go into radio because Wall Street has radio interests and wouldn't let you."

"Well," said Barbara, "do you suppose Wall Street can prevent me from sitting right here looking at the waves?"

Barbara's attorney maintained that she had fulfilled her three-picture contract with Columbia, that *Illicit,* the picture she'd made for Warner Bros. on loan-out, was Columbia's third picture. Columbia notified Warner Bros. of the injunction; Warner sent a perfunctory letter to Charles Cradick informing Barbara of Columbia's stance.

Warner was awaiting the outcome of the case and gave a copy of the script of *Safe in Hell* to the English actress Dorothy Mackaill to take over Barbara's part of Gilda Karlson. The twenty-eight-year-old blond-haired Mackaill, a former London Hippodrome and *Ziegfeld Follies* beauty, was under a one-year renewed contract to First National to make four pictures at $42,500 per picture. Mackaill appeared with John Barrymore in *The Lotus Eaters,* became a star in silent pictures—her first starring picture, *Bits of Life,* was made in 1921—and successfully made the transition to talkies. Mackaill the previous year had starred with Fay in *Bright Lights.*

She was slim and an accomplished athlete who loved to play tennis, particularly at San Simeon; William Randolph Hearst was taken with her. She had a sense of humor and was full of fun. Mackaill's face and the slope of her hazel eyes resembled Barbara's, though Mackaill didn't have Barbara's combination of gutsiness and softness, a look that made Barbara on-screen all the more touching and resonant.

Barbara was determined to make *Safe in Hell* and let the studio know she was ready to work.

In court before Judge Douglas Edmonds, Barbara testified that her contract with Columbia had expired three weeks before, that she'd made three pictures under the terms of her contract, pictures that were to be made within a certain period of time and that the time limit had expired on August 14.

When the court finally granted Columbia its injunction, Barbara and Mackaill were both in production as Gilda Karlson for *Safe in Hell.* Barbara was working with Wellman; Mackaill as backup was in wardrobe fittings. The court found that Barbara contractually owed Columbia Pictures one more film and that either she fulfill the obligation or she would be barred by court action from appearing in any other picture.

Harry Cohn had won his victory and called Barbara to ask her to come in to meet with him. "We'll see what we can do about giving you more money so you will feel better about things," he said. Barbara said, "Nuts," and hung up the receiver. Frank made Barbara call and apologize. Barbara went to see Cohn.

She agreed to make three additional pictures for Columbia, alternating with those she was to make for Warner. Barbara fought for a salary of $35,000 for the first picture and $50,000 for the remaining two but agreed to Cohn's offer to pay her $25,000 per picture instead of the contractually agreed-upon $20,000 for the first and $25,000 for each additional picture.

"Everything was very nice. He didn't have to do a thing for me," said Barbara. "He'd won the suit."

Barbara was set to make *Forbidden.* Warner tried to work out an arrangement with Columbia for her to continue with *Safe in Hell,* but negotiations fell apart.

Barbara was back at Columbia Pictures.

FOUR

"Theoretically Dangerous Overload"

Fannie Hurst's *Back Street,* originally called *Grand Passion,* was serialized in *Cosmopolitan* magazine during the fall and winter of 1930–1931.

It was said of Hurst that "no other living American woman has gone so far in fiction in so short a time." Her work was "overwhelmingly prodigal of both feeling and language . . . a succession of shocks, sparks and purple fireworks. [Hurst] mixes naked, realistic detail with simple unrestrained emotion," wrote Robert Littell in 1928, "[and] the result is lurid, magnificently lurid."

Cosmopolitan began publishing Hurst in 1914. By 1930, the magazine had published forty of her stories. *Cosmopolitan* paid $40,000 for the rights to *Back Street.* The book rights were bought by Hearst's newly formed Cosmopolitan Book Corporation for an advance of $16,500, more than double the money the author had received from her previous publishers, Harper & Brothers and Alfred A. Knopf.

Back Street, Hurst's seventh novel, was published in January 1931 and was described by *The New York Times* as "the most ambitious and carefully wrought novel Fannie Hurst has produced in years." The book was on the best-seller list, where it stayed until more than forty thousand copies had sold.

Soon after the publication of *Back Street,* Universal Pictures bought the film rights and Frank Capra, who was hell-bent on beating Universal to the screen, took the basic plot of Hurst's best seller and many of the details and wrote his own story, *Forbidden,* which Jo Swerling adapted.

At the novel's center is Ray Schmidt of Cincinnati, a girl who runs wild, living amid the solid German merchants of "Munich-on-the-Ohio," a stunning up-to-the-minute-looking girl, working in her father's concern (Schmidt's Trimmings and Findings). She entertains the traveling salesmen who come to the store to sell their goods ("she's a girl with a nest egg in her sack; never mind where she got it"). She's acquired a reputation for being "fly" without being "out-and-out fast."

At twenty years old, Ray is mourning the sudden death of her father. The store is being taken over by a St. Louis button factory, and Ray is feeling dispossessed from the world she's known forever. She is considering marrying Kurt Shendler, of Shendler's Bicycle Repair Shop (he may be crude, but he has a future and he's of her own kind). Ray's life is solidly, if passionlessly, falling into place until she meets Walter Saxel, a young Jewish man from a good family, and suddenly for Ray nothing else matters except Walter.

Her days are punctuated by their being together, planning their meetings, and being inconspicuous about being seen together. Walter worries about his mother finding out he is seeing a shiksa. An introduction between Mrs. Saxel and Ray is arranged, but Ray's sister, always so proper around boys, finds herself "in trouble," and Ray is there to help. The long-awaited meeting with Walter's mother is postponed and never takes place. As a result, Ray's life is changed forever.

Walter marries someone of his own "race"; Ray leaves Cincinnati for New York. And when they meet accidentally, six years later, Walter is a junior partner in the midst of a brilliant banking career and married with two children. Ray is rooming on West Twenty-Third Street at a boardinghouse and working at a firm on Greene Street buying dressmaker's findings, ribbons, veilings, and the like. They come together again (Walter to Ray: "My feeling for you and my feeling for my wife and children are things separate and apart. I can be loyal to both these feelings because they are so different").

Soon Walter takes an apartment for Ray, and she gives up her promising job. Ray turns away from friends and family and lives in a corner of Walter's life, her isolation becoming more complete as their affair becomes more clandestine. As the days and months turn into years, Ray is barely getting by on the meager amounts of money that Walter gives her (he sees her sparse existence as an emblem of the purity of their love). He relies on Ray's counsel for his own ever-growing success and spends money lavishly on his own flourishing family. As the novel moves to its final moments in Aix-les-Bains, Ray's life of love and sacrifice is tragically portrayed in Hurst's "courageous," ambitious novel.

Hurst's melodramatic writing lent itself to motion pictures. In Hurst's worlds, *Vanity Fair* said, "shop girls appear as heroines." The combination of character and large incident made the books successfully adaptable to a dramatic visual medium.

Hurst wrote about working men and women determined to rise out of their class. At the heart of her writing was the experience of the Jewish immigrant in American society. Hurst was herself a Jewish girl from the Midwest. F. Scott Fitzgerald proclaimed her and Edna Ferber "the Yiddish descendants of O. Henry." Hurst's writing had more of the feel of Theodore Dreiser and Sinclair Lewis than of O. Henry, in the people Hurst wrote about, in the airless circumstances of their lives, in the flatness and constancy of their struggle.

By the time *Back Street* was published in 1931, the studios had made sixteen pictures from Hurst's stories, plays, and novels. Famous Players–Lasky bought the rights to *Humoresque* in 1920, a year after the novel was published. United Artists distributed *Lummox* in 1930, based on Hurst's novel, directed by Herbert Brenon. The same year Warner Bros. made *The Painted Angel* from a Hurst story, "Give This Little Girl a Hand," inspired by Texas Guinan; the studio's counterpart, First National, remade *Back Pay* (originally made eight years earlier). Jack Warner, vice president in charge of production for Warner Bros., saw Hurst as someone who "knew how to reach human hearts and bring life's joys and sorrows to countless millions of readers."

Capra was familiar with Fannie Hurst's rich sensibility and subject matter. *The Younger Generation,* a picture he'd made in 1929 from *It Is to Laugh,* Hurst's play based on her story "The Gold in Fish," followed Capra's big success with *Submarine.*

The Younger Generation was a picture about assimilation, something Capra had experienced firsthand. It centers on the son of a junk dealer, a Jewish immigrant, who grows up in New York's Lower East Side ashamed of what he is and where he comes from—his past, his family, his Jewishness—and is determined to get a piece of the American dream. He changes his name from Goldfish to Fish, becomes a successful antiques dealer, and soon is traveling in a moneyed fast (non-Jewish) crowd. He bestows upon his old-world parents what he sees as the gift of freedom—a life away from their Delancey Street ghetto—and moves them into his new Fifth Avenue apartment. He cannot escape his shame and, in a terrible moment, introduces his parents to his friends as his servants. Rather than finding freedom living on Fifth Avenue, the father longs for the old neighborhood whose ways he cherishes and, out of his profound sense of loss for their former life, becomes ill. The family, once so close and rooted in their origins and traditions, begins to fracture as both generations become stranded between two worlds.

Capra's *Younger Generation* starred Jean Hersholt, Rosa Rosanova, Ricardo Cortez, and Lina Basquette. Capra originally shot it as a silent picture but reshot sequences to make use of the new technology on a soundstage located on Santa Monica Boulevard.

As an immigrant, Capra understood the impulse to turn away from the past—and his differentness—and become Americanized and successful.

With Hurst's *Back Street,* Capra understood the dilemma of falling in love with someone who was married (as was Barbara) and unwilling to leave her husband (as she was with Fay) and, despite himself, being helpless to end the affair. Capra was inspired by his deep feelings for Barbara and was free with an adaptation to take the basic plot of *Back Street* and project his own intimate feelings and fantasies onto his characters and story. It was in the borrowed nature of the piece that Capra was able to show his emotions about Barbara, himself, and Frank Fay.

In the character Lulu in *Forbidden,* Capra created the woman of his dreams: loyal and ready to sacrifice everything for love. She is a small-town librarian who sees that life is passing her by and one day breaks out of her dreary routinized existence to go off on a cruise to Havana, the city of romance, fall in love with a married man, and stay with him for a lifetime. Capra went one step further with the character: he has her sacrifice her love to her ideal and then admit that she was wrong to do so. That the woman loves the married man is the first of Capra's big wish fulfillments; the second is her fidelity to true love and to the lover.

Bob Grover, with Lulu's selfless and wise counsel, has worked his way from successful lawyer to district attorney to gubernatorial candidate. Years into their secret life together, he is about to win the victory he's worked decades to achieve, but realizes he no longer cares about appearances, about his career, about what his wife—or the voters—will think; his pursuit has become meaningless to him. Of single value to him now is his love for Lulu. He wants to be with her openly.

Lulu had willingly sacrificed their illegitimate child to help Grover's political climb, allowing Grover and his wife to adopt the little girl. Even with her daughter grown and engaged, when Grover begs Lulu to go off with him just before the start of the gubernatorial campaign, Lulu is still hell-bent on noble self-sacrifice; she cares about appearances for *his* sake, even if Grover no longer does, and refuses his offer. Later, as Grover lies dying, Capra has Lulu say that she was wrong not to have allowed them an open life together and risk the consequences.

Capra created a woman who, throughout years of secrecy and shame—giving up her child for the man she loves, marrying a man she doesn't care about to protect the man she does, committing an act of murder to defend her lover's career—remains utterly faithful to her lover, and to their forbid-

The book jacket for the picture's novelization. (GROSSET & DUNLAP)

den love, and finally, too late for both of them, sees the mistake of her willful self-sacrifice.

Capra added a third element to the story: another man who is in pursuit of the truth of Grover's secret life and also in love with Lulu. Holland is a star investigative reporter on the newspaper where Lulu works and is determined to get the goods on Grover. He's smitten with Lulu from the moment he sees her. She isn't at all flustered by his attention, by his flirting; Holland never goes beyond the acceptable with her, but it's clear she wouldn't care if he did; she is in control of their (to her) meaningless flirtation. Holland remains devoted despite Lulu's jokey, loving indifference. He doesn't press her, but he doesn't give up, and oddly he doesn't settle for less—he doesn't marry anyone else.

The years pass; Grover rises in political life, and he and Lulu are still together. Holland begins to close in on the secret of Grover's life, and Lulu, to throw Holland off the trail, agrees to marry him. When Holland realizes it is his wife who is at the center of Grover's life, his rage at the betrayal, and his wrath, set in motion Lulu's final sacrifice for the man she loves and her ultimate rejection of the man she doesn't.

Capra projected onto both men aspects of Frank Fay and divided his own impulses—parceling out his own complex feelings—between Grover and Holland. Bob Grover, the conventional husband who is also the lover, is both terrible and great. He is first seen drunk and passed out on Lulu's bed. He is introduced as dangerous, misbehaving, similar to Frank Fay. But Grover is given other qualities: he is refined, sensitive, elegant, loving, faithful, an idealized Capra.

Capra made Grover the opposite of the male stereotype who's got it all—the sexy woman on the side and a public wife with the appearance of respectability. Lulu sees that Grover isn't going to leave his wife. He wants his wife's money, and he wants the career. So far, Grover is in type as the cad. But his reversal of character—his second, after being introduced as a drunk and turning out to be charming—is revealed when he tracks down Lulu at her apartment. When they are together on the stairs of her building, it's clear that he loves her. When he is told that the little girl at the top of the stairs calling to Lulu is his own child as well, he's delighted and full of love for both mother and daughter.

Holland, the courtier who becomes the husband, is vigorous, vulgar, ruddy, also like Fay. His pursuit of Lulu over the years is appealing but becomes ruthless when he discovers her betrayal. Lulu refuses to allow her "husband" to bring ruin to her lover. Holland reminds her that she is married to him, and his rage and brutality lead to his own death as Lulu shoots him again and again to protect Grover, Capra getting his wish and doing in Fay.

Holland also has aspects of Capra in him: he's the popular, savvy media guy, the man of the people out to expose the cover-up.

Capra portrays Grover and Lulu's forbidden affair as being one of true love, unlike either of the marriages, which he makes villainous.

He also incorporates scenes that are totally modern, that have the sting of real life, and that jump out as not belonging to the formula of the genre. When Lulu and Grover attempt to break up in the park, she leaves him in the midst of a heavy rain—Capra's signature element in his love scenes to make them a "bit offbeat so people don't laugh at it"—only to turn around and come back to him, still sitting on the bench, wet and oblivious to it and stunned by his feelings of emptiness at the loss of Lulu; she finds herself incapable of leaving him because she loves him so much. In another scene, Lulu refuses to open the door to her apartment when Grover comes to find her after a year of trying to track her down, a year in which Lulu has given birth to their child. Lulu runs away from Grover on the stairs but comes back to him.

Adolphe Menjou was Grover. Menjou had already made a profession out of playing a cad, beginning in 1923 with Chaplin's *A Woman of Paris,* in which he played the dapper boulevardier who seduces, keeps, and discards a woman who ends up being a prostitute. Menjou went on to star in the first French all-talking movie and then worked in Italian, Spanish, and German talking pictures before returning to Hollywood. He had just had a big success as Walter Burns in the picture of Ben Hecht and Charles MacArthur's *Front Page,* directed by Lewis Milestone. Bill Wellman referred to Menjou as "the debonair Frenchman from Pittsburgh."

The newspaperman Al Holland was originally to have been played by Paul Muni, but Ralph Bellamy, a leading man in stock who was brought to

Hollywood in 1930 and who'd appeared in three pictures since, was borrowed from Fox for the role of the reporter.

Shooting on *Forbidden* began at the end of September 1931, two weeks after Barbara's dispute with Cohn was settled and a month after Capra finished shooting *Gallagher.*

As *Forbidden* started shooting, Fay went to New York to appear as the headline at RKO's Palace, his first appearance there in a year. He was to replace Edward G. Robinson and Kate Smith for $4,000 for the week. Fay, known as the King of Vaudeville Gulch, was coming into the Palace after Kate Smith's eleventh consecutive week there, breaking his own ten-week record in 1927, which Barbara had commemorated by giving Frank a cigarette case with a royal crown of jewels. Now, after the disaster of *God's Gift to Women* and the poor showing of Fay's appearance at the Strand, his drinking had progressed. He was getting drunk more frequently and staying drunk for longer periods of time. Barbara refused to give up on him; she was determined to make the marriage work.

Barbara and Menjou were shooting a scene on horseback at Laguna Beach that was to take place during their two-week idyll in Havana. They were to ride their horses on the windswept beach along the water's edge of what was to be Emerald Bay. The cameras were set up on a cliff high above the water in order to shoot them riding below and, said Joe Walker, Capra's cameraman, to capture "the morning light shimmering in a path on the ocean."

For the long shot Capra used a double. "I have always been afraid of horses," said Barbara. Capra wanted a closer shot, and Barbara, still wearing a brace from her last fall, agreed to get on the horse if Capra shot the scene quickly. Barbara shut her eyes tight and climbed on the horse. "He sensed, as horses do," said Barbara, "that I was afraid."

They were set to go. "The grips turned reflectors to catch the morning sun," said Walker. "The horse was high-strung. Barbara began to ride the horse at a canter through the heavy wet sands. The sudden flash of light directed toward the horse, startled [the animal]," said Walker. It reared, lost its footing in the loose sand, and fell backward, falling on Barbara and rolling over on her. The sand absorbed most of the force of the fall and the weight of the horse. Barbara said, "While [the horse] was trying frantically to rise, his hoofs kept striking my back."

Menjou and the crew pulled Barbara free. She was unconscious for fifteen minutes. When she finally came to, she felt the muscles in her legs tightening. Capra wanted her to go to the hospital. "Hurry," she said. "We'll have to finish this scene, my legs are stiffening."

Menjou and Barbara walked into the water as called for, swam fifty yards offshore, and returned to the beach. As Barbara walked out of the water, she lost consciousness and was taken to the Laguna Beach hospital. No bones were broken, but she suffered two sprained ankles and a dislocated coccyx.

After Barbara's fall, some of Fay's New York friends doubted he would stay in New York and open at the Palace, despite a signed contract. They took bets that Frank would cancel the engagement, which he did and returned to Los Angeles by train two days after Barbara's accident. The press, ready to describe Fay as difficult, called the circumstances surrounding his decision to cancel "strange" since Columbia's press department had minimized Barbara's accident by calling it "almost a slide off the horse" and said that she was "unhurt." In truth, the doctors told Barbara that she might not walk again and that if she did, she would have to use crutches.

Barbara refused to miss a day's work. At the end of each day's shooting, she went to the hospital to spend the night in traction. Capra had a slant board built for her to lean against between takes.

One of the camera assistants, Al Keller, who'd been with Capra for two years, said of Barbara, "Her courage, to me, was inspirational. This gal had that much integrity that she wouldn't leave the film." He thought she was "something else."

Barbara recovered slowly and continued to work, even attending the premiere of George Arliss's *Alexander Hamilton* at Warner's new theater on Wilshire Boulevard along with others, including James Cagney, Carole Lombard, Jean Harlow, and Joan Crawford.

Capra rehearsed Barbara with the rest of the actors and crew of *Forbidden* in a walk-through to go over the moves so the camera could follow her. The rehearsals were sketchy; Barbara spoke her lines, but they were barely audible. Ed Bernds, the head of the sound crew on the picture, who'd worked with Capra on three other pictures, described his rehearsals with Barbara as done at "half speed." Bernds knew the pace would be faster for camera and sound and the dialogue louder. "We were not given a sound rehearsal," he said. "When Western Electric designed the sound system, they put the mixers in a monitor booth, and you couldn't see the set. It was a glass-fronted case, hung on the wall of the stage, or maybe, in the case of Stage 1 at Columbia, pierced through the wall."

During the making of *Forbidden,* the mixers, in the upstairs monitor room, often recorded a scene they couldn't see. "We were supposed to be able to look down from our monitor room and see the set," said Bernds. "But that would have been wasteful of stage space, and often we'd be looking at the back wall of a set. When it came time to shoot the scene, camera and sound were put at great pressure to get the scene right. We were the best that Columbia had, and we coped pretty well."

"Everyone was trying to do his best," said Al Keller. "Capra inspired 110 percent from his crew. We felt that working for him, we were the elite. But he wouldn't tolerate anyone who couldn't cut it. Boy, you did it the first time or you weren't there."

"Menjou and Bellamy performed dutifully in the strange, subdued rehearsals," Bernds said. "When the cameras turned and [Barbara] responded with searing, emotional performances, [Menjou and Bellamy] responded brilliantly." Capra was a director who wanted his audiences to forget they were watching a picture. He wanted "interesting characterizations" and wanted his cast to "ad-lib, to build up little personal traits in character and story to create vitality and warmth."

Capra might shoot a scene many times over without stopping the camera. The camera was kept rolling while the actors would be called back again and again to redo the scene. This was to get around Harry Cohn's ironclad rule that, as Capra said, "no director could order more than one 'take' printed of any scene, regardless of how many takes the director had shot." Cohn even told his directors to turn off the lights in the men's room. "Why are you wasting my electricity?" he'd say. Cohn was not fooled by Capra's ruse, but it saved time and money, so Cohn went along with it.

Capra found that shooting this way not only allowed him to get as many takes as he wanted. By the second or third take, without time to be coiffed and polished by makeup people and to lose the mood, the actors, Capra said, "lost their superficial aplomb . . . they began sweating, mussing their hair, rumpling their clothes." The perfect looks were gone, "forgotten were the minutiae of cues, position tapes on the floor . . . they became real human beings playing scenes—and believing it."

In the picture, Lulu goes from being a young girl to an elderly woman. The makeup man, Monte Westmore, made sketches, experimented, and then spent two hours working with Barbara each morning to age her for her scenes as an older woman.

Barbara said, "I just ask the cameraman, in great humility, to please make me look human. You know, just make me look human, that's all."

In the early days of sound, three cameras were used to help in the difficult process of cutting sound track. By the time *Forbidden* was in production, sound track was easy to cut.

"Capra wanted to keep [the shot] just long enough to hold the two actors," said Bernds. "And we followed Barbara as it became a two-shot when she was close to Bellamy."

With Capra and Adolphe Menjou during *Forbidden,* 1931. "What those two [Capra and Willard Mack] saw in me," said Barbara, "I still don't know." (PHOTOFEST)

Capra liked to shoot a lot of angles; they gave him flexibility in cutting.

"The scene where Barbara shoots Bellamy is dynamite acting at a high intensity, very high intensity," Bernds said. "[Barbara's] voice was tough on sound because at times when she screamed, the Western Electric sound system went into a state of theoretically dangerous overload."

Bernds watched Capra with Barbara. He was aware that the director was interested in her more than just as an actress. "It showed in subtle ways," said Bernds. "In the way he looked at her, the way he talked to her. It was unmistakable."

"It is true," said Capra, "that directors often fall in love with their leading ladies—at least while making a film together. They come to know each other so intimately—more so than some married couples—and their relationship is so close emotionally, so charged creatively, it can easily drift into a Pygmalion and Galatea affinity; or, as true in some cases, it can slip into a hypnotic Svengali and Trilby association."

Bernds, as the head mixer, could hear "an awful lot of stuff through the microphone," he said, "that nobody else heard." It was clear to Bernds that Barbara admired Capra, that she "revered him as a director. But I'm not sure that she welcomed his love," said Bernds. "He seemed more smitten with her than she was with him."

Between scenes Bernds heard Menjou talk to Capra about the upcoming 1932 election and about Menjou's concerns that the "communists—the Democrats—would win the election, raise taxes, destroy the value of the dollar," and deprive Menjou of some of his wealth. In response to a rumor that the country, with Hoover out of office and a new, Democratic administration in power, might abandon the gold standard, as had Europe and England, Bernds heard Menjou tell Capra, "I've got gold stashed in safety deposit boxes all over town—they'll never get an ounce from me."

Menjou and Capra railed against the governor of New York, Franklin Roosevelt, whom they hated and who was in the running as the Democratic candidate for president of the United States. Capra was a Republican, as was Frank Fay. Each man reinforced Barbara's Republican Party beliefs; her family had been longtime Republicans. Capra, Fay, and Stanwyck believed that if they had risen up from extreme poverty and made something of themselves, why shouldn't everyone be able to do the same. The government had no business meddling in their financial affairs. The country's going off the gold standard would create havoc; money would be devalued; recession and more unemployment would result. The Hoover administration denied federal responsibility for relief of the unemployed. Governor Roosevelt in a speech before the New York State Legislature in which he asked, "What is the State?" put forth the idea that "modern society, acting through its Government, owe[d] the definite obligation to prevent the starvation or the dire want of any of its fellow men and women who try to maintain themselves but cannot . . . [A]id must be extended by Government, not as a matter of charity, but as a matter of social duty."

Mae Clarke was at Columbia making *The Final Edition* and trying to make some sense of the split in her friendship with Barbara. "I wish we could get together and straighten things out," Mae said. Barbara told Mae she didn't have time to see her.

During production on *Forbidden,* Frank Fay was aware that something was happening between his wife and Capra. His drinking grew worse as his angry rages intensified.

The last day of shooting of *Forbidden* was November 3. That evening Barbara and Fay went to a party in Los Angeles. Frank's father was staying with his son and daughter-in-law and called, frantic: their house was on fire. By the time Fay and Barbara got to Malibu, the house was a smoldering pile of ashes and debris. The fire was still going, being fanned by a strong sea wind; houses nearby were burning. A bucket brigade of more than twenty members of the Malibu colony had struggled to overcome the blaze before the fire departments of Malibu, Santa Monica, Las Flores, and Topanga Canyon arrived and fought to control the fire for the next hour.

Nothing of the Fays' house was left. It was in a state of blackened rubble. The fire had mysteriously started next door at the then-unoccupied home of their neighbor, F. Nash Carton, a banker, and went unchecked, destroying three houses, including the Fays'.

The damage to Barbara and Frank's house amounted to $35,000. Most of Barbara's valuables were destroyed. They were of little importance to her. "I'm not proud about possessions," she said. After the fire, two of Barbara's diamond bracelets were found. "Diamonds don't burn," she said. But the diamond bracelet given to her by Willard Mack for her opening in *The Noose* was lost.

"I'm not crying about the house. That's gone and it's not worth crying over." What upset Barbara more than the loss of the house and all of her valuables was losing a photograph of her sister Millie, "my sister who died— and—I'm not sure I can get another one like it."

Capra finished filming *Forbidden* and left for Europe for eight weeks, his first long holiday in four years since going to work for Harry Cohn.

Capra had been "steadily dating" a widow, Lucille Warner Reyburn, "a smallish, attractive young lady with short, dark hair and perky bangs." Lu Reyburn was the daughter of a California fig rancher, had attended two years of college at Berkeley, and, as Capra said, had "read every book ever written."

Capra met Lu when she'd come to San Diego to visit a friend on the set of *Flight,* his fourth picture for Harry Cohn. He had driven Lu back to the Hotel del Coronado and walked her to the door of her room and kissed her good night. "I knew," Capra said. "She knew."

They saw each other regularly during the next two years. Lu never brought up the subject of marriage, but "what the hell," Capra said. "You don't have to spell it out. She wanted to marry me."

Capra had been married before, to Helen Howell, an actress, as he'd begun writing gags for the Our Gang comedies at Mack Sennett. The marriage ran into trouble as Capra worked longer hours at the Sennett studio writing Harry Langdon pictures and spent less time at home with his wife. Helen felt that her husband was "more married to work than to her . . . [She] wanted a full-time companion," Capra said. "Not a part-time successful one." The marriage took a turn for the worse when Helen was told by her doctors that she was unable to have children. "Nothing can depress an Italian more," said Capra, "than finding out he can't have children."

Lu Reyburn wasn't in show business. Before she met Capra, she'd worked as a stenographer and secretary. Capra said, "She liked movies [and] was a good audience." She championed Capra and wasn't jealous of his work. But after the failure of his first marriage, he was wary about remarrying.

Lu wanted Frank and a home and children. Capra wanted Barbara. Barbara didn't want to leave Fay. Capra's shifting moods were almost as intense as Fay's. "The Irish go through their black depressions too," said Barbara. "I know. I'm an Irisher. And you can ask that Irish person why and he can't tell you, it's just a black cloud that comes over us. Well, the Italians are a very emotional race," she said. "You can say hello to an Italian and they might go into an explosion. But that's part of their charm. Mr. Capra was not afraid to show emotion. He understood it."

As a director, Capra was there for Barbara in a way other directors weren't. "He was my 'angel,' " she said. "He babied me and pampered me." No one worked with Barbara as a director the way Capra did. But could she support him, the way he did her, as a man and a woman rather than as director and actress, working separately? She knew she couldn't be a housewife; she'd tried to be that for Fay, and it hadn't worked. Despite Fay's possessiveness, his worsening alcoholism, and his explosive rages, he'd known from the beginning that Barbara couldn't have children of her own. He accepted that—in fact, he didn't want children—and adored Barbara anyway.

Capra went off to Europe without Lu, or Barbara, and instead took his friend Al Roscoe. Lu saw both men off on the train for New York. During his travels, Capra wired her from London and Paris telling her how much he missed her.

Before Capra left on his holiday, Lu had been unaware of his feelings for Barbara. She was equally unaware that while Capra was telling Lu he was nervous about getting remarried, he was trying to persuade Barbara to leave Fay and marry him. Somehow Lu found out. Capra received an angry telegram from her. She was hurt and felt betrayed. Capra begged her to forgive him. Lu refused to respond to his wires. Finally, Lu wired him that she was going to be married to someone else. Capra became frantic. He wired back, pleading with her to reconsider, even suggesting they marry upon his return to New York. Lu wired back accepting Capra's proposal. Capra cut his holiday short and returned to New York. It was reported in the New York press that Frank Capra "likes actresses and enjoys working with them but when it came to picking a second bride, he chose a home girl."

Capra (left) with his wife, "Lu," and Robert Riskin, circa 1937.
(PHOTOFEST)

Cohn made the wedding arrangements, and Capra and Lu were married by Cohn's friend the Brooklyn Supreme Court judge Mitchell May. The Capras' honeymoon was to have been a cruise to Cuba, the same cruise that changes the course of Jo Swerling and Capra's mousy heroine of *Forbidden;* instead, Capra and Lu went to the Adirondacks' Lake Placid for the 1932 Winter Olympics. On Capra's return, he was to begin work on a picture called *Tampico,* set in Mexico about a corrupt American oil driller and based on the 1926 novel by Joseph Hergesheimer. Swerling was at work on the script.

After the Malibu fire Fay and Barbara took an apartment in town and began to look for land to build a house, which Frank wanted to design himself. They agreed to appear for a week on the stage at the Paramount Theatre in Los Angeles to accompany the feature playing there, George Bancroft's *Rich Man's Folly,* directed by John Cromwell and based on Dickens's *Dombey and Son.* The movie was considered somber, but the Fays' singing, dancing, and wisecracks, which they had performed together before leaving the East for Hollywood, were a hit. Fay said, "We've both missed the audience reaction which means so much to anyone who has been on the other side of the footlights as much as we have . . . the audience is always lacking in a studio."

Fay's script for a picture called *A Fool's Advice* from his own story had

Mr. and Mrs. Frank Fay, January 1934. (CULVER PICTURES)

been turned down by every studio in town. He decided he would produce the picture himself and so needed the $8,000 he and Barbara were being paid to perform. In their act for the Paramount, Barbara incorporated the acrobatic dancing of her club days before going on the Broadway stage. At the conclusion of the dance, Barbara cartwheeled off the stage. The columnists referred to the cartwheels as "vulgar exhibitions." "[That] statement seemed entirely unnecessary," said Barbara, "and I sent [a reporter] word that if he would visit me, I'd black his eye. He never visited me." "People were horrified because the mean old Frank Fay forced his wife to do cartwheels," said Barbara. "Frank had nothing to do with it. In fact, he argued against my doing a vaudeville turn and said, 'you're a dramatic actress now.' 'Well I can still hoof. Is there any law that says a dramatic actress can't have the use of her legs?' I *made* [Frank] let me. It was *all* my idea.

"I suppose, to be a perfect lady," said Barbara, "I should have made an entrance and told the audience about my latest starring picture. That's novel isn't it? Then I could have finished by doing one of the dramatic scenes. That would have been different too.

"In the first place, I wouldn't be caught doing such an idiotic act, and especially in a movie theatre. No one can possibly hear you beyond the twelfth row. Of course, Frank got all the blame from those who do not want a dramatic actress to show any versatility. I was so proud of those cartwheels," said Barbara. "I was proud of my dance when I was in vaudeville; I am still proud of it. I regard the dance as an old friend—and I have not forgotten old friends because good fortune has befallen me. But I suppose Frank was right—they weren't very lady-like."

Critics were equally upset that onstage Barbara was the straight man for Frank's jokes and acted as his stooge, feeding him lines for comedy. "Mr. Fay is essentially a comedian," said Barbara. "I am not. Therefore, to provide entertainment, I played 'straight man' and he supplied the laughs. I fed him lines for comedy the way I did in our act at the Palace. Audiences appeared to enjoy [it]; otherwise, we would have changed it."

Barbara was "getting almighty sick of [Frank] being on the spot" because of her actions.

"I am a star today," she said, "but give me one or two bad pictures and Hollywood will consider me a flop again. It isn't what you do or have done that counts here. It's what happens. That's why I have never understood the minds of the picture brains. And never will.

"The same is true nowhere else," she said. "On the stage, if an actress is once great, she is always great. Alice Brady hasn't had a good play in five years in New York. But Alice Brady is still considered a splendid actress by the producers. If they have what they think is a fine play, they still call Miss Brady and not somebody unknown and unskilled."

Barbara defended Fay against Hollywood and was angry about the way the town was treating him. Her outspokenness led to the press calling her "temperamental" and "hard to manage." She was quoted as saying that she "would rather live happily ever after and quietly with Frank Fay than be the biggest star in the business."

As Fay's drinking worsened, Barbara was caught between her husband, whom she fiercely loved and whose binges were beginning to frighten her, and the town whose false values she resented and whose continuous prediction of the demise of her marriage made her fight even more for her husband. In the midst of all this was her own deep ambition to work and keep working as an actress and to be perfect at it in an industry she was coming to love.

A Fool's Advice, which Fay was producing from his own story, was to be shot at Columbia at the same time that Barbara was filming *Zelda Marsh;* Fay's leading lady, Ruth Hall, was borrowed from Warner Bros.

Fay said of producing and making movies with his wife, whom he affectionately called Red or Shorty or Smack: "I want to use Mrs. Fay in as many of my own pictures as I am able to, but there are her contracts with other studios to be considered . . . Only a short time ago I approached a studio executive with the idea of borrowing her for a picture I have in mind and was told I couldn't have her at any price."

To remain in Los Angeles and enable Fay to work, Barbara and Frank were considering putting together a new edition of the *Nine O'Clock Revue* with Eddie Lambert, Eddie Borden, and Al Herman.

"If Frank is happy [in Los Angeles]," said Barbara, "nothing else matters."

FIVE

F•A•Y

1931–1932

Barbara's first picture under her new Warner contract was a remake of Edna Ferber's *So Big.* The novel was originally made into a picture in 1924 by First National, starring Colleen Moore as Selina Peake, Ben Lyon as Dirk DeJong, and Wallace Beery as Klass Poole. Warner remade it six years later as a two-reel short. A new contract between Ferber and Warner Bros. was signed in early December 1931 giving Miss Ferber an additional $20,000 for the rights to remake the picture and approval over the director. Ferber okayed Bill Wellman as the director, but she didn't want Barbara for the part of Selina Peake and refused to meet with her.

Production was to begin in mid-January 1932 following Barbara's work at Columbia making *Zelda Marsh,* based on the Charles G. Norris novel.

Barbara wanted the role of the sexual beauty and got it. The studio was set to adapt Norris's novel, published in 1927, but in the spring of 1931 the Production Code Association pronounced Norris's novel "full of dangerous material [abortion included] and immoral relations." *Zelda Marsh* was a sensational, melodramatic book about a young woman whose father dies and who goes to live with her aunt and uncle, falls in love with a young man, is driven by desire to sleep with him, is found out, and is sent away for three months to an institution for the disciplining and regeneration of fallen girls. When she gets out, she marries a man she doesn't love and begins a downward spiral, only to regain her life and make her way as a young actress, until she re-meets her first love, now terminally ill, and begins a life of redemption, choosing to give up everything she holds dear, to "leave her heart behind in order to gain her soul" and to care for the man she loves in his last months of life.

A story loosely based on the novel was written by the actress and writer

Sarah Y. Mason. A draft of the script was finished in December. The title of the picture was changed to *Shopworn*. The Production Code Association still thought the script "a very grave problem," given the lead becomes a prostitute after her release from the reformatory. The Code criticized the underlying sentiment of the script, which, it said, saw "prostitution and its reward as attractive" and found "decent and conventional society unsympathetic, narrow, selfish and insincere." In addition, the Code accused Columbia of trying to include "incidents of fornication, prostitution and a 'kept' woman." The Code suggested that the female lead struggle against other unscrupulous characters to "justify the sympathy and final admiration of the audience and of the people who represent the cleaner and conventional side of life in the story."

As with the dialogue Jo Swerling wrote for *Ladies of Leisure,* his script of *Shopworn,* with dialogue by Robert Riskin, ended up being a picture about class warfare, pitting the purity and honesty of the working class against the conniving, meddlesome ways of the selfish, hypocritical rich, thereby giving the Code the element it asked for. "Other unscrupulous characters" provided enough injustice for the audience to sympathize with the female lead.

Swerling and Riskin's script showed the precariousness of life, the poverty of life lived at the back of the store, and how hard most people except the rich have to work. At the heart of the script is the ennobling and wish-fulfilling quality of ordinary people—the dream of revenge: He treated her badly. She is sent to jail. They're all heels. She'll make them sorry. She'll be a star. Poof— she's a star. Swerling and Riskin tapped into the longing of the audience and made their dreams come true. Without Barbara's instrument of feeling and authenticity, the picture wouldn't have worked.

Kitty Lane is the daughter of an engineer who dies in an avalanche caused by one of his own explosions for a construction camp (his dying words of advice to his daughter: "You're going to find the world a tough place. Be tough yourself, then they can't hurt you . . . not if you learn to take blows on the chin").

To placate the Production Code Association, Swerling and Riskin show Kitty's rise as an acclaimed actress (as close to prostitution as Swerling and Riskin could get, at least in the eyes of society). By removing any hint of Kitty's sexual avidity, the picture lost its point: that the notorious young woman becomes shopworn not of her own accord but through necessity, when the young man fails to believe in her innocence (the inverse of Swerling's *Ladies of Leisure*), and that those who point the finger of scorn have little reason to brag of their own decency.

Harry Nicholas "Nick" Grinde was directing. Grinde, whose training was in vaudeville, where he wrote sketches for the foremost two-a-day stars of variety, was a screenwriter (*The Divorcee*) who'd worked as an assistant director (*Excuse Me; Upstage; Body and Soul*) for three years before becoming a full director. *Shopworn* was his eleventh picture in four years. Grinde was competent as a director, but Barbara didn't like the script or the experience of making the picture.

Regis Toomey, who played the college student who falls in love with Kitty Lane, said, "Barbara was not too happy about [the picture] from the beginning." Toomey wasn't sure if the cause of her unhappiness was "the script, the director—who was known as a 'B' picture director—or her leading man."

The picture's cameraman, Joe Walker, described the production as a "low budget affair." Barbara saw it, she said, as "one of those terrible pictures they sandwiched in."

She was on her own again as an actress. She could handle Riskin and Swerling's dialogue and fill it with heart. She creates a woman who is brave, open, simple, and plain. She summoned up the girl of Capra's *Ladies of Leisure, Miracle Woman,* and *Forbidden* and the tough, no-nonsense, brawling spitfire of Wellman's *Night Nurse.*

While Barbara was filming *Shopworn* at Columbia, Fay was on the same lot filming *A Fool's Advice* with half a million dollars given to him by the studio to make his picture. Fay's name was listed in *Variety* as someone whose popularity at the box office was waning. Also listed in their decline were John Barrymore, John Gilbert, William Haines, Ramon Novarro, Clara Bow, Mae Murray, Douglas Fairbanks, Mary Pickford, and Marion Davies.

A Fool's Advice was Fay's attempt to show himself as a true leading man. The roles that Warner Bros. had consistently given him, that of the Latin lover, the sophisticated, irresistible ladies' man, had met with disastrous audience results. Fay had written the script and was the picture's producer and was no longer at the mercy of studio executives who were trying to make him into something that couldn't work on-screen. Fay understood his audience, what constituted a well-made plot, and the craft of moving pictures. He was banking on this as the movie that would show audiences what he could do, that his appeal—and control—were as powerful on-screen as they were on the stage of the Palace.

A Fool's Advice was a series of scenes, like Fay's monologues onstage, in which he put himself at the center of the frame and talked. To direct him, Fay chose Ralph Ceder, a second-unit director new to Columbia. The plot was about a small-town yokel, Spencer Brown, a young man in his thirties, a bumpkin, an innocent, beloved by all, who, through naïveté, goodness of heart, and belief in what he knows to be right, prevents a crooked politician from running for mayor and destroying the town by selling it off to the railroad bosses.

Fay's Spencer Brown was a Candide—"a youth whom Nature had endowed with a most sweet disposition. His face was the true index of his mind. He had a solid judgment joined to the most unaffected simplicity." The Spencer Brown of *A Fool's Advice* was the opposite of Fay's public persona; it presented a character who thinks solely of others yet who is romantically unloved. It was an attempt by Fay to redeem himself in the public's—and Hollywood's—eyes. He is both beloved and a loner, someone who belongs and is an oddball.

The budget for *A Fool's Advice* was tight; the schedule was demanding. Ed Bernds, the head sound mixer on the picture, described the production as "murderous, the worst of any picture" he ever worked on. "The picture was shot with everything Columbia," said Bernds. "Columbia sound, Columbia photography." Bernds saw Fay's script as "a haphazard, pointless story. Mainly a vehicle for a couple of Frank Fay monologues.

"Fay was the leading man and the producer," said Bernds. "We worked 105 hours from early Monday morning to late Sunday night; we finished on Sunday at three or four o'clock in the morning." Bernds was getting paid $85 a week regardless of the number of hours he worked. "I didn't get paid overtime," he said, "not a nickel."

Bernds described Fay as "sluggish until he was about to do a scene. Then he would come to life. We shot some of the picture in Encino Park," where the RKO Ranch was located, one of the lowest spots in the valley.

"There were rain scenes," said Bernds. "It was midwinter. The mist from Columbia's rain towers produced a kind of spray. It was so cold the spray froze on our sound truck, and on us," said Bernds. "[The picture] was done in six miserable days of shooting."

Fay's lyrical vision was an evocation of an idealistic forward-moving America, an America of promise and principle. There are no heroes, just simple, hardworking people, a community full of eccentrics and the fellow who loves them all, people who press onward with dignity and conviction, each in his or her own way.

The picture was not a great work of art—it was static, and except for Fay no one has a real character—but it tapped into a feeling that was beginning to make its way across the country as a result of the Depression. The picture embodied the common touch—small-town values, simplicity, and innocence—that was missing from most pictures coming out of the studios.

The gymnasium at 441 Bristol Avenue, the house that Fay built and built and built—and that Barbara continued to pay for. The dining room he designed was large enough to accommodate a thirty-foot table with six chairs on either side and a chair at each end. (COURTESY TONY FAY)

While B. P. Schulberg, then production chief at Paramount, had discovered that the public wanted family pictures with real characters and down-to-earth themes and that the trend was away from sophistication with its sex and frankness, the studios were much more apt to make pictures like *Shopworn* and *Safe in Hell*—with sex, sin, and redemption—than *A Fool's Advice*.

Production on *Shopworn* ended four days after Christmas (the studio gave each of its employees a $10 gold piece to celebrate the holiday).

Barbara was working at the studio, while Frank was busy overseeing the construction on their new house in the Brentwood Heights section of Los Angeles. The estate was situated on four acres of land on Bristol and Cliffwood. A large white wall enclosed 441 Bristol Avenue.

The house had originally been built in 1926. Fay was adding a fifty-yard swimming pool, one of the largest in the colony, with a cabana in Spanish style and a red tile roof. He was overseeing as well the building of a large separate gymnasium with wood interior and exposed wood rafters and beams. Windows and French doors were to line the walls looking out on the lawn. The main room was designed to be expansive, with exercise apparatus, billiard tables, and a full-size punching bag to accommodate Fay's lifelong wish of being a prizefighter. He frequently walked through the house wearing green running trunks and bedroom slippers. Both Barbara and Frank frequently went to the fights. Barbara's favorite boxer was Jimmy McLarnin. A six-car garage was being built to house the Fays' two Fords, one opened and one closed, their Lincoln Phaeton, and their Cadillac limousine. A wooded landscape surrounded the house. A garden was being put in that would be illumined at night.

Fay ordered large religious statues of Jesus and the Virgin Mary to be placed on the grounds in and among the flower beds. Other statuary, five feet tall, was placed near the house. There were grottoes, bridges, and in the shrubbery behind the house a miniature two-foot-high stone Italian castle. A separate building was built to house the servants, who included a butler, cook, chauffeur, and night watchman.

The living room of the main house was done in Spanish decor. A den, outside Barbara's bedroom and across from Fay's, was designed by Fay to look like an English pub and was where Fay and Barbara preferred to spend time after dinner. The den's walls, ceiling, and floor were paneled in dark mahogany. Red leather sofas and chairs filled the room, with a portrait of Shakespeare hanging over the imposing mantelpiece. Four walls with screened-in floor-to-ceiling mahogany bookcases, Prairie-style, held the Fays' collection of first editions, many of which had been signed by the authors.

Fay designed the bedrooms himself, including the drapes and the furnishings. The towels, washcloths, and linens were each monogrammed with the letters *FAY,* as was Fay's bedspread.

Frank specially designed the entrance to Barbara's bedroom. Instead of being the standard dimensions, it was a small doorway that Fay designed to fit Barbara's diminutive size. The bedroom was furnished in white. A gold vanity with a tray had a special gold plaque from Fay that read: "Barbara, just to remind you I love you." The large dining room accommodated a thirty-foot table with six chairs on either side and a chair at each end. Opposite the table was an equally imposing buffet that held a large sterling silver tea and coffee set. The kitchen was hotel-like.

The surrounding grounds took up the entire block. Joan Crawford lived up the street on Beverly; Helen Twelvetrees was across from the Fays. Hal Roach had a house down the block.

The newly acquired land adjoining the Fays' house at Bristol Avenue, photographed from the top of the surrounding wall; the property now totaled four acres. Left to right: Will (Pop) Fay, Barbara, and Frank, circa 1932. (COURTESY TONY FAY)

. . .

When *Forbidden* opened at the Rialto in New York in early January 1932, *Variety* described it as a "cry picture for the girls . . . [with] a good chance of going out and getting itself and the theatres some coin." The reviewer called it "a conglomeration of many pictures" but "the best film Miss Stanwyck has made for Columbia . . . [who has] at no time looked so well on the screen." The New York *Daily News* called Barbara "splendid"; the *Los Angeles Examiner*, "compelling" and said that she gives "further demonstration that she is one of the truly great personalities of the screen."

The studios were being affected by the economy. Unemployment was severe; movie attendance fell away. The president of RKO said that unless drastic steps were taken, the industry would be bankrupt within three months. At Warner Bros., staff cuts were put into effect along with salary cuts.

Barbara wanted to play Madame Bovary and to follow Sarah Bernhardt and Maude Adams in Rostand's *L'Aiglon*. She wanted to play Mother Goddam in John Colton's *Shanghai Gesture*. Colton, with Clemence Randolph, had dramatized Somerset Maugham's *Rain*. *The Shanghai Gesture*'s underworld life and concern for respectability and degeneracy were not that far from the stuff of *Rain*.

Florence Reed had taken over the part of Mother Goddam after Mrs. Leslie Carter broke it in and was fired from the production in Newark, New Jersey. Reed created the role on Broadway of the daughter of a Manchu prince lured from her home by an Englishman, then betrayed and cast aside, becomes keeper of the most exclusive "far-famed house" in Shanghai, biding her time for revenge. The original 1926 production played for more than two hundred performances at the Martin Beck Theatre. Reed then starred in the revival two years later. Whenever Barbara began to think about a part, she imagined how Reed and Jeanne Eagels would play it.

SIX

Salt of the Earth

Edna Ferber said of *So Big,* her eleventh novel in more than a decade, "Not only did I not plan to write a best-seller, I thought I had written the world's worst seller. I didn't think anyone would read it."

Ferber sent off the finished manuscript with a note to Russell Doubleday of Doubleday, Page: "I feel very strongly that I should not publish it as a novel. Its publication as a book would hurt you, as publisher, and me, as an author. If you decide that it will be better not to publish it I shall be entirely satisfied."

Doubleday, Page brought out *So Big* in the spring of 1924. *The New York Times* called it "a novel to read and remember"; Burton Rascoe in the *New-York Tribune* said, "To Miss Ferber's narrative and descriptive powers I genuflect in homage."

The novel that she described as a "queer sort of book," written against her judgment, sold 323,000 copies and received the Pulitzer Prize for the American Novel in 1925.

So Big, Edna Ferber said, is the story of "a material young man, son of his earth-grubbing idealistic mother." Ferber described the youth of America before the Depression as having "Money. Furs. Jewels. Automobiles. Radios. Palm Beach. California. Europe. No generation of American boys and girls ever had so much money and received so little in return for it." She used that as the core of Dirk DeJong's character and set it against the courage and splendor of his mother ("Life has no weapons against a woman like that").

So Big, said Ferber, "was the story of a middle-aged woman living on a little truck farm just outside Chicago. Nothing ever really happened in the book. It had no plot at all. It had a theme—it was a story of the triumph of failure."

Edna Ferber was gutsy and idealistic and made her way out of the Wild

West. At seventeen, she was the first woman reporter on the *Appleton Daily Crescent* in Appleton, Wisconsin, a small town outside Milwaukee where her father ran a general store. In 1902, women wrote special columns for the large papers—advice to the lovelorn, society columns, articles on the women's pages; Ferber covered a regular news beat like any male reporter, earning $3 a week. During the eighteen months she worked for the *Crescent,* she "learned to read what lay behind the look that veiled people's faces, how to sketch in human beings with a few rapid words. I learned to see, to observe, to remember." *"So Big,"* said Ferber, "was all invented. The characters, situations; the theme, the dialogue, the color, the movement. I had never spent a day on a farm and certainly never had borne a son."

Barbara read Ferber's book and loved it. Selina Peake, Ferber wrote, was a woman with "a dash of fire . . . wholesome wickedness . . . adventure," a woman who "took the best and [made] the most of it," who was able to take a "worn-out and down-at-the-heel truck farm whose scant products brought a second-rate price in a second-rate market" and turn it into "a prosperous and blooming vegetable garden whose output was sought a year in advance."

Like Barbara, Selina Peake was a motherless girl whose father sent her away after her mother's death to live with two aunts. Like Barbara, Selina read armsful of books. Her "years of grinding work," Ferber wrote about Selina, "had failed to kill her zest for living." Her will and spirit (she "used none of the artifices of a youth mad day") were similar to Barbara's, and Barbara saw in Selina's soil-encrusted hands the symbol of the character's beauty and strength.

"Edna Ferber's story and character have an epic quality that is truly great," said Barbara. "Selina became a farmer's wife, and her hands became soil worn," she said. "She lost her girlish prettiness, but she became a beauty instead. And there is beauty in fine, strong hands that have not been ashamed to work in the earth."

So Big had all the elements that interested Bill Wellman: the epic span of the story; the stripped-down truth of hard country life versus the fancified ways of big-city living; a rugged, valiant woman following her dream, pitting herself quietly, firmly against convention.

When B. P. Schulberg had left Preferred Pictures to join Famous Players–Lasky, he'd taken Wellman with him. And when the newly named Paramount Pictures wanted a Great War epic, Wellman was the only director in Hollywood with combat experience as a flier and was assigned to direct John Monk Saunders's *Wings.* It was Wellman's first big success. The picture was visually dazzling; Wellman's cameramen—fifteen in all—photographed the aerial battles. Twenty-eight hand-cranked cameras recorded planes swooping and circling and diving through cloud formations and open Texas land that was meant to be the "far-stretching fields of glorious France and inglorious Germany" pocked by "innumerable ugly, dark scars from recent wounds."

Wellman said of Ferber's *So Big*, "Both story and character were made for Barbara. [Her] spirit, her sense of fair play, her capacity for hard work were similar to the character of Selina Peake," the kind of passionate determined woman Bill Wellman understood and admired.

"Lots of actresses are getting by with good looks and practically nothing else," said Wellman. "And there are other actresses who have brains and no beauty. A few of them do pretty well, though they work under a severe handicap. But when you get beauty and brains together, there's no stopping her—and the best example of that is Barbara."

This was the second picture in which Barbara went from girlhood to old age. Unlike Lulu Smith in *Forbidden,* Selina Peake didn't simply age in a genteel and elegant fashion as she moved up in economic class. She goes from being a pretty young wife, steel-strong, married to a dull fellow in High Prairie, to a sallow, too-thin middle-aged woman approaching elderliness, in shapeless garments, "her skin tanned, weather-beaten, her hair rough and dry."

The idea that Barbara had to appear drab, dowdy, middle-aged wasn't at all off-putting to her. Monte Westmore, Warner's makeup man, was able to age Barbara forty years in forty minutes. "Very few actresses would be willing to make up as a woman of advancing years," said Westmore. "Most actresses know that nine-tenths of their public appeal is due to their youthful looks. Barbara didn't worry about that. She didn't have to. She is a real actress."

Selina Peake was based on Julia Neumann Ferber. Edna Ferber wrote of her mother, "Julia Ferber as a human being was so dimensional, sustaining, courageous and vital . . . a humorous gay shrewd woman . . . She had . . . a gigantic capacity for enjoying life and for communicating that enjoyment."

In the last scene, Dirk, or So Big, brings to the DeJong farm the young bohemian painter with whom he's fallen in love and also Roelf Pool, now an internationally acclaimed sculptor who long ago had loved Selina.

Dirk calls his mother in from the fields—the west sixteen—to welcome his friends. The three see "a small dark figure against the background of sun and sky and fields, wearing a dark skirt pinned up about her ankles to protect it from the wet spring earth . . . on her head . . . a battered soft black hat. Her feet, in broad-toed sensible boots." Selina is a source of shame for her son. But for Dallas O'Mara, the young, ambitious painter who wants to "do portraits [but] [n]ot portraits of ladies with a string of pearls and one lily hand half hidden in the folds of a satin skirt," Selina DeJong is the kind of "distinguished looking—distinguishably American" woman the young painter wants to portray. He admires her "fine splendid face all lit up with the light that comes from inside . . . the jaw-line like that of the women who came over in the *Mayflower;* or crossed the continent in a covered wagon; and . . . her eyes! [H]er hands! She's beautiful."

So Big started shooting in mid-January 1932.

Ferber said, "The title had been only a tentative working one. While the title exactly expressed the book's theme, it seemed in itself to be pretty stomach-turning and I didn't for a moment mean to keep it."

Bill Wellman was interested in directing every type of picture there was to make, and to be a studio director, he had to direct fast. He had twenty-two days to make *So Big,* which was fine with him. "No man in the business is loaded with so much energy," said Barbara. If he'd had months to make a picture, he would have been "so bored," he would have "blown his top and wouldn't have been able to finish it."

Wellman had an explosive, unpredictable temper, as did Barbara, but she rarely displayed it in front of a crew. He had piercing blue eyes that looked right through you. If he sensed phoniness, he'd cut you in half. He turned his back on the bullshit of the town and ran the show his way.

Barbara's portrait of Selina Peake doesn't have the authenticity and range that Capra got from her in *Forbidden.* On her own she reverted to a mild childlike patter in her speech, slightly singsong, which Capra had been able to smooth away. But with Wellman, Barbara did her best to portray the salt-of-the-earth character.

Barbara knew her lines—and the other actors' lines—perfectly before she went in front of the camera. Wellman loved that about her. She didn't care about her makeup or getting dirty. Barbara was a perfectionist, and Wellman marveled that she never missed a line. For Barbara, though, "Nothing ever seems secure," she said. "No matter how much you may be praised for acting a certain part, you always know in your heart that there is someone else who could have done it better than you."

"Some players are able to study the page of a script for a few moments and retain a mental photograph of every line," she said. "My own method is rather different. I arm myself with a half a dozen pencils and a pad of paper and set about copying every word of the scene I'm studying." Barbara wrote out the scene, word for word, four or five times and learned the speeches of

As Selina Peake De Jong with her son, Dirk (Dickie Moore), on their way to market from High Prairie, unaccompanied, to sell their harvest in *So Big*. "It was in 1897," said Ferber, "that I glimpsed the first faint flicker of that form of entertainment which was to encircle the world with a silver sheet. We all went to see the newfangled thing called the animatograph . . . The audience agreed that it was a thousand times more wonderful than even the magic lantern."

all the other characters. "It takes a lot longer," she said, "but I'm sure of myself when I'm finished."

"The role of my son—a young fellow—needed careful casting," said Barbara. "Out of the search came a six-year-old child by the name of Dickie Moore— a little boy with fabulous brown eyes, who looked at me sincerely. I fell head over heels in love with Dickie and luckily he took to me too." After they worked together for a day or so, their scenes were not acting. "They were real," said Barbara.

Dickie Moore had started in pictures when he was eleven months old, and by the time of *So Big* he'd appeared in more than twenty of them. Each night before he was to shoot, his mother explained what the next day's scene was about. Dickie couldn't read, and his mother read his lines and his cues, which he said back to her and memorized. The boy was a quick study. He knew his lines and the lines of the adults; if they said the wrong line, Dickie would stop the scene and let them know. He thought that Barbara "was very dear, very sweet" to him.

During her scenes with the boy, Barbara said to Wellman, "Give Dickie the close-up. It will mean so much to him."

Wellman wanted Dickie to cry for one scene and asked the boy if he thought he could do it. Dickie was quiet for a few minutes and then asked, "Do you mean really true tears?" Wellman said, "Yes—that's what they have to be."

"He didn't have to threaten [the boy]," said Barbara. "He didn't have to play tricks on Dickie. Dickie said earnestly, 'Gosh, that's hard—but I'll try.' " Dickie looked long and searchingly at Wellman, and his enormous eyes filled with tears.

Two new Warner contract players were featured in the picture. George Brent, a handsome Dubliner and former actor with the Abbey Players, was Roelf Pool, the artist as a young man. Ten days before production began on *So Big*, Brent signed a twenty-six-week contract with the studio, getting $250 a week.

Bette Davis, twenty-four years old, in her eighth picture, played Dallas O'Mara, the Texas-born painter with whom Dirk DeJong falls in love. Davis described O'Mara as the "artist who leads [DeJong] back to his destiny and his mother's dream." The Davis character is both beautiful and ugly, indifferent to convention and appearance, a woman with twenty beaux and no lover. Her ambition as a painter is to work in oils; her values—not those of the rich and spoiled—are more like Selina Peake's than her son realizes. Bette Davis's performance as the bohemian artist was like a flash of electricity.

Davis had one scene in *So Big* with Barbara. Like Barbara, she had been determined to be a dancer in the style of Isadora Duncan and a serious actress. Davis, though, had studied acting formally at the John Murray Anderson–Robert Milton School of the Theatre.

She of "the drooping eyelids and sullen mouth" (*Silver Screen*, September 1930) from Lowell, Massachusetts, was the daughter of a frustrated actress with huge ambitions for her little girl and a Harvard-educated lawyer who left his wife and two daughters when Bette was seven. On being told of the divorce, Bette said to her mother, "Good, now we can go to the beach and have another baby."

Davis had worked for half a season with the George Cukor and George Kondolf Stock Company in Rochester until she was fired. "I was too talented

From *So Big,* 1932. Left to right: Hardie Albright, unidentified, Bette Davis. Davis spent her early days under contract at Warners posing in bathing suits and evening dresses for fan magazines; her nights were spent at Grauman's or the Pantages watching the movies ("If I couldn't learn on the set I'd learn from the finished pictures themselves.") As far as Bette and her mother were concerned, "the world would not be a safe place to live until I conquered it."

for Mr. Cukor to mold," she said. Mr. Cukor saw it differently and said, "She was a stubborn young lady," who "liked to disrupt rehearsals by giving her interpretation of the author's thoughts—not only for her characters, but for the other roles as well. It was useless to argue with her."

Davis had studied diction at the Anderson–Milton School with George Arliss and movement and dance with Martha Graham. "I worshipped her," said Davis. "She was all tension-lightning! Her burning dedication gave her spare body the power of ten men. She was the true modern."

At twenty-three, Davis had made her way as a stage actress from the Provincetown Playhouse in New York City to a touring company with Blanche Yurka in *The Wild Duck* to Broadway in Martin Flavin's *Broken Dishes,* where Samuel Goldwyn caught up with her and arranged for a screen test ("Whom did this to me?" Goldwyn said after seeing the young actress on film).

Another producer said she had no more sex appeal than Slim Summer-

Ruth Chatterton, with new husband, George Brent, whom she married the day after her divorce came through from English actor Ralph Forbes, circa 1932.

ville. Universal Pictures put Davis under contract at $300 a week. She made six pictures (three for Universal; three on loan-out) in six months, until Carl Laemmle dismissed her as "a cotton-dress girl"; "the kid might be all right in certain roles but what audience would ever believe that the hero would want to get *her* at the fade-out?"

She was set to give up on Hollywood and return to New York, trunks packed, car sold, when George Arliss called to say he'd been having difficulty finding a leading lady for his new picture and wondered if Miss Davis could be at Warner Bros. that afternoon. "Universal had asked to see my legs; Mr. Arliss examined my soul," she said. She got the part and was put under contract to Warner Bros. for one picture; the studio then picked up her option.

Before *So Big,* Davis had come from her first starring role in the not-yet-released *The Man Who Played God.* She had three scenes in *So Big* and got the cream of the novel, unlike the Selina Peake role, which didn't get the time in the movie to show the change from urban girl to schoolteacher who comes to love the earth. "The discovery [in *So Big*] of our bedrock made a deep impression on me," said Davis.

During the day Davis shot her scenes for *So Big* as a bohemian artist and at night played a flapper in the drawing-room comedy *The Rich Are Always with Us* ("I never knew who I was," she said). Starring in *The Rich Are Always with Us* was Ruth Chatterton in her first picture for Warner. Chatterton had her choice of stories and was being paid $8,000 a week, and Davis, under her new twenty-six-week contract with Warner, was earning $400. The young Bette Davis thought that Chatterton, "the First Lady of Hollywood," "was magnificent . . . She was a star from the top of her head to the tips of her toes." Davis modeled her acting after Chatterton.

Near the end of production of *So Big,* Barbara wanted to give Dickie Moore a gift. She knew he loved dogs and that his mother was Irish and took great pride in it. Barbara suggested she give the six-year-old boy an Irish terrier. "No, no," Dickie said. "I don't want a dog, thank you. It might fight with my cat." Instead, she gave the young actor a small rectangular gold wristwatch with an inscription on the back that read: "To Dickie Moore, my favorite picture son, in appreciation for his grand work in 'So Big' from BARBARA STANWYCK FAY."

Production for the picture was completed in early February and cost $228,000.

Edna Ferber's millions of readers were eager to see her Pulitzer Prize–winning novel up on the screen. The studio had sold *Cimarron* as Ferber's epic of American manhood; *So Big* was her "monument of American womanhood." The script re-created the large moments of the novel, and as Ferber herself said, there weren't many. The novel was too beloved for the picture to veer away from the book's big scenes; the price of sticking to the novel was the inability to develop the characters cinematically and to capture the grittiness—without sentimentality—that gave Ferber's book its truth and simplicity.

Barbara and Fay were about town, attending the premiere of Gene Fowler and Joe Laurie's *Union Depot,* directed by Alfred Green, starring Douglas Fairbanks Jr. and Joan Blondell. James Cagney acted as master of ceremonies to the regal audience that included Fairbanks and his wife of two years, Joan Crawford, Clark Gable, Marie Dressler, Ruth Chatterton, Mary Pickford, Howard Hawks, Laurence Olivier, and William Wellman.

Barbara's wardrobe for all occasions—clothes were of little importance to her—continued to be in Fay's preferred color scheme for her: black and white. She dressed quietly, neatly, comfortably and didn't enjoy getting into evening clothes. She liked to buy clothes and to look at them, but she had no interest in glamorizing herself.

Studio photographers saw Barbara as uncooperative when she was called upon to pose for sittings. She was not comfortable with the idea of being a glamour girl or a movie queen; lavishly designed clothes that were delivered to the house for her to pose in were sent back to the wardrobe department in favor of her own clothes. "Save those other things for somebody who's got the style," Barbara said. "I just haven't and I know it."

When Barbara wasn't working, she wore no makeup, only red lipstick set against her red-gold hair, no powder or rouge offscreen. She claimed her face didn't take makeup well. "When I put rouge on my cheeks, invariably it spreads itself down to my chin. It just happens that make-up won't stay on my face. This sounds absurd but it's the truth," she said. Besides, Fay didn't want her to wear makeup or to use mascara against her deep violet eyes and fresh-scrubbed skin. "I don't want people to say," said Fay, " 'she's a good actress but she never takes off her make-up.' " He also didn't want Barbara to wear red nail polish on fingers or toes. She didn't.

Barbara's desire was still to please Fay. She noticed, though, that in addition to drinking, her husband was beginning to behave in odd ways. Reading a newspaper or book, he might cry out, "Lord help us," "Oh God Amen," "Lord, have mercy on us." Just as suddenly he might begin to swear. He couldn't help himself. If Barbara asked him why he was praying one minute and violently swearing the next, Fay got angry and didn't see a problem with what he was saying. "I can do as I please," he would say.

For as long as Barbara had known Fay, he had crossed himself when he passed a church. Now, if he and Barbara passed a church, he bowed his head, closed his eyes, raised his right hand to his hat, lifted the brim up and down several times, and muttered sounds as if in prayer. If Barbara and Frank were in a car and he was driving, Barbara would warn him to watch out, that he'd get in an accident. "No harm will come to me while I'm praying," he would say. "God will protect me."

Often when driving, Fay would be in the midst of railing against someone until he saw a church. Then he would stop talking and begin his ritual of bowing his head, closing his eyes, raising his right hand to his hat, lifting the brim up and down, and muttering sounds as if in prayer. As soon as he'd passed the church, he continued with his vicious rant.

Frank wanted to return to New York. Barbara was determined to be with him despite his drinking, violent outbursts, and curious ways. They'd decided to bring the act that they'd put together the previous December to Fay's old theater, the RKO Palace in New York, ignoring the criticism they'd received about Barbara's unseemly onstage acrobatics when the show opened in Los Angeles at Christmas.

The Fays left for New York to make arrangements for their two-week appearance as Barbara was being mentioned for the lead in First National's *Week-End Marriage,* from the Faith Baldwin novel, which was set to go into production at the beginning of April. Two other Warner stars, Ruth Chatterton and Kay Francis, were also mentioned as possibilities for the starring role; Loretta Young got the part.

The Fays were being jointly paid $8,500 a week at the Palace. Frank needed the money. His first (and second) wife, Frances White, had attached his Palace salary of $4,000 per week in favor of the $25 a week Fay had been paying her for thirteen years.

Performers on the circuit like Eddie Cantor, Maurice Chevalier, and Ed Wynn were making twice what the Fays were earning. Cantor was being paid $8,800; Chevalier, $10,000; Ed Wynn, $7,500. Those being paid in the Fays' range included Morton Downey ($4,500), George Jessel ($4,000), Beatrice Lillie ($4,500), and Ruth Etting ($4,500).

Barbara insisted Fay receive top billing over her on the Palace marquee.

Back in Los Angeles, Fay premiered *A Fool's Advice.* As he and Barbara were leaving the theater, he saw a Warner executive standing in the lobby. "Nice of you to come over," Fay said.

"Nice little picture, Frank."

"Very nice little picture my hat," said Barbara. "It's a great picture. Now what do you think of that?"

"Barbara, your tact and diplomacy astound me," said Fay, all the while amused by her advocacy of his work.

It tickled Fay to see Barbara shock people with her outbursts, particularly when they were on his behalf; she didn't care who heard them. Barbara had no patience for evasion or conceit. The angrier she was, the more well-mannered and cool Fay appeared. Barbara put Fay forward with the press. When the *Los Angeles Examiner* asked her about her hopes and ambitions, Barbara answered, "You tell them, Frank," which he did and then talked about her pedigree.

"Well, Miss Stanwyck was one of the Virginia Stanwycks and was—"

"You mean the Brooklyn Stevenses," Barbara interrupted.

He arched an eyebrow at his wife and continued.

"She was raised in seclusion and went to a very exclusive private school . . ."

Barbara said, "Yes, they called it the Everglades Café—and there were only six girls—all dancers."

Fay could be playful and loving with Barbara, but he could be equally possessive and jealous. He decided who their friends would be in the way that he was instrumental in Barbara's calling off her long-standing close friendships with Walda Mansfield and Mae Clarke. He argued as well with Barbara about whom she saw or talked to. Barbara was described in the press as someone "whose name spells box office wherever it is flaunted on a theater marquee, who is pretty, attractive, charming," yet who doesn't have many close friends in the industry. She was written about as "one of the mysteries of Hollywood; more mysterious in her way than Garbo."

Just before Barbara and Frank were to open in New York, Barbara approved her second picture for Warner Bros. It was based on a 1932 novel by Arthur Stringer called *The Mud Lark,* originally published as a short story in *The Saturday Evening Post.*

Hal Wallis was the producer. It was Barbara's third picture with Bill Wellman. He enjoyed working with her and requested her for his pictures. He liked how spirited Barbara was, how much she was like a "tomboy"—one of the guys—at the same time that she was so feminine. Barbara was the rare actress who created the kind of presence on the set that Wellman wanted. She joked with the men on the cameras and mikes, the electricians and grips, and took an interest in their lives.

Barbara admired them; there was nothing fake about them. "They know a lot about making pictures," she said. "They know more about this business than a lot of people sitting in the front offices. They're closer to it. You can learn something from every one of them."

Barbara and Fay took the train back to New York and were met at the station by the press and photographers. Those who called out to Barbara as "Miss Stanwyck" were told, "Please, I am Mrs. Frank Fay off-screen." Fay was delighted by her admonishment. The Fays went to the Waldorf Astoria, where they were staying for the run of the show.

Broadway's Favorite Son was back on the stage of the Palace. Fay was where he belonged, onstage for thirty minutes, twice a day as master of ceremonies as well as performing a whole new set of bits: his Boris Karloff–like Frankenstein's monster as an audience scarer; a comedy newsreel that showed former president Coolidge in a series of miens supposedly gagging in collo-

At the Waldorf Astoria, New York City,
February 1932.

quial language about going to see Frank at the Palace; film clips of Mahatma
Gandhi and Hindu followers with sound effects and Yiddish interpolations
praising Fay's talents. Fay was picking up on Gandhi's having been arrested
months before by the government on the eve of a new civil disobedience
campaign and the outlawing of the Indian National Congress.

He included in the evening a fourteen-minute playlet for Barbara that he
wrote and directed and set in a department store during Christmas in which
Barbara is picked up by two store detectives for shoplifting tin soldiers. The
manager is irate until it is revealed that she's stolen the toys for her baby
brother, who is crippled, and she is given the toys—and a job.

The main part of Fay's act involved three fireman stooges, and in a bit
that opened the second half, Fay, in a double-breasted tuxedo, teased Barbara about how he had given her an extensive cast for the Christmas skit
that closed the first half of the show—"a million actors, lighting effects, a
rich Hollywood wardrobe that she keeps changing each time she reappears
onstage, a fancy stage set"—and, Fay goes on, would she now let him do his
own act onstage in peace?

The show was to have included Benny Rubin and Jack Haley, but each was in a dispute with RKO, and neither was willing to appear. A grand after-piece had Barbara surrounded by eight clowns, including Fay, in different states of undress, each with a red nose and fake mustache, with Barbara once again playing a stooge to Fay's comedy.

Variety said, "[The show] is ragged and punctuated by marked let-downs. Overboard on hoofing in the fore part . . . lightweight on everything in the second half. The Final stanza merely comprises Irene Bordoni and Fay doing a solo act with the aid of Miss Stanwyck and a flock of stooges. Fay's torch patter is strong lyrically, the straight vocalizing is rather blah."

Other critics said, "Miss Stanwyck is being badly handled for a non-vaudeville actress in a vaudeville show." "The most promising young star in pictures . . . in active practice, [is] deliberately playing 'stooge'—foil—butt—for a vaudeville comedian who she trustingly adores," said *Photoplay.* "Helping him with her name, talents, her young beauty."

Following the show's opening, Barbara and Frank went to the launching of the Pierrette Club with Billie Dove, Pola Negri, Eddie Foy, Basil Rathbone, Jimmy Walker, and Barbara's former guardian, Anatol Friedland. After the late-night supper Barbara and Frank went back to the Waldorf. Frank's upset with the audience's cool response to his act was made worse by the enthusiastic applause Barbara had received, and soon they were in the midst of an argument until Frank left to get drunk and didn't return.

Reviews for their two-week run were generally negative.

Newspapers and readers were preoccupied with the story of the kidnapping, the night before Barbara and Frank's opening, of the twenty-month-old Lindbergh baby from the family's farm near Hopewell, New Jersey. State troopers, detectives, and police were on a massive hunt for two men in a dark sedan with New York license plates who, the day of the kidnapping, had stopped a man in Princeton, New Jersey, ten miles south of Hopewell, for directions to Colonel Lindbergh's farm.

The second day of the Palace run, Barbara went onstage alone and told the press that her husband had dropped out of the show because of a cold. Fay's name was taken off the Palace marquee.

She was furious with him but told reporters, "My marriage means more to me than anything else. Frank comes first with me and always will."

When one reporter suggested that it might not be wise to place all of one's happiness on one man's love, Barbara said, "Well, what about movie fame? In pictures I'm a success just as long as people like me. When they stop coming to see me, I'm just a failure. It isn't that way with love. You may lose some one's love, yes, but it's something you never quite get out of your heart once you've known the real thing."

Fay was back the next day, but the Palace booking office had hired Gus Van for Fay's slot and paid Fay for two days' work. When Fay went back into the show, he and Barbara were playing to half-full houses. *Variety* said, "The show's second week [at the Palace] wasn't any better than the first. Fay is again a disappointment."

Barbara was rated in *Variety,* as were other female performers appearing onstage at the Palace and the State, on, among other attributes: "Modishness"—8 points; "Neatness"—10 points; "Make-up"—8 points; "Coiffure"—9 points; "Personality"—10 points; "Applause"—9 points. Her total: 80 points out of 100. The overall comment: "Submerges her own ability in back chat with Frank Fay and contributes sincerely and movingly to a badly written sketch." This despite a fall Barbara sustained, slipping backstage and once again injuring her spine.

Fay dropped Barbara's "Christmas" skit from the show for another that he'd written for her called "The Interview." In it he had to resort to something Barbara wanted to avoid: reenactments of scenes from two of her pictures. He also changed one of his bits that was to center on his being in bed with a young woman under the sheets, using blackouts to punctuate their commingling.

"Something has happened to or with the Palace's ex–best m.c.," *Variety* said in its review the second week. "Fay, who used to have Palace audiences eating out of his hand, now has to struggle to keep them interested. Or maybe nothing has happened to Fay, and that's what's wrong."

Columbia Pictures was not making headway booking *A Fool's Advice.* Fay was thinking of staying behind in New York in an effort to sell the rights to the picture but decided instead to travel west with Barbara, who was due to return to Hollywood to go to work on *The Mud Lark.*

Money had never been an issue for Fay. Whether he had it or not, he spent it as if it were a constant. He'd made light in the press about how he could lose $5,000 worth of clothes a year, leaving overcoats in restaurants or other people's homes, losing trousers and countless pairs of gloves, misplacing four rings and seven wristwatches in washrooms. His absentmindedness and seeming indifference to possessions and the value of money belied a more serious problem: he could drink himself into a stupor and stay that way for weeks.

On the way back to Los Angeles, Barbara and Frank planned to stop over in St. Louis, where they'd married four years before during Fay's stint as master of ceremonies at the Missouri Theatre.

The just-released *Shopworn* was playing in St. Louis at the Ambassador Theatre. Barbara and Frank were booked to make an appearance at the theater. One reviewer called the picture's plot "shopworn," ("It belongs in the bone age of the silent drama. It is about as sophisticated as servant-girl fiction in the middle 90's"). *Variety* called the picture "the clumsiest kind of literary hoke, trashy in the last degree but somehow made fairly endurable by the curious knack of Barbara Stanwyck for investing even the most theatrical roles with something of earnest sincerity." In the same paper, one columnist wrote, "Barbara Stanwyck's temper will never atrophy from disuse. Since it was discovered Miss Stanwyck is what's known as an 'emotional actress' her pictures have always contrived somewhere to have her make a scene. Miss Stanwyck's low combustion point in *Shopworn* may be the inside on how she became a world famous actress. Temper and dramatic temperament have always been closely allied in the public mind."

The Fays told the press when they left New York that they were returning to "the Coast by way of St. Louis because we were married there" and would have a second honeymoon there.

The promotional ad for *Shopworn* and the Fays read: "Hello, St. Louis. We're coming back to the city that holds the happiest memories in our lives." The billboard advertised in large type: "*In Person,* Frank Fay, Barbara Stanwyck." Below, in much smaller type, it read: "The Gifted Screen Beauty with Her Popular Husband."

SEVEN

Prophets of a New Order

Fit as a fiddle and ready for love.

I like pictures better than any business in the world," said Frank Fay. "It's like a crap game. You can never foretell tomorrow. You make a trip to Palm Springs. The butler will ask you for your name at your own door when you return. Whenever you leave Hollywood, you are forgotten. You return to start all over."

So Big opened in Los Angeles at the Warner Bros. Hollywood Theatre along with a stage show headed by Al Kvale, Jeffrey Gil, David and Hilda Murray, and the Dancing Grenadiers with Gaylord Carter at the organ. With the picture were also a Merrie Melodies cartoon, *Freddy the Freshman,* and a Universal newsreel. Louella Parsons called the picture "infinitely better than its silent predecessor," saying that William Wellman "has maintained an excellent balance, eliminating the nonessentials and keeping the big moments . . . intact." Parsons called Barbara's Selina Peake "beautifully portrayed . . . there are few actresses whose emotional ability equals that of Miss Stanwyck." Also mentioned was the work of Bette Davis, though Parsons said Miss Davis had "far too much rouge on her mouth and too much mascara on her eyes."

The *Variety* critic said of Bette Davis, "[She] has undergone a complete transformation since she appeared as a timid little ingénue with unstudied coiffure and make-up. She used to be 'Alice Ben.' Now she has discovered the chic of smart costumes, meticulous blonde waves . . . [F]ormerly terrified of her own shadow [she] has suddenly developed the most alarmingly pretentious personality."

One critic said of Barbara's Selina Peake, "She puts the words in the mouth of Colleen Moore . . . the consensus is that she doesn't add much to the memory of the silent version." Another wrote, "Barbara Stanwyck's gradual transformation through the years . . . is a gem of insight and a marvel of make-up. She never resorts to the tricks of calculated 'sob-stuff.' " Still another reviewer recognized Barbara's ability to be funny: "The first part of the picture contains some of the best comedy of the season; Barbara in her fussy furbelows . . . Barbara at her first basket supper . . . anyone who has ever lived in a country town will rock with laughter."

Edna Ferber felt that it was Colleen Moore who best captured Selina and gave the "true performance."

Fay was admitted to the Merrill Sanitarium near Venice, California, for treatment of alcoholism. It was the second time in six months that he'd been ordered under the care of doctors from excessive, prolonged intoxication.

Bill Wellman knew of Barbara's troubles with her husband. She didn't speak about them much. Work and focus got her through. Wellman was crazy about her, and he didn't like too many actresses. She was lusty, bantered about, was full of wit. She played tennis, went to the fights, didn't gossip, and took trouble on the chin. She minded her own business, smoked with an unaffected pleasure thought of as masculine, exuded plenty of sex, but never used it to further her career.

Neither Wellman nor Barbara was interested in the social world of Hollywood, nor were they engaged in the political games of the town. She admired Wellman. Both stood apart from Hollywood society.

Barbara didn't like the showiness of picture stars. "I wouldn't wear an ermine coat to a Hollywood opening if I was offered the coat and a thousand dollar bonus," she said. "All of the ermine coats the furriers had in stock were rented to movie people for the [recent] opening of *Grand Hotel.* Imagine putting on a show like that just to let people think you're more prosperous than you are. Not for me."

Wellman saw Barbara as intelligent, resourceful, tough: "a magnificent actress."

"Wild Bill" was one of Barbara's "best-beloved" people. He studied his script hard, prepared for his day's work, and always did his best. His work was sure and fast. Wellman took chances. He would try anything that made sense to him regardless of whether it made sense to anyone else. He risked his actors' lives and limbs, but, said Louise Brooks of working with him in *Beggars of Life,* "good old Bill was always safe behind the camera."

• • •

As a "girl of the night" and torch singer, with Lyle Talbot as Eddie
Fields, club owner and gangster, *The Purchase Price* (originally called
The Mud Lark), 1932. (PHOTOFEST)

Wellman had just finished making *Love Is a Racket* with Douglas Fairbanks,
Ann Dvorak, Lee Tracy, and Frances Dee about a Broadway gossip columnist
caught up in a murder cover-up.

With the success of *So Big*, Warner put Bill Wellman together with Barbara again in another picture that had them going back to the land. The new
picture with Barbara, *The Mud Lark*, began production at First National
studios in mid-April 1932. Robert Lord's screenplay took the young English-
woman of the novel—who is educated at convent school in Switzerland (she
comes from a family of some means that summers at Cannes and Biarritz),
is orphaned by the death of her father, and by necessity becomes an "unconsidered appendicle, something between a traveling-companion and a lady's
maid"—and made her into an American girl, a torch singer in a New York
nightclub. Barbara saw her as "a streetwalker." When she asked Lord how he
dared take such liberties with Stringer's book, Lord told her, "You can't play
a lady."

"My response to that insult was termed 'temperamental,' " Barbara said.
"I am Irish. I have a temper. I do not flare into silly displays."

In Lord's script, the "streetwalker"-singer, Joan Gordon, flees her New
York nightclub life and her former racketeer boyfriend and becomes the "picture bride" of a wheat farmer in North Dakota, a man she's never met. She

With George Brent as Jim Gilson, North Dakota farmer. The movie's premise—and advertising teaser: "Can a night flower step from orchids to apron strings, from penthouse to farm house, from silk lingerie to flannel nighties—and like it . . . ?" (PHOTOFEST)

ends up in the wilderness prairie town after her maid confesses that she's answered an ad for a matrimonial agency with the singer's picture instead of her own. The farmer is expecting to see someone who looks like the nightclub singer, so Joan gives the maid $100 and decides to go in her place.

George Brent is Jim Gilson, the grim, taciturn wheat farmer who sends for his mail-order bride. On their first night together, after her long train ride west and their marriage by a justice of the peace, Gilson tries to kiss his new wife, and she, wary and repulsed by him, reflexively strikes him across the face. He becomes angry, goes to the barn to sleep in the hay bin, and from then on only tolerates her, having as little to do with her as possible. She tends to her housewifely chores, he works his fields and wheat crops. The picture is taken up with her coming to know the stranger who is her husband—and his vast stark world—falling in love with him, and winning him back.

Wellman, who was drawn to women who were tough and gutsy and resilient, gave his female character the more male role and the male character a more feminine response to his wife. Jim Gilson is rebuffed by his wife on his wedding night. Instead of "taking" her, as is his "legal right" now that she's wearing his wedding ring, he becomes hurt and sullen and withdraws. He shies away from any of her attempts to make it up to him or her advances. It

From *The Purchase Price*, 1932. (PHOTOFEST)

is up to her to woo him out of his hurt feelings—slowly, gently—in order to allow her the chance to love him.

What interested Wellman was the education of the girl. She proves herself to be tough, not by her city ways, but by the strength of her character to hold firm against the grittiness and loneliness of her new homesteading life. What she faces is a "prairie landscape as flat as the ocean floor, and ranchers' houses so far apart the skyline stretches from east to west as level as a windless sea."

In the picture, Wellman kept the feel of the small, simple novel. Its plot is secondary to the series of scenes in which he shows people being real—quirky, odd, comic, ornery, conniving, demented. They're pioneer stock, slightly teched by the brutal sun, the battle against unpredictable seasons, and the constant threat of drought or frost that can bring ruin to any hard-working farmer.

Wellman was after character. He wanted to show a gentleness underneath the crustiness of the scorched, battered plains people.

In the scene where Gilson marries the girl, the justice of the peace at Elks Crossing, Elmer (Clarence Wilson), is a plucked old bird, balding and hook-nosed. He speaks the words of the marriage ceremony with a wad of tobacco

With William Wellman, director of *The Purchase
Price,* his twenty-ninth picture, their second movie
together, circa 1932. (PHOTOFEST)

stuffed inside one cheek. His wife, Ma (Lucille Ward), large and homey looking, is called to witness the ceremony with a bowl of batter tucked under her
arm, held up by her ample stomach (she's baking a sponge cake). Then there's
Clyde (Victor Potel), the other witness, who's inbred and looks it.

As the justice of the peace reads the words, a dogfight is going on outside.
Clyde wanders over to the window and watches wide-eyed through the pane
of glass as the mutts tangle and tear at one another. Late in the picture, when
Clyde sees Gilson and his wife in town, he barks and howls, like the dogs that
fought during the Gilsons' marriage ceremony.

Wellman wasted no time. The entire picture was in his head from the day he
started shooting and was cut in the camera as he shot. He didn't appreciate
star grandstanding. "They'll hold you up every time," he said. He didn't like
fussiness and appreciated Barbara's disdain for all that.

Barbara was friends with the crew, the painters and electricians, property
boys, makeup artists, and men handling the microphone boom. "They talk

The first time she sings on-screen.

my language," she said. "Their problems are the same kind that I have had all my life. They have babies and landlords and loads of trouble and lots of fun. I'm more interested in how the property boy on this set is going to meet the eight-dollar installment on his radio this week than I am in all the gossip one could hear in the Brown Derby in a month." Barbara's closest friend was her hairdresser, Hollis Barnes. Barbara called her Barnsie.

Wellman wasn't at all subtle about what he wanted from his actors or his crew, but on-screen he summoned up telling details that were infused with a deep love of people.

He framed some of his scenes at odd angles, sometimes to show point of view: Gilson picking up the mess after a party, down on all fours, with Barbara's character, Joan, looking at him longingly, tentatively, from the doorway of the bedroom, the camera taking in his backside. Other times Wellman framed his scenes to summon up the work of painters, like N. C. Wyeth or Thomas Hart Benton, whose style reflected the contemporary look of the moment: Gilson out back in the frigid cold, bent over as he saws, windblown, a determined dark figure set against the snow, framed by the jutting teeth of the two-man saw that leans against the shed; a buggy rig holding the horizontal line that frames Gilson's bent-over body. Behind him off to the right, the darkened barn doorway giving shape to the curve of the car's trunk inside.

Barbara was given her first number to sing on-screen, "Take Me Away." Its words ("Take me away, my heart only belongs to you, knowing you love me too, take me away") set the picture's theme.

The Mud Lark was mostly shot at First National studios. The prairie snowstorm and the fight in the saloon were shot at the Vitagraph studios. The production traveled to Vincent, California, to shoot the Elks Crossing Railroad Station, where Joan Gordon first arrives in North Dakota. The interior scene in the barbershop was shot at the Ambassador Hotel. The long shots of the fire in the wheat fields took place in one of the largest wheat belts in the United States. The field of shocked and stacked wheat, the exterior of the farmhouse, and the climactic fire were shot at the Warner Bros. Ranch.

The fire at the ranch was filmed at night on the next-to-last day of the shoot, in heavy winds as the script required. A double was to be used for Barbara. "After the first take," said Sidney Hickox, Wellman's cameraman, "when the double did not show enough action, Miss Stanwyck said she would do the scene herself."

The day had started at ten in the morning. The crew broke for supper at seven and began the fire scene forty minutes later.

To fight the fire, Barbara and Brent were to use wet blankets. The scene was set. The fire was started; both actors began to fight the flames, hitting the blazing wheat with the blankets. After a few minutes it was clear that they were drawing back the blankets too soon. The actors were spreading the fire rather than smothering it. Soon they were fighting for their lives. Bill Wellman called for them to jump through the flames and get out, but Barbara and Brent continued in the midst of the heat and smoke until the fire was put out. Hickox kept the camera turning. It was two in the morning when they finished shooting.

Barbara's legs were scorched, and she was taken to the hospital. For the next few days she applied grease to her seared skin.

Wellman brought in the picture for $202,000. He shot two takes for most scenes, rarely more. "One for the take I wanted," he said. "One in case something went wrong in the lab." One print was for domestic distribution; a second was for distribution abroad.

The Mud Lark's title was changed to *Night Flower.* The previous year, Warner had announced that Barbara would star in a rags-to-riches high-society story, *The Purchase Price,* based on a novel by S. K. Morehouse. The movie was never produced. The studio took the title, used it for Arthur Stringer's *Saturday Evening Post* story published months later by Bobbs-Merrill, and released *The Mud Lark* as *The Purchase Price.*

While Barbara was making the picture, Mae Clarke had finished work on two pictures for Universal with Lew Ayres, *The Impatient Maiden* and *Night World.* During both productions Mae, ill from overwork and exhaustion, though a trained performer like Barbara, showed up for work despite fever

and infection. She was also a Christian Scientist and had minimized the effects of her symptoms from sinusitis. Soon her face began to swell. The pain
intensified; she began to hallucinate. Mae needed "intravenous feeding and
blood and rest" and drove to Palm Springs, where "only millionaires" lived,
thinking she would find the best doctor there. She found a hospital, was
admitted, and was given an injection. She woke in the middle of the night,
"raving. Out of my mind."

The following day an ambulance took her to another hospital in Pasadena, where they wrapped her "in canvas and stuck [her] in a long tube of
very hot water with my head poking through a hole at one end, like hanging
you from a tree." They gave her shock treatment "without sedation. I smelled
death coming out of my pores," Mae said.

No one was allowed to see her. Lew Brice's sister, Fanny, refused "to be
told no," said Mae. "Fanny had a way. She appeared in the doorway of my
little room where I was strapped down to the bed. Fanny said, 'Thought I'd
drop in for tea. I'm going to shampoo your hair and . . . I'm going to do your
nails.'"

Mae was able to survive, she said, through her "love of God" and her
desire to live and was finally released. "They released me because surely they
thought I was about to die. They did not want to have any investigation on
the premises of Miss Mae Clarke from the movies."

Mae weighed ninety-nine pounds.

An article in the *Los Angeles Times* said that Mae would be recovering from
an illness and spending the next two or three weeks in Honolulu. Instead, her
mother and family took care of her round the clock. During the months of
Mae's illness, she was unable to work. The studio formally dropped her; she
was on suspension.

A headline in *Variety* read: "SCARFACE $20,000 Looks Holdover for LA;
'BIG TIMER' OK at $14,000; Stanwyck helps SO BIG, $13,500."

So Big led Boston at the Metropolitan. The picture packed in audiences
in New York at the Strand, and Chicago reported its best grosses in weeks.
A full-page ad in *Variety* had as its banner: "Barbara Stanwyck in SO BIG;
It's Gone Straight to This Mark" (showing a head shot of Barbara smiling and,
underneath it, a large dollar sign). The ad's tagline read: "Another reason why
this industry has staked its future on Warner Bros."

People were scavenging for food while bankers and corporate executives
were receiving huge salaries and bonuses. Some 750,000 people were living
on city relief efforts that averaged $8.20 a month per person, while 160,000
additional people waited to get on the rolls. Henry Ford was refusing to

help those who were out of work, and the Detroit bankers would only lend the city money if it cut relief pittances. Thousands of farmers lost their land for nonpayment of taxes or mortgages. In 1932 alone a quarter of a million families lost their homes.

"Here we are in the midst of the greatest crisis since the Civil War," wrote John Dewey. "And the only thing the national parties seem to want to debate is booze." The Republican National Convention was dominated by Hoover. The main debate concerned the Eighteenth Amendment. The president was adamant about its enforcement, even though most Americans wanted it repealed.

The delegates of the Democratic convention voted in favor of its repeal and for immediate modification of the Volstead Act to allow the manufacture and sale of beer. Franklin Delano Roosevelt, the three-year governor of New York, was nominated on the fourth ballot over the four-term governor, Al Smith, whom Roosevelt had twice nominated to be the Democratic candidate for president and who held much of the Northeast, along with Speaker of the House John Nance Garner of Texas.

Governor and Mrs. Roosevelt boarded a plane in Albany for Chicago to personally accept the nomination, rather than waiting for a committee from the convention to call upon the candidate weeks later and inform him of their party's nomination. Roosevelt's appearance at the convention was breathtaking. He spoke on the floor of the convention hall in Chicago, before the applauding delegates:

> The appearance before a National Convention of its nominee for President, to be formally notified of his selection, is unprecedented and unusual, but these are unprecedented and unusual times . . .
>
> Our Republican leaders tell us economic laws—sacred, inviolable, unchangeable—cause panics which no one could prevent . . . We must lay hold of the fact that economic laws are not made by nature. They are made by human beings . . .
>
> On the farms, in the large metropolitan areas, in the smaller cities and in the villages, millions of our citizens cherish the hope that their old standards of living and of thought have not gone forever. Those millions cannot and shall not hope in vain.
>
> I pledge you, I pledge myself, to a new deal for the American people . . . This is more than a political campaign; it is a call to arms. Give me your help, not to win votes alone, but to win in this crusade to restore America to its own people.

Barbara was a lifelong Republican. Frank Fay hated Franklin Roosevelt with a passion. Both Barbara and Frank had every intention to cast their votes, again, for their president, Herbert Hoover.

Barbara was set to make her final picture under her contract with Columbia. It was to be her fourth picture working with Capra, a daring love story of a Chinese warlord and a sheltered American missionary.

The profits from Capra's most recent pictures, *Platinum Blonde* and *Forbidden,* were sizable but not large enough to offset Columbia's financial problems. During the time Capra was in Europe, production at Columbia had stopped. Most people at the studio were being laid off. Columbia was in the midst of a power struggle. Jack Cohn and Joe Brandt, both financial overseers of the studio in the East, weren't interested in making the large-budget pictures Harry Cohn was determined to produce: the risks were too large, and Jack Cohn and Brandt were planning to oust Harry as head of production. Harry was warned by A. P. Giannini, head of the Bank of America, that a plan was afoot.

Joe Brandt grew weary of the struggle and, at the urging of his wife, who wanted him to retire, offered to sell his Columbia stock for $500,000. Harry Cohn borrowed the money, bought the stock, and with it acquired 50 percent ownership of the company. Cohn, forty, became president and remained production chief of Columbia Pictures; his brother, Jack, vice president and treasurer. The Cohn brothers, who had viciously sought to undo each other during Brandt's tenure, continued to fight just as heatedly after his departure.

Jack Cohn was sitting across from his brother's desk and said one day, "Harry, why don't we do a Bible story?"

"A Bible story, why?"

"I don't know," said Jack. "It's kind of like a Western; there's no royalty and a big audience out there, don't cost a lot of money."

"You run the New York office," said Harry. "And let me make the pictures. Anyway, what do you know about the Bible? I bet you don't even know the Lord's Prayer."

Jack insisted he did.

"For $50, you don't know the Lord's Prayer," said Harry. "So let me hear you say it."

Jack began, "Now I lay me down to sleep." Harry said, "That's enough. I didn't think you knew it. Take the money."

• • •

Frank Capra at thirty-five had directed sixteen pictures for Columbia in four years. The studio was able to use the demand for Capra pictures as a way around owning theaters. If the theater chains wanted a Capra picture, they had to take Columbia's other films as well.

Capra came back from his honeymoon to begin work on *Tampico,* from a Joseph Hergesheimer novel. Instead, he was hired to take over the direction of *Faith* from the directors Allan Dwan and Roy William Neill. Ed Bernds, the sound engineer on *Faith,* said, "Dwan sat impassively on the set. He accepted whatever the actors gave him in performances. Something was needed to spark intensity."

After several days of shooting, Cohn shut down production, fired Dwan, hired Roy Neill as director, and then gave the picture to Capra. "It was the return of the conquering hero," said Bernds. "Capra refilmed everything Dwan had shot, scenes that had been slow picked up pace, characters came alive. Capra was at his best."

Faith was about an idealistic banker (Walter Huston) who lends money to people on their character, not their collateral. During the course of a twenty-four-hour period, the idealistic banker goes up against the bank's directors, hell-bent on merging the bank with a larger one, and heroically staves off a run on the bank set off by a rumor.

The picture was about fear and hysteria, money and banking, integrity and greed. Its ideas—radical, populist, based on the banking collapse and the country's devastation—were those of Robert Riskin. "Riskin brought to Capra a slangy, down-to-earth humor, almost a cracker barrel philosophy," said a mutual colleague.

Riskin was a supporter of Roosevelt's plan for a New Deal for America. He, like Capra, was the son of immigrants, but Riskin was a liberal Democrat who maintained an affinity with the working class. Capra, like Barbara, was a lifelong Republican and a supporter of Herbert Hoover. Capra believed that if he had made his way up from under, the American dream was there for anyone.

Robert Riskin had been a poor boy but stayed connected to "the proletariat." He put his dialogue—smart, witty, ennobling—into the mouths of working men and women. Through his edgy dialogue, the workers were able to stand up for themselves; they were more than a match for the educated and the rich. To Riskin, the decent values of ordinary (small-town) people would win out over the rich (city) sophisticates.

"Frank [Capra] provided the schmaltz and Bob [Riskin] provided the acid," said a mutual friend.

The Frank Fays, circa 1932.

Barbara had been in three pictures of Riskin's. Like Riskin and Capra, Barbara had come out of poverty. Riskin was of the left; Barbara of the right and loved two men who were Republicans. Capra's drive, which allowed him to break free from poverty and make his name as a director, is what spurred him to be a Republican. Barbara's drive steered her toward her Republicanism as well. As an actress, she'd come out of her childhood poverty on her own, arrived at by hard work and without help from family. She wanted to get enough work and not have to worry about being poor again.

Capra had been infatuated with Barbara for most of the three pictures in which he'd directed her. This was to be their fourth picture together in two years, their first since she'd chosen to remain with Fay and Capra had married. He was now a married man of five months.

When Barbara married Frank Fay, it was for keeps. When she loved, it was with an elemental intensity that was almost bitter. She was reserved, seemingly undemonstrative, direct, a good sport, and unlike the characters she created on-screen, in life, black was black and white was white with no vague shadings in between. Barbara was a straight shooter, honest, and would go through hell for someone she loved. If it was clear what was expected of her, she was able to find the physical and mental endurance to accomplish it. Loyalty and service, which she never disassociated from affection, were at the heart of her being.

Fay had been there for her in a way no one else had. It had taken her a long time to get used to having someone she could take her "troubles to when we were first married," she said. She would sit off in a corner and think things out by herself. Frank used to say, "What's the trouble, kid?" Barbara would answer, "Nothing." It bothered him because he thought Barbara wasn't happy with him. One day he said to her, half joking but hurt, "Don't you know who I am? I'm the guy you married. And that means for worse as well as for better. Tell your troubles to old Doc Fay and get [them] out of your system." It was difficult for her, but she learned to confide in him. "And I've done it ever since," said Barbara. "It is [wonderful] to have someone who can stand between you and the world."

EIGHT

Object of Desire

The Bitter Tea of General Yen was from the 1930 novel by Grace Zaring Stone, about a New England woman, the daughter of a college president who in the late 1920s arrives in a China torn apart by civil war to marry a medical missionary, Chinese scholar, and translator of the *Odes;* his sole intent in life is to relieve the suffering of others. The missionary, Doctor Strike, sees the Chinese as "the most tragic people . . . for hundreds of centuries they have enjoyed the highest plane of living and thinking . . . Like the Greeks they have been permitted to miss the one essential truth—the existence of a God of love." Doctor Strike's much-admired former colleague, from one of the oldest Mandarin families, is the powerful and elusive General Yen Tso-Chong, a scholar turned warlord. Yen is considered dissolute by the Europeans and the Americans. ("We have to apply our standard to them," the missionary says. "And make them accept it.") General Yen's troop trains have special cars for his concubines.

The day after Megan Davis arrives in Chapei, the native city falls to the Communists, and Megan is "rescued"—abducted—carried across the country by train, under the protection of the great general Yen, leader of the Republican forces against the Communists, ruler of a province who maintains an arsenal managed by an American. Megan is brought to Yen's house, "made for a life which began and ended with the rising and the setting of the sun."

Yen's adviser and financial procurer is Mr. Shultz, an American "dedicated to himself, first, last and always," says Yen. "My interests are his interests. As long as that remains so I can count on him absolutely. While Doctor Strike would betray me to please his God any time," Yen tells Megan. "Shultz has all I want of the West. Doctor Strike has nothing."

· · ·

Grace Zaring Stone was the great-great-granddaughter of Robert Owen, a social reformer of the Industrial Revolution as well as a pioneer of British socialism whose work inspired the trade union movements and who founded the cooperative colony of New Harmony in Indiana. Stone had lived in many societies; she was born and raised in New York and had traveled to Australia, Java, France, and England. She'd written *The Bitter Tea of General Yen* during the two years she lived in China, when her husband, Ellis Stone, was commander of the U.S. Navy ship *Isabel,* stationed on the Yangtze River. Within three years of its publication, *The Bitter Tea of General Yen* had been published in twenty editions.

What interested Grace Stone in the writing of *The Bitter Tea,* as it did Edith M. Hull in her 1921 novel, *The Sheik,* and William Archer in his play of the same year, *The Green Goddess,* was the idea of taking a white woman of good standing out of her safe milieu, putting her into a wild, exotic setting, still under the rules of "civilized" society and the protection of white men, and then thrusting her into a world where most (white) men would dare not venture, or could not gain entry; a world beyond white colonial law.

At the heart of the novel are two civilizations, two people who come together from different worlds: an American with a belief in a Christian ethic instilled through generations of teaching, brought up to cherish the notions of goodness and mercy and forgiveness; and a Chinese warlord of rarefied tastes—elegant, educated, wise, unsentimental. For three days Megan comes up against Yen's superior mind ("Have you read any of our poetry?" he asks her. "Do you understand our music? Do you know that there has never existed a people more purely artist and therefore more purely lover than the Chinese?").

Megan is shaken by the violent ways of the unchristian general Yen and at a critical moment in his campaign begs him to forgive one of his traitorous concubines rather than execute her. Megan offers him the promise of his soul's salvation. Yen asks Megan if what she is after is understanding or changing him, "to make me over into some new image, the image of God, but also, slightly, the image of Miss Davis."

The questioning of her Christian ethic and her attempt to make Yen over into a humanist, or sentimentalist, comes at little cost to Megan, but her self-discovery and enlightenment come at a high price for General Yen—his empire and his life.

Stone's novel has no hint of romantic attachment between the two. But the script by Edward Paramore is about their impossible love: a sheltered New England woman from the West and a romantic, worldly, "inscrutable"

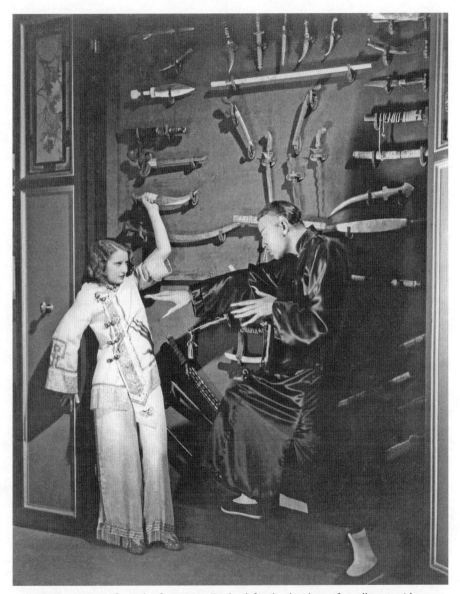

As Megan Davis, from the finest New England family, daughter of a college president, who arrives in a China torn apart by civil war, with Nils Asther as General Yen Tso-Chong, appearing to her in a sexual dream, at first as a terrifying (Oriental) figure (above), from *The Bitter Tea of General Yen,* 1933. (PHOTOFEST)

man from the East who briefly shatter the barriers of convention, race, and custom but cannot thrive in a conventional world.

Yen treats the object of his desire with an Oriental deference that Megan finds hateful and revolting. "You yellow swine," she says to him in her erotic

The costumes were designed by Robert Kalloch, his fourth picture, and Edward Stevenson, who began designing clothes in pictures in 1924 and who worked with Capra on *Ladies of Leisure* and *Forbidden*. (MARGARET HERRICK LIBRARY, ACADEMY OF MOTION PICTURE ARTS AND SCIENCES)

dream when her Christian teaching spills out and she reaches for a knife on the desk behind her. She recoils and is repulsed, then is comforted by his presence and desires him. She is stunned more by the dream that she has just awakened from in which Yen rescues her from an evil Chinese ghoul lying on top of her than by Yen's presence in her room.

In the dream a horrifying man in embroidered brocade robes, with hideous, distorted Oriental features, breaks down the door of Megan's room. He is trying to caress her body with long talons as fingers. First she sees Yen's face, but then it changes into a face with large buck teeth and drawn-back eyes.

At the wall-size octagonal window is a man in Western dress, white slacks, dark blazer, shirt and tie, white panama. He has a dark mask over his eyes. He punches the attacker; the hideous Oriental man falls to the floor, far, far below the bed, and vanishes. The man with the mask takes Megan in his arms. She is relieved, reassured; she is being whirled around and around in ecstasy. Slowly, she lifts the mask away from the stranger's face. It is Yen in another guise but dressed as she can love him: in Western garb. They lie back on the bed, he on top of her. Their mouths are touching; she belongs to him.

During the course of three days she forgets the missionary worker she's traveled to China to marry. She finds Yen alluring; her bigoted, puritanical ways disappear as she feels a sexual yearning she never felt before. Yen is warned by Jones (Shultz in Stone's book), "Don't forget she is a white woman." Yen playfully tugs the brim of Jonesy's hat and says, "I have no prejudice against her color." He is captivated and willing to risk ruin for her.

Frank Capra shot the dream sequence as a silent. To make it more dream-like and unusual, he put Nils Asther (General Yen) on a dolly, rather than the camera. At the end of Stone's novel, Yen is killed by the Communists after helping Megan escape with Mr. Shultz in a sampan headed back to Shang-hai. The end of Paramore's script for Herbert Brenon, the picture's original director, adhered to Stone's novel. But the screenwriter added a penultimate scene, in which General Yen, believing that Megan can never love him, pre-pares a cup of "bitter" tea to end his unbearable pain. As he is about to drink it, Megan comes to Yen's room and confesses her love for him, and he throws away the poisoned drink.

In Harry Cohn's fashion of putting actors and directors under contract on their way up or their way down, Herbert Brenon had been borrowed from RKO by Walter Wanger, the picture's producer, to direct *The Bitter Tea*. Brenon's most successful films, *Peter Pan* and *Beau Geste,* had been silent, and he hadn't fared well with talkies. While at work on *The Bitter Tea*, Brenon missed story conferences and fought with Cohn about money and was soon fired. Capra let it be known that he wanted to direct the picture and was hired.

Constance Cummings, who appeared in Capra's previous picture, *Faith,* was to play Megan Davis. Instead, Capra gave the role to Barbara and turned the picture into a fantasy of a thwarted love that becomes ruinous for the one who seems to make the rules.

In keeping with Capra's thwarted feelings for Barbara, he had Paramore change the scene in which Megan confesses her love for Yen and puts aside the poisoned tea. In the rewritten scene, Yen has ceremoniously prepared his tea and adds the poison powder. He is seated in a chair. His bearing is that of a prince on a throne. His palace is empty; the servants and soldiers have deserted him. The money Jones has amassed in the boxcars of Yen's train has been commandeered by enemy forces. All is lost; the game is over.

Megan comes to Yen's room dressed in Chinese sequined pajamas and makeup. She places a pillow behind Yen's back as she had watched his concu-bine Mah-Li do on the train and covers him with a silk throw. Megan kneels before him. They are close and still.

"I had to come back," she says quietly. "I couldn't leave. I'll never leave you." Yen looks into her eyes and wipes away her tears. She kisses his hand and holds it against her cheek. He sips his bitter tea. He closes his eyes and leans his head back in the chair to die.

She is saved from ruin and dishonor by Yen's death.

For the part of General Yen, Capra wanted a tall, commanding presence. He considered thirty of Hollywood's (white) leading romantic actors before narrowing it down to six possibilities, among them Leo Carrillo, Leslie Banks, and Chester Morris. Each of the six was asked to make a test, studying the part for days without pay. Each test required three hours for makeup to transform the Caucasian faces into that of the warlord General Yen Tso-Chong.

Capra was taken with three of the performances. He saw *The Bitter Tea* as a "woman's picture" and decided to let the women of the studio pick his General Yen. Sixty-five Columbia stenographers were called to the projection room. Each was given a slip of paper to vote for her choice of the most persuasive General Yen. The votes were three to one in favor of Nils Asther, the tall, suave, delicately restrained Swedish actor who was first discovered in 1916 by Mauritz (Moshe; later Moje) Stiller when Asther was in the National Cross-Country Skijoring Race, near Stockholm, something he'd been trying to win since boyhood. Asther lost the race, but Stiller, the film virtuoso called by Emil Jannings "the Stanislavski of the camera," was overwhelmed by Asther's exotic beauty and put him in his picture *The Wings*. Asther traveled to America in 1925, the same year that Stiller and his "Dream woman" creation, Greta Garbo, were brought over from Stockholm by Metro-Goldwyn-Mayer. Asther was put under contract to United Artists, where he appeared in Herbert Brenon's *Sorrell and Son* and in *Topsy and Eva,* the 1927 screen adaptation of *Uncle Tom's Cabin.* He then went to Metro and was starred opposite the studio's biggest names: Marion Davies in *The Cardboard Lover;* Joan Crawford in *Dream of Love* and *Letty Lynton;* and Greta Garbo, to whom he'd proposed three times and to which she'd replied each time, no. Asther was thought of as "the masculine version of that mysterious fascination that is Garbo's." Together they'd attended Stockholm's Kungliga Dramatiska Teatern—the Royal Dramatic Theatre Academy (Asther had said she was "always shy")—and they had co-starred in Metro's *Wild Orchids* and *The Single Standard.*

Asther spoke fluent Swedish, French, and German, but with his English as unpolished as it was, he was going to have to speak his lines phonetically as General Yen.

Once on the set, Asther was reserved. "The make-up may have had something to do with it," said Ed Bernds, Capra's sound engineer on *The Bitter*

The extraordinary look of *The Bitter Tea of General Yen* was designed by Stephen Goosson, Columbia's art director, who worked with Capra before on *Platinum Blond* and *American Madness*. This is one of the quint-essential images from *Bitter Tea*. (PHOTOFEST)

Tea, their sixth picture together. "Asther didn't fraternize with the crew." He said of himself, "I am not gay and amusing and social. I am ingrown, intro-spective, analytical."

Early in the script of *The Bitter Tea,* the missionary wife (Clara Blandick) hosting Megan and Dr. Strike's wedding party says about the Chinese, "They are all tricky, treacherous, immoral. I can't tell one from the other. They are all Chinamen to me." And of General Yen himself she says, "That's what we call our gangsters here—generals."

The portrait of China is that of empire. The West is seen as civilization, and the rest of the world, primitive and savage. In the picture, the disdain for life is everywhere: the hostage taking; the firing squads shooting at prisoners in the midst of the bucolic beauty of Yen's palace garden. Yen is shown to be a man who doesn't care a whit for human life. His car runs down a man transporting Megan through the crowds in the war-torn district of Chapei, Shanghai. Rebel troops are attacking a railroad station, burning houses, shooting at those fleeing. Megan says to Yen when he gets out of his car, unfazed by the death, "What kind of a man are you? You've run down my rickshaw boy." Yen replies, "If that is so, it is very fortunate. Life even at its best is hardly endurable."

The priest in the temple sings out descriptions of arms and transports and money instead of prayer. The Chinese are portrayed as ancestor worshippers for whom life doesn't matter; Buddhism, Taoism, Confucianism—all of the great wisdom of China—are nowhere to be seen. Instead, there is Christianity and self-sacrifice.

During the chaotic scene in Chapei, Barbara, Nils Asther, and Gavin Gordon (Doctor Strike) were supposed to walk past a flaming structure that was wired and doused in kerosene to burn in sections; it was timed to fall sixty seconds after they had passed the spot. During the shooting of the scene, the wood snapped, the kerosene caught fire, and a thirty-foot square of board, lath, and plaster fell seconds before Barbara, Asther, and Gordon were to pass under it.

"Well," said Asther. "You might say that was ashes to ashes, dust to dust."

"I'll take dust," said Barbara.

During the making of the picture, Grace Stone was living in San Diego. Her husband, Commander Ellis Stone, was stationed there, in charge of the destroyer USS *Barry*. The studio invited the writer, her husband, and their fourteen-year-old daughter, Eleanor, to spend a day in Hollywood and visit the set. Stone was introduced to Barbara, Asther, and Walter Connolly, Jones in the movie. She marveled at the realism of the set and felt she was back in China.

Stone didn't say anything but thought the movie was "grotesquely miscast," that Barbara was all wrong for the New England young woman, that her accent was "crude" and her voice "uneducated," and she wasn't at all happy that a Swede was playing the role of a Chinese general.

Capra had wanted Walter Connolly for the part of General Yen's American financial adviser and aide, Jones, who warns the general of the betrayal of his concubine and military aide to the Communist forces. Each of the major Hollywood studios had been trying to lure Connolly away from Broadway for fifteen years without success. He had appeared steadily on the Broadway stage beginning in 1916 and had worked with Ruth Chatterton, Mae Marsh, Billie Burke, and his future wife, Nedda Harrigan, daughter of Edward Harrigan of the vaudeville team Harrigan and Hart. Paramount had wanted Connolly for the first Charlie Chan picture; United Artists had wanted him

With Frank Capra and Grace Zaring Stone, author of *The Bitter Tea of General Yen,* whose first novel, *The Heaven and Earth of Doña Elena,* was published in 1929. At the time of this photograph, Stone was at work on her second, *The Cold Journey.* "I try to write the kind of books that I like to read. That is, tight, with plenty of incident. I know my stories don't resemble in the least the books of Virginia Woolf or *Wuthering Heights.* Must I be called slick because I can't write like Emily Brontë?"

for the innkeeper in *Rain.* Connolly was such a surefire stage actor—the appealing, exasperated, lovable curmudgeon—that he'd been under contract for years to the biggest New York theatrical producers such as George M. Cohan, A. H. Woods, and Jed Harris.

Capra was in luck.

Connolly's two-year contract with Gilbert Miller had expired three days before, when the extended run of *The Good Fairy,* starring Helen Hayes, had closed in Chicago. Capra tracked down Connolly in a Chicago hospital following a hernia operation, still groggy from the effects of the anesthesia. Connolly's wrists were tied to the bed, and a nurse had to hold the phone for him while he listened to Capra describe the part of Jones, Yen's American mercenary adviser. Capra assured Connolly he wouldn't have to learn Chinese for the role. Before Connolly fell back asleep, he agreed to take the part.

Connolly saw being a character actor as being similar to a country doctor carrying powders and pills. He believed that character actors got their training through long years of stage experience, experimenting with characteris-

With the versatile Walter Connolly as Jones, Yen's American financial advisor. "I kept away from pictures for nearly sixteen years," he said, "and I am not sorry that I finally yielded." From *The Bitter Tea of General Yen.* (PHOTOFEST)

tics, foibles, mannerisms, and eccentricities that make one character different from another.

The Bitter Tea of General Yen was a lavish picture for Columbia. Capra took great pains with it, carefully planning each detail of the production. The sets, designed by Steve Goosson—the interiors and exteriors of the palace, a reproduction of a palace a hundred years old; the huge four-block railroad station; an entire street in the Soo Chow Creek district of Shanghai, another in the Chapei section—required 500,000 square feet of lumber, 5,000 square yards of muslin, 500 gallons of paint, and 24,000 hours of union labor.

More than $200,000 worth of Chinese antiques, tapestries, vases, statues, rugs, chairs, paintings, bureaus, and shrines were used. Wine-red velour was used on the doors, as were gold-finished figures and muslins in pink, beige, and red. One bronze incense burner that took ten years of the life of a Chinese craftsman and then drove him crazy from the monotony of the work cost $7,000. The set dresser even found an opium bed, carved in ebony and ivory, that had never been used by anyone but its owner in Shanghai.

Several endings of the picture were shot. Grace Stone was informed that they hadn't been able to decide which one to go with until an ending had

With General Yen and Mah-Li (Toshia Mori), his concubine, on his train traveling from Shanghai, across China to his compound. Weeks before the picture was to start shooting in early July 1932, the *New York Times* announced that Anna May Wong, who had appeared in *Daughters of the Dragon* and the recent *Shanghai Express,* had been hired by Columbia for one of the leads in the "appropriately Oriental *The Bitter Tea of General Yen.*" (PHOTOFEST)

been chosen which was thought to be "finally right." It was the ending Stone had written in the book.

Joe Walker was once again Capra's cameraman. It was their seventh picture together. The mystical look of *General Yen* was unlike that of most of Capra's pictures. "People want to see things as they really are," Capra said. "Reality is what is wanted in pictures, not symbolic touches and beautiful settings for mere beauty's sake." Capra was after an Academy Award. He still didn't understand why his pictures, which he felt were better than those of other directors, weren't winning awards.

Harry Cohn said, "They'll never vote for that comedy crap you make. They only vote for that arty crap."

Capra decided to make one of "those arty things." He didn't like "fancy shooting," as he called it. He believed the camera should see life as it is and the microphone hear it as it is.

The look of *The Bitter Tea of General Yen*—dreamy, exotic, otherworldly— was achieved through Joe Walker's camera work and innovation and Capra's direction. "A cinematographer can do more than any other individual,"

Capra said, "in portraying the mood of the story. The good cinematographer portrays that mood, lights his picture so that the audience doesn't realize he has lighted it, gets over the proper effect so that the audience doesn't realize he has done it."

Walker darkened the foreground of each shot and highlighted the background farthest away from the camera, and he emphasized this by placing a piece of furniture, tiny Buddha, vase, or intricate Chinese statue in front of and closer to the camera than the action of the scene. In addition, Walker improved the technique of diffusion. Up to that time diffusion was difficult to work with. Once it was on a lens, it couldn't be changed mid-scene. Walker's invention of "variable diffusion" made it possible to change the diffusion freely while the camera was running. The sheen to the picture came from using silk stockings over the camera lens in different moments. When Capra wanted something to be seen clearly, a hole was burned in the stocking with a lit cigarette.

Fourteen days of shooting were done at night. They began at 7:30 each evening and quit before dawn. Barbara went to bed at 5:30 each morning and woke at noon. Asther could only sleep for an hour or so. Connolly, who was used to the hours of the theater and didn't usually go to bed before four in the morning, had no problem adjusting to the production's odd hours.

The look of *The Bitter Tea* was influenced by Josef von Sternberg's most recent picture, *Shanghai Express,* released five months earlier. *Shanghai Express* was about faith and rebirth, *Bitter Tea* about loss, convention, and clash of cultures. Each picture puts forth the notion of a violent, exotic country where "time and life count for nothing" (*Shanghai Express*); where "human life is the cheapest thing" (*The Bitter Tea*). Each suggests an atmospheric magic—as well as a sense of the ominous, the foreboding—associated with a late-nineteenth century Western view of the Orient.

The settings of *Shanghai Express* and *The Bitter Tea* are similar: China during a civil war in which a train carries the principals to their fate. Each production is rich, lavish, stylized: the lighting of each is diffused and alluring.

Each features a Chinese concubine. In *Shanghai Express,* Anna May Wong is Hui Fei, a "coaster" who lives by her wits. She is raped by the commander in chief of the revolutionary forces (Warner Oland), who has waylaid the train in search of a hostage important enough to exchange with the government for the commander's top aide. The Anna May Wong character is so dishonored and debased by the commander that she stabs him to death, heroically saving the passengers on the train and presumably thousands of others who would have died at his hands.

In *General Yen,* the twenty-year-old Toshia Mori is Mah-Li (Anna May

Joseph Walker was director of photography for *The Bitter Tea of General Yen*. He started in 1921 and worked with Capra on each of his pictures at Columbia.

Wong was originally to have played the part; Toshia Mori, who came from a family of sixteen generations of doctors, won the part of the Chinese concubine). Mah-Li is General Yen's favorite concubine. She pampers him and receives his gifts of luxury and precious jade, only to betray him by her clandestine love for Yen's closest adviser and her revelations of the general's plans and strategies.

The almost still photographic shots of Barbara in *General Yen* were similar to those von Sternberg used for Marlene Dietrich. *Shanghai Express* was a great success for both Sternberg and Dietrich.

The shadows on Dietrich's face, the power struggle between Dietrich and von Sternberg, being submissive and dominating at the same time, were nowhere in Capra's *Bitter Tea*. The undercurrents of the Dietrich/von Sternberg relationship that seem to fill every shot of each movie the actress and the director made together were not present between Barbara and Capra in *The Bitter Tea*. Where von Sternberg was an artist who could easily destroy himself for art and an idea, Capra was more pragmatic. His renunciation of Barbara as he attempts to deify her disarms her of her energy, independence, wit, openness. He gives her courage but not nobility in the form of sacrifice as von Sternberg gives Dietrich.

Joe Walker's use of his newly designed special portrait lenses that allowed Capra to get a beatific close-up of Barbara with light surrounding her hair didn't help to create a sexual tension; Capra's infatuation with Barbara was over.

"For me, *Bitter Tea* is unforgettable," said Ed Bernds. "It was colorful, full of action: the riots, the Chinese civil war . . . There were battles in the crowded streets of Shanghai, and there was a dramatic night sequence, an attack on General Yen's gold train made possible by Mah-Li's treachery," for which a thousand extras were hired.

The night sequence was shot with dozens of arc lights, two complete trains belching smoke and every once in a while jets of steam, and two armies. Hundreds of soldiers on both sides. "Capra, very calmly, was in charge of everything," said Bernds. "Not excited, patient; people [were] coming from all directions, asking questions, wanting a decision. [Capra] was like a general in the midst of battle, issuing orders right and left, three or four people at the time wanting an answer. He handled the big scenes with all these soldiers expertly; he was unflappable."

Bernds said there was a great deal of tension around the scene of Yen's suicide. "Usually, on a Capra set there was a lot of camaraderie. Capra liked making bantering remarks about people." The crew was "an instrument of Capra's," said Bernds. "The head cameraman, his first assistant, the mike man, the head grip, the head electrician, when there was going to be a tense, demanding scene, we became tense and keyed up doing it."

Capra tried everything to take the pressure off an actor. He tried not to show annoyance, knowing that if he did, it would only make the actor more tense. He knew when an actor was about to blow the line; the eyes would change, and he would yell "cut" to talk about a shadow on the back of the wall. "Walker was in on it," said Bernds. "And Joe would fiddle with the lights, and then they would shoot again." Usually, the actor regained his or her composure and would do the scene perfectly. When an actor blew again, Capra would pick up a handful of double-headed nails used on sets for braces and toss the nails behind him, making sure that no one was standing in back of him.

Capra would pretend to be angry at the noise and demand to know who had made the racket. The actor then had time to cool off and think it wasn't his fault.

Barbara was letter-perfect with her lines even if a scene had been rewritten the night before and she was handed the pages in the morning.

For one of the scenes, Capra rehearsed an actor over and over again.

"I'm no novice," the actor said. "I don't need an all-day rehearsal."

"You don't know Stanwyck. When she goes into an emotional scene, she'll sweep you with her like a chip on a tidal wave. She'll stir you until you'll blow and forget everything you ever knew. But once she's done that scene, she's shot. She can't do it over and give it the same stuff."

In spite of Capra's warning, the scene started, and the actor instead of reacting to Barbara began to watch her and blew his line.

"She gets them all," one assistant director said. "Even hardened grips and electricians flood the set with their tears when she gets going."

The Purchase Price was released during the shooting of *The Bitter Tea.* Zanuck sent Barbara a note he'd received criticizing Warner Bros. for producing such an inferior picture.

"I chose that picture," said Barbara. "How I fought for it. I just knew it would make a good picture. There is no one to blame but me."

NINE

A Path to Motherhood

Barbara wanted to adopt a child. "I want one so badly that it amounts to a phobia," she said. "I can't wait any longer. If I do, I'll become morbid on the subject—and no mother should be morbid."

After five years of marriage to Frank Fay, Barbara was determined to have a child. "All my life, I think I have wanted a baby," she said. "When I dream, I dream that I have a baby in my arms—I can see its little face and feel it." Barbara told her friend and business acquaintance Ann Hoyt that she was interested in adopting a baby.

"I suppose I could go to some orphans home," Barbara said. She was concerned, though, that the public might think she was doing it for publicity purposes.

Hoyt went several times to the Children's Home Society on East Thirty-Fifth Street in Los Angeles and saw one baby she thought Barbara would like. The child wasn't up for adoption, but after several visits Ann was told the baby was available. Hoyt gave Barbara the news, and early one evening, after Barbara finished working for the day, she and Hoyt went to the home to see the child.

Barbara looked at "the babies there, unwanted, unclaimed, born into a world that had no place for them," and thought of her own childhood. "I knew those babies belonged to me almost as preciously as any child of my own could belong. It didn't need the physical act of motherhood to make our hearts open or to give us love for these babies who were ours just because they were babies."

Barbara hadn't discussed with Fay that she was taking steps to adopt a baby, but now she would have to. A woman couldn't legally adopt a child without her husband's approval. Fay was perfectly content not having children; he was preoccupied, in a fight for his professional survival.

A Fool's Advice was still without a distributor. Joe Brandt of World-Wide was interested in distributing the picture but hadn't yet agreed to do so. Fay was trying to get theaters to book the picture with the added enticement of his personal appearance with Barbara.

Barbara was adamant about wanting a baby. She was determined to adopt a child regardless of Fay's objections, or his drinking. Frank finally agreed to go with her to the Children's Home Society to see the baby. They were told that Vivian Greene had given birth to John Charles Greene in Los Angeles on February 5, 1932. The infant boy was five months old.

"I wonder if the baby isn't really the only important thing—the care of the baby," said Barbara.

Soon after, Fay was admitted for the third time to a sanitarium to dry out, this one near El Monte. On his release he was to go into a new show being produced by Felix Young called *Tattle Tales.*

Barbara finished shooting *The Bitter Tea,* and Ann Hoyt brought the six-month-old baby boy to the Fays' house to stay for good. She brought a nurse along with her. Miss Richter put the baby in his crib in the nursery, which was across the hall from her room. Barbara's room was at the opposite end of the hall; Fay's was across from hers and up one step, in the back next to the den.

Frank started to go into the nursery to see the baby and was stopped by Nurse Richter, who said the child shouldn't be disturbed. It was past the baby's bedtime; he'd been taken out of the residence and was nervous and tired. Fay didn't understand why in his own home he couldn't see the child whenever he wanted; after all the child was his. Miss Richter said, "If I'm going to be responsible for the child's health, I forbid you or anyone else from going in to see the child."

Barbara fired Miss Richter the next day.

Ann Hoyt and several doctors recommended another nurse, the Scottish-born Nellie Banner, who was thought to be an outstanding child specialist and who had previously worked as a nanny for a banking family in San Francisco. Barbara hired her.

Barbara changed the baby's name from John to Dion, after Dion Boucicault, the seminal, scandalous nineteenth-century playwright, actor, translator, revolutionary theater designer (New York's Winter Garden), and manager.

"All I wish for him," Fay said of his new son, "is that he will grow up to have the sweetness, the mentality and genius of Boucicault and the guts of Dion O'Banion [underworld boss, bootlegger equally famous as a florist and rival of Al Capone]."

Dion Anthony Fay, Bristol Avenue, Brentwood, California, 1932. (COURTESY TONY FAY)

• • •

Barbara had been discussing with her sister the idea of her coming to live in Los Angeles. She wanted Maud to be near her because of Fay's drinking. Maud finally agreed to move out west with Bert and their son, Al, who was three years younger than his aunt Barbara.

Bert would leave his job at Merkent's Meat Market, where he'd worked for almost two decades, and look for something in Los Angeles. Mabel's son, Gene, was away at Boy Scout camp until late August, but the Merkents decided to drive cross-country in July. Gene would join them at the end of the summer and finish his last year of high school in Los Angeles.

Maud, Bert, and Al drove west to California in their 1932 Ford Tudor Sedan. Barbara rented a small two-bedroom house for them from Dorothy Sebastian on Carmelina Drive in Brentwood, two miles from North Bristol. The Sebastian house was a modest one-story Spanish-style red-tiled house near the Brentwood Country Club. Barbara made arrangements for Gene to attend University High School in Sawtelle.

During the shooting of *The Bitter Tea,* Warner Bros., like other Hollywood studios, announced it was cutting the salaries of its stars and featured players, including Ruth Chatterton and William Powell, each of whom was earning $7,500 a week, and Barbara, who was earning $5,000 a week.

Greta Garbo and Maurice Chevalier, according to a survey of box-office reaction to movie actors, were the two biggest moneymakers in Hollywood;

Al Merkent, driving his parents from Brooklyn to Los Angeles. Barbara had rented Dorothy Sebastian's small Spanish-style house for her nephew, sister, and brother-in-law; it was close to the Brentwood Country Club and only a couple of miles from Bristol Avenue. (COURTESY JUNE D. MERKENT)

each listed in the AA class. The A class consisted of Warner–First National's George Arliss, United Artists' Ronald Colman, and Metro's Joan Crawford, Norma Shearer, Marie Dressler, Wallace Beery, and Clark Gable. Radio Pictures and Fox followed with the BB stars Will Rogers and Janet Gaynor, and Constance Bennett, Ann Harding, and Richard Dix were listed for RKO. B actors included John and Lionel Barrymore, Jackie Cooper, and Ramon Novarro. Columbia started with C actors with Barbara Stanwyck, the only actress listed. The D list included Helen Twelvetrees, Joel McCrea, Dolores del Río, Adolphe Menjou, Polly Moran, and Jimmy Durante.

Warner told Barbara that her option was being renewed for another year. As far as Barbara was concerned, the studio had allowed its option period to lapse. Her original contract with Warner had been signed on August 1, 1931, but was set back fifteen days before it went into effect. The option renewal was called for August 1, 1932; the studio had failed to notify Barbara before August 15, and to her her option was canceled.

She insisted on a new contract. Part of the agreement was contingent on the studio contracting with Fay for the sale of *A Fool's Advice* minus British rights, which Frank had previously sold to Sterling Film Company. Warner agreed to pay Fay $50,000 against 50 percent of the net, plus prints and advertising costs and 35 percent of the gross receipts of distribution cost. There was talk of Fay making three pictures for Warner, including one based on the life of the composer Stephen Foster, none of which was reflected in Frank's contract for *A Fool's Advice*.

Warner agreed to a new contract for Barbara that would go into effect following the completion of her third picture for the studio, *Women in Prison;* Archie Mayo, who had directed Barbara in *Illicit,* was to direct the picture. Barbara's new arrangement with Warner was for an exclusive one-year contract for three pictures, with the understanding that there would be "no more back to the farm" roles. Barbara was to be paid $150,000: fifty installments of $3,000. Warner had three one-year options: three additional pictures for the first year at $175,000; $225,000 for the second year; $275,000 for the third.

Fay was finally free from trying to sell *A Fool's Advice.* Now he had other problems. He'd been brought up on charges for a hit-and-run incident. Bail was posted at $1,500; the charges were ultimately dropped when the driver of the other car refused to testify against him in court.

Barbara was besotted with their son. Dion Anthony had his first two teeth; he was healthy and loved, and Barbara was considering adopting more children.

"Did you ever notice the expression on the faces of orphans?" asked Barbara. "They're all alike. There's a deadness, a dreariness about them that to anyone who has ever lived in an orphanage marks them at once. Their eyes are lonely. As if they're searching for someone to belong to."

TEN

A Most Dangerous Man Menace

1932–1933

A product of crowded places and jammed-up emotions . . .
—Barbara Stanwyck

Yes, we could smell the depression in the air . . . which chilled so many of us like a world's end . . . It was like a raw wind; the very houses we lived in seemed to be shrinking, hopeless of real comfort.
—Harold Clurman

Barbara was determined to move away from the linsey-woolsey roles of *So Big* and *The Purchase Price*.

"Thalberg has the right idea for Norma Shearer," she said. "She does *Strange Interlude* and then *Smilin' Through* and that's going from the bedroom to the garden with a vengeance."

Barbara's third picture under her old Warner contract, originally called *Women in Prison*, then *Lady No. 6142*, then *Betrayed*, began production the first week in October 1932.

It was from a play by Dorothy Mackaye and Carlton Miles, based on Mackaye's years in prison as a result of the murder of her ex-husband by Mackaye's present husband, Paul Kelly. Working with Barbara were Lyle Talbot, the poor man's Clark Gable, a lead in stock and a popular supporting actor; Preston Foster, Lillian Roth, Dorothy Burgess, Maud Eburne, Ruth Donnelly, and Robert Warwick.

Instead of a nightclub singer who sheds her city (sullied) ways and is reborn by the toil of the land, or the selfless librarian transformed into a woman of the world who sacrifices all for (forbidden) love, Barbara's character in *Lady No. 6142* picked up where she left off with *Night Nurse* and *Illicit*.

"I'll be glad to get away from asparagus and wheat for a while," she said, "even if I do have to go to jail to do it. I'm not depending on sex to put me over. People are tired of seeing me a frump and I'm tired of being one. In *So Big* I raised asparagus and suffered in an asparagus bed. In *The Purchase Price,* I did my suffering in a wheat field."

Now her character would do her suffering, or most of it, behind bars. "But believe me," she said, "I'm going to do my suffering so they'll like it. I think people would rather see a woman sin and suffer in a pair of silk pajamas than in a flannel night gown."

"Barbara Stanwyck is going sexy again," said the press. "Off with the muslin and on with the satin. The Stanwyck girl is trading her flannel nighties for clinging silk . . . she's going sophisticate, bag and baggage."

Lady No. 6142 is tough and knowing; she's been to hell and back. She's a member of an underworld mob, a gangster's moll who turns decoy for her bank-robber boyfriend, is caught mid-heist, and is sent up the river, serving "two to five" in San Quentin.

It was exactly the kind of Victorian story that Darryl Zanuck, Warner's production head, gravitated toward and had written many times before. Zanuck consistently produced great box-office successes for the studio and was considered Jack Warner's heir apparent. Zanuck was thin, wiry, a two-goal polo player ("From Poland to polo in two generations," said the Broadway playwright and screenwriter Arthur Caesar of Zanuck), and a challenger of Irving Thalberg's for the title of "young genius of the films." He was a story writer from way back.

He'd left Omaha, Nebraska, a discharged soldier (private first class) of sixteen who survived the Great War, and headed for California with dreams of being a writer. Once out west in a "lousy rooming house" in the downtown part of Los Angeles, he wrote story after story, sometimes two a day, which he sent off to the pulp magazines looking for fiction about tough heroes brought to their knees by drink, women, and dope, who are reborn by their courage, fortitude, and the love of a decent woman.

The tough-guy hero primed for a fall in *Lady No. 6142* is the seen-it-all gun moll who long ago began her descent; she's the daughter of a small-town deacon ("Too much deaconing took all of the sweetness out of me," she

As Nan Taylor, serving time for being a decoy in a bank heist, in *Lady No. 6142*, the third in a trio of Warners prison tales. The others recently released: *I Am a Fugitive from a Chain Gang*, mid-November 1932, and *20,000 Years in Sing Sing*, December 24, 1932. (PHOTOFEST)

says) who does time in reform school before the story starts, goes to the state pen, and is reborn through the love of a God-fearing evangelist, who happens to come from the same small town she does and is the son of the town drunk.

"I never was the type to make men think," said Barbara about the part of Nan Taylor, "but perhaps I can make them react. I've known women who plodded through life, just as my character did in *So Big*, but the women I knew did their plodding on the pavement and not the soil. I know very little about the simple life. I'm a product of crowded places and jammed-up emotions, where right and wrong weren't always clearly defined and life wasn't always sweet, but it was life."

The moll is trapped in the bank while robbing it, and underneath her platinum wig a cop recognizes the "elegant lady" playing at-a-loss-without-her-maid as the cool, cold swagger of Nan Taylor. ("For a dumb dick," she tells him in a slow, world-weary way, "you have a memory like an elephant.")

During Nan Taylor's first day in San Quentin (to her cell mates, she's just another "new fish") she turns off the inmates' communal radio. She's told in no uncertain terms that she can't just walk in and take over the joint. "Yeah," says Nan, her hand on her hip. "When they add you up, what do you spell? And that goes for all of you." Barbara as Nan is all punch and guts.

Later Nan says, "I've gone around with almost everything, but it was baby's milk compared to coming through here with all these dames staring at you."

Warner wanted to shoot inside San Quentin, but the state prison board refused the studio's request, and the prison scenes were to be shot in Burbank.

John Seitz, the cameraman for the picture, was borrowed by Zanuck from Fox. Seitz shot without making any preliminary tests of Barbara. She trusted Zanuck's eye and didn't need to see how she would look.

Shooting on the picture began right away.

Preston Foster had made almost a dozen pictures, but this was his first time working with a star. Barbara gave Foster a Saint Genesius medal. "If Genesius was the patron saint of actors," said Foster, "[Barbara] is the patroness. Nobody else is quite like her."

Lyle Talbot, as Barbara's menacing bank-robber boyfriend, played the same part he played in Michael Curtiz's not-yet-released *20,000 Years in Sing Sing*, which starred Spencer Tracy and Bette Davis.

Lady No. 6142 is a fantasy—a jail fantasy that shows women in prison living in neat little rooms, playing records, throwing pillows, as if they're in a girls' school. Lillian Roth is the pretty, cute "good-girl" prisoner who shows Nan Taylor the ropes. Roth plays a ukulele and sings to her heartthrob Joe E. Brown, whose photograph is tacked on a wall in her cell ("All I do is dream of you the whole night through"). A society dowager (Helen Ware), doing time for murder (in a fit of jealousy she ground up glass and served it in the caviar to her "special guest"), is in prison with her lapdog and her black servant, who does her laundry. There's tough old Aunt Maggie (Maud Eburne), cigarette hanging from her mouth, in for having what she calls a "beauty parlor," until a detective sergeant comes for a manicure and busts up her whorehouse. The touch of real danger comes from a cigar-smoking gal inmate with short slicked-back hair, shirt, and tie, with a propensity for wrestling.

Barbara gives Nan Taylor energy and spirit. The challenge was for her to take something unbelievable and make it plausible, which she does by the sheer force of her personality. She plays it with wit and intelligence. She's free from Capra's fantasy and what he projected onto her, not that she was uncomfortable with it; it just wasn't that much fun to work with, which is exactly what *Lady No. 6142—Ladies They Talk About*—is: jazzy and fun.

The picture was shot in twenty-four days and cost $176,000 to make.

Barbara was taking home more than $4,700 a week. Fay was spending it as quickly as it came in. She returned from the studio one day to find a wall of their house knocked down to enlarge the game room and a crew of ten workmen swarming throughout.

Barbara was finished shooting *Ladies They Talk About* when Zanuck sent over a synopsis of a story for her next picture, about a small-town girl, a hash slinger in her father's rough-trade Pittsburgh speakeasy who's pawed by the customers and, after her father dies in an explosion, is forced to go to the big city to earn a living. She finds work in the lowest rung of a banking company and seduces her way up the company hierarchy, from the humble doorman to the pompous president, destroying the lives of each of the twelve men she leaves behind, draining them of money and honor. Each is bewitched by her ways and devastated when she leaves, including the elderly head of the banking firm, who falls under her spell.

Of the kind of woman Barbara was about to play, she said, "The baby-face type was the champ home wrecker from the gay nineties down to the shot that killed the Austrian Archduke. The petit enfant terrible, with her childish voice and helpless clinging ways, was the prize package of naughty femininity during pre-war days. She's coming back, along with other pre-war fashions. (Long slinky dresses, ruffs and frills and corsets—even if they don't call them corsets any more—and leg o' mutton sleeves, and little capes and jackets and muffs.)"

Baby Face was an original short story by Cosmo Hamilton, published in *Hearst's International* magazine in 1917 and bought by First National a decade later for $1,000.

Barbara was once again delighted to move away from the motherly and farmer's wife roles. Baby Face was a daring role for her: from Madonna to deadly vamp in one quick elevator ride to the top. Lily Powers is ruthless, deliberate, cold-blooded, entrancing. She is the way men have been for ages.

In early November 1932, Zanuck and Barbara met to develop the story.

"Zanuck could write ten times faster than any ordinary man," Jack Warner said. "He worked Saturdays, Sundays and nights. He could leave on Friday and come back on Monday with a script."

Zanuck had started at Warner Bros. as a scriptwriter when Jack Warner decided to make Rin Tin Tin a star. Zanuck had come up with a story and acted it out for Warner, with Zanuck playing the part of the dog. It was 1923; Zanuck was twenty-one. From his first script, *Find Your Man,* he took the basic ideas he'd used for the pulp magazines and in *Rin Tin Tin* replaced the redemptive element of a good and pure woman with a dog—the tough, courageous hero who saves his master from destruction by his constancy and love.

Zanuck wrote six more Rin Tin Tin scripts, one a month.

By 1925 the dog was an international star, and the success of the Rin Tin Tin pictures was responsible for turning around the financial state of the Warner Bros. studio.

Zanuck didn't write just dog adventures. He could write anything: a gangster comedy for Dolores Costello; a dual role for Montagu Love; a comedy about gold diggers (it took four days to write and reappeared as *The Life of the Party* and still later as *Havana Widows*). Zanuck adapted a melodrama about the Spanish-American War (*Across the Pacific*). He wrote about the San Francisco earthquake (*Old San Francisco*) and the first horseless carriage (*The First Auto*).

In one year Zanuck had written nineteen Warner Bros. features. His name appeared on the screen so frequently that a stockholder stood up at a meeting and asked Jack Warner about the expenses for the story department: "Why the hell do you spend so much money? You've only got one writer." The studio had two or three other writers under contract, but Zanuck admitted he wrote "half of the pictures." Jack Warner decided that he should write under different names. Zanuck came up with the names Melville Crossman, Mark Canfield, and Gregory Rogers—and put each under contract, increasing his weekly paycheck to $1,000. Crossman wrote class pictures (*Tenderloin*); Canfield, melodramas (*The Black Diamond Express; The Desired Woman*); and Rogers, comedies (*Hogan's Alley; The Midnight Taxi*). Jack Warner referred to Zanuck as Three Charming Fellows.

Melville Crossman "became a star," said Zanuck. "Every time his name was on a picture, it was a hit." Louis B. Mayer offered "Crossman" a writing contract. "He isn't available," Zanuck said, "but I think I could get Darryl F. Zanuck for you. He's just finished *Old San Francisco,* which I believe you saw at the sneak last night."

"Not interested," said Mayer.

For *Baby Face,* Zanuck's secretary, Molly Mandeville, plump and motherly, sat at the side of Zanuck's desk and took notes of everything he and Barbara discussed. Barbara thought it was important to establish the opening atmo-

BARBARA STANWYCK—Warner Bros. & Vitaphone Pictures

As Lily Powers, "the sweetheart of the nightshift"; "the baby faced siren as fickle as the famed Helen of Troy," . . . Lily's teacher, an elderly German cobbler, advises her: "A woman, young, beautiful like you, can get anything she wants in the world. Because you have power over men . . . You must be a master, not a slave. Look here—Nietzsche says, 'All life, no matter how we idealize it, is nothing more nor less than exploitation.' Exploit yourself. Go to some big city . . . Use men! Be strong! Defiant! . . ." (AMERICAN HERITAGE CENTER, UNIVERSITY OF WYOMING)

spheric idea of the mills, to show how the girl is forced to dance for a few shekels almost nude with the low-down characters of the mining town. The men give her money, which the father instantly takes from her. She and Zanuck thought the father should beat the girl and force her into a room where he knows a man is waiting for his daughter—and then turn the key in the lock after her.

Baby Face learns her ways from her father ("Yeah, I'm a tramp," she says, "and who's to blame . . . A swell start you gave me. Nothing but men! Dirty rotten men. And you're lower than any of them"). He sees her beauty as a lure to attract the mill workers to his speakeasy, and she sees men as mere stepping-stones on the road to wealth, luxury, and security. She ruthlessly takes from each man in turn everything he has to give her, rapidly going on to the next, making sure that each succeeding man is more powerful than the last, leaving ruined and broken lives in her wake.

Beauty and charm are her sole stock-in-trade. Jealousy, murder, and scandal are her trademarks, until the survival of the bank is at stake. To avoid further scandal, and as a payoff, the devil-temptress is shipped off to Europe to work in the Paris office, where she instantly seduces the new president of the bank, marries him, and, when he is about to lose everything, realizes she's fallen in love with him and gives him the one thing that means everything to her, her hard-acquired jewels: her way out should all else fail. She remembers her father and what he put her through and tells the banker in an impassioned scene that if she gives him the money, he will be sending her back to the hell from which she escaped and that without money she will be forced to "suffer the indignities of man's bestiality."

Together, Barbara and Zanuck worked out the idea of the girl newly arrived in the city, coming to the bank: the opening shot being the facade of the bank; the camera panning from the basement to the top floor, showing the majesty and imposing power of the institution.

Actress and writer/producer worked out the notion that Baby Face's early affairs were to be played in a comedy vein. Once she's in Paris and living with the banker, the tone was to shift and become more romantic in feeling to make it clear that she is falling in love.

Zanuck wrote the original story and for one dollar assigned all rights of *Baby Face* to Warner Bros. Warner had released the title of *Baby Face* to Universal months before and arranged with the studio to have the rights reverted.

Gene Markey, novelist, short story writer, and screenwriter, was brought over from Paramount to work on the script. Markey had sold four stories to the movies and had written seven pictures, among them an adaptation of a Pirandello play, *As You Desire Me,* that starred Greta Garbo and Melvyn Douglas. Markey had been in Hollywood for a couple of years and had recently married Joan Bennett.

The screenwriter, who was as well a witty caricaturist, was "thrilled," Zanuck wrote to Barbara, to be working on "the picture."

Zanuck wanted Barbara's auburn hair to be dyed a flaming titian gold, but she refused. Each step up the ladder of men and money was supposed to be reflected in the way Lily Powers looks. Since Barbara wouldn't allow her hair to be dyed, seven specially designed wigs were constructed, each the same color and texture but designed in different styles to reflect Lily Powers' growing social position and accumulation of money.

Gone was the prison garb of *Ladies They Talk About,* the hopsack of *The Purchase Price* and *So Big,* and the flimsy dress Barbara wears throughout *The Bitter Tea.* For *Baby Face,* Orry-Kelly put Barbara in a series of extravagant dresses—twenty-five in all—velvets, clinging sheer materials, furs, and the

Gene Markey wrote the script of *Baby Face* with Kathryn Scola. He's seen here with his new bride, Joan Bennett, 1932. Markey was a deft caricaturist (his portraits of literary figures were published by Alfred Knopf) as well as his being a novelist whose subjects included the jazz age (*Anabel* and *Stepping High* among them). (PHOTOFEST)

latest in soft negligees, each among the most feminine Kelly had made for any star.

Kelly was able to show the character as a plain, illiterate little barkeep and "build her up, step by step," he said, "until the climax shows her as a cultured, gorgeous, eminently smart woman."

Barbara's co-star was the dark, handsome George Brent. Brent was becoming a somewhat stodgy actor whose life before coming to Hollywood was one of surprising high-wire daring. He'd served in the British army and cast his lot, he claimed, with the Irish revolutionists after the Great War carrying dispatches for two years in the secret service of the Sinn Fein, from Dublin to Belfast and Glasgow, successfully eluding the Black and Tans as he traveled across the country. Now he was newly married to his frequent leading lady and star, Ruth Chatterton. In the picture as well was Donald Cook, Warner's contract player, who'd set out to be a farmer rather than an actor and who went from the lumber business in Kansas City to being discovered by Mrs. Fiske, then touring in *The Rivals*. Warner Bros. put Cook in *The Mad Genius* and *The Man Who Played God*.

Also in *Baby Face* was twenty-six-year-old John Wayne, who'd appeared in a

As Lily Powers with Henry Kolker as Carter, first vice-president of Gotham Trust Company, *Baby Face,* 1933. "Here's a drama for those who can *take* it—with the only woman on the screen who isn't afraid to *let herself go!* . . . A picture that gives you everything—*except their right names!*"

series of Westerns with Duke, his devil horse. Alphonse Ethier, who appeared in more than thirty-five silents before working in talking pictures, played Cragg, the cobbler who reads and preaches Nietzsche while he mends shoes and gives Lily the advice that shapes her life: it is the strong who take and the weak who give. It is the messianic cobbler who counsels Lily to use men to her advantage.

Alfred Green, the director, was a former actor who two decades before had started out with the Selig Polyscope Company, maker of wild animal films; he had made more than fifty pictures, beginning in 1916, among them *Little Lord Fauntleroy* with Mary Pickford and *Disraeli* with George Arliss.

Barbara was the gold-digging baby-faced doll deluxe. Reputation and ethics have no place in her world.

"It is a new line of parts," said Barbara. "A hard woman who wants everything and takes it whether it hurts somebody else or not." She was "a little

With John Wayne as Jimmy McCoy Jr., an "under manager" whose infatuation with Lily helps her ascend at the bank until he is warned, "Wake up, kid, Baby Face is moving out of your class." *Baby Face,* 1933.

nervous over it. All my other roles have had sympathy. I hope the public likes me in it."

During the weeks Barbara and Zanuck developed the script for *Baby Face,* President Hoover and Vice President Charles Curtis of Kansas were defeated by Franklin D. Roosevelt and Speaker of the House John Nance Garner. Roosevelt and Garner carried forty-two states, receiving twenty-two million popular votes to Hoover's more than fifteen million.

Barbara was dead set against Roosevelt. "Every time his name was brought up," said her nephew Gene, "why, she was just up and down."

Most studio heads had supported Hoover. Jack, Harry, and Albert Warner, "faithful Republicans," had championed Roosevelt. Harry Warner had said to Jack, "The country is in chaos. There is a revolution in the air, and we need a change." Jack Warner had organized a three-hour spectacular rally at the Olympic Stadium attended by more than seventy thousand people, twenty marching bands, a polo team, Charlie Chaplin, Clark Gable, and the Warner stock company and was told by his brother Harry to persuade William Randolph Hearst, who'd initially supported Roosevelt's running mate, John Garner of Texas, to support Roosevelt. Hearst reluctantly came around. Cecil B. DeMille, who'd given Hoover in 1928 the largest contribution he'd ever made to a political campaign, voted for Roosevelt for president for one reason: Prohibition, which, said DeMille, had brought "so many evils into American life."

· · ·

Weeks after the election, Barbara and Fay filed a petition in Superior Court of the State of California in Los Angeles for a formal hearing regarding Dion's adoption. It was set for December 1. Barbara reminded Fay that the hearing was coming up and to make sure to leave the date free; she didn't want anything to prevent him from being there.

On the morning the Fays were due in court, Frank told Barbara he wasn't going. The adoption couldn't be formalized without both parents present in the courtroom to testify and consent to it. When Fay refused to be there Barbara went without him.

In the courtroom with Barbara were Dion and his nurse; her lawyers, George Hooper and Charles Cradick; her brother, Byron Stevens; Ann Hoyt; and the lawyers from the Children's Home Society. Barbara testified before the court. Judge Samuel R. Blake then called Fay to the stand. The judge was told that Fay wasn't present and called a halt to the hearing, saying it would reconvene the following Tuesday at 10:00 a.m. with Mr. Fay in the courtroom.

Barbara was furious. During the next few days she made it clear to Fay that unless he went to court with her and consented to the adoption under oath, she was going to leave him.

On December 6, Barbara and Frank appeared before Judge Blake and testified that they wanted to adopt the ten-month-old baby John Charles Greene, whose name would now be Dion Anthony Fay.

The legally adopted boy would join a household that consisted of Barbara and Fay; Nellie Banner, the nurse; a cook; butler; chauffeur; two maids; an Irish terrier called Shanty Irish; and a Boston terrier called Punky.

Fay was starring as master of ceremonies in Felix Young's extravagant "sophisticated musical revue," *Tattle Tales,* and drinking steadily. The show was to open in Los Angeles at the Belasco on Christmas Day. It opened four days later, replacing the newly released feature film *Mädchen in Uniform.* Two shows of *Tattle Tales* were booked for New Year's Eve.

Felix Young had great plans for his show and hoped its success would make it a national institution like *Earl Carroll's Vanities.* To that end, he'd hired Howard Jackson, Leo Robin, Harry Akst, Eddie Ward, and Richard Whiting to write the music. Edward Eliscu was to write the lyrics, and the humorists Herman and Joe Mankiewicz, Moss Hart, Arthur Kober, and Edwin Justus Mayer were to write comedy sketches. Starring with Fay in the show were Janet Reade, torch singer and star of Ziegfeld's *Whoopee!* and *Hot Cha!,* and the Broadway musical idol Guy Robertson. LeRoy Prinz staged the musical numbers.

Tattle Tales was a lavish production made up of 125 people, featuring vaudeville's Miller and Mack—Uncle Buck, Millie Stevens's old stage friend—and the Three Blazes. Also appearing was sixteen-year-old Betty Grable, who'd moved to Los Angeles two years before and appeared in the studio chorus line of Fox films and Goldwyn's musical *Whoopee!,* starring Eddie Cantor. Grable had then been hired to work in Norma Talmadge's *Kiki.*

Barbara's twenty-two-year-old nephew, Al Merkent, was dancing in the show and performing with the orchestra. Al had played trombone, saxophone, and clarinet with Fred Waring's orchestra.

Putting a revue together, said Felix Young, "requires the balance of a goldsmith's scales." Young had produced *The Marriage Bed* and *Top o' the Hill* before *Tattle Tales*. "You need the judgment of the best managing editor in the world, and 100 percent imagination . . . The experience is worth everything, but like anything that's valuable, it must be earned at tremendous cost."

Part of the "tremendous cost" for Young was having Frank Fay as his "chief nonsense dispenser" and main box-office draw. *Tattle Tales* previewed in Santa Barbara at the Lobero Theatre three days before the show's Los Angeles opening.

Fay made his way home drunk from Santa Barbara to Bristol Avenue and went to Dion's nursery. Nellie Banner heard Fay come in, and just as he was about to fall across the baby's crib, she rushed in and whisked Dion out from under Fay's dead weight. Dion was frightened and couldn't sleep for the rest of the night.

Nellie Banner had quickly come to worship Barbara, but she didn't believe in drinking or carousing, and she didn't like Mr. Fay. He frightened her.

The opening night for *Tattle Tales* was a hit. The show was "bulg[ing] with talent"; Fay was "comedy plus," "worthy of a lot of attention."

Frank Fay and Felix Young got into an argument. Arguing with producers was not unusual for Fay. A few years before, he had set out to produce his own show in New York called *Frank Fay's Fables*. The revue had been in rehearsal for weeks when it was time for Fay to put down deposits for scenery and costumes; it turned out that he had no money or credit. Two men who had seen the show in rehearsal were willing to back *Fay's Fables* on the condition that they received 51 percent of the revue. Fay refused to give up control and turned down the offer.

Fay then had to court potential investors and would meet with them in the rehearsal hall, with a borrowed camel hair coat belonging to his tenor draped over his shoulders, thinking it would make him appear more prosperous.

When the actors in the show asked to draw some money to get something to eat, Fay gave out cans of corn and tomatoes that had been given to him by a grocer who had been approached as an investor.

Ultimately, Fay preferred to let the show fold rather than give up any of his share of it. It had closed with Fay owing the cast $4,000.

Fay refused to perform in *Tattle Tales* on New Year's Eve. Felix Young ordered Fay out of the theater. Young put Richie Craig Jr. and Benny Rubin on in Fay's place for the next week, until Craig was replaced by Jans and Whalen. By the end of the first week the show had broken even, bringing in $8,000.

"A good revue is just what the public needs now," said Young. Almost a third of the country's workforce—twelve million people—were out of work.

ELEVEN

Bold and Bad

As Steel Goes . . .

Fay was fired from *Tattle Tales,* and Barbara went to work on *Baby Face* in early January 1933. A week into production, *The Bitter Tea of General Yen* opened in Los Angeles at the RKO Hillstreet with a newsreel and a Charlie Chaplin comedy, *The Cure.*

In New York, the debut of *The Bitter Tea of General Yen* inaugurated a big change for the newly opened $8 million Radio City Music Hall, which went from being the world's largest two-a-day theater (seating 6,250) to a motion picture house with a newly installed screen, seventy by forty feet.

The music hall had taken two years of intensive labor to build and filled the entire block between New York's Fiftieth and Fifty-First Streets, extending halfway from Sixth to Fifth Avenue.

Soon after the theater opened, it was decided that the stage of the music hall, though designed by Peter Clark under the genius of the showman Roxy himself, was too cavernous for variety performers. The stage for the music hall was the largest ever built for indoor entertainment, 144 feet wide and 80 feet deep.

"I believe in creative dreams," said Samuel Lionel "Roxy" Rothafel, who dreamed his theaters. "The picture of the Radio City theatres was complete and practically perfect in my mind before artists and architects put pen on drawing paper."

The theater was part of the greatest single building project ever undertaken at one time by private capital. It began in boom times, and the major partners, John D. Rockefeller Jr., Owen Young, and David Sarnoff, continued with the project despite the dire state of the economy. The original site of three acres, owned by Columbia University, had been intended for a new home for the Metropolitan Opera Company. The notion of three acres grew into twelve as the plan expanded. A single opera house was replaced by a complex of twelve structures. It was to include the world's largest office building, a complete Fifth Avenue frontage devoted to international buildings, a group of offices, broadcasting studios, and theaters for Radio Corporation of America and its affiliates, National Broadcasting Company and Radio-Keith-Orpheum Corporation. One of the buildings held the headquarters of the broadcasting studios of NBC; another, the recently opened RKO Roxy Theatre (with a seating capacity of thirty-seven hundred); and still another, Radio City Music Hall. NBC occupied twelve floors of the RCA building; RKO's president, M. H. "Deak" Aylesworth, took seven floors above Radio City for RKO offices. The Rockefellers themselves had acquired 100,000 shares of stock in both RCA and RKO.

After the opening of Radio City, President Hoover sent a letter of congratulations to Deak Aylesworth for his "courage and vision," as did President-elect Roosevelt, congratulating Aylesworth on the "completion of the great undertaking" and the employment of so many when it was so badly needed.

The first showing at the Music Hall of *The Bitter Tea of General Yen* was jammed; most of the lower-priced seats were sold before one o'clock in the afternoon, with lines later in the grand foyer and along Fiftieth Street.

On the program were excerpts from *Faust* sung by Alida Vane, Aroldo Lindi, and Max Ratmiroff; the Radio City Roxyettes; *The Story of the Waltz* performed by Patricia Bowman, Gomez and Winona, and the Roxy ballet corps, with the Roxy's choral ensemble; the Tuskegee Singers; Ray Bolger; and an organ recital.

Of *The Bitter Tea of General Yen,* one critic said, "No picture half so strange, so bizarre, has ever before passed outward through the astonished doors of the Columbia Studio" (*New York World Telegram*). The reviews were admiring of Capra's work ("a triumph of repression; the more spectacular sequences [are] irreproachably conceived"), as well as Nils Asther's and Walter Connolly's "unusually clever performances" (*New York Times*). Thornton Delehanty in the *New York Evening Post* hailed the story's "poetry and beauty" and singled out the photography and the "cunning authenticity of its atmosphere."

The critics unanimously praised Nils Asther and Walter Connolly, but they picked up on the effects of Capra's feelings for Barbara that quietly deprived her work of its usual energy and force. Richard Watts wrote that her performance "hardly adds to the liveliness of the work" (*NY Herald Tribune*).

Thornton Delehanty said Barbara was "a brittle impersonation of the mission-ary girl, a portrait which lacks warmth and depth." Louella Parsons thought Barbara "miscast," and Philip Scheuer in the *New York World-Telegram* said, "The complexities of the role engulf her."

Will Hays had invited the Chinese chargé d'affaires in Washington to see the picture at the Keith. The Chinese legation wanted deleted certain "gruesome scenes," primarily the shooting of war prisoners, and "objection-able phrases," such as "yellow swine" and the statement that the Chinese "are treacherous and immoral." The Motion Picture Producers rebuffed the requests of the Chinese government and saw no reason for the scenes to be removed. They saw the story as "a eulogy of the Chinese philosophy, fair deal-ing, morality and graciousness"; said that "while soldiers are executed before the firing squad, there is no indication that these are summary executions; there is just the fact that they are executed." Hays was more concerned about the "missionary angle" but found that it was "very slight" and that their work was portrayed as "commendatory."

Cuts to the picture were made state by state. In New York, *The Bitter Tea* was released without the scenes of prisoners falling to the ground after execu-tion and a soldier shooting a prisoner running away from the firing squad. In Massachusetts, the firing squad scene was cut entirely, as was the scene showing Megan in lingerie playing cards with Yen. In Ohio, Clara Blandick's dialogue was cut in which she describes the Chinese as "tricky, treacherous, immoral. I can't tell one from the other. They are all Chinamen to me," as was Megan's calling General Yen "You yellow swine." The state of Kansas took the picture in its entirety.

"I think it one of my best pictures," said Frank Capra. "I don't really know why audiences didn't like it. The ingredients are already there for trouble, because of the racial question, the religious question, and to try to tell that kind of love story, I think I just flew over my head on that. It came off, in my mind, an artistic triumph but it was certainly not a public success."

Baby Face finished production late in January at a cost of $187,000. It was shot in eighteen days. Barbara pushed her scenes through so she could get home to see Dion. She tried to arrange her days in order to bathe him and put him to bed. And she was helping Fay to cope with the mess of *Tattle Tales* and put in $10,000 of her own money to buy the show out from Felix Young. Headlines in the press told the story: "Barbara Stanwyck Buys Show for Fay." She was now the show's producer though she denied it. "I [don't] have a penny invested," she said. "Fay financed it all himself. Fay has been a Broadway stage star for many years. I wish I had as much in the bank as he has at this moment! It is all Mr. Fay's. He wrote it. He secured the backing. He directed it. He manages it."

Fay stayed out of *Tattle Tales* for its two-week run at the Belasco but returned to the show in mid-January, when it moved to the Hollywood Playhouse. The first three days were a disaster due to lighting problems from insufficient wiring. New transformers were ordered; the show reopened and finished out the week earning $4,300.

By the end of the month Fay had paid Young a token $1,000 and officially taken over as the show's producer. Barbara, who had wanted to come into the show earlier but couldn't because of *Baby Face,* now planned to open with it in San Francisco at the Curran Theatre. Rather than put on her old act with Fay and face criticism from the press as they had when they appeared together onstage the year before, Barbara planned to perform dramatic scenes from *Ladies of Leisure* and the big opening scene from *The Miracle Woman.*

Tattle Tales' first week in San Francisco brought in $17,000 with most of the audience buying balcony seats rather than paying $2.50 for the orchestra. Barbara and Frank's hotel room at the Mark Hopkins was full of flowers.

Fay had been drinking for three successive days and continued to be so drunk he couldn't go onstage. By the middle of the second week's run in San Francisco, Barbara decided to bring down the curtain, saying she was ill, and called off performances for the next two days. At the week's end, she closed the show. Money was refunded. *Tattle Tales* had been booked at the Curran for three more weeks until *Of Thee I Sing* was to come in from Los Angeles's Biltmore Theatre.

Barbara struggled with the effects of Fay's drinking and hired an escort to travel with him to Los Angeles, where he was admitted to the Glendale Sanitarium for treatment.

Ladies They Talk About, Barbara's thirteenth picture, opened in Los Angeles at the Warner Bros. Downtown and Hollywood Theatres. In New York, the picture opened at the Capitol Theatre, and with it for a week onstage was Helen Morgan, re-creating her role as Julie in a condensed version of Ziegfeld's *Show Boat* with the original Joseph Urban scenery and a cast of eighty that included Jules Bledsoe.

The critics called *Ladies They Talk About* "undistinguished," though still enjoyable and amusing. *Variety* said, "Barbara Stanwyck and a good supporting cast, plus careful direction and snappy dialog saves the story from being ridiculed off the screen."

Reviewers couldn't help but poke fun at the portrait of San Quentin, describing it "as a retreat, the sort of a place where a lot of gals might like to spend a vacation." Louella Parsons called the prison like "a girl's seminary" but was gratified that Barbara was "back in the type of role in which she excels. Barbara as a milk-and-water character is a mistake." Other critics found Barbara's gun-moll jailbird to be a "new role for her . . . bold and bad."

Two weeks later, Fay was home from Glendale Sanitarium and was determined to take *Tattle Tales* back on the road. He made arrangements for the show to open in Portland, Kansas City, and Vancouver and then go east to Philadelphia, Washington, and New York.

In mid-February, the governor of Michigan declared an eight-day bank holiday to prevent a further run on the banks in his state. Ten days later, Maryland's governor declared a three-day bank holiday. On March 1 the governors of Kentucky, Tennessee, California, Louisiana, Alabama, and Oklahoma followed suit. By early the following morning, the governors of New York and Illinois had suspended the banks of their states.

Eleven thousand of the nation's twenty-five thousand banks had failed.

During Hoover's last days in office, Agnes Meyer, writer, lecturer, and wife of the *Washington Post* publisher and chairman of the Federal Reserve, Eugene Meyer, wrote, "Hard on H[oover] to go out of office to the sound of crashing banks. Like the tragic end of a tragic story . . . The history of H's administration is Greek in its fatality."

Jack Warner was invited to the presidential inaugural. To promote its latest film sensation, *42nd Street,* a backstage musical that had cost an astronomical $400,000, the studio sent some of its stars, contract players, and chorus girls cross-country on the 42nd Street Special, a six-coach express of silver foil and gold leaf that was to stop in thirty cities and towns along the way. Warner's actors and actresses were to speak to crowds of thousands from the platform of the train, disembark, broadcast live on radio, tour a General Electric showroom, ride through the town on floats, check into a hotel, shower, change, and appear in a live stage show to sell the premiere of the picture.

The 42nd Street Special was made up of private rooms for each of the actors, a luxury dining car, with a stateroom for Tom Mix and a stall for his miracle horse, Tony Junior. On the train, compliments of General Electric, were a portable radio station, outdoor lights and speakers, and a fully electric "health kitchen" with futuristic appliances—oven, refrigerator, and dishwasher. Among those on board were Joe E. Brown and the contract players Lyle Talbot, dubbed by the press the "Romeo of the Train" with his blue eyes, slicked black hair, and widow's peak; Bette Davis with her new husband,

The Warners 42nd Street Special starting out on its tour across America, publicizing the studio's sensational new picture, scheduled to stop in more than one hundred cities. Its final destination was Washington, D.C., in time for the presidential inauguration of Franklin Delano Roosevelt in March 1933. (PHOTOFEST)

Harmon Nelson; Preston Foster; and Jack Dempsey. With them as well were Laura La Plante, Claire Dodd, Miss California, and a dozen Busby Berkeley girls.

Tom Mix told a reporter at one of the stopovers, "What this country needs is just one big man to pull us out of trouble. Just give Roosevelt a chance and time and he will do things."

By March 4, the day Franklin Roosevelt took the oath of office at the Capitol Plaza before a crowd of 100,000 and became the thirty-second president of the United States, banks in thirty-eight states had shut their doors. The New York Stock Exchange was closed, as were the New York cocoa, metal, and rubber markets. The Chicago Board of Trade closed for the first time in eighty-five years. One woman wrote of Chicago, "As we saw it, the city seemed to have died. There was something awful—abnormal—in the very stillness of those streets."

In Roosevelt's inaugural speech he reassured the nation that it "will endure as it has endured, will revive and will prosper." He explained that "the measure of the restoration lies in the extent to which we apply social values more noble than mere monetary profit . . . I am prepared," he told the country, "under my constitutional duty to recommend the measures that a stricken nation in the midst of a stricken world may require."

The following day, to prevent additional bank closures, Roosevelt declared a three-day bank holiday. The White House drafted the Emergency Banking Act that would close insolvent banks and reorganize and reopen those banks that could survive, and outlaw the hoarding of gold, giving the Treasury the right to confiscate all privately held gold, paying for it with cash.

At the end of the first week in March, the major studios, except for MGM, were unable to meet their payrolls and were facing a general shutdown. Each studio head said that because of the "national emergency and business at the theatres" an eight-week 50 percent pay cut across the board was the only way to deal with the crisis. Actors, writers, directors, cameramen, and all the other employees of the studios agreed to the cuts; they had little choice but to go along with the pronouncement.

President Roosevelt assured the nation by radio that it was safe to redeposit money in the banks. The following day, deposits exceeded withdrawals. Some had thought that Roosevelt would nationalize the banks. Instead, his Emergency Banking Act had offered government assistance to private bankers. "Capitalism was saved in eight days," said one of Roosevelt's policy advisers.

In Hollywood, electricians, engineers, grips, and musicians who were unionized under the International Alliance of Theatrical Stage Employees, or IATSE, refused to accept salary cuts from the studios and threatened to strike. Harry Warner said, "They'd never dare." He called their bluff and persuaded the other studio heads to do so as well. The following day the studios shut down for the first time ever.

The International Alliance of Theatrical Stage Employees was not intimidated. It refused to go along with a cut in salary and demanded that lower-paid employees—union members or not—be protected from pay cuts. If not, the union would call a strike, and the projectionists—part of the union— would walk and shut down movie theaters across the country.

Louis B. Mayer of the Association of Motion Picture Producers—he had succeeded Cecil B. DeMille as president—met with members of the Academy of Motion Picture Arts and Sciences, which Mayer had helped to found, to reach a settlement that was acceptable to union and nonunion members alike. It was decided that the high-salaried contract employees would take the biggest cuts in salary. Those who were middle salaried would take a 25 percent cut, and those on small salaries would take no cut. Some of the higher-paid contract players, such as Maurice Chevalier, Constance Bennett, and Clara Bow, chose to go off salary for several weeks rather than risk a pay cut, which they feared might become permanent. The unions that were part of IATSE went back to work but refused to accept pay cuts.

The academy and Price and Waterhouse were to decide when to end the cuts at each studio. Jack and Harry Warner refused to take pay cuts and told the press about it. Zanuck hadn't been told of their decision and was furious. His own salary had been cut by 50 percent.

Barbara, like others, was to receive 50 percent of her salary for eight weeks. Her attitude about it was to "do nothing. I have a contract," she said. "I expect to fulfill its terms and I expect the studio to do likewise. Had my pictures made twice the profits my employers anticipated when my contract was signed, I doubt if they would have offered me a voluntary raise. After three years of depression we are all managing to eat and keep clothed. I think recent steps taken by President Roosevelt are wise; such steps should have been taken years ago. I am most optimistic about conditions generally."

Barbara asked for and received an advance of $10,000 against the $7,500 she was to be paid for eight weeks of work at a 50 percent reduction.

The studios reopened; production schedules continued.

Only Warner Bros. had a reserve of completed pictures. Given Zanuck's production schedules, twenty-six pictures were ready to be released. All the other studios were rushing to complete production on their films to make up for lost time.

Admission prices had been lowered, but movie audiences had decreased by 25 percent. A third of the country was unemployed. The U.S. Steel Corporation, one of the nation's largest companies, employed more than 224,000 full-time workers in 1929. Three years later it had in its employ 18,000. By April 1933, it employed none. "As steel goes, so goes the nation . . ."

With the Warners' announcement to the press that they were not cutting their own salaries, Zanuck realized he was never going to get to the top of Warner, that Jack Warner had been stringing him along with false promises.

Warner would have welcomed a strike over salaries and was only too happy to cut them. Zanuck didn't support the cuts; he wanted raises to be given to most of the technicians. If any salaries were to be cut, Zanuck thought they should be those of the studio bosses. "They weren't worth half of what they were getting," he said.

Zanuck issued his own statement to the press announcing that he was restoring studio salaries to their original amounts without running it by either Jack or Harry. He told the press that in addition he would be giving bonuses to some. Jack Warner had no intention of restoring salaries and certainly didn't want to give out bonuses. Warner issued another statement saying that all salary cuts would continue for nine weeks instead of the originally agreed-upon eight.

. . .

The Hays Office was hearing complaints about *Baby Face* from churches and women's organizations upset about seeing a story based on a prostitute. *Baby Face* wasn't the only picture that some found offensive. *Bed of Roses* with Constance Bennett, *Hold Your Man* by Anita Loos with Jean Harlow and Clark Gable, and *Bondage* were also arousing the ire of Christian audiences.

Will Hays went to the Warner lot to discuss *Baby Face,* specifically cuts that had been restored to the picture on Zanuck's orders. At the meeting were Jack Warner, Zanuck, and Sam Schneider, the home office auditor. Hays pressed Harry Warner to leave out the offending sequences. Zanuck insisted on keeping *Baby Face* as it was.

The subject came up of the emergency salary cuts. Harry Warner had no intention of complying with the academy's position that salaries be fully restored by April 10. Jack and Zanuck insisted the company had pledged to abide by the academy's ruling; Harry argued his company would conduct its business as it saw fit and that Warner would restore full pay after nine weeks instead of eight. Hays left the meeting to allow the Warners and Zanuck to thrash it out. Zanuck threatened to resign. If he remained at the studio—he had been there a decade—he insisted on full production powers without home office interference and the right to hire whomever he considered necessary for production work at salaries he felt appropriate.

Jack and Harry Warner formally accepted Zanuck's resignation.

Zanuck issued another statement to the press. "On April 10th," it read, "as Head of Production of Warner Brothers Studios, I announced that the salary cuts decided upon on March 15 last would be restored immediately. This promise has now been repudiated, and since a matter of principle is involved and I obviously no longer enjoy the confidence of my immediate superiors, I have today sent my resignation to the Chairman of the Company, Mr. Jack Warner."

Before Zanuck left Warner for good, he looked at eight pictures and gave each its first cutting. Zanuck walked away from a four-and-a-half-year contract at $4,000 per week as President Roosevelt put to work a vast army of 250,000 unemployed Americans, men between the ages of seventeen and twenty-four, to help restore America's largely forgotten national and state parks. The men were being paid $30 a month and were grateful for the work.

The day after Zanuck resigned as production head of Warner Bros., Jack Warner telephoned Hal Wallis, head of production at First National until the studios had merged. Wallis had moved his offices to Burbank and had become a producer under Zanuck. Warner asked Wallis to come to his bungalow on the Burbank lot. Both Harry and Jack rose from their chairs to greet Wallis and shake his hand. "Well, Hal, you're it," said Jack. Wallis was Zanuck's replacement as general manager of productions at Warner Bros.

A decade earlier Hal Wallis had been publicity director at Warner Bros., making up a press book for each picture, writing and making the trailers for forthcoming pictures, supervising their editing, plotting their campaigns, arranging interviews, greeting important performers arriving in Pasadena from New York, having red carpets laid for them and limousines take them back to Los Angeles.

When Warner took over First National, a beautiful new studio in Burbank, Wallis had become production manager and, to meet the demand for pictures that talked, oversaw such projects as *The Dawn Patrol, The Last Flight,* and *Little Caesar.*

Zanuck signed an agreement with United Artists and Joseph M. Schenck to become vice president in charge of production of a new company called 20th Century Pictures. He had been besieged by offers, among them one from Louis B. Mayer, who offered the former Warner executive his own production unit similar to David Selznick's. Other studios offering Zanuck a deal were Paramount, Radio, and Fox.

Zanuck agreed to make eight pictures for 20th Century Pictures (Metro had offered him twelve), budgeted from $210,000 to $225,000 a picture for the first year, and to receive a $4,500 weekly salary plus 50 percent of the net profits on each picture with a 26 percent distribution fee paid to United Artists.

Jack Warner wrote to Will Hays complaining about Zanuck's hasty resignation and his agreement with Joe Schenck, saying that "it is common rumor that Twentieth Century Pictures has been chiefly financed by a loan from Nicholas Schenck, President of Loew's Inc. and by Louis B. Mayer, head of Production at Metro-Goldwyn-Mayer, to the President of Twentieth Century Pictures who is the brother of Mr. Schenck." The letter also complained that Zanuck had tried to hire numerous Warner employees, not only actors, directors, and writers, but even stenographers and "William Goetz, who is the son-in-law of Mr. Mayer." Goetz was hired to be Zanuck's executive assistant, and Raymond Griffith, a former star, was to be Zanuck's production supervisor.

Zanuck left Los Angeles to hunt grizzlies in British Columbia and took with him most of Warner's directorial staff, including Lloyd Bacon, Michael Curtiz, Ray Enright, and Sam Engel.

Joe Schenck felt it was "absolutely none of [Jack Warner's] business" whom he, Schenck, borrowed money from. Both Nicholas Schenck and Mayer had put up $375,000 for the competing 20th Century Pictures: Schenck for his brother, Joe; Mayer for his son-in-law Bill Goetz. Both Schenck and Mayer received company stock. Mayer set up the Mayer Family Fund for the stock, keeping 50 percent for himself and dividing the other 50 percent among his two daughters, Irene and Edith, and Edith's husband, Bill Goetz.

Wallis, between Warner and First National, would now be in charge of forty or sixty features a year. He loved making pictures and "was on top of the world."

TWELVE

Entrances and Exits

On April 17, Metro restored the studio's salary cuts. Metro stockholders received the highest dividend in years. "Oh, that L. B. Mayer," one writer said. "He created more communists than Karl Marx."

A week later Paramount resumed full salaries.

The wage cut made it clear to studio employees that their contracts were not binding, that producers didn't have to abide by them, that the academy was not going to protect them, and that those who were part of the International Alliance of Theatrical Stage Employees were immune to the demands of the studios. Dorothy Parker said, "Looking to the Academy for representation was like trying to get laid in your mother's house. Somebody was always in the parlor, watching."

The writers came to see that the existing organization called the Writers Club, a subsidiary of the Dramatists Guild, did not have the power to help its members. A meeting was called at the Hollywood Knickerbocker Hotel to discuss how conditions could be improved for Hollywood writers.

The writers—among them John Howard Lawson, Samson Raphaelson, and John Bright—agreed that the only way to get what they wanted from the producers was to organize so that they too could shut down the supply of screenplays, as the projectionists could shut down movie theaters. It was decided to hold a series of meetings in which each of the ten writers would bring one guest who was qualified to be a member and who would be willing to stand up to the producers.

Roosevelt's bank holiday and the Association of Motion Picture Producers' call for pay cuts of 50 percent for all studio employees inspired actors as well to better protect themselves. Six met secretly in the Hollywood home of the well-known supporting actor Kenneth Thomson and his wife, Alden Gay Thomson, to discuss the idea of starting a self-governing independent

organization of film actors that would fight for fair economic conditions and be open to all, unlike the Academy of Motion Picture Arts and Sciences, which received new members by invitation only. Ralph Morgan hoped that the organization could be effective. Morgan was a character actor of serious roles under contract to Fox, unlike his brother Frank, at Metro, who was a stage and screen musical comedy star. Ralph had appeared in more than sixty plays, working onstage with Lynn Fontanne, Laurette Taylor, and Florence Reed. He'd appeared in O'Neill's *Strange Interlude* and had re-created the role of Charles Marsden in the Metro picture that starred Norma Shearer and Clark Gable.

Ralph had got his law degree decades before at Columbia University and, a presence in Actors Equity in New York, Morgan hoped that an independent self-governing organization for actors could do "the greatest good for the greatest number" and protect them.

Of primary concern, in addition to salaries and the forced salary cuts, were the hours actors were expected to work: twelve hours a day, usually late on Saturday night and often Sunday morning. During productions, meals would come at the producer's whim. Actors were often told to sleep on a couch rather than be allowed to go home at night and were promised a free breakfast in the morning; there was no overtime.

"You worked any kind of hours," said Ralph Bellamy. "Any number of days . . . it was brutal. The lights were enormously hot and the lesser people, not having stand-ins, standing in day after day, hour after hour, for weeks."

Fay Wray, when making *King Kong,* worked twenty-two hours straight through. "It was supposed to be test footage for the money-people back east to look at," she said. "But that material went into the film. I don't even know whether I got paid." Lyle Talbot said, "Michael Curtiz worked us till midnight Saturdays. We [would] say, he must hate his wife because he never wants to go home."

Actors worked on several pictures at a time. Talbot rode a bicycle between soundstages and productions, carrying scripts in the front basket of pictures he was making and scripts in the rear basket of pictures he was about to make.

To discuss bringing about these changes, Robert Young and others "met at night, in private homes, in the basement if there was one." They had to be very careful. Actors would go to someone's home for a party, go through the back door, walk down the alley to someone else's house, and have a meeting in the garage. "The actors unionizing were verboten as far as the studios were concerned," said Young. "It was risky for us. They hired ex-cops and had spies all over the place, so we were secretive . . . It could cost us our contracts.

The average person like myself, under contract to the studio with a family, was extremely scared."

Some actors argued against organizing. "MGM and Louis B. Mayer have been very good to us. I'm not going to do this to him," they said. Others warned, "You guys are crazy; you're going to get us all thrown out of the industry."

Through the late winter and spring, Barbara and Fay traveled with *Tattle Tales,* "a gay gorgeous musical revue," on its "trans-continental" tour, to Portland, the Metropolitan in Seattle, Spokane, playing each city two or three nights and then moving east to Billings, Cheyenne, Colorado Springs, Denver, Omaha, Kansas City, the Shubert in Cincinnati, the Hanna in Cleveland, Wilkes-Barre, the Lyceum in Rochester, Philadelphia, the Capital in Albany, making their way to the Broadhurst Theatre in New York. The plan was to open on Broadway before going to Chicago. Fay continued to make changes to the revue, adding performers along the way, even changing the orchestra and its conductor.

Richie Craig Jr., one of the *Tattle Tales* performers, and Western Costume Inc., were suing Fay in superior court, both claiming that he owed them money for services and material and for the cost of costume rentals.

The Bitter Tea of General Yen opened in London at the Regal Theatre. *The Times* of London said of the picture, it "breaks convention bravely [but] repents of its rashness at the last."

Dion was at home on Bristol Avenue with his nurse. Barbara's nephew Gene, then sixteen, had moved to Barbara and Frank's to finish the school year at University High School and was living happily with the Fays' cook, butler, chauffeur, Nellie, and Dion. Gene's older cousin, Al, then twenty-three, had worked for Barbara and Fay's decorator until he was fired.

Maud, Bert, and Al were returning to Brooklyn, driving cross-country from Hollywood to Flatbush. Bert had tried unsuccessfully to get a job in a butcher shop in Los Angeles, there was no work to be found, and he was returning to work with his brother Ray at Merkent's Meat Market. The trip took eight days and, Al noted in his daily log, two hundred gallons of gas.

Hal Wallis wired Barbara at the Shubert Theatre in Kansas City about a script he wanted her to consider for her next picture. *Female* was similar to *Baby Face* in its portrayal of love being bought by power and money. The picture was intended to reunite the *Baby Face* cast of Stanwyck and George Brent with the writers Gene Markey and Kathryn Scola. William Dieterle was to direct. *Female* was from a novel by Donald Henderson Clark about an

TATTLE TALES

BROADHURST THEATRE

industrialist—a woman—the president of an automobile company, who goes through a string of tepid affairs, each lover quickly cast off out of boredom, until a renowned engineer comes to work for her who is not amused by either her money or her power. She falls in love; he rebuffs her, and what ensues is their dance to end up together.

Barbara wired back to Wallis; she liked the script and agreed to go ahead with the picture.

In Philadelphia, Barbara was onstage at the Stanley Theatre in *Tattle Tales* performing her second monologue of the evening, the emotional pulpit scene from *The Miracle Woman.* During her fiery condemnation of the hypocritical parishioners, she became so excited she gestured with her hand, cutting it as she broke one of the microphones. Barbara was unaware of it until she came offstage all smiles; though exhausted from the emotion she'd created for the scene, and saw that her hand was bleeding. "I still can't figure out how I could have done it," she said.

Tattle Tales opened at the Broadhurst on Thursday, June 1, amid such other Broadway shows as *Gay Divorce* at the Shubert with Fred Astaire and Dorothy Stone, Ring Lardner and George S. Kaufman's *June Moon* at the Ambassador, and *Of Thee I Sing* with William Gaxton and Lois Moran at the Imperial.

The response to *Tattle Tales* was mostly cool except for *The New Yorker,* which said a "reviewer must have acid in his blood to be other than enthusiastic about the revue. *Tattle Tales* is outstanding in taste and intelligence."

Most reviewers thought the show was "a product of the urban suburbs" and "sluggish."

Barbara didn't appear onstage in the evening until ten o'clock. Reviewers accused Fay of "hogging the show by the mere lifting of his eloquent eyebrows, his wardrobe of pretty dressing gowns and witty colloquies." Burns Mantle said of Barbara, "She is blessed with that certain subtle something that distinguishes the real from the imitation; a sort of unconscious self-consciousness . . . classified most frequently as poise."

"Newspapers have been mean to *Tattle Tales*," said Barbara. "But audiences like it. We . . . have been playing it since December. Played it across the continent, seven months. The representatives of a London theatre were here with an offer to take *Tattle Tales* to London intact. Unfortunately we could not go." Fay had radio engagements: he'd been signed for a spot on *The Fleischmann's Yeast Hour.* Barbara had to be in Hollywood in mid-July to begin work on a picture.

"It won't be *Female* as planned," she said. Ruth Chatterton, now Mrs. George Brent, was set to co-star in *Female* opposite her husband of less than a year. "I shall do *Ever in My Heart,*" said Barbara, "by [Bertram Millhauser and] Beulah Marie Dix."

From *Tattle Tales,* Curran Theater, San Francisco, 1933 or '34. Frank Fay fourth from left. Stanwyck on his left, almost center stage.

Louella Parsons wrote, "I hope Barbara Stanwyck is finished trouping through the country with Frank Fay . . . Most of the people who like her and admire her artistry shudder at the idea of her playing stooge to the Frank Fay comedy."

"Fay has always stolen the act," said Barbara. "I have always been his feeder. It has always been that way. It's our act. We did the identical act in which we toured vaudeville for years. The critics used to like the act. But that was before I was The Movie Actress. The critics did a complete about-face. It wasn't that they panned me. I can stand that. What made me mad was the assertion that Fay made a stooge of me so that he could steal the act. I danced in the act, the same routine I used to use in vaudeville. Yet they said Fay made me dance. Just as though I haven't been dancing ever since I was three."

Fay ended his first weekend at the Broadhurst too drunk to perform onstage. Richie Craig was back in the show in Fay's place. The revue ran for three weeks. One day it was announced the show would close; the next, that it would run indefinitely.

Barbara's new movie, *Baby Face,* opened in New York at the Strand and in Los Angeles at the Warner Bros. Hollywood and Downtown Theatres with six vaudeville acts in addition to the picture. "She played the love game with everything she had for everything they had and made 'it' work" was the picture's teaser. "A woman without a conscience, she used her power over men to get what life denied her."

Will Hays won out with *Baby Face* after recommending that the picture be pulled from theaters for violation of the code. Now that Zanuck had left the studio, Jack Warner agreed to clean up the picture to Hays's satisfaction—it was even okayed for children—by taking out any references to Lily's being a kept woman, by reshooting the sequences that showed Lily losing the jewels she had amassed, and by adding the final two scenes that depict Lily returning to the grime and dust of Pittsburgh to show that "vice was not rewarded."

Variety noted in its review, *Baby Face* "is reputed to be a remake of the first print, which was considered too hot. Anything hotter than this for public showing would call for an asbestos audience blanket." Another critic warned movie audiences not to "take children to see [*Baby Face*]. It is hot enough to set the office files on fire. Fans will go for this picture head-over-heels." Jimmy Starr in the *Evening Herald Examiner* wrote, "Miss Stanwyck's performance [is] brilliant . . . clever and most intriguing." The *New York Herald Tribune* said there was "truth in its psychology and a genuine conviction in the performance of its star." *Variety* said that Barbara makes "Lil a beautiful bum . . . *Baby Face* and Lil are just too bad all the way."

The *Hollywood Reporter* proclaimed it "the best and by far the most entertaining picture that Barbara Stanwyck has made in years and should put her right back in the big draw class. The picture is nearly all Stanwyck." Louella Parsons said, "Miss Stanwyck hasn't had a vehicle that gives her as much of a break as *Baby Face* since *Illicit* put her name in electric lights."

Warner's ads for the picture ran with provocative taglines that promised a hot and dangerous time: "She loves as furiously as any woman/Forgets as cruelly as any man/Has more daddies than the daughter of the regiment/And is the most dangerous man menace at large today . . . You know Edward G. Robinson as LITTLE CAESAR—Ruth Chatterton as MADAME X—James Cagney as PUBLIC ENEMY—Now You'll Know Barbara Stanwyck as BABY FACE."

The picture helped spur box-office sales for *Tattle Tales* but didn't act as a deterrent to Fay's drinking.

Nancy Bernard Levy went to the Broadhurst to see her old friend from Ziegfeld days. She hadn't seen Barbara in a couple of years and got tickets for the first row. "Barbara came onstage and saw me," said Nancy. "There was no response from her. She kept turning to look at me. She knew I was there. She

With Frank Fay, Hollywood Boulevard, February
1933. (CULVER PICTURES)

acted so peculiar. It was as if she was in a daze. I thought, 'Maybe she doesn't
want to have dealings with any of her old associates.' "

At intermission, Nancy went back to say hello. At the stage door, Pops,
who knew Nancy from other shows, said, "I advise you not to go in. She's in
a terrible way. Frank is very abusive to her, and I don't think she'd be happy
to see you now. Call and get in touch with her later."

Barbara's willpower, organization, and management carried her through
the run of the show. Loyalty, self-sacrifice, and service, which she never disassociated from affection, enabled her to stick by Fay.

"A couple can't be in love without fighting," she said. "I hope Fay and
I always fight. And just as I fight *with* Fay, I'll put up an awful scrap *for* him.
Not that he needs me as a defender. He is well able to take care of himself. He wants to laugh off all this talk, but it makes me see red and I can't
laugh."

Barbara denied press reports and rumors that she was going to leave him:
"All this talk, talk, talk. . . . It's like rain on a tin roof. You don't mind it at

first. Then it seems that if it doesn't stop for a moment, you'll go insane. In Hollywood it never stops—gossiping.

"They can jabber as much as they please. Say whatever comes into their heads, gossip from now till Doomsday. But the fact remains: I'll never divorce Frank Fay. If I can't stay married and stay in pictures, I'll get out of pictures. I will too, unless they lay off Fay.

"Fay and I try to live our own lives. We never are seen in public, seldom leave our home in Brentwood. We have no friends among the movie crowd, which means we don't attend their parties or give parties for them. What few friends we have are old acquaintances from Broadway.

"Under ordinary circumstances, an attitude such as ours would be respected. But Hollywood is not an ordinary community and has utterly no respect for anything."

Tattle Tales folded on June 24 after playing to small audiences for three and a half weeks and losing $110,000; the production showed losses during the seven months that it toured. The final week cost the show $11,000 to cover the fares home for thirty-nine company members. Fay's refusal to change the revue was at the heart of the show's problem, as were his erratic stage appearances from booze.

Barbara returned to Los Angeles to start work on *Ever in My Heart.*

PART THREE

Valor and Fire

If you're mistaken, be terribly *mistaken.*

—Marguerite Young

Photograph: George Hurrell, circa 1934.

ONE

Adjusted Angles of Vision

1933

Hollywood, where gossip flourishes like fungus in a swamp.

—Joan Crawford

Barbara's sixteen-year-old nephew, Gene, was living at Bristol Avenue during the months that she and Frank were touring with *Tattle Tales.*

Gene one day took some of his friends through the house and made a point of showing them his aunt's all-white bedroom. The servants told her about it. "She didn't like it," he said. "She was a taskmaster with me. She looked right at me and said some of the darnedest things, as if what I did was the worst thing in the world. Her eyes were piercing. You were just glad to get out of her sight."

Barbara and Frank more often enjoyed having Gene live with them. "We'd be in the living room," said Gene, "and Frank would start to sing vaudeville tunes. He was a great entertainer. We'd stand by the piano and sing along with him."

Barbara made sure that Gene was unaware of Frank's drinking exploits. There were times when Frank went away and didn't show up for a couple of days until someone would call from as far away as San Francisco and tell Barbara, "He's in the gutter up here." Other times, Barbara would get a call from Catholic Charities telling her that Fay had just donated his Cadillac and that someone should come and get it.

Fay's father often stayed with Frank and Barbara. "Pop Fay was a charming old guy," said Gene. "He told me stories about the Indian Wars."

With Frank Fay and his father, Will (Pop) Fay, circa 1933.

• • •

Ever in My Heart started shooting the third week in July.

The script was about an American woman who falls in love and marries a German, educated at Oxford, who has come to America to teach at a small New England college. He becomes a citizen and loves his new country and works hard for his wife and baby until the war against Germany breaks out and, because of national fervor, he loses his teaching position. Socially demonized by patriotic frenzy, he leaves his wife to spare her from further ostracism, is driven to return to his country of birth, and joins the enemy ranks to fight for the fatherland. The young woman, brokenhearted, volunteers as a canteen worker in France, sees her husband there posing as an American, and realizes he is a German spy. Rather than turn him in, she takes his life—and her own ("Du, du liegst mir im Herzen," he sings to her when they are courting, and later as they are dying: "Du, du liegst mir im Herzen / Du, du liegst mir im Sinn / Du, du machst mir viel Schmerzen, . . . You are ever in my heart/ You are ever in my thought/You, you, make me hurt so . . .").

The New England girl whose marriage is torn apart by the outbreak of the Great War was a role more like the puritanical girl of *The Bitter Tea of General*

With Otto Kruger as Hugo Wilbrandt, from *Ever in My Heart*, 1933.
(AMERICAN HERITAGE CENTER, UNIVERSITY OF WYOMING)

Yen than the gold-digging vamp of *Baby Face*, the gangster-moll and convict of *Ladies They Talk About*, the cabaret singer and girlfriend of the bootlegging proprietor of *The Purchase Price*, and the rough, streetwise taxi dancer of *Ten Cents a Dance*.

Hal Wallis, the executive producer, had considered Kay Francis as Mary Archer, the New Englander, and Paul Muni as the young German professor. Francis had finished making *The Keyhole, Storm at Daybreak,* and *Mary Stevens, M.D.* and was at work opposite Ricardo Cortez and Gene Raymond in *The House on 56th Street.* Paul Muni, who had been nominated as Best Actor by the academy for his last picture, *I Am a Fugitive from a Chain Gang,* which was nominated as Best Picture, was making *The World Changes.*

Archie Mayo and Wallis chose Otto Kruger, under contract at Metro, for the part of the young German émigré. Kruger was the suave, sleek romantic Broadway star who had spent more than twenty years on the stage as a sophisticated farceur, debonair leading man, best known for his work in *The Royal Family, Private Lives, Counsellor-at-Law,* and *The Great Barrington.* Metro agreed to loan out the forty-eight-year-old actor to Warner for four weeks.

Kruger had worked in Hollywood for a year—he'd appeared in *Turn Back the Clock* and *Beauty for Sale*—but still wasn't used to making pictures. "The props, lights, cameras, people standing around and other minor things combine to cheat a performer," said Kruger.

Barbara believed there was "little difference between film and stage. Acting is acting. Period. One has to cut down on facial expressions and gestures but the main thing is acting and that comes from within oneself."

Ralph Bellamy was playing Barbara's cousin and fiancé coming home from Germany with his German friend to marry his childhood sweetheart. Bellamy disagreed with Barbara about acting onstage as opposed to acting for the camera. "There is a marked difference [between the two]," said Bellamy. "On the stage, you're playing to the last row in the gallery. In pictures, you're appealing to someone across the desk from you. It's more intimate, quiet."

Ever in My Heart was budgeted at $248,000. Archie Mayo was paid $16,000 for directing the picture; Barbara, $50,000; Otto Kruger, $4,550; Ralph Bellamy, $6,000; Laura Hope Crews, $1,750; Ruth Donnelly, $3,600.

Ever in My Heart was a portrait of the havoc and violence wrought by patriotic frenzy and xenophobia. It showed Germans to be loving husbands and fathers rather than the torturers and baby killers they were portrayed as during the war.

Millhauser's script was almost an apology to Germany for the ugly claims put forward about it as part of wartime propaganda. The Germany of the previous decades was of little interest to most moviegoers, unlike the Germany of 1933, which was much more on their minds.

Six months before *Ever in My Heart* went into production, the chancellor of Germany, General Kurt von Schleicher, resigned and was succeeded by Adolf Hitler. A month later the Reichstag caught fire and burned down. The president of the Weimar Republic, Paul von Hindenburg, passed an emergency decree in Berlin suspending all constitutional articles guaranteeing private property, personal liberties, freedom of the press, and the right to hold meetings and form associations. A week later, on the day Roosevelt declared a bank holiday, the National Socialists in Germany won a majority of the Reichstag in the parliament elections. The new government was voted into power; American Jews were attacked in Berlin. Reports by the foreign press that atrocities were being inflicted on German Jews by the Nazis were called "pure invention" by the Central Union of German Citizens of the Jewish Faith.

In New York City, twenty thousand rallied at Madison Square to protest alleged Hitler-Nazi atrocities against Jews.

Ever in My Heart was to start shooting as the German cabinet decreed the confiscation of property of all "hostile" persons and corporations and the alienation and property seizure for all German critics of the government living abroad who refused to return to Germany. The Ministry for Popular

Hal Wallis, circa 1940.

Enlightenment and Propaganda in Berlin announced that German Jews were no longer allowed to be involved in the production of German films or any American films being produced in Germany.

As executive producer on the picture, Hal Wallis looked at Archie Mayo's dailies and for the most part thought what he was seeing was "splendid," but he sent notes to the director and to Robert Presnell, the supervisor, commenting on all aspects of the picture, from Otto Kruger's hairpiece ("too fluffy on one side, [it looks] like a pompadour," the style of the second decade of the twentieth century), to Mayo's camera shots ("don't shoot these group things without giving me something to cut on"; "there must be at least five different angles on this two-shot . . . cut down on your angles and put the time in on getting more scenes"), to the use of the word "Huns" ("The Hays office . . . have agreed to wink at this one, particularly as it is a comedy scene, providing we are careful not to use [the word] elsewhere . . . They tell me that every time the word 'Hun' is used on the screen, they receive violent protests from the German Ambassador in Washington").

Executives at Warner found Barbara difficult to talk to. "People think I'm stand offish and they stand off," she said. Those who didn't know her saw her as tough, cynical. "People usually detest me on sight. They think I'm sullen and sulking . . . that I'm bitter or bored. I'm neither. I can't give myself until I know what 'gifts' are wanted of me," she said. "I'm afraid of making a fool of myself. I'm interested in watching people. I'd get a great kick out of it if I could be invisible."

On the set, those who watched Barbara work and who worked with her—the property men, grips, electricians, cameramen, and others—confided in her, trusted her. To the crew Barbara was unassuming, hardworking, generous.

She walked into the makeup department one day and saw the makeup women putting bottles of milk in the watercooler. The next day, a Frigidaire arrived. The package was marked, "For the make-up girls to keep their milk cool for lunch-time." The card was unsigned.

On one Saturday when the company was working until daylight on night sequences, the prop boy came back drunk from midnight dinner. Barbara knew he would be fired if he was found in that condition and sent him on an errand at the far end of the lot. When he returned, he was still drunk. She sent him back again on another pretext. This time he returned sober.

The script girl on the picture, Virginia Moore, was someone Barbara had worked with seven years before in the chorus of the Shuberts' *Gay Paree* and hadn't seen since. Because Barbara was at work, she allowed their friendship to resume as if it had never been interrupted.

One of the electricians talked to Barbara about wanting to adopt a child. She quietly watched to see if he and his wife would make good parents; she decided they would and wrote a letter of recommendation on his behalf, helping him with the adoption.

Barbara demanded perfection of her work, but she was often sentimental about others. The five-year-old boy in the picture who played Barbara's son had to shoot some scenes with a dachshund puppy. Boy and dog played together on the lawn of the set of the New England house. At the end of a week, their sequences were completed; the boy asked about the puppy and was told that the dog's work was finished, that he wouldn't be back. The little boy was upset, but he had a big scene to do, his final scene on the picture. In it, he was to be taunted and ridiculed: his German father has left America to fight on behalf of the enemy. During the scene, the boy began to cry. It was clear to Barbara that neither the teasing in the scene nor his screen father gone to war was the cause of the upset. Barbara spoke to the director; the Eastbrook kennels were called.

When the boy's work on the picture was completed, Barbara hugged him good-bye and told him that there was a "little present" in the backseat of his

With Otto Kruger (left) and Ronnie Crosby as Teddy (Sonny)
Wilbrandt, *Ever in My Heart,* 1933. (PHOTOFEST)

mother's car. "It's from all of us who think you are a pretty swell guy. Now
you'd better run along and see if you like it."

Midway through the picture, Barbara wrenched her leg and was in great
pain from it and from a back injury she'd sustained in Boston on tour with
Tattle Tales. "It won't hurt the picture if my face is drawn," she told the director. "In fact it should make it more realistic." They had finished shooting "the
cheerful part," she said. "Now we are going into the tragedy and I can just be
myself and do whatever suffering I have to do before the camera."

Barbara reported to work so ill one morning that Mayo told her he was
going to dismiss the company for the day. Her discipline was almost military;
she refused the offer. It was past midnight when the final day's scene was shot.
After it was okayed, Barbara fainted from pain and exhaustion.

In the last few scenes of *Ever in My Heart,* Barbara's character chooses country
over her own life and that of the husband she adores.

She played the scene in stillness and with the simplest of movements.
Days before the scene was to be shot, she worked out placement with Mayo
and the cameraman, Arthur Todd, so that she wouldn't have to be distracted
discussing it with them the day they were to film.

Anytime Barbara had a big emotional scene, she needed to be left alone.
"I'm building it up from scratch," she said. "By then, that's not me. I'm some-

body else. I'm within somebody else's body and mind and I don't want to be pulled out again."

Barbara's character has recognized her husband in the canteen where she is stationed in France. He is sitting in uniform with his back to her; she realizes he is trying to pass as an American soldier. Instead of turning him in to military authorities, she becomes giddy with fear and diverts the attention of the American (the Bellamy character) who is trying to capture "the spy" (Bellamy's former beloved friend) in their midst. She enables her husband to vanish into the crowd of Allied soldiers milling about. Outside, hundreds of young men are marching in formation going off to fight. It is the "big push"; the Rainbow Division is heading into battle. The din of artillery and soldiers' boots in the muddy terrain is deafening and doesn't let up.

Her character is stunned by having seen her husband, by the recognition that he is a spy, and by having colluded with the enemy, allowing him to escape. She returns to her room, dazed. He is there, waiting for her.

She realizes the nightmare of their situation. Her body is taut. "I didn't know what I was doing," she tells him. "I won't help you again. I've got to give you up."

"Give me just a few minutes," he whispers in her ear. "It's been so long, so long. Have you forgotten everything we had together? The tears. The laughs."

He is lying on her bed, his head in her arms. Her love for him washes over her. At early dawn, he must try to make it back to enemy lines. If she lets him go, thousands of soldiers will die.

She watches as the young men march past her window and turns to the photograph of her brother in uniform: he could easily be one of those soldiers.

Barbara, with hardly a gesture or movement, makes it clear that she is as trapped as Hugo; she can't betray her husband or her country or the young soldiers going to battle. Her once innocent love is no longer theirs to have; it's doomed by duty and sacrifice and a war they had nothing to do with.

She suggests they drink some wine before they part and secretly adds poison to each glass. They drink, arm in arm: he, unknowing, happy to be with his wife; she, loyal to husband and country and resolute in her decision to betray neither.

"Rest awhile," she tells him. "I'll call you when it's light." She holds him in her arms to help him through the end.

They are in profile, his head on her shoulder, holding hands. Her face is still, radiant.

"My throat is burning," he says, unaware that he is dying.

"Only for a minute."

The camera is on her face.

She caresses him with her gentle voice. "Only for a minute."

The pain of the poison traveling through her body is on her face, even in its stillness.

"A little longer," she says to him, unbuttoning the collar of her uniform to catch some air.

He can no longer hear her, lifeless in her arms.

She looks down at him and closes her eyes to wait. There are tears for what they've lost, for their little boy, for a world at war that has taken everything from them, for the choice she's had to make between self and country.

With the simplest gesture, the smallest physical movement, Barbara reveals force and heroic truth.

The final five minutes of a picture "were comparable to 'next-to-closing,' " said Barbara. "In vaudeville," she said, " 'next-to-closing' is the star spot. A real entertainer has to hold the interest of the audience. They're keyed up to a real punch and the star must deliver."

In her fifteen movies, this was the first part that allowed Barbara to put across the picture's big ideas and to deliver its power in its final moments. *Ever in My Heart* was completed in mid-August. The studio planned to sell the film as "the greatest women's picture Barbara Stanwyck has ever made . . . [it] tops every woman characterization and stamps her as one of the most dramatic actresses of the screen." Women's clubs and societies were to be blizzarded with a direct-by-mail campaign; German communities were to be approached and ads translated for German newspapers.

The world war had ended in 1918 and xenophobia had been rife, but fifteen years later Congress was about to pass a law—the Dickstein Bill—that would prohibit the bringing of foreign actors, directors, writers, or technicians into the country "unless they are proven worthy and have genius in their line."

Roosevelt's special assistant secretary of labor, Murray W. Garsson, was investigating the immigration papers of every foreign actor or actress in Hollywood. Actors' Equity Association and the Lambs Club of New York had pressured Washington to stop the influx of foreign performers to the United States who, they declared, "were taking jobs that belong to Americans." The investigation was causing a panic in Hollywood's foreign colony.

"We will not have an underpaid clerk pass judgment on anyone who claims to be a genius," Garsson said. "We will not meet the boats and test foreign actors for genius. We will take the word of the picture company—but the company had better be sure it is telling the truth about it."

Those actors in the country illegally were being asked to leave, others were searching for immigration papers, and still others had already agreed to go. The special assistant secretary of labor would not "even venture a guess as to the number of foreign players illegally in Hollywood. We are now 'requesting' them to leave. If they do not do so, we will arrest them and deport them. We mean business."

Those foreign-born actors being investigated included Charles Chaplin, Elissa Landi, Marlene Dietrich, Maureen O'Sullivan, Anna Sten, Maurice Chevalier, Leslie Howard, Benita Hume, and Boris Karloff.

The first week of the investigation, John Farrow, an Australian-born writer, was dancing at a nightclub in Hollywood, when an immigration officer asked him to step outside and put him under arrest for illegal entry into the country. "We object to hordes of players coming here and settling, many of them illegally, and, while claiming allegiance to another flag, taking the work that is so badly needed by our own players. With the passage of the Dickstein Bill, there won't be such a thing as a lot of 'extras' over here who are foreigners."

Frank and Barbara returned to New York. Fay was too drunk to go on *The Fleischmann's Yeast Hour,* and William Morris sent Lew Cody from Los Angeles to appear in his place. But Frank was hired to appear for a week at New York's Broadway Paramount in a new act put together around him called "Frankie and Junie" with June Knight. He was being paid $2,000 for the week. The act was set to open on the Friday of the first weekend in September. Days before, he was at the Sands Point club in Long Island and became embroiled in a fight in which Senator Huey Long was punched. Frank left and went into hiding. By Thursday, the Paramount house manager, Boris Morros, was beside himself, calling everywhere, beginning with Barbara, in an attempt to find him. Morros had no choice but to rebuild the show without Fay and booked Al Trahan, along with Fay's frequent stand-in, Richie Craig Jr. Three different ads were put together for the Friday papers depending on which entertainer would perform. On Thursday night at 11:00, Fay reappeared and begged Morros for another chance; the theater manager relented.

Barbara and Fay were booked on separate tours of the East Coast and the Midwest. The week following Fay's engagement at the Broadway Paramount, he was in Buffalo playing five shows a day. Barbara was in New York for a week appearing in the stage show at the Capitol Theatre for $4,000 against a fifty-fifty split beyond box office of $55,000, performing scenes from *Ladies of Leisure* and *The Miracle Woman.* The picture showing at the Capitol was W. S. Van Dyke's latest, *Penthouse,* starring Warner Baxter, Myrna Loy, Phillips Holmes, and Mae Clarke.

The New York Times called the stage show at the Capitol "excellent variety . . . and smartly turned out . . . except in two spots. The weak links in the chain of genuine diversion are the badly conceived personal appearance of Barbara Stanwyck . . . and the musically energetic singing of Morton Downey."

"Five shows a day, from 11 am to 11 pm," said Barbara. "At night it took me an hour and a half to get back to my hotel because of the crowds at the stage door. I loved the attention, the flattery, the fact that they cared enough to see me."

Barbara lost her voice the second day. "Yelling on the stage did it. The strain was bad," she said. A doctor was backstage during the five days of the engagement helping to treat her voice.

Barbara appeared in Philadelphia for Warner Bros. for a week at the Earle Theatre; Fay was in Philadelphia with her, appearing at the Warner Bros.' Stanley. The picture at the Earle was *One Man's Journey,* starring Lionel Barrymore with May Robson, Joel McCrea, and Frances Dee. Barbara said, "It isn't me that's drawing [the audience]. It's Lionel Barrymore. What a break for me. I've seen the picture and I think he deserves better. It's too bad to waste experience and real ability on poor stories. Besides, the supporting cast is inadequate. I think [Barrymore] has just about everything. That man is a genius with an invaluable background of experience. I know all his little tricks and I love them."

By the time Barbara got to Washington, D.C., she was exhausted, and her voice was beginning to go again. She asked the manager if there wasn't some way she could leave the theater without the hour-and-a-half delay in getting back to the hotel and her bed. "Tell you what," he said. "You go out the front entrance; there won't be anyone there. I'll have a taxi waiting and you won't have any trouble."

The first night went according to plan. Knowing the cab would pass the stage door on its way to the hotel, Barbara got set to view the waiting crowd. "It would be fun to see all those people standing around while I was whizzing by them unrecognized," she said.

Barbara drove by the stage door. No one was there. "Not one stale person. The next night the manager offered to escort me to the waiting taxi and I said, 'Don't bother, honey.' I went out the stage door. Matter of fact, there wasn't anybody at the stage door the whole damned week."

Fay was canceled at the Michigan Theatre in Detroit. During the second show of the opening day, he made a scene involving the piano player. Fay didn't like him and refused to work with him or any other piano player. He was told that the theater had invested $20,000 in his appearance; in addition, he was being paid $2,000 a week. He refused to appear for the third show. No act replaced him.

In Boston's RKO Keith Theatre, Barbara collapsed twice while performing the pulpit scene from *The Miracle Woman*. She hurt her spine, throwing out three vertebrae, and injured her right hand, but she was determined to finish out the week. Each day, for four days, she rested flat on her back between shows. The bandages were removed so she could be X-rayed while doctors searched for a bone sliver. She decided to cancel the last two weeks of the RKO tour and return home. Doctors prepared her for the train to Los Angeles, her X-ray plates with her. Once in Hollywood, Barbara was admitted to the hospital for exhaustion and a couple of weeks of rest.

Frank was on his way back to Los Angeles. Barbara knew he'd been on an extended bout of drinking and thought it better if her nephew returned to Brooklyn; she didn't want him to witness Fay's possibly violent behavior and arranged for Gene to return to Brooklyn by boat via the Panama Canal with a stopover in Havana.

Fay had been drinking since he'd left Detroit. On his return to 441 Bristol Avenue, he fell down a flight of basement stairs and hit his head so badly he was admitted to Glendale Hospital, where he stayed for some time. After his release a nurse was brought in to help care for him.

Amid gossip of trouble in the Fays' marriage, Barbara and Frank posed for an advertisement for Mobil oil with a headline that read: "Barbara Stanwyck & Frank Fay in a Mobil Oil Movie, *Double Anniversary.*" Six panels of photographs showed the Fays, husband and wife, very much in love, celebrating their anniversary, driving into town in their roadster convertible to see a movie. They stop at a Mobil oil station and reminisce about the wedding trip they took in their car and realize it is the car's anniversary as well (the secret of the car's longevity: Mobil oil).

After Frank's fall on the basement stairs, he changed for the worse. He could become irrational, ranting without provocation and becoming enraged. When taking a cigarette, instead of lighting it, he would put it on a table, close his eyes, and act as if he were praying to it, then smoke it. If Barbara asked him why he was praying over his cigarette, he replied, "Because I want to."

With Maud and Dad Merkent back in Flatbush, Barbara was alone with Frank, and despite his erratic fits she was determined to believe things would get better. She still wanted to do everything, have everything, *be* everything

Fay wanted her to be. Where Frank was concerned, Barbara described the feeling "of having no self of your own left, of being nothing but blind desire to be what he wants you to be, to serve, to please."

Despite that, Frank's jealousy and possessiveness of Barbara resulted in violent arguments late into the night. Dishes were broken, windows were smashed, and the police were frequently called to 441 Bristol Avenue.

If Fay left the house, Barbara would eventually beg him to return. "I love you just as much as it is possible for a woman to love a man," she wrote to him during one separation. "If I was born with anything fine in me, and I choose to think I was, from what I know of my mother and father, you have brought that fineness to the surface. I cannot imagine life without you and I am not being melodramatic."

To the press and in public Barbara was adamant about the solidity of their marriage. To Barbara, marriage was "being in the same room with another person everyday for twenty-four hours a day, three hundred and sixty five days a year," and while husband and wife would "see things differently at some time or many times," Barbara said, if they "adjust[ed] their angles of vision . . . and talk[ed] it out," things would be okay.

"Most couples don't do that," she said. "They are afraid of each other and of newspaper opinion. They hide what they believe. Or . . . reveal it only piecemeal. One of the married pair keeps quiet and lets matters drift, though inwardly protesting. I believe in free speech for the married. If anything is discussed long enough, an agreement is reached. A smothered conviction or feeling is likely to burst at last into flame.

"There must be sportsmanship in marriage to make it permanent. And religion. I had no interest in religion until I met Frank Fay. He is deeply religious. He has more books on the different religions of the world than anyone I know."

Barbara believed that Hollywood couldn't bear the thought of a man and a woman living together in lawful wedlock—and actually being happy. "Themselves having made a mess of marriage," she said, "it's as if they were determined nobody else should make a success of it. I have to smile as I read the published reports of the great sadness that overshadows Hollywood because of the Pickford-Fairbanks split. I dare say the good people of Japan and England and the farmers in the middle west who also don't know what's going on are truly sorry to learn of the end of that 'romance.'

"But Hollywood isn't sorry. It hasn't time to be sorry. It's busy telling all who will listen that I-told-you-so line. Now that their predictions have been fulfilled they're gloating. Now they can turn their destructive attention to some other noted couple."

Ann Harding with her husband, Harry Bannister, and their daughter, Jane, in happier times as a family, March 1932. Soon after, she dissolved the six-year union in divorce court in an effort to salvage the couple's love and to help Bannister, being referred to as "Ann Harding's husband," from "further losing his identity."

Barbara referred to the gossips as "venomous tattlers" and defended Fay, her marriage, and herself against Hollywood's poisonous intrusion:

"Marriage can be destroyed by scandal mongers. I know it can. I've seen it happen. Had Carole Lombard and Bill Powell lived anywhere in the world except in Hollywood, they'd have been gloriously happy together until death did them part.

"As it is the gossips drove Carole off to Reno where for no good reason she legally tore herself away from the man who adores her and whom she adores.

"Hollywood did the same thing to Ann Harding and Harry Bannister. I know Ann loves Harry devotedly. I know Harry loves her no less wholeheartedly. But Hollywood made it impossible for them to remain married."

Ann Harding had supported her actor husband, who was earning $1,000 a week as an RKO contract player. When he visited his wife on the set, he offered unwanted commentary to her directors and was eventually barred from his own studio. After six years of being "blissfully" married, Harding and Bannister divorced in a bitter custody battle over their three-year-old daughter.

Barbara's anger at Hollywood and those who'd "gloated" at the Fays from the time they first arrived in town—"we were easy meat for them they thought," said Barbara—made her more determined to stick with Fay.

She was waging war on two fronts. Will and blind desire held her firm against the onslaught of Fay's drinking, his erratic violence, and fits of anger. Loyalty and a determination to show up "the rats" of Hollywood for what they were spurred her on to publicly denounce the town and to stand arm in arm with her desperately troubled husband against those who predicted the demise of their marriage. Barbara found little comfort in either camp.

TWO

Sinister Provisions

Emotion is Miss Stanwyck's meat. She can serve it in any style.
                                    —*Variety,* October 1933

Walda Mansfield, one of Barbara's trio from New York, had married Walter Donaldson, the songwriter. His songs "How Ya Gonna Keep 'Em Down on the Farm," "My Blue Heaven," "Makin' Whoopee," "Love Me or Leave Me," and others had brought him to Metro, and he and Walda were living in Beverly Hills.

They were at a party given by MGM's vice president and general manager, Eddie Mannix, and his wife. Mannix was Metro's watchdog, in charge of all large expenditures. Mae Clarke had recently signed a long-term contract at Metro and was at the party as well. Mae was two weeks into production on a picture called *Made on Broadway* with Robert Montgomery. The party went on late into the evening, and Mannix asked the actor Phillips Holmes to drive Mae back to her house; she had an early call for the morning.

Holmes dropped off Mae and returned to the Mannix party. Mae decided it was too early to be home for the night and called a cab to take her back to the party. Mannix asked Holmes to drive her home again.

A heavy fog had set in. Holmes was hugging the right side of the curb. A block from Mae's house, he drove into the back of a parked car. Mae went onto the dash and lost seven teeth. The next day she had to call the studio and tell them that she wouldn't be coming in.

"There wasn't a person to blame it on," she said. "I had this great chance opposite one of the very big stars—and I had a great part. I was heartbroken to have missed the picture." Sally Eilers took over the part.

Mae went off salary. No money was coming in; nor was there insurance. Mae's jaw, dislocated in the accident, was wired for twelve weeks. She was confined to her home in Westwood with her family. "We counted our blessings," she said. "One day a knock came at the door. It was a florist with a box . . . about four feet long and two feet wide. I opened it, and layer upon layer of beautiful cut spring flowers were inside. And a little card: 'To Mae Clarke, because I admire you. Joan Crawford.' "

The Roosevelt administration was taking major steps to turn the country around. The banking system was overhauled under the Glass-Steagall Act. Banks could operate state to state; depositors were insured by the Federal Deposit Insurance Corporation.

Congress passed the National Industrial Recovery Act, in which Roosevelt set up a series of codes of fair practice for more than five hundred industries, as well as a maximum-hour workday and a minimum wage. Employers were allowed to regulate their own industries, but as a result many of the codes reflected antitrust practices. Lawyers, doctors, newspapermen, and writers all wanted to unionize.

The newly formed Screen Writers Guild was fighting to be included in the writing of the National Recovery Administration's Motion Picture Code, but producers wanted both the Writers Guild and the Actors Guild kept out of the discussions so they could maintain control of industry practices.

Among the troubling provisions being put forth by the producers as part of the NRA Motion Picture Code were stipulations that no actor, writer, or director could earn more than $100,000 a year and that no agent would be able to practice without being licensed by producers. A blacklisting provision, put forth by Irving Thalberg to keep salaries low, stated that no studio could approach a writer or actor whose contract had expired until the former contract holder had decided to approve the release.

Once actors became aware of the proposed article fixing salaries, a mass meeting was called at the De Mille Drive home of Frank Morgan, attended by some of the most important actors in Hollywood.

Word had spread during the summer that the newly incorporated guild (among its original members: James Gleason, Boris Karloff, and Alan Mowbray, whose personal check for $50 covered the cost of filing articles of incorporation) was "an autonomous organization composed solely of actors" whose purpose was to protect and "better the working conditions" of those who belonged. No guild member could enter into a contract with a producer unless the contract conformed to the guild's code. The guild's motto: "He best serves himself who serves others."

It was clear that the Academy, which was supposed to represent actors as well as producers, was backing the producers on the issue of salary fixing. Actors resigned from the Academy out of anger, including its vice presidents, Fredric March, Adolphe Menjou, and Robert Montgomery, and the members Groucho Marx, James Cagney, Ann Harding (the first of the big female stars to join the new guild), Jeanette MacDonald, George Raft, and Otto Kruger. They, and other academy members such as Chester Morris, Paul Muni, Lee Tracy, and Charles Butterworth, were determined to be part of an independent organization that would represent their needs.

"You may stop an army of a million men, but [you] can't stop a right idea when its time has come," said Ralph Morgan, quoting Victor Hugo, at one of the Guild discussions.

The night before the meeting at Frank Morgan's house, all twenty-one of the original members of the guild resigned their board positions so that new members—prominent actors all—would be able to help shape the organization. "We must have a Hollywood organization for Hollywood actors and actresses," said Eddie Cantor, who succeeded Ralph Morgan as the guild's president. During the meeting two kinds of memberships were defined: class A for the higher-paid actors; class B for those lower salaried. New officers were chosen: Menjou and March were named first and second vice presidents; Ann Harding, third vice president; Groucho Marx, treasurer.

The new slate of officers voted to call a mass meeting four days later at the El Capitan Theatre in Hollywood. More than 250 actors were admitted into the Guild; among the class A actors were Mary Astor, Pat O'Brien, Edward Arnold, Cary Grant, Ginger Rogers, Bing Crosby, and Jean Hersholt. "Those of us . . . under contract to the studios," said Robert Montgomery, "put our contracts in jeopardy by supporting the Guild and organizing it." Montgomery was appointed chairman of the producers committee. "The studios required you to either work on Christmas Day," Montgomery said, "New Year's Day or Thanksgiving, any real legal holiday, and if you insisted that you did not wish to work on that day, you had to work the following Sunday in order to make up for it."

Barbara, who with Fay was a member of Actors' Equity, did not join the guild.

"No actor of importance will work in a studio which signs the code," said Eddie Cantor. "These provisions are un-American." Actors said they would walk out if a salary-fixing board were put into effect under the code. "The days of slavery are over," said Cantor. "The guild is out to protect the little fellow that the administration should protect." Cantor, representing the

Screen Actors Guild, and John Howard Lawson, the Screen Writers Guild, wired Roosevelt to protest the "sinister provisions" of Article 5 of the NRA Motion Picture Code. What had bankrupted motion picture companies, the wire said, was not the players' salaries but "the purchase and leasing of theatres at exorbitant rates, caused by the race to power of a few individuals desiring to get a stranglehold on the outlet of the industry, the box office."

The headline pay of actors ranged from $3,000 to $10,000 a week, with Wallace Beery, Marie Dressler, Joan Crawford, and Ann Harding receiving the former and Greta Garbo the latter. Actors who produced their own pictures, such as Mary Pickford, Charles Chaplin, and Harold Lloyd, were paid between $500,000 and $2 million per picture.

Cantor, Fannie Hurst, and Robert Sherwood traveled to Warm Springs, Georgia, to meet with the president. Regarding the issue of salary fixing at $100,000, Roosevelt asked, "Why should an actor make more than I make?" Cantor explained that the president's salary came out of the pockets of the American people, but it was producers who paid actors and writers. Roosevelt issued an executive order eliminating salary fixing from the proposed code. He also called for the formation of the "five and five committees"—five writers, five actors, five producers—to draft the amendments to the Motion Picture Code.

Ever in My Heart opened in mid-October in Los Angeles.

The response was mixed. Critics in New York called the picture "a mild little film" and "sentimental, hackneyed"; in Los Angeles, reviewers were moved by it, calling it "tender, heart-touching, tragic." Reviewers on both coasts were in agreement about Barbara's work. The *New York World-Telegram* called Barbara's performance "one of the most searching and authentic characterizations she has yet offered"; W. E. Oliver in the Los Angeles *Evening Herald Examiner* wrote, "Both Miss Stanwyck and Kruger achieve a remarkably sincere, tender conviction in their roles." *Variety* said, "Emotion is Miss Stanwyck's meat. She can serve it in any style, restrained, despairing, smoldering, hysterical."

THREE

Leading with Your Ace

Barbara was still recuperating from her personal appearance tour. Her contract with Warner, extended because of the tour, was due to expire the third week in December.

Harry Warner sent a telegram to Jack: "Keep Stanwyck/These days cannot afford to let anybody go/Harry." Warner exercised its option and extended Barbara's contract for a year, paying her the contractually agreed-upon $175,000—$3,500 a week for fifty weeks.

For the final picture under her Warner contract, Barbara accepted the lead in a three-generation theatrical story, *Broadway and Back,* with a script by Sheridan Gibney, in which she was to play the part of a young girl who ages to a grandmother. The studio thought the idea—a cavalcade of theaterdom—worth the effort and expense, but it was concerned about the flatness of Gibney's treatment. Of concern as well was the similarity to Metro's *March of Time* (released as *Broadway to Hollywood*), from a story, and directed, by Willard Mack. The picture followed a performing family from vaudeville's heyday to their Hollywood triumph.

Barbara decided to turn down the Gibney script. Wallis next offered her *Blood of China,* and the part of a Chinese girl. Three months later the script was still being written.

The studio took note of the many doctor pictures that had recently been made—*Emergency Call, One Man's Journey, Arrowsmith, The Crime of the Century*—and offered Barbara its own medical story, a picture called *Dr. Monica* that would go into production in early January 1934. Barbara rejected it. Warner sent it to Kay Francis, who agreed to do it. Wallis looked over the gambling pictures around, including *Street of Chance, No Man of Her Own,* and *Show Boat,* and offered Barbara *Gambling Lady,* based on a story by the screenwriter Doris Malloy.

As Jennifer "Lady" Lee, a one-in-a-million card shark with a code of ethics as straight as a die. Pat O'Brien (bottom) as Charlie Lang, hooked into the syndicate; Joel McCrea as Garry Madison, scion of industry who stoops to marry the *Gambling Lady*, 1934.

Malloy, before even writing the story, thought Barbara ideal for the part of Jennifer "Lady" Lee, a female card shark who plays in the most elegant society circles and wins on the up-and-up. Lady Lee is the daughter of a legendary straight-shooting gambler, the last of a dying breed. To write the story, Malloy had visited undercover games up and down the Pacific coast, talking with professional gamblers and racetrack habitués.

Wallis budgeted the picture at $235,000 and assigned Henry Blanke as its supervisor. Archie Mayo was the director. Wallis borrowed Joel McCrea from RKO for four weeks to play opposite Barbara as the society boy she marries, and hired C. Aubrey Smith as McCrea's elegant gambler father, who fast falls under Lady's spell. The studio used the contract feature star Pat O'Brien to co-star with McCrea as Lady's longtime family pal who is in love with her and is gently rebuffed when he asks Lady to marry him; he's enmeshed with the syndicate and plays a crooked game.

Joel McCrea was in demand at RKO; *Gambling Lady* was his sixth picture that year. McCrea had been an extra in pictures and danced with Garbo in *The Single Standard;* Gloria Swanson had sent him home in her Rolls-Royce one day and tested with him the next. He'd worked with Pickford and Colleen Moore, Lillian Gish and Crawford, and had a bit in Lon Chaney's only talkie. His big break came when DeMille put the young actor under contract until the great showman went back to Paramount and turned him over to Metro. The twenty-eight-year-old actor had been featured in *The Five O'Clock Girl* with Marion Davies and *The Single Standard* with Greta Garbo.

He'd appeared opposite Constance Bennett (*Born to Love*), Dolores del Río (*Bird of Paradise*), and Irene Dunne (*The Silver Cord*).

Louis B. Mayer let McCrea's option lapse, and William Randolph Hearst wrote, "Dear Louie, You've just dropped an all-American boy . . . who Miss Davies and I thought had great possibilities. I just want you to know that I don't approve of this action . . . In my business, running three hundred newspapers and several other businesses, we never hire anyone without thinking that they have possibilities and we never let them go until we have found out whether they do or not."

Warner paid RKO $7,000 for McCrea ($3,000 for its standard carrying charge; $1,000 a week for McCrea himself). Aubrey Smith was paid $2,500 for two weeks of work, and Pat O'Brien, who unhappily agreed to share billing with McCrea, got $7,500. Barbara was paid $50,000.

For the part of Lady Lee, Barbara, who was neither a cardplayer nor a gambler, had to learn how to deal and shuffle as a professional. A tutor was brought in, and in three weeks she learned roulette, faro, craps, twenty-one, and poker as if they were a natural part of who she was. She used her imaginative powers to get into the nature of the game and chose to play Lady Lee with the lightness, grace, and skill a master cardplayer must have.

Gambling Lady was the first picture in which Barbara's wardrobe, by Orry-Kelly, was extensive and lavish. Kelly had designed costumes in New York for the Shubert and George White revues before designing costumes for Warner Bros. in 1932, beginning with *So Big,* in which he dressed Barbara in the plainest of hopsack. The clothes for *Ladies They Talk About* were almost as simple. For *Baby Face,* Kelly's third picture with Barbara, the clothes were luxurious. With *Gambling Lady,* her wardrobe was extravagant.

In the picture Barbara wears at various times a chinchilla-trimmed cape, a beaded chiffon gown with scrolls of bugle beads, a white velvet nap of Oriental cut, and a satin dress negligee, trimmed on the neckline with a fan-shaped train and bands of pink marabou. Kelly also designed for her a suit of wide-wale cloth of cadet blue, with a royal-blue georgette and gold threads in a horizontal stripe. She looked equally glamorous in Kelly's black-crepe five o'clock two-piece gown and wedding dress of off-white panne velvet with a cowl clipped at the neckline with brilliants. She wore the clothes well, except her waist, which became problematic in the noticeable width of her seat with her back to the camera.

During the first days of shooting, a stills photographer was called in to take pictures of a scene at a gambling table. The photographer began with the ex-

Draped in an Orry-Kelly silver design with white marabou, March 1934. His first job in pictures was for Fox Films in their East Coast studios, drawing titles. Soon he was designing costumes for *George White's Scandals* and Ethel Barrymore and, with his sketches shown to Warners by Cary Grant, he was assigned *So Big* and became the studio's chief designer.

tras, then photographed Aubrey Smith, Barbara, and Pat O'Brien—all Warner players.

McCrea, on loan-out, figured no one would care if he was photographed and left for lunch.

When he got back, Barbara said, "Where the hell were you? For stills? Where the hell were you?"

The crew watched and listened, including Mayo and George Barnes, the cameraman.

"You think just because you're tan and pretty you come here and coast along," said Barbara. "You think this is a picnic. When I was doing road shows, I'd be sweating so much I'd have to go in the men's room on the train and take my chances taking a shower so I'd be ready to get on and perform again when we got to the next town. I'd sleep sitting up in coaches. That's what you call a trouper."

McCrea apologized.

"Well, then, get off your fat ass, California sunshine boy, and do it."

Joel McCrea was strong, beautiful, athletic, born and bred in Los Angeles. He'd grown up a California golden boy, delivering newspapers to Valentino, William S. Hart, Sessue Hayakawa, and Wallace Reid. He had attended Hollywood School for Girls with the daughters of Louis B. Mayer and Cecil B. DeMille with classes out of doors under oak trees, even in a tree house.

Barbara could have had McCrea fired from *Gambling Lady,* but instead she took the time to teach him what was right and what was expected of him. Afterward, they went on to a scene in which Barbara as Lady tells McCrea's father, Aubrey Smith, that she loves his son. Smith tells her that she wouldn't be happy with their pompous people and that his son won't fit in with the gangsters she goes around with. Barbara has a big scene in which she cries and says, "Just tell your son that I don't love him and to hell with all your class and your money and your breeding and your blue bloods." For the scene, Barbara was to say, "I don't love you and I don't want to marry you!" McCrea was to kiss her, and then they were to cut.

Mayo said to McCrea, "Now, listen, when you grab her, you're going to lose her for life. You grab her with all sincerity in the world and kiss her. Grab her by the ass and pull her to you so she knows it isn't your pocket knife you've got there. Make it the goddamnedest kiss ever, do everything but screw her, and if that's necessary, go ahead and do that."

They did the scene.

When it was time, McCrea kissed Barbara, "practically [doing] everything." The kiss went on for four and a half minutes. The electricians were falling down laughing. Finally, McCrea said, "Isn't it cut?" Barbara looked up at him, laughed right in his face, and said, "You son of a bitch!" Then she grabbed him and kissed him back in the same way, though the cameras had stopped running. That was the end of the war.

With Archie Mayo (left), director of *Gambling Lady,* and Joel McCrea. (AMERICAN HERI-
TAGE CENTER, UNIVERSITY OF WYOMING)

McCrea's wife, the actress Frances Dee, came to the set each day to watch
her new husband work and supervise his lovemaking, shouting "Bravo! Good
work!" after McCrea and Barbara's love scenes.

McCrea was six feet two inches to Barbara's delicate, slim, five feet three.
She was diminutive, but when it came to her work, she had power and size.
She gave off an ease despite being in severe pain from her collapse onstage a
month before in Boston. McCrea was boisterous, carefree, to her cool self-
possession.

Barbara came to work one day with her back taped. Mayo asked her how
she'd hurt it.

"I fell down the stairs," she said.

Mayo didn't say anything more about it. He figured that Fay had probably
thrown her down a flight of stairs.

This new accident didn't help the leg she'd sprained while filming *Ever in
My Heart.* During production on *Gambling Lady,* Barbara was strapped onto
a board each night at home to relieve the pressure on her hip and to prevent

Frank Fay with Dion Anthony, 1934.
(PHOTOFEST)

any movement as she slept. During the day at work, between story conferences, gown fittings, and shooting, she was put under quartz lights for four hours at a time to help lessen the pain.

McCrea asked Barbara about Fay. "I'm still nuts about him," she said. "That's a man's life. And the girl he picks up out of nowhere is not gonna walk away from *him*."

She went on, publicly coming to Fay's defense, but she no longer felt that she could be alone in the house with him. He was often irrational. Servants were present in the house, as well as Nellie Banner to take care of Dion, but Barbara needed someone she felt comfortable with, someone she could trust. She asked James "Buck" Mack, of the vaudeville team of Miller and Mack, to move in with them.

Buck Mack had traveled with the Fays in *Tattle Tales*, and he agreed to make the move. Mack had been around Barbara since Broadway days. He'd encouraged her to dance when she was a girl; she'd called him Uncle Buck. Now that he was living with Barbara and Frank on Bristol Avenue, he saw how Fay drank, often nonstop for days, sometimes weeks. After he had drunk himself into a stupor, Buck would try to sober him up. He saw how Fay yelled at his two-year-old son, how his uncontrollable rages could be set off at any time, in the midst of an ordinary conversation if something favorable

With Dion, age two. (COURTESY
TONY FAY)

was said about someone Fay didn't like. It was clear to Buck that Frank was
mentally unstable.

Early in the filming of *Gambling Lady,* a lien was put on Fay and Barbara's earnings. The federal government claimed that the Fays owed more
than $6,000 in back taxes. Two weeks later Warner Bros. was summoned
by the Internal Revenue Service to appear before the Sixth District Court of
California to turn over Barbara's contracts with the studio.

Fay was still overseeing the remodeling and rebuilding of Bristol Avenue
and spending money recklessly. He'd put in a tennis court and a bicycle track
and added a party house to the gymnasium.

Barbara looked through her purse one day and realized she had no money.
Frank had taken it. She was going out that night and had to borrow $5 from
her maid.

There wasn't enough money to pay off the taxes owed the government,
and Barbara, through Warner, arranged for a $15,000 loan with the Bank
of America National Trust and Savings Association. The bank was directed
as well to pay off two real estate loans the Fays had taken in 1929 and in
January 1932. The government freeze on the Fays' bank account made it
necessary for the Bank of America loan to be made under the names of John
Doe Co., Richard Roe Co., and Henry Poe Co. Frank and Barbara put down
as collateral the deed to their property. The money for the loan was to be

repaid from Barbara's $3,500 a week salary. The Bank of America paid the IRS the $6,102 plus interest that the Fays owed in back taxes and made available to Barbara, who was unable to have access to her own money due to the government's lien on her account, an additional $6,000 at 7 percent interest.

FOUR

A Beautiful Ghost

1934

Warner Bros. was looking for a project for Barbara for her first picture under their option agreement. In the late fall, Barbara had rejected Wallis's offer of *Dr. Monica*. The year 1934 began with Barbara turning down a script of *Madame Du Barry*.

A month later, in March, Wallis sent Barbara a script called *Housewife* by Manuel Seff and Lillie Hayward from a story by Robert Lord; two days later Barbara called to say she wasn't interested. Bette Davis agreed to take the part of the successful advertising writer caught between her colleague at the office (George Brent) and his wife (Ann Dvorak). Production began in early April.

Ever in My Heart didn't do well at the box office, barely making back its cost of just under a quarter of a million dollars and Barbara was "in the doghouse with the studio" for turning down script after script, but she didn't care. "I worry night and day over stories," she said.

The Depression was changing what audiences wanted to see. Individual movie stars were no longer the draw; studios were teaming up actors—Marie Dressler and Wallace Beery, Jean Harlow and Clark Gable, Ruby Keeler and Dick Powell—and were starring ensemble casts for pictures such as *Grand Hotel* and *Dinner at Eight*. Moviegoers were willing to see fewer and fewer pictures. The federal government was supporting twenty-one million people through relief. The big moneymakers for 1933 included Dressler and Beery in *Tugboat Annie; State Fair;* Mervyn LeRoy's *Gold Diggers* and *42nd Street,* in which Warner had gambled $400,000 on an unpopular style of picture. Mae West's pictures *She Done Him Wrong* and *I'm No Angel* set records, playing as many as twelve returns in one theater.

Fewer male stars were able to draw audiences to the theaters. Those who did included Clark Gable, Robert Montgomery, and Mickey Mouse. The handful of big stars holding on included Joan Crawford, Jean Harlow, Katharine Hepburn, Janet Gaynor, and Marlene Dietrich. Katharine Hepburn in *Morning Glory* and *Little Women* and Bing Crosby in *Too Much Harmony* and *College Humor* were the newest stars of the year to take hold.

In addition to Barbara, the lead roster at Warner Bros. included Edward G. Robinson, Joe E. Brown, Paul Muni, Kay Francis, William Powell, Richard Barthelmess, and Ruth Chatterton. Among the featured players were Joan Blondell, Bette Davis, George Brent, and Pat O'Brien.

Barbara was given Ruth Chatterton's dressing room, the last remaining of two bungalow dressing rooms on the Warner lot. Chatterton's dressing room had originally been built in the 1920s for Colleen Moore, the *Flaming Youth* girl; the second Warner bungalow, for its other big star of the time, Corinne Griffith, had been converted into a steam room and bathhouse for studio officials.

Barbara and Chatterton had a cordial but cool relationship left over from New York when Barbara, then twenty and in her first hit on Broadway, was testing for *Broadway Nights,* as Chatterton, who'd come to test for the same part, walked onto the set. Barbara had been given an onion by the director to get her to cry, and Chatterton had derided the notion that anyone would need anything other than concentration and acting to bring on tears, or any emotion. This when Barbara was making audiences weep by the power of her work during every performance of *The Noose.*

Two weeks after seeing *Housewife,* Hal Wallis sent her a script from a novel by R. H. Bruce Lockhart, based on his experiences as a British agent and acting consul in revolutionary Russia from 1914 to 1917. Leslie Howard was set to play Lockhart, a former rubber plantation owner and Fleet Street journalist.

Barbara found Lockhart's book so absorbing she read it twice. "But it's the man's story," she said. The part being proposed for Barbara was of an ardent Communist, secretary to Lenin, who falls in love with the British agent. "Howard was made to order for the part," said Barbara. "But . . . I [see] no reason why I should play second fiddle to anyone. I've worked too hard to get to the top to give up top billing for no good reason. I don't mean the actual billing, because that is unimportant. I mean the top spot in the picture. In a few years, I suppose, I'll have to resign myself to leads and supporting parts—we all come to that eventually—but I don't feel I've reached that point yet."

Barbara received the script, read it, and turned it down the same day.

Wallis next sent her a comedy called *Traveling Saleslady,* about an industrialist's daughter determined to go to work against her father's wishes, with a scheme to boost the sales of the family toothpaste. The script arrived on April 24. Barbara rejected it on the twenty-fifth.

Gambling Lady had opened at the end of March. "See the flashing Stanwyck at the peak of her form—playing a man's game with the heart of a woman—in the love story for which every other Hollywood star would have given a king's ransom."

Reviewers described *Gambling Lady* as "Tailored smartly to suit [her] talents . . . Barbara Stanwyck is the picture throughout holding it up all the way." *Variety* called the picture "high entertainment [with] superb performances"; audiences responded. *Gambling Lady* was a hit at the box office and earned more than double its cost of $230,000.

A week after the picture opened, Hal Wallis wrote to his production supervisor, Henry Blanke, about another script he had in mind for Barbara. The script of *Firebird* was based on a Hungarian play set in Vienna and centered on a murder mystery. "We don't want to lose any more time," Wallis wrote. "We want to get Stanwyck's acceptance and go into production as soon as possible." Wallis sent the script to Barbara on May 3; she turned it down the following day.

A week later Wallis sent over a script for a remake of Willa Cather's *A Lost Lady*, originally made into a Warner Bros. picture a decade before with Irene Rich. Alfred Knopf had published *A Lost Lady* in the fall of 1923, months after Cather had won the 1923 Pulitzer Prize for her novel *One of Ours*. The 1924 picture had its premiere in Red Cloud, Nebraska, Cather's hometown since girlhood.

It had been five months since Barbara's last picture. She approved Gene Markey and Kathryn Scola's rewrite of the script. Production on *A Lost Lady* began in June. Al Green, who'd worked with Barbara on *Baby Face,* was the director. Green was a modest little man who smoked big cigars, collected rare books, first editions and rare manuscripts, and was known to whisper his directions to the actor so that even the cameraman couldn't hear him.

Willa Cather based Mrs. Forrester, the lost lady of her novel, on the glamorous wife of the ex-governor of Nebraska. Edith Lewis, Cather's longtime companion, wrote, "It is doubtful if anyone in Red Cloud at that time saw [Lyra] Garber . . . in the poetic light of the lost lady of Willa Cather's tale." Mrs. Forrester was a "beautiful ghost . . . for twenty years before it came together as a possible subject" for Cather.

In writing about Marian Forrester, Cather created a woman seen through the eyes of others: Captain Forrester, her much older husband; the "admiring middle-aged men of the railroad aristocracy who visit" the Forrester place, known for its "certain charm and aristocracy"; and the young boy Niel Herbert, who is first brought into the Forrester house after being knocked out cold from a fall while trying to rescue a blind woodpecker in a tree. The boy is placed on a "white bed with ruffled pillow shams" and opens his eyes to see Mrs. Forrester kneeling beside him "bathing his forehead with cologne." To Niel, Mrs. Forrester is "an excitement that came and went with summer." Even as a boy Niel recognizes Mrs. Forrester "as belonging to a different world from any he had ever known."

"There was no fun in it," wrote Cather, "unless I could get her just as I remembered her and produce the effect she had on me and the many others who knew her."

"I didn't try to make a character study," she wrote, "but just a portrait like a thin miniature painted on ivory . . . I wasn't interested in her character when I was little, but in her lovely hair and her laugh which made me happy clear down to my toes. Neither is 'Niel' a character study. In fact, he isn't a character at all; he is just a peephole into that world . . . he is only a point of view."

After Niel has grown up and moved away and Marian Forrester's world has closed in on her, left her without means—her husband, the Captain, dead; the Forrester house sold; her health failing; and she, "sadly broken"— Niel learns that Mrs. Forrester has gone west, "people supposed California." A long-ago witness to a desperate moment in which Mrs. Forrester was at the frantic end of an illicit liaison, the young man, who was not able to think about her for years "without chagrin," is pleased, finally, "that she had had a hand in breaking [Niel] in to life. He has known pretty women and clever ones since then, but never one like her, as she was in her best days. Her eyes, when they laughed for a moment into one's own, seemed to promise a wild delight that he has not found in life. 'I know where it is,' they seemed to say, 'I could show you!' "

The 1924 Dorothy Farnum script of *A Lost Lady* kept somewhat to Cather's novel. A revised script for a remake, to be called *The Reckless Hour,* saw Marian Forrester as a "beautiful, sexy young woman" and Niel as "just out of college, a youth of fine ideals, loving Marian hopelessly but with respect and reverence."

Henry Blanke was assigned the supervision of the picture for Wallis but was overwhelmed with too many productions, so Wallis turned over the picture to James Seymour.

Gene Markey thought *A Lost Lady* could be made with "dignity and great

As Marian Ormsby with Frank Morgan as Daniel Forrester. *A Lost Lady*, 1934. (AMERICAN HERITAGE CENTER, UNIVERSITY OF WYOMING)

dramatic power" but felt there was "much to be done with it." Markey took the aspect of Cather's writing that to her was the "high quality of the novel—its inexplicable presence of the thing not named, of the overtone divined by the ear and not heard by it, the verbal mood, the emotional aura of the fact or the thing or the deed"—and eliminated it altogether.

The unfolding of the story was now literal, chronological, so that the meeting and courtship of Captain Forrester and Marian Ormsby, mentioned in one sentence toward the end of the novel, becomes the first third of the picture. There is no boy who grows up and watches Mrs. Forrester for the audience. The picture is about a girl who is heartbroken; an older man who tries desperately to bring her back to life, who marries her and saves her from herself; a lover who almost takes her away; and her resolve to remain with her loving, stalwart husband.

Markey wrote a new ending "to avoid the low-key depressing effect of the last half of the novel." But, he assured Wallis, "we can get a splendid picture out of it." In a memo to Wallis, Jim Seymour wrote, "In as much as we have taken some liberties with Willa Cather's prize-winning novel in modernizing it, it would be a mistake to mention the novel and or the novelist's name on the first main title."

For their work on the script, Gene Markey was paid $10,125; Kathryn Scola, $2,775. Production for *A Lost Lady* began in mid-June 1934 and was finished in early July. The picture cost $230,000.

About the script, Jack Warner wrote to Seymour saying, "If there are any more references of any Wall Street bandits or any bankers being robbers in the script, please see that [they are] cut out at once . . . I've already instructed the cutter not to use that particular dialogue."

Mentions of Wall Street bandits weren't the only lines cut from the picture. The Legion of Decency had been formed two months before *A Lost Lady* went into production. The previous October, Archbishop A. G. Cicognani, the apostolic delegate to the United States, had addressed the National Conference of Catholic Charities at the Metropolitan Opera House in New York City. He decried the "massacre of innocent youths taking place hour by hour" and asked, "How shall the crimes that have the direct source in motion pictures be measured?" The bishops pledged to stay away from all "offensive" motion pictures and those theaters that showed such pictures. More than one hundred Catholic dioceses in the United States enrolled in the legion.

"Protests against salacious films and offensive advertising swept across the country in a rising tide," said Will Hays. "The movement was like an avenging fire, seeking to clean as it burned. It had become clear [to Hays] that a thorough house cleaning could not be done without something resembling police power. Our industry metropolis had grown too large for good behavior by mutual agreement only." Joe Breen, by acclamation, became the head of the Studio Relations Department, renamed the Production Code Administration. "At last we [have] a police department," said Will Hays. Any member company that released a picture without the Picture Code Association certificate and seal of approval would be fined $25,000.

Breen was shown a print of *A Lost Lady,* and he wrote to Jack Warner asking for a shot of a nude statue in the opening sequence to be "deleted entirely from the picture" as well as a line spoken by the wronged husband who shoots Marian Forrester's fiancé. The line "I found this cigarette case in my wife's bedroom" was taken out. Finally, and most crucially to Breen, was a scene in which Marian Forrester looks at herself in the mirror of her bedroom, wondering what madness has overtaken her as she prepares to meet her lover. Breen wanted a fade-out between it and the next scene, when wife and lover meet, to indicate different times.

Just before Barbara began work on the picture, for which by contract she was being paid $50,000, Fay's financial mess once again caught up with them. Warner Bros. informed Barbara that the Internal Revenue Service was seizing her salary and any other moneys owed her, or Fay, by the studio for back in-

come taxes for 1930 and 1932. Warner Bros. was to pay the Internal Revenue Service $600 a week until the entire $19,543.69 was paid.

Barbara persevered and got through her work on the picture.

A Lost Lady previewed at Warner's Beverly Hills Theatre on a Friday in late August. Warner production supervisors, writers, directors, and department heads were invited to attend.

Willa Cather had received letters from what she perceived were uncultured people regarding the 1924 version of *A Lost Lady* that only confirmed her belief that movie audiences were made up of the lower classes. With the picture's remake, she was so angered by what was done to the script that she added a stipulation to her will that said none of her novels could be dramatized "whether for the purpose of spoken stage presentation or otherwise, motion picture, radio broadcasting, television and rights of mechanical reproduction, whether by means now in existence or which may hereafter be discovered or perfected."

Cather "kept her distance from the world," wrote a longtime friend, "and [she] expected the world to keep its distance in return."

FIVE

Normal People Leading Normal Lives

Nothing so tempts us to approach another person as what is keeping us apart, and what barrier is so insurmountable as silence? . . . But what an even greater torture than that of having to keep silence it is to have to endure the silence of the person one loves!

—Proust, *The Guermantes Way*

The Midwest was suffering from drought; dust storms were destroying more than a million bushels of wheat daily. Three hundred million tons of topsoil were blown away, darkening the air all the way to the Atlantic Seaboard. By 1934, huge rocks, once buried deep in the soil, stood out like monuments on the bare plains. Roosevelt asked Congress for $525 million for drought relief—for emergency work camps and to relocate destitute farmers and their families. Six million dollars a day was already going to drought relief started by Harry Hopkins, head of the Works Progress Administration. Congress approved Roosevelt's request in less than three weeks.

In July, President Roosevelt went on a four-week trip to Hawaii and took a cache of not-yet-released pictures with him, including *The Scarlet Empress, Twentieth Century, Bulldog Drummond Strikes Back,* and *Gambling Lady.*

Barbara loved to go to the pictures. She was mostly interested in "their technical side," figuring out camera angles. "How the lights were placed to get a certain effect on this or that player's face," she said. "It isn't what's going to happen, but *how* it is going to happen. You instinctively know the what of the situation but the how of presenting it becomes of terrific importance.

"There are only a few actors who can get me sufficiently to make me lose myself in the story. Ann Harding is one of them and . . . my idol, Lionel Barrymore. Miss Harding is so entirely natural at all times that she makes me believe in her and what she is doing. I have always hoped that my own work shows the same degree of sincerity. When I see an Ann Harding picture nothing but her work and the story interests me."

The work of the small patrician blonde Harding, onstage and on the screen, had been so revered that critics described her as an actress to whom the wise men carried their literary frankincense and myrrh.

A Fool's Advice, which Fay had sold to Warner Bros. in 1932, was at last set to open in September after languishing unreleased for two years.

Warner had the rights to the picture but hadn't yet done anything with it. Fay was desperate to start negotiations with another company. Jack Warner wasn't interested in picking up the option; he wanted to let the situation go on indefinitely in the hope that Fay would agree to an independent release and the studio could avoid having to bring out the picture as a Warner Bros. production.

Frank was finding work here and there. He worked as the master of ceremonies for shows like Irving Strouse's *Frolics* at the Wilshire Ebell Theatre, a series of six shows modeled after the old Sunday night concerts of a decade before at New York's Winter Garden. Occasionally, he gave a concert performance. The New York vaudeville circuit was winding down.

Barbara and Fay were more aloof from Hollywood than ever. They rarely went out; few people saw them.

They had to take out another loan from the Bank of America, this time for $10,000, with Barbara's Warner salary once again as collateral and the studio paying the bank $1,000 a week until the loan was repaid.

Rumors about their marriage continued to infuriate Barbara. The gossips were ever more vicious, provoked by Fay's cockiness, his brutal wit. "If the rest of Hollywood was as lovely as the climate," Barbara said, "I'd never want to leave it." But she found the Hollywood gossips unrelenting. "They seem to be determined that nobody shall have any private life that is immune from chatter and scandal. You feel that people are watching you all the time," she said, "looking for the slightest word, or movement that will give them material to talk. And if they don't see anything to gossip about they make it up just the same. That is why Frank and I never go out except to visit a few close friends in their own homes. All we ask is to be allowed to live our own lives in peace. But some people resent that. Well, they'll just have to go on resenting."

• • •

Wallis had two new pictures in mind for Barbara, *The Right to Live* and *Concealment. The Right to Live* was to be a remake of a 1929 picture called *The Sacred Flame,* directed by Archie Mayo, from Somerset Maugham's play of the same name. Pauline Frederick and Conrad Nagel had starred in the original. *Concealment* was based on an unproduced play by Leonard Ide. The studio considered the play problematic ("Dialogue feeble," said the reader's report. "Dramatic action only implied . . . characters . . . , without exception, poorly drawn . . . the central idea could be effectively salvaged if the entire play were thrown out"). Wallis was having the script rewritten by Tom Buckingham and F. Hugh Herbert. He asked Buckingham and the producer, Henry Blanke, to tell Barbara the story. "Sell this to her," Wallis said, "and make clear to her that we are changing the play so much it would not do for her to read it. Don't, under any consideration, give her the play." Wallis knew that if Barbara read it in its present form, she would reject it straightaway.

The studio asked her to come in to discuss her situation with Buckingham; she was being evasive and wasn't showing up. They phoned her at home and were told that she was in the garden and would return the call when she came in. She didn't return the call. Wallis was furious.

Barbara was unhappy with *A Lost Lady* and with Warner Bros. The pictures Warner was giving her were getting "lousier and lousier," she said.

Her lawyer, Charles Cradick, told the studio that she would be there by eleven the following morning. The next day, Barbara, who was always prompt to the minute, didn't show up. Nor did she appear by mid-afternoon. Wallis told his staff that if she didn't appear by the end of the day, a letter of suspension was to be sent to her by special messenger. A studio lawyer advised him to phone her; if she was evasive about coming in, he suggested Wallis send a letter informing her that the studio expected her to appear the following day.

Barbara finally met with Buckingham to discuss the pictures Wallis had in mind for her.

The Right to Live was about an American girl who marries a wealthy Englishman, paralyzed as the result of an airplane accident. His brother, owner of a Brazilian coffee plantation, is sent for. Eventually, wife and brother fall in love. Her husband will never recover the use of his legs, and she decides to stay and care for him until he is found murdered and she becomes the accused. The self-sacrificing wife was too much like Marian Forrester of *A Lost Lady;* Barbara turned down the picture.

Buckingham also told her the story of the revised version of Ide's play

Concealment: a murder mystery involving political intrigue, congressional investigations, impeachment proceedings, a trial, suicide, and corruption, and at its center the daughter of the governor who marries the district attorney only to find out that her father is implicated in a high-stakes kickback scandal. Her marriage to the DA suddenly becomes a time bomb as he struggles to get to the truth without destroying his father-in-law or betraying his new wife.

After being the wilted love object brought back to life in *A Lost Lady,* Barbara agreed to make the murder mystery. *Concealment* was to be her second picture for Warner under their option agreement. Wallis's letter suspending Barbara, typed up and ready to go, wasn't sent. Instead, he showed Barbara a script of an adaptation of Mignon Eberhart's novel *The White Cockatoo,* which he hoped would be her third picture for Warner under their option agreement. The picture was a convoluted murder mystery set on the French coast. Barbara wasn't impressed with the script and turned it down.

Concealment was to be directed by William Dieterle, under contract to Warner. The picture's budget: $215,000.

Buckingham and Herbert were at work on the script when Buckingham became ill and was rushed to Queen of Angels Hospital. He was operated on but died soon after coming out of the anesthetic. He was thirty-nine years old.

Wallis assigned Mary McCall Jr., a former magazine writer, to help with the script. McCall had just finished writing dialogue for the remake of the 1924 picture *Babbitt,* based on the Sinclair Lewis novel. Mary McCall was a "corpse ranger" at Warner Bros. She saw the studio as trying "to own you . . . They wanted to make sure you weren't dawdling or doing other work on company time," and she became involved in the formation of the Screen Writers Guild. She went to work on *Concealment* and did the best she could to finish the script quickly; shooting started two months later, early in November.

"The script was bad," Dieterle said. But he couldn't refuse it for "contractual reasons"; he was paid his salaried wage of $12,000. Barbara was paid $50,000.

"Why Miss Stanwyck did not reject the script," Dieterle said, "I can only guess." The reality was that Barbara couldn't afford to go on suspension. She wanted to get out of her Warner contract, but she needed the income to support Fay, Dion, the staff, the house, and the cars and to get out of their financial bind with the Internal Revenue Service.

In the picture were Warren William, Glenda Farrell, and the feature players Grant Mitchell, Arthur Byron, Henry O'Neill, and Douglass Dumbrille.

. . .

Fay wanted Barbara with him at all times. He was possessive and argued with her from the moment she got home from the studio, questioning her repeatedly about whom she'd been with, to whom she'd spoken at the studio, why it had taken her so long to get home.

One day she was outside taking a photograph of Dion. She put the boy on the bench and went to frame him in the camera. Dion wouldn't keep still, and Fay pushed him to the ground.

Barbara knew "the agony of quarreling and trying to make up," she said. After an argument, Fay might not speak to her for days. She called it "the dull pain of making little pretexts for going into the room where he is, hoping against hope that he'll break the heartbreaking ice and say something."

Barbara would sit with Fay across a wordless table. In what she called a "final surrender," she'd break down and say, "I'm sorry. I was wrong. I'll do anything you say if you'll only speak to me again."

"The humiliation of such a surrender," she said, "knowing I wasn't wrong," felt like being bound in chains of slavery.

When Dion was two and a half years old, Barbara arranged for him to be baptized at a church in Santa Monica. In attendance were Buck Mack; Ann Hoyt; Fay's longtime business adviser and friend Nick Copeland and his wife; Dion's new nurse; and Fay and Barbara. After the service the party returned to Bristol Avenue in the early afternoon for a celebratory Sunday dinner. Everyone, except Frank, went to Dion's room to play with him.

Fay reappeared at dinner. The guests were seated at the table. Frank began a conversation with the nurse, who was new to the United States and was still unfamiliar with English. Fay asked her if she understood the meaning of the words "whorehouse" and "fucking." Barbara got up and left the table. Fay talked about what happens at whorehouses and was laughing at the nurse, who was at a loss to understand what was being said at her expense.

Later, a small cake for Dion was brought to the table. A piece was put on his plate, and the boy was enjoying it when he dropped some crumbs next to his plate. Fay screamed at him about the tablecloth. Dion dissolved into tears. The nurse took him away. When Fay, in the past, had dropped food at the table, he'd blamed Dion and yelled at him because of it.

Barbara felt as if she had "no life of her own at all, even in little inconsequential things," yet she only wanted to please Fay. If she moved a chair in the living room and Fay gave her a look, she would "run, hastily, to put it back again," she said. "You lose your life for love," she said, "this kind of love, though you are living." Barbara's allegiance to Fay extended to all things, including politics; she voted as he voted.

She wanted to surprise Frank for his forty-third birthday with a gift she lovingly thought he would enjoy. Money was tight. Fay's library consisted of an extensive collection of first editions. Barbara bought him a signed limited edition of Galsworthy's *White Monkey*, the fourth book of the Forsyte Saga, published in 1924.

Returning home from work one evening, she saw Fay in the library, the present opened, and the book being read. The butler explained that when the book arrived, he'd unwrapped it and put it on the shelf in the library and Fay had picked it up. Barbara also gave him a Dictaphone and a rare crystal paperweight for his desk. With the gifts was a birthday letter dated November 17, 1934:

Dear Kid:

I haven't any grand present to give you this year, no diamonds, no watch, no nothing!

I feel kind of funny not sending you anything but it just has to be.

However I can wish you many, many more of them and may they be happy and healthy, and full of content.

My personal wish, that they be spent with me.

But, when prayers are heard in heaven, and I hope that mine are, they are still with you and for you. And so Frank, all I have to give you today is my prayers that all will go well with you. And whatever you do shall be right, and that God will keep your path well-lighted so that you will never hurt yourself.

God bless you and spare you always. My love to you. Barbara.

Dieterle described the work on *Concealment* "[as] not [being] very pleasant."

During the first few days of the picture's production, the crew had spent an hour fixing a scrim. To see if it was right, they called Barbara's stand-in, of whom Barbara was quite fond. Katie Doyle couldn't see without her glasses and rarely wore them. She walked onto the set and walked right through the scrim.

Dieterle was furious and started to berate her. Other people were there working. Barbara quietly walked up to Dieterle and said, "Don't you ever dare talk to anybody on any set that I am on, don't you ever dare talk to anybody like that again. The next time you do, I walk. I go right up to the office and I will not finish the picture under your direction."

She didn't care if it was a stand-in or another actor; she wouldn't tolerate that kind of behavior. Dieterle was Prussian. "You know, iron rule, iron rule," said Barbara. "Well, screw that."

It was the third day of production; they had weeks to go.

Barbara looked her most glamorous in the picture, but it demanded little of her.

During production, Wallis sent her a script called *North Shore,* based on a novel by Wallace Irwin. It was to be her third picture under the Warner option agreement, which was up at the end of September. If she rejected Warner's second option, the studio was legally within its rights to restrain her from working in pictures for the next two years. If Warner chose not to exercise the option, Barbara was free and clear to work for any studio. Jack Warner wanted it both ways. He wanted her to go on making pictures for him, and he wanted to know what offers were coming in from other producers. In order for Warner to be notified of other offers, Barbara had to reject Warner's option, at which time the studio would file a notice with the Association of Motion Picture Producers and Warner would then be entitled to be told of other offers.

Warner made the offer for an additional option; Barbara, through Charles Cradick, rejected it. Warner was now in a position to be notified of each incoming offer that Barbara received for the next six months. Her dealings with Warner were further complicated by Fay being written into her contract with the studio and his still-unreleased picture, *A Fool's Advice.*

A Lost Lady opened on September 29. Warner advertised it as "*A Lost Lady* from the novel by Willa Cather, America's greatest woman writer; the world branded her a lost lady but a million women will see in her the woman they wanted her to be."

Reviewers were appalled by what Gene Markey and Kathryn Scola had done to Cather's novel ("Don't go to see *A Lost Lady* . . . under any misapprehension that you are going to see Willa Cather's fine and moving novel on the screen," said the *Los Angeles Examiner.* "It may bear the same title, it may give Miss Cather credit for story, but it is something else again"). Critics called the picture "a dismal drama" and "handicapped"; "it fails almost ludicrously to capture anything of the spirit or letter of the original [novel]." Reviewers were kind to Barbara ("As usual, [she] almost saves the day by giving one of her earnestly honest performances"). Barbara's wardrobe seemed to overwhelm the picture ("Everything and everybody is subservient to Miss Stanwyck's style parade. Even Miss Stanwyck's acting").

. . .

Barbara and Fay had a dinner party one evening. The topic of college fraternities and sororities came up and whether they were good or bad. Barbara, who hadn't gone to school beyond eighth grade, stayed out of the discussion except to say, "Sororities may be all right for people with money—but where do the poor come in? Why isn't there a sorority for working girls for example? I could have used one when I was a kid starting out to work."

The next day, Barbara and Charles Cradick asked the women in his office what they thought of the idea of a sorority for working girls. They liked the idea, and Cradick had Barbara help to form a sorority designed to give working girls social advantages, education possibilities, and friendship. They called it Athena, from the Greek goddess of wisdom, weaving, crafts, and war; an armed warrior goddess, never a child, always a virgin, associated with mentoring heroes. Her shield bore the head of the Gorgon Medusa.

SIX

Another Routine Job

1934

Before the studio bought the rights to *North Shore,* it was proposed as a "pretty good vehicle for Bette Davis" and was offered to her in the summer. When Davis didn't work out, Wallis was hopeful Barbara would accept the role of Shelby Barrett, expert equestrian, forced to earn a living by riding the horses of society folk in competition. A cameraman was sent to the Hollywood Breakfast Club to film a horse show in progress and to get on film some of the West Coast's finest-blooded horses.

Joseph Breen looked at Mary McCall and Peter Milne's script and found nothing "objectionable from the Point of View of the Production Code or censorship." *North Shore* was to begin production on November 6.

Hal Wallis wanted Joel McCrea or Robert Young for Johnnie Wyatt, the scion of a great old (penniless) Long Island family who plays professional amateur polo and pursues and marries Shelby Barrett in a whirlwind courtship. Neither actor was available. Three weeks before the start date, the platinum blond Gene Raymond—born Raymond Guion and a stage actor from the age of five, who started in pictures at twenty-three, appearing in *The House on 56th Street, Ex-lady,* and *Zoo in Budapest*—was tentatively cast as the young Wyatt, who'd played polo since he was able to sit on a horse, as had his father and his father's father. Henry O'Neill and Ralph Morgan were considered for Gene Fairchild, the arriviste with "oodles of money" determined to buy his way into society, who rides his own horses in competition, invariably placing second to Shelby Barrett's first and who is in love with her.

The production supervisor, Harry Joe Brown, thought Ricardo Cortez would be perfect for Fairchild ("It seems to me this is the type of role Rick is most suited for," Brown wrote to Wallis). John Eldredge, who'd just ap-

With Gene Raymond shooting *The Woman in Red,* from Irwin Wallace's novel, *North Shore.* The book was bought for Bette Davis; the part of Shelby Barrett went to Barbara only weeks before production began in early November 1934.

peared in *The White Cockatoo,* got the part. Eldredge invariably played spineless men, the opposite of the Cortez character.

Wallis wanted Barbara to come in for wardrobe fittings. "If there is going to be any squawk on the script," Wallis wrote to Lester Koenig, his assistant, "or any trouble on the wardrobe or due to the fact that she has to work with horses or anything else," he wanted it ironed out sooner rather than later. Barbara hadn't been near a horse in three years, since a horse fell on her during the making of *Forbidden.* She was terrified of horses and for *North Shore* had to ride again; this time on a demanding, powerful show horse.

"I kept thinking of that second vertebra," she said after riding Magna McDonald, the American saddlebred blue-ribbon mare, for the horse show scene, "and wondering if this horse would find a convenient gopher hole to step into." In addition to Barbara's regular stand-in, two doubles—expert riders—stood in for her during the demanding jumps the horse had to take on the course.

Robert Florey was directing the film. He'd directed the Marx Brothers in their first feature, the movie version of the Irving Berlin, George S. Kauffman hit play, *The Cocoanuts,* the first musical to be made into a picture, and on the East Coast ("There was little you could do with [the Marx Brothers]," said Florey. "They had performed the show a thousand times. My main job was to keep them in the camera frame. Luckily I had five cameras going at all times.")

Florey had worked with Mary Pickford and Douglas Fairbanks and with Al Santell, King Vidor, Robert Z. Leonard, and Edmund Goulding. He had written, directed, and designed other pictures before going to Warner Bros. and being forced to submit to the studio's dictates of picture making. Florey had been the set and costume designer on King Vidor's *The Big Parade.*

As a Warner contract director, Florey "didn't have the power to choose a scenario." He had to go along with what was given him to direct by the studio. He thought *North Shore* another in a string of Warner Bros. "contract assignments."

Florey had no say "in the final cutting and editing of *North Shore.* The producer and the studio boss," he said, "would do as they please . . . sometimes changing the order of the sequences, suppressing favorite scenes."

With Sol Polito as cameraman, Florey was able to give *North Shore* the right polish and old-money atmosphere of excess and entitlement and capture the right mustiness of decaying grandeur.

North Shore, by virtue of Barbara's presence, became "more than a routine job," said Florey. He thought she was "the greatest."

In the picture Barbara is at ease, stylish, seductive. She didn't complain about the script. "She was always cooperative, pleasant, helpful," Florey said.

Her quarrel was not with the director; it was with the studio.

To the press, Barbara was still difficult to know, indifferent to her "fellow players"; on the defensive, "ready to battle at the drop of a hat." "I have been accused of being anti-social," she said, "which seems to be a Hollywood sin. These allegations are a constant surprise to me." She admitted that she was not a "particularly tactful person" but someone who spoke her mind "quite frankly." She couldn't understand why anyone would say she was "indifferent to her fellow players. That is the last thing I could be." Barbara made friends slowly, cautiously. She wanted to be sure she wasn't making a mistake. "It would be the same with me if I were a waitress in Peoria or a chambermaid in Oshkosh instead of a film actress in Hollywood."

Gene Raymond suggested that Barbara hire his publicist, Helen Ferguson, former celebrated stage and silent-screen actress. "I think she could help you," he said. When sound arrived, Ferguson had given up acting and opened up a theatrical and public relations office. Helen had appeared in more than fifty silent pictures, among them *Gift o' Gab* (1917); *Just Pals* with John Ford (1920); *The Call of the North* (1921); *Hungry Hearts* (1922); *The*

Unknown Purple (1923); and *In Old California* (1929), perfecting the role of the winsome, tomboy outdoors girl—the opposite of the Mary Pickford role.

Ferguson understood actors and understood the need for publicity. The previous year, in 1933, Ferguson had opened a small one-room office in Hollywood for $15 a month and furnished it with three chairs, two installment-purchased fire-sale desks, a borrowed carpet, unframed photographs of her theatrical friends, and a small typewriter and, using a lipstick, wrote her name on the door of her first office. Within four months, business had improved, and Helen moved to an office with one and a half rooms; in ten months she had a five-suite agency at 6615 Sunset Boulevard, an associate, Jewel Smith, a secretary, and a switchboard. Ferguson's first client was Johnny Mack Brown, former all-American halfback from the University of Alabama turned actor, who appeared opposite Greta Garbo in *The Divine Woman* and Joan Crawford in *Our Dancing Daughters.* Ferguson, in addition to representing Gene Raymond, and his wife, Jeanette MacDonald, worked with Constance Bennett, Pat O'Brien, Joan Blondell, and Loretta Young. Helen was religious. She believed in prayer, and when speaking for her clients to reporters, she made sure to interweave her religious beliefs in their quotes.

Helen had married Richard Lewis Hargreaves, president of the First National Bank of Beverly Hills and the father of four children from his nineteen-year marriage to Grace Bryan, the daughter of William Jennings Bryan. Hargreaves was forty-one; Helen, twenty-nine.

Helen Ferguson was now the wife of a bank president and at the center of the Los Angeles social establishment. Her days of earning a living were over until two years later, in June 1932, when Hargreaves was accused of misusing funds—amounting to $70,000—from the First National Bank of Beverly Hills. With deposits of more than $4 million, the bank was forced to close its doors. Hargreaves was indicted on four major counts of asserted misapplication of funds and fourteen counts of false statements. He was found guilty of ten of the counts and was sentenced to serve three years in federal prison.

Helen had to help support a family in financial disaster. Her friends told her to return to acting, but she was determined to go into business for herself. She was full of explosive energy, was earnest and felt blessed with a sixth sense. She saw actors as the most important and fragile aspect of the film industry and thought stars had a responsibility to their audiences, and she expected them to accept that responsibility.

Barbara hired her.

Ferguson's girlhood was not unlike Barbara's. Helen had started to work at the age of nine doing odd jobs. Her father and grandfather had lost their

William (Big Bill) Russell and Helen Ferguson, circa 1920.

fortunes in the panic of 1907, the year Barbara was born. Helen's parents separated, and her mother took her two daughters to Chicago and was earning a living as a dressmaker. At thirteen, Helen went to get a job at the Essanay Studios in Chicago. Soon, Helen was in demand at the studio and by the age of fifteen was a leading lady in New York. Samuel Goldwyn brought Helen to Hollywood in 1920 for her first starring role in *Going Some.* She was set to return east, when she was offered an important part opposite William Russell, the hero of Western thrillers and her childhood movie idol. They appeared together in five pictures from 1920 through 1925. A year after working with her, "Big Bill" Russell (he was six feet two inches and weighed two hundred pounds) was so smitten with Helen he divorced his wife, the actress Charlotte Burton, with whom he'd made fifteen pictures from 1916 to 1918, and in 1925 married Helen.

By 1927, Helen's popularity in pictures was waning, and she decided to go on the stage, making her debut at the Hollywood Playhouse in *Alias the Deacon* and appearing in stock companies with actors such as Jason Robards (in *The Mutiny of the Elsinore,* based on a story by Jack London) and Louise Fazenda (*The Alarm Clock*).

Russell died in 1929 at the age of forty-four.

After Barbara's four-year stint at Warner Bros., she wanted to be able to choose her own scripts.

"In New York," she said, "you simply wait until a manager sends for you.

He hands you a script and you read it. If you like the part, you play it. If you don't like it, you turn it down. There isn't this constant battle for suitable vehicles."

Barbara was fed up with the scripts she was getting. In addition, there was the issue of Fay; she insisted he be included in any new contract.

"Hollywood knows so little about us or how we live," she said.

During the final week of shooting *North Shore,* a fire broke out one evening at the Warner Bros.–First National studios in Burbank. It began in one of the machine shops, near the New York and Chinatown sets, and, given high winds, spread to film vaults, destroying hundreds of thousands of feet of stock shots, including tens of thousands of feet just brought back from West Point by Frank Borzage. The following day production continued as if nothing had happened, but the fire had swept across fifteen acres of Warner's land, turning antique furniture, research material, and precision machinery into tinder and twisted steel. More than forty people were burned. Jack Warner was determined to rebuild the devastated areas.

North Shore continued to shoot.

In a few of the scenes, Barbara wore, as she did in *A Lost Lady* and every movie she made, the crystal medallion on a gold chain that she cherished, given to her by her sister Millie; it was her good luck piece. At the end of the production, the cast and crew gave Barbara a tiny mosaic figure of Saint Anthony for her car inspired by her lack of formality and self-complacency.

Joe Breen, director of the Production Code Administration, in a letter to Jack Warner, singled out one line in *North Shore* that he wanted removed in compliance with the code. Barbara's character is in the bath and says to her husband, in the bedroom: "I think you can come in and dry my back because I love you and we are going to be big business successes."

Warner wrote back to Breen the next day and said, "I cannot understand why any man who does not have to think right, and I know you do, objects to the line . . . they are *legally* married. What is objectionable to this? . . . I know you did not read the script and you just signed this letter as I know you personally would not find fault with lines of this nature." Breen "edited" three thousand scripts a year and responded to Warner, writing, "Between you and me and the four walls, as we Irish say, I think your point is well taken regarding this back-rubbing business . . . Of course I did not read the script myself, and I am glad to know that you did me the kindness to suggest that this particular detail would not be likely to disturb me . . . Here's for better and finer back-rubbing—married or unmarried!"

Irving Thalberg, like Barbara, was from Brooklyn (his father, an importer of lace). He was reserved, soft-spoken, with a boundless capacity for work. After two years at Universal, first as secretary to Carl Laemmle and then general manager of Universal City (though still too young to legally sign checks, he took charge, he said, because there was no one else left to do so), and after four years at Metro-Goldwyn-Mayer as executive production manager, he was known as "the little genius" and referred to by the *New York Times* as "an old head on young shoulders." (PHOTOFEST)

• • •

Barbara and Fay went to Metro to see Irving Thalberg. Years before, in New York, Thalberg had watched them perform at the Club Richman. He'd asked Barbara to his table, told her he was interested in her work, and wondered if she'd ever thought of appearing in pictures. She'd cut him short—he hadn't inquired about Fay—let him know that her husband had just signed a contract to make pictures for Joe Schenck.

Thalberg's gracious response: "Ah, when you come to Hollywood, drop in to see me."

Thalberg had been on the train that first brought the Fays to Hollywood.

Now the Fays needed Thalberg. Barbara had learned his correct name.

They were kept waiting at Metro for forty-five minutes. Once they were in Thalberg's office, he suggested that Barbara might possibly make a picture or two for the studio.

Frank had warned Barbara to keep quiet and let him do the talking, "*all* of it." When it came time to "talk terms," Barbara said, "Mr. Thalberg inquired how much money I should have to have."

"Fifty thousand dollars a picture—and the right to choose her own directors and stories," Frank replied without batting an eye.

Thalberg had deep penetrating eyes and shoulders that hunched forward slightly. He gave the usual producer's gasp. "Why, my dear, we don't do that for Greta Garbo!"

There was a pause, and then Frank said, "I'm still not impressed."

Barbara couldn't control herself another minute and blew up. "All I did was to laugh," she said. "But such a laugh. And at such a moment! Can you imagine Frank's feelings."

Thalberg was interested in testing Barbara for Metro's *Good Earth,* an ambitious production for the studio. He had overseen its development since Metro had purchased the rights to the Pearl Buck novel three years earlier, in 1931, before its publication and prior to the Theatre Guild's production that starred Claude Rains and Alla Nazimova. At the time, Louis B. Mayer couldn't understand Thalberg's determination to make the novel into a movie and said, "Who the hell [is] interested in a film about Chinese farmers, for God's sake?"

Thalberg had hoped to shoot the entire picture in China with an all-Chinese cast and had hired Pearl Buck as consultant to advise the studio about locations. Frances Marion, one of Thalberg's most esteemed writers, who had written the best of Mary Pickford's silent pictures as well as the scripts for Metro's *Anna Christie, Min and Bill,* and *Dinner at Eight,* had written a treatment for the picture. Marion had won two Academy Awards for her scripts of *The Big House* and *The Champ.*

Thalberg had given up the notion of using an all-Chinese cast. "There were not enough suitable Chinese actors," he said. He'd tested stage actresses such as Katharine Cornell and was now testing Barbara for the leading part of O-Lan, the kitchen slave sold into slavery by her parents and freed into marriage and whose struggle, side by side with her husband, Wang Lung, as they build farm and family and battle the effects of drought, famine, and revolution, is at the heart of the book.

Anna May Wong had been passed over for the part of O-Lan despite a publicity campaign on her behalf by the Los Angeles Press, started in 1933, two years before the picture was cast. Wong's reputation in China was questionable, cautioned the Nanking government official, General Ting-Hsiu (Theodore) Tu, friend of Chiang Kai-shek, and advisor to Metro on the picture; her previous roles as prostitute, unwed mother, slave, and coaster, among others, had rankled the people of China, who believed the actress was continually losing face on-screen and misrepresenting the women of their country.

Barbara spent days at Metro working out makeup for the test. Thalberg had sent for Nils Asther, who was coming from Europe to be tested for the part of Wang. Asther hadn't worked with Barbara since *General Yen.*

With the casting of a white man as Wang, the role of O-Lan would be closed to any Chinese actress. The production code's strict antimiscegenation rules prohibited a Chinese woman from playing opposite a white man, even if he was playing a Chinese character.

• • •

A Los Angeles billboard in support of Frank Finley Merriam in the race for Governor of California and opposing Upton Sinclair, 1934. (CORBIS)

California was in the grip of a bitter campaign to elect a new governor. Upton Sinclair, one of the candidates, had attacked Roosevelt's New Deal at its heart and ripped apart the Democratic Party. Sinclair's campaign was built upon the idea that in a land of plenty millions of people had nothing and that instead of the government putting people on relief, they should be put to work and given the chance to produce their own goods.

Sinclair envisioned the state buying or leasing lands for people to grow their own food and renting unused factories for workers to manufacture their own goods. Workers were to be paid in scrip, which would buy those products produced within the plan. He called it EPIC (End Poverty in California), and it caught on with voters. In the August primary Sinclair won an almost two-to-one victory against George Creel: Sinclair, 436,000 votes; Creel, 288,000.

Sinclair repeated to reporters a statement he'd made to Harry Hopkins, who after twenty years of social service was given the task by Roosevelt of feeding and clothing the needy and finding work for the unemployed and was heading up the Federal Emergency Relief Administration. Sinclair had warned Hopkins, "If I am elected, half of the unemployed will come to California, and you will have to take care of them."

The Democratic machine along with Republicans panicked and set in motion a campaign to destroy Sinclair's chances of becoming the next governor of California. The Los Angeles press, ruled by Hearst, refused to cover Sinclair's comings and goings. Those out to defeat him used his own writing against him, distorting his words and quoting him as dismissing marriage as a bourgeois institution and the Roman Catholic Church as "the Church of the Servant Girls." New Deal Democrats closed ranks with Democratic conservatives in support of Governor Frank Merriam, the archconservative Republican candidate. Merriam won 1,139,000 votes to Sinclair's 880,000.

Despite the win in California, the Republicans, instead of gaining seats in an off-year election as anticipated with the party not in power, lost thirteen seats in the House and more seats in the Senate. Democrats now had a two-thirds majority in the Senate, the biggest margin either party had held in its history. The reason: Franklin Delano Roosevelt.

After the win, Harry Hopkins said, "Boys—this is our hour. We've got to get everything we want—a works program, social security, wages and hours, everything—now or never."

"He has been all but crowned by the people," said William Allen White of President Roosevelt in *Time* magazine.

Others were working against the president and the New Deal and the populist spirit that had taken hold of the country. In November, at a hearing before the House of Representatives Committee on Un-American Activities in New York City, Major General Smedley D. Butler, retired Marine Corps officer, a Quaker, and two-time recipient of the Medal of Honor, beloved by the troops he commanded, testified about a plot of Wall Street interests to overthrow President Roosevelt, establish a Fascist dictatorship backed by a private army of 500,000 ex-soldiers and others, and reinstate the gold standard, which Roosevelt had abandoned in the beginning of the year.

Butler testified about how he'd been approached by Gerald MacGuire, a bond salesman and a former commander of the Connecticut American Legion, who'd traveled to Italy to observe the state under Mussolini and had come away impressed.

Butler was to deliver an ultimatum to President Roosevelt. The plan was for Roosevelt to pretend he was incapacitated because of polio. A newly created cabinet officer, a secretary of general affairs, was to run the government in Roosevelt's stead. If the president refused, he was to be forced out by an army of war veterans from the American Legion. MacGuire had told Butler, "You know the American people will swallow that. We've got the newspapers." MacGuire said, "We need a fascist government in this country to save the nation from the communists who want to tear it down and wreck all that we have built in America."

Implicated in the plot were Robert Sterling Clark, banker, stockbroker, art collector; Grayson Murphy, director of Goodyear and Bethlehem Steel; and Irénée Du Pont, whose family was one of the leading armament producers in the world, dubbed the merchants of death from the huge profits they'd made in the Civil War and the War of 1812. Du Pont was the founder of the American Liberty League, a propaganda machine whose purpose was to discredit Roosevelt in the public's eye once the president was overthrown. Other co-conspirators implicated but never subpoenaed were Al Smith, former governor of New York and co-director of the American Liberty League, and General Douglas MacArthur.

Will Rogers topped the theater owners' list of the ten stars with the biggest box-office draw. Clark Gable was next, followed by Bing Crosby; Shirley Temple, age six and the first child ever to be included; the beloved Marie Dressler, who'd passed away in the summer at age sixty-five with flags at Metro flown at half-mast and production stopped during her funeral. Norma Shearer, Katharine Hepburn, and Joe E. Brown tied for tenth place; Garbo with 73 percent of the vote was in twenty-ninth place. Gary Cooper, Zasu Pitts, John Boles, and Johnny Weissmuller were tied with 35 percent of the vote. Barbara received 17 percent of the vote, along with Paul Muni and Irene Hervey.

Jack Warner wanted a new title for *North Shore* ("In my opinion this don't mean anything in box-office value"). Hal Wallis thought it was a mistake ("Everyone I have talked to feels that NORTH SHORE is a swell title and I don't think we should let anybody stampede us into changing the titles of published books . . . especially when the titles are really good"). Warner suggested *The Girl in the Court Room; Peggy's Bustle;* and *The Girl Behind the Headlines.* The title eventually chosen was *The Woman in Red,* a title similar to *The Secret Bride,* which opened in New York at the Roxy Theatre just before Christmas. It was another inferior picture for Barbara. *The New York Times* called it "a dashing homicide melodrama but a minor product of the racy Warner studios"; the *Post* pronounced it "often in need of a tonic," with Barbara's natural charms as the perfect "builder-upper."

Barbara had still not joined the Screen Actors Guild. A new contract for actors was worked out between the Academy and the studios, but it was barely an improvement over the previous one of five years before. The earlier Guild said it was as unenforceable as ever. Whatever improvements to the contract were the result of pressure placed on the Academy by the Guild.

Workers across the country were organizing. The labor leader John L. Lewis, head of the United Mine Workers, had increased his union's membership in 1934 from 150,000 to 500,000 and set out to destroy the monopoly the American Federation of Labor had on organized labor.

A series of violent strikes took place—in Milwaukee, Philadelphia, New York—as cabdrivers rioted for better wages. Workers struck from California's lettuce farms to New Jersey's tomato fields. Electrical workers in Des Moines shut down the city's electricity for almost 200,000 residents; workers in Terre Haute picketed, as did copper miners in Butte, closing down the mines for months. In New York, the Waldorf Astoria's cooks, waiters, and busboys picketed on Park Avenue, carrying placards and singing "The Internationale." In Minneapolis truck drivers walked out, establishing the Teamsters as the most powerful union in the Northwest; in San Francisco, ship dockers shut down plants, theaters, and restaurants, blockaded highways, and stopped incoming shipments of food and fuel oil. The largest strike ever started on Labor Day; textile workers shut down the industry in twenty states.

Members of the Screen Actors Guild were warned not to agree to academy arbitration of disputes under the new studio-player contract.

Frank Fay hated Roosevelt, Communism, unions, and Jews. Frank Capra backed the academy against the guild and admired Mussolini and his stance against Communism. "[Capra] adored him," said John Lee Mahin. He "had a picture of the Prime Minister on his bedroom wall."

In addition to being tested for *The Good Earth,* Barbara was approached by New York's Theatre Guild for a stage production of James M. Cain's novel of deceit, violence, love, and death, *The Postman Always Rings Twice.* Metro had bought the rights to the novel in the spring of 1934 for $35,000. When the Motion Picture Code banned Cain's story of adultery and murder for the screen, the Theatre Guild picked up the dramatic rights from Metro.

Cain had written the play, and Barbara was at the top of his list for the part of Cora, wife of Nick Papadakis, owner of a roadside sandwich joint and gas station. Cora is sulky, a former high school beauty-contest winner from Des Moines who wins a trip to Hollywood, tries her hand at pictures ("On the screen they knew me for what I was, a cheap Des Moines trollop"), and two weeks later winds up in a Los Angeles hash house where she stays for the next two years. Desperate to get away from the diner's leg pinching and nickel tips, she ends up married to Nick the Greek, cooking at his Twin Oaks luncheonette twenty miles outside the city. Cora's a hellcat; she falls for a drifter who falls for her. She's desperate to get out of her marriage (she says of her husband, "He stinks. He's greasy and he stinks") and desperate to be with the drifter ("That's it, Frank, that's all that matters . . . You and me"); and together they set out to kill the Greek.

Cora is tough and raw and angry in the way Barbara's women are in *Ladies of Leisure, Night Nurse, Ten Cents a Dance, Shopworn, Ladies They Talk About,* and *Baby Face.* Much of Cora's dialogue sounds like characters Barbara played in each of her Warner pictures, with Barbara's inflection and sexual come-on, sultriness, and control.

Cain saw Barbara as "a saucy little number" and talked to her about the part. Between Barbara's demand that the studios allow her to pick the story and director for her pictures, her insistence that Fay be included in any contract she sign, and Fay's string of failed pictures, Barbara couldn't "give herself away," she said. She thought seriously about Cain's offer to return to the stage.

SEVEN

Average Screenfare

1935

You can't be bubbly when the man you love is more often enchanted by alcohol than you.

What is needed to hold a married couple together is horse intelligence . . . Lasting marriage is not a question of geography. The chances are as good, and as bad, in Hollywood as in any other town. No more. No less.

—Barbara Stanwyck

Dion, at three years old, saw his father at his most frightening. He and his nurse, Nellie Banner, were playing on the lawn one day when Frank walked over to join them. He was drunk and fell on his face in a stupor. Another time Dion and Nellie were returning from an outing. Dion walked into the house. There was a terrible noise. Nellie looked up to see Fay falling down the stairs, drunk, and she grabbed Dion just as Fay was about to land on him.

She was upset and jangled by the "vile language" Fay used around the child and was terrified of him but stayed on at Bristol Avenue out of affection for Barbara and her devotion to Dion.

Fay went into the nursery at odd hours, usually early in the morning, and woke the sleeping boy. Nellie was awakened as well and would try to persuade Fay to leave the nursery.

Dion was about to go to sleep one night when Nellie saw that the rug next to his bed was on fire. She grabbed some water and rushed into the room to

Nellie Banner with Dion Fay, then three years old, 1935. (COURTESY TONY FAY)

put it out. A cigarette was on the rug where the fire had started. Frank was the only person who smoked in the nursery.

Warner had dropped Barbara. Fay was too difficult. The word was out. There was no work; no studio would hire her.

Barbara was trying to keep it together—her home, her marriage, her work. She pleaded with her brother, Byron, to leave the merchant marine and come and live with her. Byron had no interest in living in Hollywood.

Warner Bros. continued to list Barbara as one of its stars along with James Cagney, Kay Francis, Dick Powell, Leslie Howard, Ruth Chatterton, and others.

Sam Jaffe, Barbara's agent, along with Arthur Lyons, was in negotiations with Fox for a picture called *Orchids to You,* a title taken from Walter Winchell's column. William Seiter was to direct; Clive Brook, to co-star. The picture was to go into production sometime in April. Fox was offering Barbara $7,000 a week with a five-week guarantee. Jaffe was asking $50,000 for the picture; Barbara wanted $55,000.

Carl Laemmle Jr. was negotiating with Lyons for Barbara to play the lead in *Hangover Murders,* based on a novel by Adam Hobhouse, to be directed by James Whale. At issue was money.

Lyons and Sam Jaffe were also in negotiation on Barbara's behalf with Metro-Goldwyn-Mayer, Paramount Pictures, Walter Wanger Productions, Monogram Pictures, Columbia Pictures, and Radio Pictures.

Other films were being discussed. Jesse Lasky had an idea that appealed to her for a picture about a department store. The novelist, playwright, and short story writer Viña Delmar (Alvina Croter) also had something for Barbara. Delmar had written two novels that were considered "daring realism"— *Bad Girl* and *Kept Woman* ("Is it daring to tell the simple facts of living and getting along in the world?" Delmar asked)—about couples living unconventionally. Delmar and her husband, Eugene, wrote scripts under her name.

Barbara was performing on radio. The studios had first resisted radio, seeing it as a competitive medium, but they came to use it as a way to help promote their "players" and help sell theater tickets. For the first time shows about motion pictures were being put on the air. The program *45 Minutes in Hollywood* dramatized soon-to-be-released pictures and featured interviews with the stars of the films. *Hollywood Hotel,* a variety show, was broadcast direct from Los Angeles and included dramatized excerpts from upcoming pictures using the actual stars. During 1934, more than 150 top actors appeared on radio, from Katharine Hepburn and Carole Lombard to Paul Muni, Jean Harlow, Joan Crawford, John Barrymore, and Joel McCrea. Frank Fay was appearing regularly on Rudy Vallée's *Fleischmann Hour.*

Barbara was taken with the medium. "Radio puts you into higher gear mentally," she said. "Everything you do must be done perfectly . . . You concentrate on every word, on every line, you rehearse and rehearse modulation, inflection. Radio does not tolerate error, even the slightest."

Barbara and Fay were on the air together during the broadcast of an industry banquet with Eddie Cantor and Harry Einstein as radio hosts. In attendance, and chatting over the air during the evening, were Mary Pickford, Charlie Chaplin, Will Hays, Jack Benny, David Selznick, Irving Berlin, Howard Hughes, Sam Goldwyn, and Merle Oberon.

In mid-March, *The Woman in Red* opened at the Warner Bros. Downtown Theatre in Los Angeles and at the Roxy in New York. It was Barbara's nineteenth picture in five years. She may have been deemed unhireable by the studios, but in the press she was "still the screen's mistress in the art of telling the world where to get off." The *Los Angeles Examiner* summed it up: Barbara Stanwyck "waves bye-bye to Warner Brothers as *The Woman in Red.* [Her] last is not her best vehicle. Neither is it her worst. [It] is average screenfare."

"Average screenfare" is what she was making, and no work was coming her way.

Barbara was introduced to Marion and Zeppo Marx. Zeppo (Herbert Manfred Marx) had been the youngest member of the Four Marx Brothers, ap-

The Marx Brothers minus Milton (Gummo), 1924 (from left to right): Adolph, later Arthur (Harpo), at thirty-six years old; Herbert (Zeppo), at twenty-three; Leonard (Chico), at thirty-seven; and (seated) Julius Henry (Groucho), at thirty-four.

pearing in vaudeville; on Broadway in *I'll Say She Is* and in the hit sensation *The Cocoanuts;* and in five Marx Brothers pictures, including *Animal Crackers, Monkey Business,* and *Horse Feathers.* After being one of the Brothers for seventeen years, he had quit and opened a theatrical agency called Zeppo Marx Inc.

Zeppo originally joined the Four Marx Brothers when his next older brother, Gummo, his senior by eight years, was conscripted by the army to fight in the Great War. Zeppo was sixteen and working as a mechanic for the Ford Motor Company when the call came from his mother, Minnie Schönberg Marx, instructing him to quit his job, come home immediately, pack his bags, and go to Rockford, Illinois. "I want the name of the Marx Brothers intact," she told Zeppo in German, the language spoken in the house. "We started that way and we're getting along pretty good," she said.

Zeppo had performed a little onstage—singing and dancing—but like Gummo before him, Zeppo, as the fourth Marx Brother, was to be the straight man. After the war, Zeppo officially took Gummo's place in the act. Said Gummo, "I preferred to sell dresses," which he did in New York at 1375 Broadway. "I never felt at home on the stage," Gummo said. "I was only on for eleven years. I was goddamn lucky to get out."

Five years after joining the Marx Brothers, Herbert, along with Leonard, Adolph, Julius, and Milton, became Zeppo, Chico, Harpo, Groucho, and Gummo. Zeppo explained the derivation of their names: "Chico because if you chased girls a lot, they were called 'chicken chasers'; Harpo because of the harp; Groucho ('impudent cad') because of his funereal look; Gummo wore rubbers—gumshoe, because he was always afraid it was going to rain and his regular shoes had holes in them. Zeppo was from the zeppelin, the graf zeppelin." It is also said that Zeppo's name came from the way he dealt cards—with a rapid spin that dropped the card in front of the player like a golf ball falling dead to the pin.

Of Zeppo's character onstage, one critic wrote, "I wonder what Zeppo thinks about as he watches his brothers in their popular pranks, while he himself is not permitted to play with them." Groucho described Zeppo's character in the act as the "handsome, wooden, slightly obtuse, fill-in . . . [who] brought logic to a basically illogical story and was often an intrusion" and who most of the time only had to say "Yes, sir" and "No, sir." "It's not that he didn't have the talent," said Groucho, "he simply had three older brothers."

During one vaudeville circuit tour, Jack Benny was to go onstage after the Marx Brothers ("Nobody could follow the Marx Bros.," said Benny. "It was impossible.") Throughout the tour, Benny roomed with Zeppo. "Zeppo off stage was like Groucho on," said Benny. "He was the funniest of the four." Benny laughed so hard around Zeppo he could hardly catch his breath.

Zeppo was handsome, athletic, a bodybuilder. He was "completely different from the rest of us," said Gummo. Zeppo was the most independent of the five brothers (there had been six Marx boys: Minnie's firstborn son, Manfred, died at seven months). Zeppo had an explosive temper, like his mother, that could be set off at any time.

"I was a real bad boy," Zeppo said. Becoming the fourth Marx Brother saved his life. "Good thing I did," he said. "Else I'd have gone to jail. I was a kid, but I carried a gun and I stole automobiles," he said. "I was real bad."

Zeppo was adept with his hands and with things mechanical. "Zeppo could take an engine apart," said Groucho. "Grind the valves, adjust the timing and clean out the carbon with no more fuss or effort than I would use in sharpening a pencil." He had a talent for invention, coming up with the idea of a single-blade shaver and shaving cream that came out of an aerosol can instead of soap in a jar that had to be whipped. He designed a bottle that was filled with a cream that rolls on under the arm to control perspiration.

By January 1934, after seventeen years as "an appendage to a fraternity already overladen," being paid a salary rather than being an equal partner in the Four Marx Brothers, Zeppo had had enough.

Production was about to begin at Metro on *A Night at the Opera,* Zeppo's sixth picture. "I'm sick and tired of being a stooge," Zeppo told Groucho.

After Zeppo left the act, he knew he had to do something related to show business, which he'd come to know so well. He bought out a partnership in a theatrical agency with Frank Orsatti and Milton Bren, which became Bren, Orsatti & Marx. Orsatti's family and Frank Capra's had come from Italy together in steerage.

Zeppo worked with the Bren, Orsatti & Marx agency for four months until the partners' arguing forced them to dissolve the business and Zeppo started his own agency. Within seven weeks he set up Zeppo Inc. at 9201 Sunset Boulevard.

Zeppo, Harpo, and Gummo, along with Beatrice Kaufman, wife of George and former press agent for the Talmadge sisters, wanted to incorporate as a producing organization for Broadway plays. Kaufman was a reader for Al Woods and was as well a playwright and editorial director for Boni & Liveright. She had been the editor of T. S. Eliot, Djuna Barnes, Faulkner, Steinbeck, O'Neill, and others. Marx hired Donald Friede, former editor at Liveright and co-founding publisher of Covici, Friede, as his story editor in Los Angeles; Gummo was in charge of the New York branch of the office.

Zeppo's first client was Alexander Woollcott, the drama critic and editorial writer. Marx negotiated a deal for Woollcott with Radio Pictures, which wanted him not as a writer but as a radio personality for its upcoming picture *Radio City Revels,* starring Fred Astaire and Ginger Rogers. There were those who saw Woollcott less as a critic than as an amusing hysteric.

Within a short time Zeppo's clients included Moss Hart, George S. Kaufman, and the comedy writer Norman Krasna.

Barbara liked Zeppo. He could be brusque, cutting, rude, but he could just as easily be charming and the funniest man at the party. Zeppo and Barbara shared a similar past. They'd both grown up on the streets (she in Brooklyn; he in Chicago); they'd each appeared onstage on Broadway and traveled across the country playing in one city after another. For Zeppo, the days on the circuit were "hectic . . . difficult." The Marx Brothers worked "in the cheapest vaudeville theaters," he said. They did their act five times a day. Every hour or every hour and a half they'd come onstage again because they'd be continuous. Later, when the theater became a movie house, the Marx Brothers did their act, and the theater would run a movie. The next live show would start again with four or five shows a day.

Zeppo and Marion Marx, Ambassador Hotel, Los Angeles, 1933.
(CORBIS)

Barbara and Zeppo considered themselves "change-of-life babies," each with much older siblings. Barbara liked Zeppo's wit, his drive, his unstoppable need to prove himself, which was similar to hers.

He never finished grammar school, and like Barbara, whatever education he had, he "learned from travelling and meeting people and picking up things."

And like Barbara's mother, Zeppo's mother wanted her boys to perform. "She couldn't do a damn thing," said Zeppo. "Couldn't sing, couldn't dance, couldn't act. But she had that bug for someone." Zeppo's grandfather and grandmother were performers in Germany, gypsies. His grandfather was a wandering magician and legerdemain artist; his grandmother, a harpist—who passed her instrument on to her grandson Adolph, who taught himself to play on it—would play the harp while her husband performed magic. "He'd carry the harp on his back from small town to small town," said Zeppo. "They'd get out on the street some place and do a little thing and people would throw coins at 'em."

Zeppo and his wife, Marion, seemed a perfectly matched couple. She was spontaneous, spirited, a jokester like Zeppo. On a lark, they once borrowed a car from a member of a Los Angeles country club where they were playing cards, drove to the farmers' market on Fairfax, removed a large street clock, put it in the backseat of the car, drove back to the club, and resumed playing cards. The Los Angeles police tracked the thieves to the country club, found the clock in the car Marion and Zeppo had taken, and arrested the unsuspecting owner for stealing public property.

The Marxes were expert bridge players. He loved to play cards and shoot craps; she was a champion tennis player and was frequently at the racket club. Winning was all to Zeppo. He was quick to get into brawls—which he won. Zeppo gambled as feverishly as Chico, but unlike his older brother of fourteen years who bet to beat the odds, Zeppo bet to win. Growing up, Chico had been a god to Zeppo, but he came to see Chico as a "schmuck" who lost his money, who bet against gamblers and gave them odds he shouldn't have.

Marion loved clothes and liked to shop, including shopping for Zeppo and making sure he was impeccably dressed. Each day Zeppo left the house, Marion made sure he was wearing the most beautiful suit or sport coat, shirt, and shoes.

Barbara and Marion were drawn to each other instantly, though Marion found Barbara "somewhat baffling." She thought Barbara was "natural, unaffected; as straightforward as a man; not like many glamour queens," and was surprised by the actress's lack of artifice.

The two women looked somewhat alike; they had the same easy manner; each was quiet with a similar sense of humor; each had the same dramatic trick of lowering her eyes; each was shy and had a hard time making conversation. "On screen Barbara is emotional and demonstrative," said Marion. "Off screen she's inclined to be withdrawn and remote except with close friends." Marion found Barbara "talkative, especially on any theatrical topic," with one or two people. In a group of people Barbara was "the best listener present. She talks little and quickly."

After Walda Mansfield and Mae Clarke, Barbara hadn't made too many women friends.

Marion saw how upset Barbara was with her marriage. "Her eyes lacked luster," said Marion. "Barbara acted like she was walking around dead, like a regular Zombie."

Barbara was drawn to both husband and wife for their sense of fun. Zeppo saw the situation Barbara was in with Frank, and her career, and wanted to help her.

He set out to find a picture for Fay. It had been five years since he'd made the still-unreleased *A Fool's Advice*.

In addition to clients like Barbara and Fay, Zeppo found clients who were undiscovered. He'd just settled a suit over a client involving Barbara's longtime agent, Arthur Lyons, regarding a young musician, Fred MacMurray, who Marx thought had great potential as an actor and wanted to represent.

Arthur Lyons had been the president of the Theatrical Artists Representatives Association and had become one of the biggest agents in Hollywood, representing everyone from Jack Benny and Mary Livingstone to George and Ira Gershwin and Kurt Weill. He'd represented the Fays in New York. When Lyons had taken MacMurray on as a client, he was getting $61 a week as a saxophone player. Lyons negotiated a contract for MacMurray with Paramount Pictures for $250 a week.

Zeppo met MacMurray, liked his looks, and thought he could help the fledgling actor. MacMurray left Lyons and signed with Marx.

The actor was then earning $600 a week at Paramount, but the studio wasn't using him; they had no idea Fred MacMurray was on the lot. "This boy has a great, great potential," Marx had said to one of the Paramount executives. The studio said it didn't have any parts for the actor.

Marx went to RKO and told Cliff Reid, a producer of inexpensive pictures, about MacMurray. "If you could find a little something for him to do in a picture," Marx said, "you can borrow him from Paramount. It'll help this boy. It'll help me."

"Bring him over and let me look at him," Reid told Marx.

The producer liked MacMurray's looks.

"He had never acted," said Marx, "never said a word before."

Marx had Reid call Paramount. "You have a boy over there," Reid said, "that we would like to use in a movie."

"We've never heard of him," Paramount said of MacMurray.

"Well, he's on the lot," said Reid.

RKO and Paramount made the deal. MacMurray went to RKO and was put in *Grand Old Girl* with May Robson.

Marx then had Cliff Reid call over to Paramount to see if the studio would sell MacMurray's contract. "Paramount said, 'Of course not,'" said Marx. "They still didn't know who MacMurray was but they renewed his contract for another year. I bought a year's time to do something with him."

In addition to MacMurray, Marx had signed Ray Milland as a client and now suggested both actors for a picture with Claudette Colbert to be directed by Wesley Ruggles. Each was hired; the picture, *The Gilded Lily,* was a big hit. Afterward, Marx went to the front office at Paramount and got each actor a new seven-year contract. "Both of them for a million and a half," said Marx.

Much to Fay's fury, Barbara began to spend evenings with Marion and Zeppo. The Marxes and others were invited to the Fays' for dinner one evening. The guests had just arrived at Bristol Avenue, and Barbara was greeting them in the foyer. Fay came in through the kitchen and was on his way to his bed-

Fred MacMurray, Claudette Colbert, and Ray Milland, in Wesley Ruggles's *The Gilded Lily* (1935), a romantic lark intended to duplicate the warmth, humor, and merriment of *It Happened One Night,* released a year earlier. MacMurray's charm and naturalness on screen promised to make him, said the *New York Times,* "one of the most popular of the cinema's glamour men within the next few months." (PHOTOFEST)

room using the back stairs. He looked down from the second-floor landing, unzipped his fly, and relieved himself on the heads of Barbara's guests.

Fay had started to hit her. He criticized his son at every turn. Dion and Nanny were near the swimming pool one day. Fay, sober, told Nellie to put Dion in the water.

"He was already in the water," she said.

Fay looked at Dion and said, "Get in the water."

Dion moved closer to Nellie.

"God damn you," said Fay. "You never do anything I tell you to do."

Fay picked up the three-year-old boy and threw him in the pool. Dion went under. He was wearing a harness, and Nellie pulled him out of the water up to the wall of the pool. Dion was crying, terrified.

Things deteriorated to such a point with Frank that Barbara one day took Dion and Nanny and checked into the Beverly Hills Hotel without officially registering. She was wearing clothes to disguise herself. She, her son, and Nellie got into the hotel elevator. Gene Raymond and his wife, Jeanette

MacDonald, also in the elevator, weren't taken in by Barbara's disguise and said how happy they were to see her; small talk was exchanged. Nothing was said of Barbara's getup. She realized, though, that word would spread that she was in the hotel and, not wanting to attract any publicity, checked out with Dion and Nellie in tow. Believing she had few options, she returned to Bristol Avenue.

Afterward, Barbara told Nellie to keep a bag packed at all times.

During another bout with Frank, Barbara ran to Joan Crawford's North Bristol Avenue house. Joan and Barbara had shared New York days together when each was a floor show dancer in clubs. Joan kept a framed hand-tinted small photograph of Ruby Stevens from those early days when the high-kicking Billie Cassin, Shubert chorine with bangs and frizzy hair in the too-tight over-the-hip dresses, danced the Charleston, said Louise Brooks, like "a lady wrestler." Billie was now living in Brentwood, in a seven-room house, originally styled with grilled Spanish doorways and arches remade in a Georgian formal style. The house had been expanded to ten rooms, not including servants' quarters, with a theater that seated twenty-five for Joan's workshops of one-act plays, which she performed with her husband, Franchot Tone.

The house's living room, playroom, and dining room, much like Barbara's bedroom, were done in austere white—white walls, white furniture, white flowers. Joan was now elegantly dressed, correct to the last pearl. Joan had a special affection for Barbara and was able to comfort her—for the moment—about her troubles with Frank.

EIGHT

"Little Sure Shot"

1935

Eddie Small, an independent producer, asked Barbara to make a comedy called *The Runaway Daughter*. Small was a former talent agent who, with his brother Morris, ran his own agency in the 1920s and had started Reliance Pictures in 1932, distributed by United Artists. Small was an ignorant man with good instincts and hunches who had produced several films, among them *I Cover the Waterfront* and *The Count of Monte Cristo,* that had made him rich.

Barbara hadn't worked in six months.

"[Eddie] called me," said Barbara, "because Constance Cummings, whom he really wanted, refused to be separated [that] long from her husband, Benn Levy, who was in England."

The Runaway Daughter was Reliance's answer to Capra's recent hit *It Happened One Night.* Capra's picture about a runaway heiress who falls in love with a tough out-of-work newspaper reporter desperately in need of a story and who sees in her the scoop he's after to get back his job had, said the critics, "plenty of laughs" but was called "improbable" and "preposterous."

It Happened One Night set a house record on its opening day at Radio City Music Hall in February 1934 and grossed $90,000 its first week. The picture was considered a disappointment and after the second week was pulled in cities across the country. Its success was made in small towns across America, where the picture continued its run for weeks. It played for the next year, into 1935, bringing in $1 million, more money for Columbia than any other picture in the studio's six-year existence.

Eddie Small's Capra-like production of *Runaway Daughter* was a romantic comedy about a spoiled young woman, expelled from college after falling in love with a fellow classmate and campus agitator who wins her over to the radical side. Her father, a U.S. Army general, has her whisked off against her will to a Mexican border town in the hope of separating the two lovers and saving the young heiress from youthful folly and further scandal. She's hell-bent on getting back to Washington and to her comrade-in-arms and, after losing her last $5 at a gambling house, tricks a handsome young American buck private, returning from leave, into helping her get across the border and back to Washington. Their means of travel: a ramshackle auto trailer being driven by a henpecked husband in on the adventure and happily on the lam from his nagging wife, also in hot pursuit, along with the law, who are after the runaway daughter. On the bumpy road to the USA and points north, madcappery ensues, and buck private and general's daughter fall head over heels.

It Happened One Night had been released a year and a half before and had been nominated for five Academy Awards, including Best Picture. In a stunning victory for Capra it had been the winner in each of the five catego-ries: Capra for Best Director; Robert Riskin for Best Writing, Adaptation; Clark Gable for Best Actor; Claudette Colbert for Best Actress (against Grace Moore in *One Night of Love,* Norma Shearer in *The Barretts of Wimpole Street,* and Bette Davis in *Of Human Bondage*). Davis had been added to the list (the academy had overlooked nominating her) only after the press had demanded to see the tabulation (the academy refused) and after the write-in ballots were so persistent the academy was forced to change its rules and allow a write-in candidate to be included on the list of nominees.

Barbara wanted and needed to work, but she hesitated playing comedy; she didn't know if she could do it. Marion Marx said of her new friend, "[Bar-bara] has a terrific sense of humor—she's forever flinging verbal barbs at her-self." It took Zeppo weeks to persuade her to try comedy on the screen.

Zeppo had an instinct for knowing who could play for comedy. He was so funny himself that Groucho was competitive with him. Their humor was alike. Zeppo was an uncanny mimic; once, in Chicago, Zeppo went onstage in Groucho's stead when he was sick with the flu. Zeppo was so convincing as Groucho the audience was unaware that the best known of the Marx Broth-ers was in a hotel room sick in bed. Groucho got word of what had happened onstage, got himself up, and went back to work. Zeppo was never again given the chance to fill in for his brother.

Capra said, "Actors don't like comedies much. They're not dynamic like melodramas—nobody gets hurt, nobody gets killed, nobody gets raped."

The romantic aspect of Barbara's relationship with Capra had ended a year before he made *It Happened One Night.* Claudette Colbert was offered the picture after Capra was turned down by Myrna Loy, Miriam Hopkins, Margaret Sullavan, Constance Bennett, Bette Davis, and Carole Lombard. Colbert agreed to make the picture "mostly to work with Clark" (Gable's part was originally written for Robert Montgomery, who had turned it down). Columbia was desperate to find a female lead and agreed to pay Colbert $50,000 out of a $325,000 production budget.

Runaway Daughter tried for all of the elements of *It Happened One Night*: the sharp-tongued rebellious daughter; the father in control of police, politicians, even an army of men, yet helpless in the face of his impossible, indulged little girl; the unassuming young man caught up in the whirlwind of the spoiled girl's mess who, with his toughness and disdain for everything she's championing, takes matters in hand the way her father never could (she to the soldier: "Are you giving me orders, Uncle Sam?"; he: "You've been giving orders all of your life. Now it's about time you found out how to take them yourself"); the jabs and wisecracks back and forth between the two (she: "I'm beginning to hate you"; he: "Oh gee. That's terrible. I think I'll kill myself"; she: "Why only think about it?") as he pulls and prods her away from her folly and misguided notions and then falls in love with her; the proletariat means of travel that brings her down from her highfalutin ways and exposes her to common folk whom she comes to love; a cat-and-mouse chase involving the law—and her father—that results in a series of mishaps, missteps, and misunderstandings; even the walls of Jericho, as young soldier and general's daughter bed down in a barn with only a few rough-hewn boards of an open stall between them.

Robert Young was the soldier, under contract to Metro and on loan-out (Mayer's advice to Young to improve his career: "Put on a little weight and get more sex"). Hardie Albright was the campus radical; Cliff Edwards ("Ukulele Ike," who'd sold more than eleven million records of his songs) was the henpecked husband, owner of the trailer. Ruth Donnelly was his ornery wife. Sidney Lanfield, former vaudeville performer brought to Hollywood to be a gag writer at Fox, was the director.

The Runaway Daughter had a surprising element that Capra's picture didn't have—a story line involving politics, radicals, campus agitators, "long-hairs," "Communists" (never addressed as such), attempting to, in her father's words, "undermine the government, and pervert the minds of the younger generation."

At the heart of the picture is a general's daughter who loves a man whose

With Robert Young (left) and Cliff ("Ukulele Ike") Edwards in *Red Sa-lute*, 1935. Edwards played his ukulele on Broadway in *Lady Be Good!*, appeared in *The Ziegfeld Follies,* and introduced "Singin' in the Rain" in his first picture, *The Hollywood Revue of 1929.* (PHOTOFEST)

political ideas go against everything her father represents. The general to his daughter about her hero lover: "I'm part of the system he's fighting. The system hasn't been so bad for us. It's given us this home, your dresses, your cars, everything we've got." At a May Day rally, the young man, introduced as "Comrade" before a crowd, says, "As students of a great college you are re-sponsible for the leadership of tomorrow . . . Destroy the old order and take the new. Militarism must be stamped out. To the young men I say, don't let anyone ever put a soldier's suit on you."

The buck private's response is the picture's message: "Sure I work for thirty dollars a month. I joined the army just because I happen to be full of that stuff they call—Americanism. The army's just full of guys like me, guys from the middle west, Yankees from up north. Some of 'em would stick in the army even if they got no pay at all. They think it's something to be proud of, being an American soldier. They took the job to protect you and your country in case of trouble and there isn't a one of them that wouldn't come through for you."

The studio made sure a disclaimer went out in its publicity about the picture stating that "*Red Salute* [its final title] is not intended to be a propaganda film in any sense of the word . . . it may start a cycle of similar films which will arouse both the man of the street and the intellectual to discussion of modern day modes of living, but this was not our aim and should not be your selling attack to the public."

There is a moment in the picture when the girl's father is pressuring a high government official to get the young man thrown out of the country. The general is told that the young man has four months left on his one-year student visa, even though the official has "more than a suspicion [the agitator] is a paid propagandist." The general is outraged that the "student" is allowed to stay in the country and "preach revolution." The official quietly interjects the one true subversive moment in the picture: "You're forgetting, General, that some very wise Americans once preached revolution. Of a different sort, I grant you, but Washington and Patrick Henry left us the sacred right of free speech."

What *Runaway Daughter* didn't have was the spirit and buoyancy, the wit and sexy kick, of Capra's *It Happened One Night.* The journey of general's daughter and buck private isn't one toward freedom; her notions don't transform him or set him free from his regimented small thinking. Instead, his beliefs—conventional to the core—ideas she's been raised on and attempted (almost successfully) to flee, reel her back. *It Happened One Night* is full of hope and promise of new ideas. *Runaway Daughter* is a warning not to stray from the conventional, as rigidly set as the military; those who conform and abide by rules and regulations will be rewarded.

Barbara seemed unsure of herself in the picture: her wisecracks, which she says from the perch of a worldly, rich, anointed sophisticate, seem too lofty to be funny or felt; and while she moves with ease from humor to tenderness and feeling, she doesn't seem engaged in it, in large part because she wasn't challenged by Robert Young. His character wants to go west toward Singapore; hers, east to Washington; and that's the route their sparring takes, each going in an opposite direction, bypassing the other, not clicking. Young's barking and he-man stuff aren't playful or sexy, and his Scoutmaster conventionality takes the shimmer out of Barbara. The flatness of her work made it seem as if she were hardly in it at all instead of being the heartbeat of the piece.

During production of *Runaway Daughter* at United Artists, Barbara signed a contract with Paramount. She would be working with Lewis Milestone, director of *All Quiet on the Western Front, The Front Page, Rain,* and *Hallelujah, I'm a Bum,* and have her choice of two pictures: *Invitation to Happiness* by Franz Schulz and Arnold Belgard or Ferenc Molnár's *The Pastry Baker's Wife* [*The Guardsmen*].

The two-year-old 20th Century Pictures merged with the Fox Film Corporation. The new 20th Century–Fox had Joseph Schenck as chairman of the board (at a salary of $130,000) and Sidney Kent as president (at $180,000). Darryl Zanuck at thirty-two became the sole head of production of 20th Century–Fox and owner of 20 percent of the company with a salary of $265,000, responsible for producing sixty pictures a year with a budget of $20 million.

Those remaining at United Artists were Edward Small, Samuel Goldwyn (Schenck and Goldwyn hadn't spoken in months), and Charles Chaplin. Mary Pickford and Douglas Fairbanks had no films in the works. Small was producing a few, among them *Red Salute*.

Zanuck said of his first year and a half at his former fledgling company 20th Century, "The pictures I was working on had to carry the entire United Artists distributing organization. I had to carry the whole goddamn load." Zanuck and Schenck realized that a large share of receipts for their eighteen pictures—*The Bowery, The House of Rothschild, Cardinal Richelieu, Les Misérables,* among them—was being appropriated by United Artists. "While King Fairbanks was worrying about how best to dump Queen Pickford," said Zanuck, "there was no one around the place making films but us. Meanwhile they were helping themselves to our profits and socking us for their expenses."

Fox Movietone City on the outskirts of Beverly Hills, with its ninety-six-acre lot (nearly twice the size of Metro's)—house fronts, gardens, a synthetic jungle, five miles of Manhattan streets, midwestern streets, a replica of Berkeley Square in London—was part of the new company. There were twelve soundstages (seven new stages were to be built once 20th Century moved from the United Artists lot to the Fox lot; Warner Bros. had seventeen soundstages with six more under construction). Fox owned fifteen hundred theaters in the United States and England as well as its distribution facilities. The studio had thirty-seven cameras (rented from Western Electric), which were to be replaced, and forty-two artists, of which only three—Shirley Temple, Will Rogers, and Janet Gaynor—were box-office successes. It also had Warner Oland, whose Charlie Chan pictures were dependable moneymakers.

From 20th Century, Zanuck brought with him Fredric March, Ronald Colman, Loretta Young, Wallace Beery, George Raft, and Jack Oakie.

The newly merged 20th Century–Fox moved into second place after Loew's Inc., which netted around $7.5 million a year. Had Paramount not gone bankrupt in 1933, it would have followed Loew's in terms of earning power. Warner Bros. had just begun to show a small profit. RKO was in receivership.

. . .

Zeppo Marx heard that Jean Arthur had turned down the role of Annie Oakley for RKO's *Shooting Star*. Arthur had just finished her fourth picture in seven months. Marx suggested to the RKO producer Cliff Reid that Barbara play the part of the legendary "Little Sure Shot."

Reid had been overseeing pictures at Radio Pictures for a year, twelve in all, including *The Three Musketeers* and John Ford's *Lost Patrol* and his latest, *The Informer,* just released.

George Stevens was directing *Shooting Star*. Reid liked the idea of Barbara as the backwoods girl who became the world's renowned champion marksman. Barbara was taken with the part. She saw Annie Oakley (Phoebe Ann Moses), the Quaker girl from Darke County, Ohio, as a "woman of the ages, deeply feminine in spite of all of her shooting ability," who used her talent with a gun to support her family and become "better at [shooting] than anyone else, male or female . . . She was a show-woman of the highest type and did much to raise the status of all professional women."

Reid offered Barbara the part, and Marx was able to get her $7,000 a week with a five-week guarantee.

Annie Oakley was the first role to come Barbara's way since *Red Salute*. She was desperate to work. "I have to work," she said. "I have people to support." Frank and their household were expensive to maintain. In addition, Fay was being sued by Los Angeles County for not declaring $50,000 in stocks and $8,000 in bank deposits. The U.S. government had filed four liens against Bristol Avenue during a four-month period as a result of unpaid back taxes.

Barbara was in negotiations with the rival studios Paramount and Radio-Keith-Orpheum, for one picture each. She wasn't happy with the contract her longtime agent Arthur Lyons had negotiated with Paramount; neither *Invitation to Happiness* nor *The Pastry Baker's Wife* had been mentioned in her agreement, and as a result the studio felt it wasn't legally obligated to provide Barbara with either picture. Barbara let Lyons go as her agent and officially hired Zeppo Marx. She notified RKO and now Fox that Zeppo and Walter Kane would be taking over the negotiations for both contracts.

Barbara was on her own, outside the protection of a single studio that built actresses and created them to last, that provided movies one after the other, shaped publicity, created a singular look, and sold the image. Barbara wasn't protected by that sense of belonging or reassured by it. She found it a constraint.

. . .

The Fays went east for a month of stage appearances to help publicize Barbara's new contracts with Paramount and RKO. They opened first at the Palace Theatre in Chicago.

Paramount decided not to go ahead with either of the pictures that Barbara had been promised. The studio put forth two additional pictures. One of them, *Guns,* a story of a prison breakout with Fred MacMurray, was to precede *Shooting Star.* The other, about an adoption home, based on the Cradle, an institution where Hollywood adopted its children, was not acceptable to Barbara; she didn't want to appear as if she were capitalizing on Dion's adoption. She asked for—and was given—her release from her Paramount contract.

In reading about Annie Oakley, Barbara could see parallels between her life and Oakley's. "I have a sketchy idea of how she felt though I grew up in Brooklyn," said Barbara. Each woman had been on her own from girlhood. Oakley's father died when she was six; at eight or nine, she moved in with another family that cared for the elderly, orphans, and the insane. She was indentured; her education was in exchange for caring for unwanted children. Oakley referred to the cruel family as "the Wolves." "I went all to pieces under the care of a home," she said.

Oakley, at the age of fourteen, supported herself and her family. She taught herself to hunt small game with her father's rifle (the first time she shot it, the kick fractured her nose, but she killed the bird). She was so good at not ruining the meat with pellets—she aimed for the head—the game was sold to restaurants and hotels as far as a hundred miles away. She earned enough money from the sales to pay off in cash the mortgage on her mother's farm.

Both actress and champion shooter wanted to be the best they could be, man's world or not. Oakley at sixteen was able to outshoot the Irishman Frank Butler shot for shot. Butler was one of the best marksmen in the country. Oakley married him, defying her own statement "You can't get a man with a gun, that's for sure."

Each woman became more famous than her celebrated husband. Oakley got top billing in Buffalo Bill's Wild West show. The great Western scout and showman signed her up in fifteen minutes and always called her "Missy." The Butlers traveled with the show from 1883 to 1913, and on a tour in England during Queen Victoria's Golden Jubilee it was Annie Oakley the crowds came to watch; as in France, Italy, Germany, Spain, and finally Russia, at a shooting match with Grand Duke Michael.

Oakley could shoot a playing card in midair thirteen times before it hit the ground; she could hit a dime with her rifle held high above her head. She

Miss Annie Oakley, 1899, champion rifle shot at thirty-nine years old. She used, at various times, two Lancaster guns, one Scott, one Parker, each with twenty-eight-inch barrels. Her famous Killdeer rifle was a gift from Buffalo Bill (he called her "Missy"). "Shooting is a splendid exercise," she said. "You can figure it out this way. My gun weighs seven pounds and I shoot somewhere around 150 shots a day. That means I lift 1,000 pounds a day." She fired more than two million shots in her lifetime. (PHOTO BY RICHARD K. FOX, AUTHOR'S COLLECTION)

once shot flying balls for nine hours straight, using three 16-gauge hammer shotguns, which she loaded herself, breaking 4,772 balls out of 5,000; and in Berlin, she shot a cigarette from the mouth of Crown Prince Wilhelm.

She was known as Annie Oakley, Sharpshooting Star, but in private she was always Mrs. Frank Butler. Each woman guarded against having her fame interfere with her marriage; each felt as if her husband had "really reared" her; that husband and wife were outside society. ("We're not fashionable," said Mrs. Frank Butler. "We've never been to Reno.")

Each woman was childless; each had felt like an orphan; each embraced children who were unwanted; it was said that Oakley raised and educated eighteen orphan girls.

"She wasn't born with a silver spoon," said Barbara. "She earned her own living and provided for her widowed mother and four siblings by shooting quail and sending them to Chicago markets. It couldn't have been much fun," she said, "but it was the only thing that she could do and she managed to do it better than anyone else." Barbara "wanted so much to play Annie Oakley," she said, "because she had courage."

Annie Oakley performed for crowned heads across Europe, "but it didn't turn her head," said Barbara. "I have been successful within a smaller scope, but I don't think I'm high-hat because of it."

Barbara had loved the Westerns as a child. The idea of the West being settled thrilled her and she'd read countless books about it. It was even more exciting

To make the picture, Barbara was loaned the saddle Annie Oakley used during her fourteen years with Buffalo Bill, which she left after her death to her longtime friend Fred Stone—they'd ridden in the circus together—and which he left to his daughter, who at age twelve was taught to shoot by the champion markswoman. (THE KOBAL COLLECTION)

for her to re-create it on film, "to become a part of the past," she said, with spectacle, showmanship, and all the action in those lives.

"The immigrants coming over on covered wagons, and atop the trains were America's royalty. Our aristocracy," said Barbara. "They broke the trails through unbelievable hardships to conquer the land."

Production on *Shooting Star* was to start the first few days in August. The script had been okayed by the Breen Office with only two suggestions: take out a scene of a spitting contest and Sitting Bull's "burp." Each was cut.

Despite Barbara's having been gun-shy all her life, in the weeks before she was to start work, she learned to shoot a shotgun and rifle from Captain A. H. Hardy, one of America's best pistol, rifle, and trick shots. Hardy had an unequaled record of successfully hitting more than thirteen thousand two-and-a-quarter-inch wooden balls twenty feet in the air with a Marlin .22 repeating rifle.

Barbara would be using Annie Oakley's own saddle, with its silver mountings and hand-carved leather, lent to her for the picture by the daughter of one of Oakley's closest friends.

As Barbara prepared for *Shooting Star,* her marriage was slipping out of her control.

One night in July, she had dinner at Zeppo and Marion Marx's. Afterward, the three went to Minsky's burlesque show, which was playing in Hollywood. The next day Barbara and Dion were standing near the pool. Frank was angry with her for having spent the evening with Zeppo and Marion. He began to argue with her and punched her in the face. She collapsed on the ground. Nellie grabbed Dion and ran into the house.

Barbara was terrified of Fay, but she was about to start a new picture and couldn't afford to disrupt her life. She did nothing to change things and showed up for work on *Shooting Star.* A few days into production, Barbara went home at the end of the day. Fay was drunk and argumentative. He hit her and knocked her down the staircase.

She knew she had to get out. She was lucky to be alive.

She waited until Dion was asleep. Fay was nowhere around. She told Nellie to get the boy. A high cement wall with a side gate surrounded the Bristol Avenue estate. Barbara told Nellie to meet her there. She went to the garage and started one of the cars. She drove it to the outside corner of the property and waited for Nellie and Dion.

Barbara took with her only what she was wearing. In her six years in pictures from 1929 to 1935, Barbara had earned more than $1 million, most of it spent on their elaborate compound. Money and possessions had no meaning to her now. She and Dion had to get out before Fay discovered what was happening.

Nellie came to the gate, and the sleepy boy and nurse got into the car. Barbara drove off; her only thought: to get away from Frank and Bristol Avenue and make it to Marion and Zeppo's and to safety.

NINE

Practical Policies

1935

I'm only brave when I'm being paid for it.
—Barbara Stanwyck

As soon as Barbara, Dion, and Nellie arrived at the Marxes', Barbara called her sister Maud back east. It was early in the morning in Brooklyn. Gene Vaslett, Barbara's nephew, was home from Notre Dame and was staying with the Merkents for the summer. Fay had helped Gene get into Notre Dame, writing, on his behalf, to Frank Hering, founder of the Eagles fraternal organization and a former Notre Dame football coach.

Gene answered the phone and put Maud on right away. Barbara told her sister what had happened and asked her to come out to California. Maud agreed and later that day flew out to Los Angeles.

Fay returned to Bristol Avenue and realized that Barbara had taken the boy and left. In the midst of his ranting, he reassured himself that she would come back, as she had the other times she'd left him.

Barbara felt safe with the Marxes (to Dion, the Marxes were Aunt Marion and Uncle Zipper), but she was devastated about the breakup of her marriage. She wanted her brother to be with her. She was terrified but went back to work as if nothing had changed in her life.

"You pay a price for everything in this world," she said. "The price you pay for being a star is that you must learn to leave all your personal troubles behind you when you walk on to a set. Invariably, the star's mood is reflected on the entire company. He or she, as the case may be, sets the pace."

Barbara behaved accordingly. She was thrilled to be playing Annie Oakley—she was a great character—and saw the role as a new start.

Oakley had been called *Watanya Cicilla*—Little Sure Shot—by Sitting Bull, the great Sioux medicine man who successfully led three thousand Sioux and Cheyenne against General Custer's attack in 1876 of the great Sioux camp near the Little Big Horn. Sitting Bull was awed by what Oakley could do and became her lifelong friend and adopted her as a member of the Hunkpapa Lakota and as a daughter.

Firsthand reminiscences were incorporated into the script. Sitting Bull was played by the sixty-nine-year-old chief Thunderbird of the Cheyenne, who, as a boy of ten, had known Bull during the time of the Custer massacre and whose older brother had traveled with the original Annie Oakley in Buffalo Bill's Wild West show. In 1860, Thunderbird's father had been priest-chief of all the North American Cheyenne, consisting of five thousand warriors; his mother was a warrior priestess of the Cheyenne Dog Soldiers.

George Stevens, at thirty, was considered one of the best young directors in Hollywood. *Shooting Star* was his second major picture. Stevens had come to RKO by way of Universal and minor features. He'd been a cameraman on two-reel comedies for Hal Roach, among them Laurel and Hardy pictures, when the two comics were hacks on the Roach lot and were paired to make a picture. At RKO, Stevens directed six pictures in exchange for the chance to direct one big feature. Months before making *Shooting Star,* he was directing Wheeler and Woolsey comedies for RKO.

Stevens had just finished his first big film, *Alice Adams,* with RKO's major star, Katharine Hepburn, a job that had come to him by virtue of a coin toss between Hepburn and Pandro Berman, the head of the studio. The first toss had come up William Wyler. Berman suggested they toss the coin again. It came up George Stevens, which was what Hepburn and Berman wanted from the start.

Alice Adams was a different kind of part for Hepburn. Until then she'd played on-screen strong and stalwart women. Playing a simple, purposely romantic girl was something new for her, and she believed that Stevens would be the best director to help her bring it off.

Every young actor in Hollywood had been considered for the part of the young society man Arthur Russell, who is smitten with her, among them George Brent, Robert Young, Cary Grant, Randolph Scott, Franchot Tone, Robert Taylor. Zeppo Marx intervened on behalf of his client Fred

From George Stevens's *Annie Oakley,* 1935. (PHOTOFEST)

MacMurray with the picture's associate producer, Cliff Reid, and the twenty-seven-year-old actor, just out of *Men Without Names,* got the part.

Hepburn was paid $55,000 for the picture; Stevens, $11,000; MacMurray, $12,000.

Shooting Star was a chance for Stevens to re-create aspects of the American West he'd experienced firsthand and come to love. He had traveled to Utah at the age of seventeen with Hal Roach as part of a camera crew; he had helped to photograph Rex the wild horse with the compact, rugged Eyemo camera and had befriended the Comanche Indians.

Stevens wanted to make *Shooting Star* as accurate and realistic as possible; period books and magazines were used to inspire the look of the picture. More than three hundred Indians, recruits from the reservations of the Southwest, were hired by Jim Thorpe, America's Indian athlete, for the picture. Archival photographs, lent by Oakley's brother, of Annie Oakley enabled Stevens to reproduce her inspiring feats shooting pennies from the hand of an assistant and puncturing the aces on cards pitched high into the air; other photographs, owned by a bronco rider, trick roper, and arena director who toured with Buffalo Bill for fourteen years, authenticated various scenes.

Preston Foster was Toby Walker, the sharpshooting star of Buffalo Bill's

Wild West who outshoots Annie, falls in love with her, and pretends to be her dead-shot rival. Foster had worked with Barbara two years before in *Ladies They Talk About*. He had just starred in five successive pictures for RKO, among them *The Informer, The Arizonan,* and *The Last Days of Pompeii*. Melvyn Douglas was Buffalo Bill's talent scout who brings Annie Oakley into the troupe and falls in love with her. Douglas had appeared on the stage in Belasco's *Tonight or Never* and was brought to Hollywood by Samuel Goldwyn to make a picture from the same play with Gloria Swanson.

Stevens liked his actors to sit and discuss the characters and read through the script. Barbara played Annie as the unassuming country girl unaware of just how extraordinary her ability is: guileless, full of optimism, going about her business modestly, yet a legend to everyone in the country and beyond. Stevens liked the women of his pictures to be good, simple, true.

In Joel Sayre and John Twist's script, unlike the historic story, Annie would rather lose the shooting match against Toby Walker than have him risk losing his job. Barbara's characterization had the same girlish openness, simplicity, and innocence that she used with Edna Ferber's Selina Peake in *So Big*.

When one of the crew, a former member of Buffalo Bill's troupe, first saw Barbara as Annie Oakley on the RKO lot, he could have sworn he was "seeing 'Little Sure Shot' again in the flesh, except for the color of her hair."

Much of *Shooting Star* was filmed at the RKO Encino Ranch as well as the Tarzana Golf Course. For the spectacular re-creations of Buffalo Bill's Wild West, the studio rented space on the Prudential Studios lot across the street and built an arena.

Barbara was exhilarated to be in the midst of the production. Stevens was a gentleman who brought out the best of his actors. His parents had been a leading acting team; his first memory was of actors. Barbara thought Stevens "kind, gracious, patient, an excellent director." "He was quiet," she said, "serious, wonderfully gentle, and in the flush of excitement about *Alice Adams*. It's always nice to have somebody happy with their work."

Barbara's sister Maud went to the studio each day, even accompanying Barbara on location shooting. Barbara was frightened of Fay and what he might do to her. Charles Cradick, their attorney, had worked out a property settlement with Fay and a visitation agreement regarding Dion.

Barbara had paid for most of the house at 441 Bristol and the furnishings, the books, the cars. She didn't want any of it. Fay could keep it all.

It was arranged for Fay to see Dion once a week. Nellie was to bring the boy to 441 Bristol in the morning, stay with him during the day, and return with him at the end of the afternoon.

In late August, Fay went to work at Warner Bros. for two days making a picture from a story by Mildred Cram that was starring the popular singer and tenor James Melton and Jane Froman, both radio personalities making their screen debuts. It was the first film work Fay had had in five years, since making *A Fool's Advice*. Zeppo had arranged with Warner Bros. for Fay to appear in *Stars over Broadway* for $1,000; Warner was to make out a check in Zeppo Marx's name so there would be no record of Fay receiving the money—this because of the outstanding IRS liens on Bristol Avenue and Barbara's and Fay's bank accounts.

In exchange for giving Fay the part in *Stars over Broadway*, Warner Bros. was free to release *A Fool's Advice*—it had purchased the rights to Fay's film in 1932—in any manner Jack Warner wanted. Fay had sold the studio the picture on condition that it be released under the Warner Bros. banner. Once Jack Warner actually screened it, he decided it couldn't be released under the agreed-upon terms. Albert Warner couldn't even remember what they'd done with it. Now that the studio was free to sell *A Fool's Advice* any way it saw fit, the picture's title was changed to *Meet the Mayor* and was sold for $5,000 to a film distributor in Chicago. Warner was to get 50 percent of the gross receipts once the distributor, B. N. Judell, had recouped his initial payment.

William Keighley—a favorite director of Hal Wallis's—was at work on *Stars over Broadway* from the Jerry Wald and Julius Epstein backstage script. Keighley had directed *G-Men* and Barbara in *Ladies They Talk About*. He was a pleasant man but didn't have the humor of a Busby Berkeley, who, with Bobby Connolly, was overseeing the musical numbers of *Stars over Broadway*. Fay was playing the radio announcer.

At work on the Warner lot were Mervyn LeRoy, directing Kay Francis in *I Found Stella Parish;* Bette Davis, Franchot Tone, and Margaret Lindsay shooting *Hard Luck Dame;* Paul Muni in *Enemy of Man;* Errol Flynn and Olivia de Havilland, paired for the swashbuckling *Captain Blood* (when they first met—he, twenty-five, she, eighteen—de Havilland had been "struck dumb" by Flynn's looks, his bearing, his aura).

After two days of work in late August on *Stars over Broadway*, Fay went to New York to try out for Jack Curtis's production of *The Postman Always Rings Twice*, the same production in which James Cain originally wanted Barbara to star. Cain had been at work on the script for a year. Barbara had decided against taking the part; she needed to have money coming in. It would have taken the Theatre Guild six months to get the play ready, cast, and into production, and Barbara didn't have the luxury, she said, of waiting "around that long."

One of the objects of Fay's hate, President Roosevelt, in June 1934, had appointed a committee to come up with proposals for comprehensive social security legislation that would include an old-age pension system, workmen's compensation, national health insurance, and unemployment insurance.

Shortly after Roosevelt took office in March 1933, he had made Frances Perkins his secretary of labor, the first woman to serve in a U.S. president's cabinet. Roosevelt wanted a comprehensive social security system that would protect Americans from "the cradle to the grave." He told Perkins: "I see no reason why every child, from the day he is born, shouldn't be a member of the social security system. When he begins to grow up, he should know he will have old-age benefits direct from the insurance system to which he will belong all his life. If he is out of work, he gets a benefit. If he is sick or crippled, he gets a benefit." Five years before, Roosevelt as governor had signed into being New York State's Old Age Security Act.

Roosevelt believed hunger and unemployment in America were "personal affronts." He wanted the Social Security Act to be a joint federal-state program financed by an "offset" tax that allowed states to collect 90 percent of the tax themselves and run their own programs; the retirement insurance was financed by a new federal payroll tax of 1 percent.

Roosevelt cautioned Americans, "A few timid people, who fear progress, will try to give you new and strange names for what we are doing," he said in a fireside chat. Sometimes they will call it 'Fascism,' sometimes 'Communism,' sometimes 'Regimentation,' sometimes 'Socialism.' But, in so doing, they are trying to make very complex and theoretical something that is really very simple and very practical . . .

"I believe that what we are doing today is a necessary fulfillment of what Americans have always been doing—a fulfillment of old and tested American ideals."

Roosevelt wasn't interested in "piecemeal" social security legislation. Harry Hopkins, director of the Federal Surplus Relief Administration and the Works Progress Administration, had hoped that "with one bold stroke we could carry the people with us for sickness and health insurance." The American Medical Association denounced the notion of national health insurance as "socialized medicine," as Roosevelt had predicted.

In early August 1935, after making its way through Congress, the Social Security Act—what was left of the original legislation—was signed into law by the president. To get southern support for the bill, congressional leaders drafted the law to deny coverage to many who needed it the most, farm laborers and domestic workers. But it was set up in a way to withstand the test of politics. "We put those payroll contributions there," said Roosevelt, "so as to give the contributors a legal, moral and political right to collect their pensions and their unemployment benefits. With those taxes in there, no damn politician can ever scrap my social security program."

Fay believed that anyone who voted for Roosevelt was a son-of-a-bitch Communist.

Barbara and Fay's separation was unknown to the press. After years of defying Hollywood's predictions that the Fay-Stanwyck marriage wouldn't last, Barbara was not ready to publicly admit that "they"—the Hollywood gossips—had been right. The Fays were still linked at social functions such as the opening night of the Shubert Festival at the Shrine Civic Auditorium of Noël Coward's operetta *Bitter Sweet*.

When the news of the Fay-Stanwyck separation finally leaked out, Barbara said to the press, "I feel that we are better apart."

Fay said, "We are still together under the same roof."

Fay was sure Barbara would come back to him; it was a matter of time.

The *Shooting Star* crew was on location. It was before lunch. Barbara was about to sit down and paused midair as she looked down and saw a tarantula on the ground next to her foot. Her screams pierced the quiet of the forest where they were shooting. A propman killed the spider. Barbara was shaken up and couldn't eat. "I'm scared stiff of snakes, spiders, flies, of anything that crawls," she said. It took hours before she was able to calm down.

"I'm only brave when I'm being paid for it," she said.

At heart Barbara was deeply shaken about Fay: his uncontrollable violence toward her, the way she'd had to flee Bristol Avenue, and the desperate end of their marriage.

Barbara's hairdresser on the picture—a hairdresser on the RKO lot—was Hollis Barnes. Barbara didn't pay attention to how her hair looked; she left its design to Holly, who studied the costuming, the period, and the character of Annie Oakley and came up with her own hairstyles using hot curlers or pin curls. To Holly, Barbara had thick, wonderful auburn hair that could take any kind of set or do anything she wanted with it.

With Hollis (Holly) Barnes, Barbara's hairdresser at RKO, who became her secretary and close friend, 1935. Holly's younger sister, Louise, also a hairdresser at RKO, did Ginger Rogers's hair, including bleaching it blond each week. Louise started cutting hair at age fifteen, and taught Holly as well.

Barbara felt comfortable with Holly and had Holly pick her up each morning on the way to work and drop her off at home at night.

Holly's sister, Louise, also a hairdresser at RKO, did Ginger Rogers's hair, including bleaching it blond each week. Rogers's hair was so curly that Louise had the RKO prop department make rollers for her using door screening that she covered with flannel to protect the scalp when straightening her hair.

Holly and her husband, Jimmy Barnes, were drinkers, as were Louise and her husband, Lloyd Nobles, a paymaster at 20th Century–Fox. Holly, like Fay, could get nasty when drunk. Even when sober, Holly could be ornery and had no problem telling people what she thought.

Soon Barbara was confiding in Holly, and they began to run lines together. Barnsie became Barbara's secretary and constant companion.

• • •

Alice Adams premiered two weeks into production of *Shooting Star.* Katharine Hepburn came onto the set of *Shooting Star* one day in a burst of excitement to tell George Stevens about the notices for his first big picture. James Agee of *Time* magazine had called Hepburn's performance "a masterpiece." Agee said that Stevens was "the youngest important director in Hollywood" and called his direction of *Alice Adams* "almost flawless."

Barbara was furious at the intrusion. Hepburn was stunned at Barbara's response and fled the set. Minutes after the disruption, Hepburn apologized to Barbara for "butting in . . . I can quite sympathize with your reception of me . . . at my own gaucherie. Please forgive and try to forget my lack of tact . . . I admire you too much to have you remember me as a complete fool."

Alice Adams crowned Katharine Hepburn's career in pictures; she was now the star on the RKO lot.

Barbara needed *Shooting Star* to be successful. Her work was admired by critics, had been called "magnificent." But the feeling from reviewers was that she had been "an invalid in pictures . . . with a chronic attack of bad stories," that she'd been wasted in "light society flim flams or shoddy underworld tales." *Shooting Star* was seen as a picture that could "bring [Barbara] back . . . reestablish her as one of the screen's dramatic actresses . . . and one of the biggest box office bets."

After the completion of the picture, Barbara wanted to get away to the desert so she wouldn't "bother anyone. There's nothing so boring to people," she said, "as a moping woman," and she "didn't want to be a bore."

"It's hard when you've trusted someone for years," she said, "believed in someone implicitly, to find out it's all a bubble and yourself the sucker."

Barbara, Dion, and her brother, By, went to the B-Bar-H Ranch in Palm Springs. The ranch owner's little girl was Dion's age, and the children played together as Barbara tried to rest and clear her head and enjoy having her brother back in America and living with her.

Byron loved the sea and had traveled the world—to the Orient, then lived in England—but he was sensitive to Barbara's being hurt. She'd played on his sympathies to get him to come to California and had persuaded him to move in with her and Dion. Byron loved the beach and spent his days by the water in Malibu or Newport.

During Barbara's time away in Palm Springs, her determination of the past two years to make things right with Fay, at any price, lifted. She thought about his constant badgering and questioning of her, about his jealousy and their repeated arguments. "More than beauty or 'having fun' or brains or fame, men want sincerity from women," Barbara said. "Men ask women

With her brother, By, and Dion at the B-Bar-H Ranch Palm Springs, recuperating from Frank Fay, 1935. (COURTESY TONY FAY)

'but do you really mean it? Are you telling me the truth? Can I depend on what you say?' over and over again. They want to be convinced of sincerity. They are like children appealing to their mothers for assurance that all is well and as it seems to be. It's rather pathetic, really, this need for stability in an unstable world."

It "ate away" at Barbara that "a ton of bricks had to fall on [her] head before" she understood what she had to do. She'd been in love with Fay, and "when a woman is in love," said Barbara, "her famous instinct goes to pot. Emotion makes her believe only what she wants to believe, to see in the man only what she wants to see."

"Love floors women," said Barbara. "Independent, strong-minded women go down like blades of grass in a story when they're in love. We lose our wits. We lose our sense of humor. Women who had battled life with their bare hands; women who have faced joblessness and hunger and death and illness and all of the major catastrophes and faced them standing up, collapse, fall to pieces, turn to water when they fall in love. It hits them between the eyes and takes the heart right out of them and plays ball with it."

Her bewilderment about Fay and how things had turned so ugly began to fade. It became clear that she had to file for divorce.

Barbara saw that "the only safe test at all is *time*—give enough time to any person or emotion," she said, "and you'll get the answer eventually, one way or the other. Sometimes it takes years—and if you get the breaks that's swell and if you find yourself a sucker there's nothing you can do about it but take it on the chin."

Zeppo was able to negotiate a new contract for Barbara with Radio for three pictures with options, to be made during the course of a year. The first picture, *Volcano,* written by Adele Buffington, was being turned into a script by Rian James. The recently formed 20th Century–Fox wanted Barbara for a picture called *A Message to Garcia,* based on a true story of high adventure, a critical moment in history involving an urgent dispatch from President William McKinley to a revolutionary leader "in the mountain vastness" of Cuba, on the eve of the Spanish-American War.

Barbara arranged for Morgan Maree, her business adviser, to set up trust funds and annuities on her behalf. She never intended to be as financially desperate as she had been when she was Mrs. Frank Fay.

TEN

Scar Tissue

An early version of *A Message to Garcia,* made by Edison in 1916 and filmed on location in Cuba, was based on the inspirational essay of the same title by the writer and publisher Elbert Hubbard ("Life is just one damned thing after another"). The essay had been published in 1899 and was known to tens of millions of readers. "Someone said to the President, 'There is a fellow by the name of Rowan will find Garcia for you, if anybody can.' Rowan was sent for and given a letter to be delivered to Garcia. How the 'fellow by the name of Rowan' took the letter, sealed it up in an oil-skin pouch, strapped it over his heart, in four days landed by night off the coast of Cuba from an open boat, disappeared into the jungle, and in three weeks came out on the other side of the island, having traversed a hostile country on foot, and delivered his letter to Garcia, are things I have no special desire now to tell in detail. The point that I wish to make is this: McKinley gave Rowan a letter to be delivered to Garcia; Rowan took the letter and did not ask, 'Where is he at?' "

Elbert Hubbard died on the *Lusitania* a year prior to the making of the Edison picture.

Ten days before production was to begin on the 20th Century–Fox remake of *A Message to Garcia,* Barbara's lawyer, Charles Cradick, served Fay with a summons to appear in superior court. Barbara was suing Fay for divorce and asking for custody of Dion. The complaint charged Fay with "grievous mental suffering" and harassment over trivial matters that resulted in Barbara becoming "extremely nervous and ill and . . . unable to properly attend to her various duties." The court date was set for the end of December.

Barbara had rented a house at 707 North Arden and then moved to a small house with English gardens in Beverly Hills at 615 North Bedford Drive across from Marion and Zeppo.

Barbara stayed home at night. During the day, she went to bookstores in a simple tailored suit with a no-nonsense hat pulled low over her face and bought as many books as she could. Reading assuaged Barbara's loneliness; it always had.

Before Fay went to New York, Nellie Banner brought Dion to 441 Bristol as agreed on, though Fay paid little attention to the four-year-old boy. Nellie would bring Dion to the house by 9:10 in the morning. On one visit Frank told Nellie to come back at five in the afternoon. She insisted that she stay with the boy, to which Fay replied, "Get the hell out of the house." Nellie was terrified and left. Dion could be made so upset and nervous by visiting his father that he would be sick for a week.

Often, when Nellie brought Dion to visit, Frank left the house at ten in the morning and wouldn't return until four in the afternoon. At other times, Fay might be friendly to the boy until Nellie left, then he would ignore the child. After a couple of months, Fay asked Dion about "Mommy's house" and what was going on there and whom she was seeing at night. "Did you go to church last Sunday and what did you wear?" Dion stared at his father as he was asked one question after another. The boy didn't answer Fay's questions except to reply that he had worn his raincoat to church. Fay wasn't satisfied and asked Dion the same questions over and over again.

The script for Zanuck's *Message to Garcia,* by W. P. Lipscomb and Gene Fowler, used the Elbert Hubbard essay, as well as an account by Colonel Andrew Summers Rowan, *How I Carried the Message to Garcia,* published in 1922. The Spanish minister in Washington let it be known to 20th Century–Fox that if the picture was "in the least bit considered offensive to Spanish-speaking people," all of Zanuck's films would be banned in Spain.

The picture takes place before the Spanish-American War. Rebels in Cuba are fighting for independence from Spain. Leading the guerrilla warfare is General Garcia. The battleship *Maine* is blown up, and President McKinley makes the decision to send men to Cuba to support Garcia and to go to war against Spain.

For Zanuck and Gene Fowler, McKinley's letter to Garcia and getting it to him, which changed the destiny of three nations, had all the elements of great adventure: a courageous American officer in the line of duty carrying a fateful message telling a rebel leader where American forces will land to join him and his troops in their just fight; a president of the United States poised to send in an army; a perilous mission through death-ridden jungles and a maze of danger to the battle lines of a rebel camp; spies betraying spies; guerrilla

Wallace Beery (left) as Sergeant Dory ("His loveable villainy was never more uproarious," said the 20th Century-Fox ad for the picture) and John Boles as Lieutenant Rowan crossing a swamp-infested Cuba on his daring mission to deliver *A Message to Garcia,* 1936. Rowan's actual journey to Garcia's camp was considered at the time to be one of the most gallant and brilliant exploits in U.S. military history. (PHOTOFEST)

executions; near escapes; alligator-infested swamps; and the passionate love between a guerrilla warrior's daughter and a courageous American soldier.

John Boles was the man delivering the message. Zanuck saw the character "as a cross between Franchot Tone and Warner Baxter, or an American Ronald Colman . . . with all the attributes of a West Pointer, an intense patriot with a fierce determination to carry through all his work; he's a soldier no matter how he is dressed."

Wallace Beery was the illiterate, conscienceless scoundrel who betrays each side for the other, who agrees to take the American soldier to Garcia's closest lieutenant, the only man who knows the whereabouts of Garcia's camp and who will escort the American to Garcia. The Beery character for Zanuck was "always looking for some new form of larceny with which to turn a dishonest dollar." Beery looked the part, exactly as Zanuck had envisioned him: "close cropped hair, bull neck, broken hands and overhanging gut." Beery was funny on-screen and a big draw with moviegoers, but in life he was seen as a tough old grouchy son of a bitch.

Zanuck's idea was for the clash of the two men to be the center of the pic-

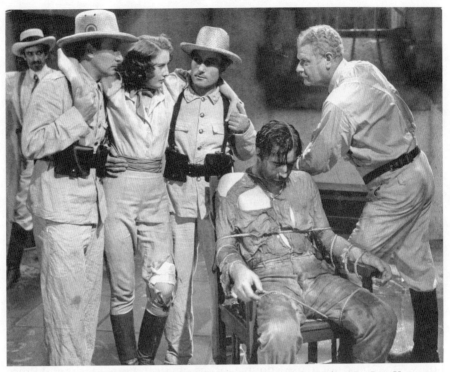

As Señorita Raphaelita Maderos, with Boles (tied up) and Alan Hale as Dr. Ivan Krug.

ture, in which each man comes to respect the other: the American with breeding and a sense of honor, determined to see his job through, chancing death and the perpetual top sergeant adrift in Cuba who believes in nothing—his flag, principles; a gunrunner and deserter; a murderer who would do anything for money and as the buffoon-like, gluttonous, lovable guide who sells out each side against the other and ultimately saves the American soldier and the Cuban rebel daughter.

Barbara was the daughter of Garcia's adjutant who witnesses her father's execution and agrees to take the American soldier to Garcia's hiding place. ("My father died for his country," she tells the American, "can I do any less?")

Zanuck wanted Roy Del Ruth to direct the picture following *Thanks a Million,* from one of his stories and a Nunnally Johnson script. Instead, Zanuck put Del Ruth on *It Had to Happen* with George Raft and Rosalind Russell. Zanuck considered John Ford for *Garcia* once the director returned from a holiday in Florida. Instead, he put Ford on *The Prisoner of Shark Island* and gave *Garcia* to George Marshall, a longtime Fox director who'd just directed *The Crime of Dr. Forbes.* Marshall had been at the studio since 1925, in the days when it was the William Fox Vaudeville Company.

Zanuck borrowed Beery from Metro for $75,000 instead of Beery's usual $6,000 a week. Of Louis B. Mayer and Metro, Beery said, "You can't tell nothing to this god-damned studio. Louis B. Mayer, why he was a god-damned blacksmith. He would blow up ships in the Boston Harbor. He's full of shit and we're working for him. How do you like that?"

For the part of the rebel daughter, Zanuck had originally wanted Simone Simon and then planned to put her in a remake of *Under Two Flags,* an adaptation of the successful stage play about the French Foreign Legion based on the novel by Ouida. Zanuck used Claudette Colbert for the part of Cigarette, a part for which Barbara had been suggested and that Zanuck had dismissed; he felt Barbara was "too American in appearance" and that the "French accent she would have to assume for the role . . . would be bad for her as well as for ourselves."

For the role of the rebel daughter, Barbara had to speak Spanish and began to take lessons with the technical director François De Valdes. Barbara had to wear boots and riding britches throughout the picture and went on a celery diet to lose weight in her hips and thighs, eating celery salads, celery soup, cooked celery, and celery stalks.

During the making of the picture, Barbara was in muddy water for hours—she chose not to use a double for the physical shots—as she and Boles were shown fleeing the Spanish army in the swamps of the Cuban interior.

Rita Cansino was to play Barbara's sister because of her fluency in Spanish and English; Zanuck instead put her in *Paddy O'Day.*

The rebel daughter of *Garcia* was a small part, but that made no difference to Barbara. "When you're in a picture with two other stars like John Boles and Wally Beery, you can't expect to have your part dominate theirs." She was just grateful "to Mr. Zanuck," she said, "for his confidence in her."

And for the work.

Fay's picture *Stars over Broadway* opened in mid-November. Louella Parsons called it "topnotch" and told her readers it was not to be missed. She noted that Fay had returned to the screen "after a long absence."

Capra called Fay a genius. "He can dominate any audience," he said. "He can do what he likes with them—in person. But he does it by superiority. By being bigger and smarter and faster than his audience. He's fresh and superior. That's great in the theater or a night club. But for some reason it just won't work in pictures. Picture audiences resent it."

Fay, the once Favorite Son of Broadway, left for New York on Thanksgiving. The government had slapped another tax lien on Barbara and Fay for asserted arrears of $22,000 each.

• • •

Runaway Daughter, retitled *Red Salute,* opened in New York at the Rivoli Theatre, which showed it with a Mickey Mouse cartoon, *Pluto's Judgement Day.* The main attraction was greeted with protests from the antiwar National Student League, who picketed in front of the theater giving out handbills and calling for a boycott of the picture because of its anti-left-wing politics.

The New York Times leveled the picture, describing it as "one of the weirdest exhibits to come out of Hollywood since that wartime masterpiece, 'The Beast of Berlin.' With the subtlety of a steamroller and the satirical finesse of a lynch mob, the film goes in for some of the most embarrassing chauvinism of the decade." The reviewer, however, thought the Mickey Mouse cartoon "brilliant . . . [s]uperb in its craftsmanship and endearingly comic" and said it "ought to win a place among the distinguished films of the year."

Picketing against *Red Salute* continued on the East Coast. In New York more than a hundred people—half of them young women—were arrested. In Baltimore students from Johns Hopkins and Goucher College presented the manager of the Baltimore Loew's Century with a petition denouncing the picture. In New Orleans, picketers from the American League Against War and Fascism carried posters declaring the film war propaganda approved by W. R. Hearst ("Who got us into the Spanish American War?" the posters read).

President Roosevelt was fishing off the coast of California and asked the Hays Office to send a print of the movie along with nineteen other pictures, among them *Shanghai, Reckless, Bright Lights,* and *The Call of the Wild.*

Shooting Star, now called *Annie Oakley,* opened in December for Christmas while Barbara was at work on *A Message to Garcia.*

A month before *Annie Oakley* opened, Barbara and Preston Foster appeared as guests on Louella Parsons's radio broadcast and performed a scene from the picture.

At an advance showing of *Annie Oakley* at the Pantages, the preview cards were mostly positive. "Authentic atmosphere—all the glamour of the wild Wild West, good love, comedy angles, a fine cast." "Stanwyck never better," said another. "Stanwyck was so natural, unaffected, charming and yet subtle with fine technique."

"A picture worthy of her talents," said Carol Frink in the *Chicago Herald and Examiner.* "Miss Stanwyck [as Annie Oakley] has a chance to exploit her own most salient characteristics; her forthright honesty and tenacious loyalty; her genuine simplicity and level-headedness." *Variety* was not as taken with the picture or with Stevens's direction. "If the picture misses as outstanding," said the reviewer, "it's because the script and direction are not up to the star."

• • •

Barbara was now one of the leading actors at RKO, along with Fred Astaire, Ginger Rogers, Katharine Hepburn, William Powell, Ann Harding, and Irene Dunne. The studio relied heavily on its featured players, who included Preston Foster, Gene Raymond, Anne Shirley, Helen Westley, Lucille Ball, Betty Grable, and Margaret Hamilton.

The only thing Barbara wanted to do was work. She was lonely and broke. She had devoted herself to Fay with all of her intensity and will for seven years. When she fled in August, she'd left everything behind, everything they'd built together, along with her possessions—clothes, jewelry, furs, the first editions and silver she'd collected, the antiques. The property. Possessions never interested Barbara, and she learned early not to cling to them.

She still loved Frank, and to get over him, she had to "somehow kill time," she said. "To kill the time that must inevitably elapse between now and the time when scar tissue will have formed over my hurt.

"I didn't want it to happen, but now that it has, I want to forget and I want to be allowed to forget."

Barbara was working hard and steadily, "but it's not enough," she said. "I want more. I want so much work that I won't have time to think."

She was alternating pictures between RKO and 20th Century–Fox. Her next picture was for RKO, called *Volcano*. Rian James had written the treatment fast, as requested, but was being held up waiting for story conferences to discuss the pages.

After *Volcano*, Barbara was to go into a remake of *Four Devils*, the F. W. Murnau picture made in 1929 about four orphans raised by a circus owner who forms a high-wire act, with Barbara in the Janet Gaynor role. Barbara was enchanted by the circus; she'd never been to it as a child, and the spectacle of it—and the clowns—seemed magical to her.

After *Four Devils*, Barbara was to go back to RKO for another picture and then "back [to Fox] again," she said. "I'm calendared right up to the hilt—and if I have my way, it'll be for months after that."

"Barbara may be exhausted when she finishes a picture," said Marion Marx, "but three days later she's asking Zeppo to hurry up and find another picture for her."

Barbara was set to make the John Ford picture *The Plough and the Stars* for RKO from the Sean O'Casey play with a script being written by Dudley Nichols. Production had been postponed; Radio Pictures was concerned its themes were too similar to Ford's *Informer* and that it would follow too soon after its release. Ford was going to make *Mary of Scotland* instead with Katharine Hepburn in the lead.

Through Zeppo, Barbara was being introduced to many new people: the Jack Bennys; Moss Hart; Alexander Woollcott, who wrote to Barbara just before Christmas to thank her for flowers she'd sent him and to wish her luck in 1936.

In between working, Barbara went to the movies.

Fay was in New York performing.

On the day before Christmas, Fay wired $50 to his housekeeper, Paget Lloyd, with instructions to buy Christmas presents for his mother, his father, Dion, and herself. Lloyd bought Dion a ski suit and had it delivered to Barbara's.

Fay phoned his housekeeper from New York four times a week; each call costing $50. He didn't ask about Dion or the present Lloyd had picked out for him, only if Lloyd had seen Barbara or heard anything from her.

Christmas came and went, and days after it Barbara appeared in superior court at 9:30 in the morning wearing dark glasses. She took the stand before Judge Dudley S. Valentine and testified to the many arguments she'd had with Fay. Barbara, in a tailored suit and a fedora, was composed as she recounted the litany of explosive fights they'd lived through.

"It was mostly during the time when I was working," she said. "I would come home and find him very sullen and cool toward me. He wouldn't talk to me. He would argue almost throughout the entire night about some unimportant matter so much that I could not sleep."

Judge Valentine listened to Barbara's testimony. Her voice quavered. "Fay [treated] my friends as coolly and his conduct caused me to become nervous and lose weight," she said.

The judge granted Barbara an interlocutory decree of divorce and custody of her son. The judgment also said that Fay would "have the right to visit with said child at such reasonable times and places as the parties hereto may agree from time to time." Barbara wanted no alimony. Fay had little money. The money to be had was hers.

"When it comes to men and women," said Barbara, "there is some equation between the sexes which makes for a natural enmity. If you fight a man he'll either call forth all of his latent cruelty and mastery and beat you down or he'll turn to some clinging beauty with a body which forgot to include brains. Or," she said, "if you start right out by surrendering your will to his he's apt to lose interest."

Barbara was twenty-eight; Fay almost forty-four. They'd married on August 26, 1928; she'd fled her marriage on August 6, 1935. The first Mrs. Fay had lasted two years; the second, three months. The third, who was the first, had wanted to try it again. Barbara was the fourth Mrs. Frank Fay in a marriage that she willed into lasting almost seven years.

ELEVEN

High Schemes and Misdemeanors

I know I have reached the stage where I wouldn't place my whole trust in any man. Not unreservedly," said Barbara. "I do trust women. I really believe that women are capable of disinterested friendship, of undivided loyalty, of keeping faith."

Barbara and Marion Marx were becoming the closest of friends. Barbara had Marion, who wanted the finest furniture for the finest home, decorate her new house. Marion filled Barbara's house with Early American maple furniture, antique samplers, and ruffled glazed chintz draperies, all done according to Barbara's wishes and Marion's taste.

Marion's attitude about life was based on money, prestige, and whom you knew. It mattered to her how much money one had and how important someone was. Marion shopped for Barbara's clothes since Barbara rarely went on her own. "Partly because I haven't the time," she said. "And partly because I detest it anyway." Chic to Marion was a "matter of the mind . . . poise, self-confidence . . . the knowledge that [one is] correctly attired to suit [one's] own individuality." Without sophistication, "I don't see how any one can be smartly dressed," she said.

When Marion and Barbara first met, Marion was alarmed at how unkempt Barbara looked. "You should have seen her hair," said Marion. Barbara was now wearing her auburn hair in a seventeen-inch bob and was proud that it was "the longest in town."

Without Fay in her life, Barbara was now free to indulge her whims, which extended to having her hair done three or four times a week. She had a self-described "complex" about clean, shining hair. "My hair is my only vanity," said Barbara, as well as a "mania for shoes."

Barbara loathed hats. Now and then she compromised and wore a beret, but that "usually came off" before she got home.

Marion Benda, later Marx, photographed by James Hargis Connelly, former Signal Corps photographer who set up a studio in Chicago in the 1920s, photographing dancers, singers, and actors. (COURTESY TIM MARX)

Marion and Barbara were looking more and more alike, though Barbara's stance was cockier; they even dressed alike.

Marion Marx, like Barbara, had appeared on the stage of the New Amsterdam Theatre in Ziegfeld's *Follies.* The former Marion Bimberg Benda and her sister, Jessica, both showgirls, were known on Broadway as "the beautiful Bimberg girls." Marion had appeared in *The Cocoanuts*—one of the Cocoanut Beach Octette—after the show left the Lyric Theatre and was playing at the Shubert. Before *Cocoanuts,* Marion had appeared in Ziegfeld's production of *Rio Rita* and his 1925 *Follies,* which featured Will Rogers and W. C. Fields, with Louise Brooks, Lina Basquette, Vivienne Segal, and Barbara's Ziegfeld pal Dorothy Van Alst.

Marion's heart-shaped face was framed by dark lustrous hair. Her luminous large eyes were set wide apart and like Barbara had a face that showed character and strength.

Marion had dated Rudolph Valentino for six months, but it was Zeppo who made her laugh and won her heart. Zeppo saw women in terms of conquests and pursued them as relentlessly as Chico, but to Zeppo, Marion was different. She was someone with whom he could pal around. She was spontaneous in the way Zeppo was.

For Marion's thirty-third birthday, Barbara insisted on taking her and Zeppo to dinner at the Trocadero. Marion walked into the restaurant—dressed somewhat for the occasion—and found 150 people there to celebrate her birthday. Barbara had taken over the restaurant without giving Marion a hint of what she'd planned.

Marion's father, Louis, had owned an oilcloth factory with his brother, Albert. In the early spring of 1914, when Marion was eleven, her father was arrested for conspiring to burn down the Bimberg factory—the American Oilcloth Company—for the insurance money. The plant manager was to destroy the building and be paid $10,000. The Bimberg brothers had their alibi planned: when the fire was discovered, the brothers would be on a train en route to White Plains, where they lived. The plant manager went along with the scheme until the last moment, when he turned in both men to the prosecutor's office. Louis Bimberg went to prison for ten years. When he got out, he returned to his family, who shunned him.

Years later Louis Bimberg killed himself at home. It was a family scandal involving homosexuality and Louis's romantic involvement with a sailor and a letter written in Chinese; Louis had committed suicide in the bathroom by stabbing himself in the stomach. Marion's mother renounced the Bimberg name and took back her maiden name of Miller. Marion changed her last name to Benda. Her brother, Alan, followed his mother's lead and changed his last name to Miller.

Marion and Zeppo were married in 1927 at the Hotel Chalfonte in New York City; *The Cocoanuts* was playing in Newark, and Marion was living on West Eighty-Sixth Street with her parents.

Zeppo, like most of the Marx brothers, had countless affairs. Marion knew about them but seemed unfazed. If another man looked at Marion, Zeppo became furious. There was the time when Marion and Zeppo were coming back from Hillcrest and stopped in Santa Monica to go on the carousel. A man started to flirt with Marion, and Zeppo, still in his golf shoes, chased him around the carousel.

Marion and Zeppo slept in separate bedrooms. "I can't stand to sleep all night with anybody," she said. "I just need my own space. I can't stand another person in the bed."

Marion liked to sit in the bathtub, a cigarette dangling from her mouth, and complete the toughest crossword puzzle in less than an hour. She was resourceful and, like Barbara, self-educated and a loyal friend. And, like Barbara, if she was crossed, the friendship was ended; there was no going back.

Fay was appearing on *The Fleischmann Yeast Hour* and on *The Magic Key of RCA,* making a hit with the popular "Darktown Strutters' Ball" ("I'll be down to get you in a taxi, honey").

With Barbara and Dion gone, Fay kept company at Bristol Avenue with professional boxers like Lou Nova and Slapsie Maxie Rosenbloom. Fay could still become enraged without provocation and start fistfights, which he frequently lost.

Fay had a new set of upper false teeth. The day after they were put in, he and his houseman, Albert Lloyd, went to a football game at the Memorial Coliseum in Los Angeles. Lloyd was told to speak on Fay's behalf to people he knew, to smile if anyone looked in Fay's direction, and to call their attention to him. Fay was sober when he asked this of Lloyd. Lloyd knew that Fay, drunk or sober, could become angry if his requests were ignored, so Lloyd bowed at people he didn't recognize and gestured toward Fay, as instructed. Fay smiled and showed off his new false teeth.

After the game, Fay and Lloyd went to the Brown Derby for dinner. At the restaurant, Ted Healy, comedian, former vaudevillian, originator of the Three Stooges, came over to the table and invited Fay and Lloyd to his house. They decided to go in one car; Healy's business agent was driving. As they approached Santa Monica Boulevard, Fay, in the backseat, leaned forward and called Healy's agent "a dirty Jew son of a bitch."

"Don't talk like that," said Healy. "He's a nice fellow and he hasn't done anything to you."

"I am going to knock you on your ass," Fay warned Healy.

Healy had his agent stop the car. They were in front of a gas station.

Fay and Healy got out of the car.

"Put up your dukes," Fay said to Healy. "I'm going to knock you right on your ass."

Fay swung his fist at Healy's face. Healy dodged the blow and struck Fay in the mouth. Fay's upper false teeth went flying onto the ground.

"He's knocked my teeth out," cried Fay.

Healy's agent got out of the car to help Fay look for his new teeth. Two Beverly Hills police officers came over and ordered Healy and Fay to the Beverly Hills jail. The following morning both men were released. Fay went home and got drunk and stayed in a drunken stupor for weeks.

Barbara, now on her own, was unburdened, living life "as I please." She could shop, dance, "cut up" if she wanted. It was Barbara, Dion, Buck Mack, and her brother, By. Fay no longer controlled her or told her how to dress, whom to see.

She had longed for a house in which she could do what she wanted without causing anyone apoplexy—put her feet on the chairs, spill ashes on the rugs. She wanted white walls and colonial fixtures, colorful colors and comfortable chairs, divans and rugs. "I can move that lamp there over

Barbara with her brother, By, and son, Dion,
1935. (COURTESY OF TONY FAY)

here if I want to—and there is no-one to give me a black look of disapproval."

The living room of her Beverly Hills house was all greens and browns
and blues against white walls. The only photograph was of Dion. French
windows looked out on a garden where Barbara's four-year-old son would
play with his nurse.

Barbara went out when she wanted and came in when she pleased. "I entertain or do not entertain as I feel inclined," she said.

She had so many dogs that she had to take up the carpets and get rid of
various chairs. A visitor walked into her house, looked around at the lack of
rugs and chairs, and asked, "Housecleaning?"

"No, dogs," said Barbara. "Don't sit there. The dogs have just about
chewed the legs off of that chair too. It'll crash the next time anyone sits on
it. I'm saving it for a producer."

In the midst of her dog menagerie was a Persian cat called Velvet who
could stand on her hind legs indefinitely.

With James Cagney and Alice Faye, circa 1936.

Barbara had emerged from the darkness of her life with Fay. She was consoled by the presence of her son. "I'm glad I've got *him* left," she said. "I don't know what I'd do without him. Thank God he's got a sense of humor. I have my own ideas about Dion and can put them into practice unmolested."

Barbara wanted to travel with her little boy, to live in different parts of the world "to see what it's all like," she said. "Twice I've gotten as far as Pasadena on my way to Europe." That's what happened when she made plans. "So I'm not making them anymore," she said.

She felt free. "There's such romance in living my own life as I wish to live it," she said. "And it's dangerous because no woman can live in marriage this way. Perhaps, no one can live this way, for long, safely. There's such passion in peace, that I can't believe it isn't dangerous. And even if it is, life *is* dangerous."

Barbara was relieved her brother was living with her. By was a plain man, simple, elegant, gallant, charming. He was well-spoken with a slight English accent. By's travels, leaving Barbara behind when she was a child, haunted her.

He talked to Barbara softly, calling her "love" or "dear"; his presence calmed her. He didn't speak harshly or get angry the way she could. Once Barbara started to get angry, she couldn't stop and wouldn't be calmed down. Byron was gentle, sensitive, but strong. Barbara worshipped her brother as a child, and she worshipped him still. He was her idea of a man.

Carole Lombard circa 1932, around the time she was making Wesley Ruggles's *No Man of Her Own,* costarring Clark Gable, from Val Lewton's novel *No Bed of Her Own,* purchased originally by Paramount for Gable and Miriam Hopkins.

Byron, at thirty, was six feet two. His hair had changed from blond to silver. Other than the red cast of Barbara's hair, she and By resembled each other; they had the same wry sense of humor; each loved to read. By looked distinguished; Barbara, girlish, sometimes tomboyish; together they made a handsome couple.

Barbara bought By clothes to wear as her escort. She gave him money and was trying to get him work as an extra. By, like their father, drank heavily. He had many girlfriends and brought them home to Barbara's, which made her angry. Barbara was possessive of her brother and questioned him about whom he was seeing. She was sure that one day he'd "get shot in the tail from so much running around."

Barbara came home one evening and walked into her living room to find By entwined with Alice Faye.

"Have you ever heard of knocking?" By said later.

"You're in my house," she yelled back.

"I'm not married to you," he said. "You're my sister."

He threatened to move out, and did. But Barbara begged him to return, and he relented.

Fay was in New York and phoned Barbara.

"I don't care to listen to anything you have to say," she said and hung up.

A few minutes later the phone rang again. Barbara asked her brother to answer it.

"If it's Fay," she told By, "tell him I don't want to talk with him."

By told Frank not to call again; it was upsetting Barbara, and she didn't want to talk to him.

The next day she changed her telephone number.

Barbara went out for the evening with the Marxes. Marion was three years older than Barbara and, like an older sister, watched out for her.

"Barbara is a moody person," said Marion. "I've never seen anyone whose spirits can go higher and lower in ten minutes time. She's intense about everything she does. And she has to be doing something every minute."

Marion's great friend was Carole Lombard, whom Marion adored. She thought Lombard was the most beautiful woman she'd ever met. Through Marion, Barbara came to know Carole and grew just as fond of her.

Men were wild about Carole and frightened of her. They thought she was promiscuous because of the way she talked. They'd give her champagne and expect to go to bed with her. Carole's response: "Why don't you go fuck yourself." One friend said of her, "She was flying all the time. Fast and light."

Barbara admired Carole for being such an extraordinary athlete. She was proficient in tennis, basketball, baseball, and boxing; she'd won medals in high school for sprinting and high-jumping, was an expert diver and crack shot, and had studied dance with Ruth St. Denis and Martha Graham. Barbara's brother, Byron, thought Carole the only woman he knew who could use rough language and sound like a lady; "she could say 'fuck,'" he said, "and make it sound like poetry."

People thought Carole was wild, an overbred, overtrained racehorse. She loved a laugh and was warmhearted, but there were those who felt that beyond the incessant gags and wisecracks, there was something of hers—a haunting terror—they wouldn't want inside them. They referred to her as "the profane angel"; she looked like a spirit and swore like a ditchdigger.

Carole may have talked a slangy American idiom all her own, but she was from a good family, from the Wilshire District, where Los Angeles society lived before Beverly Hills became popular. When a fortune-teller gave Jane Alice Peters, originally from Fort Wayne, Indiana, the name Carole Lombard, she told her it had to have an *e* on the end of it.

Lombard was hosting a White Mayfair gala for the Mayfair Club at the Victor Hugo in Beverly Hills, and Barbara went with the Marxes. In the spirit of the ball, Lombard, whose idea the evening was, wore white maline, with two bunches of artificial white flowers and a star sapphire the size of a hen's egg.

Six footmen bearing candelabra announced the 350 guests as they walked down the stairs. There were those with old money: Alfred Vanderbilt, Mr. and Mrs. Kyle Bellew, Coningsby Dawson, Mr. and Mrs. A. M. Botsford. And those with Hollywood money: W. R. Hearst, Marion Davies, Clark Gable, Mr. and Mrs. Harry Rapf, Helen Ferguson, B. P. Schulberg, Marquis and Marquise de Portago, Mr. and Mrs. W. S. Van Dyke, Mr. and Mrs. Harmon Nelson, Mr. and Mrs. Bing Crosby, Mr. and Mrs. Ernst Lubitsch.

The men wore white top hat, tie, and tails.

Merle Oberon was in a white studded dress with gold dots. Dolores Costello Barrymore wore a white wig with two white gardenias, white satin, and lace in Victorian fashion. Barbara was in a white ermine wrap with a shoulder cape of silver foxes. Norma Shearer was in red crepe.

Two months after Barbara's divorce decree, she was back in superior court, this time to answer a complaint filed against her by her former agent, Arthur Lyons, for $3,500 plus interest he claimed was due him as his commission for work he'd negotiated on Barbara's behalf during a two-year period.

Lyons and John McCormick each took the stand to testify about the negotiations the agency had conducted for Barbara. Then Barbara took the stand in her defense, followed by Buck Mack. Barbara maintained that she hadn't gone ahead with her contract at Paramount since the studio hadn't found a picture she'd wanted to do. Judge Charles Bogue listened to the testimony and dismissed the case.

Fay was in New York and appeared on NBC's *Royal Gelatin Hour.* Fay was the whole broadcast, including the plug for gelatin ("Buy lots of gelatin," he pleaded, "because if you don't, Frankie won't have a job"). He was on the air for the entire half hour with Eddie Kay and his orchestra. "The Great Faysie" was in top form—impish and winning and, even on radio, able to put over the famous Fay air of intimacy. *Variety* said, "It is a yeoman's task for a comedian to hold the interest for a half hour in person on a stage, it's doubly so in the abstract via mike transmission."

Royal Gelatin was pleased with the show and renewed Fay for an additional thirty weeks, changing the show's spot from Saturday to Friday at 8:30. It was a big boost for Fay, but he was more preoccupied with Barbara than with Royal Gelatin. In the past, whenever there'd been a row, Barbara had begged Fay to come back, and he knew she would again. Fay was sure things would be back to the way they were, despite the divorce. He'd married his first wife twice; why not his fourth.

Fay returned to Los Angeles determined to see Barbara. He devised a

Dion Fay, four years old, Bristol Avenue, 1936. (COURTESY TONY FAY)

plan. Before Dion arrived for one of his visits, Fay told his houseman, Albert
Lloyd, to get the car greased, the oil changed, the tank filled with gas, and to
put the top on.

"At four in the morning, we will be on our way across the state line," Fay
told Lloyd.

When Lloyd asked where they would be headed, Fay said, "I will tell you
once we get going."

"Don't you think we'll get into trouble?"

"No," said Fay. "I'll pretend to take the baby riding and as I am as much
entitled to the baby as she is, it cannot be called kidnapping."

Lloyd asked Fay why he was doing this. Fay's response: "It's my decoy, and
when I get the baby out of the state, she'll have to come to see me."

Lloyd told Paget, his wife and Fay's housekeeper for many years, to watch
at the front gate for the black Packard bringing Dion to the house and to
warn Nellie Banner and Bill, Barbara's chauffeur, of Fay's plan.

Lloyd drove Fay's car to the gas station, had the car greased, the oil changed, the tank filled, as Fay had asked, and returned the car to Bristol Avenue. Everything appeared to be in place for Fay's plan.

Dion's arrival time came and went.

Three hours later, Dion was still not at the house. Fay was in a rage. At mid-afternoon he called his former lawyer, Charles Cradick, who had acted as the Fays' lawyer for four years, taking care of everything from negotiating production contracts for *Tattle Tales* and Barbara's agreements with Warner Bros. and Columbia to representing Fay in court for various assault and drunk-driving charges; paying fees to the Internal Revenue Service and traffic fines to the court clerk at the Beverly Hills police station. Cradick had also advanced Fay thousands of dollars.

Now Cradick represented only Barbara.

He assured Fay that Dion would be at Bristol Avenue in the morning.

Early the next day, Fay told Lloyd to go to the airfield on West Pico Street and arrange for a private plane that could carry four passengers with a pilot ready to go at all times to fly from Los Angeles to Salt Lake City. When they left for the field, Lloyd was to call the pilot and tell him they were on their way.

Again Lloyd told his wife to go to the gate at the end of the driveway and warn Nellie of Fay's new plan, that Dion was still in danger.

Lloyd went through the motions of preparing for Fay's new scheme: going to the airport; hiring a pilot to take four passengers from Los Angeles to Salt Lake City and bring one or all back for $175. Lloyd returned to Bristol Avenue and told Fay the arrangements were set. Fay told his chauffeur, Nicholas Gyory, that once Dion arrived, he was to drive Lloyd, Fay, and Dion to the airport and bring the car back to the house.

Dion was to arrive at 9:00 a.m. Once again, Barbara's driver failed to deliver the boy to Bristol Avenue.

Fay, Lloyd, and Gyory waited in the library. By three o'clock Fay said, "It looks like the gag is off. Do you think the telephone has been tapped or that someone has placed a Dictograph in here and found out what I was going to do?"

Lloyd acted as if he were mystified by it all.

Fay had one of his servants search the house. He was convinced there was a tap in the fireplace in the library and had the servant look for wires or evidence of a Dictograph.

Barbara was unnerved by Fay's schemes. She stopped Dion's visits to Bristol Drive and started proceedings to legally change Dion's name from Fay to Dion Anthony Stanwyck.

TWELVE

This Side of the Sphinx

Marion and Zeppo were worried about Barbara. She refused to go out and be with people. On the rare occasions when she did, her escort was her brother.

The Marxes were going to a dinner party at the Trocadero given by the actor Walter Kane and asked Barbara to join them. One of the guests was Robert Taylor, Metro's new romantic sensation whose popularity was sweeping the country.

Taylor was handsome, beautiful in fact. His face was almost perfect, with a fulsome, ready smile. His olive skin set off the corn blue of his eyes; his dark brown hair was framed by an accentuated widow's peak.

Barbara and Bob spent the evening "talking shop," she said. "What else can you talk about to an actor?"

Barbara thought Bob was fun.

It was Universal's *Magnificent Obsession,* released three months before, that was causing the furor about Taylor and had caught Metro by surprise. Women moviegoers were finding Robert Taylor's beauty and vigor, energy and boyish gentleness, irresistible. His freshness and innocence gave him an air of the boy next door who grew up and made good; he had an aura of sophistication—the fancy clothes, pomaded hair—but there was a simplicity about him, a carefree sense of fun. Taylor walked with an energy, one hand in his trouser pocket, his coat tucked back just so. His stride was swift and eager, taking him up steps two at a time and down in jumps of three or four.

Barbara had seen Taylor in *Magnificent Obsession* and *Broadway Melody of 1936,* admired his work, and told him so.

Magnificent Obsession was the John Stahl picture from Lloyd C. Douglas's best-selling novel. In it Taylor was the selfish rich boy who becomes a great doctor in order to care for the woman—Irene Dunne—he accidentally blinds in a drunken selfish state and whom he comes to adore.

Robert Taylor circa 1935, age twenty-four. He was born
in Filley, Nebraska, on August 5, 1911; population as of
1910: 194. His family's wood-framed house was without
insulation and had a hand-pump for water, a wood- or coal-
burning stove, and an outhouse.

In the picture Taylor is warm, loving, dimensional. He ages from early
manhood to midlife and ably shows the maturation. Taylor saw Irene Dunne,
then thirty-seven years old, as "dignified." He had "felt the strength of her
great experience" and said that her "confident poise could not fail to help
anyone with whom she played." Taylor's assurance, agility, and depth surprised critics.

Women by the hundreds of thousands were fantasizing about Robert Taylor as the dream combination—the perfect lover (beautiful to look at, full of
spirit and play, cocky but not rough) and husband (knowing, presentable,
steady, caring). Robert Montgomery, frequently given the society playboy
roles, didn't have Taylor's prettiness. Montgomery's world-weary sophistication seemed acidic and faded next to Taylor's openness and purity.

Taylor with Irene Dunne, *Magnificent Obsession,* his eighth picture, 1935. Lloyd C. Douglas's novel was brought to John Stahl's secretary by Joel McCrea, who was tested for the part with Rosalind Russell. The director felt that neither actor was right and instead cast Taylor and Irene Dunne, then thirty-seven years old.

Women, who had been drawn to the dangerous rough-trade quality of Clark Gable or James Cagney's spitfire-like energy, saw in Taylor's beauty, openness, and loving affect a new romantic ideal. Following the release of *Magnificent Obsession* thousands of fan letters were delivered to Metro addressed to Robert Taylor written by women across the country, until ten thousand letters were arriving each week.

Magnificent Obsession was a sellout and played to held-over business, as did Taylor's next picture, *Broadway Melody of 1936,* from the Moss Hart story "Miss Pamela Thorndyke," in which Taylor danced with the rangy twenty-three-year-old Eleanor Powell in her first major picture and sang Nacio Herb Brown's "I've Got a Feelin' You're Foolin' " to June Knight.

Taylor was at work now on *Small Town Girl,* his twelfth picture in two years; William Wellman was directing.

Newspapers and magazines were pursuing Taylor; movie stars were demanding he be their leading man. Louella Parsons called him the most promising actor of the moment.

In the midst of all the fuss being made over Robert Taylor, he was still in awe of Clark Gable's rugged good looks and sex appeal; Nelson Eddy's voice; Spencer Tracy's acting. Everything that was happening to the twenty-four-year-old Taylor seemed mostly like luck.

During the dinner party at the Trocadero, Bob thought Barbara was "cute with her reddish hair; her tan, her figure"; that she was "quiet and hard to get." Taylor knew Barbara hadn't been out for some time, that it was the first time in seven years she'd been to a party and been paired off with a man.

Robert Taylor was self-possessed but self-effacing. His modesty impressed Barbara; he seemed so regular in the midst of the irregularity of Hollywood and the fuss being made about him.

Barbara noticed that Bob spent a good deal of the evening with his eye on the door. He asked Barbara to dance. Someone took a photograph of them walking out to the dance floor. Barbara enjoyed herself but didn't want to be written about by the press and didn't dance with Taylor again. Throughout the evening she referred to the actor as Mr. Taylor; he called her Miss Stanwyck. She was "non-committal," Taylor said, "the hardest gal to get talking this side of the Sphinx."

Barbara, ever cautious, saw no special reason to rave about Bob. She'd enjoyed herself and thought he seemed like "a good man." She was impressed with Bob "mainly because he was not impressed with himself," she said. She liked his unself-conscious modesty.

Bob had been voted the most popular movie star ahead of Nelson Eddy, Joan Crawford, Ginger Rogers, and Loretta Young. Clark Gable was eighth on the list; Greta Garbo, tenth; Fred MacMurray, eleventh.

During the previous five months Barbara had barely been open to the most "casual companionship of other people." She was "coming out of an emotional black hole of Calcutta," so to her Taylor seemed "hilarious."

He called her the next day. An item in the morning paper announced that Barbara Stanwyck "was being seen at all the night spots with Robert Taylor." Barbara and Bob joked on the phone about the mention in the columns and passed it off, though Barbara noted there was a "trace of uneasy formality in the conversation."

Bob asked if he could see Barbara; she put him off. Bob called repeatedly during the next few weeks. Barbara found excuses not to see him. The next time Bob called, Barbara's brother, By, answered the phone. When Bob asked what Barbara was doing, By suggested Bob come over.

Marion Marx had said to Bob that if he was going to ask Barbara out, he should suggest they go for a ride instead of going dancing.

Barbara and Bob sat for a while at her house, not saying much. "I felt like a school girl with her first date," Barbara said. Bob asked if she would like to go for a drive. She agreed to go.

Barbara wasn't drawn to Bob. Nor ostensibly he to her. He was in love with Irene Hervey, a Metro contract player.

During the drive, Bob told Barbara all about Irene. She was twenty-six, a California girl who, like Bob, had been picked by Ben Piazza, Metro's scout and casting director, and placed in Oliver Hinsdell's studio dramatic school. Bob and Irene had been seeing each other for quite a while, and Irene wanted to get married. Once the studio saw what it had in Bob Taylor, Mr. Mayer had made it clear that it was better for Bob's career to remain unmarried. It was more important for his fans to think of him as an "eligible bachelor" than it was for him to be married—and unavailable to women. Irene was impatient with the situation and had started to see Allan Jones. It was Irene and Jones that Bob had been watching for at the Trocadero the night of the Marxes' party.

Metro wanted to ensure that Bob was seen as a man-about-town, and the publicity department, under Howard Strickling, put out several stories about Bob's seeing other women, including Jean Parker, who appeared with him in *Murder in the Fleet;* Ginger Rogers; and Janet Gaynor, with whom he was finishing *Small Town Girl.* Irene was upset that Bob was giving in to the studio's demands.

Bob Taylor's feelings about Irene were clear, but so were his feelings about Mr. Mayer, whose words of advice so far had proven true. During Bob's drive with Barbara they talked of nothing else but his romantic and career problems.

Bob had been taken by surprise by all the hoopla about him. He went from a salary of $35 a week to $750. At the preview of his first major picture for Metro, *Society Doctor,* nobody had stirred when the lights went up. "They were waiting of course for L.B. to hint at his reaction," said Taylor. Mayer finally rose from his seat and marched up the aisle smiling. "The real clincher," said Bob, was when "Clark Gable, who was sitting about five rows in front of me, turned and gave me the 'OK' signal." Clark was Mr. Gable to Bob. "He set the style and the pace."

Louis B. Mayer was like a father to Bob, and he didn't want to be an ungrateful "son." Bob's own father had left the family grain business to study medicine late in life and had become a doctor in order to care for Bob's mother, whose weak heart and frail constitution had eluded available treatments. Bob saw up close the abiding love his parents had for each other. He admired his father's dedication, his return to medical school in his mid-thirties with classmates much younger than he in a field of medicine considered risky and out of the norm.

Bob saw his father graduate from medical school and saw the ways in which his treatments brought new vigor and strength to his mother. The smells of home and childhood emanated from his father's office and his mother's kitchen: "the warm mixed odors of iodoform, corn bread and hot chocolate." Bob, then Arly Brugh, had traveled with his father when he went to see patients. He saw how his father never showed anger, how he had an instinctive flair with people.

Spangler Arlington "Arly" Brugh was an only child who'd been given everything a boy could want and in return had been on his honor to be a good son. He was heartbroken when, four months after his graduation from Pomona College, his father died of cancer. Bob discovered that aside from some property and a small insurance policy his father was owed more than $25,000 in outstanding patient fees that he'd never tried to collect.

At twenty-two, Arly Brugh, who always had everything he wanted, "never thinking where it came from or wondering if you could have it," was now broke. As the head of the family, he tried to collect enough money from his father's former patients to cover funeral costs. He felt it his duty to remain in Beatrice, Nebraska, with his mother and found a job at an oil station. His mother, Ruth, insisted Arly return to Los Angeles and agreed to live with him there. Back in Hollywood, Bob rented a three-room apartment for them both on Franklin Circle and tried to make last what little money he had.

Now Taylor's name was on Hollywood's Ten Best Dressed list in the company of Cary Grant, George Brent, Fred Astaire, and William Powell. On-screen, Robert Taylor appeared dashing, entitled, rich, the driver of fast cars and possessor of custom-fitting three-piece suits. In truth, Universal was withholding a check for $2,000 until Taylor returned the six made-to-order suits, dress coat, slacks, and tuxedo coat and vest he'd worn making *Magnificent Obsession.*

Taylor had come to Hollywood with a name full of pomp and pretense and with an air that was simple, unassuming, small town. Bob Taylor was a "plain American" farm boy from prairie stock, a boy from the Midwest who grew up without running water and with an outhouse as a bathroom. Filley, Nebraska (population in 1910, 194), was his birthplace; Beatrice, his hometown. Filley was a crossroads, with nothing more than a grain elevator, a hardware store, and an undertaking establishment.

As a boy back home, nicknamed Buddy, he'd attended the Centenary Methodist Church every Sunday with his parents, said grace at table, and had neighbors who were just that, neighbors, and not strangers in some mad whirl. His parents were Republicans, nondrinkers, nonsmokers and never used profane language.

The Brugh family circa 1915, Kirksville, Missouri. Standing: Robert Flaws with his wife, Ethel, Ruth Brugh's sister. Seated: Ruth Adela Stanhope Brugh, twenty-seven years old; Spangler Arlington Brugh, age four; and Spangler Andrew Brugh, thirty-four. The Flaws and the Brughs were married in Filley, Nebraska, in a double ceremony in January 1904. (PHOTOFEST)

THIRTEEN

The Making of a Man

Barbara understood how things worked in Hollywood and was willing to listen to Bob's confusion. She was wiser than he and had been around the town longer.

"He was all mixed up," she said. "Mixed up about romance and about his career. For a long time we talked of nothing else."

Bob said he'd been given advice from everyone—"how to invest your money, what kind of movies to make, how to dress for a preview, how to zip up your fly; everything but, 'Are you happy?' They think they know the answer because anyone who is rich has to be happy."

Barbara was sympathetic, "an ear and a shoulder." She told Bob that he should go ahead, ignore what the studio wanted, and marry; "the devil with it," she said. Mayer's-Ganz-Mispochen—Yiddish for "Mayer's whole family"—was how people often referred to Metro-Goldwyn-Mayer. To some, Metro was an "insane place," filled with egomaniacs and frightened people terrified that someone superior might end their careers in a split second if they made a false move.

Going to Metro was a seamless transition for Bob. He revered his father ("He was my exhibit A, the pattern I wanted to copy"), and he revered Louis B. Mayer. There were those who saw Mayer as an uneducated, illiterate man, frightened of those who had less than he had, jealous of those who had more. Mayer (Lazar Meir) was from the Ukraine and lived as a boy in Saint John, New Brunswick. Like Dr. Brugh, he had provided for Bob and promised him everything, and so far Mr. Mayer, who at times could be vengeful and cruel as well as wise, generous, and loyal, had come through for the twenty-four-year-old actor. He'd given Taylor his start: a contract with a salary of $35 a week, which was security and the means to support Bob's failing mother.

He talked to Taylor as a son ("God gave me two lovely daughters," Mayer had said to Bob one day when the new actor was asking for a raise, "and they are a great joy to me. But for reasons, in His infinite wisdom," Mayer went on, "He never saw fit to give me a son. But if I had a son, Bob—if He had blessed me with such a wonderful gift—I can't think of anything I would have wanted than that son to be exactly like you").

Taylor didn't get the raise he was after, but the studio extended his contract and soon increased his salary from $50 to $75 a week, with a bonus of $125 per week. Mayer was making $10,000 a week, plus bonuses, prerogatives, and deductions that came to $1 million a year, making him the highest-paid executive in American industry.

"Money isn't everything," Mayer would say to his employees.

He had promised Bob that Metro would do great things for the young actor, that the studio would make Bob a star with an exceptional career (the year before, in 1935, Mayer had given Bob a bonus of $3,000 and then, four months later, an additional bonus of $1,500). He advised Taylor about clothes ("Maybe you can't act very well, Bob," he said, "but at least you can dress decently") and sent the young man to his own tailor to get his first custom-made suit, his first dinner jacket, his first white tie and tails.

The studio head had given Taylor his name. Louis Mayer's secretary, Ida "Kay" Koverman, who'd served as secretary to Herbert Hoover during his days as an engineer in San Francisco, had suggested that Brugh take the name of Taylor. Koverman, who'd worked for Mayer for eleven years and who was similar to his mother despite Koverman's being Catholic and Scottish, had insisted Mayer put Clark Gable under contract and ignore his big ears and bad teeth, just as she'd persuaded Mayer to hire Nelson Eddy and overlook the young singer's prettiness and lack of talent.

Bob suggested that he and Barbara drive down to Ocean Park. Barbara said, "Fine," thinking they would "roll down to Santa Monica, walk on the Venice Pier, take in the sea breeze and the sea view and maybe the moon."

Instead, Bob said, "Let's go on the roller coaster."

"Love to," she said, knowing she would hate every minute of it. "Every horrible up and down."

Bob took pleasure from being up in the air away from people. Frequently, on the soundstages, he climbed up to the rafters. "The biggest set doesn't look so big from a cat-walk forty feet up," Bob said. "No player looks big. It isn't an urge for privacy that lures me upward. It's just an urge to keep moving."

In Venice, Bob and Barbara went on the carousel, tossed darts into balloons, shot clay pigeons. Afterward, some boys saw Barbara standing in front of the shooting gallery and said, "Come on, Annie Oakley, let's see you shoot."

Barbara was willing to go along with the dare, but Bob picked up one of the guns and began to shoot at the targets. A crowd started to gather and became so large the police were called to help. Barbara and Bob had to escape into a hotel lobby and were escorted by two officers to Bob's car, but the crowd was overwhelming. Bob and Barbara were separated and didn't find each other for an hour and a half.

After that evening the two frequently had dinner together—mostly at Barbara's house. They put on a stack of records and listened to jazz, "St. Louis Blues"; to swing; to Cab Calloway on the red-hot "Minnie the Moocher in Chinatown who learned how to kick the gong around." "That's our dinner music," said Bob, explaining that they sat and screamed at each other across the table, "trying to make ourselves heard above Duke Ellington's band or Benny Goodman's."

After dinner Barbara and Bob went to the movies and watched the Movietone newsreels of Hitler sending fifty thousand troops into the demilitarized Rhineland in violation of the Versailles Treaty that forbade a union between Austria and Germany. They saw newsreels of the sudden floods sweeping over parts of Pennsylvania, Maryland, and West Virginia, fourteen feet of water swirling in the streets of Johnstown, Pennsylvania, and Pittsburgh, causing thousands to flee and creating widespread damage in the Ohio, Allegheny, and Susquehanna valleys. They watched on film as the new airship *Hindenburg* left Friedrichshafen at 4:00 p.m. for the United States with fifty-one passengers and arrived in Lakehurst, New Jersey, three days later at 5:23 a.m., traveling at seventy miles an hour. And they watched as Mussolini annexed Ethiopia and King Victor Emmanuel became emperor.

Bob liked to go dancing. Barbara preferred to limit their public appearances to movies or automobile rides. Bob demanded to know why Barbara didn't want to be seen with him in public. She had her reasons: privacy; the press (she hated to be gossiped about); she was twenty-nine, he, 25 (the age difference could be a problem); and there was Dion, and Fay.

Barbara had seen Fay at the extravagant premiere of Metro's *Great Ziegfeld*. The studio had spent more than $2 million on the three-hour picture; Ziegfeld's set designer, dance director, and scenarist had been brought to Hollywood to reproduce the extravagant, legendary production numbers. Taylor was mobbed by fans. Barbara and Fay didn't speak.

"It is unfortunate," Barbara said, "but that's the way it ended." After Fay's thwarted plan to kidnap Dion, Barbara was more wary of Frank than ever.

With Franchot Tone, Joan Crawford Tone, and Bob Taylor, 1936. The Tones were married in October 1935, months before this picture was taken; Barbara and Bob were newly involved but Joan and Barbara were deeply connected as seen in this photograph.

Driving home from a movie one night, Bob stopped the car in front of the Trocadero. The Troc was like the "clubhouse." Bob told Barbara that they were going in to dance. Her refusal, he said, would mean that she didn't want to be seen with him in public.

As they walked through the aisle of tables, Barbara thought her "knees were going to buckle" under her. She was that frightened. After a few minutes, it was clear to her that no one was paying any attention to them. Bob ordered two martinis. "You'd better hang on to me," Barbara said. "I'm not sure I can get up off this chair."

Barbara and Bob played tennis together, went horseback riding, and danced at the Cocoanut Grove. They had dinner and a movie with Joan Crawford and Franchot, still newlyweds after six months of marriage. Sometimes Bob played the piano, and Joan and Franchot sang; Barbara was the audience.

Bob was at work on *Small Town Girl.* The production had been problematic with a series of delays. The John Lee Mahin and Edith Fitzgerald script had required numerous rewrites; Mildred Cram, Manny Seff, Horace Jackson, Frances Goodrich, Albert Hackett, and Lenore Coffee all worked on the script.

The picture's star Jean Harlow was to be the girl who, on a lark and to get out of her humdrum small-town life, goes off with an up-and-coming surgeon who's had a fight with his fiancée after a big football game and is on a binge. He insists that the girl he's just picked up marry him; she refuses and tries to talk some sense into him, but he prevails. He awakens in the morning to find himself married to a girl he doesn't know rather than to the worldly society woman to whom he is engaged. His new wife consents to wait six months to annul the marriage and goes away with him to avoid a scandal. During their time on the family yacht, they fight and rail against one another, hate each other, fall in love, and ultimately decide to live happily ever after and stay married.

Harlow dropped out of the production, and Maureen O'Sullivan, who had made her mark in more than thirty pictures and as Jane Parker in *Tarzan the Ape Man* and *Tarzan Escapes,* was considered for the part.

Metro next wanted Janet Gaynor. She'd just appeared in Fox's *Farmer Takes a Wife* with Henry Fonda. Gaynor resisted, thinking she wouldn't be any good in a role that was intended for Jean Harlow, even with rewriting.

Robert Montgomery was to be the society doctor, but Gaynor didn't want to be billed second to Montgomery, who was being talked about for *Romeo and Juliet* (Bob Taylor had been considered for the picture, but the studio thought better of it). Franchot Tone was mentioned as Montgomery's replacement for *Small Town Girl.*

Taylor had finished *Magnificent Obsession* two months before and got the role of the young surgeon. Janet Gaynor, who had never been on loan-out in her eight years with Fox, was starring opposite Bob as Metro's new small town girl.

Bob and Barbara often went out with the Marxes.

People watching Taylor and Stanwyck found them to be quiet, absorbed, sufficiently unto themselves.

Bob was free from Irene Hervey; Barbara from Frank Fay.

"We amused each other," said Barbara. "We danced well together. We were good friends, had a marvelous time."

Bob was direct, open, and honest with Barbara. He appreciated her in big ways and little, was loving to her. After Fay, Bob seemed so normal to Barbara. He made it clear to those around them that he had great admiration for her.

They were from opposite ends of the universe, though their grandparents were Scotch-English (his) and Scotch-Irish (hers); their ancestors had come to this country in time to serve in the American Revolutionary War.

From left to right: Zeppo and Marion Marx with Barbara and Bob, 1936. (COURTESY TIM MARX)

Taylor was the grandson of a grain merchant who'd emigrated from Holland to Nebraska by way of Pennsylvania. The Brughs were members of the Church of Brethren, Republicans, and, like most people in Nebraska, of German descent. His grandmother's family, the Stanhopes, had come from Scotland to Michigan and were devoted Methodists.

Taylor was the son of a farm boy, Spangler Brugh (the fastest corn husker around), who'd grown up on a working ranch that was all light, blank horizons, and routine drudgery and who lived out his own father's dream of becoming a doctor.

As a boy, Bob had been given everything by his parents: a pony he called Gypsy—Gyp—that he'd ridden alone for hours at a time; a pony cart, harness, and saddle; a dog; and guns of various sorts. At family holidays he hunted with his father, grandfather, and uncle for rabbits and skinned them; his mother cooked the meat and served it with dumplings and prune rabbit gravy.

In high school, Arly was given a series of cars, including a convertible sports coupe and a 1929 beige-and-orange Buick. His parents bought him the books of knowledge and encouraged him to study the piano and cello (he'd wanted to study the saxophone, but his mother thought it too "noisy and jazzy").

The Brughs passed their high ideals on to their only son, teaching him honor, self-reliance, and respect for authority. As a boy, Arly had his chores at home, keeping the wood box organized and mowing the neighbor's lawn for twenty-four cents an hour. "I cleaned and kept my own room in order," Bob said. "I did my own homework. I understood that that was my job and that a man did his job alone." The Brughs were strict ("There were not many spankings," Taylor said, "but as sure as they were due, I collected").

The family took summer vacations together—to the lakes of Minnesota, to Lake Okoboji in Idaho, out west as far as Denver—and Arly went pole fishing with his father.

Bob and Barbara came from different worlds, but in basic ways they found likenesses: when they were children, circumstances led them to be alone, Barbara because she didn't have a mother, Bob because he didn't like to play with other children. "I was almost always alone," he said. "I never ran with a group. I wasn't unhappy. I went to school. I was a good little boy . . . I never played hooky. I was usually the room monitor and the president of the class . . . After school, I didn't play with other kids. I liked to be by myself . . . I always had a flock of animals to care for. I preferred being alone on the prairie or in the woods . . . I had just enough to do on my own and that's how I preferred to do and be."

Like Barbara, Bob was remote. Barbara was shy and assumed she was not really welcome. Bob was private, not outgoing or talkative; he too assumed he wasn't liked. Ruth Brugh had made sure her son in grade school and high school was well-groomed, first dressing him in short black velvet pants, a white shirt, and a huge straw hat. He'd been teased in elementary school and called Little Lord Fauntleroy. When he was older, Ruth made sure her son was immaculately dressed in slacks, sweaters, and silk clothes. The combination of Arly's beauty, which made his classmates jealous and taunt him with names of "pretty boy," and the differentness caused by his overprotective mother led him to believe that people wouldn't like him. "I've always taken it for granted that they won't," he said. "I can't make advances. I don't mix easily."

Bob, like Barbara, found solace during his school years in Hugh Walpole's *Fortitude:* "Blessed be all Sorrows, Torments, Hardships, Endurances that demand Courage . . . Blessed be these things—for of these things cometh the making of a Man."

Bob had been a star tennis player in high school; run the 100- and 220-yard dashes on the track team; was elected president of his class and of the dramatics club. He'd chosen a college that was church endowed and forty miles from home, surrounded by elms and maples on the edge of a small Nebraska

The two Spangler A. Brughs: son, age sixteen, and
father, forty-six, 1927, six years before his death in
1933 from an infection following emergency surgery;
father and son worshipped one another. (PHOTOFEST)

town; big cities and big universities frightened him. He decided he would
follow his father's path, become a doctor, and join the family practice—his
first interest, orthopedic surgery; then, psychiatry. His nickname Buddy soon
became Doc.

Bob acted in college theatrical productions and spent hours practicing
the cello and playing in the school orchestra. When he started to yearn for
something bigger and to leave his parents, and Nebraska, and small-town
life, he followed his cello instructor to a bigger college in a bigger small town,
Pomona, California; it sounded like Utopia. Once there, Bob could easily
be spotted in his brilliant yellow coupe. Arly Brugh became "Home" Brugh
and was dubbed "the Sheik"; his shyness misunderstood for conceit; his good
looks in place of brains.

Bob took over where his father left off in caring for his frail mother (there
were those back in Beatrice who said Ruth Brugh "enjoyed her illness"). Bob
had always been the object of Ruth's cloying love.

When they lived together in Los Angeles, Ruth Brugh wanted Arly with
her as much as possible. Religion took hold of Ruth; she was a strict Method-

Ruth Brugh with her son, Spangler Arlington, Robert Taylor,
1936. The people of Beatrice saw her primarily as someone who
"enjoyed her illness."

ist and couldn't abide Catholics, Germans, Jews, or Democrats. Ruth Brugh
saw sex as an evil force and girls as the instrument of that evil. There were
times when she asked her boy to sleep beside her, to hold his hand over her
left breast to make sure her heart was still beating. Bob did as he was asked.

As soon as he had enough money, he moved to his own home—a seven-
room one-story Spanish house on a tree-shaded street in Beverly Hills, four
blocks from his mother. There was no wall surrounding the house. The porch
was decked with flowering plants; the home was furnished in warm brown
shades and Monterey furniture. Bob hired a French-Hungarian manservant,
Joe Mondue, to take care of it, and him, his clothes, his car, and anything
else that came up.

Ruth Brugh was concerned that her son would "get too wild," that he
wouldn't be able to afford two houses ("We'll end up in the poorhouse,"
she said), and that she would be alone. Arly assured Ruth that he would
find someone to take care of her ("Don't worry, Mother, I'll make sure she
isn't anyone but a white Protestant"). His grandmother, cousin, and secretary
moved in with Ruth. His grandmother addressed envelopes for fans who
requested Bob's picture; his mother answered postcards; and Virginia, his
secretary, answered letters. Bob telephoned every day or dropped by; Ruth
said that what she liked best about her son was that he "treated her like his
best girl friend."

The first party Bob gave in Hollywood was for his mother, in honor of her forty-ninth birthday—a small dinner dance at one of the hotels. Ruth Brugh had outwardly changed from the woman of Beatrice, Nebraska. Her clothes were fashionable, her hair was dyed and done in a "stylish hairdo," and for her birthday dinner she wore her new diamond and sapphire bracelet, a gift from her son.

Bob was drawn to women who were older and more experienced than he, who could show him how things were done. At college, an older coed, Dorothy Forster, had taught Bob how to be with girls. When he first started in pictures, Virginia Bruce had advised him about how things should be. Virginia was a year older than Bob, but she was more sophisticated and mature and a much more experienced movie actor. She'd been on the stage in New York, appearing in the *Ziegfeld Follies,* hailed as "America's Most Beautiful Show Girl"; in Hollywood, she was one of the original Goldwyn Girls. She'd made her screen debut in 1929. *Society Doctor* was her thirtieth picture; it was Bob's sixth.

Barbara was older than Bob as well and had been on her own forever, without parents, cars, piano lessons. She'd watched and learned how to be in the world by her own fight and will; it came out of a lifetime of watching and sorting things out for herself. She'd been wary of advice or help and thrown herself into her work. She'd allowed herself to be taken in hand by wiser, more experienced professionals like Willard Mack, Arthur Hopkins, Fay, and Capra who taught her and showed her the way. Frank Fay, she believed, had taught her everything, but in the end their marriage had almost killed her, nearly destroyed their son, and just about finished her career. With Bob she may have been the older, more experienced of the two—she didn't want anyone telling her what she could or couldn't do, whom she should or shouldn't see—but he was showing Barbara for the first time how to play. They laughed together, ate together, danced together.

Barbara was teaching Bob about acting, about business, about sex. Barbara wanted to advise and guide Bob; it was clear to her he was mixed-up, overwhelmed. "His sense of values have been pushed around so quickly in the past year," she said, "that it is excusable."

Bob got a kick out of being recognized and giving autographs. He was out at nightclubs watching people watch him. Rumors wreaked havoc before friendships could even get under way. Barbara understood how dangerous fame could be—especially fame that came so quickly one didn't know what to do with it.

She was teaching Bob humility. "If you want to stay up there [on the mar-

Chester Morris, Virginia Bruce, and Robert Taylor, *Society Doctor,* 1935.

quee]," she said, "you've got to learn something every time a camera gives you the evil eye. When you can't learn anything more, you're through."

Until *Magnificent Obsession,* Bob hadn't been considered much of an actor. He was on time to the set and knew his lines. He had been in a number of pictures. His first, *Handy Andy,* with Will Rogers, was made at Fox. Bob was disappointed it hadn't been a Metro picture ("Why couldn't I make my first picture in my own studio; wasn't I good enough?"); in it he'd had three lines and whistled. In *Buried Loot,* his next picture, for Metro, one of the studio's Crime Does Not Pay series, he was given the lead. In it he was handsome and slick.

In *Society Doctor,* Taylor was the best friend of, and junior intern to, the star of the picture, Chester Morris, in love with the staff nurse Virginia Bruce; she's beguiled by the Taylor character, but her heart belongs to Morris (at the time, Taylor and Bruce were secretly having an affair—she, just recently divorced from John Gilbert, with a young child. Bruce had married Gilbert in her early twenties—his third marriage. Their two-year marriage had ended six months before making *Society Doctor.* She was Taylor's first serious romantic involvement; he thought Bruce "exquisite, graceful, an exotic flower").

In *Society Doctor,* Taylor was cocky and brash as the handsome intern, even playful at times, but not yet able to carry the difficult moments on-screen.

Taylor and Bruce were teamed up again in Bob's next picture. She was the

Times Square Lady who comes from the Midwest (Bruce was born in Minneapolis, the daughter of an insurance broker, and grew up in Fargo, North Dakota) to claim her father's empire after his death. It becomes clear that her father's vast holdings are a network of crooked sports events watched over by racketeers. Taylor is the racketeer assigned to seduce her into selling out fast to those who want full control of her father's syndicate.

Jean Hersholt worked with Taylor in *Murder in the Fleet* and said of the young actor, "I've been in Hollywood for twenty years and if I ever saw a newcomer who was marked for stardom, it is Robert Taylor. Can you see something of Gilbert in that turn of the head, and the sudden smile?"

In *Magnificent Obsession,* Taylor is beautiful, polished, worldly; his performance has a depth, thoughtfulness, and emotional undercurrent that made his prettiness seem beside the point. John Stahl, the director, was known for the care he took with his pictures.

"Once more," Stahl would say to the actors while the film was still running and not bother to say "cut." Stahl exposed more film than any other director, and he made only one picture a year: *Back Street; Only Yesterday; Imitation of Life,* among them. William Wyler worked as Stahl's script boy and learned about endless retakes from him.

Stahl had started in pictures in Brooklyn in 1913 as a bit player and extra and "approached the responsibility of a director with infinite care and painstaking slowness," said Taylor.

It was not uncommon for the director to do thirty, forty, or fifty takes on a relatively simple scene at the same time that Bob was filming retakes on *Broadway Melody of 1936,* directed by Roy Del Ruth. Woody Van Dyke, who shot certain scenes of *Melody,* "cut as he shot," said Taylor. "Van Dyke used his camera as if it were a six shooter and he was the fastest gun in Hollywood."

"With Stahl you acted," said Bob. "Woody can't stand acting; give him acting and he kicks it right out of you. [We] rarely got more than one take on any scene, then the camera was moved rapidly to another set-up."

Going from endless retakes with Stahl to rapid-fire scenes with Van Dyke "was going from the sublime to the ridiculous," said Taylor. "But it seemed normal."

Bob admired Barbara's long years of experience as an actress. "She's been a trouper since she was a kid," he said, "older in experience." Often when Bob left the studio at night, "all temperamental and steamed up about something," he would talk things over with Barbara. "When I've finished my recital," he said, "I'm feeling ashamed of myself and that the matter in hand wasn't very important anyway." Bob was reassured by Barbara's having both feet on the ground and felt that she knew the answers.

Barbara was becoming Bob's greatest influence for improvement. "I used to get into an awful state, listening to everybody," he said. "I know players of experience who still get almost frantic over the things people tell them and don't know whom to believe or what to do."

Barbara gave Bob the confidence to trust his impulses; he was carefree, buoyant. She was showing Bob how "to sort [it] out. How to judge," he said, "what's the right or the wrong thing to do." She not only gave Bob good advice but demonstrated, in her own career, how it works. Bob believed that there never had been, or ever would be, a greater "pro" than Barbara.

"She's taught me more with her knowledge," he said, "than I would have learned in a lifetime. She's the grandest sport alive."

Barbara was happier than she'd been in years.

FOURTEEN

Exactly Like Anybody

1936

Let me tell you about a boy I know
They all call him Jitterbug Joe.

Bob Taylor hated to quarrel; he hadn't grown up around it. His mother and father had loved each other without reservation, selfishness, bickering, or jealousy. "My father," Bob said, "used to say to my mother almost every day of his life, 'You are the most beautiful woman in the world to me. Every day we live together, I love you more.'"

Barbara didn't get angry easily or publicly; she rarely showed it; instead, it festered, and she didn't forget. When Barbara did get angry with Bob, he didn't argue back. Barbara suffered from moods; she called them her "black Shanty-Irish gloom." She would get up in the morning feeling fine. By noon she would begin to sink "right down." If Bob called her from the studio, he'd ask how she was. She would answer, "Fine."

"Feeling all right?"

"Fine," she'd say.

"Anything happen this morning?"

"No."

"Well, I see you're in one of those things again. I'll call you later."

From years of experience with his mother, Bob understood erratic behavior.

He admired how little effort Barbara wasted in her life; except for her moods, high or low ("extremes always," she said), how quietly she lived; how she stayed away from nightclubs; wore no makeup besides red lipstick, kept her hair color her own. Clothes held little interest for her, on-screen or off. When she was considering a script, the clothes never entered her decision. She didn't pay attention to them until it was time to put them on. Some thought Barbara looked as if she were from a small southern town, and when asked if she was, she said, "Ah's sho is, honey; South Brooklyn." "She's so completely natural. So real," Bob said. It was a relief to him that Barbara looked like a well-scrubbed child of twelve.

Bob wasn't much of a reader, but reading was like breathing to Barbara. He began to tease her about it.

Bob was shy but he liked people and liked to be around them. Barbara seemed to cut them off. With Fay, Barbara was thought of as shy, distant, unapproachable; the press saw her as impulsive, hot-tempered, always in trouble. Barbara would freeze up when meeting someone new; parties with three or more people were uncomfortable for her; even with friends and acquaintances, she'd snap out a dismal "hullo" and sink in the nearest chair—with thoughts of "Do these people want me here? I'm sure they only invited me out of sympathy. I know those two women are talking about me over there"—until she could muster enough courage to leave.

With the people Barbara did like, "it was all the way overboard," Bob said. The differences between them didn't pose a problem.

Once Bob was finished with Bill Wellman's *Small Town Girl,* he was lent to Fox for *Confessions of a Servant Girl* with Loretta Young, from the 1915 play about class and society *Common Clay,* by Cleves Kinkead. Gene Markey and William Conselman had written the script; Roy Del Ruth was directing. This was the third remake of the play.

Bob Taylor once again had the role of the scion of an aristocratic family. Loretta Young was the maid in his parents' household with whom he falls in love and secretly marries.

Bob was assigned to co-star with Clark Gable and Wallace Beery in a remake of the 1913 spectacle *Quo Vadis,* from the Henryk Sienkiewicz novel. Irving Thalberg was planning the remake with sound and dialogue. The picture was to go into production once Taylor finished shooting *Confessions* at Fox.

Bob finished production on *Confessions of a Servant Girl* just as Barbara was to start her second film for Eddie Small at Radio. Leigh Jason was directing.

Small Town Girl opened in Los Angeles at Grauman's Chinese Theatre and Loew's State in time for Easter and was held over an additional week by popular demand. Bob took Barbara to the preview.

A Message to Garcia, which opened as well, didn't fare as successfully. Frank Nugent in *The New York Times* called Gene Fowler's screenplay "ridiculous." *Variety* said Barbara was "no more a Cuban patriot's daughter than Carnera is a ballet dancer. She's a Cuban girlie who speaks her native language with an English accent and English with no accent at all."

Twenty-two actresses were considered for the star role in Eddie Small's production of *Marry the Girl* before the part went to Barbara despite their having worked together on *Red Salute*.

The woman in the picture is a successful fashion model with no interest in getting married despite her numerous suitors but somehow agrees to marry the most persistent (and the poorest)—an engineer, who insists she quit her job and they live together as man and wife on his meager $35-a-week salary.

Among those considered for the part before Barbara: Jane Wyatt, Frances Dee, Wendy Barrie, Mae Clarke, Claire Trevor, Gail Patrick, Nancy Carroll, Dixie Lee. Barbara's name was not on the list.

Radio-Keith-Orpheum was in the throes of being reorganized and redesigned for the fourth time in eight years. As part of its reorganization, Sam Briskin, former vice president and general manager of Columbia Pictures, was hired as the new head of production. Briskin increased the number of "A" pictures from fifteen a season to twenty-four "A" and "B" pictures and hired box-office names.

Into this new RKO, flush with ambitious plans and large expectations, with two new owners, Floyd B. Odlum and John D. Hertz, and a new president, Leo Spitz, Briskin signed Herbert Marshall to a five-year contract and brought John Boles and Gene Raymond to the studio. Briskin welcomed Eddie Small's production unit and worked out a schedule with Fox that would allow Barbara to make two pictures with RKO within the year, the first time in history that a star was under contract to two studios at once.

A radio operator with the Byrd Antarctic expedition on the SS *Bear of Oakland* wrote to Barbara telling her that her photograph hung over his bunk "in Little America all through the long winters night, taking the place of home and mother." The radio operator went on to say in his letter that Barbara's photograph had accompanied him "on more than 2000 miles of tractor travel over the Antarctic snows. If it had been you in person, it couldn't have been more prized . . . you might be interested to know your spirit did such great things at a distance of even 10,000 miles."

• • •

Zeppo Marx was sure Barbara could do comedy regardless of the difficulties of *Red Salute*. She was naturally funny, and her timing was good. Barbara had thought about it, but she couldn't connect herself with comedy. "It's always seemed to me there's something too heavy about me," she said and thought she should stick with what she called "the Get Outs," the point in every one of her pictures where she told someone, "Now get out!"

It took Zeppo many weeks to convince Barbara to take another chance with comedy on the screen and make *Marry the Girl*.

The picture, Barbara's twentieth in six years, was standard fare, but the dialogue by P. J. Wolfson and Philip Epstein was clever and amusing. Wolfson's twelve pictures included Selznick's *Dancing Lady* with Joan Crawford, Clark Gable, and Franchot Tone and *Reckless,* from Selznick's story, with Jean Harlow, William Powell, and Tone. Philip Epstein was just starting out and had worked with Wolfson on *Love on a Bet*.

Sam Briskin informed Leo Spitz, the new president of Radio-Keith-Orpheum, that shooting was to start on *Marry the Girl* with Barbara, Gene Raymond, Ned Sparks, Robert Young, and Helen Broderick. "I would trade all five of them," Briskin wrote to Spitz, "for one really big name, but that being impossible, I think the cast outlined above will do the trick."

The studio considered it "dangerous to use Stanwyck as a comedienne instead of [as] a woman with a baby in her arms."

Briskin assured Spitz that Leigh Jason, who'd just directed Gene Raymond in *Love on a Bet,* "ought to be able to get a fine and very exciting comedy out of it." Leigh Jason, born Jacobson, had started out in pictures as an electrician and progressed to screenwriting before becoming a director.

Briskin knew *Marry the Girl* depended on Barbara's performance. "We will have to hope she pulls through in this new type of role for her."

Barbara was getting $42,500 for four weeks of work; Gene Raymond, $14,500; Ned Sparks, $14,000; Robert Young, once again borrowed from Metro, $8,750; Helen Broderick, $9,550; and Eric Blore, $450.

The story of *Marry the Girl* reflected the dilemma facing many urban American couples: working girl marries poor boy—just starting out—who insists his wife quit her well-paying job and be a stay-at-home bride. The girl in the picture relents and allows him to be the breadwinner until the leasing company comes to reclaim the furniture for nonpayment and then she secretly goes back to work. Their marriage is bliss until he finds out his salary alone has not bought them their self-satisfied happiness. He is furious; she refuses to give up her work and leaves him—until she realizes that poverty and true love win out over money and the prettier things of life.

"THE BRIDE WALKS OUT" — An RKO Radio Picture

PERMISSION IS HEREBY GRANTED TO NEWSPAPERS, MAGAZINES AND OTHER PERIODICALS TO REPRODUCE THIS PHOTOGRAPH.   Printed in U. S. A.
Copyright 1936, RKO Radio Pictures, Inc. Property of RKO Radio Pictures, Inc. Loaned for individual use only; must be returned to RKO Radio Pictures, Inc. and must not be sold, leased or given away by any other party.

With Ned Sparks, Robert Young, and Helen Broderick, *Marry the Girl* (later, *The Bride Walks Out*), 1936. "5 brilliant stars in a laughable drama of love on a budget . . . the story of a girl who married in haste and repented on 35 a week." (RKO PICTURES LLC)

Barbara's character was literal and grounded, and she played it that way. She may not have had the elegance of Carole Lombard in *The Princess Comes Across* or the lyricism of Claudette Colbert in *She Married Her Boss* or the vulnerability and quirkiness of Jean Arthur in *Mr. Deeds Goes to Town,* but Barbara brought to the character in *Marry the Girl* a lightness, modesty, and intelligence and held her own against the banter and charm of the supporting actors, who were the vitality of the picture and were given whatever humor there was in the piece. (Ned Sparks in his steely twang, stogie between clenched teeth, to Gene Raymond, on marriage: "Listen, pal, when a dame gets you going, keep on going"; Sparks to Helen Broderick: "When I married you, you didn't have a rag on your back"; Broderick back to Sparks, "Well, I've got them now"; Hattie McDaniel to Broderick, about life and deception: "Well, you know what Mr. Lincoln said: 'You can fool some of the people all the time and some of the people some of the time, but you can't fool some of the people some of the time' "; Broderick, in response, bemused and nibbling on an olive: "He certainly did.")

Leigh Jason found Barbara to be "a real craftsman. She . . . would dig to the bitter end of what you really wanted—and then give it to you," he said.

There were times when Jason had to make two or three takes because

Barbara would be laughing at the comedic blustering and exquisite dim-wittedness of Billy Gilbert, former vaudevillian, Laurel and Hardy foil, and master of the "take 'ems."

Metro assigned Bob the role of his career to date, that of Armand Duval, opposite Greta Garbo as Marguerite Gautier, the tragic Dumas heroine of *Camille*. The studio believed it was to be Garbo's greatest role, and by casting Taylor as the young man in love with "the lady of the camellias," the dazzling courtesan of her day, it was making it known that Robert Taylor was one of its most important male stars.

Bob was making *The Gorgeous Hussy* from the popular Samuel Hopkins Adams novel about General Andrew Jackson's rise to power and about Peggy Eaton, a Washington innkeeper's daughter who becomes Jackson's unofficial First Lady (mistress) after he is elected the seventh president of the United States. She so scandalized Jackson's presidency that the whole episode was called the "Eaton malaria."

Melvyn Douglas played the senator from Virginia who secretly loves the woman he's watched grow from girlhood to beautiful woman. Taylor is her first husband; Franchot Tone, her second; Lionel Barrymore, arthritic and often in pain, Andy Jackson.

Taylor's role in *The Gorgeous Hussy* was small, but he was playing opposite Joan Crawford. *The Gorgeous Hussy* was the first costume picture for both Crawford and Taylor. Taylor and Melvyn Douglas had been cast early. Crawford's casting came later and was hard-won.

She was determined to break free from the tired up-from-under pictures she was given, such as *Dancing Lady* and *Sadie McKee,* in which the Crawford character triumphs over poverty, class, and a dubious past, "Cinderella stories," she called them. Crawford had returned from the East after secretly marrying Franchot Tone in Fort Lee, New Jersey, a change from her first wedding, at twenty-four, to Doug Fairbanks Jr., then nineteen, in New York City's Parish House of St. Malachy's Church on West Forty-Ninth Street.

Joan's succession of modern glamour stories assigned to her by the studio—*Chained, Forsaking All Others, No More Ladies,* and *I Live My Life,* each identical in plot and characterization—were dismissed by critics as "Crawford formula" pictures. "In the first reel," said Crawford, "I'm a poor girl. In the second, things have happened and I'm wearing gorgeous clothes."

Hollywood's big stars were making elaborate costume pictures: Norma Shearer, *Romeo and Juliet;* Katharine Hepburn, *Mary of Scotland;* Garbo, *Camille* as soon as George Cukor was finished directing *Romeo and Juliet.*

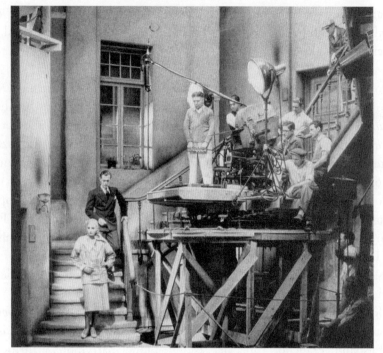

Clarence Brown, standing on raised platform, with Greta Garbo and
Robert Montgomery on stairs, 1930. The picture was *Inspiration,* from
the Alphonse Daudet novel *Sapho,* adapted for the screen by Gene Markey. William Daniels is the cameraman. (PHOTOFEST)

Crawford desperately wanted to make a period picture; she had no intention of being left out of the costume picture craze. She was going to do her
"darndest," she said, "to get away from modern pictures" and make herself
"worthy of real and vital roles."

The Franchot Tones—he, the handsome, erudite, socially prominent
young actor, potentially the best actor of his generation, member of the
Theatre Guild, a founding member of the radical, adventurous Group Theatre, who also loved the New York stage and hated Hollywood; she, influenced by her new husband's artistry, breeding, curiosity, and boldness and
hungry to improve herself in all ways cultural (a professor from one of the
local universities came each week to tutor her)—were planning to take a
few months' leave to go east and work together onstage in a small theater
in Connecticut. Joan planned to learn "everything that could be learned
about acting."

Crawford told David Selznick that she wanted to play the part of Peggy

Eaton. Selznick laughed at the notion. "You can't do a costume picture," he told her. "You're too modern."

The picture's director was Clarence Brown, who'd helped Joan in her transformation from Jazz Age dancing daughter to serious dramatic actress. It wasn't a fluke that Brown had directed Greta Garbo in five pictures—*Flesh and the Devil, A Woman of Affairs, Romance, Anna Christie,* and *Inspiration*—before he started to work with Crawford. She admired Garbo more than any other actress.

Crawford spotted the Swedish actress walking down steps and saw it as "a real inspiration. She seems to fly like a bird. Seeing her thrills me," said Crawford. "When I look at myself up there on the screen, I seem to be galumphing all over the place and wonder why I thought I could ever be an actress."

Clarence Brown had directed Crawford in *Possessed, Letty Lynton, Chained,* and *Sadie McKee.* Crawford believed that she and Brown were "attuned in spirit," that he understood the way she worked and "made allowances for her idiosyncrasies."

Metro had originally purchased the rights to *The Gorgeous Hussy* for Jean Harlow after RKO had wanted to make the picture two years before with Katharine Hepburn. Crawford went to Joe Mankiewicz, the picture's producer, and asked him to give her the part.

Mankiewicz had just started to produce at Metro. With his brother Herman's insistence, Joe got a job as a junior writer at Paramount writing dialogue; four years later he landed at Metro as a screenwriter. Two years after that he was producing, overseeing *Three Godfathers* and *Fury.*

As a Metro producer, Mankiewicz said, "The livin' was easy, the fish were bitin' and the tennis was good," but he found the job "a sad and unhappy waste." Mankiewicz wanted to write, and at Metro, where producers were forbidden writing credits, he was forced to write anonymously.

Mankiewicz had written a number of pictures at Metro, including *Manhattan Melodrama* with Myrna Loy and Clark Gable and two Crawford pictures, *Forsaking All Others* (also with Gable) and *I Live My Life.*

The Gorgeous Hussy was his next assignment.

Joan knew Mankiewicz well. Mankiewicz summoned up Crawford's sexual energy when he wrote for Robert Montgomery sharing a campsite with Joan in *Forsaking All Others,* "I don't need matches. I could build a fire by rubbing two boy scouts together." Joan was "madly" in love with Mankiewicz and said of their time together, "It was lovely. He gave me such a feeling of security, I felt I could do anything in the world."

She begged and pleaded with Joe to let her do *The Gorgeous Hussy.* Crawford saw the picture as her chance to prove she was "an actress and not a clothes horse." Mankiewicz relented.

Joseph Breen went over the script and wanted changes. In a letter to L. B. Mayer, Breen asked for no unnecessary drinking or rowdiness in any of the scenes. "Abusive and profane expressions such as 'Lord!' and 'God' should be avoided throughout . . . You should not speak hypocritically about the language of the cloth."

The Gorgeous Hussy started shooting just as Margaret Mitchell's *Gone with the Wind* was published.

Robert Taylor was uncomfortable in costume and felt "too dressed up, too showy . . . I don't like being on parade," he said. But in the part of the young, besotted suitor of *The Gorgeous Hussy,* "so alive; always laughing," Taylor was fresh and winning. Clarence Brown described Bob as "the new heart beat of America. 'Pretty Boy' was the fans' conception of him," Brown said. "Bob had classic features and some studio expert unwisely decided to make him still handsomer. Bob objected strenuously but vainly to the weeding out of the heavy eyebrows that almost met over his nose."

Joan made her entrances on the set in full costume, greeting her co-star Melvyn Douglas "in a distinctly Southern manner, less as I was a fellow player," he said, "than a guest in her home." Crawford's new dressing room was a perfect re-creation of a New England clapboard house with picket fences, grass mats, and steeply pitched roof, "presumably," said Douglas, "to withstand the weight of whatever northeastern snows might accumulate in-side the studio." Douglas had heard stories of Joan "being a hail-fellow-well-met sort of person whose language was not exactly sanitary," and he was somewhat surprised by her affect.

In response to Norma Shearer's being seen as the gracious lady of the MGM lot, attended to between takes by a maid in black uniform with cap and apron who handed the star a mirror and powder puff from the makeup tray, Joan decided to become Metro's "cultured" queen, wearing large horn-rimmed glasses, knitting between setups, with a ball of yarn tucked in her midriff and listening to opera. Joan, like Barbara, knew the name of every electrician and grip.

A special phonograph in Crawford's dressing room played music during each day of production to accompany Joan's moods. The records were chosen by a music expert out of the five thousand he kept on file for her, includ-ing those by Bing Crosby, Benny Goodman, Eddy Duchin, Paul Robeson, and Lawrence Tibbett. The records played most frequently were *La Traviata,*

With Joan Crawford, during the filming of *The Gorgeous Hussy,* with "Garbo's director," Clarence Brown, in charge. He described himself as "a company man who shot the story as well as [he] could and went on to the next thing."

Tosca, Madame Butterfly, Verdi's *Requiem.* Joan and Franchot were taking singing lessons with a well-known Los Angeles operatic voice coach, the tenor Otto Morando, for the moment when Joan would sing on the concert stage.

During production on *The Gorgeous Hussy,* Joan was impressed with Bob Taylor's easy, graceful naturalness as an actor, but she was baffled by Barbara

Bob Taylor as Lieutenant John "Bowie" Timberlake, navy purser, with Joan Crawford as the "gorgeous hussy," Margaret "Peggy" O'Neal Timberlake Eaton, called by Andrew Jackson "the smartest little woman in America."

and Bob as a couple. Joan knew what Barbara had been through with Fay, and he and Bob were different in so many ways. Joan didn't see Bob as Barbara's type.

Mankiewicz said of Joan's moods, "You'd have to watch the way she came in. If Joan was wearing a pair of slacks, that meant you could slap her on the ass and say, 'Hiya Kid. You getting much?' In turn she'd be as raucous as possible. She could come back the next day wearing black sables and incredible sapphires and by Jeses, you'd better be on your feet and click your heels, kiss her hand and talk with the best British accent you had; but never in any way indicate she was different in any respect from the way she was yesterday because the following day she'd come in in a dirndl or a pinafore and you'd be down on the floor playing jacks with her."

Joan at thirty-one was beautiful. As Peggy Eaton, the young, dewy innkeeper's daughter of simple demeanor, supposed to look fresh and innocent, Crawford, with her face framed by ringlets and a wide-brimmed nineteenth-century bonnet, belied any trace of modesty or purity. Her head looked too large, her face too square-jawed, her features too hard. Selznick's assessment

With Crawford, circa 1936.

of Crawford in a costume picture had been correct. Her features looked too modern for the part of the woman whose affairs scandalized nineteenth-century Washington and helped to shape the Democratic Party ticket of 1832 and change the course of American politics.

Crawford and Franchot had been married for less than eight months. During that time they'd given a series of dinner parties for eight or ten each Saturday night at their house on Bristol Avenue, the house Joan bought after the release of *Our Dancing Daughters,* which she changed and redecorated when she married Doug Fairbanks. Barbara and Bob were invited to the Crawford-Tones' for dinner, as were the Fred Astaires, the Clarence Browns, the Gary Coopers, Luise Rainer and Clifford Odets, Jean Muir and Jerry Asher. Asher was an escort and RKO press agent who looked out for Joan in her early Hollywood days and was one of her closest friends. After each dinner—the men wore sack coats; the women, backless dinner gowns—games were played—Ping-Pong, anagrams, backgammon, "Secrets," "Guess Who I Am," psychoanalytic word games—and the knitters went back to knitting until a new picture was shown in the projection room.

The Franchot Tones gave a Sunday afternoon reception (a first for Joan) for Leopold Stokowski, the director, for almost a quarter of a century, of the Philadelphia Orchestra. Stokowski was in town to make *The Big Broadcast of 1937* for Paramount Pictures. Invited to the Ambassador Hotel for tea were three hundred, among them Jimmy Cagney, Irene Dunne, Henry Fonda, Judith Anderson, the Otto Klemperers, Clifton Webb, Ginger Rogers, the Metropolitan Opera contralto Ernestine "Tini" Schumann-Heink, Louis B. Mayer, and Barbara and Bob.

• • •

Bob was set to fly to New York to do a radio appearance for the studio. He'd bought an acre and a half of land in Coldwater Canyon and was working with an architect on what was to be a French Colonial farmhouse.

A few days before he was to leave for New York—his first real separation from Barbara—he picked up Dion and drove eighteen miles north of Malibu to be with Barbara at the end of the day's shooting on *Marry the Girl*. Bob kept stopping along the way to buy the four-year-old popcorn, lemonade, candy, and ice cream. By the time they arrived at the shoot, Dion was sick with an upset stomach.

Bob didn't want to leave for New York and fought with Metro about going; he didn't want to be away from Barbara. The studio was insistent. Bob thought it was Metro trying to meddle in the relationship, but the studio wanted to see how his New York fans would react to the actor, to gauge how seriously the studio should take Taylor's fan mail.

Bob had never been to a big city. It was his first trip east of Michigan and his first trip in an airplane. The TWA plane, carrying fourteen passengers, made a stopover in Wichita. The field was mobbed with people. Bob assumed they were there to see him, but the American hero Clarence Chamberlin had just landed and was the cause of the furor. Chamberlin had broken Lindbergh's distance record, flying nonstop from New York to Germany, two weeks after Lindbergh's 1927 flight from New York to Paris. Chamberlin had recently started an airline whose route was between New York and Boston.

In New York, Bob wanted to make sure he saw the sights—Grant's Tomb, the aquarium, Central Park, the Brooklyn Bridge. He was mobbed by fans, and getting anywhere in the city became difficult. It took him half an hour to get from the lobby of the Waldorf Astoria to his suite. To make his way through the mob of women, Taylor pulled down his hat and turned up the collar of his coat "like a G-man." One fan managed to get through the guards and climbed thirty-eight flights of stairs to the floor of Bob's suite. He graciously let her in for an autograph and tea.

Bob couldn't wait to see the city and the next day got up at five o'clock in the morning to take a walk down Broadway. He realized that New York at that hour was "quieter than Beatrice, Nebraska, on a hot Sunday afternoon."

A while later, when the city awakened "to a turmoil of activity," Bob was "utterly awed," he said. "I've lived in small towns all my life." He got "exactly the same kick out of New York [that] any other Main Streeter would."

He went to see Sidney Kingsley's *Dead End* at the Belasco Theatre, and at intermission, when somebody called out Bob's name, an army of "youngsters still up 'way past their bedtime' " began to push forward; those up close were helpless to do anything about it; soon everyone was getting torn apart. Bob "hadn't been cautious enough," he said, and was in the center of a "shouting, laughing stampede." He couldn't escape back inside, and before he was able to get in the theater, his tie had been pulled from his neck and the buttons and pockets ripped from his jacket. With a New York crowd on his tail, he felt like a "dog just introduced to a tin can" and was "knocked cold with fear."

The radio broadcast was in the Radio City building. *Private Number* (*Confessions of a Servant Girl*), Bob's new picture with Loretta Young, was due to open there within a few weeks. Bob was escorted by two policemen to the Radio City theater and then brought up to the rooftop, where the Rockettes and the Radio City ballet corps congregated between shows.

Afterward, he was safely escorted to the seventeenth floor of the complex to do the radio broadcast. As he left, the corridor and stairway were jammed with people extending down seventeen flights waiting to see him, and he ducked out another way. Someone started to push forward, and in an effort to get to Bob, the crowd broke down one of NBC's studio doors.

Boys rode on the back bumper of Bob's taxi for miles, and when he got out, they were on "his neck." Girls called his hotel room pretending to be his mother; others called and said they were Barbara Stanwyck. When Barbara did call, Bob was so sure it was a fan he shouted in her ear that he wasn't in.

Fifteen police had to rescue him from the entrance of the Loew's State Theatre building in Times Square. He got out of a cab in front of the theater, where he was to be on an MGM radio club broadcast, and was mobbed by a thousand autograph seekers, who picked him up, taking his shoe, grabbing at him, and causing him to be escorted in and out of the building.

He felt a little foolish that the police had to hustle him through crowds as if he were a prisoner, but with their help he saw the Statue of Liberty, Grant's Tomb, Central Park, the *Queen Mary*, and the aquarium, which impressed him more than anything else.

Bob left New York before getting a chance to eat at the Automat or walk across the George Washington Bridge. He dropped in on three nightclubs and saw Helen Hayes in *Victoria Regina* and Ray Bolger in *On Your Toes*.

While he was in New York, Barbara appeared on Louella Parsons's radio show, *Hollywood Hotel*, to do a scene with Gene Raymond, Helen Broderick, and Ned Sparks from *Marry the Girl*. The picture's title had been changed from *Marry the Girl* to *They Came Back Married* to *The Bride Misbehaves*. At that point the Hays Office intervened.

In a telegram to Sam Briskin, Hays said that while *The Bride Misbehaves* lent itself "to mischief rather than evil . . . serious suggestions require careful consideration." The next day Briskin wired back, "Astonished your wire stop My personal assurance to you . . . picture contains nothing salacious . . . titles you suggest have no box office value whatsoever . . . stop With record studio has for clean pictures feel your position very unfair stop."

Hays held firm. "Opinion still prevails here," he wired back to Briskin. "Will consult board members further and advise you."

The Bride Misbehaves became *The Bride Revolts, The Bride Takes Command, She Was Independent,* and finally *The Bride Walks Out.* Hays was mollified.

Metro decided to make use of the Taylor-Stanwyck romance being written about daily in the press. The studio was excited about the prospects of pairing Bob and Barbara in a picture; it knew audiences would be titillated by seeing Robert Taylor make love to his real-life romance. Once Bob returned from New York, he and Barbara were to star together at Metro in *My Brother's Wife.*

The script by Leon Gordon and John Meehan had been kicking around MGM for two years, a variation on *Red Dust* and *China Seas,* originally meant for Jean Harlow and Clark Gable. Then it was to be for Harlow and Franchot Tone, similar to *The Girl from Missouri,* their previous picture together. The director was to be Richard Boleslawski. Leon Gordon, John Meehan, and six other writers had their hand in the script, including Zelda Sears, Lenore Coffee, and Tess Slesinger.

Three weeks before production began on *My Brother's Wife,* Harlow was off the picture, and Metro decided to put Bob in opposite Barbara.

Bob and Barbara were concerned about their "friendship" being exploited and nervous about arguing during the making of the picture, but Barbara knew it would be good for both of their careers, and they agreed to go ahead.

Bob was the screen's most popular star, along with Clark Gable, Shirley Temple, and Fred Astaire and Ginger Rogers. Bob was the object of America's magnificent obsession; Barbara was struggling to salvage her career. She needed the picture.

Woody Van Dyke was assigned to direct it. Van Dyke—Metro's trusted director—had just completed production on *San Francisco,* the studio's most expensive picture to date, budgeted at $4 million.

Van Dyke was known in the industry as one of its most commercially successful directors—his range as a director was impressive—and one of its most sophisticated and dynamic. Van Dyke was six feet tall, all bone and muscle, with steel-blue eyes that looked right through you. He was one of the toughest guys in Hollywood. Van Dyke was a hard-boiled drinker who'd served in the marines as a major in the Great War.

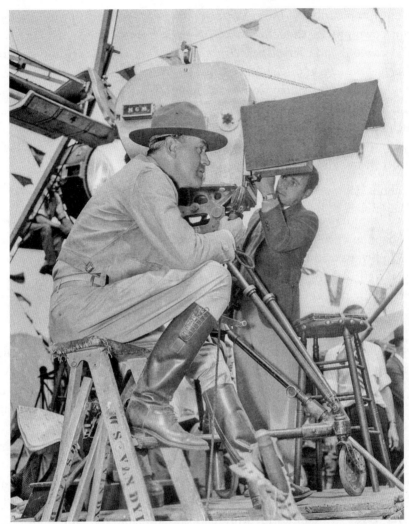

W(oodbridge) S(trong) Van Dyke II made Metro's first sound picture in 1929, based on the daring exploits along the Ivory Coast of the great African adventurer Alfred Aloysius Smith, alias "Zambesi Jack," alias "Trader Horn." The director, with more than two hundred actors and workers, and ninety tons of equipment in twenty-five trucks, traversed more than nine thousand miles of African soil through Tanganyika, Uganda, Kenya, and the Congo, crossing the equator eighteen times, all for the sake of authenticity, photographing the beauty of the sun-blistered veldt land and returning to Metro with 450,000 feet of film that caught the beauty and terror that was Africa. (PHOTOFEST)

Van Dyke never turned down an assignment even if he thought the picture was lousy ("It's their funeral, not mine," he said). He could direct anything and did: from a drama of doomed lovers living in an alien culture (*Never the Twain Shall Meet*) to one of an alien culture that brought together the most implausible of lovers (*Tarzan the Ape Man,* which included the director's own process shots from *Trader Horn*); from a comedy romance with Joan Crawford and Clark Gable (*Forsaking All Others*) to two frothy operettas (*Naughty Marietta* and *Rose-Marie*), one set in eighteenth-century Louisiana, the other on the Canadian frontier, each with Jeanette MacDonald and Nelson Eddy; from the just-completed epic about San Francisco's Barbary Coast, which culminated in a spectacularly staged twenty-minute re-creation of the 1906 earthquake that devastated the city, to a light comedy (*Penthouse*) with Warner Baxter and Myrna Loy.

It was Van Dyke who insisted to the Metro front office that Myrna Loy, a redhead of Montana pioneer stock, though until then typed as an "Oriental siren," "the subject of a thousand poems and stories of the Orient," wrote Carl Sandburg, could play a typical American girl and do comedy.

Van Dyke saw the spark and sexy ease between William Powell and Myrna Loy, directing them in *Manhattan Melodrama,* and set out to find a vehicle for a picture that could capture his notion about romance after marriage—a twist on the "they lived happily ever after" ending.

Van Dyke went through the MGM library of properties and found what he thought was the perfect story—one no director wanted to touch because of its ordinariness—a murder mystery about a detective and his wife. Van Dyke had Albert Hackett and Frances Goodrich, who faithfully re-created the humor and mystery of the book, write additional domestic scenes, and he had his script of *The Thin Man.*

It was Van Dyke who insisted on William Powell for Nick Charles against studio wisdom; Powell had been stuck in the dead-end Philo Vance series for years. The director set about using Powell's own distinct charm and friendliness, and the actor's improvised antics, to create the character of Nick Charles.

Van Dyke was famous for working fast and made *The Thin Man* in sixteen days. D. W. Griffith so admired the picture he saw it four times.

Van Dyke had started out in pictures in 1916 at the age of twenty-six as a makeup man for D. W. Griffith's *Intolerance.* Van Dyke, then the most promising young leading man on the legitimate stage, was the only one of Griffith's crew who knew how a Babylonian king should be made up (the makeup of biblical characters had been Van Dyke's hobby since childhood). He was given a week's job of daily transforming fifteen hundred extras into warriors and appeared in the picture as well—as a high priest, a groom, and a charioteer.

Soon he became Griffith's first assistant ("I was just one of Griffith's 10,000 messengers," Van Dyke said), making $3 a day. "Working under Griffith meant everything," said Van Dyke. "It was a case of hero-worship, pure and simple . . . I'm still trying to do the things I learned from him."

Griffith thought Van Dyke was an adventurer. ("Everything that man did," Griffith said, "he made into an adventure. Why, just to know him was an adventure.")

Van Dyke made his mark in 1928, when David Selznick assigned him to direct *White Shadows in the South Seas.* The picture was about a white man's redemptive journey to the Marquesas in the South Pacific—"a living fragment of the childhood of our Caucasian race"; a lost paradise over the rim of the world where Gauguin fled to paint ("Your civilization is your disease," Gauguin wrote to Strindberg, "my barbarism is my restoration to health").

Selznick saw *White Shadows* as "an ethereal love idyll"; his boss, the Metro producer Hunt Stromberg, saw it as "tits and sand" and sent off his own man, Robert Flaherty, to Tahiti to co-direct with Van Dyke.

Selznick denounced Stromberg as "tasteless"; Thalberg insisted Selznick apologize or leave the studio. Selznick cleared out his desk and was hired by Famous Players–Lasky to be assistant to B. P. Schulberg, the head of production.

When the rushes from the South Pacific arrived at Metro, it was Van Dyke's scenes of *White Shadows in the South Pacific Seas* that charmed Thalberg; Flaherty was recalled to Hollywood, and Van Dyke became the picture's sole director.

Metro was touting Robert Taylor as the "most sensational box-office draw since Clark Gable first leaped to fame."

Taylor's role in *His Brother's Wife* was that of a young research scientist, Chris Claybourne (it was Taylor's fourth role in a year as a doctor), the playboy son of an acclaimed medical doctor, about to embark on his first expedition to the jungles to find a serum for spotted fever. The role, written with Gable in mind, had many of the qualities of a Gable character: a sophisticated seducer of women, an adventurer ready to kiss civilization good-bye for untamed places and primitive jungles, a rugged man equally at home in white tie and tails or heat and sweat and dust-stained linen. The role was softened by Taylor's demeanor and at the insistence of the Breen Office, which pronounced both of the movie's leads "immoral people of loose habits and conduct" surrounded by "the inescapable flavor of loose sex."

Barbara was Rita Wilson—a professional "mannequin"—worldly, beautiful, out for a lark, who meets the young scientist just before he is to set sail for South America. Their high romance is a fling, days and nights of nonstop fun

From *His Brother's Wife,* 1936. (AMERICAN HERITAGE CENTER, UNIVERSITY OF WYOMING)

and high jinks. No questions asked, no attachments. At the end of ten days, each has been drawn into a web of feeling for the other, and hours before his departure Chris decides to abandon his mission, and the promising career that will come from it, and marry Rita.

It is his brother, Tom (John Eldredge), who dismisses Chris's ardor as nothing more than a momentary distraction, a last-minute romp, and not even with a girl of the family's standing. Tom insists his brother set sail for the sake of career and family honor and uses Chris's gambling debt as the way to prevail: Tom will pay the debt only if Chris sails for South America.

Chris's departure sets in motion the drama of the picture.

Rita—proving she's as powerful as the lofty Claybournes—seduces Chris's brother into falling in love and marrying her and walks out on her vows minutes after the ceremony. The righteous Tom Claybourne—earnest, responsible, hardworking—is desperate, unable to work or think of anything but Rita, and his own rising star as a brilliant doctor is suddenly in free fall.

Betrayal between brothers and lovers, the heat and hell of the jungle, a double dose of vengeance, a desperate fight to discover the elusive cure for the deadly spotted fever—all converge as the story moves toward its sweat-filled,

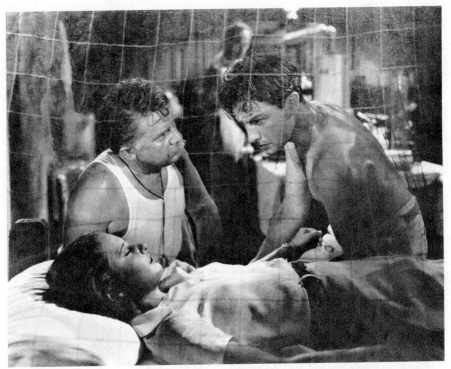

Jean Hersholt and Bob in the jungles of South America holding vigil as their antidote serum takes hold and (they hope) reverses the deadly spotted fever destroying Stanwyck's body. (AMERICAN HERITAGE CENTER, UNIVERSITY OF WYOMING)

tick-riddled climax in a steamy melodrama that caused Barbara to observe about *His Brother's Wife:* "We set pictures back 50 years."

The Breen Office insisted the studio take "the greatest care in showing scenes of physical contact" between the two characters, emphasizing in its letter to Louis B. Mayer that *"this is important."* There was to be "no *passionate kissing* between Chris and Rita at any time." And with Jean Harlow still being thought of as the star, Breen insisted "there should be no suggestion that Chris [leaning over Rita's chair] is looking down at Rita's breasts."

His Brother's Wife started shooting in early June 1936.

Van Dyke wanted his pictures vital and spontaneous; he was known as the high priest of directorial vigor and had an inexhaustible energy. He'd spent two years in the early 1920s shooting serials and making quickies for Poverty Row studios. Each scene had to be right the first time; there was no money for retakes; a few feet of wasted film could mean a man's job.

Actors were hired at fantastic salaries but on a daily basis; they had to be kept moving all day and into the night to get every one of their scenes on film. Van Dyke's one basic instruction to his cameraman was to "keep moving. No matter what the scene is," he said, "the audience should view it from as many angles as possible." Tempo was everything. At the end of the twenty-four hours, when the actor was half dead from exhaustion and all of the face-on scenes were shot, hot coffee was poured into him, and smelling salts were applied to his nose; he was sent on his way, and a double was brought in to finish the work.

Van Dyke wanted his actors to speak without self-consciousness or coyness. Writers were known to cry out when they saw what Van Dyke was doing to their words, how he was causing actors to mumble lines with their backs to the camera.

The reckless pace that Van Dyke shot was not just about saving money for the studio. He wanted an atmosphere of hurry and alertness that would give a "crisp, vital, quality to the final production." He didn't want actors wearing themselves out going over and over a scene. "The first rehearsal, the first shot, is always the best," Van Dyke said. "It may be imperfect but the general effect is superior."

He never looked at the daily rushes. Van Dyke's theory was simple: "Figure out how you would naturally do a thing and then do it naturally some other way."

During the shooting of *His Brother's Wife,* Van Dyke would pull a gag in the middle of a scene to catch an actor off guard and get a reaction or element of surprise he was after; at other times he would film actors who were only half rehearsed.

As a boy, Van Dyke, like Bob Taylor, was dressed by his mother as Little Lord Fauntleroy—in black satin and white lace with long beautiful curls. Van Dyke not only had to wear the clothes but had to act the part onstage and was sent from school to school, dressed as Fauntleroy; he let it be known he was no "sissy," but boys tortured him in one town after another, and by the age of nine Woody viewed the world with deep suspicion and distrust. At ten, he was appearing with his mother on the Pantages Circuit; he'd perfected his sense of timing and action and learned about costuming and sewing.

At fourteen, Van Dyke was in business school supporting himself by clerking in a grocery store, working as a janitor, oiling engines, selling vacuum cleaners door-to-door, driving an express wagon, and singing in vaudeville.

By twenty, he'd been just about everything: horseman, boxer, miner, electrician, newspaper reporter, switchman, sailor, a mercenary in Mexico, a gold prospector in the Klondike, a lumberjack in Washington. He'd been a socialist, a Communist, a Christian Scientist, and a Wobbly. He'd made colonel and major, gone to jail for agitating against capitalism, and then agitated against socialism when he protested the gubernatorial campaign of Upton Sinclair.

Van Dyke's trick of directing was to talk fast as he gave instructions to the actors. To get the tempo for the picture, he'd say: "You come on the set. You walk toward the table. You pick up a cigarette. You start saying your lines. You walk towards the door. And you should be finished with the speech when you open the door. Come on, let's do it."

Woody Van Dyke's pictures had an ease, a naturalism, and a sophisticated glitter. They were distinguished by beautiful photography, split-second action, and perfect continuity of story. And an authenticity.

His picture *Manhattan Melodrama* was so realistic it lured John Dillinger out of hiding to see it, setting in motion the circumstances of his death when he was killed by the FBI in front of the theater. During production of *His Brother's Wife,* the mood around Van Dyke was one of good humor and lots of laughter. Van Dyke was exact in his work and his schedule. Lunch was from twelve to one—one hour and no longer. At exactly six each evening, Van Dyke reached for his hat and signaled to the crew and actors the day was done.

Bob was thrown by the change in Barbara for the first two weeks on the picture.

"Being together socially and on the set are two different things," said Barbara. "I usually don't have any inhibitions, but when I work I'm quieter. I don't want anyone to talk to me before a scene and I don't like people to look at me when I'm crying."

Bob watched Barbara work "like a Trojan" and never complain. "She gives everybody in the studio a feeling that the picture in hand, is the most important job ever undertaken," said Bob.

Three days into the shoot, Barbara gave Bob a platinum watch with rubies as number markers on the face. Bob gave her a gift as well, a bracelet inscribed, "With Love—Robert Taylor." Barbara opened the box and said, "Oh, Bob, I'm not the type." Barbara didn't wear jewelry; Fay hadn't liked her to.

"What do you mean you're not the type?" Bob said. "To me you're beautiful and you're lovely."

Bob's kindness and attentiveness were transforming Barbara. She felt "warm and glowing and happy and wanting to be loved." She was barely recognizable to herself but still ever wary and questioned if Bob really meant what he'd said. "It's stupid to be cynical," she said. "It's more that I have grown wise; I can't be cheated if I don't trust."

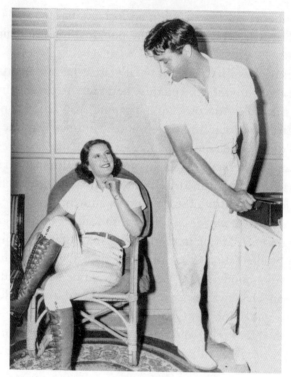

On the set of *His Brother's Wife,* 1936.

Barbara and Bob went to the studio together by car. He sent flowers to her dressing room, as he had with Janet Gaynor and Joan Crawford. He lunched daily in Barbara's dressing room and left with her at the end of the day. On Saturdays they went riding in the late afternoon or early evening and ate at the Brown Derby or at a drive-in sandwich stand near Bob's house.

When not filming, Barbara and Bob stayed in their dressing rooms. Bob brought a Victrola to the set and kept it there during the fourteen-day shoot so Barbara would be able to listen to her favorite records, among them Ray Noble, the Ambrose and Hylton orchestras, and Ellington's and Goodman's bands.

After four months of seeing each other, Bob thought Barbara "one of the great women of the Twentieth Century, a great woman and a very great actress."

Camille was to start filming as soon as *His Brother's Wife* was completed. Each night after work, Bob went to Barbara's so she could help him with the part of Armand.

Bob quoted Barbara as having said that he was the lousiest actor who ever was. She denied having said it.

The highest compliment Barbara could pay Bob, she said, was to state, positively, that "he is the same Bob he was when he was a thirty-five-dollar-a-week actor in the MGM stock company. He has risen with such dizzy speed," she said, "that he might have bumped his head against the stars and been stunned into a superiority complex, god knows. And if he hasn't blown his hat now, he never will. He's truthful with himself, with what counts. He knows just how far he can go and where to stop. He won't change and that's stability of character—and pretty fine. Bob has never become unfit for human intercourse, not for one moment."

In *His Brother's Wife*, Barbara was glamorous as Rita Wilson—lighthearted, vulnerable, assured, with none of the somber, stiff quality of *The Bride Walks Out*. She quietly gave Bob the picture.

On the last day of shooting *His Brother's Wife*, Barbara gave out lapel watches to the crew. The whole company signed a scroll naming Barbara their favorite actress.

Metro paid Bob a $5,000 bonus for making the picture.

Van Dyke gave Barbara a signed copy of his self-published book, *Horning into Africa*, about his adventures making *Trader Horn*, which she was thrilled to have. Needless to say, MGM did not give Barbara a bonus of any sort. Metro sold *His Brother's Wife* as the coming together of "America's exciting new sweethearts" and "America's Grand New Love Team."

Barbara was out, engaged with the world: dancing at the Grove, the Beverly Wilshire, the Palomar; joining the dachshund craze that had taken over the town with other dachshund lovers, including William Powell, Marion Davies, Dorothy Parker, and Donald Ogden Stewart. Barbara bought two puppies with Bob (his was black, he called it Pretzel; hers was red, she called it Lady).

After eight years of Fay's tyrannical, possessive ways, and months after Barbara's divorce, she felt free to "go where I please, with whom I please, dress as I please, talk as I please, go home when I like. I'm probably the last person in Hollywood to know what to do with freedom," she said. "Diversion of this sort would be deadly boring in time, but as a novelty it's great," she said.

Barbara was socializing with people she'd previously shunned, playing doubles tournaments at Claudette Colbert's, attending parties with Clark Gable and Carole Lombard, Ginger Rogers and the Jack Bennys, and having "peace and quiet and some fun."

With Bob and Spencer Tracy at the premiere of the film version of *Lloyd's of London* at the Carthay Circle Theatre, November 1936.

During her marriage, Fay had told her whom she could or couldn't know, and she'd ceded to his dictates, in part because she didn't make friends easily. Barbara was not one to make advances to people, gush, show that she was glad to see them even when she genuinely was. "I can't burst into a group and establish intimate terms right off the handle," she said. "I've lived too much within myself. I have no acquaintances. I don't want any. Smatterings never interest me."

Metro sent Bob to Dallas to attend the Texas Centennial on July 4 and paid him $1,000 for expenses. Barbara saw Bob off at the airport. When he arrived in Dallas, fans almost tore him apart, climbing all over him, ripping at his clothes, insisting on autographs.

On the way to the Texas Cotton Bowl, his car was stuck in traffic. An elderly farm woman came to the window and put her head inside the car to gaze at Taylor. "Why I've got two sons about your age," she said. "You're no different from them. You're exactly like anybody." Bob shook her hand and said, "You never said a truer word, ma'am."

Thirty thousand people showed up and jammed the stadium to see Robert Taylor, more people than turned out for President Roosevelt, who'd traveled to Dallas, Houston, San Antonio, and Austin to take part in the state's centennial celebrations. Roosevelt was up for reelection.

His longtime friend and supporter the four-time former governor of New York, Al Smith, denounced the president at the first dinner of the American Liberty League. Smith called Roosevelt and his administration socialistic and traitorous to many of the 1932 Democratic platform pledges and warned that if the upcoming Democratic National Convention endorsed the administration's treasonous acts, he and other old-time Democrats would "take a walk . . . There can be only one capital," said Smith, "Washington or Moscow."

Hearst's newspapers accused Roosevelt of surrounding himself with a "Communist entourage"; the *Chicago Tribune* headline said, "Moscow Orders Reds in U.S. to Back Roosevelt."

At the Republican National Convention in Cleveland, former president Herbert Hoover compared the New Deal to the "march of socialism and dictatorships" in Europe and called on the American people to enter a "holy crusade for liberty." To that end, Alf M. Landon, forty-eight, governor of Kansas, unanimously was named the Republican candidate for president. Landon was in the progressive tradition of Roosevelt.

Days before the Democratic convention in Philadelphia, five Democratic critics of the New Deal, led by Al Smith, asked the convention delegates to repudiate President Roosevelt and to nominate in his place a "genuine Democrat," Landon, "as the remedy for all the ills" of the country. Instead, the convention passed a platform that endorsed the New Deal and by acclamation renominated Roosevelt and John Nance Garner.

"America will not forget these recent years, will not forget that the rescue was not a mere party task," Roosevelt told the 100,000 cheering Democrats on the convention floor. "In our strength we rose together, rallied our energies together, applied the old rules of common sense, and together survived . . . But I cannot, with candor, tell you that all is well with the world. Clouds of suspicion, tides of ill-will and intolerance gather darkly in many places . . . We are fighting to save a great and precious form of government for ourselves and for the world."

In New York City, the Communist Party of the United States opened its national convention and nominated Earl Browder for president and James W. Ford for vice president. Ford was the first black man to be nominated for vice president of the United States.

FIFTEEN

Good Luck at Home

Barbara was set to make Sean O'Casey's *The Plough and the Stars.* John Ford was to direct. He'd just finished shooting *Mary of Scotland* with Katharine Hepburn, who had reluctantly agreed to be Mary.

"I never cared for Mary," said Hepburn. "I thought she was a bit of an ass."

The life of Mary Stuart fascinated Barbara. As a child, without mother or father, Barbara had spent endless hours dreaming of a family—a royal family—to which she imagined she rightfully belonged.

Mary's father, James V, dying when Mary was six days old, her accession to the throne to become queen of Scotland, being sent at age six to live in France at the center of one of the richest and most powerful monarchies in Europe, barely knowing the mother she adored—all of it captivated Barbara.

Mary lived with the forces dealt her in a life marked by bravery, adventure, boldness. Before her eighteenth birthday, she had lost her father, her mother, and her husband, with whom she had grown up and who had been her constant companion since childhood. She was alone.

Mary was a horsewoman of style: dressing like a man, riding with a pistol in her belt, and, even when pregnant, leading an army of thousands to defeat oncoming rebel forces. She was emotional, impetuous, headstrong. She had the ability to govern, but unlike her rival cousin, Elizabeth, queen of England, Mary had been educated to be a consort to a king, rather than a ruler in her own right. Where Elizabeth toyed with marriage, Mary was fully engaged with men and married three times. Marriage for Elizabeth was synonymous with death and disempowerment. She remained the Virgin Queen, married to England.

The life of Mary Stuart had all of the drama, size, and emotional pitch that held Barbara enthralled: heroism, passion, adventure, loss, sexual intrigue, murder, imprisonment, martyrdom; Mary's claim to the throne of England;

her imprisonment in her own country; her forced abdication in favor of her son; fleeing Scotland for England only to be incarcerated by Elizabeth and kept prisoner for seventeen years amid plans of escape and constant plotting; being implicated in a trap and found guilty of a plot to assassinate Elizabeth, and finally beheaded on Elizabeth's own order; living as a Catholic queen and dying as a Catholic martyr. Barbara had read every book written about Mary and was intrigued by how she was portrayed by different biographers.

It was Mary's rival cousin, Elizabeth I, who fascinated Bette Davis and compelled her to read every biography or play written on the subject. Davis desperately wanted to be in Ford's picture and to play the Virgin Queen to Hepburn's Mary Stuart. Katharine Hepburn was practically the only woman for whom Davis had "admiration and envy. I would have given anything to look like Katie Hepburn." Davis saw Hepburn as a Hollywood star "to be reckoned with."

Warner was adamant in its refusal to let Bette Davis work at the rival studio following the critical success she'd won for *Of Human Bondage*. Davis took it upon herself to go straight to John Ford to discuss the part. Ford laughed in Davis's face and told her she "talked too much."

Ginger Rogers wanted the part of Elizabeth as well and, after she'd finished production on *Swing Time,* began to campaign for it. The studio dismissed the idea of Rogers as the English queen. Rogers was not to be put off and disguised herself as a British Shakespearean actress—Lady Ainsley—visiting America, willing, for the fun of it and as a favor to John Ford, to make a silent test for the picture. Rogers made up for the test in full Queen Elizabeth garb: skullcap, wig, white face, and large stiff ruff. Hepburn, in her Mary costume, was there as well. Both Ford, who was delighted by the prank—and its cost to the studio—and Hepburn, who was not amused by Rogers's high jinks, were in on the ruse.

Pandro Berman, RKO's head of production, was so impressed with Lady Ainsley's test that he ordered it to be reshot with sound, until someone (Hepburn?) spilled the beans about the actress's true identity. Berman was a sport about the prank but told Rogers to stick to her high-heeled slippers and promptly put her in her seventh picture opposite Fred Astaire, *Shall We Dance.*

Ford wanted the part of Elizabeth to go to Tallulah Bankhead. Florence Eldridge was ultimately cast as Elizabeth I (Eldridge's husband, Fredric March, was Bothwell; when March was having difficulty with his character, caught in a tragic set of circumstances, Ford advised the actor to "play him for comedy").

John Ford (reflected in the mirror), Pandro S. Berman, and Katharine Hepburn during the filming of *Mary of Scotland.* Berman was producing the picture, 1936. (PHOTOFEST)

· · ·

Maxwell Anderson, George Jean Nathan, and Eugene O'Neill all had thought *The Plough and the Stars* to be one of the greatest plays of the twentieth century. "Oh, if I could write like that!" O'Neill had said about O'Casey.

John Ford had to fight to make *The Plough and the Stars,* even after receiving the Academy Award and the New York Film Critics Circle Award for *The Informer.* Ford had started directing at nineteen and made thirty-one serials at Universal and twenty-five feature pictures.

"They *may* let us do it as a reward for being good boys," said Ford of the prospects of making the O'Casey play into a movie.

Ford finished shooting *Mary of Scotland* in late April and left on a two-week holiday with Katharine Hepburn, visiting his parents in Maine and hers in Connecticut. He was back in early May and went to work on *The Plough and the Stars* the day after his return.

Sam Briskin, RKO's new production chief, was mystified about O'Casey's play. He didn't understand why, during the Great War, the Irish were fighting the British.

"What did George Washington want?" Ford said to Briskin. "They wanted liberty."

"They've got liberty," Briskin said of the Irish struggle and told Ford he thought the idea of the picture was "an entirely wrong premise."

Barbara had read the script of *The Plough and the Stars* and saw pages of dialogue for other characters and only a line here and there for Nora. It seemed such a minor role that she was skeptical about taking it.

"I can walk through this part," she told Ford the day she appeared for rehearsals. "It isn't as good as the role I had in *Message to Garcia;* in that at least I had a horse."

It was a part more emblematic than dimensional.

Thereafter, when Ford wanted her for a scene, he'd say, "Come on, Barbara, and walk through."

Up to ten days before the picture was to start shooting, Spencer Tracy was to play Jack Clitheroe at a salary of $27,500. Spyros and George Skouras "had a fit" about casting Tracy in the part. Spyros said that Tracy was "absolute poison at the box office; [that] he actually keeps people away from the theatre." The press reported that it was Tracy who bowed out of the part, saying that after reading the script, he'd decided "the part wasn't good enough."

Ford wanted the Abbey Theatre actors for the picture. In exchange, the studio insisted Barbara star as Nora Clitheroe, the young woman who runs the Dublin boardinghouse.

Cliff Reid, one of the picture's two associate producers, who'd worked with Barbara on *Annie Oakley,* put her together again with Preston Foster, RKO contract player, who had worked with Ford in Liam O'Flaherty's *Informer* and with Barbara in *Ladies They Talk About.*

Foster was given the role of the idealistic young man who accepts a command in the Irish Citizen Army, under the flag of the Plough and the Stars, and goes to fight for Ireland's sovereignty.

The plow on the flag is a primitive piece of equipment used by Irish farmers; above it, in deep green, on the field of the flag, is a constellation of Ursa Major, "the Plough," symbol of the aspiration of the Irish Labour Party, whose banner it became.

The uprising begins on Easter 1916; in the picture, the Irish Citizen Army mobilizes and is ready to strike. General James Connolly and thirty men capture the Dublin post office and barricade themselves inside; Jack Clitheroe, a commander, is among them.

Sean O'Casey, 1934, who taught himself to read and write at age thirteen; a former builder's laborer, dock hand, and railway worker. ("My chest measured 46, my arms were as big as tree limbs and I had a great ball of muscle on my hand where I gripped the pick handle . . . I worked all day and was ready to live joyously through the night.") He was down to his last shilling weeks before his first play, *Juno and the Paycock,* opened in London. (THE GRANGER COLLECTION)

Throughout Easter week, the British send in forty thousand troops; the uprising spreads through the city. Communication between those barricaded in the Dublin post office and the other strongholds throughout Dublin is cut off by the British; without contact they are lost. The post office falls; Connolly is executed by firing squad. Those fighters who make it out flee to the Dublin rooftops and, in a last desperate effort, snipe at the British troops below; Clitheroe manages to evade their hunt and make it back over the rooftops to his house and to safety.

Sean O'Casey had witnessed the uprising firsthand; he'd fought in it, was captured, and was sentenced to be shot before a firing squad. Just as the British soldiers were about to fire at him, a shell burst overhead, and the soldiers ran for cover. O'Casey escaped.

Ford considered the opportunity of making the picture "the greatest honor which has befallen me in twenty somewhat active years of picture making," he wrote to the playwright.

In a separate letter to O'Casey, Ford wrote that for years the stage had "represented our people as either comic characters or maudlin sentimentalists." *The Plough and the Stars* captured the spirit of rebellion, the fight against injustice, and the laughter and anguish of human life. Ford saw it as the showcase of "the greatness and superb achievement of our national sacrifice" and a way to mark the "awakening of the Irish national consciousness."

He asked O'Casey to add a sentence or two at the picture's end for Nora or Clitheroe or possibly Fluther after the uprising has failed. Ford wanted

The Plough and the Stars to make the point that "what they fought for would some day come true, that one day the flag of a Free Ireland might fly again."

O'Casey was a man without pretense. He had traveled to New York two years before to accompany his play *Within the Gates,* and had brought so few possessions—a brown suit and cap, a few shirts, socks, and underwear—that when unpacking, he put one sock in one drawer and its partner in the other.

O'Casey didn't want the theme of the play altered, and he didn't want Clitheroe to make a speech in the midst of the child Mollser's funeral. Ford assured the playwright that the "production would remain as close to the original as possible." Despite O'Casey's wishes and Ford's assurances, the director had Dudley Nichols, the scriptwriter, make the additions.

Ford and O'Casey corresponded about the revisions from January through March 1936. Perhaps the hopeful finish Ford sought was to honor his father, who had taken Ford at age eleven—the youngest of thirteen children—on the Red Star Line to Ireland, where the young boy had fallen in love with his father's childhood country.

Ford had been brought up to speak Gaelic, respect the Catholic Church, and hate the British, who ruled Ireland. His father, John Feeney, had lived through the famine. He grew up in a time when he'd had to sneak out at night with the other Catholic schoolboys to get his education with the help of the priests, despite the British governors, who, under the British Penal Laws, had outlawed parochial schools.

Ford's father had come to America at the age of sixteen at the end of the Civil War. He made his way to Portland, Maine, opened saloons and restaurants, became a successful politician, and rose to a position of power in the city.

Weeks after Ford's last visit with his father and just before the director was to start production on *The Plough and the Stars,* his father died.

In the final scene of *The Plough and the Stars,* Nora and Jack watch as the Irish tricolor flag is thrown down from what remains of the Dublin post office; the Union Jack is run up in its stead; the uprising is over.

"Oh, my darling, what was it all for?" Nora says to Jack in Ford's additions.

"Thousands dead—homes in ruin—what for?"

"Ah, Nora, we'll live to see Ireland free and go fighting till we do."

"Aye," she says, "and we'll go on weeping."

The haunting anguish and delicate quality of the final moments of O'Casey's play were replaced by Ford's rousing, hopeful rallying cry.

Ford wanted O'Casey to make revisions in the play to comply with the British censors, who wanted certain changes made, among them the removal

Left to right: J. M. Kerrigan, Barry Fitzgerald, Una O'Connor, Barbara, and Dennis O'Dea, from *The Plough and the Stars,* 1936. (AMERICAN HERITAGE CENTER, UNIVERSITY OF WYOMING)

of references to God. O'Casey wrote to Robert Sisk, the picture's second producer, calling the cuts, "God damn ridiculous. I may say that some of the cuts are the actual words spoken by Patric Pearse, Commander-General of the Irish Volunteers, at a meeting which I helped to organize. I can't see why they should object to this."

Four members of the Abbey Players were brought over for the picture: Barry Fitzgerald (Fluther Good), who already had an offer from Metro; Denis O'Dea (the Covey); Eileen Crowe (Bessie Burgess); and Arthur Shields, Fitzgerald's brother (Padraic Pearse). Shields, like O'Casey, had lived through the Easter week turmoil in Dublin and had been one of those holed up in the Dublin post office.

RKO wanted to reduce Barry Fitzgerald's salary from $1,000 to $750 (he settled on $850) and to get the use of the Abbey name for $750 and a four-week guarantee rather than six weeks.

As a director, Ford had a commanding presence and drove himself and his crew. One of the men working with Ford thought he was a "despot and professional Catholic," another thought he was a "sadist" who liked to terrify actors and provoke them into good performances. He created a tension on the set and would choose a patsy, ridiculing him or her. Philip Dunne, a screenwriter, thought Ford "a very temperamental, feisty character [who'd] flare up over any kind of criticism."

Others thought of him as fatherly.

Katharine Hepburn, then in the waning months of a romantic relationship with Ford, thought him "enormously rough, terribly arrogant, enormously tender, never smug, never phony . . . truly sensitive." She found him "fascinating but impossible. He was definitely the skipper of his own life and you had better not disagree with him too often."

Ford had won his first Academy Award for direction for the modestly produced *The Informer,* against Henry Hathaway's *Lives of a Bengal Lancer* and the two-time Academy Award–winner Frank Lloyd for Thalberg's production of *Mutiny on the Bounty,* the most expensive movie made since Metro's *Ben-Hur.*

The Informer had been turned down by Fox, Columbia, Metro, Paramount, Columbia, and Warner Bros. No one at RKO except Joseph P. Kennedy had actually read O'Flaherty's novel or was interested in having Ford make it into a picture. The book, set after the Irish Civil War, is about a man who sells out his former comrade and shifts the blame to another.

Kennedy, who had started RKO with David Sarnoff in 1928 in order to make talking pictures with the RCA Photophone sound process and had sold his remaining shares of the studio in 1934 to become a member of the Securities and Exchange Commission, no longer had any direct power at the studio, but he told the RKO staff producers about Ford and O'Flaherty's novel. "Let him make it [*The Informer*]," said Kennedy. "It won't lose any more than some of those you made."

The studio's minimal expectations and investment—RKO put up $234,000 for *The Informer* ("In Hollywood," Ford said, "that's considered the price of a cigar")—combined to give Ford the freedom to direct the picture as he pleased. As a result, he won the Academy Award for Best Director, his first award in twenty years of making motion pictures. Dudley Nichols won as well for Best Screenplay, but the Hollywood guilds—the Screen Actors Guild, the Screen Writers Guild, and the two-month-old Screen Directors Guild—had called for a boycott of the academy's eighth ceremony.

The president of the Screen Writers Guild called the academy a "company union with nothing in common with the Guilds"; the Screen Directors Guild pronounced the academy "a failure in every single function it has assumed. The sooner it is destroyed and forgotten, the better for the industry."

The academy had sided with producers over the pay cut of 1933 and continued to side with producers against the unions in labor negotiations.

For Best Picture, the academy was putting forward Thalberg's extravagant production, *Mutiny on the Bounty;* the guilds were pushing the modestly made *Informer.*

The heads of the studios had sent telegrams to their employees instructing them to attend the academy's ceremony, which only helped to rally support for the boycott ("You have probably been asked by your producer to go to the dinner," a telegram from the Guilds announced to their members. "The Board feels that since the Academy is definitely inimical to the best interests of the Guilds, you should not attend"). In an effort to avert a showdown with the Guilds, the academy revamped its voting procedure for Best Picture: instead of the vote being available to producers, it would now be open to the academy's full membership. In addition, Frank Capra, president of the academy, had hired an outside accounting firm, Price Waterhouse, to count the ballots.

Capra hoped to get around the boycott by announcing that a special award would be given to D. W. Griffith.

No one knew where Griffith had disappeared to. "We finally found him," said Capra, "in a Kentucky saloon."

Chaplin described Griffith as "the teacher of us all"; Cecil B. DeMille called him "the father of film." Joel McCrea, who'd been around Hollywood seeing movies get made since 1914, had stood on the corner of Vermont Avenue as a boy and watched the building of the Babylon set for *Intolerance:* D. W. Griffith sitting there overseeing it all like a king, wearing white gloves, white Stetson and carrying a walking stick.

By the late 1920s, Griffith's pictures were dismissed as old-fashioned; he no longer had artistic control of his movies, of which he believed he was the heart, soul, and mind. Following *The Struggle,* Griffith's last picture, from an Émile Zola novel, *The Drunkard,* which United Artists pulled from general release after a week, the great director was "washed up" in the business he'd helped to create. The D. W. Griffith Corporation went into bankruptcy, his pictures auctioned off, and Griffith bought the rights to twenty-six of his films for $500. A friend of his said, "D.W. made the virginal the vogue and it reigned until Volstead, gin and F. Scott Fitzgerald gave birth to the flapper."

"We used him," Capra said of the annual presentation of awards. "But we had to have a hell of a drawing card to keep the Academy alive."

D. W. Griffith (second from left), Special Award recipient at the eighth award ceremony of the Academy of Motion Picture Arts and Sciences. With him, left to right: Frank Capra, Jean Hersholt, Henry B. Walthall, Frank Lloyd, Cecil B. DeMille, Donald Crisp, at the Biltmore Bowl, Biltmore Hotel, March 5, 1936. (MARGARET HERRICK LIBRARY, ACADEMY OF MOTION PICTURE ARTS AND SCIENCES)

Griffith was delighted by Capra's invitation to accept the award and by the prospect of making the trip west. At sixty-one, Griffith was on his honeymoon with his twenty-six-year-old bride (he'd first met her when she was thirteen) and felt the trip to Hollywood would be a welcome wedding gift.

"Strangely enough," said Capra, "he did bring the crowd in. Everybody was anxious to see D. W. Griffith."

Among the thousand or so guests who attended the academy's ceremony at the Biltmore Hotel were secretaries and other seat fillers who'd received the "liberally distributed" tickets.

John Ford and Dudley Nichols were among those who did not attend. Ford, treasurer of the Screen Directors Guild, accepted his award for Best Director a week after the ceremony ("If I had planned to refuse it," he said, "I would not have allowed my name to go in nomination"). Dudley Nichols, one of the highest-paid writers in Hollywood who didn't need the protection of the Screen Writers Guild but was one of its founding members, sent back his award for Best Screenplay. In an accompanying letter to Capra, Nichols wrote, "The Screen Writers Guild was conceived in revolt against the Academy and born out of disappointment with the way it functioned against employed talent in any emergency . . . To accept [the academy's award] would be to turn my back on nearly a thousand members of the Writers Guild, to desert those fellow writers who ventured everything in the long-drawn-out fight for a genuine writers' organization, to go back on convictions honestly arrived at, and to invalidate three years' work in the guild."

After the academy ceremony, there was talk that Griffith, once again at the town's center, might be hired to remake *Way Down East*, a picture he'd made in 1920; nothing came of it.

John Ford didn't like producers. They were to stay off his set while he was shooting a picture.

A producer had once told Ford in the midst of production that he was behind schedule; Ford ripped out ten pages from the script. "Now we are three days ahead of schedule," he said and never shot the sequences.

Producers, to Ford, had one purpose: to deal with money. Ford had only contempt for money and refused to walk around with it.

"They've got to turn over picture-making into the hands that know it," Ford said. "Combination of author and director running the works: that's the ideal."

"Ford was always a cop hater," said Robert Parrish, Ford's cutter, "by religion, by belief. He had a big streak of contempt for any kind of authority, any kind of paternal influence on him—all the producers, all the money—they were the enemy."

When Cliff Reid, associate producer on *The Plough and the Stars*, went to the set to tell Ford how great the previous day's rushes were, the director said that there must be something wrong if Reid liked them and spent the next two days reshooting the scenes at an additional cost of $25,000.

John Ford was almost blind and wore dark prescription glasses that prevented his eyes from being seen. He constantly chewed and sucked on a corner of his handkerchief. He pulled his slouch felt hat down all the way around. He wore a sport coat over a sweater and shirt without a tie, with the collar of the coat turned up—a studied form of casual negligence.

Barbara didn't get along with Ford. She thought he was putting on an act.

Ford had a good luck shirt and wore it always.

"Why don't you have it laundered once in a while. You smell of perspiration," said Barbara.

"That's part of my good luck," he said.

"You have your good luck at home. Take it home with you," she said.

For the part of Nora Clitheroe, Barbara was paid $5,312.50 per week—more than twice what Ginger Rogers, the third most popular actress in America, was making. Barbara was getting $42,500 for the picture with an eight-week guarantee; Ford, $63,580. *The Plough and the Stars* was budgeted at $483,000.

Shooting on the ten-week production started in early July; Barbara began three days later.

Ford had the actors work without makeup; he wanted them to look human.

For authenticity in *Plough,* Ford used photographs of the city taken on the day of the uprising as well as news photographs from London's *Daily Mirror* and *The Illustrated London News* taken during that Easter week. Van Nest Polglase oversaw the design of the interior and exterior sets of the post office, St. Stephen's Green, and the narrow cobbled streets that led from it to the pubs, the tobacco shop, and the sets re-creating the Dublin tenements.

Barbara worked relentlessly to perfect her accent. One night in the projection room, one of the producers decided that somebody in the picture had to be understood. The Abbey Players couldn't change their dialect. Barbara was chosen, but the early sequences in which she used a heavy brogue were never reshot.

Barbara and Preston worked well together. Neither could work if spoken to before the shooting of a scene. If Barbara, who knew everyone else's lines as well as her own, prompted Foster at a slipped line, he would become frantic and stop and get the line himself.

Bonita Granville played Mollser Gogan, the consumptive girl whose death is the Clitheroes' salvation as Jack seeks refuge, in the midst of her wake, from the British soldiers searching for him and Nora hides his rifle, Sam Browne belt, and hat in Mollser's pine coffin.

Granville, whose father, Bernard "Bunny" Granville, had been a Broadway musical star before working in pictures and whose mother was a dancer on the stage, thought Ford "casual" as a director; he didn't try to "form a performance" with her. William Wyler had just directed the twelve-year-old in *These Three* and was meticulous with her about every line, every look, every thought. Ford was more interested in "the feel, the mood; he taught you about mood," she said. "He would never try to change a line or tell you anything that you should do specifically." Ford gave Granville "almost no direction. The one or two things that he would tell you," she said, "would be impressive. When he said something, he knew what he wanted. Mr. Ford let me start out as a child and kind of ramble and feel it. Then he would bring it into shape."

Barbara insisted on doing her own stunts. Foster, in one scene, throws her to the ground when she tries to prevent him from going off to fight. Ford said, "We'll show him throwing you off and then we'll cut to you lying on the street."

"We'll do no such thing," Barbara said. "We'll show the whole action."

Barbara may have had only a few lines, but Nora Clitheroe was a strenuous part; the emotion, the movement, the symbolism of her character, were more demanding than if there had been pages of dialogue. The other characters talked, but Barbara dominated. It was impossible for her to "walk through" the part.

Ford saw Nora Clitheroe as life affirming; life-giving but suffering, carrying the burden of war and death; holding the man back from a cause larger than any one man or woman or love—the fight for freedom. It is the woman who selfishly fights for the life of the man she loves and fights off madness as she awaits his return; it is she, in the play, who will mourn for his martyred death (in the Nichols script Jack Clitheroe escapes death as Nora escapes the madness that would have come in the wake of his useless dying; "Aye, you'll do the fighting," Nora says to Jack, "but the women will do the weeping").

Ford's cameraman, Joseph August, photographed Barbara in one scene as a Madonna figure—shrouded in mourning shawl—a Byzantine icon against an orb of golden light.

Ford's notion of how the picture was to look dominated every scene. With *The Informer,* he created a dreamlike world. With *Mary of Scotland,* darkness and shadow show the danger and treachery of Mary's court, the primitive harshness of her Scotland, and the inevitability of her destiny, shaped by her own willfulness and the forces of history.

Dudley Nichols, who wrote the script for *Mary of Scotland* from the Maxwell Anderson play, said of Ford, "He had the true eye of the film-maker. His sight was not very good, but he had the surprising power of an inner vision."

Darkness and shadow were central to Ford.

"I can take a thoroughly mediocre bit of acting," said Ford, "and build points of shadow around a ray of strong light centered on the principals and finish with something plausible. You don't compose a film on the set. You put a redesigned composition on film."

Barbara, seated third from left. From *The Plough and the Stars*, 1936. (AMERICAN HERI-
TAGE CENTER, UNIVERSITY OF WYOMING)

Ford's crew understood what he had in mind. "He didn't want big camera movement [or] standard close-ups. [Ford] had a thing about the eyes,"
said Robert Parrish, his cutter. " 'Look in people's eyes, see what they're telling you.' "

Ford wanted what was honest and real and simple. He went for the truth.

His main influence was Griffith. "I wouldn't say we stole from him," said
Ford. "I'd say we copied from him outright. D.W. was the only one then who
took the time for little details."

Ford often worked with a silent camera—without a microphone—in
order to be able to talk to the actors as he shot the scene. The first seven
hundred feet of *The Informer* were silent. He believed that sound was not of
primary importance to picture making. "I am a man of the silent cinema,"
he said. "That's when pictures and not words had to tell the story . . . Sound
wasn't the revolution most people imagine it was."

Darryl Zanuck had produced *The Prisoner of Shark Island* in between
Ford's making *The Informer* and *Mary of Scotland* and thought the director "could get more drama into an ordinary interior or exterior long shot
than any director . . . [Ford's] placement of the camera almost had the effect

of making even good dialogue unnecessary or secondary . . . He painted a picture—in movement, in action, in still shots."

Mary of Scotland opened in New York midway through production of *The Plough and the Stars. Mary of Scotland,* which cost RKO $864,000—the studio's most expensive production after *Swing Time*—received negative reviews; "a great treat for scholars but a bit boring for the ordinary picture audience," said *The Hollywood Reporter; Variety* faulted the film's "length and finish"; another critic summed up the picture as "a mass movement from one prison to another."

Two of Barbara's pictures opened soon after.

The Bride Walks Out opened in early July in New York at Radio City and in Los Angeles at the Pantages. "One of the merriest, most natural and human comedy romances," said one critic; important, said another, "for sending Barbara Stanwyck further on a frolicsome road to the status of comedienne, a style of acting she shows increasing aptitude for since dropping the emotional drama which made her famous."

His Brother's Wife opened weeks later at Loew's State and Grauman's Chinese. On the picture's first day, moviegoers were lined up at seven in the morning to see America's No. 1 male draw ("Hold on to your hearts, girls") make love to Barbara Stanwyck ("It's Romantic Dynamite"). Early morning patrons waited on line to get into Grauman's while the theater served them coffee and doughnuts. Bob and Barbara slipped into a preview showing. Sneak previews had taken on the excitement and devotion of religious meetings, and the unwritten law dictated attendance.

Outside Grauman's several MGM publicity people circulated in the crowd and let it be known that Taylor and Stanwyck would soon be leaving the theater. When Bob and Barbara emerged, police had to escort them through the swarms of fans.

Richard Watts referred to Bob as "the beautiful Mr. Robert Taylor, the loveliest screen hero of the season," and the "characters, the most annoying and generally unpleasant of the season . . . Miss Stanwyck," Watts said, "plays her role with her characteristic dull sincerity and Mr. Taylor never lets you forget his charm."

"Overplotted; filled with hokum," said *The Hollywood Reporter,* which called Taylor's performance "nothing short of dynamite" and, together with Barbara, "a smash." Jimmy Starr in the *Evening Herald Examiner* said, "Only the grand work of Taylor and Stanwyck, guided by that Van Dyke person, make [the picture] worth while."

Despite the reviews, Taylor's box-office draw was so strong audiences wanted to see anything in which he appeared. Universal reissued Bob's second picture, *There's Always Tomorrow,* which starred Frank Morgan and Binnie Barnes and in which Bob had only a small role.

Zeppo Marx arranged for Barbara and his discovery Fred MacMurray to appear together in the *Lux Radio Theatre* presentation of Sinclair Lewis's *Main Street.* Barbara had been under contract for eight years with the J. Walter Thompson Company for magazine advertisements for Lux soap ("Nine out of ten screen stars use Lux Toilet Soap"); this was her first radio broadcast for *Lux Theatre.*

The show had just moved to Hollywood from New York, where it had started two years before, broadcasting from Radio City, sponsored by Lever Brothers. In New York, it was made up weekly of adaptations of Broadway productions: *Smilin' Through, Berkeley Square, Counsellor-at-Law.*

In Los Angeles the broadcast had its own theater—the Music Box on Hollywood Boulevard—with an audience capacity of just under a thousand people. Cecil B. DeMille had recently been chosen as the master of ceremonies over other possible hosts, among them George M. Cohan, D. W. Griffith, Walter Huston, and Frank Morgan.

Danny Danker, vice president of Thompson's West Coast operations, was in charge of borrowing stars from the studios and worked out the details of Barbara's appearance with RKO and MacMurray's with Paramount. MacMurray, at twenty-eight, was starring in *Champagne Waltz,* his eleventh picture in two years.

Barbara was excited about being part of the *Lux Radio Theatre* program. "No one identified with stage or screen can listen to radio without [wanting] to become a part of it," she said.

The *Lux Radio Theatre* was lavishly produced, with a weekly budget of $20,000. Barbara and the other actors met on an empty stage at the Music Box, sat around a large conference table, and read from the script several times until they had the feel of it. "We spent five hours on it the first night," Barbara said. "Six hours the next."

Before the show was broadcast over the CBS nationwide network, the cast had spent twenty-five hours in actual rehearsal. It was assumed by listening audiences that Mr. DeMille was the show's producer and director, though DeMille didn't arrive at the theater until dress rehearsal. It was Frank Woodruff, described as "an actor's director," who oversaw the production.

Main Street had just been released by First National under the title *I Married a Doctor,* from the Sinclair Lewis novel that had been made into a silent in 1923, based on the 1921 Broadway adaptation.

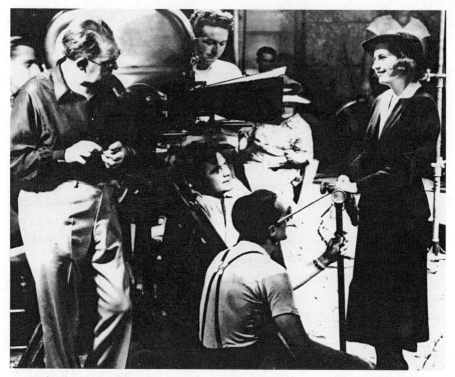

With John Ford (left). Joseph H. August (underneath the lens) was the cameraman on both *The Plough and the Stars* and *Mary of Scotland,* 1936.

The *Lux Radio Theatre* presentation used Lewis's novel, rather than the silent picture or the Broadway play.

Radio, to Barbara, "staggers the imagination. Man comes near approaching infinity in service," she said. "Radio is a hard job but I like it, because it demands more of my talent and ability than any other business, and it is my job to make a perfect delivery. At least that is my sincere ambition."

When finished with the Lux broadcast, Barbara was back at work on *Plough.* Bob Taylor called her each morning. Ford stuck his head through the open window of Barbara's bungalow and said, "Don't let that Taylor make you late on my set!"

At the end of the production, Ford gave Barbara an old Gaelic cross. On the back he had inscribed in Gaelic: "To Barbara. God and Mary always be with you. Jack Ford." Ford told her, "Always wear it inside your clothes." She did.

Despite that, Barbara said she wouldn't work with Ford again. "And he wouldn't want me, either," she said. "That's old fashioned crap, what he does.

I don't want any acts like that. I'll take some young guy who doesn't know anything and try and do it."

Robert Sisk, an associate producer on the picture with Cliff Reid, sent O'Casey a set of stills from the picture ("All in all," Sisk wrote to O'Casey, "it is certainly the best production the play has ever had and though it has been a costly affair, and though we have certainly taken a risk on the English market, I suspect we will sneak out on it"). He let O'Casey know that he and Ford were trying to secure the rights for *Juno and the Paycock.*

Sam Briskin, the picture's executive producer, wasn't happy with the finished picture. "Why make a picture where a man and a woman are married?" he asked. "The main thing about pictures is love or sex. Here you've got a man and a woman married at the start—who's interested in that?" Briskin wanted the scenes between Nora and Jack to be reshot with them unmarried.

Ford refused to reshoot the scenes, as he had five years before on *Arrowsmith* after arguing with Sam Goldwyn about retakes. Now, on *The Plough and the Stars,* Ford proceeded to get so drunk that Cliff Reid called on Kate Hepburn for help. Hepburn went to Ford's house, helped get him into her car, and drove him to her dressing room on the RKO lot, where she plied him with a large whiskey and a heaping dose of castor oil that made him so ill he thought he was going to die. When he finally passed out, Hepburn thought he had died. She somehow got him to the Hollywood Athletic Club, where he often went and where he could recover.

Ford soon left Los Angeles for the San Pedro harbor and set sail on his 106-foot ketch, the *Araner,* named for the Aran Islands, and headed west toward the translucent waters of Honolulu.

"After I had shot it exactly as it was written," Ford said, "they tried to make a love story of it."

In the reshooting of *The Plough and the Stars,* the uprising is kept in the background. The struggle between the newly married Jack and Nora Clitheroe is brought to the fore—hers to keep him safe, alive, and at home ("A woman's nature is to love just as it is a man's nature to fight," Nora says to Jack, "and neither one can help it more than the other"), his to be a freedom fighter ("Ireland is greater than a mother," Jack says to her, "Ireland is greater than a wife").

Pan Berman had the assistant directors George Nichols and Ed Donahue direct retakes on two weekends when Barbara and Preston were at work during the week on two other pictures: she on *Banjo on My Knee* at Fox; Foster on *Sea Devils* for RKO.

The O'Casey play showed the futility of war and the waste of human life in the fight for freedom; it was also alive with the wit, spirit (O'Casey's dedication to the play read, "To the gay laugh of my mother at the gate of the grave"), and crackle of the characters of the boardinghouse—old Peter, Fluther Good, the handyman, the teasing young Covey, Bessie Burgess, and Mrs. Gogan, constantly at it with one another—and the others, Rosie and the Barman. In the picture, both threads—the love story and the comic chatter of the Dubliners—run parallel with the third, the uprising itself. With the varying notions of director and writer and studio executives, the picture was pulled in too many directions.

"The final result wasn't any good," said Barbara. "John should not have left the sinking ship but stayed behind and fought for us. Only John could have saved it, and he should have."

SIXTEEN

Fresh Passion, Fresh Pain

Barbara owed 20th Century–Fox two pictures after *A Message to Garcia,* and the studio coordinated shooting schedules with RKO. Fox planned to use Barbara for eight weeks following *The Plough and the Stars,* from the end of August through the end of October.

John Cromwell was directing a romantic character-comedy adventure set on the Mississippi River written and produced by Nunnally Johnson. The story was about a loopy shanty boat colony and the ornery, cheerful patriarch, Newt Holley, determined to "git" himself an heir from the last of his six sons (the other five drowned in the river) to carry on the family name. The son marries a land girl—the daughter of a renegade river man—rather than one of his own kind, and the newlyweds, through mishaps, the law, chases and escapes, arguments and equally matched bullheadedness, can't seem to get together even for one night.

The part of the girl, Pearl Elliott was seen as "a Janet Gaynor character," in fact was to be played by Gaynor, but she was shooting *Ladies in Love* with Loretta Young, Constance Bennett, and Simone Simon and wasn't available.

John Cromwell thought Barbara would be a "natural for the role." Zanuck dismissed the idea; Barbara had "no sex appeal." He wanted Sylvia Sidney, Jean Arthur, or Margaret Sullavan. Zanuck's take on Barbara had more to do with how "he couldn't catch me," she said, than it did her allure or her acting ability. "He ran around the desk too slow," she said.

Zanuck, like Bill Wellman, was known as a drunk and whore hound. Zanuck interviewed his actresses, tested them, then made his play. Sometimes he opened a desk drawer and took out a genuine gold casting of his genitals and showed how admirably hung he was. If actresses resisted him, he could be vindictive.

John Cromwell, a former stage actor who'd appeared in the American

With Joel McCrea (left) and John Cromwell, the director of *Banjo on My Knee,* 1936.
(PHOTOFEST)

premiere of *Major Barbara* as well as an outstanding theatrical director, had appreciated Barbara's work before they'd both left New York for Hollywood. Cromwell had seen Barbara on Broadway in *The Noose* and wanted her for a new play he was then directing. Barbara had read a play called *Burlesque* and chose to go into it instead. When Cromwell co-directed with Eddie Sutherland the picture based on *Burlesque—The Dance of Life*—Nancy Carroll was in the role Barbara had made her own in its run on Broadway.

Cromwell believed Barbara had "just the right quality" for Zanuck's picture. The producer held firm against using Barbara until weeks before production was to start and then relented, saying she "would be perfect for the part."

Fox paid RKO $45,000 for Barbara's services.

Pearl Elliott marries Ernie Holley, a hardheaded, hard-lovin' shanty boat man, a Mississippi catfish, a "Spencer Tracy type." Zanuck wrote "Henry Fonda" next to the description of the character. He wanted Fonda or Fred MacMurray or Jim Stewart. Henry Fonda had been under a nonexclusive contract to Fox, appearing in *Way Down East* and *The Farmer Takes a Wife,* before Zanuck merged 20th Century with Fox. While not particularly won over by Fonda's screen presence or the money the actor was asking, Zanuck kept Fonda on.

Barbara and Joel McCrea had become friends during *Gambling Lady,* and Fox borrowed the thirty-year-old McCrea from Samuel Goldwyn for $25,000 for six weeks. In exchange, Goldwyn was to get either the three Ritz Brothers or Jack Haley for one picture. McCrea wasn't fond of Zanuck; he thought the producer "an egotistical little bastard; a gutty little guy and a chaser, but smart."

McCrea was natural as an actor, and underplayed as much as he could. Gary Cooper was his idea of a romantic leading guy.

Together McCrea and Stanwyck had a quality: they looked like pioneer stock; she was full of pluck, ready to pitch in, and game for life; he was tall, athletic, all-American, and homespun with a sincerity and innocence and a readiness to take care of her. McCrea's sexuality was in his beauty and build, his simplicity, poise, and shyness. He didn't drink or smoke or gamble. Stanwyck didn't play for being sexy; it was all around her. She didn't flaunt it but it was there, underneath everything she did, and she drew on it.

Walter Brennan was being considered for the part of Newt Holley, head of the clan. Brennan, at forty-two, had appeared in more than a hundred pictures in bit and supporting parts as the stubble-faced codger, the sailor, the sidewinder. He was a young man but played older characters—cranky, ratty, eccentric figures—with a comedic flair that made his work impossible to ignore.

Brennan was known as one of the most democratic men in Hollywood, without a "fake sense of values," said one of the sound mixers. His characterizations were picked up from friends he made along the way—street sweepers, garbage collectors, truck drivers, postmen.

He had started in pictures in 1925 "purely from hunger," he said, an extra getting paid $7.50 a day. Soon he was making between $25 and $100 a day until he got his big break with Goldwyn in Howard Hawks's *Barbary Coast,* working with Joel McCrea. Hawks, who directed Brennan in *Come and Get It,* thought the actor had "an amazing quality . . . able to play anything and do it right."

Fox decided to use Brennan for Newt, and in exchange Goldwyn was to get both the Ritz Brothers and Jack Haley. Brennan had just finished making Goldwyn's *Come and Get It* from the Edna Ferber novel, playing the logger Swan Bostrom. Brennan considered the Goldwyn Studio the country club of the motion picture industry and stayed with Goldwyn for ten years. "Sam was class," said Brennan. "He did nothing cheap."

Walter Brennan circa 1935. He left engineering school to work in vaude-ville, raise pineapples, speculate in real estate, and work as a stuntman. As Newt Holley, he had to learn to play a one-man band with harmonica, a xylophone of bottles, cow bells, and bass drum, and mastered the contrap-tion without a hitch.

As Newt, Brennan had to learn to play a one-man-band contraption, a jungle gym of branches tied together that had tethered to it a harmonica and a xylophone of bottles, cowbells, and bass drum. Brennan mastered the musical contraption without a hitch and learned as well to play the piccolo, accordion, and banjo. Brennan was nimble with his fingers and had an un-canny ear; he could imitate car horns, wasps, bees, birds, cows, roosters, dogs, and cats. He made "goofy sounds," as he called them, "just like a high school kid, simply for the hell of it," which he learned living on his farm in the San Fernando Valley with his wife, three children, dogs, horses, and cows.

Brennan decided to play Newt without his false teeth; he'd lost the origi-nals several years before in an accident.

Katherine DeMille was set to play the boat woman in love with Ernie who determines that no one else should get her man if she can't have him. Buddy Ebsen, the former *Ziegfeld Follies* dancer of *Broadway Melody of 1936,* was Newt's nephew, Buddy, the shiftless, shambling young man, as vague in intel-ligence as he is on everything; he sings and dances an odd shuffle. Anthony "Tony" Martin, in his second picture, was a New Orleans crooner down on his luck and unsure of his talent who falls hard for Pearl.

The Holley clan on board their Mississippi houseboat, *Banjo on My Knee.*

The picture was based on a novel of the same name by Harry Hamilton, recently published by Bobbs-Merrill in February 1936. Hamilton had co-written the play—called *From Now On*—ten years before with Norman Foster. Fox had bought the motion picture rights to the novel for $10,000.

Stories of the Deep South had taken hold in Hollywood since the publication of *Gone with the Wind*, which to date had sold 600,000 copies. Studios were making a picture about New Orleans, and Warner was planning a sequel to *Anthony Adverse* set in the South.

Zanuck assigned Nunnally Johnson to produce *Banjo on My Knee*, intended to be a kind of lighthearted, musical *Tobacco Road*, then running on Broadway in its third year and still shocking audiences with its comic brutality of life lived by the dissolute Lester family. If the Lesters of Georgia's *Tobacco Road* are a foul and lazy clan living in filth, Zanuck wanted the Holleys of *Banjo on My Knee* to be a merry, pride-of-folktale bunch, odd but decent sorts, who are banded together in a Mississippi shanty boat colony, folk who work hard and play harder.

Nunnally Johnson had worked with Zanuck since 1933, when the producer had left Warner Bros. to form 20th Century Corporation with Joe Schenck and Bill Goetz. Each of Johnson's pictures captured the complexity of the subject; each was visually powerful and dramatically told; and each earned large amounts of money for Zanuck. Johnson had worked as a reporter in New York City, first on the *Tribune,* then on the *Brooklyn Daily Eagle,* the *Herald Tribune,* and the *New York Evening Post.* A year after going to Hollywood, he was hired by Zanuck at the newly formed 20th Century Corporation. When 20th Century merged with Fox, Zanuck made Johnson a producer. He took the job because Zanuck asked him to, and, Johnson said, "If he asked me to jump off the bridge I'd have done it."

Banjo on My Knee was set in the South above Memphis and in New Orleans. Johnson hired William Faulkner to work on the story. Faulkner was in Hollywood; he'd been back and forth from Oxford, Mississippi, since 1932 to augment his income, after finishing *Light in August.* Sam Marx at Metro had hired Faulkner to write original stories for $500 a week, more money than the writer had ever seen, "more money than there was in all of Mississippi," he said. Faulkner had written a script for Metro's biggest star, Wallace Beery.

Following *Flesh,* Faulkner wrote a treatment and screenplay for Howard Hawks from Faulkner's story "Turnabout," which became *Today We Live* and was made with Joan Crawford and Gary Cooper. Faulkner wrote the treatment in five days; Thalberg read it and said to Hawks, "Shoot it as it is. I feel as if I'd make tracks all over it if I touched it." When Hawks left Metro after a year and a half (he was glad to get out of that "goddam place") and went to Movietone City for 20th Century–Fox, he took Faulkner to work with Joel Sayre on a script called *The Road to Glory.*

Faulkner was at work on a new novel, *Absalom, Absalom!,* when Nunnally Johnson approached him about *Banjo on My Knee.* Faulkner needed money and agreed to write a treatment, which he turned in in March 1936; Zanuck thought it full of "great possibilities" and proceeded to lay out his own ideas about the script.

Faulkner was getting paid $1,000 a week and living at the Beverly Hills Hotel. While at work on *Banjo on My Knee,* he was lonely and wrote in a letter, "I wish I was at home, still in the kitchen with my family around me and my hand full of Old Maid cards."

Faulkner's pages for *Banjo* were "magnificent," said Dave Hempstead, Nunnally Johnson's associate producer. "[He] wrote practically blank verse, sometimes two or three pages long. They were beautiful speeches." But impossible for an actor to perform. One of Pearl's speeches, written by Faulkner:

Then he left me before we were even married. He fixed it so that his people could say the things about me they wanted to say. Then he left me, because when I left I wasn't running from him. I was running after him. If he had loved me he wouldn't have known that. If he had loved me he would not have left me. If he had loved me he would have followed me and overtaken me. He could have because no woman ever runs too fast for the man she loves to catch her, but he didn't.

Faulkner said of writing scripts, "It ain't my racket. I can't see things. I can only hear."

The language could be heard on the page, but it wasn't conversational dialogue.

The picture's producer next gave *Banjo on My Knee* to Francis Faragoh, a scriptwriter whose work ranged from *Little Caesar* and *Frankenstein* to *Becky Sharp*. Faulkner was loaned out by RKO to work on George Stevens's *Gunga Din*. Zanuck trusted Faragoh but thought his screenplay for *Banjo on My Knee* "terrible . . . must have been on strike," Zanuck wrote. "Audience will laugh at drama."

Zanuck believed *Banjo on My Knee* could "easily be a comedy riot and very romantic," but Faragoh's script had turned the book into "an old fashioned rural melodrama like *Way Down East . . .* the script was terribly censorable—unnecessarily so." Zanuck doodled in a note to himself, "Censors kill us."

Zanuck made it clear to Nunnally Johnson that Pearl was the star of the story and that the underlying theme of *Banjo on My Knee* had to be the father doing everything he could to get his son and daughter-in-law into bed so he could have a grandchild.

The Breen Office objected to Zanuck's running gag in the final script—written in the end by Johnson—of "showing Newt's efforts to have Pearl and Ernie sleep together so that the marriage may be consummated and his hopes of an heir fulfilled." Zanuck wrote back: "Your reader has injected smut and sex where none was ever intended. It is not a case of trying to get them to climb into bed with each other. He wants them to be in love with each other because he knows that if they are, eventually they will have children and he will have an heir. In God's name, what is wrong with this?"

John (born Elwood Dager Cromwell in Toledo, Ohio) was an easy director to work with, trained as he was for the stage. He was not, however, an imaginative director.

Cromwell had sought out the little-known Bette Davis at Warner Bros. for the part of the insolent, intoxicating Mildred in *Of Human Bondage*. He did not believe in deviating from the script, even with a misprint on the page. When an actor complained that a line didn't make sense as it was typed,

Cromwell's response was: "Not a word, not a line, not a single syllable will be changed without the personal approval of Darryl Francis Zanuck."

Despite Cromwell's literalness, Barbara's Pearl has just the right energy and spirit; her work was simple and fresh with an optimism that reflected the buoyancy of the Roosevelt recovery. There was a new tenderness in her that came through on-screen that wasn't only about acting.

She was being loved, openly, adoringly, by Bob Taylor without the twisted darkness or fear that had been so entwined in her love with Frank Fay. She seemed softer, with a peacefulness that gave her work a fulsome quality.

In *Banjo*, Barbara had to sing for the first time in front of the camera and did so to McCrea's harmonica. Barbara wanted someone to dub her, but Zanuck insisted she sing herself.

"I have a deep husky voice without a high note in it," Barbara warned the soundman. "What are we going to do?" She was told how to make her voice sound as if it had range. "The result wouldn't make anybody cheer," she said. "But it was better than if I'd never asked the sound man anything."

Barbara's alto voice was sure and openhearted as she sang Harold Adamson's lyrics to Jimmy McHugh's music: "Oh, I never want to roam/Let me live and make my home/Where the lazy river goes by." Her voice was smoky, soulful, and intimate. Later in the picture, she reprises the song as a duet with Tony Martin and dances for the first time on-screen—a jig. Barbara was light of step, modest, the way Pearl Holley would be.

From Walter Brennan's first scene with Newt's one-man contraption, the picture was stolen out from under both Barbara and Joel and belonged solely to Brennan. McCrea and Barbara knew it. "We're supporting you, Walter," they teased. "Be nice to us. Remember to give us a nice present at the end of the picture."

Barbara's brother, By, was living with her and wasn't working. He stayed out late, dating actresses, escorting them around town, and showing up at as many parties as possible. When Barbara wasn't at the studio, she would wake him in the morning, furious that he was still asleep. "It's ten o'clock. I don't know why you don't have more get up and go."

"I would if I didn't have to stay in this town." By hated Hollywood.

"Well, I want you to," said Barbara. "I'll get you a contract."

By had met a young actress at the Cocoanut Grove, Caryl Lincoln, who resembled Louise Brooks. Caryl was a dancer, lithe with slim hips. She was flamboyant, sexual, extravagant in her gestures. She was the opposite of By's first wife, Elizabeth, his soul mate; Caryl was rowdy, raucous, and funny. Her titian hair was the color of Barbara's. By got a kick out of Caryl.

Caryl had been a WAMPAS (Western Associated Motion Picture Advertisers) Baby Star of 1929—a last-minute substitution for Sharon Lynne when Caryl's then husband, George Brown, director of publicity at Columbia Studios, picked her for the slot. As a WAMPAS star, Caryl was put across as someone who could one day become a full-fledged star. It had happened with other WAMPAS Baby Stars: Colleen Moore, Evelyn Brent, Clara Bow, Joan Crawford, Janet Gaynor, Jean Arthur, Loretta Young, Ginger Rogers, Helen Ferguson.

Caryl, a Universal starlet, had appeared in small roles in more than twenty pictures, including her first feature, *Wolf Fangs, A Girl in Every Port, Only Yesterday,* and *The Merry Widow.*

Barbara didn't think Caryl was good enough for By—she thought Caryl had no taste—and argued with him about their seeing each other. Caryl was thirty-three, two years older than By, and from a well-to-do family; her father was an executive with the Union Pacific Railroad. She was a spoiled girl who didn't have the wherewithal to take care of herself but who was smart in many ways and, when it came to being an actress, was a hard worker. After Caryl's divorce from George Brown, she'd dated Bob Cobb, owner of the Brown Derby.

By was torn between his love for his sister and his desire for Caryl. He continued to see her despite Barbara's feelings. And then Caryl told By she was pregnant; they'd been on Catalina Island one night and had too much to drink. Caryl was upset about her "condition" and blamed By, who said he would do the right thing.

"You're going to marry some dumb little extra?" asked Barbara.

She offered to pay for an abortion.

Caryl had had an abortion once before and a baby who'd died at two months. There would be no abortion.

By had had enough of Barbara's meddling and anger. The more she yelled, the quieter he became, and the more resolute. By didn't raise his voice; he moved out for good and found an apartment in West Hollywood.

Barbara believed that "if [life] gives you something with one hand, she takes something away with the other. Life is a jealous wench," she said. "I've never known it to fail. You can't have everything. You're not supposed to have everything. And it's like that with love. If you get love you usually lose somewhere else along the line."

Barbara was disgusted about By's marriage to Caryl, but if she wanted to keep him close to her, she knew better than to continue to be obvious about her feelings. By and Caryl went to Catalina for their honeymoon. After they were married, Barbara made peace with her sister-in-law, though Barbara would walk out of the room to get away from her. Caryl could get loud and argumentative when she drank. Barbara referred to Caryl as "that mouth." Sister and wife came to an understanding.

A few weeks after Barbara started work on *Banjo on My Knee,* she received a letter, the latest of several, from the Screen Actors Guild, inviting her to join the union.

Barbara had joined Actors' Equity in New York because of her work on the stage. She had no choice. Barbara didn't approve of organized labor. She had no interest in joining the Screen Actors Guild, even if it didn't call itself a "union." She did not intend to be pulled into a strike, and the possibility of an actors' strike was in the air. There was talk at the weekly guild meetings, under the auspices of the guild's president, Robert Montgomery, that it was time to have a showdown with the producers. Each guild meeting ended with members being asked to pledge their support for the planned action.

The guild's latest letter to Barbara informed her that if she didn't join the organization, she would be suspended by the Equity Council of Actors' Equity. The Screen Actors Guild and Actors' Equity became affiliated in 1934 with the mutual understanding that all members of one union had to join the other in order to appear in motion pictures or on the stage.

At Metro-Goldwyn-Mayer, 1936.
(PHOTOFEST)

Similar letters of warning were sent to Elizabeth Allan, Rosalind Russell, and Claire Trevor.

Barbara didn't respond to the guild's threat.

Finally, the guild sent Barbara's name to Actors' Equity and requested that the Equity Council suspend her. She had no choice but to join the guild, and soon after she, along with Claire Trevor and John Barrymore, were elected senior members of the guild with the guild's board of directors, Jimmy Cagney, Humphrey Bogart, Paul Harvey, and others, conducting the guild meeting.

During the day Barbara was in production making *Banjo on My Knee* as the simple bride in the world of shanty boat people living life along the banks of the Mississippi. At night she was a young Frenchman besotted with the most glamorous courtesan in the nineteenth-century Paris demimonde, as she spent her evenings helping Bob prepare for the crowning role of his young career.

Taylor was bewildered, overwhelmed, when he learned that Thalberg had picked him for the part of Armand Duval in *Camille* opposite Greta Garbo's Marguerite Gautier. Garbo, at thirty, was at the height of her career, worshipped by most of the Western world as the greatest actress of her day. She'd made twenty-eight pictures on two continents during a career that spanned almost two decades; she was idolized as "a revelation of exquisite beauty and artistry," proclaimed by critics "a flaming genius," celebrated for her intelligence, unerring instinct, grasp, and control as an actress.

Bob had played Armand in the Pomona Masquers' production at the Padua Hills Playhouse; that was Pomona, and this was Metro-Goldwyn-Mayer.

Bob was new to Hollywood, new to fame, new to acting. "The whole thing's like a madhouse," he said. "It doesn't make sense. Most of the time you don't know where you stand—or how!" At twenty-five, he'd made eleven full-length features in two years, playing romantic leading parts of spoiled adolescent men thrust into adulthood.

To cope with the rush of it all and the idea of working with Garbo, Bob took a plane to Salt Lake City, boarded a bus, rode to the end of the line, and started walking. He stopped at a ranch where he wasn't recognized, asked for a drink of water, and spent the rest of the day talking about farming, the world, anything except Hollywood, and left feeling like a human being.

Irving Thalberg had offered George Cukor his choice of pictures with Greta Garbo: Marie Walewska, the mistress of the emperor Napoleon I who bore him a son; or Marguerite Gautier, of Dumas fils's *La dame aux camélias,* based on Alphonsine Plessis—Marie Duplessis—mistress of Dumas and Liszt and the most cultivated courtesan of her day, who died of consumption at the age of twenty-three.

"Napoleon stumps me," Cukor said to Thalberg of the first choice. "He's fascinating to read about but he's a Great Man—and they all come out like waxworks in the movies." Cukor chose to make *Camille.* "I'd seen the play," he said, "and I felt it would be a perfect meeting of the actress and the role."

It was Garbo who had suggested *La dame aux camélias* to the studio. It was a role that Bernhardt had made her own. Eleonora Duse had transformed the part and performed it throughout Europe and brought the play to St. Petersburg and Moscow.

Marguerite Gautier was the one role Garbo wanted to play. But she thought it best to do Walewska first. "*Camille* [is] so like *Anna* [*Karenina,* which Garbo had just made with Fredric March] that I'm afraid," she wrote to Salka Viertel from Sweden, where Garbo was on holiday. "The Walewska story [is] a newer thing—because Napoleon isn't a usual figure on the screen, like my other fifty thousand lovers."

The premise of *Camille*—that a man could be ruined by marrying a courtesan—was archaic; Thalberg himself knew many men who had successfully married courtesans, but he also knew Dumas's *La dame aux camélias* was special. Henry James wrote of the Dumas play, it "remains in its combination of freshness and form, of the feeling of the springtime of life and the sense of the conditions of the theatre, a singular, an astonishing production . . . The play . . . has never lost its happy juvenility, a charm that nothing can vulgarise. It is all champagne and tears—fresh perversity, fresh credulity, fresh passion, fresh pain."

Garbo wrote of the Dumas heroine, "She is such a tragic figure. I do not know. I have not yet read the script. It may please me very much."

James Hilton, author of the 1933 novel *Lost Horizon* and the 1934 novel *Good-Bye, Mr. Chips,* was given *Camille* as his first screenwriting assignment. Frances Marion was assigned the script with him. Also hired along the way to work on it were Mercedes de Acosta, Vicki Baum, Ernest Vajda, Tess Slesinger, Mordaunt Shairp, Carey Wilson, and the playwright and casting director for the Shuberts, Zoë Akins.

The Breen Office made clear to Louis B. Mayer its guidelines for code approval: Marguerite Gautier was to be the only courtesan in the picture; the Baron de Varville, Marguerite Gautier's lover and benefactor, was not to live in the same house with his mistress; the awareness that Marguerite profited from her "sinful life" was to be kept at an "absolute minimum"; there was to be little physical contact between Armand and Marguerite and between Marguerite and de Varville; and, finally, there was to be a repentance and re-generation scene in which Marguerite was to make clear to Armand the "utter folly of her ways in a sin-doesn't-pay speech."

Romeo and Juliet premiered on August 20. It was a $2 million production that brought back Norma Shearer to the screen after the birth of her second child. Cukor said of the picture, "It lacked the garlic and the Mediterranean." *The Gorgeous Hussy* opened at Grauman's Chinese Theatre eight days later and was pronounced "one of the finest pictures of the year." Beulah Bondi, as Mrs. Andrew Jackson, and Lionel Barrymore, as Old Hickory, "walk[ed] away with acting honors."

Thalberg was overseeing a new set of revisions to the script of *Marie Antoinette* by Ernest Vajda, editing *The Good Earth,* and looking at drafts of *Good-bye, Mr. Chips* and *Maytime.* In between he came up with a notion for Zoë Akins to update Dumas's *La dame aux camélias;* instead of the outmoded idea of respectability and ruination being at the heart of the picture, Thalberg wanted Akins to use jealousy as the source of Armand's torment.

Akins's script caught the drama of the period and had a modern flavor. Thalberg felt the James Hilton and Frances Marion script was overwritten, badly conceived—almost comic opera—more a dramatization of their own love affair than the story of Marguerite Gautier's affair with Armand Duval.

Akins, who was in her late forties and had lived all over the world, had

Zoë Akins and pals circa 1930s. She was the daughter of a St. Louis politician; a staff writer, at age seventeen, for *Reedy's Mirror,* writing poetry, stories, criticism. At twenty-one, her play, *The Learned Lady,* went into rehearsals with May Robson. She was ordered to change scenes and rewrite one whole act. When she was asked to rewrite another, she tore up the script and promised herself that she would never rewrite another play. "And I've stuck to my vow," she said. (CORBIS)

"managed" in her script, said Cukor, "to create a whole language, a kind of argot for the story." Thalberg, Cukor, and Garbo loved Akins's script. In the end, although her script was used for *Camille,* Akins had to share the writing credit with Frances Marion and James Hilton.

Armand is a role that supports Marguerite; Armand is a foil to Camille's infatuation.

Cukor said of Armand: "It is historically a terrible part, usually played by middle-aged men. As a result [Armand] seemed stupid doing the things he did. When you get someone really young playing Armand, you understand him; he becomes appealing, with a kind of real youthful passion; whereas if he were thirty-eight, you'd think, 'Oh, you ass, why do you do that?' "

To prepare Bob for the role, the studio thought it wise for him to be privately coached by the Metro dramatic teacher, Oliver Hinsdell. Hinsdell had directed on Broadway in the mid-1920s and was theatrical director of the Dallas Little Theatre for eight years until 1931, when a Metro talent scout lured him out to Hollywood, along with the Dallas sports reporter, actor, *Black Mask* short story writer, and novelist, Horace McCoy, author of *They Shoot Horses, Don't They?*

Once at Metro, Hinsdell came to feel that the studio schools had taken the place of vaudeville, the legitimate stage, and silent pictures as a way of finding new actors. He predicted that in the future the stars would come from "talent schools."

Hinsdell worked with Bob. But the line-by-line work for the part of Armand came from the hours Bob spent with Barbara going over Akins's script. Barbara's nephew Gene was on summer holiday from Notre Dame and staying with her and watched as Barbara sat with Bob, night after night, talking over the scenes, telling Bob how to say each line.

Barbara read Armand's lines, her voice soft, almost a whisper, a caress. She spoke the lines as if in a rush of feeling. Barbara gave Bob the phrasing, the emphasis, the small gestures for the next day's scenes. "What she's done for me can't be measured in ordinary terms," said Bob. "She's taught me more with her knowledge than I would have learned in a lifetime."

Bob gave Barbara a large sapphire brooch.

The Baron de Varville was originally intended for John Barrymore. Cukor went to see the actor and bring him a copy of the script. Barrymore had put himself in a home to stop drinking, an old frame house that called itself a rest home. Cukor went into "some dreary depressing room," he said, and noticed something that struck him as "very shabby . . . they hadn't changed the table cloths." Barrymore came in with an aide and asked him, "Can we sit in here, Kelley? Nobody's going to come through and disturb us by pretending to be Napoleon?"

During much of the filming of *Romeo and Juliet,* Barrymore had been drunk and impossible. Thalberg tried to replace him with William Powell, but Powell declined the role. For Mercutio's Queen Mab scene, Barrymore, ever drunk, got through the thirty-one lines in one take. At the end of the scene the crew applauded. Barrymore's response: "Fuck the applause. Who's got a drink?"

Thalberg refused to give Barrymore the role of the Baron de Varville. Barrymore fell apart and was once again locked away at Kelley's Rest Home, this time behind bars. Henry Daniell, who made his Broadway debut in a play with Ethel Barrymore and his film debut in *Jealousy* with Jeanne Eagels, played the soigné and cynical, the enamored and possessive Baron de Varville. The supporting cast included Lionel Barrymore, Laura Hope Crews, Lenore Ulric, and Jessie Ralph.

Garbo was thought of as unapproachable, aloof. Following her return from Sweden, she was open and relaxed. When preparing for *Camille,* she allowed the designers to fit her with hoops, stays, taffetas, crinolines, furs, and velvets and spent hours with Adrian helping to perfect a taffeta silencer—a thick layer of silk beneath the material that wouldn't make too much noise on the screen.

George Cukor with Garbo shooting *Camille* throughout the summer and fall of 1936. (CORBIS)

She allowed herself to be smeared with greases and paints and her hair to be pulled and twisted. When a hairdresser created a coiffure of puffs and curls that turned out to be grotesque, Garbo made fun of it, laughing and mimicking the ridiculousness of the look. One gown was so laden with jewels that after wearing it for less than an hour when shooting, Garbo almost fainted from the heat, but she refused to rest or hold up production. A large open icebox was rigged up with a wind machine blasting icy air over the set and onto the actress.

William Daniels, the cameraman, wanted to experiment with a new screen makeup; Garbo agreed to try it out in the picture. When Daniels became ill, Karl Freund took over on the camera.

Camille began production the last week in July.

Bob was nervous the weekend before shooting was to start, wondering if Miss Garbo would like him, wondering what would happen.

"Look, she's human, isn't she?" said Barbara. "I think she'd like to be treated exactly like you treat everyone else."

Bob appeared for work on Monday and was told his introduction to Garbo was postponed until Tuesday; Miss Garbo was making tests. The next day the first scene being shot was at the Théâtre des Variétés, Paris, 1848. Gaily dressed crowds were assembled on the set. Cukor was going over his plans with the technicians. Garbo walked in. No one seemed to notice her. Bob had to look several times before he recognized her. She had long curls about her shoulders. She was slender, graceful, smiling as she greeted the cameraman and the electrician. Cukor noticed her and called Bob to her.

"I am very pleased to know you," said Garbo. Bob felt she meant it and was happier to find her so friendly.

Bob called her Miss Garbo; she called him Mr. Taylor.

The set on Stage 19 was locked, barred, guarded by a policeman at the front door. No outsiders were permitted on the set without the personal approval of Mr. Mayer. Four hours later, Garbo and Taylor were going through intimate scenes together as if they'd known each other for years.

"Well, how was the Swede?" Barbara asked Bob after the first day. Taylor went on for twenty minutes about how she wasn't rude or condescending or upstaging.

"Listen, I grant you that Miss Garbo is the most beautiful woman in Hollywood," said Barbara, "and that she is a brilliant actress, but she brushes her teeth in the morning just like everyone else."

In Bob's first love scene rehearsal with Garbo, he held her in his arms and said the line "You are the most beautiful . . ." Out of nerves, he let Garbo slip from his arms and fall on the floor. Before he could say or do anything, she jumped up and passed off the incident without anger or temperament. Garbo treated Bob much less like a schoolboy than she had some of her sixteen previous leading men. By the time the scene was shot, he'd carried her safely to the divan.

Between shots Garbo was polite but remained aloof from Bob. As soon as a take was completed, she went to her dressing room, its door marked by a single *G*, and stayed there until her next scene.

Bob felt Miss Garbo disapproved of him. "She wouldn't even acknowledge my presence off the set," he said. She had nothing to say to her Armand that wasn't to be spoken in front of the camera. This went on for weeks. Bob was miserable and started stumbling around.

In the first scene in which they kiss, Bob was sitting on the side of a love seat, next to Garbo. In the midst of the passionate scene, the love seat tipped, and Bob and Garbo fell, in front of the camera. Everyone waited. Garbo laughed and went back to kissing Bob.

Garbo had a funny laugh. "Just explodes all of a sudden," said Bob. "Before anyone else can readjust his features, she's all business again."

He was struck by how "practical a person" she was.

She kept her distance from Taylor. "If I [get] to know him too well," said

Metro-Goldwyn-Mayer's Armand Duval with his Marguerite Gautier.

Garbo, "it would only confuse the images I've been making of myself as Camille and of Armand."

"She carried herself with total assurance," said the picture's associate producer, David Lewis. "She was magnetic. She could imply a great sense of intimacy, all the time keeping a cool distance."

Bob noticed Garbo didn't upstage the other actors or ask any favors.

He was so stiff as an actor that Cukor said to him, "This isn't Pomona, this is Paris in 1850." And to Garbo, the director said, "Kiss him as if you were going down on him."

One morning Garbo smiled at Taylor. "Not only that, she said 'Hello, Bob' in that husky, intimate voice she usually reserved for the chaise longue scenes." Bob practically fell over himself getting to his place alongside her. From then on he was an awakened man, and an awkward actor. It got so that while waiting for new setups, Garbo wouldn't retire to her dressing room alone but spent time with Bob.

For one scene, Garbo and Taylor were seated at a table outside an inn in the Bois. "It's hard to be angry with you, but don't talk like a fool," Marguerite tells Armand. He kisses her. Garbo laughed instead of getting angry. "That was beautiful, lovely," said Cukor, "but you are forgetting to show anger."

"I try to get angry, but he does not give me a chance."

Garbo's quality was her beauty, her remoteness, and when she finally gave her affection to someone, it was explosive.

"There's something about Garbo's silence and her concentration that gets you, way down inside," said Taylor. "The woman is one of the most powerful personalities in the world. She wears a sort of flat colorless make-up that gives her a suggestion of something out of this world . . . There's a radiation from her when you're playing an intense scene that makes you play up to it, whether you have the stuff in you or not. She simply makes you find it and give."

Thalberg saw the early rushes of the scene where Marguerite Gautier is at the theater, sitting in a box, and said of Garbo, "She's never been quite like that, she's never been as good."

"Irving, how can you possibly tell?" asked Cukor. "She's just sitting there."

"I know but she's unguarded."

Cukor was fascinated by Garbo. He thought her manners were "beautiful," that she was "a creature of the greatest distinction in bearing and every other way. Her movement is exceptional throughout the picture. Even when she's quiet," said Cukor, "completely still, she conveys a sense of movement." When he had a close-up of her, he would often say without stopping the camera, "One more, Greta," and each time she would give him something different. Cukor might get eight or ten takes with her before he had exhausted all that she had to give.

Bob hardly had time to visit Barbara on the set of *Banjo*. He visited once when Barbara had noticed a ring that Arline Judge was wearing. Instead of a stone set in it, it had a small watch. Barbara was called for the scene, and Bob asked Arline where she got the watch. The next morning a watch ring arrived on the set for Barbara.

Bob disliked wearing fancy dress clothes in pictures. During the making of *Camille,* he had to wear fourteen different costumes.

Garbo described Taylor as "a fine actor—and handsome, too." Another time she said of him, "So handsome—and so dumb."

The actors and crew set up a softball team, called the Camillas. Garbo was their sponsor and stood at the baseline coaching her players and telling them

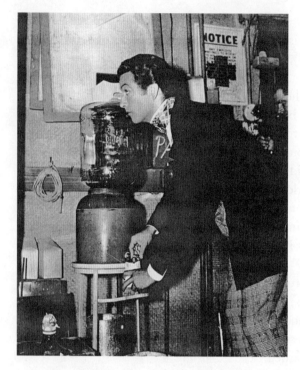

A long way from Beatrice, Nebraska, where as a boy his chores included keeping the wood box organized and cutting the lawn, and to earn extra money, shocking wheat and painting cars. (CULVER PICTURES)

how to play their positions. Taylor played second base. The Camillas played against the studio office team.

When shooting on the back lot, after finishing a scene, Garbo, instead of going to her dressing room as she had on previous films, went to a little screened-off place and sunbathed.

On location in Griffith Park, she and Bob went for walks in the woods, "holding hands," said Bob.

"She . . . was very funny and sweet and, I think, fairly happy [shooting *Camille*]," said Cukor.

Toward the end of the picture Garbo gave Bob a gift. When he opened the box, he found in it a small carved Buddha, a good luck piece from his Marguerite.

President Roosevelt toured the country on the campaign trail; thousands stood along the railroad tracks for a chance to see the president. People cried out, "He saved my home"; "He gave me a job."

Bob Taylor, W. S. Van Dyke, John Ford, Humphrey Bogart, and Paul Muni gave their names to the National Democratic Committee in support of the president. Eight million Americans were still without jobs, but prosperity was in the air. The apple sellers and breadlines were gone from the streets.

Irving Grant Thalberg, who died at the age of
thirty-seven, 1936. (PHOTOFEST)

"Four years ago and now" was the theme of Roosevelt's campaign. Working people believed that Roosevelt spoke for them, that he was their friend.
"Mr. Roosevelt is the only man we ever had in the White House who would
understand that my boss is a sonofabitch."

Shooting on *Camille* was within a couple of weeks of completion when, over
Labor Day weekend, Irving Thalberg became ill. He and his wife, Norma
Shearer, were spending their wedding anniversary at Del Monte Lodge, the
idyll of their honeymoon.

Thalberg caught cold, and they returned to Los Angeles early. Five days
later Thalberg was dead from pneumonia at the age of thirty-seven.

Once the word was out that Irving Thalberg had died, people at Metro
began to weep. They were shocked; no one knew what to do.

Thalberg had been at Metro for twelve years, from the age of twenty-
four, when he became production supervisor for the newly formed Metro-
Goldwyn-Mayer. His taste, standards, and understanding of motion pictures
combined to make Metro-Goldwyn-Mayer the most profitable and admired
studio in the industry. Thalberg was polite, respectful, and willing to listen
to others' opinions. He had three rules: Never take any man's opinion as
final. Never take your opinion as final. Never expect anyone to help you but
yourself. He refused to have his name on the screen credits ("Credit you give
yourself isn't worth having," he said). He did the unthinkable and encouraged Metro's producers and directors to shoot endless retakes of scenes that
hadn't played well in the projection room or with preview audiences.

The actor William Haines described Thalberg as "a great man; the opposite of Louis B. Mayer." "Thalberg was much respected and loved by the ordinary people in the studio," said the associate producer David Lewis. "In many ways, he [was] the symbol of MGM's greatness."

On the day of Thalberg's funeral, Metro was shut down. Cukor, Taylor, Garbo, Laura Hope Crews, Adrian, and fifteen hundred other mourners attended Thalberg's services at Temple B'nai B'rith. As the funeral service began, a five-minute industry-wide silence was observed by the other studios. A crowd of seven thousand stood on Wilshire Boulevard and Hobart Boulevard to watch as those attending the service passed by.

A great sheaf of white gardenias with hundreds of sweet peas and fresh white roses covered Thalberg's burnished copper casket, placed by his widow. MGM sent a massive wreath of orchids and gardenias with roses and lilies. Flowers stood along the bier sent by the Zukors, the Zanucks, William Randolph Hearst, the Goldwyns, Greta Garbo, the Nicholas Schenks, and hundreds of others.

Douglas Fairbanks and W. S. Van Dyke, Clark Gable and Moss Hart, Cedric Gibbons and Sidney Franklin, were ushers and helped to seat those who came to pay tribute, among them John and Lionel Barrymore, Mary Pickford, King Vidor, Spencer Tracy, Michael Curtiz, Chico, Harpo, and Groucho Marx, B. P. Schulberg, Frank and Ralph Morgan, the Hunt Strombergs, Gloria Swanson, Cecil B. DeMille, Wallace Beery, Charles Chaplin, Otto Klemperer, Ernst Lubitsch, Carole Lombard, Victor Fleming, Jean Harlow, Dr. A. H. Giannini, the Franchot Tones, Jesse Lasky, and Erich von Stroheim. Norma Shearer and Thalberg's parents sat apart from the others near the altar, behind a screen.

Rabbi Edgar Magnin, who had married the Thalbergs, gave the eulogy: "He was a great man, a good man, a simple man . . . He gave of his money and his strength—which was more important from one so frail—to every cause of good in this city, his state, his nation and in other nations where our people are oppressed . . . His love for Norma was greater than his greatest motion picture." The rabbi told of the tributes that had come from all over the world and read a telegram from President Roosevelt.

One of Thalberg's closest friends, Bernie Hyman, who'd been at Thalberg's bedside as he lay in a coma in an oxygen tent, made sure his own name went down on studio records as the producer of *Camille*.

"Everyone wanted to diminish Thalberg," said David Lewis, "to obliterate his distinctive stamp of perfectionism. The entire MGM upper echelon wanted to erase the fact that there had ever been an Irving Thalberg."

Louis B. Mayer got rid of the executives with "high brow interests" who worked with Thalberg.

During production of *Camille,* Bob began to think of his hometown, Beatrice, and scenes of his boyhood. It was three years to the month that his father had died. Bob had then been living in a room in Hollywood, taking an acting course with a Miss Dixon at her dramatic school, and going to MGM to test or try out. He'd returned to Nebraska to help his mother arrange the funeral and settle his father's estate.

Now, three years later during the shooting of *Camille,* through the wall of the big MGM soundstages, he could almost see "the golden shocks of grain in the fields," Bob said, "and very nearly taste the fried chicken" his aunt Jameson prepared "farmer style with oceans of country gravy."

Ruth Brugh was visiting friends in Beatrice, and her letters evoked in Bob a keen wish to see her again in the places he remembered so fondly.

When he was told he wouldn't be needed on *Camille* for a few days, Bob let out a "whoop" and telegraphed his mother that he was coming on the first plane and would be joining her in Beatrice to help celebrate his grandmother's eightieth birthday. Barbara had finished *Banjo* the month before but didn't accompany Bob to Nebraska; she and Ruth Brugh did not get along. *Banjo* was to open in early December; Barbara was already set to make her next picture, also with Joel McCrea, *Internes Can't Take Money,* this time for Paramount.

Bob left for Beatrice with an executive from Metro, Dean Dorn, and two other men, one, a friend of Bob's, as his bodyguard. The plane landed at the Lincoln Municipal Airport. Hundreds were there to welcome the local boy who'd made good.

Above the crowd, Bob saw a man with whom he'd gone to school standing on top of the hangar and yelled hello. The man yelled back and waved his arm. It was the signal for the steam whistle at the box factory. The whistle hadn't been blown since the armistice. "The sound symbolized so much good will from all these folks I liked so well," said Bob, that he almost cried.

He was brought into town in a Packard. Stores and banks were draped with bunting and were closed in his honor. A large banner read, "Beatrice Welcomes You Arlington Brugh."

More than twenty thousand people came from Kansas, Missouri, Iowa, and all the Nebraska counties to welcome one of their own. Bob was perched on top of the backseat of a yellow car and was driven in a parade two miles long through the streets of Beatrice. A motorcycle police escort flanked one

Bob atop Packard convertible, returning to his hometown (1936); Beatrice High School star tennis player, class president, student of oratory, and winner of the oratory city, county, district, and state championship for his lecture—"The Position of the Public School Teacher in Life." (GAGE COUNTY HISTORICAL SOCIETY)

side of his car; on the other was an American Legion color guard. Ahead of the car was the municipal band; behind it, the legion's drum corps, the Beatrice High School band, and the Doane College girls' drum and bugle corps. Flags flew everywhere.

The procession stopped at the Rivoli Theatre, where *The Great Ziegfeld* was playing. The theater marquee read in big letters, "ARLINGTON BRUGH"; below it, in smaller letters, the name "Robert Taylor." The governor of Nebraska was there to introduce the hometown hero. Later, Bob was brought before an assembly of twelve hundred students at the junior high auditorium, where he spoke a few words and was given a standing ovation.

Bob stopped off in Filley, his birthplace, to see his grandfather Jacob A. Brugh and give him $20 and a $15 grocery credit.

During the next few days Bob had dinners at the homes of family friends; went rabbit hunting with his cousin; was photographed at Penner's Pharmacy with the soda jerk who'd been behind the fountain when Bob was a boy; went to a Nebraska-Missouri football game where women chanted, "We want Taylor"; attended a reception at a hotel in Omaha; was mobbed by a crowd of fifty women; and, with his mother, was driven onto the field of the Omaha Airport to avoid a crowd of a thousand well-wishers waiting to wave off his plane.

It was the first time Bob had been back to Nebraska since 1933, when he'd graduated from Pomona. He heard his old friend Russ Gibson play the piano with Eddie Jungbluth's orchestra and remembered when he and Russ and Gerhart Wiebe were at Doane College and had toured the state as a trio and sold fly spray on the side. He reminisced with old friends about when he'd had the measles and how he'd behaved in high school when he was in love with Helen Rush. Now Helen was married and had a family.

"I felt so old," Bob told Sheilah Graham of his visit back home. "Everyone I knew was married and had children. It was all very depressing."

It was clear to Bob how much his life had changed. At twenty-five, he was under contract to the most glamorous movie studio in Hollywood with a new seven-year, million-dollar contract guaranteeing him more than $3,500 a week, with increases up to $5,000 a week. He was on a quick getaway from a picture in which he was starring opposite Greta Garbo. He had a house in Beverly Hills, a duck-hunting camp in the Sierras that he owned with Clark Gable, Sam Wood, Eddie Mannix, and Jack Conway; two secretaries and a valet tended to his needs. He drove a Ford to work and a Packard for pleasure. He'd placed first in a nationwide poll of women ages sixteen to twenty of most desirable men; thirty-six thousand fans were writing to him each month. He was in love with one of the most extraordinary and popular actresses around, four years older than he and a great deal wiser, who'd been in Hollywood since the end of the silents and had made more than twenty-five pictures in seven years, and who was helping him with his acting, advising him about his career, teaching him so many things, and who admired his levelheadedness in the face of the tremendous fan worship he inspired.

The Beatrice, Nebraska, paper had run a front-page editorial titled "Is Bob Taylor the Same Boy He Used to Be?"; the paper decided he was. Beatrice, Nebraska, was pretty much as Bob had left it, and though the lives of his boyhood friends had changed by marriage and the presence of children, what was happening to Taylor—a career he'd barely dreamed of—was carrying him along so fast he could just about maintain his bearings.

SEVENTEEN

Sea of Grass

On the eve of the presidential election, on the last day in October 1936, Franklin Roosevelt spoke at a rally in Madison Square Garden and defended the Social Security Act from the attacks being made against it by the Republicans, saying that most Republicans had voted for the legislation. "Never before in history," said the president, "have these forces been so united against one candidate as they stand today. They are unanimous in their hate for me—and I welcome their hatred. I should like to have it said of my first administration that in it the forces of selfishness and lust for power met their match. I should like to have it said of my second administration that in it these forces met their master."

Roosevelt's campaign manager, James Farley, predicted from preelection reports that the president would carry every state but Maine and Vermont. Farley's assessment was correct. Roosevelt was reelected by the largest electoral margin of any candidate since James Monroe—523 electoral votes for FDR; 8 for Landon. Pennsylvania, Delaware, and Connecticut voted Democratic for the first time in eighty years, since James Buchanan's victory in 1856. The president won the popular election by a margin of eleven million votes. He told the press, "I knew I should have gone to Maine and Vermont."

When *Camille* finished shooting, Bob was given a few weeks of holiday. He decided to go to Honolulu by boat; Barbara planned to race him there. Douglas Fairbanks gave her his reservation on the *China Clipper* since he'd been forbidden by his physician to make the trip. Barbara said that even though Bob was traveling by boat, he'd have the advantage since he'd be sailing days before she took off.

Barbara and Bob fought for the three days before he left; he went off to the Brown Derby to sulk, a heavy growth of beard on his face.

In matters of being in love, Barbara steeled herself. She had "no expectations," she said. To avoid hurt and disappointment, she believed women should have their own lives, "to build a wall of interests around their hearts that while love may find a chink in the wall it can't completely capture the fort. Love only happens once in the sense that it tears the heart right out of you, knocks you down on your knees, makes a slave out of you, abject and crying 'Surrender.' Love may come again, more than once. It may be just as sweet and fine and strong. But never the same."

Bob sailed to Hawaii alone and arrived in Honolulu to throngs at the pier, there to see America's most popular male star of the year. Bob was without studio protection; he disembarked and started to make his way through the crowd only to be pushed and jostled by adoring fans tearing at his hair and clothes. The police tried to get through the mob but couldn't control it. Women fainted. Bob pleaded for breathing space. He tried to calm the crowd by promising to sign autographs and pose for pictures but couldn't be heard over the noise and chaos.

He spent the night in Hawaii and realized his holiday would be a repeat of the nightmare of his arrival. The following day he got back on the boat that had brought him to Hawaii and sailed for home.

Zeppo and Marion Marx owned real estate in Beverly Hills. Zeppo was planning on building a house on one of the lots; the architect's plans for the Marx house had already been drawn. Barbara was thinking of buying some land as well. She was having dinner with the Marxes one night when Marion balked at the notion of a house in town. She'd always wanted to raise Thoroughbreds and be in the business of breeding racehorses. She felt now was the time. The Marxes also had property in the San Fernando Valley, above Encino, in Northridge.

"It's kind of silly to have all that property out there if we're going to live in town," said Zeppo.

Marion was an expert horsewoman. She'd ridden horses as a child and had broken her back in a riding accident. Marion thought horses were the dumbest animals that ever lived but the most beautiful.

"Don't people lose their shirts, going in for racehorses?" asked Barbara. "Maybe we could go into the breeding end and have a sideline for ourselves if I bought some land next to yours out in the valley."

The idea of a breeding and stud operation seemed like a wonderful adventure to Marion. She and Barbara decided to investigate.

Barbara talked to Joel McCrea about his ranch in Camarillo. He'd bought it in 1930, when he was twenty-five and had just finished making *The Silver Horde*. McCrea was unknown then, making $150 a week with $2,500 to his name. *The Silver Horde* hadn't even been cut, and he'd been asked to play the juvenile lead in *Lightnin'* with Will Rogers. Beyond that, McCrea's future was uncertain.

Will Rogers had advised McCrea to buy land. "They can always make more people," said Rogers, "but they can't make any more land . . . it can't go anywhere but up." McCrea was impressed with the advice. He wanted open land to ride across and found the perfect piece—more than nine hundred acres—which he was able to buy for $12,500 with a loan, without collateral, from Will Rogers's banker. McCrea told everyone he owned a thousand acres; he thought it sounded more impressive.

Zeppo consulted with Harry Hart, the accomplished trainer from the Swingalong Farms in Kentucky, and asked him what he thought of the valley property for horse breeding. Hart thought the area was perfect for it.

Northridge, in the San Fernando Valley, called itself the Horse Capital of the West with dozens of working ranches. From 1919 to 1926 the entire swath of land between the block below Devonshire (called Lassen) and the block above it was owned by the B. F. Porter Estate. In 1919 the land was worth $63,000; by 1926, $129,500; a decade later, $160,000. William Mulholland had land nearby. It, and the entire valley, had grown rich and fertile from the water Mulholland had brought to the city of Los Angeles and the San Fernando Valley by way of his historic aqueduct system, which he designed and oversaw as first superintendent and chief engineer of the Los Angeles Bureau of Water Works and Supply. Mulholland's aqueduct began at the Owens River in Mesa, California, and extended south more than two hundred miles to Los Angeles, ending at the northern tip of the San Fernando Valley, bringing water from the streams and lakes fed by the snows of the Eastern Sierras.

Barbara was hesitant about moving thirty miles outside town, even though it was less than an hour's drive from Hollywood Park. Zeppo felt the move would be good for Dion.

Barbara had worked all her life. She didn't know how to play. To help get over the breakup of her marriage, she made five pictures in a row without a week off. The roles had become "an obsession" for her. She hadn't thought of anything else, didn't want to think of anything else. It was clear to her that if she didn't buy the ranch and relax, her health would begin to crack. It already was.

The purchase of the land and the idea of the ranch came out of the blue. "Just like that," she said.

Barbara decided she would live at the ranch most of the time. "It's peaceful and quiet," she said. She could have gardens, and she agreed with Zeppo that it would be wonderful for Dion. She allowed herself to have visions of her son, tall, bronzed, and strong, handling spirited horses, riding over her acres of California land.

Barbara and the Marxes paid $200,000 for Marwyck Ranch. The land, roughly 130 acres—mostly weed patches and bean vines, set against the Santa Susanas—part of Rancho Ex-Mission San Fernando, "the choicest lands of the San Fernando Valley," bordered Lassen Street on the south, Devonshire on the north, Reseda on the east, and Wilbur Wash on the west.

To get to 10127 Reseda Boulevard, Barbara had to drive through Tarzana, past the post office of Triunfo, and on through the citrus groves and alfalfa fields at the foot of the Santa Susana Mountains. Some of the roads were paved; some were just dirt. To ride on horseback to Van Nuys and back from Reseda Boulevard took most of a day.

The plan for Marwyck was to build the stables and paddocks first. After that, the respective houses were to be built atop two hillcrests facing each other, overlooking the entire valley.

Marwyck was to duplicate the finest horse-breeding facilities of Kentucky with a three-quarter-mile training track. Harry Hart was hired to design and oversee the operation; his wife, Bertie, was to be the operation's secretary. Dick Arlen was hired to be the farrier. Arlen worked out of a streamlined trailer and did the shoeing on most of the horses in the valley.

Fifty Thoroughbreds were brought up from Kentucky and were boarded in Pomona while the stables were under construction. Barbara and Marion got up at 4:30 in the morning to get to Pomona by 6:30 for the Marwyck horses' workout. Barbara liked to stand on top of the stable roof and watch the horses be walked along the track, then saddled and raced. Afterward, she and Marion helped walk out the horses until they were cooled down. Sometimes Bob went along with them, as did Clark Gable, who also helped to walk out the horses.

About acting and being a part owner in a horse farm, Barbara said, "I think back to those one-night stands, and ask myself, 'How did I ever get out here with all this grass?' About the only grass I ever got close to before was on the backdrop of a show."

Thanksgiving was held on a hilltop in the fields of Marwyck overlooking the San Fernando Valley. Barbara and Bob and Zeppo and Marion invited the ranch's manager and his wife, Harry and Bertie Hart, as well as Carole Lombard and Clark Gable.

Carole Lombard and Clark Gable at their farm in Northridge, California, with Bon Pepper and colt, May 1938. (CORBIS)

Gable always liked "the dishy dame," said Joan Blondell, and Lombard, a former Mack Sennett beauty who repeatedly got it in the face with a pie, was beautiful, glamorous, feminine, and dishy in every way. Before Carole and Gable were a couple, Marion had had a brief affair with him. "He certainly has got a small one," she said about the actor.

Carole Lombard was one of the highest-paid actresses in the business without ever having had a top ten box-office hit. It was clear she was in love with Clark from the way she spoke about him and about his being married, which, she said, was going to be handled properly in every way.

Marwyck had no ovens with which to cook a turkey, so Carole sent over a crew to build a barbecue pit in one of the fields. When Lombard focused on something, it happened. Carole had enormous energy; she played tennis too hard, chain-smoked, and drank Coca-Colas nonstop. For the holiday feast at Marwyck, steaks and potatoes were cooked and eaten, and the party dozed off in the afternoon sun. "First time I ever ate Thanksgiving dinner lying on my stomach," said Barbara, "but it turns out to be the ideal way to cope with a barbecued steak."

Thanksgiving day, Marwyck, 1936. Left to right: Bertie Hart, wife of Harry, Marwyck's manager; Bob, Barbara, Zeppo and Marion Marx, Clark Gable, Carole Lombard. (COURTESY TIM MARX)

• • •

Banjo on My Knee was released two weeks later; *Camille* was to have its premiere the following day. Cukor was reshooting the picture's final love scene two days before the premiere, changing the death scene from one in which Garbo gives a long speech to one in which she hardly speaks.

"The screen is just too realistic for a long aria when someone's dying," said Cukor. "It seemed unreal for a dying woman to talk so much."

When the final scene was shot and the director waved his satisfaction, Bob turned eagerly to Garbo, but she was already walking away. "I called to her but she took no notice," said Bob. "As Armand I was a dead weight in front of the camera and Garbo figured that I could use some real-life stimulation. Once the picture was finished, so was I."

Despite the modest claims 20th Century–Fox made for *Banjo on My Knee,* the critics discovered the charm of the picture and called it "great entertainment," "outstanding . . . hilarious . . . eloquent . . . it will spellbind average folk and delight cultivated audiences," said *Daily Variety.*

As Barbara and McCrea predicted, Walter Brennan was called the "hit of the picture," in "one of the best pieces of acting seen on the screen in some time." *Daily Variety* said Brennan's work was "a standout in a distinguished, hilarious delivery"; the picture "makes him a top ranker among character comedians."

Louella Parsons said Barbara Stanwyck was "as full of surprises as a Christmas pudding. She sings—she dances—and how she acts . . . with all the glamour of a musical comedy queen plus genuine talent as an actress." A "sterling artist at the top of her screen career," said *The Hollywood Reporter*, whose "performance is more fluent than any she has ever enacted."

Moviegoers and newspapers throughout the country—and the world— were mesmerized by the unexpected twist of another love story: that of Edward VIII and Mrs. Wallis Warfield Simpson. As the Prince of Wales, he was seen as progressive and open to new ideas. As the king of England, he was called a modernist. "All I try to do is to move with the times," he said.

The uncrowned king of the United Kingdom, Ireland, and the other British Dominions and emperor of India had asked to be legally married to Mrs. Simpson, then awaiting her formal decree of divorce from her second husband.

Emergency sessions were called with the prime minister and the cabinet. A request was put forth before the Commonwealth's prime ministers that the king be allowed to marry Mrs. Simpson morganatically ("I'll try anything in the spot I'm in now," said Edward VIII). All except for Eamon de Valera denied the request. "This is a nice kettle of fish, isn't it?" said Queen Mary, who had always put country first and was made miserable when she learned of her son's intended marriage and abdication. During the eight days of the crisis, the king slept with a loaded pistol under his pillow; his desperation and outbursts prompted those around him to question his sanity.

His letter of formal abdication, heard over the radio—"Further delay cannot but be injurious to the people whom I have tried to serve"—ended his 325-day reign as king of England. When it was over, the former king stood up and said to his aide, "Walter, it is a far better thing I go to."

The front-page headlines of the *Los Angeles Times* told the story as it unfolded: "King's Plan to Abdicate Rumored About London"; "Mrs. Simpson and Queen Dine"; "King May Abdicate Today and Flee with Mrs. Simpson"; "Wide Choice of Titles Open in Abdication."

Bob and Barbara flew to Palm Springs for the world premiere of *Camille* at the new Plaza Theatre. The theater held eight hundred seats and was sold out for the occasion.

Cukor was "staggered by [Garbo's] lightness of touch—the wantonness, the perversity of the way she played Marguerite. Garbo had this rapport with an audience," said Cukor. "She could let them know she was thinking things and thinking them uncensored . . . She was rather cool, but seething underneath. You know that she's reckless and nothing will stop her."

(KOBAL COLLECTION)

Bette Davis said of Garbo's performance, "Her instinct, her mastery over the machine, [is] pure witchcraft. I cannot analyze this woman's acting. I only know that no one else so effectively work[s] in front of a camera."

Cukor thought that Bob "rose to Garbo in those scenes when he denounced her, threw things at her."

Norma Shearer had said of George Cukor, "He could be wonderful for you or he could be the kiss of death." Cukor understood how to help Bob and thought that as Armand, Bob was able to convey the right sort of innocence and naïveté.

The critics were awed by Garbo's work ("the most interesting [Marguerite] from Bernhardt and Duse to Jane Cowl and Eva Le Gallienne"; "Miss Garbo has never done anything better"; "in the finest tradition: eloquent, tragic and restrained") and they were equally taken aback by Bob ("His Armand will surprise you . . . the best thing he has done . . . possessing surprising authority and charm for one of little experience"; "[he] plays with surprising assurance and ease . . . [and] holds up his end of the story with distinction").

Billboards proclaimed, "Garbo loves Taylor." Garbo's response: "Why don't they say 'Taylor Loves Garbo.' "

Sam Goldwyn had plans to remake his 1925 sensation from an Olive Higgins Prouty novel. The producer was in an all-out search, testing actresses, mostly unknown, for the perfect strange creature who would be his next Stella Dallas. Barbara wanted the part of the seemingly vain, careless mother who selflessly loves her devoted, loyal daughter.

The London *Observer* described 1936 as "the year of Edward VIII, the Spanish War and Robert Taylor."

Nineteen thirty-six was the year Barbara Stanwyck turned twenty-nine, a dangerous age to be in Hollywood.

PART FOUR

A Larger Reach

Third person—and singular. That's Stanwyck . . .

—Barbara Stanwyck

From *Stella Dallas,* 1937 (AMERICAN HERITAGE CENTER, UNIVERSITY OF WYOMING)

ONE

Feelings of Uncertainty

The New Year began for Barbara with the final decree notice of divorce from Frank Fay and the formal incorporation of Marwyck. Barbara's seven-year marriage was over, "she was out of that," as she put it. "I'll never have to go through it again." "When I married Frank Fay, Mr. [Arthur] Hopkins said it was a bad marriage. And he was right."

Barbara was different now, "immunized," she said, against the kinds of feelings that caused "the total eclipse, the complete collapse; against the feelings" that knocked her "down on her knees and tore the heart out of you."

When asked by reporters if she planned to marry Robert Taylor, she replied, "No. Or anybody else."

She was still picking herself up from Fay. She had no intention of marrying again; she wasn't ready for it. She wanted to see her friends "and see them often" and be able to "go dancing with some fellow without reading [the] next day in the papers that I'm engaged to him."

Bob was in love with her; he was four years younger than she and prettier, the most sought-after male actor of the moment, bigger than Gable.

Bob was romantic, "just as most men are at first," said Barbara. "Of course he has a lot of quaint ideas about being romantic. He thinks, for instance, that a gift doesn't become a gift until it costs at least five thousand dollars. Money doesn't make a gift important. Actually, as far as I'm concerned, it takes away from its importance."

She told Bob that anyone with money could stop at a jewelry store and pick up a diamond bracelet in five minutes. "It might take ten times as long to pick out a rag doll with hair just the color of mine," she said. "Money is new and important to him. His sense of values has been pushed around so quickly that it is excusable. I suppose he once dreamed of giving a girl a diamond bracelet some day, so it is easy to see why that is exactly what he

He was six feet tall, loved riding and ranch work, eating rare steak and onions, his work on the stage: *M'Lord the Duke,* at Hollywood Playhouse; *Camille,* and *The Importance of Being Earnest* at Padua Hills. The person in history who impressed him the most: Voltaire. "Not only was he a great writer, philosopher and diplomat, but a man who did as much good for his country as anyone has ever done. And he remains the perfect example of a free thinking man." (PHOTOFEST)

wants to do when he suddenly gets the money. Soon perhaps, he will learn the importance of the unimportant little things."

Barbara never understood why the foremost impression of Hollywood was glamour. "Glamour has actually nothing to do with pictures at all," she said. "Working in pictures is one thing. Glamour is a separate thing entirely. In Hollywood you don't have to buy a certain car, a certain coat. There's nobody to demand that of you. All pictures really ask of you is that you do your best."

Bob was being called the hottest "screen lover" since Rudolph Valentino and laughed off the comparison as "hooey." Valentino "was a marvelous actor and a great picture personality," he said. "They can't really think of me as being like him."

As far as marriage to Bob Taylor was concerned, Barbara's response: "Skip the romance."

Barbara would be thirty in July. Most actresses in Hollywood were in their teens or early twenties. Barbara knew she wasn't beautiful; more "average, nice-looking," she said. She knew she didn't have the beauty of "Dietrich, or the glamour of Lombard, or the grandeur and mystery which is Garbo's. It's a good thing," she said, that she could "crack through with honesty."

She was popular with the public and admired as an actress. She'd been acting for more than a decade. She knew how to fight her fights with the studios, pick the stories that were good for her, and keep on working. "If you feel a thing strongly enough," she said, "you should have the courage of your convictions to carry it through. That's my philosophy, and it's gotten me into plenty of hot water."

She and Bette Davis were considered the most "suspended" people in pictures. She knew talent wasn't enough; neither was opportunity. What was needed was discipline, hard work, patience, stubbornness, and determination.

Barbara was constantly learning her craft; she knew there was no instant way to learn it but to learn it, and she delivered the best job she could.

King Vidor was testing actresses for Samuel Goldwyn's remake of his 1925 hit *Stella Dallas*, directed by Henry King, that had starred Belle Bennett. Goldwyn had been planning to remake the movie for two years. His search for an actress to play Stella was as extensive as it had been in 1925. It was almost comparable to the search for Scarlett O'Hara, which had taken on a frenzy in the town all its own.

Barbara was at Paramount at work on *Internes Can't Take Money*, based on a story by Max Brand (Frederick Schiller Faust), working with Joel McCrea on their third picture together. McCrea was playing a young intern, Dr. Jimmy Kildare, who falls in love with her character.

King Vidor wanted Barbara for the role of Stella Dallas. Goldwyn was intent on using unknown actors and creating a new group of stars, as he had eleven years before with the original *Stella Dallas*.

Goldwyn in 1925 claimed he'd tested more than seventy-five actresses before he'd found his Stella. Many, among them Laurette Taylor, had turned down Goldwyn's offer for the part of a woman who ages from young girlhood to middle age. Belle Bennett, a stock company actress who had appeared in forty-five pictures—two for Goldwyn—and who'd received top billing in many of them but had so far failed to distinguish her career, wanted to play Stella Dallas "more than anything" she'd wanted in her life, she wrote in a letter to Abe Lehr, Sam Goldwyn's old friend from the glove trade and his head of operations for Goldwyn Pictures.

"I have kept the book near me," she wrote to Lehr long before the company had even started to cast the picture, "reading her [Stella Dallas] over and over until she has crept into my heart and soul. I feel that she is what I have been waiting for all my life and I have built her up bit by bit until I feel sure that I have what Henry King, Samuel Goldwyn want."

To Bennett, *Stella Dallas* was her " 'comeback' in pictures . . . To own and be worthy of a great part," she wrote to Lehr, "satisfies my soul as food saves the life of a starving woman."

Bennett's Stella was so exquisite (Goldwyn had agreed to test her as a last

Belle Bennett as Stella Dallas with Lois Moran as Laurel. From the original Goldwyn production, 1925.

resort) that he gave her the part. It was the role of her career; Bennett died seven years later in 1932 at the age of forty-one. Goldwyn had brought Lois Moran from Paris at the age of fifteen and a year later had her make her screen debut as Laurel Dallas; Ronald Colman was a young actor under contract to Goldwyn who'd starred in several Goldwyn pictures but who only came to real prominence as Stephen Dallas; the 1925 *Stella Dallas* gave Douglas Fairbanks Jr. his first grown-up role and Belle Bennett her first important appearance on the screen.

Goldwyn had intended his 1925 *Stella Dallas* to be his "masterpiece." The picture had cost $700,000, twice the amount of Goldwyn's credit line at the Bank of America. The film's protracted shooting schedule was nine weeks.

Goldwyn wanted the 1937 remake to be as exceptional. If he couldn't find the right unknowns, three acclaimed actresses interested him for the part of Stella Dallas: Gladys George, at thirty-seven, under contract to Metro and impossible for Goldwyn to get because of his feud with L. B. Mayer and Mayer's refusal to loan out anyone to Goldwyn; Ruth Chatterton, who shattered hearts in *Madame X* as the noble mother risking execution to shield her

(GROSSET & DUNLAP)

son from the truth and who played the middle-aged Mrs. Dodsworth fleeing the mediocrity of the Midwest, frantically seeking her fast-slipping youth (Chatterton was forty-four), in the just-completed Goldwyn picture *Dodsworth;* and Bernadene Hayes, at thirty-four the youngest of the three, who had appeared with James Cagney in *Great Guy* and at the El Capitan Theater in *Three Men On a Horse.*

Barbara at twenty-nine was frightened of many things, personal and professional. She felt intensely about most things. By her own admission, she was shy and silent and worried endlessly about situations that usually didn't happen. She "climbed the wall inside," she said, when far worse things happened—things she hadn't worried about at all. "There are things I know I can do. And other things I can't do," she said. "I know myself."

Barbara saw Stella Dallas as a woman "moved primarily by unselfish motives . . . her life was a study of mother love and of devoted sacrifice. Part of [Stella's] tragedy was that while she recognized her own shortcomings, she was unable to live up to the standards she so painstakingly set for herself."

Some of Barbara's friends discouraged her from going for the part. They thought she was crazy for wanting it; the role of a mother who ages was not a part Barbara should be playing at the time when she was about to be moved to supporting roles. Playing a mother as a young actress was different from playing a mother when she herself was thirty. Actresses often became unhinged at this age. "What would the public think of seeing me fat and sloppy in those horrible clothes?" Barbara said. "Probably they would decide that was exactly the way I would look in a few years!"

Gloria Swanson refused to touch the role. It was dangerous to play a mother, and thirty was an age when actresses became frightened, feeling that their youth, their power, their allure, and their ability to work were slipping away.

Ruth Chatterton chose to do *Louise of Coburg* onstage.

Zeppo warned Barbara, "If you really want to do the picture, you'll have to make a test." Barbara was determined to have the part but said, "Screw them. I won't test. Either they want me or they don't want me."

She'd made pictures for William Wellman, George Stevens, and John Ford. Goldwyn could see what she could do.

Mary Pickford was looking for a picture and thought *Stella Dallas* a "good character part." Pickford had tried her hand at radio in a show called *Parties at Pickfair*, which took place at Mary's celebrated home. It was a show designed to make listeners feel as if they were at the center of the court of Pickfair. The show didn't work; the public was no longer enthralled with Little Mary, who told the press that she was finding it "pleasant to shrink in the public eye, to recede from view, to get over the highest hurdles of fame." Despite her claim that she was enjoying private life and fading from public view, Mary was busy writing three books, eleven magazine articles, and two short stories and producing two unsuccessful pictures with Jesse Lasky: *One Rainy Afternoon* and *The Gay Desperado*. Mary was unfazed by the pictures' losses and dissolved her partnership with Lasky. "I have a constitution of iron," she said. "I'm as hard as rocks."

Mary stepped into the role of president of United Artists, the company she'd helped to found seventeen years before, and replaced Al Lichtman, who'd left United Artists for the newly formed Selznick International Pictures. *Stella Dallas* was Goldwyn's first picture under the auspices of United Artists. In the end Miss Pickford said, "I shall never try to be both an actress and a producer again."

Nothing further came of her interest in playing Stella Dallas.

Zeppo and Marion pleaded with Barbara to test for the part. Barbara stood firm. She'd been a star—though she didn't like that word; she preferred "actress"—for seven years and been on her own forever. She loved her work, her job. To survive and get where she was required indestructible faith, devotion, and irrepressible hope. Whatever sacrifices she made in the line of duty were part of the job. She understood that these demands on her life were the

King Vidor began directing in 1913 at nineteen years old. By the time he started work on *Stella Dallas* in 1937, he'd directed more than thirty-five pictures, among them *The Jack-Knife Man, Wild Oranges, The Big Parade,* and *The Champ.* "Man is as old as God when it comes to understanding human emotions," he wrote. "And because of that truism, I have always attempted to adhere to the 'earthier' themes in the pictures I have directed . . . [and] appeal to the heart rather than the head." (CULVER PICTURES)

price of success. "Some people are too fragile for this business," she said. "You have to be hard. This business can kill you if you're not driven."

Finally, Zeppo went to Joel McCrea and asked him to intervene. Zeppo knew that Stella Dallas would be the most important part of Barbara's career. "She'll listen to anything from you," Zeppo said. "She won't listen to us."

During their three pictures together, Barbara and McCrea had become friends. McCrea thought Barbara "a trouper, a hell of an actress."

He liked Barbara and wanted her to get ahead.

"Listen, honey," Barbara said to McCrea about testing for *Stella Dallas,* "if they want me, they know what I can do. If I'm not good enough, to hell with them, let them get who they want. I'm not going to go up with three other people and make a test as though I couldn't get a job, and have one of them that I don't think's as good beat me."

McCrea went to Vidor and asked him whom he wanted.

"I want her," Vidor said, "but Goldwyn insists upon the test."

More than forty-five actresses had already tested for the part.

McCrea went back to Barbara and urged her to make the test.

The actor had been under contract to Goldwyn for five years. "I'm paying him three thousand a week, fifty-two weeks a year," said the producer, "and he's going to the beach, so use him." In between *These Three* and *Come and Get It,* McCrea was loaned out to Universal, Columbia, and Fox, with Goldwyn getting $60,000 per picture; McCrea, $3,000 a week. "He was making $42,000 on me every time," said McCrea.

Joel McCrea circa 1930. (DOCTOR
MACRO.COM)

Goldwyn insisted on referring to the actor as Joe McCreal.

"The L is on the first name, Sam," said Abe Lehr. "It's Joel McCrea."

"When I sign him for five years with no options," said Goldwyn, "don't tell me how to spell his name. It's Joe McCreal."

McCrea told Goldwyn he thought Barbara was a great actress and put her forth for the part of Stella.

"Oooh, she's good," said Goldwyn, "but she hasn't got any sex appeal. I want a girl like Merle Oberon that has sex appeal."

McCrea knew Goldwyn never answered a question or listened to anyone's opinion. When asked "What do you think, Sam?" his response was, "I think you'll have to do what I said in the first place."

McCrea persevered.

"Sam," he said, "[Barbara] *is* Stella Dallas. I don't give a shit if she has sex appeal or not. She must have something because she's going with a guy named Robert Taylor who every girl has been after and she's *got* him."

Goldwyn insisted Barbara test for the part. Finally, she relented.

Victor Heerman and Sarah Y. Mason, then at work on the script for *Stella Dallas,* put together the sequences for the test.

Stella is the daughter of a mill hand desperate to get away from the squalor of her life and eager to marry the handsome, well-bred, and well-scrubbed assistant mill owner of another social class. Throughout the picture, she ages twenty years. The test was made up of the four phases of her characterization: young girlhood; new wife and mother, indifferent to her days-old baby, yearning to cut loose after long months of being cooped up in the hospital; separated wife shunned as extravagant, slovenly, spirited but with a love for her daughter that is pure and boundless; middle-aged adoring mother who realizes that her flamboyant ways—seen as garish, coarse, vulgar (says one of Laurel's friends about Stella as she walks across the main lawn of the elegant resort in search of Laurel, "Did you see the makeup on her, and those shoes? I didn't know they let that kind of woman loose anymore")—are ruining her daughter's chances in society.

Stella pushes away her child, who fills her with joy and purpose and whom she loves more than anything in the world. Hiding the love that is breaking her heart, she steals out of her daughter's life to end up as she always was, a solitary figure, alone, outcast, but triumphant in her pride and love for her child and uplifted by the supreme gift she has given her: Laurel's freedom to soar and escape her mother's commonness and exile; her daughter's baptism into the aristocratic world Stella had always dreamed of and never dared inhabit; and deliverance into the arms of an adoring husband, where Laurel will receive the blessings of the conventional (happy) life her mother was unwilling to accept.

"She wasn't me, that woman," said Barbara of Stella Dallas. "But she was a woman I understood completely. She was good; cheap but good, and I could play her." Barbara saw Stella as "a woman who cheated failure. One who eagerly paid the full measure for what she wanted from life."

Goldwyn let Barbara know that she was "too young for the part," that he didn't think she was capable of doing it, and that she "didn't have any experience with children."

The day of the test for *Stella* was the coldest day of the year. Barbara had a 102-degree temperature. Her nose was running. "I looked awful," she said. Anne Shirley was testing for the part of Laurel and was also sick "with her nose running too," said Barbara.

Vidor spent an entire day, "instead of the customary few hours," said Barbara, shooting the scene of Laurel's long-anticipated birthday party in which mother and daughter await the guests who never arrive. The parents of Laurel's classmates have been warned away by Laurel's teacher, who has deemed Mrs. Dallas an improper mother and her house unfit for upstanding children; mother and daughter are left to make the best of it, each for the sake of the other and to celebrate Laurel's birthday together.

Barbara acted various crucial scenes.

Vidor had tested actresses from stock companies across the country, from Hollywood to the New York stage. Miriam Hopkins tested for the part around the time of Barbara's test.

Goldwyn had each of the forty-eight tests edited into a short reeler.

"Stanwyck's test was undeniable," said Vidor. "She put everyone else to shame." Barbara's versatility was undisputed.

Goldwyn told his production manager, Robert McIntyre, then in New York testing actresses, to return to Hollywood; they had found their Stella Dallas.

Barbara was outwardly charming and funny and full of energy, but there were feelings of uncertainty, the fear that "it" wouldn't last, that something would take it away, that she would end up "a wardrobe woman, or a scrub woman." Movie fame lasted as long as people liked her. When they stopped going to see her, that would be that.

There were feelings of bitterness deep inside that wouldn't go away: the anger at having a mother who had left her; the rage at having a father who'd taken off, leaving her and her brother stranded as small children and apart at a time when they needed each other most; the longing to be with her brother, who'd left her first when she was a little girl and then again, most recently, for a woman Barbara didn't like and didn't think was right for him; the sudden deaths of her beloved sisters Millie and Mabel (these weren't seen as deaths to Barbara; everyone had left her); and finally, her marriage, and the ugly, violent nightmare it had become in which she'd surrendered her pride, her dignity, her self, in order to serve and to please. Out of blind desire, she'd willed the marriage to work and failed, despite her discipline, her devotion, her hope. She'd been humiliated, lived with desperation, felt as if she were "in chains of slavery," and, still loving Fay, had been forced to flee into the night in order to save herself and her son.

"Someone has said that 'pain is the keenest of the pleasures,' " said Barbara, "and certainly you'd better not face love unless you can also face pain and hard work and sacrifice which are component parts of love, along with the clouds and the halos and the harps.

"Don't expect the man you love to be a combination of Mussolini, Gable, Lindbergh, King Edward Eighth or a Robert Taylor. If you do, you're riding for a fall . . . All men are human, mortals, and, if they do exhibit a few god-like traits that's velvet."

Internes Can't Take Money—originally published in *Cosmopolitan* magazine and bought by Paramount for $5,000—had started production days before

Christmas. Barbara was getting paid $55,000 to play a young woman desperately looking for her baby who is being held by gangsters. The character is a laundry worker, the estranged widow of a two-bit bank robber. A racketeer knows where the child is and has a yen for the young woman. The price for the information: $1,000 (he might as well be asking her for a million) or the young woman herself.

Joel McCrea was the idealistic, hardworking Dr. Jimmy Kildare, who believes in the goodness of medicine. He earns $10 a month in training at the hospital plus three meals a day and clean "whites."

When Kildare saves the life of a badly wounded big-time mobster at the local saloon where the doctor stops each afternoon for his two beers, he's given an envelope stuffed with money, $1,000, as thanks. Interns can't take payment for their work, and despite his dire need for cash Kildare returns the money.

Rian James, known for his books about hospitals, including *The White Parade,* and Theodore Reeves were hired to adapt Max Brand's story and added two elements: a mother's search for her missing child and her romantic involvement with Dr. Kildare.

Al Santell was hired for $42,000 to direct *Internes.* Santell was a Fox director and former short story writer and actor who, the year before, had done an impressive job with Maxwell Anderson's *Winterset.*

Internes was budgeted at just over half a million dollars and cost more than $600,000 to make. Benjamin Glazer was in charge of production. Glazer—former lawyer, newspaperman, and adapter of stage plays that included *Liliom, The Swan, The Merry Widow, Flesh and the Devil,* and *Anything Goes*—was interested in accuracy and authenticity, and he wanted both for *Internes Can't Take Money.* He used an entire soundstage 150 feet by 50 feet in order to re-create a fully equipped clinic as well as an operating room, outer room, and waiting room. He hired the chief resident physician at Hollywood Hospital to be the picture's adviser and sent McCrea there to observe surgeons at work in the operating theater.

To Santell's relief, Glazer was never on the set. "Good directors need producers like they need a third leg," said Santell. "What does one do with it? Where does it hang?"

Paramount's head costume designer, Travis Banton, passed over the picture. Barbara's wardrobe as a working woman didn't interest him. "After all, Dietrich was at Paramount," said Barbara, who didn't have the kind of glamour that appealed to Banton; he designed for Claudette Colbert and Mae West.

With Theodor Sparkuhl, the cameraman on *Internes Can't Take Money*, who gave the picture its distinctive expressionistic look, 1937. His more than fifty German pictures, made from 1916 to 1930, included many with Lubitsch; he was the cameraman as well for Jean Renoir's first talking picture, *On purge bébé*.

Banton assigned the picture to his assistant, Edith Head, a former high school teacher of Spanish grammar from Bishop, California, who knew nothing about sketching and designing. Head had wanted to be a landscape or seascape painter and had started to study at the Chouinard Art Institute. To get a job at Paramount, she borrowed the drawings of her fellow classmates, put her name on the work, combined them with her own sketches, and brought them to the studio. Head showed up with a portfolio made up of landscapes, portraits, and costume designs. Howard Greer, Paramount's designer, who said he'd never seen so much "talent in one portfolio" and hired her, soon realized that Edith couldn't draw.

Barbara was insulted that Banton didn't want to dress her and that he'd passed the job off to his assistant. Banton dressed the stars; Edith Head dressed the "grandmothers," the "aunts," and the relatives. She did the clothes for all of the "horse dramas," dressing the horses and the cowboys.

When it was time to do Barbara's wardrobe, a little lady came in with bangs and dark glasses, bubbling with enthusiasm. She wanted the two suits Barbara was to wear to be more feminine than the current vogue.

Barbara said, "Look, Edith, let's understand each other. I can't wear fancy feminine trappings."

"Of course you can wear them," said Edith.

"Not that Edith doesn't always consider the story first," said Barbara. "But she wanted the suits to do something for me." They did.

"She gave me the kind of care Banton gave the big stars," said Barbara.

With Alfred Santell, director of *Internes Can't Take Money.*

Head was able to make an actress look taller or shorter, or thinner, combined with her ability to be motherly or sisterly. She made Barbara glamorous.

The look of *Internes,* photographed by Theodor Sparkuhl, belied its mundane story of a young doctor in love with a woman desperately searching for her little girl, caught in the middle of a mob world. Sparkuhl and Santell gave the picture the gritty look of a crime movie and interwove throughout a German expressionist feel, using a deliberate blend of silent and talking techniques, "held together," Santell said, "by mood, intensity and sincerity."

Photographer and director captured the shadowy, dreamlike state of the Max Brand story and caught the loneliness of Jimmy Kildare's interior life.

Sparkuhl had photographed more than twenty of Ernst Lubitsch's German pictures. Santell was trained as an architect and was fascinated by the techniques used in *The Cabinet of Dr. Caligari,* by the shadows of *Caligari* painted on the floor instead of being cast naturally by objects or protrusions. When Santell wanted a long shot of a hospital corridor for *Internes,* he borrowed the idea used in *Caligari* of violated perspective: as the perspective diminishes, so do the objects. Instead of building a set eighty feet long, Santell worked out, architecturally and mathematically, the reduction of the arches all the way to the end of the corridor and then used midgets and children dressed in nurses' and doctors' uniforms to give the illusion of distance.

Director and cameraman caught the darkness and solitary feeling of the saloon where Kildare drinks and where he saves the gangster's life. Sparkuhl photographed it as a kind of netherworld of loneliness. The scenes in the orphanage were photographed in the dreamlike religious light of a medieval cathedral. The staircase in the tenement where the young woman lives was filmed from overhead, reversing the principle of violated perspective, fore-shortening the flights of stairs, creating a framed geometric image, an expres-sion of the dangerous maze the young woman has entered in a frantic blind search for her child.

Of Barbara, Santell said, "She knew the whole script and memorized all the other parts. Occasionally, in rehearsal, she'd toss a floundering actor his next line."

McCrea watched Barbara work and marveled that she could be as good as she was.

Paramount thought of making a series of Dr. Kildare pictures if McCrea agreed to play Jimmy Kildare; the actor wasn't interested.

Bob and Jean Harlow began production on a remake of *The Man in Posses-sion* a week into the New Year. Bob was in the Robert Montgomery part from Metro's original 1931 production. Woody Van Dyke was directing; Harlow had just signed a long-term contract with Metro. Jean called the picture *How Not to Buttle*—Bob played a butler in the picture—and one day showed him, in her own style, how to look more ridiculous than he was feeling. "I don't think I ever laughed more than I did on that day," said Bob.

Taylor was listed on *Variety*'s ten most popular international box-office draws. Shirley Temple topped the list; Gary Cooper followed; Laurel and Hardy were ninth; Taylor, tenth. Following *The Man in Possession,* Bob was to make *Three Comrades* with Spencer Tracy and Jimmy Stewart. R. C. Sherriff was finishing the script.

Three weeks into production of *The Man in Possession,* Bob and Jean Har-low were asked by the studio to attend the president's fifty-fifth birthday. Five thousand birthday balls were being held around the country and in seven hotel ballrooms in Washington to help raise funds to fight the disease that had crippled Roosevelt and to help care for the more than 300,000 children and adults afflicted with polio.

Production stopped on *The Man in Possession.* Bob and Jean—sick with the flu—took the train to Washington for two days and nights. She'd nursed her mother through an attack of it, and it hadn't helped that Bob came down with it as well. Jean was miserable but agreed to go east and took her mother and her hairdresser with her.

Bob in Washington for President Roosevelt's birthday and to help support the fight against polio, January 1, 1938. Left to right at the White House: Frederick Jagel, Marsha Hunt, Bob, Maria Gambarelli, First Lady Eleanor Roosevelt braving the cold without a coat, Jean Harlow, Mitzi Green.

After more than three days on the Santa Fe Chief, they arrived at the Washington station; Howard Hughes had just broken the transcontinental airspeed record from Los Angeles to Newark in seven hours, twenty-three minutes, and twenty-five seconds without refueling in his Hughes H-1 plane.

The Santa Fe Chief was met by more than a thousand well-wishers. State troopers on motorcycles accompanied Bob and Jean and the others to the hotel. Later, they were given the keys to the city, before seven hundred fans and guests, and attended a formal dinner in their honor with government officials and the diplomatic corps. The official hostesses of Washington society were appropriately stately and formal until they saw Bob and then began to swoon and shriek as they surged forward to touch America's heartthrob and tear off his necktie.

The next day Bob and Jean posed for pictures with the First Lady at the White House and lunched with the Roosevelt family in celebration of Roosevelt's birthday. All of Roosevelt's children were there, but the president was rewriting his birthday broadcast speech as a result of the disastrous flooding of the Ohio River. Mrs. Roosevelt told the guests how "disappointed the President was to miss you" and suggested that Bob and Jean and Marsha Hunt go to his office upstairs and say hello. "Down the hall from the top of the stairs, third door on the right."

Bob was nervous as they went up the stairs. Harlow asked the others to go ahead of her. Marsha Hunt opened the door to the office. The president was sitting behind his big desk and was friendly and welcoming.

The birthday balls—all seven of them—began at 9:30. The limousines with Bob Taylor and Jean and the others, flanked by motorcycle escort, made their way from hotel to hotel. The movie stars were rushed past screaming crowds and ball goers, through hotel kitchens, service elevators, and back corridors, and made their way into the ballrooms, where they heard the music of Guy Lombardo and his Royal Canadians, George Olsen, Ted Weems, Benny Goodman, and Ted Fio Rito. Bob and Jean were introduced from the stage or bandstand, greeted the crowd, said a few words about the need to support the fight against polio, and were whisked off to the next ball. More than a thousand Washington police were on hand but were unable to control the crowds of people pushing, screaming, dancing. Finally, the district National Guard, the U.S. Marines, and the U.S. Navy Reserve were called in to help.

Bob and Jean and the others were to leave for the gold-plate breakfast dance at the Carlton Hotel, from two to five in the morning, and instead were brought back to the White House at 11 pm to a room below the main floor. The president sat in front of newsreel cameras, lights, and microphones, about to deliver his birthday broadcast to the nation that would be carried on all three radio networks. He had rewritten his speech to address the disastrous flooding of the Ohio River. Just before he was to begin the broadcast, the president looked up from his notes and gave Bob and Jean a big wave. "Is my toupee on straight?" he asked.

On the train back to Hollywood, after twenty-two personal appearances in one day, Bob's cold returned. Jean and her mother, both still sick from the flu, stayed in their compartment during the trip west.

The cost to MGM for halting production on *The Man in Possession*: $100,000.

TWO

Goddamned Sinkhole of Culture

Bob and Barbara were nervous about money, about having it and spending it. Bob never carried it with him, and when he needed it, he borrowed it from Barbara, writing her a check at the end of the week. Bob returned from Washington to a story in the press that said his paternal grandfather, Jacob Brugh, was on county relief in Holmesville, Nebraska. Brugh's two surviving sons, both farmers, and his two daughters couldn't contribute to their father's welfare. Bob and his mother told the press they were unaware of the situation and that they would make sure Brugh wouldn't need to seek other assistance. Bob arranged with his uncle Roy for his grandfather to live with his son. Two weeks later Brugh, at eighty-three, was dead from influenza.

Barbara was set to star in *Private Enemy* from Lamar Trotti and Allen Rivkin's screenplay about a federal undercover agent and a bank robbery ring at the time of President McKinley's assassination. William Seiter was to direct. Zanuck had originally wanted Franchot Tone or Tyrone Power, Fred MacMurray or Clark Gable for the part of the agent and Alice Faye or Claire Trevor for the café singer. Once Barbara was cast, the plan was to star Don Ameche opposite her. But 20th Century–Fox decided it wanted Bob Taylor instead.

It was Bob's first time back at Fox since making his debut in Will Rogers's *Handy Andy*. Metro paid Bob a $10,000 bonus for the picture. Fox paid Metro $75,000 for Taylor. Barbara saw it as an important picture for Bob; playing the part of a federal secret agent would get him out from under the beautiful glamour boy roles that were becoming a problem for him.

The lure for audiences who wanted to watch Barbara Stanwyck and Robert Taylor together on the screen was so great *His Brother's Wife* had broken box-office records and started a new fad. It was all the rage for studios to feature couples in pictures who were romantically connected or recently disconnected. Margaret Sullavan appeared opposite Henry Fonda in *The Moon's Our Home;* Carole Lombard and William Powell, following their divorce, made the just-released *My Man Godfrey;* Metro teamed Harlow with Powell in *Libeled Lady* now that they were seeing each other. The studio was trying to pair Lombard with Clark Gable. Joan Blondell and Dick Powell, newly married, made *Colleen, Stage Struck,* and *Gold Diggers of 1937,* and Ginger Rogers and Jimmy Stewart were set to make *Vivacious Lady.*

The Plough and the Stars opened at Radio City Music Hall in New York days before Barbara and Bob were to start on *Private Enemy,* now called *This Is My Affair.* In the wake of the acclaim and box-office appeal of John Ford's *Informer* and the four Academy Awards the picture received for Best Actor, Director, Music, and Writing, the notices for *The Plough and the Stars* were full of praise. Critics called the picture "a masterpiece" and "one of the most artistic pictures ever seen on the screen," Ford's direction "magnificent."

Dudley Nichols's adaptation was both praised ("notable" for its "rich texture of melancholy and laughter, heroism and cowardice," said one reviewer) and criticized ("The tragic original has been modified into a romantic melodrama," said another).

Barbara was equally praised and criticized: "Barbara Stanwyck reaches new heights"; "the picture [calls] for an actress of considerable more gifts"; she "varies between a shrill insistence and puzzled bewilderment"; "a remarkably vivid portrait . . . unforgettable." After the unexpected success of *The Informer,* critics hedged their bets and only passingly questioned the picture's interest among moviegoers.

Within its first month at Radio City Music Hall, *The Plough and the Stars* brought in $62,128, just under $1,000 less than *The Informer.* Several reviewers called attention to the brogue used by the actors and criticized Barbara for the inconsistency of hers throughout the picture. She was furious about the way reviewers raved about the Abbey Players and criticized her for her now-you-hear-it-now-you-don't Irish accent.

Twentieth Century–Fox heralded its new production *This Is My Affair* as a great romance set against the backdrop of a large historical drama. The studio proclaimed its stars to be the "film colony's Number One off-screen romantic team" and said the picture gave Barbara and Bob a chance "to be together, to act together, to become greater together."

They had been seeing each other for more than a year, and the town, in its quest for fairy-tale turns, continued to pose the question of when they were going to be married.

"I'm not going to marry now," said Barbara. "I'm not going to marry for a long time. Maybe never. I don't *feel* like marriage. I couldn't even tell you why I don't want to marry. I haven't a reason—not one. All I want now are peace and quiet."

Bob and Barbara were together most of the time. Bob loved swing rhythm and listened to Benny Goodman's orchestra and Lud Gluskin and the Casa Loma band. He loved "I'll Get By," "Avalon," "China Boy," "When Did You Leave Heaven?" They rarely entertained or went to nightclubs, though they often ate out. Bob, as a boy in Beatrice, Nebraska, had frequently eaten out with his family. His tastes were simple—steak, potatoes, succotash. He'd only just tasted champagne and didn't know what an artichoke was.

This Is My Affair was originally intended to be about the McKinley assassination; then the career of the detective Allan Pinkerton; and then the sinking of the *Maine.* It ended up a romantic secret agent saga called *The McKinley Case* from a story by Melville Crossman, a.k.a. Darryl F. Zanuck, set at the turn of the century in the midwestern United States.

A Washington newspaperman had told Zanuck of an incident involving a Secret Service operative at work on a political mission so dangerous that only the president of the United States knew of it, but before the work could be completed, McKinley was assassinated, and the agent, dishonored and unsung, in the line of (secret) duty lost his life after being court-martialed. Zanuck used it to write a story about the young nation's stability being threatened by a gang of bank robbers, about President McKinley enlisting the help of a young naval officer (Taylor) in a secret mission to find the robbers, with those in government believed to be involved.

Barbara was the nightclub singer implicated in the plot. Twentieth Century–Fox felt that her singing voice had fared well in *Banjo on My Knee* and gave Barbara three songs to sing. Though somewhat rough around the edges, her voice had the richness and mystery, the smoky tease, of Marlene Dietrich's.

Barbara bought a trailer to use as a dressing room, which she had outfitted and rolled onto the soundstage at Fox. Though the studio would have given her use of a trailer, she wanted her own that she could move from studio to studio and take on location to the San Fernando Valley and Pasadena.

Barbara and Bob looked glamorous on the screen together: dark, intense, radiant. Bob's beauty reflected on Barbara and made her more so. Barbara did her best to help Bob, but her intelligence and strength overpowered him and made him seem diminished. She was much more solid in her scenes opposite Brian Donlevy and Victor McLaglen.

As Lil Duryea, singer at the Capital Café, St. Paul, with Bob as Lieutenant Richard L. Perry, on a top-secret mission direct from President McKinley, Douglas Fowley (second from right) as Alec, and John Carradine as Ed in *This Is My Affair,* 1937. "Thrillingly these real-life sweethearts achieve their true greatness in the most important story either one has ever had" read the studio's advertising teaser. ". . . their fire and power given full scope for the first time!" (AMERICAN HERITAGE CENTER, UNIVERSITY OF WYOMING)

• • •

Many of the most successful actors in the industry were following the path Barbara had braved four years before, when she refused to be under exclusive contract to any one studio. Barbara was under contract to Fox and Radio.

Other actors were under term contracts and could work elsewhere; some had signed up with one producer for one or two pictures. The only actress at Metro who had the right to decide where she would make pictures was Norma Shearer.

Gary Cooper had left Paramount for Goldwyn and was under contract as well with Emanuel Cohen. Claudette Colbert, at Paramount, made pictures at 20th Century–Fox (*Under Two Flags*) and Columbia (*She Married Her Boss*) and was about to make a picture at Warner Bros. (*Tovarich*). Carole Lombard refused to sign a new contract with Paramount until she was given permission to make pictures at other studios, and both Metro and Radio were bidding for her.

Irene Dunne was under contract to Universal (*Show Boat*), Paramount (*High, Wide, and Handsome*), Columbia (*Theodora Goes Wild;* and was preparing to make *The Awful Truth*), and Radio (*Roberta*). Janet Gaynor, who'd been under contract to Fox for years, was freelancing and had just finished making *A Star Is Born* for Selznick International. Ronald Colman had moved from 20th Century–Fox to Columbia to Selznick International. Jean Arthur was at Columbia, Paramount, and Radio and was under contract to Walter Wanger.

Barbara's twenty-sixth movie, *Internes Can't Take Money,* was released in mid-April 1937. Reviewers liked the re-pairing of Barbara and Joel McCrea and thought they were "aptly matched" and the picture "affecting; genuine." Max Brand's agent, Carl Brandt, saw the picture and wrote to his client, "A lot of tears were shed by Barbara Stanwyck, but that can't be helped. She weeps easily." *Cue* called the picture a "fast-moving, tense, thrilling melodrama in the best Alfred Hitchcock tradition . . . gripping film entertainment."

Bob's new picture—his seventeenth—was released in Los Angeles at Grauman's Chinese and Loew's State Theatres and in New York at the Capitol.

At the preview for *The Man in Possession,* now called *Personal Property,* the MGM studio publicity advance men let it be known that Barbara and Bob were at the theater, and as they tried to leave, they were mobbed by several hundred people and had to run back into the theater and climb down a fire escape.

Critics found *Personal Property* "a hilarious piece of screen fun"; others weren't amused. Lucius Beebe thought the picture "pedestrian . . . heavyhanded . . . designed for the delight of the half-wit Croatian peasants." But Beebe found Bob's performance "peerless" and Miss Harlow "ineffable."

Irene Dunne and Bob appeared on the *Lux Radio Theatre* in a reprise of *Magnificent Obsession.* Bob was introduced as "Metro-Goldwyn-Mayer's sensational personality." On the show as special guests were Dr. Lloyd C. Douglas, author of *Magnificent Obsession* and other best-selling novels, and John Arnold, head of Metro's camera department and president of the American Society of Cinematographers. Arnold had started cranking his camera back in 1903, when he worked for Thomas A. Edison, and had since shot more than a billion feet of film.

Barbara and Anne Shirley were borrowed from RKO for *Stella Dallas.* Barbara's contract was split between Radio Pictures and 20th Century–Fox. King Vidor was getting paid $60,000 to direct the picture, $15,000 less than Goldwyn had paid Henry King twelve years earlier; Barbara was getting $50,000;

John Boles $35,000; Anne Shirley, at age nineteen, was paid $3,500. *Stella Dallas* was budgeted at $660,000. In the end it cost $677,000.

A few weeks into the filming of *Stella Dallas, A Star Is Born,* also to be released by United Artists, previewed in Los Angeles at Grauman's Chinese and opened in New York at Radio City Music Hall.

There had been a great deal of talk about the picture.

It was Selznick's third picture under his new company, David Selznick International, and cost more than $1.2 million. Selznick had first approached George Cukor to direct the picture—he directed Selznick's *What Price Hollywood?* for RKO in 1932—but Cukor declined the offer. Bill Wellman directed instead. Wellman and Selznick had collaborated in 1929 at Paramount Famous Lasky on *Chinatown Nights* and *The Man I Love* and again in 1932 at RKO on *The Conquerors.*

Four years later, Wellman had been under contract at MGM, "picking up his weekly check," he said, but not being given anything to direct, only write (he referred to Louis B. Mayer as L. B. Napoleon). Wellman had directed forty-five pictures, among them fifteen silents.

Wellman had asked Metro for a young writer to help him with the typing and chose Robert Carson.

Wellman and Carson were sprung from MGM with the start, in July 1936, of Selznick International. They brought with them two stories that MGM had turned down: a sequel to *The Public Enemy,* called *Another Public Enemy,* and, Wellman's favorite, a story based on his memories, in which everything in it happened to somebody Wellman knew. "Sometimes a little too well," he said.

Carson and Wellman first worked out the story of *It Happened in Hollywood* in detail, and then Carson went away and wrote it. "Wellman read it, when he got around to it," Carson said, "because he didn't read anything— but he read it and we discussed it again. He didn't do any of the writing. [Wellman] was engaged socially, emotionally and alcoholically in many other endeavors, and he had, in addition, his directing chores," among them directing Robert Taylor and Janet Gaynor in *Small Town Girl* and Johnny Weissmuller and Maureen O'Sullivan in a portion of *Tarzan Escapes.*

Selznick read the pages and felt that stories about Hollywood were too much of a gamble. His *What Price Hollywood?* had been one of the few successful pictures about Hollywood.

Wellman, not to be put off, went to see David's wife, Irene ("Brilliant, fascinating, wonderful," Wellman said of her, "with no fear whatsoever of her titanic father; Mayer was both scared and crazy about her, a dilemma").

Russell Birdwell, director of publicity for
David O. Selznick, circa 1938. (GETTY IMAGES)

Wellman told Irene his story ("with no overtones of enthusiasm; no fakery of any kind, just the simple telling of a story I loved").

Irene and David were going to Honolulu for six weeks; she told Wellman not to worry.

"Six weeks later to the last day marked off" on his calendar, Wellman got a call from Selznick telling him to get over to the studio right away.

Selznick gave Wellman the "fakiest explanation of a change in attitude" that he'd ever heard. Selznick said he hadn't been able to get the story out of his mind—night or day. "It's a gamble worth taking," Selznick said. "We'll get Gaynor and March and Menjou, we will make an epic of Hollywood—the real truth, we'll tear down all the tinsel, people will know the gutty Hollywood, the tragedy, the humor."

"Selznick was never satisfied with one script or with the original writers," said Wellman. "Other writers, great writers arriving in sets as if from department stores, young blossoming writers, sons of famous dead writers, idea men who will talk fast but who couldn't write a script to save their lives."

There were three teams of writers on *It Happened in Hollywood*. In the end, Dorothy Parker, Alan Campbell, and Robert Carson received screenwriting credit. John Lee Mahin wrote the final scene. Budd Schulberg, son of B. P. Schulberg—who'd "made 'Willy' Wellman a big-time director with *Wings*," and whose career was ruined by alcohol, and who was the model for Oliver Niles, the producer in *A Star Is Born*—was, along with Ring Lardner Jr., on Selznick's payroll.

Schulberg, at twenty-two, was a reader in the story department; Lardner, at twenty-one, was assistant to Selznick's publicity director, Russell Birdwell. Carson and Wellman used Birdwell as the model for Matt Libby, the studio publicity hack who obsequiously obliges Norman Maine his every whim and demand and endlessly bails him out of trouble until Maine has slipped in popularity and is weakened by booze and failure. Matt Libby then turns on Maine with full loathing and cunning in a vengeful campaign that will publicly finish off the actor's career.

Schulberg and Lardner—both good, beginning writers—were used as "trouble shooters and were brought in to fix up the picture's ending," said Schulberg. Adela Rogers St. Johns, uncredited, worked on the script, as did Ben Hecht.

Bill Wellman spent most of the preproduction putting back the material that had been replaced by the bevy of writers who came as quickly as they seemed to go. Wellman would read his memos "from God" (Selznick), tear them up, and throw them away.

Selznick's legal department drafted a twenty-page brief that spelled out the script's similarities to well-known situations and real-life people, such as Barbara and Frank Fay and John Barrymore.

It Happened in Hollywood was about success and failure, comebacks and downfalls, love and sacrifice, about a destroyed marriage and a tragic death. It was about the rise of one star set against the demise of another and about how, despite personal heartbreak and tragedy, the rising star, as the price of movie greatness, must persevere. At the heart of the story was another toll exacted: the wreckage of lives that comes with too much alcohol.

Wellman, at forty, had seen what too much booze could do to those he knew and loved: failure, humiliation, loss, and death. He knew firsthand the insanity that came with too much drinking; he'd fallen in and out of hell-raising brawls his entire life, almost as easily as he'd fallen in and out of his four marriages ("for a while," Wellman said, he thought "the world was populated entirely by mothers-in-law"). With his last marriage, in 1933, his twenty-year-old wife, Dorothy Coonan, had straightened him out "fast," and Wellman was on the wagon.

Some of the incidents in the story had happened to Wellman himself, such as the scene in which the actor is brought up on drunk-driving charges and comes before a judge who berates him.

Wellman had seen the havoc caused by alcohol in those he and Carson had chosen to write about—the silent-screen actor John Bowers; John Barrymore, the most inspired actor of his time; the silent director Bernard J. Durning and his wife, the silent star and former child actress Shirley Mason (sister

John Bowers appeared in more than ninety silent pictures, beginning in 1914; his twenty-one-year career did not survive talking pictures. (PHOTOFEST)

of Viola Dana)—and in the career and marriage of Wellman's good pal Barbara Stanwyck to Frank Fay. Also drawn upon were the marriages of John McCormick and Colleen Moore, and John Gilbert and Virginia Bruce.

The silent star John Bowers, a Hoosier from Indiana, an extra in 1914 in a Tom Mix picture, *In the Days of the Thundering Herd,* and two years later an overnight success was a leading man playing opposite Mary Pickford in *Hulda from Holland.* More than eighty pictures and two decades later, Bowers was washed up as an actor, done in by alcohol and by sound pictures.

When Bowers's old friend Henry Hathaway failed to give the former star a major part in Hathaway's new picture, Bowers, an avid sailor who'd threatened to "sail into the setting sun" several times before, made good on his threat.

Bowers rented a sixteen-foot boat and sailed out into the ocean. A few days later, the boat was found drifting off Santa Monica, its sails set with no one aboard. Bowers's body was found floating in the surf near Las Flores, south of the Malibu Colony, dead at fifty. Wellman was two weeks into production with *A Star Is Born.*

One of the most beloved and influential figures in Wellman's life was Bernie Durning, Wellman's teacher and boss for two years at Fox. Durning was in his late twenties and a top director making silent action-adventure pictures and melodramas when Wellman, in 1922, left Goldwyn for Fox Film Corporation. To get a job with Durning, Wellman waited for three days in the great director's reception room, along with another hopeful, Adolphe Menjou.

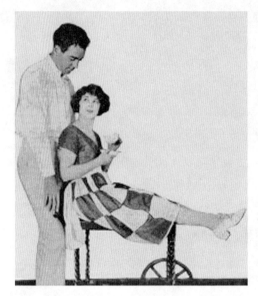

Bernard J. Durning, actor/director, with his wife, Shirley Mason, who began in films when she was eleven and who retired at twenty-nine, having appeared in more than one hundred pictures, circa 1922. (PHOTOFEST)

Wellman was "nuts" about Durning from their meeting. "Quite frankly," said Wellman, "he was my God."

Durning was "a big, handsome, hard-drinking, tough, lovable guy with a terrific temper. He was well over six feet, dressed immaculately." He was also an actor, "and a bad one," said Wellman. Durning was "so tall that he breathed different air." He was the handsomest man Wellman had ever met.

Durning was married to "a little bitty gal" called Shirley Mason, also at Fox Studios. Mason started on the stage when she was four. She was so full of pranks she was called the "boy of the family."

Wellman was hired as Durning's assistant and was warned by the director that he was "a periodic drunk . . . the worst drunk you ever saw, and the most helpless." When the time came, Durning would need Wellman "goddamned badly."

The first year Durning and Wellman made five pictures together. Wellman never saw Durning give in to the "sickness that was supposed to possess him." Durning's only overindulgence, said Wellman, was chocolate ice-cream sodas. "Three whoppers at a sitting," said Wellman, "and [he] never bat[ted] an eye or add[ed] . . . a pound to his sit-down."

It was in the second year, while shooting *The Eleventh Hour,* that Wellman saw Durning become the "slave to whatever you call it" and go into an "alcoholic hibernation for a week, just coming to often enough to replenish the burning wick." Durning asked Wellman to finish shooting *The Eleventh Hour,* which he did. Afterward, Durning told the heads of the studio that he'd been on one of his "pilgrimages to the land of nod and had been gone for five mislaid days," that Bill Wellman had finished the picture, and that Wellman deserved to be given his own picture to direct. The studio listened and complied.

Durning had taught his assistant well; he'd given Bill the confidence of "a pit bull-dog." A month into Wellman's picture, he got word while shooting a scene that Durning was dead. "The King of Terrors had reached out and grabbed him," said Wellman. "Bernie wasn't ready for that." He was thirty years old; Wellman was twenty-seven. It was 1923.

John Barrymore's drunkenness and outrageous behavior were, along with Frank Fay's, the model for the doomed matinee idol Norman Maine. Barrymore and Fay, each in his own way, had been celebrated as the most innovative, electrifying, and nuanced performers of their generation.

Ben Hecht and Charlie MacArthur called Barrymore "the Monster"; he was celebrated as a theatrical genius who'd created the first postwar modern Hamlet. Greta Garbo, after working with Barrymore in *Grand Hotel,* called him "a perfect artist. He had that driven madness without which a great artist cannot work or live."

Barrymore and Frank Fay had each fallen ill from alcoholism; each had been in and out of sanitariums in an effort to dry out from booze. The scene of Norman Maine in the "rest home" was inspired by George Cukor's visit to see Barrymore at Kelley's Rest Home, where he was struggling, once again, to get out from under the Barrymore curse.

"Lollipop Hollywood bastards" was the way Barrymore described the film world. A "goddamned sink hole of culture. The good die young because they see it's no use living if you have to be good."

To David Selznick, Barrymore *was* Norman Maine, and he was determined to use the fallen theatrical idol in the role. "If we use him," Wellman warned, "we'll have to blackboard him." Selznick wanted to chance it, but he didn't want to be the one to tell Barrymore about the blackboard.

America's greatest Shakespearean actor, whose Hamlet the English critic James Agate had called "nearer to Shakespeare's whole creation than any other I have seen," had for the past few years become unhinged by lapses of memory. After years of too much alcohol, Barrymore at fifty-four was having trouble remembering his lines.

Three years earlier Barrymore had delivered one of the most startling screen performances in Elmer Rice's *Counsellor at Law.* In it Barrymore had spoken his lines at rapid fire with speeches that went on for pages, and he'd finished the picture without a problem. Weeks later, after completing *Long*

Lost Father for RKO, Barrymore was recalled by William Wyler to reshoot a sequence for *Counsellor at Law.*

It was a simple scene between Barrymore and the actor John Qualen. Barrymore finished his longish speech; Qualen said his lines. Barrymore started to give what was a few short lines and stumbled over the words. He made a silly face, people laughed, and they started the scene from the beginning. Again Barrymore missed the line. He looked at the script. They started again. The words still escaped him. Barrymore was somewhat tired but not drunk. After several more tries, he was angry and upset, and then Qualen blew his lines. Barrymore persisted. Hour after hour, take after take, Barrymore blew his lines at the same place. Fifty-six takes later he asked for the scene to be shot the following day.

That night Barrymore was called on to help his neighbor John Gilbert, who was threatening suicide; Gilbert's fourth wife, Virginia Bruce, had announced she was taking their three-month-old baby daughter and leaving him. Barrymore stayed with Gilbert until seven the following morning and, without any sleep, went before the cameras and shot the *Counsellor at Law* scene perfectly.

Two months later Barrymore began tests for a Technicolor screen version of *Hamlet.* The picture was to be directed by his friend Robert Edmond Jones and financed by Jock Whitney. For the test, Barrymore was to perform the "rogue and peasant slave" soliloquy. He began the speech from act 1, scene 5, a speech he'd made onstage hundreds of times. He came to the line "Yea, from the table of my memory," and he couldn't find the lines that began, "I'll wipe away all trivial fond records." Barrymore tried to do the scene again but was still unable to remember the lines. He was neither drunk nor ill.

The *Hamlet* production was canceled.

Two months later Barrymore created the inspired performance of the demented manic Oscar Jaffe, adapted for the actor by Hecht and MacArthur from their play *Twentieth Century.* Barrymore was brilliant and had no problems with his memory.

During the next couple of years, as Barrymore attempted to work in other pictures and contracts were canceled, he was diagnosed with Korsakoff syndrome, toxemia affecting the brain brought on by excessive alcohol. Barrymore could at times be vital and alert; at other times he was listless and unable to sustain attention. The lapses of memory had panicked the actor, and he'd progressed to a point where in order to work, he required a blackboard with the scene's lines out of camera range. The Selznick office called Barrymore and asked him to come in regarding the role of Norman Maine.

Selznick's business manager told the actor they wanted him for the part of the fading movie idol.

Barrymore listened as he was told that the part of the doomed actor was his but that he would have to use a blackboard. He said nothing and left the office.

The model for the Vicki Lester–Norman Maine marriage was Barbara's marriage to Fay, which by this point had become Hollywood lore. Fay had come to Hollywood a huge Broadway star; Barbara's big Broadway success in *Burlesque* had carried no weight in Hollywood. She was an unknown girl married to one of the biggest draws in vaudeville and on Broadway. For the first few years in Hollywood, after Fay changed his mind and allowed Barbara to work, he'd guided and supported her career; it was Fay who had Harry Cohn hire his wife for *Mexicali Rose* and arrange to pay her salary. Fay brought Capra a copy of Barbara's test scene from *The Noose,* shot by Alexander Korda, when Barbara, after making eleven unsuccessful tests, refused to make another for Capra's new picture, *Ladies of Leisure,* and it was Fay who insisted that Capra watch the test. Capra, watching it, had fallen in love with Barbara and starred her in four of his pictures, launching her career. Wellman and Carson used this in the picture when Norman Maine insists that the producer, Oliver Niles, watch Esther Blodgett's screen test.

It was part of Hollywood lore that as Barbara's star began to rise in picture after picture, Fay's godlike stature as Broadway's Favorite Son began to collapse. Warner Bros. had put Fay in one improbable movie role after another in an attempt to make the red-haired, brilliant monologuist into the screen's most irresistible Latin lover.

Bill Wellman had watched much of this unfold. He adored Stanwyck and she him. They'd made three pictures together—*Night Nurse, So Big, The Purchase Price*—during the years—1931–1932—when Barbara's marriage was starting to come apart. In many ways Bill felt that Barbara was a female version of himself: the leanness, the energy, the passion, the toughness, the fierce loyalty.

Hollywood had watched appalled and sniggering as Barbara stood steadfast by Fay's side ("I'm Mrs. Frank Fay," she'd insisted to reporters at the height of her stardom and the low point of his): through his publicized brawls, his string of failed pictures, and his disastrous return to Broadway's Palace, where once he'd played the longest engagement in the theater's history.

Wellman knew about Barbara's troubled marriage. He'd watched, though she hadn't spoken about it, as Barbara supported Fay, fighting his decline

John McCormick, head of production, First National, and his wife, Colleen Moore, circa 1923. Her mother cut off her long curls, shaped her bangs to look "like a Japanese girl's haircut," she said, and the vision of flaming youth took hold. "We were coming out of the Victorian era and in my pictures, I danced the Charleston, I smoked in public and I drank cocktails. Nice girls didn't do that before." (MARGARET HERRICK LIBRARY, ACADEMY OF MOTION PICTURE ARTS AND SCIENCES)

every step of the way, signing studio contract after contract with the stipulation that Fay be part of the deal and be given money to make his pictures. She'd appeared with Fay in his act—as his straight man and performing her old cartwheeling dance numbers—much to the horror of the press, who accused them both of denigrating her image as a serious actress. Barbara had invested in Fay's extravagant revue that crisscrossed the country, even appearing with him in it when he was often too drunk to go onstage. The press wrote about the marriage, about how it wouldn't last, how it shouldn't last, which made Barbara fight harder to keep it alive, until Fay's illness—his alcoholism and violent rages—forced her to flee it for good.

Interwoven in the portrait of the Maine-Lester marriage was that of John McCormick and Colleen Moore, a producer-star team that fused into being one artist. McCormick, the former publicity chief of First National, became production head when First National went from a distribution company to a producing studio, and he set out to make his wife into America's No. 1 box-office draw. Moore, neither beautiful nor glamorous, had starred in a string of treacly pictures. Through McCormick's persistence and Moore's pragmatism, she cut off her hair and went from being a modestly successful sweet young thing to America's Jazz Age flapper with Dutch bob and boyish figure. Colleen Moore's straight hair took the place of Mary Pickford's curls. With *The Perfect Flapper* and *We Moderns,* the convent-educated Colleen Moore became bigger than Pickford, Swanson, Chaplin, and Tom Mix.

Throughout the 1920s, John McCormick was making $100,000 a year.

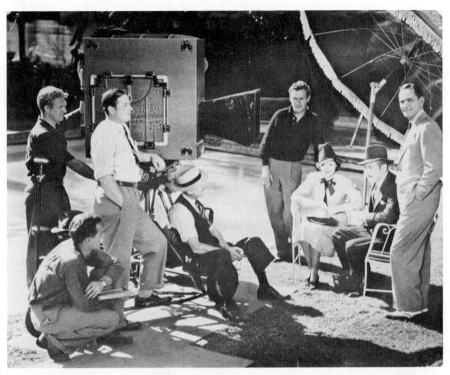

William Wellman (in black sweater to the right of the camera), Janet Gaynor, Adolphe Menjou (seated), Fredric March, and W. Howard Greene, the cameraman (seated, with hat), on the set of *A Star Is Born,* winter 1936.

McCormick and Moore made twenty pictures together; their collaboration seemed to be at its height. Moore's pictures were bringing in millions. As she became the idol of the nation, McCormick's alcoholic binges grew more frequent and destructive. America's wide-eyed flapper stood by her husband through his hospitalizations and covered for him at the studio until she realized he was set on his own destruction and Moore filed for divorce to save her life. The girl with the Dutch bob and the short shorts, who became on-screen the symbol of the Roaring Twenties, made the transition to sound pictures and flourished, making several successful movies, among them *The Power and the Glory* by Preston Sturges and *The Scarlet Letter.* Americans, though, still yearned for their perfect flapper, and in 1934 Colleen Moore left pictures altogether.

In *A Star Is Born,* love was the heroine; drink was the destroyer.

Wellman was so drawn to the lore of those whose careers were done in by drink and by the coming of sound that he cast several actors undone by both in small parts in the picture: Owen Moore, Mary Pickford's first husband, was cast as a director. Marshall Neilan, a former silent director, was given a small part as someone who bumps into Norman Maine at the Santa Anita racetrack. Bob Perry, who had appeared in three of Wellman's pictures, beginning with the 1928 *Beggars of Life,* as well as *Night Nurse* and *The Purchase Price,* was given a role as a boxing referee. Even Wellman's first wife, the silent star Helene Chadwick, appeared in the picture. Chadwick first met Wellman at a dinner party in New York when he'd returned from the Lafayette Flying Corps before the United States entered the Great War. Throughout the 1920s, Chadwick had made more than seventy pictures, including *The Cup of Fury, Dangerous Curve Ahead,* and *Brothers Under the Skin;* Wellman, as a twenty-four-year-old studio messenger, had delivered Chadwick's fan mail.

In its own way, *A Star Is Born* was a love letter to Hollywood. Scenes were shot at Grauman's Chinese Theatre, the Trocadero, the Hollywood Legion Stadium, the swimming pool of the Ambassador Hotel, the Santa Anita racetrack, and the Hollywood Bowl.

The picture's first sneak preview was in Pomona, where there were technical difficulties. Next it was shown in Huntington Park.

"The audience," Wellman said, "did everything but dance in the street—they laughed, cried and shook the ceiling with applause."

Selznick had told Wellman he was a lousy writer; Wellman expected an apology. Instead, Selznick jumped up and down "as awkward looking as a kangaroo leaping around with his front paws against his chest" and grabbed Wellman in a bear hug and repeated hysterically, "What did I tell you, what did I tell you." Selznick wrote a memo saying that *A Star Is Born* was much more his story than either Wellman's or Carson's. Selznick went on to say, "The actual original idea, the story line and the vast majority of the story ideas of the scenes themselves are my own. If, however, I am wrong in my recollection of our contract, and it states that Wellman is entitled to a bonus on *Star Is Born,* as it is his story, I would not for a moment quibble on whose story it is, and we should by all means pay him."

A coast-to-coast hookup nationally broadcast for the first time the world preview of the all-color production of *A Star Is Born* at Grauman's Chinese Theatre. Grandstands lined both sides of Wilshire Boulevard. A twenty-piece orchestra played as hundreds of stars, directors, studio executives, civic leaders, and Los Angeles society arrived. The event was broadcast over the radio.

George Fisher, of *Hollywood Whispers,* introduced the stars as they arrived: Fredric March, who earlier in the evening had had his footprints taken in cement at the forecourt of Grauman's; Janet Gaynor in white summer ermine;

Adolphe Menjou, Andy Devine, Lionel Stander, Bill Wellman, Robert Carson, Selznick, and Jock Whitney were there, as was almost everyone else in Hollywood from Louis B. Mayer, Jack Warner, and Cecil B. DeMille to Jean Harlow and William Powell, Ethel and Lionel Barrymore, Myrna Loy, Cary Grant, Charles Chaplin, and Marlene Dietrich. Also there were P. G. Wodehouse, at work at Metro, who had allowed Selznick to appropriate the title of *A Star Is Born* from one of his short stories; Clark Gable and Carole Lombard; and Jack Benny and Mary Livingstone. Noticeably absent from the evening were John Barrymore, Frank Fay, and Barbara Stanwyck.

Barbara was just starting production on *Stella Dallas*.

THREE

Stella Dallas

Stella is real.
—Barbara Stanwyck

You may say that Stella is crude and noisy and vulgar," said Barbara. "She is. But when you get through with the play you also must say, 'That was a woman.' And it means something to play a real person. I've had so many of the other kind to do; pretty women who didn't matter. Stella is real."

Being beautiful and romantic in the theater was all very well, but Barbara understood that sooner or later an actress had to see that it was the "unlady-like role" that would give her an opportunity to achieve greatness. "Helen Hayes scored her greatest screen triumph in *The Sin of Madelon Claudet*," said Barbara. "Ruth Chatterton created the greatest of all her characterizations in *Madame X*. Her work in *Dodsworth* proved that a portrayal may be repellent yet so finely turned that it is beautiful to watch. Miss Chatterton is versed in the ways of acting for it has been the unattractive roles that have meant her greatest successes."

Barbara admired character actors; they were constantly working. She saw how character actresses playing type roles were being rewarded with substantial recognition. Gale Sondergaard as the female heavy in *Anthony Adverse* had won the Academy Award and was the outstanding character in the picture; Beulah Bondi's homely Rachel Jackson in *The Gorgeous Hussy* had been acclaimed, while the performances of two newcomers to the screen, Estelle Winwood and Fay Bainter, in the just-released *Quality Street* were notable successes.

"Give me a good supporting role," said Beulah Bondi, "that's all I ask."

Barbara saw the deep dramatic possibilities inherent in those roles, which to her "did not preclude unrestrained acting." An ordinary leading role, "even though good," she said, didn't offer the chance to "slough off the restraints of glamour." To Barbara, the average leading lady had been "built up" and was forced to act in type, "to hew the line laid down for her," and was unable to "realize the full potentialities of her acting ability." Barbara believed that character roles allowed an actress to "sink her teeth into the part and extract the last bit of flavor. Forgotten twists in characterization come to the fore." Barbara had been looking for a part "of that kind for some time" before she won the role of Stella Dallas.

Stella, ambitious, illiterate, with her misguided social ambitions, wearing frightful clothes and too much makeup, is undone by her generous but pre-posterous manners, her flamboyant, vulgar self. Her beloved daughter takes after her father, with his refined taste, bearing, and curiosity, as Stella learns of the enormity of the handicap she is to the one person she loves.

Goldwyn's *Stella Dallas,* the 1925 silent and the 1937 remake, were about mother love, about marriage and divorce between two people of different social backgrounds: he, rich and educated; she, poor and striving.

Stella Dallas is a punitive movie in which the woman is tortured with class, propriety, and the split between husband and child. Stella Martin, the ambitious seventeen-year-old daughter of a mill hand, aching to get out from the squalor of her upbringing, finds escape through impulsive love and mar-riage. Stella Dallas, in both play and movies, flaunts an exaggerated notion of a woman. She is a spectacle and is oblivious of its effect. The production code did not allow sexuality in a family picture, and the women in *Stella Dallas* aren't sexual, including the slinky good debutante widow.

Olive Higgins Prouty, author of the novel *Stella Dallas,* was pleased that Barbara avoided "any attempt at sex appeal in Stella," she said. "This inno-cence was one of Stella's outstanding characteristics."

Olive Higgins had shocked her family when she announced she was going to Smith. "College was apt to make a girl opinionated, undomestic, unmanage-able and also unmarriageable in the opinion of many a young man who didn't want a 'blue stocking' for a wife."

Higgins graduated from Smith and married Lewis Isaac Prouty, whose family ran a shoe and boot company. They lived in Brookline, Beacon Hill, and Buzzards Bay. Prouty's first book, *Bobbie, General Manager,* was a big success.

Olive Higgins (Prouty), circa 1904. (SMITH COLLEGE ARCHIVES, SMITH COLLEGE)

Stella Dallas, Prouty's fifth book, was a novel inspired by a conversation the author overheard at a dinner party in Boston. One of the guests was curious about her dinner partner. "Evidently," the guest said to the hostess, "a member of an old Boston family. He referred to a daughter he was taking with him on a camping-trip this summer. Where is his wife?"

"Separated," the hostess said. "He married someone beyond the pale socially when he was very young and was sent by his business to a branch office somewhere a long way off from Boston. They have been separated ever since the child was born—a girl twelve or thirteen now, quite lovely in spite of her mother—really terribly ordinary. The child lives with her mother in a dreary little apartment out in the suburbs somewhere but spends a month every summer with her father . . . It was really pathetic last August, all the plans that man made for the child—packing into one month, a whole year's devotion."

That night, after the party, as Prouty was falling asleep, she thought about the "lovely" child and the "terribly ordinary" mother, "beyond the pale socially," left behind in her "dreary apartment" when the little girl went to visit her aristocratic father, and about why "such an apparently discriminating man" had married such an inappropriate woman. The next day Mrs. Prouty began to write a book about them. For her, the novel was never about "mother love." It was a much more daring subject in 1923: about "the paths of the sensitive child of separated parents of different backgrounds with the resulting conflict."

Stella Dallas was serialized in the fall of 1922 in *The American Magazine* and published in April 1923 by Houghton Mifflin Company.

Soon after the book's publication, Prouty had a nervous breakdown. She was forty-one years old and had lost two baby daughters within a period of three years.

In the novel, Prouty wrote about courageous themes: a woman—a mother—who refuses to be restrained by the conventions of marriage; who forsakes her child to go dancing with her husband and flaunts herself before other men; who refuses to follow her husband when he is given a promotion and assigned a big job in New York; who brings into her house a crude, over-affable "other man" who is shunned by the society she so venerates.

Mrs. Prouty wrote about divorce; about a child balancing her relationship with her mother and father and the fierce loyalty the child feels toward the mother as a result of the father's leaving; about the mother's struggle financially to give everything she can to the child and the vast disparity between the way the parents live.

"A novel of absolutely first rate importance," said the *New York Herald Tribune*. *The New York Times* saw Prouty's novel as "a book written with sophistication . . . there is no attempt at fine writing, and yet . . . the reader has the impression that all the effects of fine writing have been attained. There is no reason why *Stella Dallas* should not place Mrs. Prouty immediately amid such writers as Zona Gale and Willa Cather."

Stella Dallas was produced as a play by Selwyn and Company with Mrs. Leslie Carter in the title role. It was not a pleasant experience for Mrs. Prouty, who watched helpless as *Stella Dallas* was turned into a play she barely recognized. The playwrights, Harry Wagstaff Gribble, a former actor who'd toured the American West with Mrs. Patrick Campbell in *Pygmalion,* and Gertrude Purcell, transformed Stella Martin—despite Prouty's protestations—from a respectable woman who had attended the State Normal School—an innocent woman misjudged—into a wily, sexual, blowsy dame whose gaudiness and killing manner were played up in order to bring in laughs for the seventy-year-old Mrs. Carter. Mrs. Carter's dressing room was locked shut so that none of the other actors could see her making up or see that her hair was a wig, then a taboo subject.

Edward G. Robinson was Mrs. Carter's Ed Munn, Stella's sometime lover and, later in the play, her husband. Robinson, as a teenager, had watched Mrs. Carter onstage, then a mature woman. Now, years later, Mrs. Carter would doze onstage and wake just in time to step on Robinson's line.

Mrs. Prouty liked Harry Gribble and Gertrude Purcell "well enough,"

Mrs. Leslie Carter, in her sixties, circa 1924. She was called the "American Bernhardt" and rose to stardom under the tutelage of David Belasco. (ROBINSON LOCKE COLLECTION, NEW YORK PUBLIC LIBRARY FOR THE PERFORMING ARTS)

she wrote to her husband. "But I do not think they are to the manner born when it comes to fine points of feeling and etiquette in play-writing. They're rough-hewn. The play is a mess."

Mrs. Prouty realized early that Mrs. Leslie Carter "herself, is the problem. She's pretty coarse," she wrote, "and will 'damn and gosh-darn' and 'golly'— till I'm wondering *what* sort of character I wrote about, anyway."

Mrs. Carter was desperate for a solid characterization and a good director. "If [the director] had any of Mr. Belasco's talent," Mrs. Carter said to Mrs. Prouty one day during rehearsals, "he could make me *your* kind of Stella without all this agony. Mr. Belasco could make me a saint or a devil, a nun or a harlot, a lady or a slut, just as he chose. Such a director! Such an artist! And oh such a man!"

The feud between Mrs. Carter and Mrs. Prouty over the characterization of Stella continued.

"Mrs. Carter is acting pretty badly," Mrs. Prouty wrote to her husband. "Showing unfortunate traits—ugly, teary, soft—hard—loyal—disloyal— all in one half-hour. Whenever she's off-stage I *like* the play but when she's on—I have to *try* and like it. Well, it isn't my fault."

Mrs. Prouty said later, "There are two things I want to avoid in my writing: sentimentality and melodrama." The play, unlike her novel, was accused of both. Selwyn's *Stella Dallas* was received by critics as "claptrap" and an "incongruous combination of burlesque and melodrama."

• • •

For the silent picture of *Stella Dallas,* Frances Marion struggled to find the "thin line between convincing sentimentality and lachrymose melodrama." For the remake, the Marion script, her first assignment for Goldwyn, was mostly unchanged. It was basically Gribble and Purcell's script of the play.

During the filming of the silent *Stella Dallas,* Goldwyn kept Mrs. Prouty informed about the picture's progress. He sent her stills that "puzzled" her. "There were characters I did not recognize and scenes I could not place," she said. As a result of the play, there were gaping inconsistencies with Stella's character and with the plot of the movie script.

In the movie, Stella Martin, as the young girl living with her parents, with her heart set on the handsome, dashing Stephen Dallas, is lovely, well-spoken, with energy and spirit; her clothes are modest with touches of color in contrast to the drabness of her mill-town family. She flirts shyly, with upward glances, with reservation. After she becomes Mrs. Stephen Dallas and has attained the stature she's yearned for—married to a blue blood with a fine apartment on the other side of the river—she flirts outrageously with other men, dresses in outlandish clothes, and speaks in a shrill voice with a harsh mill-town accent.

In the silent version, there is the sequence when Stella and Stephen are courting. They sit on the veranda swing in front of Stella's living room window. Behind them, from the other side of the window, are Stella's brother and her father mugging and making fun of what to them is laughably fake—her modest demeanor when they know that their Stella is fun loving and playful, a cutup. She is holding herself back as a way to win Stephen's heart.

In the Vidor remake, Stella, who had her heart set only on Stephen Dallas, is now, a year later, home from the hospital with their new baby, bored (inexplicably in story terms) with her husband, bored with his "iceberg-y" ways of doing things, his lectures about how she should walk and talk and comport herself.

She comes home with her new baby from the hospital an altogether different person. Gone are her modest clothes; instead, she is wearing a foolish hat of extreme design and an equally silly coat. Where before she wanted only to be Mrs. Stephen Dallas, now she's fed up with having to adapt to his ways ("How would it do for *you* to do a little of the adapting, Stephen, a little of the giving up?" And when he asks her why she married him, she—bravely—returns the question, "Why did you ever marry *me?*"). When Stephen leaves for New York to take a big job, Stella (oddly in terms of the story but again as an interesting, brave choice) refuses to go with her husband and chooses instead to stay behind in Millwood (Millhampton in Prouty's novel) with their baby.

Stella Martin is the ambitious girl who has married up and has arrived as Mrs. Stephen Dallas; why would she choose to stay behind in Millwood when her husband leaves for New York? The reason given: "I'm not going to leave here just when I'm getting in with the right people." In the Vidor version, Stella's decision to stay behind dislocates the story. Does she choose to stay behind as a small-town girl, frightened of leaving what is familiar and her childhood fantasy of an adult world?

On a date with Stephen while they are courting, they are at the movies. Stella watches transfixed as the screen lovers (they are watching Belle Bennett in the 1925 version of *Stella Dallas*) dance off to a private place where they turn toward each other and embrace; the picture ends with a they-lived-happily-ever-after kiss. Stella is so carried away by the power of the movie story it takes her a few seconds to come back to her real life. As they walk home, Stella tells Stephen, "I don't want to be like me. I want to be like the people in the movies, everything well-bred and refined."

Olive Higgins Prouty's Stella makes the decision to stay behind when Stephen Dallas leaves for New York, and it makes sense. Prouty's Stella Martin is the belle of her town, the girl who far outshines all the others; she has "stacks of style" and can "drape a straight piece of cloth about her hips and shoulders and [make] it assume fashionable lines all by itself." She's a girl with ambition who makes it through high school and completes a course at the State Normal School. She knows she's different from the other girls, most of whom are content after ninth grade to work in the weaving rooms at the mills or else marry "some raw half-awake young man from the mills and have children, and children and children."

Stella's got confidence in her "personal charm."

When Stephen marries her, he sees her limitations and crudities. He sees how she occasionally makes mistakes with grammar and in taste. But to Stephen, Stella is wonderfully sweet-tempered, always amiable, always gay; and he's moved by the fact that she doesn't pity him because of the family scandal he's fled (the discovery that his father has embezzled and has subsequently committed suicide). Stephen is ready to "rub down [Stella's] rough edges."

In the novel, Prouty charts their class differences and shows how their marriage is undone by the inevitable: Stephen is tall and slight, aristocratic in bearing; Stella is plump and constantly nibbles on candy. Stephen loves the beauty of the outdoors and finds it exhilarating. Stella doesn't enjoy the outdoors but uses it for practical purposes, as a means to reduce her weight. Stephen takes pleasure from reading and listening to music. "That dead, old-fashioned high-brow stuff" gives Stella "the fidgets" and "horribly bores her."

As Stella Dallas with John Boles as her husband, Stephen, and an unidentified child as their daughter, Laurel, 1937.

Stella's only interest in books is in their decorative quality (she arranges them on the shelves according to the color of their bindings). She prefers movie magazines and finds comfort in them.

Stella doesn't know Thackeray or Eliot or Trollope or Meredith ("Lord, what did he [Stephen] find in those old birds?" she asks); a violin makes her "want to scream" it's so "squeaky"; she likes to go to a vaudeville show and a good play with "modern actors."

Stephen, as the blue blood, is conventional; he is adaptable, approachable, accorded the advantages of his breeding and class, but to Stella he is glum and ill-humored ("What is he, an undertaker?" asks Ed Munn, to which Stella breaks into shrieks of laughter in recognition of the truth about her husband). To Stella, Stephen is someone who wants to tamp down her spirit and style. She may not have his breeding, she may be loud and conspicuous, but she's got energy, and she wants to have "some fun in life."

As Prouty shows how Stephen's breeding comes to the fore, how his love of success cannot be denied, she shows as well how Stella's lack of breeding does her in. Stephen, in horror, comes to see that he has married a woman

With Alan Hale, the towering hearty 220-pound actor as Ed Munn, with whom Barbara had worked in *So Big* and *Message to Garcia*. He began in one-reel, ten-minute Lubin pictures in 1912, appeared in Rex Ingram's *Four Horsemen of the Apocalypse* and John Ford's *The Lost Patrol*, among others, but it was his small role in *It Happened One Night* that propelled him into another realm: *Of Human Bondage*, John Stahl's *Imitation of Life*, and *High, Wide, and Handsome*, among them. (AMERICAN HERITAGE CENTER, UNIVERSITY OF WYOMING)

he does not love and that the loneliness he feels is his burden to bear for his hasty choice. Prouty shows how, once Stella is received and accepted as Mrs. Stephen Dallas by certain Millwood prelates and officials, her innocence is turned into disastrous self-confidence, "how the limelight of recognition turns her into something hard and brittle that flies to pieces at his slightest touch."

Stella's transformation throughout Prouty's novel is interwoven so that when Stephen leaves for New York, Stella's choice to stay behind makes sense. Barbara's Stella shows up basic problems with the script that Belle Bennett's Stella was able to hide. Barbara's Stella, so tender with her child, is not at all the same Stella who laughs at Ed Munn's pranks.

Jean Hersholt as Ed Munn in the Henry King silent production is much less of a blowhard than Alan Hale. Hersholt's Munn has a humanity Hale's doesn't have. Hale played Munn as wide and loud as he could.

Belle Bennett was able to evoke a real-life vulgarity, a woman not elegantly brought up; she evokes a woman with unsuitable responses to things.
Bennett had the life to fill out her Stella Dallas. When Bennett stays behind
in Millhampton, it feels right. Barbara saw playing Stella as a "double challenge." There was Bennett's performance "beautifully played." Barbara saw
that the way to play Stella was "on two levels, almost making Stella two
separate women."

As an actress, Barbara makes one expect subtle, delicate responses. It is the
way her face moves, a sharpness, a strength that comes through, and an intelligence that make it hard to believe her Stella is unaware of the way people
are responding to her.

"On the surface," said Barbara, Stella "had to appear loud and
flamboyant—with a touch of vulgarity. Yet while showing her in all commonness, she had to be portrayed in a way that audiences would realize that
beneath the surface her instincts were fine, heartwarming and noble."

Barbara accomplished what she set out to do with Stella.

"Portraying surface vulgarity" is a thin dividing line "between tragedy
and comedy," said Barbara, who made sure that "all of the facets of Stella—
a great woman in spite of jangling bracelets and bobbing plumes—were never
confusing to the audience." It wasn't confusing, just inconsistent with who
Stella was. The constant in the character is the love Stella feels for Laurel, a
love that, for Stella, supplants all others.

In one scene Stella and Ed Munn are on the train to Boston to pick up
party favors for Laurel's tenth birthday celebration. Ed has played a practical
joke on the other passengers in the car: he's duped them into thinking he's
a big winner on a horse race and shakes their hands, unbeknownst to them,
with itch powder. Stella is quietly sipping sarsaparilla and, even as she objects to Ed's antics, is drawn into the prank. The hapless passengers are now
scratching every which way. Ed is delighted with the joke, and Stella is shrieking with laughter so much that they both flee the car before they are found
out and stumble into the next car, where Laurel's teacher, Miss Phillibrown,
is sitting. Miss Phillibrown is aghast at what she sees: Laurel's mother with a
man who is not her husband and carrying on in a rowdy, vulgar way. Stella
doesn't notice Laurel's teacher; nor does she see the disapproval on her face
or anyone else's. (In the silent picture, Miss Tibbets spots Stella in Boston
leaving a boardinghouse with Ed and assumes they've shared a room when
they had innocently stayed in separate bedrooms.) It is hardly believable that
Stella doesn't recognize Miss Phillibrown when she's recently come to Stella's
house; it is equally hard to believe Stella doesn't notice how she and Ed are
being looked at by the other passengers.

Ed becomes serious and tells Stella once again how he feels about her. She explains to him, with nobility and with Barbara's full-throated softness and resonance, "It's not personal, Ed. There's not a man living that could get me going anymore. Lollie just uses up all the feelings I got. I don't seem to have any left for anyone else." That Stella is believable, and real.

Other inconsistencies occur when Dallas surprises Laurel on Christmas Day and asks Stella if Laurel can spend the day with him. Stella and Laurel have planned to open presents and then "take in a show." Stella is glad to see Stephen, and when he asks her to join them for dinner before they are to catch the train back to New York, Barbara's Stella sees in Stephen the man she fell in love with. Gone is the blowsy, loud common woman; she is modest and quiet and excuses herself to get ready to join them for dinner. She removes the frills and extras from the dress she's made in order to please Stephen. She comes back into the living room wearing a simple dark long-sleeved dress.

When, later in the picture, Stella is summoned to the office of Dallas's lawyer, she is once again strident, brusque, dressed to the tens in outlandish hat and coat speaking in a more outlandish lower-class accent and a shrill voice to tell the lawyer what for.

When shopping for her resort wear before she and Laurel go off to the Mirador, Stella buys the kinds of tacky shoes no one but a nineteenth-century London trollop would wear, and not the modest Stella who greets Stephen on Christmas Day or who tells Ed Munn she doesn't have feelings for anyone but Laurel. Stella at the resort, getting out of her sickbed all dolled up to go and find Laurel, has put on such an assortment of clothes, jewelry, and makeup to toddle across the manicured lawn that one young man remarks, "She isn't a woman; she's a Christmas tree."

The silent *Stella Dallas* was directed by Henry King. The picture had a simplicity and an honesty, King's signature. His interest was American life. His pictures were infused with an idealization of place and captured a loneliness that came from King's boyhood life in the South, where he was raised on a farm in Montgomery County, Virginia. His grandfather, a plantation owner, had fought under Lee in the Civil War. King quit school at fifteen and joined a theatrical stock company and toured as an actor throughout the South. Before becoming a motion picture actor, King worked in the circus, vaudeville, burlesque, and the New York stage. He'd always thought of himself as an actor, but by 1907, at the age of twenty-one, he was directing stage plays. King acted in pictures from 1913 to 1925. While he appeared in more than

Henry King circa 1915. Of his work, a leading producer said, "Run twenty new pictures and I will pick out immediately the one of the twenty which was made by Henry King." By the time he was forty, he had made two hundred films, including *The White Sister, The Winning of Barbara Worth, Romola,* and *Stella Dallas.* (MOTION PICTURE MAGAZINE)

a hundred pictures, by 1915 he was directing them as well and had directed thirty before making his big picture for Thomas Ince, *23½ Hours' Leave.* King and Richard Barthelmess started their own production company, Inspiration Pictures, funded by the Harriman Bank and located at the Biograph studio. Inspiration Pictures was started with $250,000 and, after only six pictures, ended up with assets of more than $6 million. "I didn't have a position in the company," said King. "I just did everything. I was producer, director, head of the scenario department, business manager, head of casting." King's big hit was based on Joseph Hergesheimer's novel about the rural South called *Tol'able David,* shot on location in the mountains of West Virginia, a few miles from King's childhood home. "A lot of my boyhood days went into it."

"You're too good," said D. W. Griffith to King. "You're giving me a tough race."

King sold his interest in Inspiration Pictures and directed two inexpensive pictures for Famous Players–Lasky, *Sackcloth and Scarlet* and *Any Woman,* and was approached by Goldwyn to make *Stella Dallas.*

King was told two things about Goldwyn: "Sam may have, no Sam does have—his idiosyncrasies, but to Sam Goldwyn, his word is his bond and a contract is something to be lived up to." And, "Goldwyn will do anything in the world that he signs his name to, but don't pay any attention to any of the promises he makes that are not in writing." King received a percentage of the profits of *Stella Dallas.*

• • •

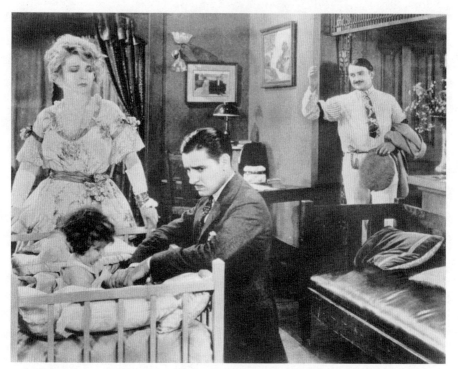

From the original *Stella Dallas,* 1925. Left to right: Belle Bennett, Ronald Colman, and Jean Hersholt, one of the best-known juvenile actors in Denmark. (PHOTOFEST)

King had discovered Ronald Colman. Colman was acting on the stage with Ruth Chatterton and Henry Miller in *La Tendresse.* King was casting *The White Sister* to be filmed in Rome—it was 1922–1923—and he needed an actor to play a young Italian. He had Colman's ruffled hair slicked down, painted on a mustache and lipstick, and made a test of him that confirmed King's hunch. After *The White Sister,* Colman was a sought-after leading man.

While King was making *Stella Dallas,* Goldwyn went to him in tears. He'd just watched some rushes from the picture (the scene where Stella gives a birthday party for Laurel and no one shows up: Stella and Laurel, trying to make the best of it, sitting together alone at the festive party table set for many; Stella laughing to keep away her desire to weep; Laurel pretending to be excited by her presents until she is overcome, burying her head on her mother's breast). Goldwyn said to King, "I've never seen anything like this in pictures."

Goldwyn wanted *Stella Dallas* to have its premiere in New York at George White's Apollo Theatre on Forty-Second Street in honor of Ethel Barrymore. For the showing he hired Louis Gottschalk to write a special musical score for the picture.

After the premiere, Ethel Barrymore wrote to Goldwyn that she thought it "the best moving picture I have ever seen. Best in its direction, acting, restraint, taste and appeal." Cecil B. DeMille told Goldwyn, "*Stella Dallas* is, in my opinion, one of the few great screen achievements."

Belle Bennett prepared for eleven months before she was given the part of the 1925 Stella Dallas. She bought the clothes, wigs, and accessories for every period of Stella's life to get ready for the test. Frances Marion had suggested Bennett to Henry King ("This woman has just what it takes," Marion wrote to King. "She is a mother, she has two children, and she has had everything on earth happen to her. Both on stage and off, she *is* Stella Dallas"). Bennett had once played a twelve-year-old child who grows to be a seventy-five-year-old woman.

As a child Bennett had led a nomadic life—she was born in Coon Rapids, a village in Iowa—appearing with her father's troupe in plays and tent shows. It was Bennett's early marriage that prompted the change in the marriage laws of Minnesota. She was married at twelve and had a child by the time she was thirteen.

After appearing in pictures until Triangle Studios went out of business, Bennett returned to the stage a star at the Alcazar Theatre and was called San Francisco's Sweetheart. Soon afterward, she decided to return to pictures. The studios wanted only young girls as leads. Belle, at twenty-eight, knew that she could pass as one but had to hide the fact that she had a fifteen-year-old son. She pretended the boy was her brother and once again was able to get work in pictures.

Bennett got the part of Stella, and production was to start right away. She was being paid $500 a week; Colman, $2,000; Lois Moran, $500. King was paid $75,000 plus 25 percent of the profits. Frances Marion was paid $10,000 for the script.

No sooner had Bennett got the part than her son—her "brother"—became deathly ill. Belle remained at his bedside round the clock. Three weeks later the boy was dead. He died in the morning; that afternoon Belle was called to the studio for a costume fitting. She was stunned by the loss of her child. He was buried on Saturday. Bennett had waited almost a year to get the part of Stella, and now production was to start on the picture. The afternoon of her son's funeral, Bennett had to leave with the *Stella Dallas* company to go on location.

Bennett loved the picture; she felt there was no villain, no bad women, just real people enmeshed by fate, trying to do and live their best. For the role, Bennett used padding to make her look thirty pounds heavier and added makeup to make her look older. At thirty-four, Bennett, unadorned, looked more like the seventeen-year-old Stella.

. . .

Olive Higgins Prouty saw in Laurel "a character as heroic as Stella, and far more unusual." In King's version, Lois Moran's freshness and innocence as Laurel were dazzling.

The picture's opening in Los Angeles was attended by Chaplin, Mae Murray, Jack Gilbert, Vilma Banky, Betty Bronson, von Stroheim, Lubitsch, King Vidor, Lillian Gish.

Marion Davies, Jane Cowl, and Jeanne Eagels were all overwhelmed by the magnificence of Bennett's performance.

Morris Gest said of Bennett's Stella Dallas, "At last America has produced a great actress." Following the success of the picture, Bennett was frustrated with Goldwyn's choice of roles for her. "I don't want young parts," she said. "I am 35 and I want to portray women of my own age—past the sweetheart age, but not yet arrived at old age, the saddest time in a woman's life . . . I am ranked among men in the picture trade as a character actor, like [Emil] Jannings. I always have the love of women."

Belle Bennett died in 1932, seven years after the release of the silent *Stella Dallas.* Bennett was a follower of Mary Baker Eddy. She was forty-one years old. Among the friends at her funeral: Mary Pickford, Norma Shearer, Jean Hersholt, Thelma Todd, and Zasu Pitts.

Goldwyn said, "I make my pictures to please myself."

King Vidor had directed *Street Scene* for Goldwyn a few years before. Soon after they started shooting the remake of *Stella Dallas,* Vidor realized it was going to be a good picture. "We had a good cast, great photography [by Rudolph Maté] and everything seemed to work well. I decided to give it a sense of reality."

Vidor was called into Goldwyn's office. Goldwyn had just seen the daily rushes and was ready to fire Vidor and the entire cast and call a halt to the whole project. Vidor was shocked. He thought they were "getting a fine picture and that the cast were giving their best performances." He was so upset he couldn't shoot anymore that day. Vidor left the studio in "utter dejection" and went home to eat nothing but milk toast and Ovaltine for dinner and to try to get some sleep. At about one in the morning, the phone rang. It was Goldwyn.

"Hello, King—how are you feeling?"

"Not so good," Vidor said.

"I just ran the rushes again and they look wonderful," said Goldwyn.

"What happened to them since this afternoon? Did the actors change their performances?"

"They're giving great performances," said Goldwyn.

"Well, I'm glad to hear it."

"I just wanted to call you up and tell you to have a good night's sleep. Good night."

To make the picture, Vidor wanted to go back to the aesthetics of the silents and use the sequences that showed the deep love between mother and daughter.

As a boy, Vidor had crawled under the canvas fence around the Babylonian set of *Intolerance,* one of the largest sets that had ever been built. Griffith used a camera in a balloon that went up and down and approached the high walls. "Griffith was everything I looked up to," said Vidor. "He was mentor, teacher, idol." Vidor never got that close.

"Griffith went beyond the usual or obvious moving picture technique of the time. He seemed to be able to combine a feeling of tempo, music, crescendo . . . he captured a symphonic feeling. Technically he was using new techniques, such as bigger close-ups and some sort of dissolves or irises . . . he was the master."

To get the silent sequences past Goldwyn, Vidor showed them with a musical accompaniment, scoring each to the same poignant music to punctuate the emotional moments.

In one scene, Laurel gets furious with her mother for getting cold cream on the treasured photograph of Mrs. Morrison. Without use of dialogue Stella is hurt by Laurel's obvious infatuation with the new woman in Stephen's life and is embarrassed by her own carelessness. Stella sits at her dressing table, in a dressing gown, stunned by her daughter's rebuke, staring into the mirror, unseeing, until she takes in that her roots are beginning to show and, to distract herself from her hurt, starts to touch them up. Laurel is ashamed of the way she's screamed at her mother; she gently takes the coloring stick from her mother's hand and begins to part the back of Stella's hair with almost professional assurance—she's done it for her mother a thousand times before—and lovingly dabs the peroxide on Stella's hair. All without a word of dialogue.

In another scene, Stella has taken Laurel to a resort as fancy as any that Stephen could afford. Laurel is off with her new friends, blissfully happy. Stella is seen in a mussed-up bed, sick (or hiding out) in bed jacket with caribou, hair stuck up in curls, reading confession magazines and eating chocolate creams. Laurel, in a sequence of moments, is having the time of her life: playing tennis; riding a bike on a country road, four abreast, with her newfound friends, each from a fine old family; sitting on a rock by a lake with her new young man, a Grosvenor, feeling the heat of the sun and the coolness of

With Anne Shirley as Laurel (Lollie) Dallas.

the breeze as she leans against him. The air is clean, they are in love, she feels free, their life is ahead of them. He gives Laurel his pin. They kiss without self-consciousness, and Laurel runs off, suddenly overcome with shyness. A montage done without dialogue.

In another scene, Vidor used silent film to show Laurel and Stella on the train after Laurel has packed up their bags and fled the resort. At the hotel Stella had risen from her sickbed and dressed to introduce herself to the parents of Laurel's new fine friends. Stella sees herself as glamorous a figure as the people in the movies and the fashion magazines. She is wearing the most outrageous ensemble of furs, feathers, shoes, and clanking bracelets, with makeup an inch thick. She sees herself as the height of chic.

On the night train home, Laurel looks in on her mother, in the lower berth, asleep, and then climbs into the upper berth. As Laurel is drifting off to sleep, she overhears a conversation among some of the girls from the resort, sitting across the aisle from them in the car.

The girls are talking about "the strange-looking woman parading around the grounds" at the resort who was so outrageous "she can't be described," says one of them. The strange, common woman "had bracelets up to here that clanged and bells on her shoes that tinkled," and, she tells the other two, she is the mother of Laurel Dallas.

Stella and Laurel, in their separate berths, overhear the girl say, "Isn't it weird to have such a common-looking thing for a mother?" Laurel leans down to make sure Stella has not heard the comment. Stella has heard every word but pretends to be asleep. Laurel lowers herself onto the bottom berth. She caresses her mother's cheek with her own. It is clear she loves her mother more than anyone in the outside world, even though she knows her mother is ridiculed. She knows the truth about her mother, but Laurel's love for Stella goes far beyond what anyone else thinks of her.

Stella pretends to awaken and acts surprised to see Laurel near her. "It's lonely up there, Mother, I want to come down here and cuddle with you." Stella pulls back the covers so Laurel can slip into bed beside her. Laurel lies with her head on her mother's outstretched arm and curls up against Stella's body. Stella strokes Laurel's hair as she thinks of what she must do to free her daughter from the burden she's realized she's become.

It was a difficult scene to rehearse; the set had been silent as Barbara and Anne Shirley went through it. Afterward, to diffuse the tension, as well as the strong feelings summoned by the scene, Barbara turned to Anne and said, "All these years I spend in movies, and I have a scene in bed with someone, and who do I end up with? You! Not Clark Gable, *not* Gary Cooper . . ."

In another scene, Vidor used silence to show Stella, at home, after she has carried out her plan and sent Laurel to New York to live with her father and the new Mrs. Dallas. In the sequence, Stella is reading a telegram in which Laurel informs her that she is coming home to be with her mother. Stella is beside herself with upset. She realizes that she must come up with another plan, this time more wrenching, more final, if she wants to push away her daughter for good and send her back to her father, freeing Laurel from any responsibility for her mother.

King Vidor had a natural affection for people. He didn't accept the glamorous, well-smoothed-over attitude of the rich. His sympathies lay at the lower half of the class struggle, although *Stella Dallas* is a picture that abuses ordinary people. Vidor's family had been in the cotton business in Texas. He grew up in Galveston, "a place strange for Texas and strange for the United States," he said. Galveston was an island, a cotton port that attracted people of all nationalities. Vidor grew up in an atmosphere of many languages and cultures. "Galveston was considered beyond the law," he said. Gambling and prostitution went on long after they were outlawed in other Texas towns. As a boy, Vidor was interested in photography and movement. What interested him was the telling detail that reveals the way people are with one another. At the age of six Vidor lived through a hurricane. The island was covered in ten feet of water. Out of a population of twenty-nine thousand, ten thousand were drowned or killed. Vidor took the first tugboat out. He walked to the boat's bow; when he looked down from it, he saw dead bodies—horses and other animals, and people.

"Images remain over everything else," Vidor said.

What comes through in *Stella Dallas* is Vidor's own kindness and modesty. He was fascinated by locales in the Midwest and the Mississippi valley, especially Indiana. He'd read everything by Booth Tarkington and admired James Whitcomb Riley.

Vidor, unlike some directors who did lots of talking and lots of acting, tried to make it clear to the actors exactly what he wanted from them. If something developed during a scene, he kept the camera going. "Those actors who had been on the stage were like children," Vidor said. "They missed the applause. The director had to take the place of the audience."

"If love exists, admiration, love, exists between director and actress," Vidor said of working with Barbara, "which I felt—I felt a deep feeling of love. It's like a family functioning. It's like a husband and wife functioning."

During the making of *Stella Dallas,* Vidor never spoke to his Laurel. Anne Shirley was given no direction from him. He let her shift for herself and didn't say whether she was doing well or not.

Anne Shirley had grown up at RKO and graduated from the studio high school. She lived through two RKO regime changes and saw the company go in and out of receivership. Through it all, she continued to support her mother and collect her paycheck every Saturday night with a slight salary raise every six months. Anne had worked in a succession of parts, playing the young version of Myrna Loy, Janet Gaynor, and Fay Wray. She appeared with Barbara in William Wellman's *So Big* and *The Purchase Price*—billed as Dawn O'Day—and made ninety-five other pictures as well.

Shirley had brown eyes, and her once brown hair was now corn colored. She was born Dawn Evelyeen Paris. At three, when she was cast in Herbert Brenon's *Miracle Child* with William Farnum at the Astoria, Long Island, studios, her name was changed to Dawn O'Day ("You've a career ahead of you," said Jimmy Ryan, Brenon's casting director. "It's the dawn of a new day—so I dub you Dawn O'Day"). Dawn and her mother were advised to go west to follow the future of movie work. RKO legally changed Dawn's name to Anne Shirley at fifteen after the character she made famous in *Anne of Green Gables.*

Three years later (she celebrated her eighteenth birthday on the set of *Stella Dallas;* Goldwyn gave her her first car for the occasion) and with almost two decades of screen experience, Anne Shirley was making $1,750 a week. She had been her mother's sole support from the time she was eighteen months old. "Be nice to the director, dear," she was told by her mother. "If Mommy has to work, then she'll be separated from her baby. But if the baby works, then they can be together all the time."

Anne went to professional school with Mitzi Green, Anita Louise, Mickey Rooney, Judy Garland, and Virginia Weidler and worked for every studio in town until RKO put her under a long-term, eight-year contract. Up to that point Anne and her mother lived in a tiny three-room apartment above a neighborhood hardware store.

When Dawn Paris first arrived in Hollywood, she and her mother had come upon apartment houses with posted signs that read, "No Dogs or Actors Allowed." After Anne signed her contract with RKO, she and her mother moved to a six-room bungalow, still on the wrong side of town but five blocks from the studio.

A month before production began on *Stella Dallas,* Vidor was still looking at tests for an actress for the part of Laurel. Bonita Granville's test was convincing for the older Laurel. But Vidor felt that Granville lacked "something in gentleness and softness," he wrote to Merritt Hulburd, associate producer for *Dodsworth* and *Stella Dallas.* "I would be happier if we could get the perfect girl, but as yet I haven't seen one."

Lois Moran sent both Goldwyn and Vidor letters asking them to consider her younger sister, Betty, for the part of Laurel. "Knowing something about the character Laurel," she wrote Goldwyn, "and knowing Betty's capabilities as I do, I cannot but feel she would do a grand job of the part in your forthcoming production of *Stella Dallas.*"

During production on the picture, Anne did her work, went to her dressing room, and went home and cried every day. She was sure she would be fired at any moment. She knew she was the second or third choice for the part, and it was clear to her that she wasn't wanted. Despite Vidor's sense of it being family, Barbara felt as Anne did; neither felt wanted.

Anne wasn't used to this kind of treatment and made an appointment to see Goldwyn. She was ushered into his office and burst into tears.

"Mr. Goldwyn, you've got to replace me," she said. "I can't finish this picture. I can't work like this."

Goldwyn told Anne to dry her eyes and go back to the set. He was sure she wouldn't have any more problems.

As soon as Anne left the office, Goldwyn picked up the phone.

"I don't care what you tell the kid," he told Vidor. "Tell her she's lousy if

Left to right: Anne Shirley, Barbara, Rudy Maté (on camera), unidentified (behind Maté and in plaid jacket), and King Vidor, *Stella Dallas,* spring 1937.

she's great or great if she's lousy. Tell her any damn thing you please. I just can't cope with hysterical females and I don't want to be bothered again!"

After looking at the first day's rushes, Vidor wasn't happy with Barbara O'Neil in the Mrs. Morrison role. "I want to repeat what I said about ten days ago," Vidor wrote. "I am very much worried about [O'Neil's] appearance, which isn't offset by her great ability as an actress. I don't think we should go too far with her until Mr. Goldwyn has seen the first two days rushes and put his approval on them. It would be too bad starting this picture off with an actress looking the way she does in the first scene with Boles."

This was Barbara O'Neil's first picture. O'Neil was a stage actress who'd been brought to Hollywood by a Goldwyn scout specifically for *Stella Dallas.* She'd won the part of Helen Morrison over Mary Astor, then embroiled in a court case against her ex-husband for custody of her four-year-old daughter. Out of the messy legal battle had come Astor's most intimate sexual disclosures, which made front-page headlines across the country. *Stella Dallas's* Mrs. Morrison, the elegant society widow, couldn't possibly have been played by an actress who "willfully abandoned" her young daughter for a married man and whose "stray thoughts" told of her "gross immoral conduct" (so claimed Astor's husband).

. . .

The start of *Stella Dallas* had been delayed by a makeup artists' and hairdressers' strike in an effort by the Federated Motion Picture Crafts unions to win recognition from the producers as a guild shop; when production finally began on *Stella Dallas,* there was only a skeletal crew to cover for those artists on strike.

Barbara O'Neil was unhinged that she had to cross a picket line each morning and was further upset when she wasn't allowed to put on her own makeup as she had each night at the theater in the privacy of her own dressing room backstage.

Months before, O'Neil was appearing on Broadway at the St. James Theatre in Sidney Kingsley's *Ten Million Ghosts* along with twenty-one-year-old Orson Welles, who'd just come from adapting, directing, and starring in several plays. Barbara O'Neil had been on the Broadway stage for a few years, working with Melvyn Douglas in his production of *Mother Lode;* with Tallulah Bankhead in *Forsaking All Others;* and with Josh Logan, James Stewart, and Esther Dale in Blanche Yurka's staging of *Carry Nation.*

Now at the Goldwyn Studio, O'Neil was greeted each morning by Bob Stephanoff, the head of the United Artists makeup department, who applied O'Neil's makeup and because of the strike was forced to do it behind drawn curtains while his fellow makeup men and women were picketing outside the studio walls. As Stephanoff applied O'Neil's makeup, she became more agitated, knowing just how dangerous it was for him to be working at all.

By the time O'Neil arrived on the set "in the presence of Miss Stanwyck, Mr. Vidor and Rudy Maté," the cameraman, she said, she was an "already shattered, New York–imported commodity" who knew little about acting before cameras.

Vidor wasn't happy after looking at the first day's rushes, in which Helen Morrison and Stephen Dallas are engaged. (The picture's opening was originally shot as the Henry King silent had been but wasn't used. The scenes that show Dallas fleeing the family scandal—his father's suicide because of the front-page headlines that tell the world he has been caught embezzling and has brought ruination and shame to his family—were replaced with the establishing shot of the town of Millwood and the young, pretty Stella Martin waiting at the gate of her parents' simple house to be seen by the oblivious, to her, Stephen Dallas.)

When things became particularly rocky for O'Neil, Barbara went to the actress's dressing room and encouraged her to keep in there pitching and to try not to let Mr. Goldwyn bother her. O'Neil saw Barbara as a life raft in the tension-ridden atmosphere created by the strike and Sam Goldwyn.

O'Neil said of watching Barbara, "I understood the depth and strength of her work. She is an actress [who] works from the inside out. This privacy makes her performances . . . last."

For Barbara to age fifteen or twenty years as Stella, she had to wear five pairs of hose to make her ankles thick and use padding to fill out her girth, which was needed even more so after she'd lost twenty pounds. Barbara practically collapsed from the heat during production. In addition, she put sags in her cheeks by stuffing cotton in her mouth as Helen Hayes did during her run as Queen Victoria.

"It was a matter of upholstery," said Barbara, who said she felt like a football player. The pouches under her eyes and the lines and wrinkles on her face and on her hands were done with paint and brush.

Barbara was offered the use of wigs in the picture, which she rejected. Wigs would have prevented her from doing anything with her hands, "like running them through my hair," she said. "Furthermore in Stella's home her hair was neglected, unkempt—and that just can't be done realistically except with one's own hair."

Barbara agreed to have her hair bleached blond.

Her hairdresser, Holly Barnes, had been with Barbara for two years, moving with her from production to production, from RKO to Fox. Barbara and Holly worked together six days a week. On Sundays, Holly went to Barbara's to go over her fan mail and to do Barbara's nails. Barbara felt comfortable with Holly; Holly was always there with Barbara. Their closeness annoyed people.

Holly and the other hairdressers and makeup artists were on strike along with scenic artists, art directors, and draftsmen. To bleach Barbara's hair, the studio brought in hairdressers out of a Los Angeles beauty college. The inexperienced hairdressers tested Barbara's hair to get the right shade of blond for Stella's hair and to see how various tints photographed. Nine tints were tested before they found the right shade of blond, damaging Barbara's hair in the process.

A few days before she was to film the scene at the train station, where Stella says what she believes will be her final good-bye to Laurel, Barbara and Bob and Marion and Zeppo Marx had been riding on a mountain trail above Marwyck. One of Barbara's favorite horses, Buck, stumbled into a gopher hole. The horse tripped, Barbara was thrown, and the horse fell heavily across her body. Her legs and right arm were badly bruised and bandaged, and it was suggested she stay in bed and rest. Barbara insisted on returning to work.

The good-bye scene between Stella and Laurel was to be shot at the Santa Fe station in downtown Los Angeles. Barbara was to walk alongside the train as Laurel leaves for New York for what she thinks is her annual summer visit; Stella has arranged with Stephen and his new wife for her daughter to live with her father and stepmother. Laurel is unaware of the arrangement; Stella knows this is the last time she will see the child she adores.

Barbara was limping and put aside the cane for the shot. As Stella, she tearfully held on to Laurel; the train started to pull away from the platform. It lurched forward. Anne Shirley lost her balance. Barbara, still in pain and banged up from her fall, had to walk alongside the train holding on to Shirley to keep the young actress from falling until the porter could help stabilize her.

Vidor shot the last scene of the picture with few words of dialogue. Stella is outside the Dallas apartment, standing in the street close to the wrought-iron fence with the other onlookers watching the grand guests inside in the warmth and comfort of the town house, the bride and groom—Laurel Dallas and Richard Grosvenor III—stand together aglow with happiness in front

The final scene of the original *Stella Dallas:* Belle Bennett gazes into the living room window of the Morrison/Dallas home as her daughter, Laurel, is wed to Richard Grosvenor III.

of the picture window. Stella, watching with the throng, is worn, seared, outcast.

What she sees has a fairy-tale quality. She is watching the lovers as if it were a movie. She is transfixed, crying at the picture's happy ending, rapt, a corner of her handkerchief in her mouth, as the lovers embrace.

The only line of dialogue comes from the cop who drives away the crowd and tells Stella and the others to "move along."

"I had to indicate to audiences, through the emotions shown by my face," said Barbara, "that for Stella, joy ultimately triumphed over the heartache she felt. Despite her shabbiness and loneliness at that moment, there was a shining triumph in her eyes, as she saw the culmination of her dreams for her daughter."

Barbara didn't try to pretend or signal that she was acting, or overact. She exceeded the bounds of good taste and suspended sex appeal of any sort.

Stella Dallas is a woman whom the audience suffers for every step of the way; she is humiliated, unseeing, silly, or pretentious, but she loves her child. Barbara makes the character endearing, even though terrible things happen to her and she is punished. The film plays off the illusion about parenthood and class. Vidor embraced naïveté and put audiences on the side against the hypocrisy of the society Prouty wrote about. The punishment of trying to

Twelve years later, the same scene with Barbara Stanwyck in King
Vidor's 1937 version of *Stella Dallas*. (PHOTOFEST)

change class is that in the end one doesn't belong anywhere. Laurel is permitted to change class because she has the makings of it from the father's genes.
Prouty punished Stella Dallas, and Barbara punished her as well, by being so
relentless, so tough on her.

"It is difficult with that sort of performance," said Vidor, "to keep from
going overboard in getting funny and comical. [Barbara] knew how to handle
it. She won admiration and sympathy in spite of the broad strokes of her
character."

Vidor admired Barbara's "humanness and ability and the way she came
over as a down-to-earth person." She made "everything entirely believable—
makes you think it is really happening when she does it. And this to me," said
Vidor, "is the test for all acting and directing—if someone watching in the
audience can entirely forget that he's looking at a movie."

Barbara was "prepared to the very top of her ability," said Vidor. "Dialogue learned perfectly. Hair, clothes, energy ready. There was no 'I am not
feeling well today.' Or 'I have a personal problem' and then a request to be
excused for the day, as happens with so many actresses. She felt she was in a
business . . . You gave a day's work for a day's pay."

"King was very nice," said Barbara. "But there wasn't any great affinity
there, not the kind I felt for Capra, and Wild Bill Wellman. King did his job
and I did mine."

"Sam Goldwyn made sure everything was first-class," she said. "He may have come out of the penny arcade, but he took a lot with him—and what he took he used."

" 'The Goldwyn touch' is not brilliance or sensationalism," said Alva Johnston, the Pulitzer Prize–winning journalist who wrote about Goldwyn for *The New Yorker*. "It is something that manifests itself gradually in a picture; the characters are consistent; the workmanship is honest; there are no tricks and short cuts; the intelligence of the audience is never insulted. With his background, the most impressive fact about him is his development of taste and artistic conscience."

Vidor tried to cut the picture with the camera; there weren't a lot of ways to put the picture together, and he decided on the set which shot he was going to use. One night Goldwyn called up Vidor and said, "You told me you were going to take close-ups, but you didn't take them!"

Vidor told Goldwyn the close-ups were there, that perhaps Goldwyn had turned away to talk to someone when the close-ups were on the screen. Goldwyn said, "Well, I didn't see them and I was watching all the time!" "Go watch them again!" Vidor said.

As they were making the picture, Barbara said she was "scared to death." She even blew up in one scene, "went all to pieces," she said, "and had to go home. That's not like me. I usually can take a lot. But when the time came for me to give up my daughter Laurel, I couldn't go through with it. Not that day. Neither could she." Barbara had no mother who fought or sacrificed for her; she knew no mother love; she was unable to have children of her own.

Anne Shirley had worked for sixteen years to become a star and make her mother happy. Mrs. Harry Paris had changed her name to O'Day when her daughter did. When Mrs. O'Day married her second husband and became Mrs. Quirk, she still went by the name Mrs. O'Day so she would be recognized as Dawn O'Day's mother. When Dawn became Anne Shirley, her mother changed her own name to Mimi Shirley. During the early years, daughter and mother struggled and were "dreadfully poor." After the success of *Anne of Green Gables*, Anne's new five-year contract with the studio gave her the means to have the home her mother had never given her daughter and the things Anne wanted. Anne's devotion and loyalty now extended to RKO as well as to her mother. Her years of acting—the only life Anne knew—had all been for her mother.

During production, Anne and her close friend Phyllis Fraser went on a double date to the Trocadero. Anne's escort was Lee Bowman. Phyllis Fraser, cousin of Ginger Rogers, had been invited by Anne's mother to live with the Shirleys (it had been more than a year now) in the hopes of furthering Anne's career; Ginger's mother, Lela Rogers, was the head talent coach at RKO.

Lee Bowman took Anne home early the following morning and invited her to a cocktail party he was having at his house later that day. Anne was set to go on a picnic with her friend Phyllis and didn't think she'd be able to attend Bowman's party. She slept until three that afternoon and decided to go to the party for a while, get to bed early, and be on the set Monday morning.

At Bowman's house, she saw John Payne putting records on the Victrola and went to sit next to him. Payne, at twenty-five, was an up-and-coming Warner leading man. He was six feet four, broad shouldered, narrow waisted, with the looks of a movie star. Both Anne and Payne liked the songs "Now" and "Slaughter on Tenth Avenue" and continued to select records for a couple of hours. Payne invited Anne to the Tropics for dinner. She accepted. He called her several days later, and they went out again. Payne was a former Columbia University student at the School of Journalism who earned extra money as a male nurse, ran an elevator, operated a switchboard, and had been a boxer and wrestler—"Alexei Petroff, the Savage of the Steppes," and "Tiger Jack Payne." He was from a moneyed family and was raised on a former plantation outside Roanoke, Virginia. Soon Anne and Payne were engaged.

Barbara saw Stella as "a woman who cheated failure. One who eagerly paid the full measure for what she wanted from life."

Barbara and Anne had spent so much time together, "studied our lines in my dressing room. Got to understand one another, really, instead of being just acquaintances on the set. You must, you know, to play such a friendship." Barbara thought that Anne played "the exquisite Laurel very sensitively."

When production closed, Barbara inscribed a photograph to her Laurel that said, "For Anne, whose loveliness helped so much during *Stella Dallas*. My love, always, Barbara."

Olive Higgins Prouty felt Anne Shirley's "interpretation of the shy sensitive Laurel was exactly as she had written her."

Joseph Breen begrudgingly approved the picture. He wasn't happy that the Christmas scene in Stella's apartment with Ed Munn drunk with a raw goose under his arm couldn't be cut because of its importance to the story. The Breen Office certificate of approval was granted only with the assurance that the shot of Alan Hale squeezing Barbara's thigh had been removed from the picture. Breen wasn't happy with any part of the scene. "May I not say again that [it] . . . is at best, a border-line scene, with respect to the resolution of the Board of Directors of this Association, condemning unnecessary or excessive drinking and drunkenness. We regret that this particular scene was not toned down."

Stella Dallas grossed more than $2 million; Goldwyn's profit was more than $500,000.

Vidor found Goldwyn a warm, appreciative friend who could be unpredictable, impulsive, difficult. After making *Stella Dallas,* Vidor wrote a note to himself and put it in a desk drawer: "No more Goldwyn pictures."

Goldwyn said, "The trouble with directors is that they're always biting the hand that lays the golden egg."

Olive Higgins Prouty was unhappy about what had become of *Stella Dallas.* It "has been crammed and jammed into so many different mediums," she wrote, "and has been mauled over by so many producers, playwrights, script-writers, tragediennes and would-be tragediennes that she has been worn pretty thin . . . and I for one, shall thank heaven when she no longer exists even as a memory or a by-word. I feel about *Stella Dallas* a good deal as Gillette Burgess [spelling OHP's] felt about his Purple Cow when he wrote in despair,

> *Yes, I wrote the Purple Cow,*
> *I'm sorry now I wrote it,*
> *But I can tell you anyhow*
> *I'll kill you if you quote it."*
> —Gelett Burgess

FOUR

"Clean Labor Unionism"

1937

There'd been talk for months of a strike by the Screen Actors Guild to win a guild shop contract from motion picture producers. Actors, meeting in weekly small gatherings, were asked to pledge to support a strike. More than 98 percent of those asked had said yes.

The actors willing to strike had little to gain and everything to lose; they had contracts with major studios; by walking out, they would be in violation of their contracts and open to lawsuits. Many were former stage actors, members of Actors' Equity, who benefited from the power and influence wielded by Equity-negotiated contracts that had set fair wages, hours, and working conditions. Soon after its full recognition as the bargaining agent for actors eighteen years before, in 1919, Equity had tried unsuccessfully to unionize Hollywood. The union had since recognized the Screen Actors Guild as the legitimate representative for screen actors.

Actors' Equity, during its 1919 strike, had called on—and received—the support of the stagehands' union, the International Alliance of Theatrical Stage Employees and Motion Picture Machine Operators of the United States and Canada, the most powerful trade union in Hollywood.

The International Alliance had come to the support of Hollywood actors and pledged its undivided support of the Screen Actors Guild. In 1935, the guild also joined the American Federation of Labor. Two years later, more than a thousand members of the Screen Actors Guild had agreed to support a strike. Some who opposed a strike were silent-film actors who'd survived the transition to sound; others were opposed out of loyalty to the heads of the studios ("MGM and Louis B. Mayer have been very good to me. I'm not going to do this to him"); still others feared that they, and everyone striking, would be banned from the industry.

There were those who'd held out against joining the Screen Actors Guild al-together: Marlene Dietrich, Greta Garbo, Norma Shearer, Jean Harlow, Lionel Barrymore, Wallace Beery. Barbara had resisted as well; she didn't believe in organized labor. If the guild voted to go on strike, Barbara would have to cross the picket line ("Work was work," she said), just as she'd crossed the hairdressers' and makeup artists' picket line to show up for work each day on *Stella Dallas*. Other actors and actresses—Garbo, Jean Harlow, Bing Crosby, Herbert Marshall, and Jack Benny, among them—had passed through picket lines as well.

Barbara had been invited to join the Screen Actors Guild seven months before, an invitation she'd ignored. When the guild threatened to have her expelled from Actors' Equity if she didn't join the fledgling union, she relented and became a member.

Gary Cooper said, "I've been figuring and I think we should belong. Maybe we don't need a Guild, but a lot of those who haven't been so lucky as us, do. We should help them out."

Guild members, the heads of the studios, and the entire country had watched six months before as the United Automobile Workers of America, in mid-November 1936, had challenged the National Labor Relations Act and waged a series of sit-down strikes against General Motors to win recognition as the sole bargaining agent for GM's workers. The strike had started at a Fisher Body plant in Atlanta and spread to GM plants in Kansas City, then Cleveland; two days later, a Fisher Body plant was struck in Flint. By January 1937, 135,000 men from thirty-five cities in fourteen states were on strike against General Motors; 90 percent of GM's factories were shut down because of parts shortages. GM's president was against the union, but the company's vice president, William Knudsen, recognized that collective bargaining had arrived and that the UAW had to be reckoned with.

During the weeks that followed, riots ensued; four thousand National Guardsmen were ordered to Michigan; the autoworkers called in reinforcements to help defy a court injunction; GM threatened to withhold food deliveries to striking workers; the workers threatened hunger strikes in retaliation. Finally, in early February 1937, General Motors recognized the UAW as the sole bargaining agent for GM's employees and agreed to a contract guaranteeing a thirty-hour workweek, a six-hour day, with time and a half for overtime, and a minimum rate of pay commensurate with an American standard of living.

The screen actors' fight to win union recognition and a union shop contract from producers had been ongoing for three and a half years. The Screen Ac-

Members of the Screen Actors Guild, meeting at Legion Stadium to discuss the striking motion picture craftsmen, May 1937. Top row: Warren William; Fredric March; Larry Steers (bending down, mostly obscured); Donald Woods (SAG board member); Robert Young; Aubrey Blair (Guild staff member who oversaw extras' issues); Frank Morgan (in background); and Robert Montgomery. Bottom row: Joan Crawford, who often knitted at meetings, with husband, Franchot Tone.

tors Guild had allied itself with the newly striking Federated Motion Picture Crafts, made up of fifteen unions, among them hairdressers, makeup artists, scenic artists, plumbers, engineers, molders, boilermakers, machinists, blacksmiths, and sheet-metal workers. After Federated voted to strike, twenty-five hundred hairdressers, makeup artists, scenic artists, draftsmen, art directors, and painters walked out; a thousand workers were on picket lines in front of the studio gates of twelve companies. While strikers picketed, the major movie production plants were rushing out more pictures than in any spring in the last four years.

Paramount was in production with *Angel* with Marlene Dietrich and *Souls at Sea* with Gary Cooper; Metro was at work on six pictures, including *Madame Walewska* with Greta Garbo and *Saratoga* with Gable and Harlow. Warner was in the midst of making seven pictures, among them *The Life of Emile Zola* with Paul Muni and *Varsity Show* with Dick Powell. RKO had four pictures in the works, including *Vivacious Lady* with Ginger Rogers; Columbia had five, and United Artists was five weeks into production with *Stella Dallas*.

Twenty-four hours after the strike began, the costumers' union, the second-largest group in the Federated Motion Picture Crafts, withdrew from the strike in an effort to independently negotiate with the producers.

The Screen Actors Guild called a mass meeting at the Hollywood Legion Stadium for Sunday, May 2, to consider whether its members should join forces with the eleven striking unions of the fifteen that made up Federated Motion Picture Crafts. If the guild vote was to strike, British Actors' Equity from across the Atlantic pledged to support the action and would ask its members to refuse to work at any of the Hollywood studios.

The night of the May 2 meeting, the stadium's weather-beaten hall was jammed with four thousand guild members, who listened to Robert Montgomery, the guild's third president after Ralph Morgan and Eddie Cantor. Montgomery was one of Metro's leading romantic male stars, often cast as the glib society rebel, the restless man-about-town on-screen, but deadly serious off, in his efforts on behalf of actors. Montgomery spoke to the crowd and laid out the guild's plan of action: the producers had one week to recognize the Screen Actors Guild and agree to a guild shop contract. If the Association of Motion Picture Producers failed to reach an agreement with the guild within six days, its sixty-five hundred members would strike.

The vote to support the guild's plan was unanimous.

The next five days were frantic with meetings; during the days the negotiating committee met with those representing the Association of Motion Picture Producers: Joseph Schenck, president of 20th Century–Fox; Eddie Mannix, production manager of MGM; Hal Wallis, production manager of Warner Bros.; and Sam Briskin, production manager of RKO. Following its meetings with producers, the guild's negotiating committee reported back late in the evenings to the guild board at the homes in Beverly Hills of Frank Morgan, Chester Morris, and Jimmy Cagney. Countless hours were spent, until three or four in the morning, planning the following day's strategy with the producers.

In addition to Robert Montgomery, the negotiating committee for the Screen Actors Guild consisted of Kenneth Thomson, the guild's executive secretary and veteran actor from the mid-1920s who appeared in more than sixty pictures; and Franchot Tone, scion of an industrialist fortune, who'd fled his privileged upbringing for the stage to become the handsome, genteel leading man of the Group Theatre. Tone decided to leave the stage for a year when an offer came from Hollywood; the other Group Theatre founders were heartbroken to see him go; they believed Tone had the makings of a great stage actor. Twenty pictures later and with a long-term contract with

Metro, Tone was married to one of the studio's—and Hollywood's—most glamorous stars and had himself become the ultimate of urbane movie idols. Tone, ever ambivalent in his choices, saw his defection from the stage as a fall from grace.

Advising the committee was Willie Bioff, head of IATSE, which represented ten thousand studio technicians and thirty thousand projectionists.

By the end of the week, producers and the guild had failed to come to an agreement. In addition to fighting for guild shop recognition, the guild was fighting for better wages and working conditions for extras and bit players. Fifty percent of the actors, excluding extras, had earned less than $2,000 in 1936.

Robert Montgomery called for another mass meeting at Legion Stadium on Sunday, May 9, this time to vote on a walkout that would send the sixty-five hundred members of the Screen Actors Guild out to join the striking Federated Motion Picture Crafts unions against the nine or ten major studios and paralyze the industry.

A walkout by the actors would shut down the major studios—Paramount Productions, Inc., RKO Radio Pictures Corporation, 20th Century–Fox, Warner Bros.–First National, Metro-Goldwyn-Mayer, Columbia Pictures Corporation, United Artists Studio, Hal Roach Productions, and Universal Studios. The night before the Legion Stadium rally, the guild's board of directors held a special meeting at Frank Morgan's and formally elected as guild senior members Greta Garbo, Luther Adler, George Burns, Gracie Allen, Dolores Costello Barrymore, Alice Faye, Constance Collier, and others.

A strike by the actors seemed inevitable.

In an effort to head off the walkout, Willie Bioff arranged for a last-minute meeting between the guild's Montgomery, Tone, its business manager, Aubrey Blair and the studio heads Louis B. Mayer and Joe Schenck at Mayer's beach house. The meeting began on Sunday morning and continued through the late afternoon.

From there the guild's negotiating committee met with the board at Fredric March's and formally elected Jean Harlow, Frances Dee, and Joel McCrea as senior guild members.

Five thousand actors filled Legion Stadium—character actors, bit players, and stars, representing millions of dollars in annual salaries—among them James Cagney, Carole Lombard, Boris Karloff, Fredric March, Gary Cooper, Miriam Hopkins, and the Metro actors Clark Gable, Spencer Tracy, Luise Rainer, Robert Young, William Powell, and Bob Taylor.

Among those on the rostrum were the guild board members Joan Crawford, knitting at a fierce clip, her husband, and Frank Morgan.

Montgomery opened the meeting. The crowd was braced to hear the latest word on the committee's progress with negotiations and to take a vote to strike. Kenneth Thomson, the guild's executive secretary, came before the thousands of seated actors who were fully prepared to strike the major studios on Monday and go on picket duty at 8:00 the following morning.

Thomson began to read a statement: " 'After a number of conferences with the committee appointed by you and with Mr. William Bioff, of the I.A.T.S.E., we wish to express ourselves as being in favor of Guild [union] Shop . . . We have also conferred with Mr. Briskin of R.K.O., Mr. Zukor of Paramount, and Mr. Harry Cohn of Columbia and assure you that they are in entire agreement. We expect to have contracts drawn between the Screen Actors Guild and the studios before expiration of this week . . . Very Truly.' Signed Louis B. Mayer and Joseph M. Schenck."

The crowd in Legion Stadium went wild. The guild had been fighting for this moment for years. Robert Montgomery came forward and warned those in the stadium that the guild shop agreement had not been signed by all studios and that the audience should still take a vote on whether to strike in case a contract was not forthcoming. (Montgomery had come from a fallen moneyed family back east; his grandfather had lost his fortune, as did his father, who killed himself when Bob was sixteen.) The vote was taken; 99 percent were in favor of a walkout. The board now had the power to call a strike if necessary.

Montgomery announced that extras doing "mob stuff" would be earning a minimum of $5.50 a day instead of $3.20. The audience shouted its acclaim. Montgomery went on: extras getting $7.50 to $15 a day would get a 10 percent increase, and the records of the Central Casting Bureau would finally be open to the guild. The audience rose in spontaneous cheering to thank the guild's negotiating committee for what Ralph Morgan called "honest, clean labor unionism."

Newspaper war-size banner headlines in Los Angeles read: "Actors Win! AFL Guild Wins!"

Extra players and bit players received the biggest gains from the agreement. The new agreement provided for minimum pay of $50 a week for stock players and an increase from $15 to $25 a day for bit players. All actors were to be paid for travel to locations; stand-ins won an increase from $20 to $33 and a daily wage of $6.50 a day plus overtime.

The makeup artists, hairdressers, and painters of the Federated Motion

Picture Crafts were still on strike. Now that the Screen Actors Guild had come to a separate agreement with the Association of Motion Picture Producers, the striking crafts' unions were without the power of the guild's participation.

Hundreds, including longshoremen, supported the eleven striking units of the crafts' unions and picketed outside movie theaters in Los Angeles and Hollywood, including the Warner Bros.' Pantages and Egyptian.

Some in the guild were angry that it had abandoned the crafts' unions.

Charles Lessing, business agent for the Federated Motion Picture Crafts, said to the press, "I've learned never to depend on an actor. It was a sellout. The heat is on tomorrow. I'll break every star who passes through the picket lines."

Federated was not to be undone by the actors' pact with producers and called on the support of the CIO and AFL unions in the East. Federated announced a nationwide boycott in New York, Detroit, Chicago, Cleveland, Pittsburgh, Philadelphia, Minneapolis, and St. Paul of theaters showing films produced by the major Hollywood studios. Unless Federated's demand for a union shop was met, more than 300,000 men and women were expected to go on picket lines. If the strike continued, Federated threatened to extend the boycott and involve more than 2 million pickets.

Within the next few days each of the individual unions began to talk to the producers.

FIVE

Starry Skies Above

Making *Stella Dallas* had been an exhausting two months for Barbara. The part was emotional, and the work was made more strenuous by her having to wear so much padding in the sweltering heat. As a result, she had lost 20 pounds during the course of production and weighed 103 pounds.

For her next picture, Barbara wanted to do something different, a farce comedy, "something diametrically opposed to *Stella Dallas*," and agreed to make a picture for RKO—*A Love Like That*—and be directed again by Al Santell. She had three weeks off between *Stella Dallas* and *A Love Like That* and was under doctor's orders to rest and go on a strength-building diet to gain fifteen pounds.

Barbara had made nine pictures since her separation from Frank Fay in August 1935, one right after the other; *Stella Dallas* was the toughest and almost brought her to the breaking point. She'd already committed to her next picture after *A Love Like That*; 20th Century–Fox's *Wife, Doctor, and Nurse* with Loretta Young and Warner Baxter from a story by the Fox writer Kathryn Scola, who'd written *Baby Face* and the script for *A Lost Lady.*

Other studios, aware of the working conditions on *Stella Dallas,* wanted to make sure their stars wouldn't go through a similar near collapse. The Metro director Dorothy Arzner and the producer Joe Mankiewicz were careful with Joan Crawford during *The Bride Wore Red.*

In the picture, originally intended for Luise Rainer, from the Ferenc Molnár play *The Girl from Trieste,* Crawford was to wear a beaded gown by Adrian that cost $10,000 and weighed thirty pounds. Crawford's moods were reflected in the choice of English, German, and French opera recordings she played daily in her portable colonial dressing room as she prepared for the day she would sing onstage in concert. During rehearsals for the scenes with the beaded gown, Crawford wore regular clothes. The sequences were shot the following day and were broken up by frequent rest periods.

. . .

Barbara played tennis regularly at the Beverly Hills Tennis Club. She was a strong player and played with Marion and Zeppo and Groucho. The eight-year-old club had reinforced-concrete courts as well as two Davis Cup En-Tout-Cas courts from England. Behind the courts was a view of the mountains to the north. Capra belonged, as did Janet Gaynor and Edmund Goulding, who'd designed the locker rooms with David Burton and Robert Riskin. Mervyn LeRoy, Fredric March, and Florence Eldridge were members, as were Pandro Berman, Howard Dietz, Helen Hayes, Norman Krasna, Ernest Vajda, and Charles Lederer.

This Is My Affair opened on Memorial Day weekend in Los Angeles at Grauman's Chinese and Loew's State Theatres. The picture opened in New York at Radio City Music Hall on a program that included a Donald Duck cartoon and performances on the stage by the Music Hall Symphony, the Music Hall Glee Club, the Music Hall Corps de Ballet, and the Music Hall Rockettes.

Reviewers were captivated by the picture's history and by what they saw as a "smart hard-paced colorful entertainment." The pairing of Stanwyck and Taylor, "Hollywood's No. 1 romantic team," was 20th Century–Fox's "box-office bonanza," although some called the love scenes between Barbara and Bob not as "palpitating as might be expected"; others said it "some of their best work." Howard Barnes aptly described the problem for Barbara when he said there was "almost no mobility in her performance." Dorothy Manners described Barbara as "nothing short of beautiful; a sheer optical and dramatic delight." *Variety* thought the picture "slow and weak," the production, directing, casting, and photography "near perfect," and Barbara's work "the most flattering spot in the film." But the picture achieved its goal for Bob; he was seen for the first time as a "tough guy," a man among men instead of an irresistible face for women to swoon over.

There were rumors that Jean Harlow was sick; she'd complained of severe abdominal pain and left the set of *Saratoga* to go home. Her doctor diagnosed her condition as cholecystitis and attended to her throughout the week, administering dextrose injections and sulfa drugs. Private nurses tended to her as well.

Harlow's last-released picture had been *Personal Property* with Bob Taylor. "She was so full of life and such a good sport," he said of her.

The press was assured Jean was improving. The opposite was true. She was under the care of a doctor, though her mother refused to send her daughter to the hospital, claiming they were Christian Scientists.

William Powell, second from left, with his mother at the funeral service of Jean Harlow, his fiancée, at Wee Kirk o' the Heather, Forest Lawn Memorial Park. The organ played "None but the Lonely Heart"; words were spoken from the Gospel of John and Book of Revelation. Jeanette MacDonald sang "Indian Love Call" and Nelson Eddy, "Ah, Sweet Mystery of Life," June 1937.

Louis B. Mayer went to the house and suggested that his own personal physician be called in. Mrs. Bello refused the offer. When Mayer returned to the studio, he was furious and described Harlow's condition as "nothing but legalized murder."

Finally, Mrs. Bello called in another doctor. By the time he examined Harlow, he was helpless to do anything; it was too late to treat her. She'd been misdiagnosed. She was suffering from acute nephritis, originally brought on by scarlet fever when Harlow was fifteen, and not cholecystitis. Nephritis had developed into uremia. Dextrose injections had only exacerbated the kidney failure; diuretics would not have helped. With her kidneys completely gone, Harlow was taken to Good Samaritan Hospital, put in an oxygen tent, and given two blood transfusions. Three days later, on June 7, she slipped into a coma and died.

Clark Gable and Lionel Barrymore were filming scenes for *Saratoga,* with Harlow as the lead, when word came that she had died. The studio went into mourning. The MGM commissary, newly redesigned by Cedric Gibbons, was deathly quiet. "It wasn't a star passing away," said Mickey Rooney. "It wasn't 'Jean Harlow.' It was one of our family."

"She was gay and humorous, always," said Bob. "Her vivacity and sincerity remain to inspire those of us who knew her and admired her as one of the most truly beautiful of all Hollywood's beauties."

Her funeral was held two days later at Forest Lawn Memorial Park. Harlow's casket was covered with fifteen hundred lilies of the valley and five hundred gardenias paid for by Metro-Goldwyn-Mayer. Two hundred and fifty stars, producers, directors, screenwriters, designers, cameramen, agents, bankers, musicians, and hairdressers came to pay tribute to the twenty-six-year-old beloved actress, thought of as "one of the dearest, sweetest, most adorable human beings ever."

One of the honorary pallbearers said, "It was the first big Hollywood funeral. Thalberg wasn't a public figure and Valentino had died in New York. It was quite a scene."

The day of Harlow's funeral, Barbara's brother, By Stevens, was starting his first picture as an extra. Stevens, at thirty-two, was about to become a father and had to earn some money. Barbara adored her brother and thought he could do anything. She thought he might be able to teach. Acting wasn't By's calling. He didn't take it seriously, but this was the best way he knew how to make a living.

By was to appear in *Stage Door*, shooting at RKO, Barbara's studio of the moment. Gregory La Cava was directing the adaptation of the Edna Ferber and George S. Kaufman play that had opened on Broadway eight months before. La Cava, who liked to drink heavily but never while working, was an inspired director who didn't give much direction. He often started a picture with only a few pages of a script, never planned out anything, but knew exactly what he wanted and made his actors feel as if they could play any part.

The Broadway production of *Stage Door* had starred Margaret Sullavan and Phyllis Brooks as the two aspiring actresses from opposite ends of the social spectrum who share a room in a theatrical boardinghouse and who have nothing but contempt for each other and vie for the same man.

The picture was to star the equally rivalrous actresses of the RKO lot, the imperious Katharine Hepburn, whose last few pictures, including *Mary of Scotland,* were box-office failures and who was nothing if not dismissive of her counterpart, Ginger Rogers. Rogers, who was flying high with one Astaire-Rogers hit after another—*Follow the Fleet, Swing Time,* and *Shall We Dance*—was desperate to do a picture without Astaire and one in which she could show that she could act.

Barbara's brother had a bit role in the picture, as did Florence Reed and the choreographer and Ballets Russes dancer Theodore Kosloff.

The construction of Marwyck was almost completed. Harry Hart was involved in every detail of its design. Marwyck was designed and built to be one

Marwyck Ranch, 1937. (COURTESY TONY FAY)

of the premier breeding and stud farms in the country and to surpass even
the old bluegrass farms.

Gone were the weeds and overgrown vines of the original landscape. Five
miles of winding macadam drives took their place and made their way between twenty-two buildings: broodmare barns for twenty horses, training
stable, manager's cottage, tool and machine shed, quarters for the stable help,
and a six-furlong training track. The fencing surrounding the property was
put in before construction on the buildings was started. Barbara, Bob, and
Marion invited Carole Lombard and Clark Gable to see the land. A decent
interval of time went by during the day, and Barbara and Marion took out
paintbrushes and paint cans and started to paint the redwood fences. "There's
something hypnotic about painting," said Barbara. "You see someone waving
a brush, and pretty soon you want to be painting too."

Bob offered to help Barbara, as did Uncle Buck and Dion and his nanny.
Paintbrushes and paint cans appeared. Soon Clark and Carole offered to
help. Barbara placed each painter a half mile away from the next so serious
attention could be paid to the task at hand.

In the end, though not solely by those who attended the mad paddock

With Dion on the six-furlong training track at Marwyck, Northridge, 1937.

party, miles of white fencing, made of redwood planks—each post set in cement—enclosed the fields and paddocks. Beyond the cross fencing was an eleven-gauge link wire-steel fence with steel posts set every ten feet.

Each paddock was double fenced to make sure the horses or colts didn't get into adjacent paddocks. Marwyck's training stables were large and roomy with heavily planked boundary floors; each stall had a cabinet for grooming tools so pitchforks, rakes, and brooms could be put away instead of hung on posts. The tack and feed rooms were combined with rows of saddles, bridles, and martingales carefully hung. The feed bins, conveniently placed, were vermin-proof. The shed row was high and wide to prevent horses from damaging themselves; the loft was screened with galvanized wire netting. Every second stall had a new device called an electric fly killer. A veterinary surgeon was on duty full-time with a room devoted entirely to veterinary supplies. The entire stable was treated for termite control and had a modern automatic fire sprinkler system. In addition, every building was earthquake-proof, with steel-reinforced foundations sunk deep into the ground and girders and beams and uprights of bolted oak.

The quarters for the stable help were close to the training stable. The

With Marion Marx (left), Marwyck, 1937. (CULVER PICTURES)

building had all of the modern conveniences, including electric lights, shower baths, and steel lockers, as well as a recreation room containing a card table, pool table, and library. An oil painting of the Four Marx Brothers, from *I'll Say She Is,* greeted those who entered the building.

The office, a bungalow, was done in knotty pine and had overstuffed chairs and divans. Built-in bookcases, filled with books about horses, stood on either side of a fireplace.

The ranch was designed to be irrigated at any location to keep the grass and alfalfa green for grazing. Barbara and Marion hoped to bring in 130 acres of hay at the end of each season.

The training track was to be of a loam that would not "cup out from under." Its stretches were fifty-five feet wide and its turns ten feet wider. A chute stood at the head of each stretch; each chute had regulation starting stalls. The center field was planted with alfalfa but at any time could be turned into a polo field.

There were utility horses and pleasure horses for Barbara and Marion and a pony for Dion, called Beauty. Horses could be boarded there for breeding. Barbara and Dion rode their horses from Marwyck into Van Nuys with nothing along the way but dirt paths.

Josef von Sternberg and Paul Kelly owned houses close by. Bob Taylor and Clark Gable were thinking of buying farms in the vicinity. Bob was living at 510 North Roxbury Drive down the road from Jack and Mary Benny and Benita Hume and Ronald Colman and was making plans to buy land (thirty acres) six miles from Barbara's. Bob's idea was to build a modest Early American farmhouse of four rooms. Gable was thinking of boarding his horse there. Raoul Walsh had a breeding stable in the valley, as did Winnie Sheehan. Charles Bickford owned a hog ranch there. Barbara was impressed with Bickford's real estate ventures. He'd owned garages and a women's wear shop, and he bought what he called "corners" all over the city. It took her a while to figure out that "corners" were gas stations.

Barbara and the Marxes sent out invitations for an all-day opening to officially inaugurate Marwyck Ranch. On the Sunday of the opening, Marwyck's first filly foal was dropped, its first Thoroughbred, of Sun Beau.

Barbara said, describing the event, "I don't know that the birth of the Quintuplets [four years before] was any more exciting to the Dionnes than Marwyck's first foaling was to me."

SIX

Well, Who Am I?

1937

"**B**rian Stanwyck Stevens. This is what I want his name to be," said Barbara to her brother, By, of his newborn son.

Barbara didn't have a child of her own blood; she wanted to be a part of By's. Barbara had become friends with Brian Donlevy on *This Is My Affair* and admired him. They were both loners who stayed away from Hollywood. Donlevy was a shy man who liked to retreat to his Brentwood farm, take off his toupee, and write poetry. He was an adventurer as well. In between pictures, he mined for gold in the Panamint Mountains of Death Valley. As a young man, he'd run away from school and joined the army. He was a bugler in General Pershing's 1916 campaign against Pancho Villa and a pilot in the Lafayette Escadrille in the Great War and was awarded the Croix de Guerre.

Barbara liked the name Brian, as did By. And she wanted her name—though invented—to be part of her nephew's. It was. He was called Brian Stanwyck Stevens.

By's wife, Caryl, was afraid to hold her new son. Her baby from her first marriage had died at two months. She was terrified it might happen again. Nannies were hired to take care of Brian. Caryl wasn't easy to work for; nannies came and went, but By patiently, steadily waited on his wife, cooking, cleaning, shopping, doing the laundry.

Barbara was living at 615 North Bedford Drive. The foundation for her permanent home at Marwyck was excavated in April. Her classic English manor house was almost completed, as was Marion and Zeppo's white pillared southern plantation. Each house cost about $30,000 to build.

Barbara's house was designed by the Southern California architect Paul

With Dion; Barbara's sister-in-law, Caryl Stevens; and her nephew,
Brian Stevens, 1937. (COURTESY TONY FAY)

Williams, winner of the Beaux-Arts Medal. Williams was changing the look
of Los Angeles through his designs of apartment houses (the Sunset Plaza
Apartments); hotels (the Knickerbocker in Hollywood); movie theaters (the
Fox in Huntington); churches (Pleasant Hill Baptist Church and the Second
Baptist Church, both in Los Angeles); car showrooms (Packard of Beverly
Hills); schools and fire and police stations.

Williams's style was defined by dramatic spaces and shapes: sweeping
open-air foyers, coffered ceilings, curved staircases, massive windows with
garden views—Hollywood's idea of English aristocratic country living. It
was a style gleaned from the Virginia plantation houses of Nancy Lancaster's
youth—bold, elegant, unpretentious—a style Lancaster transposed to the
Palladian Kelmarsh Hall in Northamptonshire, England, and the eighteenth-
century Ditchley Park of Oxfordshire. Lancaster's ability to make a grand
house seem less grand and her sunny disregard for the preservation of "important furniture" were exactly what Barbara wanted for Marwyck.

Williams, like Barbara, had been orphaned at four and was raised separated from his brother. Williams had managed to triumph over the issue of
race and prejudice. His instructor at Polytechnic High School had said to
him, "Whoever heard of a Negro architect?"

By the time Williams was thirty, he'd designed an estate for the horse
breeder Jack Atkin and a thirty-two-thousand-square-foot home (Cord-

Barbara and Marion Marx in 1937 with Harry Hart, Marwyck's manager, who chose the location of the ranch because its air currents helped the horses to flourish throughout the year. (CULVER PICTURES)

haven) for Errett Lobban Cord, head of the Auburn Automobile Company, introducer of the Model J Duesenberg and the Cord L-29, the first American car made with front-wheel drive. The openness and sweeping grandeur of Williams's design were hallmarks of the stage sets of the celebrated theatrical scenic designer Jo Mielziner, with their signature double-storied windows.

Bob's proposed new house—a rambling Early American farmhouse—was to be built up the road from Marwyck. In the meantime, he was living at 510 North Roxbury. Barbara planned to supervise the furnishing of Bob's house when he was in England making a new picture. Helping her would be the former silent star Jetta Goudal, who, after her lawsuit against Cecil B. DeMille for breach of contract, became an interior decorator with her husband, the art director Harold Grieve. Bob wanted the furniture to be modern. Barbara's own house, except for the few rooms in which she, Dion, Nellie, and Uncle Buck were to live, was barely furnished.

Barbara hadn't moved into the house, but Marwyck was officially open for business. The stables were up, and the training track was finished. Marwyck had one stallion, a bay called the Nut, a son of Mad Hatter from Afternoon by Prince Palatine. The Nut had won the Latonia Championship.

Bing Crosby as official ticket taker, opening day of his Del Mar
Race Track with its first patron, July 5, 1937. (DEL MAR THOR-
OUGHBRED CLUB)

Marwyck had twenty broodmares, each selected by Harry Hart, including
Granny's Trade, daughter of Axenstein; Jane Packard, by the stallion Spanish
Prince 2d, out of Lamplight, who'd won twenty-five races; and Maylite, half
sister of Chase Me. Among the two-year-olds, yearlings, and weanlings were
Sun Beau, Sunador, Ladkin, Tick On, Distraction, Golden Broom, and Rev-
eille Boy. The ranch had already sold a number of yearlings.

Barbara was thrilled when Bing Crosby opened his $1,000,0000 Del Mar
track. (Crosby's slogan: "Where the turf meets the surf.") The Del Mar track
was a hundred miles from Los Angeles, twenty miles from San Diego, with a
landing strip for planes and a harbor for yachts. Del Mar's purses were $5,000
a day with eight races daily and a grandstand that sat four thousand people.

The Del Mar track was a boon for Marwyck. More and more Hollywood
people were getting involved with horse breeding and racing. Crosby was
president of the Del Mar Turf Club with stockholders who included George
Raft, Wesley Ruggles, Oliver Hardy, and Harry Cohn. Bob Taylor owned
eight Thoroughbreds and had just bought his ninth. Spencer Tracy and his
wife, Louise, had more than half a dozen horses, as did Wallace Beery.

For the track's opening day on July 3, Harry Cohn's horses, Best Bid,
En Masse, and Papenie, were running, as were Constance Bennett's Rattle-
brain, and Sam Briskin's Lady Florine and Gertie. Finer horses were run-

Opening day at Del Mar, July 3,
1937.

ning there as well: King Saxon, two-time winner of the Excelsior Handicap;
Grey Count, winner of the Louisiana Derby; and Lloyd Pan, which won
the $10,000 Catalina championship for California-bred horses at Santa
Anita.

Barbara and Bob went to Del Mar's opening with Zeppo and Marion
Marx and were given an ovation by the crowd. Gail Patrick was there with
Bob Cobb, as were Lucille Ball and Lee Tracy, who left his boat at the Coro-
nado Yacht Club; Oliver Hardy; George Jessel; the Jack Warners; the Pandro
Bermans; Walter Connolly and his wife, Nedda Harrigan. Walter Connolly
loved horses and was interested in having them bred at Marwyck.

Crosby, unshaven and in work clothes, opened the gates of his new racetrack and served as ticket taker.

Barbara was to start *A Love Like That,* working again with Al Santell, who'd
directed her in *Internes Can't Take Money.* RKO had hoped to get Bob for *A
Love Like That,* but Metro was starring him, at $3,571 a week, in one of its
new productions to be made in England. Barbara and Bob were about to face
a big moment: a four-month separation.

They had been together every day, every evening, for the past two years. They weren't sure whether they could live happily without each other.

"Perhaps it is the best thing that could happen to us, this separation," Barbara said. Bob was leaving for England in mid-August to make *A Yank at Oxford* after the opening of his new picture, the lavish *Broadway Melody of 1938*. Barbara believed that friendship was more powerful than love, that when one reached the heights of romantic love, there was no place to go but back, but with friendship there was a goal that could never be completely attained. It could be built upon by years of devotion, but it was always possible to intensify it; friendship grew with the years, "while love can only lose," she said. She believed her friendship with Bob could withstand the inevitable loss of the passionate nature of their love. "If you could fall in love with your best friend," she said, "I suppose such a marriage would come as close to perfection as marriage can come."

The issue of Barbara's marrying was a sore one. She had petitioned the court for an order of a division of property that she'd acquired with Frank Fay—five parcels of Brentwood Heights land that were considered community property. She wanted to sell the property and divide the proceeds. Fay in response filed a $31,364 suit against her claiming that she had relinquished all rights to the property, stating that because she'd failed to pay income tax in 1932 and 1934, Fay's property had been attached for that amount and he'd countersued for a half-share claim of $40,000 in community property and $7,500 in personal property in her possession when they separated.

Barbara was wary of marriage, even in her present state of happiness. Bob's idea of marriage was based on his memory of his parents' love for each other. He wanted a married life to be as happy and loving as theirs had been.

"I'm finding it a little difficult," said Barbara, "to keep from being skeptical that such marvelous happiness can last—but I'll try not to tempt Fate."

A Yank at Oxford was the first of Metro's four international pictures. MGM British Studios announced it intended to produce "quality" pictures in England with British subject matter. Each of MGM's four pictures was to be produced by Michael Balcon, former partner of Victor Saville and head of Gainsborough Pictures as well as the former head of Gaumont-British. The forty-one-year-old Balcon, from a "respectable but impoverished" Jewish Birmingham family, was a first-generation Englishman. Balcon was modest and quintessentially English, as were his films. From the age of twenty-seven, he had produced almost 150 pictures, including *Woman to Woman,* about an amnesiac British army officer whose dark past is revealed to him, *A Gentleman of Paris,* and *The Constant Nymph.* He'd discovered the young art director Alfred Hitchcock and produced *The Man Who Knew Too Much, The 39 Steps,* and *Secret Agent.*

Balcon was finishing up a four-month tour in Hollywood observing MGM's production techniques and was to sail back to England.

A Yank at Oxford was a big production for Metro with a budget of $800,000. Both the studio and Balcon had chosen Jack Conway, director of Metro's *A Tale of Two Cities* and *Libeled Lady,* to direct the picture.

The story of *A Yank at Oxford* had been suggested by John Monk Saunders, who, after winning a Rhodes scholarship, was himself a Yank at Oxford. Twenty-three writers worked on the script, among them Sidney Kingsley, Charles Lederer, Joe Mankiewicz, Gottfried Reinhardt, Hugh Walpole, and a depressed Scott Fitzgerald under a six-month Metro contract ("Very few lines of mine are left," Fitzgerald wrote. "I only worked on it for eight days, but the sequence in which Taylor and Maureen O'Sullivan go out in the punt in the morning is mine, and one line very typically so—where Taylor says, 'Don't rub the sleep out of your eyes. It's beautiful sleep.' I thought that line had my trade mark on it"). George Oppenheimer received final screen credit along with Malcolm Stuart Boylan and Walter Ferris.

Louis B. Mayer was going to London to personally launch Metro's new enterprise, whose other planned pictures included *Finishing School* by Tennyson Jesse, *And So—Victoria* by Vaughan Wilkins, and *Good-Bye, Mr. Chips* by James Hilton. At home, Metro's roster for the four months Bob would be away included W. S. Van Dyke, in preproduction for *Rosalie;* Clark Gable, scheduled to make *Test Pilot;* Robert Montgomery in *Under the Flag;* Spencer Tracy and Joan Crawford in *Mannequin.*

Comedies such as *My Man Godfrey, Marry the Girl, Mr. Deeds Goes to Town* were the mainstay of pictures at the moment.

Barbara saw *A Love Like That* as a respite. Comedy to her was like "a vacation," she said. Irene Dunne, considered by Hollywood the first real lady the town had seen, went from playing difficult emotional character roles that spanned from youth to old age (*Magnificent Obsession; Show Boat*) to playing comedy. The "dignified" Miss Dunne wanted to do something besides look cool or cry. She wanted to laugh and show her crazy sense of humor. Comedy to Dunne was easy, "very natural," and to remind herself to keep it natural, she repeated over and over to herself before shooting a scene, "Corned beef and cabbage." Dunne believed that comedy, with the right director, could be a "hilarious occupation." To Barbara, it was "relaxation." She was "playing. Not working."

Critics and audiences were getting their fill of comedies going toward farce, hence the success of David O. Selznick's *Star Is Born.*

"I couldn't possibly have followed *Stella* with another emotional role," Barbara said. "It had run the gamut. I had to let down and give the boys a chance."

Breakfast for Two, the final title of *A Love Like That,* struggled to be in the style of the current cycle of screwball comedies. It was called a comedy romance, sparkling, full of wit and high sophistication, involving an untamed oil heiress from out west and a spoiled shipping magnate whose reckless boozy ways have brought his ancestral company to receivership. The picture promised ventriloquism, a boxing match between heiress and playboy (her glove is rigged with a doorknob but so is the choreographed fight to make Barbara's character flail helplessly like "a girl" and Herbert Marshall, playing the weary "he-man," who waits her out at arm's length; the final KO belongs to the heiress), a black-and-white Great Dane called Pee-Wee, an English butler called Butch (Eric Blore), and a wedding ceremony with a giddy gold-digging actress in which bride and groom can't seem to clinch their vows and the officiating justice of the peace (Donald Meek) is interrupted by everything from a persistent window cleaner scraping against glass and a fainting bride, to a surprise (forged) marriage certificate listing an altogether different intended.

Al Santell said of Barbara, "[She] is all things a performer should be. She arrives on the set ready and equipped to do her chores. And she does them."

"I do very little in *Breakfast for Two,*" said Barbara. She saw it as "practically Herbert Marshall's picture."

Marshall, at forty-seven, looked elegant as the charming idler, though he appeared somewhat ragged and puffy from alcohol.

As the urbane leading man—reserved, unaffected, slightly melancholy—Marshall had appeared in a string of pictures opposite the biggest stars in Hollywood: Lubitsch's *Trouble in Paradise* opposite Kay Francis; von Sternberg's *Blonde Venus* ("quite adorable," Marshall said of Dietrich); *Riptide* with Norma Shearer; Maugham's *Painted Veil* opposite Garbo ("a very nice lady"); *The Flame Within* with Ann Harding; *If You Could Only Cook* with Jean Arthur; *A Woman Rebels* with Katharine Hepburn.

Marshall had served in the Scottish Rifles in the Great War and suffered the loss of his right leg. He was comfortable wearing a prosthesis, it was only barely detectable, and in the picture with Barbara he was willing to do physical humor—pratfalls, knockouts, boxing, ducking a marshmallow cake aimed at his face—using a stand-in. Production would be stopped to allow Marshall to rest. His artificial limb would be removed, the stump massaged and powdered, and then he went back to work.

Santell shot *Breakfast for Two* in sequence exactly as a stage production. He called it a "swing" production since the actors "got the swing into their parts each day." Marshall and Barbara ate lunch together daily, and he drove her home each evening. Marshall had come from a theatrical family in London and graduated from St. Mary's College in Harlow. He'd worked as a chartered accounting clerk—he vowed never to go on the stage—until he joined a stock company in Brighton and made his debut in 1911 at the age of twenty-one. In 1929 he went to Hollywood to star opposite Jeanne Eagels in *The Letter.*

While Barbara and Marshall looked right together on the screen, their pairing didn't work for what was supposed to be a zany comedy. Despite Marshall's cultivated, polished air—he was wry, lean, wistful—he didn't have the lightness for comedy. The intensity of Barbara's yearning for him, while believable from her, seemed misplaced given Marshall's surface demeanor and sallow elegance.

A week after production started, Barbara and Bob went to a preview of *Stella Dallas* at the Warner Bros. Hollywood Theatre. Uncle Buck joined them. Bob parked the car while Barbara and Buck waited in front of the theater. Barbara was shy of people and didn't want to be recognized. She turned up the collar of her plaid jacket and pulled down her hat to cover her eyes. A crowd of two thousand fans waited. By the time Bob got to the theater, a mob of women surged toward him. Bob and Barbara and Buck began to make their way into the theater, but the crowd had Bob. He pushed and shoved his way through the lobby, past the special studio police Goldwyn had hired to keep order and protect the actors. Barbara held on to Bob's coattails as he made his way through the jam.

One of the cops saw a woman pulling on Taylor's coat and said, "Oh, no you don't. None of that stuff." The six-foot cop grabbed Barbara and pulled her away, shoved her through the doors and out onto the street. She tried to pull away from the cop's grip, but he held on, roughing her up.

Bob was unaware of what was happening. He continued through the mob until he turned around and saw a strange girl with him instead of Barbara. He heard Barbara's voice and pushed his way back through the crowd to Barbara who was weeping and disheveled and trying to free herself from the cop's hold. The cop weighed more than 200 pounds to Barbara's 105.

Bob went at the officer and threatened to punch him in the jaw. The cop, one of ten hired by the Goldwyn Studio for the night, let Barbara go. The other police and studio people cut in and broke up the skirmish.

After the preview, a doctor treated Barbara for bruises on her arms and shoulders. Bob wanted her to file charges against the cop. Barbara refused. Goldwyn said, "[The officer] did what he was paid to do."

Later, Buck said to her, "Are you crazy? Why didn't you tell him who you were?"

"Well, who am I?" she said.

Barbara was terrified of crowds and felt suffocated around them. The incident only intensified her fears. She was sure it had been a publicity stunt arranged by the Goldwyn press department that went awry, but no one would own up to it.

After the *Stella Dallas* previews, telegrams of congratulations were sent off to Goldwyn from Norma Shearer ("I have never seen a more touching picture"), Gary Cooper ("Congratulations on a fine picture that has something to say"), Charles Boyer ("A credit both to Samuel Goldwyn and to the entire industry"), and Sophie Tucker ("*Stella Dallas* has everything. I loved every minute of it"). Barbara had put everything she had into the picture and was proud of it, a luxury she'd never before permitted herself.

It was said to be Vidor's best picture: eloquent; memorable; an inspiration; retaining the power of the book and the silent picture released more than a decade before; a picture that Goldwyn was bold enough to make despite its being a remake of a silent-era hit and a tearjerker, and at a time when crazy comedies were the vogue. It was the kind of role that Barbara Stanwyck had long needed but had never been given; it was being talked about as the best work of her career.

The picture opened in New York at Radio City Music Hall two weeks after its previews.

It was a smash. The *Herald Tribune* saw Vidor's consummate staging as a "personal triumph of one of the few really great directors." Other papers declared *Stella Dallas* "as great a picture today as it ever was"; "a triumph both artistically and as a potential moneymaker . . . utterly simple in structure and without a single descent into banality or dramatic trickery."

At Radio City, when Barbara appeared on the screen in Stella's outlandish clothes, the audience burst into laughter. But they loved the picture. Barbara's work was called "courageous," "outstanding," "superb" ("By innumerable little touches she creates in two hours the character of an entire class of society . . . hers is a delineation of a caste system that exists despite the tenets of freedom and equality of which we in the United States are so proud"; "tops in Miss Stanwyck's screen repertoire; she makes the sordid sublime"). Anne Shirley's performance was called "remarkable," "flawless"; Alan Hale's, "outstanding."

Frank Nugent, in *The New York Times,* saw all of the weaknesses of the Prouty novel and the silent version. "On the practical surface," he wrote, "we cannot accept Stella Dallas in 1937. She is a caricature all the way. [But] even that realization is no insurance against a blow to the heart. Mother love and sacrifice are durable dramatic commodities, as irresistible and compelling today as they were in 1923. "Vidor's *Stella Dallas* is the most satisfactory of all remakes the screen has attempted."

Barbara had turned thirty just as shooting started on *Breakfast for Two.* After ten years in Hollywood and twenty-nine pictures, she was being recognized as a major actress of big emotions, an actress of range and courage. She'd done what was necessary to survive and had taken her sorrow, rage, and fear and compressed them into one winning, forceful, controlled performance after another. Her audience admired her, feared her, and rooted for her, and she held them at her command, enthralled.

SEVEN

Bull in the Afternoon

Bob didn't see himself as an artist. "To my mind," he said, "you need years of experience before you can even think of yourself as a great actor. There are plenty of people in it really for art's sake. It is their life, and every word in every part is vitally important to them. But I'm not an artist. How can I be?"

Bob was mobbed by women and cast opposite one glamour queen after another. Women moviegoers found him irresistibly handsome and romantic, the epitome of physical perfection: handsomely poised, handsomely dressed, handsomely scrubbed and polished. Bob was called "Pretty Boy" and "Beautiful Robert Taylor." It began to show at the box office. He was desperate to be in something other than a young-lover role.

The studio hoped *A Yank at Oxford* would turn around the public's perception of him. The idea was for Taylor, playing a midwestern American football hero who falls for a coquette, to be seen as physical, rugged, mussed up, doing something besides being attentive to Janet Gaynor, Joan Crawford, or Greta Garbo.

To squelch the image of Bob as a beautiful effeminate man, MGM released stories about him as ranch owner, avid hunter, fight fan, as rival to Clark Gable. Gable dismissed the idea of a competition and said, "No good actor is a rival, he's an asset. Everyone has his own individual way of doing things and I never felt I had something that no one else had."

Gable was grateful Bob was at Metro. For a long period, Gable and Bob Montgomery were the only leading men on the Metro lot. Gable, from the first, hadn't the "faintest notion" of ever becoming a star. "Such a possibility never entered my head," he said. "My looks, romantically, weren't worth a nickel. I didn't even think I could even be a leading man. The studio didn't think much of stage actors then. They'd rather have a good-looking doorman or a truck-driver," he said. If it hadn't been for gangster pictures, "I'd never have got my foot in at all," said Gable. "All that saved me was that I could look tough. I was lucky to get anywhere." He went on, "We were kept going from one woman star to another." When Bill Powell went to Metro and then Spencer Tracy, the leading men numbered four; Taylor's arrival at the studio made five.

"Bob has taken some of the burden off my shoulders," said Gable.

Bob was in awe of Gable, who in turn was "mighty proud" of Bob. "He has come along like no other actor in the business," said Gable, who saw himself as a "home grown, garden variety, actor." Gable came out of the back hills of Ohio, as "green as they come," and went to Akron, where he trained in theatrical stock companies. "There's no other place where an actor can get such valuable training," said Gable. He saw Bob's training, from college and the dramatic society to studio dramatic class, as "valuable." Taylor said of Gable, "Clark is so big that all I can do is look up to him. Gable is in a class by himself," said Bob. "He isn't like any other actor."

After the skirmish at the *Stella Dallas* preview, Barbara realized it was part of her job to dress more dramatically for public appearances and talked with Edith Head—they'd first worked together on *Internes Can't Take Money*, got along instantly, and become friends—about designing a wardrobe for her. Barbara felt her clothes were neat and of good material. Edith thought they were "too stern; too grim," she said. "Your clothes can be simple and tailored, but they can be feminine too."

Edith set about designing suits for Barbara without their having a suggestion of menswear. She designed dresses for evening that were dramatic and daring, and Barbara was delighted to wear them. Head kept in mind for whom she was designing: her clothes for Barbara were neat, tidy, and plain.

She finished *Breakfast for Two* on a Monday in mid-August. Two days later Bob's new picture, *Broadway Melody of 1938,* opened at Grauman's Chinese and Loew's State. In *Melody,* directed by Roy Del Ruth, Bob plays a producer/composer of popular songs down on his luck trying to put on a new Broadway show. The specialty numbers are performed by Eleanor Powell, George Murphy, Sophie Tucker, Buddy Ebsen, and thirteen-year-old Judy Garland, who steals the picture with "Everybody Sing" and her fan letter "Dear Mr. Gable." The critics felt the twenty-six-year-old Robert Taylor was lost against the fast-moving musical talent. Bob was not surprised. Eleanor Powell, at twenty-four, was a big star at Metro and was taken with Bob. She'd worked with him in *Broadway Melody of 1936* and thought him very handsome. At the time, Eleanor had just come to Hollywood and was over-

The cast of *Broadway Melody of 1938* appearing on *Hollywood Hotel,* July 16, 1937. Left to right: Billy Gilbert, George Murphy, Judy Garland, Charles Igor Gorin, Sophie Tucker, Eleanor Powell, Bob, Vilma and Buddy Ebsen, and (between them) Frances Langford.

whelmed by it all. Now, two years later, she felt Bob was interested in her, and she wrote to her mother that there might be a romance. Ellie Powell was naive and a virgin. Her whole reason for being was to dance.

A Yank at Oxford was one of the few pictures Bob balked at having to make. He left for New York and arrived there four days later—flying first to Oklahoma City and then to Kansas City, where crowds of fans swarmed the airport. After two days in New York, Bob boarded the *Berengaria* bound for Southampton. Hundreds of women charged through the police lines in a mass frenzy. The liner's officers and staff and the police were needed to clear the ship's deck.

New York reporters kidded Bob and asked him if he thought he was "a beautiful boy," if he had hair on his chest, and if it was real.

The question came from a newspaper story about Ernest Hemingway that had run the previous week. Hemingway had been in New York to sail to war-torn Spain. He'd dropped in unannounced on his publisher, Charles Scribner's Sons, to see his editor, Maxwell Perkins, and ended up in a fight with another Scribner's writer, Max Eastman, who was there discussing a new edition of his book *Enjoyment of Poetry* with Perkins, also his editor.

The trouble started with a four-year grudge over a review Eastman had written of Hemingway's book on bullfighting, *Death in the Afternoon.* Eastman's review, titled "Bull in the Afternoon," which ran in June 1933 in *The New Republic,* took Hemingway to task for the "unconscionable quantity of bull," wrote Eastman, that Hemingway "poured and plastered all over what he writes about bullfights. By bull," Eastman wrote, "I mean juvenile romantic gushing and sentimentalizing of simple facts. A bull fight . . . is men tormenting and killing a bull." Eastman went on to say that Hemingway's "red-blooded masculinity [is] made obvious in the swing of the big shoulders and the clothes he puts on . . . and in the stride of his prose style . . . Our full-sized man," wrote Eastman, "lacks the serene confidence that he *is* a full-sized man."

Eastman wrote about how "this trait of character has been strong enough to form the nucleus of a new flavor of English literature, and it has moreover begotten a veritable school of fiction writers—a literary style of wearing false hair on the chest."

Hemingway wrote to *The New Republic* challenging the magazine to "have Mr. Max Eastman elaborate his nostalgic speculations on my sexual incapacity." Eastman apologized in what Hemingway called a "kissass letter."

Four years later, in the sweltering heat of a mid-August day, when Hemingway walked into Charles Scribner's Sons and found Perkins in a meeting with Eastman, Hemingway was friendly enough, shook Eastman's hand, and ripped open his shirt to show Eastman the plentiful real hair on his chest. Then he opened Eastman's shirt; his chest was smooth and hairless. It was all in fun until Hemingway said, "What do you mean by accusing me of impotence?" Eastman denied that he'd written that in the review. Scribner's had published Eastman's essays and a copy of the collection happened to be on Perkins's desk. Eastman showed the piece to Hemingway to prove his denial.

Hemingway started to read the review and became enraged all over again. He took the open book and hit Eastman with it. Eastman lunged at Hemingway. Perkins got up to stop Hemingway from hurting Eastman. Books and papers spilled onto the floor. Perkins shouted at Hemingway to stop and grabbed him to pull him off Eastman, but to Perkins's surprise it wasn't Hemingway who was hurting Eastman. Perkins was pulling Eastman off Hemingway.

The press got wind of the story—through Eastman, who read aloud his account of what had happened at a dinner party attended by a number of newspaper people. The story made the evening papers. The next day, Hemingway was sailing for Spain and was questioned by reporters about the fight. He described it as ending with his bashing Eastman with a lightweight book and went on to warn, "When I come back I'll take his pants down and spank him."

A week later Bob Taylor, in New York and sailing for England, got the tail end of the chest hair joke. Bob was unaware of the Hemingway-Eastman fracas and was angry about the question. The press went on to ask him if he would rather have beauty or brains.

Bob, to show how manly and rugged he was, told reporters that he didn't read because he didn't like to be indoors and that he hoped one day to retire from pictures to his new ranch and raise cattle. Taylor talked about getting a ranch in Northern California or Wyoming. "I like the seasons," he said. "You know—winter, spring, fall—the sort of thing you don't get [in Los Angeles]."

"Aren't you interested in anything but Barbara Stanwyck, your job and your ranch?" he was asked.

Bob smiled and said, "That's enough for anyone."

Two days out at sea aboard the *Berengaria,* Bob shouted into the radio telephone to Barbara, "Do you love me?"

"Yes, I love you," she shouted back. She had rushed home from the Ray Millands' to get Bob's call.

"Dear, I'm counting the moments until I can get back to you—and my new ranch home."

"I'll watch out for your new home until you get back."

Barbara was planning on leaving town as soon as she could. She finished work on *Breakfast for Two,* and *Stella Dallas* opened in Los Angeles the following Monday. That Wednesday she and Holly Barnes flew to Sun Valley for a long weekend.

Stella Dallas had the biggest opening on record, beating *A Star Is Born.* The picture was held over for a second week. Howard Barnes saw both pictures in terms of a "society at a critical point in a period transition where what was needed was fundamental aspects of human relationships."

A Star Is Born worked not because of the inside view of Hollywood but because of its sentiment, and, wrote Barnes, "*Stella Dallas* is the very apogee of screen sentiment."

EIGHT

Rearing Up

1937

For Robert Taylor I whistle and stamp:
That's why the lady is a tramp!

—Lorenz Hart, "The Lady Is a Tramp"

Three days after Bob sailed for England with the director Jack Conway and his co-stars in *A Yank at Oxford,* Lionel Barrymore and Maureen O'Sullivan, Barbara and Holly Barnes, resting in Sun Valley, Idaho, decided to travel to the Pacific Northwest and make their way east. Barbara needed a break from the endless speculation about whether she and Bob were getting married.

A week before they were to leave for Canada, Barbara went to a preview of Selznick International's fourth picture, *The Prisoner of Zenda.*

She was leaning out of her car, after the picture, signing autographs, when the door shut and caught two of her fingers. She postponed her holiday for a few days to make sure no infection set in, and then she and Holly left for the Château Frontenac in Quebec and went into seclusion. A few days later, they furtively left for Montreal. Barbara was besieged by the press about whether or not she was sailing to England to marry Bob (she wasn't). She and Holly left Montreal sooner than planned and went to New York to see her sister and brother-in-law Maud and Bert Merkent.

Bob arrived in Southampton to hundreds of women waiting for him thanks to MGM's publicity department. He boarded the boat train from Southampton and arrived at Waterloo to be greeted by cheers of three thousand women.

The stationmaster came solemnly toward Bob in frock coat and striped trousers. "I thought he must be at least the Duke of Westminster," said Bob.

Extra police were called to control the crowd. Bob left the platform flanked by six policemen, three in front of him and three behind.

As the station manager maneuvered Bob, the crowd massed behind the barrier and pushed him into a milk lift, and said, "Sorry if it's a bit stuffy here, and hope you don't mind," said the station manager. "Mind?" said Bob. "I'm only too thankful to be delivered with the milk." He was then driven to the hotel with crowds of women still at the station cheering each car that left.

At Claridge's, he was met by crowds in the street in front of the hotel going wild. To appease the mob that was blocking traffic, he had to appear at the balcony like royalty. He had missed the fanfare of the coronation of George VI by three months, but the attention aimed at him was too much. The crowd below his window was still hollering for him late into the night. After being cooped up in the hotel for hours, Bob was desperate to get out for some fresh air.

At midnight, he and Howard Strickling, MGM's publicity chief, who'd come over ahead of Bob, sneaked down Claridge's back stairs and got into a cab. A man on a bicycle was trailing them. They tried unsuccessfully to shake him off in Hyde Park, and finally the cab pulled over. The pursuer leaped off his bike and pulled out a pencil and paper. He was a journalist who asked a few questions and politely went on his way. Bob walked around the park for an hour or so and then returned to the hotel.

Alexander Korda's discovery Vivien Leigh, of *Fire over England, Dark Journey,* and *Storm in a Teacup,* was to play the English girl opposite Bob. Vivien Leigh, at twenty-three, had enough fire, darkness, and turbulence to have made her mark along with Korda's other discovery, Merle Oberon.

Metro rented a twelve-bedroom fifteenth-century house for Bob at High Wycombe near Denham, along with a Rolls-Bentley. Bob was in training—sprinting and running a quarter mile and learning to scull on the Thames with a rowing club.

L. B. Mayer arrived in London soon after to officially inaugurate Metro's plans to make pictures in England with a luncheon at the Savoy hotel that included Bob, Maureen O'Sullivan, Sir Hugh Walpole, Lord Sempill, Lord Lee of Fareham, Alexander Korda, and Ivor Novello.

A Yank at Oxford didn't begin filming until late September, when Mayer

Bob in the Thames while shooting *A Yank at Oxford*, fall 1937.

returned from Paris, where he was elected an officer of the Legion of Honor for his work in pictures.

Barbara wasn't about to get married again. She knew what could happen. She saw what was happening with Joan Crawford's marriage to Franchot Tone, how they'd been married for two years, and though Joan had been changed by Franchot (Joan had hoped their marriage would be like that of the Lunts, joined onstage and off—longtime, loving friends and actors), she was already wearying of him and their endless arguments, in which Tone occasionally, in a drunken rage, beat her, and she would go to work wearing dark glasses to hide the bruises on her face.

Joan and Franchot had finished making *The Bride Wore Red*, and Joan was working on a picture with Spencer Tracy. Barbara knew that Joan was mixed up with Tracy. Barbara had tremendous admiration for Spencer Tracy as an actor; he could do no wrong. She admired the way he subordinated the technical perfection of his tricks to naturalness. What Joan was doing with her marriage infuriated Barbara. It was only a flurry with Tracy, but Joan would come home after being with him and call people at two or three in the morning asking if Franchot was there. "Well, I don't know where he is. He's out . . . and I can't find him. And I'm desperate."

Franchot was out drinking and, said Barbara, "wearing his heart on his sleeve and staying in some lousy bar" because he'd found out "about Joan and

Tracy." Barbara knew what a superb actress Joan was, on-screen and off. "She would look you in the eye," said Barbara, "and make you absolutely believe whatever she was saying," but "not me, she won't."

Barbara hadn't been to New York in two years, since her days with Fay on the circuit for *Tattle Tales.* Now, back in the city, she went to some of the second-rate nightclubs she'd spent so much time in before her success in *The Noose* and *Burlesque.*

She saw Rodgers and Hart's new show, *Babes in Arms,* at the Shubert. During the performance, she noticed the violinist conducting the orchestra. She stared at the back of his neck and looked at the program to see his name. It was Gene Salzer, her sister Millie's fiancé from when they'd worked together years before—Salzer conducting the orchestra and Millie performing onstage. Barbara's earliest awareness of the theater began with Gene and Millie.

On weekends Millie and Gene had brought Barbara from Brooklyn to the city, where they'd let her stand in the wings of the theater and watch the performances. "Everyone looked so happy out there," said Barbara, "dancing and singing for the audience. When the applause broke out it thrilled me. The music and lights . . ." Barbara was seven, but she "remembered every second of it."

Millie's memory was sacred to Barbara. Millie was the most beautiful woman Barbara had ever seen, "with all of the real talent, the beauty, and the emotion an actress should have," she said. "She was very good to me," said Barbara. "Millie and Gene bought me clothes and little luxuries I had never known existed. Whatever unhappiness I may have suffered, it was all made up to me when they called for me and took me back to the city."

Barbara hadn't seen Gene in more than twenty years. He was graying now; she was thirty. Barbara had wanted for so long to find him to thank him for everything he'd done for her.

During the show she tried to catch Gene's eye; when he saw her and recognized her, he went white. Barbara began to cry. The curtain came down on the first act. Barbara walked to the orchestra pit. She put her arms around Gene and wept on his shoulder. He promised to go to Barbara's hotel. "There was so much to say; so many years to cover."

Barbara remembered how when she was little, after the theater, Gene would take her to get something to eat. He always ordered cream puffs and coffee. Barbara had Holly call bakers and restaurants at that late hour in search of the long-remembered cream puffs.

Barbara's English-style manor house, Marwyck, designed by Paul Williams, with French Normandy and Tudor Revival details. The 6,500-square-foot house had eight bedrooms, four fireplaces, a three-car garage, and eventually a swimming pool (out of camera range, right) and tennis court. (CULVER PICTURES)

Gene and Barbara talked through the night, he telling her things about Millie she hadn't known and about her own early childhood she'd forgotten.

Their evening together "was one of those things that happen once in a lifetime," said Barbara, "filled with heartbreaking memories and the joy of having found the one connecting link" between her sister and their past.

Barbara and Holly sailed home on the *Virginia* by way of the Panama Canal. Seven days later, in Los Angeles, Barbara received an urgent letter from Frank Fay that she refused. She knew it was about Dion. Fay had been trying to see the boy, and Barbara wouldn't allow it.

Barbara, Dion, Uncle Buck, and Nellie had moved from Los Angeles to Northridge, a town made up of a post office and a laundry. At Marwyck, Barbara had a new house, the first she'd owned by herself. Long and rambling but "a small house at that," she said. "We don't need a lot of room."

The Paul Williams design was an ornate manor house of brownish-gray stone with tones of yellow and with high English gables. The porch with its flagstone floor was as long as the house, with comfortable chairs in rust color and driftwood. The living room was in chintzes of brown, yellow, and green against a canary-yellow carpet and gamboge tapestries. The fireplace was a brown marble. Bob had put in a tennis court in April as an early birthday present to Barbara.

The playroom had redwood beams; the carpet was a hand-braided gray, the furniture chromium and scarlet leather.

The garage and servants' quarters were still being built.

Flagged promenades and porticoes surrounded the compound with grassy terraces that sloped away. An ornate sixty-foot swimming pool was being put in. Zeppo and Barbara supervised the replanting of giant trees that had been hauled great distances and would grow to forty or fifty feet; the area dug out for each tree was large enough for a swimming hole.

Bob called Barbara across the Atlantic and the continent every Sunday morning. She hadn't put in a phone yet at Marwyck; she hated the telephone—couldn't stand it ringing and always picked it up after the first ring. If the phone on the set of *Breakfast for Two* happened to ring and Barbara was studying her lines, she answered it. If it rang and she was shooting a scene, it made her so nervous the phone was finally removed altogether. In town her friends knew that if the phone rang twice, Barbara wasn't home. Barbara, like Crawford, changed her telephone number every few weeks to keep away salesmen and fans and those actors and crew members trying to forge a friendship Barbara didn't want.

The only way to reach Barbara by phone at Marwyck was to call the stable office a half mile from the house. The stable hands were given strict instructions not to bother Barbara unless the call was an emergency or to phone Zeppo Marx, who lived a quarter of a mile away.

Barbara rarely went out when Bob was away. For the most part she stayed at the ranch, only sporadically going into town. She held a wedding at Marwyck for one of the stable boys and happily agreed to be a bridesmaid.

Between Sundays, when Bob called, he wrote letters and sent Barbara flowers. Uncle Buck noted that "she missed him pretty bad." Bob repeatedly asked Barbara to join him in England. "Can you imagine what would happen if I went?" she said. "It's bad enough here alone with reporters. We wouldn't have a moment's peace."

When production on *A Yank at Oxford* was stopped because of bad weather, Bob called Barbara and asked her to marry him. She thought he should experience more before he settled down. She understood how impor-

"Lux presents Hollywood! . . ." For Lux Radio Theatre's *Stella Dallas,*
left to right: Anne Shirley, John Boles, Barbara, and Cecil B. DeMille,
October 11, 1937.

tant it was for him to remain single for his career, how marriage might damage his standing with the moviegoing audience. At the heart of it, though,
the lure of marriage and its promise of happiness and contentment seemed
remote to her.

Barbara appeared on the third-anniversary show of *Lux Radio Theatre* performing *Stella Dallas* with most of the cast (minus Alan Hale; Ed Munn was
played by Lou Merrill).

Cecil B. DeMille was the host. John Boles, Stephen Dallas in the picture, was performing again with Barbara, as were Anne Shirley and Barbara
O'Neil. Boles had appeared on the first *Lux Radio Theatre* presentation that
aired three years before. DeMille congratulated *Lux* on its third birthday and
the players on their year of success: Boles for his busiest and most successful
year on the screen; Anne Shirley for her newly acquired stardom and husband, John Payne; and Barbara for "at last coming into her own through her
magnificent performance as Stella Dallas.

"I know of no one in Hollywood," said DeMille to the theater audience
and to listeners at home, "who merits success more than Barbara Stanwyck."
DeMille described her rise and how "Barbara, now on top, can indulge a
lifelong ambition. She's purchased a farm in the San Fernando Valley and will
spend her off-screen life raising horses."

. . .

Following *Breakfast for Two,* Barbara had been waiting for a script revision from RKO for a picture called *Condemned Women.* The picture was originally intended for Sally Eilers; it was about a former nurse in prison for larceny who falls in love with a doctor who performs psychological experiments on the women prisoners. Barbara was to make the picture with Anne Shirley following their success together in *Stella Dallas.* When Barbara finally read the script for *Condemned Women,* she wasn't happy with it and turned down the project.

Radio Pictures was about to remake *Holiday,* the 1930 Pathé release that had starred Ann Harding and for which she'd been nominated as Best Actress for an Academy Award. Barbara wanted the Ann Harding role of Linda Seton, the rebel sister.

Harding hadn't wanted to do the original picture, because it was a comedy role; she'd practically been forced into it when Ina Claire, for whom the screen rights of the play had been bought, began to film a remake of the 1925 silent *The Awful Truth* from Arthur Richman's Broadway play in which Claire had starred.

Linda Seton, in *Holiday,* is the misfit younger daughter of a financier who rebels against the family's "reverence for riches," its solid conservative standing, and its relentless pursuit of things conventional and deadening, and she sees in her older sister's fiancé a kindred spirit. He is an up-from-under young man, "a man of the pee-pul," at work since the age of ten. He is about to make a small killing of his own, becomes engaged, and discovers, after the fact, that it is one of *the* Setons he is to marry. He says from the outset he isn't interested in "all this luxe"; he doesn't want "*too* much money"; he wants to "retire young, and work old" to save part of his life for himself, "the young part." He wants to take the money he makes and go off on an extended holiday until he's spent every penny he's earned to find out who he is and what he is about, to dream his dreams, see the world, and find out "what goes on and what about it."

In the original picture with Ann Harding were Mary Astor as Julia Seton, the older sister, and Robert Ames as the young man, Johnny Case. RKO had acquired the rights to *Holiday* in 1930 when the studio absorbed Pathé for $5 million, along with its library, its trademark, and its contracts with Helen Twelvetrees, Constance Bennett, and Ann Harding.

At the heart of Philip Barry's play: two rich girls, sisters, each the mirror image of the other. The older, Julia, appears to be the unconventional one who returns from a winter holiday having fallen in love with an unlikely young man without background or breeding (his "mother wasn't even a Whoozis"). What Julia loves in him is that she thinks he can become just like her father. Julia Seton is the good girl, seemingly appealing, womanly, and playful on the surface; underneath, she is tradition-bound, deeply hard, soulless.

The younger sister, Linda, is rebellious and brusque but at heart is soft, empathetic, human, fragile. She wants out from the money, her father's stuffiness and plutocratic view of the world, but doesn't quite have the guts to take the leap. She wants to save the young man from her family, from the fate he is being seduced into. Out of loyalty to her sister, whom she adores, she holds herself back from warning the young man that to enter into her family is to be stunted humanly. Along the way, Linda realizes she's fallen in love with him.

The person who gives away the truth of the family is the brother, a broken man caught between his two sisters. The more sympathetic and likable the brother, the more frightened the audience is for the fiancé, who, starry-eyed and sincere, doesn't see what he is getting himself into.

The picture asked: What is human quality? What is class?

Barbara was excited about *Holiday*. She had enormous admiration for Ann Harding, the passion, the fire, the freedom in front of a camera, the naturalness of her work. *Holiday* was considered Harding's best work on the screen. Barbara was drawn to Philip Barry's writing—elegant, light, playful, comical. It had a melancholy about it under the surface; it was charming and heartbreaking at every moment. The misfit aspect and gallantry of the Linda Seton character suited Barbara.

She had played upper-class women but as the interloper, as was Philip Barry himself, born an outsider of Irish Catholic descent in Rochester, New York. Barry came to inhabit the worlds of the rich and wellborn, though he remained wary of the type and used what he saw of his adopted society as the setting in his plays. Barbara admired *Holiday*, which Barry wrote as a drawing room comedy for Hope Williams and which Barbara's champion Arthur Hopkins directed on Broadway.

RKO wasn't happy with Barbara for turning down *Condemned Women* and put her on suspension. The remake of *Holiday* was set to bring together again Irene Dunne and Cary Grant and to be directed by Leo McCarey. Instead, George Cukor was directing the picture and hired Katharine Hepburn for the part of Linda Seton. Irene Dunne was heartbroken that she didn't get it.

"A lot of times," said Barbara, "a studio knows better than a star whether or not a picture will be a success." Barbara insisted on going with her instincts. "Sometimes I've been wrong," she said, "but more often I've been right."

RKO and Fox had both raved about two pictures they wanted Barbara to do. "They were rabid about these 'great' pictures," said Barbara, who had no intention of making either.

The roles coming to Barbara were too similar. *Condemned Women* said it all. If Barbara continued to play small drab, respectable roles of resignation and reverie, there would only be more like them ahead of her. To rear up now was going to cost her a contract and a fortune in lost salary, but she had to take the stand. If she didn't, varying roles wouldn't come to her and her career would be over.

Barbara had no backlog of savings. She had to earn money somehow while on suspension and not receiving her salary.

Danny Danker, who oversaw *Lux Radio Theatre,* assured Barbara not to worry, that she was welcome in radio, and that he would cast her in the *Lux* shows. She was profoundly grateful to him for giving her the work. Danker hired her right away, and she appeared on *Lux Radio* with Mary Astor in *These Three* with Errol Flynn.

Breakfast for Two opened the day before Thanksgiving in Los Angeles at the Paramount and in New York at the Palace. The picture, of "the intermediary classification," had enough zany antics and screwy situations to hold its own against the string of other comedies just out, from *LIVE, LOVE, AND LEARN* with Robert Montgomery, Rosalind Russell, and Robert Benchley to *True Confession* with Carole Lombard, Fred MacMurray, and John Barrymore.

"Cunning . . . clever . . . and good entertainment," said the *New York Herald Tribune,* which described Barbara's work as "cocky and demure, assured and sorrowfully frustrated." *The New York Times* was baffled by the audience's explosive laughter and called the picture a "drab little comedy."

The screen comedy of the season that outdid the others with comic spins, wit, and slapstick fun was Leo McCarey's remake of *The Awful Truth* with the radiant, irrepressible duo of Irene Dunne and Cary Grant.

NINE

Charges of Contempt

1937–1938

With Bob out of town, Frank Fay was circling Barbara. In October she had petitioned the court for a division of property—five parcels of Brentwood Heights land—that she'd acquired with Fay. Barbara wanted to sell the property and split the proceeds. Fay saw the court petition as an opening.

In the first week in December, a process server tried unsuccessfully to deliver court papers to Barbara. When the server rang the bell at 615 North Bedford Drive, the door was opened slightly. The server was told that Barbara was not at home; that she was, or was not, out of town; that she may, or may not, be coming home for dinner. The process server left his card and asked Miss Stanwyck to call him on her return. The server went to RKO and was told that she wasn't working at the studio but could be found at home. During the next few days the server tried unsuccessfully to deliver papers to Barbara at North Bedford Drive and at RKO.

Fay had been trying to see Dion, as spelled out in Barbara and Fay's divorce agreement, which stated that he was to see his son at least once a week. After Barbara learned of Fay's plan to take Dion out of California as a ploy to make her go to him, she put a stop to Dion's Bristol Avenue visits.

Finally, at a loss, the server called Barbara's lawyer, Charles Cradick, who said he would not help make arrangements to have the papers served.

Barbara was being charged with contempt of her divorce agreement. Fay had waited until Bob was out of the country to set the court challenge in motion and have his lawyer draw up papers.

A Yank at Oxford finished shooting, and Bob had wanted to see something of Europe—it was his first time abroad—before returning to Hollywood. MGM gave him a big private plane, and Bob went to Paris for the weekend.

"Each time we arrived somewhere the pilot circled around several times before landing," he said. "And I could never figure out why so many people always collected. Then I discovered they'd painted a damn great MGM lion under the belly of the plane with my name in huge letters beside it."

After four months away in England, Bob sailed for New York on the *Queen Mary* and arrived in mid-December. Several reporters were allowed to go on board to Taylor's stateroom for a brief interview. Taylor was asked about the British press in relation to the American press.

"[British reporters] don't grab you on the street or interrupt you while you [are] eating dinner," Bob said. "And they weren't allowed on the set."

Bob joked with reporters about how the U.S. press had predicted the end of his career. "Don't think I don't remember reading your releases about my trip to England and how I was 'through' in the movies. You boys buried me. Maybe I was dying a slow death," said Bob. "But you could have given me one last chance," he said, referring to *A Yank at Oxford*.

As reporters left Bob's stateroom, they saw Lionel Barrymore, walking slowly with the use of a cane. Barrymore had also made the crossing on the *Queen Mary* and was asked about his health, and about Bob Taylor. Barrymore's response: "I haven't had a drink in a long time. And it's not Bob's fault he's so handsome. Good day, gentlemen."

Bob disembarked from the boat with Barrymore. Barrymore got into a car and was driven off. Bob was surrounded by more press who shouted questions at him: "Hey, Bob, do you still think you are beautiful?" "Who was the hairdresser who created your widow's peak?" "How does it feel to be more beautiful than Garbo?"

Bob answered in rapid succession: "I resent that question." "It runs in the family." To the Garbo comment, he finally got annoyed: "For God's sake, that's ridiculous and I've said it a hundred times, how can you compare me to Garbo or any other woman, for that matter? If we have to continue this, get off the subject of my face and my chest and I know God damn well you'll get around to that. Why the hell don't you ask me how the voyage home was—or about *Yank at Oxford?*"

When a reporter tried to pull down Bob's sock and photograph the hair on his legs, Bob said, "That's enough, damn it to hell. I have a train to catch."

On the train west, he told a friend from Metro, "I shave twice a day because I have to. I don't wear my mother's dresses when she's not at home. I ride a horse better than Gary Cooper, and shoot straighter than Randolph Scott. I like to get laid and can screw better than Errol Flynn. Trouble is I can't act as good as Spencer Tracy or drink as much as Bogart."

Louis B. Mayer told Bob that he had seen the rushes of *A Yank at Oxford* and assured the actor that the studio would do everything it could to publicize the picture. "Nothing happens overnight, son," said Mayer, "but you will see a change, not only in your fans, but in yourself." Mayer told Bob that he was now "a man."

Barbara was at the ranch. Bob couldn't wait to see her. They hadn't seen each other in months.

He asked her to marry him, this time without an ocean or continent between them. Barbara felt they should wait but agreed to be secretly engaged. Bob gave her a charm that read, "Luck to you from Lucky Me."

Bob had missed her, as well as his mother and his friends. And he missed his car, a stripped-down racer without fenders and with specially braced wheels, a red exhaust pipe, and no floorboard. Back at the studio, Bob was clapped on one shoulder by Gable and by Tracy on the other. Jimmy Stewart yanked Bob's hair; Tyrone Power hullooed to him; Reginald Gardiner made welcome-home noises; Myrna Loy, Sophie Tucker, Rosalind Russell, Fanny Brice, Maureen O'Sullivan, and Judy Garland blew him kisses. He had missed the studio prop boys and carpenters and electricians. "I wasn't homesick," he said. "I'm not the homesick type. I adjust easily and happily to any environment. I'm the adaptable kind who could be equally content in a hovel or in a palace, in Paris or Peoria. Doesn't matter a hoot in hell to me where I live."

Barbara had been ordered to appear at city hall in Los Angeles Superior Court. Judge Goodwin Knight, a superior court judge for two years, had a caseload that ranged from the mundane to overseeing Hollywood weddings and divorces, including the scandalous Mary Astor custody case. Knight had called for Miss Astor's diary, in which she described in ecstatic detail her love life while married, including her affair with the playwright George S. Kaufman ("the perfect lover," she'd written of him).

The Astor/Kaufman case took on larger ramifications.

The heads of the studios were terrified the contents of Astor's diary would wreck the careers of those mentioned in it and destroy the movie industry. Will Hays fought to make sure the diary was not presented as evidence. After four hours of reading the two hundred pages of entries from beginning to end, Judge Knight ordered the diary, written in lavender ink, sealed and impounded with the court. George Kaufman was subpoenaed to appear before Judge Knight's court but fled California and was smuggled to New York. A headline in *The New York Times* read: "Warrant Out for Kaufman." Judge

Knight said, "I'll put him away for a while to cool off . . . He could write quite a play about life in jail."

It was arranged with the court that Barbara did not have to appear when Fay was present. Hy Schwartz, Fay's lawyer, tried to have Barbara brought into the courtroom to settle who would have Dion on Christmas Day. Fay went before Judge Knight and asked that Barbara be held in contempt for refusing to let him see their five-year-old adopted son.

Fay told the judge how he had tried to make arrangements with Barbara to see the child. He'd phoned, written letters, and repeatedly called Barbara's lawyer and presented to the court a returned letter as evidence. In it Fay had written, "I have been put off and put off and ignored and I have only stood for this treatment because of my great love for the boy and my desire not to involve him in any publicity or to confuse his young mind, but I do not intend to permit anyone to cause him to forget me.

"You subjected me to every indignity and humiliation by making me phone through a theatrical switchboard agency office," Fay wrote. "I have spent amounts ranging as high as $100 a week to hear the boy say, 'Hello, Daddy.' It finally became so difficult and so unsatisfactory, not to mention the expense, that I gave it up for the time being."

Judge Knight postponed the hearing until after Christmas. Cradick assured the judge that his client would be there when the case resumed.

No sooner had Bob returned from England than he was helping Barbara transport Marwyck's horses in a new trailer from the ranch to Santa Anita for the track's opening on Christmas Day. Six horses were running under the Marwyck colors. After a few weeks' rest, Bob returned to Metro, wiser about the world. His excitement about travel—and his understanding of affect— were evident.

"When people mention the Champs Elysees I can look intelligent. When folks speak of the Place Vendome or the white cliffs of Albion I can adopt that bright expression of one who is in-the-know. I can act discriminating about roast beef and Yorkshire pudding. When the low fogs of California chase me off the tennis court, I can wave it away with dour comments about the pea soup fog of dear ole Lunnon. In other words, I can lie more convincingly now than I ever could before."

Bob's next picture was to be from the Erich Maria Remarque novel *Drei Kameraden, Three Comrades,* which Remarque had written as part of a trilogy that began with *All Quiet on the Western Front* and continued with *The Road Back.*

Three Comrades was about the lost generation of soldiers returning to civilian life in a shamed and defeated Germany after the Great War.

Nazi Germany had condemned Remarque for "cultural internationalism and intellectual treason." Einstein, Freud, Heinrich and Thomas Mann, Heinrich Heine, Bertolt Brecht, even Bertha von Suttner, author of the pacifist novel *Lay Down Your Arms,* were among those blacklisted. Remarque had fled Nazi Germany for Switzerland, just barely escaping arrest. He was "without a country," he said, "like an animal that gets nothing more to eat."

Two months after Remarque left Germany, his novels were burned as students from Wilhelm Humboldt University, participating in a national "Action Against the Un-German Spirit," emptied the library's shelves and hauled truckloads of books to Franz-Joseph-Platz for Säuberung, "public annihilation in the lambent flames of the all-purging Nazi fires." In a torchlight procession, a chain of students passed books hand to hand and threw them on a pyre to burn as a band played marching songs and the names of those whose books were being burned were called out: "Erich Maria Remarque for degrading the German language and the highest patriotic ideal . . . Sigmund Freud for falsifying our history and degrading its great figures."

Before a crowd of forty thousand Germans, Dr. Goebbels, Nazi minister for popular enlightenment and propaganda, proclaimed the death of "the age of Jewish intellectualism . . . National Socialism has hewn the way. The German folk soul can again express itself. The old goes up in flames, the new shall be fashioned from the flames in our hearts . . . Our vow shall be: The Reich and the Nation and our Führer Adolf Hitler."

Throughout Germany—in pyres in Frankfurt, Munich, Breslau, Kiel—more than twenty-five thousand books were destroyed.

The following day Helen Keller wrote in an open letter to German students, "History has taught you nothing if you think you can kill ideas. Tyrants have tried to do that often before, and the ideas have risen up in their might and destroyed them . . .

"Do not imagine your barbarities to the Jews are unknown here. God sleepeth not, and He will visit his Judgement upon you."

A hundred thousand marched in New York City in a six-hour protest that extended from Madison Square Garden to the Battery. Similar protests took place in Philadelphia, Chicago, St. Louis, and other cities.

Remarque was so despondent over leaving Germany that it took him four years to finish *Three Comrades*. The book, finally published in the United States in May 1937 by Little, Brown, had been sold to Metro-Goldwyn-Mayer ten months earlier.

Three Comrades was to start shooting after the first of the year. F. Scott Fitzgerald worked on the script for six months with the picture's producer, Joe Mankiewicz, who brought in Fitzgerald thinking that he would be able to summon up Germany's postwar generation.

The book was set in contemporary Berlin in the 1920s and 1930s—its cabarets and nightlife—a city about to erupt in political upheaval. It was about three friends, former soldiers together, who run a garage. "A slice of life of young people who have often sacrificed something and begun anew," Remarque wrote, describing the novel. "People who have to fight hard for their existence. People without illusions who nevertheless know that comradeship is everything and fate is nothing."

Fitzgerald's script was long and slow, and Mankiewicz hired Edward Paramore to collaborate and help shape the pages. Paramore's first big writing job was on *The Bitter Tea of General Yen*. The collaboration between him and Fitzgerald was not a happy one ("Ted," Fitzgerald wrote to him, "when you blandly informed me yesterday that you were going to write the whole thing over yourself, kindly including my best scenes, I knew we'd have to have this out"). Both Fitzgerald and Paramore received screen credit for the script. Joe Mankiewicz rewrote what became the final script. Fitzgerald, reading one of Mankiewicz's changes, wrote, "This isn't writing. This is Joe Mankiewicz. So slick—so cheap."

Bob Taylor's comrades in the picture were to be Spencer Tracy and Jimmy Stewart. Joan Crawford was to be in it as well but backed out, thinking that the male stars would overwhelm the picture; Luise Rainer was to appear in Crawford's stead.

Metro announced that Bob was to star in *Northwest Passage* with Spencer Tracy; W. S. Van Dyke, who'd worked with Bob on three pictures—*Broadway Melody of 1936, His Brother's Wife,* and *Personal Property*—was to direct.

Bob had just been named the second most popular movie star of 1937 after Gable (and Myrna Loy) in a nationwide poll of fifty-five newspapers conducted by the Chicago Tribune–New York News Syndicate. Tyrone Power followed, with William Powell, Nelson Eddy, and Spencer Tracy bringing up the rear. After Loy came Loretta Young, Jeanette MacDonald, with Barbara, still on suspension from RKO, fourth in the poll. Sonja Henie and Shirley Temple followed.

As Christmas was approaching, Barbara and Bob saw friends. Bob didn't like nightclubs, parties, "that hey-hey stuff," as he called it. He liked to take

With Bob and his mother, Ruth Brugh, circa 1937. (PHOTOFEST)

trips in the car and ride horses. He and Barbara, with Zeppo's clients the Fred MacMurrays and the Ray Millands, spent evenings playing Quotations, the most popular game in Hollywood. The player would take a quotation, a slogan, or a title and act it out for his or her team. Bob, one night, was on the same team as Barbara and was having trouble with a difficult quotation. "What's the matter," said Barbara, "can't you act?"

Four days before Christmas, Barbara was served with a subpoena by the sheriff's office. It was an order to appear at city hall before the Los Angeles Superior Court on December 28 to show why she had violated her custody agreement of 1935 or face contempt charges.

It wasn't Dion Fay wanted to see; he was determined to get to Barbara and implicate Bob Taylor in a public scandal. Barbara knew Fay was trying to see Dion to "harass and annoy" her into changing their property settlement.

Her response: "I'll fight him all the way."

She was determined not to allow Dion to be a "little emotional football tossed about this way and that. I can't," she said.

Barbara went on with her Christmas plans as scheduled.

Bob gave his mother a Christmas present of a trip to Idaho Falls to spend the holiday with relatives. Barbara referred to her as a "miserable old bitch" and started arguments with Ruth who didn't know what to say or how to respond.

Ruth often complained to Bob that she was frail and sickly; she controlled her son through her constant illnesses and the threat of her imminent death.

Before she left for Idaho, Ruth and Bob and Barbara had Christmas dinner and unwrapped presents around the tree. Among the presents Bob gave Barbara was a cow that mooed when its tail was pulled. Barbara gave Bob a set of magic tricks. On Christmas Day, they went with Marion and Zeppo to the fourth annual Christmas Stakes at the Santa Anita racetrack on the old Lucky Baldwin ranch. Dion stayed at home with Nanny, as he usually did.

The Santa Anita track was considered the most luxurious and, since its opening, had attracted the country's best horses: Cavalcade, Time Supply, Top's Boy, Equipoise, Twenty Grand, Seabiscuit. The track was the talk of the country. Santa Anita was the place to be on Christmas: Spencer Tracy, Jeanette MacDonald, Gene Raymond, Anthony Quinn and his new bride, Katherine DeMille, were there, as were Edward Arnold and his son; Virginia Bruce and her husband, the writer and director J. Walter Ruben; George Raft and Virginia Pine. Also watching the Christmas Stakes were the Leo McCareys, the Ernst Lubitsches, the Darryl Zanucks, and the Clarence Browns.

Loretta Young was giving a Christmas party for the Sisters of Nazareth Orphanage—she'd decorated the tree herself—and wasn't at the track.

Bing Crosby's High Strike won the opening race—the $5,000 Christmas Mile—as forty-eight thousand fans cheered on. High Strike was now in the company of Cornelius Vanderbilt Whitney's High Glee, who'd taken the prize the first year of the Christmas Mile; Bert Baroni's Top Row and Goldeneye had won it the two succeeding years.

One of Marwyck's horses came in first, and Barbara, still on suspension at RKO, said, "I'm glad someone in the family is working."

Myron Selznick was there with Ginger Rogers to watch his horse Pasha run in the sixth race. Pasha was scratched, but He Did, who'd triumphed in the 1936 Santa Anita Derby, led the field practically all the way and won by a length and a half.

Three days after Christmas, Barbara went down to city hall, accompanied by Marion and Zeppo Marx. Marion and Barbara looked so much alike spectators mistook Marion for Barbara.

Barbara entered Judge Knight's courtroom to defend herself against charges by Fay that she had refused to permit him to visit their son. Barbara was sick with a cold and headache and was exhausted from lack of sleep, pacing the floor throughout the night and falling asleep only hours before she had to get up. The courtroom was overflowing with spectators. Barbara sat in the last row wearing a black fedora, a mink coat, and under it a gray tailored suit and blouse.

She listened as Fay testified: "I wasn't in favor of a divorce in the first place, but . . ." Judge Knight cut him off. "That will do," the judge said. "This hearing has nothing to do with the divorce case."

The judge asked Fay if it would be agreeable for him to visit the boy at Barbara's house.

"I think my presence in her house might be difficult for both of us," said Fay. "I would like to have the boy brought to my Brentwood Heights home. I have everything fixed up so he could enjoy himself. I have a nursery and I would engage a nurse for him."

Then it was Barbara's turn to take the witness stand. Fay's lawyer asked her, "Isn't the reason you are barring Mr. Fay from visiting the child because you want the boy to become accustomed to someone else—say Robert Taylor, for instance?"

"No," answered Barbara.

"Wasn't it a fact that you were having Mr. Taylor to your house frequently so that the child would forget Fay?"

"Certainly not. Mr. Taylor was at the house frequently, but it was not so the boy would forget Fay," she said.

"Did not Mr. Taylor give the boy gifts on numerous occasions?"

"Yes."

Fay's lawyer asked her about a check for $50 that had been made out to Dion and signed by Taylor.

The judge had the question withdrawn.

"I was trying to show that a deliberate attempt was being made to alienate this boy's affections from his father," said Fay's lawyer to Judge Knight.

"I don't care how many times Mr. Taylor came to her house," said Knight. "This is her personal life and has nothing to do with this proceeding."

Barbara's personal life was the sole reason Fay had brought the court order against her.

Barbara testified before the courtroom that Fay was unfit to spend time with their son. She told the court about Fay's drinking, about how he hadn't wanted to adopt a child, that Fay had failed to show up in court for the adoption proceedings, and that she'd threatened to leave him if he didn't appear with her in court for the legal proceedings. She testified how once they had the boy, Fay's anger frightened the child; how Fay had pushed the boy so that he had fallen on the ground; that Fay used vile language in front of the boy and was "wandering around the house and his condition was none too good," she said; and how she saw Fay leaving the nursery when he was drunk. "I found the carpet beneath my son's crib burned from a cigarette stub," Barbara testified.

She testified about Fay's bouts of violence, about how at the Trocadero he had accused her of drinking too much champagne and knocked her down. "I only had one glass of champagne," she said.

She told the court about how Fay had become upset because "she'd had dinner at the home of Mr. and Mrs. Marx and then," after she had accompanied "them to Minsky's burlesque," how Fay "had struck" her "with his fist here," pointing to her chin. "I fell over a chair," she testified. "The baby was much upset."

Then Barbara's lawyer, Charles Cradick, asked Fay if he recalled an incident at his home in Brentwood when he was "gathered at the side of the pool with the nurse and baby." He wanted to know if Fay had "asked the nurse to place the baby in the water" despite her protests that the child was frightened of water; if Fay had "picked up the child and tossed him into the pool."

Fay's lawyer intervened, and through technicalities he was not required to answer the question, though he did say about Dion, "I just want to see the little fellow, and they can have the marines there if they want."

Fay hadn't seen Dion in sixteen months. He blamed Barbara for their divorce; she'd insisted on it against his wishes. He said he hadn't contributed to Dion's support because Barbara hadn't asked him to.

Cradick proceeded to file ten affidavits with Judge Knight. There were sworn statements by Barbara, Dion's nurse, Fay's chauffeur and his wife, about Fay and Barbara's marriage; about Fay's erratic and violent behavior; about how he'd toppled onto Dion's crib and shouted at the boy and frightened him; and about how, after the separation, Fay's only interest in the child was to find out information about Barbara, whom she was seeing and what she was doing.

Judge Knight called the charges against Fay serious. Fay's attorneys protested. Judge Knight recessed the case until January in order to give Fay and his lawyers a chance to build a reply to Barbara's charges against him.

As a once motherless child, Barbara had said at different times that no one had been there, no one to fight her battles. She'd chosen to star in four pictures about mother love: the devoted mother in *Forbidden* protecting her illicit child; the mother in *So Big* struggling on a hardscrabble farm to earn a living for her son and build an empire for his future; a frantic woman willing to trade her body to find her lost baby in *Internes Can't Take Money;* and, as Stella Dallas, a sacrificing mother willing to relinquish her daughter's love for the child's happiness.

Sam Goldwyn had questioned Barbara's ability to feel the part of Stella Dallas.

Testifying before Judge Goodwin Knight in Superior Court regarding Fay's visitation rights of Dion. January 1938.

"Have you ever suffered over a child?" he'd asked her.

"No, but I can imagine how it would be," she'd answered.

Now Barbara was locked in a real-life fight to protect herself and her boy. She and Bob were together for the New Year to welcome in 1938.

When the custody case resumed days later, it was standing room only in the courtroom. Barbara took the stand. She testified that Fay was unfit to see her little boy, that he'd endangered the child's well-being while they lived together. Her lawyer, Charles Cradick, requested that Fay be examined by a psychiatrist. Fay laughed in response. Fay's attorney Philip Stein said, "We question Miss Stanwyck's fitness to keep the child, and we think it would be a good idea to have a psychiatrist examine her."

Barbara testified that she didn't believe Fay was insane when she was his wife. "And I don't think he is insane now."

Barbara sat aloof and erect. She told the court, though, about Fay's peculiar rituals when lighting a cigarette, of folding his hands, closing his eyes, and muttering a prayer; how he did the same as he passed a church, even when driving a car, frequently letting go of the steering wheel to pray and often narrowly avoiding a crash; how his newspaper reading was punctuated with profanity about murder stories and prayers over reports of death; how he had chased a doctor with a knife from their house; and how he'd been in and out of sanitariums.

On cross-examination Barbara admitted that the many things she accused Fay of—throwing Dion in the pool and saying prayers over cigarettes—had happened while they were married.

Fay's lawyer said to the court, "Miss Stanwyck is being prompted in her answers by counsel."

Barbara's attorney stood, his face flushed. "I just want to say, mister, that you are a liar." Cradick was on the verge of hitting Stein.

Judge Knight called for order and suggested both lawyers stay away from personalities.

Fay's attorney continued with his cross-examination.

Barbara admitted that when she and Fay went through an elaborate church wedding on their seventh wedding anniversary, she hadn't loved him. "He promised to quit drinking and live a different life if I would remarry him in his church," said Barbara. "His church seemed to mean so much to him that I agreed to give up the Protestant faith and remarry him in a church ceremony. We were married on a Friday in Sierra Madre. On Monday he came home drunk. I saw that it meant very little to him after all, so I left him."

"Was he celebrating his wedding, perhaps?" asked Fay's attorney.

"I hardly think so," said Barbara. "The wedding was on Friday and he waited until Sunday to start drinking."

She was asked if it was true that she owned fifty racehorses and if she'd spent most of Christmas Day at the races instead of at home with her child.

Barbara lowered her head and nodded.

Fay was the final witness. He took the stand and told the judge he hadn't had a drink until he was twenty-one; that he'd been drunk "about fifteen times in my life. But, Judge, I have been absolutely 'on the wagon' for the last year." He admitted he prayed over cigarettes but said he "always held on to the cigarette so nobody could snatch it while" he was praying. As to the question of throwing Dion in the pool and almost drowning him, Fay said, "Even Man Mountain Dean couldn't drown under those conditions. [Dion] was a big, husky, overweight kid, big enough to push me in. All I did was to fix him in one of those contraptions so he couldn't sink and put him in the water."

Judge Knight handed down his decision days later. Fay was given the right to visit Dion at Barbara's house each Tuesday from 9:00 a.m. to 5:00 p.m.

Frank Fay at Marwyck, showing that he is attempting to gain entrance to see his son, 1937.

and was given custody of the boy, who was to be accompanied by his nurse, one weekend each month from 9:00 a.m. Saturday until 5:00 p.m. Sunday. If Fay had liquor on him "externally or internally," he was not to see the child, nor was he to have any friends present who had been drinking.

Fay was all smiles. "I won everything I asked for," he said.

Barbara showed no emotion.

Her lawyer filed an appeal with the state supreme court on uncontradicted evidence offered in court that Fay had planned to kidnap Dion and take him out of the state. Cradick thought the appeal would keep Fay away until it was heard. Judge Knight issued Fay an official order granting him the right to visit his son. Cradick advised Barbara in writing not to comply with the court order to let Fay see Dion, saying, "The appeal automatically nullifies the order."

Dion was to be brought to Fay's house for a visit at 9:00 a.m. on Saturday. The time came and went without Dion's arrival.

One of Fay's lawyers said that after the weekend they would go to Barbara's house and demand to see the "child in accordance with the court order.

If we are refused there," said Hy Schwartz, "we will demand that the appeal he dismissed and seek a contempt of court citation against Miss Stanwyck."

Barbara received thousands of letters and wires from supporters telling her that her court fight with Fay would not hurt her at the box office. Other well-wishers drove to her ranch and dropped letters in her mailbox.

A few days later, Fay and his attorneys traveled to Northridge and appeared at the gates of Marwyck. They got as far as the barn; a servant had been ordered not to let anybody in and told Fay he couldn't enter the grounds. Fay stood outside the Stanwyck property, blocked by its surrounding wall.

In addition to losing the custody battle for Dion, Barbara was still on suspension for refusing to make *Distant Fields* (released as *Married and in Love*). Her argument was with Jesse Lasky.

"It was the difference of opinion of an artist and a producer," said Barbara. The script was too similar to "the aging woman role" of *Stella Dallas*. "The two roles would tend to type me," she said. "I understand they've already got someone else to play the part."

RKO wrote off the cost of developing *Distant Fields* for Barbara—more than $34,000.

"I am really the loser," said Barbara. "They have taken me off the payroll temporarily and I am being disciplined for not obeying orders."

TEN

Wins and Losses

Somebody told me the other day," said Barbara, "that Bette Davis and I were the most suspended people in pictures, and wanted to know why we argued so. I don't know about Bette, but the reason I argue is because I believe in myself."

Davis, just finished shooting *Jezebel,* was eager to make a picture about the legendary nineteenth-century French actress Rachel from a Jean Negulesco script already at Warner. Davis had won an Academy Award for *Dangerous.* She was being critically recognized and celebrated, with large box-office receipts, though she'd been described as "loaded with ice-cold New England sex." Davis was about to turn thirty. She'd had it with "haggling" over scripts and money.

A week after Davis finished *Jezebel,* Hal Wallis sent her a script for a Busby Berkeley picture, *Comet over Broadway,* about a small-town girl married to a garage owner who, to help her husband, becomes a Broadway success. Davis was incensed. "I know that every star has her night," she said, "but I wasn't prepared to kill myself off in one fell swoop." She refused to make the picture. Kay Francis took the part. Warner next sent Davis a script for another Berkeley production, this one called *Garden of the Moon,* about a girl who works as a secretary for a nightclub manager and is caught between the manager and an unknown bandleader whom she hires and who soon becomes famous.

The second Berkeley script was enough for Davis to prepare for a good fight. She'd just returned from a six-week unpaid "rest period," actually recovering from an abortion; it was William Wyler's child. Their affair had ended, and he had married. The script for *Garden of the Moon* was sent back to Wallis, and Margaret Lindsay was cast as the girl. Davis went into combat with the studio, combat that she viewed as "damn good character development."

She appeared on the cover of *Time* magazine, but rather than help her cause, Wallis put her on suspension the day after the magazine hit the newsstands.

Warner Bros. took out a full-page ad in *Motion Picture Daily* for Davis's new hit picture, *Jezebel*. Next to it was another full-page ad from Warner Bros. that read, "Bette Davis Suspended." Wallis appealed to the Screen Actors Guild to intervene; it refused. Davis remained on suspension for four weeks until she was sent a script for *The Sisters*, originally bought for Kay Francis, to be directed by Anatole Litvak.

Barbara would have loved to have played the lead in *Jezebel*. She saw Davis in it and called Warner and said to the operator, "This is Barbara Stanwyck. I know it doesn't mean anything to Bette Davis but I want to tell her how much I admired her in *Jezebel*."

The operator rang Miss Davis's room and came back on the line and said, "So sorry, Miss Stanwyck. Miss Davis is sleeping and can't be disturbed."

Barbara called the studio the next day and again asked to speak to Miss Davis. Again she was told, "Miss Davis is sleeping. Miss Stanwyck, do you care to leave a message?"

"Oh, don't bother," Barbara said. "Miss Davis is evidently rehearsing for Snow White."

Barbara, still on suspension, sent Holly on vacation to a dude ranch. Barbara was desperate to work. She had to work to keep happy. "They could work me every day and I'd love it," she said. Barbara knew what parts were right for her and what weren't, what she could do and what she couldn't, and she "wasn't afraid to say, 'Wait a minute, this stinks.' "

The Santa Anita racetrack, in addition to the $10,000 San Juan Capistrano Handicap, added a new feature, the Marwyck purse, a grade D allowance event. As a result the six-furlong training track at Marwyck was being remodeled; sand-soil was being used, the same kind of soil being used at the new two million dollar dream track in Inglewood, Hollywood Park.

A Yank at Oxford previewed toward the end of January. Bob and Barbara were there, as were his mother and grandmothers.

The lead was a new kind of role for Bob. In place of the beautiful, sophisticated lover, Metro presented Bob as the exuberant, virile young man—a brash, boyish athletic American from the Midwest who runs, rows, and fights and who blunders, Stars and Stripes, into the tradition-bound world of ancient Oxford. Reviewers who formerly, but politely, dismissed Bob as a mere beauty now talked about his work seriously and called his portrait of the cocky American athlete abroad "disarming." Howard Barnes wrote, "Judging on this performance, it is my suspicion that Mr. Taylor may be an actor."

Bob started work on *Three Comrades.*

Less than a week into production, Hitler's long-feared *Anschluss* took place as his army forces massed along the German-Bavarian frontier, preceded by thousands of uniformed Nazi storm troopers, exiled Austrian Nazis, and other Nazi Party workers, who took control of village after Austrian village. Hitler installed an Austrian Nazi cabinet and a new minister of the interior, who announced, "Austria free and independent." Austria ceased to exist and was merged with Germany. Jubilant Viennese Nazis by the tens of thousands shouted, "One Reich—one Führer."

In December, when the script for *Three Comrades* was being written, Joseph Breen received a letter from Dr. George Gyssling, consul of Germany: "As [*Three Comrades*] deals with conditions as they allegedly existed in Germany after the war and during the 'inflation period,' I would be grateful to you if you would give this matter your attention, so that future difficulties might be avoided. With my best wishes for a happy and prosperous New Year, I remain . . ." Early in January, Breen wrote to Metro-Goldwyn-Mayer saying, "The story, while dramatically sound and entertaining is, inescapably, a serious indictment of the German nation and people and is certainly to be violently resisted by the present government of that country." The scenes about anti-Semitism were removed from the script, as were any portrayals of Nazi brutalities and the lines "Here is one country where a Jew is not homeless—where the Fatherland belongs to him as well as to the others. For that I am proud and happy."

The picture was set a year or two after the Great War rather than in 1930. Breen suggested the Communists be the heavies instead of the Nazis; Nazi uniforms were not to be shown, nor was the swastika; the script was not to mention Felix Mendelssohn, whose music had been banned in Germany by the Nazi regime by virtue of his being Jewish. Metro's longtime cameraman Joe Ruttenberg, an American, replaced Karl Freund. Franz Waxman, who scored the picture, asked to have his name omitted from all publicity for "personal reasons." Despite the request, his name remained on the picture's credits.

Bob, under Barbara's tutelage, turned to radio: she for the work; he to be showcased. Barbara appeared on NBC's *Chase and Sanborn Hour,* then in the title role of *Anna Christie* and a week later in O'Neill's early play *The Straw,* inspired by his six-month stay in his early twenties at a tuberculosis sanitarium. O'Neill agreed to sell for $500 the rights to a ten-minute excerpt of the play—the first time he ever granted radio broadcast rights. The show's advertising agency, J. Walter Thompson, guaranteed the playwright that it would use Barbara for the young woman.

The Straw was about a girl at a TB hospital who falls in love with a writer there (Don Ameche) who does not return her feelings. She wastes away after he is cured and leaves, and when he returns he gives her one straw of hope for life: the promise of his love as he sees that he does indeed love her.

Barbara was powerful as the consumptive Irish girl.

Bob Taylor hosted the Maxwell House–Metro program called *Good News of 1938,* a showcase for Metro actors and actresses. Other Metro stars, such as James Stewart and Robert Young, rotated as the show's host. Each week the show featured the dramatization of a new Metro picture with its stars. Jack Benny appeared one week and stole the show from everyone else ("This show needs all the help I can give it," Benny said as part of the gag). Bob did bits with his *Yank at Oxford* co-star, Maureen O'Sullivan, and director, Jack Conway. Allan Jones sang "My Heaven on Earth," and Fanny Brice was Baby Snooks.

Other actors were appearing on radio as well. Jeanette MacDonald, Nelson Eddy, Tyrone Power, Claire Trevor, and Rosalind Russell appeared on consecutive weekly shows. Bette Davis, Eleanor Powell, Randolph Scott, and Olivia de Havilland were on *The Campbell Playhouse;* Frances Farmer, Gary Cooper, Joan Bennett, and Robert Montgomery appeared on *Lux Radio Theatre;* Leslie Howard on *Texaco Star Theatre.*

Radio didn't really hold much interest for Bob; he had no desire to become "a radio personality," he said, "like a Jack Benny or a Don Ameche."

Bob appeared at a fund-raiser at the Warner Bros. Hollywood Theatre in honor of the late comedian Ted Healy, who had died December 21, 1937. In the show were Judy Garland, Bob Hope, Al Jolson, Roy Bolger, Fanny Brice, Martha Raye, Spencer Tracy, and Jack Benny. Healy had been named in the custody suit against Barbara; a few years before he'd become irritated by Fay's behavior over his set of brand-new teeth and punched Fay so hard that Fay's uppers and lowers were knocked out of his mouth. Fay and Healy had stopped fighting long enough to look for Fay's teeth. Despite the fracas, Fay was one of the pallbearers at Healy's funeral.

Barbara's suspension at RKO was finally over. It had cost her more than $75,000, her salary per picture. Her new RKO contract, in conjunction with Fox for five additional pictures, was to go into effect in March 1938. She was to make two pictures for Fox during the first and last three months of the year and one picture for RKO in between. Fox paid RKO $55,000 for the first picture, $60,000 for the second, and $65,000 for the third.

No sooner did Barbara go off suspension than her house at Marwyck was robbed of almost $10,000 worth of jewelry, furs, and clothing.

"Those seven months away from the studio I didn't know what to do with myself," said Barbara. "But if the same argument came up tomorrow, I'd probably go on another suspension."

Barbara was to be one of the stars in *The Saint in New York,* from the Leslie Charteris novel about a celebrated rogue, Simon Templar, a.k.a. the Saint, foe of criminals and the law, "a twentieth-century privateer," whose clear idea of justice inspires him to pilfer from the rich to help the poor.

In the novel, Templar comes to New York to bust up a criminal organization protected by corrupt politicians. Charteris—Leslie Charles Bowyer-Yin, the son of a Chinese father and English mother, who grew up in the British Crown Colony of Singapore—like Simon Templar, was forever the outsider. *The Saint in New York* revealed a darker, more violent Templar.

The story had originally been bought for Fredric March. The role of the girl had been built up by Charles Kaufman and Irwin Shaw. Kaufman had worked uncredited on the script of Barbara's previous picture, RKO's *Breakfast for Two.*

For the first time in her eight years in pictures, Barbara was nominated for an Academy Award for her work in *Stella Dallas.* The nomination by the academy was vindication of the work she'd put into the picture and of her triumph over her childhood and the years she'd defied Hollywood's indirect dismissal of her.

Marion and Zeppo Marx gave a party in honor of his client Moss Hart, in town for the opening at the Biltmore Theatre of his comedy *You Can't Take It with You.* Hart was in Los Angeles to see if the company needed a rehearsal after its three-thousand-mile trek following a fifteen-week run in Boston. It didn't; the cast was giving a "flawless performance," he said.

For the Marxes' party, Hart brought along his movie camera and asked people to act scenes: Carole Lombard and Gable, Phyllis Brooks and Cary Grant, Barbara and Bob.

Hart and Barbara talked about her nomination, about awards and plaques.

"You won't get one," he said to Barbara.

"I won't? How do you know?" she asked.

"Because you make things look too easy."

She did make it look easy; it was her skill as an actress, her ability to tell the truth. She knew that honesty was her draw. She was able to use her shoals of loss and regret, her feelings of being an orphan, the outsider, her big emotions—highs and lows always, as she said—her sexual tension and control, a lifetime of defiance and daring, her need to connect and deliver perfection, and focus these things, adapt them, to create women on the screen whom audiences admired and knew to be true.

As Capra said, when she turned it on and went into an emotional scene, she carried others along like specks on a wave; actors blew their lines and watched her; grips and electricians stopped what they were doing and teared up.

Barbara was the favorite to win the Academy Award for Best Actress against the other nominees: Janet Gaynor for *A Star Is Born;* Irene Dunne in *The Awful Truth;* Greta Garbo in *Camille;* and Luise Rainer for *The Good Earth.* Gaynor, thirty-one, Greta Garbo, a year older, and Barbara were all of an age. Dunne was at the extraordinary age for a romantic ingenue of thirty-nine; Rainer, the youngest, was twenty-eight.

Gaynor had been nominated and won ten years earlier in 1929—the first year of the academy's awards—for her performance in *Seventh Heaven.* Irene Dunne had been nominated in 1931 for the epic saga of the Oklahoma land rush *Cimarron;* Marie Dressler had taken home the statuette for *Min and Bill.* Garbo had just won her second New York Film Critics Circle Award for *Camille.* Luise Rainer had received the Academy Award for Best Actress the previous year, at age twenty-seven, for playing Anna Held, the legendary musical-comedy star, in *The Great Ziegfeld.*

The scene that won Rainer the award in her second American movie was one in which she is on-screen alone, talking on the telephone with her former husband, Florenz Ziegfeld (Louis B. Mayer found the scene "dreary" and tried to cut it). Rainer had seen Cocteau's play *La voix humaine,* in which a woman talks on the telephone for the entire one-act, and used it to rewrite the scene, telling the director, Robert Z. Leonard, to "do it in one take."

In the scene, Held desperately hopes for and believes that Ziegfeld's phone call will lead to a reconciliation; instead, she learns that their life together is over. Rainer, ever wistful, with enormous haunted eyes, played it with a frenetic stillness like the dying Odette from Petipa's *Swan Lake.* ("I never acted," Rainer said. "I felt everything.") Audiences wept, as did the jaded studio electricians on the soundstage catwalks at Metro who watched Rainer shoot the scene.

Rainer had fled Vienna in 1935, at the age of twenty-five, with the rise of the Nazi Party, despite having been given the special title Honorary Aryan (she'd instructed the brown-shirted soldier-stagehands to get rid of their "blasted boots and [wear] slippers as stagehands normally do"). Rainer had been in America only two years before winning the Academy Award for her portrayal of Held ("I never dreamed of becoming a movie actress," she said).

She mystified Hollywood; she defied simple analysis. At sixteen, Rainer left behind her upper-middle-class bourgeois family (her father was an oil and soybean importer-exporter) to become an actress—"a low and vulgar profession," her father had called it—and she'd flourished in Max Reinhardt's repertory company "playing something else every night surrounded by great artists."

The academy's award, Rainer claimed, was of no interest to her. ("In Europe we did not need these accolades," she said.) Her interests lay elsewhere. She wanted good scripts and better parts, though to her, acting in pictures was not acting.

Capra, as president of the academy, had dissolved its nominating committee of fifty men and opened the vote to all members of the guild, whether they belonged to the academy or not. For the first time, the Screen Actors Guild was actively involved with the proceedings; in addition, extras were allowed to vote for Best Picture, Best Acting, and Best Song. Instead of a vote of eight hundred, the awards were to be voted on by fifteen thousand, and it was impossible to predict how they would cast their ballots.

The academy's banquet awards ceremony at the Biltmore Bowl was originally set for Thursday, March 3. The evening was postponed due to severe storms that caught many involved with the ceremony in the floods, among them Capra, who was marooned in Malibu. The banquet's hundreds of dollars' worth of flowers were donated to hospitals.

A week later, on the evening of the awards dinner at the Biltmore Bowl, extras stood outside the affair due to the exorbitant cost of tickets at $15 per couple; inside, the eighteen hundred seats were filled.

Mrs. Spencer Tracy was there to represent her husband, recuperating from appendicitis at Good Samaritan Hospital. Tracy was nominated for outstanding performance for his role in *Captains Courageous,* Metro's most financially successful picture of the year and *Photoplay*'s most popular. Fredric March, nominated as Best Actor for his performance in *A Star Is Born,* was east, recuperating with his wife, Florence Eldridge, from their aborted Broadway run of *Yr. Obedient Husband.*

Paul Muni, nominated for outstanding performance for *The Life of Emile Zola,* made sure to be out of town. He'd won the Academy Award the year before for best performance for *The Story of Louis Pasteur* and wanted to steel himself against the inevitable. "It will be less embarrassing for everybody," Muni said, "if I'm in Palestine or Greece. Nobody wins two years in a row."

Greta Garbo was absent from the proceedings, traveling abroad; she'd spent Christmas in Sweden with her family on the thousand-acre estate outside Stockholm that she'd bought for her mother and brother. She had then traveled to Rome to join Leopold Stokowski, conductor of the Philadelphia Orchestra, for a month together in Ravello at a villa overlooking the Bay of Salerno. "No, no—I will not marry Mr. Stokowski," Garbo had told the press before leaving America.

As for performances that the academy had overlooked, Carole Lombard's in the antic *Nothing Sacred* was among them ("You wanted comedy," Selznick had wired to Jock Whitney. "Boy you're going to get it, and be it on your own head"). Lombard was nominated the previous year as the screwball sensation of *My Man Godfrey* and had lost to Luise Rainer.

Comedy and comic actors and actresses were rarely recognized for their work by the academy. Lombard saw comedy as more difficult than heavy roles. "In a straight role," she said, "you react as you would in life—in comedy, you have to do the unexpected."

Cary Grant's work in *The Awful Truth*—his first real shot at comedy in pictures—was also overlooked, though the movie received six nominations, among them Ralph Bellamy for Best Supporting Actor, Viña Delmar for best-written screenplay, and Leo McCarey for Best Direction.

McCarey had preceded *The Awful Truth* with another picture made earlier in the year for Paramount called *Make Way for Tomorrow*, a film much closer to the director's heart. The McCarey pictures were opposites in every way except for their humanness; each was from a screenplay by Viña Delmar in collaboration with McCarey. For *The Awful Truth*, McCarey had his actors improvise, invent bits of business, and rewrite scenes.

McCarey, at thirty-nine, had directed eighty-odd pictures, including *Six of a Kind* with W. C. Fields, *Duck Soup* with the Marx Brothers, and *Belle of the Nineties* with Mae West, as well as more than three hundred shorts for Hal Roach (McCarey had brought together Stan Laurel and Oliver Hardy as a comedy team). He was considered one of the funniest directors at work, writing each day's shooting on the set after playing ragtime for an hour or two. He was an irresistible storyteller who liked a "little bit of the fairy tale" and thought that someone else "should photograph the ugliness of the world."

Make Way for Tomorrow was an exception, a labor of love for McCarey: his father had just died when he made the picture, and the director took a cut in salary to make the film. It was about "old folks" and the burden they become for their children. The elderly couple was Victor Moore and Beulah Bondi (at forty-eight and athletic, Bondi was far from the elderly, frail woman she'd made a career of playing for two decades).

In the picture, Ma and Pa are forced to live apart (she with their daughter; he with their son). Pa refuses to accept that he can no longer find work and support his wife. Their adult children are torn between their love and sense of duty for their parents and their need to have their own families.

Ma and Pa meet one last time: she is being sent away to the old-age home; he to California to live with another daughter. They meet in New York City at the same hotel where, fifty years before, they'd spent their honeymoon. When they say good-bye at the train station—Pa promising to get a job and send for Ma—they know it will be the last time they see each other.

The picture was called "one of the finest films to come out of Hollywood in years." It was hailed for its "three qualities rarely encountered in the cinema: humanity, honesty and warmth." Orson Welles said of it, "My God, it's the most moving picture; a stone would cry."

Despite its critical acclaim, it did little business at the box office, and Paramount bought out McCarey's contract. He was out on the streets until he was hired by Columbia to make *The Awful Truth*.

Robert Montgomery was in attendance at the academy banquet in two guises: as a nominee for best performance in Emlyn Williams's suspense thriller, *Night Must Fall* (Louis B. Mayer had objected to the project from the outset, saying, "We make pretty pictures"; despite that, *Night Must Fall* received two nominations); and as the president of the Screen Actors Guild.

King Vidor was representing the Screen Directors Guild; Dudley Nichols, the Screen Writers Guild.

Under Capra's leadership, the academy had voted for a new charter that removed itself from any further involvement with labor-management disputes; as a result, Nichols agreed to accept the Oscar for *The Informer* that he'd turned down two years before.

The first part of the awards evening—the banquet—ended at 10:30. The awards ceremony followed. Bob "Bazooka" Burns, the Arkansas Sage, filled in as master of ceremonies for George Jessel, who was sick.

Frank Capra introduced Cecil B. DeMille, one of the academy's original founders ten years before and a director of the board, who announced that the academy was "free of all labor struggles" and continued to speak for the next thirty-five minutes.

For the first time, the names of the winners of the twenty-one awards had been kept secret from those guests seated in the packed Biltmore Bowl. Some learned who the winners would be from the reporters and newspapermen in the audience who had been told at 8:35.

A new award was to be presented, the Irving G. Thalberg Memorial Award, in honor of the late producer. The award, a bronze bust of Thalberg mounted on a marble base, was to be given for "the most consistent high quality of production achievement by an individual producer, based on pictures he has produced during the preceding year." Those in the running were Darryl F. Zanuck, Hunt Stromberg, David O. Selznick, Pandro Berman, and Samuel Goldwyn.

Zanuck had made fifteen pictures for the year, including *In Old Chicago* and *Wee Willie Winkie* as well as Barbara and Bob's *This Is My Affair.* Stromberg crashed through with *Maytime* and *Night Must Fall.* Selznick had *A Star Is Born, The Prisoner of Zenda,* and *Nothing Sacred.* Pandro Berman, *Stage Door, A Damsel in Distress,* and *Shall We Dance.* Samuel Goldwyn had released *Dead End, The Hurricane, Woman Chases Man,* and *Stella Dallas.*

The Thalberg Award committee was chaired by Capra and included Lionel Atwill, Jean Hersholt, Henry King, William Wellman, Robert Riskin, Leo McCarey, and Douglas Shearer. Capra wanted Zanuck to receive the award. Zanuck was head of 20th Century–Fox and, more immediately important, head of the producers committee negotiating with the Screen Directors Guild; Zanuck's receiving the award might make him sympathetic to the directors then negotiating with the producers.

Hal Wallis, head of production at Warner Bros., wanted the award for himself, but if he wasn't going to get it, as a loyal Warner employee he certainly didn't want it to go to Zanuck; nor did Wallis's boss, Jack Warner, who was still sore about Zanuck's walking out of the studio in protest over the way the brothers had handled the 1933 salary crisis.

Despite Warner's objections, the Thalberg Award committee voted to give the award to Zanuck, and it was presented to him during the awards ceremony by Douglas Fairbanks Sr.

The Life of Emile Zola, Warner's most successful picture of the year, won as outstanding production; Spencer Tracy won for *Captains Courageous.* Louis B. Mayer accepted the award and said, "It is a privilege to be the stand-in for Spencer Tracy. Tracy is a fine actor, but he is most important because he understands why it is necessary to take orders from the front office."

Capra presented the Best Director Award and said, "A director must strive always to make great pictures and think of something besides their salaries." The award went to Leo McCarey for *The Awful Truth.* McCarey, still wounded by the fate of *Make Way for Tomorrow,* accepted the award and said, "Thanks, but you gave it to me for the wrong picture."

Two special comedy awards were given: a miniature wooden statuette to Edgar Bergen "for his outstanding comedy creation," to which Charlie McCarthy, in tuxedo, said, "Carved out of wood! A bit of sarcasm, I suppose . . . Well, thanks, even if it isn't gold. But if you've got a gold one leftover at the end of the night, I'd like to have it"; W. C. Fields presented Mack Sennett, comedy producer, with a standard-size gold-plated statuette as "the master of fun, discoverer of stars, comedy genius . . ." Sennett was each of these things, but his kinds of pictures had passed out of fashion, and the "comedy genius" was out of work and broke.

Joseph Schildkraut, nominated as Best Supporting Actor for his portrayal of Dreyfus in *The Life of Emile Zola,* had been told by his agent not to bother attending the academy banquet, he didn't have a chance; the race was between Ralph Bellamy in *The Awful Truth* and H. B. Warner in *Lost Horizon.* Schildkraut beat out Bellamy and Warner and won for best performance by a supporting actor. Alice Brady won the award for Best Supporting Actress for *In Old Chicago.*

The award for best performance by an actress was being presented by C. Aubrey Smith. Barbara sat there smiling, "her heart pounding in her mouth." Smith announced that the award was to go to Luise Rainer for *The Good Earth.*

The audience was stunned.

No one had ever received the academy award two years in succession. A German Jew as a Chinese peasant, and without much make up, which Rainer had insisted on. Her face on-screen, as still and resolute as the soul of the woman she played, made clear O-Lan's every thought and feeling ("I became Chinese," Rainer said).

When the winner of best performance by an actress was announced, Barbara showed little emotion; she'd steeled herself against another loss. "Human emotions don't change," she'd said, "only situations."

Barbara had experienced too many losses to count on winning the academy's award for her work. She was merciless with the character of Stella, going all the way playing her. She was naked, honest, disturbing. It took courage to go that far with her.

The academy's vote for Rainer was Hollywood voting for its lofty notions of itself, made even more ironic given Rainer's dismissal of movie stardom and what it stood for. ("They call me a Frankenstein that will destroy the studio," she said. "It is more important for me to be a human being than to be an actress.")

Luise Rainer as O-Lan and Paul Muni as Wang Lung in Metro-Goldwyn-Mayer's three-million-dollar epic *The Good Earth,* 1937. The long-anticipated picture had its premiere at the Carthay Circle Theatre, which was done up for the event in thatched huts, fish ponds, and great bronzed Buddhas. Rainer, anxiously awaiting her next part, said, "To have a car, and money, and to do nothing is un-normal."

Rainer had sat at a Metro luncheon next to Bob Taylor and asked him what his ideas were, what he wanted to do, and was stunned when he told her he wanted "ten good suits to wear, elegant suits of all kinds." Rainer's Hollywood society was made up of European refugees living in Los Angeles—Thomas Mann and Erich Remarque—as well as George Gershwin and Harold Arlen.

Her indifference to movie stardom (her costume for *The Good Earth* had cost $1.89), to money, and to Hollywood gave her power as an actress, but it antagonized Metro (Louis B. Mayer had asked her, "Why do you not sit on my lap when we talk contracts, like my other stars do?") and provoked the press. Rainer was written about as being "difficult," "mercurial," "a great artist," "The Girl Who Hates Movies"; she was talked about as "a shrewd, phony, fake, temperamental lady with big eyes and an exaggerated opinion of herself."

Rainer's award was as well a vote for Thalberg's legacy and the production he lovingly oversaw until his sudden death. *The Good Earth* had been in the works for almost eighteen months, using the talents of twenty writers and three directors (the first director committed suicide; the second succumbed to illness; the third stepped in and somehow prevailed). The picture cost $2.5 million (100,000 feet of film were shot in China) and involved five thousand extras, the planting of real farms, and a carved replica of a Chinese landscape with the Great Wall. On the release of *The Good Earth,* it was hailed as "a real cinema epic; one of the great pictures of all time."

Barbara's independence from the studios came at a price. Warner and

Luise Rainer, nominated as Best Actress for *The Good Earth,* at the tenth Academy Awards ceremony with her husband, Clifford Odets. The Biltmore Bowl of the Biltmore Hotel, March 10, 1938. (PHOTOFEST)

Metro had more employees in the academy than any other studio, and it was reflected in the winners.

Rainer, a few days before the ceremony, had taken her husband, the Group Theatre playwright Clifford Odets, to San Francisco to show him the city she loved (he'd not fallen under its spell), and they'd just driven back the afternoon of the academy banquet.

At six that evening Rainer and Odets had a two-hour drive from Santa Barbara to Los Angeles. Odets viewed his wife as "the Thomas Mann of actresses" and told her to forget the awards dinner; he couldn't stomach the commercialism of actors. He and Rainer were written about as "two lonely, shy, music-loving intellectuals [who] spurn the usual glitter of Hollywood nightlife."

Rainer knew that she had to show up at the Biltmore and drove home fighting with Odets the entire time about going to the awards ceremony. Odets was the passion of her life, though he'd said of their idyll, "We married so that God could witness our fights."

Rainer was in jeans and sneakers when the academy committee phoned to tell her she'd won another Oscar. She quickly put on a gown—after arguing with Odets for hours, she felt miserable—and, with Odets in business suit instead of black tie, left for the Biltmore Bowl. They arrived in the rain; Luise was too upset to go in, and with Odets she walked around the hotel four or five times before entering the building.

A smiling, brown-haired, awkwardly dressed Rainer, with little makeup, stood before the Academy of Motion Picture Arts and Sciences and murmured in broken English a frightened, wispy "Thank you very much."

The ceremony ended at 2:00 in the morning.

"My heart's blood was in that film," said Barbara of *Stella Dallas*. "I should have won."

The day following the academy's ceremony, Sidney Skolsky's column was all about Barbara: about how she was under contract to two studios, and had been suspended by each; about how she hadn't permitted success to keep her from being herself; about her best friends, Zeppo and Marion Marx and Joan Crawford (and the jeweled cigarette case given to Barbara by Joan); about her devotion to her son, Dion (it didn't mention that she saw his weight as problematic); about Marwyck; Bob Taylor; about her sleeping habits (her difficulty falling asleep and reading into the night for hours); about her large bedroom, where she had on display photographs of Taylor, Dion, Marion Marx, and Joan Crawford.

ELEVEN

Golden Influences

1938

Barbara was to report to Fox the first week in April but refused to go. The studio announced that she was to make *I'll Give a Million* for Zanuck. He'd decided musicals were dead at the box office and canceled the Ritz Brothers' next musical, *Straight, Place, and Show.* He planned instead to star Barbara with Warner Baxter and Peter Lorre in a Depression fairy-tale version of *The Prince and the Pauper,* in which a millionaire rescues a bum from attempting suicide, takes his clothes, and, pretending to be a tramp, tries to give away a million dollars. It was from an Italian script, adapted for Zanuck by Niven Busch.

Barbara wasn't interested in the story. Zanuck suspended her contract.

A week later, after reading a script by Kathryn Scola and Edith Skouras, Barbara was offered the lead in *Always Goodbye,* a remake of a 20th Century film from four years before.

Always Goodbye, to be directed by Allan Dwan, was a story of mother love and sacrifice with a twist that harked back to Barbara's third movie with Frank Capra, *Forbidden:* the mother is unwed and gives up her baby for the sake of the child. In its theme of noble mother love, *Always Goodbye* was similar to *Stella Dallas,* something Barbara had wanted to avoid for her first serious picture after playing Stella, but the Scola and Skouras screenplay, from the original story by Douglas Doty and the character actor Gilbert Emery, was without moral punishment and redemption and had an interesting angle. Instead of the mother's life becoming dark and poverty-stricken after she gives up her illegitimate child, she becomes a successful, glamorous woman in the haute couture business and rises up from suicidal unwed mother to fully expressed career woman. Her happiness and satisfaction with her life are made only more complete when she accidentally meets her little boy in the lobby of an elegant hotel in Paris and determines to get him back as her son.

The sympathy remained with the movie star even as unwed mother who gives up her child, unlike *Stella Dallas,* where the mother—poor, alone, outside life—gives up her child and the audience roots for her to do so. The script had an unexpected ending as well: the man (Herbert Marshall) who at the start of the picture saves the young mother from drowning is a brilliant surgeon done in by drink and botched dreams. He starts her on her career, and she in turn helps him find himself anew to take his rightful place in his field of medical research. She is in love with him, but he's not the man she marries. Instead, she marries her son's adoptive father, Ian Hunter, whom she does not love.

Scola had written the botched script of *A Lost Lady*; she'd written as well the sharp, clever *Baby Face,* and Barbara trusted her as a writer.

There was nothing predictable about the picture's resolution: the man she loves is a wanderer who travels for years at a time, a periodic drinker, a dazzling scientific researcher with the soul of an artist who has just enough money to get by and more than enough love for her to reclaim his life; by marrying the man she doesn't love, she becomes rich, is the adored object of his genuine affection, and becomes once again—the excuse for the disingenuous choice—the mother of her son.

If there was a moral cost, it was that romance must be forfeited when it comes to mother love.

Stella Dallas and *Always Goodbye* were different enough, but with each the message was clear: virtue is associated with class and money; poverty, with sex and sin.

Barbara needed the income. She was eager to get back to work and agreed to make the picture.

She appeared regularly on the *Lux Radio Theatre* beginning in 1936 with the show's second season. She was on Radio Theater's *Main Street, Stella Dallas,* and *These Three,* and the producers continued to ask her back.

Barbara was interested in doing a dramatization of *Dark Victory* from the George Brewer and Bertram Bloch play that had had a monthlong run on Broadway in 1934. ("A curious stew of mixed vegetables," is how Brooks Atkinson described it.) Tallulah Bankhead was the spoiled, headstrong socialite diagnosed with a brain tumor who marries her doctor and learns by accident that her illness is fatal. The play's demise was due to its weak third act.

Lux Radio Theatre, since its move from New York to Hollywood, had never before presented a play on the air that hadn't been made into a movie. Barbara was intent on doing *Dark Victory* first on radio and then on the screen.

She hoped that the radio broadcast would persuade RKO or Zanuck to buy the rights for her. A society woman dying of brain cancer wasn't an easy idea to sell to any studio; in addition, it was not a Zanuck or RKO kind of picture.

Zanuck made few pictures that were carried by an actress. Those that did featured a nine-year-old Shirley Temple. The last Zanuck picture that a woman had carried had been five years before, with Barbara starring in *Baby Face,* where the woman, desperate to escape the poverty of her childhood, seduces her way to the top, destroying a string of men in her wake ("She climbed the ladder of success—wrong by wrong," said the picture's teaser line), and at the end is redeemed by love. Each of Zanuck's recent historical dramas had a hero who triumphed over self and adversity, certainly not one felled by physical infirmity and helpless in the face of it.

As for RKO, its contemporary pictures were breezy, sophisticated, carefree; they were musicals, backstage dramas, or comedies. The studio had announced at the start of the New Year that it had two of the best comedy scripts, *The Mad Miss Manton* and *Love on Parole,* with Pandro Berman, the leading producer on the RKO lot, overseeing the former.

Irene Dunne was originally to have made *Miss Manton,* as a follow-up to *Theodora Goes Wild,* to be co-starred with Herbert Marshall, after her great success with Cary Grant in *The Awful Truth.* Dunne left RKO for Universal to make *Madame Curie,* and *The Mad Miss Manton* went to Katharine Hepburn as a logical next picture after *Bringing Up Baby.* Douglas Fairbanks Jr., who appeared with Hepburn in her Academy Award–winning *Morning Glory,* was cast opposite her. Lucille Ball was to play one of the sleuthing society debutantes, as was Anne Shirley.

The Mad Miss Manton was written by Wilson Collison from a comic whodunit about a spoiled society woman who turns detective and sets out to solve a murder with her gaggle of flighty society pals.

It would be tough in the midst of RKO's comedy capers to get the studio to make a tragic story about a dissolute society woman who gets cancer, turns valiant, and dies. In addition, no writer had been able to solve the problem of the play's weakness, and the project had been shelved.

Barbara knew that the character of Judith Traherne was a great part, and she was determined to get it. She went to J. Walter Thompson, the advertising agency for Lux, the show's sponsor, and got it to agree to acquire for her the play's broadcast rights. She thought for sure that performing the play on the radio was the way to get the part in the picture. A contract between the agency and Barbara stipulated that it would do everything to obtain the rights at a reasonable cost. Barbara was to be paid $4,000 for the broadcast. If the agency failed to secure the rights, Barbara's commitment to Thompson for that airdate was to be canceled.

Several years earlier, Jock Whitney had backed the Broadway production of *Dark Victory* and had urged David Selznick to acquire the movie rights, which he did, in 1936, in an effort to beat out Katharine Hepburn. Barbara told her agents to do anything to get the picture from Selznick, who in turn wanted *Dark Victory* for Garbo. He thought it "the best modern women's vehicle since . . . *A Bill of Divorcement*" and wanted Garbo to do it as her next picture following *The Painted Veil* rather than have her make the "heavy Russian drama she was intent on making on the heels of so many ponderous similar films."

Selznick wanted Philip Barry to write the script and George Cukor to direct. Garbo wasn't interested in Selznick's ideas about her career, or *Dark Victory*. She was intent on making *Anna Karenina*. Cukor didn't want to direct another period costume picture and returned to RKO to make the modern-day *Sylvia Scarlett*.

Selznick continued on with *Dark Victory*, which he was now preparing for Merle Oberon. Four drafts later, the problem with the play's third act was still unresolved, which left Ben Hecht to remark, "The only way to save [the play] is to make it a comedy."

Over the years Selznick had been approached by Warner Bros. with offers to buy the rights to *Dark Victory*, prompted by Casey Robinson, a Warner screenwriter whose wife had breast cancer. When Hal Wallis asked what the play was about and Robinson answered, "A woman who dies of cancer of the brain," Wallis had turned pale.

Robinson was an experienced, deft screenwriter and had figured out how to fix the problems of *Dark Victory*. He'd written the titles for ten silents and the scripts of more than twenty pictures, among them *Captain Blood, It's Love I'm After*, and *Tovarich*. He saw that once the character discovers she is going to die and courageously accepts her end in the second act, there was nothing left to resolve in the play's third act. "There had to be in the middle of the piece," Robinson said, "a period of great rebellion against fate, of anger, . . . mixed up with her love for the doctor . . . and the anger that she hadn't been told" the truth that she was dying.

Robinson saw the role for Bette Davis; she, to Robinson, was the key to the picture: her vitality, her restlessness, her unpredictability.

Selznick had consistently rebutted Warner's offer to take over the rights of *Dark Victory* until *Radio Theatre* offered to pay $500 for broadcast rights for Barbara. Selznick was by then on to other projects: the just-released *Adventures of Tom Sawyer;* the completion of the Carole Lombard and Fredric March picture, *Nothing Sacred;* the casting of *The Young in Heart;* the painstaking script revision, with Sidney Howard, of *Gone With the Wind.*

The night of the *Radio Theatre* broadcast of *Dark Victory,* its host, Cecil B. DeMille, was recuperating from an operation and was replaced by Edward Arnold, who introduced Barbara as Judith Traherne and Melvyn Douglas as Dr. Frederick Steele.

Douglas was the Park Avenue doctor about to retire to a country practice who agrees to operate on the selfish, high-flying Judith Traherne. He realizes that her condition will recur and that it will be fatal.

Brilliant, serious doctor and flamboyant, spoiled patient fall in love and marry; he knows that the end may come for her at any time and protects her from knowing the truth. When she accidentally learns of her "death sentence" and doesn't reveal to him that she knows she is doomed, her triumph comes with her ultimate acceptance as she gallantly, stoically braves the end alone. Traherne: "It must be met beautifully, and finally . . . nothing can limit us now. That's our victory; our victory over the dark."

The former MGM associate producer David Lewis, who helped Thalberg produce *Riffraff* and *Camille,* had been at Warner Bros. for a year. When he first arrived, Jack Warner had said to him, "You won't find the stars here that you worked with at Metro. Our Gable is Humphrey Bogart; our Garbo is Bette Davis."

Lewis had been the associate producer of four Warner pictures, including Bette Davis's last, *The Sisters.* He'd worked with Casey Robinson on *Four's a Crowd,* and Lewis and Robinson had spoken about *Dark Victory.* The producer admired Robinson but wasn't interested in the picture. "It's just a story about a woman who's going to die and finally does so," said Lewis. But he began to see in the play what Robinson saw, and together they worked out how to shape the script.

Soon Lewis was also pushing Wallis to buy the rights to *Dark Victory.* "Christ, not that again," Wallis said.

Finally, Lewis went off on his own and approached Selznick at the right moment; Selznick agreed to sell Lewis the rights to *Dark Victory* for $15,000. Warner ultimately took over the picture. Lewis and Robinson adapted the script for Bette Davis; she was "the only person to play [Judith Traherne]," said Robinson. Hal Wallis bought the property for Miriam Hopkins, who needed a picture; she'd been promised *We Are Not Alone,* but the part had gone to Jane Bryan.

Robinson tailored the part to Davis.

Barbara might be asked by a screenwriter about a character he or she was working on, but she could never answer questions about the character until she was playing her. She trusted, though, that writers looked at the work of an actor or actress and "knew a certain part of you," she said, "and they wrote for that."

Warner "didn't want trouble from [Miriam] Hopkins," said Lewis, "but Davis was more of a threat."

Lewis and Robinson had discussed the part with Davis and prevailed on Wallis to give her the role. Wallis had some ideas about the script himself. He wanted to change the doctor from a New England type to someone French and to use Charles Boyer, referred to by one director as the "Japanese Sandman." Boyer, though, had another commitment. The French doctor went back to being a New Englander, and George Brent, whom David Lewis thought a "cold, black Irishman and a predator with women," was assigned the part.

A few days after Barbara appeared as Judith Traherne on *Radio Theatre of the Air,* Warner announced it was making *Dark Victory* as a picture with Bette Davis. The very English Edmund Goulding, director of *Queen Kelly* and *Grand Hotel,* among others, was to direct. Goulding, invariably attired in scarves and blue blazers, was thought of as a genius—extravagant, bold.

Barbara was furious.

She was paying the price—again—for not being under contract to one studio that would have steadily built her up picture after picture. Bette Davis, at Warner Bros. since 1932, had risen up through more than thirty Warner pictures, from supporting ingenue to the studio's "top rank female star," particularly once Hal Wallis had lost faith in Warner's other top star, Kay Francis. Eight months before, the thirty-three-year-old Francis had sued Warner Bros., claiming that she'd been defrauded by Jack Warner into extending her contract with the promise of being given the starring role in *Tovarich.* When the part went to Claudette Colbert, borrowed from Paramount for the lead, Francis took Warner Bros. to court. She was fed up with the roles being submitted to her and was willing to terminate her contract and forgo her $3,000-a-week salary. The case was settled; Francis remained under contract to Warner Bros., but the best roles—*The Sisters, Dark Victory*—were going to Bette Davis. And Davis had since broken through with *Jezebel.*

At Radio, Katharine Hepburn and Ginger Rogers were the stars the studio had built up over the last few years. Ann Harding, under contract to Radio, accurately described an actor's choice: "If you're under contract . . . you may get the plums, but they [the studio] own your soul. If you're not under contract, you have to take your chances."

Barbara's next picture for RKO, a screwball murder mystery—*The Mad Miss Manton*—had been purchased with Irene Dunne in mind and then passed on to Katharine Hepburn. Barbara's next picture for 20th Century–Fox, *Always Goodbye*, was one for which Zanuck had first envisioned Myrna Loy.

Bob Taylor's picture *A Yank at Oxford* opened in London and was regarded as the most solid British picture ever made. It brought in more than $40,000 its first week at the Empire Theatre, the kind of box office that was equivalent to a Garbo picture and was exceeded only by *Mutiny on the Bounty* and *The Broadway Melody*.

When Eleanor Roosevelt visited Metro-Goldwyn-Mayer in mid-March, it was Robert Taylor she asked to see first. Metro announced that it planned to make *Ivanhoe* for its new season with Clark Gable, Bob Taylor, Myrna Loy, and Luise Rainer. In the midst of all the flurry, Bob was busy planting two hundred citrus trees on his newly acquired thirty-acre ranch.

Barbara was to start production on *Always Goodbye* for 20th Century–Fox. Sidney Lanfield, who directed her three years before in *Red Salute*, was to take Allan Dwan's place as the picture's director.

On April 15, three days before Barbara was to show up for work on *Always Goodbye*, she was informed by RKO that the government had seized her salary for back taxes amounting to $61,689.02. "All property, rights to property, moneys, credits and/or bank deposits now in your possession are hereby seized and levied," read the letter from the Internal Revenue Service to RKO. If something wasn't worked out, the IRS would take her weekly paycheck until the amount was paid off.

RKO owed Barbara $4,400 after tax deductions. Twentieth Century–Fox was paying her $55,000 for *Always Goodbye*. The sale of Bristol Avenue was discussed as a way to pay off some of the taxes. It was mortgage-free, but Fay's finagling had further embroiled Barbara in a deeper financial mess. There were twelve liens against the house, each with the Internal Revenue Service, for more than $35,000 of unpaid income tax over a five-year period, from 1932 through 1937.

Fay's house could bring in $75,000 with its swimming pool, tennis court, and large grounds, not to mention its gold bathtubs. In addition to the government liens against 441 Bristol Avenue, the Bank of America was after the property.

Fay and Barbara were named in a suit, along with the United States of America, in an attempt to foreclose on the property. Four years earlier, in 1934, Fay and Barbara had signed a promissory note with the Bank of America against Bristol Avenue for $4,250. Half of the money had been repaid a year later. In its suit, the Bank of America spelled out how the defendant used "fictitious names whose true names are unknown to plaintiff," and the plaintiff "prays that when the true names of said defendants are known and discovered this complaint may be amended accordingly."

Neither Barbara nor Fay appeared in court. The court issued a foreclosure on Bristol Avenue for $2,171.75 plus interest of $146.96, attorney fees of $118.90, and expenses of $27.50. The IRS had issued a lien for more than $60,000 against Barbara's house on Devonshire Boulevard. She needed the money from *Always Goodbye* to pay the government.

Part of the allure for Barbara of *Always Goodbye* was that she was remaking *Gallant Lady*, a picture that had starred Ann Harding. There were few actors or actresses whose work on-screen absorbed Barbara enough for her to be drawn away from studying the technical aspects of a picture and become immersed in the story. Ann Harding was one of those actresses.

Harding's work on-screen was characterized by a dimensionality and ease. At the core of her softness and calm was an immutable strength, a reserve that combined with her winsomeness and patrician beauty to give her a dignity and size and a golden luminosity.

Harding (Dorothy Walton Gatley) was the daughter of a colonel, a West Point graduate, and the foremost authority on artillery fire in the U.S. Army. Harding had withstood with equal strength her father's unyielding condemnation of her choice to make a living as an actress ("Such a step is the straight and inevitable road to Hell," her father had said. Her "painted face" on-screen was there "for harlots and perverts to gape at"). George Grant Gatley disowned his daughter, and she, at eighteen, was even more determined to act onstage.

The discipline, self-confidence, and courage that made Harding's father a brigadier general of the U.S. Rainbow Division in France during the Great War were present in her temperament, on-screen and off. Harding found army life "a narrow prison cell for a woman" that forced her to "restrict [her] thoughts," she said, and to "fold her wings." She recognized the truth of military life and set off to find her own way. Once in New York City, she went from the Metropolitan Life Insurance Company as a Dictaphone operator to Greenwich Village and George Cram Cook's Provincetown Playhouse to Jasper Deeter's Hedgerow Theatre company in Rose Valley, Pennsylvania.

Harding's cool, standoffish demeanor on-screen seemed the opposite of Barbara's. The strength, energy, and anger that drove Barbara's performances were made human, familiar, by a softness from deep down and a hurt that combined to give Barbara her stature, her honesty, her likability; they made her knowable, admirable. The stillness and taut passion of the two actresses made them similar.

Harding, RKO's answer to MGM's Norma Shearer, once said, "Perhaps I am that unfortunate creature known as a high-brow."

Barbara didn't see Harding that way. She'd admired Harding since their stage days in New York. Harding became a Broadway star the same season as Barbara, though they came from opposite ends of the theater world: Barbara as a dancer from revues and clubs; Harding from the stock companies of "the Provincetown Players little theatre" and Rose Valley's Hedgerow Theatre. Harding became a star in *The Trial of Mary Dugan,* which opened on Broadway in September 1927, within a few weeks of *Burlesque.* Co-starring in *Mary Dugan,* opposite Harding, was Rex Cherryman, one of Barbara's early loves. Barbara saw Harding's work in the play and, through Cherryman, came to know her.

Her life and Harding's followed a similar track. Each actress went to Hollywood in 1928 and each because of her husband's theatrical career, when talking pictures were coming into vogue; each thought of the theater as her rightful world and resisted the lure of motion pictures. Harding, because of her golden beauty and rare voice (once compared to the sound of temple songs), as well as her eight years of New York stage experience, was put under contract immediately (at Pathé). With her first picture, *Paris Bound,* from the Philip Barry play, Harding was a sensation; a year later, years before Barbara, Harding was a full-fledged movie star, earning, in 1929, $3,500 a week. By 1931, with a new contract from RKO/Pathé, she was earning what she called "a fair salary," more than $250,000 a year, enough to order her own plane— a Bellanca Skyrocket—to appease her husband, the actor Harry Bannister, who soon got his private pilot's license. The plane's custom-built cabin and fittings matched the gold of Harding's hair. One side of the plane's exterior said, "Ann Harding"; the other, "Mr. Bannister."

Harding's acting and being had a big influence on Barbara. Harding thought of herself as an actress rather than a star; on-screen she wanted to look "like a person," she said, "not an actress." Long before Barbara became a star, Harding was written about as brilliant, superior, forthright, "with a

Ann Harding, 1934. "Work in Hollywood," she advised, "but keep away from Hollywood when you are not working . . . if you must be in Hollywood seek seclusion . . . Fight, fight, always, to avoid becoming a formula star, one who is ever the same type. Seek to be yourself at all costs. Live, laugh, and play, but do it away from the place where movies are discussed, exploited, and proclaimed about morning, noon, and night."

natural reserve of super-intelligence," someone with character and grit who hates sham and ostentation. Harding had beautiful skin; on-screen she barely used greasepaint. Offscreen she was known for wearing no makeup, just lipstick. Harding was hardworking, no-nonsense, thoroughly a member of the company. She knew studio workers by their first names and knew the names of their children. Harding's generous acts for others were legion and inconspicuously rendered. When interviewed, she invariably mentioned the name of Jasper Deeter, director of the Hedgerow Theatre, who'd taken her in hand, educated her about acting, and given her her start as an actress.

Barbara, in interviews, often mentioned Willard Mack as the man who taught her how to act. Harding had decided what mattered in life, and she was determined to maintain it at all costs. Finally, she was concerned with the business of being an actress, a good actress.

Though her childhood and Barbara's were diametrically opposite from one another—Harding, as a daughter of the regiment with much social activity, was nomadic and spoiled, competing in horse shows and, with her own uniform and pony, riding to maneuvers and never missing reveille—both were subjected to an endless number of schools (Barbara to more than ten Brooklyn public schools in eight years; Harding to exclusive private schools along the Eastern Seaboard—thirteen in all—and then a year at Bryn Mawr). Where Barbara made friends with difficulty, Harding learned a superficial adaptability, the value of friendships, and the necessity of making friends quickly.

Each stayed in a situation until it could no longer be endured, and then finally, when the tie was cut, it was abrupt and permanent.

Barbara went to the movies and watched camera angles and studied the placement of lights and how it affected this or that actor's face. When she watched Ann Harding, she was mesmerized.

"Miss Harding is so entirely natural at all times," said Barbara, "that she makes me believe in her and what she is doing. I have always hoped that my own work showed the same degree of sincerity. When I see an Ann Harding picture nothing but her work and the story interests me. I am really able to lose myself."

Harding had retired from pictures in 1936 after a bitter court fight with her husband over custody of their eight-year-old daughter. Barbara had followed the trial closely; the parallels between her marriage and Harding's were unmistakable. Harding's husband, Harry Bannister, a stage actor, much older than Harding, like Fay and Barbara, had failed to establish a successful career in Hollywood and became known as "Mr. Ann Harding."

During the Harding-Bannister marriage, they, like Barbara and Frank Fay, had built a rambling house with rolling gardens in a modest village twenty miles outside town to separate themselves from a Hollywood Harding refused to be part of and as a way to protect her marriage. Ann, like Barbara, rarely gave an interview without talking about her husband's inspired acting and how much better he was at it than she would ever be. The house the Bannisters built, like the Fays' at Bristol Avenue, which was meant to insulate their happiness, became more tomb-like as their marriage disintegrated. During the Harding-Bannister custody case, Bannister, like Fay, tried to kidnap their child.

Always Goodbye was about mother love, but Barbara played the part as differently as she could from that of Stella Dallas. Her portrait of the woman who, following the accidental death of her fiancé, gives up her baby for adoption and becomes a big success as a dress designer, accidentally meets her son five years later, and marries the adoptive father in order to become the mother to her child that she was meant to be was played for strength, gaiety, and glamour. The studio's style expert—Royer—created more than twenty costumes for Barbara. Her Margot Weston was as lighthearted and beautiful as her Stella Dallas was beset and full of feeling.

Harding in the original role of Margot Weston (Sally Wyndham) was moving, dignified, and sexy, simple and real. *Gallant Lady* had been directed in 1934 by Gregory La Cava and co-starred Clive Brook. Harding's work in the picture had been called "splendid" and "radiant."

She created a character who was serious, haunted, and, when she reveals her sense of fun, irresistible. When the moment comes for her to give up her baby for adoption just after having given birth, the feeling of loss is overwhelming. Later, when Harding is with her son (Dickie Moore), now five years old, her playfulness and banter with the boy is fresh and beguiling as she combines the easy authority and fulsome pleasure of a parent.

Barbara had told Pan Berman, executive producer at RKO, that she wanted to make a picture with Gregory La Cava, *Gallant Lady*'s director. La Cava had recently come to RKO along with Leo McCarey as a producer-director, as had George Stevens before him.

Barbara knew how inspired and brilliant La Cava was as a director. She saw it in his work with Carole Lombard in *My Man Godfrey*. She knew how assured La Cava was; he knew exactly what he wanted.

La Cava, however, didn't like to work with a finished script. He worked each day with two or three pages of script that he would type out the night before and give to the actors the day of shooting. It was an odd choice of director for Barbara, who didn't like to veer away from a script and who, from the first day of production, knew the script—every part—letter-perfect.

When La Cava directed *Stage Door,* he'd had a secretary write down the off-camera talk among the actresses and used it throughout the picture, rewriting scenes daily to get a feeling of intimacy among a group of girls boarding together. Ginger Rogers thought La Cava "masterful" as a director; Pan Berman was "amazed" by him but aged a hundred years each day from the chaos La Cava created from "not knowing where we were going, what we were doing tomorrow, how the script would turn out."

The work was tailored to bring out the actor. If something didn't fit, La Cava changed it without going to the writers. The actors improvised, as did Ann Harding and Dickie Moore in the scene in *Gallant Lady* on the transatlantic *Ile de France* in which she tells her little boy the exquisitely improvised story of how the elephant got its trunk; the child interrupts at every turn, and Harding, never getting ruffled or impatient, answers every one of his questions as if mother and boy were gliding in tandem on skates.

La Cava encouraged overlapping dialogue and gags (he'd started out as a cartoonist and animator for Walter Lantz on the Katzenjammer Kids series), but Barbara didn't enjoy improvisation.

Pan Berman liked the idea of Barbara working with La Cava. His next picture needed someone to be a Secret Service–type agent, and, Berman told Leo Spitz, RKO's president, Barbara would be "good in this type of part." He saw it as a good way "of bolstering up the picture from the name angle" without RKO's having to add to its commitment; if the studio used Barbara in the picture, it wouldn't have to "go outside to buy" another star.

A few weeks into production of *Always Goodbye,* Hollywood was stunned by a full-page ad in *The Hollywood Reporter* taken out by the Independent Theatre Owners Association of New York, with a headline that read, "Wake Up! Hollywood Producers." The ad, framed with a red border, attacked producers for paying stars huge salaries on long-term contracts that didn't return on the investment. The copy went on to say, "This condition is not only burdensome to the studios and its [*sic*] stockholders but is likewise no boon to exhibitors who, in the final analysis, suffer by the non-drawing power of these players."

Many of Hollywood's top stars were listed: Mae West, Edward Arnold, Greta Garbo, Joan Crawford, Katharine Hepburn, Kay Francis, and Marlene Dietrich, among them, and were called "box-office deterrents"; these high-salaried performers, it said, "take millions out of the industry and millions out of the box-office."

It was a bombshell dropped on moviemakers, at the expense of those actors and actresses named in the ad, and it ordered the producers to do something about the situation.

Instead of "surrounding a $5,000 a week star with any sort of vehicle," said the fifty members of the association representing 240 theaters in New York City, producers should concentrate on making good pictures. The exhibitors were in favor of "series" pictures": "the Jones Family pictures, the Mr. Motos . . . the Charlie Chans, [and] Judge Hardy pictures." The association was "not against the star system, mind you, but we don't think it should dominate the production of pictures." The statement concluded by saying, "Sound judgment and good business sense are valuable assets in an industry that is far from being an art."

Lawyers and managers of those singled out in the ad conferred at the offices of the Artists' Managers Guild. It was agreed that the ad was libelous, but the actors were unable to sue because of their contractual agreements with the studios.

Of the producers, Harry Cohn had the most at stake; two of those named as "box-office deterrents" were under contract to Columbia. The studio had just completed making *Holiday* with Katharine Hepburn and had signed Marlene Dietrich—after Paramount bought out her contract for $250,000—to star as George Sand in a picture about Chopin.

Cohn, with his policy of hiring those actors and actresses on their way up or down, issued a statement saying that all of those mentioned in the Theatre association's ad would be welcomed at Columbia.

Exhibitors had long complained about the Hollywood system of placing strong box-office names in bad pictures and then relying on the star's drawing power to bring in big receipts. They argued that those players who had saved the studios for years had been destroyed by the same system, one of the reasons that Barbara made sure she was never under contract to one studio.

TWELVE

Mother Love at Home and Abroad

Bob Taylor was in training for *The Crowd Roars,* an exposé of the fight game, in which he was to play a prizefighter who rises up from the slums, a choir singer who sells his soul to a racketeer to become a contender for the light heavyweight title. It was a story indirectly inspired by Clifford Odets's hit play *Golden Boy,* which had opened the Group Theatre's seventh season in November 1937 and was running on Broadway with Luther Adler, Frances Farmer, Morris Carnovsky, Jules Garfield, Elia Kazan, Lee J. Cobb, and Robert Lewis.

For the part of the young boxer in *The Crowd Roars,* Bob didn't want to just go through the motions of being a fighter, the old left right. He wanted to know something about the tricks of being a boxer. Metro arranged for him to be coached by the former fighter Johnny Indrisano. Indrisano had never been a champ, but he'd beaten champions in nontitle matches.

Barbara also hired an ex-fighter, Tommy Herman, to be her physical trainer, and to give Dion boxing lessons in the ring she had put up near her swimming pool.

Bob was training from nine to six, fourteen days in a row, punching bags, doing roadwork, jumping rope, shadowboxing, and learning to duck, weave, watch his footwork, lead with his left, and take the offensive. He was also training with Patsy Perroni and Mickey McAvoy. During one training fight, McAvoy broke the actor's thumb. "His head got in the way of my thumb, or vice versa," said Bob, who thought his thumb was sprained and kept on fighting.

Metro was once again presenting Bob as rugged. To show how much of a man's man he was becoming, the studio released Bob's body measurements and compared them with his body of 1935, including the measurements of his thighs (20 inches in 1935; 23 inches in 1938); wrists (6½ inches in '35; 7 inches in '38); and neck (14 inches in '35; 16 inches in '38).

In training for *The Crowd Roars*, 1938.

Bob's previous picture, *Three Comrades*, opened to bad reviews ("There must have been some reason for making this picture," *Variety* said, "but it certainly isn't in the cause of entertainment . . . despite the draught of the star names, it's in for a sharp nose dive at the box office"). Though Metro tried to gloss over what was happening in Germany and set the story in the 1920s instead of ten years later, reviewers called the story dated and said that that period had no relation to the "Reich of today."

Metro had extended Bob's contract and began negotiations on his next. He consulted a financial manager, Morgan Maree, Barbara's accountant, a partner of Alan Miller, Marion Marx's brother.

Bob still feared financial insecurity, despite his success with Metro. His new home, which he called a gentleman's ranch, in the San Fernando Valley near Barbara's Marwyck, was set up so that ten of the thirty acres were for his house, lawn, and paddocks with the other twenty being used to grow and sell alfalfa. Bob was considering whether to put up a storage barn and get $20 a ton for alfalfa or sell it immediately for $12.50 a ton. He'd bought government bonds and annuities, but he didn't yet have the kind of cash that allowed him to buy a real cattle ranch, the eight-hundred-acre ranch he'd seen in the hills with oaks and sycamores and a year-round stream that flowed through the Barley Flats.

Others had followed Barbara and the Marxes to the San Fernando Valley: Francis Lederer, Gene Autry, Wallace Beery, Will Hays, Al Jolson, and Ruby

Keeler. Each was within a ten-mile area of the other with farms that were between twenty and two hundred acres, laid out for fruit or feed or, as with Mae West, used for a trotting track.

The day after Barbara finished *Always Goodbye,* she and Bob went to a preview of Irving Berlin's *Alexander's Ragtime Band,* which starred Tyrone Power and Alice Faye. Twentieth Century–Fox held the evening at the Carthay Circle Theatre, which had been dark since the end of a two-day run of *Snow White.* Barbara wore an accordion-pleated white chiffon with a square-shouldered cape of white fox from *Always Goodbye.*

With production completed on the picture, Barbara appeared on *The Chase and Sanborn Hour.* Don Ameche was the host; Edgar Bergen and Charlie McCarthy, the comedy regulars; Ameche and Dorothy Lamour, the musical entertainment. Barbara and Ameche did a shortened version of *Magnificent Obsession;* Barbara was powerful as Helen Hudson. Later in the show she did a skit with Charlie McCarthy about his teaching her to swim, and together they drew their quota of laughs from a bit about lifesavers and then segued into a duet of "The Man on the Flying Trapeze."

Barbara was getting ready for *The Mad Miss Manton.* Leigh Jason was directing the picture.

Barbara watched as the careers of those actors and actresses denounced in the Theatre association's ad suffered the effects of being called "box-office deterrents." Pan Berman had allowed Katharine Hepburn to leave RKO for Columbia since her ranking at the box office had fallen to 189. Joan Crawford saw herself go from "being Queen one year to being washed up the next," while Louis B. Mayer assured her that the public loved her and would always love her and that he would take care of his "little Joan" as if she were his daughter ("His hand always touched my right tit," said Joan, "whenever he said the word 'daughter' ").

When Crawford's contract was up, Mayer offered her a one-year renewal at $300,000 for two pictures. Marlene Dietrich left America—Cohn canceled the George Sand picture after the exhibitors' ad ran—and the thirty-seven-year-old German actress returned to Europe. Mae West had just returned from a triumphant ten-week nationwide personal appearance tour—doing six shows a day—to drum up business for her picture *Every Day's a Holiday.* The picture had not done well at the box office. West said, "The only picture to make money recently was *Snow White and the Seven Dwarfs* and that would have made twice as much if they had let me play Snow White." West's career was considered finished, but she was determined to make a picture as Catherine the Great.

· · ·

Breakfast for Two opened to positive reviews.

Bob went to New York for a few days, and Barbara and Cesar Romero, her co-star in *Always Goodbye,* went to the Trocadero and were given dancing lessons in the shag by a group of college kids.

Always Goodbye was rushed into theaters as a summer picture. Unlike the 1934 original, *Gallant Lady,* reviewers called the remake "sentimentally sticky and maladroit" and "careless as to details, logic and reason" but wrote about Barbara's and Marshall's "fine performances in the face of the material they have to work with." Louella Parsons, always a champion of Barbara's, wrote about how Stanwyck, "one of our most attractive stars, plays with emotional understanding and feeling in the role."

In the picture Barbara was loving and patient as the mother fighting to win a place in the life of her little boy, played by five-year-old Johnnie Russell. Barbara was not as patient with her own son, Dion, only a year older than Russell. In *Always Goodbye,* the turning point in the picture comes when Stanwyck's character is told by her son's soon-to-be stepmother that the boy will be sent off to military school. Stanwyck's character, alarmed by this, asks, "Isn't six years old too young to send the boy to military school?"

Dion Fay had witnessed his father's frightening rages and drinking, but Barbara's expectations of her son were high. She wanted perfection. Dion was a freckle-faced six-year-old boy with glasses who was starting to get plump, which annoyed Barbara, who had little patience for people who were fat. Dion was not the perfect movie son of *Always Goodbye, Ever in My Heart,* or *So Big.* When Barbara and Dion were living in the city proper, he went to kindergarten at CalCurtis on Beverly Boulevard. When mother and son moved to Northridge, Dion was sent away to school, partially to protect him from Fay's winning the appeal that would uphold his visitation rights and also because Barbara thought it would be good for the six-year-old boy.

It was a damp, overcast day when Uncle Buck and Dion headed over the Santa Monica Mountains and Sepulveda Boulevard to Raenford Military Academy in Encino, five miles from Marwyck. Buck and Dion didn't talk much. The drizzle turned to a slight rain. Once at Encino, the car turned onto Louise Avenue. Dion recognized it; Gable and Lombard lived there.

As the car passed the Gable-Lombard ranch, he remembered the great times he'd had with their horses and dogs. Carole had always picked him up and kissed him on his cheek. It was the first time he'd thought about love.

He thought of where he was being driven and became frightened. He was being taken to an unknown place and was terrified he would never see home

Dion, age six, in cadet uniform, 1938. Raenford Military Academy, on Hayvenhurst Avenue, was originally the Encino Country Club, built in the 1920s and bankrupt a decade later. Dion, who learned the close-order drill and the manual of arms for rifle and saber, often watched Darryl Zanuck and others playing polo on his Hayvenhurst Avenue field. Note the inscription: "To Nany. With all my love. Dion."(COURTESY TONY FAY)

again. He'd been warned by Barbara about the school's disciplinary ways and that he'd better be good.

The sky opened up to a downpour. Raenford Academy, with its ivy-covered buildings, loomed in the distance.

Once at the school, Dion was given an olive-green wool uniform with a sand-brown belt to wear around his waist and over the shoulder. Each boy was issued a wooden rifle to be carried during morning formations and parades.

Dion's fear gave way to excitement about his new school.

He was given a small spare room to share with another boy, who was much more knowing of the world than Dion and who soon showed him how to smoke. Often the two boys wandered up in the shrub-covered hills behind the barracks to explore. Dion would take a certain kind of weed, hollow at the center, and light it up, pretending to smoke.

On weekends some of the boys went home. Dion wasn't among them. Uncle Buck came to visit on Sundays once every other month and on holidays drove him back to the ranch. The boy counted the days until Thanksgiving, when he would go home for a week. On Saturdays, those who remained at the school were taken to the movies at the La Reina Theatre in Sherman Oaks on Ventura Boulevard.

Dion graduated from first grade, which Barbara celebrated with a party at Marwyck. The party was postponed for a week as punishment for Dion's bad behavior. Barbara wanted no publicity about the party and swore each of the mothers to secrecy so there would be no cameramen and the children would be free to play.

From *The Mad Miss Manton*, 1938. Right to left: Frances Mercer as Helen Frayne, Barbara as Melsa Manton, Linda Perry as Myra Frost, Henry Fonda as Peter Ames, and Sam Levene as Lieutenant Mike Brent.

Dion hated school; he was lonely and wanted to be home, though he wasn't happy there—he saw little of Barbara—but it was better than being sent away. At home Dion had his own room with a workbench where he could make models. He swam in the pool with its clear view of the valley and spent time at the stables. He rode his horse, Beauty, and helped Uncle Buck paint the fences. Uncle Buck and Nanny took care of him, and he learned from his beloved nurse how important it was to be a good person.

RKO borrowed Henry Fonda from Walter Wanger at Fox for the role opposite Barbara in *The Mad Miss Manton*. Shooting began on the picture following the July 4 weekend. In addition to *The Mad Miss Manton*, RKO had four pictures in production: *Room Service, Gunga Din, The Castles,* and *Love Affair;* eleven more were due to start within the next two months.

The Mad Miss Manton fulfilled Barbara's nonexclusive contract with RKO. The picture was a whodunit comedy adventure with Stanwyck as a spoiled debutante who discovers a double murder and, to spite the police

With Leigh Jason, director of *The Mad Miss Manton*. (PHOTOFEST)

who dismiss her story of finding a dead body as another in a long line of charity high jinks (the corpse has vanished by the time the police get there), sets out with her Park Avenue sidekicks to prove they're not liars and parasites to the community and solve the murder on their own.

Fonda is the serious newspaper editor who, in an irate editorial on unemployment and the budget, denounces "the mad Miss Manton and her ilk" for their ermine-lined escapades wasting police time and money. He soon finds that he's landed the newspaper in a million-dollar libel suit ("Did you print that?" Melsa Manton says to him after slapping his face. And he hers. "I'll make you eat every word of it," she promises). He ends up chasing after Melsa and her dizzy deb detectives in what turns into (for him) risky business and (for editor and heiress) battling romance.

Anne Shirley was to be featured with Barbara in the picture but was instead put into *Condemned Women*, starring Sally Eilers and Louis Hayward. Frances Mercer, Vicki Lester, Eleanor Hansen, and Penny Singleton were among the flock of Melsa Manton's seven society friends.

Leigh Jason, known for his fast-paced, whimsical pictures, was to direct. Jason was married to Ruth Harriet Louise, a rabbi's daughter from New York, who, at twenty-two years old, was hired in 1925 by Howard Strickling to be Metro's official portrait photographer, the only woman employed as a photographer by a major Hollywood studio. Lillian Gish thought Louise's photographs "magnificent. I took orders from her as I would have from D. W. Griffith." Louise left Metro in 1930 to marry Leigh Jason.

From *The Mad Miss Manton* with Henry Fonda. (AMERICAN HERI-
TAGE CENTER, UNIVERSITY OF WYOMING)

Henry Fonda didn't like the script of *The Mad Miss Manton* or the picture's director. After Fonda's roles in *Jezebel, You Only Live Once,* and *The
Trail of the Lonesome Pine,* even the screwball farce *The Moon's Our Home,*
Peter Ames was a one-note—but so was the part of Melsa Manton. Fonda
is one-upped by the undone Miss Manton, who bounds and gags him and
leaves him flummoxed. Fonda—a true deadpan comedian—resented having
to make the picture. He was known to work hours, days, on a gag, and when
he'd spring it at the right moment, he didn't laugh.

On the set, Fonda was aloof and barely talked to anyone, including Barbara. When he asked Frances Mercer, one of the society sleuths, to have lunch
one day, Barbara was not happy.

The script was written by twenty-nine-year-old Philip Epstein. His twin
brother, Julius, had been in Hollywood for a few years, writing for Warner Bros. In New York, the brothers Epstein had worked as press agents for
Fatty Arbuckle and written a play, *And Stars Remain,* produced in 1936 by
the Theatre Guild and starring Helen Gahagan, called by Heywood Broun
"ten of the twelve most beautiful women in America." Philip, at his brother's
prompting, had come out to Hollywood to write. The Epstein brothers—
practical jokers and wits—did everything together; they thought of themselves as one person.

Philip was newly arrived at RKO. His script for *The Mad Miss Manton*
was smart, worldly writing, with its allusions to "communism" and "come the

revolution." At the heart of the picture was the issue of class: the rich versus the rest of the world (one character to the police detective played by Sam Levene: "I'm class-conscious, see! I don't like society dames." Ames to Melsa: "You're just a decorative, useless member of a rapidly vanishing class").

Fonda, at thirty-three and more than six feet, was boyishly handsome, fresh, clean looking, with an honest face, a midwestern drawl, and a slow grin. His innocence played well against Barbara's sexuality, her seeming glamour and worldliness.

Barbara was making $60,000 for the picture; Fonda, $25,000. Sam Levene, as the harassed police lieutenant driven to distraction by too much Melsa Manton and in need of a "bicarb" as antidote, $1,500 per week; Hattie McDaniel as Hilda, the clever, wisecracking maid, $500 a week.

The New York City scenes for *The Mad Miss Manton* were shot at the Warner Bros. Ranch in the San Fernando Valley, where the sun was brilliant, hot. More than $50,000 worth of furs were worn in 120-degree heat. The society sleuths, including Barbara, were swathed in fur for the winter scenes and were miserable. Electric fans put behind blocks of ice failed to provide relief.

Production was stopped for a week when Barbara caught a severe cold that almost resulted in pneumonia. When she returned to work, she was given the use of Ginger Rogers's new dressing room (Rogers had sent a telegram from Mexico offering it) while shooting the picture, and she spent most of the time there between scenes.

The first day into production Barbara and Bob attended the long-awaited premiere of *Marie Antoinette* at the Carthay Circle in Hollywood. The premiere was planned as the most spectacular in motion picture history.

Norma Shearer, the star of the picture and the first lady of film, arrived with Louis B. Mayer and Helen Hayes, the first lady of the theater, and her husband, Charles MacArthur. As Bob and Barbara and the others entered the theater, the crowd of more than twenty-five thousand in the specially erected grandstands gave them an ovation.

Mayer had put Bob forward for the part in *Marie Antoinette* of Count Axel de Fersen, but Shearer insisted on Tyrone Power, who was stunned when he learned that he was being loaned out by Fox to MGM to make the picture. Ty Power, from two generations of Shakespearean actors, his great-grandfather, the first Tyrone Power, an acclaimed Irish comedian, with his liquid brown eyes and dark, handsome face, had been prevented by Fox from appearing in pictures at competing studios. Fox, in exchange for the loan-out to MGM, got Spencer Tracy for its production of *Stanley and Livingstone*.

Marie Antoinette had cost the studio almost $2.5 million, more than any previous Metro picture except *The Good Earth*.

After the screening of *Marie Antoinette*, Mayer gave a party at the Trocadero for six hundred guests. Shearer arrived in a brocade coat over a low-cut white gown and went to the powder room, where her maid was waiting. The picture's star emerged in a handmade black-sequined sheath "so tight," wrote Hedda Hopper, "she had to watch not only her step but her breathing."

Marie Antoinette, according to Thalberg's plan for his wife, was to have been Norma's final picture. "Too many stars stay on camera too long," Thalberg had said. He wanted Norma to leave "at her highest point." Instead, it became his ultimate picture in a brilliant career.

Marie Antoinette was a triumph for Shearer, and rather than it marking the finale of a long ambitious run, her success in the picture prompted David Selznick to woo her for the most coveted part in Hollywood history.

Word got out that Shearer was being seriously considered for the part of Scarlett O'Hara. A group of stenographers working in the Fisher Building in Detroit wrote in to protest the choice. They wanted, they said, to see Miss Scarlett played by Bette Davis, Miriam Hopkins, or Barbara Stanwyck.

THIRTEEN

Pomp and Glory

1938–1939

Barbara was still suffering from a recurrence of the back injury she'd sustained in Laguna Beach when she was thrown from a horse while shooting *Forbidden.* She'd ridden in *The Woman in Red, Annie Oakley,* and *A Message to Garcia* but didn't want to ride in front of the cameras again and had a clause added to her RKO contract that protected her from having to do so.

She was worried about Marion Marx, who'd taken a bad fall from a horse she intended to buy for Marwyck and was flat on her back in a cast with a broken shoulder.

Marion and Barbara were both out of riding commission for the two-day horse event they helped to organize. The San Fernando Valley Fiesta Horse Show, "The Horse Show of the Stars," was held across the road from Marwyck on Northridge Estates in a specially constructed arena at Devonshire and Reseda Boulevards. Carole Lombard, Bing Crosby, Noah Beery Jr., and Harry Hart, Marwyck's manager, were co-organizers. Barbara and Marion, along with Bob, Don Ameche, Andy Devine, Clark Gable, and Carole Lombard, were to be trophy presenters.

Lombard and Gable had bought the Raoul Walsh estate nearby and transformed the twenty-one acres from a rich man's retreat into a working farm with orchard, dairy, hennery, and vineyard, staffed by secretary, butler, cook, two maids, caretaker, groom, and handyman. Lombard, manic practical joker and hostess, late of the Mayfair Balls, who had collected $50,000 worth of star sapphires and then sold the collection when she grew tired of them, became architect, agriculturalist, and economist of the Gable-Lombard venture. She tended their cows, chickens, ducks, pair of mules, goat, rabbits, and horses, including Gable's two racehorses. Lombard oversaw the growing

Carole Lombard, circa 1938.
(PHOTOFEST)

and selling of the farm's garden vegetables, its hay, alfalfa, peaches, oranges, lemons, walnuts, apricots, grapes, and turkeys, which MGM bought for its commissary. Raoul Walsh had previously rented the property to the studios at $500 for location work, but that stopped with Gable and Lombard.

Barbara and Marion entered six horses from Marwyck in the Northridge show. Their horse Heromane took second place among the Thoroughbred stallions; Little Shower, third. Gable's horse Nugget's King won first place in the stock class with the trophy presented by Lombard. Bob's copper-colored stallion, Rokhalad, won first prize in the Arabian class; his black gelding, Midnight, took third place in the silver mounted class. Watching from the boxes were Mrs. Liz Whitney, Louella Parsons, Jack Warner, Bruce Cabot, and Harry Strickling.

Bob's latest picture, *The Crowd Roars,* opened on his twenty-seventh birthday; Barbara celebrated by giving him an elaborate horse trailer. Reviews for *The Crowd Roars* were positive for him, less so for the picture. "Let it be noted at once," wrote Howard Barnes in *The New York Herald Tribune,* "that Mr. Taylor plays a tough guy with considerable persuasion. If you are keenly interested in just how virile he can be, you will find the show intriguing. If you are looking for a genuinely entertaining prizefight picture you are likely to be disappointed."

• • •

On "Reno," Marwyck, circa 1938.

Life for Barbara with Bob and the Zeppo Marxes was social. Joan Crawford, Tone, the Marxes, the Ray Millands, the Fred MacMurrays, and Barbara and Bob were a regular set.

Barbara came to love Bob. He did the things she wanted to do. If she wanted to go to the racetrack, Bob went to the track. If she wanted to go to the newsreel theater, they went to the newsreels. On the rare occasions when she wanted to join friends for a night out at one of the nightclubs, he was willing to go. Barbara enjoyed being on Bob's arm at Hollywood functions. She took pleasure when Bob got a role and asked her opinion about it and wanted to be coached by her.

The summer months of 1938 came to a close with Hollywood being targeted by Washington for political fodder, with Bob, among others, at the center of the controversy.

Professor James B. Matthews, director of research of the three-month-old Special Committee on Un-American Activities of the House of Representatives in Washington, came before Martin Dies's panel—made up of Dies, Ar-

With Bob and Dion at a horse show, part of the San Fernando Valley Fiesta, Northridge, June 1938.

thur Healey of Massachusetts, John J. Dempsey of New Mexico, Joe Starnes of Alabama, Harold G. Mosier of Ohio, Noah Mason of Illinois, and J. Parnell Thomas of New Jersey—and presented a list of actors and actresses in Hollywood who had lent their names "unwittingly" to Communist propaganda.

Matthews was a former Methodist missionary who'd covered the spectrum of radical life—as pacifist, socialist, Trotskyite, Wobbly, and Communist. A few years before, he'd made clear that big business, the government, and liberals were paving the way to Fascism; now he was before the panel warning that labor unions, the government, and liberals were making a path to Communism.

The new committee had been the idea of Martin Dies, an anti–New Deal Democratic congressman from Texas. Its mandate was to investigate subversive activities on U.S. soil, including German-American involvement with Nazism, the Ku Klux Klan, and American Communism; its intent was to protect what Dies called "Americanism" and restore "Christian influence" in America.

Despite the specter of being "investigated," the Ku Klux Klan sent a telegram to Chairman Dies saying, "Every true American, and that includes every Klansman, is behind you and your committee in its effort to turn the country back to the honest, freedom-loving, God-fearing American to whom it belongs."

Roosevelt called Dies's committee "sordid, flagrantly unfair and un-American." In Nazi Germany and in Fascist Spain and Italy, Martin Dies was hailed as a hero who would rid the United States of "Pres. Rosenfeld, the Communist Jew."

The committee's investigator accused the First Lady, Mrs. Franklin D. Roosevelt, of helping to spread Communist propaganda by speaking before the American Youth Congress at Vassar College in Poughkeepsie, New York. Among the Hollywood actors Matthews accused of being the dupes of "Reds" were Clark Gable, James Cagney, Bette Davis, and Miriam Hopkins. The name at the top of Matthews's list: ten-year-old Shirley Temple. Also named by the committee was Robert Taylor, just as he was to start filming Metro's *Give and Take* with Wallace Beery.

The list was from a French newspaper, *Ce Soir,* that had featured greetings in its anniversary issue from each of the actors Matthews named. The investigator claimed *Ce Soir* was under Communist control. The various studios responded by issuing statements that the actors were unaware the paper was owned by the Communist Party, though it turned out to be owned by a group of Paris bankers who supported the French government.

A week earlier, the Dies Committee had leveled charges against Hollywood itself, saying that actors and writers were financing "communistic" activities. Among those named were Luise Rainer, Gale Sondergaard, Joan Crawford, and the screenwriter Morrie Ryskind.

Metro-Goldwyn-Mayer responded to the attack against its actresses by saying, "No one has anything to say."

Donald Ogden Stewart, co-founder and chairman of the Hollywood Anti-Nazi League, responded on his own, calling the charges that actors and writers were supporting "communist organizations" "fiction" and stating that the charges came from "all the Hollywood rumors collected from the various anti-labor, anti-Roosevelt sources, especially those provided by the efficient Los Angeles police intelligence bureau, or, as we call them, the 'used-car squad.' I am only sorry that the story failed to include one additional and equally true rumor, which is to the effect that when Hitler has taken over Czechoslovakia, [the committee's investigator] is coming secretly to Hollywood to play the part of Scarlett in *Gone with the Wind*."

Robert Taylor was anything but a Communist supporter, socialist, liberal, or Democrat. A former member of the Boy Scouts of America and the Order of DeMolay, Taylor, foursquare Republican and "patriot," like Barbara, was anti-Roosevelt and anti–New Deal, raised a Nebraska heartland Methodist from a long line of Methodists and German Baptists and, like his mother, didn't trust Catholics, Jews, or Italians.

. . .

Bob's next picture, *Give and Take,* produced by Mervyn LeRoy, was to be directed by W. S. Van Dyke, their fourth picture together. Both Beery and Bob had been set to make *Northwest Passage* until production was delayed and then each was assigned to *Give and Take,* another picture in which Bob would be showcased as the virile, rough-and-tumble man.

At the heart of *Give and Take* was the fight between the railroads pushing west through the Alleghenies and the already established stagecoach lines. The script was by James M. Cain, Laurence Stallings, Jane Murfin, and Harvey Fergusson. Murfin had been around the picture business for almost thirty years; she'd written *Come and Get It, Alice Adams,* and *What Price Hollywood?,* among fifty other screenplays going back to 1918. Fergusson had written a couple of novels.

Bob announced to the press that he'd felt "limited" in the parts he'd played and wanted to do a Western if he could. "I want to get parts where I can wear overalls, leave my hair uncombed and unbrushed, forget to shave for a few days." To make *Give and Take,* Bob stopped going to a barber and, like Barbara, who didn't like to wear wigs, grew his hair so it could be tied back in a pigtail in the look of the 1850s.

Bob's mother heard the title of the picture, now called *Stand Up and Fight,* and said out of concern, "O, dear God, dear God." Bob assured her the picture had nothing to do with boxing. "I'm gonna play the part of a guy who just wants to build a railroad. Mr. Mayer picked me, Mother, and he knows exactly what he's doing. Anyway, so far he's kept us out of the poorhouse."

Barbara had agreed to make *Falling Star* for Zanuck from a script, similar to *A Star Is Born,* by Richard Sherman. Sherman had adapted *Alexander's Ragtime Band* for Zanuck and had just finished writing *The Story of Vernon and Irene Castle.* Warner Baxter was to play the down-and-out movie star.

Barbara and Bob were planning a holiday in South America after finishing their current pictures. Bob loved to travel; Barbara was not as enthusiastic about it. Mayer had suggested a story that MGM was already planning as Bob's picture after *Give and Take. Hands Across the Border* was about a fifteen-year competition between hockey teams representing West Point and the Royal Military College of Canada, in which Bob was to co-star with Jim Stewart. Bob's new contract with Metro, to go into effect with the New Year, increased his salary to $5,000 a week and guaranteed him two holidays: one a month long; and the other for two weeks. Bob had just been named the sixth most popular box-office star by the *Motion Picture Herald* exhibitors poll; the previous year he'd ranked third on the list.

. . .

The Mad Miss Manton opened at the Pantages in Los Angeles and at Radio City Music Hall in New York. Reviewers had had their fill of the string of wild comedies about giddy Park Avenue heiresses and cynical newspapermen and had hoped they'd seen the last of that kind of picture. Despite that, *The Mad Miss Manton*'s madcappery ("screwball comedy and screwball murder mystery," said *Time*) surprised and (begrudgingly) seduced the critics who were disarmed by Leigh Jason's light, adept direction, Barbara and Fonda's comic work, and the cavorting whimsy of Melsa Manton's posse of Junior League sleuths. It was Philip Epstein's clever script, Sam Levene's zealous theatrics, and Hattie McDaniel's perfect timing and delivery that stole the picture.

Moviegoers didn't want to be buoyed by films that showed up the rich and that made clear, through zaniness and giddy hoopla, how Park Avenue types needed the common touch to be made part of the human race. The desperate times of the Depression had been supplanted by uncertainty and danger, and what audiences wanted on the screen was real emotion.

At President Roosevelt's suggestion, Germany, England, France, and Italy had met in Munich to decide the fate of Eastern Europe, in an effort to stave off a second world war. It was agreed that Germany would take over Sudetenland with 3.5 million Sudeten Germans, enlarging the Nazi empire in the Danube valley; that German troops would occupy the most German areas; and that Hitler, in exchange, would become part of a new European concert of nations. The less German areas would hold a plebiscite to decide if they wanted to remain a part of the Reich. The agreement nullified the Versailles Treaty that had ended the Great War and created Czechoslovakia.

Dorothy Thompson, syndicated columnist, said, "Czechoslovakia was disposed of by four men who in four hours made a judgment of the case in which the defendant was not even allowed to present a brief or be heard [neither Czechoslovakia nor its protector, the Soviet Union, was asked to the meeting] . . . What ruled that conference was Nazi law."

Newspaper headlines and radio commentators fed a mood of fear. The hope was that things would turn out all right just as long as the United States didn't get mixed up in it.

Now that Washington had turned its attention to Hollywood, Lela Rogers and her daughter, Ginger, gave a party for J. Edgar Hoover, who was visiting Los Angeles. Irene Dunne was there, as was Jack Benny. The Rogerses ended the evening by showing Hoover and his associates from the Federal Bureau of Investigation Barbara's new picture, *The Mad Miss Manton*.

Barbara and Bob's trip to South America was postponed. With *Give and Take*, Metro had tried to rush out the picture about the battle between the railroads' westward expansion and the stagecoach lines ahead of what the studio knew was coming: Cecil B. DeMille's epic new picture about the building of the country's first transcontinental railroad, *Union Pacific.*

Barbara was signed to play the lead opposite Joel McCrea.

DeMille's picture was to be the "titanic story of the American empire builders who found their way to destiny conquering mountains and deserts . . . savage red men and ruthless white, forging an iron road built on stout hearts and reckless courage."

Barbara saw the Western as honest and true with simple story lines. To her the people of the West were "America's 'royalty.' Sure there were the good guys and the bad guys," she said. "But didn't the royal families have the same? You bet they did! Those marvelous men and women and, yes, even children broke the trails through unbelievable hardships to conquer the land for all of us. It is a wonderful history to read and even more wonderful to be given the opportunity to recreate it on film."

The day before Halloween, Orson Welles's Mercury Theatre on the Air put on an adaptation of H. G. Wells's *War of the Worlds.* Welles, twenty-three years old, wrote the show as a news broadcast with break-ins to dance music; the news bulletins told of a Martian invasion taking place near Grover's Mill, New Jersey. The broadcast was periodically interrupted with disclaimers that listeners were not hearing actual news bulletins, but many who tuned in between announcements thought they were hearing news accounts of an invasion from Mars, just as they'd recently heard other regularly scheduled broadcasts interrupted to report real-life developments concerning Czechoslovakia. Police, radio stations, and newspapers coast-to-coast were flooded with calls about an invasion from outer space; thousands fled their homes.

The next day the *Los Angeles Times*'s headline read: "Radio Story of Mars Raid Causes Panic." H. G. Wells said he had not given permission to turn the novel into a news broadcast.

In the *New York Herald Tribune,* Dorothy Thompson wrote, "All unwittingly, Mr. Orson Welles and the Mercury Theatre on the Air . . . have proved that a few effective voices, accompanied by sound effects, can convince masses of people of a totally unreasonable, completely fantastic proposition as to create a nation-wide panic. They have demonstrated more potently than any argument . . . the appalling dangers and enormous effectiveness of popular and theatrical demagoguery . . . Hitler managed to scare all of Europe to its knees a month ago, but he at least had an army and an air force to back up his shrieking words. But Mr. Welles scared thousands into demoralization with nothing at all."

Since the early radio days in New York when Barbara had read poetry over the WHN airwaves, she'd understood the power of radio and the actor's voice.

The state supreme court's long-awaited decision came down regarding Barbara's appeal to prevent Fay from seeing Dion. The court had ruled in Fay's favor. Barbara was adamant that Fay not be permitted to see the boy at her house—or at Fay's. Cradick, her lawyer, made clear that her stance was for the "welfare of the child." The court had believed Fay when he said he hadn't had "a drop of liquor, including beer or cider," since November 1936. Barbara's statement to the court that she didn't think Fay was unfit to see Dion right after she and Fay had separated, combined with her having entered into a property settlement that said that as long as Dion lived near Fay, the boy would be taken to visit with Fay once a week, worked against her appeal. Barbara's charge in the appeal that the court was acting on the "pleasure of the defendant and not the welfare of the child" had not worked. Her appeal to prevent Fay from seeing Dion was denied. In addition, she was ordered to reimburse Fay and the court for charges of the appeal.

Dion was away at school, and Fay was getting ready to return to Broadway after the New Year to do straight vaudeville: ten acts with Elsie Janis as his star and Eva Le Gallienne making her debut in vaudeville doing the balcony scene from *Romeo and Juliet*. For Fay it was back to seven nightly shows with a Saturday matinee. He had leased the Hudson Theatre; it was not by accident. In his own way, he was still trying to seduce Barbara back to him. Twelve years before, Barbara had had her first big success at the Hudson Theatre when, at nineteen, she'd opened on Broadway in *The Noose*.

The idea of making a picture about the empire builders who conquered mountains and deserts to forge an iron road to the West came to DeMille while traveling by train from Hollywood to New York. For two days he watched vast stretches of America flash by him. He thought of the building of the railroad and was overwhelmed with the courage, vision, and hard work of the men and women who, some seventy years before, had made the dream of spanning the continent a reality. The idea for the picture came to DeMille in Omaha, Nebraska, where the Union Pacific began its route west to Sacramento. In Cleveland, DeMille telegraphed the Paramount office in Hollywood: "Story of building of Union Pacific railroad to be my next work."

. . .

DeMille, in 1938, was as powerful a man in the film business as D. W. Griffith in 1918. No director was able to command the money DeMille could to make the movies he wanted to make.

DeMille, a quarter of a century before, in 1913, with Jesse Lasky, a disappointed gold seeker from Alaska and cornetist (the first white man in the Royal Hawaiian Band), and Lasky's brother-in-law Samuel Goldfish, a glove salesman, formed Jesse Lasky Feature Play Company to produce feature-length motion pictures. DeMille went west to make *The Squaw Man* and ended up in Hollywood, a town of orange and lemon groves and dust-covered roads, rented a barn on Vine Street, and made the movie, one of the first five-reeler motion pictures.

DeMille was made the director general of Jesse Lasky Feature Play Company in 1914. He wrote and directed his own pictures and oversaw the company's productions. He wore a holster and gun and rode a horse to and from the studio; there were no banks, and checks were cashed at Hall's grocery store on Hollywood Boulevard.

Three years later Jesse Lasky Feature Play Company merged with Adolph Zukor's Famous Players to form Famous Players–Lasky, which distributed pictures through Paramount Pictures Corporation, and then took control of Paramount. DeMille was still director general. Eight years later, in 1925, DeMille set up his own company at the former Thomas Ince Studio in Culver City; three years later he went to Metro, and in 1932 he returned to Paramount. By 1938, DeMille had produced and directed more than sixty (mostly) action-crammed pictures in twenty-five years, including *The Buccaneer, The Plainsman, Cleopatra, The Sign of the Cross, The Godless Girl, The King of Kings, The Ten Commandments, Manslaughter, The Affairs of Anatol, Male and Female, Joan the Woman, The Cheat, The Warrens of Virginia,* and *The Squaw Man.*

His pictures educated moviegoers about the rich, class divisions, marriage, etiquette, history, God, sex, the Bible, and the life of Christ. DeMille's father was a lay Episcopal minister; his mother was from an Orthodox Jewish Liverpool family. Motion pictures to DeMille were the universal pulpit.

The forces that shaped DeMille as an artist—his father's Episcopalianism and his mother's Jewishness and heritage, which the family denied—were at odds with each other. DeMille made pictures on a large canvas, and when the moment came to choose between art and commerce, the scholarly William, DeMille's older brother, chose art; Cecil, like his mother, who converted to the Anglican church, chose practicality and commerce.

DeMille's pictures were dismissed by critics as pandering to the masses.

DeMille would say, "Nobody likes me but the people"; he knew what they wanted, and his pictures were considered easy to watch. Like Griffith's, they moved; they were alive, beautifully designed, and well cast with memorable faces. They were exciting, rich in detail, and directed with gusto. DeMille could create viable drama out of mundane material. He said of D. W. Griffith, "He taught us how to photograph thought"—a sign in DeMille's office said, "Say it with props"—which "enabled us to tell stories in a new way and not just by action. Up to that time pictures had been all motion; after Griffith, we could photograph the soul and the mind, and that opened the gates that gave us the world."

From DeMille's days on the road as an actor, where he'd met his wife, Constance, and where he often had to dig ditches for the funds to get home ("I dug more ditches than anyone else west of the Mississippi," he said), he got a feel of and for America. "That America is still there," said DeMille, "and now it goes to the movies."

DeMille was following the family tradition. His father was a touring stage actor and playwright, one of the founders of the American Academy of Dramatic Arts in New York; he in fact named the institution and taught there for seven years.

Few directors were on the scale of Cecil B. DeMille. He was a showman, a master of the spectacle. Gloria Swanson, his greatest star, described DeMille entering the set like Caesar, with assistants following in his wake and everyone silent while he looked at each detail; when he was ready to sit down, a chair carrier was there to put the seat under him as the great director descended.

DeMille's demeanor came directly from watching his father's old friend, partner, and producer, David Belasco, who many believed was the greatest figure in the American theater and who towered over two generations. "To me," said Mary Pickford, "David Belasco was like the King of England, Julius Caesar and Napoleon rolled into one."

DeMille admired Belasco's handling of actors and his showmanship and made Belasco's style his own. Like Belasco, DeMille surrounded himself with pomp and glory. There was always a crowd of dignitaries to watch DeMille shoot one of his big scenes; he loved to have an audience as long as they were quiet and paid attention to the work at hand. DeMille even re-created Belasco's cathedral-like office, where more than a decade before Barbara had been brought by Willard Mack and Belasco had changed her name from Ruby Stevens to Barbara Stanwyck.

To both Belasco and DeMille, the minute attention to detail was directed toward a single objective: the production. DeMille's pictures may have been dismissed as lavish blobs of color with streaks of action, but they made mil-

lions. Barbara, for the first time in nine years of making pictures, was working with one of the most powerful and successful directors in Hollywood.

DeMille dressed like a director; he wore puttees and riding boots and
western dress with ruby, diamond, or sapphire cuff links and matching tie-
pin. He was flamboyant, learned to fly in 1917, and, when flying his own
plane—a Curtiss "Jenny" with a wingspan of forty-three feet and a top speed
of seventy-five miles per hour—wore goggles and leather helmet. In 1919, at
the age of thirty-seven, DeMille rented forty acres at the southwest corner of
Fairfax and Melrose Avenues with an option to buy at $1,500 an acre and cre-
ated a flying field there. He bought a number of Curtiss "Jennys" and started
Mercury Aviation, the first commercial transport company to carry passengers on scheduled flights to other cities, including San Diego, Salt Lake City,
and San Francisco (an eight-hour flight from Los Angeles). Three years and
twenty-five thousand passengers later (without an accident), DeMille had to
choose between Mercury Aviation and picture making. He sold the airline to
Rogers Airport and the planes to the government of Mexico, where they were
soon captured by the Zapata revolutionists.

Barbara and DeMille had worked together during the past couple of years
on *Lux Radio Theatre*. She enjoyed C.B.—he wasn't corrupt—and he loved
her; she was thrilled to be working with him.

"You certainly knew where his pictures were going or why they were
made," Barbara said of DeMille. He had "a style of his own," she said. "Something you don't see too much of."

Barbara was devoted to DeMille's ideals of the theater, despite their being
considered old-school; she was loyal to what she called "the ham."

DeMille, like Barbara, was a Republican. He'd voted for Roosevelt in
1932 "for one reason," he said. "Prohibition." It was Herbert Hoover whom
DeMille still held in the highest "esteem for his sheer brain power and his
dogged, uncompromising, selfless honesty." DeMille didn't like "the Jewish
people" in Los Angeles, though he would remind himself that he "was one
of them."

Barbara had played midwestern farm women, New England factory girls,
Park Avenue society women, business owners, prisoners, con artists, mis-
sionaries, mistresses, generals' daughters, gamblers, wives, mothers, and sluts.
She'd been in one Western as Annie Oakley, the best sharpshooter of the
American West, and loved the freedom of the role. She'd loved Westerns as a
child, had read countless books on the country's pioneers, and wanted to play
a real frontier woman, "not one of those crinoline-covered things you see in
most westerns," she said. "I'm with the boys. I want to go where the boys go."

Cecil B. DeMille, master showman who dressed and acted it; DeMille Drive, Los Angeles, circa 1936. "When you have a hundred electricians and a thousand extras waiting," said DeMille of moviemaking, "it's no time to begin worrying about the story. There's a devil on your back and he's riding with whip and spurs." (PHOTOFEST)

. . .

The building of the transcontinental railroad had been a dream of giants, and Cecil B. DeMille's re-creation of it would be almost as heroic a spectacle.

The United States was less than one hundred years old when the first transcontinental railroad was built. The country had been held together, North and South, with the winning of the Civil War, and the transcontinental railroad connected its coasts, East and West, and bound the country together.

It took fifteen thousand mostly Irish laborers—the size of the Civil War armies—to build the Union Pacific with picks, shovels, and mule-drawn scrapers, from the outer edges of civilization through prairie, desert, and mountains of wilderness.

At work DeMille was never without a finder around his neck. Like his parents, DeMille had been a stage actor; he made his debut at the age of nineteen and was in six Broadway productions, including *To Have and to Hold, Hamlet,* and his brother's semi-biographical *The Warrens of Virginia,* based loosely on the capture during the Civil War of their grandfather by the enemy. In it, Cecil appeared with Mary Pickford, then known as Gladys Smith. DeMille toured as an actor from Florida to Alaska and never lost the actor's flair; when directing, he performed for those on the set. All eyes were to be on DeMille; he didn't tolerate any competition from his actors or his crew.

Union Pacific, 1939. Left to right: Joel McCrea as troubleshooter Jeff Butler; Barbara as Mollie Monahan, postmistress at "end of track"; Robert Preston as Dick Allen, agitator. "A lot of actors thought he was hammy," McCrea said of DeMille, "but they were hammy actors so they shouldn't have worried about it. And Coop [Gary Cooper] wasn't hammy. He liked the old man and I did too." (PHOTOFEST)

"You are here to please me," DeMille said to his crew. "Nothing else matters."

Barbara was playing Mollie Monahan, the postmistress—the daughter of the Union Pacific's first engineer—who handles the Union Pacific mail at "end of track" and is the eyes and tongue for Irish immigrants who hadn't learned to read or write. Mollie belongs to the railroad, though with her orneriness and fight she acts as if the railroad belongs to her.

DeMille had originally wanted Claudette Colbert for the part of Mollie, but Colbert turned down the role.

He had wanted Gary Cooper for the part of Jeff Butler, the heroic troubleshooter sent from Washington to help keep law and order along the right-of-way. DeMille loved Cooper; he was DeMille's favorite actor. He'd just directed him in *The Plainsman*. Cooper had too many commitments with Goldwyn and Warner Bros. and wasn't available for the picture. He told DeMille, "Get McFee," Joel McCrea, the poor man's Gary Cooper.

DeMille had known McCrea socially. As a boy, McCrea had visited the DeMille family regularly, going to Sunday suppers there. DeMille had hoped

McCrea would marry his daughter Cecilia. McCrea had attended his daughters' school, a girls' school; the only boy other than McCrea there was the grandson of Harriet Beecher Stowe. DeMille's brother, William, sent his daughters, Agnes and Margaret, to the school, as did Louis B. Mayer his daughters, Irene and Edith. (DeMille himself had gone to a girls' school. When DeMille was eleven, his father died, and his mother, to support the family, turned the DeMille house into a girls' school. One of the students was Evelyn Nesbit, sent there by Stanford White to separate the sixteen-year-old from Jack Barrymore and other admirers. Nesbit described Cecil as a "pie-faced mutt." DeMille went to the Henry C. De Mille School for Girls for four years and at fifteen was sent to a military academy. To help his mother with expenses, DeMille rode the ninety miles to the Pennsylvania Military College on bicycle—clothes, equipment, and all, strapped on the back—his mother accompanying him on her own bike. It was at military school that DeMille's passion for detail, order, self-discipline, and physical fitness, instilled by his father's teachings, took shape and where the artist versus military regimentation was first played out.)

A treatment of *Union Pacific* was written for Fredric March, Joel McCrea, and Irene Dunne. Charles Bickford was cast as the gambler/saloon owner who was to bring drink, women, and trouble to the end of track and delay the Union Pacific's progress. Bickford dropped out of the picture because he didn't like the part and was replaced by J. Carrol Naish, who dropped out as well, because of a scheduling conflict. Brian Donlevy was hired for the job.

DeMille could be dictatorial. He had his quirks, but he was loyal to those who worked with him. He gave work to silent-screen actors long after their prime. He would give his crew hell and berate them if they made trouble or joked around when he was directing, but he invariably hired them back.

"If there were 500 people up on a mountain," said Barbara, "Mr. DeMille knew who the hell each one was. He could hear the train long before he could hear the whistle."

John Ford had made a triumphant epic in 1924—almost fifteen years earlier—about the building of the transcontinental railroad. It was the biggest picture Fox had ever made.

To make *The Iron Horse,* Ford had set up a base of operations in the Nevada wilderness. Five thousand extras played the Irish and Chinese railroad laborers; a regiment of the U.S. Cavalry was brought in; eight hundred Pawnee, Sioux, and Cheyenne Indians were used. A hundred cooks were needed

William Jeffers, center; with (left to right) Governors John Vivian of Colorado, Earl Warren of California, Ronald Sparks of Alabama, Prentice Cooper of Tennessee, 1943. Jeffers
taught himself telegraphy and rose through the ranks of the Union Pacific: a dispatcher at
nineteen, switchman, yardmaster, trainmaster, and onward. Twenty-eight years later, he
was made president of the railroad.

to feed the vast army of people involved in the making of the picture. "The
actors arrived wearing summer clothes," said Ford. They lived and worked
through blizzards with temperatures twenty degrees below zero; the women
lived in circus railroad cars; the men made homes on the sets. Ford worked
from a private railroad car hired from the Ringling Brothers. "We had a hell
of a time," he said.

Union Pacific had a budget of a million dollars. The West was America's
empire, and Cecil B. DeMille was considered as American as Mount Rush-
more. DeMille wanted to tell the story as an epic adventure, a "thundering
drama" of the men and women who "worked, fought, suffered to make the
American dream come true."

More often than not, it was said of DeMille that he ignored the facts of
history and cared less about character. DeMille's credo became: "Legend rides
the trail with history; truth rides a lonely trail." It was DeMille's lonely trail.
He was obsessed with historical accuracy and steeped himself in the period

With Holly Barnes and unidentified. (AMERICAN HERITAGE CEN-
TER, UNIVERSITY OF WYOMING)

before he was ready to go into production. He insisted that every significant
episode of *Union Pacific* was documented despite a popular ditty that said:
"Cecil B. DeMille/Much against his will,/Was persuaded to keep Moses,/Out
of the War of the Roses."

The Union Pacific's railroad lines went from the banks of the Missouri
River at Omaha, through the trackless prairie lands, to the endless reaches of
the West and met up with the Central Pacific Railroad at Promontory Summit, Utah, where the tracks were joined and the last tie was laid. With the
meeting of the tracks, the two companies, the Central Pacific and the Union
Pacific, had brought the country together; every city and town in America
was linked by railroad and telegraph line. When the last spike was hammered
in, church bells rang, fire alarms went off, people cheered passing parades,
and thousands knelt in prayer. "The future is coming. And fast," was the cry.

The Central Pacific originated in Sacramento. The mostly Chinese laborers laid track, ten miles of it a day, that went eastward across the Sierra
Nevada Mountains, fourteen thousand feet high, making a line 1,848 miles
through a country that for the most part was uninhabited.

DeMille went to York, Nebraska, to visit the last surviving witness of the
driving of the golden spike at Promontory Summit, Utah, in May 1869,
which marked the completion of the road and the linking of the continent.

To make the picture, DeMille enlisted the help of William Jeffers, the president of the Union Pacific Railroad. DeMille thought Jeffers "hard-fisted and outspoken," a man with "a big, heavy frame topped by a face that matched it and a cigar clenched in his strong teeth." Jeffers had started to work at the Union Pacific when he was fourteen and rose to be its president. He lent DeMille the company's fast track-laying crew to re-create the race between the Union Pacific and its rival, the Central Pacific, and arranged for DeMille to have the use of six locomotives and fifty-five cars, each of 1860–1870 vintage, and a right-of-way of fifteen miles of track, and he made available the railroad's resources, including the Union Pacific archives.

Natalie Visart designed the picture's costumes. Some felt she wasn't qualified to be a designer, that she was there as a friend of the DeMille family; she'd attended school with DeMille's daughter Katherine. But Visart and others had designed the clothes for DeMille's *Cleopatra,* with Travis Banton designing the costumes for Claudette Colbert. DeMille was a perfectionist; everything had to be just so. Visart would sit with DeMille and try to think of all the things he could possibly say against the design. If he didn't like something such as a hat or a wrap, she would offer up another. DeMille would put the other hat on a paper doll, and, said Visart, "it would slip the way it does and [DeMille] would poke it one way and another . . . and we'd spend hours poking paper dolls."

His office was filled with miniature trains and dollhouse-size sets. DeMille used Mathew Brady photographs to capture the period. He re-created the entire town of Cheyenne, Wyoming, complete with banks, saloons, livery stables, hotels, and railroad station.

A real trestle was built and weakened at key points, and a full-size locomotive rode through and toppled over like some great wounded dinosaur, hissing steam. DeMille got permission from the Interstate Commerce Commission to run and operate a railroad and had it licensed as a full-fledged railroad company.

He wanted real Indians, not overweight Cheyenne—"not in my pictures," he said. Some of the beer-bellied Indians did get through, and ultimately it was a good thing. No sooner did they arrive on location than it started to snow. The cold and wet and mud resulted in an outbreak of the flu. More than five hundred people were down at one time and had to be treated in emergency clinics.

The British director Arthur Rosson spent almost three weeks overseeing for DeMille a second unit of four hundred on location, first in Iron Springs, Utah, where six miles of railroad track were laid, and then in Oklahoma and the Mojave Desert. Rosson, former stunt actor and screenwriter, had worked as one of DeMille's associate directors, beginning in 1926 with *The King of Kings.*

If one wanted to talk with Barbara on the set, Holly Barnes was always there, sitting with her, watching, never excusing herself. As Barbara's secretary and on-the-set hairdresser, she was described as Barbara's shadow. Barnes went where Barbara went, regardless of the studio. Holly was making $65 a week with a weekly bonus of $17.50.

Barbara didn't have a studio maid; her maid had quit. Holly thought Barbara should have one. All the stars had maids whom they paid for themselves. Holly interviewed various people and recommended Harriett Coray, a longtime friend then working for another actress. Harriett had started as a studio maid working for Myrna Loy, a job she took on from one of Harriett's adoptive aunts, who also worked for Loy.

Harriett Coray was twenty-seven, fair-skinned with straight hair and green eyes. Her mother was part Irish, part black, and passed for white. Her father, a miner who panned for gold, traveled with Harriett's mother throughout the Southwest after placing Harriett in a convent in St. Louis where she was raised by nuns. When her family relocated to Los Angeles and Harriett graduated from Thomas Jefferson High School, she applied for a job working as a cartoonist with a new artist—Walt Disney—whose company was in Burbank. But Harriett got cold feet and went to work for Myrna Loy. Harriett was married and had a six-year-old girl called Peggy Jean.

Barbara said to Harriett about the job, "Why don't you try me?"

At first Harriett was scared to death of Barbara. Harriett knew how to do her job, but Barbara was businesslike and seemed to have "an aura all her own," said Harriett. She got Holly to clue her in to the things that Barbara liked, such as tea every afternoon at four o'clock served on big trays brought by uniformed waiters in white coats. Barbara soon put Harriett at ease and made her feel comfortable. Harriett thought Barbara was "the least actress-y of any star" she had known. "It's too much of an effort for her to put on an act, so she's simply herself—real—and real means self-reliant."

Barbara moved fast, and Harriett had a hard time keeping up with her. No sooner would Harriett say "Miss . . ." than Barbara was out of earshot across the set, which only exasperated Harriett. After a day or two of that, Harriett just yelled, "Missy," and that stopped Barbara. The name stuck.

DeMille told Barbara that as Mollie Monahan she could use an Irish brogue. Barbara recalled what had happened with *The Plough and the Stars,*

Harriett Coray, circa 1939. She grew up in Chicago and went to convent schools. When she started to work for Barbara she was living in a segregated Los Angeles neighborhood, on East 54th Street, with her husband, Simon, and six-year-old daughter from a previous marriage. Barbara would read ten books a week and pass them on to Harriett, who, after reading each, would take them to the Motion Picture relief home.
(COURTESY MICHAEL CORAY)

where mid-picture she was told to drop her Irish accent and was then accused by reviewers of not being able to sustain one. She bet DeMille $50 that she wouldn't lose her accent during the production.

Barbara arranged for her brother, By—screen name, Bert—Stevens, to get a bit part in the picture as one of the patrons in a Cheyenne gambling tent.

Robert Preston, at 21, was hired to play Brian Donlevy's fast-talking, slick gambling partner at odds with his old war pal Jeff (McCrea); they had fought, bled, and "died" together as Union soldiers; each is in love with Mollie Monahan.

Preston had worked in the Pasadena Community Theater for two years, where he appeared in more than forty productions, including *Idiot's Delight,* which had helped to bring him to Paramount.

Preston was new. No one had heard of him, but he was sure of himself. He'd been told by a character actor, "Whenever you're acting, you reach up and take hold of the proscenium arch and you pull it down around your shoulders."

Just before DeMille was to start shooting the picture, his prostate acted up, and he underwent an emergency operation. It didn't stop him, though, from going forward with the first day's shooting. The day following the operation the fifty-seven-year-old director was brought to the set with a fever of 102. Barbara, Joel McCrea, and Robert Preston rehearsed while DeMille directed

With Robert Preston, *Union Pacific,* 1939. DeMille was described by Evelyn Keyes as "a tyrant . . . a despot in his own world, perched high above on a giant boom, [giving] his orders through a microphone whose projection filled every corner of the stage." (AMERI-CAN HERITAGE CENTER, UNIVERSITY OF WYOMING)

from a stretcher. For ten days, DeMille's stretcher was fixed to the camera boom, and he swung with it up in the air and down to check camera angles.

Preston believed that DeMille only understood the spectacular crowd scenes, that as soon as those shots were finished, DeMille didn't know what he was doing. "In the small interior shots," said Preston, "DeMille would yell, 'Cut! Print it.' And that was it. No direction. No retakes."

For more than two weeks of shooting, Barbara and Bob Preston were alone in a boxcar. "Because there were no crowd scenes, no special effects, just two people acting," said Preston, "you'd never have known the old man was on the set." DeMille believed that making a picture was not "an acting school." He hired an actor because he trusted him or her to be "professional. *Professional.*" He said, "When you do something wrong, *that* is when I will talk to you."

DeMille thought Barbara was one of the most sensitive, least temperamental artists that he'd worked with. "She is a human being as well as a great artist," he said of her.

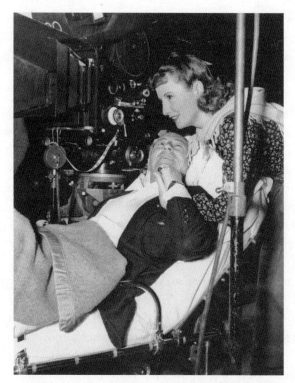

With DeMille, shooting on *Union Pacific*. He returned to the studio, against doctor's orders, the day after his emergency operation from a prostate flare-up that had caused him to collapse, seen here directing from a stretcher with a fever of 102, January 10, 1939.

There was never a "better workman." DeMille believed that no woman could be an actress until she'd had her heart broken.

He expected his actors and actresses to act with courage and to be willing to do whatever the role required without "squalls of temperament or temper" and to do it well; Barbara was the most willing, the least actressy; he could count on her to do "her work with all her heart." DeMille was equally impressed with how, in making *Union Pacific,* Barbara willingly exposed herself to danger to do the most extraordinary stunts: leaping from railroad cars; lying on her back in a boxcar while sulfur and molasses spilled over her.

DeMille never allowed his actors to read the script. "It only confuses them and they get their ideas mixed up with mine." He outlined each scene as the actors came to it, explained the business, gave them their lines, and rehearsed the action. "The first thing every one of them has to learn is to do exactly what they are told." This was the way other silent directors worked—John

Ford, Henry Hathaway, Henry King, and the others—who survived sound. John Ford's advice for a director setting up a scene: "Don't look at the fucking script. That will confuse you. You know the story. Tell it in pictures. Forget the words."

While Barbara had proved she could do light comedy, Bob's railroad picture, *Stand Up and Fight* ("for the muggs more than the dames," said *Variety*), once again set out to show moviegoers that Robert Taylor was all man ("another two-fisted role for Taylor and a smash hit for MGM").

In the picture, which opened early in 1939, Bob was transformed into Clark Gable; he walked like Gable, talked like Gable, smiled like Gable, even looked like Gable.

Bob's next picture was a light comedy, this time with Myrna Loy, called *Lucky Night*.

Myrna Loy viewed picture making as "a tiresome necessity in a chaotic world," and she thought *Lucky Night* was "a lame bit of whimsy." Loy was supposed to first make a new *Thin Man* with William Powell, so Bob left Los Angeles for New York to see as much theater as possible. No sooner had he arrived at Grand Central than Metro called him back to the studio. Bill Powell was being operated on because of an intestinal obstruction. *The Thin Man Returns* was postponed; *Lucky Night* was to start shooting right away.

Myrna Loy thought Bob somewhat stuffy. The first day on the set Loy put on some Cuban records to fill the hours between shots. Bob approached her and said, "Do you have to play that sexy stuff all the time? It's the dirtiest music I ever heard."

"Oh, brother," Loy said to herself.

Myrna and Bob got on during the picture, but she was further put off when Bob tried to "cook up a little triangle" to make Barbara think Myrna was interested in him. Holly Barnes asked Myrna's maid, Theresa, about Myrna's interest in Bob, and she assured Holly that it wasn't true.

"I'm not sure Barbara believed that," said Myrna. On the last day of shooting "Barbara came by in a limousine," said Loy, "and whisked Bob off."

The final scene of *Union Pacific* showing the driving of the golden spike joining the track-laying teams and completing the transcontinental railroad was shot in Canoga Park, near Hollywood. DeMille was at the helm. The actual golden spike of the 1869 ceremony—removed from a special vault in the Wells Fargo bank in San Francisco—was used in the picture. The two trains were perfect replicas in every detail. The Chinese and Irish laborers flung their hats to the wind and cheered to the tune of the locomotives' whistles.

With Joel McCrea, *Union Pacific*, 1939. As photographed, they embodied DeMille's vision of the men
and women who worked, fought, and suffered to
make the American dream come true.

As they were setting up the shot, DeMille told his assistant to have the
Indians lined up along the track. "Their lands have just been sequestered,
progress and civilization are triumphant," said DeMille. "And this scene is
symbolic of their plight. So they should look sad."

The scene was shot. The Indians sat quietly by the side of the tracks amid
all the hoopla, looking sad-eyed. The sadness was real; two steel rails lay
across the breadth of their once holy hunting grounds like dead black snakes,
and the fire-breathing "iron horse" that slithered along would soon forever
chase away the buffalo.

DeMille shot much of *Union Pacific* in Cedar City. The location work
with McCrea and Barbara was shot in Sonora and at Woodland Hills in the
western area of the San Fernando Valley, including the scene with the Indians tearing down water tanks and the scene with the golden spiking. Some
of the picture was shot in an icehouse in Los Angeles. Much of it was shot
on soundstages at Paramount; the studio had no back lot, and DeMille used
process shots.

DeMille shot 200,000 feet of film on a $1 million budget.

Barbara was getting $7,500 a week (actresses, though not Barbara, often worked with "the great DeMille" at half their salary for the privilege of working with him and the chance at stardom; Claudette Colbert, making *Midnight* at the same time, was getting $15,000 a week); McCrea, $5,000; Preston, $250; Akim Tamiroff, $1,000 per picture.

Barbara was on location for five weeks, eating cookhouse food, going without hot water, sleeping on a cot. "Just trying to re-create our history, to the best of my ability, was more than enough job for me," she said. She felt as if she were a part of the American past.

From her days as a child in Brooklyn, watching the fearless Pearl White—the modern Joan of Arc—jump off bridges, cliffs, railroad trains, yachts, doing her own stunts in the serials, Barbara respected stunt people, understood how hard they worked, and marveled at what they could do, and she was determined to do most of her own stunts. Pearl White had been Barbara's model: a woman without temperament who worked ten hours a day, disliked flattery, was frank, with plain common sense, and regarded her acting more as work than as art.

To make *Union Pacific,* Barbara stepped out of the Park Avenue gowns of *The Mad Miss Manton* into the dust-covered boots and britches of Mollie Monahan. Her glamorization didn't stop from one picture to the next. As scruffy as she was, done up to look like the postmistress at "end of track," the refinement of Barbara's beauty and her burgeoning radiance on-screen were there to see. Her thick brogue softened her edgier self; she played Mollie Monahan with the spirit of an innocent and the wisdom of an experienced soul. At last, she was the girl "with the boys" in an epic saga of the American West, and she reveled in it.

FOURTEEN

Champion of the "Cockeyed Wonder"

Where do you come from? You look like you don't have parents.
—Joe Bonaparte to Lorna Moon, *Golden Boy*

No tricks, Miss Moon.
—Eddie Fuseli, *Golden Boy*

Dream lover, fold your arms around me
—"Dream Lover," from the film *The Love Parade* (1929)
(Clifford Grey/Victor Schertzinger)

January started off with Hollywood spinning from the aftershocks of a *Photoplay* article that revealed the names of those movie couples who were living together in unwedded bliss. The exposé was on the stands weeks before Christmas.

The article, "Hollywood's Unmarried Husbands and Wives," struck dumb Will Hays, the former postmaster general under Warren G. Harding and guardian of motion picture movie morals. His code of movie "don'ts and be carefuls" had been devised to limit sex on-screen, banish scandals off, and keep the government out of filmdom's business.

The article caused havoc with the studios and with those whose living arrangements were openly written about for the moviegoing public.

"Nowhere has domesticity, outside the marital state, reached such a full flower as in Hollywood," said the article by Kirtley Baskette. "Nowhere are there so many famous unmarried husbands and wives."

The Hays Office issued a statement calling the article "pretty bad. The title is even worse than the story itself but it's all bad." The article described the intimate details of the living arrangements of Hollywood's biggest names: Carole Lombard and Clark Gable; George Raft and Virginia Pine; Charlie Chaplin and Paulette Goddard (no marriage certificate existed to prove they were husband and wife); Constance Bennett and Gilbert Roland ("in a perfect design for living," said the article, "with a titled husband in Europe and . . . her devoted slave [Roland] in Hollywood"); and Barbara Stanwyck and Robert Taylor.

The article described how most of the couples could not marry since one or both were already married. These "unwed couples . . . go everywhere together; do everything in pairs. No hostess would think of inviting them separately, or pairing them with another. They solve one another's problems," the article went on, "handle each other's business affairs . . . build houses near each other . . . father or mother each other's children . . . Consider the results," it said, "strictly out of wedlock."

Of Barbara and Bob, the piece described how "they've been practically a family since Bob bought his ranch estate in Northridge and built a house there . . . No coincidence can possibly explain his choosing that site . . . right beside Barbara Stanwyck's place . . . [W]itness how quickly their interests— deep and expensive, *permanent* interests—merged after they slipped into the unique Hollywood habit . . . Just as Dad gives Mother an electric icebox for Christmas and she retaliates with a radio, Bob Taylor presents Barbara Stanwyck with a tennis court for her birthday, with Barbara giving Bob a two-horse auto trailer for his!"

Following the publication of the piece, Metro-Goldwyn-Mayer insisted Bob and Barbara get married.

Newspapers ignored the article, but within a few weeks Clark Gable and Carole Lombard announced they were to be married as soon as Gable's divorce came through from his second wife, Rhea Langham, and Barbara and Bob publicly announced their engagement. Bob had given Barbara a diamond and ruby engagement bracelet for Christmas, along with a Saint Christopher medal engraved, "God Protect Her Because I Love Her."

Barbara and Bob had been seeing each other for three years. Barbara knew she was in it for the long haul and in certain ways knew that marrying Bob was going to be tough. Barbara was attractive, but there were many other women in Hollywood who were far more beautiful. She knew she was going to have to vie for Bob's attention, and "how in hell am I supposed to do that?" she said.

The *Los Angeles Examiner* banner headline, December 14, 1938, soon after the *Photoplay* article "Hollywood's Unmarried Husbands and Wives" appeared on the stands, creating an industry-wide scandal. (*LOS ANGELES EXAMINER*)

When Barbara and Bob had started to see each other, she was much more experienced sexually than he. She taught him about making love, as she taught him everything she'd learned about Hollywood; coached him with his roles; advised him in his dealings with Metro; sent him to her publicist, Helen Ferguson, and to her financial managers, Morgan Maree of Miller Marx, headed by Marion's brother, Alan Miller.

Morgan Maree had taken over Barbara's finances and investments after Zeppo became her agent. She and Maree had become friends, as he set about undoing the web of chaos created by Fay's schemes and dealings, from which she was still trying to get free. Barbara thought Maree an astute businessman and gave him the latitude to invest her money in long-term plans as he saw fit. Barbara required a business manager "just to stop all silliness" and plan for the future. Money was important to Barbara, but security was more important; she didn't want to be dependent on anyone.

Once Barbara and Bob were married, the plan was to have Bob and his horses and Great Dane, Hager, move to Marwyck while they looked for a house in town. Bob was selling his eight-room cottage made from rock and his twenty-eight-acre ranch. With it were a two-car garage, dog kennels for twelve dogs, a mile-long practice track, and thirty acres. The racers Barbara

had given him were to be moved to a stable in town; he would find good homes for all the other horses, and he was hoping to buy a 160-acre ranch near Chatsworth.

Barbara had put her share of Marwyck up for sale: the house, tennis courts, pool, and ten acres. The rest of the ranch the Marxes would keep.

Barbara had owned Marwyck for three years. The farm had thirty-nine racehorses—each from celebrated bloodlines—Brief Moment, Irish Broom, Little Shower, among them. The Nut, by Mad Hatter from Afternoon by Prince Palatine, had won more than $100,000 and was from the family of Top Flight, Spot Cash, Candy Kid, Whisk Broom 2nd, Crusader, and Fayette.

They'd sold one horse called Mad Sue to Mervyn LeRoy and another, Co Step, to Harry Warner. As a breeding farm, Marwyck was a success. It was a profitable year for the ranch. "We haven't made a lot of money," said Barbara, "but probably about as much as we could have got in interest from the banks. And look at the fun we've had."

Barbara had spent afternoons with Dion by the pool, looking out over the fields and marveling at how "wonderful [it was] that we own this? When I was a child," she said, "if I'd had a pool like this I'd have thought I'd died and gone to heaven. I thought a squirt from a garden hose was wonderful."

Dion wasn't as thrilled about it as Barbara was; he'd grown up with it. Barbara felt she'd been too extravagant with him.

Their ranch house was simple, unpretentious, comfortable, with a lived-in feeling. Its only extravagance: her bathroom with its large marble tub. Barbara had always wanted a fancy bathtub. She'd only found out what a bathtub was when she was an older child. To make up for the times when she'd toured on the road staying "in tank town boarding houses" and bathing in awful tubs, she'd given herself a bathroom the size of a movie set.

The ranch was too far out of town for friends to visit. The long drive to and from the studio was too much for Barbara. Before she'd started to see Bob, she'd disliked socializing. Now she'd come to enjoy it, and several nights a week she and Bob were out at parties, premieres, and nightclubs. She still suffered from shyness and the feeling that she didn't measure up. She would arrive at the Trocadero or Ciro's in an evening gown, her hair done up, and would see Claudette ("looking divine") or Dietrich ("looking like something out of this world") or Hedy Lamarr and feel awful about herself, like a shop-girl. "It's no use," Barbara would say. "I know what I look like. I like comfort too well to fix and fuss."

Barbara and Bob had permanent ringside seats for fight night at the Hollywood Legion Stadium and went regularly to Hollywood Baseball Park to watch a game and eat hot dogs and peanuts, often taking Dion with them.

Through Bob Cobb, president of the Brown Derby, Barbara and Bob were part owners of the Hollywood Stars, a decades-old baseball team, originally the Vernon Tigers, that had joined the Pacific Coast League in 1909. The team had moved to San Francisco and become the Mission Reds, or the Missions.

In 1938, the Missions' owner, Herbert Fleishhacker, brought the team back to Los Angeles, reclaimed its Hollywood name, and after one season sold the Stars to a syndicate of Hollywood and Los Angeles businessmen, among them Bob Cobb, who enlisted the energy and financial backing of Barbara and Bob, Gary Cooper, and William Powell, as well as the former silent actor and director Lloyd Bacon (*42nd Street, Footlight Parade, San Quentin,* and eighty-odd additional pictures) and others. Wade "Red" Killefer was the team's manager.

For its first season, the Stars—the press called them the "Twinks"—had charity exhibition games with actors like Bob, playing against studio supporting players. The fans loved the games and filled the stands.

Bob threw the first pitch for the team's debut game against the Chicago White Sox; Gary Cooper was catcher; Lloyd Bacon, umpire. Barbara, Bob, and Dion sat behind home plate. The Ritz Brothers sat nearby. When the Stars made a good play or a home run, the Ritz Brothers climbed the screen and put on their act for seven-year-old Dion, who was delighted with their antics.

The team's financial backers soon recouped their investment and went out

With Franchot Tone and Joan Crawford at a polo match with actors and the Uplifters Club to benefit the Children's Convalescent home, June 1936.

to hire serious players: Floyd Caves "Babe" Herman of the Brooklyn Robins; Bill Cissell; the Chicago "Black Sox" spitball ace Frank Shellenback; Bobby Doerr; and Vince DiMaggio.

Barbara and Bob's circle of friends was made up of Ty Power and Annabella, the Fred MacMurrays, the Bennys, the Marxes, the Wellmans. Dinner parties were on Saturday nights in rotation, at the Bennys', Barbara and Bob's, the Millands', sitting around the fireplace or the patio after dinner, getting into arguments about pictures, listening to Jack Benny tell stories, or playing the Game, Tripoli, bingo, or geography. Barbara still had a horror of going to a party and not knowing anyone there, and if everyone was asked to get up and perform, she avoided it. She would leave the room to make a phone call or powder her nose. Barbara loathed parlor games, particularly when they were played so seriously. She played in order to be sociable and, when she did play, felt like "committing manslaughter." She rarely knew the answers—the capital of Utah or the biggest city in South Dakota—and people would get annoyed with her for not knowing. Barbara had traveled with shows all over the United States. "But who knows where you are in shows?" she said. "All you're interested in is counting up the house. I think you're lucky if you know what state you live in these days."

On other occasions the Bennys, Millands, Marxes, and MacMurrays went to the movies together.

Barbara gave Zeppo a party at the Cafe Lamaze for his thirty-eighth birthday. Bing Crosby sang, Bob Hope told jokes, Jack Benny played his violin, and Fred MacMurray played the saxophone. The press assumed Barbara would use the event to announce the date of her wedding; city desks checked in to see if there was any news. No announcement was made.

After *Union Pacific* was finished shooting, Barbara and Joel McCrea were called into DeMille's office. He was preparing a script, *North West Mounted Police,* and wanted Barbara and McCrea to star in the picture. Barbara was thrilled, as was McCrea. When Gary Cooper became available—he was unhappy with the picture Warner Bros. had for him—DeMille wanted Cooper to star in the picture as well. McCrea and Cooper were both right for the same role. McCrea decided to bow out and let Cooper take the part. DeMille hired Preston Foster to replace McCrea, and he dropped Barbara and hired Paulette Goddard, then in the press for being the unwed, unofficial Mrs. Charlie Chaplin as well as one of Selznick's final choices for Scarlett O'Hara, along with Jean Arthur and Joan Bennett until Vivien Leigh appeared as "the dark horse."

McCrea advised Barbara not to be angry. "It's just another picture," he said, and reassured her there would be others.

"Well, he loved us until he could do better," she said.

Moviegoers were staying at home, mesmerized by their favorite radio shows. Attendance at the box office was dropping off; double features weren't drawing audiences the way they had. The average moviegoer was twenty-seven years old, earning $28 a week.

Barbara renewed her contract with the J. Walter Thompson Company for *Lux Radio Theatre.* She frequently used radio as a showcase for her work and asked a producer to tune in to her next broadcast.

Nothing lighthearted had come her way in a long time. Barbara wanted to prove that she could do something happy. She gave the lines everything she had. "The audience in the theater seemed to like it," she said. "And I was feeling pretty good about the whole thing." One of the technicians told Barbara that for the broadcast's last forty minutes the show had been off the air in Los Angeles. "A week's work shot to hell," said Barbara. "The station has to break down just when I have a chance to prove I can do something besides woebegone mothers with fourteen children at their skirts, heading over the hill to the poorhouse."

In that vein, Barbara performed *So Big* on *Lux Radio Theatre* with Preston

Foster, Fay Wray, and Otto Kruger. At intermission, the show's guests were Sara Delano Roosevelt, the president's mother, and Edna Ferber.

Barbara appeared on *The Chase and Sanborn Hour*. With the host, Don Ameche, she did an adaptation of Universal's 1936 hit *Next Time We Love*, which had starred Margaret Sullavan and James Stewart. On the same show, Barbara did a comedy skit with Edgar Bergen and Charlie McCarthy in which she marries Charlie so he can go to Niagara Falls (she's honeymooning in London; they're "modern") on "the Twenty-Cent Limited" ("And they charged me $8.20 for a ticket," said McCarthy).

Barbara signed a contract with Columbia to star in the film version of Clifford Odets's hit play *Golden Boy*. The play was the Group Theatre's greatest success; when it opened in November 1937 at the Belasco, *The New York Times* hailed the company as "our leading art theater."

Golden Boy had the patina of "official art": hallowed, reverential, self-important. It had the seriousness and the suffering of its moment.

Its subject: the working class, talent, family virtue; the conflict between artistic aspiration up against brute force and money; sexual suffering, political suffering, social suffering, exotic suffering.

The play ran for 250 performances in New York and was sold to Columbia Pictures for $100,000. Harry Cohn wanted it to be the studio's biggest movie of the year. Columbia was still in search of its golden boy to be the lead. More than five thousand possible golden boys had been interviewed in three months; almost a hundred actors were tested, including Elia Kazan, Alan Ladd, Richard Carlson, and Tyrone Power.

Alan Ladd blackened his hair with mascara to look Italian for his test. It was a hot day, and the mascara and sweat ran down his face. Richard Carlson was on Broadway in the musical comedy *Stars in Your Eyes* with Jimmy Durante and Ethel Merman; Fox refused to loan Columbia Francis Lederer, who'd starred in the West Coast company of *Golden Boy*.

Cohn wanted John Garfield for the role of Joe Bonaparte, but after Capra had picked Darryl Zanuck to be the first recipient of the Irving Thalberg award, Jack Warner refused to lend Garfield to Columbia for the picture.

Odets's play was about Hollywood, about success and fame, about a musician fighting for self-expression; a prizefighter out to conquer (his name is Bonaparte); a first-generation American, son of an Italian immigrant, refusing to be kept down, fighting to get out, to be 100 percent American, and searching for his place in a world that ignores those without success and money. To have it all, he abandons his art, his intellect, his family, his soul.

Barbara was to play Lorna Moon, girlfriend of Tom Moody, former top fight manager around town who takes his 10 percent; he's desperate to find a winner again who can turn things around for him.

Moody won't divorce his wife and marry Lorna until he's achieved a "resurrection." ("I've been off the gold standard for eight years," he tells Lorna. "Find me a good black boy and I'll show you a mint.")

Lorna Moon, like Barbara, is an orphan, but untouched by love. Odets saw in Lorna a "quiet glitter" despite her eyes that "hold a soft, sad glance"; she is feminine, vulnerable, alone in the world, but tough in her ability to take care of herself. She's been reared by a father incapable of raising a child; she's got by with no feeling.

She's the girl over the river ("My father's still alive, shucking oysters and bumming drinks," says Lorna). Her side of life is lonely, abandoned; she's "a lost baby," Joe Bonaparte says of her. Odets took her first name from "forlorn" and "lovelorn." She's a drifter, brought up with the war in the streets; nothing can touch her. She understands cruelty; she had no dolls, no birthday parties.

Her last name is Moon. The moon is made of rock, lifeless. Lorna wants to marry Moody, though she doesn't love him; she wants to be protected by him. Moody needs Joe Bonaparte to stop holding back with "his mitts" and fight with fists "mightier than the fiddle" and win. Moody's partner says, "Bonaparte used to have a punch like dynamite; now even a mosquito stings harder."

Without Bonaparte's soul in the ring, he won't win.

"It's our last chance for a decent life," Moody says to Lorna. "For getting married—we have to make the kid fight! He's more than a meal ticket—he's everything we want and need from life!"

Lorna goes on their behalf to stir Joe up. "I'm a tramp from Newark," she reassures Moody about being able to seduce Joe into taking the fighting road. "I know a dozen ways."

Lorna makes it clear to Bonaparte she's a whore and doesn't much like him; she doesn't need anybody, unlike Moody, who tells Lorna how much he needs her. "Success and fame!" Lorna says to Joe as they sit alone one night on a park bench. "Or just a lousy living." That sums it up for Lorna. Joe is complex and tough and proud. Lorna has never been protected by life and family; her world has no values; fame and success are the answers for her; she sees it the way society sees it—winning and losing—and she's rooting for the fighter. Joe knows money won't get him a soul or culture; he is literate, educated by the *Encyclopaedia Britannica* ("from A to Z"), with a desire to learn; he knows that fighting is brutal, that it tears down life.

Luther Adler as Joe Bonaparte with Frances Farmer as Lorna Moon, in the Group Theatre's production of Clifford Odets's *Golden Boy,* directed by Harold Clurman; it played for two hundred and fifty performances, opening in November 1937 and closing in June 1938. In the cast were the Group's actors Morris Carnovsky, Lee J. Cobb, Howard Da Silva, Jules Garfield, Elia Kazan, Robert Lewis, and Martin Ritt.

Joe has it all except for love. Bonaparte's trainer says to him, "Your heart ain't in fightin'—your hate is."

Golden Boy was about to start filming, and Columbia still didn't have its Joe Bonaparte. The studio was casting Bonaparte's sister and sent for a test of a girl under contract at Paramount. Rouben Mamoulian, the picture's director, watched the test and spotted in it a young man.

Harry Cohn sent for the actor. He was a twenty-year-old contract player, a member of Paramount's Golden Circle of promising actors, who included Betty Field and Robert Preston.

Cohn asked the blond twenty-year-old William Beedle if he could act.

"I'm not sure," said Beedle.

"Can you box?" Cohn asked.

"No."

"Can you play the violin?"

"No."

Nor had he ever studied an Italian dialect or been photographed with darker hair or had his hair curled.

Cohn asked, "Then what the hell are you doing here?"

"I'm here because you sent for me," Beedle said.

The actor was given a script on Thursday and told he would be tested the next day.

Barbara and Adolphe Menjou agreed to work with Beedle on the test Mamoulian was ready to direct.

Barbara saw that the young actor had a certain quality. She saw his dedication and thought he would be good as Joe Bonaparte. He was six feet tall with blue eyes and blond hair. She thought he had what it took to be a big star and pushed Mamoulian to hire the young actor.

On April 1, April Fools' Day, Mamoulian took a big chance and agreed to give Beedle the part. Mamoulian told the young actor he had twelve days, when the picture was to start, to be made over into a boxer, a violinist, and an Italian. Beedle wondered why they hadn't mentioned the acting.

The name William Franklin Beedle Jr. was changed to William Holden, an associate editor of the *Los Angeles Times*. ("I've got a boy here I'd like to use your name for," said Terry DeLapp, the head of Paramount's publicity department. "Will he get me into trouble?" asked the namesake. "I'll vouch for him," said DeLapp.)

Columbia bought out half of Beedle's contract from Paramount. His salary, which he had negotiated himself, was $50 a week; Columbia was paying $25 of it. Beedle was making "less than a waitress at a drive-in," he said.

Lorna Moon is the unattainable. Joe says to her, "You're half dead and you don't know it." Lorna says later, "You make me feel too human, Joe. All I want is peace and quiet, not love . . . I don't mind being what you call 'half dead.' In fact it's what I like."

Frances Farmer had starred as Lorna Moon in the original stage production of *Golden Boy*. At twenty-three, Farmer was under contract to Paramount and made a success in *Come and Get It*. She'd left Hollywood to go east on a leave from the studio to work in summer stock with the hope of becoming a more serious actress. Harold Clurman, directing the stage production of Odets's play and head of the Group Theatre and one of its founders, and Clifford Odets were both drawn to Farmer's perfect beauty and hired her for the part of Lorna Moon.

Elia Kazan, Odets's best friend, who played Eddie Fuseli, the gangster who takes over managing Bonaparte's career, said Farmer "had a special glow, a skin without flaw, lustrous eyes—a blonde you'd dream about. She also had a wry and rather disappointed manner, a twist of the mouth, that suited the part. She was a dramatic contrast to the dark up-from-under men she was going to play with."

"You want your arm in gelt up to the elbow," Lorna says to Joe. "You'll take fame so people won't laugh or scorn your face. You'd give your soul for those things. But every time you turn your back your little soul kicks you in the teeth."

Lee J. Cobb (left) as Mr. Bonaparte in the screen version of *Golden Boy* (he played Mr. Carp in the original stage production) with William H. Strauss (silent picture actor as well as in *The Public Enemy* and *I Am a Fugitive from a Chain Gang,* among other sound films) as Mr. Carp. (AMERICAN HERITAGE CENTER, UNIVERSITY OF WYOMING)

Clifford Odets was drawn to women who would permit him to "combine the best features of both married and single life without the woman being unhappy about it." Odets wanted it "hot and cold, north and south." He believed a wife should keep house for him, cook for him, give him children and care for them, and, at the same time, look after and protect his genius. The character of Lorna Moon is there to serve as a mirror of male virtue, male aspiration, male sensitivity and conflict.

Most of the time is spent on the male characters, even the minor male characters: Lee J. Cobb; Adolphe Menjou; his partner, Sam Levene, as the brother-in-law. The daughter, Beatrice Blinn, has nothing to do except beg for her husband to go to bed with her. She admires him; she admires the father; the women are there to admire the men. The nuance and the character are in the men.

Odets wrote Fuseli as a predator on the hunt. "It is the background of the downtrodden Wop," wrote Odets. "It develops a furtiveness . . . His homosexuality may be only partly conscious. He is a bird of prey. Eddie should be the most stylized performance in the play. The reason he is anxious to have a champ is that he would be Eddie's boy to be proud of. He would have dominance over him." Kazan said he played the part of the mobster, "circling the young fighter" that he wanted a piece of, "like a hawk then stooping to pick him up. I couldn't take my eyes off Luther [Joe Bonaparte]; he was what I craved." Kazan gave the part "an elegance of manner and dress" that he'd observed in top gangster figures. "I also made myself like a homosexual."

"Don't ask me which is worse," Fuseli says, "women or spiders." When Kazan looked at Frances Farmer onstage, he "felt this disgust," he said. "I couldn't understand what the man I wanted saw in her."

Bonaparte finally erupts and says to Fuseli, "You use me like a gun. Your loyalty's to keep me oiled and polished."

Kazan played the part with passion; eventually, he took over the part of Joe Bonaparte on the stage, and Lee J. Cobb took on the role of the father that Morris Carnovsky had played. Cobb at twenty-six years old was playing the elderly Mr. Bonaparte.

"What Odets was trying to say," wrote Harold Clurman, "was that the old world of money and power was fast becoming decrepit and desperate, while the new world of the future, which belonged to the mass of people, was, in America, still raw, unclear, undisciplined, mentally and morally clumsy."

Frank Capra recognized himself in Joe Bonaparte and intended to direct *Golden Boy* as soon as he finished directing the picture of the Moss Hart and George S. Kaufman Pulitzer Prize–winning play, *You Can't Take It with You*. Capra had convinced Harry Cohn to buy the film rights to Odets's play as a way to entice Jean Arthur back to Columbia, to star in *You Can't Take It with You* (replacing Olivia de Havilland, whom Warner had decided not to loan to Columbia). Arthur was then to star as Lorna Moon, the blonde who would be the dramatic contrast to the dark up-from-under men Kazan spoke of.

Jean Arthur announced that she was retiring from the screen, or Cohn planted the story in the press as part of his attempt to win Arthur back to Columbia. She was "completely worn out," she said, "more mentally than physically," from the six pictures she'd made in a year, one right after the other, including Capra's *Mr. Deeds Goes to Town*, *The Ex–Mrs. Bradford*, DeMille's *Plainsman*, and Frank Borzage's *History Is Made at Night*. "Three too many," she said. She was bushed from her yearlong legal battle with Columbia over Cohn's bullying picture assignments for her. She was "physically numb" from her fight with Cohn.

Instead of retiring, Arthur signed a new three-year contract with Columbia that allowed her to make only two pictures a year for Cohn and gave her the right to make one film a year with another studio. Most crucial of all for Arthur, her new contract stipulated that she would not be required to talk to the press or make public appearances for any of the pictures.

Rouben Mamoulian didn't want Jean Arthur for the part of Lorna Moon. He wanted Barbara Stanwyck. Barbara could much more project Lorna Moon, cynical and sexual, "a tramp from Newark" rescued by Tom Moody, fight manager ("He loved me in a world of enemies," says Lorna, "of stags and bulls. He stiffened the space between my shoulder blades. Misery reached out to misery"). Jean Arthur was cast in Howard Hawks's *Only Angels Have Wings.*

Mamoulian saw in Barbara "the essence of a personality. The capacity to stir the imagination of the audience, to make them feel that there is much more to the actor or actress than meets the eye and the ear."

Mamoulian, like the members of the Group Theatre, was drawn to the techniques of Stanislavsky and the Moscow Art Theatre, to realism and naturalism in acting. As he directed on the stage, he came to see, as did the Group, that though dramatic plays like DuBose and Dorothy Heyward's *Porgy*—Mamoulian's first production in New York—were realistic (the play was acclaimed as a triumph of realism), what gave the production its feeling of realism was highly stylized, even choreographed. Mamoulian came to see that stage poetry, rhythm, integration, and style were much more effective than stage realism. What was important was the inner truth, not the logic of life.

Harry Cohn had wanted Mamoulian to come to Columbia for some time. He had directed ten pictures, among them *The Song of Songs* with Marlene Dietrich; *Queen Christina* with Garbo, with whom he'd had an affair; and *Becky Sharp,* the first Technicolor picture, starring Miriam Hopkins. His last picture had been *High, Wide, and Handsome,* and he'd recently finished directing the West Coast stage production of Gershwin's *Porgy and Bess.* Cohn wanted Mamoulian to direct a story called *The Gentleman from Montana* by Lewis R. Foster about a young man who goes to the U.S. Senate and sees the stuff of American politics at work. The Production Code thought the picture an "unflattering portrayal of our system of government . . . [that] might lead to being a covert attack on the democratic form of government." As a result, Cohn changed his mind about wanting to make the picture; Capra had seen the *Montana* script and turned it down, but when he learned that Mamoulian was going to make the picture with or without Cohn's backing, Capra read the script again. He decided he liked it after all and wanted to do it.

Rouben Mamoulian, circa 1939.

Mamoulian went to Cohn and said, "The one thing I like here is *Golden Boy.*" Capra decided to trade Mamoulian the Odets play for *The Gentleman from Montana.*

Mamoulian had enormous charm; he was old-world, an Armenian from Tiflis, Georgia, a theatrical country. He was sent to the University of Moscow to study law and instead studied writing, rehearsing, and directing with the Moscow Art Theatre studio; he learned music and spoke Russian, Armenian, Georgian, French, Italian, German, Spanish, and English. He understood and talked easily of electronics, painting, botany. At twenty-seven, he was invited by George Eastman to come to America and organize and direct an opera company at the Eastman Theatre in Rochester, New York.

In *Golden Boy,* Mamoulian, whose two heroes were Napoleon and Buffalo Bill, wanted to show the savagery of those who attended boxing matches, more so than the people who boxed.

Odets's plays were an indictment of America and were about the underdog. Odets wrote for actors; his dialogue had power and urgency. It was sharp and ungrammatical, full of jargon and imagery, natural and easy for actors to speak, not at all the kind of language that was heard from most playwrights; there was a rhythm in it. The dialogue was stylized, written to be played with speed and energy. The trick was for the actor to throw away the lines, not hit them; otherwise they would sound phony.

Odets wrote in his notebook the words heard in the streets of half-educated

Clifford Odets in Sidney Kingsley's first play, *Men in White,* directed by Lee Strasberg, 1933. As an actor, Odets was "strictly stock, as though in a straitjacket," said Franchot Tone. But Odets watched the director work on *Men in White,* made suggestions about how the play could be reshaped—and Strasberg incorporated the actor's notes.

Jews, Italians, and Irish and made them unique. He found something "elevated and poetic," he said, "in very common scenes in the way people spoke."

Odets was originally a stock company actor who felt he should have been a composer (his conversation was punctuated with arias; he improvised on the piano, often in the middle of the night; a bust of Beethoven sat over his writing table). As an actor, Odets was barely adequate on the stage; "too tense," he said, he couldn't relax. He was one of the original members of the Group Theatre, a theater collective inspired by Konstantin Stanislavsky and the Moscow Art Theatre that used an ensemble approach to produce plays that were emotionally true and more realistic than anything being produced in America. Stanislavsky had said, "The whole theatrical business in America is based on the personality of the actor."

Those in the Group Theatre made up a permanent company of actors; there were no stars. Each was trained in Stanislavsky's technique. Clurman, Cheryl Crawford, Lee Strasberg, and the others created a new kind of theater where the actor expressed true emotional life onstage and where the play's lines no longer carried him.

From the Group's beginning, Odets was taken on as an actor despite the misgivings of the Group's heads, Harold Clurman and Lee Strasberg. Clurman said of Odets at the time, "Something is cooking with him. I don't know if it's potato pancakes or what, but what's cooking has a rich odor. Something will develop from that man."

Two seasons into the Group's existence, Odets, in the background as an actor, began to write plays in a large kitchen closet, "crouched over his type-writer," said Kazan, "like a lion over prey, pounding away, accompanying himself with roars and grunts and snatches of dialogue—he spoke the actors' roles as he wrote them." Odets wrote his plays for the Group and for its method of acting, its ensemble idea; all the parts were important to him. He wrote as an actor and a director.

Odets's plays went unproduced for two years until the Group put on *Waiting for Lefty* and followed it with his *Awake and Sing!* and *Till the Day I Die.* He had three plays on Broadway and a fourth about to be produced—*Paradise Lost.* He was celebrated as the most promising young playwright in the country—his own kind of "cockeyed wonder"—who was as well a radical, a revolutionary. He was written about, sought after, courted by Hollywood, where he soon went ("with a sense of disgrace," he said) and wrote *The General Died at Dawn* to earn enough money—$2,500 a week—to send back half to the Group.

He appeared on the cover of *Time* magazine, was hailed as the most exciting playwright since Eugene O'Neill, and was compared to O'Casey and Chekhov.

Within three months Odets was not the same young man he'd been before: the parties to which he was invited, the people who took him up, the noise of it. He wasn't prepared for the onslaught of fame ("Well, who doesn't want to be famous? Who doesn't want to be successful?" he asked. "But you want it on your own terms"). Odets said of his boyhood growing up in the Bronx: it was "ordinary, middle-class"; everything about it was "typical, typical, so typical."

Odets was the spoiled Jewish boy whom everyone expected to do great things. Stella Adler once said to him, still a minor actor in the Group, "Clifford, if you don't become a genius, I'll never forgive you." The choice for Joe Bonaparte is, will he be a great violinist or a champion boxer? *Golden Boy* in part is a male fantasy of choice, of virtue, of filial devotion, of success.

Odets said of the society that embraced him, "Is this all? Stendhal kept asking," said Odets, " 'Is this all?' How well I understand that question!" He saw the acclaim as empty, even harmful; it "blunted his impulses," he said, took away his "appetite and zest." "I could be a better and broader man if I were not known, if I could wear a mask or change my name."

Accolades isolated Odets and cut him off from the things he was trying to get to. "He wanted to be the great revolutionary playwright of our day," said Harold Clurman. "And the white-haired boy of Broadway. He wanted the devotion of the man in the cellar and the congratulations of the boys at '21.' "

In Hollywood Odets worked on a screenplay for Lewis Milestone about the Spanish Civil War. Milestone took him to his first prizefight to see the great boxer Tony Canzoneri fight Lou Ambers for the lightweight title. Canzoneri was a two-time champion by the age of twenty-two, considered the best fighter in the world, winning in one year the lightweight title in sixty-six seconds and the junior welterweight championship and beating the reigning lightweight champion, the dazzling Cuban two-handed puncher Kid Chocolate.

From the preliminaries of the Canzoneri-Ambers fight, Odets avoided looking at the ring and spent the fight—Canzoneri lost to Ambers—writing in his notebook, which he was never without. Milestone complained that the tickets had been expensive and that Odets should write at home; the playwright said, "You have just given me a very fine play and what's more it will make money for the Group," which was then about to fold from financial difficulties.

Odets's play, originally called *The Manly Art*, or *Golden Gloves*, then *A Cockeyed Wonder*, and finally *Golden Boy*, was about how to live and unify the soul in an indifferent—American—society, its artists, seen through the corruption of a young musician—Joe Bonaparte—who wants to be a concert violinist. "With music," he tells Lorna, "I'm never alone when I'm alone— Playing music . . . that's like saying, 'I am man. I belong here. How do you do, World—good evening!' When I play music nothing is closed to me. There's no war in music. It's not like the streets. When you leave your room . . . down in the street . . . it's war."

Bonaparte feels compelled to choose between his music and the bare life of a serious artist ("I don't like myself, past, present, and future," Bonaparte says to his immigrant father. "Do you think I like this feeling of no possessions?"), and the shattering brutality of the fight ring ("I'm out for fame and fortune, not to be different or artistic! I don't intend to be ashamed of my life!"). Bonaparte is fighting for his soul, but he wants both his art and big success, and when he destroys his musician hands, he shouts, "Hallelujah! It's the beginning of the world!" When he murders his opponent, the Baltimore Chocolate Drop, in the ring, he yearns to clear his head and in the play kills himself and Lorna in his high-powered Duesenberg, the car that's poisoning his blood, the symbol of his American dream come true ("When you sit in a car and speed," Bonaparte says to Lorna, "you're looking down at the world. Speed, speed, everything is speed—nobody gets me!").

John Garfield, then on Broadway in Arthur Kober's *Having Wonderful Time*, had been led to believe by Odets that he would play Joe Bonaparte.

Holden (center) with Harry Cohn (left) and Lee J. Cobb, 1939.
(PHOTOFEST)

Odets had written the part with Garfield in mind, but the playwright realized, watching Garfield in Kober's play, that the actor didn't have the complexity for the part and thought it should go to Elia Kazan. Instead, Clurman gave the part to Luther Adler; Garfield played the minor comedy part of Siggie, a fast-talking taxicab driver, desperate to own his own cab, who is married to Joe Bonaparte's sister. Siggie is described by Odets as "the Halvah king of Brooklyn." At his son's bar mitzvah party, Siggie prominently displays a bust of his son in halvah.

Rouben Mamoulian wanted Odets to write the script for the picture; Odets refused, not because of his marital troubles with Luise Rainer, but because Mamoulian was the only director Odets "loathed" and refused to work with. Many commented that Odets and Mamoulian looked alike.

Years before, when Mamoulian was directing Capek's *R.U.R.* for the Theatre Guild, Odets had been hired to do a walk-on. Someone had suggested during the course of rehearsals that Odets be given a few lines. Mamoulian dismissed the idea and said, "He is no good."

Harry Cohn hired Sarah Y. Mason and Victor Heerman, a husband-and-wife writing team, to write a draft of the script of *Golden Boy* before Mamoulian had been hired to direct the picture. Mamoulian hated the script and told Cohn he couldn't possibly work from it and went to the Bureau of New Plays playwriting course, financed by the studios, in the hope of finding new talent.

The course was run by Theresa Helburn, who, with Lawrence Langner and Armina Marshall, had founded the Theatre Guild. Mamoulian hired two students from the course to write another draft of the script as a team: Daniel Taradash, twenty-five, just out of Harvard Law School, and Lew Meltzer, twenty-six, both there through scholarships at the Bureau of New Plays. Mamoulian hired them to write the script as a team. Each was signed to a seven-year contract, with six-month options, getting paid $200 a week. When Harry Cohn heard about Mamoulian's new writers, he screamed over the phone, "You're out of your God damned mind. Forget these kids. Find a five thousand dollar a week writer!" Cohn referred to the writing team as "Hector MacArthur" and "those f——ing Theater Guild writers."

Mamoulian took Taradash and Meltzer to Yucca Loma Ranch in the desert for a month and came back with a finished script.

Mamoulian was not Harry Cohn's kind of director. Mamoulian disliked Cohn, and Cohn sensed that the director had no respect for him. Where politics was at the center of Odets's play, Mamoulian couldn't have been less interested. Art was his god. Mamoulian was known for using the camera at odd angles in his pictures. "In Frank Capra's pictures," Cohn said to Mamoulian, "you don't see a camera coming out of somebody's ass." (Capra thought of a picture as an electric current that must not be broken; once the audience was more conscious of the photography than the actors, the current was snapped.)

Shooting for *Golden Boy* began in mid-April 1939.

Barbara was up at 5:30 each morning to get to Columbia, get her makeup on, be on the set in time. Bob didn't have to leave until 7:30. They never had breakfast together, seldom ate lunch together, though occasionally Bob would rush over to the studio to have lunch with Barbara, and seldom saw each other before nine at night.

Odets's play ended with Joe and Lorna dying in a car crash; the picture ends with them going home to the Bonapartes and Joe embracing his father. "It was a phony ending," said Daniel Taradash. "We had to leave the audience happy, or at least happier with some kind of feeling that life is good."

For *Golden Boy,* Holden spent three hours a day learning how to bow and finger a violin from Julian Brodetsky and how to box from Cannonball Green. Holden had been living at home in South Pasadena, but he was far too busy to commute between there and Hollywood. Columbia took a room for him at the Hollywood Athletic Club and moved a voice coach in with him.

Each morning Holden got up at 5:30 to get to the studio at 8:00 and

Holden trained to fight with James Cannonball Green, then twenty-two years old, from Cape Town, who also played Chocolate Drop in the picture. (CULVER PICTURES)

have his hair curled. He arrived on the set feeling less than sure of himself. After each day's shooting, interviews were set up with the press for him to talk about having been "discovered." Holden was working seventeen hours a day and calling his mother every few hours for help in calming his fears. He reassured himself by asking, "What would Fredric March do? What would Gary Cooper do?" They and Spencer Tracy were his heroes.

Holden turned twenty-one at the end of the first week of shooting. He was ready to quit the picture—and the studio was ready to fire him. Barbara went to Harry Cohn and persuaded him to call off Holden's interviews and close the set to visitors.

The tension needed for the character of Joe Bonaparte was in Holden; he was at odds with himself: he wanted to be the good boy, the choirboy as his mother had taught him, but he moved toward danger. In his hometown of O'Fallon, Illinois (population seventeen hundred), Holden was considered a wild man riding on his motorcycle at high speeds, standing in the saddle, both hands aloft. He was an expert horseman and rifle shot and a trained gymnast like his father, an industrial chemist. Holden, by the age of eight, could tumble like a circus performer.

While he was fearless in certain situations—walking on his hands along the outer rail of Pasadena's "suicide bridge" with its 190-foot drop—on the first day of shooting of *Golden Boy* he was pale with fear. At moments his terror of appearing before the camera was so great he had to drink to show up for work. He found acting an emotional drain; this picture was his big break,

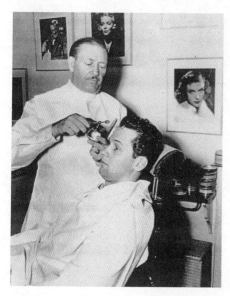

Beedle, now Holden, becoming Joe Bonaparte,
Golden Boy, 1939. (CULVER PICTURES)

and he couldn't afford to blow it. The most demanding part of it was keeping
up the level of his performance.

"If audiences don't like my characterization of *Golden Boy,*" Holden said,
"I'll go back to choir singing on Sunday, the chemistry 'lab' [he studied at
South Pasadena Junior College], and little theaters. I won't earn much, but
it will be fun."

Barbara was tired at the end of each day's shooting, but she would say to
Holden, "Okay, Golden Boy, get your ass into my dressing room. We've got
to go over the scenes we'll make tomorrow."

She spent hours digging beneath the surface of scenes to drag out some
experience of Holden's that would help him. She taught him what she'd
learned from Willard Mack about stagecraft and timing and made sure in
their scenes together that Holden looked good.

Bob would sometimes come to the studio to pick up Barbara, but he
waited as she rehearsed with Holden night after night and read lines with
him for the next day's scenes, helping him with his emphasis and timing and
phrasing.

"She pulled me through," said Holden.

Barbara knew he would be a star and believed he would have made it
without her help.

Mamoulian shot the picture in sequence.

He worked first with a loose rehearsal, then another to tighten the scene;

"He was a dedicated young actor," said Barbara. "I sensed this when he first started." (AMERICAN HERITAGE CENTER, UNIVERSITY OF WYOMING)

the third he called a take, but rather than waste film, he did the final rehearsal without film. To get the actors to give more, Mamoulian would sometimes tell them the camera was rolling when no film was being exposed. Mamoulian tried the ploy on Barbara. She gave a great take and found out no film had been exposed. "You ask me as a professional to perform for you," Barbara told Mamoulian. She expected the director to behave as professionally. "Don't tell me it is rolling when it isn't."

"She would never expose herself to a poor take," said Holden. "Barbara's so consistent, she rarely deviates from the level she's set for herself. She would have whatever was awkward ironed out before. He lost a damn good performance."

Mamoulian drove Holden—he was "bewildered, nervous, awkward," said Mamoulian—and was pleased with the results. He used Holden's irritability and exhaustion from long hours of work to shoot the tense scenes, and the director turned Holden's faults into acting virtues. Holden's sincerity came through.

Holden asked Barbara how she could be so calm on the frenzied set. "Don't let me fool you," she said. "I wear myself out keeping myself calm."

During production of *Golden Boy,* with the Omaha world premiere of *Union Pacific* days away, April 1939.

Barbara's lack of temperament on the set had to do with hating to be the center of attention. "I couldn't bear that. I couldn't be temperamental even if I wanted to be," she said. She was comfortable with people on the set when she was working and was unaware they were there. She was full of poise and confidence. Off the set, she was fearful and shy and still beset by a dread of strangers. A familiarity that she fostered at work was ended when she finished a picture. She invariably changed her telephone number and retreated.

Holden's performance was awkward, but his intelligence came through. In the picture, as with Bob Taylor in *Camille,* Holden's emphasis and the rhythms of his dialogue were Barbara's.

Lorna Moon is the girl with the tough background, tough choices, tough exterior, heart of gold; the girl from the school of hard knocks, with a secret longing for refuge in home and family that she never had; the archetype of the character Barbara played. Mamoulian filmed her so that she looked much older than Holden; he was twenty-one; she, a decade older.

Barbara was playing the part from a Broadway hit that was considered art. As Lorna, she is earnest in a way that makes her heavy; the character is a persona with no reality except for the needs of the other characters and the plot. The kinds of color, nuance, and tone that Barbara is able to bring to a character aren't here. Instead, she is walking on eggshells because of the stature of the piece. Her intensity is about the pleasure of being in a work of

Barbara as Lorna Moon, Holden as Bonaparte, Adolphe Menjou as Tom Moody, and Joseph Calleia as Eddie Fuseli, *Golden Boy,* 1939. (PHOTOFEST)

official art. *Golden Boy* was an "important picture," not a commercial picture, and it saps the vitality out of her—the quickness and lightness on her feet. She was playing the part as written and doesn't feel free, playing wet-eyed loyalty at face level.

Paramount's publicity department was gearing up for the world premiere of *Union Pacific,* which was to take place during a three-day celebration of Golden Spike Days in Omaha, Nebraska, commemorating the seventieth anniversary of the Union Pacific.

The picture's premiere was to be held simultaneously in three first-run theaters in Omaha. Paramount joined forces with Union Pacific and was spending $50,000 on its advertising campaign.

Barbara and Bob were to be part of the celebrations.

For the premiere, Bill Jeffers had given DeMille a special Union Pacific train drawn by two engines: the railroad's latest steam-electric turbine and its wood-burning Old 58, or General McPherson, from the railroad's early days, which had been used in the picture. Old 58 was in perfect working order but had to stop every fifty miles to take on water.

The *Union Pacific* train was to stop at every major station along the route from Los Angeles to Omaha where there were to be parades or decorated platforms near the train set up for speeches. Those who gathered from the surrounding towns for the event and to celebrate the picture were expected to dress in pioneer clothes. Barbara and Bob were to meet up with the train in Omaha.

A week into shooting *Golden Boy,* Paramount's publicity department suggested to Barbara that she and Bob get married amid the fanfare of *Union Pacific's* publicity tour.

"You're not going to make a three-ring circus out of our marriage," said Barbara. She and Bob had planned to get married in six or eight weeks, after *Golden Boy* finished shooting. Bob had promised his mother a church wedding with bridesmaids.

At Metro, Bob had just started filming *Lady of the Tropics* with Hedy Lamarr. The studio was grooming Lamarr for stardom in an effort to make her into an exotic European. To that end, Louis B. Mayer was giving her the benefit of "the biggest stars, the finest writers, and the most talented directors." Metro to Bob was "the campus"; even the seasons became semesters. "Only Garbo remained aloof," said Bob. "Always arriving alone in her chauffeured Packard."

There was nothing predictable about Metro to Bob Taylor except perhaps sunrises and L. B. Mayer, "and not necessarily in that order," said Bob. "L.B. was the most important person" in Bob's career, as he was in hundreds of others. "In his way," said Bob, "he was a great man. Moreover, he was not a 'desk jockey.' He was consistently on the move around the lot—he knew every department. He knew everyone's problems." And he knew that while Bob was a big star, and that the studio had resisted the idea of Taylor's getting married, following the publication of the *Photoplay* article it had reversed its position. The notion of America's heartthrob living in "unwedded bliss" was untenable.

Mayer had put Hedy Lamarr in *A New York Cinderella,* written by Charles MacArthur, one of the highest-paid screenwriters in Hollywood. Spencer Tracy, following his success with *Boys Town,* was in the picture as well and was unhappy with the script and working with Lamarr. *A New York Cinderella,* budgeted at $700,000, was in trouble, and months into it and $900,000 later production was stopped; the picture, now called *I Take This Woman,* was shelved.

Bob didn't like the script for *Lady of the Tropics,* but rather than turn down the part, he figured it was his turn to support the newcomer. He remembered

Hedy Lamarr and Bob, from *Lady of the Tropics,* 1939.

how the bosses had seen to it that he was given the breaks when he was new and was put into *Small Town Girl* with Janet Gaynor and *The Gorgeous Hussy* with Joan Crawford.

Hedy Lamarr had been named Glamour Girl of 1938, called the "Dream Girl of 50 Million Men," all on the basis of one picture, *Algiers,* made on loan-out to Walter Wanger and United Artists. Lamarr, while shooting *Lady of the Tropics,* taught Bob how to kiss more convincingly for the cameras. "His usual kiss seemed much more like a school-boy's when photographed in close-up," she said.

The picture was directed by Jack Conway, Bob's frequent coyote-hunting partner, and written by Josef von Sternberg, Jules Furthman, Dore Schary, John Lee Mahin, and Ben Hecht, with Hecht getting final screenplay credit.

The press exclaimed that Lamarr was more beautiful than Taylor. The two looked eerily alike and reflected each other's beauty. Barbara wasn't jealous of Bob working with Lamarr; she would have been jealous had he been working with Spencer Tracy in *Northwest Passage.*

The word on *Union Pacific* was that it was a "box-office winner; a socko spec," said *Variety,* "surefire for big grosses right down the line." *The New York Times* called it a "little opus . . . colorful, spectacular; easily the best DeMille has made in years." And *Time* said it was "a full payload of first-rate screen

Welcoming the *Union Pacific* train at Omaha's Union Station for the three-day celebration. Large crowds had gathered along the train route to watch Old 58 traveling from Hollywood northeast to Nebraska. Barbara on the platform in Omaha is in dark hat, holding flowers. Evelyn Keyes, near her on the platform, is in white dress with white flower on hat. April 1939. (COURTESY: EVELYN KEYES)

entertainment." It was Barbara's last picture under her Paramount contract. *The Mad Miss Manton* had already made close to $600,000 worldwide.

The monthlong tour for *Union Pacific* was given a send-off with a party at Ouida and Basil Rathbone's Bel Air estate.

On the *Union Pacific* train were DeMille, Akim Tamiroff, Lynne Overman, George Raft in McCrea's stead, Madeleine Carroll, Lloyd Nolan, Betty Grable, Mrs. DeMille, Anthony Quinn, and dozens of reporters and columnists, including Ed Sullivan, Sheilah Graham, and Lucius Beebe. Evelyn Keyes, at twenty-two, who was under personal contract to DeMille, had just finished shooting her last scene for *Gone With the Wind* as Scarlett O'Hara's younger sister. Keyes was from Atlanta (DeMille described her as being "as beautiful as the South itself"). She flew eleven and a half hours, from Los Angeles to Omaha and, with a police escort, met the *Union Pacific* train for the tour just as the train pulled in to the station.

The first night out of Los Angeles, DeMille called Robert Preston into his private car and told the actor that as master of ceremonies at the *Union Pacific* events he knew everybody else on the train but didn't know anything about Preston. "How will I introduce you?" asked DeMille.

The actor told DeMille that before *Union Pacific* he'd made three pictures.

"No before that," DeMille said.

Preston said he'd been at the Pasadena Community Theater and had acted in more than forty plays in two years. DeMille didn't seem interested in that either. The actor mentioned that he'd once been a parking attendant at the Santa Anita racetrack. DeMille introduced Preston to movie audiences by saying that he'd found the actor parking cars at Santa Anita and immediately put him into *Union Pacific* and made him a star.

To kick off the three-day commemoration of the Golden Spike Days, President Roosevelt pushed a key in his White House office and the city of Omaha erupted in festivities. The cast rode through the streets in carriages. Two hundred thousand people cheered them on; the confetti in the air made it seem like a New York ticker-tape parade. Bands played and people hung out of windows to see the passing spectacle, all in celebration of DeMille's *Union Pacific* and the commemoration of the Golden Spike. Tribes of Sioux and Cheyenne who appeared in the picture were there for the premiere, and the parking area of Omaha's Union Station had been transformed into an Indian stockade of seventy-five years before.

Omaha had built false fronts on one street to re-create a street of the 1860s. Parking meters were removed to make way for water troughs for horses. The courthouse lawn was turned into an Indian reservation for thirteen Sioux from Pine Ridge Reservation. Men were in beards, string ties, buckskin jackets, and Prince Albert coats; they wore beaver hats and fringed gauntlets. Women dressed in bonnets and wore high-buttoned shoes and pantaloons under crinolines.

A special train from the East brought Averell Harriman, the chairman of Union Pacific's board of directors, and other industrialists to the celebration. A banquet dinner at the coliseum for three thousand guests was served by more than five hundred Union Pacific waiters. DeMille spoke before his audience. "*Union Pacific* is a picture of events in American history that occurred 70 years ago," he said. "But it is timely and has a message for us right now . . . it shows the ideal cooperation between capital and labor that built this country, and that this country should have today.

"It is not the supremacy of labor over capitalism," he said, "nor capital's uncontrolled tyranny over labor. It is the triumph of cooperation between the two."

The premiere of *Union Pacific* at Omaha's Opera House, April 27, 1939.

DeMille's words had more to do with the present labor situation than they did the truth of the building of the Union Pacific Railroad.

In the midst of the dinner, Evelyn Keyes received a telegram from David Selznick recalling her to Hollywood to shoot an additional scene for *Gone With the Wind*. Keyes left the way she arrived, with a police escort that accompanied her back to the Omaha airport.

On the third day of the festivities another grand parade was held with more than eighty floats and thirty marching bands. Averell Harriman and William Jeffers were at the head of the procession. Barbara and Robert Preston were next, riding on the backseat of a convertible waving to the crowds.

Union Pacific had its grand premiere that night and was seen by ten thousand moviegoers. Two train car loads of flood, search, and klieg lights had been brought in for the premiere. The beams of light could be seen for thirty miles. DeMille and the cast were at each screening and said a few words.

Barbara didn't get much sleep, but it was a trip she wouldn't have missed.

The tour continued. Barbara and Evelyn Keyes, who had returned to Omaha after shooting her additional scene for *Gone With the Wind*, were on the same plane back to Los Angeles, seated together. Barbara didn't say a word to Evelyn—at the airport or on the plane. The pilot invited Barbara, who hated to fly, to the cockpit. She accepted and stayed there for the duration of the trip.

Reviewers criticized Barbara's brogue in *Union Pacific* as being incomprehensible. When she was panned in *The Plough and the Stars* for her on-again, off-again brogue as well as for her seeming to have confused Brooklyn with Dublin, Barbara went into a state of despair. She'd worked hard in *The Plough and the Stars* to perfect her accent in the early sequences. Her response to the criticism of her brogue in *Union Pacific* was to shrug it off with a laugh and say, "Oh, well, you can't win."

Barbara finished her publicity appearances for *Union Pacific* and returned to work on *Golden Boy*.

The admired cameraman Karl Freund had been assigned to the picture. Freund had been the cameraman on more than twenty pictures, from *Dracula* and *Murders in the Rue Morgue* to *Camille* and *The Good Earth*. After three weeks of shooting, Freund resisted setting up the lights as Mamoulian had asked and was replaced. "Karl, you are a great cameraman," Mamoulian said. "And you have your own ideas, but this is not your picture." Freund had directed eight pictures for Universal. "I don't want pretty photography," said Mamoulian. "I want something that to me fits the story I have, the cast I have." Freund was replaced with RKO's master cinematographer Nick Musuraca, who started as a cameraman in the early 1920s and whose harsh, dark low-key lighting setups produced a dramatic, stylized effect of blacks and whites with powerful shadows, an ominous expressionistic look of images set in geometric patterns of light and shadow.

Barbara was on call one Saturday afternoon for the studio. She waited at home all day. Finally, she telephoned Bob and suggested they plan to go someplace for the evening. Bob said, "Okay, let's get married."

Barbara and Bob had driven to San Diego three days before to take out a marriage license without having any specific date in mind. The license was under their own names, Ruby Stevens Fay and Spangler Arlington Brugh, as a way to throw off the press. Clark Gable and Carole Lombard had married six weeks before in Kingman, Arizona; Tyrone Power and Annabella, three weeks before in Bel Air. Louis B. Mayer's secretary—and Bob's champion from his earliest days at the studio—Ida Koverman was part of the wedding party.

Bob gave Barbara ten minutes to pick a dress for her wedding gown. Bob was wearing a brown business suit. Barbara conformed to sentiment. "Old shoes," she said. Her crepe silk dress was new and blue; her hat was borrowed from Holly Barnes; Barbara was "the old couplet come to life," she said.

Barbara and Bob met Zeppo and Marion for dinner that night at the Bar-
clay Kitchen. Barbara barely touched her shrimp and steak. Afterward, they
discussed what to do next. Bob suggested a movie. They searched the ads for
a picture they hadn't seen. Marion suggested they go to the Palladium. Bob
and Barbara thought that was a good idea. At 8:30 they were still sitting and
talking in the restaurant.

Marion said, "We'd better go or we'll miss the show."

They got into Bob's car and set off.

After a few minutes Zeppo said, "Aren't you heading in the wrong direction?"

"I just remembered," said Bob, "I have an appointment with a man in San
Diego tonight."

"Are you kidding?" said Zeppo. "Why San Diego?"

"For this," said Bob. "The man is going to marry Barbara and me."

He took a piece of paper from his pocket and handed it to Marion.

When Bob and Barbara first started to see each other, Zeppo and Marion
would babble double-talk for hours in front of Bob. "He'd never met anyone
like us," said Marion. "He told Barbara he was sure I was crazy." But Bob and
Marion had become great friends.

Marion looked at the certificate and screamed.

They picked up Uncle Buck, Ida Koverman, and their friend the actor
and musician Dalies Frantz and drove to the home of Thomas Whelan, a
former San Diego district attorney who, as deputy county clerk, had issued
Bob and Barbara's marriage license a few days before.

The wedding party ate a buffet supper in the Whelans' living room overlooking San Diego Bay. Twenty minutes after midnight, Judge Phil Smith married Barbara and Bob in a room filled with roses from the Whelans' garden.

Barbara was thirty-one; Bob, twenty-seven.

Marion Marx was Barbara's matron of honor; Uncle Buck gave away the
bride and acted as Bob's best man. "Who'd figure Spangler Brugh and Ruby
Stevens?" said Buck. "Seeing that pair like I do, you'd know as a team they're
a solid act. No valentine patter, maybe, but they back each other up all the
time."

During the ceremony Judge Smith was so nervous he kept clearing his
throat and almost lost his voice.

Bob was equally nervous; he wasn't sure he was in love and mumbled his
responses in a husky voice. Barbara was cool and clear. Bob put a wedding
band on her finger. It was a thin gold ring surrounded by rubies, similar to
her engagement ring made up of heart-shaped rubies; both rings matched the
bracelet Bob had designed and given Barbara for Christmas.

At a press reception at the Victor Hugo Restaurant, newly married and just back from San Diego, April 14, 1939. "Here I am married today," said Bob, "and tomorrow I've got to be back at work making love to another woman, Hedy Lamarr."

Bob loved jewelry—gold, rubies, sapphires, emeralds; he disliked the coldness of diamonds and platinum—and often designed pieces that Bill Ruser, a jeweler in town, made up for him.

Bob had asked Barbara if she would like to give him a wedding ring to put on his finger. She happily put a gold band on Bob's finger to go with the cabochon ruby ring she'd given him for their engagement.

Barbara's steely tones in accepting the wedding vows belied her emotions. She was full of sentimental feelings about Bob. She'd marked every one of their anniversaries: the day they'd first met three years before; the music they'd first danced to; the flowers Bob had first sent her. She felt secure in her happiness, safe, not hell-bent as she had been with Frank Fay to overlook his drinking to make the marriage work.

After the ceremony, Barbara and Bob called their family and friends.

William Holden sent a telegram that said, "Gosh, what a blow!" and signed it "Golden Boy."

Ninety minutes later the wedding party drove back to Los Angeles. Barbara and Bob took a few days off before going back to work—Barbara to *Golden Boy,* Bob to *Lady of the Tropics.* Husband and wife appeared at a press reception at the Victor Hugo Restaurant in Beverly Hills and posed for pictures.

On her first day back at work on *Golden Boy* after being married, the crew put up a sign on the door of her portable dressing room, which she stuck upside down and put on a shelf.

Barbara returned to Marwyck.

Bob went to see his mother; it didn't help that it was Mother's Day. He knew Ruth would be heartsick about his marriage. Barbara and Ruth had disliked each other from their first meeting. Ruth didn't like the woman who'd won her son's heart, didn't know what to make of her. Barbara wasn't any more receptive to Ruth. Barbara knew that Bob was a mama's boy and didn't like it. She wanted Bob to "stand on his own two feet" and "get some balls."

When Bob walked into his mother's house, Ruth buried her face in her hands and sobbed. He tried to reassure her nothing would change because of his marriage.

Ruth said she felt sick, and weak, and asked Bob to stay and check her heartbeat every now and again during the night, "just to make sure." As he had during childhood, Bob spent the night in bed next to his mother, holding her to make sure her heart was pumping and making sure that she didn't die of a heart attack.

Ruth was so distraught by Bob's wedding that she refused all food. Her doctor gave her a sedative and warned her that if she didn't eat, he would hospitalize her.

At Bob's ranch after being
recently married, 1939.

Bob and Barbara spent a few magical days together at Bob's ranch, and then Barbara went back to work on *Golden Boy*, where a wedding party was held on the set. Later she and Bob went to the season's opening day of Hollywood Park racetrack, owned by Jack Warner, and watched Bing Crosby's horse Don Mike outrun Louis B. Mayer's Main Man in the feature race.

Barbara wrote to DeMille to thank him for "my beautiful nickels. If they bring me as much luck as the others," she wrote, "everything will be alright. I am still counting the time until I work for you again and always I shall be grateful to you for your kindness. Devotedly, Barbara."

If Barbara adored DeMille, she was not as won over by Rouben Mamoulian. He was not her kind of director. "Technically," she said, Mamoulian was "fine, you couldn't ask for more, but there was no affinity there, no joy. To me, the essence of a good director is not to say, 'Walk to the table, then turn around and face to the left.' The good director will walk you through gently and give you some air . . . I had to have the feeling that the director was with me because I sure as hell was with him."

Barbara was busting to feel free again. She was free from her contract with RKO and Columbia and didn't want to be tied down to the responsibilities of the ranch. "I don't want us to settle down," she said. "That settling down business is more dangerous for men, than for women.

"We want to go places and do things," said Barbara. "I don't know what places, specifically, or what things. We just want to be near, to be in everything."

Barbara and Bob were making no plans; they didn't know where they were going to live and didn't have a permanent home to live in. They drove around Beverly Hills looking at houses to rent but didn't find one they liked. They made no plans for a family or to adopt another child. "I know that if you make plans and they don't work out," said Barbara, "they break your heart. The only plan we have calls for our being together as much as possible. Plan for nothing and be prepared for everything, that's the Taylor motto.

"I'm so thrilled, so absolutely happy right now, I'm not concerned about the next hour or the next day."

FIFTEEN

Ain't She a Peacherino

Now that Barbara and Bob were married, Uncle Buck assumed it was time to move on. Barbara wouldn't hear of it. Buck was family to her, and she insisted he stay. He loved Dion and continued to look after him.

Eddie Mannix sent flowers to the newly married Mrs. Robert Taylor. Barbara wrote to thank him the same day ("I do appreciate your kindness to me. I sincerely hope I shall please all of you as much as I know Bob has"). Nick Schenck gave the Robert Taylors a silver coffee service. Emily Post wrote to Barbara from Edgartown, Massachusetts, over the Fourth of July to tell her how much she hoped Barbara's "new found happiness" would be "as complete and enduring" as Barbara so "richly deserved." "Mrs. Post" added that it was her first fan letter. Moss Hart wrote to tell her he was sending Barbara a Picasso for a wedding present. The package arrived, and Barbara quickly opened it. She was stunned for a moment. It was the white Picasso *Harlequin.* Barbara didn't know what to expect, "but it certainly wasn't that," she said.

Barbara and Bob found a large house to rent in Beverly Hills at 1101 North Beverly Drive. Colleen Moore had built it for her mother ten years before. The house was white brick with weathered oak trim and protected by a wall around the property. Inside, a large stairway was on the immediate right. Bob liked to slide down the winding banister. A step-down living room ran the length of the house. Off the entryway of the living room were the breakfast room, pantry, and kitchen. Off the dining room was a den with built-in bar, bookcases, and a place for Bob's gun case, which was filled with his rifles. Opposite the bookcases was a fireplace.

Upstairs on the right, over the garage, was Dion's room with a bath. Uncle Buck's room was to the left of the staircase. Barbara and Bob's bedroom was at the front of the house.

Bob's twenty-eighth birthday given by Barbara at the Victor Hugo restaurant, August 5, 1939. Seated (left to right): Ann Dvorak, Barbara, Fred MacMurray. Standing: Bob and Jack Benny.

A large covered patio extended out to a grassy area and tennis courts, where a fifteen-year-old Budge Patty would be giving Barbara tennis lessons. Beyond the courts was an expansive lawn that surrounded the house.

Barbara didn't know how to cook and didn't care about learning. "I gave up fooling around with recipes," she said, "when I came home and found the cook pasting paper on the shelves with my rice pudding."

They planned to move from Northridge before leaving for a trip abroad and packed each night after they got home from the studio.

Being a stepfather was a new role for Bob. He was not fully comfortable with children, but he was kind to Dion. "He couldn't have been nicer and more loving," said Barbara's son.

Bob tried to teach Dion about baseball and football. On Sundays, Bob often drove Dion from Marwyck in his black woody station wagon to the Church of the Good Shepherd in Beverly Hills. On their way to church one day, Dion got out of the car to open the wooden gates at the back of the

Bob with Dion, then age seven, 1939. (COUR-
TESY TONY FAY)

Marwyck driveway and, as he got back in the car, caught one of his fingers in the door.

Bob comforted him and didn't lecture him the way Barbara did. In private, Bob defended the boy against the way Barbara was raising him. He saw Dion's sadness and believed that he should be at home with his family instead of being sent away to school.

But Bob was not at ease with most children. When Barbara's nephew Brian came to the ranch, Bob was curt with him until Barbara walked in the room. Brian didn't like Bob and didn't like being at the ranch. He was often there without his parents and didn't feel comfortable. He had nothing in common with Dion, who was five years older. Barbara would send Brian off to play with the horses, but he often felt stuck out at the ranch and found Barbara and Bob cold.

During Dion's first year at Raenford Academy, his class would go into town on weekly Saturday excursions to the movies. After the picture, Dion would spend time in the Reina drugstore waiting for the bus to take them back to school. On a lark, one time, Dion pocketed a cigarette lighter. One of the other boys told on him. Barbara was furious and made Dion go back to the drugstore and apologize for taking what didn't belong to him.

At seven years old, Dion would have preferred to be home at Marwyck for the summer. But no sooner had Dion come home from school at the end of the semester than he was packed off with new clothes for camp, driven by Uncle Buck to Terminal Island, south of Long Beach, where he was put onboard a canvas-canopied boat—his first boat ride—and taken with thirty other children and camp personnel to an island with cliffs and beautiful sand at Howland's Landing.

Catalina Island Boys Camp had football and baseball fields, archery, swimming, spearfishing, boating. Meals were cooked on the beach and eaten under an old shade tree. Dion collected shells and driftwood and slept with the other boys under the stars.

Each was given the responsibility of caring for a horse for the duration of the summer. Dion was considered one of the better riders at the camp and won a black kerchief for his riding skills along with merit badges for other activities. For those campers who could handle a horse, there was a trip on horseback around the island.

Dion was on his own, but he felt cared for by the three men who ran the camp, Al Madden, Gloomy Gus Henderson, and Arnold Eddy. They were kind to the boys; each was made to feel important, something Dion didn't get from either his school or Barbara.

Bob had grown up on a farm and still loved to hunt and fish. He, Clark Gable, Carole Lombard, Gary Cooper, Andy Devine, and Morgan Maree often hunted together. Barbara was afraid of guns and hated the idea of hunting; it gave her the shudders, and she refused to go along.

Bob and Gable went to the skeet fields at the Los Angeles–Santa Monica Gun Club, half a mile south of the Douglas airplane plant on Ocean Park Boulevard, and were joined by Devine, Cooper, and Robert Stack. Skeet shooting, originally designed to simulate upland game hunting, was practice for quail and pheasant hunting. The hunter walked through the field with the gun down, and clay targets were thrown in the air.

The Los Angeles–Santa Monica Gun Club had been around since the turn of the century and now belonged to Harry Fleischmann, the black sheep of the Fleischmann family, whose fortune came from butter and yeast. Harry Fleischmann was the best shot in town and taught most of the stars how to shoot: Gable, Bob Taylor, Fred MacMurray, Fredric March, Michael Curtiz, Cooper, Jack Conway, Jack Holt, Victor Fleming, Frank Morgan, Gene Raymond, and Ginger Rogers.

Fleischmann also ran a duck-hunting club near Bakersfield, where he, Gable, Bob Taylor, Jack Conway, and others would go for the weekend.

Bob Stack, at twenty, was an expert shot and had been since boyhood, when he was accepted by Fleischmann for the California five-man team. At seventeen, Stack was one of the five best shots in the world, winning in 1936 the national 20-gauge crown and the Del Monte pistol championship and holding the world's long-run skeet record with 364 straight hits. Stack's grandfather had won the 1910 Los Angeles blue-rock championship, breaking 58 targets without a miss.

Stack, whose father died when he was nine, met Clark Gable skeet shooting, and Gable became one of his surrogate fathers. Through Harry Fleischmann, Stack met Gene Raymond, Howard Hughes, Hemingway, and others. To the teenage Stack they were just a "bunch of older guys" whom he could "whip with a shotgun."

Stack got to know Bob Taylor before he began to date Barbara and thought him one of the nicest guys. "A country boy," said Stack. "A small-town guy and a darned good actor." Stack thought Taylor "probably the handsomest man alive, and the least actorish actor, without any feeling about being a matinee idol. What he looked like was not who he was. He was just a guy who looks like a god with a widow's peak."

Soon Taylor was seeing Barbara, and she and Stack came to know each other. "She had no bullshit about her," said Stack.

He thought Barbara was not an obvious beauty but a "nifty" actress with "boundless energy." She had "banked fires" in her, he said. To Stack, she had "second level."

Stack and Barbara and Bob had Helen Ferguson in common. Helen was a friend of Stack's glamorous mother, Betzi, and took Stack on as a client when he was nineteen. Helen helped Stack project his career, advising him that he was driving the wrong kind of car: Bob drove souped-up hot rods and held the record for four-cylinder poppers. "If you get a more sedate car," Helen said, "the studios will take you more seriously."

Ferguson was like family to Stack, as well as to Barbara and Bob, Loretta Young, Anita Louise, Ida Lupino, Vincent Price, Gene Raymond, and Jeanette MacDonald and to her other clients, including Lew Ayres, Fay Wray, Irene Dunne, and Franchot Tone. Helen was considered loyal—devoted—to those she represented. She was aware of details, "all of which had nothing to do with getting a job in pictures," said Stack, and he followed her motherly advice. He and Helen spoke regularly on the phone for at least half an hour a call with one earring (always) clipped to Helen's dress.

Bob Taylor, Bob Stack, and Andy Devine one day were shooting doves in El Centro. It was a hot day, and they'd been drinking beer. Bob Taylor and

Andy were peeing. Devine looked down at Bob and said in his cracked drawl, "I don't know. For the world's biggest, greatest lover, that doesn't look like a helluva lot to me."

Bob said, without hesitating, "Don't tell my wife. She thinks they're all the same size."

From DeMille's Irish postmistress at end of track to Clifford Odets's world-weary "tramp from Newark," Barbara, in her next picture, was to play a seen-it-all, light-fingered jewel thief on trial in New York for shoplifting a blindingly sparkling bracelet.

Mitchell Leisen, one of Paramount's leading directors, was assigned the picture. Each of Leisen's fourteen pictures had been a box-office success. Leisen was in great demand with actors. He was Paramount's answer to George Cukor. If Leisen snapped his fingers, he got what he wanted. And he wanted Barbara for the part of Lee Leander, jewel thief. He felt the part was written for her.

Fred MacMurray was to be the hard-driving assistant district attorney prosecuting the case who, instead of sending her to jail, falls in love with her. Leisen thought MacMurray a good-looking actor—with a beautifully built body and great legs, six feet four, tall and lanky—but MacMurray was quiet, genial, modest, and inexperienced. Carole Lombard, who believed all the actors in a picture had to be good or it wouldn't matter how good she was, worked with Leisen and MacMurray in both *Hands Across the Table* and *Swing High, Swing Low*. MacMurray had made only four pictures before *Hands Across the Table*—and didn't project much sex.

For one scene in *Hands Across the Table*, Lombard was to walk in, kiss Fred, and then walk out of the frame. She walked in, kissed Fred, walked out past the camera, looked at Leisen, and shrugged her shoulders as if to say, "So what?" MacMurray had an appealing reticence, projecting small-town boy making good in the big city, which is exactly what he was. While making *Hands Across the Table*, MacMurray was living with his mother in a little apartment in Hollywood and, as he was able to move up and rent a rambling house, lived with his mother, grandmother, aunt, and uncle.

Before Leisen was assigned the picture, Ray Milland and Franchot Tone had been suggested to Preston Sturges, whose script it was, for the part of the district attorney.

MacMurray in his early pictures with Leisen was shy and afraid to try anything. He didn't presume he was acting; he just did what he was told. Leisen helped him along and tried to draw out the actor. Lombard's way of getting

MacMurray to relax in front of the camera was to kick him in the shins, grin, and yell, "Loosen up, you big ape! It isn't going to hurt."

MacMurray had never thought of being an actor, never intended to be one. He'd planned on being a musician like his father, a concert violinist who had taught MacMurray to play the instrument. MacMurray, like the character in Preston Sturges's script, was from the Midwest, Kankakee, Illinois. His grandfather had been the leading minister of the town; his grandmother, the head of the local telephone exchange. But one fluke followed another until he found himself being an actor and had to learn to get over his horrible stage fright.

Leisen trusted MacMurray's work and felt that in the end he could be counted on to come through. If he got bogged down, a line or a movement was changed, and Fred got around it.

Leisen had just directed Claudette Colbert, Don Ameche, and John Barrymore in *Midnight,* a picture he'd wanted Barbara to star in after Carole Lombard had turned it down, having worked with Jimmy Stewart in *Made for Each Other* and resting while Gable shot *Gone With the Wind.* Instead of making *Midnight,* Barbara went to work for DeMille in *Union Pacific.*

Leisen thought Lombard's comedic sense superb, as he did Jean Arthur's and Claudette Colbert's.

A year before, Leisen had wanted Barbara to star in *Swing High, Swing Low,* a remake of *The Dance of Life,* based on her Broadway success *Burlesque.* When Barbara wasn't available for it, Leisen tried to get Irene Dunne. Instead, Carole Lombard starred in it.

Leisen had helped launch Carole Lombard's career when he'd recommended her to Cecil B. DeMille for his production of *Dynamite.* DeMille rehearsed Lombard for two weeks and then let her go; she was out too late at night and didn't concentrate on her work.

Beyond These Tears was from an original screenplay by Preston Sturges written for the Paramount producer Al Lewin, based on a love story from a Scottish poem ("Beyond these tears, sweet bairn/So needful to a better ken/Of light and shade and happiness and pain/We'll scamper doon a better geen/Your eyes aspark/Your lips like roses in the rain").

Two years before, the studio, under Lewin's supervision, hired Rebecca West (born Cicely Fairfield; her adopted name, the designing woman of Ibsen's *Rosmersholm,* was taken for the stage when West studied acting at the Royal Academy) to write an original outline for a picture, for either Carole Lombard or Claudette Colbert. West met with Adolph Zukor and asked for a two-month extension on the outline's delivery date; she was at work on a nonfiction book on Yugoslavia. West looked at several of Lombard's and Colbert's pictures and in August 1938, six months after her extended due date, turned in an outline of *The Amazing Marriage.* The studio paid West $5,000 for her outline instead of the $15,000 she would have received had she been given a writing credit, and the rights to the material reverted to Paramount. *The Amazing Marriage* was the working title of the picture that became *Remember the Night.*

Preston Sturges hated deadlines; he put off working for as long as he could and much preferred to play, but he needed money to do so.

Sturges grew up having money one day and being broke the next. Whether his mother was rich or poor, Sturges was always in the flush of the beau monde in the gayest of cities. He took money for granted; it was somehow there for him when he needed it, and he was accustomed to living by the seat of his pants. "Men of intelligence need very little," Sturges said. "And writers have always worked better hungry."

Paramount had to prod pages out of Sturges, and he was still at work on the script weeks before the picture was to start shooting.

Sturges had written a number of plays, most of them unsuccessful. His play *Strictly Dishonorable,* written in six days, a month before the stock market crashed, ran in New York for two years. (Brooks Atkinson called it a well-nigh perfect comedy. "Mr. Sturges has not only an extraordinary gift for character and dialogue but for the flow and astonishment of situation.") The play made Sturges one of the most acclaimed playwrights of the moment— and $300,000, which he quickly spent. He came to see the theater "as a little old man, the last living member of a once rugged dynasty," and saw the movies as "a big twilly with high-button shoes," beckoning him to "come up and see me some time."

Sturges had grown up in a world of privilege, surrounded by artists, café society, who found large sums of money for their art and millionaire benefactors to provide it. His upbringing, chaotic but enchanted, took place in Europe part of the time; his mother, Mary Dempsey, thought of herself as an Italian princess and used the name Mary d'Este Dempsey. She came to know Isadora Duncan, and they became lifelong intimates until Sturges's mother, indirectly, became the instrument of Isadora's death when d'Este's gift to her beloved friend of a bright red batik silk shawl, which Isadora instantly wrapped around her neck, got caught in the spokes of the wheel of Duncan's open Amilcar and instantly killed her.

• • •

Sturges finished the script of *Beyond These Tears* in nine weeks; it was 148 pages long, too long for Paramount's maximum running time of a hundred minutes. Barbara loved the script.

"There's only one thing I want," she said, "a good story. I don't care about clothes or production values or the rest of those things. If it's a good yarn, the other things will take care of themselves."

Though Sturges came from the top and Barbara from the bottom—he from a European bohemian aristocracy and she from a showgirl street life— Barbara felt a great compatibility with Sturges.

She thought him enormously talented and his script one of the best she'd ever read. "What's on paper is on the screen," she said. "If it isn't there, it isn't on the screen."

Sturges had worked as a writer at various Hollywood studios, being fired almost as soon as he walked through the door: a month at Metro adapting Michael Arlen's *Green Hat* for Thalberg; four days at Columbia on *Twentieth Century* for Harry Cohn; a quick round for B. P. Schulberg on *Thirty-Day Princess;* a quicker round on Universal's *Imitation of Life* and a turn on Tolstoy's *Resurrection* (it became *We Live Again*) for Goldwyn, who each day asked Rouben Mamoulian, the director, "When can we get rid of this fellow, Sturgeon?" Sturges also wrote a few scenes for *The Buccaneer* until DeMille saw that his Napoleon was being turned—"Sturgeon"-style—into a comedian.

In between writing (*Hotel Haywire; Never Say Die; If I Were King*), being hailed as a genius, being fired, and running an engineering company, Sturges opened a restaurant on Sunset Boulevard called Snyder's that served steaks, chops, and liquor and stayed open past ten o'clock. After that he built and opened the Players, also on Sunset.

Sturges felt that Mitch Leisen didn't get his humor. When Sturges went to work under contract at Paramount, he was given a Vera Caspary story to adapt called *Easy Living*, which he hoped to direct himself. Instead, the script was given to Leisen, a man Sturges thought arrogant, without a sense of pacing or a knack for comedy.

Everything Leisen knew about making pictures he'd learned from Cecil B. DeMille, with whom he had worked for twelve years. Leisen started working with DeMille at the age of twenty-one on *Male and Female* without knowing anything about costume design or set decoration. In the end, he designed the look of seven of DeMille's most stylized pictures, including

The Godless Girl, Dynamite, Madam Satan, The Squaw Man, and *The Sign of the Cross.*

Leisen set DeMille's cameras—the lighting, setup, the actors' movements—for each of the pictures. DeMille wanted to get as much production value as possible out of Leisen's sets to compensate for his own natural inclination to shoot a master take straight on. When DeMille's master shot was broken down for close-ups and over-the-shoulder shots, the angle would be reversed, and there would be no set behind the actors, no matter how lavish or big Leisen's sets. Long after Leisen stopped supervising DeMille's pictures, he stayed on the set with DeMille to help him stage the action.

When Leisen left to direct his own pictures, DeMille hired ten people to do what Leisen had accomplished himself.

Because of Leisen's obsessive concern with the look of his pictures and with authenticity and his years as a costume designer, Sturges felt that the director was more interested in the sets than the material. Leisen, with his training as an architect at Washington University, had designed his own house as well as that of the Metropolitan Opera mezzo-soprano Gladys Swarthout, also under contract to Paramount. He designed the Palm Springs Racquet Club. His pictures were considered equally elegant. Their light touch was compared to those of Lubitsch's; their charm, to Capra's.

Leisen was able to make the unusual transition from art director/costume designer to director. He'd studied at the Art Institute of Chicago and started directing pictures in 1933 at the age of thirty-five with *Cradle Song* and *Death Takes a Holiday.*

Sturges and Leisen were an interesting combination of sensibilities. Sturges believed that Leisen threw away lines he should have held on to and kept lines that should have been tossed.

Sturges wrote comedy with flashes of feeling and warmth; Leisen directed pictures that were warm with bursts of comedy.

Barbara was five feet three, with broad shoulders and back, a long waist, and flat buttocks that then extended outward. She refused to "glamorize" or care how she looked on-screen. The problem of how she looked in clothes on-screen was the designer's, not hers. She wanted her mind to be free for her performance. It didn't matter to her what she wore in a picture. "People don't remember what you wear," she said. "And if they do, you're fading." Leisen could dress his actors beautifully—both male and female. He designed the costumes on many pictures, among them *The Thief of Bagdad, Dorothy Vernon of Haddon Hall,* and DeMille's *Sign of the Cross.* For *The Thief of Bagdad,*

Leisen designed a different costume for each of the picture's three thousand extras. With *Dorothy Vernon,* he designed a dress embroidered with real pearls for Mary Pickford that was so heavy he had to carry her onto the set each morning to conserve her strength.

Barbara would rather wear a piece of gunnysack for "wardrobe" and have people remember her for one scene she did. She knew she was supposed to set the standards of glamour higher, not lower, that if she were on the screen, she had to try to be glamorous. "The trick," she said, "is to stay natural doing it. The only thing that counts in the long run is the ability to be natural and believable and interesting on the screen."

Naturalness, to Barbara, was "as appealing as glamour," she said. "Maybe more appealing." Her clothes had to be simple, unadorned, well made with good fabrics: man-tailored suits of hard fabrics for daytime and work; tweeds for topcoats; draped gowns, dinner gowns in print, hostess gowns, and afternoon dresses in black, designed by Monica, for evening.

If Barbara didn't wear a dress for a few weeks, she gave it away. She hated hats but bought them, as long as they were "sit-ons," hats that could be crushed and then worn.

Most designers coped with the problem of Barbara's long waistedness by creating clothes for her that had a slightly higher waist and a full skirt. Edith Head did this as well but devised another way to cope with the problem. Head designed belts for Barbara that were wider in the back than in the front and gave the appearance of lifting her waist.

"Nobody understands my figure as well as Edith Head," said Barbara, who called Edith "Jug Head" and thought she was a great designer.

Barbara arrived for a fashion sitting one day in a dress that was three inches off the floor. It was neither a dinner dress nor a street dress. Barbara didn't know what to make of it, but the tailor had lifted it three inches off the floor, and that was that. She coped with it by sitting down on the davenport and draping the skirt over the seat so no one would know how long it was. "And what difference did it make anyway?" she asked.

Hollywood had a wonderful standard of beauty, and most women paid attention to their looks. Barbara didn't. "I have the face that sank a thousand ships," she said. She held on to the theory that what's on the surface isn't as important as what comes from within. "And so far I've managed to make a living."

For a modern-dress picture, actors were to wear their own clothes. Fred Mac-Murray didn't have the right clothes for the part of the assistant DA; he owned very few clothes at all. Mitch Leisen, however, was one of the best-

Edith Head, Paramount Studio designer, with Claudette Colbert, 1939. For the new season, Head wrote, "I shall use a lot of white for whole costumes and for accents, but am deserting navy and black for shades of green in sage, sap, heather and yellowish greens."

dressed men in Hollywood, with perfectly cut suits and specially designed shoes. He and MacMurray were the same size, and Leisen had lent Fred various suits for both *Hands Across the Table* and *Swing High, Swing Low.*

Leisen asked MacMurray why he didn't buy more clothes. MacMurray was so sure he wouldn't last as a movie actor that he'd waited to cash his first few payroll checks. He'd worked at Paramount for a year as a day laborer, helping to construct Stage 5, putting the soundproofing boards in place, painting signs, and doing other odd jobs.

MacMurray was known to be tight with money. Both Barbara and Leisen said that Fred still had the first penny he'd earned. He brought his lunch to the studio: a hard-boiled egg in a brown paper bag. MacMurray was adept at getting by with little money (he'd grown up in near poverty after his parents had separated). In Chicago, studying at the Art Institute at night, MacMurray sold golf clubs during the day and kept his living expenses below minimum. He cooked every meal in his room.

Beyond These Tears was a comedy romance.

It starts out more as a wisecracking comedy: a callous beautiful jewel thief (Anna-Rose Malone, sometimes known as Lee Leander), on trial for stealing

Fred MacMurray circa 1939, six foot three and painfully shy, called "Mr. Normal" by his friends. As a boy in Beaver Dam he dreamed of having a wood lathe, a leather-punching outfit, and an Irish setter.

a priceless bracelet, is about to be acquitted by a sentimental jury (it's the day before Christmas). Her ("windbag") lawyer's defense: she'd suffered a temporary loss of will and consciousness known as . . . hypnotism! "Consider the jewel scene between Mephistopheles and Marguerite in *Faust,*" he tells the jury; she's overcome by the jewels' dazzling light and walks out of the store with the bracelet on her wrist not knowing what she's doing. Of the legal ploy put forward by her lawyer, the Stanwyck character says, "That gag's so old, it's got whiskers." Trying to send the ravishing thief to prison for a good long time is the fast-rising assistant DA (John Sargent) with a big future in politics. He's known for his smooth courtroom technique with women and an unbroken record for winning convictions. He asks for, and is granted, a continuance until after New Year's, knowing that he will get his conviction after the sentimentality of the Yuletide season has passed.

The DA is getting ready to drive home to Wabash, Indiana, for the holidays to the family farm to see his mother and aunt. In the spirit of Christmas, he bails out the girl he's about to prosecute so she won't have to spend the holiday behind bars. The bondsman delivers her—with his compliments and

As Lee Leander, shoplifter, with Chester Clute as salesman behind the counter, *Remember the Night,* 1940. (AMERICAN HERITAGE CENTER, UNIVERSITY OF WYOMING)

a wink—to the DA's apartment, the last thing he wants or expects ("What are you doing here?" he asks her. "I don't know," she says, "but I've got a rough idea"). Now he's stuck with her; she's been locked out of her hotel; she's got nowhere to go, and she's in his custody.

He takes her to dinner, and as they dance to "Back Home in Indiana," he learns they're both Hoosiers, from towns not fifty miles apart ("When I dream about the moonlight on the Wabash/Then I long for my Indiana home"), and offers to drive her to her mother's for a Christmas visit. She hasn't seen her mother since she ran away years ago; he offers to drop her off and pick her up on his way back to New York.

In a wistful moment full of yearning, she agrees to go.

He asks her about her past as a thief, and she assures him she's not a kleptomaniac; it's just that her mind works differently. She makes clear the difference between them. "Supposing you were starving to death," she postulates, "and you didn't have any food and you didn't have any money and you didn't have a place to get any, and there were some loaves of bread out in front of a market—now remember, you're starving to death—and the man's back is turned, would you swipe one?"

"Of course I would."

"That's because you're honest," she says. "You see, I'd have a six-course dinner at the table d'hôte across the street and then say I'd forgotten my purse."

What starts out as sophisticated whimsy as the two drive through Pennsylvania and Ohio and experience a series of detours and mishaps, adventures and near escapes, turns darker and darker as they reach her hometown in Indiana. They arrive at her mother's house late at night; it's on the other side of the tracks, a bleak, forbidding Gothic bathed in blackness and shadow—and the jewel thief comes face-to-face with the past that has held her in its grip.

Walking up to the house, she's buoyant, she's glad to be home, and then she's scared.

Somehow believing that she will be welcomed home, as John Sargent has assured her she would—as he will be with his mother—they are instead brought into a dark, bleak parlor, lit by the light of an oil lamp (no one had electricity in rural America) carried by her mother, who is somber, stone-faced, rigid (played by Georgia Caine), partly enveloped in a shawl, and the girl's joyless past washes over her. Her mother—grim, punishing—asks her what she's come home for, as if the years had meant nothing, as if their argument were still in place.

"Good riddance to bad rubbish, I said the day she left," the mother tells her daughter. "We weren't good enough for her here, a hardworking mother with a crook for a daughter. Stealing my mission money that I put by with the sweat of my brow. You didn't pay me back and you never paid me back."

"How could I?" the Stanwyck character says. "I couldn't get a job after you called me a thief in front of the whole town."

Later, on the porch of her house, she weeps and says to the DA, "I'd forgotten how much that woman hates me and how much I hate her. Ever since I was little, she was always so right and I was always so wrong. She was always so good and I was always so bad."

Her longing in that moment for home, for a childhood with happy memories—for love—makes it clear that she has been living out, frozen to the persona, her mother's unforgiving view of her: rebellious and criminal.

It is a powerful scene—surprising, chilling, melancholy. Unlike the rest of the script, which is done with the lightest of touch and thrown away, this scene is emphatic, underlined. Though there is foreshadowing of trouble at the prospect of visiting her mother, the harshness of the encounter between mother and daughter seems like a nightmare from another story.

And it is: it's the arrival of Jane Eyre at Lowood.

Not only did Sturges inject a bit of Charlotte Brontë into the script, but later he uses the familiar element of *Camille* (the tainted woman willing to sacrifice herself for the man she loves who's too besotted to see his ruination in their love). In addition, *Beyond These Tears,* with Leisen's cutting and re-shaping of the script, became a *Wizard of Oz* in reverse. L. Frank Baum had been Sturges's neighbor in Coronado; Baum's sons, Sturges's playmates. Metro-Goldwyn-Mayer's *Wizard of Oz,* directed by King Vidor and Victor Fleming, was about to have its premiere with Sturges still at work on the script of *Beyond These Tears* weeks before Leisen was to start shooting.

Instead of Kansas, the picture starts in the fast-paced, glittering city, not exactly Oz, but where anything's possible. The story leads back toward a simpler life where man and woman are cleansed: she's no longer the bad girl with a disregard for the law; he's not the cynical DA. There's the bad witch, *her* unloving mother; the good witch(es), *his* mother and his aunt Emmy; Willie, the hired hand, is Hickory; and the others.

Lee Leander, self-admitted thief, and John Sargent, hard-driving but naive district attorney, go on a three-state junket through (seemingly bucolic) small towns and pastures fraught with unexpected twists and turns (the MacMurray and Stanwyck characters spend the night in their car marooned in a field; try to milk a cow for breakfast; are arrested for trespassing on posted property and charged with petty larceny and wanton disregard for the law) until they arrive at Sargent's boyhood home, which is bathed in snow, where cookies are baking in the oven and wood is being set in the bedroom fireplace. Mother (Beulah Bondi) and Aunt Emma (Elizabeth Patterson) are aflutter with excitement that their boy is home for the holiday; all is safe, wholesome, restorative.

His mother welcomes the girl and tells her, "It's a joy to have you here."

And Willie (Sterling Holloway) adds, as an aside to the DA, "Ain't she a peacherino."

On their way west to Wabash, Barbara's and Fred's characters—she, the wary, glib, seen-it-all thief "whose mind works differently"; he, the earnest, decent, hardworking, straight-and-narrow letter-of-the-law lawyer—get a taste of what it's like to see the world as the other does. She sees his sweetness, is touched by his goodness and generosity. He feels what it's like to be exploited, to defy the rules, to give a false name ("Henry Wadsworth Longfellow") to the justice of the peace. And, when they are under arrest and she sets fire to a wastebasket so they can make a getaway in the confusion, he becomes a fugitive from justice and like her is on the lam, trying to make it safely across the state line.

The difference between them is clear when he finds out that she's deliberately set the fire. "I suppose you know that's called arson," he tells her.

"No," she replies, feigning jokey ignorance. "I thought that was when you bit somebody." And then, her knowing, realistic self: "Well, it's better than going to jail. I told you my mind worked differently."

"What's that got to do with the morals of the case?" he asks her.

"What have morals got to do with it?"

She pauses and says under her breath, the real outrage, "And you treated me like a sister."

Leisen cut Sturges's speech about marriage being God's greatest gift to man and woman, which the district attorney says in response to the farmer who arrests him and accuses him of not "even being married" and traveling with "whatever she is." In an effort to put some zip in the story, Sturges tried various approaches to make sense of why the Fred MacMurray character, a district attorney, would take the Barbara Stanwyck character, a girl on trial for theft that he was attempting to put in prison, with him during the Christmas holiday.

First Sturges wrote it so the district attorney took the girl to the mountains to reform her, then he took her out of guilt, for winning a continuance until after Christmas, then out of feeling for the Christmas spirit. Finally, Sturges had the DA take her along with him for "the purpose of violating the Mann Act; this has always been a good second act," said Sturges. "It is an act enjoyed by all, one that we rarely tire of, and one not above the heads of the audience."

The reference to the Mann Act stayed in the script but was later cut.

The studio felt the picture's title was wrong for the box office. *Beyond These Tears* had little bearing on the script. It was decided that a contest might produce a better title. A synopsis of the script with the title *Remember the Night* was sent around. Suggested titles included *The Fortunate Sinner, I Love a Thief, State Versus Love, Romance on Probation, Love Convicted, Out on Bond.*

It was finally decided that the title *Remember the Night* would do. "The title doesn't do violence to the story," said A. M. Botsford of Paramount, "and has attractive box office quality."

The picture was sophisticated, clever, tender. The studio couldn't decide if Sturges had written a "crime melodrama" or a "quiet homey comedy." It finally settled on "romantic drama."

Stanwyck's first line to MacMurray when Fat Mike, the bail bondsman, delivers her to the DA's apartment: "One of these days, one of you boys is going to start one of these things differently, and one of us girls is going to drop dead from surprise." It's a line that has everything; it's light, amused, cynical, sophisticated, trashy, elegant. It's mysterious and rich.

When Stanwyck and MacMurray are home with his family after their travels together, and just when it seems as if they are in a romance, he makes the choice to tell his mother the truth about the girl he's brought home for Christmas. If he hadn't told her, he would have been a heel and seen to be taking advantage of his mother as he palmed off a criminal as an ordinary person. To save him and keep him pure, Sturges has him tell his mother that she is a thief. ("It's not even her first offense," he says. His mother can't believe it and says that if she—the girl—did take anything, it must have been by mistake, she must be a "hypochondriac.") It also makes his betrayal that much more poignant when, later in the courtroom, he deliberately tries to lose the case and spare the accused.

At the end of the scene, his mother reminds her son of the time when he was a little boy and stole her egg money that she was going to use to buy a new dress. She reminds him of how hard he worked to pay it back once he understood what he'd done wrong.

He tells her, "You made me understand." And she replies, "No, dear, it was love that made you understand."

The picture's lesson: "there's no place like home" coupled with "there's nothing as powerful as love."

The scene between Barbara and Beulah Bondi after the New Year's Eve barn dance is nuanced. Here Barbara is at her absolute best; she's not self-pitying but a woman in love. She plays shame in front of the mother, but she rises to the occasion, and there's much nobility of soul. There's no anger or bitterness at the mother for asking the Stanwyck character not to ruin her son's chances by allowing him to fall in love with her, only nobility of heart; both women love the man, and they meet on the ground of love. Barbara is noble and gorgeous. After Beulah Bondi has thanked her for not getting involved with her son and has walked away to leave the room, she turns in the doorway and says, "You love him, though, don't you?" Barbara says, "I'm afraid so."

Bondi had always admired Barbara. They worked well together, though Bondi thought Barbara was somewhat impersonal when the day's work was finished.

Leisen understood about timing and rhythm, about using the actors' spontaneous reactions. He favored his female stars, was drawn to them, which is

With Beulah Bondi, John Sargent's mother, in *Remember the Night,* 1940. Mitchell Leisen's direction and Ted Tetzlaff's camerawork made Barbara look her most beautiful. (PHOTOFEST)

why many actresses wanted to work with him. He was attracted to strong women, women who were audacious, who didn't play by the rules, and who made up their own: Claudette Colbert, Irene Dunne, Jean Arthur, Carole Lombard, Barbara Stanwyck.

Colbert adored Leisen as a director. She appreciated that he didn't impose his will on actors. "Mitch left the acting to the actors." Leisen built sets specifically for Colbert so he could easily film only the left side of her face. She had a notion that her nose was crooked on her right side and used to shade it with green, adding a highlight down the center to straighten it. Leisen photographed his actors with Ted Tetzlaff as his cameraman so that they looked more beautiful than they did in other pictures.

Leisen preferred a first take rather than counting on four, five, six, seven takes to produce an ideal take. While the soundmen and the cutters wanted the actors to pause between sentences so there would be a natural place to cut, Leisen had the cutters find the pause in the sentence. He understood how to create atmosphere and how to use it to bring a sense of reality to the audience.

He kept certain scenes long and deliberately slowed up the pace once the DA and the girl arrive at the Sargent farm to show the effect on the Stanwyck character of the family's warmth, love, and coziness. In the scene in which the family has gathered in the parlor around the Christmas tree, MacMurray plays the piano and sings "Swanee River," and Barbara plays "A Perfect Day" on the piano as Willie (Sterling Holloway) sings.

Leisen knew how to use visual business in a scene to create character, mood, story. His subtle eloquence and deftness was called the Leisen magic.

He admired how Barbara never moved her head or her hands. He liked to have actors play a scene with their backs to the camera. He thought Lombard knew how to do it. Barbara's scene in her bedroom with the Beulah Bondi character ends with Barbara turning her back to the camera, facing the vanity, absently brushing her hair, gazing in the mirror, and seeing how once again she can't be loved; she has to give up the one good thing that has happened to her. The sadness, the defeat, the inevitability, come through as she holds herself up by the dresser and gives in to the tears, expressed by a lovely downward cast of her head.

A simple response but full of color, full of depth.

When Barbara and MacMurray are at Niagara Falls (they return to New York by way of Canada to avoid the law in Ohio), MacMurray, who has been equally transformed by romantic love, does what for him would have been unthinkable: he offers her her freedom and the easy way out. "You're in Canada now," he says. "If you didn't go back now, I couldn't make you." He kisses her and tells her she is in love with him; she denies that she is. He kisses her and she melts; she comes out of it and says to him, simply, "Be fair." She's promised his mother she wouldn't be with him and is trying to keep her word.

It is such a deep line, and Barbara gives it a beautiful reading of vulnerability, common sense, and integrity. It is a line that isn't anticipated—and is dead-on of the character in the moment. That is the brilliance of Sturges's writing, and there are flashes of it throughout the script.

The Fred MacMurray character tells her that after she has been acquitted and he pulls out the marriage license, they will march into the judge's chambers and be married, and for their honeymoon they will return to Niagara Falls.

"But, darling," she says, "we're there now."

He takes her in his arms and they kiss; it isn't a kiss about getting married. It's about sex.

It was Sturges's genius to come up with a title for the picture, which seemed so curious to the studio—*Remember the Night* to replace *Beyond These Tears*—with an ellipse. Sturges is saucy and irreverent; to title a picture from a night of illicit sex is outrageous, but he gets away with it, as well as the scene itself; he is piquant, and he has good taste.

Sturges's genius is to be both high and low, never middle-class, not official art, as with Odets's *Golden Boy.* Sturges always has more than one thing happening, unlike Odets, who has a self-preoccupation with being smarter than everyone else. Sturges can play the violin *and* knock you out.

Sturges had what few screenwriters had. He was upper-class and Europeanized; elegant and sophisticated, he could be colloquial and slapstick without ever being vulgar. He could take slang and the vernacular and vulgarity and give them panache, energy, wit, and brains.

Sturges's setup is artificial: a DA who bails out a crook for Christmas because he feels guilty that he got a continuance and drives her to Indiana. This would never happen. The realism is in its emotionalism, character, people, and humor. Whereas Odets—who was so careful to summon up real life with the taxicabs and the grocery store and was considered so deep and human—is artificial and stylized, Sturges is high elegance and high sophistication while being banana peel low, and Barbara as an actress is freed up by it.

Remember the Night was scheduled to be completed in forty-two days. It was finished in thirty-four, including the scenes Leisen shot and cut from the final print. Leisen was able to shoot quickly by avoiding rewrites. He was also helped by the pace Barbara set.

She learned the entire script to help her with the way movies were made— bits and pieces here and there. "They begin anywhere," she said. "Usually at the end. Never a performance straight through." At first—eleven years before—she'd found it hard to snap into the required mood. Then she caught on to the trick.

"Memorize the script, the whole thing," she said, "so you can think of any place in it, then work backward or forward from there—like a sailor boxing the compass." Before shooting started, Barbara knew her part completely, and all the other actors' so she could prompt them. She never blew one line; the other actors worked harder trying to outdo her.

Barbara had a bad back, but she was dressed and on the set by eight thirty in the morning.

Leisen came on the set at a quarter to nine, having lined up the sets the night before. Barbara's voice came out of the fly gallery saying, "Come on, you sonofabitch, let's get this show on the road—where the hell have you been?"

Leisen was able to shoot more than four pages a day, the fastest he'd ever shot.

Just before shooting a scene, Barbara called for a hat she was to wear and put it on.

"Okay, let's go," she said.

Leisen asked Barbara if she wanted to look in the mirror.

"Why? Isn't the hat on right. This is the front I hope. Looking in the glass won't help."

Leisen couldn't believe that Barbara never looked in the mirror. He'd waited hours for other actresses who'd held up scenes looking at themselves in the mirror.

"Suppose I don't look good in it," said Barbara. "Nothing can be done about it. Just looking won't help. Come on, let's shoot."

Barbara was willing to withstand great physical discomfort and saved Leisen time. In one scene she and Fred, having spent the night in a pasture, try to milk a cow for breakfast. The scene was shot at the Paramount Ranch during the hottest time of the summer. In the picture, it's supposed to be the day before Christmas.

For the scene Barbara had on a wool suit, a sweater, a fur coat, galoshes, and a scarf; the crew was wearing as little as possible. In between scenes, instead of changing out of the hot, heavy clothes, Barbara refused to take off any of the layers; it would take too long, she said, to get them back on when they were ready to start again.

For the New Year's Eve barn dance scene, Barbara had to wear a wedding dress with corsets. Edith Head, who designed the clothes for the picture, created a 1900-type wedding gown that had corsets, petticoats, chemises, and underskirts, which Barbara had to wear in hundred-degree heat.

Leisen wasn't going to be using Barbara for an hour and said, "For God's sake, why don't you loosen up those corsets?"

"No, you may need me." Barbara sat on the set by Leisen the whole time. When he was ready for her, she was there. Leisen never had to wait for her to finish with the hairdresser or the makeup man.

Leisen told Barbara he wouldn't need her anymore that day, and she left. He continued to work with the other actors until about an hour later, when he realized that to wrap up the set, he would need one more shot of Barbara and sent someone to see if she was still on the lot. Leisen's assistant, Chico

With Fred MacMurray as John Sargent, camped in a pasture, on their way back home to Indiana, *Remember the Night*, 1940. (AMERICAN HERITAGE CENTER, UNIVERSITY OF WYOMING)

Day, ran to her dressing room. Barbara was still in costume with her makeup on. "I knew you would need me again," she said.

Every time Leisen dismissed Barbara early, she waited in her dressing room in costume and makeup, just in case.

In another scene Barbara had to pack a suitcase and had to do several takes. Each time she had to redo the scene, she put everything back before the propman could get there. In every take, she put things in the suitcase exactly the same way.

Leisen admired Barbara. "She's a perfectionist if ever I saw one," he said.

She was up in the gallery talking to the electricians when Ted Tetzlaff, Leisen's cameraman, called up to the crew to tell them how he wanted the lights adjusted. "Down a litte," he said. "Turn it to the left, turn that one to the right." Over and over. Finally, Barbara, hands on hips, called down, "For Christ's sake, Ted, make up your mind!"

Barbara and Fred were great friends, though they hadn't worked together in a picture.

From *Remember the Night*, 1940. In the midst of the New Year's Eve barn dance scene. Left to right: Elizabeth Patterson, Beulah Bondi, unidentified cast and crew, Barbara with Fred MacMurray, Ted Tezlaff, Mitchell Leisen, and unidentified child.

She teased MacMurray for being shy about filming love scenes. Everyone on the set dreaded having to shoot the scene at the end of the picture. Barbara handled it by saying to the crew, "This is really going to be something, I am supposed to be kissed passionately by Fred." She kidded Fred about it, as did the crew. When the day arrived, MacMurray gritted his teeth, determined to show them he wasn't such a bad lover, and did the scene perfectly.

MacMurray had appeared in twenty-four pictures as a leading man. He made actresses look good without stealing their scenes, and actresses asked to work with him because of it. His modesty, reserve, and affability made real the lightest romance.

MacMurray worked repeatedly opposite several actresses: Claudette Colbert in three pictures (his screen debut in *The Gilded Lily, The Bride Comes Home,* and *Maid of Salem*); Carole Lombard in four (*Hands Across the Table, The Princess Comes Across, True Confession,* and *Swing High, Swing Low*); and Madeleine Carroll in two (*Cafe Society* and *Honeymoon in Bali*). By the time he made *Remember the Night*, he'd starred opposite Hollywood's top actresses, including Ann Sheridan (*Car 99*), Katharine Hepburn (*Alice Adams*), Sylvia

With Mitch Leisen (left) and Fred MacMurray in the final scene of *Remember the Night*, 1940. When making *Honeymoon in Bali*, MacMurray mumbled to the director, "Let's do the love scenes first. I can't work for weeks with that hanging over me."(COURTESY OF DAVID CHIERICHETTI)

Sidney (*The Trail of the Lonesome Pine*), and Irene Dunne (*Invitation to Happiness*).

MacMurray wasn't temperamental; he didn't blow up or get excited. He spent hours at home oiling and polishing his guns. He and Claude Binyon, a Paramount writer, liked to shoot doves together.

At the end of the picture, after the Stanwyck character has pleaded guilty and is about to be taken away by the matron, she and MacMurray are in a catacomb. In the scene MacMurray was to say how much he loved her.

MacMurray was shy and reserved, particularly with women. Leisen thought his lack of ease with women "pitiful." Leisen was drawn to both men and women; he was married with a mistress and flaunted his homosexuality.

He couldn't get the scene with Fred in the catacombs, and then MacMurray disappeared. Leisen asked his assistant where Fred was and was told he was behind the set. Leisen went around to the back of the set, and MacMurray was crying.

"I've never said that to anybody in my life," he told Leisen. "I just can't."

"You must have loved a dog, or your mother," said Leisen.

"I've never said, 'I love you' to anybody. I just can't say it.'"

Leisen did away with the line, and MacMurray got through the scene.

The picture's producer, Al Lewin, suddenly left the studio. Leisen became the picture's producer and could do what he wanted with Sturges's script. He shaped the script to fit Barbara's and Fred's personalities. He cut MacMurray's longer speeches since the actor had difficulty with his lines, and the story became more the girl's picture. Unlike Barbara, who could do anything and pace herself according to what was needed—and does in this picture—MacMurray was a slow and gentle actor. Leisen used MacMurray's natural flair for comedy and sense of timing and the actor's leisurely pace to help build Sargent's character.

Sturges was on the set and resented that so much of the dialogue was cut. He felt the cuts were unnecessary. Had Sturges directed the picture, he would have made the pace faster and would have made it, as he'd written it, more John Sargent's story with a different emotional quality.

Leisen took Barbara into the projection room one day after shooting to look at the picture. It was still rough in spots, still minus the musical score. Barbara watched it all and said, "God help me. After all these years. I'm turning into a first class ham."

Remember the Night was budgeted at $634,000 and came in at $588,000, $46,000 under budget. Barbara was paid $67,500 for forty-eight days of work; MacMurray, $60,000. Beulah Bondi was paid $5,000 for two weeks of work; Elizabeth Patterson, $2,500; Sterling Holloway was paid $750 a week. Sturges, $47,000; Leisen, $50,000.

When Leisen directed women, he dominated them in a masculine way and was attracted to them, and it shows on-screen. MacMurray took on Leisen's look—literally wearing Leisen's clothes—but Leisen was able to direct women, flirt with them, draw performances out of them because he admired women in a male way. Barbara never looked more beautiful, more luminous, than she does in *Remember the Night.*

In the end of Sturges's script, "love reformed her and corrupted him, which gave us the finely balanced moral," said Sturges, "that one man's meat is another man's poison, or caveat emptor."

In *Remember the Night,* Barbara is both classy and shopgirlish. Sturges was a loner, as Barbara had been before Bob came into her life. Sturges, like Barbara, was wary of people in the industry. Both were possessive of those around them.

In the picture it is acknowledged that her character, Lee Leander, is hot, that she knows about sex, that she's not a good girl, and yet she's not vulgar or tainted or soiled or bitter. She is sexy and good-hearted and smart. Sturges allows her to be all of these things, and somehow it brings Barbara's own persona together in a way that is light and appealing, buoyant and still full of substance.

The combination of Sturges's nuanced writing and comedy released Barbara. Her attraction to melodrama had become her signature, though in ways it confined her. With Sturges's brilliant writing, she was freed up. On-screen she is a person with weight and power, and comedy lightens her. Sturges was able to write with tone and color, and Barbara was able to play the nuance.

In previous work, Barbara, playing full-out vulgar, full-out tragedy, full-out noble, put all her power into it and at times could get overloaded. In the hands of Sturges and Leisen, the pace is light and up. Barbara is full of vitality and quick on her feet, and she blazes.

Barbara operates on many levels in *Remember the Night:* she is a believable crook; believably vulgar; believably sensitive and vulnerable; rebellious (in the scene with her mother, it is clear her defiance is bonded to her mother's take on her). What Sturges gives Stanwyck is her longing for roots, her longing to go home for Christmas, the way it comes up when she hears "Back Home Again in Indiana." She melts at his mother's house because he has everything she's ever wanted and she basks in the warmth of it, allows herself to be corseted, and becomes noble.

Sturges's best lines are simple, colloquial, sayings that people use all the time, but because of circumstance and character they resonate.

The morning after Niagara Falls they are in a cab on their way to the New York courthouse, where he is about to prosecute her and send her to jail. He is all goofy from the night before because he's inexperienced; she has taken on the role of being the sensible one because she's experienced. She insists on going to jail so he won't be tainted and so that their relationship will be evenly weighted. If she had allowed him to get her off, she would have been indebted to him ("If you still want me afterward," she says to him, "I'd be all squared"), and it would have falsified everything between them. Their pact is not at all superficial; it is quite deep. "When you make a mistake," she says, "you've got to pay for it, otherwise you never learn."

The combination of Barbara and MacMurray works: he is light and a good egg; she is breezy, grounded, larcenous, with a heart of gold and a yearning for home, like Sturges himself, who had such an uprooted childhood.

"As it turned out," said Sturges, "the picture had quite a lot of schmaltz, a good dose of schmerz and just enough schmutz to make it box office."

It was Leisen's best picture to date and Barbara's best performance.

After *Remember the Night,* Leisen wanted Barbara to star in *Night of January 16th,* based on the Ayn Rand Broadway courtroom hit of 1935–1936. For each of its more than two hundred performances, the play drew its jury from the audience and had alternate endings depending on the jury's verdict ("Elaborate melodrama," wrote Brooks Atkinson of Rand's play. "Routine theater with the usual brew of hokum"). Ayn Rand was working at RKO as an extra and wardrobe woman when, at the age of twenty-eight, she wrote the play, modeled on the death of the Swedish financier Ivar Kreuger, the "Match King," this after Rand worked as an extra at age twenty-two in DeMille's *The King of Kings.* Rebecca West had written a play in the 1920s about Kreuger and the financial scandal that shook the world. Nothing came of West's play until she lent it out to an old friend, an American who used it to produce his own play.

RKO bought the rights to Rand's play with Claudette Colbert and Lucille Ball in mind to star as the accused, lover of the swindler who has stolen millions from investors and, facing bankruptcy and ruin, falls, or is thrown, from a New York skyscraper to his death. Paramount took over the rights from RKO as a picture for Don Ameche and Barbara.

The Paramount publicity department came up with two stunts to help promote *Remember the Night.* The first was to have Bob Taylor sue the studio because he didn't want Barbara doing a scene in a corset. The second was to have Barbara pose for photographs hugging a cow.

"I must be lousy in the picture if you can't sell it any other way," said Barbara. The studio pressed her about the promotional ideas; she rejected them out of hand, saying simply, "They're phony."

SIXTEEN

Darkening Lands

Bob loved to design jewelry for Barbara, such as a pair of matching gold bracelets set with sapphires, which he then had made at Bill Ruser's store on Rodeo Drive. Bob's chief hurdle was to get Barbara to wear the pieces—she preferred not to wear jewelry.

Bob began production on a picture called *Remember?*, written and directed by Norman McLeod, who directed the *Topper* features for Hal Roach. Starring with Bob and Lew Ayres was Greer Garson, who'd been on the London stage for three years and was considered one of the most promising young British actresses of her generation. She'd been brought to Metro eighteen months before by Louis B. Mayer. Garson didn't think she was particularly photogenic; Mayer told her there's no one who can't be photographed. Garson negotiated her contract and got $500 a week, the biggest salary ever paid a beginner in pictures.

Garson was Scots Irish ("Greer," the Irish contraction of the Scottish "McGregor"). Her green eyes, red hair, and alabaster complexion resembled a Burne-Jones painting. At the University of London, which Garson completed in three years on full scholarship, she was described as "a unique blend of La Belle Dame Sans Merci and Goldilocks and the Three Bears"; her beauty was rich and kind. Garson's friend Noël Coward said to her, "You're lucky, you have the best possible mask for an actress—everything goes up—it should." There were those in London who called her "Ca-Reer Garson."

Joan Crawford and Robert Young were to have starred in *Remember?*; then Margaret Sullavan. Crawford instead was put into Rachel Crothers's *Susan and God,* which Greer Garson had asked to do when she found out that Gertrude Lawrence, star of the Broadway production, wouldn't be reproducing the role on the screen.

Louis B. Mayer had originally brought Garson over and groomed and tested her for months, looking for the right vehicle for her. Nothing came of it; Garson became depressed. She lived on work, and the limbo, combined with a deep loneliness, caused her to stay indoors for months.

Two weeks before her MGM contract was to expire, Garson was assigned to play opposite Robert Donat in Metro's *Goodbye, Mr. Chips* since Myrna Loy had left the studio for 20th Century–Fox.

It was a small part. Garson was angry that she'd been offered a supporting role; she saw the character as a "sparrow," but she took the part in order to get away from Hollywood and get back to London. She soon came to see the part of Mrs. Chipping as a "dove," a woman in love whom every man would like to marry.

"If anything glowed through Mrs. Chips," said Garson, it was the actress's own deep delight that "after fifteen months of miserable, humiliating idleness," she was finally working. Garson left for London for four months to make the picture and had no intention of returning to Hollywood; the place had broken her.

It was clear that *Goodbye, Mr. Chips* was about to be a hit. And Greer Garson a big star.

Garson was seen as the epitome of the dignity and beauty of mature womanhood. Mayer wanted her back at Metro and asked her to return. She wired back, "I will gladly come and make a picture with you when you have one ready for me. A repetition of the past eleven and a half months I spent in Hollywood would kill me. All I have to show for it is eighteen thousand miles of travel, a few tests, and an almost infinitesimal part in *Goodbye, Mr. Chips.* Now that I am fortunate enough to be away, it would take wild horses to drag me back."

Garson's contract was renewed and her salary increased. She was given a new dressing room, and while she returned to Metro triumphant, she still was made to wait months for another part.

The picture *Remember?* was a comedy with a good deal of slapstick, which Garson enjoyed. "I've always wanted to jump into the water fully dressed," she said, "but never dared to."

Garson had come from London, where gas masks hung in every home and were present at the studio. Each afternoon at 4:30 she invited Bob and Lew Ayres and others to tea (two bags; the cream in first).

Remember? was the hardest work Garson ever did. She knew the picture was bad and that she was bad in it, but somehow she got through it.

During the production Bob was given a surprise party on the set for his

Lew Ayres, Greer Garson, and Bob, *Remember?*, 1939. (PHOTOFEST)

twenty-eighth birthday that was attended by Eddie Mannix, Benny Thau, Bill Powell, Myrna Loy, and Woody Van Dyke.

Metro wanted Bob to appear in one of the starring roles in a remake of the 1912 Italian silent epic *Quo Vadis?* The novel, a best seller published in 1896 by Henryk Sienkiewicz, tells the story of the religious conversion of a noble Roman warrior set against the emperor Nero's persecution of the early Christians. It had been made into one of the most ambitious pictures of its time, running twelve reels—almost three hours—and paved the way for D. W. Griffith's *Birth of a Nation.* When *Quo Vadis?* came to America, shortened to eight reels, it was a sensation; it opened at the Astor Theatre in New York and ran for an unheard-of twenty-two weeks. The remake, with Hunt Stromberg as producer, was to be Metro's big spectacle for the 1939–1940 program.

Bob and Barbara had made a date for Bob's twenty-eighth birthday. On Barbara's July 16 birthday Bob had had a 7:00 a.m. call to reshoot scenes for *Lucky Night* and hadn't been able to put together a party for her.

For Bob's birthday, Barbara and Bob decided to have a candlelit dinner, just the two of them. They went out to a restaurant and got back to the house early. Bob told Barbara to go upstairs and put on her prettiest nightgown.

The lights in the house were off. Barbara went up to the bedroom, changed, and then stood at the top of the stairs. "Here, Dad," she called down to Bob. "Come and get it."

The lights went on. A roomful of people looked up at Barbara and yelled, "Surprise! Happy birthday!"

Barbara stood there naked, a birthday present for Bob. She ran into their bedroom and locked the door. She refused to speak to Bob, who tried to apologize. "I didn't dream . . ." he said.

"Well, I didn't dream there were going to be people there."

A week after Nazi Germany and Soviet Russia signed a nonaggression pact, Nazi Germany invaded Poland from the west; Soviet Russia invaded from the east. More than a million German soldiers—thirty-two divisions—crossed the borders of Silesia, East Prussia, and Slovakia into Poland and overran an army of half a million Polish soldiers.

England and France announced they were at war against Germany; the British liner *Athenia,* with more than a thousand passengers on board, two hundred of them Americans, was attacked by German torpedoes off the Hebrides.

The headlines in the *Los Angeles Times* read: "*Three Nations War* on Hitler"; "Liner Torpedoed—1400 Aboard"; "British Planes Bomb Nazi Fleet."

President Roosevelt addressed the nation over the radio: "Tonight my single duty is to speak to the whole of America . . . I had hoped against hope that some miracle would prevent a devastating war in Europe and bring to an end the invasion of Poland by Germany . . . This nation will remain a neutral nation, but I cannot ask that every American remain neutral in thought as well. Even a neutral has a right to take account of facts. Even a neutral cannot be asked to close his mind or his conscience."

Roosevelt proclaimed a state of "limited national emergency," safeguarding and enforcing the United States' neutral position. All U.S. military forces were told to increase enlistments; reservists were called to active duty.

America was neutral, but Hollywood had been making pictures for the past year that led audiences to feel they were as much at war as Europe was.

Metro's pacifist picture *Idiot's Delight* with Clark Gable and Norma Shearer was about the imminence of war. *Thunder Afloat* with Wallace Beery was about German submarines invading America's coast. Warner Bros. *Confessions of a Nazi Spy,* released in the spring, months before the start of the war in Europe, was about the dangers of the Nazi-run German American Bund and how it threatened to overthrow the American government. The picture's message: Wake up, America! *Blockade,* originally called *The River Is Blue* from a script by Clifford Odets, written ultimately by John Howard Lawson, was about the Spanish Civil War and the resistance, about Loyalists and Fascists;

it starred Madeleine Carroll and Henry Fonda, who asks the audience directly into the camera, "Where's the conscience of the world?"

Studios were frantic to have those actors and actresses traveling in Europe return to America as soon as possible. Norma Shearer, Tyrone Power and his wife, Annabella, and Edward G. Robinson were in France. Douglas Fairbanks and Robert Montgomery were in London. Maureen O'Sullivan had been one of only ninety-six passengers out of a possible two thousand on a crossing of the *Queen Mary* to London.

The Tele-View newsreel theater in Hollywood increased its business, one of the few theaters to do so. Barbara and Bob were among the many who went to the newsreels to find out what was going on with the war in Europe.

Their plans for a European trip, including bicycling for part of it, were canceled because of the war. Bob suggested South America as an alternative. Barbara wanted to see Europe first; if she couldn't go to Europe, she preferred not to go anywhere—and didn't.

A week after completing *Remember the Night,* Barbara appeared on *Lux Radio Theatre* in *Wuthering Heights,* from the Ben Hecht and Charles MacArthur adaptation of Samuel Goldwyn's picture. Brian Aherne was her Heathcliff; Ida Lupino, Isabella. William Wyler's picture had been released five months before and was a big hit. *Radio Theatre* listeners had sent in letters requesting that Lux present *Wuthering Heights* on the air. J. Walter Thompson paid Barbara her usual $4,000 for the broadcast.

The Englishness of the novel, its underscoring of gentry and class, seemed to be an intimidating element for Barbara and kept her from capturing the more nuanced, challenging aspect of Cathy's character: the "perverted passion and passionate perversity" of her attachment to Heathcliff, lower-class, illegitimate, a black gypsy who falls in love above himself.

Barbara seemed more concerned about her English accent than portraying Cathy's passionate love ("I *am* Heathcliff") for her demonic stepbrother. For someone who read as much as Barbara did, there was an awe of English society and an England that existed in the hearts and minds of novelists and in the movies.

Barbara's Catherine Earnshaw, a nineteenth-century English girl of the moors, was too modern, too contemporary—a rare off note in Barbara's many *Lux* appearances. Her voice was too strident, too shrill. There wasn't a nineteenth-century bone in Barbara's body.

Cathy's marriage to Linton as an escape from her incestuous love for Heathcliff is a rush to convention, a turning away from her uproarious emotions toward order, comfort, kindness, civility, all the gentler virtues that society has to offer. It was impossible for Barbara to play a weak-willed woman, a woman who turns her back on emotion for convention.

Cathy and Heathcliff's love for each other is a contract of childhood so intense, so binding, that they cannot outgrow it ("He's more myself than I am; whatever our souls are made of, his and mine are the same"), as the Brontës could not get out of their contract of childhood, they could not prolong the idyll of it. Barbara is not a conventional woman. She understood the deep feelings forged in childhood and its bond; she had that pact with her own brother.

Always the up-from-under girl, Barbara was not someone who could act against her true feelings or run from them if they challenged family life. She could never turn away from passion because she didn't want it. Barbara is about surviving. Love may get in the way, or be the way; she can sacrifice herself because of love but not sacrifice love because of pleasantness, courtesy, and comfort.

After the "curtain," DeMille called the actors back onstage to the microphone to take a bow and say a few (scripted) words to the audience. Barbara said of *Wuthering Heights,* "It's a moving play, C. B. But more than that, I think it has a lesson today for every woman. It shows the necessity of holding on to one's ideals." As for the moors, Barbara said, "It's no place for my Irish imagination."

The move from Marwyck into town caused Barbara to lose too much weight. She was down to 106 pounds and was on a regimen to gain back some of it. Barbara was disciplined about food; she didn't approve of people being fat. It implied negligence. She ate little—roast beef au jus; steak, rare ("Just let it bow to the broiler on the way over"); hamburger, raw. She could be ravenous until she sat down to eat, and then her appetite vanished. Other times she would eat something she shouldn't. She drank up to twelve cups of coffee a day and ran on nervous energy.

If she couldn't fall asleep until five in the morning and had to be at the studio early, she was up an hour after she fell asleep and sometimes went as long as twenty-eight hours without a catnap.

During the move from Marwyck, cartons of liquor and wine were stacked on the patio to be brought into the house the next day. Bob and Barbara's Great Dane and golden retriever knocked over the cartons, which fell and broke on the patio floor. The dogs lapped up the wine that spilled and the following morning were hungover.

Barbara brought most of her furniture from the ranch. It was simple, contemporary, comfortable. Two couches faced each other in their new living room. Looking down on the furniture was a six-foot painting by Paul Clemens of Barbara in a red velvet full-length gown. An imposing phonograph, given to her by RCA for doing an advertisement for the company, stood in the living room; at Christmas, a large tree took its place.

The bedroom and sitting room on the second floor overlooked sycamore boughs and a garden at the back of the house. The bedroom had a tufted flowered-chintz bed; the sitting room was simple, without dressing table, elaborate mirrors, or perfume bar. Around a white brick fireplace were a Victorian sofa and a large wing chair, unadorned lamps, and tables piled with books.

Bob loved to cook. When he wasn't cooking, Barbara ordered the meals and planned the menus, something she never did before knowing Bob. She didn't care what she ate, but Bob was particular about food.

Barbara loved to clean; ashtrays were emptied as fast as they were used. "You were never royalty," said Bob to Barbara on her fanatical cleaning. In another age, he told her, she would have been the scullery maid, never the princess, although his affectionate name for her was Queen. If the kitchen was a mess or a toilet had to be scrubbed, even with a cook or a maid in the house, Barbara did the cleaning and scrubbing.

The gardeners who tended the grounds were out every Saturday mowing the huge lawns. The smell of newly cut grass was so intoxicating to Dion it made him want to get on his bike and ride forever.

Two weeks after moving into the house in Beverly Hills, Barbara was trying to open a window that had been painted shut. It wouldn't give. She hit the frame with the heel of her right hand. The glass broke; her wrist was cut. She was bleeding badly and was taken to Cedars of Lebanon Hospital and rushed into the operating room. For the next hour, the doctor, whose patients included other actors and performers—Sylvia Sidney, Alice Faye, Mickey Rooney, Al Jolson—sutured Barbara's severed tendon with fifty-five stitches. Bob was at work shooting retakes of *Remember?* Barbara didn't call him; she didn't want to worry him or interrupt his work.

Barbara went through trouble alone. At Marwyck, one night in the midst of the move, she awakened in the early morning hours in horrible pain from food poisoning and paced in darkness for the rest of the night instead of waking Bob, who was working the next day, or asking Uncle Buck to drive her to the hospital. In the morning, she went to work with spasms of pain rather than cause a delay in shooting.

After putting her arm through the window, Barbara spent the night in the hospital and went home the next day with a splint on her wrist and a special glove to protect her hand.

After the accident, there was talk of what had happened and why Barbara hadn't told Bob about it. Barbara's response: "I'm not the morbid type, and if I were, what in heaven's name have I to be morbid about? I'm lucky and happy and I know it." DeMille sent Barbara a telegram telling her how sorry he was about her hand. The success of *Union Pacific* resulted in the director's signing a new four-year contract with Paramount. Barbara wrote back thanking DeMille and said that she'd wanted to call but knew he wasn't feeling well—he was still having prostate difficulties—and didn't want to bother him.

"I can't write very good yet so please do forgive me," she wrote. "My hand is healing nicely. The stitches were taken out a few days ago. Could I please have an autographed picture of you C.B.? I hope you are feeling better and may I please work for you soon again. Devotedly Barbara."

Barbara worked with DeMille on *Lux Radio Theatre* when she starred in the Margaret Sullavan part in Universal's *Only Yesterday,* first directed in 1933 by John Stahl. It had been Sullavan's screen debut and was from the Stefan Zweig novella *Letter from an Unknown Woman* and Frederick Lewis Allen's "informal" history of the 1920s. George Brent performed on the air opposite Barbara.

The same night marked the premier broadcast of *The Hedda Hopper Show,* also on CBS; the show was fifteen minutes long and was to run three times a week.

Barbara's picture *Golden Boy* and Bob's *Lady of the Tropics* opened within a few weeks of one another: *Lady of the Tropics* at the Capitol in early August; *Golden Boy* in New York at the Music Hall on Labor Day weekend.

Reviewers were full of praise for Mamoulian's translation of Odets's play and his portrait of the brutality of prizefighting. They wrote of William Holden's "at times perfect" interpretation of Joe Bonaparte. It was Lee J. Cobb, at twenty-seven, also a newcomer to pictures from the Group Theatre, as the senior Bonaparte, and Sam Levene, as the taxi driver brother-in-law, who walked away with the picture and the reviews.

Barbara, who captured Lorna Moon so thoughtfully and worked so hard to coach Holden to build a difficult role, was passingly acknowledged by critics ("A solid performance," *The Hollywood Reporter;* "Stanwyck has supplied just the proper note of cynicism and frankness," said *The New York Times*). Reviewers took their cue from Odets's setup and regarded Lorna Moon in the piece as a character there to support the men instead of seeing how central she is to the play and how delicate a role it was to create. *Variety* called Barbara's performance "a standout . . . [it] does much to provide a sincere ring to the picture." Barbara's deftness made it look too easy.

Lady of the Tropics was called "hokum" by Louella Parsons, "grand opera tragedy; more droll than deadly" ("The fact that Mr. [Ben] Hecht emerges with his reputation intact," wrote Frank Nugent in *The New York Times,* "is something which belongs among his own recently published 'Book of Miracles' "). Bob Taylor's work was acknowledged despite the picture ("Taylor turns in a good performance under the circumstances," said *Variety*). Hedy Lamarr was dismissed ("It is necessary to report that Lamarr is essentially one of those museum pieces, like the Mona Lisa, who are more beautiful in repose").

Bob was slipping in popularity. Pictures like *Lady of the Tropics* weren't helping his career. The *Motion Picture Herald*'s annual poll listed Mickey Rooney as the top motion picture personality of 1939, with Shirley Temple falling from first place after holding that spot for four years. Gable, Tyrone Power, Spencer Tracy, Bette Davis, Errol Flynn, James Cagney, and Sonja Henie were among the top ten American stars. Bob was now in the category of honorable mentions, along with Bing Crosby, Deanna Durbin, Wallace Beery, Myrna Loy, Gary Cooper, Henry Fonda, Ginger Rogers, and Cary Grant.

A month after Barbara's accident, she and Bob, just back from a week in Mexico City, flew to New York for a ten-day belated honeymoon, to rest, Christmas shop, buy clothes, and see every show they could. Barbara still had a splint on her wrist.

She didn't have to start work at United Artists on *Cheers for Miss Bishop* until January. She would be working with Archie Mayo on their fourth picture together. The script, by Stephen Vincent Benét, was from the Bess Streeter Aldrich novel *Miss Bishop,* published in 1933, about a dedicated midwestern schoolteacher from pioneer stock who sacrifices the richness of conventional life for service.

Bob was to start work soon on *Flight Command* by Commander Harvey Haislip and John Sutherland. Haislip had written a picture—*Thunder Afloat*—about German U-boats invading American waters in the Great War that opened in mid-September 1939, weeks after Europe was at war. Haislip's new picture was a propaganda story about preparedness. Metro made clear it did not advocate war, though the studio was hoping to get the cooperation of the navy for the picture.

Barbara and Bob flew into Newark Airport and went to the Pierre, where they were staying. While in New York, they went to see Tallulah Bankhead in *The Little Foxes*. The curtain went up, and a woman turned around and whispered so the entire house could hear, "Look, there's Barbara Stanwyck and Robert Taylor!"

Their presence caused such a commotion in the theater that during the first intermission Barbara and Bob moved to the back row. The next morning a friend called to ask if it was true that they had walked out on Tallulah's play. Barbara wrote a letter to Miss Bankhead explaining what had happened. "I wanted her to know that we didn't walk out," said Barbara. "I have too much respect for actors who are trying to do their best, to be the cause of upsetting them."

Miss Bankhead wrote back saying that the story hadn't reached her but that if it had, she would not have given it any credence.

Barbara and Bob saw Katharine Hepburn in *The Philadelphia Story*, then running in its eighth month. Joseph Cotten was C. K. Dexter Haven; Van Heflin, the journalist; Shirley Booth, the photographer. Barbara and Hepburn had been accused in the press of feuding. Barbara thought Hepburn wonderful in the play and wrote to tell her so.

In between going to the Billy Conn–Gus Lesnevich bout at Madison Square Garden, Barbara and Bob went to a party given by Moss Hart on their behalf. Hart's play with George Kaufman, *The Man Who Came to Dinner*, had opened on Broadway a month earlier.

A guest at the party went on about how badly movie stars behave in New York. Barbara sat and listened. "Aren't you going to defend Hollywood actresses?" "No I am not," said Barbara. "There's no excuse for those girls. They know better than that. They are rude and someone should tell them so. Just because we've been lucky enough to make money and get our names in lights doesn't give us the right to be rude." Edna Ferber overheard the exchange, rose to her feet, and bowed to Barbara, who smiled back and turned to Moss Hart and said, "Be sure and invite me back again sometime, if you want to break your lease."

After the party, Hart, Barbara, and Bob drove to Bucks County for the weekend. Hart's eighty-odd-acre farm was an hour-and-a-half drive south of New York. He referred to his eighteenth-century fieldstone house, Fairview Farm, as "my Pennsylvania extravagance, my appalling little dream-farm, my beautiful white elephant," and dubbed himself the "Jewish Ethan Frome." Fairview Farm's regular guests included Ferber, Alexander Woollcott, and Katharine Cornell.

Hart's neighbors, George and Beatrice Kaufman, lived a mile down the road on Barley Sheaf Farm, which Kaufman called Cherchez la Farm. The Kaufmans, who rented an apartment on East Sixty-Third Street, had bought the house in Bucks County following his much-publicized scandal involving Mary Astor.

Moss Hart was an avid shopper of colonial antiques. "When I go into a store," he said, "I'm convinced that every piece of merchandise on every shelf is trembling with desire to belong to me." During the weekend Hart took the Taylors antiquing for their new house.

Barbara and Bob flew to South Bend to go to the Notre Dame–USC game and watch, along with fifty-six thousand other spectators, the Fighting Irish battle the Trojans and lose in the last three minutes of the game to USC's two battering-ram running backs, Grenville Lansdell and Ambrose Schindler, 20–12.

Barbara and Bob arrived back in Los Angeles in time for their prize-winning German boxer, Princess Ondra, to give birth to her first litter of eight puppies, which were to be given away as Christmas presents.

Barbara made it clear to her friends that if they planned to give Dion presents, they shouldn't spend more than $1.95 and that if the gifts cost more, Dion wouldn't get them. The year before Dion had received thirty or forty expensive presents from Bob and Barbara and their friends. Barbara felt that no child could cope with that much and disciplined herself not to give Dion a surfeit of things. She was trying not to be extravagant with him. Though she wanted him to have the things she didn't have as a child, she thought she'd overdone it and that it wasn't helping him.

The piles of presents under the tree with Dion's name on them were, by Christmas Eve, diminished by half. Dion had shaken and felt each wrapped present in an effort to guess what was inside. Barbara explained to him that there were many poor people in the world and that he could have five of the presents; the rest were to be sent to orphanages.

Barbara's generosity with others was legendary. She didn't speak of it and didn't want it mentioned. She never went to charity bazaars or benefits but sent anonymous gifts to those who were in need—wheelchairs, crutches, and braces to a local clinic for paralyzed children whose parents couldn't afford to buy the equipment. She redid a hospital room for a short story writer and playwright who, months before, had been severely burned all over her body when her dress caught fire and she was forced to spend months recovering in the hospital.

Barbara felt that too many possessions for her son would deprive him of a proper perspective on what was important. She saw it as a way of building Dion's character; he saw it as an inexplicable punishment.

With Europe at war, Hollywood stayed home for the Christmas holiday. Clark Gable and Carole Lombard ate turkey. Barbara, finally free from the splint on her arm, and Bob had their first open house on Beverly Drive.

Ronald Colman and Alan Mowbray, president of British War Relief of Southern California, and Charles Boyer of French War Relief organized a Franco-British war relief dinner dance at the Cocoanut Grove with the help of Claudette Colbert, Herbert Marshall, Edgar Bergen, Basil Rathbone, Mary Pickford, and Norma Shearer.

W. H. Auden's "September 1, 1939" caught the tone of the time:

I sit in one of the dives
On Fifty-second Street
Uncertain and afraid
As the clever hopes expire
Of a low dishonest decade:
Waves of anger and fear
Circulate over the bright
And darkened lands of the earth,
Obsessing our private lives;
The unmentionable odour of death
Offends the September night.

"You can't put blinders on and refuse to see what's happening," said Bob Taylor of the war across the ocean. "You can't plug up your ears and refuse to hear what's happening. You've got to stop, look and listen and ask yourself, 'What kind of part do I want to play in all this?' "

SEVENTEEN

On the Brink

1940

And if ever I'm left in this world all alone
I shall wait for my call patiently
For if heaven be kind
I shall wait there to find
Those two eyes of blue
Come smiling through . . . at me . . .

—Arthur Penn, "Smilin' Through"

Barbara started the New Year with an appearance—her first—on *The Jack Benny Hour.* His was among her favorite radio shows, along with *Information Please,* Orson Welles's dramatic series on Sunday nights, and the music of Andre Kostelanetz.

Barbara was close to both Mary and Jack Benny. She thought Jack the dearest man in the world. He wasn't particularly funny off the radio, but nevertheless the way he would tell her about something that happened to him would have her "falling off her chair," she said.

Jack was equally crazy about Barbara. "For my money," he said, "along with all the nobler virtues, such as loyalty and integrity, Barbara has the greatest sense of humor in Hollywood." Her friendship was invaluable to him.

In photographs, Mary Benny and Barbara resembled each other, with similar hairstyles and a similar cast to the face. Barbara often sent her hairdresser, Holly Barnes, to Mary Benny's to do her nails. Holly still did Barbara's nails every Sunday and answered her fan mail. The first time Holly went to Mary Benny's, Barbara felt Mary hadn't paid Holly enough and called Mary to tell her so. To make amends, Mary gave Holly one of her jeweled evening bags.

Mary Benny was beautiful, glamorous, and fun. She was down-to-earth, amusing, strong, the kind of woman Jack was drawn to, women like Barbara, Ann Sheridan, and Carole Lombard.

Mary and Jack were uneducated, but Jack, like Barbara, read and wanted to learn. For Mary, being Mrs. Jack Benny was the be-all and end-all. What interested Mary was learning to buy the right silver, the right jewelry (the bigger, the better), the right clothes (she shopped incessantly). Mary had taste, but most of it was copied from Edie Goetz, older daughter of Louis B. Mayer and one of the leading hostesses of Hollywood.

Mary was Sadie Marks, a shopgirl from Seattle with no credentials and little sophistication. She strove to be a great Hollywood hostess like Edie. Mary wanted to *be* Edie Goetz (when the Goetz cook died, Edie's response: "How could she do this to me?"). If Edie Goetz fired her butler, Mary fired hers.

Mary could be cruel and unpredictable; at times she threatened to send her adopted daughter back to the orphanage, and Joanie Benny found it difficult to relax around her mother.

The Bennys lived in a Georgian mansion in Beverly Hills with roses and pansies lining the front walk and a large swimming pool and playhouse in the rear. Mary would look at their spiral staircase and say, "Joan will look lovely coming down those stairs, a bride."

The Bennys' parties, particularly their New Year's Eve celebrations, were lavish, filled with people who to Mary were the right crowd: Barbara and Bob; Frank and Nancy Sinatra; George Burns and Gracie Allen; Jimmy and Gloria Stewart; Ray and Mal Milland; Clark Gable and Carole Lombard; Errol Flynn; Gary and Rocky Cooper; the Humphrey Bogarts; the Robert Montgomerys; the Ronald Colmans; Ann Sheridan; Bob and Dolores Hope; and others.

The Jack Benny Hour, sponsored by Jell-O ("Jell-O again," Jack would say at the opening of each show), had aired on Sunday nights at seven since 1934.

Benny had created a radio family that seemed real to his listening audience. His comedy was sophisticated and childlike. Jack was the butt of most of the comedy situations, the guy the others picked on. Benny's style of comedy had been influenced by Frank Fay; each had headlined at the Palace in New York. Like Fay, Benny sauntered onstage, without props or funny suits or a stooge. Like Fay, Jack didn't tell jokes but told stories around events of the day that seemed ad-libbed. And like Fay, Benny took his time and never rushed the punch line; his humor, like Fay's, was put across by his voice, its inflection and pauses.

The Jack Benny Hour, by 1937, had forged ahead of *Major Bowes' Original Amateur Hour* and was the No. 1 show in the country; more than thirty-seven million American families tuned in each week to listen to Jack and Mary, Phil Harris, Dennis Day, and Mel Blanc. Benny was earning $400,000 a year from radio and pictures, a far cry from his first act in vaudeville as "Ben Benny—Fiddleology and Fun," in which he told jokes and sang "After the Country Goes Dry, Good-Bye, Wild Women, Good-Bye" and "I Used to Call Her Baby but Now She's Mother to Me."

The Jack Benny Hour was the first to spoof best-selling novels, hit plays, and motion pictures, starting with *Grind Hotel.* The Benny show did a take-off of *The Crowd Roars* with Jack in the role played on-screen by his good friend Bob Taylor. In the Benny script, Taylor's father says, "And don't forget your toupe, son." Jack answers, "I won't, Pa. I'm going to wear it on my chest so everyone will know I'm a man"—a play on the press's teasing Taylor about his questionable manliness. Benny hesitated about getting a laugh at his friend's expense, but Taylor called Jack after the show to tell him how much he'd loved it.

The Benny show with Barbara as Jack's guest centered on her new picture, *Golden Boy.* Jack had promised the audience the week before that he would present a sketch based on the just-released picture.

The show begins with Mary Livingstone explaining to the announcer Harry von Zell, filling in for Don Wilson, that Jack won't be doing *Golden Boy* after all, much to Jack's denials, embarrassment, and pooh-poohing.

Mary explains how she and Jack had run into Barbara Stanwyck a few days before at the Wilshire Bowl. The music signals a flashback to the Bowl . . .

"You know *Barbara Stanwyck?*" Mary asks Jack when they spot Barbara sitting at a ringside table. "Of course I know her," says Benny. "And say, Mary, I've got a great idea . . . as long as we're doing *Golden Boy* on the show, wouldn't it be marvelous if I could get Barbara to play her original role on the program?"

Jack, full of confidence and open affection, approaches Barbara's table and gives her a big "Well, well, hello, Barbara" as if they were the best of chums.

Barbara gives Jack a clipped "Hello" and goes on talking with her dining companions.

Benny interrupts again. "Where's Bob [as if they too were great pals] and will he be joining you?" Barbara barely answers. Jack, eager to engage Barbara Stanwyck in conversation, and ever the stooge—with nothing really to say, except to ask her to appear on his show—asks again about Bob.

Finally, Barbara asks Benny, "Are you working here?" as if he is the waiter.

Barbara introduces him to her friends as "Ben Bernie," confusing him with the vaudeville comedian. (Jack had changed his name from Benny Kubelsky to Ben Benny. He and Bernie were often confused for each other, much to Jack's annoyance. Bernie's most famous hit, "When Polly Walks Through the Hollyhocks," led the way, months later, for Nick Lucas's hit song, "Tip Toe Through the Tulips.")

Jack asks Barbara to dance and, while he is tripping over her on the dance floor, says, "I don't know what's the matter with me tonight. I'm generally very graceful. In fact, I got medals for dancing."

"Well, take them off. They're tearing my dress," she says.

Jack ignores Barbara's snarl and talks her into appearing on his show. They make a plan to rehearse the play. Tuesday afternoon, three o'clock, at Jack's house . . .

The day arrives; Jack is excited. A new brown suit for the occasion; tea sandwiches made by Rochester from the "Thanksgiving turkey they'd served for Christmas."

Mary Livingstone comes for the event ("Jack, you ought to take that sign down in front of your house," she tells him. "It looks awful. The one that says, 'Today in Person, Barbara Stanwyck' ").

When Barbara arrives, Jack introduces her to Mary.

"How do you do, Miss Livingstone."

"I knew Bob Taylor before you did," says Mary.

Jack apologizes for her: "Pay no attention to her. She's always like that."

"I know," says Barbara. "She used to sell me hose at the May Company." (Before Mary was Mrs. Jack Benny, she worked in the department store behind the hosiery counter.)

Barbara tells Jack that she has selected the scene from *Golden Boy* for them to rehearse in which Lorna Moon pleads with Joe Bonaparte to give up fighting and go back to his violin.

"I see. And I'm Joe."

"Unless you'd rather be Lorna," says Barbara.

Benny is endearing and funny as the desperately bad wannabe actor who reads Joe Bonaparte's lines with a tin ear, an effeminate inflection, and the voice of a high-pitched Groucho Marx. Barbara holds her own as the straight man: serious, dutiful, doing her best as her acting partner hams it up, causing

Joan Benny, age six, with Richard, the Bennys' chauffeur; Dion, age seven; and Henrietta (Joan called her "Henny"), Mary Benny's personal maid, Palm Springs, circa 1940. (COURTESY JOAN BENNY)

the studio audience to burst into laughter while she ignores how hopelessly inept he is as an actor.

Barbara can't help herself and progresses steadily into the character of Lorna as she pleads with Joe ("I didn't care whether you lived or died or what happened to you . . . I didn't care if I ever saw you again . . . Joe, you must listen to me") while Benny, in monotone, punctuates her pleas with his one line, "I'm going, Lorna."

Barbara gets more heartfelt, more emotional. Benny, bored with saying his one line the same way, finally says, "I'm going, Lorna?" with the emphasis on the question mark.

They go on until Barbara tells Jack the scene is hopeless ("Believe me, Jack, rehearsing won't help any"). Jack pleads with Barbara to stick it out with him. There's no point, she tells him. On the way out the door, Barbara says, "Oh, by the way, Jack, you can take that sign down now."

Barbara refused to be paid for the show, and Benny, who adored her, gave her a sable coat.

Barbara and Dion—then called Skip—often stayed with the Bennys in Palm Springs. Their daughter, Joan, was impressed that Barbara sunbathed nude on the roof of their house. Joanie Benny played with Skip and the two went to the movies together, learned to ride two-wheel bicycles around the same time, and rode off toward the mountains to explore the desert. Joanie thought Skip's blond hair and freckled face cute. He was her first romance. Dion talked at home about Joanie and told Barbara and Uncle Buck that he was going to marry her. Barbara told Uncle Buck that Skip couldn't marry Joan. "She's Jewish," Uncle Buck reported.

Remember the Night opened in mid-January. It was Barbara's thirty-fifth picture.

"Barbara Stanwyck at her magnificent best." The critics were unanimous in their praise.

The reviews were equally celebratory about the picture: "Memorable; the best picture of 1940," Frank Nugent in *The New York Times*; and about Leisen's direction: "Its character drawing is splendid and in splendid proportion"; Sturges's script: "Simple, eloquent," *NY Times* and the cast, "Not a false note; not a bad performance," said Hedda Hopper; "Fred MacMurray gives one of his best performances; Barbara Stanwyck is thoroughly Grade A," Archer Winston in the *New York Post*.

The picture's first week at New York's Paramount Theatre took in the record amount of $45,000.

Barbara and Bob took stock of industry salaries for 1939: Joan Crawford was paid $305,000 for the year; Clark Gable, $272,000; Robert Montgomery, $209,000; Ginger Rogers, $208,000; Irene Dunne, $405,000; Jean Arthur, $136,000; Claudette Colbert, $125,000; Lionel Barrymore, $136,000; Spencer Tracy, $212,000.

Barbara had earned $117,000 in 1939. She thought a lot about fame, staying power, and the craft of being an actor or actress. "Fame is a wonderful sensation," she told Bob. "The attention you get in Hollywood can be a very heady thing. It can make you believe audiences are interested in anything you do, no matter what—if you don't know better. It's a thrill to look at a marquee and see your name in electric lights. But the real thrill lies in being able to say, 'Well, I think I earned it. It wasn't all luck. I've served an apprenticeship, learned my trade.' "

Too many, Barbara felt, wanted to get into pictures who didn't have any great drive to learn their trade; their thoughts were on the fanfare, the luxuries, the limousines, the pretty clothes. "That's all very nice," said Barbara. "But you can't appreciate it without earning it. And you can't hang onto it without earning it."

Frank Capra had been an important teacher for Barbara, as were Frank Fay, Willard Mack, and Arthur Hopkins before him. No matter what she was taught by others, learning was something that had to be done alone, following head and heart.

Barbara and Bob, soon after they met, were one night looking up at a marquee of the Chinese Theatre on Hollywood Boulevard. Taylor's name was in lights for the first time—"ROBERT TAYLOR AND LORETTA YOUNG" in *Private Number,* with his name first. Bob was impressed with it all. "Don't let it go to your head," said Barbara. "Loretta has been working for years to get her name up there; you've been at it for six months. The trick is to keep it up there."

Barbara learned that in the theater she couldn't kid herself about her ability to interest an audience. "You've got to be good—or else. And you've got to be good on the first take because there isn't a second. You have two weeks of tryouts, and then the opening night—and that's it. You have to sell yourself as a performer."

In Hollywood, it was done differently. Before a picture played a single theater, everyone in the picture was sold to the public as being interesting. If the picture was good, the fans flocked to it.

"Popularity befalls popularity," said Barbara. "And when that happens, youngsters who aren't trained as actors don't stop and wonder how much of their popularity they owe to publicity, and how much to their performances. They rush headlong into the assumption that they must be good. They're bolstered in that belief by their long-term contracts. Even if their next pictures are flops," said Barbara. "For a time they'll still keep their jobs. And still draw their salaries.

"In the theater, you get your salary only as long as a play runs. You have a job only if you're good."

Barbara knew that without stage training, she would have been lost in the movies. It was important to have a "thorough understanding of the business of acting," to start at the bottom and build up. She believed that Flaubert's observation to de Maupassant about writing was true about acting: "Talent is long patience." A career was a battle of wits; those who were educated about acting and the business had the advantage. Real acting to Barbara wasn't based on spontaneity. It was based on craft and the solidity of a foundation; it developed inside by growth of that talent, by working on it, thinking about it, doing it, and studying it more and more.

In a poll of the most popular stars of Hollywood, Bob fell from sixth place and was no longer listed among the top ten. His next two assignments were important pictures for him and important parts; in his sixth year of stardom, he needed both. Metro had put him in *Stand Up and Fight,* a good script and a picture that made money for the studio but one that "conked me on the head to the count of nine," he said. *Lady of the Tropics, Lucky Night,* and *Remember?,* all bad pictures, were equally bad roles for Bob.

He was set to appear opposite Vivien Leigh in Metro's remake of the romantic tragedy *Waterloo Bridge* and then to star with Metro's queen of the lot, Norma Shearer, in *Escape,* from Ethel Vance's just-published best-selling suspense thriller about Nazi Germany.

Mervyn LeRoy finished producing the lavish *Wizard of Oz,* his first picture at Metro as (unofficial) director, stepping in between stints of the picture's four directors: Richard Thorpe, who was fired; George Cukor, who was reassigned; Victor Fleming, following in Cukor's wake to take over *Gone With the Wind;* and King Vidor, who came in at the last. LeRoy was brought over to MGM as head of production following the death of Irving Thalberg in 1936 and the departure of David Selznick in 1935 to start his own company. LeRoy, after eleven years of directing at Warner Bros., was to direct Metro's *Waterloo Bridge* and *Escape.*

"Be versatile" was Barbara's rule. She'd learned firsthand that those actors who varied their acting experience were "the only ones who stood a chance of being remembered."

"People won't forget Bette Davis," said Barbara that winter. "She didn't become memorable without any training. She put herself through the long, hard school of experience. She learned her trade."

And varied the roles she undertook.

Barbara had settled into a groove only once, from 1933 to 1934, under contract to Warner Bros. playing a series of parts that were alike: poor, suffering women living under shabby conditions who rise up any way they can, in such pictures as *Ladies They Talk About, Baby Face,* and *Gambling Lady.* She had refused to make similar pictures and paid a heavy price, but it was worth it to break free. Warner Bros. put her on suspension when she could ill afford it, and later the studio dropped her as her marriage fell apart. After Eddie Small's *Red Salute* at Reliance, Barbara broke through to play Annie Oakley in the kind of picture she'd been dreaming of for a long time, a Western.

Bob was assigned the lead in *Waterloo Bridge* only weeks before it went into production. He was to play an aristocratic officer from one of Britain's finest regiments, scion of an old Scottish family who, on the eve of his departure to France to fight in the Great War (with overtones of the present war in Eu-

Bob and Vivien Leigh, *Waterloo Bridge,* Leigh's first picture after *Gone With the Wind,* 1940.

rope), falls in love with a young ballet dancer he meets by chance on Waterloo Bridge. Their whirlwind courtship causes her to lose her position in the ballet company, and he is called to the front before they can marry.

She reads he has been killed in battle, and she, unable to find work and in desperate straits, resorts to prostitution to survive. A year later, he returns to London and sees her at the train station, where she regularly picks up soldiers. He assumes she has come to meet him and, seeing her only as the girl he loves, takes her home to his family estate. When she realizes her past can only destroy him, she flees and is drawn back to Waterloo Bridge and to the tragic end that seals their doomed love.

The role of the officer was one Bob could easily have turned down; the captain at first seemed only a stooge part: uncomplicated and another in the string of juvenile roles from which Bob had been trying to escape. He took the part knowing that Vivien Leigh, at twenty-six the biggest movie star in the world, would turn the film, her first since *Gone With the Wind,* into a sensation. Bob was going through the painful experience of "slipping." "I went up in a rocket, exploding and coming down like a stick," he said. He needed *Waterloo Bridge* to break the jinx on his career and his four previous pictures.

Metro had bought the rights to *Waterloo Bridge,* the Robert Sherwood play, from David O. Selznick.

S. N. Behrman and Mervyn LeRoy worked on the script for more than a year and a half with help from Gottfried Reinhardt, Hugo Butler, Claudine West, Hans Rameau, and George Froeschel. The script of *Waterloo Bridge* was still being revised weeks before the picture started to shoot. The final result was different from both the Sherwood play and the 1931 James Whale picture from Universal that had adhered to Sherwood's play and had starred Mae Clarke and Kent Douglass.

"The only part that was [left intact]," said LeRoy of the script, "was the bridge."

Included in the deal between Selznick and MGM was Vivien Leigh. *The New York Times* had said of her as Scarlett, "She is so beautiful she hardly need be talented, and so talented she need not have been so beautiful; no actress was as perfectly suited for the role." Leigh had been nominated for an Academy Award for Best Actress.

Vivien Leigh could have done anything for her next film, but she was drawn to the love story of *Waterloo Bridge.* She was about to be granted a divorce from her present husband, Leigh Holman, and would be free to marry the man she adored, Laurence Olivier.

Selznick was lending Leigh to Metro as a way of paying Mayer back for his help with *Gone With the Wind.* Leigh was intent on following Scarlett O'Hara with a theatrical twenty-week tour of America with Olivier in *Romeo and Juliet,* much to Selznick's dismay and displeasure. She would be one of the youngest Juliets of her time.

Leigh's previous contract with Alexander Korda at London Films allowed the actress the freedom of stage work. Selznick believed motion pictures were much more important than theatrical productions and argued against the *Romeo and Juliet* tour. He was hoping *Waterloo Bridge* would equal the success of *Gone With the Wind.*

Metro originally wanted Michael Redgrave for *Waterloo Bridge,* but the studio had offered him the lowest amount of money possible, and he'd turned it down. Leigh wanted Olivier to co-star with her in the picture. Olivier was about to make *Pride and Prejudice,* also for Metro, and he wanted Vivien to be his Elizabeth Bennet instead of Greer Garson. Sidney Franklin, producer of *Waterloo Bridge,* also wanted Olivier for the part of the British officer, and the actor agreed to do it. Mayer would not hear of it. He was adamant that Olivier appear with Greer Garson in *Pride and Prejudice.*

Bob had worked with Vivien three years before in Metro's first picture

Vivien Leigh, Olivia de Havilland, and Bob on the MGM set of *Waterloo Bridge,* 1940.

made in Denham, England. In *A Yank at Oxford,* Bob was the twenty-six-year-old star. Vivien, in a supporting role, had agreed to make the picture to win attention in America and the role of Scarlett O'Hara.

Before shooting started on *Waterloo Bridge,* Vivien Leigh wrote to her then husband, Leigh Holman, "Robert Taylor is the man in the picture and as it was written for Larry, it's a typical piece of miscasting. I am afraid it will be a dreary job but I won't think about it, and just concentrate on *Romeo and Juliet.*"

Vivien spent her lunch hours on the picture working with Dame May Whitty, soon to be the nurse in the forthcoming *Romeo and Juliet,* who was helping Vivien with her voice.

Despite Vivien's feelings about Bob as the lead in the picture, she was generous and gracious to him. Their different sensibilities were summed up in their birthplaces: she was born in Darjeeling, India; he, in Filley, Nebraska.

Between scenes Vivien got Bob to play Chinese checkers and battleships. When Olivier came to visit, she served both men tea in her dressing room. Vivien's easy, friendly manner helped Bob. On the set, he was neither stiff nor self-conscious and could calmly think about his character. In their scenes together, "Vivien didn't have to help," said Bob. "She would have been a help even if she hadn't wanted to be." Bob thought she was one of those rare workers, like Garbo, who knew what she was doing every minute.

Mervyn LeRoy had Bob grow a mustache for the picture for verisimilitude: English officers of the Great War wore mustaches; at the picture's end, Bob appears middle-aged. Barbara had been telling Bob for three years that he would look good with a mustache, that it might take away from some of his beauty, give him some authority, and make him seem more real, less perfect. Now that he had grown a mustache, he liked the look of it, as did the studio.

LeRoy's final whispered comment to his actors each time before he shot: "Now let's have a nice scene with a lotta feeling."

While shooting *Waterloo Bridge,* LeRoy got the flu and was laid up for five days. Woody Van Dyke stepped in. Bob was working late and asked Barbara to visit him on his set. She had never been on one of Bob's sets. She hesitated and said, "Miss Leigh might not like it." Bob assured her that Vivien wasn't like that, that it would be fine. Barbara agreed to have Bob drive her onto the Metro lot. She had Bob park his car a short distance from the soundstage where he was shooting. At the last minute Barbara thought it better for her to stay in the car and read a book while Bob worked.

Barbara was an insomniac and read throughout the night. When not working, she spent days combing the shops for books. She subscribed to book clubs, looking for stories that would make good movies for her. The managers of the bookstores in town knew Barbara's taste and sent her the latest books, which she read, one a night, and then sent on to friends.

When Barbara wasn't working, she still got up early each morning to see Bob off at the front door. She didn't join him for breakfast, sensitive to how annoying it would be for her if she was on her way to the studio and had to converse when she was in a hurry and preoccupied with the day's work.

Barbara's appearance on *Lux Radio Theatre* in late March was her first job in two months. She reprised *Remember the Night* with Fred MacMurray, Beulah Bondi, Elizabeth Patterson, and Sterling Holloway. A week later Barbara and Bob were on *The Gulf Screen Guild Theater.* The script was about a couple who take a cab ride and forget to stop at their church for their own wedding before taking the boat on their honeymoon. Franklin Pangborn appeared on the broadcast. They rehearsed at the Earl Carroll Theatre from 11:00 on a Sunday morning until the show went on the air that afternoon at 4:30 and donated their salaries to the Motion Picture Relief Fund.

Barbara, Bob, and Clark Gable; photographed by Gable's wife, Carole Lombard, summer 1940.

Barbara was learning to play golf. She didn't much like the game, but Bob had asked her to take it up. She bought all the paraphernalia—clubs, clothes, shoes. They practiced every day.

Barbara was trying to do what Bob liked: joining him on his Sunday expeditions with the Moraga Spit and Polish Club; riding on the back of Bob's motorcycle, despite the pain it caused her from old back injuries.

Bob enjoyed playing golf on Sunday, but he didn't want to play without Barbara. She thought Bob a fairly good player, "not bad; not bad at all." He played in tournaments with Gable, Mickey Rooney, Spencer Tracy, Eddie Mannix, and other MGM actors, executives, and workers.

Barbara knew she was never going to be much of a golfer. She seldom hit the ball and didn't really care. Her pro kept telling her to keep her head down and her eye on the ball, but she constantly lifted up her head.

She hit bucketfuls of balls. Bob was patient with her, but after six solid days at a driving range Barbara told Bob that she just wasn't the type, that work was play to her and play, work, and that he should play golf either alone or with someone who would be as intent as he was on cutting down his score.

Her scores, she said, read like the "national debt and, like the debt, were getting higher and higher." She thought bowling might be more for her; "a high score is something to work for there."

While in production on *Waterloo Bridge,* Vivien Leigh received the Academy Award for Best Actress for *Gone With the Wind,* winning against Bette Davis in *Dark Victory.*

The awards ceremony, held on February 29 at the Ambassador Hotel, was being filmed for the first time by Frank Capra, the academy's outgoing president; the overseeing cameraman was Charles Rosher, who filmed the twelve hundred guests. Vivien Leigh arrived at the Cocoanut Grove on the arm of David Selznick; also with her was Laurence Olivier, nominated for Best Actor for *Wuthering Heights. The Hollywood Reporter* described the couple—Leigh as Scarlett O'Hara and Olivier as Heathcliff—as being, "for the moment, just about the most sacred of all Hollywood's sacred cows."

Bob Hope was introduced as "the Rhett Butler of the air waves" and made his debut as the evening's master of ceremonies.

Gone With the Wind won eight Academy Awards—for best picture, direction, screenplay, actress, supporting actress, photography, art direction, and editing—and two special awards, with Selznick receiving the Irving G. Thalberg Memorial Award and the late Douglas Fairbanks Sr. being honored as the first president of the academy. William Cameron Menzies received a special plaque for his outstanding work in the use of color on *Gone With the Wind.*

The evening's biggest excitement was Hattie McDaniel's winning the award for best supporting actress for her role as Mammy against Olivia de Havilland's Miss Melanie. The audience cheered. Olivia de Havilland fled from the Selznick table to the kitchen and burst into tears. McDaniel was the first "of her race to receive an Award," said *Variety,* and the first "Negro," the paper reported, "ever to sit at an Academy banquet," though McDaniel and her escort were put at a table for two in the rear of the Cocoanut Grove.

Ethel Vance's novel *Escape* took place in an unnamed—but recognizable—totalitarian country: Germany ("We meet in an evil land/That is near to the gates of Hell"). It was a novel about a people caught up in the war in Europe desperately trying to get to freedom; its story involved the rescue from a concentration camp of one of Germany's stage idols by her American son and their perilous attempt to flee the country.

Bob found the notion of the book "a little ironic," he said. "There isn't a place in the world today where anyone can go and escape what's happening."

The war in Europe was intensifying: the British were rationing food; German planes were shot down over England; the Soviet Union had invaded Finland and was expelled from the League of Nations; the United States repealed the arms embargo in favor of a cash-and-carry policy.

Louis B. Mayer's concern about what was happening to the Jews in Europe overrode his desire to hold on to the German market, and MGM was rushing *Escape* into production. The studio was concerned that peace might happen before the picture would come out and undercut its timeliness.

George Cukor had been intrigued by the prospect of directing *Escape* and by the complex nature of the actress at the book's center, a woman both noble and vain (after she comes out of the concentration camp, her first request is for her makeup case). Lawrence Weingarten, the picture's producer, didn't think Cukor right for the picture and offered it instead to Alfred Hitchcock, who wanted to work with Norma Shearer. Hitchcock was wary of Metro's interference with his work and turned down the offer. Weingarten, much to Cukor's disappointment, offered the picture to Mervyn LeRoy, who Cukor thought a "melodramatic" director.

Escape was Ethel Vance's debut novel. It had sold more than 200,000 copies in its first three months of publication and was a selection of the Book-of-the-Month Club. Metro had bought the film rights to the book knowing that Ethel Vance was a pseudonym. Those who speculated on her identity rightfully assumed it was a woman who'd taken another name to protect some relative or friend living in Germany. Among those thought to have written the novel were Erika Mann, Dorothy Thompson, and Rebecca West. Ethel Vance was Grace Zaring Stone.

The novel's timeliness made its portrait of Nazi Germany more terrifying. As Hitler's troops marched across Western Europe, Vance's novel seemed eerily prophetic, though *Escape* ends in hopeful triumph and there seemed to be no end to Hitler's reign of terror.

L. B. Mayer had appealed to Norma Shearer's sense of public duty to make *Escape*; she'd just finished shooting *The Women* and before that Robert Sherwood's picture *Idiot's Delight,* with Clark Gable, about the last gasp of frivolity and the imminence of war. Shearer had mistakenly turned down the starring role in the film version of Rachel Crothers's Broadway hit comedy, *Susan and God,* in which Gertrude Lawrence had given a virtuoso performance onstage and which Joan Crawford had tried with relentless gusto to re-create on film. Shearer decided to follow Mayer's urging and agreed to play Countess von Treck in *Escape.*

Shearer, a widow of thirty-eight, had, at the insistence of L. B. Mayer, ended her romance with twenty-year-old Mickey Rooney, who, as Andy Hardy, was Metro's balm to a scared and vulnerable America in need of reassurance and buoyancy now that Britain alone stood between the United States and Hitler's Third Reich.

Two months before production started on *Escape,* Metro was trying to get Laurette Taylor for the part of the legendary German actress Emmy Ritter. Blanche Yurka campaigned for the role. After twenty years on the stage, Yurka had become a star in a 1928–1929 production of *The Wild Duck* and made her film debut six years later as Madame DeFarge. Instead of winning the part of Emmy Ritter, Yurka was cast as the sadistic concentration camp nurse who tortures the actress. Alla Nazimova was tested twice for the role of the celebrated actress at the center of *Escape* and was signed for the part two weeks before production started. Nazimova, of the Moscow Art Theatre, who brought Ibsen and Chekhov to America, was an acclaimed silent star and discoverer of Rudolph Valentino. Judith Anderson was tested for the part as well but was felt to look "too sinister" and "too Jewish." "That tickles me pink," wrote Nazimova, "considering [Anderson] hasn't a drop of it." *Escape* was Nazimova's first talking picture.

Barbara and Bob appeared together for the first time on *Lux Radio Theatre.* They performed *Smilin' Through* from a play by Allan Langdon Martin, a pseudonym for Jane Cowl and Jane Murfin.

Smilin' Through—a haunted love story of two generations set in England during the world war—had been made into a picture in 1922 with Norma Talmadge and Harrison Ford and remade ten years later by MGM, starring Norma Shearer, Fredric March, and Leslie Howard. In the *Lux Radio* broadcast, Barbara and Bob played the double parts, both young and old lovers.

After the performance, Barbara and Bob were called onstage together to chat. The subject of discussion was the Hollywood Stars, then playing at Gilmore Field. "Keep your fingers crossed for us stockholders," said Barbara. "We may have a pennant winner."

Barbara was referred to as Miss Stanwyck, never Mrs. Taylor. She'd gone through that once when she'd insisted on being called Mrs. Frank Fay. Bob introduced her as Miss Stanwyck. She was Miss Stanwyck to her servants. Dion referred to her as "my mother, Barbara Stanwyck."

Barbara had been waiting to make *Night of January 16th.* In the end, Don Ameche refused to make the picture—he didn't want to play the unlikable financier—and the project fell apart. Paramount had borrowed Ameche from

At a Hollywood Stars game, Gilmore Field, circa 1940.

20th Century–Fox and claimed its deal with Fox didn't give Ameche the right of script approval. Paramount filed suit in superior court against Ameche for $170,000 to cover the costs of script, sets, and costumes, until he agreed to appear in Paramount's *Kiss the Boys Goodbye* with Mary Martin from the Clare Boothe Luce hit play, and the suit was settled.

Barbara decided to make two pictures with Bill Wellman at Paramount— *F.O.B. Detroit,* re-titled first *The City That Never Sleeps,* then *Reaching for the Sun,* and another picture called *Pioneer Woman.* Joel McCrea was to star opposite Barbara in both pictures.

Barbara and Bill Wellman hadn't worked together since he'd directed her eight years before in *So Big* and *The Purchase Price.*

The script for *F.O.B. Detroit* was based on Wessel Smitter's novel about the auto industry, the story of a lumberjack who takes a job in a car factory and dreams of returning to the north woods to start his own business.

Paramount had purchased Smitter's novel for Wellman two years before to star Fred MacMurray and Robert Preston with Jean Arthur as the likely choice for the female lead. Wellman had wanted Jean Gabin instead of MacMurray, but the French actor was too expensive. Instead of Jean Arthur,

Wellman was interested in Carole Lombard for the female lead, but Lombard was at RKO making Garson Kanin's *They Knew What They Wanted* from the Sidney Howard play. Wellman settled on Barbara and McCrea.

Bob and Barbara went to see the Hollywood Stars play at Gilmore Field, as did Bing Crosby, Humphrey Bogart, Clark Gable, Bill Frawley, George Raft, and Gail Patrick. Barbara and Bob had their regular seats, behind the netting back of home plate, a mere thirty-four feet away. Barbara wore the ruby and topaz bracelet Bob gave her to celebrate their first wedding anniversary.

This was the first season the Hollywood Stars were being televised in the West. Cameras were placed in boxes near first and third bases for the few hundred people who owned television sets within a thirty-mile radius of the station.

Bob, Mervyn LeRoy, Norma Shearer, Ilona Massey, and Ann Rutherford went to San Francisco to see Vivien Leigh and Olivier on opening night in *Romeo and Juliet.* Clark Gable wanted to go as well but was filming *Boom Town.* Leigh and Olivier planned to give the proceeds of one night's performance to the Finns, who were in great need of aid.

Waterloo Bridge previewed at Grauman's Chinese and opened in mid-May. Reviewers called it Bob's strongest performance. Barbara thought it his best picture and that he and Vivien Leigh looked beautiful together.

Bob and Barbara nightly talked about the war. Often they ate dinner as fast as possible to get to their favorite newsreel theater in time for the first show each time the bill changed, sitting last row center.

Bob went back to see the newsreels again and again. He was ready to go to war. Of course he wanted to do his job six days a week, play golf on Sunday, and spend every evening with his wife. He had no more use for war than the next guy, but he was ready to fight to keep America "a country where the little guy has a break; to keep America a democracy," he said.

"We think of ourselves as a nation too big and too powerful and too far away for any aggressor to tackle," he said. "We're big all right. Most of Europe would fit inside Texas. We have all kinds of room here, all kinds of natural resources, all kinds of wealth. But we're not too far away to tackle, not if they can get control of the seas, not if they can get a foothold south of us.

"I don't like war," said Bob, "but if we have to go to war, I'm enlisting."

In April, Nazi troops crossed the Danish border and invaded along the Norwegian coast. A month later Hitler launched his blitzkrieg against the

Low Countries. Neville Chamberlain resigned; Winston Churchill became the new head of England's wartime coalition government.

The question plaguing America was war or peace; should the country help the British, or should it send aid and remain aloof from the war overseas? The British had fewer than nine hundred fighters to the Luftwaffe's almost two thousand bombers and twelve hundred fighters.

There were those Americans who wanted an immediate declaration of war against Germany and others who wanted us to help European democracies while staying neutral. The playwright Robert Sherwood took out an advertisement saying that whoever thought the Nazis would hold back until America was ready to fight was "either an imbecile or a traitor."

The isolationists included the Irish and Germans, college students, and the Republican Party. The America First Committee, made up of midwestern businessmen like Robert Wood of Sears, Roebuck and Jay Hormel, the meat packer, believed there was a Jewish-British-capitalist-Roosevelt conspiracy to get America into the war and that it was much more prudent to learn to do business with Hitler. Charles Lindbergh said that accommodating Germany "could maintain peace and civilization throughout the world as far into the future as we can see."

Churchill went before the House of Commons and appealed to the United States in a speech that made clear what had been accomplished at Dunkirk and paid tribute to the young airmen of the Royal Air Force who'd fought the German air forces: "Every morn brought forth a noble chance/And every chance brought forth a noble knight." Churchill promised his country that they would "prove ourselves once again able to defend our Island home, to ride out the storm of war, and to outlive the menace of tyranny, if necessary for years, if necessary alone."

In the speech he sent a message to Roosevelt and America: "We shall go on to the end . . . we shall never surrender, and even if . . . this Island or a large part of it were subjugated and starving, then our Empire beyond the seas, armed and guarded by the British Fleet, would carry on the struggle, until, in God's good time, the New World, with all its power and might, steps forth to the rescue and the liberation of the old."

Hollywood did what it could to help, donating money to various causes. Cary Grant gave his salary of $62,000 from *The Philadelphia Story* to the American Red Cross war relief, as did Myrna Loy and William Powell their earnings of $10,000 from *Lux Radio Theatre*. Walt Disney's premier showing of *Fantasia* in New York raised money for British War Relief to be used for rolling kitchens to feed the homeless, firefighters, and rescue crews in bombed areas of Britain.

The newly organized Theatre Guild of Southern California put on a Bundles for Britain benefit production of Noël Coward's series of nine plays, *Tonight at 8:30,* with the proceeds going to the British War Relief Society. Constance Bennett, Douglas Fairbanks Jr., Rosalind Russell, Binnie Barnes, and others made up the casts; the plays were directed by George Cukor, Edmund Goulding, and Margaret Webster. A production of *Cavalcade* premiered at Billy Wilkerson's new club, Ciro's, with the money being sent to the British Red Cross. Noël Coward went to see the productions and adored them. He had an eye for detail; on a stage with four hundred people, in a show set in 1900, Coward would spot the man with the watch that wasn't of the day.

The English colony came together to make a picture to help British war charities from a story by Robert Stevenson. Edmund Goulding, Victor Saville, and Herbert Wilcox were directing; among those starring in the picture were Brian Aherne, Anna Neagle, Ray Milland, Charles Laughton, Merle Oberon, and Claude Rains; the picture was being produced and distributed by RKO. Each week, the English colony sent a fully equipped ambulance to the British Red Cross; Robert Montgomery donated an ambulance and went to England to drive it himself.

On June 14, 1940, the German army formed a great ring of steel around Paris. The city was outflanked by German spearheads of tanks and men. More than a million and a half Parisians fled the city and hid in the Bois de Boulogne and the surrounding woods. The news that the German armies were inside the gates of Paris was broadcast over the radio. Swastika banners of Nazi Germany were raised over the Arc de Triomphe, the Eiffel Tower, and Versailles, where, in the Hall of Mirrors, the First Reich was born and where it died a "shameful" death in 1919. It seemed impossible that Paris had fallen to the Germans. Eight days later France formally surrendered to Germany.

England's ships, ports, and coastal towns were under attack from the Luftwaffe. It was suddenly made clear that America was vulnerable to foreign invasion. The United States had only 160 P-40 planes for the more than two hundred pilots waiting to fly them; it had no anti-aircraft ammunition. Most Americans wanted to stay out of war, but they were arming to defend themselves.

The California legislature organized a guard inspired by the Swiss Home Guards; Chicago rifle clubs formed a civilian army of modern minutemen; New York's National Legion of Mothers of America organized the Molly Pitcher Rifle Legion to shoot at attacking parachute troops.

The U.S. Army consisted of half a million men, including the National Guard.

In June, President Roosevelt signed the Smith Act that required more than three million aliens to register at local post offices and to be fingerprinted.

The feeling in many parts of America was, "What the hell's the use of writing a column? Who gives a damn if so-and-so breaks her neck or marries a man with vegetable juice in his veins?" And in Hollywood it was, "Why kill myself making this scene. What can it possibly matter in a world gone mad?"

Bette Davis's new picture, *All This, and Heaven Too,* premiered at the Carthay Circle Theatre the day newspaper headlines read, "Nazi Trap Closes on Paris." Bleachers built around the circle were filled with crowds of people. Charles Boyer was there, sick from the news. The studio insisted Davis attend the premiere. Newspapers bannered headlines: "France Falls."

As the picture started, a shudder went through the audience when, to set the scene of the nineteenth-century romantic drama, the words "Paris, France" appeared on the screen imposed over a view of a city that was soon to be overrun with Nazi soldiers.

For the first time in Hollywood since the Great War, something was happening that was more important to the industry than itself.

Bette Davis went back to work the day after her picture opened and said, "Your routine may not seem important. What is important is that we keep on going. If the British can do it with their world in literal ruins around them, then phooey to us for whining before we're touched."

Frank Capra asked Barbara if she would take a chance and make a picture with him without seeing a script.

"Is it an honest role?" she asked.

"I give you my word," said Capra.

"I'll do it," she said.

Gary Cooper, Barbara, Spring Byington, Edward Arnold, James Gleason, and Walter Brennan all agreed to make Capra's new picture before there was a script. Cooper, like Barbara, had said, "It's okay, Frank. I don't need a script."

Capra's picture was a chilling cautionary tale about the rise of Fascism in America and the endangerment of democracy. Each character was tailored to the actor. Capra was interested in characters that did what human beings do, or "would do if they had the courage and opportunity," he said. He wanted his cast members to be, in real life, the nearest thing possible to the characters they were playing so that their performances required the least acting.

Capra was at work on the script with Robert Riskin, who'd written for

With Frank Capra during production of *Golden Boy,* visiting the set of *Mr. Smith Goes to Washington;* both Columbia Pictures, 1939. Capra's next picture, his first with Barbara in eight years, would be their fifth collaboration.

Barbara before: *Illicit,* his first screenplay; *The Miracle Woman,* her second Capra picture; and *Shopworn.*

In each, Barbara was the hard-boiled girl, on her own, rich or poor, full of spirit, living outside convention, daring to break society's hypocritical rules, toughing it out. Barbara took the high, low, and middle classes; they and Riskin were awed by her.

Capra and Riskin collaborated to make Barbara, in each picture, the girl who, as Capra said of Barbara herself, has "bounced off the floor and come back better each time, has never let herself down. It just isn't in her to let anyone else down either."

Barbara was to be a hardworking newspaper columnist, an ambitious girl who's worked her way through with the "courage to crusade for a good idea and with enough intelligence to spoof those that aren't." She's been fired by the paper, and she dreams up a stunt to keep her job and hold on to her salary. Like Barbara, Capra said, "Ann Mitchell has humor, a sense of news and human understanding, a bit of idealism for things worthwhile and loyalty to friends. She has beauty and charm and likes pretty things."

In the picture, Mitchell goes for the money and through her cynicism becomes the instrument of a windfall plot to help an oil magnate, trying to crash national politics, circumvent the principles of American democracy and double-cross his way into the White House—until she is called up short and sees what she is truly fighting for. Barbara saw Capra's picture as a "social history of our times, about an Everyman—caught in the web. Doesn't know what it's all about—no more than the rest of us."

Of the actresses with whom Capra liked to work—Jean Arthur, Claudette Colbert, and Barbara Stanwyck—he thought Barbara "the most interesting" and "the hardest to define," he said. "She's sullen, she's somber, she's the easiest to direct . . . she could suffer from her toughness and really suffer from the penance she would have to pay."

Capra admired Barbara's honesty; he saw her as earnest, simple, real. Barbara had a capacity for honesty and discretion but not necessarily for gentleness. A flippant remark by her could be misunderstood, and she might spend the day worrying about it. She rarely said yes when she should say no. She was not an indecisive woman—fluttering, coy, flitting from one uncertainty to another. She knew her mind and spoke it.

The only make-believe Capra saw in Barbara was what she projected in her art. She was a brave enough actress to let her audience see her think, something Capra had taught her from their earliest picture together, *Ladies of Leisure*.

Barbara was so excited about starting *The Life of John Doe* that she was "not of this earth"; she could "hardly contain herself," she said.

She took nothing for granted, neither poverty nor plenty, talent or ambition. Plenty could be taken from her at any time; poverty she'd overcome with hard work. She didn't believe in taking bad breaks for granted. If she did, she might stop fighting for the things she had it in her to accomplish. She didn't believe that life should be lived easily and softly or that people should crave the easy way. She'd made her own breaks and knuckled against the hard times and didn't regret it. She'd grown up in a world of loneliness that had forced her to create her own world. She'd built it of her dreams and hidden it jealously from everyone and learned to lose herself in it. For a long time, it was the only home she felt she had.

The Fourth of July came and went with quiet fanfare. To Barbara hard work with the prospect of rich reward was the American way. "If any country was ever developed by harder work, I don't know what country it could possibly be," she said. Bob Taylor said about democracy and the fight for it, "Any other set-up [system of government]—no matter what you call it—puts the power in the hands of the few. The little guy has to obey laws that he had no hand in making. If he's hauled into court, he has no guarantee of justice, because he doesn't get a trial-by-jury. If the heads of state don't want him going to church, assembling with his fellows, he can't go to church. "I'm a little guy but I'm free to enjoy the life God gave me. I live in America."

In Frank Capra's new picture, Barbara was playing a character who is almost undone by an industrialist press lord manipulating the goodwill of the people to ride to power and undo the democratic state.

"America was developed by blood, sweat, and tears," said Barbara. "And now it is blood, sweat, and tears, which will keep America alive."

After the holiday weekend, Barbara went into Warner Bros. for makeup tests. Production on *The Life of John Doe* began four days later.

Alfred Hitchcock's *Foreign Correspondent* was released during the height of the summer. It was about a young newspaper crime reporter (Joel McCrea; Hitchcock originally wanted Gary Cooper for the part), chosen because he isn't a foreign correspondent, "somebody who doesn't know the difference between an ism and a kangaroo, a good honest crime reporter; that's what the Globe needs; that's what Europe needs. There's a crime hatching on that bedeviled continent." The reporter is chosen in the hope that he will be able to get some facts, any kind of facts (the paper's editor—Harry Davenport—says, "There must be something more going on in Europe [in August 1939] besides a nervous breakdown"), and he is sent off by the paper's editor to a Europe about to blow up.

The young man is drawn into a "fifth-column plot" that takes him from London and Amsterdam and back again as he chases down Nazi agents, kidnappers, and spies, tracking the assassin of an international political leader, a keynote to the European situation, fighting for peace in Europe, a man who knows too much as the world is closing in and who fights to keep the terrifying darkness at bay.

The final explosive scene of *Foreign Correspondent* is Hitchcock's rallying cry to America.

Joel McCrea as the small-town crime reporter is broadcasting from a London radio station: the Nazi plot has been uncovered; the love interest fulfilled . . . Hitler's planes are in the skies over London; additional German bombers are on their way . . . everyone has fled. The station microphone is still live, but the lights have gone out in the building. McCrea is speaking "off the cuff" because he can't see to read his speech. The city is going up in flames . . .

"All that noise you hear isn't static," he says. "It's death coming to London. Yes, they're coming now. You can hear the bombs falling on the streets and the homes. Don't tune me out. Hang on a while. This is a big story and you're part of it. It's too late to do anything here now except stand in the dark and let them come. It's as if the lights were all out everywhere—except in America. Keep those lights burning there. Cover them with steel, ring them with guns, build a canopy of battleships and bombing planes around them. Hello, America, hang on to your lights. They're the only lights left in the world!"

APPENDIX I: STAGE CHRONOLOGY

Ziegfeld Follies (1922–1923)

Touring production: Colonial Theatre, Boston; Forrest Theatre, Philadelphia; Ford's Opera House, Baltimore; National Theatre, Washington, D.C.; Pittsburgh; Cleveland; New Detroit Theatre, Detroit; Colonial Theatre, Chicago; Davidson Theatre, Milwaukee; American Theatre, St. Louis; Sam S. Shubert Theatre, Kansas City, Mo.; English's Opera House, Indianapolis; Grand Opera House, Cincinnati; Dayton; Royal Alexandra Theatre, Toronto; Majestic Theatre, Buffalo. Four hundred twenty-four performances, June 5, 1922–June 23, 1923. Book: Ring Lardner, Gene Buck, Ralph Spence. Music: Victor Herbert, Louis A. Hirsch, David Stamper. Choreography: Ned Wayburn. Scenic design: Joseph Urban. Opening night: New Amsterdam Theatre, New York. Cast: Babs Aitlen, Jean Arundel, Leonora Baron, Michel Barroy, Clara Beresbach, Eva Brady, Margery Chapin, Thelma Connor, Velma Connor, Dorothy Conroy, Dolly Daggars, Marie Dahm, Peggy Dana, Audrey Darrell, Nellie Davage, Ellen de Lerches, Hazel Donnelly, Alma Drange, Betty Dudley, Marcelle Earle, Mary Eaton, Pearl Eaton, Dolly Evans (Ruby Stevens; Ensemble), Victoria Gale, Ed Gallagher, Helen Gates, Alexander Gray, Gilda Gray, Ivy Halstead, Netta Hill, May Howard, Frances Howden, Virginia Howell, Ada Hughes, Sonia Ivanoff, Beatrice Jackson, Brooke Johns, Naomi Johnson, Virginia King, Teddy Knox, Frank Lambert, Evelyn Law, Helen Lee, Phoebe Lee, Mary Lewis, Doris Lloyd, Jean Lloyd, Martha Lorber, Alma Mamay, Pansy Maness, Hallie Manning, Irene Marcellus, Pauline Mason, Lulu McConnell, Mary McDonald, Beulah McFarland, Blanche Mehaffey, Kathryn Mehaffey, Madge Merritt, Hilda Moreno, Madelyn Morrissey, Polly Nally, Cora Neary, Jimmy Nervo, Al Ochs, Olive Osborne, Rita Owin, Annie Patron, Serge Pernikoff, Miss Ray, Jessie Reed, Betsy Rees, Anastasia Reilly, Frances Reveaux, Marion Rich, Will Rogers, Addie Rolfe, Rita Royce, Nellie Savage, John Scott, Gertrude Selden, Sonia Shand, J. J. Shannon, Al Shean, Marie Shelton, Grant Simpson, Beatrice Singleton, Nellie Smith, Miss Starhill, Kathryn Stoneburn, Muriel Stryker, Avonne Taylor, the Follies Four, Frank Tierney, Tiller Girls, Irene Todd, Andrew Tombes, George Truscott, Brandon Tynan, Vangie Valentine, Albertina Vitak, Irene Wales, Marie Wallace, Betty Webb, Hazel Webb, Fay West, Edna Wheaton, Miss Whittington, Elsie Woodall, Lillian Woods, Helen Lee Worthing.

Ziegfeld Follies (Summer Edition) (1923)

Touring production: Colonial Theatre, Boston; Forrest Theatre, Philadelphia; Ford's Opera House, Baltimore; National Theatre, Washington, D.C.; Pittsburgh; Cleveland; New Detroit Theatre, Detroit; Colonial Theatre, Chicago; Davidson Theatre, Milwaukee; American Theatre, St. Louis; Sam S. Shubert Theatre, Kansas City, Mo.; English's Opera House, Indianapolis; Grand Opera House, Cincinnati; Dayton; Royal Alexandra Theatre, Toronto; Majestic Theatre, Buffalo. Ninety-six performances, June 25–September 15, 1923. Book: Ralph Spence, Eddie Cantor. Music: Victor Herbert, Louis A. Hirsch, David Stamper. Choreography: Ned Wayburn. Scenic design: Joseph Urban. Opening night: New Amsterdam Theatre, New York. Cast: Babs Aitlen, Leonora Baron, Michel Barroy, Clara Beresbach, Emma Beresbach, Nina Byron, Erla Calame, Eddie Cantor, Betty Carsdale, Dorothy Clarkson, Thelma Connor, Velma Connor, Dolly Daggars, Ethel Dale, Helena D'Algy, Eleanor Dana, Audrey Darrell, Mae Daw, Alma Drange, Marcelle Earle, Mary Eaton, Pearl Eaton, Dolly Evans (Ruby Stevens; Ensemble), Victoria Gale, Ed Gallagher, Joan Gardner, Alexander Gray, Gilda Gray, Ivy Halstead, Netta Hill, May Howard, Ada Hughes, Sonia Ivanoff, Beatrice Jackson, Hazel Jennings, Brooke Johns, Naomi Johnson, Simeon Karavaeff, Kello Brothers, Lily Kimari, Virginia King, Julia Kingsley, Sylvia Kingsley, Teddy Knox, Frank Lambert, Evelyn Law, Mary Lewis, Kitty Littlefield, Jean Lloyd, Martha Lorber, Pansy Maness, Hallie Manning, Irene Marcellus, Ilsa Marvenga, Pauline Mason, Beulah McFarland, Constance McLaughlin, Janet Megrew, Madge Merritt, Hilda Moreno, Polly Nally, Cora Neary, Jimmy Nervo, Al Ochs, Joe Opp, Olive Osborne, Elaine Palmer, Annie Patron, Ann Pennington, Serge Pernikoff, Elsa Peterson, Pearl Prosser, Jessie Reed, Anastasia Reilly, Frances Reveaux, Marion Rich, Addie Rolfe, Nellie Savage, John Scott, Gertrude Selden, J. J. Shannon, Al Shean, Marie Shelton, Grant Simpson, Beatrice Singleton, Nellie Smith, Kathryn Stoneburn, Muriel Stryker, the Follies Four, Tiller Girls, Irene Todd, Andrew Tombes, Brandon Tynan, Ruth Urban, Vangie Valentine, Miriam Vandergriff, Shirley Vernon, Vivian Vernon, Blossom Vreeland, Irene Wales, Marie Wallace, Betty Webb, Hazel Webb, Madlyn Wells, Fay West, West and McGinty, Edna Wheaton, Margie Whittington, Lois Wilde, Betty Williams, Elsie Woodall, Helen Lee Worthing.

Ziegfeld Follies (1923–1924)

Touring production: Colonial Theatre, Boston; Forrest Theatre, Philadelphia; Ford's Opera House, Baltimore; National Theatre, Washington, D.C.; Pittsburgh; Cleveland; New Detroit Theatre, Detroit; Colonial Theatre, Chicago; Davidson Theatre, Milwaukee; American Theatre, St. Louis; Sam S. Shubert Theatre, Kansas City, Mo.; English's Opera House, Indianapolis; Grand Opera House, Cincinnati; Dayton; Royal Alexandra Theatre, Toronto; Majestic Theatre, Buffalo. Two hundred thirty-three performances, October 20, 1923–May 10, 1924. Book and lyrics: Gene Buck, Eddie Cantor. Music:

Victor Herbert, Rudolf Friml, David Stamper. Choreography: Ned Wayburn. Scenic design: Joseph Urban. Opening night: New Amsterdam Theatre, New York. Cast: Bernice
Ackerman, Ethel Allis, Ruth Andrae, Wilma Ansell, Mary Bancroft, Virginia Beards-
ley, Doris Bennett, Mildred Billert, Lois Blackburn, Fanny Brice, Dorothy Brown, Lilly
Burgess, Catherine Burke, Marie Callahan, Cynthia Cambridge, Louise Carlton, Joan
Carter Waddell, Gladys Coburn, Hettie Cooper, James J. Corbett, Roy Cropper, Mar-
garet Cummings, Marie Dahm, Helena D'Algy, Mae Daw, Claire DeFitamiere, Fer-
ral Dewees, Harland Dixon, Helen Dobbins, Andre Dumont, Paulette Duval, Dorothy
Ellis, Gladys Ellison, Helen Ellsworth, Alberta Faust, Hilda Ferguson, Mme. Florianne,
Harriet Fowler, Catherine Gallimore, Millie Glossop, Florentine Gosnova, Hetty Gra-
ham, Roberta Grant, Sarah Granzow, Nelle Greasley, Beryl Halley, Marion Hamilton,
Helen Henderson, Jean Henderson, Lew Hern, Norah Jackson, Brooke Johns, Mary
Julian, Bob Karna, Elizabeth Kay, Winnie Keane, Dorothy Kelsall, Flo Kennedy, Emma
Klige, Alice Knowlton, Florence Kolinsky, Margaret Langhorne, Edna Leedom, Mar-
jorie Leet, Virginia Magee, Maud Mansfield, Harriet Marned, Phyllis Mawer, Irma
McShane, Lily McWilliams, Janet Megrew, Goodie Montgomery, Inez Moreno, Rita
Moriarty, Polly Nally, Alma Nash, Raymond O'Brian, Gladys Peterson, Martha Pierre,
Robert Quinault, Violet Regal, Billy Revel, Addie Rolfe, William Roselle, Iris Rowe,
Gertrude Selden, Peggy Shannon, Heloise Sheppard, Harry Short, Margaret Sloan, Dave
Stamper, Olga Steck, Ruby Stevens (Ensemble), Charlotte Suddath, Beatrice Thorburn,
Billie Tichenor, Dorothy Van Alst, Feon Vanmar, Hazel Vergess, Vivian Vernon, Hap
Ward, Betty Warrington, Nondas Wayne, Marjorie Weaver, Arthur West, Elsie Westcott,
Bert Wheeler, Betty Wheeler, Paul Whiteman, Paul Whiteman's Orchestra, Lois Wilde,
Doris Wilson, Dottie Wilson, Imogene Wilson, Lily Winton, Stella Wooten, Helen Lee
Worthing, Alexander Yarkovleff, Ruth Zoakay.

Keep Kool (1924)

Morosco Theatre, New York, 148 performances, May 22–July 6, 1924. Producer:
E. K. Nadel. Book: Paul Gerard Smith. Music: Jack Frost. Lyrics: Paul Gerard Smith.
Choreography: Earl Lindsay. Cast: Hazel Dawn, Johnny Dooley, Charles King, Ethel
Bryant, Ann Butler, Val De Mar, Helen Fables, Maerena Grady, Lillian Harnack, Lon
Hascall, Rita Howard, Dick Keene, James Kelso, Ruth Laird, Jessie Maker, Isabelle
Mason, Claire Miller, Lucille Moore, Walter Morrison, Helen Paine, Hal Parker, William
Redford, Ruby Stevens (Ensemble), Mildred Stewart, Mimi Tattersall, Dorothy Thattel,
Edward Tierney, Dorothy Tiller, Ethelyn Tillman, Dorothy Van Alst, Ina Williams.

Keep Kool (1924)

Globe Theatre, New York, July 7–August 31, 1924. Producer: E. K. Nadel. Book: Paul Gerard Smith. Music: Jack Frost. Lyrics: Paul Gerard Smith. Choreography: Earl Lindsay. Cast: Ruby Stevens (Ensemble).

Keep Kool (1924)

Earl Carroll Theatre, New York, September 1–September 27, 1924. Producer: E. K. Nadel. Book: Paul Gerard Smith. Music: Jack Frost. Lyrics: Paul Gerard Smith. Choreography: Earl Lindsay. Cast: Ruby Stevens (Ensemble).

Gay Paree (1925)

Majestic Theatre, Buffalo. Book: Harold Atteridge. Lyrics: Clifford Grey. Music: J. Fred Coots, Alfred Goodman, Maurie Rubens. Cast: Winnie Lightner, Billy Van, Mae Clarke, Ruby Stevens.

Gay Paree (1925)

Everglades Café, New York. Book: Harold Atteridge. Lyrics: Clifford Grey. Music: J. Fred Coots, Alfred Goodman, Maurie Rubens. Cast: Winnie Lightner, Billy Van, Mae Clarke, Ruby Stevens.

Gay Paree (1925)

Club Anatol, New York. Book: Harold Atteridge. Lyrics: Clifford Grey. Music: J. Fred Coots, Alfred Goodman, Maurie Rubens. Cast: Winnie Lightner, Billy Van, Mae Clarke, Ruby Stevens.

Gay Paree (1925–1926)

Shubert Theatre, New York, August 18, 1925–January 30, 1926. Book: Harold Atteridge. Lyrics: Clifford Grey. Music: J. Fred Coots, Alfred Goodman, Maurie Rubens. Cast: Newton Alexander, Betty Allen, Lucille Arden, William Baden, Dorothy Barber, Pauline Blair, Frances Blythe, Richard Bold, Ilsi Bott, Alice Boulden, Carol Boyer, William Brainerd, Lorraine Brooks, Camille, Jean Caswell, Chandler Christy, Helen Claire, Mae Clarke, Eddie Conrad, Claire Daniels, Isabel Dawn, Claudia Dell, Johnny Dove, Louise Dove, Clarice Durham, Mabel Earle, Beth Elliott, Byrdeatta Evans, Florence Fair, Rosemary Farmer, Margie Finley, Walton Ford, Ruth Gillette, Florence Golden, Viola Griffith, Texas Guinan, Jack Haley, Ruth Hamilton, Thalie Hamilton, Edith Higgens, Alice Hooke, Edna Hopper, Florence Horne, Gus Hyland, Katherine Janeway, Frank Kimball, Marty Kolinsky, Lillian Lane, George LeMaire, Fern LeRoy, Winnie Lightner, Martha Linn, Gertrude Lowe, Viola Marshall, Betty Maurice, Arthur May, Verdi Milli, Marie Price, Prosper & Maret, Dorothy Rae, Nora Reed, Camille Renault, Charles

"Chic" Sale, Salt and Pepper, Wilfred Seagram, Winifred Seale, Dorothy Sheppard, Jeanette Simard, Bartlett Simmons, Marie Simpson, Bernadette Spencer, Louise Taylor, Billy B. Van, Lorraine Weimar, Margaret Wilson.

The Noose (1926)
Hudson Theatre, New York, 197 performances, October 20, 1926–April 1927. Playwright: Willard Mack. Cast: Ralph Adams, George W. Barnum, Charles Brown, Harry Bulger Jr., Rex Cherryman, Carolyn Clarke, Mae Clarke, Jack Daley, Helen Flint, Maryland Jarbeau, Ralph Locke, Lester Lonergan, Wilfred Lucas, George Nash, Hans Robert, Dorothy Sheppard, Ann Shoemaker, Barbara Stanwyck (Dot), George Thompson, Erenay Weaver.

The Noose (1927)
Selwyn Theatre, Chicago, April 18–June 4, 1927. Playwright: Willard Mack. Cast: Barbara Stanwyck (Dot).

Burlesque (1927–1928)
Plymouth Theatre, New York, 372 performances, September 1, 1927–July 14, 1928. Playwrights: Arthur Hopkins, George Manker Watters. Choreography: Mary Jennings. Scenic design: Cleon Throckmorton. Cast: Charles D. Brown, Mitty De Vere, Pauline Dee, Wilkie Dodsworth, Ruth Holden, Oscar Levant, Paul Porter, Jack B. Shea, Hal Skelly, Barbara Stanwyck (Bonny), Ralph Theodore, Eileen Wilson.

Burlesque (1928)
Newark, N.J., August 27, 1928. Playwrights: Arthur Hopkins, George Manker Watters. Choreography: Mary Jennings. Scenic design: Cleon Throckmorton. Cast: Barbara Stanwyck (Bonny).

The Conflict (1929)
Palace Theatre, New York, February 11, 1929–February 19, 1929. Playwright: Vincent Lawrence. Cast: Barbara Stanwyck, Frank Fay.

The Conflict (1929)
Club Richman, New York, February 20, 1929. Playwright: Vincent Lawrence. Cast: Barbara Stanwyck, Frank Fay.

A Night in Venice (1929)
Shubert Theatre, New York, 175 performances, May 21, 1929–September 1929. Producers: Lee Shubert, J. J. Shubert. Music: Lee Davis, Maurie Rubens. Lyrics: J. Keirn

Brennan, Moe Jaffe. Choreography: Busby Berkeley, Chester Hale. Cast: Ted Healy, Ann Seymour, the Dodge Sisters, Arthur Havel, Morton Havel, Stanley Rogers, Betty Allen, Walter Armin, Barbara Stanwyck (unconfirmed).

A Night in Venice (1929)
Majestic Theatre, New York, September 16, 1929–October 19, 1929. Producers: Lee Shubert, J. J. Shubert. Music: Lee Davis, Maurie Rubens. Lyrics: J. Keirn Brennan, Moe Jaffe. Choreography: Busby Berkeley, Chester Hale. Cast: Ted Healy, Ann Seymour, the Dodge Sisters, Arthur Havel, Morton Havel, Stanley Rogers, Betty Allen, Walter Armin, Barbara Stanwyck (unconfirmed).

Tattle Tales (1932)
Belasco Theatre, Los Angeles, December 28 or 29, 1932. Producer: Frank Fay. Book: Frank Fay, Nick Copeland. Lyrics: George Waggoner, Leo Robin, Edward Eliscu, William Walsh, Frank Fay, Willard Robison, Howard Jackson. Music: Edward Ward, Ralph Rainger, Willard Robison, Howard Jackson, Eddie Bienbryer. Choreography: John Lonergan, Danny Dare, Leroy Prinz. Cast: Frank Fay, Betty Grable, Barbara Stanwyck (Herself, Kay Arnold).

Tattle Tales (1932)
Touring production: Portland, Oreg.; Spokane; Billings, Mont.; Cheyenne, Wyo.; Colorado Springs; Denver; Omaha; Kansas City, Mo. March 6–April 10, 1932. Producer: Frank Fay. Book: Frank Fay, Nick Copeland. Lyrics: George Waggoner, Leo Robin, Edward Eliscu, William Walsh, Frank Fay, Willard Robison, Howard Jackson. Music: Edward Ward, Ralph Rainger, Willard Robison, Howard Jackson, Eddie Bienbryer. Choreography: John Lonergan, Danny Dare, Leroy Prinz. Cast: Frank Fay, Betty Grable, Barbara Stanwyck (Herself, Kay Arnold).

Tattle Tales (1933)
Broadhurst Theatre, New York, 28 performances, June 1–June 24, 1933. Producer: Frank Fay. Book: Frank Fay, Nick Copeland. Lyrics: George Waggoner, Leo Robin, Edward Eliscu, William Walsh, Frank Fay, Willard Robison, Howard Jackson. Music: Edward Ward, Ralph Rainger, Willard Robison, Howard Jackson, Eddie Bienbryer. Choreography: John Lonergan, Danny Dare, Leroy Prinz. Cast: Lois Ackerman, Jerry Archer, Mary Barnett, Beauvell, Eddie Byrnbriar, Les Clark, Ione Collombe, Nick Copeland, Don Cumming, Dorothy Dell, Betty Doree, John Dyer, Helen Eades, Edith Evans, Frank Fay, Wilma Flannigan, Betty Grable, William Hargrave, Jane Hayes, Collece Legget, James Mack, Lucille Matthews, Ray Mayer, Jane Morgan, Barbara Near, Charlotte Neste, Betty Norton, Betty Nylander, Evelyn Page, Lillian Reynolds, Beverly Royde, Sylvia Schiller, Barbara Stanwyck (Herself, Kay Arnold), Miss Tova, Elsa Walbridge, Wilma Wray.

The Interview (1933)

Playlet, New York, September 1933. Based on the book by Arthur Somers Roche. Cast: Morton Downey, Barbara Stanwyck.

Tattle Tales (1934)

Broadhurst Theatre, New York, June 1, 1934. Producer: Frank Fay. Book: Frank Fay, Nick Copeland. Lyrics: George Waggoner, Leo Robin, Edward Eliscu, William Walsh, Frank Fay, Willard Robison, Howard Jackson. Music: Edward Ward, Ralph Rainger, Willard Robison, Howard Jackson, Eddie Bienbryer. Choreography: John Lonergan, Danny Dare, Leroy Prinz. Cast: Frank Fay, Barbara Stanwyck (Herself, Kay Arnold).

APPENDIX II: FILM CHRONOLOGY

Broadway Nights (1927)
Director: Joseph C. Boyle. Screenplay: Forrest Halsey. Story: Norman Houston. Photography: Ernest Haller. Editor: Paul F. Maschke. Production: Robert Kane Productions. Distribution: First National. Release date: May 15, 1927. Running time: 72 minutes. Cast: Lois Wilson, Louis John Bartels, June Collyer, Sam Hardy, Georgette Duval, Philip Strange, Henry Sherwood, Sylvia Sidney, Francis "Bunny" Weldon, De Sacia Mooers, Lee Armstrong, Ann Sothern, Barbara Stanwyck (Dancer).

The Locked Door (1929)
Executive producer: Joseph P. Kennedy. Director: George Fitzmaurice. Based on the play *The Sign on the Door* by Channing Pollock. Adaptation: C. Gardner Sullivan. Dialogue: George Scarborough. Photography: Ray June. Editor: Hal C. Kern. Production: Feature Productions. Distribution: United Artists. Release date: November 16, 1929. Running time: 70 minutes. Cast: Rod La Rocque, Barbara Stanwyck (Ann Carter), William "Stage" Boyd, Betty Bronson, Harry Stubbs, Harry Mestayer, Mack Swain, Zasu Pitts, George Bunny, Purnell Pratt, Fred Warren.

Mexicali Rose (1929)
Producer: Harry Cohn. Director: Erle C. Kenton. Story: Gladys Lehman. Screenplay: Gladys Lehman, Norman Houston. Photography: Ted Tetzlaff. Editor: Leon Barsha. Production and distribution: Columbia. Release date: December 26, 1929. Running time: 60 minutes. Cast: Barbara Stanwyck (Mexicali Rose), Sam Hardy, William Janney, Louis Natheaux, Arthur Rankin, Harry J. Vejar, Louis King, Julia Bejarano.

Ladies of Leisure (1930)
Producer: Harry Cohn. Director: Frank Capra. Based on the play *Ladies of the Evening* by Milton Herbert Gropper. Adaptation: Jo Swerling. Photography: Joseph Walker. Editor: Maurice Wright. Production and distribution: Columbia (Frank Capra Productions received production credit). Release date: April 5, 1930. Running time: 98 minutes.

Cast: Barbara Stanwyck (Kay Arnold), Ralph Graves, Lowell Sherman, Marie Prevost, Nance O'Neil, George Fawcett, Juliette Compton, Johnnie Walker.

Illicit (1931)

Producer: Darryl F. Zanuck. Director: Archie Mayo. Based on a play by Edith Fitzgerald, Robert Riskin. Adaptation: Harvey F. Thew. Photography: Robert Kurrle. Editor: William Holmes. Production and distribution: Warner Bros. Release date: February 14, 1931. Running time: 79 minutes. Cast: Barbara Stanwyck (Anne Vincent Ives), James Rennie, Ricardo Cortez, Natalie Moorhead, Charles Butterworth, Joan Blondell, Claude Gillingwater.

Ten Cents a Dance (1931)

Producer: Harry Cohn. Director: Lionel Barrymore. Screenplay: Jo Swerling. Photography: Ernest Haller, Gilbert Warrenton. Editor: Arthur Huffsmith. Production and distribution: Columbia (Lionel Barrymore Productions received production credit). Release date: March 6, 1931. Running time: 75 minutes. Cast: Barbara Stanwyck (Barbara O'Neill), Ricardo Cortez, Monroe Owsley, Sally Blane, Blanche Friderici, Phyllis Crane, Olive Tell, Victor Potel, Al Hill, Jack Byron, Abe Lyman, Pat Harmon, Martha Sleeper, David Newell, Sidney Bracey, Harry Todd, Aggie Herring, Peggy Doner.

Night Nurse (1931)

Director: William A. Wellman. Based on the novel by Dora Macy. Adaptation: Oliver H. P. Garrett. Photography: Barney McGill. Editor: Edward M. McDermott. Production: Warner Bros. Distribution: Warner Bros., Vitaphone. Release date: July 16, 1931. Running time: 72 minutes. Cast: Barbara Stanwyck (Lora Hart), Ben Lyon, Joan Blondell, Clark Gable, Blanche Friderici, Charlotte Merriam, Charles Winninger, Edward J. Nugent, Vera Lewis, Ralf Harolde, Walter McGrail.

The Miracle Woman (1931)

Producer: Harry Cohn. Director: Frank Capra. Based on the play *Bless You, Sister* by John Meehan and Robert Riskin. Adaptation: Jo Swerling. Photography: Joseph Walker. Editor: Maurice Wright. Production and distribution: Columbia (Frank Capra Productions received production credit). Release date: July 20, 1931. Running time: 90 minutes. Cast: Barbara Stanwyck (Florence Fallon), David Manners, Sam Hardy, Beryl Mercer, Russell Hopton, Charles Middleton, Eddie Boland, Thelma Hill.

Forbidden (1932)

Producer: Harry Cohn. Director: Frank Capra. Story: Frank Capra. Adaptation: Jo Swerling. Photography: Joseph Walker. Editor: Maurice Wright. Production and distribution:

Columbia (Frank Capra Productions received production credit). Release date: January 9, 1932. Running time: 85 minutes. Cast: Barbara Stanwyck (Lulu), Adolphe Menjou, Ralph Bellamy, Dorothy Peterson, Thomas Jefferson, Myrna Fresholt, Charlotte Henry, Oliver Eckhardt.

Shopworn (1932)

Director: Nicholas Grinde. Story: Sarah Y. Mason. Screenplay: Jo Swerling, Robert Riskin. Photography: Joseph Walker. Editor: Gene Havlick. Production and distribution: Columbia. Release date: March 25, 1932. Running time: 72 minutes. Cast: Barbara Stanwyck (Kitty Lane), Regis Toomey, Zasu Pitts, Lucien Littlefield, Clara Blandick, Robert Alden, Oscar Apfel, Maud Turner Gordon, Albert Conti, James Durkin.

So Big (1932)

Director: William A. Wellman. Based on the novel by Edna Ferber. Adaptation: J. Grubb Alexander, Robert Lord. Photography: Sid Hickox. Editor: William Holmes. Production: Warner Bros. Distribution: Warner Bros., Vitaphone. Release date: April 30, 1932. Running time: 81 minutes. Cast: Barbara Stanwyck (Selina Peake De Jong), George Brent, Dickie Moore, Bette Davis, Mae Madison, Hardie Albright, Alan Hale, Earle Foxe, Robert Warwick, Dorothy Peterson, Noel Francis, Dick Winslow.

The Purchase Price (1932)

Director: William A. Wellman. Based on the novel *The Mud Lark* by Arthur Stringer. Adaptation: Robert Lord. Photography: Sid Hickox. Editor: William Holmes. Production: Warner Bros. Distribution: Warner Bros., Vitaphone. Release date: July 23, 1932. Running time: 68 minutes. Cast: Barbara Stanwyck (Joan Gordon), George Brent, Lyle Talbot, Hardie Albright, David Landau, Murray Kinnell, Leila Bennett.

The Bitter Tea of General Yen (1933)

Director: Frank Capra. Based on the novel by Grace Zaring Stone. Screenplay: Edward Paramore. Photography: Sid Hickox. Editor: Edward Curtis. Production and distribution: Warner Bros. (Frank Capra Productions received production credit). Release date: January 6, 1933. Running time: 88 minutes. Cast: Barbara Stanwyck (Megan Davis), Nils Asther, Toshia Mori, Walter Connolly, Gavin Gordon, Lucien Littlefield, Richard Loo, Helen Jerome Eddy, Emmett Corrigan.

Ladies They Talk About (1933)

Directors: Howard Bretherton, William Keighley. Based on the play by Dorothy Mackaye and Carlton Miles. Adaptation: Brown Holmes, William McGrath, Sidney Sutherland. Photography: John Seitz. Editor: Basil Wrangel. Production: Warner Bros. Distribution:

Warner Bros., Vitaphone. Release date: February 4, 1933. Running time: 69 minutes. Cast: Barbara Stanwyck (Nan Taylor), Preston Foster, Lyle Talbot, Dorothy Burgess, Lillian Roth, Maud Eburne, Ruth Donnelly, Harold Huber, Robert McWade.

Baby Face (1933)
Director: Alfred E. Green. Story: Darryl F. Zanuck (as Mark Canfield). Screenplay: Gene Markey, Kathryn Scola. Photography: James Van Trees. Editor: Howard Bretherton. Production: Warner Bros. Distribution: Warner Bros., Vitaphone. Release date: July 1, 1933. Running time: 71 minutes. Cast: Barbara Stanwyck (Lily Powers), George Brent, Donald Cook, Alphonse Ethier, Henry Kolker, Margaret Lindsay, Arthur Hohl, John Wayne, Robert Barrat, Douglass Dumbrille, Theresa Harris.

Ever in My Heart (1933)
Executive producer: Hal B. Wallis. Director: Archie Mayo. Story: Beulah Marie Dix, Bertram Millhauser. Screenplay: Bertram Millhauser. Photography: Arthur Todd. Editor: Owen Marks. Production and distribution: Warner Bros. Release date: October 28, 1933. Running time: 68 minutes. Cast: Barbara Stanwyck (Mary Archer Wilbrandt), Otto Kruger, Ralph Bellamy, Ruth Donnelly, Laura Hope Crews, Frank Albertson, Ronnie Cosby, Clara Blandick, Willard Robertson, Nella Walker, Harry Beresford, Virginia Howell.

Gambling Lady (1934)
Associate producer: Robert Presnell Sr. Director: Archie Mayo. Story: Doris Malloy. Screenplay: Ralph Block, Doris Malloy. Photography: George Barnes. Editor: Harold McLernon. Production: Warner Bros. Distribution: Warner Bros., Vitaphone. Release date: March 31, 1934. Running time: 66 minutes. Cast: Barbara Stanwyck (Lady Lee), Joel McCrea, Pat O'Brien, Claire Dodd, C. Aubrey Smith, Robert Barrat, Arthur Vinton, Phillip Reed, Philip Faversham, Robert Elliott, Ferdinand Gottschalk, Willard Robertson, Huey White.

A Lost Lady (1934)
Producer: James Seymour. Directors: Alfred E. Green, Phil Rosen. Based on the novel by Willa Cather. Screenplay: Gene Markey, Kathryn Scola. Photography: Sid Hickox. Editor: Owen Marks. Production: Warner Bros. Distribution: First National, Vitaphone. Release date: September 29, 1934. Running time: 61 minutes. Cast: Barbara Stanwyck (Marian Ormsby Forrester), Frank Morgan, Ricardo Cortez, Lyle Talbot, Phillip Reed, Hobart Cavanaugh, Henry Kolker, Rafaela Ottiano, Edward McWade, Walter Walker, Samuel S. Hinds, Willie Fung, Jameson Thomas.

The Secret Bride (1934)

Associate producer: Henry Blanke. Director: William Dieterle. Based on the play *Concealment* by Leonard Ide. Screenplay: Tom Buckingham, F. Hugh Herbert, Mary McCall Jr. Photography: Ernest Haller. Editor: Owen Marks. Production: Warner Bros. Distribution: Warner Bros., Vitaphone. Release date: December 22, 1934. Running time: 64 minutes. Cast: Barbara Stanwyck (Ruth Vincent), Warren William, Glenda Farrell, Grant Mitchell, Arthur Byron, Henry O'Neill, Douglass Dumbrille, Arthur Aylesworth, Willard Robertson, William B. Davidson, Russell Hicks, Vince Barnett.

The Woman in Red (1935)

Producer: Harry Joe Brown. Director: Robert Florey. Based on the novel *North Shore* by Wallace Irwin. Screenplay: Mary McCall Jr., Peter Milne. Photography: Sol Polito. Editor: Terry Morse. Production and distribution: First National. Release date: March 25, 1935. Running time: 68 minutes. Cast: Barbara Stanwyck (Shelby Barret Wyatt), Gene Raymond, Genevieve Tobin, John Eldredge, Phillip Reed, Dorothy Tree, Russell Hicks, Nella Walker, Claude Gillingwater, Doris Lloyd, Hale Hamilton, Edward Van Sloan, Forrester Harvey, Bill Elliott, Frederick Vogeding, Eleanor Wesselhoeft, Brandon Hurst.

Red Salute (1935)

Producer: Edward Small. Director: Sidney Lanfield. Story: Humphrey Pearson. Screenplay: Humphrey Pearson, Manuel Seff. Photography: Robert H. Planck. Editor: Grant Whytock. Production: Reliance (Edward Small Productions received production credit). Distribution: United Artists. Release date: September 13, 1935. Running time: 77 minutes. Cast: Barbara Stanwyck (Drue Van Allen), Robert Young, Hardie Albright, Cliff Edwards, Ruth Donnelly, Gordon Jones, Paul Stanton, Purnell Pratt, Nella Walker, Arthur Vinton, Edward McWade, Henry Kolker, Allan Cavan, Ferdinand Gottschalk, Selmer Jackson, David Newell.

Annie Oakley (1935)

Associate producer: Cliff Reid. Director: George Stevens. Story: Joseph A. Fields, Ewart Adamson. Screenplay: Joel Sayre, John Twist. Photography: J. Roy Hunt, Harold Wenstrom. Editor: Jack Hively. Production and distribution: RKO Radio Pictures. Release date: November 15, 1935. Running time: 90 minutes. Cast: Barbara Stanwyck (Annie Oakley), Preston Foster, Melvyn Douglas, Moroni Olsen, Pert Kelton, Andy Clyde, Chief Thunderbird, Margaret Armstrong, Delmar Watson, Adeline Craig.

A Message to Garcia (1936)

Producer: Darryl F. Zanuck. Director: George Marshall. Based on the book *How I Carried the Message to Garcia* by Lieutenant Andrew S. Rowan. Screenplay: W. P. Lipscomb,

Gene Fowler. Photography: Rudolph Maté. Editor: Herbert Levy. Production and distribution: 20th Century–Fox ("A Darryl F. Zanuck Twentieth Century Production" received credit). Release date: April 10, 1936. Running time: 77 minutes. Cast: Wallace Beery, Barbara Stanwyck (Raphaelita Maderos), John Boles, Alan Hale, Herbert Mundin, Mona Barrie, Enrique Acosta, Juan Torena, Martin Garralaga, Blanca Vischer, José Luis Tortosa, Lucio Villegas, Frederick Vogeding, Pat Moriarity, Octavio Giraud.

The Bride Walks Out (1936)

Producer: Edward Small. Director: Leigh Jason. Story: Howard Emmett Rogers. Screenplay: Philip G. Epstein, P. J. Wolfson. Photography: J. Roy Hunt. Editor: Arthur Roberts. Production and distribution: RKO Radio Pictures ("An Edward Small Production" received credit). Release date: July 10, 1936. Running time: 75 minutes. Cast: Barbara Stanwyck (Carolyn Martin), Gene Raymond, Robert Young, Ned Sparks, Helen Broderick, Willie Best, Robert Warwick, Billy Gilbert, Wade Boteler, Hattie McDaniel.

His Brother's Wife (1936)

Producer: Lawrence Weingarten. Director: W. S. Van Dyke. Story: George Auerbach. Screenplay: Leon Gordon, John Meehan. Photography: Oliver T. Marsh. Editor: Conrad A. Nervig. Production and distribution: Loew's ("A W. S. Van Dyke Production" received credit). Release date: August 7, 1936. Running time: 90 minutes. Cast: Barbara Stanwyck (Rita Wilson Claybourne), Robert Taylor, Jean Hersholt, Joseph Calleia, John Eldredge, Samuel S. Hinds, Phyllis Clare, Leonard Mudie, Jed Prouty, Pedro de Cordoba, Rafael Storm, William Stack, Edgar Edwards.

Banjo on My Knee (1936)

Executive producer: Darryl F. Zanuck. Director: John Cromwell. Based on the novel by Harry Hamilton. Screenplay: Nunnally Johnson. Photography: Ernest Palmer. Editor: Hanson Fritch. Production and distribution: 20th Century–Fox ("Darryl F. Zanuck in charge of production" received credit). Release date: December 11, 1936. Running time: 95 minutes. Cast: Barbara Stanwyck (Pearl Elliott Holley), Joel McCrea, Walter Brennan, Buddy Ebsen, Helen Westley, Walter Catlett, Tony Martin, Katherine DeMille, Victor Kilian, Minna Gombell, Spencer Charters, the Hall Johnson Choir, George Humbert, Hilda Vaughn, Cecil Weston, Louis Mason.

The Plough and the Stars (1936)

Associate producer: Cliff Reid. Director: John Ford. Based on the play by Sean O'Casey Screenplay: Dudley Nichols. Photography: Joseph H. August. Editor: George Hively. Production and distribution: RKO Radio Pictures. Release date: December 26, 1936. Running time: 78 minutes. Cast: Barbara Stanwyck (Nora Clitheroe), Preston

Foster, Barry Fitzgerald, Denis O'Dea, Eileen Crowe, F. J. McCormick, Una O'Connor, Arthur Shields, Moroni Olsen, J. M. Kerrigan, Bonita Granville, Erin O'Brien-Moore, Neil Fitzgerald, Robert Homans, Brandon Hurst, Cyril McLaglen.

Internes Can't Take Money (1937)

Producer: Benjamin Glazer. Director: Alfred Santell. Story: Max Brand. Screenplay: Rian James, Theodore Reeves. Photography: Theodor Sparkuhl. Editor: Doane Harrison. Production and distribution: Paramount. Release date: April 16, 1937. Running time: 78 minutes. Cast: Barbara Stanwyck (Janet Haley), Joel McCrea, Lloyd Nolan, Stanley Ridges, Lee Bowman, Barry Macollum, Irving Bacon, Steve Pendleton, Pierre Watkin, Charles Lane, James Bush, Nick Lukats, Anthony Nace, Fay Holden, Frank Bruno.

This Is My Affair (1937)

Producer: Kenneth Macgowan. Director: William A. Seiter. Screenplay: Allen Rivkin, Lamar Trotti. Photography: Robert Planck. Editor: Allen McNeil. Production and distribution: 20 Century–Fox ("Darryl F. Zanuck in charge of production" received credit). Release date: May 28, 1937. Running time: 101 minutes. Cast: Robert Taylor, Barbara Stanwyck (Lil Duryea), Victor McLaglen, Brian Donlevy, John Carradine, Douglas Fowley, Alan Dinehart, Sig Ruman, Robert McWade, Sidney Blackmer, Frank Conroy, Marjorie Weaver, J. C. Nugent, Tyler Brooke, Willard Robertson, Paul Hurst, Douglas Wood.

Stella Dallas (1937)

Producer: Samuel Goldwyn. Director: King Vidor. Based on the novel by Olive Higgins Prouty. Dramatization: Harry Wagstaff Gribble, Gertrude Purcell. Screenplay: Sarah Y. Mason, Victor Heerman. Photography: Rudolph Maté. Editor: Sherman Todd. Production: Howard Productions. Distribution: United Artists. Release date: August 5, 1937. Running time: 106 minutes. Cast: Barbara Stanwyck (Stella Dallas), John Boles, Anne Shirley, Barbara O'Neil, Alan Hale, Marjorie Main, George Walcott, Ann Shoemaker, Tim Holt, Nella Walker, Bruce Satterlee, Jimmy Butler, Jack Egger, Dickie Jones.

Breakfast for Two (1937)

Producer: Edward Kaufman. Director: Alfred Santell. Based on the novel *A Love Like That* by David Garth. Screenplay: Charles Kaufman, Paul Yawitz, Viola Brothers Shore. Photography: J. Roy Hunt. Editor: George Hively. Production and distribution: RKO Radio Pictures. Release date: October 22, 1937. Running time: 67 minutes. Cast: Barbara Stanwyck (Valentine Ransome), Herbert Marshall, Glenda Farrell, Eric Blore, Donald Meek, Etienne Girardot, Frank M. Thomas, Pierre Watkin.

Always Goodbye (1938)

Associate producer: Raymond Griffith. Director: Sidney Lanfield. Based on the film *Gallant Lady* by Gilbert Emery and Franc Rhodes. Screenplay: Kathryn Scola, Edith Skouras. Photography: Robert H. Planck. Editor: Robert L. Simpson. Production and distribution: 20 Century–Fox ("Darryl F. Zanuck in charge of production" received credit). Release date: July 1, 1938. Running time: 75 minutes. Cast: Barbara Stanwyck (Margot Weston), Herbert Marshall, Ian Hunter, Cesar Romero, Lynn Bari, Binnie Barnes, Johnny Russell, Mary Forbes, Albert Conti, Marcelle Corday, Franklin Pangborn, Ben Welden, Eddie Conrad.

The Mad Miss Manton (1938)

Associate producer: P. J. Wolfson. Director: Leigh Jason. Story: Wilson Collison. Screenplay: Philip G. Epstein. Photography: Nicholas Musuraca. Editor: George Hively. Production and distribution: RKO Radio Pictures ("Pandro S. Berman in charge of production" received credit). Release date: October 21, 1938. Running time: 80 minutes. Cast: Barbara Stanwyck (Melsa Manton), Henry Fonda, Sam Levene, Frances Mercer, Stanley Ridges, Whitney Bourne, Vickie Lester, Ann Evers, Catherine O'Quinn, Linda Perry, Eleanor Hansen, Hattie McDaniel, James Burke, Paul Guilfoyle, Penny Singleton, Leona Maricle, Kay Sutton, Miles Mander.

Union Pacific (1939)

Executive producer: William LeBaron. Director: Cecil B. DeMille. Based on the novel *Trouble Shooter* by Ernest Haycox. Adaptation: Jack Cunningham. Screenplay: Walter DeLeon, C. Gardner Sullivan, Jesse Lasky Jr. Photography: Victor Milner. Editor: Anne Bauchens. Production and distribution: Paramount. Release date: May 5, 1939. Running time: 135 minutes. Cast: Barbara Stanwyck (Mollie Monahan), Joel McCrea, Akim Tamiroff, Robert Preston, Lynne Overman, Brian Donlevy, Robert Barrat, Anthony Quinn, Stanley Ridges, Henry Kolker, Francis McDonald, Willard Robertson, Harold Goodwin, Evelyn Keyes, Richard Lane, William Haade, Regis Toomey, J. M. Kerrigan, Fuzzy Knight, Harry Woods, Lon Chaney Jr., Joseph Crehan, Julia Faye, Sheila Darcy.

Golden Boy (1939)

Producer: William Perlberg. Director: Rouben Mamoulian. Based on the play by Clifford Odets. Screenplay: Lewis Meltzer, Daniel Taradash, Sarah Y. Mason, Victor Heerman. Photography: Nick Musuraca, Karl Freund. Editor: Otto Meyer. Production and distribution: Columbia ("A Rouben Mamoulian Production" received credit). Release date: September 5, 1939. Running time: 99 minutes. Cast: Barbara Stanwyck (Lorna Moon), Adolphe Menjou, William Holden, Lee J. Cobb, Joseph Calleia, Sam Levene, Edward Brophy, Beatrice Blinn, William H. Strauss, Don Beddoe.

Remember the Night (1940)

Executive producer: William LeBaron. Director: Mitchell Leisen. Screenplay: Preston Sturges. Photography: Ted Tetzlaff. Editor: Doane Harrison. Production and distribution: Paramount. Release date: January 19, 1940. Running time: 94 minutes. Cast: Barbara Stanwyck (Lee Leander), Fred MacMurray, Beulah Bondi, Elizabeth Patterson, Willard Robertson, Sterling Holloway, Charles Waldron, Paul Guilfoyle, Charles Arnt, John Wray, Thomas W. Ross, Snowflake, Tom Kennedy, Georgia Caine, Virginia Brissac, Spencer Charters.

The Lady Eve (1941)

Executive producer: William LeBaron. Director: Preston Sturges. Story: Monckton Hoffe. Screenplay: Preston Sturges. Photography: Victor Milner. Editor: Stuart Gilmore. Production and distribution: Paramount. Release date: March 21, 1941. Running time: 93 minutes. Cast: Barbara Stanwyck (Jean), Henry Fonda, Charles Coburn, Eugene Pallette, William Demarest, Eric Blore, Melville Cooper, Martha O'Driscoll, Janet Beecher, Robert Greig, Dora Clement, Luis Alberni.

Meet John Doe (1941)

Director: Frank Capra. Based on the short story "A Reputation" by Richard Connell. Screenplay: Robert Riskin. Photography: George Barnes. Editor: Daniel Mandell. Production: Frank Capra Productions. Distribution: Warner Bros. Release date: May 3, 1941. Running time: 123 minutes. Cast: Gary Cooper, Barbara Stanwyck (Ann Mitchell), Edward Arnold, Walter Brennan, Spring Byington, James Gleason, Gene Lockhart, Rod La Rocque, Irving Bacon, Regis Toomey, J. Farrell MacDonald, Warren Hymer, Harry Holman, Andrew Tombes.

You Belong to Me (1941)

Director: Wesley Ruggles. Story: Dalton Trumbo. Screenplay: Claude Binyon. Photography: Joseph Walker. Editor: Viola Lawrence. Production and distribution: Columbia. Release date: October 22, 1941. Running time: 94 minutes. Cast: Barbara Stanwyck (Helen Hunt), Henry Fonda, Edgar Buchanan, Roger Clark, Ruth Donnelly, Melville Cooper, Ralph Peters, Maud Eburne, Renie Riano, Ellen Lowe, Mary Treen, Gordon Jones, Fritz Feld, Paul Harvey.

Ball of Fire (1941)

Producer: Samuel Goldwyn. Director: Howard Hawks. Story: Billy Wilder, Thomas Monroe. Screenplay: Charles Brackett, Billy Wilder. Photography: Gregg Toland. Editor: Daniel Mandell. Production: Samuel Goldwyn. Distribution: RKO Radio Pictures. Release date: December 2, 1941. Running time: 111 minutes. Cast: Gary Cooper, Barbara Stanwyck (Sugarpuss O'Shea), Oskar Homolka, Henry Travers, S. Z. Sakall, Tully Marshall, Leonid Kinskey, Richard Haydn, Aubrey Mather, Allen Jenkins, Dana Andrews, Dan Duryea, Ralph Peters, Kathleen Howard, Mary Field, Charles Lane, Charles Arnt.

The Great Man's Lady (1942)

Director: William A. Wellman. Based on the short story "The Human Side" by Viña Delmar. Story: Adela Rogers St. Johns, Seena Owen. Screenplay: W. L. River. Photography: William C. Mellor. Editor: Thomas Scott. Production and distribution: Paramount ("A William A. Wellman Production" received credit). Release date: April 29, 1942. Running time: 90 minutes. Cast: Barbara Stanwyck (Hannah Sempler), Joel McCrea, Brian Donlevy, K. T. Stevens, Thurston Hall, Lloyd Corrigan, Etta McDaniel, Frank M. Thomas, William B. Davidson, Lillian Yarbo, Helen Lynd, Mary Treen, Lucien Littlefield, John Hamilton, Fred "Snowflake" Toones.

The Gay Sisters (1942)

Producer: Henry Blanke. Director: Irving Rapper. Based on the novel by Stephen Longstreet. Screenplay: Lenore J. Coffee. Photography: Sol Polito. Editor: Warren Low. Production and distribution: Warner Bros. Release date: August 1, 1942. Running time: 108 minutes. Cast: Barbara Stanwyck (Fiona Gaylord), George Brent, Geraldine Fitzgerald, Donald Crisp, Gig Young, Nancy Coleman, Gene Lockhart, Larry Simms, Donald Woods, Grant Mitchell, William T. Orr, Anne Revere, Helene Thimig, George Lessey, Charles Waldron, Frank Reicher, David Clyde, Mary Thomas.

Lady of Burlesque (1943)

Producer: Hunt Stromberg. Director: William A. Wellman. Based on the novel *The G-String Murders* by Gypsy Rose Lee. Screenplay: James Gunn. Photography: Robert de Grasse. Editor: James E. Newcom. Production: Hunt Stromberg Productions. Distribution: United Artists. Release date: May 1, 1943. Running time: 91 minutes. Cast: Barbara Stanwyck (Dixie Daisy), Michael O'Shea, Iris Adrian, Charles Dingle, J. Edward Bromberg, Frank Conroy, Victoria Faust, Gloria Dickson, Marion Martin, Frank Fenton, Stephanie Bachelor, Pinky Lee, Eddie Gordon, Janis Carter, Lou Lubin, Gerald Mohr, Bert Hanlon, Claire Carleton, George Chandler, Lee Trent, Don Lynn.

Flesh and Fantasy (1943)

Producer: Charles Boyer. Director: Julien Duvivier. Story: Ellis St. Joseph (segment 1), Oscar Wilde (segment 2), László Vadnay (segment 3). Screenplay: Ernest Pascal, Samuel Hoffenstein, Ellis St. Joseph. Photography: Stanley Cortez, Paul Ivano. Editor: Arthur Hilton. Production and distribution: Universal. Release date: October 29, 1943. Running time: 94 minutes. Cast: Edward G. Robinson, Charles Boyer, Barbara Stanwyck (Joan Stanley; segment 3), Betty Field, Robert Cummings, Thomas Mitchell, Charles Winninger, Anna Lee, Dame May Whitty, C. Aubrey Smith, Robert Benchley, Edgar Barrier, David Hoffman.

Double Indemnity (1944)

Director: Billy Wilder. Based on the novel by James M. Cain. Screenplay: Billy Wilder, Raymond Chandler. Photography: John Seitz. Editor: Doane Harrison. Production and distribution: Paramount. Release date: April 24, 1944. Running time: 107 minutes. Cast: Fred MacMurray, Barbara Stanwyck (Phyllis Dietrichson), Edward G. Robinson, Porter Hall, Jean Heather, Tom Powers, Byron Barr, Richard Gaines, Fortunio Bonanova, John Philliber.

Hollywood Canteen (1944)

Executive producer: Jack Warner. Director: Delmer Daves. Screenplay: Delmer Daves. Photography: Bert Glennon. Editor: Christian Nyby. Production and distribution: Warner Bros. Release date: December 15, 1944. Running time: 124 minutes. Cast: the Andrews Sisters, Jack Benny, Joe E. Brown, Eddie Cantor, Kitty Carlisle, Jack Carson, Dane Clark, Joan Crawford, Helmut Dantine, Bette Davis, Faye Emerson, Victor Francen, John Garfield, Sydney Greenstreet, Alan Hale, Paul Henreid, Robert Hutton, Andrea King, Joan Leslie, Peter Lorre, Ida Lupino, Irene Manning, Nora Martin, Joan McCracken, Dolores Moran, Dennis Morgan, Janis Paige, Eleanor Parker, William Prince, Joyce Reynolds, John Ridgely, Roy Rogers, Trigger, S. Z. Sakall, Zachary Scott, Alexis Smith, Barbara Stanwyck (Herself), Craig Stevens, Joseph Szigeti, Donald Woods, Jane Wyman.

Christmas in Connecticut (1945)

Producer: William Jacobs. Director: Peter Godfrey. Story: Aileen Hamilton. Screenplay: Lionel Houser, Adele Comandini. Photography: Carl Guthrie. Editor: Frank Magee. Production and distribution: Warner Bros. Release date: August 11, 1945. Running time: 102 minutes. Cast: Barbara Stanwyck (Elizabeth Lane), Dennis Morgan, Sydney Greenstreet, Reginald Gardiner, S. Z. Sakall, Robert Shayne, Una O'Connor, Frank Jenks, Joyce Compton, Dick Elliott.

My Reputation (1946)

Producer: Henry Blanke. Director: Curtis Bernhardt. Based on the novel *Instruct My Sorrows* by Clare Jaynes. Screenplay: Catherine Turney. Photography: James Wong Howe. Editor: David Weisbart. Production and distribution: Warner Bros. Release date: January 26, 1946. Running time: 94 minutes. Cast: Barbara Stanwyck (Jessica Drummond),

George Brent, Warner Anderson, Lucile Watson, John Ridgely, Eve Arden, Jerome Cowan, Esther Dale, Scotty Beckett, Bobby Cooper, Leona Maricle, Mary Servoss, Cecil Cunningham, Janis Wilson, Ann E. Todd.

The Bride Wore Boots (1946)
Producer: Seton I. Miller. Director: Irving Pichel. Based on the play *The Odds on Mrs. Oakley* by Harry Segall. Screenplay: Dwight Mitchell Wiley. Photography: Stuart Thompson. Editor: Ellsworth Hoagland. Production and distribution: Paramount. Release date: May 31, 1946. Running time: 85 minutes. Cast: Barbara Stanwyck (Sally Warren), Robert Cummings, Diana Lynn, Patric Knowles, Peggy Wood, Robert Benchley, Willie Best, Natalie Wood, Gregory Marshall, Mary Young.

The Strange Love of Martha Ivers (1946)
Director: Lewis Milestone. Story: Jack Patrick. Screenplay: Robert Rossen. Photography: Victor Milner. Editor: Archie Marshek. Production: Hal Wallis Productions. Distribution: Paramount. Release date: July 24, 1946. Running time: 117 minutes. Cast: Barbara Stanwyck (Martha Ivers), Van Heflin, Lizabeth Scott, Kirk Douglas, Judith Anderson, Roman Bohnen, Darryl Hickman, Janis Wilson, Ann Doran, Frank Orth, James Flavin, Mickey Kuhn, Charles D. Brown.

California (1947)
Producer: Seton I. Miller. Director: John Farrow. Story: Boris Ingster. Screenplay: Frank Butler, Theodore Strauss. Photography: Ray Rennahan. Editor: Eda Warren. Production and distribution: Paramount ("A John Farrow Production" received credit). Release date: February 21, 1947. Running time: 97 minutes. Cast: Ray Milland, Barbara Stanwyck (Lily Bishop), Barry Fitzgerald, George Coulouris, Albert Dekker, Anthony Quinn, Frank Faylen, Gavin Muir, James Burke, Eduardo Ciannelli, Roman Bohnen, Argentina Brunetti, Howard Freeman, Julia Faye.

The Two Mrs. Carrolls (1947)
Producer: Mark Hellinger. Director: Peter Godfrey. Based on the play by Martin Vale. Screenplay: Thomas Job. Photography: Peverell Marley. Editor: Frederick Richards. Production and distribution: Warner Bros. Release date: March 4, 1947. Running time: 99 minutes. Cast: Humphrey Bogart, Barbara Stanwyck (Sally Morton Carroll), Alexis Smith, Nigel Bruce, Isobel Elsom, Patrick O'Moore, Ann Carter, Anita Sharp-Bolster, Barry Bernard.

The Other Love (1947)

Director: André De Toth. Based on the short story "Beyond" by Erich Maria Remarque. Screenplay: Ladislas Fodor, Harry Brown. Photography: Victor Milner. Editor: Walter Thompson. Production: Enterprise. Distribution: United Artists ("The David Lewis Production" received credit). Release date: May 14, 1947. Running time: 95 minutes. Cast: Barbara Stanwyck (Karen Duncan), David Niven, Richard Conte, Gilbert Roland, Joan Lorring, Lenore Aubert, Maria Palmer, Natalie Schafer, Edward Ashley, Richard Hale.

Cry Wolf (1947)

Producer: Henry Blanke. Director: Peter Godfrey. Based on the novel by Marjorie Carleton. Screenplay: Catherine Turney. Photography: Carl Guthrie. Editor: Folmar Blangsted. Production and distribution: Warner Bros. ("A Thomson Production" received credit). Release date: August 19, 1947. Running time: 83 minutes. Cast: Errol Flynn, Barbara Stanwyck (Sandra Marshall), Geraldine Brooks, Richard Basehart, Jerome Cowan, John Ridgely, Patricia Barry, Rory Mallinson, Helene Thimig, Paul Stanton, Barry Bernard.

B.F.'s Daughter (1948)

Producer: Edwin H. Knopf. Director: Robert Z. Leonard. Based on the novel by John P. Marquand. Screenplay: Luther Davis. Photography: Joseph Ruttenberg. Editor: George White. Production and distribution: MGM/Loew's ("A Robert Z. Leonard Production" received credit). Release date: April 2, 1948. Running time: 108 minutes. Cast: Barbara Stanwyck (Pauline "Polly" Fulton Brett), Van Heflin, Charles Coburn, Richard Hart, Keenan Wynn, Margaret Lindsay, Spring Byington, Marshall Thompson, Barbara Laage, Thomas E. Breen, Fred Nurney.

Sorry, Wrong Number (1948)

Producer: Hal Wallis. Director: Anatole Litvak. Based on the radio play by Lucille Fletcher. Screenplay: Lucille Fletcher. Photography: Sol Polito. Editor: Warren Low. Production: Hal Wallis Productions. Distribution: Paramount. Release date: September 1, 1948. Running time: 89 minutes. Cast: Barbara Stanwyck (Leona Stevenson), Burt Lancaster, Ann Richards, Wendell Corey, Harold Vermilyea, Ed Begley, Leif Erickson, William Conrad, John Bromfield, Jimmy Hunt, Dorothy Neumann, Paul Fierro.

The Lady Gambles (1949)

Producer: Michael Kraike. Director: Michael Gordon. Story: Lewis Meltzer, Oscar Saul. Adaptation: Halsted Welles. Screenplay: Roy Huggins. Photography: Russell Metty. Editor: Milton Carruth. Production and distribution: Universal. Release date: May 20,

1949. Running time: 99 minutes. Cast: Barbara Stanwyck (Joan Boothe), Robert Preston, Stephen McNally, Edith Barrett, John Hoyt, Elliott Sullivan, John Harmon, Philip Van Zandt, Leif Erickson, Curt Conway, Houseley Stevenson.

East Side, West Side (1949)

Producer: Voldemar Vetluguin. Director: Mervyn LeRoy. Based on the novel by Marcia Davenport. Screenplay: Isobel Lennart. Photography: Charles Rosher. Editor: Harold F. Kress. Production and distribution: MGM/Loew's ("A Mervyn LeRoy Production" received credit). Release date: December 22, 1949. Running time: 108 minutes. Cast: Barbara Stanwyck (Jessie Bourne), James Mason, Van Heflin, Ava Gardner, Cyd Charisse, Nancy Davis, Gale Sondergaard, William Conrad, Raymond Greenleaf, Douglas Kennedy, Beverly Michaels, William Frawley, Lisa Golm, Tom Powers.

The File on Thelma Jordon (1950)

Producer: Hal B. Wallis. Director: Robert Siodmak. Story: Marty Holland. Screenplay: Ketti Frings. Photography: George Barnes. Editor: Warren Low. Production: Wallis-Hazen. Distribution: Paramount ("Hal Wallis' Production" received credit). Release date: January 18, 1950. Running time: 100 minutes. Cast: Barbara Stanwyck (Thelma Jordon), Wendell Corey, Paul Kelly, Joan Tetzel, Stanley Ridges, Richard Rober, Minor Watson, Barry Kelley, Kasey Rogers, Basil Ruysdael, Jane Novak, Gertrude Hoffman, Harry Antrim, Kate Drain Lawson, Theresa Harris, Byron Barr, Geraldine Wall, Jonathan Corey, Robin Corey.

No Man of Her Own (1950)

Producer: Richard Maibaum. Director: Mitchell Leisen. Based on the novel *I Married a Dead Man* by William Irish. Screenplay: Sally Benson, Catherine Turney. Photography: Daniel L. Fapp. Editor: Alma Macrorie. Production and distribution: Paramount ("A Mitchell Leisen Production" received credit). Release date: May 3, 1950. Running time: 98 minutes. Cast: Barbara Stanwyck (Helen Ferguson), John Lund, Jane Cowl, Phyllis Thaxter, Lyle Bettger, Henry O'Neill, Richard Denning, Carole Mathews, Harry Antrim, Catherine Craig, Esther Dale, Milburn Stone, Griff Barnett.

The Furies (1950)

Producer: Hal B. Wallis. Director: Anthony Mann. Based on the novel by Niven Busch. Screenplay: Charles Schnee. Photography: Victor Milner. Editor: Archie Marshek. Production: Wallis-Hazen. Distribution: Paramount. Release date: August 16, 1950. Running time: 109 minutes. Cast: Barbara Stanwyck (Vance Jeffords), Wendell Corey, Walter Huston, Judith Anderson, Gilbert Roland, Thomas Gomez, Beulah Bondi, Albert Dekker, John Bromfield, Wallace Ford, Blanche Yurka, Louis Jean Heydt, Frank Ferguson, Charles Evans, Movita, Craig Kelly, Myrna Dell.

To Please a Lady (1950)

Director: Clarence Brown. Screenplay: Barré Lyndon, Marge Decker. Photography: Harold Rosson. Editor: Robert J. Kern. Production and distribution: MGM/Loew's ("A Clarence Brown Production" received credit). Release date: October 13, 1950. Running time: 91 minutes. Cast: Clark Gable, Barbara Stanwyck (Regina Forbes), Adolphe Menjou, Will Geer, Roland Winters, William C. McGaw, Lela Bliss, Emory Parnell, Frank Jenks, Helen Spring, Bill Hickman, Lew Smith, Ted Husing.

The Man with a Cloak (1951)

Producer: Stephen Ames. Director: Fletcher Markle. Story: John Dickson Carr. Screenplay: Frank Fenton. Photography: George J. Folsey. Editor: Newell P. Kimlin. Production and distribution: MGM/Loew's. Release date: October 19, 1951. Running time: 81 minutes. Cast: Joseph Cotten, Barbara Stanwyck (Lorna Bounty), Louis Calhern, Leslie Caron, Joe De Santis, Jim Backus, Margaret Wycherly, Richard Hale, Nicholas Joy, Roy Roberts, Mitchell Lewis.

Clash by Night (1952)

Producer: Harriet Parsons. Director: Fritz Lang. Based on the play by Clifford Odets. Screenplay: Alfred Hayes. Photography: Nicholas Musuraca. Editor: George Amy. Production: Wald-Krasna Productions, RKO Radio Pictures. Distribution: RKO Radio Pictures. Release date: June 16, 1952. Running time: 105 minutes. Cast: Barbara Stanwyck (Mae Doyle D'Amato), Paul Douglas, Robert Ryan, Marilyn Monroe, J. Carrol Naish, Silvio Minciotti, Keith Andes.

Jeopardy (1953)

Producer: Sol Baer Fielding. Director: John Sturges. Based on the radio play *A Question of Time* by Maurice Zimm. Screenplay: Mel Dinelli. Photography: Victor Milner. Editor: Newell P. Kimlin. Production and distribution: MGM/Loew's. Release date: March 30, 1953. Running time: 69 minutes. Cast: Barbara Stanwyck (Helen Stilwin), Barry Sullivan, Ralph Meeker, Lee Aaker.

Titanic (1953)

Producer: Charles Brackett. Director: Jean Negulesco. Screenplay: Charles Brackett, Walter Reisch, Richard L. Breen. Photography: Joe MacDonald. Editor: Louis Loeffler. Production and distribution: 20th Century–Fox. Release date: May 27, 1953. Running time: 98 minutes. Cast: Clifton Webb, Barbara Stanwyck (Julia Sturges), Robert Wagner, Audrey Dalton, Thelma Ritter, Brian Aherne, Richard Basehart, Allyn Joslyn, James Todd, Frances Bergen, William Johnstone.

All I Desire (1953)

Producer: Ross Hunter. Director: Douglas Sirk. Based on the novel *Stopover* by Carol Brink. Adaptation: Gina Kaus. Screenplay: James Gunn, Robert Blees. Photography: Carl Guthrie. Editor: Milton Carruth. Production and distribution: Universal. Release date: July 3, 1953. Running time: 79 minutes. Cast: Barbara Stanwyck (Naomi Murdoch), Richard Carlson, Lyle Bettger, Marcia Henderson, Lori Nelson, Maureen O'Sullivan, Richard Long, Billy Gray, Lotte Stein, Dayton Lummis, Fred Nurney.

Blowing Wild (1953)

Producer: Milton Sperling. Director: Hugo Fregonese. Writer: Philip Yordan. Photography: Sid Hickox. Editor: Alan Crosland Jr. Production: United States Pictures. Distribution: Warner Bros. Release date: October 17, 1953. Running time: 90 minutes. Cast: Gary Cooper, Barbara Stanwyck (Marina Conway), Ruth Roman, Anthony Quinn, Ward Bond, Ian MacDonald, Richard Karlan, Juan García.

The Moonlighter (1953)

Producer: Joseph Bernhard. Director: Roy Rowland. Story and screenplay: Niven Busch. Photography: Bert Glennon. Editor: Terry Morse. Production: Abtcon Pictures/J.B. Productions. Distribution: Warner Bros. Release date: September 19, 1953. Running time: 77 minutes. Cast: Barbara Stanwyck (Rela), Fred MacMurray, Ward Bond, William Ching, John Dierkes, Morris Ankrum, Jack Elam, Charles Halton, Norman Leavitt, Sam Flint, Myra Marsh, William Kerwin, Tom Keene.

Executive Suite (1954)

Producer: John Houseman. Director: Robert Wise. Based on the novel by Cameron Hawley. Screenplay: Ernest Lehman. Photography: George Folsey. Editor: Ralph E. Winters. Production and distribution: MGM/Loew's. Release date: April 20, 1954. Running time: 104 minutes. Cast: William Holden, June Allyson, Barbara Stanwyck (Julia O. Tredway), Fredric March, Walter Pidgeon, Shelley Winters, Paul Douglas, Louis Calhern, Dean Jagger, Nina Foch, Tim Considine, William Phipps, Lucy Knoch, Edgar Stehli, Mary Adams, Virginia Brissac, Harry Shannon.

Witness to Murder (1954)

Producer: Chester Erskine. Director: Roy Rowland. Screenplay: Chester Erskine. Photography: John Alton. Editor: Robert Swink. Production: Chester Erskine Pictures. Distribution: United Artists. Release date: April 15, 1954. Running time: 83 minutes. Cast: Barbara Stanwyck (Cheryl Draper), George Sanders, Gary Merrill, Jesse White, Harry Shannon, Claire Carleton, Lewis Martin, Dick Elliott, Harry Tyler, Juanita Moore, Joy Hallward, Adeline de Walt Reynolds.

Cattle Queen of Montana (1954)

Producer: Benedict Bogeaus. Director: Allan Dwan. Screenplay: Robert Blees, Howard Estabrook. Photography: John Alton. Editor: James Leicester. Production: Filmcrest Productions/RKO Radio Pictures. Distribution: RKO Radio Pictures. Release date: November 18, 1954. Running time: 88 minutes. Cast: Barbara Stanwyck (Sierra Nevada Jones), Ronald Reagan, Gene Evans, Lance Fuller, Anthony Caruso, Jack Elam, Yvette Duguay, Morris Ankrum, Chubby Johnson, Myron Healey, Rodd Redwing, Paul Birch, Byron Foulger, Burt Mustin.

The Violent Men (1955)

Producer: Lewis J. Rachmil. Director: Rudolph Maté. Based on the novel *Smoky Valley* by Donald Hamilton. Screenplay: Harry Kleiner. Photography: Burnett Guffey, W. Howard Greene. Editor: Jerome Thoms. Production and distribution: Columbia. Release date: January 26, 1955. Running time: 96 minutes. Cast: Glenn Ford, Barbara Stanwyck (Martha Wilkison), Edward G. Robinson, Dianne Foster, Brian Keith, May Wynn, Warner Anderson, Basil Ruysdael, Lita Milan, Richard Jaeckel, James Westerfield, Jack Kelly, Willis Bouchey, Harry Shannon.

Escape to Burma (1955)

Producer: Benedict Bogeaus. Director: Allan Dwan. Based on the short story "Bow Tamely to Me" by Kenneth Perkins. Screenplay: Talbot Jennings, Hobart Donavan. Photography: John Alton. Editor: James Leicester. Production: Filmcrest Productions/RKO Radio Pictures. Distribution: RKO Radio Pictures. Release date: April 9, 1955. Running time: 86 minutes. Cast: Barbara Stanwyck (Gwen Moore), Robert Ryan, David Farrar, Murvyn Vye, Lisa Montell, Robert Warwick, Reginald Denny, Robert Cabal, Peter Coe, Alex Montoya, Anthony Numkena, John Mansfield, Gavin Muir.

There's Always Tomorrow (1956)

Producer: Ross Hunter. Director: Douglas Sirk. Remake of 1934 film of same name. Based on a story by Ursula Parrott. Screenplay: Bernard C. Schoenfeld. Photography: Russell Metty. Editor: William M. Morgan. Production and distribution: Universal. Release date: February 1956. Running time: 84 minutes. Cast: Barbara Stanwyck (Norma), Fred MacMurray, Joan Bennett, William Reynolds, Pat Crowley, Gigi Perreau, Jane Darwell, Race Gentry, Myrna Hansen, Judy Nugent, Paul Smith, Helen Kleeb, Jane Howard, Frances Mercer, Sheila Bromley, Dorothy Bruce, Hermine Sterler, Fred Nurney, Hal Smith.

The Maverick Queen (1956)

Producer: Herbert J. Yates. Director: Joe Kane. Based on the novel by Zane Grey. Screenplay: Kenneth Gamet, DeVallon Scott. Photography: Jack Marta. Editor: Richard L. Van Enger. Production and distribution: Republic. Release date: May 3, 1956. Running time: 90 minutes. Cast: Barbara Stanwyck (Kit Banion), Barry Sullivan, Scott Brady, Mary Murphy, Wallace Ford, Howard Petrie, Jim Davis, Emile Meyer, Walter Sande, George Keymas, John Doucette, Taylor Holmes, Pierre Watkin.

These Wilder Years (1956)

Producer: Jules Schermer. Director: Roy Rowland. Screenplay: Frank Fenton. Story: Ralph Wheelwright. Photography: George J. Folsey. Editor: Ben Lewis. Production and distribution: MGM/Loew's. Release date: August 17, 1956. Running time: 91 minutes. Cast: James Cagney, Barbara Stanwyck (Ann Dempster), Walter Pidgeon, Betty Lou Keim, Don Dubbins, Edward Andrews, Basil Ruysdael, Grandon Rhodes, Will Wright, Lewis Martin, Dorothy Adams, Dean Jones, Herb Vigran.

Crime of Passion (1957)

Producer: Bob Goldstein. Director: Gerd Oswald. Story and screenplay: Jo Eisinger. Photography: Joseph La Shelle. Editor: Marjorie Fowler. Production: B.G. Productions. Distribution: United Artists. Release date: January 9, 1957. Running time: 84 minutes. Cast: Barbara Stanwyck (Kathy Ferguson Doyle), Sterling Hayden, Raymond Burr, Fay Wray, Virginia Grey, Royal Dano, Robert Griffin, Dennis Cross, Jay Adler, Stuart Whitman, Malcolm Atterbury, Robert Quarry, Gail Bonney, Joe Conley.

Trooper Hook (1957)

Producer: Sol Baer Fielding. Director: Charles Marquis Warren. Based on the short story "Sergeant Houck" by Jack Schaefer. Screenplay: Martin Berkeley, David Victor, Herbert Little Jr. Photography: Ellsworth Fredericks. Editor: Fred W. Berger. Production: Fielding Productions/Filmaster Productions. Distribution: United Artists. Release date: July 12, 1957. Running time: 81 minutes. Cast: Joel McCrea, Barbara Stanwyck (Cora Sutliff), Earl Holliman, Edward Andrews, John Dehner, Susan Kohner, Royal Dano, Celia Lovsky, Stanley Adams.

Forty Guns (1957)

Director: Samuel Fuller. Screenplay: Samuel Fuller. Photography: Joseph Biroc. Editor: Gene Fowler Jr. Production: Globe Enterprises. Distribution: 20th Century–Fox. Release date: September 1, 1957. Running time: 79 minutes. Cast: Barbara Stanwyck (Jessica Drummond), Barry Sullivan, Dean Jagger, John Ericson, Gene Barry, Robert Dix, Jidge Carroll, Paul Dubov, Gerald Milton, Ziva Rodann, Hank Worden, Neyle Morrow, Chuck Roberson, Chuck Hayward.

Walk on the Wild Side (1962)

Producer: Charles K. Feldman. Director: Edward Dmytryk. Based on the novel *A Walk on the Wild Side* by Nelson Algren. Screenplay: John Fante, Edmund Morris. Photography: Joseph MacDonald. Editor: Harry Gerstad. Production: Famous Artists Productions. Distribution: Columbia. Release date: February 21, 1962. Running time: 114 minutes. Cast: Laurence Harvey, Capucine, Jane Fonda, Anne Baxter, Barbara Stanwyck (Jo Courtney), Joanna Moore, Richard Rust, Karl Swenson, Don "Red" Barry, Juanita Moore, John Anderson, Ken Lynch, Todd Armstrong, Sherry O'Neil, John Bryant, Kathryn Card.

Roustabout (1964)

Producer: Hal B. Wallis. Director: John Rich. Story: Allan Weiss. Screenplay: Allan Weiss, Anthony Lawrence. Photography: Lucien Ballard. Editor: Warren Low. Production: Hal Wallis Productions. Distribution: Paramount. Release date: November 11, 1964. Running time: 101 minutes. Cast: Elvis Presley, Barbara Stanwyck (Maggie Morgan), Joan Freeman, Leif Erickson, Sue Ane Langdon, Pat Buttram, Joan Staley, Dabbs Greer, Steve Brodie, Norman Grabowski, Jack Albertson, Jane Dulo, Joel Fluellen, Wilda Taylor.

The Night Walker (1964)

Producer: William Castle. Director: William Castle. Based on a story by Elizabeth Kata. Screenplay: Robert Bloch. Photography: Harold Stine. Editor: Edwin H. Bryant. Production: Castle. Distribution: Universal. Release date: December 30, 1964. Running time: 86 minutes. Cast: Robert Taylor, Barbara Stanwyck (Irene Trent), Judi Meredith, Hayden Rorke, Rochelle Hudson, Marjorie Bennett, Jess Barker, Tetsu Komai, Lloyd Bochner.

APPENDIX III: RADIO CHRONOLOGY

Lux Radio Theatre (1936)
Episode 92: "Main Street"
Director: Frank Woodruff. Based on the novel by Sinclair Lewis. Radio play: George Wells, Sanford Barnett. Production: Lux. Distribution: CBS. Recorded at the Music Box Theatre, Hollywood, Calif. Original broadcast: August 3, 1936. Running time: 60 minutes. Host: Cecil B. DeMille. Cast: Barbara Stanwyck, Fred MacMurray.

Lux Radio Theatre (1937)
Episode 145: "Stella Dallas"
Director: Frank Woodruff. Based on a screenplay by Sarah Y. Mason and Victor Heerman. Based on a novel by Olive Higgins Prouty. Radio play: George Wells, Sanford Barnett. Production: Lux. Distribution: CBS. Recorded at the Music Box Theatre, Hollywood, Calif. Original broadcast: October 11, 1937. Running time: 60 minutes. Host: Cecil B. DeMille. Cast: Barbara Stanwyck (Stella Dallas), John Boles.

The Charlie McCarthy Show (1937)
Episode 26: "Guest: Barbara Stanwyck"
Production: Chase and Sanborn Coffee. Distribution: NBC. Original broadcast: October 31, 1937. Running time: 60 minutes. Host: Jim Ameche. Cast: Barbara Stanwyck, Charlie McCarthy, Edgar Bergen, Dorothy Lamour, W. C. Fields, Nelson Eddy.

The Charlie McCarthy Show (1937)
Episode 27: "Guest: Barbara Stanwyck"
Production: Chase and Sanborn Coffee. Distribution: NBC. Original broadcast: November 7, 1937. Running time: 60 minutes. Host: Jim Ameche. Cast: Barbara Stanwyck, Charlie McCarthy, Edgar Bergen, Dorothy Lamour, W. C. Fields, Nelson Eddy.

Lux Radio Theatre (1937)

Episode 153: "These Three"

Director: Frank Woodruff. Based on a screenplay by Lillian Hellman. Radio play: George Wells, Sanford Barnett. Production: Lux. Distribution: CBS. Recorded at the Music Box Theatre, Hollywood, Calif. Original broadcast: December 6, 1937. Running time: 60 minutes. Host: Cecil B. DeMille. Cast: Barbara Stanwyck, Errol Flynn.

Lux Radio Theatre (1938)

Episode 170: "Dark Victory"

Director: Frank Woodruff. Based on a screenplay by Casey Robinson. Based on a play by George Emerson Brewer Jr. and Bertram Bloch. Radio play: George Wells, Sanford Barnett. Production: Lux. Distribution: CBS. Recorded at the Music Box Theatre, Hollywood, Calif. Original broadcast: April 4, 1938. Running time: 60 minutes. Host: Cecil B. DeMille. Cast: Barbara Stanwyck (Judith Traherne), Melvyn Douglas.

The Charlie McCarthy Show (1938)

Episode 56: "Guest: Barbara Stanwyck" Segment: "Barbara Stanwyck's Swimming Pool"

Production: Chase and Sanborn Coffee. Distribution: NBC. Original broadcast: May 29, 1938. Running time: 60 minutes. Host: Jim Ameche. Cast: Barbara Stanwyck, Charlie McCarthy, Edgar Bergen, Dorothy Lamour, W. C. Fields, Nelson Eddy.

The Charlie McCarthy Show (1939)

Episode 92: "Guest: Barbara Stanwyck and Sterling Holloway" Segment: "Honeymoon Around the World"

Production: Chase and Sanborn Coffee. Distribution: NBC. Original broadcast: February 5, 1939. Running time: 60 minutes. Host: Jim Ameche. Cast: Barbara Stanwyck, Sterling Holloway, Charlie McCarthy, Edgar Bergen, Dorothy Lamour, W. C. Fields, Nelson Eddy.

Lux Radio Theatre (1939)

Episode 210: "So Big"

Director: Frank Woodruff. Based on a screenplay by J. Grubb Alexander and Robert Lord. Based on a novel by Edna Ferber. Radio play: George Wells, Sanford Barnett. Production: Lux. Distribution: CBS. Recorded at the Music Box Theatre, Hollywood, Calif. Original broadcast: March 13, 1939. Running time: 60 minutes. Host: Cecil B. DeMille. Cast: Barbara Stanwyck (Selina Peake De Jong), Preston Foster.

Lux Radio Theatre (1939)

Episode 229: "Wuthering Heights"

Director: Sanford Barnett. Based on the novel by Emily Brontë. Radio play: George Wells, Sanford Barnett. Production: Lux. Distribution: CBS. Recorded at Vine Street Playhouse, Hollywood, Calif. Original broadcast: September 18, 1939. Running time: 60 minutes. Host: Cecil B. DeMille. Cast: Barbara Stanwyck (Cathy Earnshaw), Brian Aherne.

Lux Radio Theatre (1939)

Episode 236: "Only Yesterday"

Director: Sanford Barnett. Radio play: George Wells, Sanford Barnett. Production: Lux. Distribution: CBS. Recorded at Vine Street Playhouse, Hollywood, Calif. Original broadcast: November 6, 1939. Running time: 60 minutes. Host: Cecil B. DeMille. Cast: Barbara Stanwyck, George Brent.

The Jack Benny Show (1940)

Episode 11X14: "Golden Boy"

Production: Jell-O. Distribution: NBC Red. Original broadcast: January 7, 1940. Running time: 29 minutes. Cast: Barbara Stanwyck, Jack Benny, Mary Livingstone, Eddie Anderson.

Lux Radio Theatre (1940)

Episode 256: "Remember the Night"

Director: Sanford Barnett. Based on a screenplay by Preston Sturges. Radio play: George Wells, Sanford Barnett. Production: Lux. Distribution: CBS. Recorded at Vine Street Playhouse, Hollywood, Calif. Original broadcast: March 25, 1940. Running time: 60 minutes. Host: Cecil B. DeMille. Cast: Fred MacMurray, Barbara Stanwyck (Lee Leander).

Screen Guild Theater (1940)

Episode 50: "Allergic to Love"

Production: Gulf Gasoline. Distribution: CBS. Original broadcast: March 31, 1940. Running time: 30 minutes. Cast: Barbara Stanwyck, Robert Taylor, Franklin Pangborn.

Lux Radio Theatre (1940)

Episode 261: "Smilin' Through"

Director: Sanford Barnett. Radio play: George Wells, Sanford Barnett. Production: Lux. Distribution: CBS. Recorded at Vine Street Playhouse, Hollywood, Calif. Original broadcast: April 29, 1940. Running time: 60 minutes. Host: Cecil B. DeMille. Cast: Robert Taylor, Barbara Stanwyck.

Screen Guild Theater (1941)

Episode 84: "Meet John Doe"

Based on a screenplay by Robert Riskin. Production: Gulf Gasoline. Distribution: CBS. Original broadcast: September 28, 1941. Running time: 30 minutes. Cast: Gary Cooper, Barbara Stanwyck (Ann Mitchell), Edward Arnold.

Screen Guild Theater (1941)

Episode 87: "Nothing Sacred"

Based on a screenplay by Ben Hecht. Production: Gulf Gasoline. Distribution: CBS. Original broadcast: October 19, 1941. Running time: 30 minutes. Cast: Barbara Stanwyck (Hazel Flagg), Robert Taylor, James Gleason.

Lux Radio Theatre (1942)

Episode 362: "The Lady Eve"

Director: Sanford Barnett. Based on a screenplay by Preston Sturges. Story: Monckton Hoffe. Radio play: George Wells, Sanford Barnett. Production: Lux. Distribution: CBS. Recorded at Studio A, Hollywood, Calif. Original broadcast: March 9, 1942. Running time: 45 minutes. Host: Cecil B. DeMille. Cast: Barbara Stanwyck (Jean Harrington), Ray Milland.

Note: Program was 45 minutes due to Roosevelt administration broadcast.

Lux Radio Theatre (1942)

Episode 349: "Penny Serenade"

Director: Sanford Barnett. Based on a screenplay by Morrie Ryskind. Story: Martha Cheavens. Radio play: George Wells, Sanford Barnett. Production: Lux. Distribution: CBS. Recorded at Studio A, Hollywood, Calif. Original broadcast: April 27, 1942. Running time: 60 minutes. Host: Cecil B. DeMille. Cast: Robert Taylor, Barbara Stanwyck (Julie Gardiner Adams), Beulah Bondi.

Lux Radio Theatre (1942)

Episode 354: "Ball of Fire"

Director: Sanford Barnett. Based on a screenplay by Charles Brackett and Billy Wilder. Story: Billy Wilder, Thomas Monroe. Radio play: George Wells, Sanford Barnett. Production: Lux. Distribution: CBS. Recorded at Studio A, Hollywood, Calif. Original broadcast: June 1, 1942. Running time: 60 minutes. Host: Cecil B. DeMille. Cast: Barbara Stanwyck (Sugarpuss O'Shea), Fred MacMurray.

Lux Radio Theatre (1942)

Episode 361: "This Above All"

Director: Sanford Barnett. Based on a screenplay by R. C. Sherriff. Based on the novel by Eric Knight. Radio play: George Wells, Sanford Barnett. Production: Lux. Distribution: CBS. Recorded at Studio A, Hollywood, Calif. Original broadcast: September 14, 1942. Running time: 60 minutes. Host: Cecil B. DeMille. Cast: Tyrone Power, Barbara Stanwyck (Prudence Cathaway).

The Jack Benny Show (1942)

Episode 13X2: "Jack Takes Two Cadets to Barbara Stanwyck's House"

Production: Grape Nuts Flakes. Distribution: NBC Red. Original broadcast: October 11, 1942. Running time: 30 minutes. Cast: Barbara Stanwyck, Jack Benny, Mary Livingstone, Eddie Anderson.

Screen Guild Theater (1942)

Episode 116: "My Favorite Wife"

Based on a screenplay by Bella Spewack and Samuel Spewack. Production: Lady Esther. Distribution: CBS. Original broadcast: November 2, 1942. Running time: 30 minutes. Cast: Barbara Stanwyck (Ellen Arden), Robert Taylor.

Lux Radio Theatre (1942)

Episode 371: "The Gay Sisters"

Director: Sanford Barnett. Based on a screenplay by Lenore J. Coffee. Based on the novel by Stephen Longstreet. Radio play: George Wells, Sanford Barnett. Production: Lux. Distribution: CBS. Recorded at Studio A, Hollywood, Calif. Original broadcast: November 23, 1942. Running time: 60 minutes. Host: Cecil B. DeMille. Cast: Barbara Stanwyck (Fiona Gaylord), Robert Young.

The Charlie McCarthy Show (1943)

Episode 287: "Guest: Barbara Stanwyck" Segment: "Charlie's Manager"

Production: Chase and Sanborn Coffee. Distribution: NBC. Original broadcast: May 2, 1943. Running time: 30 minutes. Host: Jim Ameche. Cast: Barbara Stanwyck, Sterling Holloway, Charlie McCarthy, Edgar Bergen, Dorothy Lamour, Edward Arnold.

Lux Radio Theatre (1943)

Episode 402: "The Great Man's Lady"

Director: Sanford Barnett. Based on a screenplay by W. L. River. Based on the short story by Viña Delmar. Radio play: George Wells, Sanford Barnett. Production: Lux. Distribution: CBS. Recorded at Studio A, Hollywood, Calif. Original broadcast: June 28, 1943.

Running time: 60 minutes. Host: Cecil B. DeMille. Cast: Barbara Stanwyck (Hannah Sempler), Robert Young.

The Jack Benny Show (1943)
Episode 14X8: "Dennis Wants a Raise"
Production: Grape Nuts Flakes. Distribution: NBC. Original broadcast: November 28, 1943. Running time: 29 minutes. Cast: Barbara Stanwyck, Jack Benny, Mary Livingstone, Eddie Anderson.

The Jack Benny Show (1944)
Episode 14X24: "Dennis Dreams He Has a Radio Program"
Production: Grape Nuts Flakes. Distribution: NBC. Original broadcast: March 19, 1944. Running time: 29 minutes. Cast: Barbara Stanwyck, Jack Benny, Mary Livingstone, Eddie Anderson.

The Jack Benny Show (1944)
Episode 189: "Why Jack Is Not Going to Appear on Show"
Production: Lady Esther. Distribution: CBS. Original broadcast: March 27, 1944. Running time: 30 minutes. Cast: Jack Benny, Basil Rathbone, Barbara Stanwyck, Jean Hersholt.

Screen Guild Theater (1945)
Episode 235: "Double Indemnity"
Production: Lady Esther. Distribution: CBS. Original broadcast: March 5, 1945. Running time: 29 minutes. Cast: Fred MacMurray, Barbara Stanwyck, Walter Abel.

Screen Guild Theater (1946)
Episode 313: "Waterloo Bridge"
Based on the play by Robert E. Sherwood. Production: Lady Esther. Distribution: CBS. Original broadcast: September 9, 1946. Running time: 30 minutes. Cast: Barbara Stanwyck (Myra), Robert Taylor, Isabel Jewell.

Lux Radio Theatre (1947)
Episode 568: "My Reputation"
Director: Fred MacKaye. Based on a screenplay by Catherine Turney. Radio play: George Wells, Sanford Barnett. Production: Lux. Distribution: CBS. Recorded at Vine Street Playhouse, Hollywood, Calif. Original broadcast: April 21, 1947. Running time: 60 minutes. Host: William Keighley. Cast: Barbara Stanwyck (Jessica Drummond), George Brent.

Lux Radio Theatre (1947)

Episode 576: "The Other Love"

Director: Fred MacKaye. Based on a screenplay by Ladislas Fodor and Harry Brown. Radio play: George Wells, Sanford Barnett. Production: Lux. Distribution: CBS. Recorded at Vine Street Playhouse, Hollywood, Calif. Original broadcast: June 16, 1947. Running time: 60 minutes. Host: William Keighley. Cast: George Brent, Barbara Stanwyck (Karen Duncan).

Screen Guild Theater (1948)

Episode 382: "One Way Passage"

Based on a screenplay by Wilson Mizner and Joseph Jackson. Production: Camel Cigarettes. Distribution: CBS. Original broadcast: April 5, 1948. Running time: 30 minutes. Cast: Barbara Stanwyck (Joan), Robert Taylor, Ward Bond.

The Jack Benny Show (1948)

Episode 19X3: "Sorry, Wrong Number"

Radio play: Lucille Fletcher. Production: Lucky Strike. Distribution: NBC. Original broadcast: October 17, 1948. Running time: 29 minutes. Cast: Barbara Stanwyck (Leona Stevenson), Jack Benny, Mary Livingstone, Eddie Anderson.

The Jack Benny Show (1949)

Episode 19X28: "Dennis Dreams He's a Star"

Production: Lucky Strike. Distribution: NBC. Original broadcast: April 10, 1949. Running time: 30 minutes. Cast: Barbara Stanwyck, Jack Benny, Mary Livingstone, Eddie Anderson.

Screen Guild Theater (1949)

Episode 424: "Undercurrent"

Based on a screenplay by Edward Chodorov. Story: Thelma Strabel. Production: Camel Cigarettes. Distribution: NBC. Original broadcast: May 5, 1949. Running time: 30 minutes. Cast: Barbara Stanwyck (Ann Hamilton), Robert Taylor.

Screen Director's Playhouse (1949)

Episode 41: "Remember the Night"

Based on a screenplay by Preston Sturges. Production: Pabst Blue Ribbon Beer. Distribution: NBC. Original broadcast: October 31, 1949. Running time: 29 minutes. Cast: Barbara Stanwyck (Lee Leander), Gerald Mohr.

Lux Radio Theatre (1950)

Episode 684: "Sorry, Wrong Number"

Director: Fred MacKaye. Radio play: Lucille Fletcher. Production: Lux. Distribution: CBS. Recorded at Vine Street Playhouse, Hollywood, Calif. Original broadcast: January 9, 1950. Running time: 60 minutes. Host: William Keighley. Cast: Barbara Stanwyck (Leona Stevenson), Burt Lancaster.

Screen Guild Theater (1950)

Episode 452: "Double Indemnity"

Based on the novel by James M. Cain. Production: Camel Cigarettes. Distribution: NBC. Original broadcast: February 16, 1950. Running time: 30 minutes. Cast: Barbara Stanwyck (Phyllis Dietrichson), Robert Taylor.

Screen Director's Playhouse (1950)

Episode 74: "The Strange Love of Martha Ivers"

Based on a screenplay by Robert Rossen. Production: RCA. Distribution: NBC. Original broadcast: June 23, 1950. Running time: 30 minutes. Cast: Barbara Stanwyck (Martha Ivers).

Lux Radio Theatre (1950)

Episode 684: "Double Indemnity"

Director: Earl Ebi. Based on the novel by James M. Cain. Radio play: George Wells, Sanford Barnett. Production: Lux. Distribution: CBS. Recorded at Vine Street Playhouse, Hollywood, Calif. Original broadcast: October 30, 1950. Running time: 60 minutes. Host: William Keighley. Cast: Barbara Stanwyck (Phyllis Dietrichson), Fred MacMurray.

Lux Radio Theatre (1950)

Episode 724: "B.F.'s Daughter"

Director: Earl Ebi. Based on the novel by John P. Marquand. Radio play: George Wells, Sanford Barnett. Production: Lux. Distribution: CBS. Recorded at Vine Street Playhouse, Hollywood, Calif. Original broadcast: December 11, 1950. Running time: 60 minutes. Host: William Keighley. Cast: Barbara Stanwyck (Pauline "Polly" Fulton Brett), Stewart Granger.

Screen Director's Playhouse (1950)

Episode 81: "The Lady Gambles"

Based on a screenplay by Roy Huggins. Production: RCA. Distribution: NBC. Original broadcast: December 14, 1950. Running time: 60 minutes. Cast: Barbara Stanwyck (Joan Boothe), Stephen McNally, William Conrad.

Screen Director's Playhouse (1951)

Episode 94: "The File on Thelma Jordon"

Production: RCA. Distribution: NBC. Original broadcast: March 15, 1951. Running time: 60 minutes. Cast: Barbara Stanwyck, Wendell Corey, William Conrad.

Screen Director's Playhouse (1951)

Episode 94: "No Man of Her Own"

Based on a screenplay by Sally Benson and Catherine Turney. Production: RCA. Distribution: NBC. Original broadcast: September 21, 1951. Running time: 60 minutes. Cast: Barbara Stanwyck (Helen Ferguson).

Lux Radio Theatre (1952)

Episode 773: "Goodbye, My Fancy"

Director: Earl Ebi. Based on the play by Fay Kanin. Radio play: George Wells, Sanford Barnett. Production: Lux. Distribution: CBS. Recorded at Vine Street Playhouse, Hollywood, Calif. Original broadcast: January 14, 1952. Running time: 60 minutes. Host: William Keighley. Cast: Barbara Stanwyck (Agatha Reed), Robert Young.

Screen Guild Theatre (1952)

Episode 525: "Hold Back the Dawn"

Based on a screenplay by Charles Brackett. Production: Screen Guild Theatre. Distribution: CBS. Original broadcast: June 15, 1952. Running time: 30 minutes. Cast: Barbara Stanwyck (Emmy Brown), Jean Pierre Aumont.

Lux Radio Theatre (1954)

Episode 872: "Jeopardy"

Director: Earl Ebi. Based on a screenplay by Mel Dinelli. Story: Maurice Zimm. Radio play: George Wells, Sanford Barnett. Production: Lux. Distribution: CBS. Recorded at Vine Street Playhouse, Hollywood, Calif. Original broadcast: March 15, 1954. Running time: 60 minutes. Host: Irving Cummings. Cast: Barry Sullivan, Barbara Stanwyck (Helen Stilwin).

APPENDIX IV: TELEVISION CHRONOLOGY

The Ford Television Theatre (1956)
Episode 5.2: "Sudden Silence"
Producer: Jack Denove. Director: Lewis Allen. Story: William Heuman. Teleplay: Larry Marcus. Production: Ford Motor Company, Screen Gems. Distribution: ABC. Original air date: October 10, 1956. Running time: 30 minutes. Cast: Jimmy Baird, Trevor Bardette, Jim Hayward, Mort Mills, Jeff Morrow, Barbara Stanwyck (Irene Frazier).

Zane Grey Theatre (1958)
Episode 2.15: "The Freighter"
Creators: Luke Short, Charles A. Wallace. Producer: Hal Hudson. Director: Christian Nyby. Teleplay: Fred Freiberger. Photography: Guy Roe. Editor: Thomas Neff. Production: Four Star, Pamric, Zane Grey. Distribution: CBS. Original air date: January 17, 1958. Running time: 30 minutes. Cast: Barbara Stanwyck (Belle Garrison), Robert H. Harris, John Archer, James Bell, Jason Johnson, Bill Catching, Thomas Peters, Robert F. Hoy, Charles Tannen, Troy Melton.

Alcoa Theatre (1958)
Episode 1.21: "Three Years Dark"
Producer: Vincent M. Fennelly. Director: Robert Florey. Writer: Fred Freiberger. Photography: George E. Diskant. Editor: Arthur D. Hilton. Production: Four Star, Screen Gems, Showcase. Distribution: NBC. Original air date: June 23, 1958. Running time: 30 minutes. Cast: Barbara Stanwyck (Midge Varney), Malcolm Atterbury, Russ Conway, Valerie French, Gerald Mohr, Richard Reeves.

Goodyear Theatre (1958)
Episode 1.19: "Three Dark Years"
Director: Robert Florey. Writer: Fred Freiberger. Photography: Joseph F. Biroc. Production: Four Star. Distribution: NBC. Original air date: June 23, 1958. Running time: 30 minutes. Cast: Barbara Stanwyck (Midge Varney), Russ Conway, Gerald Mohr.

Decision (1958)

Episode 1.5: "Sudden Silence"

Producer: Jack Denove. Director: Lewis Allen. Teleplay: Larry Marcus. Photography: Frederick Gately. Production: Ford Motor Company, Screen Gems. Distribution: NBC. Original air date: August 3, 1958. Running time: 30 minutes. Cast: Malcolm Atterbury, Jimmy Baird, Trevor Bardette, Ralph Dumke, Robert Easton, Jim Hayward, Charlotte Knight, Jeff Morrow, Barbara Stanwyck (Irene Frazier).

Zane Grey Theatre (1958)

Episode 3.1: "Trail to Nowhere"

Creators: Luke Short, Charles A. Wallace. Producer: Helen Ainsworth. Director: William D. Faralla. Teleplay: Aaron Spelling. Editor: Thomas Neff. Production: Four Star, Pamric, Zane Grey. Distribution: CBS. Original air date: October 2, 1958. Running time: 30 minutes. Cast: Barbara Stanwyck (Julie Holman), David Janssen, Paul Genge, Irene Calvillo, Stephen Chase, Ian MacDonald, Allen Pinson, Dick Powell, Bill Quinn, Richard Shannon, Guy Wilkerson.

Zane Grey Theatre (1959)

Episode 3.15: "Hang the Heart High"

Creators: Luke Short, Charles A. Wallace. Producer: Helen Ainsworth. Director: William D. Faralla. Teleplay: John McGreevey. Editor: Thomas Neff. Production: Four Star, Pamric, Zane Grey. Distribution: CBS. Original air date: January 15, 1959. Running time: 30 minutes. Cast: Barbara Stanwyck (Regan Moore), David Janssen, Paul Richards, Lane Bradford, Margarita Cordova, Frank Harding, Dick Powell.

Zane Grey Theatre (1959)

Episode 4.2: "The Lone Woman"

Creators: Luke Short, Charles A. Wallace. Producer: Helen Ainsworth. Director: James Sheldon. Teleplay: Richard Fielder. Editor: Thomas Neff. Production: Four Star, Pamric, Zane Grey. Distribution: CBS. Original air date: October 8, 1959. Running time: 30 minutes. Cast: Barbara Stanwyck (Leona Butler), Martin Balsam, George Keymas, Joel Crothers, Shari Lee Bernath, Veronica Cartwright, Tom Masters, Dick Powell.

The Barbara Stanwyck Show (1960–1961)

Series, 37 Episodes

Executive producer: Louis F. Edelman. Producer: William H. Wright. Directors: Jacques Tourneur, David Lowell Rich, Richard Whorf, Robert Florey, Arthur Hiller, Don Taylor. Teleplays: Albert Beich, Jerome Gruskin, A. I. Bezzerides, Margaret Fitts, Blanche Hanalis, Leonard Praskins, John Hawkins. Photography: Hal Mohr. Editors: Carl Pierson, Bruce Shoengarth. Production: ESW Productions. Distribution: NBC. Original air dates: September 19, 1960–July 3, 1961. Running time: 30 minutes. Cast: Barbara Stanwyck (Herself, Hostess).

Wagon Train (1961)
Episode 5.3: "The Maud Frazer Story"
Director: David Butler. Story: Alford Van Ronkel. Teleplay: Norman Jolley, Alford Van Ronkel. Editor: Gene Palmer. Production: Revue Studios. Distribution: NBC. Original air date: October 11, 1961. Running time: 60 minutes. Cast: Robert Horton, John McIntire, Denny Miller, Barbara Stanwyck (Maud Frazer), Frank McGrath, Terry Wilson.

G.E. True Theater (1961)
Episode 10.8: "Star Witness: The Lili Parrish Story"
Director: Jacques Tourneur. Teleplay: James P. Cavanagh. Production: Revue Studios. Distribution: CBS. Original air date: November 8, 1961. Running time: 30 minutes. Cast: Ronald Reagan, Barbara Stanwyck (Lili Parrish), Bennye Gatteys, Ted Knight, Jack Mullaney, Lloyd Nolan, Paul Tripp.

Rawhide (1962)
Episode 4.14: "The Captain's Wife"
Producer: Endre Bohem. Director: Tay Garnett. Teleplay: John Dunkel. Photography: Jack Swain. Editor: Roland Gross. Production and distribution: CBS. Original air date: January 12, 1962. Running time: 50 minutes. Cast: Eric Fleming, Clint Eastwood (credit only), Sheb Wooley (credit only), Paul Brinegar, James Murdock, Steve Raines, Rocky Shahan, Robert Cabal, Barbara Stanwyck (Nora Holloway), John Howard, Robert Lowery, Nestor Paiva, Eugene Mazzola, Dennis Cross, Don C. Harvey, Bill Walker.

The Dick Powell Theatre (1962)
Episode 2.1: "Special Assignment"
Creator: Richard Alan Simmons. Producer: Aaron Spelling. Director: Don Taylor. Teleplay: Bob O'Brien, Ben Starr. Photography: George E. Diskant. Editor: Desmond Marquette. Production: Four Star. Distribution: NBC. Original air date: September 25, 1962. Running time: 60 minutes. Cast: Dick Powell, June Allyson, Edgar Bergen, Frances Bergen, Jackie Cooper, Lloyd Nolan, Mickey Rooney, Barbara Stanwyck (Irene Phillips), Lauren Gilbert, Kurt Russell, Gina Gillespie, John Newton, Michael Hinn, King Calder, Joe Conley, Bobby Johnson, Frank J. Scannell, David Armstrong, Wendy Russell, Everett Chambers.

Wagon Train (1962)

Episode 6.2: "The Caroline Casteel Story"

Director: Virgil W. Vogel. Teleplay: Gerry Day. Editor: Sam E. Waxman. Production: Revue Studios. Distribution: NBC. Original air date: September 26, 1962. Running time: 60 minutes. Cast: John McIntire, Denny Miller, Frank McGrath, Terry Wilson, Barbara Stanwyck (Caroline Casteel), Charles Drake, Roger Mobley, Robert F. Simon, Richard H. Cutting, Alice Frost, Kathleen Freeman, Dennis Rush, Renee Godfrey, Dal McKennon, Charles Horvath, Kenneth MacDonald.

The Untouchables (1962)

Episode 4.8: "Elegy"

Producer: Alvin Cooperman. Director: Robert Butler. Teleplay: Herman Groves. Photography: Charles Straumer. Editor: Ben Ray. Production: Desilu, Langford. Distribution: ABC. Original air date: November 20, 1962. Running time: 60 minutes. Cast: Robert Stack, John Larch, Peggy Ann Garner, Barbara Stanwyck (Lieutenant Agatha Stewart), Edward Asner, Walter Winchell, Woodrow Parfrey, Ernest Mason, William Bramley, William Sargent, Steve Harris, Virginia Capers, Andrea Darvi, Hope Summers, Edward Holmes.

The Untouchables (1963)

Episode 4.13: "Search for a Dead Man"

Producer: Alvin Cooperman. Director: Robert Butler. Teleplay: Harold Gast, Herman Groves. Photography: Charles Straumer. Editor: Axel Hubert Sr. Production: Desilu, Langford. Distribution: ABC. Original air date: January 1, 1963. Running time: 60 minutes. Cast: Robert Stack, Sheree North, Tom Reese, Edward Asner, Barbara Stanwyck (Lieutenant Agatha Stewart), Walter Winchell.

Wagon Train (1963)

Episode 7.1: "The Molly Kincaid Story"

Producer: Howard Christie. Director: Virgil W. Vogel. Teleplay: Gene L. Coon. Photography: Bud Thackery. Editor: Richard G. Wray. Production: Revue Studios. Distribution: NBC. Original air date: September 16, 1963. Running time: 75 minutes. Cast: John McIntire, Robert Fuller, Frank McGrath, Terry Wilson, Denny Miller, Carolyn Jones, Ray Danton, Barbara Stanwyck (Kate Crawley), Fabian, Brenda Scott, Michael Burns, Harry Carey Jr., Richard Reeves, Myron Healey, James Griffith, Michael Fox, Pamela Austin.

Calhoun: County Agent (1964)

Episode: "Pilot" (unaired)

Producers: Robert Alan Aurthur, Everett Chambers. Director: Stuart Rosenberg. Teleplay: Merle Miller. Production date: 1964. Cast: Ken Berry, Jackie Cooper, Howard Duff, Beverly Garland, Robert Lansing, Barbara Luna, Barbara Stanwyck (Abby Rayner).

Wagon Train (1964)

Episode 7.19: "The Kate Crawley Story"

Producer: Howard Christie. Director: Virgil W. Vogel. Teleplay: Norman Jolley. Editor: Gene Palmer. Production: Revue Studios. Distribution: NBC. Original air date: January 27, 1964. Running time: 75 minutes. Cast: John McIntire, Robert Fuller, Denny Miller, Frank McGrath, Terry Wilson, Michael Burns, Barbara Stanwyck (Kate Crawley).

The Big Valley (1965–1969)

Series, 112 Episodes

Executive producers: Arthur Gardner, Arnold Laven, Jules V. Levy. Creators: A. I. Bezzerides, Louis F. Edelman. Photography: Wilfred M. Cline, Charles Burke. Editors: Sherman Todd, Arthur Hilton, Desmond Marquette, Tom Rolf, Sherman A. Rose, Anthony Wollner. Production: Levee-Gardner-Laven, Four Star, Margate. Distribution: ABC. Original air dates: September 15, 1965–May 19, 1969. Running time: 60 minutes. Cast: Richard Long, Peter Breck, Lee Majors, Linda Evans, Barbara Stanwyck (Victoria Barkley).

The House That Would Not Die (1970)

TV Movie

Producer: Aaron Spelling. Director: John Llewellyn Moxey. Based on the novel *Ammie, Come Home* by Barbara Michaels. Teleplay: Henry Farrell. Photography: Fleet Southcott. Editor: Art Seid. Production: Aaron Spelling Productions. Distribution: ABC. Original air date: October 27, 1970. Running time: 74 minutes. Cast: Barbara Stanwyck (Ruth Bennett), Richard Egan, Michael Anderson Jr., Kitty Winn, Doreen Lang, Mabel Albertson.

A Taste of Evil (1971)

TV Movie

Producer: Aaron Spelling. Director: John Llewellyn Moxey. Teleplay: Jimmy Sangster. Photography: Archie R. Dalzell. Editor: Art Seid. Production: Aaron Spelling Productions, ABC. Distribution: ABC. Original air date: October 12, 1971. Running time: 73 minutes. Cast: Barbara Stanwyck (Miriam Jennings), Barbara Parkins, Roddy McDowall, William Windom, Arthur O'Connell, Bing Russell, Dawn Frame.

The Letters (1973)

TV Movie

Executive producers: Leonard Goldberg, Aaron Spelling, Tony Thomas. Directors: Paul Krasny, Gene Nelson. Teleplay: James G. Hirsch, Ellis Marcus, Hal Sitowitz. Photography: Leonard J. South, Tim Southcott. Editors: David Berlatsky, Carroll Sax, Robert L. Swanson. Production: ABC Circle Films. Distribution: ABC. Original air date: March 6, 1973. Running time: 74 minutes. Cast: John Forsythe, Jane Powell, Lesley Ann Warren, Trish Mahoney, Gary Dubin, Mia Bendixsen, Dina Merrill, Leslie Nielsen, Barbara Stanwyck (Geraldine Parkington), Orville Sherman, Pamela Franklin, Ida Lupino, Ben Murphy, Shelly Novack, Frederick Herrick, Ann Noland, Brick Huston, Charlie Picerni, Gilchrist Stuart, Henry Jones.

Charlie's Angels (1980)

Episode 4.23: "Toni's Boys"

Creators: Ivan Goff, Ben Roberts. Producers: Leonard Goldberg, Shelley Hull, Aaron Spelling. Director: Ron Satlof. Story: Robert Janes, Katharyn Powers. Teleplay: Katharyn Powers. Photography: Richard M. Rawlings Jr. Production: Spelling-Goldberg. Distribution: ABC. Original air date: April 2, 1980. Running time: 45 minutes. Cast: Jaclyn Smith, Cheryl Ladd, Shelley Hack, David Doyle, Stephen Shortridge, Bruce Bauer, Bob Seagren, Barbara Stanwyck (Toni), Robert Loggia, Andy Romano, Tricia O'Neil, Roz Kelly, Jenny Sherman, James Brodhead, Ken Scott, Fil Formicola, Patti Townsend, Asa Teeter, Yulis Ruval, Dusty Deason.

The Thorn Birds (1983)

TV Miniseries

Executive producers: Edward Lewis, David L. Wolper. Director: Daryl Duke. Teleplay: Carmen Culver, Colleen McCullough, Lee Stanley. Photography: Bill Butler. Editors: Carroll Timothy O'Meara, Robert F. Shugrue. Production: David Wolper–Stan Margulies Productions, Edward Lewis Productions, Warner Bros. Television. Distribution: ABC. Original air date: March 27, 1983. Running time: 460 minutes. Cast: Richard Chamberlain, Rachel Ward, Christopher Plummer, Bryan Brown, Brett Cullen, Stephanie Faracy, Barry Corbin, John de Lancie, Barbara Stanwyck (Mary Carson).

Note: Barbara Stanwyck only appears in the first episode of this four-episode miniseries.

Dynasty (1985)

Episode 6.3: "The Californians"

Creators: Esther Shapiro, Richard Shapiro. Executive producer: Douglas S. Cramer. Director: Gwen Arner. Story: Diana Gould. Teleplay: Edward DeBlasio. Photography: Richard L. Rawlings. Editor: George W. Brooks. Production: Aaron Spelling Productions, Richard & Esther Shapiro Productions. Distribution: ABC. Original air date: October 9, 1985. Running time: 60 minutes. Cast: John Forsythe, Linda Evans, Joan Collins, Pamela Bellwood, John James, Emma Samms, Jack Coleman, Gordon Thomson, Michael Nader, Catherine Oxenberg, Diahann Carroll, Heather Locklear, Maxwell Caulfield, Barbara Stanwyck (Constance Colby Patterson).

Dynasty (1985)
Episode 6.4: "The Man"
Creators: Esther Shapiro, Richard Shapiro. Executive producer: Douglas S. Cramer. Director: Don Medford. Story: Diana Gould, Scott Hamner. Teleplay: Dennis Turner. Photography: Richard L. Rawlings. Editor: Larry Strong. Production: Aaron Spelling Productions, Richard & Esther Shapiro Productions. Distribution: ABC. Original air date: October 16, 1985. Running time: 60 minutes. Cast: John Forsythe, Linda Evans, Joan Collins, Pamela Bellwood, John James, Emma Samms, Jack Coleman, Gordon Thomson, Michael Nader, Catherine Oxenberg, Diahann Carroll, Heather Locklear, Maxwell Caulfield, Barbara Stanwyck (Constance Colby Patterson).

Dynasty (1985)
Episode 6.6: "The Titans"
Creators: Esther Shapiro, Richard Shapiro. Executive producer: Douglas S. Cramer. Director: Irving J. Moore. Story: Diana Gould, Scott Hamner. Teleplay: Edward DeBlasio. Photography: Michel Hugo. Editor: Kenneth Miller. Production: Aaron Spelling Productions, Richard & Esther Shapiro Productions. Distribution: ABC. Original air date: November 13, 1985. Running time: 60 minutes. Cast: John Forsythe, Linda Evans, Joan Collins, Pamela Bellwood, John James, Emma Samms, Jack Coleman, Gordon Thomson, Michael Nader, Catherine Oxenberg, Diahann Carroll, Heather Locklear, Maxwell Caulfield, Barbara Stanwyck (Constance Colby Patterson).

The Colbys (1985–1987)
Series, 24 Episodes
Creators: Esther Shapiro, Richard Shapiro, Eileen Pollock, Robert Pollock. Executive producer: Douglas S. Cramer. Producers: William Bast, Paul Huson. Photography: Tony Askins, Richard L. Rawlings, Roland "Ozzie" Smith, Hugh K. Gagnier. Editors: Chuck Montgomery, Larry Strong, Chuck McClelland, Richard M. Burlatsky. Production: Aaron Spelling Productions. Distribution: ABC. Original air dates: November 20, 1985–March 26, 1987. Running time: 60 minutes. Cast: Charlton Heston, John James, Katharine Ross, Emma Samms, Stephanie Beacham, Tracy Scoggins, Maxwell Caulfield, Ricardo Montalban, Claire Yarlett, Ivan Bonar, Kim Morgan Greene, Barbara Stanwyck (Constance "Conny" Colby Patterson), Ken Howard, Adrian Paul.

ACKNOWLEDGMENTS

Many people have helped in the writing of this book, some directly, some in an offhand way. As an editor, I have spent most of my adult life reading manuscripts—and authors' acknowledgments, not truly understanding how important those are who have given assistance in the writing of a book. I now know what that generosity of spirit means.

I would like to thank:

John Kobal, who spent many afternoons at the Knopf offices at 201 East 50th Street regaling me with enchanted bedtime stories about actors and actresses, designers, cameramen, photographers, and directors he had come to know during his many decades as a fan and then collector for a book we were working on together, I as his editor. It was John who talked to me about Barbara Stanwyck with the excitement, appreciation, and thrill that made me see Miss Stanwyck in a way I hadn't before. That appreciation stayed with me, long after John and I had worked together on several books, long after John had died.

James Curtis, early on, opened an important door that led me to Walda Mansfield, the third in the triumvirate of show girls—Ruby Stevens, Mae Clarke, and Walda—who banded together in New York's 1920s and made a pact to work together onstage no matter what—in nightclubs, musical revues, and on Broadway. It was Walda Mansfield, through extensive interviews, who first made Ruby Stevens real to me. She was no longer abstract, an actress on the screen.

Jim Curtis's perceptive, thorough interviews with Mae Clarke (*Featured Player,* Scarecrow Books, 1996) and movie producer David Lewis (*The Creative Producer;* The Scarecrow Filmmakers Series, Book 36, 1993) were an invaluable help. Anthony Slide and his pathfinding press, Scarecrow Books, have performed a great service over many decades, making available an important, perhaps arcane but vital history of Hollywood.

Barbara Stanwyck's family—Gene Vaslett, an adorable, loving man— believed in this book and spent many hours telling me stories of his life with his aunt Barbara and entrusting me with photographs, letters, and notes and making available Barbara Stanwyck's archives at the University of Wyoming. Gene's wife, the effusive, supportive Barbara Vaslett, daughter of one of the busiest character actors in Hollywood's great age, Irving Bacon; Barbara and Gene's children, Christine, Kathleen, and Victoria, and grandchildren, Megan and Darcey, have all been supportive and generous.

A special appreciation to Tori Burns for leading me to June D. Merkent, wife of Barbara Stanwyck's nephew, Al Merkent. June, at first wary and formal, became an insightful, beloved friend to this book.

Judith Stevens, former wife of Brian Stevens, nephew of Barbara Stanwyck, somehow found me and gave of her time, telling me a side of the Stevens story I hadn't yet been able to find.

Suzanne Frasuer, avid fan and staunch sentry, opened an important door into the Stanwyck inner sanctum.

Barbara Stanwyck's closest friends—her adopted family who spent holidays with her year in and year out, each pal as much a mensch as was Barbara Stanwyck—all were generous with their time and thoughts, willing to open up about their adored friend.

Larry Kleno, former assistant to Helen Ferguson, amanuensis and longtime confidante to Barbara Stanwyck, was steadfast and generous, loving and supportive in so many ways.

The distinguished Dick Wells and David Janzow were always helpful, fun, full of impish talent, invention, and insight.

John Testa was generous with his time and stories about Stanwyck and the years of their friendship.

Barbara Stanwyck's closest friend (theirs was indeed the perfect blendship), the beautiful, sublime Nancy Sinatra Sr. Her faith in this book meant more to me than she could ever know.

Alicia Smith, longtime friend of Harriett Coray, was steady-as-she-goes; Alicia's help and support were crucial in the writing of this book as was her double-dose of wry humor.

Dion Anthony Fay, adopted son of Barbara Stanwyck and Frank Fay, who opened his heart and his memory to me during the course of many years when it would have been much easier, and less painful, to have kept both locked away.

Michael Coray, son of Harriett Coray, gave of his time and family history and helped me with a crucial aspect of Barbara Stanwyck's story. I am grateful for his assistance, his honesty, his trust.

Tim Marx, for telling me about his parents, Marion and Zeppo, so central to Barbara's life—as actress and adventurer, and for sharing family photographs.

Bobbie Poledouris, for her generosity and her stories.

David Chierichetti, for the use of his photographs and for his eminent knowledge of movies; of the men and women who worked at the studios, and about studio photography, negative retouching, and prints; about Edith Head, Mitchell Leisen, and many others.

Tom Toth, film collector extraordinaire, who had in his impressive library of 16mm films every Stanwyck picture no one else owned or knew where to find—this, years before most were available, as they are now, on DVD. Tom was more than generous in making the films available to me and screening 16mm pictures other than Stanwyck's, films I'd never seen before, or had never seen on a large screen.

The Mandelbaum brothers, Howard and Ron, for continuing on with the great stock archive, Photofest, founded by Carlos Clarens, and for their service above and beyond on so many books, including the one in your hands.

John Slotkin for his many stories of Barbara Stanwyck as Shirley Eder's closest friend, and for making available to me Stanwyck's letters to her, as well as their taped conversations.

Ella Smith for offering her time when she had so little left and for sending on her vast correspondence with the many directors, cameramen, and actors who worked with Barbara Stanwyck.

Ursula Thiess, for her perspective and her time. And her son, Terry Taylor, for being so gracious and open.

Lois Wilson and John Henderson, for their wisdom and for providing the way.

I'd like to thank the following for their conversations about acting, Hollywood, and all things Barbara Stanwyck: Ellen Adler, Steve Allen, Jacques d'Amboise, Army Archerd, Lauren Bacall, Joan Benny, Milton Berle, Nancy Bernard Levy, Edward L. Bernds, A. I. Bezzerides, Peter Bogdanovich, Patti Bosworth, Peter Breck, Norman Brokaw, Tom Capra, Frank Capra Jr., Leslie Caron, Stan Cohen, Jerry Cohen, Nancy Coleman, Jackie Cooper, Wendy Cooper, Alvin Cooperman, Mara Corday Long, Cheryl Crane, Christina Crawford, Luther Davis, Frances Dee, Bruce Dern, Edward Dmytryk, Kirk Douglas, Lynn Duddy, Daryl Duke, Yvette Eastman, Doris Eaton Travis, Kate Edelman, Shirley Eder, Jeannie Epper, Linda Evans, Irving Fein, Lucille Fletcher, Nina Foch, Jane Fonda, Christa Fuller, John Gallagher, Peter Gardiner, Arthur Gardner, Irvin Gelb, Herbert G. Goldman, Farley Granger, James Gregory, James Grissom, John Guare, Dolores Hart, June Haver,

Harry Hay, Dorothy Herrmann, Charlton Heston, Daryl Hickman, Charles Higham, Leonora Hornblow, Kim Hunter, Josephine Hutchinson, Maria Janis, Fay Kanin, Elia Kazan, Evelyn Keyes, Richard Kiley, Joann Koch, Kurt Kreuger, Diane Ladd, Gavin Lambert, Betty Lasky, Arthur Laurents, Piper Laurie, Ernest Lehman, Joe Lewis, Michael Lindsay-Hogg, Joan Lorring, Sidney Lumet, A. C. Lyles, Kathy Mackay, Sharon Madearia, Randal Malone, Dorothy Manners, Jacques Mapes, Andy Maree, Stan Margulies, Bill Marx, Maxine Marx, Virginia Mayo, Joseph McBride, Todd McCarthy, Gavin MacLeod, Roddy McDowall, John Miehle, Nolan Miller, Juanita Moore, Dick Moore, Ivy Mooring, Patricia Neal, Dana O'Connell, Maureen O'Sullivan, Robert Osborne, Barry Paris, Julie Payne, Eleanor Perenyi, Christopher Plummer, Abraham Polonsky, Jane Powell, Ellen Pucky Violet, Tom Purvis, Anthony Quinn, José Quintero, Nancy Reagan, Rex Reed, Art Reeves, Michael Ritchie, Jill Robinson, Peter Rogers, Betty Rowland, Tom Del Ruth, Ted Sannella, Budd Schulberg, Daniel Selznick, Jean Simmons, John Slotkin, Edward Slotkin, Ann Sothern, Aaron Spelling, Robert Stack, Leonard Stanley, George Stevens Jr., Dr. Michael Taylor, Studs Terkel, Phyllis Thaxter, Lee Thuna, André de Toth, Catherine Turney, Dorothy Van Als, Michael Vollbracht, Robert Wagner, Jane Ellen Wayne, J. Watson Webb, Dorothy Wellman, William Wellman Jr., Jesse White, Oona White, David Wolper, Fay Wray, Teresa Wright, Jane Wyman, Richard Ziegfeld, and Victoria Danzig.

A special heartfelt thanks to Marilyn Goldin, beloved pal, the most dazzling of thinkers and storytellers.

Irene Diamond, age eight-five when I met her and still a knockout, former head of the story department under Hal Wallis at Warner Bros., then with Wallis at Paramount from 1941 through 1971. Irene, unsung but deserving of great accolades, who chose many of the pictures Stanwyck made at Warner Bros. and Paramount, was walking on the Warner lot one day when Barbara Stanwyck stopped her and said, "You know we look alike . . ."

E. A. Kral for his diligent research and reporting on the history of Nebraska and on Robert Taylor, boy Nebraskan.

Nils Hanson for being the keeper of the Ziegfeld flame, and for his hard work and generosity.

I am grateful to those who assisted in research: Peter Bankers, Maria Ciaccia; Ellen Martin, Don Tango, Anat Soloman, Bradley Friedman (when he got out of bed), and especially, the dogged and reliable duo, East Coast and West, Stephen Bowie and Jonathan Ward.

Katherine Hourigan, longtime pal, trusty editor, who came forth with suggestions, notes, and wisdom and her famous Hourigan enthusiasm. She was there at every stage of this book and patiently answered, or rightfully pooh-poohed, my annoying relentless questions.

Helen Brann, Colorado cowgirl, fellow dog lover, ace handicapper at Inner Track, true friend, literary agent, who gave of her time and read the manuscript—and read it again—during its many stages.

At Knopf, Sonny Mehta graciously allowed me to undertake this book, and over the years, never inquired about its completion, which could be read two ways; either way, I'm grateful for it and to him; Andy Hughes and Romeo Enriquez for their supreme production expertise and for their enduring friendship; Carol Carson, the best of jacket designers, for her perfect jacket—and for being game; Lydia Buechler, copy chief, for her wise suggestions; Anke Steinecke, Senior Vice President and Associate General Counsel, for just that, her much appreciated counsel; Kathy Zuckerman for her expert publicity know-how, years of experience, and sense of fun; Paul Bogaards, amidst all the dust and commotion of his uber-self, for his good heart; Nicholas Latimer, elegant hard worker, longtime Borzoi standard-bearer; Altie Karper for her appreciation of Barbara Stanwyck, and for her anticipation and excitement about this book; my assistants, past and present, each of whom crucially helped at various stages of its making: Lee Buttala, there at the outset, Zachary Wagman, Daniel Schwartz, and, in particular, Carmen Johnson and Charlotte Crowe, valiant and indispensable. Interns Nick Naney, Christina Sontag, Audrey Silverman, Gene Tajada, and Eric Herskovic, who worked so diligently to get the job done, whatever it was. Anne Diaz, wise soul who could manage the world—and should. Most of all, Shelley Wanger, who knows everyone who is anyone on the planet, and perhaps on a few others nearby, and who generously vouched for me to those from her Hollywood childhood past.

Jill Ciment for her offhand comment at lunch one day that sent me in a new direction.

Foster Hirsch, quiet impresario, master interviewer, admired cultural historian and biographer, for his time and efforts.

G. D. Hamann for his research, culling of articles decade by decade, subject by subject, and for his love of the movies.

Brenda Wineapple, for her generosity and for our many conversations on the white heat of writing biography.

The American Film Institute Catalog of Feature Films, available only in book form when I began this book, now online and an invaluable tool. The AFI deserves a national medal for their valiant and important archival work.

The New York Times Archive, a researcher's dream, which should be celebrated as a national treasure.

In New York and the surrounding area, Maryan Chach, head archivist of the Shubert Archive, who made me feel at home in the stacks of her magical collection. My thanks to the staffs at the Billy Rose Theatre Collection at the Performing Arts Research Center, Lincoln Center; the Theater Collection of the Museum of the City of New York; the Columbia University Center for Oral History. Edward Cypress, Principal, P.S. 152, Brooklyn, New York.

To Eva Tucholka and Harriet Culver of Culver Pictures, for their determined efforts and generosity.

To Jeanine Basinger, Corwin-Fuller Professor of Film Studies and Founder and Curator of the Cinema Archives Center for Film Studies at Wesleyan University.

In Gloucester, Massachusetts, my appreciation to the Cape Ann Museum, Cape Ann Historical Society, Lanesville Historical Society, and Barbara Lambert, and to Fred Bodin of Bodin Historic Photographs.

The Maine Historical Society Research Library and Nancy Taylor.

The Philadelphia Theatre Collection, Free Library of Philadelphia, and Geraldine Duclow.

In Washington, the Library of Congress, Raymond Chandler Collection, and to Heather Burke for her research.

In Atlanta, the Turner Entertainment Company, which opened their archives when they could easily have maintained their policy and kept them closed.

In the midwest, State Historical Society of Wisconsin, Wisconsin Center for Film and Theater Research, and the Gage County Historical Society.

In the southwest, the Ransom Center at the University of Texas at Austin; Southern Methodist University, DeGolyer Library, Ronald Davis Oral History Collection of the Performing Arts, Dallas, Texas.

A special nod of gratitude to the University of Wyoming, American Heritage Center Archives, the Barbara Stanwyck Collection, and to Rick Ewig, Associate Director, for his help and the help of his efficient staff.

To Helen Cohen, President of Entertainment Management and on behalf of the DeMille Estate, and James V. D'Arc, Curator of the Motion Picture and Arts Communications Archive, Brigham Young University, Provo, Utah, for their help with the Cecil B. DeMille Archives, 1863–1983.

In Los Angeles, the Academy of Motion Picture Arts and Sciences; Brigitte Kueppers, Librarian and Archivist, the Department of Special Collections, the Arts Library of the University of California, Los Angeles.

At the Warners Archive at the University of Southern California Cinematic Arts Library, Edward S. (Ned) Comstock, Senior Library Assistant, the biographer's best pal and essential guide to almost everything Hollywood-related. For his boundless generosity, for his being at the crossroads of all books Hollywood in nature, for "meritorious conduct, extraordinary valor, conspicuous bravery against"—and on behalf of—needy biographers, Edward S. Comstock is hereby awarded the "Triple Cross."

The Archives Department of Los Angeles District Court; the Motion Picture & Television Country Home and Hospital.

IMDB and IBDB—the greatest movie and theater reference this side of the cyber Rio Grande.

Valerie Yaros, Screen Actors Guild and SAG-AFTRA historian, for her generous guidance with the Guild's complex beginnings.

Lynn Nesbit, literary agent, colleague, longtime friend . . . Who knows what lurks in the heart of that brusque, no-nonsense affect? Anyone knows who has worked with her—decency, honor, taste, and above all, loyalty.

Michael Korda, publisher, novelist, biographer, equestrian, photographer, illustrator, and a few other incidentals, who contracted for this book many a year ago and who continued to act as its editor long after life took him into the realms of writing military history and biography. Thank you for your patience, your eye, your constancy; your Korda sense of the heroic.

David Rosenthal, for his daring choices and for his long-standing admiration of Barbara Stanwyck.

At Simon & Schuster, Gypsy da Silva, pro of pros, upholding the long traditions of S&S's diligent sower; the ever efficient—and adorable—Nick Greene, who weathered the storm with charm and good cheer. The jazzed Jessica Zimmerman Lawrence, Senior Publicist, who spread the word with grace and zip; Elina Vaysbeyn, Online Marketing Manager, for her online energy and webmaster know-how; George Turianski, Senior Production Manager; Joy O'Meara, Director of Interior Design; Gina DiMascia, Associate Managing Editor; and Brittany Dulac, Assistant Managing Editor; Irene Kheradi, Executive Managing Editor; Jackie Seow, Executive Director of Trade Art—all first-rate book producers who did a yeoman's job with a complicated manuscript.

Ingrid Sterner, the book's copy editor, for her thoroughness and care, who dutifully tortured me with questions and more questions . . .

And Jonathan Karp, a true publisher and an elegant man, who stood at the helm of the good ship Barbara Stanwyck with a steady hand and heart, and who brought us into port and made it all fun.

To friends and family who were there through thick and thicker: Tony Chirico (good neighbor; better pal), Mike Comerford, Lynne Cox, Brenda Feigen, Jane Friedman (sister-in-heart; woman of the year; empire builder on an open road with an open soul), Faith Stewart Gordon, Gail Hochman, Melanie Jackson, Martha Kaplan, who forged the path westward into the hills of Sullivan County and led the way for the rest of us, Ruth Lippman (Miss Subways to the core and one of the book's earliest readers), Lena Mitchell (who kept me sane), Joanne Parent, Marjorie Pleshette, Alice Quinn (from black skirt and 3 Loop Road to 121 Madison and beyond), Anne Rice, writer, worker, friend (ours has to be one of the longest marriages in publishing), Ethan Silverman, John Torre, Blossom and Walter Wilson.

And to my sister, Erica Silverman, wise reader and supporter, with memories of Vineyard summers, Tisbury winters, Madame Alexander dolls, onion grass, and nifty cookouts on the opening nights of the MV Agricultural Fair.

My father, Mitchell Wilson, taught me laughter and silliness, discipline and quiet work; about how anything is possible, and how you can go from being almost thrown out of high school to becoming a physicist (seesaws to cosmic rays) assisting the likes of Enrico Fermi and I. I. Rabi; and who opened up for me the world of writing, silk scarves, and book publishing.

Regina Tierney, artist, entrepreneurial force, and computer whiz who can read a five-hundred-page manual on Unix, Boolean geometry, and C++ as if it were *Anna Karenina,* for all of our (loopy) years together and for so much more.

To the dedicatees of this book—to my mother, Helen Wilson; and to Nina Bourne; and to Bob Gottlieb. How could a person be so lucky as to have known and been taught by all three of these extraordinary people?

NOTES

Unless otherwise specified, all interviews are with the author.

PART ONE: Up from Under

One: Family History

PAGE

3 *"My grandparents on both":* BS in Gladys Hall, *Modern Screen,* November 1937.

4 *Her great-great-grandmother:* Megan Robinson in letter to author.

4 *Stephens established a business:* Maine probate records; DAR genealogy commissioned by BS.

4 *The Stephens family:* Deeds from 1852–1859.

4 *They kept their nets:* Ibid., 16.

4 *In 1862:* War Department document, February 8, 1883; *Supplement to the Official Records of the Union and Confederate Armies* (Wilmington, N.C.: Broadfoot, 1996), pt. 2, vol. 27, serial 39, 279.

4 *Months later, Stevens:* Pringle, *History of Gloucester,* 202.

5 *Women sewed black:* Barbara H. Erkkila, *Village at Lane's Cove* (Gloucester, Mass.: Ten Pound Island, 1989), 93, 94.

6 *found employment:* Autobiographical sketch by Maud Stevens Merkent, 1944, courtesy of June Merkent.

6 *Paving stones:* Erkkila, *Village at Lane's Cove,* 54.

6 *They were Presbyterian:* Leyburn, *Scotch-Irish.*

7 *The city of roughly:* Gillespie, *Historical and Pictorial History of Chelsea,* 19, 21.

7 *Shipyards still produced schooners: Dover Enquirer,* March 6, 1896.

7 *The girls would have:* Maud Merkent to June Merkent; June Merkent to author.

8 *The largest of the mills:* Cathy Beaudoin, Dover Historical Society.

8 *The harbor's 140-foot: Calamity of the Cochecho,* Dover, New Hampshire, October 1996.

9 *Snow squalls were raging: Gloucester Daily Times,* February 16, 1898, 1.

9 *Coasters, sloops, and fishing: Gloucester Daily Times,* February 17, 1898, 6; Barbara Lambert, Cape Ann Historical Society.

9 *Abby's funeral was: Gloucester Daily Times,* February 17, 1898, 6.

11 *Byron realized that employment:* Gene Vaslett to author.

11 *By 1906, when the Stevenses:* Kenneth T. Jackson, ed., *The Encyclopedia of New York City* (New Haven, Conn.: Yale University Press, 1995).

11 *Landowners had resisted:* Gertrude Lefferts Vanderbilt, *The Social History of Flatbush* (Brooklyn: Frederick Loeser, 1909), 169–74.

11 *The Stevenses moved to:* 1909 telephone directory; *Thirteenth Census of the United States: 1910 Population.*

13 *Kitty and Byron liked:* June Merkent to author.

13 *The Merkent family owned:* 1912 telephone directory with job description.

13 *Millie Stevens was being: Toledo Blade,* October 7, 1907, Billy Rose Collection, Lincoln Center Library.

13 *Byron and Ruby watched:* Byron Stevens to Judith Stevens.

13 *Five-year-old Malcolm:* Ibid.

14 *Blood poisoning set in:* Death certificate of Catherine McPhee Stevens, no. 14976.

14 *Kitty was dead:* Ibid.

14 *In another, Millie:* "Barbara Stanwyck," *Today and Yesterday.*

15 *Malcolm and Ruby were taken:* Vaslett to author.

15 *And in yet another:* According to Ruby's cousin Helen Joppeck, the daughter of Albert Merkent's sister, who played as a child during those years with Ruby, Malcolm, and Al Merkent—following Kitty Stevens's death; Helen Joppeck to June Merkent in a letter.

15 *He wept for:* Byron Stevens to Judith Stevens.

15 *The boy sensed his father:* BS to Judith Stevens.

15 *There were extra dollars:* Haskin, *Panama Canal,* 164, 165; *World Almanac and Book of Facts for 1927,* 724.

15 *U.S. military engineers had:* Lieutenant Colonel George Washington Goethals, the man overseeing the project, needed men for the Army of Panama, made up of some fifty thousand men; Haskin, *Panama Canal,* 164.

Two: The Perils

PAGE

16 *"My father loved my mother":* BS, in *Screenland plus TV-Land,* 1964; BS to Rex Reed, April 13, 1981.

16 *Ruby often slept:* Gene Vaslett to author.

16 *"There was never a family":* BS, in Gladys Hall, *Modern Screen,* November 10, 1937.

16 *He was a little boy:* BS to Judith Stevens; Stevens to author, March 5, 1999.

17 *"When you live like that":* Marcia Borie, *Radio-TV Mirror,* August 1966.

17 *"Despite her quietness":* Byron Stevens, in Gladys Hall, *Modern Screen,* November 1937.

17 *Ruby found a world:* BS to Rex Reed.

17 *Ruby thought the church:* BS to Rex Reed, interview, April 13, 1981.

18 *The teachers called her:* BS, in Gladys Hall, *Modern Screen,* November 1937.

18 *Literature was the first thing:* BS to Judith Stevens; Stevens to author, June 2, 1999, 28.

18 *Ruby acted as if:* "Barbara Stanwyck," *Today and Yesterday.*

18 *She kept her eyes level:* BS, in Virginia de Paolo, *Screenland plus TV-Land,* 1964.

18 *With the exception:* BS, in Walter Ramsey, *Modern Screen,* May 1931.

18 *The girls had known:* Byron Stevens to Judith Stevens.

18 *Ruby felt only:* BS, in Walter Ramsey, *Modern Screen,* May 1931.

18 *If she needed to get:* BS to Judith Stevens; Stevens to author, May 19, 1999.

19 *"I used to dream":* Jane Wilkie; Paul Rosenfield, Calendar, *Los Angeles Times.*

19 *Millie was the most beautiful:* Jerry Asher, "The Strangest Reunion," *Hollywood,* January 1939, 26.

19 *Her work continued: Syracuse Post,* December 6, 1912; *Toledo Blade,* January 6, 1913; Billy Rose Collection.

20 The Perils of Pauline *featured: Motion Picture,* June 1916.

20 *Pearl joined a touring: Photoplay,* July 1913.

20 *There were times when:* BS to John Slotkin; Slotkin to author, January 7, 1999.

21 *Even Madame Sarah Bernhardt: Toledo Blade,* July 5, 1917.

21 *The eighteen-year-old: New York Times,* August 5, 1938; *Moving Picture World,* May 6, 1916.

21 *Draped over her shoulders: Chicago Tribune,* December 13, 1916.

21 *Pearl had a fondness:* Pearl White, "Why I Like the Movies," September 1916.

21 *She was called a modern: New York Mirror,* March 28, 1915; *Motion Picture Classic,* March 1918; *Dramatic Magazine,* May 6, 1914.

21 *The press described her: Dramatic Magazine,* May 6, 1914.

21 *She understood that "pantomime":* Pearl White, interview with *Indianapolis Star,* March 14, 1916.

22 *Pearl White was a girl:* Ibid.

22 *After watching Pearl:* Charles Samuels, "The Search for Ruby Stevens," *Motion Picture,* October 1949, 80.

22 *"high class vaudeville": Buffalo Enquirer,* October 26, 1915.

22 *the show continuing:* Reviews in ibid.; *Rochester American,* October 30, 1915; *Indianapolis Star,* December 10, 1915.

22 *"the hit of the bill": Indianapolis News,* December 10, 1915.

22 *"an expressive comedienne": Pittsburgh Leader,* September 19, 1915.

22 *Ruby watched as the performers:* Jane Wilkie article.

22 *"I couldn't have cared less":* Ibid.

22 *Ruby experienced an ecstasy:* Asher, "Strangest Reunion," 26.

Three: Starting Life Anew

PAGE

23 *"was the only person":* BS, in Charles Warner, *TV Picture Life,* n.d.

23 *"During one Sunday sermon":* Ibid.

23 *"The hate was drained":* Ibid.

23 *Ruby was inspired by the work:* BS to Rex Reed. April 13, 1981, *New York Daily News.*

23 *On a spring day early in June:* Baptismal record, Dutch Reformed Church, 36.

23 *Without any family:* Ibid.

23 *Mabel and Harold Cohen:* Brooklyn directory.

24 *She learned to play jacks:* BS, in Gladys Hall, *Modern Screen,* November 1937.

24 *Ruby marked off the days:* Adele Whitely Fletcher, "The Stanwyck Myth," *Lady's Circle,* March 1967.

24 *After performance:* Asher, "Strangest Reunion," 26.

24 *Millie would take Ruby:* Jane Ardmore, and Claudia Clark, "I Was a Gentile Child in a Jewish Family," June 1967.

24 *The Germans had sunk three:* Kendrick A. Clements, *The Presidency of Woodrow Wilson* (Lawrence: University Press of Kansas, 1992), 139.

24 *Ray Merkent:* Gene Vaslett to author, October 19, 1996.

24 *Bert's brother and the youngest:* William Merkent to author.

24 *The Brooklyn Navy Yard: Brooklyn Almanac.*

25 *In Malcolm's and Ruby's schools:* Edward Cypress (principal of P.S. 152) to author, January 21, 1999.

25 *She understood that these:* BS, in Gladys Hall, *Modern Screen,* November 1937.

25 *She went to live with Maud:* School record, P.S. 152.

25 *Eastern Parkway with Giles's parents:* Vaslett to author.

25 *He would somehow work:* Byron Stevens to Judith Stevens; Judith Stevens to author.

25 *At fourteen, Malcolm:* BS to Judith Stevens.

25 *At thirty-two years: Glorianna* program, January 6, 1919.

25 *"well accounted for": New York Times,* October 28, 1918.

25 *Also in* Glorianna *was:* Barbara Stanwyck, *Photoplay,* 1949.

26 *"mosey up" to see Millie:* Buck Mack, *Screen Guide,* 1948.

26 *"We had a regular":* Barbara Stanwyck, *Photoplay,* 1949.

26 *In his nine years of education:* Ibid.

26 *Ruby would have given:* Samuels, "In Search of Ruby Stevens," 80.

26 *Soon after Malcolm's graduation:* Buck Mack, interview in *Screen Guide,* 1948.

26 *She acted as if:* BS to Judith Stevens; Byron Stevens to Judith Stevens; Judith Stevens to author, May 19, 1999.

26 *Maud expected:* Mack, interview in *Screen Guide,* 1948.

27 *Ruby entertained her nephew Gene:* Vaslett to author, October 19, 1996.

27 *"Here's a Japanese sandman":* "Just a Japanese Sandman," lyrics by Raymond B. Egan, music by Richard Whiting.

27 *Ray Merkent, the Merkent with the most:* June Merkent to author, February 2, 1999.

27 *Her debut was:* Vaslett to author, October 17, 1996.

27 *Ruby began appearing:* Vaslett to author, October 19, 1996.

27 *In one of the productions:* Ibid.

27 *She could see the spire:* School brochure on the Glenwood Road School, courtesy Edward Cypress.

28 *"And," she said:* Jane Wilkie article.

28 *The other girls working:* Judith Stevens to author, June 2, 1999.

28 *On Sunday mornings:* Vaslett to author, February 6, 1997.

28 *Malcolm sent Ruby postcards:* Malcolm Stevens to Judith Stevens; BS to Judith Stevens; Stevens to author, May 17, 1999.

Four: Heart and Nerve and Sinew

PAGE

29 *In 1921, Ruby: Radio-TV Mirror,* April 1966.

29 *Now that she'd finished school: Photoplay,* December 1937.

29 *"talked back to a caller": Christmas in Connecticut* press book.

29 *"got their wires so jammed up":* Barbara Berch, *New York Times,* March 21, 1943.

29 *paid $13 a week: Liberty,* August 1945.

29 *"I couldn't stand the":* Walter Ramsey, *Modern Screen,* May 1931.

29 *After many months "of this [nothingness]":* Jane Wilkie article.

29 *Frankie Chauffeur:* Gene Vaslett to author, September 2, 1999.

29 *Sometimes they would go: Modern Screen,* November 1937.

30 *When Frank mentioned marriage:* Ibid.

30 *Bert Merkent and his brother:* Gene Vaslett to author,

30 *One day Ray showed up:* June Merkent to author, May 17, 1999.

30 *"didn't have a great figure":* Ibid.

30 *Isadora danced with her: New York Times,* April 10, 1915.

30 *"a return to simplicity": New York Times Magazine,* October 15, 1922, 12.

30 *Next she worked at the Vogue:* Edwin Kennedy, in Ruth Waterbury, *TV Radio Mirror,* December 1966. Most books incorrectly say BS worked at Condé Nast's *Vogue.* I doubt this and have found no record of her employ in the Condé Nast archives.

30 *on Fifth Avenue: New York Times,* December 19, 1926.

30 *knew how to sew and cut patterns:* BS, in *Photoplay,* December 1937.

30 *She was hired: Modern Screen,* November 1937.

30 *She read "nothing good":* Ibid.

30 *Soon she was reading Conrad:* Ibid.

31 *It was a way of being:* Barbara Stanwyck, "This Is What I Believe," magazine clipping, n.d.

31 *"the debut of [her] artistic life":* Bernhardt, *Memories of My Life,* 60.

31 *the moment when Bernhardt at age fifteen:* Ibid., 71.

31 *"soul remained childlike":* Ibid., 75.

31 *"You are original":* Ibid., 332.

31 *"felt a sense": Modern Screen,* November 1937.

31 *"a knockout, sultry":* Edwin Kennedy, in Ruth Waterbury, *TV Radio Mirror,* December 1966.

31 *He knew that Ruby was a girl:* Ibid.

32 *Ruby loved to dance:* Ibid.

32 *"And then there were too many":* *Photoplay,* December 1937.

32 *began to study acrobatics:* Walter Ramsey, *Modern Screen,* May 1931.

32 *"I loved to show her off":* Ibid.

32 *The Jerome Remick music publishing company:* 1921 telephone directory.

32 *But Ruby felt at home:* Screenland plus TV-Land, 1964.

33 *The audition was over:* Ramsey, *Modern Screen,* May 1931.

33 *He could see that she:* Ibid.

33 *Ruby told Lindsay that she'd been:* Caravan, June 1943.

33 *The Strand Roof was popular:* Abel Green and Joe Laurie Jr., *Show Biz, from Vaude to Video* (New York: 1951), 134.

33 *It was charged with solicitation:* Ibid., 190, 191.

33 *dinner deluxe for $2:* Eighteen dollars in today's money.

33 *There were eight cast members:* Ibid., 16.

34 *Lindsay caught her:* James Gregory, *Movie Digest,* 1972.

34 *With her salary:* Walda Mansfield to author, September 2, 1998.

34 *The Ziegfeld girls were from all over:* Bernard Sobel, *Broadway Heartbeat: Memoirs of a Press Agent* (New York: Hermitage House, 1953), 108.

34 *Out of five hundred:* Ibid., 110.

34 *Lillian Lorraine:* Nils Hanson, *Lillian Lorraine* (Jefferson, N.C.: McFarland, 2011).

34 *Ziegfeld's set designer:* Charles Higham, *Ziegfeld,* (Chicago: Regnery, 1972), 103.

34 *had worked with Ziegfeld:* Ziegfeld and Ziegfeld, *Ziegfeld Touch.*

34 *There were twenty-five showgirls:* Nils Hanson, Ziegfeld Club.

34 *who performed the famous Ziegfeld walk:* Higham, *Ziegfeld,* 108.

35 *it was straight backed:* Ibid.

35 *a step with a slide:* Dana O'Connell to author, February 11, 1998.

35 *The chorus dancers:* Higham, *Ziegfeld,* 106.

35 *the dancers thought Fokine flighty:* Dana O'Connell to author, February 11, 1998.

35 *Sixteen ponies:* Higham, *Ziegfeld,* 106.

35 *ten girls were in musical numbers:* Doris Eaton to author, February 3, 1998.

35 *Then "Sure-Fire Dancers of Today":* Program Sixteenth of the Series, December 25, 1922.

36 *The sixteenth edition of the* Follies *cost:* Roughly $3.5 million today.

36 *Ziegfeld cut the cost:* The equivalent of going from $48 to $39.99 in 1998.

36 *He returned from Panama:* Mansfield to author, August 27, 1999.

36 *he had signed up with the merchant marine:* Judith Stevens to author.

36 *He told Ruby only that their father was dead:* Byron Stevens to Judith Stevens; Judith Stevens to author, 1999.

36 *"I learned how to dance":* Rex Reed, *New York Daily News,* April 13, 1981.

36 *performing an acrobatic dance:* Granlund, *Blondes, Brunettes, and Bullets,* 130.

36 *"I tried to outdo myself":* BS, in Hedda Hopper.

36 *Ruby thought it was a wonder:* Judith Stevens to author.

36 *The eighteenth edition of the* Follies: Dorothy Van Alst to her son, Robert Gale, n.d.

37 *Al Jolson used to stand in the wings:* Lina Basquette, in Barry Paris, "The Godless Girl," *New Yorker,* February 19, 1989, 57.

37 *One of Ruby's dance partners:* Brooklyn Standard Union, December 28, 1924.

37 *Dorothy, nineteen:* Robert Gale to author, May 1999; William Slavens McNutt, *Colliers,* December 13, 1924.

37 *By December 1923:* Ibid.

37 *another dancer who was engaged:* Ibid.

Five: Keeping Kool

38 *Nils Granlund began working:* Granlund, *Blondes, Brunettes, and Bullets,* 37.

38 *Granlund started to broadcast:* Ibid., 86.

39 *Granlund let her read one of his poems:* Ibid., 94.

40 *He thought her deep voice:* Granlund, *Blondes, Brunettes, and Bullets,* 130.

40 *He thought she was beautiful:* Ibid.

40 *Despite that, when he put together shows:* Ibid.

40 *Along Fifty-Second Street:* Sobel, *Broadway Heartbeat,* 206.

40 *There were five thousand speakeasies:* Bishop, *Mark Hellinger Story,* 60.

40 *There was the Club Lido:* Ibid., 87.

40 *Fay opened a nightclub:* Ibid., 89.

40 *Granlund finally figured out:* Ibid., 101.

40 *The authorities soon caught on:* Louis Sobol, *The Longest Street* (New York: Crown, 1968), 76.

41 *The silks on the walls:* Granlund, *Blondes, Brunettes, and Bullets,* 119.

41 *Texas—she was born in Waco:* Louise Berliner, *Texas Guinan: Queen of the Nightclubs* (Austin: University of Texas Press, 1993).

41 *She was loud:* Granlund, *Blondes, Brunettes, and Bullets,* 63.

42 *The El Fay's watered-down liquor:* Ibid., 125.

42 *was sold for $1.25:* In 1924 dollars, $1.25 was the equivalent of $16.60 in 2013.

42 *While the doctored liquor:* Ibid.

42 *Ruby Keeler at fourteen:* Ibid., 128.

42 *After that, for her own:* Ibid., 129.

42 *Often the two Rubys:* Randall Malone to author, February 9, 2001.

42 *It was when Mae Klotz was onstage:* Clarke, *Featured Player,* 13.

43 *"[Ruby] talked real low":* Ibid.

43 *"Our name was a very honored name":* Ibid., 5.

43 *"where all the theaters":* Ibid., 18.

43 *Ruby taught Mae about sex:* Malone to author, February 9, 2001.

43 *Ruby told Mae about men:* Ibid.

43 *Ruby taught Mae how to charm men:* Gil Frieze to author, May 28, 1997.

43 *Ruby told her how:* Malone to author, March 5, 2001.

43 *"You say to your date":* Malone to author, February 9, 2001.

44 *Mae tried it out:* Ibid.

44 *Ruby brought Mae home:* Gene Vaslett to author.

44 *at other times Mae brought Ruby:* Walda Mansfield to author.

44 *When Ruby's friend Claire Taishoff:* Ibid.

44 *"a cute place":* BS, in Gladys Hall, *Modern Screen,* November 1937.

44 *"Each night we washed our stockings":* BS profile (Helen Ferguson's office).

44 *"We couldn't wait to get together":* *Featured Player: An Oral Autobiography of Mae Clarke,* James Curtis (Lanham, Md., 1996), 21.

45 *"She'll go a long way":* David Bret, *Joan Crawford* (New York: Carroll & Graf, 2006), 9–10.

45 *The dressing rooms were large:* Clarke, *Featured Player.*

45 *Earl Lindsay wanted the dancers:* Ibid., 17.

45 *"I only changed it":* Ibid., 27, 28.

46 Sitting Pretty *opened at the Fulton Theatre:* Program notes, April 8, 1924, and June 9, 1924, Billy Rose Collection.

46 *In the program notes:* Ibid.

46 *It was a musical revue:* Gerald Bordman, *American Musical Theatre* (New York: Oxford University Press, 1978), 333.

46 *"The business of America is business":* Meltzer, *Brother, Can You Spare a Dime?,* 4.

46 *"the hoofiest chorus":* Newspaper clipping, n.d., Billy Rose Collection.

46 *audience applauding them throughout:* Alexander Woollcott, *Sun.*

47 Hopwood *("the Playboy Playwright") wrote:* Jack F. Sharrer, *Avery Hopwood: His Life and Plays* (Jefferson, N.C.: McFarland & Co., 1989).

47 *It was Hopwood's play:* Ibid.

47 *"high spot":* Waters, *Variety,* April 30, 1924.

47 *Ruby appeared onstage: Keep Kool* program, Morosco, June 2, 1924.

47 *mannequin wearing an evening gown:* Caption for photograph of Dorothy Van Alst, newspaper clipping, n.d.

47 Keep Kool *was more than three hours long:* Gordon Whyte, *Billboard,* May 31, 1924.

47 *"too good to be missed":* Mr. Hornblow Goes to the Play, *Theatre Magazine,* April 24, 1924.

47 *A block south of the Morosco: Sitting Pretty* program, April 1924.

47 *After the show Ruby's sisters:* Vaslett to author, September 2, 1999.

48 *During the summer* Keep Kool *moved: Keep Kool* program, July 7, 1924.

48 *by the fall it had moved again:* Earl Carroll Theatre program, September 26, 1924.

48 *Among them was Dorothy:* Mansfield to author, April 13, 1997.

48 *they were both from Flatbush:* Ibid.

48 *Ruby had confidence:* Ibid.

48 *"one of the famous kuties":* National Police Gazette, August 30, 1924.

48 *Nothing surprised people:* June Merkent to author, February 2000, 1–2.

48 *Florenz Ziegfeld agreed with the assessment:* Gordon Whyte, *Billboard,* May 31, 1924.

48 *In October 1924:* Dorothy Van Alst, notes on the tours of her career. It is usually said that Stanwyck was in the summer edition of the 1924 *Follies.* That is untrue. She was on tour with the 1923 *Follies* that Ziegfeld kept out on tour through 1925. Nils Hanson; Programs, January 25, 1925, Buffalo.

49 *Ruby was a principal in the show, earning:* Salary file, week ending March 21, 1925, Billy Rose Collection. All figures courtesy of Nils Hanson.

49 *a weekly salary of $50:* Roughly $660 in 2013 dollars.

49 *The* Follies *road show with* Keep Kool *in it:* Newspaper clipping, n.d.; telegram to Dorothy Van Alst; both courtesy of Robert Gale/Dorothy Van Alst archive.

49 *Dorothy Sheppard didn't want to leave:* Mansfield to author, August 20, 1999.

50 *The number builds to Van Alst:* Review, Dorothy Van Alst Papers, courtesy of Robert Gale. Other biographers have said that Ruby Stevens appeared in this number; she did not.

50 *After opening in Detroit, the show toured:* Nancy Bernard Levy, who traveled in *Keep Kool,* to author, March 21, 1998.

50 *months to Cleveland, Buffalo:* Dorothy Van Alst, oral history, courtesy of Robert Gale.

50 *"But I'm a Christian":* Levy to author, March 21, 1998.

51 *Ruby had a "problem":* Levy to author, March 21, 1998.

51 Gay Paree *opened in Atlantic City:* Apollo Theatre program, August 3, 1925.

51 *It starred Billy B. Van, Chic Sale:* David Ewen, *Complete Book of the American Musical Theater* (New York: Holt, 1959), 124.

51 *Earl Lindsay hired Ruby and Mae:* Mansfield to author, August 27, 1999.

Six: The Prevailing Sizzle

PAGE

52 Gay Paree *was conceived:* Gilbert Gabriel, *New York Sun,* n.d.

52 *"continental revue":* From an ad.

52 *The show was fast paced:* Review by Ashton Stevens, newspaper clipping, n.d.

52 *The chorus of* Gay Paree *danced the American crawl:* Burns Mantle, review, *New York Daily News,* n.d., 22.

52 *"There are girls and girls":* Gilbert Gabriel, review, *New York Sun,* August 19, 1925.

52 *It was the first time in the history:* Burns Mantle, *New York Daily News,* September 9, 1923.

53 *Fay's rare timing, control:* Colgate Baker, *New York Review,* August 12, 1919.

53 Artists and Models *was instantly sold out:* Ibid.

53 *"the most original":* Judge, September 13, 1923.

53 *Michael Arlen's play* The Green Hat: *The Critic Says,* 1925, 9.

54 *Its caricature of well-mannered:* The Vortex *program notes,* October 19, 1925, 30.

54 *Nils Granlund put together:* Granlund, *Blondes, Brunettes, and Bullets,* 129, 130.

55 *Dorothy, whose mother was:* Walda Mansfield to author, April 1997.

55 *She liked the idea:* Clarke, *Featured Player,* 19.

55 *When the girls thought:* Randall Malone to author, March 21, 2001.

55 *"They were both beautiful girls":* Screenland plus TV-Land, 1964.

55 *But she loved the work:* Cleveland Amory, newspaper clipping, May 28, 1967.

55 *Sally O'Neil called Billie:* Elizabeth Wilson, "Joan Crawford Projections," *Silver Screen,* October 1936.

55 *On Sundays, Ruby, Mae, and Dorothy slept:* BS, in Jane Ardmore, *TV Radio Mirror,* May 1967.

55 *During the service:* Ibid.

56 *Dorothy was content:* Mansfield to author, April 13, 1997.

57 *regularly went to Schrafft's:* Dana O'Connell to author, February 11, 1998.

57 *In 1923 chorus girls:* Dana O'Connell, in Ziegfeld and Ziegfeld, *Ziegfeld Touch,* 94, 95.

57 *The triumvirate went out together:* BS, in Jane Ardmore, *TV Radio Mirror,* May 1967.

58 *LaHiff's Tavern was the kind:* Clarke, *Featured Player,* 23, 24.

58 *Hellinger was thought to be the first:* Bishop, *Mark Hellinger Story,* 63.

58 *Winchell's column,* Your Broadway and Mine: Green and Laurie, *Show Biz,* 217.

58 *a newspaper for the "masses:":* Neal Gabler, *Winchell* (New York: 1994), Alfred A. Knopf, 60.

58 *Winchell and Hellinger were so linked:* Ibid., 70.

58 *Ruby, Mae, and Dorothy knew they could go:* BS, in Gladys Hall, *Modern Screen,* November 1937.

58 *"La Hiff and his waiter Jack Spooner":* "B Stanwyck," *Today and Yesterday,* 1949(?).

58 *"Down and out fighters":* BS, in Gladys Hall, *Modern Screen,* November 1937.

58 *"our chance to step up":* Clarke, *Featured Player,* 23, 24.

59 *Ruby was ambitious:* Ibid.

59 *Ruby was the most disciplined:* Malone to author, February 9, 2001.

59 *Dorothy wanted to make money:* Mansfield to author, April 1997.

59 *Ruby told Dorothy about the death:* Mansfield to author, 1997.

59 *"You seem as if":* Mansfield to author, April 1997.

59 *"an enemy, not a friend":* Adela Rogers St. John, *Photoplay,* January 1936.

59 *Ruby didn't want to hear:* Malone to author, February 9, 2001.

59 *"Ruby would finish books":* Ibid.

59 *It was clear that Ruby thought:* Ibid.

59 *Ruby admired that:* Gene Vaslett to author, November 2, 1999.

59 *One Christmas the whole family:* Vaslett to author, September 16, 1999.

60 *The Everglades Café was transformed:* Abel Green, review, *Variety,* October 7, 1925.

60 *"Bootlegging, speakeasies":* Clarke, *Featured Player,* 23.

60 *"Something was happening"*: Ibid.

60 *He knew she was fifteen:* Ibid.

60 *"hopping from one [supper club]"*: Ibid., 143.

60 *At other times Ruby and Mae went:* Malone to author, February 9, 2001.

60 *To Mae the gangsters were nice:* Malone to author, March 5, 2001.

61 *They got to the Everglades Café:* Barbara Stanwyck, "Moving Day," *Photoplay,* January 1949.

61 *"We worked like dogs"*: Ibid.

61 *Ruby learned discipline:* Paul Rosenfield, Calendar, *Los Angeles Times,* April 5, 1987.

61 *It didn't fit that well:* Judith Stevens to author, May 19, 1999, 8.

61 *He took his lit cigar:* BS, in Walter Ramsey, *Modern Screen,* May 1931; Judith Stevens to author, May 1999.

61 *"Ruby was tough"*: Malone to author, February 9, 2001.

61 *She was becoming more:* Ibid.

62 *"This is it"*: Ibid.

62 *She had a childlike gentleness:* Ibid.

62 *"wangle it"*: Clarke, *Featured Player,* 24.

62 *"I wouldn't have known that"*: Ibid.

62 *"We were harum-scarum"*: S. R. Mook, *Modern Screen,* October 1934, 96.

62 *"She was the Duchess"*: Clarke, *Featured Player,* 24.

Seven: On Being Actresses, Not Asstresses

PAGE

63 *became protective:* Walda Mansfield to author, April 1997.

63 *A year before he opened:* Anatol Friedland obituary, *New York Herald Tribune,* July 25, 1938; *New York Times,* July 25, 1938.

63 *"Whatever he did"*: Mansfield to author, April 24, 1997.

64 *Malcolm at twenty-one:* Gene Vaslett to author, October 17, 1996.

64 *and out of the heat:* Gene Brown, *Show Time* (New York: Macmillan, 1997), 79; $100,000 in 1926 was the equivalent of $1,283,000 in 2013 dollars.

64 *After nine months of trying:* Vaslett to author, October 1999.

64 *Each time Ruby came to visit:* Vaslett to author, October 17, 1996.

64 *Gene was thrilled:* Vaslett to author, November 17, 1999.

64 *"My sister thinks"*: Shirley Eder to author, 1997.

65 *Maud's son, Albert, would:* Vaslett to author, November 9, 1999.

65 *As spring turned into summer:* Dorothy Van Alst, scrapbook, courtesy of Robert Gale.

65 *While working for:* Mansfield to author, April 13, 1997.

65 *He had the reputation:* Ibid., 743.

65 *De Haven had built:* Slide Interview-*Silent Picture,* no. 15 (Summer 1972)—or, at the Club Airport Gardens, *Los Angeles Times,* April 2, 1933.

65 *Dorothy was tempted:* Mansfield to author, April 13, 1997.

66 *Ruby made it back to shore:* Mansfield to author, August 27, 1999.

66 *At the end of the 1926 summer:* Ibid.

67 *By late summer, theaters:* Brown, *Show Time,* 79.

67 *In the first week:* August 6, 1926.

67 *When they arrived:* BS, in Gladys Hall, *Modern Screen,* November 1937.

67 *"This made all the difference"*: BS, in Gladys Hall, *Modern Screen,* November 1937.

67 *Without Mack's knowledge:* Renée Harris to Hedda Hopper, September 3, 1947, Hedda Hopper Collection, Academy of Motion Picture Arts and Sciences. In any biographical sketch of Stanwyck's life it has been written that it was Willard Mack who hired Stanwyck, Clarke, and Sheppard. It has also been writ-

ten that Mack found the three women through the intervention of Billy LaHiff, who supposedly went over to Mack, then dining at LaHiff's Tavern, and suggested the three women. Also an incorrect story.

67 *By 1920, Van Loan:* H. H. Van Loan, *How I Did It* (Los Angeles: Whittingham Press, 1922), 129.

68 *"with human frailties":* Willard Mack, "The Writing of Plays," n.d., Shubert Press Office, Shubert Archive.

68 *The realism of his characters:* Ibid.

68 *"their ways of living":* Ibid.

68 *"handsome, wonderful actor":* Clarke, *Featured Player,* 26.

68 *Cherryman, then twenty-nine:* John Harkins, *Morning Telegraph,* November 9, 1926.

68 *"George Nash was the villain":* Clarke, *Featured Player,* 25.

68 *When the script:* Ibid.

68 *Bill Mack wanted to rehearse:* Mansfield to author, April 24, 1997.

68 *Miss Rambeau had forcefully:* "The Eternal Triangle," 1918, Star Company.

69 *By 1926, Belasco:* Samuel Spewack, *The Broadway Revolution,* no. 6, "David Belasco," January 2, 1930.

69 *Belasco had started:* H. I. Brock, "Belasco, Magician of the Theatre," *New York Times Magazine,* July 21, 1929.

69 *By 1915, Belasco was:* "Mr. Belasco and a Passing Matter of Footlights," *New York Times Magazine,* February 2, 1930.

69 *By using manually operated:* "Belasco Found Varied Lights a Big Problem," *New York American,* March 10, 1919.

70 *Another housed the:* Earl Sparling, *New York World Telegram,* n.d.

70 *And then, finally:* Sidney Skolsky, *New York Sun,* March 19, 1928.

70 *Mack had Ruby read:* Rex Reed, *New York Daily News.* April 13, 1981.

70 *"I kept wondering":* BS, in Gladys Hall, *Modern Screen,* November 1937.

70 *"Go to the zoo!":* BS, in Adele Whitley Fletcher, *Lady's Circle,* March 1969.

70 *"He sounded as though":* Rex Reed, *New York Daily News,* April 13, 1981.

71 *"bravest of all":* John Greenleaf Whittier, "Barbara Frietchie."

71 *"took up the flag":* Ibid.

71 *play was fresh:* Bill Everson notes for *Barbara Frietchie.*

71 *"Jane Stanwyck won't do":* BS, in Gladys Hall, *Modern Screen,* November 1937.

71 *Cowl was due to:* Brown, *Show Time,* 82.

71 *with Philip Merivale in a debut play:* Ibid., 62.

71 *"As one man":* Gladys Hall, *Modern Screen,* November 1937.

72 *Later, when Ruby signed:* BS to Rex Reed, 1981.

72 *Mrs. Harris cast and staged:* New York Telegraph, December 6, 1926.

72 *She'd learned from her brother:* Ibid.

72 *Henry Harris was from:* Silas B. Fishkind, "A Woman Unafraid," newspaper clipping, n.d., Shubert Archive.

72 *Shortly before Harris:* Gerald Bordman, *The Oxford Companion to American Theatre* (New York: Oxford University Press, 2004), 292.

72 *The Harrises' journey abroad:* New York Times, April 11, 1912, 1.

72 *Mrs. Harris broke an arm:* Lord, *A Night to Remember,* 12.

72 *On the fourth day out:* Ibid.

72 *Women and children were loaded:* Ibid.

72 *Henry Harris, then forty-five years old:* Fishkind, "Woman Unafraid."

72 *The boat sat forty-seven:* Lord, *A Night to Remember,* 82.

72 *Renée (listed on the ship's manifest as Irene):* Passenger list *Titanic;* Robert Landry, obituary, *Variety,* September 1969, 118.

72 *Following a long period:* Lord, *The Night Lives On,* 172.

73 *One of the first to be presented:* Ibid.

73 *Renée Harris became a theatrical:* New York Telegraph, December 6, 1926.

73 *Mack was tough and demanding:* Joseph W. Phillips, "As Willard Mack Rehearses a Play," Shubert Press Department, Shubert Archive.

73 *acted in more than 130 plays:* Julia Chandler, "The Belasco I Know," *Mid-week Pictorial,* July 13, 1929, Shubert Archive.

73 *Mack's notion of realism:* Joseph W. Phillips, "Willard Mack Talks About the Theater," n.d., Shubert Archive.

74 *Mack believed that his new play:* Willard Mack, "The New Realism of the Stage," Shubert Archive.

74 *Established standards had been thrown:* Ibid.

74 *"It is a way":* BS, in Adele Whitley Fletcher, *Lady's Circle,* March 1969, 64.

75 *"It was a big nothing":* Clarke, *Featured Player,* 25.

75 *"the girl who has":* Ibid.

75 *Mrs. Harris told Mack to rewrite:* Renée Harris to Hedda Hopper, September 3, 1947. Hedda Hopper Collection, Academy of Motion Pictures Arts and Sciences.

75 *"You've got a great":* Clarke, *Featured Player,* 25.

75 *Bill Mack left for New York:* Harris to Hopper, September 3, 1947.

75 *Renée Harris worked with:* Ibid.

75 *"I was no actress":* Rex Reed interview, April 13, 1981.

75 *"dynamic":* Harris to Hopper, September 3, 1947.

75 *Mack called several times:* Ibid.

75 *"proceeded to go":* Ibid.

75 *During the remainder:* Paul Rosenfield, Calendar, *Los Angeles Times,*

75 *Toward the end:* James Gregory, *Movie Digest,* 1972.

76 *"It's no use":* Gladys Hall, *Modern Screen,* November 1937.

76 *"dead right":* Ibid.

76 *"I told him I was":* Ibid.

76 *Mack had seen temperament:* S. R. Mook, *Modern Screen,* October 1934, 96.

76 *Then he hammered:* James Gregory, *Movie Digest,* 1972.

76 *teaching Ruby how:* Paul Rosenfield, Calendar, *Los Angeles Times,* April 5, 1987.

76 *how to sell:* Gladys Hall, *Modern Screen,* November 1937.

76 *"Mostly he taught me":* Rosenfield, Calendar, *Los Angeles Times,* April 5, 1987.

76 *Mae and Dorothy worked:* Clarke, *Featured Player,* 26.

76 *After rehearsals:* Mansfield to author, April 24, 1997.

76 *"Everything about him":* Lincoln Center Tribute, *Film Comment,* March–April 1981; *New York Times,* August 11, 1928.

76 *He'd traveled to Los Angeles:* New York Times, August 11, 1928.

76 *The cast rehearsed:* William French, *Screen Play,* June 1936, 22.

77 *"When I came out":* Ibid., 59.

77 *"didn't recognize":* Ibid.

77 *Then Dot sinks her head: The Noose,* script act 3, Billy Rose Collection.

77 *"didn't say a word":* Clarke, *Featured Player,* 26.

78 *"a simple melodrama":* Pittsburgh Post, October 11, 1926.

78 *"I did it":* James Gregory, *Movie Digest,* 1972.

78 *"It's noisy back stage":* Samuels, "In Search of Ruby Stevens."

78 The Noose *was being compared:* New York Times, October 21, 1926.

78 *"realistic as a metronome":* S. N. Behrman, *Tribulations and Laughter* (London: Hamish Hamilton, 1972), 39, 38.

78 *was a big hit:* Brown, *Show Time,* 80. Lee Tracy's understudy was James Cagney.

78 *"melodrama of a slightly old"*: *New York Times,* October 21, 1926.

78 *He assured them that:* Ibid.; *New York World,* October 21, 1926.

79 *"the most authentically teary"*: *New York Telegram,* October 23, 1926.

79 *Another time Ruby heard:* BS, in Gladys Hall, *Modern Screen,* November 1937.

79 *They were sure:* BS, in Margaret Lee Runbeck, *Good Housekeeping,* July 1954.

79 *"We both had these terrible"*: Edwin Kennedy, in Ruth Waterbury, *TV Radio Mirror,* December 1966.

80 *"he was wrong there"*: Axel Madsen, *Stanwyck* (New York: HarperCollins, 1994), 27.

80 *She and Rex began to spend:* Vaslett to author.

80 *Its competition during:* Gentlemen Prefer Blondes opened September 28, 1926; Brown, *Show Time,* 80.

80 *In November, Gertrude Lawrence:* Oh, Kay! opened November 8, 1926; ibid., 81.

80 *Ethel Barrymore was playing:* The Constant Wife opened November 29, 1926; ibid.

81 *When* The Captive *opened:* It opened September 29, 1926; Ibid., 80.

81 *"unprecedented . . . a study"*: Bourdet, *Captive,* back of jacket.

81 *"profoundly wrought"*: *New York Morning Telegraph,* n.d.

81 *Marion Davies was unfazed:* Leonora Hornblow to author.

81 *Articles condemning* The Captive: Hornblow to author, January 11, 2000.

81 *The Society for the Suppression of Vice:* Leider, *Becoming Mae West,* 152.

82 *In response to the hysteria:* Ibid., 166.

82 *Sex had been written:* Green and Laurie, *Show Biz,* 288.

82 *When it opened:* Ibid., 81.

82 *Tickets sold for the extraordinary:* Ibid.

82 *The play was making:* Leider, *Becoming Mae West,* 152.

82 *No newspaper, including:* West, *Goodness Had Nothing to Do with It,* 80.

82 *"I'm going to dig"*: Ibid., 74.

82 *The charge: obscenity:* February 9, 1927 THREE PLAYS BY MAE WEST, Lillian Shlissel (Routledge, 1997), 8.

82 *"It was no rose"*: West, *Goodness Had Nothing to Do with It,* 87.

83 The Shanghai Gesture *was about:* Brown, *Show Time,* 82.

83 *the headline in the* New York Herald Tribune: Leider, *Becoming Mae West,* 155.

83 *"an obscene, indecent, immoral"*: Ibid., 15.

83 *The jury handed down:* Grand jury indictment of Mae West, William Morganstern, James Timony, John Cort, The Moral Producing Company, and the Cast of Characters, Case 168495.

83 *The judge applauded the decision:* Leider, *Becoming Mae West,* 167.

83 *Welfare Island:* Now Roosevelt Island.

83 *pay a fine of $500:* Ibid., 168.

83 The Captive *reopened and closed:* Ibid., 164.

83 The Captive's *translator:* Hornblow to author, January 12, 2000.

83 *"She cried and she screamed"*: Mansfield to author, April 24, 1997.

Eight: Formerly Ruby Stevens of the Cabarets

PAGE

84 *Ruby tested for the part:* Broadway Nights press book, 1927.

84 *The cameraman:* Ibid.

85 *Miss Chatterton was quiet:* Account by Wilbur Morse Jr., in Ella Smith, *Starring Miss Barbara Stanwyck* (New York: Crown, 1974), 5.

85 *Kane was so impressed:* Broadway Nights press book.

85 The Noose *closed in New York:* Suzanne Fraseur, *Variety,* June 8, 1927.

85 *Business was slow:* Ibid.

85 *Ruby, Dorothy Sheppard, and Mae Clarke:* BS, in Gladys Hall, *Modern Screen,* November 1937.

85 *going in and out:* Dixie Willson, *Photoplay,* December 1937.

86 *Dorothy Sheppard was now:* Walda Mansfield to author, March 4, 2000.

86 *"lost all sense":* Mae Clarke to S. R. Mook, January 1932.

86 *Once her mood abated:* Dolores Hope to Stephen Silverman, February 29, 2000.

86 *Shurr was a short:* Ibid.

86 *Shurr suggested that Mae:* Clarke, *Featured Player,* 29.

86 *Donaldson played song after:* Ibid., 28.

86 *Next Mae called her friend:* Mansfield to author, April 1997.

86 *with little diamonds:* Clarke, *Featured Player,* 29.

86 *"Besides, he was cute":* Ibid.

86 *White liked what he saw:* Review, *Variety,* August 24, 1927. Elizabeth Hines starred in the show when it
toured out of town.

86 *Mae was given two:* Clarke, *Featured Player,* 30.

86 *Ruby was looking:* Mansfield to author, April 1997.

87 *Her ambitions of being:* Edwin Kennedy in Ruth Waterbury, *TV Radio Mirror,* December 1966, 42.

87 *"This is crazy":* Ibid.

87 *Watters had been:* Gilbert Gabriel, *New York Sun,* September 2, 1927.

87 *The play was given:* *Variety,* May 11, 1927.

87 *The producer sent the script:* Hopkins, *To a Lonely Boy,* 248.

87 *Hopkins thought the play:* Ibid.

87 *Hopkins's experience:* Ibid., 77.

87 *Writing and acting:* Ibid.

88 *Jones moved away from:* Ibid., 154.

88 *"from the unconscious":* Arthur Hopkins, "The Lost Theatre," *New Outlook,* January 1933, 21.

88 *Watters was delighted:* Hopkins, *To a Lonely Boy,* 249.

89 *"Atta boy, Skid":* Totheroh, *Burlesque.*

89 *"Yeah," Skid says:* Anyone who saw that production of *Burlesque* never forgot it. Studs Terkel, who saw the
production in Chicago in its 1929 tour, remembered the final scene, the final line of the play, sixty-nine
years later when I interviewed him in December 1997. "How could I forget that night?" he said. "I remember that moment, that line, when they were hoofing and she says, 'Marriage is for better or worse,'
and he says, 'Better for me and worse for you.' Never forgot it."

89 *"engaging, lovable":* Hopkins, *To a Lonely Boy,* 249.

90 *"sort of rough poignancy":* Ibid.

90 *He leaned back:* Madsen, *Stanwyck,* 31.

90 *Instead, he agreed to pay:* Walter Ramsey, *Modern Screen,* May 1931.

90 *"Hopkins told me his terms":* Madsen, *Stanwyck,* 31.

90 *"the perfect team":* Hopkins, *To a Lonely Boy,* 249.

91 *Four days into rehearsals:* Nancy Bernard to author, April 21, 1998.

91 *"Ruby never paid":* Ibid.

91 *Hopkins's rehearsals were known:* *New York American,* January 1928.

91 *Hopkins stayed in the shadows:* Roy L. McCardell, *New York Morning Telegraph,* April 2, 1922.

91 *Hopkins sought naturalness:* Ibid.

91 *Oddly, it was during:* Ibid.

91 *that he came to understand:* Hopkins, *To a Lonely Boy.*

91 *He saw vaudeville:* Ibid., 102.

91 *His only safety:* Ibid., 103.

91 *Hopkins watched Ruby work:* Ibid., 250.

91 *He'd first seen:* Ibid., 148.

92 *Hopkins worked as well:* Ibid., 161.

92 *During the summer months:* Variety, July 20, 1927.

92 *"a big drunken lout":* Hal Skelly, "That's Why Whitey Was Born," *New York Times,* February 11, 1934.

92 *Like Skid, Skelly: New York Herald Tribune,* June 17, 1934.

92 *"elected for the job":* Jane Ellen Wayne, *Stanwyck* (New York: Arbor House, 1985), 20.

92 *Hopkins wanted a musician:* Kashner and Schoenberger, *Talent for Genius,* 63.

92 *Levant had just returned:* Levant, *Memoirs of an Amnesiac,* 79.

93 *"full of technical ornamentation":* Ibid., 65.

93 *He studied the work:* Ibid.

93 *he and Ruby became good friends:* Walter Ramsey, *Modern Screen,* May 1931.

94 *"got through marveling":* Modern Screen, October 1934, 96.

94 *"never heard one person":* Ella Smith, *Starring Miss Barbara Stanwyck,* 11.

94 *President Coolidge announced: World Almanac and Book of Facts for 1928,* 118.

95 *"We have not yet reached":* Meltzer, *Brother, Can You Spare a Dime?,* 3.

95 *The opening night audience:* Alexander Woollcott, *New York World,* September 2, 1927.

95 *"the trick first": New York Times,* September 2, 1927.

95 *"more touching piece":* Walter Winchell, Opening Nights, September 2, 1927.

95 *"no account and palpably":* Alexander Woollcott, *New York World,* September 2, 1927.

95 *"Young Barbara Stanwyck":* Variety, September 7, 1927.

96 *Every time she moved her hand:* BS, in Jane Ardmore, *TV Radio Mirror,* May 1967.

96 *The 650-seat theater: New York Times,* September 5, 1927.

96 *The show was grossing: New York Times,* n.d.

96 *"Chorus girls stripped":* Terence O'Flaherty, *San Francisco Chronicle,* March 18, 1967.

96 *"She just looked at me":* Gene Vaslett to author, October 19, 1996.

96 *"she sat there":* Mansfield to author, April 1997.

97 *"She was the rage":* Levant, *Memoirs of an Amnesiac,* 82.

97 *Ruby sent a note to Mr. Nast:* Ibid.

98 *"the only girl who'd":* BS, in Jane Ardmore, *Above and Beyond/* "This Chorus Girl's Made It."

98 *The catcalls so agitated Ed:* Edwin Kennedy, in Jane Ardmore, *TV Radio Mirror,* December 1966.

98 *The play wasn't doing:* Variety, September 21, 1927.

98 *Ona Munson was brought in:* Ibid.

98 *He had written screenplays:* Veiller, *The Fun I've Had,* 239–41.

98 *Alexander Woollcott described the opening: NY World,* September 20, 1927.

98 *agent, who refused to read it:* Ibid.

99 Burlesque *was right behind:* Variety, n.d., 50.

99 *Two weeks after* Burlesque *opened:* Walter Ramsey, *Modern Screen,* May 1931.

99 Manhattan Mary *opened:* Featured in the play was Paul Frawley, brother of Bill, whom Mae Clarke described as "the star of the two brothers because he was younger and handsomer and a singer, therefore the love interest. In those days, your comedians were second bananas." *Featured Player,* 32.

99 *"There-it-is, one, two":* Ibid., 33.

99 *A couple of weeks later:* Clive Hirschhorn, *The Warner Bros. Story* (New York: Crown, 1979), 34.

99 *The lines went around:* Kevin Brownlow, *Hollywood: End of an Era* (Thames Television, 1980).

99 *"that when the guy opens":* Mosley, *Zanuck,* 92.

99 *"If we can get him":* Ibid.

99 *Jolson agreed to make:* Herbert G. Goldman, *Jolson: The Legend Comes to Life* (New York: Oxford University Press, 1988), 149–52.

99 *In the picture, directed by Alan: The Jazz Singer* program notes, 1927.

100 *Zanuck came up with:* Gussow, *Don't Say Yes Until I Finish Talking,* 44.

100 *"The public won't put up":* Kotsilibas-Davis, *Barrymores,* 78.

Nine: Broadway's Favorite Son

PAGE

101 *"Frank Fay's a great guy"*: Levant, *Memoirs of an Amnesiac,* 79.

101 *"the big time"*: Milton Berle to author, October 1997.

101 *"Albee's Irish Rose"*: *New York Telegraph,* July 11, 1926.

101 *"the Chairman"*: *New York American,* May 30, 1926.

101 *After a run of eight*: *New York Tribune,* July 11, 1926.

102 *"They never went after"*: Elliot Norton, *New York Times,* November 5, 1944.

102 *"You'd meet a vaudevillian"*: Irving Fern, *Jack Benny* (New York: Putnam, 1976), 18.

103 *"not what they used"*: Frank Fay, *Philadelphia Inquirer,* March 4, 1928.

103 *"The public will not stand"*: Colgate Baker, "Girl o Mine and Frank Fay," newspaper clipping, n.d., Shubert Archive.

103 *"wide open with no"*: Frank Fay, *Philadelphia Inquirer,* March 4, 1928.

103 *Then, as he was doing*: Steve Allen to author, September 14, 1999.

103 *"always finished up"*: Frank Fay, Shubert press release, 1918, Shubert Archive.

103 *"an aversion to"*: "He Never Told a Joke," press release, Shubert Archive.

103 *"natural; a human"*: Frank Fay, 1920, Shubert Archive.

103 *and another of his doing*: Allen, to author, September 14, 1999.

103 *Burns also saw Fay*: Ibid., 99. Before Ted Healy, and before he developed the Three Stooges.

103 *"stock company"*: *Boston Post,* December 21, 1926.

104 *He didn't want her*: James Robert Parish and William T. Leonard, *The Funsters* (New Rochelle, N.Y.: Arlington House, 1979), 358.

104 *After* Burlesque *opened*: Levant, *Memoirs of an Amnesiac,* 83.

104 *Fay conducted the audience*: Ken Murray, in Allen, unpublished manuscript, 30.

104 *He felt he had an advantage*: Press release, 1918, Shubert Archive.

104 *"He could give you an inferiority"*: Jesse White to author, February 1997.

104 *He had a way of making*: Gene Vaslett to author, May 30, 2000.

104 *Bob Hope and Jack Benny adopted*: Steve Allen to author, September 14, 1999.

104 *In it Fay introduced*: Jack Benny used this affect later.

104 *"He always worked"*: Allen, to author, September 14, 1999.

104 *"He had a hauteur"*: Milton Berle to author, October 1997.

105 *"the wistful comedian"*: Ada Patterson, *Screenland,* September 1933, 90.

105 *Then he would raise*: Steve Allen, to author, September 14, 1999.

105 *" 'Just picture me upon' "*: Ibid.

105 *He called it "breaking up"*: J. P. Shanley, "Frank Fay Returns," *New York Times,* October 27, 1957.

105 *Fay might stop there*: Ibid.

105 *"We just fell in love"*: Walda Mansfield to author, April 25, 1997.

105 *"something to see"*: George Burns, *All My Best Friends,* with David Fisher (New York: Putnam, 1989), 55.

105 *"incomparable"*: Berle to author, October 1997.

106 *Eddie Cantor said Fay*: Ibid.

106 *While Ed Wynn and Raymond*: Review of Frank Fay's *Intimates,* newspaper clipping, April 4, 1921.

106 *He often shepherded more*: "Why Master of Ceremonies? Ask Frank Fay, He Knows," newspaper clipping, November 16, 1929, Shubert Archive.

106 *"Fay would comment on"*: Ibid.

106 *Women saw Fay*: Colgate Baker, *New York Review,* August 2, 1919.

106 *"blonde young comic"*: *New York Tribune,* June 1, 1926.

106 *"auburn haired"*: *Boston Herald,* December 26, 1926.

106 *"I was a pugilist"*: *Boston Evening Transcript,* December 28, 1926.

107 *"had an aura":* Levant, *Memoirs of an Amnesiac,* 80.

107 *When Fay came offstage:* Berle, *Milton Berle.*

108 *"And we loved to listen":* Ibid.

109 *Frank disliked Barbara:* Sidney Skolsky, newspaper clipping, 1932, Shubert Archive.

109 *"I took it":* Walda Mansfield to author, April 1997.

109 *Claire brought the silver:* Mansfield to author, April 1997.

109 *Claire adored Barbara:* Ibid.

109 *"thought he was the one":* Nancy Bernard Levy to author, March 21, 1998.

109 *He had his own:* Colgate Baker, *New York Review,* August 2, 1919, Shubert Archive.

109 *"nobody drank because":* Mansfield to author, April 1997.

110 *"The wonderful love":* On the inside back cover of Fay's scrapbook, Lincoln Center.

110 *"had always been an addict":* New York Journal, November 11, 1944, Frank Fay Scrapbook, Lincoln Center.

110 *She had heard of:* Chorus Equity Claims Against the Frank Fay Company, June 17, 1921; "Frank Fay Fables," 1923, Actors' Equity Files.

110 *After only two months:* They met in March, married in April, and were divorced in June of the same year.

111 *Because of his cruelty:* Allen to author, September 14, 1999.

111 *"the fastest mind":* Maurice Zolotow, *No People like Show People* (New York: Random House, 1951), 204.

112 *The audience laughed:* Allen to author, September 14, 1999.

112 *When the stage manager:* Anthony Slide, *The Vaudevillians: A Dictionary of Vaudeville Performers* (Westport, Conn.: Arlington House, 1981).

112 *Fay was known to look:* Berle to author, October 10, 1997.

112 *When he came offstage:* Jesse White to author, February 1997.

112 *"He was a joy":* Mansfield to author, April 1997.

112 *"she and Fay were together":* Clara Beranger, "The Private Life of Barbara Stanwyck," *Liberty,* September 17, 1932.

112 *If Fay uttered a wish:* Vaslett to author, October 19, 1996, 14.

112 *Fay didn't like it when:* Skolsky, newspaper clipping, 1932, Shubert Archive.

112 *He preferred her in:* Radie Harris, *Silver Screen,* December 1930, 27.

112 *His formal education ended:* New York Times, September 27, 1961.

113 *Frank Fay made his debut:* Elliot Norton, "Notes on a Genius with Guts," *New York Times,* November 5, 1944.

113 *He appeared in every:* Zolotow, *No People like Show People* (New York: Bantam Books, 1952), 193.

113 *"looked forward to":* Baker, "Girl o Mine and Frank Fay."

113 *He had appeared at:* Press Department, 1918, Shubert Archive.

Ten: Having a Hunch

PAGE

114 *First National Pictures released:* January 29, 1928. The film of *The Noose* stars Richard Barthelmess as Nickie Elkins, Thelma Todd as Phyllis, the society girl, and Lina Basquette in the Barbara Stanwyck role as Dot. William Torbert Leonard, *Theatre: Stage to Screen to Television* (Metuchen, N.J.: Scarecrow, 1981).

114 *Some thought Lina and Barbara:* Nancy Sinatra Sr. to author, August 3, 2002.

114 *Lina, a featured dancer:* In 1916, Basquette was offered a six-year contract, the longest yet offered, by Laemmle. Barry Paris, "The Godless Girl," *New Yorker,* February 19, 1989, 56. The press called Lina, Pavlova Junior. Universal assigned Lois Weber to direct her in her first picture, *The Juvenile Dancer Supreme: Lena Baskette in a Group of Classical Dances.* Ibid.

114 *Ziegfeld was furious:* Ibid., 57.

114 *By the time Lina got:* Ibid.

114 *Paramount Famous Lasky: Variety,* January 25, 1928, 53.

114 *Louis B. Mayer, the general manager:* Crowther, *Hollywood Rajah,* 23.

115 *"Fay was irate":* Levant, *Memoirs of an Amnesiac,* 82.

115 *"It was instantaneous":* Clarke, *Featured Player,* 34, 31.

115 *"a handsome dresser":* Ibid., 31.

115 *"Get on that train":* Ibid., 36.

115 *"You could see he had":* Ibid.

116 *Lew Brice (1938):* Herbert G. Goldman, *Fanny Brice* (Oxford University Press, 1992), 108–9.

116 *The act was a musical:* Ibid., 37.

116 *The Brice and Clarke act: Variety,* December 5, 1928.

116 *"Our whole act":* Clarke, *Featured Player,* 38.

116 *"People are especially critical":* Contract signed February 15, 1928, J. Walter Thompson Archives, Duke University.

117 *He asked Barbara to marry:* Radie Harris, *Silver Screen,* December 1930, 62.

117 *During the crossing he: Variety,* August 15, 1928.

118 *When the boat docked: New York Times,* August 11, 1928.

118 *"Barbara's relationship with Rex":* Walda Mansfield to author, April 4, 1997.

118 *"if you see ten troubles":* Memoirs of Herbert Hoover. 55.

118 *Some worried that if:* Galbraith, *Great Crash, 1929,* 15.

118 *"Leave it alone":* Gene Smith, *Shattered Dream,* 56–57.

119 *"hadn't had a drink":* Frank Fay to Walter Ramsey, June 1931.

119 *Barbara and Frank rushed off:* Fay, in Lucy Greenbaum, *Globe Democrat,* December 8, 1928. *New York World,* August 27, 1928.

119 *With them was Spyros:* Lucy Greenbaum, *Globe Democrat,* n.d.

119 *Ruby Stevens was now: New York Times,* August 27, 1928. Frank Fay claimed that Spyros Skouras was the best man at their wedding, and it has been written in biographies of Stanwyck that Skouras did attend; Barbara Stanwyck, in a memo to Helen Ferguson, wrote: "Here's a new one Skouras was Fay's best man at our wedding." Larry Kleno to author. December 5, 2002.

119 *By 5:00 p.m., Barbara was: New York Daily News,* August 26, 1928.

119 *Barbara couldn't have cared:* Samuels, "In Search of Ruby Stevens."

120 *"of etiquette and the niceties":* Faith Service, *Motion Picture,* December 1932.

120 *"it was no way":* BS, in Walter Ramsey, "The Amazing Life of Barbara Stanwyck," *Modern Screen,* July 1931.

120 *"It was very dramatic":* John Slotkin to Shirley Eder, Detroit, November 25, 1964.

120 *After staying in the hospital:* Ibid.

121 *Barbara said that when:* Ibid.

121 *Eddie Mannix, one of:* Clarke, *Featured Player,* 135.

121 *It was a picture called:* Ibid., 39.

121 *"Are you out of":* Ibid.

121 *At Fanny Brice's suggestion:* Ibid., 43.

122 *Mae couldn't think:* Ibid., 40, 41.

122 *The word came back:* Ibid.

122 *Mae ate her first:* Ibid., 41.

123 *Gene, Mabel, and Maud traveled:* Gene Vaslett to author, June 2, 1999.

123 *They left the sanitarium:* Vaslett to author, April 5, 2001.

123 *Gene, who was:* Vaslett to author, June 29, 2000.

123 *At the end of the evening:* Vaslett to author, June 7, 1999, 11.

123 *Kingman, Arizona, had been:* Kingman, Arizona, Chamber of Commerce.

124 *Elizabeth's doctor told him:* Judith Stevens to author, January 15, 1999, 20.

124 *Goldwyn had sent a wire:* Samuel Goldwyn to Al Lichtman, telegram, December 26, 1928.

124 *Barbara responded to Goldwyn's:* Ibid.

124 *Barbara's name was mentioned: Variety,* January 29, 1920, 48.

124 *Byron was heartbroken:* Green-Wood Cemetery records, receipt BSFAY.

124 *He had traveled in a world:* Judith Stevens to author, January 15, 1999.

124 *By loved his sister:* Judith Stevens to author, January 15, 1999.

124 *Barbara and By looked:* Judith Stevens to author, January 15, 1999.

Eleven: Invitation West

PAGE

125 *Fay opened at Keith's Palace: Variety,* January 30, 1929.

125 *"Let's build a stairway to": Be Frank with Fay,* Bally Records, 1957.

125 *"and could have made": Variety,* February 6, 1929.

125 *"[Fay] is essentially":* James Fidler, "Barbara Stanwyck Answers Twenty Timely Questions," *Movie Classic,* June 1933, 23.

126 *During their second week: New York Times,* February 11, 1929.

126 *Barbara's clothes reflected:* The Skirt Jr., *Variety,* February 13, 1929.

126 *"of chief interest": New York Times,* February 11, 1929.

126 *"Frank comes first with me":* Virginia Maxwell, *Picture Play,* October 1932, 64.

126 *Buck had drifted away:* Gene Vaslett to author, October 19, 1996.

126 *He'd lost track:* Buck Mack, *Screen Guide,* 1948.

126 *"Things look good":* Ibid.

126 *"a smart looking, young lady":* Ibid.

126 *Barbara and Frank's run:* Opened February 20, 1929. *Variety,* February 27, 1929, 180.

127 *And Marion Davies made drinks:* Harry Richman, *A Hell of a Life,* with Richard Gehman (New York: Duell, Sloan and Pearce, 1966).

127 *"the most economical":* Bob Hope, in Steve Allen, unpublished manuscript, 31.

127 *"darkened stage":* Bob Hope, in Cleveland Amory, *Parade,* June 22, 1986, 4.

127 *"Everyone knows string savers": Boston Herald,* December 26, 1926.

128 *"dramatic moment":* Ibid.

128 *It was noted how much: Variety,* February 27, 1929.

128 *Barbara and Fay were held: Variety,* March 6, 1929, 59.

128 *Fay was billed as:* Program, February 18, 1929, 13.

128 *The Fays' run followed that: Variety,* January 29, 1929, 48.

128 *Ruth Etting was to appear: Variety,* February 20, 1929.

128 *Barbara and Frank's new manager:* Ibid.

128 *His radio commercials: Variety,* March 6, 1929, 30.

128 *The new technology was coming: Fortune,* April 1930, 20.

128 *Schenck, before becoming president:* Ibid., 45–50.

128 *Schenck, Russian-born:* Gary Carey, *Anita Loos* (New York: Alfred A. Knopf, 1988), 60.

128 *He'd earned his first dimes:* Loos, *Talmadge Girls,* 29.

129 *Within a few years Palisades:* Carey, *Anita Loos,* 60.

129 *In 1917, Schenck left for:* Ibid., 61.

129 *Schenck had seen Barbara: The Locked Door* press book.

129 *As chairman of the board:* Balio, *United Artists,* 56.

129 *Loew then bought Goldwyn Pictures:* "Loew's Inc.," *Fortune,* August 1939, 28–30.

130 *Barbara nodded and walked:* Helen Louise Walker, *Movie Classic,* June 1932, 62.

130 *On the train, Barbara recognized:* Ibid.

130 *For the next two days:* Wyatt Blassingame, *Great Trains of the World* (New York: Random House, 1953); Lucius Beebe and Charles Clegg, *The Trains We Rode* (Berkeley, Calif.: Howell-North Books, 1966), 53–58.

130 *Amid the luxury:* Loos, *Talmadge Girls,* 63.

131 *"in New York, he might":* Helen Louise Walker, *Movie Classic,* June 1932, 62.

131 *"Do that":* Walda Mansfield to author, April 1997.

Twelve: Panic of Self-Doubt

PAGE

132 *"Pictures have only scratched":* S. R. Mook, *Modern Screen,* October 1934.

132 *She wanted to turn right: Los Angeles Times,* June 21, 1931.

132 *Instead, she sent a Western:* Gene Vaslett to author, June 2000.

132 *Pictures were insane:* Gladys Hall, "Barbara Stanwyck's Advice to Girls in Love," unedited manuscript, 23, Academy of Motion Picture Arts and Sciences Library (hereafter cited as AMPAS).

132 *Fay was expected:* April 10, 1929, letter of agreement between Jack Warner and Frank Fay, Warner Bros. Archives, University of Southern California.

132 *A few days after Fay:* Three-color Technicolor process was not developed until 1932; *Under a Texas Moon* press book, Warner Bros. Archives.

133 *It was one of forty:* Color and Sound on Film, *Fortune,* October 1930, 33.

133 *"She was very cool":* Walda Mansfield to author, April 1997.

133 *"looked the nearest thing":* Gladys Hall, *Modern Screen,* November 1937.

133 *Fay was waiting to begin: Variety,* April 14, 1929, 55.

133 *Barbara put on a gown: Variety,* June 5, 1929, 47.

133 *"wanted a home":* Faith Service, *Motion Picture,* December 1932.

133 *"don't buy anything":* Lyle Talbot, interview with Terry Sanders, May 1989, 16, Screen Actors Guild (hereafter cited as SAG).

133 *The large, comfortable house:* Walter Ramsey, *Modern Screen,* July 1931.

133 *The Langdon character that won:* Ibid.

134 *Three of the four pictures:* Capra, *Name Above the Title,* 58–60.

134 *As soon as he insisted:* David Thomson, *Biographical Dictionary of Film* (New York: Alfred A. Knopf, 2002).

134 *La Rocque and his wife: The Locked Door* press book, Microfilm 448, reel 15, p. 68–1999[pos], Wisconsin Historical Society.

134 *The director of* The Locked Door: Ibid.

134 *George Fitzmaurice, and other:* John Cromwell, interview with Leonard Maltin, *Movie Crazy,* no. 19 (Winter 2007): 5.

134 *The camera now had:* Ed Bernds to author, June 8, 1997.

135 *The camera crews came:* Bernds, *Mr. Bernds Goes to Hollywood.*

135 *What was good for one:* Ibid.

135 *Scenes were ruined when:* Ibid., 80.

135 *or when the microphone picked: Fortune,* October 1930, 32–41.

135 *"you could light a cigar":* Brownlow, *Hollywood.*

135 *The thirty-four incandescent: The Locked Door* press book.

136 *Pola Negri: The Cheat* (1923).

136 *Betty Compson: To Have and to Hold* (1922).

136 *Anna Q. Nilsson: The Man from Home* (1922).

136 *Marie Prevost: Tarnish* (1924).

136 *Gary Cooper: Lilac Time* (1928).

136 *Several of Fitzmaurice's pictures: The Locked Door* press book.

136 *"all one big mystery":* Bernard Drew, *Film Comment,* March–April 1981.

136 *"a magnificent example":* Bernds, *Mr. Bernds Goes to Hollywood,* 74.

136 *For one set in: The Locked Door* press book.

137 *"as an average-looking":* Paul Rosenfield, Calendar, *Los Angeles Times,* April 5, 1987.

137 *Two of her teeth:* Katherine Albert, "She Has Hollywood's Number," *Photoplay,* June 1931, 69.

137 *"Look," Barbara said:* Bernard Drew, *Film Comment,* March–April 1981; Paul Rosenfield, Calendar, *Lo37Angeles Times,* April 5, 1987.

137 *What interested Barbara:* Paul Rosenfield, Calendar, *Los Angeles Times,* April 5, 1987.

137 *Its achievement was: The Locked Door* press book.

137 *Bernds saw Barbara as:* Bernds to author, June 8, 1997.

137 *"Fitzmaurice seemed at quite":* Ibid.

137 *"Fitzmaurice didn't direct":* Ibid.

137 *Barbara's frustration:* Ibid.

137 *it was difficult for her: Variety,* May 22, 1929, 52.

138 *Barbara's husband in the:* Bernds, *Mr. Bernds Goes to Hollywood,* 74.

138 *Her deep and resonant:* Bernds to author, June 3, 1997.

138 *Fay's leading woman: The Bridge of San Luis Rey* had just been released on March 30, 1929.

138 *Torres, who was educated: Stars of the Photoplay* (1930).

139 *Each day when they:* Ralph Bellamy, interview with Ronald L. Davis, *Southern Methodist University,* no. 103, May 18, 1977, 33.

139 *The regular heavy makeup:* "What? Color in the Movies Again?" *Fortune,* October 1934, 92–97.

139 *Pictures that had been made: Variety,* April 10, 1929, 4.

139 *"the gold rush of '49":* Colleen Moore, *Silent Star* (New York: Doubleday, 1968).

140 *A man with a stutter: The Locked Door* press book.

140 *"no precedents, no rules": New York World,* December 1930, 7.

140 *"It killed the time":* Clarke, *Featured Player,* 45, 46.

140 *"with the dearest friend":* S. R. Mook, *Screenland,* January 1932, 113.

140 *In New York:* Randall Malone to author, February 9, 2001.

140 *"Barbara thought I was":* S. R. Mook, *Modern Screen,* October 1934, 96.

141 *"I'm just not good for anything":* S. R. Mook, *Screenland,* January 1932, 113.

142 *"Forget it":* Mansfield to author, June 13, 1997, 7.

142 *"was an entire new game":* Malone to author, February 9, 2001.

142 *In August the movie:* August 16, 1929.

142 The Dance of Life *was a talking:* Sutherland is the theater attendant; Cromwell, the doorkeeper. *AFI Catalog,* 162.

142 *"old devil dialogue":* Cromwell, interview with Maltin, 4.

142 *Hal Skelly repeated his role:* Ibid., 2.

142 *"dramatic and wistful": Memo from David O. Selznick,* ed. Rudy Behlmer (New York: Viking Press, 1972), 22.

143 *Harry Cohn of Columbia Pictures:* Samuels, "Search for Ruby Stevens," *Motion Picture,* October 1949, 80.

143 *She tried to pretend:* Gladys Hall, *Modern Screen,* November 1937.

143 *"in a corner attracting": Screenland,* March 1964.

143 *"I was still the child": Screenland,* March 1964; Ella Smith, *Starring Miss Barbara Stanwyck,* 14.

143 *After the completion:* Ned Comstock, William Schaefer Collection, Film and Television Archives, University of Southern California.

143 *Fay was to receive:* Zanuck to Mr. Chase, memo, September 6, 1929, Warner Archives.

143 *"feel cherished":* Film and Television Archives, USC; Warner Archives.

143 *"it was too late":* Gladys Hall, *Modern Screen,* November 1937.

144 *"Barbara is unhappy":* Helen Louise Walker, *Movie Classic,* June 1932, 62.

144 *Barbara wasn't as sure:* Robert Blees, "Barbara Stanwyck," *American Film,* April 1987.

144 *Fay wanted Barbara:* Muriel Babcock, "Stanwyck-Fay Menage Plays Up-and-Down Role," *Los Angeles Times,* June 21, 1931.

144 *As a fly-by-nighter:* Capra, *Name Above the Title,* 78.

145 *There were no wardrobe:* Bob Thomas, *King Cohn* (New York: G. P. Putnam's Sons, 1967), 30.

145 *While the large studios were investing:* Dick, *Merchant Prince of Poverty Row,* 20, 21, 43, 44, 45.

145 *Harry Cohn was crude and rough:* Ibid.

145 *He could be a gambler:* Capra, *Name Above the Title,* 82.

145 *"the wandering Jew":* Thomas, *King Cohn,* xiv.

145 *"Our scenarios run about":* Ibid., 47, 48.

145 *Cohn could be tyrannical:* Ibid., xviii.

145 *"We get 'em":* Ibid.

145 *Many of the studio's supporting:* Ibid., 45.

145 *"It was Margaret":* Gladys Hall, *Modern Screen,* November 1937.

145 *Hardy was a graduate: Miracle Woman* press book.

145 *To Kenton, the spoken:* Bernds to author, June 3, 1997, 4.

146 *Bernds thought Kenton was:* Bernds, *Mr. Bernds Goes to Hollywood,* 116, 117.

146 *"he seemed overbearing":* Bernds to author, June 3, 1997.

146 *"the manner—of all of them":* Bernds, *Mr. Bernds Goes to Hollywood,* 117.

146 *"landowner talking":* Bernds to author, June 3, 1997, 6.

146 *"added little or":* Gladys Hall, *Modern Screen,* November 1937.

146 *"didn't even know how":* Ella Smith, *Starring Miss Barbara Stanwyck,* 13.

146 *"She knew she was a good":* Bernds, *Mr. Bernds Goes to Hollywood,* 117.

146 *Barbara struggled to make:* Bernds to author, June 3, 1997, 4.

147 *On Monday of the final week: World Almanac and Book of Facts for 1930,* 125.

147 *People were nervous:* Galbraith, *Great Crash, 1929,* 96, 97.

147 *By midweek, stocks:* Wednesday, October 23, 1929.

147 *Reports came back:* Ibid., 98.

147 *On Sunday, thousands of Wall: New York Times,* October 28, 1929, 1.

147 *Losses in quote values: World Almanac and Book of Facts for 1930,* 126.

147 *Stock prices virtually collapsed:* Ibid.

147 *Fourteen billion dollars: New York Times,* October 29, 1929, 1.

147 *So many stocks were: New York Times,* October 20, 1929.

148 *A merger that was: Variety,* November 6, 1929.

Thirteen: A Test in Technicolor

PAGE

149 *Barbara was certain:* John Kenneth Galbraith, *Great Crash, 1929* (Boston: Mariner Books/Houghton Mifflin Harcourt Publishing Company, 1972), 114.

149 *"They didn't fool me":* Babcock, "Stanwyck-Fay Menage Plays Up-and-Down Role."

149 *"was stuck off":* Gladys Hall, *Modern Screen,* November 1937.

150 *In Hollywood, Korda had: The Private Life of Helen of Troy* and *Love and the Devil.*

150 *He kissed Barbara's hand:* Ella Smith, *Starring Miss Barbara Stanwyck,* 14.

150 *"injustice of it all":* Gladys Hall, *Modern Screen,* November 1937.

150 *"The front office group":* Ray Rennahan to Ella Smith, May 30, 1972.

150 *Investors who, two weeks before: Variety,* October 30, 1929, 1.

150 *People were reassured: New York Times,* October 30, 1929.

151 *She went to the meeting:* Capra, *Name Above the Title,* 114.

151 *"frankly admitted her failure":* McBride, *Frank Capra,* 209.

151 *"waved a red flag": Meet John Doe* press book.

151 *"Either I'm qualified":* James Reid, *Silver Screen,* June 1941, 74.

151 *Screw it, she thought:* McBride, *Frank Capra,* 209.

151 *"Oh, hell, you don't":* Capra, *Name Above the Title,* 115.

151 *"Forget it, Harry":* Ibid.

151 *She was going back:* Gladys Hall, *Modern Screen,* November 1937.

152 *"You gotta see it":* Capra, *Name Above the Title,* 115.

152 *"underneath her sullen shyness":* Ibid.

152 *"If I'm against a girl":* Dwight Whitney, *TV Guide,* February 26, 1966.

152 *She was being paid: Variety,* November 6, 1929, 58.

152 *Barbara's first picture:* November 16, 1929, AFI Catalog.

152 *"A better bilge":* Gladys Hall, unedited manuscript, 23, AMPAS.

152 *"fine taste and elegance": Variety,* January 22, 1930, 17.

153 *"That was just wonderful":* Gene Vaslett to author, September 2000.

Fourteen: Trying to Make a Living

155 *They come onstage:* Darryl Zanuck, *Show of Shows* treatment, 1929, UA Collection Series 1.2, box 351, folder 10, Wisconsin Center for Film and Theatre Research.

155 *He had choreographed the large:* John McCabe, *Cagney* (New York: Alfred A. Knopf, 1997), 60–66.

156 *"never made an unnecessary":* Ibid., 50.

156 *Fay returned to Los Angeles: Variety,* December 11, 1929, 24.

156 *She and Fay began to:* Faith Service, *Motion Picture,* December 1932.

156 *"When I dream":* Ibid.

156 *He promised an overall: World Almanac and Book of Facts for 1930,* 129.

156 *"A very large degree":* Warren, *Herbert Hoover and the Great Depression,* 118.

156 *It was hot, but on Hollywood Boulevard:* Bellamy, interview with Saunders, 10.

157 *In Boston's State Theatre: Variety,* December 18, 1929, 14, 45.

157 *"500 horsepower entertainment": Bright Lights* (1930) press book.

157 *"The main flaw":* Gladys Hall, *Modern Screen,* November 1937.

157 *She hated it: Miracle Woman* press book.

157 *"In the eyes of":* Grace Mack, *Screen Play,* June 1932, 29.

Fifteen: A Primitive Emotional

158 *Columbia Pictures' newly released:* New York opening, September 1929; Capra, *Name Above the Title,* 110.

158 *It was Capra's second big:* Ibid., 91.

158 *He'd worked for Jack Cohn:* McBride, *Frank Capra,* 121.

158 *Before that, he had drifted:* Ibid., 123, 124.

158 *"got a real sense":* Ibid., 122.

158 *He taught ballistics mathematics:* Ibid., 103.

158 *"ate, slept, and dreamed":* Capra, *Name Above the Title,* 30.

158 *He'd worked for a:* McBride, *Frank Capra*, 40.

159 *During the year and a half:* Ibid., 150.

159 *"timing, construction":* Capra, *Name Above the Title*, 51.

159 *He wrote gags for every type:* McBride, *Frank Capra*, 151.

159 *Graves had starred in five:* Ibid., 186.

159 *"a delightful guy":* Ralph Graves, interview with Anthony Slide, quoted in ibid.

159 *But Capra was told that:* Capra, *Name Above the Title*, 79.

159 *"not a place for the weak":* Ibid., 82.

159 *"tough, brassy":* Ibid.

159 *"faults were legion":* Ibid., 85.

159 *Capra never let Cohn:* American Film Institute, "Frank Capra: One Man, One Film," in Glatzer and Raeburn, *Frank Capra*, 20.

160 *In the months that Capra:* Ibid., 93; Geoffrey T. Hellman, "Thinker in Hollywood," in ibid., 9.

160 *In the quickies for Columbia:* Capra, *Name Above the Title*, 86.

160 *"master the new":* Ibid.

160 *He trusted that D. W.:* Richard Griffith, "Capra's Early Films," in Glatzer and Raeburn, *Frank Capra.*

160 *Right away Capra brought:* Walker and Walker, *Light on Her Face*, 169.

160 *Cohn had Joseph Walker:* Walker and Walker, *Light on Her Face*, 176.

160 *"Glamour was a key":* Ibid.

161 *Capra asked Walker:* Ella Smith, *Starring Miss Barbara Stanwyck*, 17.

161 *Walker made the test:* Ibid.

161 *"With the right handling":* Walker and Walker, *Light on Her Face*, 176.

161 *"If that happens":* Ibid.

161 *Capra had written:* Hellman, "Thinker in Hollywood," 10.

161 *He sent out copies:* Capra, *Name Above the Title*, 113.

161 *At the end of the reading:* Marguerite Tazelaar, "Failure to Be 'Yes Man' Started Swerling's Career in Hollywood," McBride, *Frank Capra*, 211.

162 *Everyone thought the script:* Hellman, "Thinker in Hollywood," 10.

162 *One of the newly hired:* Tazelaar, "Failure to Be 'Yes Man,' " McBride, *Frank Capra*, 211.

162 *"The piece stunk":* Capra, *Name Above the Title*, 114.

162 *Swerling read aloud:* Tazelaar, *"Failure to Be 'Yes Man,' "* McBride, *Frank Capra*, 211, 212.

163 *He'd been a reporter:* "Sunday News of the Theatre and Its Workers," *New York Times*, February 24, 1929, sec. 9, p. 2; *Dictionary of Literary Biography*, S.V. "Swerling, Jo."

163 *He started at the* Chicago Herald: "Sunday News of the Theatre and Its Workers."

163 *Swerling took Capra's script:* Tazelaar, "Failure to Be 'Yes Man,' " McBride, *Frank Capra*, 211, 212.

163 *"long enough for":* Tazelaar, "Failure to Be 'Yes Man.' "

163 *"magnificent—human":* Capra, *Name Above the Title*, 114.

163 *"curry of sensationalism":* Alan Dale, *New York American*, December 24, 1924.

163 *"went the limit":* Ibid.

163 *"violation of the canon":* Percy Hammond, review, *New York Herald Tribune*, December 31, 1924.

163 *"the language of the gutter":* Theatre, March 25, 1925.

164 *"shrewd frame-up calculated":* Hammond, review.

164 *"the old Camille story":* Frank S. Nugent, "Jo Swerling, Scenarist," *New York Times*, February 17, 1935.

164 *Throop College of Technology:* Later California Institute of Technology. McBride, *Frank Capra*, 70.

164 *"changed his whole viewpoint":* Hellman, "Thinker in Hollywood."

164 *Swerling's Russian-born family:* Jo Swerling Jr. to author, January 2001.

164 *Swerling also sold newspapers:* "Sunday News of the Theatre and Its Workers."

165 *"a rebel against":* American Film Institute, *Frank Capra.*

165 *"goal as a youth":* Capra, *Name Above the Title*, 93.

166 *"a natural actress"*: McBride, *Frank Capra*, 213.

166 *Capra had what he thought*: Capra, *Name Above the Title*, 114.

166 *There he met Louella Parsons*: Ralph Graves, interview with Anthony Slide, *The Idols of Silence* (South Brunswick: A. S. Barnes, 1976).

166 *Graves, like Capra, trained*: Capra wrote three Sennett pictures starring Graves: *Breaking the Ice* (1925); *Good Morning, Nurse* (1925); and *Cupid's Boots* (1925).

166 *He'd become famous*: *Ladies of Leisure*, 1930 press book.

166 *Capra's first picture for*: *That Certain Thing* (1928).

166 *Marie Prevost made her mark*: *The Old Swimmin' Hole* (1921); *Cornered* (1924); *Tarnish* (1924).

166 *She was first noticed*: *The Marriage Circle* (1924); *Kiss Me Again* (1925).

167 *Sherman was one of the most*: *Ladies of Leisure* 1930 press book.

167 *"asked to play roles"*: McBride, *Frank Capra*, 190.

167 *"clear, sharp lighting"*: Ibid.

167 *"It was the first time"*: Ibid., 191–92.

168 *The cameras themselves had*: Walker and Walker, *Light on Her Face*, 171.

168 *For his work at Columbia*: McBride, *Frank Capra*, 190.

168 *"Suddenly [with talking pictures]"*: Capra, *Name Above the Title*, 101.

168 *"The silence from the studio"*: Mary Astor, interview in Brownlow, *Hollywood*.

168 *Shooting on Ladies*: January 14, 1930; Ed Bernds to author, June 9, 1997.

168 *"from the start"*: BS, in Walter Ramsey, *Modern Screen*, July 1931, 63.

168 *"was perfectly accustomed"*: Bernds to author, June 10, 1997.

169 *"didn't see anybody else"*: BS to Rex Reed, April 13, 1981.

169 *"The next day I waved"*: Ella Smith, *Starring Miss Barbara Stanwyck*, 20.

169 *"Don't you ever dare"*: BS to Rex Reed, April 13, 1981.

169 *"Only go later"*: Paul Rosenfield, Calendar, *Los Angeles Times*, April 5, 1987.

169 *"We're going to do this"*: BS to Rex Reed, April 13, 1981.

169 *"it was fun to make"*: Walker and Walker, *Light on Her Face*, 164.

169 *"different from any other"*: McBride, *Frank Capra*, 190.

169 *Capra wouldn't tell Walker*: Ibid., 192.

169 *"to let a person play"*: Ibid., 213.

170 *"ubiquitous phantom"*: Capra, *Name Above the Title*, 100.

170 *"But then she could never"*: American Film Institute, *Frank Capra*.

170 *"Barbara was rehearsing mentally"*: Ibid., 17.

170 *About the third or fourth take*: McBride, *Frank Capra*, 212.

170 *Instead of a full rehearsal*: Bernds to author, June 8, 1997.

170 *"to utter one word"*: Capra, *Name Above the Title*, 116.

170 *This presented a problem*: Bernds to author, June 9, 1997.

170 *Capra had Barbara's*: Capra, *Name Above the Title*, 116.

170 *"the points of emphasis"*: Ibid.

170 *If he agreed with*: McBride, *Frank Capra*, 213.

170 *"Barbara was silent"*: American Film Institute, *Frank Capra*, 17; McBride, *Frank Capra*, 210.

171 *"fan the smoldering"*: Capra, *Name Above the Title*, 116.

171 *He stressed honesty*: Tom Capra to author, December 4, 2000.

171 *"You can almost smell it"*: McBride, *Frank Capra*, 213.

171 *"It has to be from"*: Ibid.

171 *"could see a performance"*: Bernds to author, June 3, 1997.

171 *"attempted only one thing"*: Ella Smith, *Starring Miss Barbara Stanwyck*, 20.

171 *"to show how really"*: Ella Smith, *Starring Miss Barbara Stanwyck*, 20.

171 *"something was happening"*: Bernds to author, June 3, 1997.

171 *Barbara was "so happy":* Walter Ramsey, *Modern Screen,* May 1931.

172 *"Somehow," said Ed:* Bernds to author, June 3, 1997.

172 *"she exposed her arms":* Ibid.

172 *They shot throughout:* Ibid.

172 *"if you can* think *it":* Paul Rosenfield, Calendar, *Los Angeles Times,* April 5, 1987.

174 *"an exciting stimulant":* Capra, *Name Above the Title,* 199.

Sixteen: Life, Liberty, and the Pursuit of Love

PAGE

176 *Fay and Michael Curtiz: Variety,* February 5, 1930, 35.

176 *He had an enormous:* David Lewis, *Creative Producer,* 136–37.

176 *He was under contract: Variety,* March 26, 1930.

177 *To celebrate, a banquet:* May 11, 1927; Robert Osborne, *75 Years of the Oscar: The Official History of the Academy Awards* (Abbeville Press, 2003), 9.

177 *The nominees and the winners:* Ibid., 8, 9, 17.

177 *For the 1930 awards:* McBride, *Frank Capra,* 226.

177 *At the beginning of April: Variety,* April 9, 1930, 2.

177 *The weekly box-office receipts: Variety,* December 18, 1930, 14, 15.

177 *By March 1930:* Meltzer, *Brother, Can You Spare a Dime?,* 21.

178 *"blowsy acrobatic":* Charles Brackett, *New Yorker,* February 18, 1928, 25.

178 *"one of the great comic":* New York Times, February 10, 1928.

178 *"mad, unique":* Capra, *Name Above the Title,* 122.

178 *"only one set":* Ibid., 123.

178 *With the signing: Variety,* April 9, 1930, 2.

178 *"a delicious bit":* Los Angeles Examiner, May 29, 1930.

179 *Fay traveled to Texas: Variety,* April 9, 1930, 62.

179 *Warner was considering: Variety,* May 7, 1930, 4.

179 *Fay, in preparation for: Variety,* June 4, 1930, 65.

179 *"great box office": Variety,* May 28, 1930, 35.

179 *The headline of the review:* Regina Crewe, *New York American,* May 24, 1930.

179 *The censors gave the picture: Variety,* April 9, 1930, 8.

179 *"with a good deal": New Yorker,* May 31, 1930, 72.

179 *"that the screen version": New York Evening Journal,* May 24, 1930.

179 *"talkie version of":* Louella Parsons, *Los Angeles Examiner,* April 3, 1930.

179 *"Barbara Stanwyck's Career": New York Herald Tribune,* May 25, 1930.

179 *"Frank is a big actor":* "Barbara Sticks to Her Man," *Screen Play,* June 1931.

179 *In Los Angeles, the Fays: Variety,* April 9, 1930, 62.

180 *"Full to the brim": New York Times,* January 12, 1930, 8.

180 *First National bought it: Mothers Cry* contract, March 6, 1930, Warner Bros. Archives.

180 *During the spring of 1930:* Walter Ramsey, *Modern Screen,* July 1931, 115.

181 *She and Fay spent time:* Budd Schulberg to author, 1998.

181 *"I never demanded anything":* Jerry Asher, "In Exile and Loving It," *New Movie Magazine,* April 1935.

181 *"a new sensation": Photoplay,* July 1930, 74.

181 *"we felt our unimportance":* Asher, "In Exile and Loving It."

182 *To honor the men:* Watkins, *Great Depression,* 95–97.

182 *Fay's studio, Warner: Variety,* July 9, 1930, 30.

182 *Edith Fitzgerald and her companion:* Wray, *On the Other Hand,* 200; Riskin Papers. (Fay Wray/Robert Riskin Collection), the University of Southern California Cinema–Television Archives.

182 *The plan was to produce:* Variety, September 24, 1930, 57.

183 *$7,000 a week:* Samuel Briskin, affidavit, 2.

183 *Zanuck, in addition to:* Gussow, *Don't Say Yes Until I Finish Talking,* 42.

183 *"Anne Vincent is a girl":* Illicit press book, 9, Warner Bros. Archives.

183 *"Her drama":* Ibid.

184 *Columbia's agreement with:* Columbia Pictures to Warner Bros., memo, July 2, 1930, file 2874, Warner Bros. Archives.

185 *"butchered in [the] operation":* Grace Mack, *Screen Play,* June 1932, 57.

185 *He had shot sixteen:* Gussow, *Don't Say Yes Until I Finish Talking,* 38.

185 *directed such actresses:* Illicit press book.

185 *Before shooting a scene:* Ibid.

185 *"[Joan's] career was pre-determined":* Ibid.

185 *"I was never so":* Ella Smith, *Starring Miss Barbara Stanwyck,* 27.

185 *When Jack Warner first:* Mosley, *Zanuck,* 77.

186 *They chose Zanuck:* Ibid., 86.

186 *"Even if you don't need":* Gussow, *Don't Say Yes Until I Finish Talking,* 42.

187 *"What she did":* Ella Smith, *Starring Miss Barbara Stanwyck,* 27.

187 *Several weeks into:* Jerry D. Lewis, "Top Story Man," *Collier's,* March 29, 1941, 83.

187 *The picture cost:* Schaefer Collection.

187 *Warner Bros. in 1932:* Variety, June 25, 1930, 102.

Seventeen: On Her Own

PAGE

188 *During the early weeks:* August 2, 1930.

188 *"the city of beautiful":* The Matrimonial Bed press book, 4.

188 *"missed fire":* Variety, August 25, 1930.

188 *"preposterous and grotesque":* New Yorker, August 30, 1930, 50.

188 *"the coming big star":* Walter Ramsey, *Modern Screen,* July 1931, 115.

189 *"frozen rabbit":* Grace Mack, *Screen Play,* June 1932, 29.

189 *"The two best friends":* Ibid.

189 *Judith Anderson:* She made her debut in vaudeville at the Palace headlining in *Thieves Journal,* June 7, 1926.

189 *Ethel Barrymore:* She appeared at the Palace in the fifth act in J. M. Barrie's one-act play *The Twelve Pound Look* in 1926.

189 *Rita Mayon:* Also at the Palace in a number called *Dance Sparkles of 1926.*

189 *as well as:* They too worked as Fay's stooges. Vaslett to author, May 30, 2000.

190 *RKO threatened to cancel:* Variety, September 10, 1930, 64.

190 *The picture cost $208,000:* Warner Bros. Archives; Ned Comstock to author.

190 *Playhouses along Forty-Second:* Madsen, *Stanwyck,* 63.

190 *The Shubert brothers were:* Hirsch, *Boys from Syracuse,* 163.

190 *Soon six thousand people:* Watkins, *Great Depression,* 63.

190 *"In the years between":* Kotsilibas-Davis, *Barrymores.*

191 *"Well, this fellow ran":* Barrymore and Shipp, *We Barrymores,* 236.

192 *Mannix, who had the:* Scott Eyman, *Lion of Hollywood* (New York: Simon & Schuster, 2005), 130–31.

192 *"You're finished, Gilbert":* Fountain, *Dark Star,* 131.

192 *His Glorious Night received positive:* Ibid., 178, 179.

192 *Instead of inspiring women:* Ibid.

193 *"I watched John Gilbert":* Hopper, *From Under My Hat,* 164.

193   *Gilbert's opening speech:* Fountain, *Dark Star,* 181.

193   *"love was a comedy word":* Hopper, *From Under My Hat,* 200.

193   *"Jack's voice was not":* Colleen Moore, *Silent Star,* 206–7.

193   *"I don't know whether":* Fountain, *Dark Star,* 184.

194   *"never turned up":* Ibid.

194   *After the Gilbert picture:* Cromwell, interview with Maltin, 3.

194   *in 1929: AFI Feature Films, 1921–1930,* 662.

194   *Metro temporarily released: Variety,* August 13, 1930, 24.

194   *The picture's title:* Simple Simon opened at the Ziegfeld and ran from February 18 through June 14, 1930;
Stage, Film, and Television Scores.

195   *"Ten Cents a Dance":* Ibid., 132; Frederick W. Nolan, *Lorenz Hart: A Poet on Broadway* (New York: Oxford University Press, 1994).

197   *Ann Harding:* Ann Harding was nominated in 1931 for Best Actress in a Leading Role for *Holiday.*

197   *Two weeks into the filming:* The picture started filming on September 12; Barbara fell on September 23. *Variety,* September 24, 1930.

197   *"In my desire":* Ella Smith, *Starring Miss Barbara Stanwyck,* 27.

197   *Barbara landed on: Variety,* September 24, 1930, 3.

198   *Barbara defined her days:* Sonia Lee, *Movie Classic,* February 1934, 62.

198   *The hours between:* Ibid.

198   *"[Lionel] seems to check":* Kotsilibas-Davis, *Barrymores,* 64.

199   *"Lionel was the real":* The House of Barrymore (New York: Alfred A. Knopf, 1990), 437.

199   *"He has none of those":* Margot Peters, *The House of Barrymore,* 175.

199   *"The theatre was not":* Barrymore and Shipp, *We Barrymores,* 37.

199   *"labor for months":* Ibid., 241.

199   *"The poor man was in":* As reported to Larry Kleno to author, June 19, 2001.

199   *"very trying":* Ella Smith, *Starring Miss Barbara Stanwyck,* 27.

199   *"for her dignity":* Ibid., 29.

199   *"old fish eyes":* Kleno to author, June 21, 2001.

199   *"He gave me nothing":* Ibid.

200   *In the midst of shooting:* September 29, 1930, Warner Bros. Archives.

200   *The contract was for:* Watkins, *Great Depression,* 54.

200   *"It is further agreed":* Warner Bros. to BS, September 29, 1930, 3, Warner Bros. Archives.

200   *If the studio picked:* Agreement between BS and Warner Bros. Studio, 4, September 29, 1930.

200   *After the reception: Variety,* October 8, 1930, 12.

201   *The contract department:* Zanuck to Ralph Lewish, memo, March 19, 1931, Warner Bros. Archives.

201   *"I couldn't believe that":* Sonia Lee, *Movie Classic,* February 1934, 62.

PART TWO: Undertow

One: "Hot Speel in the Blood"

PAGE

205   *For the first time: Variety,* October 1, 1930, 1.

205   *It was rumored that Metro:* Wiley and Bona, *Inside Oscar,* 26.

205   *Joan Crawford, Mrs. Douglas:* They married on June 3, 1929.

206   *"I had my freedom":* Capra, *Name Above the Title* (Da Capo Press, 1997), 116.

206   *von Sternberg's original exotic: Variety,* December 31, 1930, 55.

206   *Barbara turned over her money:* Warner Bros. Feature Service, February 1931.

207   *Fay began filming:* January 5, 1931.

207 *In one scene in which: God's Gift to Women* press book.

207 *"Mr. Vinegar":* Barry Paris, *Louise Brooks* (New York: Alfred A. Knopf, 1989), 358.

207 *Before* Illicit *could be: AFI Catalog,* 1009.

207 *"self-control and":* Memoirs of Will H. Hays, 347.

208 *Eighty million people went:* Ibid., 352.

208 *"easily become a corrupting":* Ibid., 326.

208 *The MPPDA's fight:* Ibid., 330.

208 *But Hays had something:* Ibid., 438.

209 *They argued about:* Ibid., 329–442.

209 *Barbara traveled north with Jack Warner: AFI Catalog.*

209 *The picture was being:* Louella Parsons, *Los Angeles Examiner,* January 30, 1931.

209 Little Caesar *was based:* LeRoy and Kleiner, *Mervyn LeRoy,* 98.

210 *"the deadly first reel":* Variety, January 21, 1931, 17.

210 *"belongs in subdued":* Cecelia Ager, "Going Places," *Variety,* February 4, 1931, 66.

210 *"as smart as next year's":* Louella Parsons, *Los Angeles Examiner,* February 21, 1931.

210 *Although many of the:* The Negative Cost was $385,000; the Gross Income to August 31, 1944: $301,000; the Domestic Income was $301,000; the Foreign Total $89,000. Total earned $390,000. Ned Comstock, USC Film and Television Archive.

210 Ten Cents a Dance, *Barbara's:* The contract was due to expire on August 1, 1931.

210 *At the last minute: Variety,* September 9, 1931, 3.

210 *Warner had considered using:* John Andrew Gallagher and Frank Thompson, *Nothing Sacred: The Cinema of William Wellman* (Men with Wings Press).

210 *daring spectacle* Wings: 1927.

210 *and also* Beggars of Life: 1928.

211 *The supporting cast: Variety,* January 7, 1931, 4.

211 *Cagney was to play:* Gallagher and Thompson.

211 *Jack Warner drew up:* J. L. Warner to BS, December 18, 1930, Warner Bros. Archives.

213 Ten Cents a Dance *opened:* March 6, 1931.

213 *"out of place":* New York Times, March 7, 1931.

213 *"Columbia should be grateful":* Variety, March 11, 1931, 51.

213 The Miracle Woman *was based: Bless You, Sister* opened on December 26, 1927. It starred Alice Brady, Charles Bickford, and George Alison.

213 *"a sort of cathedral":* J. W. Krutch, *Nation,* March 16, 1927.

214 *Aimee Semple McPherson: New York Times,* September 28, 1944. The temple opened in Los Angeles in 1919.

214 *"We all know what":* Daniel Mark Epstein, *Sister Aimee* (New York: Harcourt Brace Jovanovich, 1993), 283.

214 *"You can't kid religion":* Capra, *Name Above the Title,* 129, 130.

214 *At seventeen, Riskin became executive:* Fay Wray to author.

214 *"everything, not only producing": New York Herald Tribune,* February 23, 1941.

215 *Alice Brady was the loving: Bless You, Sister,* 1–19, Lincoln Center Library.

215 *Riskin thought Capra looked:* McBride, *Frank Capra,* 277.

215 *"I wrote that play":* Lewis, "Top Story Man."

216 *Capra said he thought:* Capra, *Name Above the Title,* 130.

216 *Riskin argued that* Bless: McBride, *Frank Capra,* 228.

217 *Capra believed audiences:* Eileen Creelman, *New York Sun,* September 13, 1934; "Frank Capra, Director of Two of the Year's Biggest Hits, Talks of His Work," Box 4:2, USC Cinema–Television Archive courtesy of Ned Comstock/Fay Wray Collection.

218 *And for each soul:* "Amazing Grace."

218 *"I have to absorb"*: Frank Capra, oral history, 1956, Columbia University.

218 *It took a full hour: Miracle Woman* press book.

220 *If different shots:* American Film Institute, "Frank Capra," 17.

221 *Barbara did the scene:* Ed Bernds to author, June 8, 1997.

221 *"Multiple cameras aggravate"*: Capra, *Name Above the Title,* 116.

221 *"they were working"*: McBride, *Frank Capra,* 213.

221 *"It's all right if you have"*: Ibid.

222 *just-released* Dracula: Released February 1931, a month before shooting began on *The Miracle Woman,* *AFI CATALOG A–L,* 537.

224 *"What would you like"*: *The Miracle Woman* script 151, box 12, Barbara Stanwyck Collection, University of Wyoming.

224 *Mrs. Higgins opens the box:* The bust of Stanwyck was created by Richard Cromwell, a young actor at Columbia who had had a great success in his debut in *Tol'able David.*

224 *"I'll say I'm getting"*: *The Miracle Woman* script 164, 65, 3787, box 12, Stanwyck Collection.

225 *"But of course you were"*: McBride, *Frank Capra,* 213.

226 *"Remember, Barbara"*: Capra, *Name Above the Title,* 116.

226 *"babied and pampered"*: BS, in Gladys Hall, *Modern Screen,* November 1937.

226 *And in his understanding:* McBride, *Frank Capra,* 214.

226 *"knew nothing about camera"*: Capra, *Name Above the Title,* 115.

226 *When production started: Los Angeles Examiner,* March 5, 1931; G. D. Hamann, *Barbara Stanwyck in the 30's* (Hollywood, Calif.: Filming Today, 1997), 11; *Variety,* March 11, 1931, 44.

226 *"I'm making a pot": Los Angeles Examiner,* March 5, 1931; Hamann, *Barbara Stanwyck in the 30's,* 11.

227 *attended the opening:* April 3, 1931.

228 *"soured [them both] on"*: Fidler, "Barbara Stanwyck Answers Twenty Timely Questions," *Movie Classic,* June 1933, 23.

Two: Idealism and Fight

PAGE

230 *"I like to keep them"*: Ezra Goodman, *Fifty-Year Decline and Fall of Hollywood,* 209.

230 *At twenty-one, he'd run off:* " 'Wild Bill': William A. Wellman," interview by Scott Eyman, *Focus on Film,* March 1978, 17.

230 *Wellman was a fighter pilot:* Ibid., 10.

230 *During Wellman's months fighting:* Ibid.

230 *"of grabbing a headline"*: Frank T. Thompson, *William A. Wellman* (Metuchen, N.J.: Scarecrow Press, 1983), 107.

231 *"a crazy bastard"*: Scott Eyman interview with William Wellman, *Focus on Film* #29, 1978.

231 *"Miss one of those"*: Mosley, *Zanuck,* 28.

231 *Zanuck worked as a dishwasher:* Ibid., 33.

232 The Public Enemy *was taken from:* Lee Server, *Screenwriter: Words Become Pictures* (Pittstown, N.J.: Main Street Press, 1987), 70.

232 *"Italians, Irish, Jewish"*: Ibid., 74.

232 *Bertolt Brecht was fascinated:* Clurman, *All People Are Famous,* 137.

232 *He wanted to make:* John Bright, interview in McGilligan and Buhle, *Tender Comrades,* 134.

232 *James Cagney was under:* Warner Bros. pay ledger, Warner Bros. Archives, courtesy of Ned Comstock.

232 *"gutter quality"*: *Cagney by Cagney,* 80.

232 *"We got the wrong man"*: "Wild Bill," interview by Eyman, 13.

232 *Zanuck sent out:* Thompson, *William A. Wellman,* 112.

233 *The part of Powers's girlfriend:* Louise Brooks, *Lulu in Hollywood* (New York: Alfred A. Knopf, 1982), 21.

233 *"that's all [she] had"*: Clarke, *Featured Player*, 64.

233 *In it, Blondell, a former:* Thompson, *William A. Wellman*, 109.

233 *It was her first picture:* Clarke, *Featured Player*, 64.

233 *"Anyone working in one"*: Julian Fox, "A Man's World," *Films and Filming*, March 1973, 36.

234 *"quiet sadism"*: Brooks, *Lulu in Hollywood*, 25.

234 *He had been fired:* Bright, interview in McGilligan and Buhle, *Tender Comrades*, 134.

234 *"tough, tough, tough"*: Mosley, *Zanuck*, 115.

234 *"as tough as they come"*: Fox, "Man's World," 36.

234 *"I doubt there is"*: McCabe, *Cagney*, 82.

234 *"felt an empathy"*: Clarke, *Featured Player*, 68.

234 *"Shut your mouth"*: Mosley, *Zanuck*, 116.

235 *Powers cuts her off:* Henry Cohen, ed., *The Public Enemy*, Wisconsin/Warner Bros. Screenplay Series (Madison: University of Wisconsin Press, 1981), 129.

235 *"That was enough"*: Clarke, *Featured Player*, 68.

235 *"Bill [Wellman] and I"*: Ibid.

235 *Cagney said the omelet: Cagney by Cagney*, 45.

235 *"No, come on back"*: Clarke, *Featured Player*, 69.

236 *"I was a good sport"*: James Curtis, *Featured Player*, 69.

236 *"I put my head on her"*: Randall Malone to author, March 5, 2001, 16; Clarke, *Featured Player*, 69–70.

236 *"We needed something big"*: "Such Guys as Capra and Wellman," *New York Times*, October 16, 1938.

237 *"stole scripts, new ones"*: John Wakeman, ed., *World Film Directors* (New York: H. W. Wilson, 1987), 1:1186.

237 *"more than anybody"*: Ibid.

237 *"stayed for half"*: Ibid.

237 *"That's what I want"*: "Wild Bill," interview by Eyman, 11.

237 The Public Enemy *was shot:* Wakeman, *World Film Directors*, 1:1188.

238 *"we are renting her"*: Sam Briskin to Warner Bros. Pictures Inc., March 6, 1931, Warner Bros. Archives.

238 *A month later Cagney: Night Nurse* cast memo, February 2, 1931, Warner Bros. Archives.

238 *"I had a script"*: "Wild Bill," interview by Eyman, 17.

239 *With Clark Gable:* Harry Lang, " 'What a Man!'—Clark Gable," *Photoplay*, October 1931.

239 *"a real tough guy"*: LeRoy and Kleiner, *Mervyn LeRoy*, 95.

239 *"He was powerful, brutal"*: Ibid.

239 *"the same quality"*: Ibid., 96.

239 *"Do you know what"*: Ibid., 95.

239 *"They [the powers that be]"*: Wellman, *Short Time for Insanity*, 229.

239 *"The instant Clark walked"*: Gladys Hall, *Modern Screen*, November 1937.

240 *"That was okay"*: BS to Shirley Eder, conversation, April 1981, courtesy of John Slotkin.

240 *"resembled an actor"*: Brooks, *Lulu in Hollywood*, 25.

240 *"rough and tough"*: William Wellman, "The Birth of a Celebrated Mug Shot," Calendar, *Los Angeles Times*, November 26, 1978, 127.

241 *Wellman married Marjorie:* John Gallagher, *Nothing Sacred: The Cinema of William Wellman* by John Andrew Gallagher and Frank Thompson (Men with Wings Press), 8.

241 *Margery Chapin:* Shawna Kelly, *Aviators in Early Hollywood* (Arcadia Publishing, 2008), 41.

241 *"intelligent; womanly"*: Doris Lee, *Motion Picture*, August 1920, 44.

242 *"I was happy when"*: Thomas Dove, *National Enquirer*.

242 *Wellman finished* Night Nurse: Daily production notes.

242 *The picture was budgeted:* March 26, 1931, budget, no. 606, $289,898.

242 *Wellman brought it in at:* Warner Bros. budget, Warner Bros. Archive.

242 *appearing at the Strand: Variety*, April 22, 1931.

242 *"It's no gift"*: Ibid.

242 *"the whole show"*: *New York Times,* April 18, 1931.

243 *In early June, Warner Bros.*: *Variety,* June 16, 1931, 24; Hollywood, *Variety,* April 29, 1931, 6.

243 *"When you are up"*: Ruth Biery, "Let's Talk About 'Em," *Photoplay,* January 1933, 114.

243 *Life would be rich:* Albert, "She Has Hollywood's Number," *Photoplay,* June 1931, 69.

Three: On Being "Barbaric"

PAGE

245 *"She was gorgeous"*: BS to Shirley Eder.

246 *"Where the hell am I"*: BS to Shirley Eder, April 1981.

246 *"got to thinking"*: Helen Louise Walker, *Movie Classic,* June 1932, 62.

246 *"Good for Ann"*: Beranger, "Private Life of Barbara Stanwyck," 8.

246 *Barbara concluded that:* Helen Louise Walker, *Movie Classic,* June 1932, 62.

246 *She was delighted:* Frank Capra, affidavit, 2, *Columbia Pictures Corporation v. Barbara Stanwyck,* injunction no. 327362.

246 *"I [was to] be paid more"*: Fidler, "Barbara Stanwyck Answers Twenty Timely Questions," 23.

246 *"Fifty thousand dollars"*: Helen Louise Walker, *Movie Classic,* June 1932, 62.

247 *"You'll have to stick"*: Ibid.

247 *"In the theatre we had"*: Cagney by Cagney, 39, 40.

247 *She was ready to report:* Sam Briskin, affidavit, 8, *Columbia Pictures Corporation v. Barbara Stanwyck,* injunction no. 327362.

248 *Having made extensive plans:* Capra, affidavit, 2.

248 *"My mind is made up"*: Briskin, affidavit, 7.

248 *"Barbara Stanwyck's quiet charm"*: *New York Times,* July 25, 1931.

248 *"one of the most natural"*: *Los Angeles Evening Herald,* July 24, 1931.

248 *"The second day"*: Conversation with Shirley Eder, April 1981.

248 *"I consider it"*: Capra, affidavit, 2.

249 *Frank Fay emceed the opening:* *Variety,* July 28, 1931, 45.

249 *"Miss Stanwyck's most effective"*: Marquis Busby, *Los Angeles Examiner,* July 18, 1931.

249 *"Capra can do more"*: *Variety,* July 28, 1931, 14.

249 Photoplay *singled out Barbara:* *Photoplay,* August 1931, 57.

249 *Barbara made it clear:* *Photoplay,* September 1931, 88.

249 *The press wrote about her:* Beranger, "Private Life of Barbara Stanwyck."

249 *Harry Cohn offered Barbara's:* Bernds, *Mr. Bernds Goes To Hollywood,* 219.

250 *"turn to her husband"*: Fidler, "Barbara Stanwyck Answers Twenty Timely Questions," 22.

250 *"many of the exhibitors"*: P. S. Harrison to BS, July 23, 1931, 9, in *Columbia Pictures Corporation v. Barbara Stanwyck,* injunction no. 327362.

250 *"I asked for fifty thousand"*: Stanwyck response to Peter Harrison (publisher of *Harrison's Reports*), 9, in ibid.

251 *"I knew you had"*: Beranger, "Private Life of Barbara Stanwyck," 8–9.

251 Night Nurse *was a standout:* *Variety,* August 18, 1931, 5.

251 *"This town of supreme"*: *Los Angeles Examiner,* July 27, 1931.

251 *"If you only knew"*: Helen Louise Walker, *Movie Classic,* June 1932, 62.

251 *"cut me cold"*: Fidler, "Barbara Stanwyck Answers Twenty Timely Questions"; and Barbara Stanwyck, *Movie Classic,* June 1933, 70.

251 *Despite that and Barbara's:* *Los Angeles Evening Herald,* September 23, 1931.

251 *While driving, he hit:* newspaper clipping, Temple University.

252 *Fay went to the bank:* Zolotow, *No People like Show People,* 193.

252 *As soon as he:* Barbara Stanwyck Fay, affidavit, January 10, 1938, 6, Superior Court of the State of California.

253 *Cohn was adamant:* "Stanwyck Must Adjust with Col Before Playing for WB-Position," *Variety,* August 18, 1931, 3.

253 *"it would be difficult":* Irving Thalberg, affidavit, September 9, 1931, *Columbia Pictures Corporation v. Barbara Stanwyck,* injunction no. 327362.

254 *Columbia notified Warner Bros.:* Ralph Lewis to J. L. Warner, August 17, 1932, Warner Bros. Archives.

254 *$42,500 per picture:* Dorothy Mackaill contract, August 29, 1930.

254 *In court before Judge Douglas:* August 14, 1931.

254 *Barbara went to see:* Helen Louise Walker, *Movie Classic,* June 1932, 62.

255 *Warner tried to work:* Lewis to Warner, August 17, 1932.

Four: "Theoretically Dangerous Overload"

PAGE

256 *Fannie Hurst's* Back Street: Brooke Kroeger, *Fannie: The Talent for Success of Writer Fannie Hurst* (New York: Times Books, 1999), 161.

256 *"no other living American":* Grant Overton, *Fannie Hurst: A Biographical Sketch, Critical Appreciation, and Bibliography* (New York: Harper & Brothers, 1928), 13.

256 *"overwhelmingly prodigal of both":* Robert Littell, "Lummox," in ibid., 37.

256 *"the most ambitious":* Margaret Wallace, *New York Times Book Review,* January 18, 1931, 11.

256 *The book was on the:* Kroeger, *Fannie,* 163.

257 *"courageous," ambitious novel:* Overton, *Fannie Hurst,* 11.

257 *"shop girls appear":* Kroeger, *Fannie,* 39.

258 *"the Yiddish descendants":* Ibid., 47.

258 *Famous Players–Lasky bought:* Ibid., 163.

258 *"knew how to reach":* Modern Movies, November 1938.

258 *Capra originally shot it:* Capra, *Name Above the Title,* 101.

261 *"bit offbeat so people":* American Film Institute, "Frank Capra," 39.

261 *"the debonair Frenchman":* Wellman, *Short Time for Insanity,* 70.

262 *Vaudeville Gulch, was coming into: Variety,* October 6, 1931, 35.

262 *Barbara had commemorated by:* Sidney Skolsky, newspaper clipping, 1932, Shubert Archive.

262 *He was getting drunk more:* Barbara Stanwyck Fay, affidavit, January 10, 1938, Superior Court of the State of California.

262 *"He sensed, as horses":* Martha Kerr, *Modern Screen,* February 1936.

262 *"The grips turned":* Walker and Walker, *Light on Her Face,* 184–85.

262 *"While [the horse] was":* Martha Kerr, *Modern Screen,* February 1936.

262 *"Hurry," she said: Los Angeles Times,* October 6, 1931.

263 *In truth, the doctors told:* Martha Kerr, *Modern Screen,* February 1936.

263 *"Her courage, to me":* McBride, *Frank Capra,* 240.

263 *Barbara recovered slowly: Los Angeles Evening Herald,* October 7, 1931.

263 *"We were supposed to be":* Ed Bernds to author, June 9, 1997.

264 *"Everyone was trying to":* McBride, *Frank Capra,* 213.

264 *"Menjou and Bellamy performed":* Bernds, *Mr. Bernds Goes to Hollywood,* 146, 147.

264 *"interesting characterizations":* Forbidden press book.

264 *"lost their superficial":* Capra, *Name Above the Title,* 108.

264 *"I just ask the cameraman":* Rex Reed interview April 13, 1981.

265 *"What those two":* Paul Rosenfield, *LA Calendar.*

265 *"The scene where Barbara":* Bernds to author, June 9, 1997.

265 *"It is true":* Capra, *Name Above the Title,* 115.

266 *"communists—the Democrats":* Bernds, *Mr. Bernds Goes to Hollywood,* 147.

266 *Menjou and Capra railed:* McBride, *Frank Capra,* 254.

266 *"modern society, acting":* Message to the Legislature, August 28, 1931, in *The Roosevelt Reader,* ed. Basil Rauch (New York: Rinehart, 1957).

266 *"I wish we could get":* S. R. Mook, *Screenland,* January 1932, 113.

267 *A bucket brigade of more: Los Angeles Evening Herald,* November 4, 1931.

267 *The damage to Barbara: Los Angeles Times,* November 4, 1931, 1.

267 *"I'm not proud":* Fredda Dudley Balling, *Lady's Circle,* May 1968.

267 *"I'm not crying about the house":* Beranger, "Private Life of Barbara Stanwyck."

267 *Capra finished filming:* McBride, *Frank Capra,* 241.

267 *"steadily dating":* Capra, *Name Above the Title,* 134.

267 *"a smallish, attractive":* Ibid., 110.

267 *Lu Reyburn was the daughter:* McBride, *Frank Capra,* 207.

267 *He had driven Lu back:* Capra, *Name Above the Title,* 111.

267 *"You don't have to":* McBride, *Frank Capra,* 217.

267 *"more married to work":* Capra, *Name Above the Title,* 67.

268 *"Nothing can depress":* Ibid.

268 *"She liked movies":* McBride, *Frank Capra,* 207–8.

268 *"The Irish go through":* Ibid., 216.

268 *"He was my 'angel' ":* Gladys Hall, *Modern Screen,* November 1937.

268 *"likes actresses and enjoys":* "Frank Capra Bridegroom Today," *New York Daily News,* January 28, 1932, 42.

269 *The Capras' honeymoon was:* McBride, *Frank Capra,* 243–44.

269 *On Capra's return, he:* Ibid., 241.

269 *After the Malibu fire:* Forbidden (1931) press book.

269 *"We've both missed": Los Angeles Record,* November 21, 1931.

270 *He decided he would: Variety,* November 17, 1931, 30.

270 *"[That] statement seemed":* Fidler, "Barbara Stanwyck Answers Twenty Timely Questions," 22–23.

270 *"People were horrified":* Dick Hunt, "Barbara Stanwyck Tells Why She Turned Cartwheels on Stage," *Los Angeles Evening Herald Express,* February 13, 1932.

271 *"In fact, he argued":* Helen Louise Walker, "Barbara Stanwyck Loves a Good Scrap," *Movie Classic,* June 1932, 60.

271 *" 'Well I can still' ":* Ibid., 17, 60.

271 *"I was so proud":* Ibid., 60.

271 *"I regard the dance":* Fidler, "Barbara Stanwyck Answers Twenty Timely Questions," 22.

271 *"But I suppose Frank":* Walker, "Barbara Stanwyck Loves a Good Scrap," 60.

271 *"Mr. Fay is essentially":* Fidler, "Barbara Stanwyck Answers Twenty Timely Questions," 22.

271 *"getting almighty sick":* Hunt, "Barbara Stanwyck Tells Why She Turned Cartwheels on Stage."

271 *"The same is true nowhere":* Babcock, "Stanwyck-Fay Menage Plays Up-and-Down Role."

271 *"would rather live happily": Photoplay,* April 1932, 38–39.

272 *A Fool's Advice, which Fay: Los Angeles Evening Herald,* December 7, 1931.

272 *"I want to use": Los Angeles Record,* November 21, 1931.

272 *To remain in Los Angeles: Variety,* November 24, 1931, 2.

Five: F•A•Y

PAGE

273 *A new contract between:* Warner Bros. to Edna Ferber, December 7, 1931, specifying Wellman was to direct and giving Ferber consultation in the selection of another director if Wellman was unavailable.

273 *Ferber okayed Bill Wellman: Variety,* December 1, 1931, 6; Dick Moore to author, n.d.

273 *Production was to begin:* M. Gordon to George Crowley Jr., memo, December 18, 1931; start date January 18, 1932.

273 *"leave her heart behind":* Charles G. Norris, *Zelda Marsh* (New York: E. P. Dutton, 1927), 484.

274 *"justify the sympathy":* AFI Feature Films, *1931–40, 1926–27.*

275 *was a screenwriter: The Divorcee* (1930).

275 *worked as an assistant director: Excuse Me* (1925); *Upstage* (1926); *Body and Soul* (1927).

275 *"Barbara was not too happy":* Ella Smith, *Starring Miss Barbara Stanwyck,* 41.

275 *"low budget affair":* Ibid., 40.

275 *"one of those terrible":* Ibid., 41.

275 *While Barbara was filming:* Bernds, *Mr. Bernds Goes to Hollywood* (Lanham, Md.: Scarecrow Press, 1999).

275 *Also listed in their: Variety,* December 29, 1931.

276 *"a youth whom Nature":* Voltaire, *Candide: The Works of Voltaire,* François-Marie Arouet, Trans. E.R. DuMont, 1901.

276 *"There were rain scenes":* Ed Bernds to author, June 9, 1997.

276 *"[The picture] was done":* Bernds to author, June 3, 1997.

277 *While B. P. Schulberg: Memoirs of Will H. Hays,* 444.

277 *The house had originally:* Tony Fay to author, June 12, 2002.

278 *A separate building was:* Gene Vaslett to author, January 31, 1997.

278 *A den, outside Barbara's:* Vaslett to author, June 28, 2000.

278 *Four walls with screened-in:* Tony Fay to author, June 12, 2002.

278 *Opposite the table was:* Tony Fay to author, February 27, 1998.

279 *"cry picture for the girls": Variety,* January 12, 1932.

279 *"further demonstration that she": Los Angeles Examiner,* February 12, 1932.

280 *Whenever Barbara began: New York Times,* February 23, 1941.

Six: Salt of the Earth

PAGE

281 *"Not only did I not":* Ferber, *Peculiar Treasure,* 279.

281 *"I feel very strongly":* Ibid., 280.

281 *"a novel to read": New York Times,* February 24, 1924, 9.

281 *"To Miss Ferber's narrative": New York Tribune,* March 16, 1924, 19.

281 *"queer sort of book":* Ferber, *Peculiar Treasure,* 276–77.

281 *sold 323,000 copies:* Ibid., 282.

281 *"Money. Furs. Jewels. Automobiles":* Ibid., 276.

281 *"Life has no weapons":* Ferber, *So Big,* 166.

281 *"was the story of":* Ferber, *Peculiar Treasure,* 276–77.

282 *"learned to read what":* Ibid., 103.

282 *"was all invented":* Ferber, *Kind of Magic,* 161.

282 *"a dash of fire":* Ferber, *So Big,* 124.

282 *"took the best and":* Ibid., 173.

282 *"a prosperous and blooming":* Ibid., 217.

282 *"used none of the":* Ibid., 290.

282 *"Selina became a farmer's":* So Big press book, 5.

283 *Twenty-eight hand-cranked:* Wellman, *Go, Get 'Em!,* 243.

283 *"Lots of actresses are":* So Big press book, 4.

283 *Selina Peake didn't simply age:* Ferber, *So Big,* 172, 292.

283 *Monte Westmore, Warner's makeup:* So Big press book, 4.

283 *"Very few actresses would be":* Ibid.

283 *"Julia Ferber as a human"*: Ferber, *Peculiar Treasure,* 165.

283 *"a small dark figure"*: Ferber, *So Big,* 354.

283 *"do portraits [but] [n]ot"*: Ibid.

284 *"fine splendid face"*: Ibid., 353–54.

284 *"The title had been"*: Ferber, *Peculiar Pleasure,* 277. The book was originally serialized in *Woman's Home Companion* as *Selina,* but the title *So Big* stayed on the book.

284 *"No man in the"*: *Jeopardy* press book.

284 *"so bored"*: Wellman interview, 80.

284 *Barbara was a perfectionist*: Bill Wellman Jr. to author, February 20, 2007.

284 *"Nothing ever seems secure"*: Marion Carter, *Journal,* March 15, 1932.

284 *"Some players are able"*: *Shopworn* press book.

285 *"It was in 1897"*: Edna Ferber, *A Peculiar Treasure,* 65.

286 *"Give Dickie the close-up"*: Grace Mack, *Screen Play,* June 1932, 57.

286 *"He didn't have to threaten"*: Barbara Stanwyck, *Screen Guide,* 1946, 47.

286 *Ten days before production*: George Brent contract with Warner Bros., December 16, 1932.

286 *"artist who leads [DeJong]"*: Davis, *Lonely Life,* 123, 124.

286 *"the drooping eyelids"*: *Silver Screen,* September 1930.

286 *"Good, now we can go"*: Shaun Considine, *Bette and Joan* (New York: E. P. Dutton, 1989), 6.

287 *"She was a stubborn"*: Ibid., 20.

287 *"I worshipped her"*: Davis, *Lonely Life,* 55.

287 *At twenty-three, Davis had*: Considine, *Bette and Joan,* 14.

287 *"Whom did this to"*: Davis, *Lonely Life,* 96.

287 *Another producer said she*: Janet Flanner, "Cotton-Dress Girl," *New Yorker,* February 20, 1943, 26.

288 *"a cotton-dress girl"*: Ibid., 19.

288 *"the kid might be"*: Davis, *Lonely Life,* 113.

288 *"Universal had asked to"*: Ibid., 121.

288 The Man Who Played God: Release date February 20, 1932.

289 *"The discovery [in* So Big *]"*: Davis, *Lonely Life,* 129.

289 *"I never knew who"*: Ibid., 124.

289 *"was magnificent . . . She was"*: Ibid.

289 *"To Dickie Moore"*: Dick Moore to author, n.d.

289 *Production for the picture*: February 3, 1932.

289 *"monument of American"*: Advertisement for *So Big.*

290 *She dressed quietly, neatly, comfortably*: Steef F. Phillips, "Barbara Defies Hollywood," *Motion Picture,* March 1940, 58.

290 *didn't enjoy getting*: Grace Mack, *Screen Play,* June 1932, 29.

290 *"When I put rouge"*: Jack Grant, "I'll Never Divorce Frank Fay, Says Barbara Stanwyck," *Movie Classic,* April 1933.

290 *"I don't want people"*: Sidney Skolsky, *New York Daily News,* February 22, 1932.

290 *"I can do as"*: Barbara Stanwyck Fay, affidavit, James Mack, affidavit, January 10, 1938, 2.

290 *As soon as he'd*: Stanwyck Fay, affidavit, January 10, 1938, 9, Superior Court of the State of California.

291 *Two other Warner stars*: Los Angeles Evening Herald Examiner, January 22, 1932.

291 *His first (and second)*: Variety, March 8, 1932.

291 *Those being paid*: Ibid.

291 *Barbara insisted Fay receive*: "Vaude House Reviews," *Variety,* March 1, 1932.

291 *"Barbara, your tact and"*: Helen Louise Walker, *Movie Classic,* June 1932, 17, 60.

291 *"Well, Miss Stanwyck was"*: Los Angeles Examiner.

292 *"whose name spells box"*: Photoplay, April 1932, 38–39.

292 *originally published as a short story*: Saturday Evening Post, October 1931.

292 *He liked how spirited:* William Wellman Jr. to author.

292 *"They know a lot about":* The Purchase Price *press book.*

293 *The manager is irate:* "Vaude House Reviews," *Variety,* March 1, 1932, 28.

294 *"[The show] is ragged":* Variety, *March 1, 1932.*

294 *"Miss Stanwyck is being":* "Vaude House Reviews," *Variety,* March 8, 1932.

294 *"The most promising young":* Leonard Hall, *Photoplay,* May 1932, 47.

294 *Following the show's opening:* Variety, *March 1, 1932.*

294 *State troopers, detectives, and police:* New York Times, *March 2, 1932.*

294 *Fay's name was taken:* Virginia Maxwell, *Picture Play,* October 1932, 64.

294 *"My marriage means more":* Ibid., 26.

294 *"Well, what about movie":* Ibid., 64.

295 *Fay was back the next:* Variety, *March 8, 1932.*

295 *"The show's second week":* Ibid.

295 *"Submerges her own ability":* Variety, *March 1, 1932, 49.*

295 *He also changed:* "Vaude House Reviews," *Variety,* March 8, 1932.

295 *"Something has happened":* Ibid.

295 *He'd made light in:* Sidney Skolsky, newspaper clipping, 1932, Shubert Archive.

296 *"the clumsiest kind":* Variety, *April 5, 1932, 14.*

296 *"Barbara Stanwyck's temper":* Cecelia Ager, *Variety,* April 5, 1932, 16.

296 *"the Coast by way":* Virginia Maxwell, *Picture Play,* October 1932, 64.

296 *The billboard advertised:* Variety, *April 5, 1932, 16.*

Seven: Prophets of a New Order

PAGE

297 *"I like pictures better":* Biery, "Let's Talk About 'Em," 114.

297 *With the picture were:* Louella Parsons, April 15, 1932.

297 *"infinitely better than":* Ibid.

297 *"[She] has undergone":* Ruth Morris, Uncommon Chatter, *Variety,* May 3, 1932, 40.

298 *Edna Ferber felt that:* Colleen Moore, *Silent Star,* 158.

298 *Fay was admitted to:* Barbara Stanwyck Fay, affidavit, January 10, 1938, 6, Superior Court of the State of California.

298 *"I wouldn't wear an":* Beranger, "Private Life of Barbara Stanwyck," 9.

298 *"a magnificent actress":* Fox, "Man's World," 36.

298 *Wellman took chances:* Darryl Hickman to author, March 28, 2007.

298 *"good old Bill was":* Paris, *Louise Brooks,* 225.

299 *The new picture:* April 14, 1932.

299 *"unconsidered appendicle":* Stringer, *Mud Lark,* 14.

299 *"My response to that":* Fidler, "Barbara Stanwyck Answers Twenty Timely Questions," 70.

301 *"prairie landscape as flat":* Stringer, *Mud Lark,* 55.

302 *"They'll hold you up":* Fox, "Man's World," 37.

304 *The field of shocked:* John Gallagher, filmography and notes.

304 *"After the first take":* Ella Smith, *Starring Miss Barbara Stanwyck,* 47.

304 *It was two in the:* Gallagher, notes.

304 *Barbara's legs were scorched:* The Purchase Price *press book.*

304 *"One for the take":* "Wild Bill," interview by Eyman, 17.

304 *One print was for:* It made $299,000 domestically and $45,000 in foreign sales.

304 *The Mud Lark's title:* AFI, 1715.

305 *The studio formally dropped:* Clarke, *Featured Player,* 112–23.

305 *A headline in* Variety: *Variety,* April 26, 1932, 8.

305 *The ad's tagline: Variety,* May 3, 1932, 14.

305 *Henry Ford was refusing:* Leuchtenburg, *Franklin D. Roosevelt and the New Deal,* 21.

306 *"Here we are in":* Ibid., 9.

307 *Barbara was a lifelong:* Gene Vaslett to author.

307 *Frank Fay hated Franklin:* Jesse White to author.

307 *Jack Cohn was sitting:* Bellamy, interview with Saunders, 19, 20.

308 *If the theater chains:* McBride, *Frank Capra,* 248.

308 *"Dwan sat impassively":* Bernds, *Mr. Bernds Goes to Hollywood,* 151–52.

308 *"It was the return":* Ibid., 152.

308 *"Riskin brought to Capra":* Joe McBride, "Robert Riskin Esquire," *Magazine of the Writers Guild of America* 3, no. 1 (1999): 48.

308 *"Frank [Capra] provided the":* Philip Dunne, in Joseph McBride, "Riskinesque: "How Robert Riskin Spoke Through Frank Capra and Vice Versa," *Written By* 3, no. 1 (1999).

310 *"And I've done it":* Beranger, "Private Life of Barbara Stanwyck," 8.

Eight: Object of Desire

PAGE

311 *Grace Zaring Stone:* Stone later wrote, under the name Ethel Vance, *Escape,* which was made into a movie with Norma Shearer and Robert Taylor, and *Winter Meeting,* made into a picture with Bette Davis.

312 *William Archer in his play: The Green Goddess* was made into a movie with George Arliss in 1923 by Goldwyn-Cosmopolitan and again in 1930, also with Arliss, directed by Alfred Green, from Warner Bros.

315 *But the screenwriter added:* McBride, *Frank Capra,* 279.

315 *Capra let it be:* Ibid., 278.

315 *Instead, Capra gave the role:* Ibid.

316 *among them Leo Carrillo: AFI* Catalog of Feature Films/ *The Bitter Tea of General Yen.*

316 *Asther lost the race:* Barry Paris, *Garbo: A Biography* (New York: Alfred A. Knopf, 1994), 46.

316 *Together they'd attended:* Ibid., 41.

316 *"The make-up may have":* Ed Bernds to author, June 9, 1997.

318 *"I'll take dust":* Eleanor Barnes, *Illustrated Daily News,* July 23, 1932.

319 *fourteen-year-old daughter:* She became the writer Eleanor Perényi.

319 *"grotesquely miscast":* Eleanor Perényi to author, January 5, 1998.

319 *Connolly saw being a character:* "Walter Connolly, Actor, 53, Is Dead," *New York Times,* May 29, 1940.

320 *"I kept away from pictures":* "Film Work and Actor: Walter Connolly Discusses Some Phases of Hollywood's Artistic Problems," *New York Times,* March 18, 1934.

320 *The set dresser even: The Bitter Tea of General Yen* press book.

321 *the* New York Times *announced: New York Times,* May 8, 1932.

321 *It was the ending:* Perényi to author, January 5, 1998.

321 *"People want to see":* Hal Hall, "An Interview with Frank Capra," *American Cinematographer,* February 1931, 38.

321 *"those arty things":* Frank Capra, in George Stevens Jr., ed., *Conversations with the Great Moviemakers of Hollywood's Golden Age at the American Film Institute* (New York: Alfred A. Knopf, 2006), 98.

321 *He believed the camera:* Ibid.

321 *"A cinematographer can":* Hall, "Interview with Frank Capra," 20.

322 *Walker's invention of "variable diffusion":* Walker and Walker, *Light on Her Face,* 186–87.

322 *When Capra wanted something:* Capra, in Stevens, *Conversations,* 39.

322 *Connolly, who was used: The Bitter Tea of General Yen* press book.

323 *Wong was originally: AFI,* 171.

323 *Toshia Mori, who came from: The Bitter Tea of General Yen* press book.

324 *"For me,* Bitter Tea*":* Bernds to author, May 1997.

324 *"Capra, very calmly, was":* Ibid.

324 *"The head cameraman":* Bernds to author, June 9, 1997.

325 *"I chose that picture":* Biery, "Let's Talk About 'Em," 114.

Nine: A Path to Motherhood

326 *"I want one so badly":* Faith Service, *Motion Picture,* December 1932.

326 *"All my life, I think":* Ibid.

326 *Hoyt gave Barbara the news:* Ann Hoyt, affidavit, January 10, 1938, Superior Court of the State of California.

326 *"I knew those babies":* Faith Service, *Motion Picture,* December 1932.

327 *"I wonder if":* Ibid.

327 *Barbara's room was at:* Tony Fay to author, October 9, 2002.

327 *Barbara fired Miss Richter:* Barbara Stanwyck Fay, affidavit, January 10, 1938, 2, Superior Court of the State of California.

327 *Ann Hoyt and several doctors:* Ibid.

327 *who had previously worked:* Margaret Griffin (niece of Nellie Banner) to author, July 18, 2002.

327 *"All I wish for":* Louis Sobol, The Voice of Broadway, April 1, 1935.

328 *Maud, Bert, and Al:* Al Merkent log, June Merkent to author.

328 *Barbara made arrangements for:* Gene Vaslett to author, January 31, 1997.

328 *survey of box-office reaction: Variety,* August 23, 1932, 3.

329 *Warner agreed to pay:* Roy Obringer to Morris Ebenstein (Warner Bros., New York City), November 3, 1932.

330 *Warner agreed to a new: Variety,* September 6, 1932, 2.

330 *Warner had three one-year:* Warner Bros. contract, September 19, 1932.

330 *"Did you ever notice":* Faith Service, *Motion Picture,* December 1932.

Ten: A Most Dangerous Man Menace

331 *"Yes, we could smell":* Leuchtenburg, *Franklin D. Roosevelt and the New Deal,* 18.

332 *"But believe me":* Clarke Warren, "Barbara Stanwyck Frankly Considers Sex," *Screen Play,* January 1933, 23.

332 *"Barbara Stanwyck is going":* Ibid.

332 *Once out west:* Gussow, *Don't Say Yes Until I Finish Talking,* 21.

333 *"I never was the type":* Warren, "Barbara Stanwyck Frankly Considers Sex," 46.

334 *Warner wanted to shoot: Variety,* November 8, 1932.

334 *"If Genesius was the":* Films in Review, March 1968, 135.

335 *Barbara was taking home:* Memo from payroll office, Warner Bros. Archives.

335 *She returned from the studio:* Judith Stevens to author, June 2, 1999, 13.

335 Baby Face *was an original:* Contract between First National and Cosmo Hamilton, February 28, 1927.

336 *By 1925 the dog was:* Mosley, *Zanuck,* 68, 69.

336 *gangster comedy for Dolores Costello: The Little Irish Girl;* Gussow, *Don't Say Yes Until I Finish Talking,* 40.

336 *dual role for Montagu Love: The Social Highwayman;* ibid.

336 *comedy about gold diggers: Footloose Widows;* ibid.

336 *Jack Warner referred to:* Ibid.

336 *"He isn't available":* Mosley, *Zanuck,* 77; Gussow, *Don't Say Yes Until I Finish Talking,* 55.

338 *"suffer the indignities":* Howard Smith to Zanuck, memo, November 11, 1932, Warner Bros. Archives.

338 *for one dollar assigned:* W. B. Dover to Chase, memo, November 11, 1932, Warner Bros. Archives.

338 *Warner had released:* W. B. Dover to Roy Obringer, memo, November 23, 1932, USC Warners Archive.

338 *The screenwriter, who was:* Zanuck to BS, November 11, 1932.

339 *"build her up":* Baby Face press book, 5.

340 *Alfred Green, the director:* Green, interview with Hal Wiener, *Los Angeles Evening Herald,* May 16, 1931.

340 *"It is a new line":* "Easier to Reach Top Than to Remain There, Barbara Stanwyck Says," *San Francisco Chronicle,* February 5, 1933, 1.

341 *"Every time his name":* Gene Vaslett to author, June 7, 1999.

341 *"The country is in chaos":* Warner, *My First Hundred Years in Hollywood,* 208.

341 *Jack Warner had organized:* Stephen Talbot, "On with the Show," *Washington Post,* January 21, 2001.

341 *"so many evils into":* Cecil B. DeMille, *Autobiography,* ed. Donald Hayne (Englewood Cliffs, N.J.: Prentice-Hall, 1959), 326.

342 *Barbara reminded Fay:* Barbara Stanwyck Fay, affidavit, January 10, 1938, 3, Superior Court of the State of California.

342 *The judge was told:* Ibid., 2–3.

343 *"requires the balance":* Florence Lawrence, "Producer Finds Revue Requires Unusual Tricks," newspaper clipping, n.d.

343 *Dion was frightened:* Stanwyck Fay, affidavit, January 10, 1938, 5.

343 *He frightened her:* Margaret Griffin (niece of Nellie Banner) to author, July 18, 2002.

343 *"bulg[ing] with talent":* Relman Morin, newspaper clipping, n.d.

344 *It had closed with:* Fred Allen, *Much Ado About Me* (Boston: Little, Brown, 1956).

344 *By the end of:* Variety, January 10, 1933, 45.

Eleven: Bold and Bad

PAGE

345 *"I believe in creative":* Roxy, *Variety,* December 20, 1932.

346 *The Rockefellers themselves had:* Ibid.

346 *"courage and vision":* December 14, 1932.

346 *"completion of the great":* December 16, 1932.

346 *"No picture half so":* Philip K. Scheuer, *New York World-Telegram,* January 14, 1933.

346 *"poetry and beauty":* Thornton Delehanty, *New York Evening Post,* January 12, 1933.

347 *Louella Parsons thought Barbara:* Louella Parsons, *Los Angeles Examiner,* January 14, 1933.

347 *The Chinese legation wanted:* F. L. Herron to Will Hays, memo, January 17, 1933, AMPAS.

347 *"a eulogy of the Chinese":* Wilson to Hays, memo, January 21, 1933, AMPAS.

347 *"missionary angle":* Geoffrey Shurlock to Dr. Wingate, memo, January 19, 1933, AMPAS.

347 *In New York,* The Bitter Tea *was released:* AMPP, memo, December 28, 1932, AMPAS.

347 *In Massachusetts, the firing:* AMPP, memo, December 19, 1933, AMPAS.

347 *In Ohio, Clara Blandick's dialogue:* AMPP, memo, January 25, 1933, AMPAS.

347 *"I think it one":* Eileen Creelman, *New York Sun,* September 13, 1934; Capra, oral history, 1956, Columbia University.

347 *she was helping Fay:* Larry Kleno to author, November 27, 2002.

347 *Headlines in the press: Variety,* January 10, 1933, 3.

347 *"I [don't] have a penny":* Grant, "I'll Never Divorce Frank Fay," 26, 60.

348 Tattle Tales' *first week: Variety,* February 7, 1933.

348 *Fay had been drinking:* Barbara Stanwyck Fay, affidavit, January 10, 1938, 7, Superior Court of the State of California.

348 Tattle Tales *had been booked: Variety,* February 21, 1933, 51.

348 *Barbara struggled with the effects:* Stanwyck Fay, affidavit, January 10, 1938, 7.

348 *In New York, the picture:* Capitol Theatre Program, February 17, 1933, no. 7.

348 *"Barbara Stanwyck and a good": Variety,* February 28, 1933, 15.

348 *"as a retreat, the sort":* Ibid.

349 *"a girl's seminary": Los Angeles Examiner,* February 24, 1933.

349 *"new role for her": New York Sun,* February 24, 1933.

349 *By early the following:* Leuchtenburg, *Franklin D. Roosevelt and the New Deal,* 39.

349 *Eugene Meyer:* Meyer bought *The Washington Post* on June 1, 1933.

349 *"Hard on H[oover] to go":* Leuchtenburg, *Franklin D. Roosevelt and the New Deal,* 39.

350 *"What this country needs":* Stephen Talbot, "On with the Show."

350 *"As we saw it":* Leuchtenburg, *Franklin D. Roosevelt and the New Deal,* 40.

350 *"will endure as it":* Jack Warner to Edward G. Robinson, memo, March 9, 1933, Rudy Behlmer, *Inside Warner Bros.* (New York: Viking, 1985), 10.

351 *The following day, deposits:* Leuchtenburg, *Franklin D. Roosevelt and the New Deal,* 45.

351 *"Capitalism was saved":* Raymond Moley, in Ibid.

351 *He called their bluff:* Mosley, *Zanuck,* 125.

352 *"I expect to fulfill": Movie Classic,* June 1933, 23.

352 *Barbara asked for:* Jack Warner to BS, amendment letter, March 9, 1933, Warner Bros. Archives.

352 *Admission prices had been:* Schwartz, *Hollywood Writers' Wars,* 10–11.

352 *"They weren't worth":* Mosley, *Zanuck,* 128.

353 *"On April 10th":* Ibid., 127.

354 *Wallis was Zanuck's replacement:* Wallis and Higham, *Starmaker,* 28–29.

354 *When Warner took over:* Ibid., 23–29.

354 *Zanuck agreed to make: Variety,* April 25, 1933.

354 *Zanuck left Los Angeles: New York Sun,* April 26, 1933.

355 *Joe Schenck felt it was:* Behlmer, *Inside Warner Bros.*

355 *Mayer Family Fund:* Crowther, *Hollywood Rajah,* 190.

355 *"was on top":* Wallis and Higham, *Starmaker,* 29.

Twelve: Entrances and Exits

PAGE

356 *"Oh, that L. B. Mayer":* Schwartz, *Hollywood Writers' Wars,* 13, 10.

356 *"Looking to the Academy":* Ibid., 13.

357 *"You worked any kind":* Bellamy, interview with Saunders, 14.

357 *"It was supposed to be":* SAG Website interviews, SAG historian Valerie Yaros.

357 *Talbot rode a bicycle:* Laura Wagner, "Lyle Talbot," *Films of the Golden Age* no. 60 (Spring 2010): 20.

357 *"met at night, in private":* SAG Website interview with Robert Young conducted for *Screen Actor* magazine to commemorate the 60th anniversary of the American Federation of Labor charter of the Screen Actors Guild. Courtesy of Valerie Yaros.

358 *"MGM and Louis B. Mayer":* David F. Prindle, *The Politics of Glamour* (Madison: University of Wisconsin Press, 1988).

358 *were suing Fay: Variety,* March 28, 1933, 28.

358 *"breaks convention bravely": Times* (London), March 13, 1933.

358 *The trip took eight:* Al Merkent's log; June Merkent to author.

358 *Hal Wallis wired Barbara:* Hal Wallis to BS, telegram, May 19, 1933, Warner Bros. Archives.

358 *William Dieterle was to direct:* Dieterle was replaced by William Wellman when Dieterle became ill; Michael Curtiz took over from Wellman when he started work on *College Coach. AFI,* 623.

359 *Barbara was unaware of it:* Julia Gwin, "She's a Movie Fan Too," *Silver Screen,* January 1934, 62.

359 *"reviewer must have acid":* Florence Hayden, *New Yorker,* June 1, 1933.

360 *"a product of the urban":* Percy Hammond, *New York Herald Tribune,* June 2, 1933; Robert Garland, *New York World-Telegram,* June 2, 1933.

360 *and "sluggish":* New York Times, June 2, 1933.

360 *"hogging the show":* Percy Hammond, *New York Herald Tribune,* June 2, 1933.

360 *"She is blessed":* Burns Mantle, *New York Daily News,* June 3, 1933.

361 *"I hope Barbara":* Louella Parsons, *Los Angeles Examiner,* June 15, 1933.

361 *"Fay has always stolen":* Grant, "I'll Never Divorce Frank Fay," 26, 60.

361 *One day it was: New York Sun,* June 17, 1933.

362 *"is reputed to be":* Variety, June 27, 1933.

362 *"take children to see":* W. E. Oliver, *Los Angeles Evening Herald Examiner,* July 14, 1933.

362 *"Miss Stanwyck's performance":* Jimmy Starr, *Los Angeles Evening Herald Examiner,* April 29, 1933.

362 *"truth in its psychology":* New York Herald Tribune, n.d.

362 *"Lil a beautiful bum":* Variety, June 27, 1933.

362 *"the best and by far":* Hollywood Reporter, March 22, 1933.

362 *"Miss Stanwyck hasn't had":* Louella Parsons, *Los Angeles Examiner,* July 14, 1933.

363 *"I advise you not":* Nancy Bernard Levy to author, March 21, 1998.

363 *"All this talk":* Grant, "I'll Never Divorce Frank Fay," 26, 60.

364 *The final week cost: Variety,* June 27, 1933, 1.

PART THREE: Valor and Fire

One: Adjusted Angles of Vision

PAGE

367 *"Hollywood, where gossip flourishes":* Elizabeth Wilson, "Carnival Nights in Hollywood," magazine clipping, n.d.

367 *"She didn't like it":* Gene Vaslett to author, October 1996.

367 *"He's in the gutter":* Ibid.

367 *"Pop Fay was a charming":* Vaslett to author, June 2000.

370 *"little difference between film":* BS to Lisa Kirk in response to Kirk's letter asking for BS's help, September 1965.

370 *"There is a marked":* Bellamy, interview with Saunders, 10.

370 *Archie Mayo was paid: Ever in My Heart,* Warner Bros. Archives.

370 *the German cabinet decreed: World Almanac and Book of Facts for 1934.*

371 *"too fluffy on one":* Wallis to Koenig, memo, July 26, 1933.

371 *"don't shoot these group":* Wallis to Mayo, memo, July 29, 1933.

371 *"The Hays office":* Wallis to Mayo and Presnell, memo, August 15, 1933.

372 *"For the make-up girls":* Asher, "In Exile and Loving It," 69.

372 *This time he returned: Ever in My Heart* press book, 4.

373 *"It's from all of us":* Ibid.

373 *"I'm building it up":* Ron Miller, *Hartford Courant,* March 29, 1983, D10.

375 *"were comparable to":* Fidler, "Barbara Stanwyck Answers Twenty Timely Questions," 23.

376 *"We object to hordes":* Frank Cates, "Has America Declared War on All Foreign Players?," *Movie Classic,* April 1933, 32, 33, 66–67.

376 *Fay was too drunk: Variety,* September 5, 1933, 5.

376 *Barbara was in New York:* Variety, September 12, 1933.

377 *A doctor was backstage:* Telegraph, September 15, 1933.

377 *"It isn't me that's":* Gwin, "She's a Movie Fan Too," 47.

377 *"Not one stale person":* Article by Barbara Stanwyck, no date.

378 *No act replaced him:* Variety, October 17, 1933, 49.

378 *Barbara knew he'd been:* Vaslett to author, October 2002.

378 *After his release a:* Barbara Stanwyck Fay, affidavit, January 10, 1938, 8, Superior Court of the State of California.

378 *Amid gossip of trouble:* Saturday Evening Post, September 1933.

378 *"Because I want to":* Stanwyck Fay affidavit, 8.

379 *"of having no self":* Gladys Hall, "Barbara Stanwyck's Advice to Girls in Love," 3, AMPAS.

379 *"Most couples don't do that":* Movie Classics, September 1933, 28.

380 *Soon after, she dissolved:* New York Times, March 24 and May 8, 1932.

380 *After six years of being:* Scott O'Brien, "The Inevitable Road to Stardom," *Films of the Golden Age* no. 60 (Spring 2010), 41.

Two: Sinister Provisions

PAGE

383 *"We counted our blessings":* Clarke, *Featured Player,* 137–39.

383 *Word had spread:* Ralph Morgan and John C. Lee, "The Guild," *Screen Actor,* September 1941, 19.

383 *"an autonomous organization":* Ibid., 20.

384 *During the meeting two:* Ibid., 20, 52.

384 *New officers were chosen:* New York Times, October 10, 1933.

384 *The new slate of officers:* Valerie Yaros (SAG) to author, January 21, 2003.

384 *More than 250 actors:* Morgan and Lee, "Guild," 52.

384 *Montgomery was appointed chairman:* SAG meeting minutes, p. 57, courtesy Valerie Yaros.

384 *"The studios required you":* Robert Montgomery interview, SAG 1979, 28.

384 *"The days of slavery":* New York Times, October 13, 1933.

385 *Actors who produced:* Ibid.

385 *He also called for:* Schwartz, *Hollywood Writers' Wars,* 30–31.

385 *"tender, heart-touching, tragic":* W. E. Oliver, *Los Angeles Evening Herald Examiner,* October 20, 1933.

385 *"Both Miss Stanwyck and Kruger":* Ibid.

385 *"Emotion is Miss Stanwyck's":* Variety, October 17, 1933, 57.

Three: Leading with Your Ace

PAGE

386 *"Keep Stanwyck/These days":* Harry Warner to J. L. Warner, telegram, September 11, 1933.

386 *Of concern as well:* Wallis to Jim Seymour, memos re: *Broadway and Back,* August 8–September 19, 1933, Warner Bros. Archives.

386 *Wallis next offered her:* Variety, November 21, 1933, 29.

386 *Three months later:* David Mathews to W. G. Wallace, WB memo, March 30, 1936.

386 *The studio took note:* Roy Obringer to Jack Warner, memo, December 13, 1933, Warner Bros. Archives.

388 *"Dear Louie, You've just":* Ibid., 73.

388 *Warner paid RKO $7,000:* Roy Obringer to Mayberry, memo, November 22, 1933, Warner Bros. Archives.

390 *"Well, then, get off":* Interview of Joel McCrea with Peter McCrea.

390 *He'd grown up:* Ibid.

390 *He had attended Hollywood:* Ibid.

390 *That was the end:* Ibid.

391 *He figured that Fay:* Ibid.

392 *During the day at work: Los Angeles Post Record,* December 1, 1933.

392 *"I'm still nuts about":* Interview Joel McCrea with Peter McCrea.

393 *It was clear to Buck:* Buck Mack affidavit, January 10, 1938, 3.

393 *The federal government claimed: Los Angeles Evening Herald Record,* November 24, 1933.

393 *Two weeks later Warner Bros.:* Summons to Appear, December 1, 1933, Warner Bros. Archives.

393 *He'd put in a tennis: A Lost Lady* press book, 20.

393 *She was going out:* Judith Stevens to author, October 18, 1998, 16.

393 *Frank and Barbara put down: Bank of America v. Frank Fay, Barbara Stanwyck Fay, Corporation of America, John Doe Co., Richard Roe Co., Henry Poe Co.,* February 20, 1939, 2.

394 *The Bank of America paid:* BS to Bank of America, December 15, 1933, Warner Bros. Archives.

Four: A Beautiful Ghost

PAGE

395 Ever in My Heart *didn't do well:* Gross income breakdown of pictures, Schaefer Collection, courtesy of Ned Comstock.

396 *Among the featured players: Variety,* January 2, 1934, 127.

396 *"But it's the man's story":* S. R. Mook, *Modern Screen,* October 1934, 97.

397 *"Tailored smartly to suit": Variety,* April 10, 1934, 13.

397 *"high entertainment [with] superb": Variety,* n.d.

397 Gambling Lady *was a hit:* It cost $230,000 and made back, domestically, $478,000. Warner earnings to February 27, 1942, Schaefer Collection, courtesy of Ned Comstock.

397 *"We don't want to":* Hal Wallis to Henry Blanke, memo, May 2, 1934, Warner Bros. Archives.

397 *Wallis sent the script:* List of scripts and dates submitted to Stanwyck, memo, n.d., Warner Bros. Archives.

397 *"It is doubtful if":* Edith Lewis, *Willa Cather Living,* 24.

397 *"beautiful ghost":* Cather and Bohlke, *Willa Cather in Person,* 79.

398 *"an excitement that came":* Cather, *A Lost Lady,* 31.

398 *"as belonging to a different":* Ibid., 42.

398 *"There was no fun":* Cather and Bohlke, *Willa Cather in Person,* 77.

398 *"I didn't try to make":* Ibid.

398 *"that she had had a hand":* Cather, *A Lost Lady,* 171.

398 *"just out of college":* Graham Baker to Hal Wallis, memo, July 10, 1930, Warner Bros. Archives.

399 *"we can get a splendid":* Gene Markey to Hal Wallis, memo, February 21, 1934, Warner Bros. Archives.

399 *"In as much as we":* Jim Seymour to Hal Wallis, memo, May 25, 1934, Warner Bros. Archives.

399 *For their work:* Budget, *A Lost Lady* no. 881, 2.

399 *and was finished:* AFI Catalog.

400 *"If there are any":* J. L. Warner to Jim Seymour, memo, June 18, 1934, Warner Bros. Archives.

400 *"massacre of innocent youths": Memoirs of Will H. Hays,* 450.

400 *"Protests against salacious films":* Ibid., 451.

400 *"At last we [have]":* Ibid., 454.

400 *Warner Bros. informed Barbara:* Roy Obringer to BS, May 31, 1934, Warner Bros. Archives.

401 *Warner Bros. was to pay:* to Warner Bros. from James Lytle (Internal Revenue Service), September 10, 1934, Warner Bros. Archives.

401 *Warner production supervisors, writers:* Hal Wallis to supervisors, writers, directors, department heads, memo, August 23, 1934, Warner Bros. Archives.

401 *Willa Cather had received letters:* Janis P. Stout, ed., *A Calendar of the Letters of Willa Cather* (Lincoln: University of Nebraska Press, 2002), 163.

401 *"whether for the purpose"*: Lee, *Willa Cather,* 330.

401 *"kept her distance from"*: Fanny Butcher, in Cather and Bohlke, *Willa Cather in Person,* xxviii.

Five: Normal People Leading Normal Lives

PAGE

402 *Three hundred million tons:* World Almanac and Book of Facts for 1934, 152.

402 *By 1934, huge rocks:* Johnson, *Heaven's Tableland,* 164.

402 *Congress approved Roosevelt's request:* Ibid., 174.

402 *In July, President Roosevelt: Variety,* July 3, 1934.

402 *"How the lights were placed"*: Gwin, "She's a Movie Fan Too," 47, 62.

403 *Jack Warner wasn't interested:* Roy Obringer to Hal Wallis, memo, October 9, 1934, Warner Bros. Archives.

403 *He worked as the master: Variety,* October 16, 1934, 15.

403 *They had to take:* August 7, 1934, letter, signed Barbara Stanwyck, Warner Bros., and Bank of America.

403 *"If the rest of Hollywood"*: *New York Evening Post,* March 31, 1934.

404 *"Dramatic action only implied"*: Reader's report, Warner Bros. Archives.

404 *"Sell this to her"*: Hal Wallis to Tom Buckingham, memo, July 10, 1934, Warner Bros. Archives.

404 *The pictures Warner was:* Bernard Drew, *Film Comment,* March–April 1981, 45.

404 *Wallis told his staff:* Hal Wallis to Miss Juergens (secretary to Roy Obringer), memo, August 29, 1934.

404 *A studio lawyer advised:* Ralph Lewis to Hazel Juergens, August 29, 1934, Warner Bros. Archives.

405 *The picture's budget: $215,000:* Weekly Production Cost, September 11, 1934, Warner Bros. Archives.

405 *Buckingham became ill: Variety,* September 12, 1934.

405 *"to own you"*: Schwartz, *Hollywood Writers' Wars,* 20–21.

405 *She went to work:* September 11, 1934, Warner Bros. production notes.

405 *"The script was bad"*: Ella Smith, *Starring Miss Barbara Stanwyck,* 68.

406 *Dion wouldn't keep still:* Barbara Stanwyck Fay, affidavit, January 10, 1938, 4.

406 *"the agony of quarreling"*: Hall, "Barbara Stanwyck's Advice to Girls in Love," 2, 3.

406 *"The humiliation of such"*: Gladys Hall, 1935.

406 *The nurse took him:* Ann Hoyt, affidavit, January 10, 1938, 5–6.

407 *Barbara's allegiance to Fay: Red Salute* press book, 2.

407 *Barbara also gave him: The Woman in Red* press book, 14.

407 *"Dear Kid"*: Jane Ellen Wayne, *Robert Taylor,* 62 (New York: St. Martin's Press, 1987), and Gladys Hall Papers, 1918–1969, Margaret Herrick Library, AMPAS.

407 *"[as] not [being] very"*: Ella Smith, *Starring Miss Barbara Stanwyck,* 68.

408 *"You know, iron rule"*: BS to Rex Reed, 1981, 18–19.

408 *In order for Warner:* Roy Obringer to Jack Warner, memo, September 15, 1934, Warner Bros. Archives.

408 *"Don't go to see"*: Muriel Babcock, *Los Angeles Examiner,* October 27, 1934.

408 *"a dismal drama"*: Eileen Creelman, *New York Sun,* October 4, 1934.

408 *"it fails almost ludicrously"*: Richard Watts, *New York Herald Tribune,* October 16, 1934.

408 *"Everything and everybody is"*: *Variety,* October 9, 1934.

Six: Another Routine Job

PAGE

410 *"pretty good vehicle"*: Sam Bischoff to Hal Wallis, memo, July 26, 1934, Warner Bros. Archives.

410 *"objectionable from the Point"*: Joseph Breen to Jack Warner, November 15, 1934, Warner Bros. Archives.

410 *Hal Wallis wanted Joel McCrea:* Hal Wallis to Maxwell Arnow, memo, October 8, 1934, Warner Bros. Archives.

410 *"It seems to me this"*: Harry Joe Brown to Hal Wallis, memo, October 26, 1934.

411 *"If there is going"*: Hal Wallis to Koenig, memo, October 22, 1934, Warner Bros. Archives.

411 *"I kept thinking of"*: *The Woman in Red* press book, 14.

411 *"There was little"*: *The Marx Brothers Scrapbook,* 117.

412 *"didn't have the power"*: *Starring Miss Barbara Stanwyck,* 68, 73.

412 *"more than a routine"*: Ibid.

412 *"She was always cooperative"*: Ibid., 73.

412 *"It would be the same"*: *The Woman in Red* press book, 15.

412 *"I think she could"*: Larry Kleno to author, April 2003.

415 *In addition, there was:* Variety, December 4, 1934, 3.

415 *"Hollywood knows so little"*: Asher, "In Exile and Loving It," 69.

415 *Jack Warner was determined:* Variety, December 11, 1934, 3.

415 *In a few of the scenes:* The Woman in Red press book, 13.

415 *At the end of:* Ibid., 16.

415 *"I cannot understand why"*: J. L. Warner to Joseph Breen, November 7, 1934, AMPAS.

415 *"Between you and me"*: Joseph Breen to J. L. Warner, November 9, 1934, AMPAS.

416 *"All I did was"*: Helen Louise Walker, "Barbara Stanwyck Loves a Good Scrap," 62.

417 *"Who the hell [is]"*: Beauchamp, *Without Lying Down,* 316.

417 *Wong's reputation in China:* Hye Seung Chung, *Hollywood Asian: Philip Ahn and the Politics of Cross-Ethnic Performance* (Philadelphia: Temple University Press, 2006), 98.

417 *Asther hadn't worked with:* Variety, January 10, 1935, 1.

417 *With the casting of a white man:* Graham Russell Gao Hodges, *Anna May Wong: From Laundryman's Daughter to Hollywood Legend* (New York: Palgrave Macmillan, 2004), 151–52.

419 *"Boys—this is our"*: Leuchtenburg, *Franklin D. Roosevelt and the New Deal,* 113–16.

419 *In November, at a hearing:* World Almanac and Book of Facts for 1935, 169; the hearing was November 20, 1934.

420 *the beloved Marie Dressler:* Beauchamp, *Without Lying Down,* 319.

420 *Barbara received 17 percent:* Hollywood Citizen-News, no date.

420 *"In my opinion this"*: Jack Warner to Hal Wallis, memo, December 6, 1934, Warner Bros. Archives.

420 *"Everyone I have talked to"*: Hal Wallis to Jack Warner, memo, December 6, 1934, Warner Bros. Archives.

421 *The largest strike ever:* Leuchtenburg, *Franklin D. Roosevelt and the New Deal,* 111–13.

421 *Members of the Screen:* John C. Lee, "The Guild—the Contract—Actors Win Pact," Screen Actor, 1941, 9.

421 *"[Capra] adored him"*: McBride, *Frank Capra,* 242.

421 *the top of his list:* James Cain to BS, November 26, 1950, Alice L. Birney Manuscript Division, Library of Congress.

422 *"a saucy little number"*: Ibid.

422 *"give herself away"*: Bernard Drew, *Film Comment,* March–April 1981, 45.

Seven: Average Screenfare

PAGE

423 *"You can't be bubbly"*: Screenland, March 1964.

423 *"What is needed to"*: Ada Patterson, Screenland, September 1933, 28.

423 *Nellie looked up to see:* Nellie Banner, affidavit, 3, Superior Court of the State of California.

424 *Frank was the only:* Ibid.

424 *Byron had no interest:* Judith Stevens to author, October 15, 1998.

424 *Warner Bros. continued to list:* Variety, January 1, 1935, 37.

424 *Clive Brook, to co-star:* In the end John Boles took Brook's role; AFI, 1582.

424 *Jaffe was asking $50,000:* February 25, 1935, memo from Sam Jaffe, Stanwyck Legal File no. 2929, Special Collections, UCLA.

424 *Carl Laemmle Jr. was negotiating:* The picture, *Remember Last Night?,* starred Edward Arnold, Robert Young, and Constance Cummings. James Whale directed. *AFI,* 1765.

424 *Lyons and Sam Jaffe were also:* Bill of particulars, 3, *A & S Lyons Inc. v. Barbara Stanwyck,* no. 396667, Superior Court of the State of California.

425 *The novelist, playwright:* February 25, 1935, memo from Jaffe.

425 Hollywood Hotel, *a variety:* Billips and Pierce, *Lux Presents Hollywood,* 3.

425 *During 1934, more than 150: Variety,* January 1, 1935, 89, 105.

425 *In attendance, and chatting:* Eugene Inge, *Los Angeles Evening Herald Examiner,* July 10, 1935.

425 *"still the screen's mistress":* W. E. Oliver, *Los Angeles Evening Herald Examiner,* February 15, 1935.

425 *"waves bye-bye to":* Jerry Hoffman, *Los Angeles Examiner,* February 15, 1935.

426 *"I want the name":* Maxine Marx to author, July 8, 2003.

426 *"We started that way": Freedonia Gazette* (Winter 1981) and (Summer 1982); *The Hollywood Greats,* BBC-TV, written and produced by Barry Norman.

426 *"I preferred to sell":* A. J. Liebling, "Fifth Marx Brother Claims Credit for Success of Act," *New York World-Telegram,* August 17, 1932, courtesy Shubert Archive.

426 *"I never felt at home":* Ibid.

427 *"Chico because if you":* Zeppo Marx to Shirley Eder, tape recording 10, courtesy of John Slotkin.

427 *It is also said:* "Christening the Marx Brothers," *New York Evening Post,* December 8, 1928.

427 *"I wonder what Zeppo":* Percy Hammond, November 10, 1928.

427 *"handsome, wooden, slightly obtuse":* Groucho Marx, *The Groucho Phile* (Indianapolis: Bobbs-Merrill, 1976).

427 *"Yes, sir" and:* Marx and Anobile, *Marx Bros. Scrapbook,* 79.

427 *"It's not that he":* Stefan Kanfer, *Groucho* (New York: Alfred A. Knopf, 2000), 186.

427 *"Nobody could follow":* Marx and Anobile, *Marx Bros. Scrapbook,* 45; Liebling, "Fifth Marx Brother Claims Credit."

427 *"Zeppo off stage was":* Marx and Anobile, *Marx Bros. Scrapbook,* 44.

427 *"He was the funniest":* Ibid., 45.

427 *"completely different from":* Ibid., 25.

427 *"Zeppo could take an engine":* Groucho Marx, *Groucho and Me* (New York: Da Capo Press, 1995), 104.

427 *He had a talent:* Michael Taylor to author, June 15, 2003.

428 *"I'm sick and tired": The Marx Brothers A Bio-Bibliography,* Wes D. Gehring (Greenwood, July 1987), 70.

428 *There were those who:* Tallulah Bankhead, *My Autobiography* (Jackson: University Press of Mississippi, 2004), 82.

428 *The next live show: Freedonia Gazette* (Winter 1981) and (Summer 1982); *Hollywood Greats,* written and produced by Norman.

429 *"learned from travelling": Freedonia Gazette* (Winter 1981) and (Summer 1982); *Hollywood Greats,* written and produced by Norman.

429 *"He'd carry the harp": Freedonia Gazette* (Winter 1981) and (Summer 1982); *Hollywood Greats,* written and produced by Norman.

429 *The Los Angeles police:* Michael Taylor to author, June 2003.

430 *Growing up, Chico had:* Maxine Marx to author, July 8, 2003.

430 *Marion loved clothes:* Joan Benny to author, June 22, 2003.

430 *Each day Zeppo left:* Tim Marx to author, August 8, 2003, 8.

430 *"On screen Barbara is":* Marion Marx, "My Pal Barbara Stanwyck," as told to James Reid, magazine clipping, n.d.

430 *"Her eyes lacked luster":* Nanette Kutner, "Her Neighbors—the Taylors," *Modern Screen,* December 1939.

431 *Zeppo met MacMurray:* Zeppo Marx to Shirley Eder.

431 *"Both of them for":* Zeppo Marx to Shirley Eder.

432 *"one of the most popular":* Andre Sennwald, *New York Times,* February 9, 1935.

432 *He looked down from:* Anthony Fay to author, June 2002, 7.

432 *Dion was crying:* Banner affidavit, 3.

433 *Afterward, Barbara told Nellie:* Ibid.; Margaret Griffith (niece of Nellie Banner) to author, 9.

Eight: "Little Sure Shot"

PAGE

434 *"[Eddie] called me":* Bernard Drew, *Film Comment,* March–April 1981, 45.

434 *It played for the next:* McBride, *Frank Capra,* 309.

435 *It took Zeppo weeks:* Marion Marx, "My Pal Barbara Stanwyck."

435 *Groucho got word:* Maxine Marx to author, July 8, 2003.

436 *Columbia was desperate:* McBride, *Frank Capra,* 303–4.

436 *"Put on a little":* Leonard Maltin's *Movie Crazy* (Spring 2003), 3.

438 *Barbara signed a contract: Variety,* April 24, 1935, 3.

438 The Pastry Baker's Wife: *A&S Lyons v. Barbara Stanwyck,* no. 396667, Superior Court of the State of California, 3, February 28, 1936.

439 *"The pictures I was":* Gussow, *Don't Say Yes Until I Finish Talking,* 60.

439 *The newly merged 20th:* "Twentieth Century Fox," *Fortune,* December 1935, 138.

440 *"woman of the ages":* Helen Harrison, "Famous, but Human," *Movie Classic,* April 1935, 39, 53.

440 *"I have to work":* BS to Rex Reed. April 13, 1981.

440 *The U.S. government: Bank of America v. Frank Fay, Barbara Stanwyck Fay, Corporation of America, John Doe Co., Richard Roe Co., Henry Poe Co.,* February 20, 1939, 5.

440 *Barbara was in negotiations: Variety,* April 24, 1935, 3.

440 *She notified RKO and now Fox:* BS to studio, April 18, 1935.

441 *She asked for: A&S Lyons v. Barbara Stanwyck,* no. 396667, Superior Court of the State of California, February 28, 1936, 3.

442 *"Shooting is a splendid exercise":* "Annie Oakley Known by Gun," *New York Times,* November 14, 1926.

442 *"We're not fashionable":* "Annie Oakley Dies," *New York Times,* November 5, 1926.

442 *"She wasn't born":* Martha Kerr, *Modern Screen,* February 1936, 78.

442 *"but it didn't turn":* Ibid.

443 *"to become a part":* Buck Rainey, *Sweethearts of the Stage,* with a foreword by Barbara Stanwyck (Jefferson, N.C.: McFarland, 1992), vii.

443 *The script had been:* Joseph I. Breen to B. B. Kahane, August 5, 1935, and July 15, 1935, Margaret Herrick Library, AMPAS.

443 *Afterward, the three went:* Jim Burton, *Modern Screen,* July 1951, 98.

443 *To make the picture:* "Fred Stone to Issue Annie Oakley History," *New York Times,* November 24, 1926.

444 *Barbara drove off:* Anthony Fay to author, July 2002.

Nine: Practical Policies

PAGE

445 *"I'm only brave":* Screenland, March 1964.

445 *Fay had helped Gene:* Gene Vaslett to author. June 1997.

445 *Maud agreed and later:* Vaslett to author, October 1996.

445 *to Dion, the Marxes:* Anthony Fay to author, June 2003.

445 *"You pay a price":* Vivian Cosby, *Screenland,* June 1942, 76.

446 *Firsthand reminiscences were: Annie Oakley* press book, "F."

446 *In 1860, Thunderbird's father:* Letter from Chief Thunderbird of the Cheyennes, Herrick Library.

447 *Hepburn was paid $55,000: Alice Adams* budget estimate, May 13, 1935, courtesy Herrick Library.

447 *He had traveled to:* J. R. Silke, "George Stevens Talks About Movies," *Cinema,* January, 19.

448 *Stevens liked the women:* George Stevens III to author, December 11, 2003.

448 *"seeing 'Little Sure Shot' ": Annie Oakley* press book.

448 *For the spectacular re-creations:* Barbara Stanwyck, interview with Susan Winslow, September 24, 1981, Herrick Library.

448 *"kind, gracious, patient":* Ibid.

448 *Nellie was to bring:* Nellie Banner, affidavit, January 10, 1938, 6.

449 *In late August, Fay:* Warner daily production and progress report, August 29, 30, 1935, courtesy of Ned Comstock, USC.

449 *Zeppo had arranged:* Maxwell Arnow to Roy Obringer, memo, August 30, 1935.

449 *Albert Warner couldn't even:* to Jack Warner, memo, June 9, 1936, Warner Bros. Archives.

449 *Warner was to get:* Roy Obringer to Morris Ebenstein, memo, August 23, 1935, Warner Bros. Archives.

449 *Bette Davis, Franchot: Hard Luck Dame* was released as *Dangerous.*

449 *when they first met:* Interview with Olivia de Havilland: October 5, 2006, 13, Academy of Achievement.

449 *After two days of work:* Daily production report, August 29–30, 1935, Warner Bros. Archives.

450 *It would have taken:* Samuel Richard Mook, "Barbara Lets Go," *Picture Play,* September 1936, 84.

450 *"personal affronts":* Raymond Moley, *After Seven Years* (New York: Harper & Brothers, 1939), 391.

451 *"We put those payroll":* Leuchtenburg, *Franklin D. Roosevelt and the New Deal,* 132–33.

451 *Fay believed that anyone:* Jesse White to author, February 1997.

451 *"I'm scared stiff":* Los Angeles Evening Herald Examiner, September 11, 1935.

451 *"I'm only brave":* Article by BS, n.d.

451 *Barbara didn't pay attention:* David Chierichetti to author, May 1998.

452 *With Hollis (Holly) Barnes:* David Chierichetti to author.

452 *Rogers's hair was so curly:* Ibid.

452 *Holly, like Fay, could:* John Miehle to author, December 27, 1996, 13, 6.

452 *Soon Barbara was confiding:* Chierichetti to author, May 1998.

453 *"the youngest important director":* James Agee, *Time,* August 26, 1935.

453 *"butting in . . . I can":* BS to Larry Kleno to author.

453 *Her work was admired:* Carol Frink, *Chicago Herald and Examiner,* December 8, 1935.

453 *"an invalid in pictures":* Clark Rodenback, *Chicago Daily News,* December 6, 1935, 36.

453 *"light society flim flams":* Carol Frink, *Chicago Herald and Examiner,* December 8, 1935.

453 *"bring [Barbara] back":* Harriet Parsons, *Hollywood Studio Magazine,* n.d., 24.

453 *"bother anyone. There's nothing":* George Stevens, *Photoplay,* June 1936, 25, 90.

453 *The ranch owner's little:* Anthony Fay to author, June 2003.

453 *Byron loved the beach:* Judith Stevens to author, June 2, 1999.

453 *"More than beauty":* Faith Service, *Modern Screen,* October 1936.

454 *It "ate away" at Barbara:* BS to Judith Stevens; Stevens to author, October 1998.

455 *"the only safe test":* Faith Service, *Modern Screen,* October 1936.

455 *The first picture,* Volcano: *Variety,* October 2, 1935.

Ten: Scar Tissue

PAGE

456 *An early version:* William K. Everson, The Theodore Huff Memorial Film Society.

456 *"grievous mental suffering":* Complaint, November 8, 1935.

456 *The court date was set:* Summons to Frank Fay, November 12, 1935.

457 *Before Fay went to:* Paget Lloyd (housekeeper for Fay), affidavit, January 10, 1938, 1–3.

457 *Dion could be made:* Nellie Banner, affidavit, January 10, 1938, 6.

457 *Fay wasn't satisfied:* Lloyd affidavit, 1–3.

457 *The Spanish minister in Washington: AFI,* 1369.

458 *("His loveable villainy"):* "Lieut. Rowan's Mission," *New York Times,* May 16, 1898.

458 *"close cropped hair, bull neck":* Zanuck, story conference notes, August 17, 1935, 2.

458 *Zanuck's idea was for the clash:* Ibid., 3.

460 *"You can't tell nothing":* Interview Joel McCrea with Peter McCrea.

460 *"too American in appearance":* Darryl Zanuck to Ben Kahane (RKO Studios), January 20, 1935, RKO legal files, Turner Archives.

460 *"When you're in a":* Mook, "Barbara Lets Go," 84.

460 *The government had slapped:* govt. case 1938.

461 *"one of the weirdest":* Andre Sennwald, *New York Times,* September 30, 1935.

461 *In New Orleans, picketers: Variety,* December 10, 1935, 7.

461 *President Roosevelt was fishing off: Variety,* October 2, 1935, 4.

461 *"Authentic atmosphere":* Preview cards, October 31, 1935.

461 *"A picture worthy of her":* Carol Frink, *Chicago Herald and Examiner,* December 8, 1935.

461 *"If the picture misses": Variety,* December 25, 1935.

462 *The studio relied heavily: Variety,* January 1, 1936, 4.

462 *"To kill the time": Motion Picture,* March 1936.

463 *Ford was going to make: Variety,* November 26, 1935, 3.

463 *thank her for flowers:* Alexander Woollcott to BS, December 22, 1935.

463 *only if Lloyd:* Albert Lloyd, affidavit, January 10, 1938.

463 *"have the right to visit":* Interlocutory judgment of divorce, no. D 137906.

463 *"When it comes to men":* Gladys Hall, newspaper clipping, 1935, Gladys Hall Collection, AMPAS, 1–6.

Eleven: High Schemes and Misdemeanors

PAGE

465 *"I know I have reached":* Gladys Hall, newspaper clipping, 1935, Gladys Hall Collection, AMPAS, 1–6.

465 *Marion's attitude about life:* Maxine Marx to author, July 8, 2003.

465 *It mattered to her:* Maxine Marx to author, June 22, 2003.

465 *"I don't see how":* New York Telegram, May 22, no year, courtesy Shubert Archive.

465 *"the longest in town":* "Thank God I'll Never Be Thirty Again," *Pageant,* May 1967.

466 *Marion Marx, like Barbara: New York Telegram,* May 22, no year, courtesy Shubert Archive.

466 *The former Marion Bimberg Benda:* Maxine Marx to author, July 8, 2003.

466 *Barbara had taken over:* Marion Marx, "My Pal Barbara Stanwyck."

467 *The plant manager went along:* Michael Taylor, *New York Times,* March 29, 1914, 1.

467 *When he got out:* Maxine Marx to author, July 8, 2003.

467 *Her brother, Alan, followed:* Tim Marx to author, October 18, 2003.

467 *"I can't stand to sleep":* Ibid.

467 *And, like Barbara:* Tim Marx to author, August 8, 2003.

467 *Fay kept company:* Gene Vaslett to author, June 25, 2000.

468 *Fay went home and got:* Albert Lloyd, affidavit, January 10, 1938.

469 *In the midst of her dog:* Elizabeth Wilson, "Barbara Stanwyck," *Silver Screen,* December 1936, 26.

470 *"to see what it's all":* Jerry Lane, *Motion Picture,* November 1936, 31.

470 *"There's such romance":* Hall, "Barbara Stanwyck's Advice to Girls in Love," 6.

471 *She gave him money:* Brian Stevens to author, June 16, 1998.

471 *Barbara came home one:* Judith Stevens to author, June 1999.

471 *"I'm not married to you":* Judith Stevens to author, June 22, 1998, 1.

471 *But Barbara begged him:* Ibid., 3.

472 *The next day she changed:* Barbara Stanwyck Fay, affidavit, January 10, 1938, 11.

472 *"She was flying":* Lyn Tornabene, *Long Live the King* (New York: Putnam, 1976), chap. 28.

472 *"she could say 'fuck' ":* Judith Stevens to author, 1999, 13.

472 *"the profane angel":* Chierichetti, *Mitchell Leisen, Hollywood Director* (Photoventures Press, 1995), 96.

472 *Lombard was hosting: Variety,* January 29, 1936, 57.

473 *Judge Charles Bogue listened:* Judgement Court of the State of California for the County of Los Angeles, no. 396,667, February 28, 1936.

473 *"It is a yeoman's task": Variety,* April 22, 1936, 42.

473 *Royal Gelatin was pleased: Variety,* May 27, 1936, 34.

475 *He was convinced there:* Albert Lloyd affidavit, January 10, 1938.

Twelve: This Side of the Sphinx

PAGE

477 *Robert Taylor circa 1935:* E. A. Kral: "Robert Taylor: A Golden Era Hollywood Movie King from Nebraska," *Beatrice* (Nebr.) *Daily Sun,* October 8, 1993.

477 *"felt the strength": Evening Mail,* August 20, 1937.

479 *Bob had been voted: Screen Guide,* n.d., 1936.

480 *When Bob asked what Barbara:* Elizabeth Wilson, "Barbara Stanwyck," 66.

480 *"The real clincher":* "Robert Taylor," *Film Fan Monthly.*

481 *"the warm mixed odors":* E. A. Kral, "Robert Taylor: A Golden Era Hollywood Movie King from Nebraska," supplement to *Beatrice (Neb.) Daily Sun,* October 8, 1993.

481 *Filley was a crossroads:* B. R. Crisler, "Robert Taylor," *New York Times,* June 7, 1936.

482 *The Brugh family:* Kral, "Robert Taylor," *Beatrice* (Nebr.) *Daily Sun,* October 8, 1993.

Thirteen: The Making of a Man

PAGE

483 *"how to invest your":* Jane Ellen Wayne, *Robert Taylor* (St. Martin's, 1973, 1987) 39.

483 *To some, Metro was:* "Conversations: Marc Connelly," *Leonard Maltin's Movie Crazy* (Spring 2008), 3.

483 *"He was my exhibit A":* Robert Taylor, as told to Ben Maddox, *Screenland,* September 1937.

483 *Mayer (Lazar Meir) was from:* Edwin H. Knopf, "Over My Shoulder," unpublished manuscript, 41, courtesy of Wendy Cooper.

483 *"God gave me two lovely":* Wayne, *Robert Taylor,* 46.

484 *Taylor didn't get the raise:* MGM memo, January 6, 1935.

484 *"Money isn't everything":* Knopf, "Over My Shoulder," 43, 47.

484 *"Maybe you can't act":* Wayne, *Robert Taylor,* 51.

484 *Koverman, who'd worked for:* E. J. Fleming, *The Fixers* (Jefferson, N.C.: McFarland, 2005), 31.

484 *"roll down to Santa Monica":* BS 1947.

484 *"The biggest set doesn't":* James Reid, *Modern Screen,* June 1937, 74.

485 *Bob and Barbara were: Los Angeles Evening Herald Examiner,* July 3, 1936.

485 *the new airship* Hindenburg: *World Almanac and Book of Facts 1936,* 146.

485 *"It is unfortunate":* Harrison Carroll, *Los Angeles Evening Herald Examiner,* May 1, 1936.

486 *"You'd better hang on": Good Housekeeping,* April 1983.

486 *Sometimes Bob played:* Jerry Lane, *Motion Picture,* November 1936, 70.

487 *People watching Taylor:* Gladys Hall, "Barbara Stanwyck's True Life Story," *Modern Screen,* November 1937.

487 *"We amused each other":* "Dinner for One, Please Johns," *Photoplay,* June 1936.

488 *At family holidays:* Kral, "Robert Taylor."

489 *"There were not many":* Ibid.

489 *"I was almost always":* Ibid.

489 *"I've always taken it":* Ibid.

490 *The two Spangler A. Brughs:* Kral, "Robert Taylor," *Beatrice* (Nebr.) *Daily Sun,* October 8, 1993.

490 *"enjoyed her illness":* Ibid.

491 *Ruth Brugh with her son:* Kral, "Robert Taylor," *Beatrice* (Nebr.) *Daily Sun,* October 8, 1993.

491 *Ruth Brugh saw sex:* Wayne, *Robert Taylor,* 42.

491 *There were times when:* Ibid.

492 *"His sense of values":* Walter Ramsey, *Photoplay,* April 1937.

492 *"If you want to stay":* Nancy Cole, *Picture Play,* November 1938.

493 *"Why couldn't I make":* Robert Taylor, *Ladies' Home Journal,* September 1936, 93.

493 *"exquisite, graceful":* Daily Mail, August 20, 1937.

494 *"I've been in Hollywood":* Margaret Chute, "The New Valentino This Man Robert Taylor," *Evening News,* August 18, 1937.

494 *"approached the responsibility":* "Robert Taylor," *Film Fan Monthly.*

495 *Bob's greatest influence:* Ibid.

495 *She not only gave Bob:* Screen Book, September 1937, 32.

495 *Bob believed that there:* "Robert Taylor," *Film Fan Monthly.*

Fourteen: Exactly like Anybody

PAGE

496 *"Let me tell you about":* Dick Marshall, 1942.

496 *"My father," Bob said:* Kral, "Robert Taylor."

496 *Barbara didn't get angry easily:* Elizabeth Wilson, *Silver Screen,* December 1936, 26, 66.

496 *From years of experience with:* Barbara Stanwyck, "Things I Don't Like About Myself," as told to Sara Hamilton, *Movie Mirror,* December 1939, 36.

497 *"She's so completely natural":* Grace Mack, magazine clipping, 1936, 201.

497 *It was a relief to him:* The Maverick Queen press book.

497 *With Fay, Barbara was thought:* Martha Kerr, *Modern Screen,* February 1936, 43.

497 *Barbara would freeze up when:* Elizabeth Wilson, *Silver Screen,* December 1936, 26.

497 *This was the third remake:* In 1919, Pathé made a version of the picture directed by George Fitzmaurice starring Fannie Ward; in 1930, Victor Fleming remade it for Fox starring Constance Bennett.

497 Small Town Girl *opened:* April 6, 1936.

498 *"no more a Cuban patriot's":* Variety, April 15, 1936.

498 *Briskin welcomed Eddie Small's:* Ben Kahane to Sam Briskin, February 26, 1936, RKO legal files, Turner Archives.

498 *"in Little America":* Amory H. "Bud" Waite Jr., April 29, 1935, courtesy of Eugene Vaslett.

499 *"It's always seemed to me":* Mook, "Barbara Lets Go," 84.

499 *"I would trade all five":* Sam Briskin to Leo Spitz, April 22, 1936, Turner/MGM files.

499 *and Eric Blore:* Blore was subsequently not in the picture.

500 *"a real craftsman":* Ella Smith, *Starring Miss Barbara Stanwyck.* 80.

501 *"In the first reel":* Ed Sullivan, "Garbo Is Right," magazine clipping, n.d.

502 *"to get away from":* Katherine Albert, "What Joan Crawford Thinks of Joan Crawford," *Photoplay,* December 1936.

503 *It wasn't a fluke:* Joan Crawford, *Ladies' Home Journal,* December 1942, 125.

503 *"a real inspiration":* Albert, "What Joan Crawford Thinks of Joan Crawford."

503 *"attuned in spirit":* Joan Crawford, "The Job of Keeping at the Top," *Saturday Evening Post,* June 17, 1933.

503 *Metro had originally purchased:* AFI, 814.

503 *Crawford went to Joe Mankiewicz:* Joan Crawford, *Ladies' Home Journal,* December 1942, 125.

503 *Mankiewicz wanted to write:* Joe Mankiewicz, oral history, 11, January 1959, Columbia University.

503 *"I could build a fire":* Considine, *Bette and Joan,* 82.

503 *"It was lovely":* Ibid., 83.

504 *"an actress and not":* Sullivan, "Garbo Is Right."

504 *"Abusive and profane":* Joseph Breen to L. B. Mayer, October 7, 1935, 2.

504 *Clarence Brown described Bob:* Dorothy Manners, "Bob Taylor Sees All the Sights in New York," *Los Angeles Examiner,* July 14, 1936.

504 *Bob objected strenuously but:* Alice Tildesley, *Family Circle,* September 26, 1941.

504 *"in a distinctly Southern":* Considine, *Bette and Joan,* 93.

504 *"to withstand the weight":* Ibid.

505 *"a company man":* "Clarence Brown, Director of Garbo, Gable, Dies at 97," *Los Angeles Times,* August 18, 1987.

506 *"You'd have to watch":* Ibid.

507 *After each dinner—the men:* Wilson, "Carnival Nights in Hollywood."

507 *Invited to the Ambassador Hotel:* Sidney Skolsky, *New York Daily News,* March 4, 1936.

508 *"quieter than Beatrice":* "Robert Taylor's Own Life Story," *Lincoln Journal,* March 6, 1937, 6.

508 *"exactly the same kick":* Manners, "Bob Taylor Sees All the Sights in New York."

509 *"hadn't been cautious":* "Robert Taylor's Own Life Story," 6.

509 *"dog just introduced":* Charles Darnton, "Alright I'll Fight," *Screenland,* February 1939, 83.

509 *When Barbara did call:* Manners, "Bob Taylor Sees All the Sights in New York."

509 *He got out of a cab:* New York Times, June 6, 1936.

509 *He dropped in on three:* "Robert Taylor's Own Life Story," 6.

509 *"to mischief rather than":* Will Hays to Sam Briskin, telegram, May 14, 1936.

510 *Three weeks before production:* Joseph Breen to Louis B. Mayer, May 25, 1936. Harlow is mentioned as the actress playing Rita Wilson.

510 *Van Dyke was six feet:* Cannom, *Van Dyke and the Mythical City, Hollywood,* 181.

510 *one of the toughest guys:* Alva Johnston, "Lord Fauntleroy in Hollywood," *New Yorker,* September 28, 1935.

511 *"It's their funeral, not mine":* Howard Sharpe, "The Star Creators of Hollywood," *Photoplay,* December 1936, 71.

512 *Van Dyke saw the spark:* W. S. Van Dyke, "Rx for a Thin Man," *Stage* 14, no. 4 (1937).

513 *"Everything that man did":* Cannom, *Van Dyke and the Mythical City, Hollywood,* 24.

513 *When the rushes from:* Samuel Marx, *Mayer and Thalberg,* 103–4.

515 *"We set pictures back":* Hollywood Life Stories (1952).

515 *"the greatest care":* Breen to Mayer, May 25, 1936.

516 *At the end of the twenty-four:* Alva Johnston, "Lord Fauntleroy in Hollywood," *The New Yorker,* September 28, 1935, 20.

516 *Writers were known:* Ibid.

516 *"The first rehearsal":* John Gallagher, "W. S. Van Dyke," in *World Film Directors* (New York: H. W. Wilson, 1988), 1121.

516 *"Figure out how you":* Johnston, "Lord Fauntleroy in Hollywood."

516 *he let it be known:* Ibid., 20.

516 *By twenty, he'd been just:* Ibid.

517 *"Being together socially":* Los Angeles Evening Herald Star, 51.

517 *"She gives everybody":* Daily Mail, August 20, 1937.

517 *"warm and glowing":* Hall, "Barbara Stanwyck's Advice to Girls in Love," 4.

517 *"It's stupid to be cynical":* Ibid.

518 *"one of the great"*: Faith Service, *Modern Screen,* October 1936.

519 *She denied having: Hollywood Life Stories* (1952).

519 *"he is the same Bob"*: Faith Service, *Modern Screen,* October 1936.

519 *"Diversion of this sort"*: Ibid.; Gladys Hall, original manuscript, Gladys Hall Collection, AMPAS.

520 *"I can't burst into"*: Faith Service, *Modern Screen,* October 1936; Gladys Hall, Gladys Hall Collection, 48.

520 *Bob shook her hand:* Alice Tildesley, *Family Circle,* September 26, 1941.

521 *Hearst's newspapers accused:* Boller, *Presidential Campaigns* (Oxford Univ. Press, 2004), 240.

Fifteen: Good Luck at Home

PAGE

522 *"I never cared for"*: McBride, *Searching for John Ford,* 229.

522 *The life of Mary Stuart:* Jane Dunn, *Elizabeth and Mary* (New York: Alfred A. Knopf, 2004).

523 *Barbara had read:* Nancy Anderson, clipping, n.d.

523 *Ford laughed in Davis's face:* Davis, *Lonely Life,* 138.

523 *Berman was a sport:* Ginger Rogers, *Ginger: My Story* (New York: HarperCollins, 1991), 170–71.

523 *"play him for comedy"*: Andrew Sinclair, *John Ford,* 69.

524 *"Oh, if I could"*: Arthur Miller, introduction to *Sean O'Casey: Plays* (London: Faber and Faber, 1998).

524 *"They may let us do it"*: Eyman, *Print the Legend,* 162.

525 *"What did George Washington"*: John Ford, oral history, interview with Dan Ford, Southern Methodist University Oral History Program, July 16, 1991, August 12, 1993, Ford, J. mss., Box 30, Folder 15, Lilly Library, Indiana University, Bloomington.

525 *Thereafter, when Ford: New York Times,* July 26, 1936.

525 *Up to ten days: The Plough and the Stars* budget sheet.

525 *"absolute poison at the box"*: Ned E. Debinet to Leo Spitz.

526 *("My chest measured 46):* Bosley Crowther, "Who Is Then the Gentleman?" *New York Times,* October 14, 1934.

526 The Plough and the Stars *captured: The Plough and the Stars* press book.

527 *"what they fought for"*: John Ford to Sean O'Casey, January 27, 1936.

527 *He had traveled to:* Gish, *The Movies, Mr. Griffith, and Me,* 328.

527 *"production would remain"*: Robert Sisk to Sean O'Casey, January 27, 1936.

527 *Ford had been brought up:* Ford, interview with Dan Ford, 10, the Lilly Library, Indiana University, Bloomington, Indiana.

527 *He grew up in a time:* Andrew Sinclair, *John Ford,* 4.

528 *"God damn ridiculous"*: Eyman, *Print the Legend,* 177.

528 *RKO wanted to reduce:* Lillie Messinger of RKO/New York to Sisk in Hollywood, March 11, 1936.

528 *"despot and professional"*: Eyman, *Print the Legend,* 156.

529 *thought he was a "sadist"*: John Carradine, in ibid., 163.

529 *"enormously rough, terribly arrogant"*: McBride, *Searching for John Ford,* 232–33.

529 *"fascinating but impossible"*: Eyman, *Print the Legend,* 155.

529 The Informer *had been:* McBride, *Searching for John Ford,* 214.

529 *"Let him make it"*: Ibid., 215.

529 *"In Hollywood," Ford said:* Michael Mok, "The Rebels, If They Stay Up This Time, Won't Be Sorry for Hollywood's Trouble," *New York Post,* January 24, 1939.

529 *"company union with nothing"*: Ernest Pascal (president of the SWG) to *Los Angeles Times,* in Mason and Bona, *Inside Oscar,* 63.

530 *In addition, Frank:* McBride, *Frank Capra,* 337.

530 *"D.W. made the virginal"*: Herb Sterne, in Gish, *The Movies, Mr. Griffith, and Me.*

531 *"Strangely enough"*: McBride, *Frank Capra,* 337.

532　*"The Screen Writers Guild was"*: McBride, *Searching for John Ford*, 225.

532　*"Now we are three"*: Andrew Sinclair, *John Ford*, 53.

532　*"They've got to turn"*: E. Eisenburg, *"John Ford: Fighting Irish,"* *New Theatre*, April 1936.

532　*"Ford was always"*: Andrew Sinclair, *John Ford*, 87.

532　*He wore a sport:* Henry Fonda, oral history, 35, Columbia University, March 1959.

533　*Barbara was getting $42,500:* RKO production budget, July 8, 1936.

533　*"the feel, the mood"*: Bonita Granville, oral history II, DeGolyer Library, Southern Methodist University, August 1976.

534　*"almost no direction"*: Bonita Granville oral history, Columbia University, June 1959.

534　*"We'll do no such"*: Jerry Lane, *Motion Picture*, November 1936, 70.

534　*"He had the true"*: Andrew Sinclair, *John Ford*, 67.

534　*"I can take a thoroughly"*: Ibid., 147.

535　*"He didn't want big"*: Eyman, *Print the Legend*, 158.

535　*He went for the truth:* Darryl Hickman to author, March 16, 2007.

535　*"I wouldn't say we stole"*: Andrew Sinclair, *John Ford*, 22.

535　*Ford often worked with:* Eyman, *Print the Legend*, 162.

535　*"I am a man"*: Andrew Sinclair, *John Ford*, 37.

535　*"could get more drama"*: McBride, *Searching for John Ford*, 248.

536　*"a great treat for scholars"*: *Hollywood Reporter*, July 24, 1936.

536　*"length and finish"*: *Variety*, August 5, 1936.

536　*"a mass movement from"*: Newspaper clipping, October 1936.

536　*"One of the merriest"*: Muriel Babcock, *Los Angeles Examiner*, July 2, 1936.

536　*"for sending Barbara Stanwyck"*: *Los Angeles Evening Herald Examiner*, July 2, 1936.

536　*Sneak previews had taken:* "Robert Taylor," *Film Fan Monthly.*

536　*When Bob and Barbara:* *Los Angeles Evening Herald Examiner*, July 30, 1936.

536　*"Only the grand work"*: Jimmy Starr, *Los Angeles Evening Herald Examiner*, August 8, 1936.

537　*In Los Angeles the broadcast:* Billips and Pierce, *Lux Presents Hollywood*, 4–20.

537　*"No one identified with"*: *Liberty*, August 11, 1945.

538　*The Lux Radio Theatre presentation:* Billips and Pierce, *Lux Presents Hollywood*, 116–17.

538　*"staggers the imagination"*: *Liberty*, August 11, 1945.

538　*"Always wear it"*: James Reid, *Modern Screen*, January 1939, 74.

539　*"All in all"*: Robert Sisk to Sean O'Casey, September 3, 1936.

539　*"Why make a picture"*: Scott Eyman, *Print the Legend*, 242.

539　*Ford refused to reshoot:* James Kotsilibas-Davis and Myrna Loy, *Myrna Loy: Being and Becoming* (New York: Alfred A. Knopf, 1987), 67.

539　*She somehow got him:* Eyman, *Print the Legend*, 172.

539　*Pan Berman had the assistant:* George Nichols and Ed Donahue direct retakes (October 10, 11, 17, 18, 29), *The Plough and the Stars* dailies; David Chierichetti to author, December 2, 2005.

539　*Sea Devils:* An Eddie Small Production later titled *We Who Are About to Die.*

540　*"The final result wasn't"*: BS in Bernard Drew, *Film Comment*, March–April 1981, 44.

Sixteen: Fresh Passion, Fresh Pain

PAGE

541　*Fox planned to use Barbara:* Lew Schreiber (Fox) to George Wasson (RKO), memo, March 25, 1936.

541　*"natural for the role"*: Ella Smith, *Starring Miss Barbara Stanwyck*, 90.

541　*Zanuck, like Bill Wellman:* Ibid., 221.

541　*Sometimes he opened a desk:* Roy Newquist, *Conversations with Joan Crawford* (Secaucus, N.J.: Citadel Press, 1980), 172.

542 *"just the right quality"*: Ella Smith, *Starring Miss Barbara Stanwyck,* 90.

542 *"would be perfect for"*: Zanuck, story conference notes, August 15, 1936, 1.

543 *"an egotistical little bastard"*: McCrea, unpublished manuscript, 201.

543 *underplayed as much:* Ibid., 60.

543 *Gary Cooper was his idea:* Ibid., 373.

543 *He didn't drink:* Ibid., 93–94.

543 *"purely from hunger"*: Walter Brennan, oral history, August 11, 1971, Columbia University.

543 *"an amazing quality"*: Joseph McBride, *Hawks on Hawks* (Berkeley: University of California Press, 1982), 107, 108.

543 *Fox decided to use:* Lew Schreiber (Fox) to George Wasson (RKO), memo, August 28, 1936, file 2929, UCLA Research Library.

543 *"Sam was class"*: Brennan, oral history.

544 *"just like a high school"*: Jeanne De Kolty, "He Can Do Anything," *Silver Screen,* August 1937, 73.

545 *Stories of the Deep South: New York Times,* December 13, 1936.

546 *"If he asked me to"*: Nora Johnson, *Flashback* (Garden City, N.Y.: Doubleday, 1979), 63.

546 *"more money than"*: Tom Dardis, *Some Time in the Sun* (New York: Limelight, 1988), 88.

546 *"Shoot it as it is"*: Joseph Blotner, *Faulkner* (New York: Random House, 1984), 307.

546 *"goddam place"*: McCarthy, *Howard Hawks,* 196.

546 *Zanuck thought it full:* Conference notes with Zanuck, March 5, 1936.

546 *"I wish I was at"*: Blotner, *Faulkner,* 367.

546 *"[He] wrote practically"*: Ibid.

546 *"Then he left me"*: Tom Dardis, *Some Time in the Sun,* 107.

547 *"It ain't my racket"*: Ibid., 90.

547 *"Censors kill us"*: Zanuck notes, May 15, 1936.

547 *"Your reader has injected"*: AFI Feature Films, *1931–1940,* 114.

549 *"We're supporting you"*: Ibid., 200.

549 *Caryl, a Universal starlet:* Roy Liebman, *The Wampas Baby Stars* (Jefferson, N.C.: McFarland, 2000).

550 *By didn't raise his voice:* Judith Stevens to author, June 1998–1999.

550 *Barbara referred to Caryl:* Judith Stevens to author, November 29, 1998, 10, # 27.

551 *She had no choice:* October 19, 1936, minutes from board of directors meeting, September 8, 1936.

551 *Taylor was bewildered, overwhelmed:* Alice Tildesley, *Family Circle,* September 26, 1941.

552 *"The whole thing's like"*: Jerry Lane, *Motion Picture,* November 1936, 31.

552 *To cope with the rush:* Alice Tildesley, *Family Circle,* September 26, 1941.

552 *Irving Thalberg had offered:* Paris, *Garbo,* 330.

552 *"Napoleon stumps me"*: Lambert, *On Cukor,* 108.

552 *Eleonora Duse had transformed:* Helen Sheehy, *Eleonora Duse* (New York: Alfred A. Knopf, 2003), 108–9.

552 *"Camille [is] so like"*: Paris, *Garbo,* 329.

552 *The premise of* Camille: Lambert, *On Cukor,* 109.

552 *"remains in its combination"*: Ibid., 112.

553 *"She is such a tragic"*: Paris, *Garbo,* 330.

553 *"utter folly of her ways"*: Joseph Breen to Louis B. Mayer, May 18, 1936.

553 *"It lacked the garlic"*: Ibid., 230.

553 *"one of the finest pictures"*: Harrison Carroll, *Los Angeles Evening Herald Examiner,* September 9, 1936.

553 *"walk[ed] away with"*: Louella Parsons, *Los Angeles Examiner,* September 3, 1936.

553 *Thalberg felt the James Hilton:* David Lewis, *Creative Producer,* chap. 5.

554 *Zoë Akins and pals:* "Zoë Akins Arrives," *New York Times,* October 12, 1919.

554 *"to create a whole"*: Lambert, *On Cukor* (New York: Putnam, 1972), 109.

554 *"It is historically a terrible"*: Paris, *Garbo,* 334.

554 *He predicted that:* Oliver Hensdell article. February 10, 1938, 3.

555 *Barbara's nephew Gene was:* Gene Vaslett to author, October 1997, 16.

555 *"What she's done for me":* Jerry Lane, *Motion Picture,* November 1936.

555 *"Can we sit in here":* Ronald Haver, *David O. Selznick's Hollywood* (New York: Alfred A. Knopf, 1980), 196.

555 *"Fuck the applause":* Peters, *House of Barrymore,* 387.

556 *A large open icebox:* Annabelle Gillespie-Hayek, *Silver Screen,* December 1936, 22.

556 *William Daniels, the cameraman:* Ibid.

556 *"Look, she's human":* Jerry Lane, *Motion Picture,* November 1936, 31.

557 *"I am very pleased":* Daily Mail, August 20, 1937; Dugal O'Liam, *Modern Screen,* March 1942.

557 *"Listen, I grant you":* Liberty, August 11, 1945.

557 *"She wouldn't even":* Coronet, April 1961.

557 *"Just explodes all of":* Dugal O'Liam, *Modern Screen,* March 1942, 97.

557 *"practical a person":* Evening Mail, August 20, 1937.

557 *"If I [get] to know":* Paris, *Garbo,* 335.

558 *"She carried herself":* David Lewis, *Creative Producer,* 91.

558 *"This isn't Pomona":* Arthur Laurents to author, June 1997.

559 *Garbo's quality was her:* David Lewis, *Creative Producer,* 91–92.

559 *"There's something about Garbo's":* Dugal O'Liam, *Modern Screen,* March 1942.

559 *"She's never been quite":* Lambert, *On Cukor,* 112.

559 *"a creature of the greatest":* Ibid., 113.

559 *Cukor might get eight:* David Lewis, *Creative Producer,* 98–99.

559 *"a fine actor":* Paris, *Garbo,* 334.

560 *A long way from Beatrice:* Kral, "Robert Taylor," *Beatrice* (Nebr.) *Daily Sun,* October 8, 1993.

560 *On location in Griffith:* Coronet, April 1962.

560 *"She . . . was very funny and sweet":* Lambert, *On Cukor,* 113.

560 *When he opened the box:* Arlene Dahl to author, October 28, 2001, 2.

560 *Eight million Americans were:* Leuchtenburg, *Franklin D. Roosevelt and the New Deal,* 194.

561 *"Mr. Roosevelt is the only":* Ibid., 189.

561 *Five days later Thalberg:* Thalberg died on September 14, 1936.

561 *They were shocked:* David Lewis, *Creative Producer,* 100.

561 *He had three rules:* Fleming, *Fixers.*

562 *"Thalberg was much respected":* David Lewis, *Creative Producer,* 101.

562 *A crowd of seven thousand:* Lambert, *Norma Shearer,* 239.

562 *"He was a great man":* Los Angeles Times, September 17, 1936; *Los Angeles Examiner,* September 17, 1936.

562 *"Everyone wanted to diminish":* David Lewis, *Creative Producer,* 96.

563 *"the golden shocks of grain":* "Robert Taylor's Own Life Story."

563 *"The sound symbolized":* Ibid.

564 *Bob atop Packard convertible:* Kral, "Robert Taylor," *Beatrice* (Nebr.) *Daily Sun,* October 8, 1993.

565 *Now Helen was:* Kral, "Robert Taylor."

565 *"I felt so old":* Ibid.

Seventeen: Sea of Grass

PAGE

566 *"Never before in history":* Boller, *Presidential Campaigns,* 242.

567 *"to build a wall":* Hall, "Barbara Stanwyck's Advice to Girls in Love," 6.

567 *The following day he:* Jane Ellen Wayne, *Robert Taylor* (New York: St. Martin's Press, 1987), 64.

567 *Marion thought horses were:* Tim Marx to author, 2004.

568 *Beyond that, McCrea's:* Joel McCrea interview with Peter McCrea.

568 *"They can always":* Ibid.

568 *William Mulholland had land:* Jon Ward, May 7, 2004.

569 *She could have gardens:* Hall, "Barbara Stanwyck's Advice to Girls in Love," 5.

569 *Barbara and the Marxes paid:* Paul Cervin, *Turf and Sport Digest,* December 1937.

569 *"I think back to those":* James Reid, *Modern Screen,* January 1939, 37.

570 *"He certainly has got":* Tim Marx to author, October 15, 2003.

570 *"First time I ever ate":* Ruth Rankin, "She Has a System," *Modern Screen,* August 1937, 39.

571 *"The screen is just too":* Lambert, *On Cukor,* 114.

571 *"I called to her but":* *Coronet,* April 1961.

571 *"great entertainment":* Louella Parsons, *Los Angeles Examiner,* December 10, 1936.

571 *"outstanding . . . hilarious . . . eloquent":* *Daily Variety,* November 28, 1936.

571 *"as full of surprises":* Louella Parsons, *Los Angeles Examiner,* December 10, 1936.

572 *"sterling artist at the top":* *Hollywood Reporter,* November 28, 1936.

572 *"All I try to do":* Philip Ziegler, *King Edward VIII* (London: Collins, 1990), 218.

572 *"I'll try anything":* Ibid., 263.

572 *"This is a nice kettle":* Ibid., 218.

572 *During the eight days:* Ibid., 285.

572 *"Walter, it is a far":* Ibid., 288.

572 *"staggered by [Garbo's] lightness":* Lambert, *On Cukor,* 108.

573 *"Her instinct, her mastery":* Davis, *Lonely Life,* 116.

573 *"rose to Garbo":* Lambert, *On Cukor,* 115.

573 *"He could be wonderful":* Sydney Guilaroff, interview with Jimmy Bangley, *Classic Images,* January 1997.

573 *Cukor understood how:* Gavin Lambert to author, n.d.

573 *"the most interesting":* Beverly Hills, *Liberty,* February 6, 1937.

573 *"Miss Garbo has never":* *Variety,* January 27, 1937.

573 *"in the finest tradition":* Frank S. Nugent, *New York Times,* January 23, 1937.

573 *"His Armand will surprise you":* Beverly Hills, *Liberty,* February 6, 1937.

573 *"[he] plays with surprising":* *Variety,* January 27, 1937.

573 *Billboards proclaimed:* Sidney Skolsky, *Hollywood Citizen-News,* February 1, 1937.

PART FOUR: A Larger Reach

One: Feelings of Uncertainty

PAGE

577 *"she was out of":* Faith Service, *Modern Screen,* October 1936.

577 *"When I married Frank":* Samuels, "In Search of Ruby Stevens."

577 *"the total eclipse":* Hall, "Barbara Stanwyck's Advice to Girls in Love," 2.

577 *"No. Or anybody":* *New York Times,* January 3, 1937.

577 *She wanted to see her:* Walter Ramsey, *Photoplay,* April 1937.

577 *"It might take ten times":* Ibid., 25.

578 *"Not only was he":* Ed Sullivan, *Sunday World Herald,* November 5, 1939.

578 *"was a marvelous actor":* *Photoplay,* January 1937.

578 *"Skip the romance":* Harry Lang, "She Doesn't Say Yes, She Doesn't Say No," *Motion Picture,* March 1938, 66.

578 *"average, nice-looking":* Faith Service, *Modern Screen,* October 1936; Gladys Hall, "Stanwyck Through the Looking Glass," 48, Gladys Hall Collection.

578 *"If you feel a thing":* James Reid, *Modern Screen,* January 1939, 74.

579 *It was almost comparable:* Elizabeth Yeaman, *Hollywood Citizen-News,* April 4, 1937.

579 *"I have kept the book":* Valeria Belletti, *Adventures of a Hollywood Secretary* (Berkeley: Univ. of California Press, 2006).

579 *" 'comeback' in pictures":* Ibid.

580 *three acclaimed actresses:* Los Angeles Times, September 3, 1936; November 14, 1936.

581 *"There are things I know":* James Reid, *Modern Screen,* January 1939, 74.

581 *"moved primarily by unselfish":* Ella Smith, *Starring Miss Barbara Stanwyck,* chap. 6.

582 *Goldwyn could see what:* A. Scott Berg, *Goldwyn* (New York: Alfred A. Knopf, 1989), 293.

582 *"I shall never try":* Eileen Whitfield, *Pickford* (Lexington: University Press of Kentucky, 1997); Alma Whitaker, "Iron Constitution Aids Mary Pickford in Her Many Tasks," *Los Angeles Times,* May 27, 1936, A19.

582 *She understood that these:* Barbara Stanwyck, "Self-Discipline's Your Best 'Buy.' "

583 *"Man is as old as God":* King Vidor, "From a Vidor Notebook," *New York Times,* March 10, 1935.

583 *"Some people are too":* Judith Stevens to author, July 16, 1998.

583 *"a trouper, a hell of an actress":* Joel McCrea interview with Peter McCrea.

583 *"I'm paying him three thousand":* Ibid., 186.

584 *"When I sign him for":* Ibid., 232.

584 *"Sam," he said, "[Barbara]":* Ibid., 203–4.

585 *"She wasn't me":* Paul Rosenfield, "Saluting Stanwyck: A Life on Film," Calendar, *Los Angeles Times,* April 5, 1987.

585 *"a woman who cheated":* Ella Smith, *Starring Miss Barbara Stanwyck,* 107; *Movie Digest,* January 1972.

585 *"too young for the part":* Ella Smith, *Starring Miss Barbara Stanwyck,* 94.

585 *"with her nose running":* Bernard Drew, *Film Comment,* March–April 1981, 45.

585 *"instead of the customary":* Ella Smith, *Starring Miss Barbara Stanwyck,* 94.

586 *"Stanwyck's test was undeniable":* Berg, *Goldwyn,* 294.

586 *When they stopped going:* Faith Service, *Modern Screen,* October 1936, pp. 1–6; Hall, "Stanwyck Through the Looking Glass," 8.

586 *"Someone has said that":* Gladys Hall, 1936. Gladys Hall Collection, AMPAS.

587 *"Good directors need producers":* Al Santell to Ella Smith, April 7, 1972.

588 *She did the clothes for:* Edith Head, AFI Institute Seminar interview, November 23, 1977, 12.

588 *"Not that Edith doesn't always":* David Chierichetti, *Edith Head* (New York: HarperCollins, 2003), 39.

588 *"She gave me the kind":* Barbara Stanwyck to Shirley Eder, October 28, 1981.

589 *Sparkuhl and Santell gave:* Al Santell to Ella Smith, April 7, 1972.

589 *Instead of building a set:* Interview with Al Santell, 3/7–8, AMPAS.

590 *"She knew the whole script":* Ella Smith, *Starring Miss Barbara Stanwyck,* 93.

590 *McCrea watched Barbara work:* McCrea, unpublished manuscript, 203.

590 *"I don't think I ever":* Daily Mail, August 20, 1937.

590 *Taylor was listed:* Variety, January 6, 1937, 3.

Two: Goddamned Sinkhole of Culture

PAGE

593 *Two weeks later:* February 28, 1937.

594 *"a masterpiece":* Hollywood Reporter, December 22, 1936.

594 *"one of the most artistic":* Louella Parsons, *Los Angeles Examiner,* January 21, 1937.

594 *Ford's direction "magnificent":* New York Herald Tribune, January 1937.

594 *"notable" for its "rich texture":* Ibid.

594 *"The tragic original has been":* Variety, February 3, 1937.

594 *"Barbara Stanwyck reaches new":* Variety, February 3, 1937.

594 *"the picture [calls] for":* Louella Parsons, *Los Angeles Examiner,* January 21, 1937.

594 *"varies between a shrill":* Howard Barnes, *New York Herald Tribune,* January 29, 1937.

594 *"a remarkably vivid portrait"*: *Hollywood Reporter*, December 22, 1937.

594 *"to be together, to act"*: *This Is My Affair* press book.

595 *"I'm not going to marry"*: Molly Gardner, "I'm in No Mood for Marriage—Barbara Stanwyck," *Motion Picture*, May 1937, 32.

595 *It ended up a romantic*: *The McKinley Case*, by Melville Crossman, treatment by Allen Rivkin, May 20, 1936.

597 *Jean Arthur was at Columbia*: Elizabeth Yeaman, *Hollywood Citizen-News*, April 3, 1937.

597 *"aptly matched"*: *Variety*, May 12, 1937, 12.

597 *"affecting; genuine"*: W. E. Oliver, *Los Angeles Evening Herald Examiner*, May 7, 1937.

597 *"A lot of tears"*: Robert Easton, *Max Brand: The Big Westerner* (Norman: University of Oklahoma Press, 1970), 198.

597 *"a hilarious piece"*: Regina Crewe.

597 *"pedestrian . . . heavyhanded"*: W. E. Oliver, *Los Angeles Evening Herald Examiner*, May 15, 1937.

598 *"Sometimes a little too"*: Frank Thompson, *William A. Wellman* (Metuchen, N.J.: Scarecrow Press, 1983), 162.

598 *"Wellman read it, when"*: Ibid., 159.

598 *"Brilliant, fascinating"*: Wellman, oral history, 20.

599 *"with no overtones"*: Ibid.

599 *"Selznick was never"*: Ibid., 21–22.

599 *"made 'Willy' Wellman"*: Budd Schulberg to author. April 1997.

600 *"for a while"*: Charles Champlin, "Remembering a Wild Man Named Bill," *Los Angeles Times*, May 5, 1996.

601 *Bowers's body was found*: *Los Angeles Times*, November 18, 1936, 1.

602 *Wellman was "nuts" about*: Wellman, *Short Time for Insanity*, 57.

602 *"Quite frankly"*: Ibid., 59.

602 *"a big handsome"*: Ibid., 55.

602 *"and a bad one"*: Thompson, *William A. Wellman*, 37.

602 *"so tall that he breathed"*: Wellman, *Short Time for Insanity*, 57.

602 *"a little bitty gal"*: Hazel Shelley, *Motion Picture Classic*, October 1921, 18.

602 *"a periodic drunk"*: Wellman, *Short Time for Insanity*, 59.

602 *"goddamned badly"*: Ibid.

602 *The first year During*: *The Fast Mail, Oath-Bound, Strange Idols, While Justice Waits*, and *The Yosemite Trail*.

602 *"Three whoppers at a sitting"*: Wellman, *Short Time for Insanity*, 215.

602 *"slave to whatever"*: Ibid., 217.

603 *"The King of Terrors had"*: Ibid., 219, 218.

603 *"a perfect artist"*: Gene Fowler, *Good Night, Sweet Prince* (New York: Viking Press, 1944), 340.

603 *Weeks later, after completing*: Ibid., 352, 356.

605 *He said nothing*: Peters, *House of Barrymore*, 390.

606 *"like a Japanese girl's"*: Colleen Moore, *Silent Star*.

606 *"We were coming out"*: Mike Connell, "From Movie Stars to Radio Pioneers, . . ." thetimesherald.com, October 24, 2008.

606 *Throughout the 1920s, John*: More than $1.3 million in 2013.

608 *Scenes were shot at*: AFI Catalog, 2044.

608 *"The audience"*: Wellman oral history, 36.

608 *"as awkward looking"*: Ibid., 30.

608 *"The actual original idea"*: Ibid., 31.

609 *Barbara was just starting*: *Los Angeles Examiner*, May 21, 1937.

Three: Stella Dallas

PAGE

610 *"You may say that"*: Barbara Miller, *Los Angeles Times,* August 22, 1937, C1.

611 *"sink her teeth into"*: *Mirror,* July 27, 1937.

611 *"any attempt at sex"*: James Lee, *Worcester Evening Gazette,* September 2, 1937, Clark University Archives.

612 *"Separated," the hostess said*: Prouty, *Pencil Shavings,* 152.

612 *"the paths of the sensitive"*: James Lee, *Worcester Evening Gazette,* September 2, 1937.

613 *She was forty-one*: Prouty, *Pencil Shavings,* xii.

613 *"A novel of absolutely first"*: Ibid., xvii.

613 *Now, years later, Mrs. Carter*: Robinson, *All My Yesterdays,* 75.

614 *"But I do not think"*: Olive Higgins Prouty to Lewis Prouty, December 8, 1923, Clark University.

614 *"herself, is the problem"*: Ibid.

614 *"If [the director] had any"*: Prouty, *Pencil Shavings,* 168.

614 *"Mrs. Carter is acting pretty"*: Olive Higgins Prouty to Lewis Prouty, December 28, 1923.

614 *"There are two things"*: Prouty, *Pencil Shavings,* xvii.

614 *"incongruous combination"*: *Boston Evening Transcript,* February 19, 1924.

615 *"thin line between"*: Beauchamp, *Without Lying Down,* 169.

615 *"There were characters I"*: Prouty, *Pencil Shavings,* 172.

615 *"How would it do"*: Prouty, *Stella Dallas,* 103.

616 *"drape a straight piece"*: Ibid., 85.

616 *"some raw half-awake"*: Ibid., 86.

616 *"rub down [Stella's] rough"*: Ibid., 92.

616 *"That dead, old-fashioned"*: Ibid., 94.

617 *Stella doesn't know Thackeray*: Ibid., 95.

618 *"how the limelight of recognition"*: Ibid., 99.

619 *There was Bennett's performance*: Ella Smith, *Starring Miss Barbara Stanwyck,* 99.

619 *"On the surface"*: Ibid., 99.

621 *"Run twenty new pictures"*: "Director Praised by Producer," *Los Angeles Times,* August 21, 1927.

621 *"A lot of my boyhood"*: Henry King, interview with David Badder, *Sight and Sound* (Winter 1977– 1978), 44.

621 *"You're too good"*: Wakeman, *World Film Directors,* vol. 1.

621 *"Sam may have, no"*: Henry King, interview with Scott Eyman, *Focus on Film,* 26.

621 *"Goldwyn will do anything"*: Henry King, interview with Badder, 44.

622 *"I've never seen anything"*: Ibid., 441.

623 "Stella Dallas *is, in my"*: Berg, *Goldwyn,* 154.

623 *"This woman has just"*: Beauchamp, *Without Lying Down,* 170.

623 *Bennett had once played*: *Variety,* November 8, 1932.

623 *She pretended the boy*: "The Real Belle Bennett," *Picturegoer,* April 1926, 12.

623 *The afternoon of her son's*: Belletti, *Adventures of a Hollywood Secretary,* June 26, 1925, 55–57.

623 *Bennett loved the picture*: "Belle Bennett Adds to Fame," *Los Angeles Times,* April 4, 1926, 21.

624 *"a character as heroic"*: James Lee, *Worcester Evening Gazette,* September 2, 1937.

624 *The picture's opening*: Belletti, *Adventures of a Hollywood Secretary,* April 4, 1926, 125.

624 *"I don't want young"*: *Los Angeles Times,* July 17, 1927, C9.

624 *"We had a good cast"*: King Vidor, oral history, 205, UCLA Theatre Arts Library, January 31, 1969,

624 *"Hello, King—how are you"*: King Vidor, *A Tree Is a Tree,* 145.

625 *"Griffith went beyond"*: King Vidor, oral history, 13–15, Columbia University, May 1958.

627 *"All these years I spend"*: Ella Smith, *Starring Miss Barbara Stanwyck,* 109.

627 *She realizes that she*: King Vidor, oral history, 204, UCLA Theatre Arts Library.

627 *"Galveston was considered beyond"*: Ibid., 1.

628 *"Images remain over everything"*: Ibid., 2.

628 *He'd read everything*: George Mitchell, letter to *Films in Review,* n.d., 180.

628 *"Those actors who had been"*: King Vidor, oral history, 50, UCLA Theatre Arts Library, January 31, 1969.

628 *"If love exists, admiration"*: Ella Smith, *Starring Miss Barbara Stanwyck,* 104.

628 *During the making of* Stella Dallas: James Robert Parish, *The RKO Gals* (New Rochelle, N.Y.: Arlington House, 1974), 351.

628 *"You've a career ahead"*: Irene Thirer, "Anne Shirley, Veteran at 22, Recalls Her Past," *New York Post,* September 26, 1941.

628 *her eighteenth birthday*: Phyllis Fraser, "My Pal, Anne Shirley," *Hollywood,* October 1946, 32.

629 *"Be nice to the director"*: Julie Payne to author, May 2, 2001.

629 *Up to that point Anne*: Dan Tomas, "Sanity and Enthusiasm Held an Answer to Anne Shirley's Ascending Film Star," *New York World-Telegram,* May 16, 1935.

629 *When Dawn Paris first arrived*: Jerry Mason, *This Week,* April 11, 1943.

629 *"something in gentleness"*: King Vidor to Merritt Hulburd, March 1, 1937.

629 *"Knowing something about"*: Mrs. Clarence M. Young to Samuel Goldwyn, December 17, 1936.

629 *"I don't care what"*: Parish, *RKO Gals,* 351.

630 *"I want to repeat what"*: King Vidor to Merritt Hulburd, memo, April 29, 1937.

631 *"in the presence of"*: Ella Smith, *Starring Miss Barbara Stanwyck,* 109.

631 *O'Neil saw Barbara as:* Barbara O'Neil to Ella Smith.

632 *"I understood the depth"*: Ella Smith, *Starring Miss Barbara Stanwyck,* 109.

632 *In addition, she put sags*: Barbara Miller, *Los Angeles Times,* August 22, 1937, C1.

632 *"It was a matter of upholstery"*: BS to C. B. DeMille on *Lux Radio Theatre,* October 11, 1937.

632 *"like running them through"*: Ella Smith, *Starring Miss Barbara Stanwyck,* 100.

633 *Nine tints were tested:* David Chierichetti to author, October 1998.

633 *Barbara, still in pain: Stella Dallas* press book.

634 *"I had to indicate to"*: Ella Smith, *Starring Miss Barbara Stanwyck,* 99.

635 *"It is difficult with that"*: Vidor, oral history, 205, UCLA Theatre Arts Library.

635 *"humanness and ability"*: Ella Smith, *Starring Miss Barbara Stanwyck,* 107.

635 *"prepared to the very top"*: Ibid.

635 *"King was very nice"*: Bernard Drew, *Film Comment,* March–April 1981, 45.

635 *"Sam Goldwyn made sure"*: Rosenfield, "Saluting Stanwyck."

636 *" 'The Goldwyn touch' "*: Griffith, *Samuel Goldwyn.*

636 *"You told me you"*: Vidor, oral history, 206–7, UCLA Theatre Arts Library.

636 *When Dawn became Anne*: Edwin Schallert, "Anne Shirley at Turning Point in Her Career," *Los Angeles Times,* February 25, 1945.

637 *He was from a moneyed family*: Frances Ingram, "John Payne: Living Out the Dream," *Classic Images,* March 2011.

637 *"a woman who cheated"*: Ella Smith, *Starring Miss Barbara Stanwyck,* 107; *Movie Digest,* January 1972.

637 *"interpretation of the shy"*: James Lee, *Worcester Evening Gazette,* September 2, 1937.

637 *"May I not say again"*: Joseph L. Breen to Samuel Goldwyn, July 8, 1937.

638 Stella Dallas *grossed more*: Berg, *Goldwyn,* 294.

638 *"has been crammed"*: Olive Higgins Prouty to *New Yorker,* March 20, 1953.

Four: "Clean Labor Unionism"

PAGE

639 *"MGM and Louis B. Mayer have"*: Prindle, *Politics of Glamour,* 19.

640 *"I've been figuring"*: Joel (McFee) McCrea, "My Friend Coop," *Photoplay,* October, 1939, 85.

640 *Finally, in early February 1937: Detroit News,* 2004.

641 Madame Walewska: Released as *Conquest.*

641 *RKO had four pictures: Los Angeles Times,* May 2, 1937.

642 *Twenty-four hours after:* Ibid.

642 *If the guild vote was: Los Angeles Times,* April 30, 1937.

642 *Tone decided to leave:* Ellen Adler to author, December 20, 2004.

643 *Tone, ever ambivalent in his choices:* Clurman, *All People Are Famous,* 122.

643 *In an effort to head off: Screen Guild Magazine,* May 1937, 35.

644 *"honest, clean labor"*: Ralph Morgan and John C. Lee, *Screen Actor,* September 1941, 18.

644 *All actors were to be: Los Angeles Times,* May 11, 1937.

645 *Now that the Screen Actors: Los Angeles Times,* May 10, 1937.

645 *"I've learned never to"*: Prindle, *Politics of Glamour,* 31.

645 *Within the next few: Los Angeles Times,* May 11, 1937.

Five: Starry Skies Above

PAGE

647 *She was a strong:* Gene Vaslett to author, October 19, 1996.

647 *Capra belonged, as did:* Reine Davies, *Los Angeles Times,* May 10, 1937.

647 *The picture opened in New York:* Radio City Music Hall program, June 3, 1937.

647 *"Hollywood's No. 1 romantic"*: Dorothy Manners, *Los Angeles Examiner,* June 3, 1937.

647 *"nothing short of beautiful"*: Ibid.

647 *"slow and weak"*: *Variety,* June 2, 1937, 15.

648 *William Powell, second:* Edwin Schallert, *Los Angeles Times,* June 10, 1937.

648 *"nothing but legalized murder"*: David Stenn, *Bombshell: The Life and Death of Jean Harlow* (New York: Doubleday, 1993), 230.

648 *"It wasn't a star"*: Ibid., 237.

648 *"She was gay and"*: *Daily Mail,* August 20, 1937.

649 *"one of the dearest"*: David Lewis, *Creative Producer,* 70–71.

649 *Barbara adored her brother:* Judith Stevens to author, June 1998.

649 *Broadway eight months before:* Brooks Atkinson, *New York Times,* October 23, 1936.

650 *"There's something hypnotic"*: Rankin, "She Has a System," 74.

653 *"I don't know that"*: Hall, "Barbara Stanwyck's Advice to Girls in Love," 5.

Six: Well, Who Am I?

PAGE

654 *Nannies were hired:* Judith Stevens to author, October 15, 1998, 41.

655 *"Whoever heard of a Negro"*: Karen Hudson, *Paul R. Williams, Architect: A Legacy of Style* (New York: Rizzoli, 1993), 11.

656 *Barbara and Marion Marx: The Blood-Horse,* April 2, 1938.

657 *Among the two-year-olds:* Paul Cervin, *Turf and Sport Digest,* December 1937.

658 *Walter Connolly loved horses:* Ann Connolly to author, March 1, 2001.

659 *"If you could fall in love"*: Walter Ramsey, *Photoplay,* April 1937, 103.

659 *"I'm finding it a little difficult"*: Ibid.

659 *Balcon was modest:* Geoff Brown, "A Knight and His Castle," in *Michael Balcon: The Pursuit of British Cinema* (New York: Museum of Modern Art, 1984).

660 *Twenty-three writers worked on the script:* MGM legal files 15030-0001.

660 *"Very few lines of mine"*: Matthew J. Bruccoli and Margaret M. Duggan, eds., *Correspondence of F. Scott Fitzgerald* (New York: Random House, 1980), 498.

660 *Comedy to Dunne was easy:* Irene Dunne, interview with James Harvey, *Romantic Comedy in Hollywood,* 686.

661 *"[She] is all things"*: Ella Smith, *Starring Miss Barbara Stanwyck,* 113–14.

661 *"I do very little"*: Ibid., 113.

661 *"quite adorable"*: Alma Whitaker, "Film Lover Fascinating to His Wife," *Los Angeles Times,* July 3, 1932.

661 *"a very nice lady"*: Philip K. Scheuer, "Herbert Marshall Abhors Being Known as Gentleman," *Los Angeles Times,* March 31, 1935.

662 *His artificial limb would be:* Alfred Santell to Ella Smith, June 17, 1972.

662 *"got the swing into"*: *Breakfast for Two* press book, 11.

663 *She was sure it:* BS magazine clipping, n.d.

663 *Barbara had put everything:* Barbara Stanwyck, "My Favorite Designer Is Edith Head," magazine clipping, n.d.

663 *"as great a picture"*: *Los Angeles Evening Herald Examiner,* August 20, 1937.

663 *"a triumph both artistically"*: *Hollywood Reporter,* July 23, 1937.

663 *At Radio City, when Barbara:* Kate Cameron, "Music Hall Picture a Teary Festival."

663 *"courageous," "outstanding"*: *Hollywood Reporter,* July 23, 1937.

663 *"By innumerable little touches"*: Elizabeth Yeaman, *Hollywood Citizen-News,* August 20, 1937.

664 *"tops in Miss Stanwyck's screen"*: *Variety,* July 23, 1937.

664 *"On the practical surface"*: *New York Times,* August 6, 1937.

Seven: Bull in the Afternoon

PAGE

665 *"To my mind"*: Freda Bruce Lockhart, "Plain Facts About Taylor," *Film Weekly,* October 2, 1937, 11.

666 *"Clark is so big"*: Charles Darnton, "Gable and Taylor Rivals?," *Screenland,* May 1937, 24.

666 *Head kept in mind for whom:* Stanwyck, "My Favorite Designer Is Edith Head," 108.

667 *Her whole reason for being:* Peter Ford to author, April 5, 2010.

667 *He'd dropped in unannounced:* Bruccoli and Duggan, *Correspondence of F. Scott Fitzgerald.*

668 *"unconscionable quantity of bull"*: Max Eastman, "Bull in the Afternoon," *New Republic,* June 7, 1933, 96.

668 *Perkins was pulling Eastman:* John Kuehl and Jackson R. Bryer, eds., *Dear Scott/Dear Max: The Fitzgerald-Perkins Correspondence* (New York: Charles Scribner's Sons, 1971), 239–40.

669 *"When I come back"*: *Los Angeles Examiner,* August 15, 1937.

669 *"I like the seasons"*: *Los Angeles Examiner,* August 20, 1937.

669 *That Wednesday she and Holly: Variety,* August 25, 1937.

669 *The picture was held over:* Goldwyn to Dr. A. H. Giannini, August 10, 1937.

669 *"society at a critical"*: Howard Barnes, newspaper clipping, August 8, 1937.

Eight: Rearing Up

PAGE

671 *As the station manager:* Charles Darnton, "Stand Up and Fight," *Screenland,* February 1939.

671 *To appease the mob: Los Angeles Times,* August 29, 1937.

671 *A man on a bicycle:* Darnton, "Stand Up and Fight."

672 *She admired the way:* Ed Sullivan, *Omaha Sunday World Herald,* November 5, 1939.

673 *"She would look you":* BS to Shirley Eder.

674 *"was one of those things":* Asher, "Strangest Reunion," 26.

674 *"a small house":* Dixie Willson, *Photoplay,* December 1937, 69.

675 *If it rang and she was:* Breakfast for Two press book, 11.

675 *She held a wedding:* Lang, "She Doesn't Say Yes, She Doesn't Say No," 29.

675 *"she missed him":* Buck Mack, *Screen Guide,* 1948.

675 *Bob called Barbara and asked:* Wayne, *Robert Taylor,* 81.

676 *"at last coming into":* Cecil B. DeMille, *Lux Radio Theatre,* October 11, 1937.

677 *He says from the outset:* Philip Barry, *Holiday* (New York: Samuel French, 1929), 27.

677 *"mother wasn't even":* Ibid., 20.

679 *"They were rabid":* James Reid, *Modern Screen,* January 1939, 74.

679 *Danker hired her right:* "Barbara Stanwyck Moving Day."

679 *"the intermediary classification":* Variety, November 24, 1937, 16.

679 *"Cunning . . . clever . . . and good":* Ella Smith, *Starring Miss Barbara Stanwyck,* 113.

679 *"drab little comedy":* New York Times, November 20, 1937.

Nine: Charges of Contempt

PAGE

681 *"Each time we arrived":* Sunday Express, Manchester, U.K., December 8, 1962.

681 *"I haven't had a drink":* Wayne, *Robert Taylor,* 83.

681 *"I shave twice a day":* Ibid., 84–85.

682 *"Nothing happens overnight, son":* Ibid., 86.

682 *Bob gave her a charm:* Ibid.

682 *"I wasn't homesick":* Gladys Hall, "Has Bob Taylor Had a Change of Heart?," *Modern Screen,* 1938, 27, 78.

683 *"I'll put him away":* Time, August 24, 1936.

683 *"I have been put off":* Court documents, case no. D 137906.

683 *Cradick assured the judge:* Ibid.; affidavits filed December 3, 1937; December 15, 1937; December 20, 1937; December 21, 1937; December 23, 1937.

683 *"When people mention the Champs":* Hall, "Has Bob Taylor Had a Change of Heart?," 26.

684 *"cultural internationalism":* Hilton Tims, *Erich Maria Remarque: The Last Romantic* (New York: Carroll & Graf, 2003), 79.

684 *"without a country":* Ibid., 81.

684 *Two months after Remarque:* Walter Lippmann, "Today and Tomorrow: The Burning of Books," *Los Angeles Times,* May 13, 1933, p. 4.

684 *more than twenty-five thousand books were:* Tims, *Erich Maria Remarque,* 80.

685 *"A slice of life":* Ibid., 77.

685 *The collaboration between:* F. Scott Fitzgerald's Screenplay for "Three Comrades" by Erich Maria Remarque (Carbondale: Southern Illinois University Press, 1978), 260.

685 *Both Fitzgerald and Paramore:* F. Scott Fitzgerald to Phil Berg, Dozier and Allen, February 23, 1940, in Bruccoli and Duggan, *Correspondence of F. Scott Fitzgerald,* 498.

685 *Joe Mankiewicz rewrote what became:* Fitzgerald's Screenplay for "Three Comrades," 263.

686 *"harass and annoy":* Barbara Stanwyck affidavit, December 1937.

686 *"little emotional football":* Joan Bonner, "The Truth About the Stanwyck Court Case," *Motion Picture.*

687 *"I'm glad someone":* (ACN 3/14/38).

688 *"I wasn't in favor":* Bonner, "Truth About the Stanwyck Court Case."

688 *"I don't care how many":* Wayne, *Robert Taylor,* 87.

690 *"We question Miss Stanwyck's"*: AP, January 11, 1938.

690 *"And I don't think"*: *Hollywood Citizen-News,* January 12, 1938.

692 *"I won everything I asked"*: Ibid.

692 *"The appeal automatically"*: "Fay Waits in Vain: Stanwyck Keeps Boy," *Los Angeles Evening Herald Examiner,* January 15, 1938."

692 *"child in accordance with"*: Ibid.

693 *RKO wrote off the cost:* J. R. McDonough to George J. Schaefer (RKO NYC), memo, April 3, 1939, RKO legal files, Turner Archives.

Ten: Wins and Losses

PAGE

694 *"Somebody told me"*: James Reid, *Modern Screen,* January 1939, 74.

694 *"loaded with ice-cold"*: David Lewis, *Creative Producer,* 147.

694 *"I know that every"*: Davis, *Lonely Life,* 180.

694 *"damn good character"*: Barbara Leaming, *Bette Davis* (New York: Simon & Schuster, 1992), 152.

695 *Davis remained on suspension:* Ibid., 152–53.

695 *"This is Barbara Stanwyck"*: Elizabeth Wilson, *Liberty,* August 11, 1945.

695 *"They could work me"*: James Reid, *Modern Screen,* January 1939, 74.

695 *"wasn't afraid to say"*: Ibid.

695 *The Santa Anita racetrack: Los Angeles Times,* March 12, 1938, A9.

695 *Bob and Barbara were there: Los Angeles Evening Herald Examiner,* January 24, 1938.

695 *Reviewers who formerly:* Edwin Schallert, *Los Angeles Times,* February 17, 1938, 11.

696 *"Judging on this performance"*: Howard Barnes, *New York Herald Tribune,* February 25, 1938.

696 *"As [Three Comrades] deals"*: George Gyssling to Joseph Breen, December 29, 1937, MGM files, Turner Production File 1036, Atlanta, GA.

696 *"The story, while dramatically"*: "Off-Color Remarque," *New Masses,* February 15, 1938.

696 *"Here is one country"*: F. Scott Fitzgerald, *Three Comrades* script (1938), 122, Loew's Incorporated.

696 *Metro's longtime cameraman: Three Comrades, AFI Catalog,* 2194.

697 *The show's advertising agency:* Cal Kuhl, J. Walter Thompson.

697 *Radio didn't really hold:* Robert James, "Keeping Tabs on Robert," *Modern Screen,* September 1938, 82.

698 *Fox paid RKO $55,000:* RKO legal files, Turner Archives.

698 *"Those seven months"*: James Reid, *Modern Screen,* January 1939, 74.

698 *The nomination by the academy:* Terence O'Flaherty, *San Francisco Chronicle,* March 18, 1967.

698 *"flawless performance"*: *Los Angeles Times,* February 18, 1938, 15.

698 *"You won't get one"*: BS to Stanley Eder, vol. IV, 10, transcript of phone conversation.

699 *Louis B. Mayer found the scene:* Marie Brenner, *Great Dames* (New York: Three Rivers Press, 2000), 183.

699 *Rainer had seen Cocteau's:* Ibid.

699 *"I never acted"*: Ibid., 175.

699 *Rainer had fled Vienna:* Ibid., 180.

700 *She mystified Hollywood:* Ibid., 178.

700 *"In Europe we did"*: Ibid., 183.

700 *The banquet's hundreds of:* Wiley and Bona, *Inside the Oscar,* 79.

701 *"It will be less embarrassing"*: Ibid., 80.

701 *Greta Garbo was absent:* Paris, *Garbo,* 353, 351.

701 *"You wanted comedy"*: Memo from David O. Selznick, 116.

701 *"In a straight role"*: AP, October 2, 1937.

701 *He was an irresistible storyteller:* Leo McCarey obituary, *New York Times,* July 6, 1969.

702 *"one of the finest"*: *Newsweek,* May 22, 1937.

702 *"three qualities rarely"*: *New York Times,* May 10, 1937.

702 *"We make pretty pictures"*: Brenner, *Great Dames,* 184.

702 *Under Capra's leadership:* Wiley and Bona, *Inside Oscar.*

703 *Zanuck's receiving the award:* McBride, *Frank Capra,* 386.

703 *Hal Wallis, head of production:* Ibid.

703 *"It is a privilege"*: Wiley and Bona, *Inside Oscar,* 82.

704 *"Thanks, but you gave it"*: Ibid.

704 *Two special comedy awards:* Ibid.

704 *"I became Chinese"*: Brenner, *Great Dames,* 187.

704 *"Human emotions don't"*: Barbara Miller, *Los Angeles Times,* August 22, 1937, C1.

704 *"They call me a"*: Brenner, *Great Dames,* 184.

705 *Luise Rainer as O-Lan:* " 'Good Earth' Premiere Dazzles Onlookers," *Los Angeles Times,* January 17, 1937.

705 *"ten good suits"*: Kevin Lewis, "Luise Rainer: She Did It Her Way," *Movie Maker,* September 1, 1999.

705 *Rainer's Hollywood society was:* Kyle Crichton, "The Girl Who Hates Movies," *Colliers,* May 23, 1936, 42.

705 *Her indifference to movie:* Ibid., 36.

705 *"a real cinema epic"*: *Time,* February 15, 1937.

706 *Odets was the passion:* Ellen Adler to author, June 15, 2005.

706 *They arrived in the rain:* Brenman-Gibson, *Clifford Odets,* 500.

707 *"My heart's blood was"*: Elizabeth Wilson, *Liberty,* August 11, 1945.

Eleven: Golden Influences

PAGE

708 *to be directed by:* *Variety,* March 23, 1938, 2.

709 *"A curious stew"*: Brooks Atkinson, *New York Times,* November 10, 1934.

711 *If the agency failed:* J. Walter Thompson contract, March 10, 1938, Duke University Archives.

711 *Barbara told her agents:* Blees, "Barbara Stanwyck."

711 *wanted* Dark Victory: Haver, *David O. Selznick's Hollywood,* 162, 76–77.

711 *"The only way to"*: McGilligan, *Backstory 1,* 301.

711 *"A woman who dies"*: Ibid., 300.

711 *"There had to be"*: Ibid., 301.

712 *Selznick had consistently rebutted:* *Leonard Maltin's Movie Crazy* (Winter 2003).

712 *"You won't find the stars"*: David Lewis, *Creative Producer,* 125.

712 *"It's just a story about"*: Ibid., 147.

712 *"the only person to play"*: McGilligan, *Backstory 1,* 301.

713 *"knew a certain part"*: Rosenfield, "Saluting Stanwyck."

713 *"didn't want trouble from"*: David Lewis, *Creative Producer,* 149.

713 *the "Japanese Sandman"*: The director was Gregory La Cava.

713 *"cold, black Irishman"*: David Lewis, *Creative Producer,* 152.

713 *The very English Edmund Goulding:* Ibid.

713 *When the part went to:* September 3, 1937.

714 *"If you're under contract"*: Ann Harding obituary, *New York Times,* September 4, 1981.

714 *Barbara's next picture for:* Zanuck copy of draft of *The Lady Is a Lady—Always Goodbye—*March 4, 1938.

714 *"All property, rights to property"*: Ross Hastings to J. R. McDonough, memo, April 18, 1938, RKO legal files, Turner Archives.

715 *Fay and Barbara were named:* *Bank of America National Trust and Savings Association v. Frank Fay, Barbara Stanwyck Fay, Corporation of America, John Doe Co., Richard Roe Co., Henry Poe Co.,* February 20, 1939.

715 *"fictitious names whose true"*: Ibid., 4.

715 *IRS had issued:* Tax lien under Internal Revenue Laws no. 45480, July 26, 1938.

715 *Harding (Dorothy Walton Gatley) was:* Colonel George G. Gatley obituary, *New York Times,* January 10, 1931.

715 *"Such a step is":* Parish, *RKO Gals,* 14.

715 *Once in New York City: New York Times,* October 7, 1923.

716 *"Perhaps I am that":* James Robert Parish, *The RKO Gals* (New Rochelle, N.Y.: Arlington House, 1974).

716 *sound of temple songs:* Scott O'Brien, "The Inevitable Road to Stardom: Ann Harding," *Films of the Golden Age,* no. 60 (Spring 2010).

716 *One side of the plane's: New Yorker,* October 24, 1931, 15.

717 *"Work in Hollywood":* Edwin Schallert, "Ann Harding Reveals Road to Happiness," *Los Angeles Times,* April 7, 1935.

717 *Offscreen she was:* Parish, *RKO Gals,* 22.

718 *"Miss Harding is so":* Gwin, "She's a Movie Fan Too," 47.

718 *"splendid" and "radiant":* Mordaunt Hall, *New York Times,* January 22, 1934.

719 *Ginger Rogers thought:* Rogers, *Ginger,* 187.

719 *Pan Berman was "amazed":* Gary Morris, "Forgotten Master: The Career of Gregory La Cava," www .brightlightsfilm.com.

719 *If something didn't fit:* Joel McCrea interview with John Kobal, *People Will Talk* (New York: Alfred A. Knopf, 1985), 294.

719 *"good in this type":* Pandro Berman to Leo Spitz, memo; June 8, 1938, Turner Legal Files.

720 *"Wake Up! Hollywood Producers": Los Angeles Times,* May 5, 1938.

720 *after Paramount bought out: Los Angeles Times,* May 4, 1938.

Twelve: Mother Love at Home and Abroad

PAGE

723 *"There must have been": Variety,* May 24, 1938.

723 *"Reich of today":* Ibid.

723 *Others had followed Barbara: Variety,* May 11, 1938, 4.

724 *Barbara wore an accordion-pleated:* Ella Wickersham, *Los Angeles Examiner,* May 21, 1938.

724 *"His hand always touched":* Bob Thomas, *Joan Crawford* (New York: Simon & Schuster, 1978), 127.

724 *When Crawford's contract was:* Considine, *Bette and Joan,* 94.

724 *"The only picture to make":* Jill Watts, *Mae West* (New York: Oxford University Press, 2001), 233.

725 *"sentimentally sticky and": New York Herald Tribune,* June 25, 1938, 6.

725 *"fine performances in the face": Variety,* June 29, 1938.

725 *"one of our most": Los Angeles Examiner,* July 8, 1938.

726 *Barbara wanted no publicity:* Louella Parsons, *Los Angeles Examiner* July 3, 1938.

727 *Uncle Buck and Nanny took care:* Tony Fay to author, May 19, 2005.

728 *Louise left Metro:* John Kobal, *The Art of the Great Hollywood Portrait Photographers* (New York: Alfred A. Knopf, 1980), 93, 117.

729 *When he asked Frances Mercer:* Ella Smith, *Starring Miss Barbara Stanwyck,* 116; Frances Mercer to author, 1997, 2.

730 *"You're just a decorative":* Epstein, *Mad Miss Manton,* 32.

731 *"she had to watch":* Lambert, *Norma Shearer,* 269.

731 *"Too many stars stay":* Ibid., 220.

731 *They wanted, they said:* Ed Sullivan, *Hollywood Citizen-News,* July 16, 1938.

Thirteen: Pomp and Glory

PAGE

733 *Barbara and Marion entered six:* Ella Wickersham, *Los Angeles Examiner,* May 30, 1938.

733 *"Let it be noted":* New York Times, August 5, 1938.

734 *She took pleasure when Bob:* Larry Kleno to author, January 1, 2004.

735 *A few years before:* Walter Goodman, *Committee,* 40.

736 *Also named by the committee:* Charles Darnton, "Stand Up and Fight," *Screenland,* February 1939.

736 *The various studios responded: Los Angeles Evening Herald Examiner,* August 22, 1938.

736 *Among those named were: Los Angeles Times,* August 15, 1938.

736 *"No one has anything":* "Anti-Nazi Leaguers Fight Red Aid Charge," *Los Angeles Times,* August 16, 1938.

736 *"all the Hollywood rumors": Los Angeles Times,* August 16, 1938.

736 *A former member:* A. E. Kral, "Robert Taylor: A Golden Era Hollywood Movie King From Nebraska," Supplement, *Beatrice Daily Sun,* Oct. 8, 1993.

737 *"I want to get parts":* Hall, "Has Bob Had a Change of Heart?," 27, 78.

737 *"I'm gonna play the part":* Wayne, *Robert Taylor,* 94.

738 *The Rogerses ended the evening:* Hedda Hopper's Hollywood, *Los Angeles Times,* October 12, 1938, 21.

739 *Barbara saw the Western:* Bernard Drew, *Film Comment,* March–April 1981, 45.

739 *"America's 'royalty' ":* Stanwyck, foreword to *Sweethearts of the Sage,* by Rainey.

740 *Her appeal to prevent:* Certified copy of opinion I.A. no. 16650, D 137906, November 9, 1938.

741 *Eight years later, in 1925:* Bernard Drew, *Film Comment,* March–April 1981, 45.

742 *"He taught us how":* John Kobal, unpublished biography of DeMille, chap. 8, "Man, Woman, and Sin," 34.

742 *"Say it with props":* John Cromwell, interview with Leonard Maltin, *Leonard Maltin's Movie Crazy* (Winter 2007): 5.

742 *"That America is still":* Kobal, biography of DeMille, 216.

742 *DeMille even re-created:* Ibid., 35.

743 *He sold the airline to Rogers:* Ibid., 636.

743 *"esteem for his sheer": The Autobiography of Cecil B. DeMille,* ed. Donald Hayne (Englewood Cliffs, N.J.: Prentice-Hall, 1959), 326.

743 *DeMille didn't like:* Kobal, biography of DeMille, 142.

744 *"When you have a hundred":* Frank S. Nugent, *New York Times,* December 21, 1947.

745 *"A lot of actors":* John Kobal interview with Joel McCrea.

746 *One of the students:* Ibid., 45–46.

746 *"If there were 500 people":* Bernard Drew, *Film Comment,* March–April 1981, 45.

747 *"The actors arrived wearing":* Peter Bogdanovich, *John Ford* (Berkeley: U. of California Press, 1968, 44.

747 *Ford worked from a private:* Andrew Sinclair, *John Ford,* 34–35.

747 *a budget of a million dollars:* Roughly $16.5 million in 2013.

747 *"Legend rides the trail":* Bosley Crowther, *New York Times,* May 7, 1939.

748 *a popular ditty that said:* Kobal, biography of DeMille, chap. 8, "Man, Woman, and Sin," 8.

749 *"hardfisted and outspoken": Autobiography of Cecil B. DeMille,* 363.

749 *"it would slip the way":* Kobal, biography of DeMille, 1672.

749 *A real trestle was built:* Ibid., 1674.

749 *The cold and wet and mud:* Ibid., 1673.

750 *Barnes went where Barbara went:* Wally Westmore to R. L. Johnson, memo, October 11, 1938.

750 *Harriett was married:* Michael Coray to author, September 2006.

750 *"It's too much of an effort":* Harriett Coray, "The Woman Who'd Dare the Devil," as told to Jane Ardmore, magazine clipping, 1965.

750 *After a day or two of that:* Harriett Coray as told to Jane Ardmore, *Motion Picture,* March 1966, 70.

751 *Harriett Coray, circa 1939:* Michael Coray to author.

751 *"Whenever you're acting":* New York Times, March 23, 1987, B7.

752 *"a tyrant . . . a despot":* Evelyn Keyes, *Scarlett O'Hara's Younger Sister* (Random House, 1978), 21.

752 *"In the small interior":* Films in Review, March 1968.

752 *"Because there were no":* Kobal, biography of DeMille, 1670.

752 *He hired an actor because:* Swanson, *Swanson on Swanson,* 101.

753 *DeMille believed that no:* Chierichetti, *Mitchell Leisen,* 23.

753 *"her work with all":* Autobiography of Cecil B. DeMille, 364.

753 *"The first thing every":* Kobal, biography of DeMille, 333.

754 *"Don't look at the fucking":* Ibid., 334.

754 *"another two-fisted role":* Los Angeles Evening Herald Examiner, February 9, 1939.

754 *"I'm not sure Barbara":* Kotsilibas-Davis and Loy, *Myrna Loy,* 156.

755 *The sadness was real:* Kobal, biography of DeMille, 1675.

Fourteen: Champion of the "Cockeyed Wonder"

PAGE

758 *"pretty bad. The title":* New York Daily News, December 12, 1938, 3.

758 *Bob had given Barbara:* Wayne, *Robert Taylor,* 95.

759 *She and Maree had become friends:* Jane Ardmore Papers, ca 1920s–1960s, 6–7, Margaret Herrick Library, AMPAS.

760 *"We haven't made a lot":* G. D. Hamman, *Los Angeles Evening Herald Examiner,* 79.

761 *She would arrive:* Gladys Hall, "Information, If You Please, About Barbara Stanwyck," Gladys Hall Papers, 1918–1969, Margaret Herrick Library, AMPAS; *Modern Screen,* March 3, 1940, 14.

761 *When the Stars made:* Tony Fay to author, January 9, 2006.

762 *"But who knows where":* Stanwyck, "Things I Don't Like About Myself," 78.

763 *"Well, he loved us":* McCrea, unpublished manuscript, 254.

763 *"A week's work shot":* Ella Smith, *Starring Miss Barbara Stanwyck,* 120.

764 *It was a hot day:* June Allyson with Frances Spatz Leighton, *June Allyson* (New York: G.P. Putnam's Sons, 1982), 180–81.

765 *She understands cruelty:* Stella Adler notes on *Golden Boy.*

766 *Cohn asked the blond:* Pete Martin, "Hollywood's Most Improbable Star," *Saturday Evening Post,* September 4, 1954.

767 *"I've got a boy here":* Ibid.

767 *"less than a waitress":* Joe Hymans, "Hollywood's Busiest Leading Man," 12.

767 *"had a special glow":* Elia Kazan: A Life (New York: Alfred A. Knopf, 1988), 163.

768 *"hot and cold":* Odets, *Time Is Ripe,* 62.

768 *"It is the background":* Brenman-Gibson, *Clifford Odets,* 469.

769 *"felt this disgust":* Elia Kazan, 164.

769 *"What Odets was trying":* Harold Clurman, *The Fervent Years* (New York: Alfred A. Knopf, 1945), 174.

769 *Arthur was then to star:* McBride, *Frank Capra,* 386.

770 *Most crucial of all:* Oller, *Jean Arthur,* 101–2.

770 *Mamoulian came to see:* Mamoulian, interview with Raymond Rohauer, *A 40th Anniversary Tribute to Rouben Mamoulian, 1927–1967* (1967).

771 *Capra decided to trade:* McBride, *Frank Capra,* 401–2.

771 *In* Golden Boy, *Mamoulian:* Rouben Mamoulian, oral history, December 1958, Columbia University.

771 *It was sharp and ungrammatical:* Clifford Odets, interview with Arthur Wagner, *Lincoln Center Review,* no. 42 (Spring 2006): 13.

771 *The trick was for:* Peter Bogdanovich to author, October 5, 2005.

772 *"strictly stock"*: Margaret Brenman-Gibson, *Clifford Odets: American Playwright* (New York: Applause Books, 2002), 195.

772 *"elevated and poetic"*: Odets, interview with Wagner, 10.

772 *his conversation was punctuated:* John McCarten, "Revolution's Number One Boy," *New Yorker,* January 22, 1938.

772 *a bust of Beethoven:* Elia Kazan, 86.

772 *"Something is cooking"*: Brenman-Gibson, *Clifford Odets,* 170.

773 *"crouched over his typewriter"*: Elia Kazan, 87.

773 *"with a sense of disgrace"*: Odets, interview with Wagner, 13.

773 *"ordinary," "middle-class"*: McCarten, "Revolution's Number One Boy," 22.

773 *"blunted his impulses"*: Odets, *Time Is Ripe,* 100.

773 *"I could be a better"*: Ibid., 71.

773 *"He wanted to be"*: Clurman, *Fervent Years,* 249.

774 *"You have just given"*: Brenman-Gibson, *Clifford Odets,* 426.

775 *"the Halvah king"*: Ibid., 461.

775 *Many commented that:* Odets, *Time Is Ripe,* 294.

775 *"He is no good"*: McCarten, "Revolution's Number One Boy," 21.

776 *"You're out of your"*: Daniel Taradash to author, March 11, 12, 1998, 8.

776 *Cohn referred to the writing:* Thomas, *King Cohn,* 155.

776 *"In Frank Capra's pictures"*: Taradash to author, March 11, 12, 1998, 12.

776 *Shooting for* Golden Boy: *Variety,* April 4, 1939, 7.

776 *"It was a phony"*: Taradash, oral history, 58.

776 *Each morning Holden got:* Frank S. Nugent, "Golden Holden," *Collier's,* June 2, 1951.

777 *They and Spencer Tracy were: New Yorker,* October 21, 1961, 113.

777 *In his hometown:* Nugent, "Golden Holden."

778 *The most demanding part: New Yorker,* October 21, 1961, 117.

778 *"If audiences don't like"*: James F. Scheer, *Motion Picture,* May 1941, 70.

778 *Bob would sometimes:* Hedda Hopper, "Holden Wasn't Fooling by Starting His Career," *Los Angeles Times,* April 1, 1953, D1.

778 *"She pulled me through"*: *Time,* February 27, 1956.

778 *Barbara knew he would:* Stanwyck telephone conversation with Shirley Eder, March 28, 1983.

779 *"He was a dedicated"*: Barbara Stanwyck to Shirley Eder, n.d.

779 *"She would never expose"*: Ella Smith, *Starring Miss Barbara Stanwyck,* 133.

779 *Holden's sincerity came through: Los Angeles Times,* September 11, 1939, 8.

779 *"Don't let me fool"*: *Liberty,* August 11, 1945; Vivian Crosby, *Screenland,* June 1942, 7.

781 *The* Union Pacific *train was: Autobiography of Cecil B. DeMille,* 365.

782 *"and not necessarily"*: "Robert Taylor," *Film Fan Monthly.*

783 *"His usual kiss seemed"*: Stephen Michael Shearer, *Beautiful: The Life of Hedy Lamarr* (New York: St. Martin's Press, 2010), 59.

783 *"little opus . . . colorful": New York Times,* May 11, 1939, 31.

783 *"a full payload": Time,* May 8, 1939, 66.

785 *DeMille introduced Preston: Films in Review,* March 1968.

785 *Men were in beards, string ties: Autobiography of Cecil B. DeMille,* 366.

786 *Keyes left the way she:* Keyes, *Scarlett O'Hara's Younger Sister,* 34.

786 *DeMille and the cast:* Budington Swanson, "The Glory of Golden Spike Days," *Sunday World-Herald Magazine of the Midlands,* April 22, 1979.

787 *She accepted and stayed:* Evelyn Keyes to author, March 27, 1998, 16.

787 *"Karl, you are a great"*: Mamoulian, interview with Ronald L. Davis, August 19, 1980, 46, DeGolyer Library, Southern Methodist University.

787 *"the old couplet come"*: Gladys Hall, "Sunny Side Up," *Modern Screen,* October 1939, 97.

788 *"He'd never met anyone"*: Kutner, "Her Neighbors—the Taylors."

788 *"Who'd figure Spangler Brugh"*: Buck Mack, *Screen Guide,* 1948.

788 *During the ceremony Judge:* Wayne, *Robert Taylor,* 96.

789 *On her first day back:* Gladys Hall, "Sunny Side Up," *Modern Screen.*

789 *Bob loved jewelry:* Barbara Vaslett to author, November 13, 1996.

789 *She happily put a gold:* Julia McCarthy, *New York Daily News,* November 11, 1939.

789 *William Holden sent a telegram:* Wayne, *Robert Taylor,* 96.

794 *As he had during childhood:* Ibid., 97; and Jane Ellen Wayne to author, January 24, 2004.

794 *"my beautiful nickels"*: BS to Cecil B. DeMille, May 28, 1939, Kobal biography of DeMille, 1678.

794 *"Technically," she said, Mamoulian:* Bernard Drew, *Film Comment,* March–April 1981, 45.

795 *"I don't want us"*: Gladys Hall, *Modern Screen,* October 1939, 97.

Fifteen: Ain't She a Peacherino

PAGE

796 *"I do appreciate your"*: BS to Eddie Mannix, May 16, 1939.

796 *"new found happiness"*: Emily Post to BS, July 5, 1939.

796 *"but it certainly wasn't"*: Newspaper clipping, February 1, 1942.

797 *Barbara didn't know how:* Jim Burton, *Modern Screen,* July 1951, 98.

797 *"I gave up fooling"*: Newspaper clipping, February 1, 1942.

797 *"He couldn't have been"*: Tony Fay to author, October 15, 2005.

798 *He saw Dion's sadness:* Ibid.

798 *When Barbara's nephew Brian:* Judith Stevens to author, September 28, 1998, 16.

798 *Barbara was furious:* Tony Fay to author, August 2005.

799 *They were kind to the boys:* Tony Fay to author, October 30, 2005.

799 *Fleischmann also ran:* Robert Stack, with Mark Evans, *Straight Shooting* (New York: Macmillan, 1980), 34–35.

800 *Stack's grandfather had won:* Ibid., 41.

800 *"A country boy"*: Robert Stack to author, May 5, 2003.

800 *"She had no bullshit"*: Stack to author, May 5, 2003.

801 *"Don't tell my wife"*: Stack to author, May 5, 2003.

802 *"Beyond these tears, sweet"*: James Curtis, *Between Flops* (New York: Limelight, 1991), 124.

803 *The studio paid West $5,000:* A. M. Botsford to Albert Lewin, memos, October 11, 1937, and October 28, 1937; Manny Wolfe to Jacob Karp, memos, August 5, 1937, and August 15, 1938; AMPAS.

803 *"Mr. Sturges has not"*: Amusements, *New York Times,* September 19, 1929, 48.

803 *"as a little old man"*: Preston Sturges, *Preston Sturges* (New York: Simon & Schuster, 1990), 265–66.

804 *"There's only one thing"*: Paramount publicity notes on *Remember the Night,* October 3, 1939.

804 *"When can we get rid"*: Sturges, *Preston Sturges,* 278.

804 *Sturges also wrote a few:* Ibid., 287.

805 *Long after Leisen stopped:* Leisen, in Kobal biography of DeMille, 1396.

805 *Because of Leisen's obsessive:* Curtis, *Between Flops,* 113.

806 *With* Dorothy Vernon, *he:* Chierichetti, *Mitchell Leisen,* 32.

806 *"The trick," she said:* Thomas Lawley, "Stanwyck Warns Starlets—Don't Fall Up Hill!," *Screen Life,* October 1940, 75.

806 *Head designed belts:* Chierichetti, *Edith Head,* 42.

806 *"Nobody understands my figure"*: BS to Shirley Eder, October 28, 1981.

806 *"And what difference did"*: Stanwyck, "Things I Don't Like About Myself," 37.

806 *"I have the face that"*: Lawley, "Stanwyck Warns Starlets," 75.

807 *"I shall use a lot":* Edith Head, *Los Angeles Times,* February 17, 1939.

807 *He and MacMurray were:* Chierichetti, *Mitchell Leisen,* 86.

808 *Her ("windbag") lawyer's:* Willard Robertson is Lee Leander's defense attorney who goes on in court in a brilliant comic performance—six full minutes of film time—in an early scene of the picture. Robertson had been an attorney before becoming an actor and writer, working for the government and the railroads in the world war. *Remember the Night* publicity file, October 31, 1939.

809 *"When I dream about":* "Back Home Again in Indiana," lyrics by Ballard MacDonald; music by James Hanley.

812 *"The title doesn't do":* Memo, August 8, 1939, from A. M. Botsford.

813 *They worked well together:* Beulah Bondi to Ella Smith, August 17, 1972.

814 *"Mitch left the acting":* Chierichetti, *Mitchell Leisen,* 124.

814 *Leisen preferred a first take:* Olivia de Havilland to author, April 2010.

815 *Leisen knew how to use:* Chierichetti, *Mitchell Leisen,* 87.

816 *"Memorize the script":* Idwal Jones, *New York Times,* February 23, 1941, 4.

817 *"Come on, you sonofabitch":* Leonard Maltin, *"FFM* Interviews Mitchell Leisen," *Film Fan Monthly,* January 1970, 3–21.

817 *In between scenes, instead:* Chierichetti, *Mitchell Leisen,* 130.

818 *Every time Leisen dismissed:* Ibid.

818 *"For Christ's sake":* Ibid.

819 *When the day arrived:* Ibid., 133.

820 *"Let's do the love scenes":* Lupton A. Wilkinson, "Let's Do the Love Scenes First," *Los Angeles Times,* December 3, 1939.

820 *MacMurray wasn't temperamental: Remember the Night* press book, 5.

820 *Leisen thought his lack:* Maltin, "FFM Interviews Mitchell Leisen," 10.

821 *Leisen did away with:* Mitchell Leisen, interview with David Chierichetti, 21, AFI Archive.

821 *Leisen used MacMurray's natural:* David Chierichetti to author, December 2, 2005.

821 *Had Sturges directed:* Chierichetti, *Mitchell Leisen,* 127.

821 *"God help me. After":* Jerry Asher, "The Amazing Mrs. Taylor," *Silver Screen,* 68.

821 *"love reformed her":* Sturges, *Preston Sturges,* 288.

821 *Both were possessive:* Curtis, *Between Flops,* 89.

822 *The combination of Barbara:* Sturges's script may have been long, but it was deliberately, leisurely paced. Leisen didn't rewrite the script, but he shortened and simplified some of Sturges's scenes and chose not to film several sequences: a scene where Lee Leander goes to church with John Sargent's family and is moved to tears by the choir's singing "Holy Night"; and an organ accompaniment followed by the minister's recitation of the Lord's Prayer. Leisen shot other sequences and took them out of the final cut: a scene in which Lee Leander, in the women's detention room, is told she's been bailed out; an apple-bobbing scene at the farm where Barbara and Fred lose their balance and duck their heads in the tub; a scene in his bedroom, where he is stripped to the waist and she comes in to dry her hair in front of the fire. She brings up the court date after the New Year, which he hadn't even thought of, and she, out of affection, takes his hand and kisses it and comments, looking into the fire, that no one would believe they'd traveled this far together, slept in adjoining rooms, "and never had an evil thought."

823 *"As it turned out":* Sturges, *Preston Sturges,* 288.

823 *"Elaborate melodrama":* New York Times, September 17, 1935.

823 *Nothing came of West's play:* Rebecca West, "The Art of Fiction No. 65," interviewed by Marina Warner, *Paris Review,* no. 79 (Spring 1981).

823 *"I must be lousy":* James Reid, *Silver Screen,* June 1941, 74.

Sixteen: Darkening Lands

PAGE

824 *"You're lucky, you have":* Ruth Waterbury, "Redheaded Rebel," *Movie Mirror,* March 1941, 56.

825 *"If anything glowed through":* Michael Troyan, *A Rose for Mrs. Miniver* (Lexington: University Press of Kentucky, 1999), 98.

825 *"I will gladly come":* Ibid., 94.

825 *"I've always wanted":* Ibid., 100.

825 *Garson had come from: Hollywood Citizen-News,* April 4, 1939.

826 *When* Quo Vadis? *came to:* Hal Erickson, *All Movie Guide.*

827 *"Well, I didn't dream":* Judith Stevens to author, June 4, 1998, Dorothy Wellman to author, May 16, 1997.

827 "Three Nations War": *Los Angeles Times,* September 4, 1939, 1.

827 *"Tonight my single duty": New York Times,* September 4, 1939, 6.

829 *She ate little—roast:* Stanwyck, "Things I Don't Like About Myself," 37.

829 *She drank up to twelve:* Ed Sullivan, November 5, 1939.

830 *An imposing phonograph, given:* Tony Fay to author, November 2, 2005.

830 *The smell of newly cut grass:* Tony Fay to author, November 11, 2005.

830 *Barbara didn't call him: Los Angeles Times,* October 6, 1939, 1.

831 *"I'm not the morbid":* BS to Vivian Crosby, February 27, 1940, *Photoplay Combined with Movie Mirror,* n.d., 55.

831 *"I can't write very good":* Kobal, biography of DeMille, 1679.

831 *"at times perfect": New York Times,* September 10, 1939.

831 *"A solid performance": Daily Variety,* February 15, 1939.

831 *"Stanwyck has supplied just":* Frank S. Nugent, *New York Times,* September 8, 1939, 28.

832 *"a standout . . . [it] does": Variety,* August 16, 1939, 14.

832 Lady of the Tropics *was called: Los Angeles Examiner,* September 9, 1939.

832 *"Taylor turns in a good": Variety,* August 9, 1939, 14.

832 *"It is necessary to": New York Times,* September 8, 1939, 28.

833 *"I wanted her to know":* Asher, "Amazing Mrs. Taylor," 27.

833 *"Aren't you going to":* Ibid., 27, 66.

833 *"my Pennsylvania extravagance":* Steven Bach, *Dazzler: The Life and Times of Moss Hart* (New York: Alfred A. Knopf, 2001), 175.

833 *Fairview Farm's regular guests:* Ibid., 177.

834 *"When I go into a store":* Ibid., 175.

834 *Barbara made it clear:* Hall, "Information, If You Please, About Barbara Stanwyck," 10.

834 *The piles of presents:* Tony Fay to author February 27, 1998.

835 *"You can't put blinders on":* James Reid, "What I'll Fight For," *Motion Picture,* October 1940, 27.

Seventeen: On the Brink

PAGE

836 *His was among her:* Hall, "Information, If You Please, About Barbara Stanwyck," 2.

836 *"falling off her chair":* Jane Ardmore Papers, 6.

836 *"For my money":* Jack Benny, *Photoplay,* 1948.

837 *Mary was Sadie Marks:* Joan Benny to author, 1997.

837 *She strove to be:* Joan Benny to author, January 9, 2006.

837 *Mary could be cruel:* Hedda Hopper's Hollywood, *Los Angeles Times,* January 11, 1940.

837 *The Bennys' parties, particularly:* Jack Benny and Joan Benny, *Sunday Nights at Seven* (New York: Warner Books, 1990), 61, 201.

838 *Benny hesitated about getting:* Louis Xavier Lansworth, *New Yorker* or *Coast,* April 1939, 11.

841 *"She's Jewish":* Tony Fay to author, November 3, 2004.

842 *"Don't let it go to":* Robert Taylor, "Pleased to Meet You," magazine clipping, c. 1949. Victoria Wilson Archive.

843 *Barbara had settled into:* Edwin Schallert, "Call of Wolf Reversed by La Stanwyck," *Los Angeles Times,* July 23, 1944, 1.

844 *"I went up in a rocket":* Robert Taylor, "Why a Star Gets the Jitters," *Cosmopolitan,* September 1941, 36.

845 *"The only part that was":* Raymond Rohauer, *A Tribute to Mervyn Leroy* (New York: Gallery of Modern Art, 1967), 14.

845 *"She is so beautiful":* Anne Edwards, *Vivien Leigh* (New York: Pocket Books, 1978), 134.

845 *He was hoping* Waterloo: *Memo from David O. Selznick,* 295–96.

846 *"Robert Taylor is the man":* Edwards, *Vivien Leigh,* 136.

846 *Vivien spent her lunch:* Ibid.

846 *"Vivien didn't have to":* Roberta Ormiston, *Photoplay,* n.d.

847 *"Now let's have a nice":* Peter B. Flint, "Mervyn LeRoy, 86, Dies," *New York Times,* September 14, 1987.

847 *Woody Van Dyke stepped: Syracuse Herald-Journal,* February 6, 1940, 18.

849 *"a high score is":* BS to Vivian Crosby, June 5, 1940, *Photoplay Combined with Movie Mirror,* n.d., 55.

849 *The evening's biggest excitement:* Fay Bainter presented the award for best supporting actress, and said, "To me it seems more than just a plaque of gold; it opens the doors of this room, moves back the walls, and enables us to embrace the whole of America. An America that we love, an America that, almost alone in the world today, recognizes and pays tribute to those who give it their best, regardless of creed, race, or color. It is with the knowledge that this entire nation will stand and salute the presentation of this plaque that I present the Academy Award for the best performance of an actress in a supporting role during 1939 to Hattie McDaniel."

Miss McDaniel accepted the award and said, "Academy of Motion Picture Arts and Sciences, fellow members of the motion picture industry and honored guests, this is one of the happiest moments of my life . . . For your kindness, it has made me feel very, very humble, and I shall always hold it as a beacon for anything I may be able to do in the future. I sincerely hope that I shall always be a credit to my race and to the motion picture industry. My heart is too full to tell you just how I feel, and may I say thank you and God bless you." The 12th Academy Awards, February 29, 1940. Broadcast from the Cocoanut Grove at the Ambassador Hotel in Los Angeles, California.

849 *"We meet in an evil":* Rudyard Kipling and Wolcott Balestier, *The Naulahka: A Story of West and East* (New York: Macmillan, 1892).

849 *"a little ironic":* Reid, "What I'll Fight For."

850 *Weingarten, much to Cukor's:* Gavin Lambert, *Nazimova* (New York: Alfred A. Knopf, 1997), 370.

850 *Among those thought:* Two and a half years after the publication of *Escape,* Grace Zaring Stone revealed that she was Ethel Vance. Stone had written three successful novels, including *The Bitter Tea of General Yen.* She had chosen a pseudonym to protect her daughter, Eleanor, then living in occupied Czechoslovakia with her husband, a Hungarian, Count Perényi, as well as her husband, Ellis Stone, who was living in Paris, the U.S. Navy attaché at the American embassy there. Stone said she chose the name Ethel Vance because "it sounds like a name you were born with and can't get rid of." *New York Times,* April 5, 1942, 17.

851 *Escape was Nazimova's:* Lambert, *Nazimova,* 370–71.

851 *Dion referred to her:* Hall, "Information, If You Please, About Barbara Stanwyck," 3.

852 *Instead of Jean Arthur:* John Andrew Gallagher and Frank Thompson, *Nothing Sacred: The Cinema of William Wellman* (Men with Wings Press), 102–3.

853 *Cameras were placed in:* Bob Ray, *Los Angeles Times,* March 29, 1940, 20.

853 *"We think of ourselves":* Reid, "What I'll Fight For," 60.

854 *"either an imbecile":* Leuchtenburg, *Franklin D. Roosevelt and the New Deal,* 310.

854 *"could maintain peace"*: Ibid., 312.

854 *Walt Disney's premier showing*: *New York Times,* October 23, 1940, 20.

855 *A production of* Cavalcade: *Los Angeles Times,* July 28, 1940, D8.

855 *The English colony came together*: *New York Times,* August 4, 1940, 105.

855 *Each week, the English colony*: Kotsilibas-Davis and Loy, *Myrna Loy,* 165.

855 *The California legislature organized*: Leuchtenburg, *Franklin D. Roosevelt and the New Deal,* 300.

856 *the day newspaper headlines read*: *Los Angeles Times,* June 13, 1940.

856 *"Your routine may not"*: *Modern Screen,* January 1941, 70.

856 *"Is it an honest"*: Ella Smith, *Starring Miss Barbara Stanwyck,* 138.

856 *"It's okay, Frank"*: Charles Wolfe, "Authors, Audiences, and Endings," in *Meet John Doe,* vol. 13 of Rutgers Films in Print (New Brunswick, N.J.: Rutgers University Press, 1989), 211.

857 *"bounced off the floor"*: *Meet John Doe* press book, 29.

857 *"Ann Mitchell has humor"*: Ibid., 30.

858 *"the most interesting"*: Richard Glatzer, "A Conversation with Frank Capra," in Glatzer and Raeburn, *Frank Capra,* 35.

858 *She knew her mind:* "Letter to My God Child," magazine clipping, 1949–1951, 59, 60–87, 88. Victoria Wilson Archive.

858 *"not of this earth"*: BS to Vivian Crosby, July 3, 1940.

858 *She took nothing for:* "Letter to My God Child."

858 *"If any country was"*: "This Is What I Believe," magazine clipping, n.d. Victoria Wilson Archive.

858 *"Any other set-up"*: Reid, "What I'll Fight For."

859 *The young man is drawn:* The picture was written by the screenwriters Joan Harrison, who wrote *Jamaica Inn* and *Rebecca,* and Hitchcock's longtime collaborator, Charles Bennett, who'd written for the director since Hitchcock adapted Bennett's play *Blackmail* and made it into England's first sound picture. Bennett and Hitchcock had collaborated on numerous films, among them *The Man Who Knew Too Much, The 39 Steps,* and *Secret Agent.*

SELECTED BIBLIOGRAPHY

Adler, Stella. *The Art of Acting*. Edited by Howard Kissell. New York: Applause Books, 2000.

———. *Ibsen, Strindberg, and Chekhov*. Edited by Barry Paris. New York: Alfred A. Knopf, 2000.

Ambrose, Stephen E. *The American Heritage New History of World War II*. Original text by C. L. Sulzberger. 1966. New York: Viking Press, 1997.

———. *Nothing Like It in the World: The Men Who Built the Transcontinental Railroad, 1863–1869*. New York: Simon & Schuster, 2000.

The American Film Institute Catalog of Motion Pictures Produced in the United States: Feature Films, 1921–1930. Berkeley: University of California Press, 1997.

Astor, Mary. *A Life on Film*. New York: Delacorte Press, 1967.

Balio, Tino. *United Artists: The Company Built by the Stars*. Madison: University of Wisconsin Press, 1978.

Barrymore, Lionel, and Cameron Shipp. *We Barrymores*. New York: Grosset & Dunlap, 1951.

Barson, Michael, and Steven Heller. *Red Scared! The Commie Menace in Propaganda and Popular Culture*. San Francisco: Chronicle Books, 2001.

Beauchamp, Cari. *Without Lying Down: Frances Marion and the Powerful Women of Early Hollywood*. New York: Scribner, 1997.

Bell, Millicent. *Marquand: An American Life*. Boston: Little, Brown, 1979.

Bentley, Eric. *Thirty Years of Treason: Excerpts from Hearings Before the House Committee on Un-American Activities, 1938–1968*. New York: Viking Press, 1971.

Berle, Milton. *Milton Berle: An Autobiography*. With Haskel Frankel. New York: Delacorte Press, 1974.

Bernds, Edward. *Mr. Bernds Goes to Hollywood*. Lanham, Md.: Scarecrow Press, 1999.

Bernhardt, Sarah. *Memories of My Life*. New York: Benjamin Blom, 1968.

Bernstein, Eve. *Illicit*. New York: Jacobsen, 1930.

Billips, Connie, and Arthur Pierce. *Lux Presents Hollywood: A Show-by-Show History of the "Lux Radio Theatre" and the "Lux Video Theatre," 1934–1957*. Jefferson, N.C.: McFarland, 1995.

Birmingham, Stephen. *The Late John Marquand*. New York: Lippincott, 1972.

Bishop, Jim. *The Mark Hellinger Story: A Biography of Broadway and Hollywood*. New York: Appleton-Century-Crofts, 1952.

Bogdanovich, Peter. *Who the Devil Made It: Conversations with Legendary Film Directors*. New York: Alfred A. Knopf, 1997.

Boller, Paul F., Jr. *Presidential Campaigns*. New York: Oxford University Press, 1984.

Bordeaux, Jeanne. *Eleonora Duse: The Story of Her Life*. New York: George H. Doran, 1924.

Bosworth, Patricia. *Anything Your Little Heart Desires: An American Family Story*. New York: Simon & Schuster, 1997.

Boughton, Willis. *Chronicles of Erasmus Hall*. Brooklyn: General Organization, Erasmus Hall High School, 1906.

Bourdet, Édouard. *The Captive*. Translated by Arthur Hornblow. New York: Brentano's, 1926.

Branden, Nathaniel. *Judgment Day: My Years with Ayn Rand*. Boston: Houghton Mifflin, 1989.

Brenman-Gibson, Margaret. *Clifford Odets: American Playwright*. New York: Atheneum, 1981.

Brooks, Tim, and Earle Marsh. *The Complete Directory to Prime Time Network TV Shows, 1946–Present.* New York: Ballantine Books, 1979.

Busch, Niven. *Duel in the Sun.* New York: Hampton, 1944.

———. *The Furies.* New York: Dial Press, 1948.

———. *The San Franciscans.* New York: Simon & Schuster, 1962.

Cain, James M. *Double Indemnity.* New York: Alfred A. Knopf, 1943.

———. *Past All Dishonor.* New York: Alfred A. Knopf, 1946.

Cannom, Robert C. *Van Dyke and the Mythical City, Hollywood.* Culver City, Calif.: Murray & Gee, 1948.

Cantor, Norman F. *The American Century: Varieties of Culture in Modern Times.* New York: HarperCollins, 1997.

Capra, Frank. *The Name Above the Title: An Autobiography.* New York: Macmillan, 1971.

Carey, Gary. *All the Stars in Heaven: Louis B. Mayer's MGM.* New York: E. P. Dutton, 1981.

Carlisle, Helen Grace. *Mothers Cry.* New York: Harper & Brothers, 1929.

Caspary, Vera. *The Secrets of Grown-Ups.* New York: McGraw-Hill, 1979.

Cather, Willa. *A Lost Lady.* New York: Alfred A. Knopf, 1923.

———. *Not Under Forty.* New York: Alfred A. Knopf, 1936.

Cather, Willa, and L. Brent Bohlke. *Willa Cather in Person: Interviews, Speeches, and Letters.* Lincoln: University of Nebraska Press, 1986.

Cavell, Stanley. *Contesting Tears: The Hollywood Melodrama of the Unknown Woman.* Chicago: University of Chicago Press, 1996.

Ceplair, Larry, and Steven Englund. *The Inquisition in Hollywood: Politics in the Film Community, 1930–1960.* Garden City, N.Y.: Anchor Press/Doubleday, 1980.

Chierichetti, David. *Mitchell Leisen: Hollywood Director.* Los Angeles: Photoventures Press, 1995.

Churchill, Allen, ed. *The "Liberty" Years, 1924–1950.* Englewood Cliffs, N.J.: Prentice-Hall, 1969.

Clarke, Mae. *Featured Player: An Oral Autobiography of Mae Clarke.* Edited by James Curtis. Santa Barbara, Calif.: Santa Teresa Press, 1996.

Clurman, Harold. *All People Are Famous.* New York: Harcourt Brace Jovanovich, 1974.

Connolly, Myles. *Mr. Blue.* New York: Macmillan, 1928.

Crafton, Donald. *The Talkies: American Cinema's Transition to Sound, 1926–1931.* New York: Charles Scribner's Sons, 1997.

Crowther, Bosley. *Hollywood Rajah: The Life and Times of Louis B. Mayer.* New York: Henry Holt, 1960.

Davenport, Marcia. *East Side, West Side.* New York: Charles Scribner's Sons, 1947.

Davis, Bette. *The Lonely Life.* New York: G. P. Putnam's Sons, 1962.

De Mille, Richard. *My Secret Mother, Lorna Moon.* New York: Farrar, Straus & Giroux, 1998.

Desti, Mary. *The Untold Story: The Life of Isadora Duncan, 1921–1927.* Cambridge, Mass.: Da Capo Press, 1929.

De Toth, André. *De Toth on De Toth: Putting the Drama in Front of the Camera.* Edited by Anthony Slide. New York: Faber and Faber, 1996.

Deutsch, Helen, and Stella B. Hanau. *Provincetown: A Story of the Theatre.* New York: Farrar & Rinehart, 1931.

Dick, Bernard F. *Hellman in Hollywood.* Madison, N.J.: Fairleigh Dickinson University Press, 1982.

———. *The Merchant Prince of Poverty Row: Harry Cohn of Columbia Pictures.* Lexington: University Press of Kentucky, 1993.

Donovan, Denis M., and Deborah McIntyre. *Healing the Hurt Child: A Developmental-Contextual Approach.* New York: W. W. Norton, 1990.

Dunne, Philip. *Take Two.* New York: Limelight, 1992.

Epstein, Philip G. *The Mad Miss Manton.* New York: Frederick Ungar, 1938.

Erikson, Erik H. *Childhood and Society.* New York: W. W. Norton, 1950.

Eyman, Scott. *Print the Legend: The Life and Times of John Ford.* New York: Simon & Schuster, 1999.

Fausold, Martin L. *The Presidency of Herbert C. Hoover.* Lawrence: University Press of Kansas, 1985.

Fay, Frank. *How to Be Poor.* New York: Prentice-Hall, 1945.

Ferber, Edna. *A Kind of Magic.* Garden City, N.Y.: Doubleday, 1963.

———. *A Peculiar Treasure: An Autobiography.* New York: Literary Guild of America, 1939.

———. *So Big.* Garden City, N.Y.: Doubleday, 1924.

Fountain, Leatrice Gilbert. *Dark Star: The Untold Story of the Meteoric Rise and Fall of Legendary Silent Screen Star John Gilbert.* With John R. Maxim. New York: St. Martin's Press, 1985.

Francisco, Charles. *The Radio City Music Hall: An Affectionate History of the World's Greatest Theater.* New York: E. P. Dutton, 1979.

Fraser, Antonia. *Mary Queen of Scots.* London: Weidenfeld & Nicolson, 1969.

Freidel, Frank. *Franklin D. Roosevelt: A Rendezvous with Destiny.* Boston: Back Bay Books, 1990.

Galbraith, John Kenneth. *The Great Crash, 1929.* Boston: Houghton Mifflin, 1954.

Gardner, Gerald C. *The Censorship Papers: Movie Censorship Letters from the Hays Office, 1934 to 1968.* New York: Dodd, Mead, 1987.

Gillespie, Charles Bancroft. *Historical and Pictorial History of Chelsea, Mass.: Her History, Her Achievements, Her Opportunities.* Courtesy of the Chelsea Public Library. Chelsea, Mass.: Chelsea Gazette, 1898.

Gish, Lillian. *The Movies, Mr. Griffith, and Me.* With Ann Pinchot. Englewood Cliffs, N.J.: Prentice-Hall, 1969.

Glatzer, Richard, and John Raeburn, eds. *Frank Capra: The Man and His Films.* Ann Arbor: University of Michigan Press, 1975.

Goodman, Ezra. *Bogie: The Good-Bad Guy.* New York: Lyle Stuart, 1965.

———. *The Fifty-Year Decline and Fall of Hollywood.* New York: Simon & Schuster, 1961.

Goodman, Walter. *The Committee: The Extraordinary Career of the House Committee on Un-American Activities.* New York: Farrar, Straus & Giroux, 1968.

Granlund, Nils Thor. *Blondes, Brunettes, and Bullets.* With Sid Feder and Ralph Hancock. Philadelphia: David McKay, 1957.

Greene, Graham. *The Lost Childhood and Other Essays.* New York: Viking Press, 1951.

Griffith, Richard. *Samuel Goldwyn: The Producer and His Films.* New York: Museum of Modern Art Film Library, 1956. Distributed by Simon & Schuster.

Gunnison, Herbert Foster, ed. *Flatbush of To-day.* Brooklyn, 1908.

Gussow, Mel. *Don't Say Yes Until I Finish Talking: A Biography of Darryl Zanuck.* Garden City, N.Y.: Doubleday, 1971.

Halliday, Jon. *Sirk on Sirk.* 1971. London: Faber and Faber, 1997.

Hardy, Phil. *Samuel Fuller.* New York: Praeger, 1970.

Harvey, James. *Romantic Comedy in Hollywood: From Lubitsch to Sturges.* New York: Alfred A. Knopf, 1987.

Harvey, Rita Morley. *Those Wonderful, Terrible Years: George Heller and the American Federation of Television and Radio Artists.* Carbondale: Southern Illinois University Press, 1996.

Haskell, Molly. *From Reverence to Rape: The Treatment of Women in the Movies.* New York: Penguin Books, 1974.

Haskin, Frederic J. *The Panama Canal.* Garden City, N.Y.: Doubleday, Page, 1913.

Hays, Will H. *The Memoirs of Will H. Hays.* Garden City, N.Y.: Doubleday, 1955.

Higham, Charles, and Joel Greenberg. *The Celluloid Muse: Hollywood Directors Speak.* Chicago: Henry Regnery, 1969.

Hirsch, Foster. *The Boys from Syracuse: The Shuberts' Theatrical Empire.* Carbondale: Southern Illinois University Press, 1998.

———. *A Method to Their Madness: The History of the Actors Studio.* New York: Da Capo Press, 1984.

Hoover, Herbert. *The Memoirs of Herbert Hoover: The Cabinet and the Presidency, 1920–1933.* 1952. New York: Macmillan, 1955.

———. *The Memoirs of Herbert Hoover: The Great Depression, 1929–1941.* 1951. New York: Macmillan, 1955.

Hopkins, Arthur. *How's Your Second Act?* Introduction by George Jean Nathan. Yale Drama Library. New York: Philip Goodman, 1918.

———. *To a Lonely Boy.* Garden City, N.Y.: Doubleday, Doran, 1937.

Hopper, Hedda. *From Under My Hat.* Garden City, N.Y.: Doubleday, 1952.

———. *The Whole Truth and Nothing But.* With James Brough. Garden City, N.Y.: Doubleday, 1963.

Housman, Arthur. *Forbidden.* New York: Grosset & Dunlap, 1932.

Hurst, Fanny. *Back Street.* New York: Cosmopolitan Books, 1931.

Johnson, Vance. *Heaven's Tableland: The Dust Bowl Story.* New York: Farrar, Straus & Giroux, 1947.

Kahn, Gordon. *Hollywood on Trial: The Story of the 10 Who Were Indicted.* New York: Boni & Gaer, 1948.

Kashner, Sam, and Nancy Shoenberger. *A Talent for Genius: The Life and Times of Oscar Levant.* New York: Villard, 1994.

Keyes, Evelyn. *Scarlett O'Hara's Younger Sister: My Lively Life in and out of Hollywood.* New York: Lyle Stuart, 1977.

Kindleberger, Charles P. *The World in Depression, 1929–1939.* Berkeley: University of California Press, 1986.

Kotsilibas-Davis, James. *The Barrymores: The Royal Family in Hollywood.* New York: Crown, 1981.

Kroeger, Brooke. *Fannie: The Talent for Success of Writer Fannie Hurst.* New York: Times Books, 1999.

Lambert, Gavin. *Norma Shearer: A Biography.* New York: Alfred A. Knopf, 1990.

———. *On Cukor.* New York: G. P. Putnam's Sons, 1972.

Langner, Lawrence. *The Magic Curtain.* New York: E. P. Dutton, 1951.

Laurence, Frank M. *Hemingway and the Movies.* Jackson: University Press of Mississippi, 1981.

Lee, Hermione. *Willa Cather: Double Lives.* New York: Vintage, 1991.

Leider, Emily Wortis. *Becoming Mae West.* New York: Farrar, Straus & Giroux, 1997.

Lerner, Harriet Goldhor. *The Dance of Intimacy.* New York: Harper & Row, 1989.

LeRoy, Mervyn, and Dick Kleiner. *Mervyn LeRoy: Take One.* New York: Hawthorn Books, 1974.

Leuchtenburg, William E. *Franklin D. Roosevelt and the New Deal, 1932–1940.* New York: Harper Torchbooks, 1963.

Levant, Oscar. *The Memoirs of an Amnesiac.* New York: G. P. Putnam's Sons, 1965.

Lewis, David. *The Creative Producer.* Edited by James Curtis. Metuchen, N.J.: Scarecrow Press, 1993.

Lewis, Edith. *Willa Cather Living.* New York: Alfred A. Knopf, 1953.

Lewis, Sinclair. *Elmer Gantry.* New York: Harcourt, Brace, 1927.

Leyburn, James. *The Scotch-Irish: A Social History.* Chapel Hill: University of North Carolina Press, 1962.

Liedloff, Jean. *The Continuum Concept: In Search of Happiness Lost.* Addison-Wesley, 1985.

Lifton, Betty Jean. *Lost and Found: The Adoption Experience.* New York: Dial Press, 1979.

———. *Twice Born: Memoirs of an Adopted Daughter.* New York: McGraw-Hill, 1975.

Loos, Anita. *Anita Loos Rediscovered: Film Treatments and Fiction by Anita Loos, Creator of "Gentlemen Prefer Blondes."* Edited by Cari Beauchamp and Mary Anita Loos. Berkeley: University of California Press, 2003.

———. *The Talmadge Girls.* New York: Viking Press, 1978.

Lord, Walter. *The Night Lives On.* New York: Avon Books, 1987.

———. *A Night to Remember.* New York: Bantam Books, 1955.

Lynch, Don, and Ken Marschall. Titanic: *An Illustrated History.* New York: Hyperion, 1992.

Marion, Frances. *Off with Their Heads! A Serio-comic Tale of Hollywood.* New York: Macmillan, 1972.

Marx, Groucho, and Richard J. Anobile. *The Marx Bros. Scrapbook.* New York: Darien House/Crown, 1973.

Marx, Samuel. *Mayer and Thalberg: The Make-Believe Saints.* New York: Random House, 1975.

Mayer, Arthur, and Richard Griffith. *The Movies.* 1957. New York: Simon & Schuster, 1970.

McBride, Joseph. *Frank Capra: The Catastrophe of Success.* New York: Simon & Schuster, 1992.

———. *Searching for John Ford.* New York: St. Martin's Press, 2001.

McCarthy, Todd. *Howard Hawks: The Grey Fox of Hollywood.* New York: Grove Press, 1997.

McCullough, Colleen. *Tim.* New York: Harper & Row, 1974.

McElvaine, Robert. *The Great Depression: America, 1929–1941.* 1984. New York: Times Books, 1993.

McGilligan, Patrick. *Backstory 1: Interviews with Screenwriters of Hollywood's Golden Age.* Berkeley: University of California Press, 1986.

————. *Fritz Lang: Nature of the Beast*. New York: St. Martin's Press, 1997.

————, ed. *Six Screenplays by Robert Riskin*. Berkeley: University of California Press, 1997.

McGilligan, Patrick, and Paul Buhle. *Tender Comrades: A Backstory of the Hollywood Blacklist*. New York: St. Martin's Press, 1997.

Meltzer, Milton. *Brother, Can You Spare a Dime? The Great Depression, 1929–1933*. New York: Alfred A. Knopf, 1969.

Miller, Alice. *The Drama of the Gifted Child: The Search for the True Self*. New York: Basic Books, 1981.

Miller, Merle, and Evan Rhodes. *Only You, Dick Daring! or, How to Write One Television Script and Make $50,000,000, a True-Life Adventure*. New York: William Sloan, 1964.

Moore, Colleen. *Silent Star*. Garden City, N.Y.: Doubleday, 1968.

Moore, Dick. *Twinkle, Twinkle, Little Star (but Don't Have Sex or Take the Car)*. New York: Harper & Row, 1984.

Mosedale, John. *The Men Who Invented Broadway: Damon Runyon, Walter Winchell, and Their World*. New York: Richard Marek, 1981.

Mosley, Leonard. *Zanuck: The Rise and Fall of Hollywood's Last Tycoon*. New York: Little, Brown, 1984.

Nevins, Francis M., Jr. *Cornell Woolrich: First You Dream, Then You Die*. New York: Mysterious Press, 1988.

O'Brien, Frederick. *White Shadows in the South Seas*. New York: Century, 1919.

Odets, Clifford. *Clash by Night*. New York: Random House, 1942.

————. *The Time Is Ripe: The 1940 Journal of Clifford Odets*. New York: Grove Press, 1988.

————. *Waiting for Lefty, and Other Plays*. New York: Grove Press, 1994.

Oller, John. *Jean Arthur: The Actress Nobody Knew*. New York: Limelight, 1997.

Peary, Gerald, ed. *John Ford: Interviews*. Jackson: University Press of Mississippi, 2001.

Petroski, Henry. *Remaking the World: Adventures in Engineering*. New York: Alfred A. Knopf, 1997.

Photoplay. *Stars of the Photoplay*. 1924. Chicago: Photoplay Publishing, 1930.

Photoplay Magazine. *Stars of the Photoplay*. Chicago: Photoplay Publishing, 1924.

Photoplay Magazine. *Stars of the Photoplay*. Chicago: Photoplay Publishing, 1930.

Prebble, John. *Glencoe*. New York: Holt, Rinehart and Winston, 1966.

————. *The Highland Clearances*. London: Secker & Warburg, 1963.

Pringle, James R. *History of the Town and City of Gloucester, Cape Ann, Massachusetts*. 1892. Gloucester, Mass.: City of Gloucester Archives Committee and Ten Pound Island Book Co., 1997.

Prouty, Olive Higgins. *Pencil Shavings*. Cambridge, Mass.: Riverside Press, 1961.

————. *Stella Dallas*. Boston: Houghton Mifflin, 1923.

Rand, Ayn. *The Fountainhead*. 1943. Indianapolis: Bobbs-Merrill, 1968.

Robinson, Edward G. *All My Yesterdays*. With Leonard Spigelgass. New York: Hawthorn Books, 1973.

Rose, Billy. *Wine, Women, and Words*. New York: Simon & Schuster, 1948.

Sakall, S. Z. *The Story of Cuddles: My Life Under the Emperor Francis Joseph, Adolf Hitler, and the Warner Brothers*. Translated by Paul Tabori. London: Cassell, 1954.

Salzman, Jack, ed. *Years of Protest: A Collection of American Writings of the 1930's*. New York: Pegasus, 1967.

Schary, Dore. *Heyday*. New York: Little, Brown, 1979.

Schlissel, Lillian, ed. *Three Plays by Mae West*. London: Routledge, 1979.

Schulberg, Budd. *What Makes Sammy Run?* 1952. New York: Vintage, 1990.

Schwartz, Nancy Lynn. *The Hollywood Writers' Wars*. Completed by Sheila Schwartz. New York: Alfred A. Knopf, 1982.

Sherman, Vincent. *Studio Affairs: My Life as a Film Director*. Lexington: University Press of Kentucky, 1996.

Sinclair, Andrew. *John Ford*. New York: Dial Press/James Wade, 1979.

Sinclair, Upton. *Upton Sinclair Presents William Fox*. Los Angeles: Upton Sinclair, 1933.

Smith, Gene. *The Shattered Dream: Herbert Hoover and the Great Depression*. New York: William Morrow, 1970.

Stein, Gertrude. *3 Lives*. 1909. New York: Vintage Books, 1936.

Stone, Grace Zaring. *The Bitter Tea of General Yen*. Indianapolis: Bobbs-Merrill, 1930.

Stringer, Arthur. *The Mud Lark*. New York: A. L. Burt, 1932.

Swanson, Gloria. *Swanson on Swanson*. New York: Random House, 1980.

Tanenhaus, Sam. *Whittaker Chambers: A Biography*. New York: Random House, 1997.

Taylor, William R., ed. *Inventing Times Square: Commerce and Culture at the Crossroads of the World*. Baltimore: Johns Hopkins University Press, 1996.

Terry, Walter. *Isadora Duncan: Her Life, Her Art, Her Legacy*. New York: Dodd, Mead, 1963.

Totheroh, Dan. *Burlesque: From the Play by Arthur Hopkins and George Manker Watters*. Garden City, N.Y.: Doubleday, Doran, 1928.

Trewin, J. C., Raymond Mander, and Joe Mitchenson. *The Turbulent Thirties: A Further Decade of the Theatre*. London: MacDonald, 1960.

Van Dyke, W. S. *Horning into Africa*. Privately printed, 1931.

Veiller, Bayard. *The Fun I've Had*. New York: Reynal & Hitchcock, 1941.

Verrier, Nancy Newton. *The Primal Wound*. Baltimore: Gateway Press, 1993.

Vidor, King. *A Tree Is a Tree*. London: Longmans, Green, 1954.

Viorst, Judith. *Necessary Losses: The Loves, Illusions, Dependencies, and Impossible Expectations That All of Us Have to Give Up in Order to Grow*. New York: Ballantine Books, 1986.

Walker, Joseph, and Juanita Walker. *The Light on Her Face*. Los Angeles: ASC Press, 1984.

Wallis, Hal, and Charles Higham. *Starmaker: The Autobiography of Hal Wallis*. New York: Macmillan, 1980.

Walpole, Hugh. *Fortitude*. New York: George H. Doran, 1913.

———. *Jeremy*. New York: George H. Doran, 1919.

Walsh, Raoul. *Each Man in His Time*. New York: Farrar, Straus & Giroux, 1974.

Warner, Jack. *My First Hundred Years in Hollywood*. New York: Random House, 1965.

Warren, Harris Gaylord. *Herbert Hoover and the Great Depression*. 1959. New York: W. W. Norton, 1967.

Watkins, T. H. *The Great Depression: America in the 1930s*. Boston: Little, Brown, 1993.

Welles, Orson, and Peter Bogdanovich. *This Is Orson Welles*. Edited by Jonathan Rosenbaum. New York: HarperCollins, 1992.

Wellman, William A. *Go, Get 'Em!* Boston: Page, 1918.

———. *A Short Time for Insanity*. New York: Hawthorn Books, 1974.

West, Mae. *Goodness Had Nothing to Do with It*. New York: Avon, 1959.

Wiley, Mason, and Damien Bona. *Inside Oscar: The Unofficial History of the Academy Awards*. Edited by Gail MacColl. New York: Ballantine Books, 1986.

Winter, William. *The Life of David Belasco*. New York: Moffat, Yard, 1918.

Wray, Fay. *On the Other Hand*. New York: St. Martin's Press, 1989.

Ziegfeld, Richard, and Paulette Ziegfeld. *The Ziegfeld Touch: The Life and Times of Florenz Ziegfeld Jr.* New York: Harry N. Abrams, 1993.

INDEX

Page numbers in *italics* refer to illustrations.